CHURCHILL:
THE END OF GLORY

CHURCHILL:
THE END OF GLORY

A POLITICAL BIOGRAPHY

BY

JOHN CHARMLEY

LONDON   NEW YORK   SYDNEY   TORONTO

This edition published 1993
by BCA by arrangement with Hodder & Stoughton Ltd
CN2943

Designed by Cinamon and Kitzinger, London
Photoset by Rowland Phototypesetting Ltd,
Bury St Edmunds, Suffolk
Printed in Great Britain by
St Edmundsbury Press Ltd,
Bury St Edmunds, Suffolk

Contents

Contents

Illustrations

Illustrations

Field Marshal Sir Alan Brooke, and General Simpson at the Citadel Fortress
of Julich, 1945 (*S & G Press Agency Ltd*)

The victorious leader receives the plaudits of the crowds, 8 May 1945 (*Popperfoto*)

A Conservative Party poster from 1950 (*author's collection*)

Acknowledgments

This time there is no copious list of illustrious names to thank for telling me stories which already appear in their memoirs; I deliberately avoided seeking interviews with what Sir John Colville called 'Churchillians'. In the course of my researches over the last fifteen years it became clear to me that just about everyone of the 'war generation' to whom I talked had been touched by the Churchill 'myth'. As I already knew what that was, I deliberately avoided exposing myself to any more of its manifestations, preferring, instead, to immerse myself in the archives, Churchill's writings and the works of others – the result can be seen in the form of the bibliography.

But that does not mean that there are no acknowledgments – quite the contrary. I am grateful to everyone who has spoken to me about this period and especially to those who have let me examine and quote from their private papers. Particular thanks are due to Julian Amery (Leo Amery), John Harvey (Oliver Harvey), Paul Channon (Sir Henry Channon) and Dr B. Z. Benediktz (Chamberlain and Avon Papers). Copyright for the Churchill Papers is owned by C&T publications, but my quotations are from documents in the public domain. If I have inadvertently infringed any copyright, I hope that the owner will get in touch so that I can correct this state of affairs in any future editions. Since this book is the culmination of fifteen years' work, it seems the right place to pay tribute to two historians whom I admire not only as scholars, but also as friends. Alastair Parker of the Queen's College, Oxford, introduced me to the arcane mysteries of historical research on the Second World War, and although he will disagree with much of what follows, he can have the melancholy satisfaction of knowing that he helped set my feet on the road. To my former tutor, Piers Mackesy, I am grateful on two counts: if Alastair Parker guided me at a later stage, it was Piers who first showed me what an historian could be; he has put me even further in his debt by reading and commenting on parts of the manuscript. To my former colleague James Jones I am grateful for once more taking time from his labours to comment on the results of mine. My colleague Dr Geoffrey Searle has earned some sort of medal by reading and commenting on most of the manuscript – heroism way beyond the call of any possible duty.

I must also acknowledge an immense debt to all the other scholars who have worked in this period; there is scarcely a book in the bibliography from which I did not learn something. Of the existing biographies, Robert Rhodes

James's brilliant book was the one most difficult to keep a proper distance from. Like everyone else working this field I owe a debt to Martin Gilbert's industry; to adapt a phrase, his biography is a 'quarry' from which much of the stone for any other monument must be taken. Professor Warren Kimball's monumental edition of the Churchill–Roosevelt correspondence is both a 'quarry and a classic' and, having dogged his footsteps for so long, I should like to pay a special tribute to what is probably the finest work of its kind.

I am also grateful to another group of people – those who over the years have taken my special subject on Churchill at the University of East Anglia; their refusal to take anything I said for granted has been an immense stimulation. I am particularly grateful to Richard Grayson and Jane Cheadle. In previous books I have thanked the University of East Anglia for providing conditions in which serious historical research can be carried on, but given the philistine climate which now prevails in higher education, I should like to make those thanks more specific – for fear that bureaucrats who deserve little but scorn might be thought to be included in a more general expression of gratitude. The University Study Leave Committee, which has sanctioned a term's leave to finish this book, and the research committee of my own school, come high up on my list, but my chief debt is to my colleagues in English history, who create an intellectual climate in which debate and discussion thrive; I count myself as fortunate in having worked with them for the past decade and more.

To my publisher, John Curtis, I have to extend my warmest thanks for bearing with me through a long period of silence and for accepting a manuscript which was three times the size of the one contracted for; his advice and support have been much appreciated. To Linda Osband, who read and commented on the massive typescript, I can offer only apologies and thanks. If they will both pardon the expression, it was nice to be working with 'the old firm' again. I would also like to thank my agent, Felicity Bryan, for her efforts on my behalf.

Thanks of a more personal kind need to be conveyed with delicacy. A caesura in my private life makes it difficult to thank Dorothea adequately for her help, but I want to place on record my thanks to her – for everything. To my sons, Gervase, Gerard and Kit, I owe an immense debt for the joy which they give me. To my brothers, David and Gary, and especially to my sister, Julie Godsell, I also owe much. If it were not for one other, I would have dedicated this book to the memory of my mother and my father – to whose shades I would none the less pay homage. But since neither the author nor this book would have been here without her, it is only fitting that the final thanks should be expressed to Lorraine, to whom this book is, like its author, dedicated. Inshallah.

John Charmley, The Retreat, East Tuddenham, 1992

Introduction

At the time I was only aware that somebody terrifically important had died; it reminded me of President Kennedy's death, but it was somehow different. I had heard of Churchill. He was the man my father always mentioned whenever he talked about his time in somewhere called the 'western desert' during 'the war'. My grandmother talked about Churchill in terms usually reserved for The Almighty; my father criticised him in the way he did most 'Tory politicians'. The concept of a 'Tory politician' being spoken of in terms of hushed reverence was not one which I could grasp; maybe Churchill was The Almighty? My mother, who had been about the age I was then when 'the war' broke out, recalled listening to Churchill's marvellous speeches in 1940, and he had, I was told by other relatives, 'won the war'. Was he perhaps that 'Lord God mighty in battle' of whom my grandmother spoke? Nine-year-old boys collect information about the past in a jumbled fashion.

That was my introduction to Churchill – the day of his great state funeral. Having been born seven months after he had ceased to be Prime Minister, there were no memories of the deity as living man; he was always history to me. He had 'saved England' and 'won the war', and since these were undeniably good things, Churchill was a 'good thing'; I was all in favour of him.

There matters rested until I began to do historical research. Since my Modern History course stopped in 1939, I came across Churchill only through the medium of his career before that date; Robert Rhodes James easily convinced me that that had been 'a study in failure'. Because I was working on British policy towards General de Gaulle, I came across Churchill frequently. The picture which emerged from my work did not fit the Churchill whom I had 'inherited'. Working on Duff Cooper's biography served to confirm Rhodes James's picture and also suggested that 1940–5 might not have been as simple as I had been led to believe. When I worked on Lord Lloyd's biography, I came to have more sympathy for and understanding of Churchill's attitude towards the Empire; but the triumphalist tone which I had adopted towards Munich became clouded. As more work was done on the period 1937–41, it became apparent that the picture of Churchill which had begun to emerge from my thesis was replicated elsewhere. Churchill was as fallible as he had been before the war. Editing Sir Evelyn Shuckburgh's diaries certainly confirmed the existing view of most scholars that Churchill had not been up to the job after about 1952. Trying to write a book on some of these things led to one on Chamberlain instead. He, so it seemed, had offered the only way of preserving what was left of British power; if 1945 represented 'victory', it was, as Chamberlain had foreseen, for the Soviets and the Americans.

To write about 1940 and Churchill meant going back to explain how the man of 1940 had been created. Naïvely, I thought that this would be an easy task; I had taught a Special Subject on him for some years. But as I pulled together the material which I had collected, something changed. Churchill ceased to be an 'historical figure'. He had become an iconic Prime Minister, but he was never an icon in real life; indeed, no one can be that. It became a matter of getting the icon off the shelf and of trying to discern the lineaments of the living man.

Historians should normally stick to writing in the third person if they have to mention themselves, but in a book of this nature I thought that a note on how it came to be written would not be out of place.

The Churchill who emerged from this work was not the one I had expected. The idea of the 'great man' is not one which exercises historians much any more, only feminist historians look to the past for 'role-models'; but by any definition Churchill remained a 'great man'. If you take his own definition literally, that a man's actions must profoundly affect both his own and sub-sequent generations, this would allow monsters like Hitler and Stalin into the 'club', which would not have pleased him. But inherent in Churchill's idea of the 'great man' was the idea of virtuous action – that the figure concerned should have risen to the 'level of events'. The Churchill delineated here did so only intermittently, but he did so with such magnificence in 1940 that, at least in the eyes of his contemporaries, all else was forgiven. What was there to be said about the political skill of a professional politician who repeatedly found himself in some sort of 'wilderness', and whose personality in itself constituted a formidable obstacle to success? He was, as Harold Macmillan acknowledged, 'romantic and reactionary'. His part in the Dardanelles fiasco warranted the distrust which it aroused in contemporaries; Churchill did underestimate the obstacles in the way of success and he did treat the lives of men with undue levity.

That his 'first political career' ended as it did was due to Churchill's own choice. There was no pressure on him to resign in November 1915; he chose to go. Had he waited, perhaps Lloyd George would have taken him in before 1917. For Churchill the post-war decades were to prove the worst part of a 'disappointing' twentieth century, and he spent much of his time inveighing against the decline in British power. Yet, when he came to wield that power, he found what those whom he had criticised had found in their turn – that Britain was no longer a Great Power. Churchill chose to behave as though this was not the case. In the summer of 1940 Churchill's vision and the ghost of Britain's faded grandeur met for one last moment of glory; after that the twilight fell. At the end it was a melancholy story which emerged. There was nothing to be done by 1945, but action earlier might have averted the worst. At the end of the day there were no 'sun-lit uplands', only a 'darkling plain' where 'ignorant armies clash by night'. In the long story of British decline the part played by a failure of leadership has yet to be properly told, but that there was such a failure is hardly in doubt. Churchill's leadership was inspiring, but at the end it was barren, it led nowhere, and there were no heirs to his tradition.

I

Glad Confident Morning

1874–1915

The Subaltern's Star

Writing to his sister Ida on 2 November 1930, the Conservative statesman, Sir Austen Chamberlain, commented: 'Winston's *My Early Life* is very good reading. Don't miss it';[1] it was, and she did not. The book was a great success, not least because, as one of Churchill's old army friends, Sir Reginald Barnes, pointed out: 'It shows the world the human and cheery Winston that I know, but which so many know nothing of.'[2] Churchill was in his fifty-sixth year before such a 'human' portrait of him reached that wider public whose attention he had always sought; so how was it that another picture of him had become fixed in the public mind? The answer requires us to go behind the *Boys' Own paper* adventure yarn which comprises *My Early Life*.

As family mottos go, that of the Marlboroughs, '*Fiel Pero Desdichado*', 'Faithful but Unfortunate', was singularly inappropriate. The first Duke of Marlborough and founder of the family's fortune was the greatest soldier of the late sixteenth and early seventeenth centuries. But as every Victorian schoolboy knew, thanks to the writings of Lord Macaulay, the most eminent as well as the most readable of Whig historians, 'Duke John' was not noted for his fidelity to anything save his own career, a characteristic later historians have not hesitated to ascribe to his most illustrious descendant. The last example of a type common in the sixteenth century and earlier, John Churchill was a courtier-soldier who rose through royal favour; in this case purchased at the price of the honour of his sister Arabella, who was the mistress of James, Duke of York. Having thus risen, he abandoned his patron, now King James II, after William of Orange invaded England. He then proceeded to keep open a line to the exiled court at St Germain, just in case it should be necessary to desert the new monarchs, William III and Mary. This was Macaulay's picture, and even when Winston Churchill came to challenge it, there were times when he had to admit that the first Duke's behaviour was almost incomprehensible.[3]

So much for 'faithful'. Inhabiting a marvellous Italianate palace in the middle of thousands of acres of the finest English countryside can hardly be described as being 'unfortunate'. 'Undistinguished' would be the kindest word to apply to Marlborough's descendants. Leaving no sons, the great Duke's title passed by the female line into a branch of the Spencer family of Althorp. In the reign of George III the family was given permission to resurrect the name of 'Churchill'; but the 'Spencer-Churchills' proved no livelier for it. In so far as a duke possessed of a palace on the scale of Blenheim can be said to live in the obscurity conferred by mediocrity, generations of Marlboroughs managed so to do; the dimness of their fame being lit only by the occasional roué who managed to dissipate more of the family fortune than his predecessors.

It was into this line of dim dukes that Winston Spencer-Churchill was born on 30 November 1874. His father, in deference to his well-known view that mediocrity lurked behind double-barrelled names, was always known as Lord Randolph Churchill. The second son of the seventh Duke of Marlborough, he was the first of his line since its founder to detain the interest of his historically minded son. Winston Churchill certainly had respect for pedigrees which were hallowed by antiquity, but he preferred those who did great things to those who lived in the shadow of a great name. Lord Randolph certainly fitted the bill. His career merited the epithet, meteoric. A political unknown before 1880, by 1886 he was Chancellor of the Exchequer and he was spoken of by some as the next Conservative Prime Minister. The most popular platform orator in the Conservative Party, he was the only Tory who could meet the great Gladstone on his own ground with advantage. His enemies called him unprincipled, and even his leader, the third Marquess of Salisbury, bore him little love. Known, not least through his own speeches, as the advocate of 'Tory Democracy', there was some doubt as to what the term meant. 'A democracy which votes Tory' was the cynic's favourite; and it was certain that a policy which advocated more social reform did not have for its purpose the spurning of the votes of those who had received the franchise in 1867 and 1884. So Salisbury, acknowledging the need for the votes, bore with the erratic and wayward Lord Randolph, until he resigned in December 1886 in protest at what he considered excessive estimates for spending on the Navy. Salisbury jumped at the chance to rid himself of a colleague he had neither liked nor trusted. Lord Randolph fell like Lucifer, never to rise again.

In his life of Lord Randolph, Winston Churchill discerned a more serious purpose to his career than has found favour with later historians, who have generally concluded that 'Tory Democracy' was a device by which Lord Randolph could further his own position. But the fact that Lord Randolph's son could not write of him as a mere adventurer was due to more than filial piety; by the time he wrote his father's biography, the son himself was accused of similar proclivities, and in providing Lord Randolph with an alibi, Winston Churchill gave himself one too.

For the Victorians it was important to be earnest: morals, religion and politics, all were spheres in which public adherence to a code of strict ethical probity was not simply desirable, but essential. Those unwise enough to mock this convention by appearing to treat political life with the degree of levity which the modern age accords it were apt to suffer the consequence of being thought at best lightweight, and at worst mere adventurers. It took the great Disraeli a generation to live down his youthful debts and his Society novels; Lord Randolph, in imitating him, incurred similar censure. Winston Chur-

chill, who admired both men, fell under the same Dundreary-whiskered suspicion. If we decline to adopt the strict distinction between adventure and
high principle which is at the root of this Victorian dichotomy, then some
understanding of the roots of Winston Churchill's political career is possible.

'You know I have unbounded faith in myself,' Churchill wrote to one of
his aunts in May 1898.[4] It was as well that he had, for at the time he wrote
he was a subaltern in the Fourth Hussars, which was hardly the obvious
starting place for a political career which envisaged the highest office. Like
many famous men, Churchill was fond of enlarging the obstacles which stood
in the way of his success. By doing so he magnified the character of that
success. Out of nearly three hundred Conservative MPs in 1914, fifty-three,
or nearly twenty per cent, had served in the Army, the largest number in any
occupation save for barristers. But few such men aimed for, or reached, even
Cabinet level. Besides, in 1914, Churchill was a Liberal MP – and only fifteen
Liberal MPs (less than nine per cent of the total) came from such a background.[5] So, here is another question to answer: why did Churchill go into
politics, and why, having done so, did he change his Party? The question of
why, having changed Party, he was so successful can wait its turn.

To many observers of the young man's career the answer to the first two
questions was straightforward. He went into politics for the same reason that
he switched Party: he was intensely ambitious.[6] Churchill himself once wrote
that 'ambition stirs imagination nearly as much as imagination excites
ambition'.[7] Although he applied the aphorism to the Mahdi, who defeated
General Gordon at Khartoum, many would have applied it to Churchill
himself. In so doing they might also have recalled Lord Salisbury's comparison
of Lord Randolph and the Mahdi: 'The latter is sane but pretends to be
half-mad, whilst the former occupies precisely the opposite position'; comparing Churchills with charismatic religious leaders came naturally to some.
Ambition was (and still is) disapproved of in British politics; that is to say
that overt ambition is thought to be a plant which needs heavy pruning.
The intenseness of Churchill's ambition has been variously attributed to his
half-American ancestry ('Half-alien and wholly undesirable', as Lady Astor
put it), his unconscious need to prove himself to his disapproving father,[8] or
a psychological need to fight off his 'black dog' – the moods of depression
which, at times, came near to overwhelming his vitality.[9]

Churchill disliked psychiatrists[10] and was not given to analytical introspec-
tion. He simply accepted that 'from the beginning "personal distinction" was
his goal'.[11] His son, Randolph Churchill, took a similarly robust view in
his first volume of the official biography, the theme of which was how 'an
underesteemed boy of genius of noble character and daring spirit' seized
opportunities to rise in the world.[12] There is something to be said for most
of the explanations canvassed above. His mother, Jennie Jerome, certainly
infused into the Churchill blood-line a more robust strain than it had

exhibited for generations – even if it only showed in Winston. That Lord Randolph alternately neglected and scolded his son is as clear as the son's desire for parental approval; even towards the end of his life Churchill could dream vividly about the desire to win his father's favour. Churchill was always conscious of being something of an outsider, a 'red-haired urchin cocking a snook at anyone who got in his way'.[13] This might be thought an odd emotion for one who was born, if not into the purple, then into the top echelon of English Society; but there can be no doubt that it was genuine.

Churchill's earliest memories were of the Vice-regal lodge in Phoenix Park, Dublin, where his grandfather was Viceroy. His aunt, Lady Leslie, could write, a lifetime later, about fond memories of little Winston and his nurse, Mrs Everest, 'waddling after you' in idyllic by-gone days,[14] but it may be that Churchill's sense of being an outsider derived from this time. He was in Ireland because his father was there as secretary to his grandfather; and they were all there because of Lord Randolph's foolish impetuosity. After his marriage to the glittering and beautiful Jennie in 1872, Society should have been at Lord Randolph's feet; instead, through his own actions, it was soon at his throat.

The first part of the family motto could never have been applied to the private lives of Lord Randolph and his brother, the Marquess of Blandford. When the latter was in danger of being cited as co-respondent by Lord Aylesford who wished to divorce his unfaithful wife, Lord Randolph hit upon what seemed at the time the capital idea of getting Aylesford's best friend to persuade him to withdraw the case; this he did by telling the friend's wife that he possessed letters which implicated her husband in an affair with Lady Aylesford. It was the action of a cad, but when the friend was the Prince of Wales, it was more than a crime, it was folly. The Prince ostracised the Randolph Churchills, and Society followed his lead. Disraeli prevailed upon the Duke of Marlborough to accept the post of Viceroy of Ireland, which enabled him to take Randolph into what amounted to exile. It was a bitter blow to the newly-wed Lord Randolph, and seems to have inspired in him a desire for revenge.[15] Winston lacked his father's bitterness, but inherited a similar role as a species of political outlaw.

But parental neglect, which was compensated for in some measure by the love of his nurse, to whom he paid generous homage in his only novel, can cut more than one way. 'Solitary trees,' Churchill wrote, 'if they grow at all, grow strong . . . a boy deprived of a father's care often develops, if he escape the perils of youth, an independence and vigour of thought which may restore in after life the heavy loss of early days.'[16] Used of the Mahdi, these words have about them an autobiographical ring. A small, befreckled, under-sized, ginger-haired runt of a boy, who came to his first English school possessed of a lisp and few friends, Churchill was a natural target for bullies. But in the first sign of the willpower which was to carry him through many trials, Churchill 'set out to make himself tough and unfeeling'.[17] His doctor, Lord

Moran, was right to 'marvel at his will'.[18] From his earliest days this distinguished him from his quiet and well-behaved brother, Jack. Where the latter was 'not a bit of trouble',[19] Winston was in need of a 'firm hand' on account of his extreme stubbornness and self-will.[20]

As these comments of his grandmother's imply, such behaviour, whilst an object of admiration in a world-famous statesman, was less admirable in a growing child. To Lord Randolph it was quite intolerable that his son should not be a credit to him. He lacked the detachment to have been capable of the comment that with himself and Lady Randolph behaving like stubborn and self-willed children, there was no room in the family for anyone else to exhibit such behaviour patterns. Mathematics is of limited value to the biographer, and the fact that Winston was born only seven months after his parents' marriage does not necessarily suggest that he was the reason for what was an extremely rushed courtship. Lord Randolph was an impulsive man, had known Miss Jerome for a year and had been determined to marry her almost from the moment he met her. Whether this haste was the product, as this suggests, of passion, or whether the passion precipitated the haste, may be left to those with a taste for such speculation. But it appears probable that it was in this haste that the seeds of the disintegration of the marriage lay. Preoccupied each with their own life, the only time which Churchill's parents possessed for their son was to complain about him.

From the time Winston Churchill entered Harrow in April 1888, to the time he left it in December 1892, his career was a wearisome catalogue of complaints from his father, prompted in the main by comments from his masters, which were, in turn, the product of his own behaviour. Like his father, young Winston was adept at behaving in a manner calculated to offend against the rules which governed late-Victorian society. Lord Randolph, despite his own shortcomings (or perhaps because of them) was little pleased to be told that Winston was a model of 'forgetfulness, carelessness, unpunctuality, and irregularity in every way'. What made such reports even worse was the conviction of some of Winston's masters that 'as far as ability goes he ought to be at the top of his form, whereas he is at the bottom'.[21] In all of this he was little different from his father, but the sins that had been excusable in the younger son of a duke were unforgivable in the son of a younger son who would have to rely more upon his own talents to make a way in the world.

To trace the young Churchill down the channels of his scapegrace days is an exercise leading to little profit. Most of the accounts of his days at Harrow date from the time of his greatest fame, when the story fostered by Churchill in *My Early Life* was adopted by the grateful nostalgia of the elderly. Thus Churchill's own self-portrait of a bright youth who could not fit into an over-rigid system of education was supported by remarks such as these by Sir Cyril Norwood, then President of St John's College, Oxford, who wrote in 1941 that

The little Churchill was a tough proposition for any organised system of education. He wanted to get into the Army. His compulsory subjects were Mathematics, Latin and English, and of these, if English was a walk-over, it remained true that he could not, or would not, learn Latin, and he could not, or would not, learn Mathematics.[22]

Churchill was able to conceal his lack of progress in Latin, at least for a while, by getting a senior boy to do his work in return for providing him with essays in English. 'It all began', he later told Lord Moran, 'at Harrow', where he discovered 'that he could do what other boys could not do – he could write'.[23]

Churchill's own account, which cheered many of his contemporaries in 1930, who told him of their own similar experiences, was designed to demonstrate that it was the system, and not himself, which had failed. He regaled his readers with accounts of the three masters, Somervell, Moriarty and Mayo, who managed to make something of him. But as the first two taught him the only subjects in which he evinced both interest and talent, English, History and fencing, this need occasion no surprise, and it strengthens the suspicion that Churchill's problems were of his own making. Mayo must have been a remarkable teacher – it was he who succeeded in drilling the rudiments of mathematics into the recalcitrant youth.[24]

If, as Churchill would have us believe, it was his father who decided that he should enter the Army, then it was not against the will of his son – far from it. Churchill expressed his regret for the effect which entry into the Army class at Harrow had upon his education, cutting him off from the classical curriculum which still dominated higher education in Britain.[25] But the young Winston does not seem to have regretted the passing of *amo, amas* or even *amat*, whilst Lord Randolph's only regret was that his brat was too stupid to pass into the infantry class at Sandhurst. Hearing of his son's failure, Lord Randolph, who had complained that 'if you were a millionaire you could not be more extravagant',[26] considered trying to find him a career 'in business'.[27] Canon Welldon, his Headmaster at Harrow, helped save him from such a fate when, after Winston once more failed the examination in early 1893, he advised Lord Randolph to send him to a crammer.[28]

Churchill was fortunate that he was able to go to the crammer. During his vacation, whilst playing a game of hide-and-seek, he had, when cornered, flung himself from a bridge thirty feet above the ground, hoping that the trees would break his fall; later observers of his political career might see a certain symbolism here and wonder whether his judgment ever improved. His doctors at the time pronounced him a fortunate young man to survive. But the incident is worth noting, if only for the fact that it exhibited two of the characteristics which were most marked in his nature: an extreme stubbornness; and a constitution which was, appearances to the contrary, exceedingly tough – in less than two months he was back cramming for his exams, despite the serious nature of his injuries.[29]

Lord Randolph, whose health was now deteriorating rapidly, was less impressed by any of this than he was disappointed when Winston only did well enough to pass into the cavalry. This would cost him about £200 a year more, and all for what? He unburdened himself in a bitter letter to his mother, in which his frustration with all his son's promises to reform and do better broke out. It was, perhaps, a sign of his mental state that he could write that an expensive education at Harrow and Eton had done nothing for Winston, but there was nothing confused about his peevish complaint: 'I have told you often and you never would believe me that he has little [claim] to cleverness, to knowledge or any capacity for settled work. He has great talent for show off exaggeration and make believe.'[30] That he might have inherited just these qualities from Lord Randolph himself cannot have commended him to a bitterly disappointed father.

In his anger and frustration, Lord Randolph launched a stern warning at young Winston. His performance was stigmatised as 'disreputable', his style of work as 'slovenly happy-go-lucky' and 'harum-scarum', and his general conduct was castigated. Coming very close to washing his hands of his son, Lord Randolph warned him that 'I no longer attach the slightest weight to anything you may say about your own acquirements and exploits.' If Winston continued to lead 'the idle useless unprofitable life' he had hithertofore led, 'you will become a mere social wastrel, one of the hundreds of the public school failures'. The 'shabby unhappy and futile existence' which Lord Randolph prophesied for Winston was exactly what he had come to himself – it was no wonder that his message was expressed so fiercely and with such bitterness.[31]

It is only with hindsight that Lord Randolph's fears seem ludicrous. Despite their undoubted talents, both he and his brother amounted, in practice, to 'mere social wastrels', and the Marlborough past provided many other examples of the genus; nor were the Jeromes renowned for the regularity of their lives. Moreover, the next few years were to see Winston sail pretty close to the wind in his financial and personal affairs.

Lord Randolph died a poor man, ruined by his own extravagances and bank-rolled by his Jewish friends, the Rothschilds and the Cassells. Lady Randolph's style of life was not calculated to produce financial surpluses. So it need occasion no surprise that their son found it difficult to manage his finances. Whilst he was still at Sandhurst, Winston had been warned by his mother that 'you are spending too much money' and 'really must not go on like this'.[32] The very frequency with which this complaint was to be reiterated over the six years after 1894 is evidence of how close young Winston came to the fate which his father had feared.

The Fourth Hussars was an expensive regiment, and Churchill lived in the fastest set, finding himself both in financial trouble and accused of participating in the bullying of subalterns from humbler backgrounds.[33] Speaking frankly to his mother in 1898, he wrote that 'there is no doubt that we are both ... equally thoughtless – spendthrift and extravagant'; he was equally perceptive in noting that 'we both know what is good and we both like to have it. Arrangements for paying are left for the future.'[34] What he did not propose was any way of dealing with the situation. He was, and remained, easily satisfied with the best of everything, and his attitude towards finance was always Whiggish in the extreme.

But his mother, for all her extravagance, always had first call upon her devoted son. But in return, she did her best to foster his prospects. Soldiering in the late-Victorian era, at least for those of Churchill's class, had about it a good deal of the air of a prolonged adventure. Those with good contacts could use them to secure postings to 'interesting' billets, and Lady Randolph was second to none in pulling strings. But young Winston was not merely looking for adventure in the field. He had nurtured hopes that despite his father's disapproval, he might yet soften his heart by entering politics and working with him. But Churchill was over-romanticising when he wrote *My Early Life*; as long as Lord Randolph lived, he would go on being regarded as 'that boy'.[35] His father's early death removed this shadow and provided instead a myth: 'There remained for me only to pursue his aims and vindicate his memory.'[36] The shadow provided more encouragement than the reality ever could have done. 'Politics', he told his mother in August 1895, was a 'fine game to play' and it was 'well worth waiting for a good hand – before really plunging'; soldiering, however pleasant an occupation was not, he now felt, 'my *métier*'.[37]

But even as this ambition burgeoned, Churchill was painfully aware that finance was not the only obstacle in its way. His habitual optimism concerning money prevented that subject circumscribing him, but the other difficulty was not so easily surmounted. Thus far his education had been 'purely technical' and, as a result, he felt that 'my mind has never received that polish which for instance Oxford or Cambridge gives'.[38] This sense of being inadequately educated was to persevere, and even when he was appointed to his first Ministerial post he would write to his old history master that, 'I fear I am sadly lacking in scholarly education.'[39]

The story of how Churchill battled to overcome this handicap is, justly, one of the most famous in *My Early Life*. Posted to India in 1895, he spent the afternoons reading in his tent whilst his peers slept or played cards. As early as August 1895 he set himself the tasks of acquiring the rudiments of political economy as well as reading Gibbon and Lecky.[40] He had taken himself off into the Army and, with his father's death, had decided that that was a false move; so he now proceeded to create himself in the image of his father – as far as that was possible. He learnt Lord Randolph's speeches by heart and, through reading *Hansard* and the *Annual Register*, he came to be familiar with the political era which his father had adorned. The Army was to be a springboard, not a sofa.

The caste of mind created by this autodidact's education will be considered in the next chapter. Here we are concerned with the efforts which the young subaltern made to ensure that he became famous. With his mother's social contacts, Churchill tried to be posted to areas where he could be expected to see military action. This was not because he was a brave soldier (although he was); action provided two routes to fame: the swift one attained through some glorious feat of arms; and the slower but safer one of writing about the campaigns he had seen. The appetite of the late Victorians for heroes and heroics was formidable, and it found satisfaction in reports from the far-flung battle-lines where thin red lines of ''eroes' defended the ramparts of Empire. If, as in 1895, Churchill could not get himself to the North-West Frontier, then he was quite willing to undergo his baptism of fire elsewhere – provided he could write about it for the press. Of course there was always the possibility that he would be killed, but he did not think that likely: 'the fact of having seen service with British troops while still a young man must give me more weight politically'; and 'besides this I think I am of an adventurous disposition and shall enjoy myself'.[41]

His first adventure was one which he organised himself in late 1895, when he obtained leave to go to Cuba, where he witnessed the war between the Americans and the Cuban rebels. He enjoyed Cuba, where he celebrated his twenty-first birthday by coming under fire for the first time, and he found America exhilarating: 'a great crude, strong young people . . . like a boisterous healthy boy among enervated but well-bred ladies and gentlemen'.[42] It was a description which many would have applied to Lieutenant Churchill. Writing about campaigns was something which some soldiers did, but gallivanting off to some foreign war, and then writing about it for the *Daily Graphic* with all the exuberant self-confidence at his command, was an exercise which brought mixed results.

It certainly brought the name of Winston Churchill to a wider public, and Lady Randolph made sure that her important political friends noticed the articles, and arranged for her son to meet the great men of the Conservative Party, such as the Colonial Secretary, Joseph Chamberlain. Because of Lord Randolph's early death, his contemporaries were still in positions of power, and his son was more than willing to satisfy their curiosity to meet 'Randolph's boy'.[43] This use of his family connections to push himself into places where more conventional souls might have held that he had no business, his easy assumption that such favours were his due, and his unsoldierly excursions into journalism, were all essential components of what amounted to a personal public-relations exercise; but what the young Churchill was blind to was the effect it would all have on other people. Consideration for the feelings of others was something which he never did acquire. Henry Herbert Asquith, who as Liberal Prime Minister did more than anyone to foster Churchill's career, caught this exactly when he wrote: 'He never fairly gets alongside the person he is talking to, because he is so much more interested in himself and his own preoccupations . . . than in anything his neighbour has to contribute.'[44] The very characteristics which enabled him to push himself were equally those which raised obstacles in his path. Ambition and youth, like the ankles of a lady, were likely to arouse passions unless decorously concealed – and Churchill was seldom able to conceal anything, least of all the ambition which drove him.

But regular soldiering could not be avoided, and in September 1896 he set off with his regiment for India. Churchill did not like India. Although his father had briefly been its Secretary of State, Winston had few influential contacts there and felt far from the centre of the Empire.[45] All it did offer was a prospect of involvement in some border skirmish, polo, and the chance to enjoy a life of luxury on the cheap. To most of his contemporaries this was sufficient, but Churchill used the long periods of idleness to further his programme of reading. Gibbon and Macaulay would improve his prose style, *Hansard* and the *National Register* would give depth to the knowledge of recent politics which a study of his father's speeches had begun. Lord Randolph's example, like that of Lord Chatham who had led England to victory in the Seven Years' War, convinced the young Churchill that, far from being the harlot of the political arts, oratory gave its possessor 'a power more durable than that of a great king'; as Chatham's example had shown, the orator could survive any political setback, for whoever commanded its power would always be 'formidable'. Churchill determined to master it, despite the fact that, like his father, he suffered from a curious inability to enunciate the letter 's' clearly; it was not quite a lisp, but it sounded like one.[46] Long hours practising in front of mirrors, declaiming speeches which he had committed to memory, bore witness to Churchill's determination to succeed. He comforted himself with the reflection that 'rhetorical power is neither wholly bestowed, nor wholly acquired, but cultivated'. He was sure that the talent was his 'by nature' and that all he needed was to practise the art to make it his chief weapon.[47]

If Churchill was training his memory and his tongue, he was also acquiring through his programme of reading a caste of mind which was to remain recognisably late-Victorian. His own experiences left him with great sympathy for adult education: 'these are the very people who ought to be helped – because they are helping themselves far more than a stodgy boy of fourteen, sulkily reading his lessons'.[48] But the defect in Churchill's own programme was that it was self-education with a limited purpose; it provided no training in learning how to think, how to weigh arguments, and how to judge your own ideas against those of others. In one sense this was an advantage, for it gave a freshness and enthusiasm to his speaking and writing which was appealing. But in another sense it was a defect. The ideas he accumulated he retained, and he did not find it easy to adapt them to later changes. But what were these ideas?

2

A Victorian Frame of Mind

Most self-made men are well satisfied with the product of their labours, and Churchill was no exception. To those who accused him of changing his mind, he would reply that, on the contrary, he had seldom changed; it was the political Parties to which he had belonged who had changed.[1] He never stopped to ask himself whether his own inability to change was a good or a bad thing. But by the time *My Early Life* was published in 1930, the world it depicted had all but vanished, and to be endowed still with its caste of mind was not necessarily an advantage. As Leo Amery, his older contemporary at Harrow, noted in 1929: 'The key to Winston is to realise that he is Mid-Victorian, steeped in the politics of his father's period, and unable ever to get the modern point of view.'[2]

Modern literary critics seem to have little truck with the idea that the hero of a novel speaks the words of his author, but as they also have little truck with Churchill, their opinion need not detain us. Churchill told his mother in 1897 that 'all my philosophy is put into the mouth of my hero';[3] we may thus read his only novel *Savrola* to discern the caste of mind inculcated by all that reading in the hot Indian afternoons. Savrola's bookshelves, unsurprisingly, were identical to those of Lieutenant Churchill: 'the philosophy of Schopenhauer divided Kant from Hegel', whilst Gibbon, Macaulay, Darwin and the Bible all jostled them for space.[4] The 'armour of his philosophy' which Savrola, the leader of the forces of liberty, donned in order to gaze 'at the world as from a distance',[5] amounted, in practice, to what one historian has called 'a pagan mish-mash'[6] – or, in Churchill's own description, 'the sad, cynical, evolutionary philosophy which is so characteristic of modern thought and which claims a good deal of my sympathy'.[7]

That 'sea of faith', the ebb of which Matthew Arnold caught so hauntingly in *Dover Beach*, had receded even further by Churchill's youth, and the reading upon which he embarked did nothing to reverse the process for the young subaltern. The deism and Augustan disdain for religion in general and Christianity in particular, which he derived from Gibbon, was well expressed in his description of the plight of Lieutenant Tiro, who, in a crisis, found that 'his religion, like that of most soldiers, was of little help; it was merely a jumble of formulas, seldom repeated, hardly understood and never investigated'.[8]

These Gibbonian resonances were reinforced by his reading of that minor classic of humanistic atheism, *The Martyrdom of Man* by Winwood Reade.

Reade, drawing upon T. H. Huxley and other popularisers of Darwin, drew conclusions from the theory of evolution which its best-known discoverer failed to do. The implications of Darwin's theories were bleak, especially to generations schooled in the naturalistic theology of Paley and soothed by the pantheism of Wordsworth. Suddenly, in place of a beneficent nature and a caring God, Man was alone in the universe. Not only that, his place in the order of things was no different from that of any other species – for, as Tennyson put it, nature was 'careless of the individual, so careful of the type'. The purpose of existence was nothing more than to perpetuate the species – ethics, morals, religion, all these were no more than man-made comforters; man was no more than an 'infant crying in the night' and an 'infant crying for the light'. But men like Huxley and Reade were too much children of their age to be satisfied with the anarchic implications of such a situation – and where Thomas Hardy could write about such a world, they needed to alleviate pessimism and reinforce morality with a 'scientific' explanation.[9]

Reade's explanation carried total conviction with Churchill. Although, like Reade, he could not escape visions of the bleak side of evolutionary theory, he used them to strike Byronic poses. There were times when, like Savrola as he contemplated the deaths which his revolution would cause, Churchill was tempted to ask 'What was the good of it all?', and to get no reassuring answer back;[10] in the end the universe would die and be 'sepulchered in the cold darkness of negation'.[11] But despite this, and the insignificance of the indi-vidual, there was more purpose to life than those who held that might was right could comprehend. Like Huxley, Churchill found that purpose in the belief that 'organisms imbued with moral fitness would ultimately rise above those whose virtue is physical'; the 'motive force' in the universe was 'con-stant' and its tendency was upwards – civilisation would triumph over barbar-ism because its 'virtues' were 'of a higher type', and it was the morally 'fittest' who would survive: 'we cannot say that a good man will always overcome a knave; but the evolutionist will not hesitate to affirm that the nation with the highest ideals will succeed'.[12]

All Churchill's other reading reinforced this humanistic Darwinism, and when it was combined with the view of English history which he drew from Macaulay, the result was a powerful vision of England as the beacon of this civilising mission that made him the Whig-imperialist he was to remain. A confidence in Britain's imperial mission and in her destiny to be 'great' remained with him always; but this did not suffice to make him a Con-servative.

Churchill himself was aware that his views on the world were hardly those of the average Conservative. On the great question of the relations between the Church and the State, Churchill was a complete Erastian: 'If a Church is "established" . . . it is obvious that the State should be able to insist on effective control.'[13] This was closer to the view of the Liberation Society and the nonconformist Liberals than it was to Salisburian Conservatism. The same was true of Churchill's 'advanced' views on matters such as the extension of the franchise. In *Savrola* his sympathy with the rebels and with democratic methods of government is plain, and he took the view that 'ultimately "one man, one vote" is logically and morally certain'.[14] But he was no radical democrat. Time would be needed and the lower classes would have to be 'levelled up', presumably led by those like Savrola possessed of a 'greater soul and stronger mind'.[15] Churchill's democratic thought was of a distinctly Whiggish caste – the aristocracy leading the 'people'.

Young Winston's views were, for all their idiosyncratic acquisition and mode of expression, not dissimilar to those held by many of his Liberal-minded contemporaries. He certainly felt an affinity with Liberalism, telling Lady Randolph in March 1897 that he was 'a Liberal in all but name'. It was, he said, only that Party's addiction to Home Rule for Ireland which kept him from joining it.[16] That was true as far as it went, but it was only part of the filial piety which made him want to enter Parliament as a Conservative.

In the great schism of 1886 caused by Gladstone's commitment to Home Rule for Ireland, Lord Randolph had played a prominent role. As the Liberal Party split, so he encouraged Joseph Chamberlain, one of the leaders of the Liberal Unionists, to maintain close co-operation with the Conservative Party. The untimely demise of Lord Randolph's political career prevented anything coming of this alliance, but Winston saw himself as the inheritor of the tradition for which his father had stood. As Churchill studied his father's career, he joined the ranks of those who believed that Lord Randolph had been the true successor to Disraeli: a prophet of 'Tory Democracy' and the inheritor of 'Elijah's mantle'. Disraeli left a rich mythology to his adopted Party, one of its most important parts being the idea of 'One Nation Toryism'. The Conservative Party, this line of thought went, was the only true 'national' Party. Disraeli had carried out social reforms and given recognition to the right of trades unions to picket, during his 1874–80 administration; for Churchill, Lord Randolph represented this tradition, as opposed to the aristocratic, reactionary Conservatism of Hatfield House and Lord Salisbury.

This then was where Churchill saw himself fitting into the Conservative Party – or rather the Conservative and Unionist Party as it was after the formal alliance in 1895. Only 'obstinate' reactionaries like Salisbury, 'lack-a-daisical cynics' like his nephew, Arthur James Balfour, and 'superior Oxford prigs' such as Lord Curzon, failed to support 'Tory Democracy', with its potential for winning over the lower orders.[17] This was one view. But as all the men whom Churchill mentioned so disdainfully were the leading figures in the Party whose ranks he wished to join, it did not bode well for his political future. Lord Randolph's adherence to the Union meant that his son had to support the Unionist Party, but his own personal programme of domestic reform, accompanied by universal male suffrage and a progressive income tax, would have raised the eyebrows of Conservatives beyond the purlieus of Hatfield. But this was Churchill's policy at home. Abroad, imperialism would be pursued, but there would be no intervention in the affairs of Europe; isolation was the order of the day here: 'Peace and Power abroad – Prosperity and Progress at home' was 'the creed of Tory Democracy'.[18] Churchill recognised that most 'Tory Democrats' were 'Tories first and Democrats after';[19] the reverse was true with him.

But at the time when he was formulating these views, the possibility of their practical expression from within the Unionist Party exercised him less than the fear that he might never be able to realise them at all. He needed to make money and to produce a book on a military campaign to 'bring my personality before the electorate'.[20]

Churchill wanted his mother to use her influence to get him posted to the Sudan, where Lord Kitchener was mounting a campaign to reconquer the territory from the heirs of the Mahdi, but her charms were not the sort to prevail upon the stern, imperial warlord, so Churchill had to languish at home. But Lady Randolph finally came up trumps. Her friendship with Sir Bindon Blood secured an opportunity for Churchill to see active service on the North-West Frontier with the Malakand Field Force; it was not the reconquest of the Sudan, but it would do. Campaigning offered the possibility of military distinction, newspaper articles and even a book, all of which would bring closer the political career he longed for. War also offered the chance of an early grave, but Churchill did not think that death awaited him on the North-West Frontier: 'I have faith in my star – that I am intended to do something in the world.'[21]

The Malakand campaign allowed Churchill to show not only his bravery, but also the speed and application with which he pursued his literary ambitions. *The Malakand Field Force* was published in March 1898, having taken him five weeks to write – and he had to set aside his novel to do the job.[22] This haste, and the efforts at proof-reading of his uncle, Moreton Frewin, produced a host of errors which caused an embarrassed Churchill to dismiss the book as an 'eyesore',[23] but it did bring him offers of further work from the literary world, and praise from his mother's friends, including the Prince of Wales.[24] Churchill, however, was disappointed that 'the present edition does not reach where it is intended. It is all very well to write for democracy, but you must publish at democratic prices.'[25] He could not afford to be caviare to the general – that is why he wrote for the popular press and lost no opportunity of publicising himself. As Lord Randolph's son he was automatically of interest to the readers of the large-circulation, popular newspapers, which had come into existence in the 1880s under the impact of wider elementary education – and the commercial genius of Alfred Harmsworth, founder of the *Daily Mail*, and later, as Lord Northcliffe, the prototype of the press baron.

It was all very well for the head of the Cecil clan, in the seclusion of his library at Hatfield, to dismiss the *Mail* as 'a paper written by office boys for office boys', but young Churchill realised that with the advent of a larger electorate, the 'office boys' had the vote. The old methods of electioneering would no longer do; it was necessary, if a larger audience was to be reached, for politicians to impress a clear 'image' on the public mind. As Churchill told his mother, this was 'not so much a question of brains as of character and originality'.[26] In this, as in his tireless self-promotion, Churchill showed himself a child of the new political age which dawned after the 1884 Reform Act. 'I should never care to bolster up a sham reputation and hold my position by disguising my personality,'[27] he told his mother in January 1898. Indeed, such an exercise would have been pointless, for it was that personality, writ large for consumption by an electorate which was nearly as unsophisticated as himself, which was to become Churchill's main political tool. Lord Moran was nearly half a century out in his calculation that Churchill had allowed himself to become 'a character' in 1940 because 'none knew better that the public must see clearly the outline of their heroes';[28] this was a lesson Churchill had imbibed before his political career started.

Churchill's too overt use of 'influence' to get himself posted to spots where he could write books caused a reaction against him in parts of the Army, and he was only able to get himself to the Sudan in 1898 by courtesy of the help of the Prime Minister, Lord Salisbury. This enabled Churchill to ride in the last great cavalry charge at Omdurman – a classic moment in *My Early Life*, and a permanent topic of after-dinner reminiscence. It also provided the raw material for his next, and more controversial, book, *The River War*, which was published in December 1899.

The River War marked a considerable advance on Churchill's previous work. This time the adventure story was seasoned with philosophical reflections and downright criticisms of his superior officers, especially Kitchener. The book revealed that Churchill's imperialism was as Liberal as the rest of his views. Although he was prepared to use Salisbury's influence, he regarded the Prime Minister as 'an able and obstinate man, who joins the brains of a statesman with the susceptibilities of a mule'.[29] The Salisburian quotation with which he decorated the title page of *The Malakand Field Force* was used with the Churchillian tongue firmly in cheek. Salisbury called frontier wars 'the surf that marks the edge of the wave of civilisation', but Churchill's experience at Malakand, and then during the River War, made him draw different conclusions. Although 'no one in the world' was 'more proud of the British Empire',[30] Churchill's admiration was not unconditional. He regarded the British achievement in India with pride, as 'an accurate measure of the distance through which development aided by civilisation has carried the human species',[31] but this made him all the more critical when the British fell below what he considered the level of events. Just as Macaulay could not condone the *realpolitik* of Warren Hastings or Robert Clive, so too did Churchill regard Salisbury's 'forward' policy. Whilst describing the bravery of the British troops in both his early books, Churchill was critical, first in private but then in public, of the mainsprings of British policy.

In Macaulayesque language, he described the Malakand campaign to his mother as 'financially ruinous ... morally ... wicked, and politically it is a blunder'.[32] The whole thing would not have been necessary save for the home Government's 'forward policy', which he described as 'an awful business' as the 'tribesmen can give nothing but bullets'.[33] He was scornful of the way in which patriotism degenerated into jingoism[34] and of the way the public seemed to imagine that wars could be won without loss of life: 'the sooner they realise that this is impossible, and that no tactics can prevent bullets from hitting men, the better'.[35] He expected the British to be on the side of liberty and of progress, and when they were not he was unsparing in his criticism, hence his condemnation in the first edition of *The River War* of Kitchener's conduct in taking the skull of the Mahdi and fashioning a drinking vessel from it, and in failing to take care of the wounded properly.[36]

'Tory Democracy' was an imprecise creed, but if its formularies comprehended such impeccably Liberal sentiments, then there were perhaps grounds for asking in what particulars save Home Rule it differed from Liberalism. But ancestry had cast Churchill's lot in the Conservative Party. He had made his first political speech at a Primrose League gathering in Bath in 1897 and his second the following summer at Bradford. This last experience convinced him that he did, indeed, have a future in politics, confirming as it did that his speech impediment was no barrier to success and, most vitally, that 'my ideas and modes of thought are pleasing to men'.[37]

Churchill's popular 'fame' was purchased at two prices which he was willing to pay. The risk of death whilst in action was ever-present, but Churchill did not let it disturb him; he could not believe that 'the Gods would create so potent a being as myself for so prosaic an ending'.[38] The second price was paid in the distrust which his overt ambition aroused in others. There were, indeed, times when he questioned his own sincerity, acknowledging the truth in Cecil Rhodes's criticism that he did 'not care so much for the principles I advocate as for the impression which my words produce' and the reputation which they gave him.[39] But for all this, and his outrageous egotism, Churchill was more than a creation of his own hyperbole. A self-educated 'Tory Democrat' and Liberal imperialist, there was a tension between his imbibed views on democracy and his instincts, but he resolved it to his own satisfaction by the concept of the leadership of 'great souls' – such as Savrola, and himself. That the 'masses' might lead themselves was not an idea which ever readily occurred to Churchill.

The River War certainly brought Churchill plenty of publicity, but some of it proved that P. T. Barnum was wrong when he said that there was no such thing as bad publicity. The criticisms he so freely levelled at Kitchener aroused the hostility of the military establishment,[40] and the Prince of Wales spoke for many when he told Winston: 'I must say I think that an officer serving in a campaign should not write letters for the newspapers or express strong opinions of how the operations are carried out.'[41]

As early as 1897 Churchill had decided to spend no more than two further years in the Army,[42] but the prospect of having nothing to live on if he did resign his commission was hardly encouraging. He considered applying for a home posting, or perhaps a transfer to the Intelligence Branch, which would have allowed him to pursue his political ambitions but retain his place.[43] The financial problems besetting him were acute.[44] Despite the money earned from his despatches for the *Morning Post* during the Sudan campaign, and the money he might earn from *Savrola* and any other literary work, the outlook was not good. As he told his mother in December 1898, 'Poverty produced by thoughtlessness will rot your life of peace and happiness and mine of success.'[45] The prospect of failure appalled him: 'It will break my heart, for I have nothing else but ambition to cling to.'[46]

These were not prospects which would induce most men to resign their posts and gamble on success, but then unless he did 'unusual things' Churchill did not see 'what chance I have of being more than an average person'.[47] Even when he resigned his commission in March 1899, he had no plan of how he was going to achieve his great ambition – merely faith that he would do so. Napoleon used to ask not whether his generals were any good, but whether they had luck. Churchill's faith in his 'star' may have been nothing more than a continuation of infantile feelings of omnipotence,[48] but it is not surprising it persisted – events seemed to suggest that he had Napoleon's vital quality. His luck and courage took him through the frontier campaigns in India with no serious injuries, and he rode in the cavalry charge at Omdurman, one arm strapped up, firing his pistol at the Dervishes, and came out unscathed;[49] it was little wonder that his faith in his 'star' should have waxed.

Churchill left the Army in 1899 and, at first, it appeared that his gamble had not paid off. His own reputation, allied to his father's name and his mother's influence, was sufficient to extract from the Conservative Party the nomination for one of the Oldham seats at a by-election, but, despite a vigorous campaign, he failed to get elected.[50] Churchill's reaction to his wife's remark that the 1945 election result was a 'blessing in disguise' is well-known, but in this instance the blessing was, indeed, well-disguised. Had he won the by-election, he would have been presented with the prospect of another election within the year and how to pay both for it and his own existence; as it was, events conspired in his favour. The outbreak of the Boer War provided him with another journalistic beano, and what at first seemed another mischance turned out to be the foundation of his fortune.

Of all the events which brought Churchill's 'personality' before a wide public audience, the capture by the Boers of a military train in which he was travelling in November 1899, and his subsequent escape from captivity, were by far the most important. That Lord Randolph's son had been captured was news, albeit of a sort all too distressingly common in November and December 1899, as the British began to realise that the Boers were formidable opponents; but that he should have escaped was, in one of the blackest periods for the British, sensational news.[51] Churchill became an instant popular hero – there were not, after all, many other candidates for the post. As ever, controversy dogged his steps, and it was not long before stories began to circulate that Churchill had broken his parole with the Boers and left two of his companions in the lurch in order to make good his own escape.[52] Lord Rosslyn, who saw service at Ladysmith and was correspondent for the *Mail*, made these aspersions public in his memoir, *Twice Captured*, published in 1900.[53]

Churchill denied that he had done anything wrong, telling the Prince of Wales that the charge was 'a cruel and wicked falsehood'.[54] But the stories that he had behaved dishonourably in leaving behind the two comrades who had originally planned the escape, circulated for years afterwards, becoming, in their very vagueness, part of the 'proof' that Churchill was unreliable.[55] As late as 1930, with the publication of *My Early Life*, the charges resurfaced, but Churchill maintained that he had acted in 'strict good faith'.[56]

None of this clouded Churchill's celebrity at the end of 1899. A famous figure in every British household with access to a newspaper, he had at last come before 'the democracy'. This stood him in good stead for the contest at Oldham in the general election of October 1900, but it did more than that: it also provided him with an income. Turning lecturer, he toured first England and then the United States, amassing the tremendous sum of £10,000 by his efforts.[57] He now had, with careful management, that competence which he needed to be independent. The great war hero could hardly escape being elected for Oldham on his 'Tory Democrat' platform.[58] Those who doubted the subaltern's 'star' might have been given pause for thought by such a concatenation of circumstances: Churchill, who did not doubt, was merely more convinced than ever that he was marked out for great things.

But election to Parliament in the Conservative–Unionist interest meant that the time was approaching when the consonance between his 'Tory Democrat' ideas and the policy of his Party would be tested. In so far as anything in politics is inevitable, Churchill's quarrelling with his Party was. The ideas which have already been examined were not those of the average Conservative MP. His first try at Oldham in 1899 had revealed the sort of problems which were likely to arise.

Religion was not a topic which greatly engaged Churchill's attention, but it was one about which large sections of the electorate felt strongly. When Churchill's agent in Oldham told him that something called the Clerical Tithes Bill, which was designed to bring greater equality into clerical salaries, was an object of aversion to nonconformists, of whom there were many in the borough, he was quite willing to disown it. This brought down upon his head a flood of rebukes for abandoning a policy about which the Party felt strongly. Other examples soon multiplied.

3

A Dissident Unionist

A man who believed in universal male suffrage, progressive taxation and social reform, and who attached no importance to protecting the position of the Church of England, was always going to find life in the Conservative Party difficult. When, as in Churchill's case, these views were combined with a personal manner which could only be described as 'pushing', and a lack of respect for Conservative shibboleths and the grey-beards who led the Party, it was likely that the difficulties would become major. But that is not to say that Churchill was bound to part company with the Conservatives.

The Viceroy of India, Lord Curzon, was an accurate prophet when he warned Churchill that there was 'no more difficult position than that of being on the benches behind a Government. It is so hard to strike the mean between independence and loyalty.'[1] Grandees like Joe Chamberlain used to say that as Winston was young he could 'afford not to hurry too much',[2] but that was to mistake the nature of the beast. His Cabinet colleague, the Secretary of State for War, St John Broderick, showed more acuity when, in congratulating Churchill upon his election, he commented that it was a shame they were not going to be in opposition as 'your artillery will inevitably be directed against us'.[3]

Because Churchill crossed swords with his leaders from the start, as a prelude to crossing the floor of the House in 1903, and because of his reputation as a self-willed, pugnacious individual, it is easy to see him as a natural rebel; he was no such thing. Churchill was certainly a young man in a hurry, but young men usually are, and the art of political management is to ensure that their energy is utilised and their ambitions encouraged. Churchill's career suggests that he responded well to good management. On the whole he prospered under the aegis of a leader who gave him sympathy and responsibility: Asquith after 1908 and Stanley Baldwin between 1924 and 1929 are obvious examples. The 'tragedy', as Churchill himself later recognised, was 'that Balfour had never bothered to get hold of him when he was a young Conservative MP . . . if he had he would probably have gone down with him'.[4]

Arthur James Balfour had been associated with Lord Randolph in the early 1880s in the 'Fourth Party': a group of rebellious, young(ish) Conservatives who had harassed Gladstone in the Commons. A philosopher, the aesthetic (even slightly precious) side of Balfour's character was captured in one of his nick-names, 'Pretty Fanny'. But anyone who, seeing his languid manner, took the slim, elegant bachelor for a weak man, was wide of the mark. When his uncle, Lord Salisbury, appointed him Chief Secretary for Ireland, there had been gasps of astonishment; but by the time he left that post, he was known as 'Bloody Balfour'. By 1900 he was the obvious successor to his uncle, and with Salisbury's health failing, his accession to the Premiership would be at not too distant a date. Churchill came to have for him an admiration which he extended to few others; fascinated by his conversation and his intellect, Churchill would have willingly followed him, but no lead was given.[5]

There was, of course, no reason why Balfour should have made any great efforts in Churchill's direction. The name which Lord Randolph had left behind in the Conservative Party was one which encouraged the House of Cecil to distrust him and any heirs to the tradition which he had espoused. In the absence of any warm welcome from his leaders, Churchill was left to his own devices. This exercise was, whenever it was indulged in, seldom productive of good relations between Churchill and whichever Party he belonged to. In harness he was excellent; out of it he was a loose cannon on the deck.

There were three circumstances which militated in favour of friction between Churchill and his Party over the next two years. The one issue which, back in 1897, had tied him to the Conservative Party was the question of the union between England and Ireland, but that question had fallen into the background of Westminster politics, and the issues which replaced it were not ones which emphasised the common ground which Churchill had with the Conservatives. This sense of being out of tune with his Party was fostered by his major literary activity during this time, the writing of Lord Randolph's official biography. He started the book feeling that his father had been badly treated, and ended it with the burning conviction that he had been scurvily handled by the House of Cecil. His attachment to Party orthodoxy was not strengthened by any demands from his constituency, which, as a marginal seat, contained many Liberals who found their MP's heretical views quite acceptable.

But perhaps the greatest obstacle in the way of Churchill being accepted by the Conservative hierarchy was the shadow of Lord Randolph. Just as Randolph's personality had been unstable, and his character considered to be 'unsound', then so too were those of the son who sought to model himself so closely upon the father he idolised. The frock-coat, the stoop forward in debate, the stance at ease, with hands on hips, the love of drama, the unabashed egotism, all these resemblances may have brought Churchill closer to his father, but they did not inspire trust upon the front bench. If there was a natural interest in Churchill as Lord Randolph's son, it was accompanied by the shadow of the suspicions which were raised by his father's ghost.

As Churchill worked away at Lord Randolph's life, he came to have his own view of the relationship between his father and the House of Cecil. The

Cecils, it seemed, had used Lord Randolph for their own ends: his oratory had damaged Gladstone's Government and had destroyed Salisbury's rival for the leadership of the Conservatives, Sir Stafford Northcote. Lord Randolph's contacts with Chamberlain had been useful in 1886, and his platform speeches and 'Tory Democratic' policies had been electorally advantageous, but then in 1886 the Cecils had let him fall and made sure that he stayed out of office. There was, of course, much to be said on the other side, but Churchill did not see it. It seemed to him that his father would have been better advised, instead of struggling against the 'old gang', to have sought allies elsewhere.[6]

In the atmosphere thus engendered by Churchill's study, his own differences of opinion with the Party helped to create a climate of acrimony. His maiden speech, on 18 February 1901, was watched with interest by the many MPs who had known his father. It was a good performance, but his declaration that 'if I were a Boer I hope I should be fighting in the field', whilst attracting favourable notice from the Liberal press, earned him criticism in the Tory papers.[7] Churchill's views were, in part, a reflection of the sympathy for nationalist revolts against foreign oppression which he had expressed in *Savrola*. In *The River War*, he thought that the Mahdist revolt was, in some ways, understandable and even laudable; it was not (heaven forfend) the expression of religious fanaticism which had been alleged, rather it was nationalistic in character. He showed sympathy too for the bravery of the Dervishes, and in a passage that with hindsight is oddly prophetic, he declared his hope that 'if evil days should come upon our country' and the last British army had collapsed, 'there would be some – even in these modern days – who would not care to accustom themselves to the new order of things and tamely survive the disaster'.[8] Such sentiments were hardly those of the average jingoistic Conservative. Nor was he any closer to the species in his view that to take revenge on the Boers would be 'morally wrong'.[9]

In *The River War* and *The Malakand Field Force* there had been muted criticisms of the 'forward policy' in imperial affairs which Chamberlain's aggressive imperialism had fostered. Churchill had confined himself to noting that it had 'precluded the possibility of peace', and said that it would be for the historian to pronounce upon its correctness.[10] To be asked, as an MP, to vote for a scheme which would reorganise the Army in a manner which would make more such campaigns possible was, therefore, likely to mean asking too much of Churchill's loyalty too soon. As early as his third Parliamentary speech Churchill was attacking the Government, with St John Broderick as his target and retrenchment upon Army expenditure as his theme.[11] It was easy for the Secretary of State to respond to what became Churchill's major campaign by accusing him of an 'hereditary desire to run imperialism on the cheap',[12] but that missed the point, just as much as allegations that he was an impatient adventurer. In raising Lord Randolph's 'tattered flag', Winston was doing more than demonstrating filial piety; he was exposing the Liberal foundations of his own thought. He had two main objections to the plan to reorganise the Army so as to provide six corps, three of which would be available for foreign service, and both of them were impeccably Liberal. In the first place, to spend £31 million on the Army was 'intensely stupid'; in the second place, the desire to do so 'betrays immoral yearnings'.[13] A vast increase in expenditure on the Army would alarm other powers without increasing Britain's strength, which depended, as it had always done, upon the Navy. Over the next three years this potent combination of inherited crusade and Liberal instincts was to lead to a series of speeches opposing what Churchill called 'the great English fraud'.[14]

If attacking the Party leadership and a desire for 'imperialism on the cheap' were both family traits, then Churchill showed further devotion to his father's memory by gathering together a latter-day Fourth Party, which even had (as Lord Randolph's had) a member of the 'Hotel Cecil' on board – in this case Salisbury's youngest son, Lord Hugh Cecil, in whose honour its members were called 'Hughligans'. Rebelliousness was to be expected of Lord Randolph's boy, and no one held against him his participation in such a group, but it was one thing to criticise the Government in a debate or two, and another to make a habit of it; as Chamberlain warned, there was 'no room in politics for a dissentient Tory'.[15] But in his views on the Army Scheme, and his advocacy of lenient treatment for the Boers, Churchill's sentiments were not simply dissentient, they were Liberal, and it was radicals like John Burns and little Englanders like Gladstone's biographer, John Morley, who wrote to congratulate him on his campaign for economy,[16] and Whig grandees such as Earl Spencer who found themselves pleasantly surprised at how 'sound and liberal' his views on the war were.[17]

If debates on the Army and the Boer War exposed the Liberal foundations of Churchill's thought, and if writing Lord Randolph's biography suggested that 'Tory Democracy' might not prosper under the Cecilian Conservative Party, it was association with Lord Rosebery which first suggested to Churchill the possibilities of political infidelity. Six months before Chamberlain raised the subject upon which Churchill was to cross the floor, he was writing to Rosebery that 'if some definite issue – such as the Tariff – were to arise', it would remove the difficulties lying in the path of the formation of a 'Tory–Liberal' coalition.[18] Churchill had first sought out Rosebery because he had known Lord Randolph, but he stayed to listen because he found him fascinating.[19] Archibald Philip Primrose, the fifth Earl of Rosebery, was an enigma. Liberal Prime Minister from 1893 to 1894, he had resigned the Liberal leadership thereafter, retiring in a sulk like Achilles, but in his case not to his tent, but rather to his mansions at Mentmore, the Durdans and Berkeley Square. But in 1901–2 it seemed that he was once more emerging, and that in a fluid, political situation he might act as the rallying-point for a 'Tory–Liberal' combination which might suit young Churchill's requirements.

The Liberal Party, fissiparous at the best of times, had suffered particularly badly from the Boer War. On one side of the Party were those who agreed with the firebrand radical from North Wales, David Lloyd George, that the war was wrong and should be condemned; set against the Gladstonian and radical elements were the Liberal imperialists or 'Limps', Asquith, Sir Edward Grey and Richard Haldane. These men looked towards Rosebery as their leader and inspiration. It all meant a hard life for the official Liberal leader, an amiable Scots mediocrity, Sir Henry Campbell-Bannerman, especially when, in a major speech at Chesterfield in December 1901, Rosebery seemed to condemn the war and went on to urge the Liberal Party to 'wipe its slate clean' on Ireland, abandon the outworn radicalism of the 1893 Newcastle programme, and take its stand on the subject of 'national efficiency'. In February 1902 he established the Liberal League as an instrument for promoting his views.[20]

Rosebery's appeal met with mixed fortunes, but to a young MP who was already finding the strain of confining his imbibed Liberalism within the Conservative Party considerable, the prospect of the creation of a 'middle Party' was irresistible. Lord Hugh Cecil was sceptical – 'that may be a very proper course when there is a Middle Party to join'[21] – but for Churchill, Rosebery offered a Party 'free at once from the sordid selfishness and callousness of Toryism on the one hand and the blind appetites of the Radical masses on the other': a 'Tory–Liberal Party'.[22] The problem was that any desertion of the Conservative Party without due cause would look like treason. But in March 1903 Joseph Chamberlain's declaration that he favoured a system of imperial tariffs provided just the excuse Churchill had been looking for. As Churchill told the newspaper magnate, Lord Northcliffe, in August 1903: 'I think this is the time for a central Government and if Lord Rosebery lets the opportunity pass it may never return.'[23] Lord Hugh was cautious, but then his filial piety acted as an anchor to the Conservative Party. Churchill's growing conviction that 'Tory Democracy' would always be stifled by the 'old gang', who had destroyed his father, led him in another direction.

Churchill accepted the system of free trade which Britain had had since 1846 as one of the foundations of her imperial greatness, and, overlooking his father's flirtation with 'fair trade' in the 1880s, he took his stand against the introduction of tariffs on imports. Many Conservatives held similar views, but others rallied to Chamberlain's standard like men to a crusade. For Balfour, who had become Prime Minister in 1902, it was the last thing he needed. A Prime Minister who has not won his own position is always vulnerable, and when the most powerful figure in the Conservative and Unionist alliance chose to challenge one of the fundamental dogmas of British politics, that vulnerability increased enormously. But Balfour's danger might be Churchill's opportunity. When the matter was debated in the House on

28 May 1903, Churchill prophesied that the 'old Conservative Party' would 'disappear', to be replaced by something like the American Republican Party, 'rich, materialist and secular'.[24] It would certainly have suited Churchill's purpose if this had come to pass.

Churchill was convinced that tariff reform, or 'Protection', would result in a 'landslide' against the Government at the next election; putting taxes on basic food-stuffs seemed like evidence of an electoral death-wish. As he told Northcliffe in September 1903, 'the smug contentment and self-satisfaction of the Government will be astonished by what is coming to meet them'. With 'a little care' he thought that 'we might very easily set up a great Central Government, neither Protectionist nor pro-Boer, which will deal with the shocking administrative inefficiency which prevails'.[25] Churchill looked towards the Duke of Devonshire, who as Lord Hartington had led the Whig defection from the Gladstone Government in 1886, to repeat the performance by leading many Liberal Unionists out of their alliance with the Conservatives.[26] Devonshire certainly possessed the stature to head such a revolt, but Lord Hugh was right to doubt whether, at the age of seventy, the Duke was the man for such 'visionary' enterprises.[27]

A Whig grandee, who cultivated an image of himself as a man above ambition or intrigue, 'Harty-Tarty', as he was unkindly known in circles not far from Rotten Row where the 'pretty little horse-breakers' took their equestrian promenades, was past his best. Even at his best he, like Rosebery, lacked the energy and ambition necessary to try to create a 'Central Party'. Balfour, who tried to keep him in the Cabinet when a crisis arose on the tariff issue in September, by assuring him privately that Chamberlain was going to resign, encountered problems with the Duke's vagueness. Annoyed to receive a letter of resignation from him the following day, Balfour's feelings turned to astonishment as drama gave way to high farce. Devonshire's private secretary, Lord Stanley, assured him that the Duke did not intend to go. It transpired that Devonshire, having mislaid the key to his Cabinet box, had failed to open it and had thus never seen Balfour's letter. Upon reading it the Duke withdrew his resignation.[28] His remaining credit was expended when he finally resigned in early October.

With Chamberlain stumping the country, his tariff reform league captured most local Conservative associations and the lot of the free-trade Tory was not a happy one. To men like Lord Hugh this was a source of regret; they saw themselves being driven from the Party they loved by a wave of intolerance stirred up by a man who had never been a proper Conservative. But Churchill, who had certainly never been a proper Conservative, felt somewhat differently. 'I hate the Tory Party, their men, their words and their methods,' he declared in a letter, which, with unusual sensitivity, he did not send to Lord Hugh; he was 'an English Liberal'.[29] He may not have sent the letter, but it summed up how he felt by October 1903, which made the advice which he received upon how to prevent a breach between himself and the Party somewhat otiose.

The local Party chairman in Oldham, Mr Travis-Clegg, himself a free trader, told Churchill in October that he had no chance of retaining the Conservative nomination for the seat, but advised him on how best to avoid being repudiated by the Oldham Conservative association before the next election.[30] Lord Hugh joined in these counsels of moderation, pointing out that their attempt to organise against the 'Joeites' was beginning to show signs of success.[31] It was to no avail. Rumours abounded that Churchill would stand against Chamberlain in his Birmingham fiefdom at the next election,[32] and he received a rapturous welcome from the 'large number of Liberals' at the first meeting of the Free Food League on 24 November.[33] His actions in speaking against the Government at the opening of the next session of Parliament, and in supporting a Liberal candidate at the Ludlow by-election in December, were the final straw for his constituency organisation.[34] Lord Hugh lamented his 'instability'; this, he said, was not the way to win over 'Unionists who are in doubt'.[35] But since Churchill had neither doubts nor consideration for the feelings of others, Lord Hugh was wasting paper and ink.

Lord Hugh hoped that the Conservative free traders might 'drive a hard bargain for our votes',[36] but with the Government seemingly bent on political suicide, the Liberals were not disposed to pay too high a price for the votes of those who had nowhere else to go.[37] Whilst Devonshire tried to persuade Earl Spencer and Campbell-Bannerman to come to some sort of electoral pact, Churchill let it be known that he was 'quite ready after a gap in his parliamentary career to become a Liberal'.[38] If they could pick off individual Conservatives in this way, the Liberals had even less incentive to pay any price for Lord Hugh and company. Although he still hoped for the creation of a Roseberyite 'Centre Party', Churchill evidently realised that it was not going to come from the ruins of the Liberal Party; in choosing to attack free trade, Chamberlain had united the Liberals in a way which almost made up for his helping to split them in 1886.

Contacts with the Liberal Chief Whip, Herbert Gladstone, showed Churchill that there would be no difficulty in finding a Liberal seat; indeed, as he later said, he was in the 'enviable situation' of 'a lady with several suitors'.[39] There was, however, the problem that this 'young lady' was already attached. The pro-Chamberlain Oldham association had long been discontented with Churchill, and by the end of 1903 it was expressing votes of no confidence in him. In early January 1904 it formally disavowed him, but Churchill, secure in the knowledge that both Liberal and Labour interests would not oppose him, could challenge the association to force a by-election.[40] Since a straight fight between a tariff reformer and a free-trade candidate was the last thing which the Party wanted, Churchill could remain as MP for Oldham – at least until the election. But was he a Conservative of some sort, or was he a Liberal?

Churchill's exact position was, by the beginning of 1904, a matter for speculation. The *Daily Telegraph* reported in mid-January that he was among several Unionists to whom the Party Whip would not be sent. Churchill asked Balfour whether this was so and whether it had been done on his authority.[41] The terms of his letter were so guarded that, despite his later claim that his meaning was clear, Balfour chose (perhaps mischievously) to read it as a declaration that he was 'a loyal though independent supporter of the present administration'.[42] Churchill's response to this hardly clarified the situation. Writing on 2 February, he told Balfour that he had 'expressed no desire . . . to receive the Government Whips. . . . I neither invite them nor decline them.' Describing himself as a 'Unionist Free Trader', who was 'opposed to what is generally known as Home Rule and to Protection in any form', he told Balfour that he could not regard 'your administration as any satisfactory security against the latter . . . and I am not quite sure that its continuance is of any particular value to the cause of the Union'. He was, he wrote, a 'wholehearted opponent of Mr Chamberlain', something which might drive him to take actions which, 'though not necessarily contrary to the permanent interests of the Unionist Party, may be incidentally hostile to the existing Government'. Churchill left it to Balfour to decide 'whether it is worthwhile to forward me the Government whips. . . . I certainly shall not complain whatever your decision may be.'[43]

It was a curious correspondence; but if Churchill had been trying to provoke Balfour into precipitating him from the Party, as his original intention of publishing the correspondence suggests, he had met his match. Balfour's dialectical mastery made it look as though Churchill was simply prevaricating; so the correspondence was never published.[44] In the end Churchill had to declare his hand in a more public fashion. When he rose on 29 March to announce that he was resigning the Conservative Whip, the whole Party, including Balfour, rose and left him alone. The experience shook him. He even thought about forcing a by-election, but decided to sit tight instead.[45]

Churchill's attachment to his father's Party had been weakened by the process of writing *Lord Randolph Churchill*, shaken by disagreements over Army reform, and finally sundered by the success which tariff reform was having within its ranks; but underlying this process was the liberal caste of Churchill's mind. Where Lord Hugh Cecil would not touch the policies advocated by Lloyd George 'with a punt pole', Churchill discovered that their views had a good deal in common. It was, perhaps, tactless of Winston to tell Lord Hugh, whose views on Church matters would have been regarded as extreme in a sixteenth-century prelate, that the only thing which surprised him in the course of a discussion on religious education in schools with Lloyd George was how 'astonishingly small and petty' some of the differences were. But it is indicative, as was his agreement with Lloyd George's ideas on agricultural and trades union reform, of how easy Churchill found co-operation with even radical Liberals.[46] It was true that some Liberals found him insufficiently radical for their taste,[47] but Churchill found no problem in accepting most Liberal attitudes on the central political questions of the day.

Not yet a Liberal in name, but not a Conservative, Churchill was in a position which suited him well. Lord St Aldwyn, who, as Sir Michael Hicks-Beach, had been a Conservative Chancellor and an associate of Lord Randolph's, warned Churchill that 'Radical tendencies in a Tory, or Tory tendencies in a Radical, however agreeable to the conscience, handicap a man severely on the run.'[48] But making up his mind to 'stick to one side or the other', as St Aldwyn advised, was something Churchill would always have difficulty doing. As the Free Food League candidate for north-west Manchester, he had the promise of support from the Liberals and from Labour, but he was under none of the usual obligations entailed by membership of a political Party. Those obligations which did come his way were perfectly acceptable. If the Manchester Jewish community objected to the Government's Aliens Bill, which would have restricted the right of their co-religionists fleeing Tsarist pogroms to find refuge in England, well, so too did Churchill's Liberal instincts.[49] If the trades unions and the nonconformist conscience revolted at the thought of indentured Chinese labour being brought into the Transvaal, so did Churchill's.[50] As progressive Liberals like Charles Trevelyan and Charles Masterman opened Churchill's eyes to the sufferings and the poverty of the great mass of the English people, he came to believe that the ideals of 'Tory Democracy' could be achieved only through alliance with the Liberal Party. But as Churchill himself recognised, the process of leaving the Conservatives would have been much more difficult had tariff reform not become an issue; even now, if it subsided, his 'personal ambitions' would be left 'naked and stranded on the beach'.[51]

Despite crossing the floor of the House, Churchill avoided actually joining the Liberal Party. 'I am at this present moment', he told one correspondent in October 1904, 'entirely isolated in politics – having no sort of connection with any group of politicians.'[52] But that was whilst Rosebery's 'attempt to form a central Conservative Party comprising the free trade element'[53] was still in the air. Churchill had his name removed from the books of the Carlton Club in April 1905,[54] and rumour, in its usual abounding fashion, had it that he would be offered a seat in the next Liberal Cabinet.[55] His position, if still equivocal, was becoming increasingly defined by the reaction of others to his own actions. There was no room in politics for an independent Conservative. Every political Party values loyalty above independence of judgment, but only the Conservatives regard it as the ark of the covenant. Churchill had, from the first, offended against this code and to rebellion had added other objectionable qualities: egocentricity of an intensity which most politicians take elaborate steps to conceal, but which he seemed to flaunt; an excessive liking for the sound of his own voice; and, finally, a tendency to personalise his political

attacks in a manner which combined offence and vulgarity in equal proportions. Balfour, the butt of many salvoes, referred dismissively to the 'elab-
orately prepared personalities of the member for Oldham',[56] but after one
particularly vicious attack upon the Prime Minister, the King declared that
'Churchill is a born cad';[57] he was not alone in taking this view.

Churchill's co-operation with the Liberal association in north-west Manchester still left him free to join in any Roseberyite revival, but in even
expecting such a thing, Churchill showed his political naïveté. The 'great
imperialist' put himself totally out of court in late November 1904 with a
speech declaring that he could support no government pledged to introduce
Home Rule. John Morley reassured Churchill that there was 'no question' of
'forcing' the issue 'to the point', and urged him not to refuse office.[58]

Balfour resigned on 4 December 1905, and within four days the unregarded
Campbell-Bannerman had managed to bring even the Liberal imperialists
into his Government. The same electoral considerations which demanded
their inclusion also suggested the wisdom of inviting a prominent Conservative defector. Campbell-Bannerman's original intention was to offer Churchill
the post of Financial Secretary to the Treasury. This seems to have been
prompted by the vigour with which Churchill had combated Chamberlain's
economic arguments, but the post, although commonly held to be the ante-
chamber to the Cabinet, did not appeal. Asquith, who was to be Chancellor
of the Exchequer, was the most formidable Liberal speaker in the House, and
to be his junior would offer little scope for shining in debate. Churchill asked
the new Prime Minister for the post of Under-Secretary at the Colonial Office;
it is not without significance that his chief there, the Earl of Elgin, was not
only a peer but also a singularly taciturn one.[59] Churchill described his job as
'only a stipendiary echo' – it would have been that at the Treasury, but the
Colonial Office offered something more.[60]

4

Son of his Father?

Churchill's name had been a considerable asset to a young man bent upon making his way in Conservative politics, but it had been a mixed blessing. It had made 'young Winston's' actions noteworthy before he had really done anything, but it also made them liable to misconstruction. Lord Randolph had left behind him a reputation which was far from unsullied: adventurer, cad and opportunist were just some of the adjectives used about him by his contemporaries. Churchill's biography of his father, which was published in 1906, created a portrait in which light predominated over shade. Lord Randolph's life became an explanation of his son's career, and 'Tory Democracy' became a crusade rather than a tactical device with which to win electoral support.[1] *Lord Randolph Churchill* established its author's reputation as an historian, but that was only half its work; the other half was to establish the suitability of its hero as a role-model for his son.

During the course of writing the book Churchill had been able to come into closer contact with the great men of the political world than would have been usual for a tyro backbencher: Arthur Balfour, Joseph Chamberlain, the Duke of Devonshire and Lord Rosebery had all been free with their reminiscences and, in some instances, with their correspondence. However, Churchill's warm relations with Rosebery had been blighted by a frost when he called Lord Randolph by the opprobrious Etonian epithet of 'scug' – the whole thrust of the biography was to absolve its main protagonist from such charges. Lord Randolph's old radical crony, Wilfrid Scawen Blunt, had written in his diary following Winston's defection from the Tory Party that he expected 'to see [him] playing precisely his father's game, and I should not be surprised if he had his father's success'.[2] It was because people made such comparisons that it was essential that the true significance of Lord Randolph's career (as interpreted by his son) should be understood.

The foundation of Churchill's success as a writer was his ability to tell a dramatic story; his heroes are there to evoke sympathy and empathy, and his villains are, like those of Macaulay, men whose great gifts have been perverted to mean ends. Had Churchill still been in the Conservative Party in 1906 he would have suffered some embarrassment; the villains of the piece are clearly the Cecil clan, amongst whose members was the leader of the Tories, Arthur Balfour. The 'Hotel Cecil' had been happy to utilise Lord Randolph's considerable gifts in pursuit of its own dominance. Whilst the struggle for power had been in progress, lip-service had been paid to Lord Randolph's ideas of 'Tory Democracy'; once power was won, he had been ruthlessly discarded, along with his rhetoric. In Winston's story this becomes a great tragedy. Lord Randolph had been the true heir of Disraeli, but the bearer of the mantle of Elijah had been used by clever reactionaries for their own ends. If readers decided that it was no surprise that the son had changed Party because he too found the way to 'Tory Democracy' blocked by the same men, then so much the better. Scawen Blunt concluded that young Churchill seemed to be looking 'to a leadership of the Liberal Party and an opportunity of full vengeance on those who caused his father's death'.[3]

Lord Randolph Churchill, by casting the career of its hero in a kindlier light, suggested that the actions of its author should also be so interpreted. Before 1906 Winston Churchill's reputation rested upon foundations which suggested that parallels with his father's career were very much in order. Thus far he had been a Parliamentary gadfly, a bumptious overgrown schoolboy with the tongue of an orator and the manners of a boor; his position rested on the twin foundations of a famous name and a considerable talent for self-advertisement. Political infidelity had already made him an object of contemptuous loathing on the Unionist benches. Edward VII spoke for many in 'Society' when he labelled the young man 'a cad'.[4] Lord Randolph had attracted similar epithets. To attribute Churchill's behaviour to his 'bright red American blood'[5] explains little about his character, but it could have been said of him, as it was of Disraeli, that 'men who make their positions will say and do things which are not necessary to be said and done by those for whom positions are provided'.

'Winston Churchill' as a public figure was the product of his age. Lord Randolph had said in 1884 that 'we live in an age of advertisement', and whatever was true of the 1880s, by 1906 his verdict was accurate. Politics was still sufficiently dominated by men born to the purple for this fact to be obscured: Balfour, Rosebery, Sir Edward Grey, Earl Spencer and their like needed no advertisement; their social position gave them the opportunity and the wealth to engage in the great game. Churchill's success, and his manner of achieving it, were signs of the changing political climate. 'Winston Churchill' provided good 'copy' for the mass-circulation, popular press. Sophisticated politicians, then as now, liked to claim that politics was about 'issues' and not 'personalities', but the general public has always taken a different view. Churchill's personality was one which easily impressed itself on a wider audience; but by the same token he was bound to arouse antagonism from those who deplored the 'vulgarity' of the new age.

By birth, education, upbringing and family ties, Churchill was indubitably a member of England's aristocratic ruling elite; yet he was identifiably different from many of his colleagues in politics. He had not been through the 'staff colleges' of Oxford and Cambridge, acquiring there a social polish and a range of intellectual references sufficient to over-awe the plebeian mind. It was true that many Tory MPs came from a military background, but few Cabinet Ministers were to be counted in their number. Churchill enjoyed the advantages of being part of 'the "old boy network" that connected all parts of patrician society',[6] but his character was not one which fitted easily into its conventions. Like Savrola, his 'cast of mind' was 'vehement, high and daring'.[7] He was by instinct and military training a man of action. In the most intimate of his books, *My Early Life*, Churchill wrote that 'a man's life must be nailed to a cross either of Thought or Action';[8] there could be no doubt where Churchill was 'nailed'. He worked by intuition and instinct, and he had not had the mental training which channels the former and stifles the latter. Asquith, under whom he served for longer than he did under any Prime Minister, said of him that 'Winston thinks with his mouth'.[9] This may have been unkind, but it reflected the difference between the 'man of Action' and the 'man of Thought'; and the upper reaches of British politics were dominated by the latter group – which was why Churchill was always something of an outsider.[10]

Lord Randolph's career had soared like a meteor when he had been in opposition, for his gifts were essentially destructive in kind and thus peculiarly suited to that situation; but in office he had been unable to harness his talents to more constructive purposes and had committed political suicide by an impulsive resignation. His whole political career had effectively spanned the years 1880 to 1886; gaudy, attractive, but short-lived, he had been a political mayfly. Winston's restless career contained no suggestion that he would have greater sticking-power than his father. He had been a soldier, a journalist, a war hero and a lecturer before turning politician, and within three years he had changed from being a Unionist to being a Liberal. But the other careers had been means to the final one. A political career of half a century is not sustained by hot air alone, and the Campbell-Bannerman Government was to show that young Churchill could be a formidable 'pack horse' when it came to carrying the burden of administration.

Between the impetuous, aristocratic, former subaltern and the dour, Scottish Prime Minister there was fixed a gulf bridged only by mutual convenience. Churchill thirsted after office as a man in the desert does for water, and Campbell-Bannerman wanted to employ the brightest of the talents which the tariff reform controversy had cast up on the shores of Liberalism; but Churchill's place would depend entirely upon the success with which he adapted his talents to the demands of office. There was no place for renegade mayflies in Campbell-Bannerman's Government.

The Colonial Office was a conducive berth for an ambitious and impatient young man. One of the major problems facing the new Government was the settlement of South Africa in the aftermath of the Boer War, a task which fell within the remit of the Colonial Office. Churchill would not only be involved in trying to find a solution, but as his chief was in the House of Lords, it would fall to him to be the department's spokesman in the Commons. If Churchill represented the new era, then Victor Alexander Bruce, ninth Earl of Elgin, was a perfect specimen of the old order that was passing. A reticent, Scottish nobleman, who firmly believed that public service was the duty which the aristocracy owed in return for its privileges, Elgin was not disposed to contest his subordinate's desire for the limelight. He came to regard his brash junior Minister with a tolerant amusement tinged with respect for his extraordinary abilities. It was only after his own career had been cut short by Asquith that Elgin began to complain that Churchill had hogged the credit for work which was not solely his own.[11]

From the very start of his period of office Churchill laboured to impress himself upon both his post and his chief. An Under-Secretary can be a very minor form of political life, but Churchill showed from the start that he regarded his office as a springboard and not a sofa. Before the dust of the election had settled in January, Churchill had produced two large memoranda on the future status of South Africa, and in early February his arguments were circulated to the Cabinet.[12] His contribution to the form of the final settlement of the South African problem is easily overestimated by those looking for signs that even in his political youth the lineaments of the great man of the future could be discerned,[13] but he certainly played an active role in shaping a settlement along Liberal lines.

There was more to Churchill's Liberalism than a mere distaste for tariff reform. Behind Joseph Chamberlain's fiscal policy was a fear that Britain might be about to join the ranks of those Great Powers of the past who had been unable to hold on to their imperium. Early Edwardian Unionism was suffused with a pessimism which went beyond the usual Conservative inclination to see all change as being for the worse. The Boer War had been an attempt to stop the rot, to assert British imperial will over territories which were strategically and economically important.[14] Chamberlain saw Britain as a 'weary titan' staggering under the 'too vast orb of her fate'.[15] In the aftermath of the war the Unionist Government had struggled to find a form of constitution which would allow the British to hold on to the reins of power whilst reconciling the Boers to this fact; it was an enterprise which had enjoyed limited success. The High Commissioner in South Africa, Salisbury's son-in-law, Lord Selborne, took the view that 'Responsible Government probably means a Boer Ministry', which, in turn, meant that they would use their position 'remorselessly to diminish British influence in every possible way'.[16] He and the Unionist Colonial Secretary, Alfred Lyttelton, had laboured to come up with a constitution which bore the name of the latter and, as far as the Boers were concerned, the mark of Cain. Churchill shared neither the cultural pessimism of the Unionist hierarchy, nor the conclusions to which it had driven them.

Churchill was by nature an optimist, and nothing in his reading of British history inclined him to draw pessimistic conclusions. A study of Macaulay and of the constitutional history of the British Empire furnished both ample reason for optimism and precedents upon which to act. It had been the folly of George III in levying unconstitutional dues on the American colonies which had driven them into revolt. To treat the natural desire of men of English stock to rule themselves as though it were rebellion was to invite it. The Boers were, in this scenario, honorary Englishmen. The Durham report of 1837 was the focus of Liberal mythology on the development of the Empire; by granting greater self-government to Canada, that country had evolved into a Dominion firmly attached to the mother country.[17] Such was the Liberal view, and it was one which, as he made clear to Selborne, Churchill shared. Self-government, he believed, should be conceded now to avoid a situation where 'what we might have given with courage and distinction both at home and in South Africa, upon our terms, in the hour of our strength, will be jerked and twisted from our hands without grace of any kind'.[18]

The ideas which Churchill, Elgin and Campbell-Bannerman brought to bear on the South African problem were of impeccable Liberal provenance and were to produce, within reason, a classic Liberal solution to the problem, but they did not comprehend its racial dimension. However, racial problems were not then the touchstone of Liberalism which they were to become. But not all the difficulties facing the new team at the Colonial Office were reconcilable with Liberal promises at the election. Whilst the Cabinet committee laboured away at South Africa and her future, Parliamentary debate was much taken up by the question of what had become known as 'Chinese slavery'. Electioneering is notoriously a time when promises exceed a Party's ability to deliver their object. The Liberals had condemned the importation of Chinese labourers into the Transvaal to help with the work of reconstruction as 'slavery', and they had promised to put an end to the practice. Churchill had been as forward as any in employing the issue as a stick with which to beat the Unionists; now he had to do something to fulfil the pledges made when the blood was heated by election-fever.

Churchill and Elgin discovered that the previous administration had already issued licences for another 14,000 'slaves' and that it was not possible to end the system with the stroke of a pen.[19] Common sense has never proved very popular with ideologues, and the use of arguments about practicability cut no ice with the radicals. One of the few Unionists to get himself elected for the first time in the new Parliament, the member for Walton, one F. E. Smith, had some sport with the dilemma in which the son of his great hero, Lord Randolph, found himself. During the debate on the King's speech on 19 February Churchill admitted that, in his opinion, the terms upon which the Chinese were employed could not be described as 'slavery' without 'some risk of terminological inexactitude'.[20] This was interpreted by many Unionists as a euphemism for 'lie', and Smith, in one of the most famous maiden speeches in Parliamentary history, made reference to the wording of the Government's motion that the election result gave 'unqualified' approval to Liberal policies. To call a man an 'unqualified slave', Smith opined, was to say that he could 'be honestly described as completely servile, and not, merely, as semi-servile'. But to call a man 'an unqualified medical practitioner, or an unqualified Under-Secretary' was, he sneered, to say that 'he is not entitled to any particular respect, because he has not passed through the normal period of training or preparation'.[21]

Churchill, who never minded the give-and-take of Parliamentary debate, took no offence at these remarks, which were delivered in a manner far from his own rather laboriously constructed efforts in the House. Smith was a born orator, whose skills were sharpened on the grindstone of his legal practice. His oratory was made all the more effective for being delivered in what might be described as a 'deep brown' voice. Churchill's more highly pitched delivery was the product of hard work and a naturally good memory trained by practice. Smith could grab the House by its lapels at his first attempt, Churchill had to study the art; but he did this as he did all his political work, with dedication and perseverance. In an age of amateurs Churchill was a professional politician, and those parts of the politician's armoury which he did not possess by gift of nature he acquired by perspiration.

What Churchill was naturally gifted with was a belligerent style. Impetuous and inclined to act before weighing the consequences, Churchill's lack of sensitivity to the feelings of others was always apt to lead him into stormy waters. He wrote optimistically to Selborne in March of seizing the opportunity provided by a debate on Lord Milner to 'improve the temper' of those in South Africa who distrusted the Liberals and all their works.[22] Milner, who had been High Commissioner at the time of the Boer War, was the darling of the Unionists, but much distrusted by Liberals as its architect. It had recently been revealed that whilst Milner had been in office, some of the coolies had been flogged. Radical Liberals seized the opportunity to put down a motion condemning their *bête noir*, but, as Churchill explained to Selborne, the Government would defuse the situation by putting down an amendment which avoided naming any individual. These admirable intentions were nullified by Churchill's tactless language in the debate on 21 March; indeed, his speech could not have incensed Unionists more had it been planned with that end in mind. He spoke of Milner with a patronising condescension which sounded both 'impertinent' and 'pompous', referring to him as a 'retired Civil Servant without any pension or gratuity'; a man who 'has ceased to be a factor in public life'.[23] His words may, as the official biographer thought, have been an echo of Macaulay's famous passage on Warren Hastings, but it ill behoved the Government to seem to be standing in judgment on the great Unionist hero at the same time that it was alleging that no individual was to be condemned. Unionist opinion, predictably, was scandalised, but even the King found Churchill's language 'violent and objectionable'.[24] Churchill seems to have been the only person to have been surprised at the furore.

The fact that Milner was 'idolised' by many Unionists brought down a flood of abuse on a man already castigated as a 'traitor' and sealed the breach between Churchill and his old Party. Judas had, after all, had the decency to hang himself afterwards. What gave offence was Churchill's use of sonorous language in an inappropriate context; the spectacle of an 'unqualified Under-Secretary' patronising one of the great heroes of the imperial story had about it something smacking of bathos. Churchill had not learnt to use the instrument of his oratory with any great precision, and he would nearly always be accused of rhetorical exaggeration and of using over-inflated language. There were occasions, however, when the Macaulayesque 'grand style' was appropriate, and his happiest hours would be found at such times. The fact that these tended to be great crises led naturally to the conclusion that he was a man who, in his own words, 'liked things to happen' and 'liked to make them' when they were not.[25] But there was more to it than that. Life for Churchill was a vast heroic drama and his language, like that of Wagner's *Ring Cycle*, was an instrument for conveying that vision to an audience. Churchill's historical writings confirm a high and exalted view of life and its purpose. He would have agreed with Aristotle that 'History is what Alcibiades did and suffered.' For those who did not know that Alcibiades was the hero of Thucydides's history of the Peloponnesian Wars, Churchill's language, like Aristotle's statement, failed to hit its target.

The most obvious period in which Churchill's highly coloured rhetoric was matched with an appropriate occasion was the summer of 1940, but there were other occasions upon which the needs of the hour fitted the dimensions of a Churchillian oration. Speaking in the Commons on 31 July, announcing the decision to grant responsible government to the Boer republics, Churchill soared to heights of great rhetorical eloquence. Drawing on the model of Gladstone in his great final appeal to Conservatives to endorse his first Home Rule Bill, Churchill appealed to the Unionists to support the policy: 'With all our majority we can only make it the gift of a Party; they can make it the gift of England.'[26] After the Milner speech the King had declared with reference to Churchill that 'nowadays Party comes before country',[27] but after this speech no one could have said that.

Churchill's advocacy of greater self-government for South Africa may have placed him in the camp of Liberalism, but he was a Liberal–imperialist. There was no question for him but that the British Empire was a great engine of civilisation and an instrument for good. What he condemned were imperial actions which fell below what he regarded was the level of behaviour appropriate to those who bore the 'white man's burden'; Kipling had a 'great influence' on him.[28] Churchill might, in an ill-season when his habitual concentration on the matter in hand narrowed his view, advocate reductions in armaments, but he never, even then, espoused the cause of anti-imperialism. Party labels fitted such a man where they touched. Churchill's attachment was to his own ambition to secure personal fame and the greatness of England, and he tended to consort with those who shared such visions – to the distrust of the staid Party 'hacks' who dominated Westminster politics. Those who burn incense on the altars of a Party have a natural distrust of those freelances who take their pleasure where they find it; and, in a political system dominated by Party, the latter will always be accused of insincerity.

All political Parties have their own puritanism, but those of the left are more inclined towards the sins of self-righteousness and sanctimony. For a Liberal Minister to holiday with rich friends who owned yachts was a sin against the puritan god of self-denial, and it was one which Churchill committed with gay abandon, unconscious of his crime, for there was in him none of the puritan. But for him to form a friendship with F. E. Smith, who was such a scourge of the Liberal Government, was indeed to invite questions about his adhesion to Liberal values.

F. E. Smith was a man whose virtues commended themselves to those lacking the puritan spirit, which helps to explain the initial attraction between himself and Churchill. Bred in the 'Tory Democracy' of Birkenhead, that most spectacular of Victorian boom-towns, built on John Laird's ship-building acumen, Smith was reared in a Toryism which owed nothing to the elevated pessimism of Lord Salisbury and Hatfield House, nor to the 'lords of the pineries and vineries' of London's suburbia; anti-Popery and drink were its twin pillars. Born in Pilgrim Street, a stone's throw from the Woodside Ferry, F.E. (as he was always known) was quite as imbued with ambition for himself and his country as the scion of the Churchill clan. Lacking Churchill's connections with the 'patrician network', Smith had taken the classic method of acquiring them for a bright boy of his background – public school and then Oxford. His intellect had earned him a fellowship at Wadham, and his legal talents enabled him to make his way at the Bar. He swiftly established himself as one of the brightest stars on the Northern Circuit and he used his fame and forensic skills to cultivate political contacts in Liverpool, which brought him the nomination for Walton. Like that very different Merseyside man, W. E. Gladstone, he had acquired from Oxford culture, an entrée to the great world and an accent. Smith remained rooted in the soil of his native political culture.[29]

Smith's appeal to Churchill was obvious. Tall, dark and saturnine, F.E. had a mind of lightning quickness and a power of repartee which made his fame at the Bar and at Westminster. He was one of the greatest orators in an age when that art flourished, and he was the most accomplished Parliamentary debater since Edward Stanley in the early nineteenth century. In short, he was many of the things which the small, epicene, lisping Churchill was not, but would like to have been. In turn, Churchill represented for Smith many of the things he would like to have been. Aristocratic and well-connected, Churchill bore a name which Smith honoured and possessed literary talents and personal qualities which he could admire.

But such analysis hardly does justice to the two men and their friendship. If it was partly founded on mutual admiration for qualities which each respected and lacked, its depth owed most to a common outlook. Both had entirely absorbed the social–Darwinian view of life as a struggle in which only the fittest would triumph; both were convinced of the possession of innate talents which would enable them to win through. Later, as the first Earl of Birkenhead, Smith was to scandalise the great and the good by telling an audience of undergraduates that life's main purpose lay in winning the 'glittering prizes'. He refused to retract; indeed, he could hardly have done so, for this was his creed as it was Churchill's. They would both have agreed with Disraeli's statement that 'we are here for fame'. The *Punch* cartoon which had both men leaning eagerly over a life of Disraeli and spotting the parallels with their careers captured the spirit of their comradeship, even if its title, 'Adventurers on the make', represented the Establishment view of the pair.

F.E. had made his reputation with that maiden speech in which he had dealt Churchill a glancing blow. Before it he was a little-known MP for Walton with an Oxford reputation behind him; after it he was the great white hope of a defeated and demoralised Party. Although his detractors liked to allege that he had no principles, and F.E. liked to play up to them, the truth was otherwise. He admired the Lord Randolph Churchill depicted in the official biography – a swashbuckling adventurer with a serious purpose. The Birkenhead Unionist could not but admire the man whom he regarded as the inheritor of Disraeli's 'One Nation' brand of Toryism. He had kept his distance from the renegade son at first, but soon found that they shared a common impatience with the 'old gang' who dominated life at Westminster.

Churchill had left the Conservative Party, declaring that its leaders had betrayed Lord Randolph's legacy. Smith worked from within to revive 'Tory Democracy'. It is easy to dismiss 'Tory Democracy' with one of Lord Randolph's own jibes – as merely a means of getting the democracy to vote Tory. But there was nothing unnatural in such an activity. Political Parties exist to attract votes; if they fail to do so, they usually cease to exist. F.E. saw in reality what Churchill had seen only in theory, that is the existence of a democracy that was naturally Tory in many of its instincts. Outside the Liberal voting and often nonconformist 'respectable' working classes lay an electorate which was patriotic, monarchist, xenophobic, beer-drinking and instinctively Protestant. It might yet be captured by the 'class-based' politics of the new Labour Party or bribed by the social reforms of the 'new Liberalism', but it ought to be wooed by the Tories. It was not quite the 'angel in the marble' of Disraeli's musings, but something rougher, tougher and more untamed.

The shopkeepers and the unionised forces of labour might vote Liberal, but no man reared in Birkenhead and Liverpool could be unaware of the vast ranks of ununionised labour who worked on the docks and in the shipyards. If these men voted Tory, they did not do so because they appreciated Balfour's balancing act over tariffs. They voted for a Toryism which was firmly Unionist over Ireland and which defended the right of the free-born Englishman to drink as much as he liked. The Liberal desire to 'improve' the working man by restricting his opportunities to imbibe alcohol, and Gladstone's truckling to the Irish over Home Rule, were powerful stimulants to vote Tory in a town like Birkenhead, where there was a pub on every street corner and too many Irishmen who would underbid the English when it came to wages for casual labour. A firm commitment against Irish Home Rule and against Liberal faddism was at the heart of F.E.'s political creed.

But F.E.'s fame, like Churchill's, was not won by exercise of those virtues so beloved by the sober men in grey suits. In the green and happy days of the first flowering of their careers neither man cared about this, scorning the conventional paths to political power in favour of the unorthodox ones more suited to the exercise of their talents. But the time would come when shadows would gather, and then the cold winds of disapproval would act as a blight upon their prospects, as the grey men exacted their revenge. Only one of the two would rise again, only to find that the men in grey know when it is best to bow before the powers that be. Churchill's relationship with F.E. was the closest friendship he ever formed, with Smith taking the dominant role in it. Churchill stood in awe of his learning and his gift of oratory.[30]

F.E. was a natural Conservative who had come to 'settled and somewhat sombre conclusions upon a large number of questions, about which many people are content to remain in placid suspense'. Churchill could optimistically assume that in the elections which would be held after the grant of responsible government in South Africa, 'a clear Boer majority is outside the bounds of possibility'.[31] However, when elections were held in the Transvaal in February 1907, the Boers had a clear majority of five, and when the Orange River Colony voted in November, they won thirty out of thirty-eight seats.[32] Edward VII had feared that Churchill was 'somewhat sanguine' in his 'prognostications' and, as so often, Conservative scepticism was the justified response to Liberal optimism.[33] F.E. would not have made the same mistake as his friend, but their differences did not mar their comradeship.

The fatuity of his prophecies about South Africa did Churchill no harm within the Liberal Party, where his views were widely shared. Even if the outcome was not what had been expected, the Liberals could plausibly claim to have dealt with the problem of what to do with the Boers. The formation of the Union of South Africa in 1910, and the subsequent support which that Dominion gave to Britain during the Great War, was taken as a sign of the success of the line of policy which Campbell-Bannerman and Churchill had favoured.

Identified as he was with the successful resolution of the South African problem, Churchill's general performance at the Colonial Office marked him out for further preferment. But this did not mean that he made an entirely satisfactory junior in the eyes of his superiors. There were times when Churchill's habit of minuting his views in strong words on papers which would be read by subordinates irritated Elgin, and his ceaseless interest in all aspects of his work could lead to a lack of a sense of perspective, but there could be no doubting that the young Minister had proved himself worth his passage.[34] There were, naturally, those who dissented. On the one hand were those like the Permanent Under-Secretary at the Colonial Office, Sir Francis Hopwood, who, in response to the ceaseless stream of memoranda which issued from Churchill on his tour of the colonies in 1907, told Elgin that 'He is most tiresome to deal with and will, I fear, give trouble. . . . The restless energy, uncontrollable desire for notoriety and the lack of moral perception make him an anxiety indeed!'[35] On the other was Churchill himself, who by late 1907 felt that he had done more than enough to warrant promotion to the Cabinet.[36]

There had been rumours in late 1906 that Churchill was to be promoted, and it is testimony to Elgin's largeness of character as well as to Churchill's abilities that he should have written to him in December to say that 'I have been dreading every post to find the rumours true and that I was to lose your help.'[37] Campbell-Bannerman wrote to Churchill in September 1907 to congratulate him on his part in the settlement of the South African issue and Churchill seems to have interpreted this as a sign that he might get into the Cabinet whilst in his current post. The problem with that, however, as he told his mother in October, was that 'They are afraid that Elgin's position would become very difficult, he being such an unassertive fellow.'[38] It was characteristic of him to assume that this was the only obstacle in his way, but Churchill underestimated Campbell-Bannerman. That cautious Scotsman believed in letting youth work its passage; promotion, if it came, would do so only slowly – at least as long as he remained Prime Minister.[39]

However, Campbell-Bannerman was an old and ailing man. His obvious successor, Asquith, was more favourably disposed to the young Minister. Except in times of crisis the Yorkshire grit inherited from Asquith's background was hidden beneath an aristocratic manner acquired at Oxford and cultivated assiduously since his second marriage to Margot Tennant. Daughter of the chemicals magnate, Sir Charles Tennant, and one of the numerous clan which intermarried into most branches of political life, Margot was a woman with immense ambitions for her husband; indeed, before her marriage to Asquith, it was rumoured that she would marry Arthur Balfour, who commented, upon being informed of this: 'No, I had rather thought of having a career of my own.' She considered Asquith's first wife, Helen, as unsuitable because she lived in Hampstead and never entertained; neither charge could have been levelled against Margot.[40] At the time of his daughter's engagement,

Sir Charles Tennant had commented of Asquith that 'She has smartened him up wonderfully, you would hardly know him.'[41] Those sour puritans of ascetic habit who are always to be found amongst the ranks of the radicals were apt to dismiss him as 'a raw middle-class radical with a character deteriorated by a vulgar society of another sort and by a free use of wine which he cannot carry'.[42] But such comments ignored Asquith's formidable political skills.

The 'cold, hard, unsympathetic'[43] Asquith was bound to suffer when compared with the venerable and much loved 'C-B', but the fact was that the Government he had inherited in 1908 was in deep, perhaps even terminal, trouble. On the one hand came the criticism from the radicals and Labour that it had not done enough in the field of social reform; on the other came attacks from some of its own middle-class supporters and the Unionists that what it had done was costly and destructive.[44] An education bill, plural voting and a land reform bill had all perished at the hands of the House of Lords, and by late 1907 the euphoria of the previous year had given way to demoralisation. The ailing Campbell-Bannerman was not the man to transform this situation; the ambitious Asquith was. Even before coming to power he was giving thought to the composition of a Ministry which would regain the political initiative. His feelings for Churchill were complex and may best be described as a slightly patronising, rueful admiration. Recognition of 'genius' was accompanied by fears about his rashness; Asquith was, however, confident enough of his own powers to think that he could utilise the former whilst restraining the latter.[45]

The question of where to accommodate Churchill was not easily solved. In his last Cabinet reshuffle, Campbell-Bannerman had considered whether he might not be sent to the Board of Education, despite being 'wholly ignorant and indifferent to the subject'. He was disabused of this idea by John Morley who, incredulous at the idea of Churchill as 'umpire between Church and Chapel', told him that it would be 'both ridiculous and a scandal'. As the Prime Minister had his own doubts about appointing a 'Liberal of yesterday' whose 'tomorrow is doubtful', Churchill had remained where he was.[46] But Asquith had more radical ideas on how to employ such a figure.

In March he suggested that Churchill might care for the Local Government Board. As Churchill had recently taken to making pronouncements on social issues, this suggestion was not as odd as it sounded; but it held little attraction for its intended occupant. The work was 'laborious' and 'choked with petty and even squalid detail', Churchill told Asquith. Protesting that he knew nothing about its affairs, Churchill said that he would rather stay at the Colonial Office under Elgin.[47] 'Being shut up in a soup kitchen with Mrs Sidney Webb' is how Churchill is supposed to have responded to Asquith's suggestion,[48] but there are good reasons for supposing that Churchill was not wholly averse to such an encounter.

5

The 'New' Liberal

It used to be said of the Liberals that their Party resembled the Kingdom of Heaven – at least in so far as it was a 'house' which contained 'many mansions'; three such may be observed within the Edwardian Liberal Party and it is significant that Churchill had affiliations with only two of them. The one strand of Liberalism with which Churchill had little contact was the one to which most Liberals adhered – the Gladstonian tradition. Represented in the Cabinet by Gladstone's biographer, John Morley, the Gladstonians saw Liberalism as primarily a moral crusade concerned with peace, economy and freedom. They had been happy to support Campbell-Bannerman, who was a leader in their own tradition; they were less happy about his successor. Asquith had been identified with Rosebery and the Liberal imperialist wing of the Party, which had supported the Boer War, but he could just as easily have been associated with the 'New Liberalism' by 1908.[1] Churchill's progress in Liberalism followed a path not dissimilar to his leader.

'C-B' may have been the darling of the Gladstonians, but nothing in his period of office suggested that he and his creed had answers to the problems of the new century; it was no longer enough to utter the old war-cries of 'peace, retrenchment and reform'.[2] The work of 'social investigators' like Seebohm Rowntree and Sidney and Beatrice Webb had revealed to a shocked country the true 'condition of England', where families huddled together in slum tenements in industrial cities in the richest nation in the world, and where prostitution, poverty and unemployment were the lot of many. Churchill's own lot had been cast in a quite different England, but he could hardly avoid being aware of the work of the Webbs and Rowntree, and the picture they painted was not one which he could reconcile with England's destiny: 'I can see little glory in an Empire which can rule the waves and is unable to flush its sewers.'[3]

No single Party held a monopoly of concern about the 'condition of England'. Beatrice Webb, the most formidable of the Fabians, who concealed and constrained her passions by channelling them into social investigation and good works, believed that salvation lay in the application of the scientific method to social problems. She hoped that politicians of all Parties would be 'permeated' by the ideas which the Fabians and other 'experts' adumbrated. It was not, as Richard Haldane asserted in 1891, the function of politicians to 'mould ideas'; that was the duty of intellectuals and universities.[4] Mrs

Webb had first looked towards Balfour to carry out her ideas on how to deal with social problems, but getting little from that source, she had cast her eyes towards the Liberal Government: 'it looms as progressive in its direction and all the active factors are collectivist'.[5] Unfortunately, Campbell-Bannerman was not much inclined to favour the 'active factors'.

Asquith could not afford to remain supine. His motive in offering Churchill the Local Government Board had been to try to remove one of the main obstacles to radical social reform: its President, John Burns. The Board was the department most closely concerned with social questions and it had been natural for Mrs Webb and company to look to Burns for action. But the Board was hidebound by its own bureaucracy and unreceptive to advice from outside 'experts', whilst Burns, whose initial good intentions had come to naught, was being written off by Mrs Webb as a 'monstrosity', who 'talks incessantly and never listens to anyone except the officials to whom he *must* listen in order to accomplish the routine work of his office'.[6] But Burns did not want to move, and Asquith did not want to remove the only 'working-class' member of his Cabinet. If Churchill would not and could not have the Board, he would have the Board of Trade, which would become, *faute de mieux*, the focus of legislation on social policy.

Churchill's 'Tory Democratic' background gave him a rhetorical interest in the lot of the masses, but when Mrs Webb had quizzed him in 1904, she had found him 'completely ignorant of all social questions' and his ideas a 'quaint jumble of old-fashioned radicalism and mere Toryism', with the former in the ascendant as he wished to appear 'advanced'.[7] By 1906 Churchill had added some of the 'new' Liberalism to the ingredients noted by Mrs Webb. Speaking in Glasgow in October 1906 he declared that it was not possible to 'draw a hard and fast line between individualism and collectivism'. Having known nothing in 1904 about Mrs Webb's scheme for a 'national minimum', he was now advocating 'the universal establishment of minimum standards of life and labour'.[8] Churchill read the newspapers avidly and followed the political debate the way some of his colleagues followed the Turf guide; always eager for new knowledge, he sucked in what people like the Webbs were writing. He was a 'political linguist' of great gifts, and he picked up the language of the radicals speedily at need. He set out his ideas more fully in an article in *The Nation* on 7 March 1908 called 'The Untrodden Field in Politics'.[9] It was entirely in character for him to assume that any field he had not walked upon was 'untrodden'.

That Churchill should have published such a piece when the talk at Westminster was all of the impending political changes which would follow Asquith's succession to the Premiership was a sign of his acuteness. A few weeks before his article was published Churchill had dined with the Webbs. In sharp contradistinction to an earlier occasion, when he had been 'egotistical, bumptious, shallow-minded and reactionary',[10] Churchill was 'very anxious to be friends and asked to be allowed to come and discuss the long-term question' with the Webbs.[11] At another dinner on 20 February Mrs Webb wrote that he 'made me sit next to him and was most obsequious – eager to assure me that he was willing to absorb all the plans we could give him'.[12] What the acidulous Beatrice missed was the purpose behind Churchill's quizzing – he was preparing himself for the Board of Trade. Churchill may not have had any great insight into how to deal with the social problems of the masses, but he knew a lady who did. If Mrs Webb was anxious to be part of a secular priesthood, 'disinterested experts' devising 'a blueprint for society', then Churchill was eager to grant her wish.[13]

Churchill's article advocated Webbian solutions to the problem of unemployment and identified him with the 'new' Liberalism just as it was about to come into the forefront of Liberal politics. It also strengthened his claim to an important domestic political office. Even whilst professing his unworthiness for the Local Government Board, Churchill had sounded like a man with more ideas than its President (although it must be admitted that it would have been difficult to have had fewer ideas than Burns). It was not surprising that Asquith, who was looking for a revitalised programme of social legislation, should have responded to Churchill's statement that, 'dimly across gulfs of ignorance', he saw the 'outline of a policy which I call the Minimum Standard',[14] by making him President of the Board of Trade.

Before 1911 a change of office meant that Ministers had to submit themselves for re-election; 1908 was not a good year for a Liberal to do so. The Party was to lose eight by-elections, squeezed between the Socialists on the one hand and the resurgent Unionists on the other.[15] Contrary to Churchill's confident expectations in 1906, tariff reform was not dead as a political issue, and militant Unionism proclaimed it as the road to salvation for a country which was suffering from a growth in unemployment and a rise in imports. Moreover, the Unionists were well-placed to receive the middle-class vote, which wanted to protest against what it saw as a standard of living being eroded by Liberal concessions to organised labour. The Labour Party on the other hand was equally well-placed to pick up the votes of those disgruntled workers who felt that the Liberals were not doing enough for them.[16]

If 1908 was not a good time to be seeking re-election as a Liberal, then it was the worst possible time for a renegade Conservative to do so in the north-west. With the Unionist Free Fooders who had helped elect him in 1906 now virtually eliminated, and in the face of a revivified Unionist Party, Churchill was in trouble from the very start of his campaign. The intervention of H.G. Wells in his favour may have been a mark of how some Fabians supported him, but it counted for little else. When the result came in, Churchill found that he had lost by 429 votes; a 6.4 per cent swing had let in Mr Joynson-Hicks, who, twenty years on, would be his Cabinet colleague. Unionist delight was unbounded: 'What is the use of a W.C. without a seat?', was merely one of the *bons mots* circulated. It was a measure of how much Churchill was disliked that his old Party took such joy in his discomfiture. But Asquith wanted him at the Board of Trade and a safe seat at Dundee was made vacant for him. Churchill's mind readily drew parallels from the 1880s: for the second time in twenty-five years an English Liberal would stump a Scottish constituency declaring that there was a moral crusade to be won.[17]

Liberals of an older vintage could have been forgiven if they had thought that the great days of Mr Gladstone at Midlothian had come again. Declaring that he had come to unfurl 'the old flag of civil freedom and social justice under which your fathers conquered', Churchill set about his opponents with gusto. The House of Lords, which had killed so many Liberal bills, was 'filled with doddering old peers, cute financial magnates, clever wirepullers, big brewers with bulbous noses' and 'all the enemies of progress'. As for the Socialists, he dealt with them at the same time as rebutting charges that there was no difference between them and the Liberals: 'Socialism wants to pull down wealth, Liberalism seeks to raise up poverty'; the one was destructive, the other constructive.[18] As for Mr Scrymgeour, the prohibitionist, he was a 'hen-dim figure', worth commenting about only in retrospect. The victory was overwhelming. Churchill collected forty-four per cent of the total vote and had a majority of nearly three thousand over the Unionist.

Churchill seized the opportunity thus offered to appear in two guises. The content of his rhetoric identified him with the 'new' Liberalism, whilst his style proclaimed him as a radical scourge of his former Party. It was as an ally of Lloyd George and an advocate of the most 'advanced' social policy that Churchill took his place at the centre of Asquith's use of the 'new' Liberalism.

David Lloyd George was the 'white hope' of radical Liberalism. A Welshman (despite being born in Manchester) from a poor background, Lloyd George spoke the language of the political left as easily as he did that of his native land. As a radical solicitor he had fought the battle of the Welsh peasantry against their English and Anglicised landlords. He had sprung to national prominence during the Boer War for his bitter attacks on Chamberlain and the 'jingoes'. 'C-B' had made him President of the Board of Trade, where, contrary to the hopes of some, his radicalism had not been dimmed by the pressures of office.[19] A mercurial figure of great charm and persuasiveness, it was hardly surprising that Lloyd George should have captivated his successor at the Board of Trade. If Churchill wished to learn the language and *mores* of the 'new' Liberalism, Lloyd George was willing to teach him.

The Gladstonian tradition had no remedies for the problems of unemployment, low wages and poverty – which was where the 'new' Liberalism came into its own. With Lloyd George as Chancellor and Churchill at the Board of Trade, Asquith had equipped himself with two Ministers whose eclecticism would avoid the perils of a doctrinaire approach, but who would, by their energy, infuse life into a government which seemed to be running out of steam. The 'heavenly twins' (as the two men became known) became a conduit through which the ideas of people like the Webbs and their protégé, William Beveridge, were channelled into political life; but the conduit was not a straight one and the water which passed through it was diluted and altered by all manner of considerations. The Webbs and Beveridge were social scientists, Lloyd George and Churchill were practical politicians – a marriage of convenience could be arranged, but it was bound to end in tears for the ideologues.[20]

One of the first items on which Churchill sought the help of the 'experts' was the problem of the labour market: there were people without jobs and jobs which had no people. How could this state of affairs be altered? Churchill's practical mind was not bounded by the tenets of Gladstonian Liberalism, which shied away from government interference with the iron laws of economic reality. In this he was at one with the 'new' Liberalism, which, in the search for solutions to problems, allowed ethical and social factors to outweigh purely economic ones.[21] The question of how far the state should intervene in economic affairs and the relationship between it and the individual was still fluid.[22] Social 'scientists' and progressive thinkers like the Webbs and their peers sought to use the powers of the state in a constructive way, but they did not deny that there was a place for individual morality. Mrs Webb, for example, opposed a national system of unemployment insurance on the ground that 'the state gets nothing for its money in the way of conduct'.[23] The concept of the 'deserving poor' was far from dead. Even Ramsay MacDonald, the Labour leader, thought it necessary to declare that his Party had no sympathy with 'the loafer and shirker of work who tried to batten and fatten on public funds'.[24] The question facing Asquith and company was how to translate their social concern into policy on unemployment, poverty and associated problems: this was where they needed the intellectuals.

The impression left on Beatrice Webb after talking with Churchill and other politicians on 10 February 1908 had been of a 'scramble for new constructive ideas. We happen now to have a good many to give away, hence the eagerness for our company. Every politician one meets wants to be "coached".'[25] It was not for her *beaux yeux* that Churchill cultivated the imperious Mrs Webb's company. Eclectic in his intellectual voracity, he took ideas from her, from Beveridge, from his civil servants, from studying the German example and from talking things over with Lloyd George. He was not, as Beveridge noticed, 'at all points clear' about what was meant by concepts like 'labour exchanges', but he took them into his repertoire all the same, which meant that 'you never know what he is going to hand back to you afterwards as his version of your idea'.[26]

By the autumn of 1908 Churchill was fluent enough in his new language to impress even Mrs Webb, who thought him 'brilliantly able – more than a phrase-monger'. Her praise never came unalloyed with gall, so she wondered if it was the case that 'he puts that side forward to me'; but she did conclude that 'he could not do it so well if he did not agree with it somewhat'.[27] The question of how far Churchill agreed 'with it' is an intriguing irrelevance. He was a politician with a job to do and he needed 'experts' and information with which to do it. His generous heart revolted at the spectacle of widespread poverty, but his head still had to acquire the means of acting to solve it – hence Churchill's interest in the Webbs and their ilk. It was only when the price to be paid for such action began to appear unacceptably high that Churchill began to query where the road upon which he had embarked with such gusto was leading. It was ever his way to so immerse himself in his own concerns that his perception of what was happening outside his vision was never strong.

Churchill was not only a man of action, he was also someone who liked to have a grandiose governing idea behind that activity, and this was provided for him at the Board of Trade by the Webbs' concept of the 'national minimum'. The problems facing him at the Board of Trade were various and complex and to deal with them piecemeal would not satisfy his craving for action on a grand and heroic scale. He could not be a petty bureaucrat, but with an idea like the 'national minimum' he did not have to be. It offered a readily identifiable label, which could be attached to a complicated series of problems. The idea of 'spreading a net' to save the poorest also implied a springboard from which the industrious could launch themselves upwards. Speaking in Dundee in October 1908, Churchill asserted the Government's responsibility to provide the social organisation necessary to counteract fluctuations in the labour market. He identified three basic faults: the lack of any central organisation for industry and for controlling government spending on relief work; an increasing pool of unqualified, casual labour; and a growth in child labour. His suggested solution to the first problem was the pure milk of the Webb doctrine, the establishment of a department with responsibility for 'increasing temporarily and artificially the demand for labour during a period of temporary and artificial contraction'. On the second point it was necessary to enact legislation which would deal with wage levels to prevent 'sweated labour'; whilst on the third, more children must be educated for longer: this would not only do away with the scandal of child labour, but it would also provide a better-educated workforce.[28]

These ideas came from the Webbs and Beveridge and by themselves were worthy but dull – certainly not the fodder of a political campaign. What Churchill did was to invest them with his own, highly charged, romantic vision. Who else would have addressed the problem of child labour by referring to its victims as 'the heirs of all our exertion, the inheritors of that long treasure of history and romance, of science and knowledge – aye, of national glory, for which so many valiant generations have fought'? 'Soon', he reminded his audience, 'our brief lives will be lived' and 'uncounted generations will trample heedlessly upon our tombs. What is the use of living, if it be not to strive for noble causes and to make this muddled world a better place for those who will live in it after we are gone?' It was the rhetoric of the Victorian romantic harnessing the Victorian faith in science and progress. In his peroration Churchill declared his confidence that 'we are marching towards better days. Humanity will not be cast down.'[29]

If Churchill the orator transformed the details of social legislation into a grand vision of progress and prosperity for all, then it was the task of Churchill the Minister to cast these things into legislative form. This he did in a memorandum to the Cabinet on 11 December 1908. Drawing on ideas culled from the Webbs, Beveridge and the Germans, Churchill argued for the creation of labour exchanges as the means of mitigating fluctuations in the labour market. There would also be a system of unemployment insurance covering the three million men employed in the building, engineering and shipbuilding trades. Writing to Asquith on 29 December, Churchill put forward his arguments for 'a tremendous policy of social organisation', which would include a national system of health insurance, the establishment of state-run enterprises, a modernised Poor Law, state control of an amalgamated railway system and compulsory education of children until the age of seventeen; his aim was 'to thrust a big slice of Bismarckianism over the whole underside of our industrial system'.[30] Whether or not Mrs Webb had been right in supposing that Churchill 'hardly comprehended the philosophy' behind her ideas, she was accurate in noting that he had 'the American's capacity for the quick appreciation and rapid execution of new ideas'.[31]

What Churchill also possessed was a Prime Minister who was sympathetic to his aims and, in Lloyd George, a Chancellor who would take the lead on social reform. If Churchill's friendship with F. E. Smith centred around the private sphere, it was otherwise with Lloyd George; but in both cases Churchill was the junior partner. Lloyd George shared Churchill's obsessive interest in politics, but in their private lives they shared only a taste for the best. Churchill, who did not marry until 1908, was almost a model of marital fidelity, whilst Lloyd George was a womaniser of such assiduity that his career would have been destroyed many times in an age with a more enquiring press. Where Churchill was transparent in his political manoeuvrings, even when he thought he was being tortuous, Lloyd George was 'a veritable corkscrew'.[32] But they were both inspired by the ambition to be great men and to achieve great things and for a while they trod the same road.

Lloyd George's quest for fame left him time to pursue a consuming interest in women, but Churchill's character was very different. Lloyd George could have said with MacHeath that he liked women because 'nothing unbends the mind like them', but Churchill would not have agreed. Lloyd George had 'never met anyone with such a passion for politics' as Churchill. Even 'after his marriage he commenced talking politics ... in the vestry and was quite oblivious of the fact that he had to take out the bride'.[33] This was not untypical. Churchill suffered, like so many men, from the fact that education and employment had conspired to keep him from being comfortable in female company. He had no small talk for the dinner table, where his main topic of conversation tended to be himself.[34] His romantic dalliances had been few and chaste. Indeed, his main passion was for politics, and even his literary work fell by the wayside. Churchill wrote primarily for money and with his Ministerial salary filling his bachelor's coffers he had no need to write. The only material issuing from his pen during this period was a collection of his speeches and a book of articles about his visit to East Africa when he was at the Colonial Office. The young Minister was learning his craft and there were as few distractions as a single-minded determination to succeed could contrive.

But it should not be imagined that the young Churchill led a life of monastic seclusion; the Edwardian age allowed ample room for combining politics with a full social diary. Churchill had little interest in what might be called high culture; his programme of education had not included music or paintings, and his literary interests were confined to a few classics. Away from politics his main interests were those which required purely masculine company. He and F.E. revelled in their membership of the Oxfordshire Yeomanry, and Churchill enjoyed the comradeship which it provided as well as the opportunities for military action which it afforded. He shared with Lloyd George and F.E. a taste for the company of the Edwardian *nouveaux riches*, who spent their money ostentatiously on grand parties, yachts and on enjoying life to the full; neither Liberal saw any incongruity between this and their political activities – a view not shared by all members of their Party.

It was at a ball given at the London home of Lord Crewe (one of his colleagues in Government) that Churchill first met Clementine Hozier, the woman whom he was to marry. It was not until 1906, however, that their acquaintanceship ripened into anything more, and Clementine quickly discovered that politics was her main rival and one with which she would be wise not to compete. In August 1908 during a house-party at Blenheim, Churchill finally summoned up the courage to propose.[35] Prudence might have indicated a need for caution. Miss Hozier had a record of jilting her fiancés and, although beautiful, she was not rich – a qualification which an impecunious politician might have borne in mind. But it was hardly to be expected that Churchill's temperament, so romantic in the arid fields of social reform, would be any less so when it came to love. To those who knew only the conceited and self-advertising politician, Churchill in love would have come as a surprise. He was, as Scawen Blunt noted, 'gentle and tender, and affectionate to those he loves'.[36] A long engagement was anathema to Churchill; if he was to be married, it should be as soon as could be decently contrived. Having been accepted by Clementine on 11 August he married her on 12 September, with his old friend, Lord Hugh Cecil, as best man. It was a sign of his celebrity that the marriage was the 'news event' of the month. In *My Early Life* Churchill wrote that they then lived 'happily ever after',[37] which was a pretty romantic conceit, and the fact that nobody ever does should not disguise the happiness marriage brought him.

Churchill was a gregarious man, but he had lived his life in a series of institutions where human contact was, although frequent, relatively shallow. Public school, Sandhurst, the Army and Parliament all provided him with the audience he craved, but they did nothing to give him anything in the way of family life; marriage altered this state of affairs. For the first time he had a family life of his own and he luxuriated in the emotional comforts which it afforded to his own inner need for stability and affection. In 1909 he and Clementine bought a house – 33 Eccleston Square, near Victoria Station and the House of Commons – and later that year their first child, Diana, was born. The experience of having a person who loved him for himself and not for anything he might achieve brought out the sentimental and affectionate side of his character. 'Clemmie' was his 'Kat' and he was her 'Pug' or 'Pig', and he would adorn his signature with drawings of little pigs. Clementine's own interest in politics was limited, but she was a staunch Liberal and encouraged his friendship with social reformers like Charles Masterman (Burns's junior at the Local Government Board) and the Webbs. She was less keen on her husband's friendship with the hard-drinking F.E., whom she believed encouraged him to drink and gamble – but there are some spheres where even the best wife is ill-advised to tread, and Clementine had to accept that F.E. and Winston were inseparable. When their next child, Randolph, was christened in 1911, he took his second name, Frederick, from F.E., who was one of his godfathers; the fact that his other godfather was the Foreign Secretary, Sir Edward Grey, represented a sensible compromise. But Clementine was content to leave the political sphere to her husband; she did not seek to emulate Margot Asquith or other 'political' wives.[38]

Whether Lloyd George's tale of Clementine being kept waiting whilst he and Winston discussed politics in the vestry is true or not, it contains a symbolic truth – politics was Churchill's consuming interest. Conscious as he was of his own brilliance, Churchill was prepared to describe Lloyd George as 'the greatest political genius of the day'. It was the Chancellor who 'resolved upon the necessity for a constructive social policy' and who 'selected and "imported" with great skill four units': labour exchanges, a 'sweated trades wages scheme', a national insurance bill and an unemployment bill.[39] 'Large measures of Finance and Unemployment' would, Churchill thought, 'dignify and justify our retention of office'.[40] But they would do more than that. It would be too cynical to conclude, with Mrs Webb, that Churchill's concern with economic and social problems stemmed merely from a realisation that 'no government can now ignore them'.[41] 'Fame' and renown remained his goals and, as he reminded Asquith at the end of 1908, the enacting of an 'impressive social policy' would 'leave an abiding mark on national history'. It might, of course, fail to win elections, but 'the Minister who will apply to this country' the 'German' model in social policy 'will at least have left a memorial which time will not deface of his administration'.[42]

Not everyone, however, was enamoured of the enhanced place given to the 'new' Liberalism, or of the behaviour of the 'heavenly twins'. Charles Hobhouse, the Financial Secretary to the Treasury, disliked the 'personal discourtesy' shown by Churchill to his opponents and blamed him for the 'disappearance of that harmony' which had been a feature of Campbell-Bannerman's Cabinets.[43] But objections went deeper than personal dislike of Churchill or of Lloyd George. Commitment to social policy meant an increase in government expenditure and, at a time when a 'balanced budget' was an article of financial faith, the question of how to raise the money was bound to bring out the tensions existing between the various strands of Liberalism.

As the Unionists had already found, governing an Empire which faced challenges from abroad as well as problems at home was an expensive business. Chamberlain had sought to square the circle through tariff reform, which he said would make the 'foreigner pay'. The Liberals rejected any such course, but they still had to find an answer to the problem of how to spend money on 'guns and butter' at the same time as expenditure on both was rising. Unionists predicted that a 'cheese-paring Cobdenite Cabinet' would ruin the Empire in order to provide old-age pensions,[44] and Lloyd George and Churchill were soon identified as the chief villains in this respect. Churchill's attitude towards defence expenditure during these years has remained a source of embarrassment to his biographers as it sits so incongruously with his behaviour after 1910 and before 1939; but the explanation for it is not far to seek. To attribute it all to Lloyd George's influence is to go too far. Churchill always had a tendency to assume that his own departmental interests should come before any wider concerns, and at the Board of Trade this meant competing with Service departments for money; it was easy to predict how Churchill would react to claims for higher defence spending. Moreover, as Mrs Webb had noticed in July 1903, Churchill was 'at heart a Little Englander', who looked to 'the *haute finance* to keep the peace'.[45] Like many Liberals who believed in 'progress', Churchill liked to think that the most civilised parts of the human race had advanced beyond the point where a recourse to arms to settle disputes was necessary. From conviction and departmental self-interest Churchill was inclined to agree with Lloyd George that the defence estimates could be pruned to provide money for their own programmes.

It was at this point, where the demand for social legislation clashed with the needs of national defence and the requirements of sound finance, that the Asquith Government threatened to fall apart; that it did not do so was due almost entirely to the political and tactical skills of the Prime Minister. Asquith's talents, unlike those of Lloyd George and Churchill, were not such as to invite the enthusiasm of posterity. His oratory was good, but not inspiring, and he lacked the charisma of his two lieutenants; but he possessed what neither of them did – a massive fund of common sense and patience. Given the behaviour of some of his colleagues, Asquith was to find these qualities indispensable.

Churchill had challenged the Secretary of State for War, Richard Haldane, in May 1908 over his plans for the reorganisation of the Army, alleging that they were too extravagant; any money saved could be spent on social policy. Haldane, paranoid as only a War Minister in a Cabinet full of Liberals can be, thought that he saw the hairy hand of Lloyd George behind this. Churchill's plan would have stopped him from sending an expeditionary force to France in the event of war with Germany and thereby have dealt a blow to Sir Edward Grey's foreign policy. What the radical element in the Cabinet was unaware of was that, soon after coming to office, Grey had authorised the opening of Staff talks with the French military; so Churchill had no conception of just how much damage his proposals would do.[46] Rumours abounded, with *The Times* reporting that Haldane would soon be removed to the Woolsack to be replaced by Churchill.[47] There was no foundation in the story, but it was symptomatic of the Unionist fear that the radical element in the Cabinet would seize control.

On that occasion Churchill's challenge had come to naught. The Cabinet committee set up to examine his proposals came down against them. Haldane was able to show that in size and type, the British Army was smaller and less expensive than its foreign counterparts. He also took issue with Churchill's sanguine assumption that there was no military danger to be apprehended from Germany. Although defeated, Churchill was not convinced. Speaking at a miners' rally in Swansea on 15 August 1908, Churchill repudiated suggestions that war with Germany was inevitable. There was, he declared, no point at issue between Britain and Germany and it would be financial madness for them to fight each other.[48] This was not an attitude which boded well for Asquith's prospects of being able to get the Cabinet to sanction the increases in naval expenditure which would be necessary to keep his pledge to maintain British naval supremacy.[49]

Traditionally Britain was committed to maintain the 'Two Power' standard, which Asquith defined in December 1908 as 'a predominance of ten per cent over the combined strengths in capital ships, of the next two naval powers'.[50] The Unionists, who thought that the Government could not be trusted with such matters, kept a sharp eye on its activities. The Liberal First Lord of the Admiralty, Reginald McKenna, was one of the few exceptions to this Unionist distrust. An efficient bureaucrat, McKenna was largely in the hands of his First

Sea Lord, Sir John Fisher. Since 1905 Britain had built four Dreadnoughts a year, but with rumours abounding that the Germans were also building at this rate, the press whipped up a public agitation, encouraged surreptitiously by Fisher; the slogan of this campaign was: 'We want eight and we won't wait.' In January 1909 the Admiralty formally requested an increase in the naval construction programme for 1909–10 to eight Dreadnoughts.[51] This precipitated a political crisis within the Cabinet.

In an impassioned thirteen-page letter to Asquith on 2 February 1909, Lloyd George warned that the problem 'threatens to reopen all the old controversies which rent the Party for years and brought it to impotence and contempt'. He asked the Prime Minister not to commit himself to the 'very crude and ill-considered Admiralty demands' without listening to himself, Churchill, John Morley and others who thought like them. There were, he warned, 'millions of earnest Liberals in the country who are beginning rather to lose confidence in the Government'; for the most part this was for reasons beyond the Government's control, but if the Cabinet deliberately threw over their pledges of 'economy', then such Liberals would 'break out into open sedition'. If this happened, Lloyd George warned, it would not just be a few radicals making a noise – 'the usefulness of this Parliament will be at an end'.[52] Churchill took the same line.

From a radical Welsh solicitor who had opposed the Boer War, such sentiments were only to be expected, but for a scion of the house of Churchill to share them was something which required explanation; most of those provided were unflattering. Lord Knollys, the King's Private Secretary, opined that 'it cannot be from conviction or principle as the very idea of his having either is enough to make anyone laugh'.[53] Another courtier, though one of a more political hue, Lord Esher, thought that it was all quite simple: Churchill aspired to the leadership of the radical wing of the Liberal Party.[54] Esher did not share the Court's low opinion of Churchill. A man who prided himself upon his genius for friendship and his reading of character, Esher's political experience went back to the days of Lord Randolph, and he reminded Churchill of the fate that had awaited his father when he had resigned over a similar issue; to resign on an issue where the public were against you was to court political 'ruin'.[55]

In all political crises there is a certain amount of shadow-boxing and posturing for the benefit of supporters, and whilst Asquith was occasionally tempted by irritation at the behaviour of the 'heavenly twins' to 'summarily . . . cashier them both', he restrained himself – and kept the Cabinet intact.[56] In Asquith's eyes the issue was not really one of finance, but rather one of 'security'. 'No surplus,' he thought, 'however large, would justify the laying down of a ship that was not needed for security', and equally, 'no deficit can justify the failure to lay down any number of ships that are so needed'.[57] Asquith's forensic skills carved out a solution which avoided resignations. On

25 February it was decided that six ships would be built, with two more tacked on to the estimates for the following year. This allowed the Government to claim that it was building eight ships at the rate of four a year. Churchill was despondent, foreseeing possible defeat for the Government ahead; but he remained in office – Lord Randolph's shadow was a long one. It was, however, now necessary to find money for the new naval programme and for social reform.[58]

It might be overly cynical to say that the famous 'People's budget' was a device for pulling the Liberal Government back together, but that was certainly one of its effects. The fact was that unless more money could be found from some source, then the quarrels of 1909 would be repeated in successive years, and with the Government's unity having been preserved only with difficulty, Asquith was not anxious for that. Lloyd George's budget, by increasing income tax and introducing a 'supertax', promised a solution to the problem. Chamberlain had said let 'the foreigner pay'; Lloyd George said 'squeeze the rich'. The Gladstonians could rest easy about free trade, the Liberal imperialists could do the same about national defence, whilst the 'new' Liberals could rejoice that their social programme would be paid for. But for these things a price would have to be paid.

6

The Limits of Radicalism

Churchill's rhetoric, like his manners and his association with Lloyd George, gave an easy credibility to the charges levelled by his enemies that he was an extreme radical; after all, having fled the fold of pure Conservatism, who could put a limit to the leftward march of a Churchill in pursuit of political advantage? For this view Churchill had only himself and his name to blame. Lord Randolph's political eccentricities were still remembered, and to a generation brought up on Macaulay's picture of the first Duke of Marlborough, it was almost second-nature to adopt the view attributed to Gladstone: 'Who ever heard of a Churchill with principles?' Men who change their Party in British political life do so at a permanent cost in reputation. To this natural concomitant of political infidelity, Churchill added coals of fire which were of his own devising. For the President of the Budget League to stump the country vying with Lloyd George in devising insults to fling at the aristocracy may have been natural, but when the man doing so was the grandson of one Duke and, the cousin of another, who retired to Blenheim Palace to recuperate from his labours, it was not surprising that he was accused of 'a lack of common decency' and suspected of humbug.[1]

What such behaviour reflected was Churchill's very aristocratic disdain for the opinion of others, as well as an egotism which was purely his own. Churchill's perception of others was always very tenuous. He was concerned for the 'masses' in the way a great landowner is for his tenants, but he had little contact with them on an individual basis. He would talk to his valet, by whom he would be dressed and who would run his bath for him. He would rarely set eyes on the cook who prepared his meals or the maids who kept Eccleston Square tidy. He might address a word to the cab-man who drove him to work, but he was a stranger to public transport. Churchill lived the life normal for a man of his class; it put him in a position to improve the lot of the masses, but hardly to understand them. It was easy for his Unionist critics to accuse him of hypocrisy and of betraying the order into which he was born, but their anger blinded them to something which was clear to Liberals like Lloyd George and Masterman – that Churchill was a profoundly conservative man. He accepted the social order which gave him such privileges without question and he wanted to preserve it. He wanted to extend some of its benefits to the dispossessed and his generous nature revolted at the conditions in which some of his countrymen lived; but there were limits as to how far he was prepared to go. These were revealed by the events of 1910–11. When Lloyd George and Masterman teased him that their campaign against the Lords was the first step on the road to revolution, he replied, 'If this is what it leads to, you must be prepared for me to leave you!'[2]

Where Lloyd George had a genuine hatred of what he termed 'landlordism', which derived from his own youth and which made him relish the prospect of a full-blown constitutional crisis, Churchill was quite different. His radicalism was that of the Whig grandee who saw it as the duty of his order to ensure that those social and political changes which were needful for political stability were not blocked by vested interests; change in order to preserve. As Masterman's wife observed: 'Winston, of course, is not a democrat, or at least he is a Tory democrat.'[3] The theme of his speeches during his Lancashire campaign in December was not the budget itself, but rather the dangers of an unelected chamber frustrating the will of the people. His speeches generally struck a sober note. In contrast to Lloyd George, 'both his defence of the Budget and his indictment of the House of Lords were fair, reasoned and statesmanlike, free from vulgarity, cheap sentiment or class cat-calls'.[4]

Asquith, who was not given to cheap compliments, wrote to Churchill on 1 February to congratulate him on his work: 'Your speeches from first to last have reached high-water mark and will live in history.'[5] Nor could the ranks of Tuscany forbear to cheer. Lord Curzon, one of the leading Unionists, had told the people of Oldham that 'all civilisation has been the work of aristocracies', and had received for his pains one of Churchill's finely honed shafts of satire. There was not, Churchill said, a 'duke, a marquis, an earl or a viscount in Oldham who will not feel that a compliment has been paid to him'. Curzon freely admitted that Churchill had mounted a 'very remarkable Lancashire campaign'.[6] Margot Asquith, fearing that Churchill might slip back into his old ways, told him that the King had hinted that 'if you w[oul]d just keep up that moderation of language wh[ich] had struck so many in this election, you w[oul]d not be at all unappreciated'; 'cheap scores, hen-roost phrases and all oratorical want of dignity is out of date'.[7] Churchill was the acceptable face of radical Liberalism; it was only his past associations which blinded Unionists to this fact.

The result of the election certainly seemed to confirm that extremism was 'out of date'. In 1906 the Liberals had won 377 seats, but after the 1910 election they held only 275. The Unionists, by contrast, went up from 157 to 273. The balance of power was held by the eighty-two Irish and forty Labour MPs. Whatever lessons the result held for the Liberals, it was difficult to argue that it indicated public approval for extreme policies – or even moderate ones couched in extreme language. The part which he had played in the campaign strengthened Churchill's already substantial claims to promotion, but Asquith did not find it easy to place him. He had wanted to offer Churchill the Admiralty in 1908, but as that post was held by Lord Tweedmouth, who was his uncle by marriage, Churchill had not pressed his claims. When Churchill had gone to the Board of Trade, Asquith had promised to ensure that he had the same status and salary as a Secretary of State, but an attempt to vote him the same salary had failed; now the time had come to make reparations.[8] Writing to Churchill on 1 February 1910 Asquith offered him the post of Chief Secretary for Ireland. Given the Government's dependence upon Irish votes, this would entail bringing in a Home Rule bill. But despite the obvious importance of the job, Churchill declined it. Before a Home Rule bill could be contemplated, it would be necessary to deal with the Lords, and Churchill wanted to be in the thick of the action, not waiting in the second rank. He told Asquith that he would prefer the Admiralty or the Home Office. Given Churchill's role in the crisis over naval expenditure and McKenna's touchiness about the subject, Asquith offered Churchill the Home Office.[9]

To become His Majesty's Principal Secretary of State at the age of thirty-five was an achievement to gratify even the ambitions of Churchill. His claim to be one of the principal figures in the Cabinet had been formally recognised: only Sir Edward Grey and Lloyd George now stood ahead of him should the Prime Minister retire. He would certainly not overhaul either of them should a leader be required in the very near future, but he was a decade younger than his rivals; he could afford to wait. The prospect before him was an alluring one. In the meantime, his new position required the adoption of a certain amount of *gravitas*. Asquith delegated to Churchill the task of writing reports on Commons business to the King, a job which meant mastering the language of discretion. Moreover, the business of his office, which included the prison service, reviewing death sentences and dealing with public order, was less susceptible to the temptations of demagoguery.

These things would, in themselves, have drawn Churchill away from his radical preoccupations, but the direction taken by the constitutional crisis brought him up against the reality of what some of those on the left of politics wanted; here he found the limits of his own radicalism. Churchill had been able to accommodate himself happily to the shift towards social reform, which had been marked by Asquith's succession to the Premiership, but the desire of some radicals to move towards a 'wider goal of social reconstruction'[10] marked the point at which his conservative instincts would let him go no further. *The Times* thought that Lloyd George's budget, with its increase in taxes on land, had taken the doctrine of 'social ransom' to an extreme, whilst the Liberal *Daily News* described them as taxes on 'surpluses and luxuries'.[11] But at what point, however, did social reform become social redistribution? Churchill, who had no great liking for the budget itself, found the constitutional struggle which had been unleashed by its rejection disturbing. Before the election Mrs Webb had feared that in the event of a Conservative victory 'the whole Liberal Party would become extremists', and that Grey, Haldane and company would find themselves pushed aside: 'political radicalism would finally be merged into economic collectivism';[12] the 'Peers versus People' crisis offered another means to that end.

The radicals wanted the Government to press ahead with abolishing the House of Lords. Its rearguard action had frustrated the Campbell-Bannerman administration and it was an obvious barrier to Home Rule for Ireland and a full-scale radical programme. In the aftermath of the January election Churchill was prepared to threaten the Lords with abolition, but he was willing to settle for an elected second chamber.[13] In this he occupied a position mid-way between Lloyd George's demands for an end to the House of Lords and Grey's total opposition to the idea.[14]

Asquith's greatest strength as Prime Minister was his ability to keep together his tempestuous colleagues by finding compromises, but there were times when his evasiveness in confronting issues was politically damaging. The revelation on 21 February that he had not, as he had implied during the election, secured a promise from the King to create more peers if necessary, was one such occasion. Liberal morale in the House and the country plummeted under the realisation that if the peers proved obstinate, there would have to be another election.[15] Dependent as the election had left him on Irish and Labour votes, Asquith had to concede their demands that the veto powers of the House of Lords should be dealt with at once.[16] Churchill stuck to his moderate position, but his main attention was directed elsewhere during the post-election period.

Churchill's first priority as Home Secretary was to reform the prison system, to which end, following his usual pattern, he sought the advice of those who had views about how it might be made more humane. But he had scarcely begun to collect his information than he was faced by the beginnings of what was to become a wave of industrial unrest. A dispute between the Empire Transport Company and the dockers who unloaded their ships at Newport in South Wales degenerated into violence in May when the employers brought in 'black-leg' labour. At the Board of Trade it would have fallen to Churchill to act the part of conciliator, but at the Home Office it was his duty to maintain public order. This led to his authorising the despatch of 300 Metropolitan policemen to Newport. Churchill resisted the pressure on him to send troops and concentrated on ensuring that order was maintained and that the employers used the conciliation services of the Board of Trade. But in the next surge of unrest, in the coalfields of the Rhondda valley, matters were not so easily settled.

The dock-workers were only partly unionised and the very nature of their job, depending as it did upon the selection of 'gangs' by foremen, militated against the development of any *esprit de corps*; the same was not true of the Rhondda miners. Strikes by the Miners' Union over pay and conditions resulted in a shutdown of the pits and, during the picketing which followed, there were confrontations between the police and the miners. The Chief Constable, fearing a breakdown of law and order, asked Whitehall whether troops could be despatched to the coalfields. Churchill saw no need for the employment of the military, a view shared by Haldane. But it transpired that troops had been sent on the night of the Chief Constable's request by the general officer in command of the southern region. The two Ministers decided to keep the troops back and to follow the Newport precedent, sending in extra policemen from the Metropolitan force. But the incident provided Churchill with an example of why the Home Office has often been a thankless position to hold. On the one hand, *The Times* criticised him for interfering with the 'arrangements demanded by the Chief Constable' and employing the 'rosewater of conciliation'. On the other side, the episode went down in labour demonology as the occasion upon which Churchill called the troops out at Tonypandy.[17]

Against this backdrop the manoeuvrings at Westminster seemed, perforce, somewhat artificial. The Unionists had rejected the budget and their gamble had not been sanctioned by the electorate; on the other hand, the Liberals could hardly claim to have been given a ringing endorsement. Asquith's Irish allies were insisting on the abolition of the veto of the House of Lords as a condition of their support; this would clear the way for the introduction of a Home Rule bill. Thus it was that a 'hung Parliament' gave great power to the tail to wag the dog; it is ever thus. Asquith would have to have another election before Edward VII would consent to give promises about the creation of enough peers to ensure the passage of the Parliament Act, which would amend the power of the Lords; it was a long and bumpy road ahead. But so it was for the Unionists. Balfour was inclined to yield to the threats of the Liberals, but more radical Unionists wanted to take up the gauntlet and fight into the 'last ditch'. Under pressure from their more hot-headed supporters, both Asquith and Balfour strove to maintain a 'civilised' detachment in a political climate which was becoming over-heated. The unexpected death of Edward VII in May 1910 and the accession of the inexperienced George V led to cries for a 'truce of God'; it was one which Asquith and Balfour were glad to hear.

With the nation in mourning for 'Edward the peacemaker', arrangements were made to convene a constitutional conference at which Unionists and Liberals could attempt to find a solution to a political crisis which had seemed to be getting out of hand; between June and October the front-benchers searched for a way out.

The constitutional conference of the summer and early autumn of 1910 was barren of immediate political results, but it was pregnant with significance for the future. It proved impossible to find a mutually acceptable compromise on the issue of the House of Lords, but the most striking development during the conference was an initiative from Lloyd George. Neither Balfour, Asquith nor Lloyd George was anxious to see constitutional problems and Ireland dominate political life when there were great social and international issues which needed to be dealt with. Lloyd George put 'two alternative sets of ideas'

– 'winning ones' – to Churchill on 25 September.[18] One was to 'form a coalition, settle the old outstanding questions, including Home Rule, and govern the country on middle lines which will be acceptable to both parties but providing measures of moderate social reform'. The other was 'to formulate and carry through an advanced land and social reform policy'. Churchill plumped as unhesitatingly for the first as Clemmie did for the second.[19] Knowing that men said that he had been heavily influenced by Lloyd George, Churchill once wrote that he thought that 'sometimes I influenced him, and so to a large extent did . . . Balfour'; 'we were able to show him the other side of the picture of politics which in his youth . . . he had never been called upon to think much about'.[20] Lloyd George had certainly been attracted by Balfour's 'caressing charm', but as his two 'sets of ideas' showed, 'no policy was permanent, no pledge final'.[21] Churchill was attracted by the idea of a 'national government', but took the view that 'it is not for me to take the lead'.[22] Given Unionist hostility to him as a traitor, and Liberal suspicion of him as an 'eleventh-hour workman', he was wise to be reticent. But he told Lloyd George that if the two of them stood together, they could give a 'progressive character' to the policy of a coalition – or, by their withdrawal, destroy it if it failed to live up to expectations.

It was characteristic of Churchill's self-absorption that he did not stop to ask whether the Unionists would welcome him into any 'national' coalition. 'Hatred' is a strong word, too strong perhaps for the pallid emotions of politicians, for, as the coalition talks revealed, men who publicly denounce each other in language larded with insult may yet sit together to discuss matters of state – and the distribution of loaves and fishes; but in writing of Unionist feelings towards Churchill, it seems to be inescapable. One advantage which some Unionists perceived in the constitutional conference was that, if it prospered, 'Lloyd George will not attack the Naval Estimates'. Churchill, however, was considered to be 'implacable'.[23] His statement in May that if the peers would not come to heel then the monarch and the people would have to ally against them caused great offence to Edward VII and, after his death, there was no lack of voices to say that it had been politicians like Churchill who had harried him to his end. As Lord Balcarres, a Unionist Whip, commented: 'That Churchill is without conscience or scruple, without a glimmer of the comities of public reserve and deference, we all know, and all, even his closest friends, admit.'[24] Churchill's position was not an enviable one by the time of the December 1910 election. His erstwhile radical allies looked at him askance and remembered whence he had come, whilst Unionists regarded him with the hostility that must always pursue one regarded as a traitor.

Unionist opinion saw only the President of the Budget League, not the man who favoured the 'national government'; it took Churchill's rhetoric at face value. But with Churchill's translation to the Home Office there were not wanting signs which indicated to those who had always looked for them that his attachment to Liberalism was less firm than it ought to be. At the Home Office Churchill was responsible for public order and it was a responsibility which he discharged with great seriousness; as he did so at a time of social unrest, his naturally conservative instincts rose to the surface. The myth of Churchill calling out the troops at Tonypandy was, like that of King Alfred burning the cakes, symbolically true; it epitomised an attitude. Churchill, like many Liberals, approved of extending benefits to a grateful working class, but when organised Labour exerted itself to demand its 'rights', he shared in the feeling that having helped to 'uncork the bottle containing the *djinn*', Ministers were now unable to control it.[25] His reaction to unrest was that of the soldier: it must be stopped. Once it had been stopped he was prepared to be generous to defeated opponents – but only when they had been defeated. When, the week after Tonypandy, there was a huge demonstration by the suffragettes in London, it was broken up by the Metropolitan police with great brutality – policemen taking, so it was reported, particular delight in grabbing the demonstrators by their breasts. It seemed to be a sign that the new Home Secretary would brook no dissent. Of course Churchill was not to blame for the behaviour of the police, but he was censured all the same; his bellicose attitudes lent an easy credibility to such charges. That the Home Secretary liked a 'scrap' could hardly be doubted from the newspaper reports in early January 1911.

It says something for Churchill's reputation that the most famous incident during his period at the Home Office was not his attempt at penal reform but rather his attendance at the 'battle of Sidney Street'. On 3 January the police cornered an 'anarchist gang' at 100 Sidney Street in the East End; by late morning there were over two hundred policemen on the spot, many of them armed. It was too much for Churchill to resist and, disregarding his advisers, he took himself off to Sidney Street, impelled by 'a strong sense of curiosity which perhaps it would have been as well to keep in check'.[26] Newsreels captured what the press reported, namely a Churchill in Napoleonic vein – 'moving restlessly hither and thither among the rather nervous and distraught police, a professional soldier among civilians'.[27] With a Maxim gun called into action and a complement of over seven hundred policemen, Churchill made ready to assault the building – when it caught fire and burnt to the ground. Later the charred bodies of two men were found inside, but no trace was discovered of the leading anarchist, 'Peter the Painter'. The whole episode was faintly ludicrous. It provided acres of publicity, but Balfour summed up the view of the Establishment when he commented: 'We are concerned to observe photographs in the illustrated newspapers of the Home Secretary in the danger zone. I understand what the photographer was doing, but why the Home Secretary?'

The episode seemed to epitomise Churchill's defects. Egocentricity and boyish enthusiasm were all very well in their place, but that place was not in a responsible Minister of the Crown. Those who thought Churchill an interfering busy-body with an exaggerated sense of his own importance and a dangerous tendency to over-dramatise politics, found confirmation for their opinion. As Lloyd George put it, all politicians were 'keen on success' but most of them lacked what Churchill possessed in superabundance – 'the Napoleonic idea'.[28] To have such a man at the Home Office at a time of growing labour unrest, suffragette demonstrations and the threat of disorder in Ireland was something of a risk. Churchill's duties came to weigh 'heavily upon him' and Lloyd George thought that 'his position at the Home Office was gradually becoming intolerable to him'. Lloyd George and Asquith feared that, 'being a soldier', Churchill might 'act in a thorough and drastic manner in the event of further labour troubles', and within a year of appointing him Home Secretary, Asquith was looking for an opportunity to move him elsewhere.[29]

It was one thing for an elected government to challenge the powers of an unelected House of Lords, but quite another for workers to challenge the administration which was in the process of giving them so much; at least it was in Churchill's mind. Like many conservative members of his class, Churchill was easily persuaded that the only way to deal with the growing wave of industrial unrest in 1911 was by a show of force. The long, hot summer that year saw railway and dock strikes at a time when Britain found herself within measurable distance of war with Germany. In Birkenhead and Liverpool the mayors, alarmed by the riots which accompanied the strikes, reported that a revolutionary situation was developing. Churchill, sanctioning the use of troops, was alarmed at the rash of 'sympathy strikes' and the possibility of a general strike. 'A new force', he told the King, 'has arisen in trades unionism, whereby the power of the old leaders has proved quite ineffective.'[30] Fortunately, the old skills of Lloyd George proved up to negotiating an end to the strikes. The spectacle of an alarmed and bellicose Churchill at the Home Office in such an inflammatory situation was not one which brought much comfort to either the Chancellor or the Prime Minister; but events had already suggested to Asquith a way out of a situation which could become dangerous.

As a Minister Churchill tended to become absorbed in the work of his own department; his rhetoric often preceded thought rather than contrariwise. At the Board of Trade he had thrown himself wholeheartedly into the cause of social reform. There he had appeared in the guise sanctioned by his father's career – that of a sceptic of high naval spending. Thus it was that he had been aligned with Lloyd George and the 'little Englanders', but his assumptions were not theirs. All through the history of modern western civilisation there have been those who have held that war is morally wrong and that it is caused by arms races, profiteers and reactionary aristocrats. Men and women have held such views, sincerely failing to see that if there are fairies at the bottom of the garden, then they are heavily armed and have designs on their neighbour's ass and ox; Churchill was never in their ranks. The bellicosity which he had shown in the face of challenges to public order at home was equally evident when the Kaiser seemed to challenge the international order.

The Liberals had come to power in the middle of a crisis over Morocco and it was this second crisis which was to be decisive in changing the direction of Churchill's career. British support for French claims to a sphere of influence in Morocco was implicit in the *Entente Cordiale* of 1904. Lord Lansdowne, the Unionist Foreign Secretary, had meant the *Entente* to end Anglo-French hostility, but the Germans chose to interpret it as directed against themselves and had resolved to challenge it. When Grey had first become Foreign Secretary, he had been asked by the French Ambassador, Paul Cambon, one of the main architects of the *Entente*, whether France could rely upon the British in the event of German aggression. Grey's reply was that he could not imagine that the British would stand aside.[31] This was, strictly speaking, non-committal, but that was not how the French took it and the military talks which Grey sanctioned. As Harold Nicolson commented, 'this perfected type of British parliamentarian did not attribute any but a purely technical and conditional importance to such conversations. . . . It cannot be expected that anyone not deeply imbued with the doctrines of parliamentary liberalism will understand this point of view.'[32] The radical section of the Cabinet, which was thoroughly imbued with such doctrines, was saved from having any view on these things as they were not informed of them. Indeed, even Campbell-Bannerman seems to have been imperfectly acquainted with his Government's foreign policy. In April 1907 on a visit to Paris, he startled his hosts by saying that he did not regard Britain as being in any way committed to help France in the event of a German attack. The British Ambassador, Sir Francis Bertie, put French minds at rest by telling them that the Prime Minister had not really meant what they had taken him to mean.[33]

But in 1911 when the Germans sent the gun-boat *Panther* to the Moroccan port of Agadir to pressurise the French, the whole question of Britain's obligations came up again. Churchill, like other radicals, was surprised to learn of the Staff talks, but any indignation which he and Lloyd George might have been inclined to feel had this news been given to them earlier, was eclipsed by their reaction to German threats. A scholarly cottage-industry has grown up around the most public manifestation of Lloyd George's reaction to the crisis, his speech on 21 July when he declared that he could not stand by and let Britain be treated as a negligible quantity in an area where her interests were vitally concerned. This was taken by contemporaries as a warning to the Germans; indeed, the latter were astonished by such a proclamation from such a source. Disregarding this, some later historians have alleged that the speech was really a warning to the French that they ought to compromise with the Germans; however, since no one at the time was clever enough to figure this out, it hardly matters, save as an illustration of why some people get irritated by historians.[34]

Lloyd George was, Balfour reported, 'very bellicose, as I hear Churchill is also'. They were, he explained to his private secretary, Jack Sanders, 'bellicose' in the sense that they thought 'war must come' and that 'now is the best time for fighting'. Lloyd George declared that if war did come, the Unionists 'will have to join us', thus showing, Balfour thought, that he had 'not yet wholly given up his position of last November'.[35] The Chancellor would soon lapse back into the tongue which he could assume at will, which implied a radical condemnation of the arms race; but the Home Secretary would not follow his example.

During the Agadir crisis Churchill had been told by the Chief Police Commissioner that the Home Office was responsible for the safety of the cordite reserves stored in magazines in London. Being Churchill, he immediately enquired into this and, discovering that the reserves were not properly guarded, he persuaded Haldane to release troops for this purpose.[36] He was hardly more impressed by the attitude of the Admiralty as revealed at the important Committee of Imperial Defence (CID) meeting held on 23 August. The conversations which the British and French military had been having presupposed the despatch of a British expeditionary force to the Continent upon the outbreak of war, but McKenna did not seem very confident that this could be done speedily and without loss. Churchill, on the other hand, was a staunch supporter of the idea of an expeditionary force. He submitted a paper to the CID meeting outlining (with remarkable prescience) the likely course of the first few weeks of a major European war and showing why it was vital that Britain should intervene. He also proposed to Grey that they should enter into a Triple Alliance with France and Russia.[37] Churchill's instinctive aggressiveness in the face of challenges may have been a potential liability at the Home Office, but his performance at the CID meeting helped to convince Asquith that it could be converted into an asset at the Admiralty.

The Agadir crisis revealed a lack of consensus and co-ordination in British defence policy which worried the Prime Minister. At the CID meeting McKenna had made plain his dislike of the War Office plans and their implications for British foreign policy. Admiralty strategy was to defend the shipping lanes and mount small, amphibious attacks on Germany. The Admiralty war plans were firmly locked in the head of the First Sea Lord, Sir Arthur Wilson, whose hesitant and confused manner contrasted poorly with the self-assurance and confidence of General Sir Henry Wilson, who presented the Army case.[38] Haldane, who took the view that 'our problems of defence are too numerous and complex' to be 'locked in the brain of the First Sea Lord', pressed for the creation of a 'properly organised and scientifically based war staff' for the Navy, which could co-operate with the Army's General Staff. He threatened to resign if this was not done, and even offered to do the job himself.[39] But Asquith preferred to appoint Churchill. The usual reasons given for the choice – that Churchill was in the Commons and that

Haldane's overt criticism of the Navy at the CID would have given offence to the Admiralty, are all valid, but they failed to go to the heart of the matter.[40]

In sending Churchill to the Admiralty, Asquith tilted the balance of power in the Cabinet towards a commitment to France. McKenna objected strenuously to the military conversations with France, and by replacing him with Churchill, who did not, Asquith ensured that Grey's policy of supporting the Anglo-French *Entente* received much-needed reinforcement.[41] Solid, white-haired and impressive in mien, Asquith was less decisive than he looked. As one of his Ministers observed, 'He has little courage; he will adopt the views of A. with apparent conviction and enthusiasm, but if the drift of opinion is against A. he will find an easy method of throwing him over.'[42] But it was not simply want of courage that afflicted Asquith. Any attempt to be clear about the exact nature of the French connection would probably have destroyed the Government by exposing the differences on the subject between Grey, Haldane and the radical element in the Cabinet; prevarication, which instinct provided, was what policy demanded.

At the Home Office Churchill had occupied a position which was still close to the main reforming drive of Asquith's Government. He had been able to open the first labour exchanges and set in train improvements in the prison service. But at the Admiralty he was to find himself in a position inimical to the 'new' Liberalism which he had espoused since 1908. As one of the leaders of the attack on 'bloated armaments' in 1909, Churchill would be expected, by his radical adherents, to curb the rise in the naval estimates. Being in charge of the Admiralty or the War Office in a Liberal government was no sinecure, and as both Haldane and McKenna could bear witness, it was impossible to win much in the way of kudos. If expenditure increased, the radicals decried the Minister as the tool of the military; if it decreased, the Unionists would accuse him of being a traitor.

Churchill's tremendous ability to concentrate upon the work of his office made him a formidable departmental Minister, but his faculty of beginning each job anew, without regard for previously expressed views, was to become a political liability the longer his career became. He was to demonstrate a damaging tendency to alienate former allies without winning new ones or even propitiating former enemies. The *Spectator* took the view that he had neither 'the loyalty, the dignity, the steadfastness and the good sense which make an efficient head of a great office' and that his love of the 'limelight' disqualified him from his post. Leo Maxse's *National Review* took an even curter line, dismissing him as a 'windbag'.[43] The speed with which he was to turn his back on social reform aroused memories of his Tory antecedents. Long before the dramatic events of the Dardanelles fiasco, the way to political isolation was being signposted.

7

Young Man in a Hurry

Lord Randolph Churchill had once accused Gladstone of being 'an old man in a hurry'; at the Admiralty his son Winston was to prove to be a young man in a hurry. The news of Churchill's appointment to the Admiralty was not welcomed in what might be called 'navalist' quarters. The admirals, and those Unionists who supported them, viewed the advent of a 'little Englander' to the Admiralty with ill-concealed hostility. Unionists interpreted it as Asquith dumping an unsuccessful Home Secretary on to the Navy in order to reduce naval expenditure; they could hardly have been more wrong – at least on the last point.[1]

The Home Office was not a post Churchill had found congenial, nor was it well-suited to his talents. He was the one member of the Liberal Cabinet of whom it could have been said, 'he is evidently a soldier at heart'.[2] He enjoyed discussing military subjects and, even during his most radical phase, had been happy to attend German military manoeuvres, even if he had returned from Berlin with the idea that Germany was no threat to Britain. The view from Admiralty House was somewhat different. No First Lord could have avoided being caught up in the fears engendered by Germany's naval programme. That the Germans should have a large army was accepted as natural; but why did she need a large fleet? To 'navalist' journalists like Leo Maxse, and to Unionists who supported the idea of the 'two-power standard', there could be only one answer: Germany wanted to be in a position to threaten Britain's control of the seas. No free-born Briton could stomach that. Arriving in the wake of the Agadir crisis, Churchill was not disposed to contest this view.

Churchill came to the Admiralty in October 1911 with an agenda drawn up by the experience of Agadir. On the purely professional front, his first task was to create a naval war staff to engage in planning with the Army; on the political front, his task was to align the Admiralty with the general direction of Grey's foreign policy. He set about the first job at once, creating in the process much unrest in the Navy; but this was as nothing to the waves created by the political consequences of Agadir.

McKenna had not been happy at moving from the Admiralty. A slim, elegant figure, McKenna was a good hater and, blaming Churchill for the move, was henceforth inclined to snipe at his successor. McKenna's opposition to Sir Henry Wilson's plans for sending an expeditionary force to the Continent derived from a radical distrust of too close a connection with the French. On 20 October, whilst he was still trying to resist being moved from the Admiralty, the aggrieved First Lord demanded assurances that British troops would never be used 'in the first instance' and that the French should not be encouraged to think that they would; he had threatened to resign if conversations between the military Staffs of the two countries were continued. Asquith assured him that Wilson's views were not his own, but McKenna acutely observed that the French had already been encouraged to believe that 'we should fight on their side'; he commented that whatever Asquith's views, he might find himself 'rushed into it'. The Prime Minister, with more bluster than truth, denied that he was a 'figurehead pushed against his will and without his knowledge by some energetic colleagues'.[3]

Reassured by Grey that 'at no stage of our intercourse with France since January 1906 had we either by diplomatic or military engagements compromised our freedom of decision and action' in the event of a Franco-German war,[4] Asquith increasingly leant upon this as a defence against those who claimed that the military talks had done just that. Lord Esher, the civilian member of the CID, shared McKenna's concern. He told Asquith on 4 October that 'the mere fact' that the War Office had worked out plans with the French 'has certainly committed us to fight, whether the Cabinet likes it or not'.[5] But Asquith went on repeating that Britain had a free hand. Whether, as Esher thought, Asquith had finally realised the implications of the Staff talks with the French, but was 'lazy and hesitates to act on these views',[6] or whether he simply preferred to take the line of least resistance, the Prime Minister certainly staged a retreat under fire during November.

McKenna had told Asquith that Britain was now in a position vis-à-vis France where she could not win: 'if we failed to join them we should be charged with bad faith', whilst if 'we joined them we should be plunged into war on their quarrel'.[7] There were three possible responses to this allegation. The first was the line taken by Unionists like Balfour and Chamberlain, by General Wilson and by members of the Foreign Office, namely that national self-interest demanded that Britain should support France, in which case the sooner an alliance was concluded the better.[8] But as no Liberal espoused this in public, the debate in Cabinet centred around the other two responses. The minority, including Churchill, Haldane, Grey and Asquith, argued that there was no commitment. Others held that 'without the previous knowledge of the Cabinet', Britain had become committed to France.[9] When the matter was discussed on 15 November, opposition came from a number of directions. Old Gladstonians like Morley and the Lord Chancellor, Lord Loreburn, objected to 'foreign entanglements'. 'Loulou' Harcourt, the Colonial Secretary, spoke for many old-fashioned radicals when he expressed a distrust of the 'anti-German' bias of the Foreign Office and wanted to reassess the basis of the Government's foreign policy. Radicals of a younger generation like

Lloyd George and John Simon objected to the arms race, as did McKenna, who also had an axe to grind. All of them shared a sense of outrage at having been kept in the dark and a feeling that Haldane had been 'very slim'.[10] Despite assurances from Grey and Asquith that they still had a 'free hand', the majority of the Cabinet took the view that Britain had been 'partially' committed and demanded that, in future, no Staff talks should be considered as binding Britain to France; they demanded that there should be no further talks without their approval. Despite the claims of some historians that the Agadir crisis strengthened Britain's commitment to the French connection,[11] it did not; indeed, without Churchill at the Admiralty, the policy of the *Entente* might well have broken down.

Rumours were rife that the Liberals would 'break up in the debate on foreign policy'.[12] A 'Grey-must-go' movement in the radical and Liberal press criticised his policy towards Russia, France and Italy, and called for a move to improve Anglo-German relations.[13] The *Entente* was, in Esher's words, 'decidedly imperilled'.[14] If Churchill had leant towards the 'radical tail', then the issue might have gone badly for Grey; instead, the reforms which he instituted at the Admiralty actually helped to save Grey's policy. By early 1912 he had overridden Admiral Wilson's opposition to the creation of a war staff for the Navy and sacked the Admiral, replacing him with one who would co-operate. The new war staff would not have time to make a great impact on naval planning before war overtook it, but it did commit the Navy to transporting the Army to France upon the outbreak of an Anglo-German war.[15]

The Conservative press had greeted Churchill's advent with a mixture of criticism and insult: 'He has not the loyalty, the dignity, the steadfastness to make an efficient head of a great office'[16] was the opinion of the *Spectator*. Esher, who admired his great talents, eyed him uneasily, but the events of November seemed to show that he would 'play up' the right way: 'W[inston] thinks Germany *l'ennemi* and quite uncapturable.'[17] Speaking at the Guildhall on 9 November, Churchill made it clear that Britain would retain her existing margin of superiority over the German Navy even if the Germans stepped up their rate of building.[18] This brought him plaudits from old enemies like Lord Northcliffe, whose newspapers had been among Churchill's harshest critics: 'I judge public men on their public face and I believe that your inquiring, industrious mind is alive to the national danger.'[19] But old radicals like Scawen Blunt, who had admired Churchill in his 'little Englander' phase, now sorrowfully concluded that he was 'bitten with Grey's anti-German policy'.[20]

Grey would have denied that his policy was 'anti-German', and as a sop to the Cabinet he decided that efforts should be made early in 1912 to improve Anglo-German relations. Churchill's old friend and financial adviser, Sir Ernest Cassel, visited Germany in January to have 'unofficial' talks. Of particular interest to Churchill was the question of a 'naval holiday'. Blunt had hoped that Churchill was 'open to conversion' on Germany; the idea of a moratorium on naval construction might well allow tension to dissipate. Churchill did not think that this particular horse would run, but could hardly veto the idea.[21] It was necessary that 'our foreign policy should go to the utmost point that it could to be friendly to Germany' because it was the 'only way to preserve unity of support in the Cabinet and in the Liberal Party for the Anglo-French Entente';[22] so it was decided that Haldane should go to Germany.

But whilst the British press enjoyed speculating upon why the Government should be at such pains to pretend that Haldane was going to Germany for 'personal reasons', Churchill and the Admiralty were digesting the details of a new German naval law brought back by Cassel. Churchill told Grey at the end of January that the planned increases in the rate of production were 'serious, and will require new and vigorous measures on our part'.[23] The chances that Haldane's mission would bear fruit were always slender, but they were rendered even more so by a speech which Churchill chose to make in Glasgow on 7 February in which he described the German Fleet as 'in the nature of a luxury', and went on to proclaim that Britain would maintain her naval supremacy whatever the cost.[24] The Germans were furious at the insult which they conceived had been offered to their Navy, and many Liberals regarded the speech as unduly provocative and unnecessary; Conservatives, on the other hand, welcomed this fresh evidence that the First Lord of the Admiralty was on the right side.[25] The radical who had opposed naval estimates of £35 million in 1908 was now proposing to increase them to over £40 million. Thus it was that for the second time in succession Asquith's appointment of an 'economist' to the Admiralty ended with the First Lord advocating higher naval estimates. It may be that Asquith had hoped that Churchill would do rather better than his predecessor on this score, but if he too became a convert to the Admiralty view, then at least the Lloyd George–Churchill combination would not operate against Cabinet unity.[26] Between 1910 and 1914 the estimates were to rise from £35,142,700 to £51,550,000.[27]

The dramatic change in Churchill's position on these matters naturally gave rise to speculation about his motives. The German Naval Attaché, Captain Widenmann, had a straightforward explanation when he wrote to his master, Admiral Tirpitz, in October 1911. He thought that the new First Lord was 'clever enough' to realise that the British public would support 'naval supremacy' whoever was in charge at the Admiralty and, 'as his boundless ambition takes account of popularity, he will manage his naval policy so as not to damage that'; this, Widenmann thought, would mean dropping 'the ideas of economy' which he had preached.[28] It proved a prescient comment, but it does not mean that Churchill advocated higher naval spending just because he wanted to win popularity. The only real rival to the British Fleet was the one which Tirpitz had created; thus it became the target against which Churchill measured himself. He was willing to contemplate 'naval holidays', but he would not entertain the idea of Germany out-building Britain. There were many times when Churchill seemed to forget that he was a Liberal in a Cabinet of men who were, as a body, far from convinced that greater spending on the Navy was necessary. The fact that he, himself, had adopted such a position in 1908–9 added a certain piquancy to the disputes which marked his time at the Admiralty.

Now that Churchill was at the Admiralty, he was apt to be antagonistic towards anyone who opposed his plans for increases in expenditure; but it was not necessary to be 'pro-German' to think that the sums of money being demanded were excessive. Lloyd George, whose speech in July 1911 had made such an impact on Germany, remained aware of the danger to be apprehended from that quarter. 'In his heart', Lloyd George did 'not care a bit for economy',[29] and his junior Minister, Hobhouse, found that he was entirely lacking in the Gladstonian cheese-paring instinct.[30] He was, Esher noted, 'plucky and an imperialist at heart, if he is anything'.[31] Lloyd George had certainly left the Unionists with the impression that he might yet 'follow Chamberlain'.[32] Yet Lloyd George remained opposed to what he saw as inflated naval estimates. 'He did believe in a strong navy and was always open to arguments for greater expenditure provided the Admiralty could "prove" that the nation's security would be otherwise endangered'; he was not, however, 'prepared to squander money on building gigantic flotillas to encounter mythical armadas'. Churchill's habitual self-immersion in the outlook of his department deprived him of the ability to take a similarly critical look at the Admiralty and its policy; it also opened something of a breach between himself and Lloyd George. On a personal level the two men remained 'as close friends as ever', but by mid-1912 they were 'drifting wide apart on principles'.[33] Remembering whence Churchill had come, some Liberals saw in his changed attitude the revival of the 'Tory' in him,[34] and there were rumours that he was 'mediating ... going over to the other side'.[35]

The fact that such stories could be spread indicated how widespread was the distrust felt towards Churchill – and how little even someone like Lloyd George actually knew him. There was no likelihood of Churchill leaving the Admiralty voluntarily; it had everything he wanted. He 'felt to the quick the traditional glamour of his new office, the romance of sea-power, the part that it played in our island history' and 'the conviction that it was today the keystone of our safety'.[36] The only way he would leave the Admiralty would be if the Cabinet did not let him discharge his duties as he saw fit. He felt that no one could 'do my job ... properly. It is too big and difficult', but he did feel that, 'owing to my experience as a soldier and politician I can do it better than anyone else'; he 'loved the work'.[37] Asquith's daughter Violet recalled Churchill 'buoyantly engaged in his new context', declaring that he could 'now lay eggs instead of scratching around in the dust and clucking'.[38] But not everyone liked the 'eggs', and there were those who were disturbed by the 'clucking'.

Those who thought it odd that the critic of increased naval spending in 1909 should now be the advocate of great increases for 1912–13 had a point. Churchill and Lloyd George had been right to be sceptical of the Admiralty figures in 1908–9. Then it had been pronounced 'a practical certainty' that the Germans would have seventeen Dreadnoughts by 1912; in fact, they had only completed nine ships by the spring of that year.[39] McKenna had admitted in February 1911 that of the nine ships which it had been said would be ready by then, the Germans had taken delivery of only five. As prophets the admirals made good sailors, but they responded to demands that the estimates should be cut with the familiar story of rumours that the Germans were stepping up their rate of construction of Dreadnoughts.[40] With the 'proof' of this now in Churchill's hands, thanks to the Kaiser's generosity to Cassel, the new First Lord took the same line as his predecessor. In a rare admission of fallibility, one qualified and hedged about with caveats to be sure, Churchill managed to have his cake and eat it when writing about this period. Describing the line which he and Lloyd George had taken, he wrote that they 'were right in the narrow sense', but 'absolutely wrong in relation to the deep tides of destiny'.[41] But the 'numbers game' was not as straightforward as this made it sound.

In a memorandum in January 1914 Churchill wrote that 'in the discussion of naval details there is such a wealth of facts that the point of the argument turns rather upon their selection than upon their substance';[42] in the 'selection' of his 'facts' Churchill was heavily influenced by the navalist press and by the former First Sea Lord, Admiral Lord Fisher of Kilverstone. Writing to the Conservative leader, Andrew Bonar Law, in July 1912, Fisher admitted that 'We are very much stronger than anyone supposes', but went on to reveal the true Admiralty mind when he continued: 'but we are not too strong, for as Nelson said – *we never can be!*'[43] On this reading the whole of the nation's wealth could have been poured into the Admiralty without satisfying its voracious appetite. As Lord Salisbury once commented about the cult of the 'expert', 'If you listen to admirals, no ship is safe.' Churchill spent plenty of time listening to Fisher. 'Jacky' Fisher had introduced the Dreadnought and had committed Britain to a policy of concentrating upon their construction, despite claims from some quarters that he was neglecting other categories of ship. He looked forward to a great naval Armageddon, a modern-day Trafalgar, when two mighty battle-fleets would strive for mastery of the waves. But what came, in the end, was a whimper, not a bang, in the form of the Battle of Jutland. To boast, as Churchill did, of the number of capital ships built by 1914 is only half the story. If Britain found herself with enough Dreadnoughts, she was to be short of light-cruisers for convoy duty

– and nearly lose the war as a result.[44] The 'numbers game' can be misleading, and it may have misled Churchill.

There was a diplomatic as well as a naval price to be paid for concentration on building capital ships. With the breakdown of the Anglo-German talks which had followed Haldane's mission, by mid-April 1912 the Government found itself committed to building even more Dreadnoughts to match the increase in German construction. In order to limit Britain's commitments, Churchill decided that the squadron at Malta would have to be withdrawn to Gibraltar – and found himself criticised for neglecting the Mediterranean.[45] Surprised at the criticisms, Churchill told Haldane on 6 May that 'the actual point has been settled long ago by the brute force of facts. We cannot possibly hold the Mediterranean.' It would take 'another fleet of Dreadnoughts', which was not 'practical politics', to hold on to the Mediterranean.[46]

Churchill's absorption in the Admiralty view of the world blinded him to the political and diplomatic implications of his plan. Grey feared that such an announcement would weaken Britain's international position,[47] whilst the Foreign Office and the War Office disliked anything which would complicate existing plans.[48] When Churchill brought his scheme to the Cabinet on 19 June, he found that the navalists objected to his statement that 'we cannot afford to keep six battleships in the Mediterranean in full commission', whilst the radicals took fright at his blithe comment that 'a definite naval arrangement should be made with France without delay'.[49] Since many navalists shared Lord Esher's view that starting naval conversations with France meant 'an alliance ... under cover of "conversations"',[50] and since they and the radicals both agreed (for different reasons) that 'entangling alliances' were a bad thing, Churchill found himself faced by a 'misalliance of convenience'.[51]

Asquith's policy of constructive prevarication had worked before and it was to work again – but Churchill's attitude was to put a great strain on it. Having argued that the Mediterranean was a theatre of secondary importance, and that the withdrawal of the squadron would not matter, Churchill now switched tack and, in a paper circulated on 22 June, maintained that it would be 'very injurious' to abandon it. He now argued that a new fleet, costing '15 to 20 millions', should be built. To cover the period until this would be ready in 1916, Britain should enter into 'an arrangement with France and leave enough ships in the Mediterranean to give her undoubted superiority'.[52] By this move Churchill managed to annoy both the 'economists' and the 'little Englanders', and together these groups had a majority in the Cabinet. McKenna condemned the plan on two grounds. Firstly, an 'alliance' with France was an 'essential feature' of the Admiralty scheme; and secondly, it was unnecessary. More effective use of the reserves and a willingness to risk some inequality before mobilisation would, he contended, free several battleships for duty in the Mediterranean. An increase in spending on ships and personnel would be preferable to being 'driven by our weakness into dependence upon an alliance with any European Power'.[53]

Churchill, who did not want an alliance with the French, simply denied McKenna's assertion and went on to overwhelm his colleagues with technical detail about gunnery sizes and assurances that 'my advisers' thought that to leave a squadron of non-Dreadnoughts in the Mediterranean would be to expose it to 'certain destruction'. The burden of his message, unsurprisingly, was that there was no other course than the one he was proposing, and his advisers (who had, of course, initiated the scheme) were prepared to swear to it.[54] The Cabinet, unable to come to any decision when it met on 27 June, decided to postpone the matter until the CID had considered it on 4 July.

The situation which was developing was reminiscent of the arguments deployed in the Cabinet back in November. McKenna, urged on by Morley who wanted 'no alliance with, or without, a mask',[55] maintained that Churchill's propositions amounted to a 'policy of dependence on France' and that all the detail about ships and guns was unimportant compared to entering into 'an alliance with its obligation to fight in a war not of our own making'. McKenna wondered what price France would demand for 'protecting us in the Mediterranean'.[56] But Churchill argued, as Haldane had in November, that no *alliance* was intended, and Asquith, whose chairmanship was not directed towards clarifying such issues, presided over a 'rambling six-hour session'[57] of the CID at which McKenna's 'essential point' was buried.

Churchill confined himself to the technical arguments, and much was heard of 'margins of safety' and ratios of British to German construction. The debate on naval matters was usually carried out in terms of 'the two-power standard' and an 'adequate margin of safety', with those employing the terms using them as though they were a matter of scientific fact; in actuality they were 'the subject of endless debate and dispute'.[58] Churchill's whole case was built upon the 'necessity' of maintaining a 'sixty per cent advantage' over Germany – and a ten per cent margin over Austria. If Britain had to face Germany, Austria and Italy, her Mediterranean Fleet would be inadequate and her Home Fleet would be hard-pressed. According to this scenario, Britain would need at least six more Dreadnoughts; however, with help from the French, a mere two extra battle-cruisers would suffice to ensure Anglo-French superiority. Churchill hotly rejected McKenna's allegation that this amounted to 'an alliance' and, according to Fisher, he and McKenna were 'tearing each other's eyes out the whole time'.[59]

But how 'factual' were the Admiralty's 'facts'? It was certainly correct to state that Britain would be hard-pressed to fight the whole Triple Alliance single-handedly, but this, as Churchill admitted to Lord Roberts (outside the CID), was 'unlikely'.[60] In that case the figures which Churchill employed, comparing Britain's naval resources to the whole of the Triple Alliance and omitting the Russian and French Navies, were, as some of his colleagues pointed out, a trifle gloomy.[61] Moreover, given the Admiralty's own presentation of its case, the French connection was essential.[62] McKenna argued that it was necessary, for diplomatic and military reasons, to retain a 'one-power standard' fleet in the Mediterranean – thus opening a new area of debate. Churchill maintained that a small squadron, which was the most that could be spared, would suffice. It was a stormy meeting. To Hobhouse's disgust Churchill 'repeated before the naval and military officers his threat of leaving the Government and stumping the country if he could not get his own way'. This, however, 'fell quite flat', except 'that one or two muttered, as all felt, that they wished to goodness he would go'.[63] Churchill's protests were to no avail. With Asquith 'wobbling as he always does over to the majority', it was decided that a 'one-power standard' fleet should be kept in the Mediterranean.[64] Esher and the navalists were jubilant: 'We can hold up our heads in the Mediterranean and beyond!'[65]

The problem of how to implement the CID decision still had to be faced. Since his colleagues would not abandon the Mediterranean, Churchill impressed upon them that they would have to pay the price needed to maintain a properly equipped fleet there. In Cabinet on 10 July he argued that Malta was 'untenable' at present. He proposed a fleet of four battle-cruisers and four armoured-cruisers, to be supplemented by 1916 with three Dreadnoughts, which should be laid down at once. If the 'Admiralty mind' never missed an opportunity of pressing for more Dreadnoughts, then the radicals were equally adept at countering it. Lloyd George and company argued that in place of the usual sixty per cent superiority over the Germans, Churchill was now advocating a forty per cent superiority 'over the next two strongest fleets combined'.[66] Their position had, however, been weakened by the decision to maintain a Mediterranean fleet. If the radicals wanted this and did not want to build more ships, then the logic of Churchill's argument that an arrangement with the French was necessary was inescapable; this last point became clear when the Cabinet discussed the matter on 15 and 16 July.

The meetings were, once again, marked by the personality clash between the current and former First Lords, with Churchill being 'most abusive and insulting to McKenna'.[67] The Home Secretary argued that they needed a full-strength squadron at Malta and that the force of eight which Churchill was willing to supply would have to be withdrawn to Gibraltar in the event of a major European war. He was right, but, as Churchill pointed out on 16 July, he was offering no answer to the question of how this larger fleet was to be provided without a massive increase in the estimates. The Cabinet really had no alternative to accepting the assurance of '*some* of his naval experts' that the proposed fleet would be strong enough and that, except in some 'unforeseen emergency', it would not be withdrawn from the Mediterranean.[68] As Churchill wrote to Balfour that afternoon: 'It was settled . . . to take my advice about holding the Mediterranean with battle cruisers for the present, and not to propose the additional new construction which would have been necessary had the battle-fleet project been adhered to.'[69] It was recognised that this would mean discussions with the French, but it was agreed that they would be told that any naval conversations would not 'prejudice' Britain's 'freedom of action' in 'time of war'.[70]

Ever since the end of the Agadir crisis the French had been anxious to clarify their relations with the British. In April the French Ambassador, Paul Cambon, asked the Foreign Office whether it would not be possible to draw up a joint declaration which would reassure some of those in the French Cabinet about Britain's intentions.[71] Although the Permanent Under-Secretary, Sir Arthur Nicolson, was himself in favour of such a proposal, he had warned Cambon off; with the radical section of the Cabinet seeking an agreement with Germany, 'it would be far wiser to leave matters as they were'.[72] Although this had been done, the French were not happy with the situation. Britain's new naval dispositions gave Cambon a perfect opportunity to renew his efforts to get a firmer commitment from the British.[73]

The Cabinet's view that talks between naval experts should not be held to commit the Government was conveyed by Churchill to the French Naval Attaché on 17 July and formally embodied in a draft agreement given to the French on 23 July.[74] Churchill took the view that as the French had already deployed their fleet in the Mediterranean, they could look for no *quid pro quo* from the British;[75] but matters were hardly that simple. Bertie, the British Ambassador in Paris and a warm partisan of the *Entente*, had warned Grey that the French were unlikely to welcome the terms of the British proposals, and so it proved.[76] Raymond Poincaré, the French Premier, angrily pointed out that to begin a naval convention by saying 'it means nothing so far as the Governments are concerned, is superfluous and quite out of place'; as he put it to Bertie, in a comment that went to the heart of the matter: 'If the entente does not mean that England will come to the aid of France in the event of Germany attacking the French ports, its value is not great.'[77] The French took the view that the two nations would hardly have adopted their present dispositions unless each had been confident of the support of the other.[78] Churchill recognised that if the French were able to say that they had left their 'northern coasts defenceless', they would have a 'tremendous' weapon with which to compel Britain to enter a war; the British would have 'the obligations of an alliance without its advantages and above all without its precise definitions'.[79] Churchill was right, but it was his own short-sighted concentration on the purely naval aspects of the affair which had helped lead to the situation which he was now deploring.

Churchill, like Grey and Asquith, was under the impression, which Bertie and Cambon both attempted to dispel, that the British could have their cake and eat it. They wanted to be able to rely on the French Fleet in the Mediterranean in the event of war with Germany, but they wanted any arrangement to be contingent – only to come into effect once war had been declared. They wanted to be able to state that they had a 'free hand', but to be able to rely on the French if the worst happened. But the French did not want a free hand, they wanted commitment, and the British attitude of going so far and then pulling back was likely to put a strain on the relationship between the two countries. On the same day that Churchill wrote to him, Asquith decided that if the French objected all that much to the preamble to the agreement, it had better be dropped.[80] Cambon then took the initiative to try to ensure that the French at least received a written guarantee that the two powers would consult in the event of a major crisis. Although the British havered about the precise form this should take, the Cabinet did agree to an exchange of notes between Grey and Cambon on 22 and 23 November.[81] The notes, whilst stating that each side retained freedom of action and that the naval arrangements did not constitute an engagement 'to co-operate in war', conceded that the two countries should consult each other in the event of 'something that threatened the general peace'.[82] In January and February 1913 the final naval accords were agreed, with the British safeguarding the North Sea and the Channel, whilst the French took care of the Mediterranean.[83]

Thus it was that the final result of Churchill's strategy was to commit Britain further to a Continental commitment. Asquith, Grey and Churchill could all point out, as they did, that there was no binding commitment, but there was now more than simply a moral one. Churchill's point, that the notes should recognise that the French were responsible for the disposition of their own fleet, had been lost in the final agreements; this would allow Cambon to allege, in August 1914, that they had moved their forces to the Mediterranean at the behest of the British.[84] But even without this, the notes constituted the completion of 'the formal political evolution of the entente'.[85] As Harold Nicolson put it:

It seems almost incredible that the British Government did not realise how far they were pledged. They had, in fact, committed themselves to a guaranty which would involve England either in a breach of faith or a war with Germany.[86]

This was where the 'hysteria navalis'[87] to which Churchill had succumbed led.

Churchill had pursued naval aims as though there were no political implications to them, a view which might have been expected of the admirals, but which was short-sighted coming from the First Lord of the Admiralty. Of his devotion to the Navy there could be no doubt. For all that his manner created hostility in some quarters, Churchill threw himself into his new post with even more than his usual vigour. He took particular pleasure in having the Admiralty yacht, *Enchantress*, at his disposal. He turned it into a second office, spending nearly a third of his time at the Admiralty on it; he used it to visit almost every naval establishment in the British Isles and the Mediterranean. He felt himself to be 'in close touch with the men and ships whose destiny was his special charge'.[88] His new post also carried with it Admiralty House just across Whitehall from Downing Street, but Clementine fought a rear-guard action to prevent her growing family moving there from Eccleston Square; unlike her husband, she never forgot how slender were the financial resources with which he played the 'great game' of politics.[89]

In contrast to his own parents' behaviour, Winston took a close and adoring interest in his offspring – when the pressure of work allowed. He enjoyed being a family man, and his relationship with Clementine flourished. She was mistrustful of his extravagances and some of his friends, but it was only after he went to the Admiralty that she began to have fears about his politics. However, there was little she could do about any of these things. Churchill would continue to gamble more than he could afford and to drink more than she felt was good for him. Some of this she put down to the influence of F. E. Smith, who certainly drank more than was good for anyone, but there was nothing to be done about that. Indeed, in 1911 the two men had founded (perhaps with Lloyd George's assistance) a dining club – 'The Other Club' – at which the 'asperity of politics' could be expressed in an atmosphere made convivial by good food, wine and company; Churchill remained wedded to his masculine pursuits. If this caused Clementine a few twinges of anxiety, it was as nothing compared to her fears that her 'darling amber pug' was going to let himself be 'blinded' by the 'glamour of elegance & refinement' and the 'return of old associations'. She was, as she remained, a stern Liberal and to her the rapprochement between Unionist opinion and her 'shining progressive Winston' boded no good.[90] But here too she could do little beyond expressing her fears. And what were such small clouds on the distant horizon compared with the sunshine days of early married life and motherhood? It was to this period that Clementine would point as the 'happiest time of her life';[91] and it was good that she enjoyed it while it lasted.

8

An Isolated Liberal

The fact that Churchill was now in alignment with Fisher, the navalists and the *Daily Mail* meant that he was estranged from his former allies. The 'new' Liberals and radicals were sworn enemies of 'great armaments' and distrusted the foreign policy of Sir Edward Grey as being pro-French and anti-German, positions which Churchill was now taken to have adopted as his own. At the Board of Trade and the Home Office his eyes had been fixed upon the domestic scene and his sympathies had lain with those who wished to cut defence spending in order to provide money for social reform. But at the Admiralty his eyes were fixed on the international scene. Britain's chief naval rival was Germany, whose strength seemed, to Churchill's Whiggish eyes, a threat to the balance of power in Europe. It was a short step from seeing Germany as a rival to seeing her as a potential enemy, and it was one which Churchill took imperceptibly. The effects of this upon his career were profound. Not only did he lose his own political allies, and thus add to his reputation for political infidelity, but his new allies were men who agreed with him only on one topic – the German menace – and who had not forgiven him for deserting the Conservatives or for the role he had played alongside Lloyd George. He could try to revive his standing in the Liberal Party by espousing the Irish cause,[1] but this simply confirmed his new allies in their long-held belief that he could not be trusted. During his time at the Admiralty Churchill not only prepared the British Navy for war, but he also eroded the foundations of his position within the Liberal Party without acquiring support from elsewhere.

Such an erosion might have been expected in the position of any Liberal who held one of the Service departments and pressed for an increase in spending, but in Churchill's case it was made worse by his behaviour. His consideration for the feelings of others had always been notable by its absence and now, immersed in his own affairs, he was determined to get his own way whatever the cost. Churchill's rapid and uninterrupted rise in politics had preserved his 'rough edges', and his considerable self-confidence had hardened into something not readily distinguishable from arrogance. Naval officers were 'gentlemen' and they expected to be treated as such. Churchill's unconventional behaviour and methods quickly gave offence, and the tales about him lost nothing in the telling as they passed around the ward-rooms of the Fleet and the clubs of London.[2] Hobhouse, who had observed him at close quarters since 1908, regarded Churchill as 'ill mannered, boastful, unprin-cipled' and 'without any redeeming feature except his amazing ability and industry'.[3] Churchill's 'abusive' behaviour to McKenna during the Cabinet discussion on 15 July over the Mediterranean Fleet brought from Hobhouse the irritated exclamation: 'He really is a spoilt child endowed by chance with the brain of a genius.'[4]

It would be easy to dismiss Hobhouse as a staid, middle-aged Liberal who disliked Churchill, but the list of those who agreed with him was a long one. Men as diverse as Lord Balcarres, the Unionist Whip before 1912, Lord Hankey, the Cabinet Secretary, and his old sparring-partner, Lord Selborne, all remarked upon his egotistical behaviour; so did diplomats like Oliver Harvey and Sir Alexander Cadogan, who were joined by soldiers such as Alan Brooke: they all found Churchill exasperating and infuriating at times. There is a sense in which it hardly matters whether such a verdict was 'fair'; because it was so widely held, it became a factor in Churchill's political career whether it was true or not. No doubt, as with most people, those closest to him saw more deeply, but even some of these, for example his doctor, Lord Moran, and one of his secretaries, Elizabeth Layton, recorded behaviour which would not be out of place in the kindergarten or the palace of a pasha.[5]

The source of such irritation is easily comprehended. Success, especially won early and accompanied by an ebullience of spirit which accepts it as a right, is not likely to breed popularity. Contemporaries are apt to be envious of the success, whilst the tribal elders are likely to find their sense of propriety outraged. As the most perceptive of Churchill's biographers, Robert Rhodes James, has put it:

There is a common misconception to the effect that, in England, Youth and Ambition are regarded with approval. In reality, Youth is deemed a regrettable interlude, to be borne with appropriate patience and modesty; Ambition is tolerable only if it is decently concealed.[6]

Only an aristocratic society can tolerate the success of a Pitt, Prime Minister at twenty-four, or the rakish brilliance of a Charles James Fox. In the long after-glow of mid-Victorian bourgeois sensibility, Churchill was an unwel-come throw-back to a disregarded era.

Churchill's 'faith in his star', his unbounded assurance in himself and the 'amazing' energy with which he applied himself to his work were all calculated to inspire envy and irritation in equal measure. No doubt the man was good at his job, but did he have to interfere in departments that were not his concern? Did his Cabinet memoranda have to be quite so long? Lord Melborne once remarked that he wished that he could be as sure of anything as Macaulay was of everything; Churchill had a similar effect on many of his contemporaries. Most men are decently confused about what course of action they should take at any one moment and their doubts and hesitancies are affronted by the sort of self-confidence which Churchill exhibited. He had, to use a word which through careless application has lost some of its real force, charisma. Reminded that 'we are all worms', he could truly reply: 'Yes, but I believe that I am a glow-worm!' So he was, but it would have been asking too much of fallen human nature to have expected all the other 'worms' to have rejoiced in that fact quite as much as the 'glow-worm' evidently did![7]

Ebullient and self-centred, Churchill had little time or space for other people and their opinions. Those, like his private secretary, Eddie Marsh, who relished his dynamic strength and were prepared to yield to his will, found themselves captivated: where others saw a ruthless selfishness, Marsh saw a man possessed of a great mission. With Churchill, more than most people, you paid your money and you took your choice. One of the reasons why the Churchill marriage was a success, even if it was rather strained at times, was that for most of it Clementine had the strength of character to stand up to her husband and prevent him becoming in the domestic sphere what he too easily became in the public sphere, a petty tyrant.[8]

Churchill's desire to 'get on' with things, combined with his already poor perception of the reality of other people's needs and emotions, led others to think of him as 'stubborn and tyrannical';[9] there were times when he could be both. Unlike most First Lords, Churchill was not content to leave things to his professional advisers, and he took 'an active part in formulating all important measures and policies'.[10] Having secured the retirement of Sir Arthur Wilson, who had made such a poor showing at the CID meeting of 23 August, Churchill found that he could not get on with his successor, Sir Francis Bridgeman, so he 'persuaded' him to retire on grounds of 'ill health'. Bridgeman, who rightly felt himself badly used, never forgave Churchill, and the Unionists raised the matter in the Commons in December 1912. Balcarres, who called it 'a scandalous act of tyranny', simply expressed in private what others were saying in public.[11] The incident in which the First Lord was threatened with ejection from a ship for having asked a junior officer his opinion of his seniors was one which appeared in a number of forms and which created antagonism to the pushy young First Lord.[12]

Churchill's habit of seeking advice from any source which seemed useful led him into correspondence and contact with Lord Fisher; this may have given him access to the advice of the greatest British sailor since Nelson, but it also embroiled him in the old man's many private quarrels. The 'Malay', as the oriental-looking Admiral was known to his enemies, was that rare creature – a man whose self-confidence equalled Churchill's own. Fisher had made a host of enemies, and he was a man who loved to nurture his enmities; advised by his friends to cultivate moderation, his only reply was: 'I am going to kick other people's shins if they kick mine!' 'Yours 'til hell freezes over!', 'yours to a cinder!', the extrovert subscriptions to his long letters of advice to

Churchill (made all the longer because they were written with characters an inch in height), marked his enjoyment of his role as *éminence grise* to the new First Lord.[13] His cultivation of the press exceeded anything Churchill had ever attempted; the First Lord was content to bask in publicity, Fisher used the newspapers 'unblushingly' to promote himself and his causes.[14] During the crisis over the naval estimates in 1909, he had fed J. L. Garvin of the *Observer* with information about the naval programmes of both Britain and Germany in order to support his own case.[15] Fisher's advice was useful, and he was a figure to whom Churchill could warm, but he was not a fit companion to take on a tiger hunt.

Churchill's love of his office was evident to his new naval secretary, the future Admiral Beatty, who recorded in May 1912 that, 'Winston talks about nothing but the sea and the Navy and the wonderful things he is going to do.' He was both assiduous and energetic. Churchill improved the pay and the conditions of sailors and introduced reforms designed to secure the promotion of talent from whatever quarter it came. He supported the introduction of faster Dreadnoughts and the oil-fired 'Queen Elizabeth class'; indeed, he pioneered the switch from coal to oil in the Royal Navy.[16] As the German Naval Attaché recorded in 1914: 'On the whole the Navy is satisfied with Mr Churchill because it recognises that he has done and accomplished more for them than the majority of his predecessors.'[17] But this adoption of the Admiralty 'mind' was not without its political price. Churchill's cultivation of Garvin and the navalist (and invariably Unionist) press, the admiration expressed for him by Lord Northcliffe's jingo newspapers, and his evident delight in things military, all served to distance him from his Party. This would have been harmful enough to a man whose loyalty to his Party was unquestioned, but it was doubly so to a man whose loyalty to the Liberal Party could so easily be called into question.[18] Usually, as an ambitious and successful Minister ascends the greasy pole, he acquires what politeness terms acolytes and cynicism jackals. But Churchill hunted alone; his patronage was not sought – perhaps because his weak perception of the existence of others made him a poor patron. Lloyd George and Sir Edward Grey were tipped as possible successors to Asquith; but, as the Prime Minister was to comment in 1914, it was difficult to see where Churchill's career would go in the future.

If Churchill's antics and his policy at the Admiralty combined to isolate him within the Cabinet, he could not look outside it for support from the rank and file of the Liberal Party. The God-fearing, nonconformist proletarian, the sensible bourgeois, the cautious shopkeeper and the hard-headed businessman always saw him as an exotic. What were these people to make of the Duke's grandson, the Tory turncoat who spent his summers on the Riviera, sailing and gambling, and who divided his leisure hours between fine living at Blenheim and manoeuvres in the park with the Oxfordshire Yeomanry? What were the Party loyalists to make of the man whose closest friend was arch-Tory, F. E. Smith? Churchill's only real patron in the Party was the Prime Minister, whose support, fortunately, counted for much.

Over the next few years it became increasingly clear that Asquith's favour and his own abilities were the only two props of Churchill's career; it did not need a soothsayer to predict that the former would vanish if the latter failed to produce the goods. The Prime Minister had a difficult team to drive, and he was, perhaps, rather too prone to take shelter in prevarication. Alcohol and epistolary flirtation with young ladies were Asquith's chief refuge from the strains of high office and his wife Margot. In the eyes of his admirers these things were unfortunate blemishes which did not detract from his great qualities as leader, but to his critics they had become a source of scorn: 'What with drink, bridge and holding girls' hands, [he] is now incapable of doing anything except drift.'[19]

Asquith's patronage of Churchill is explained in part by recognition of his great abilities, but there is no doubt that Churchill's personality held an appeal to the jaded, old statesman. Churchill's bumptious enthusiasm for everything appealed to him. Where he and his circle were 'mostly scholars steeped in the classical tradition' who 'knew most of the arguments and all of the answers' on 'many themes', to Churchill 'everything under the sun was new – seen and appraised as on the first day of creation'.[20] It was true that this breath of fresh air carried with it risks, but in the days of his pomp and the plenitude of his power, Asquith knew he had the ability to harness the dynamo. But there were times when Asquith's patience was sorely tried by the First Lord's loquacity; during one particularly interminable lecture in Cabinet, the Prime Minister interjected to tell Churchill that his comments were 'pure cynicism defended by sophistry'.[21]

The First Lord was undoubtedly a Parliamentary and departmental workhorse, and a Prime Minister increasingly beleaguered on the home front by suffragettes and, far more importantly, the Irish was grateful for such a colleague. His trust was repaid. Churchill liked 'the old boy' and admired his 'intellect and his character', and when during the crisis over the Parliament Bill in 1911 Asquith had turned up to the House too drunk to deliver his speech, Churchill had covered for him.[22] There were rumours in early 1912 that Asquith, who had continued to drink more than was good for him, might well retire, and he was certainly showing the strains of seven years of high office.[23] The prospects for the succession were uncertain, but F. E. Smith, who doubted whether there was anything in the rumours, told Austen Chamberlain that Churchill and Lloyd George would probably agree to serve under Grey, as neither of them would give way to the other; Churchill, F.E. said, felt that 'his star is in the ascendant'.[24]

F.E. was correct to doubt the rumours, and by the middle of 1912 Asquith was back on form, helped in part by his *amitié amoureuse* with Venetia Stanley.[25] The Liberals certainly had need of his skills in council and the Commons.

The election results of 1910 had left the Party dependent upon John Redmond's Irish MPs, who had only one price for their support – Home Rule. With the passing of the Parliament Act in 1911, the great barrier to the passage of a Home Rule bill, the absolute veto of the House of Lords, had been removed. A bill was duly introduced in 1912 and rejected by the Lords, but under the new dispensation it would automatically become law in 1914 – unless Parliament should be dissolved before then. The next two years saw the Irish question once more convulse British politics as it had in Lord Randolph's day. But this time the Churchills were on the side of the Home Rulers.

Bonar Law, whose Unionism was of the stern and unbending variety, called the Government a 'revolutionary committee which has seized despotic power by fraud' and, in a speech at Churchill's ancestral home on 27 July 1912, declared that there were 'things stronger than parliamentary majorities'. He could, he said (ungrammatically), 'imagine no length of resistance to which Ulster can go in which I should not be prepared to support them'.[26] Sir Edward Carson, the eminent KC who had successfully prosecuted Oscar Wilde, took the lead in organising Protestant opinion in Ulster and Westminster. A situation developed in which both Unionists and Liberals attempted to face each other down, not disdaining to use the threat of a resort to force in extremities. Given that he was already involved in one controversial subject, naval expenditure, Churchill might have been well-advised to have stayed out of the Irish question; instead, he sought to restore his credit with the radical section of the Party by actions which gave rise to the belief in Unionist circles that he was prepared to use the Fleet to coerce Ulstermen who refused to accept Home Rule.

To many Unionists Churchill's vocal espousal of the Irish cause simply added fuel to their hatred; that the son of the man who had declared, 'Ulster will fight and Ulster will be right', could now call for Home Rule, seemed to add filial impiety to political infidelity. This made Churchill a particular target for Unionist displeasure, in one instance quite literally. When the Speaker had to suspend the House during the second reading of the Home Rule Bill, one enraged Unionist, Ronald MacNeil, flung a book at him, which caused a nasty gash on his forehead.[27] The fact that Churchill was, in private, trying to help broker a compromise between the two parties, was not something which he could have used in a plea of mitigation. Neither a compromise nor a solution to the Irish problem proved attainable so long as both sides took Bonar Law's view that it was 'bad for us ... but much worse for them'.[28]

Churchill's views on Ireland paralleled those of most Liberals. He did not want to see the will of Parliament flouted by Ulstermen using threats of violence; but, on the other hand, he did not want to see Home Rule forced on those who were unwilling to receive it. Imbued as he and Asquith were with the classical Liberal sentiment that all problems are sent into this world with a twin called solution, and that the art of politics is to find that twin, they imagined that it was simply a matter of bringing the Unionists to state what their terms would be.[29] They found, instead, a problem which was so shot through with passions stirred by religion and history that it evaded the nostrums of Liberal politics. By January 1914 attempts to find a compromise solution had broken down. Asquith was confident that his usual 'wait and see' approach would call the Unionists' bluff; for their part, the Unionists were confident that they could call Asquith's.

If Ireland gave Churchill an opportunity to ingratiate himself with his own Party, it was one he badly needed. If 1913–14 witnessed a worsening of the Irish problem, it saw Anglo-German relations entering a period of calm unknown since the turn of the century – a situation which gave rise to cries within the Liberal Party for a reduction in naval expenditure.[30] For Churchill to present the House with the largest naval estimates in history – £50,694,800, an increase of £3 million on the previous year – against such a back-cloth was bound to lead to friction.[31] That this friction escalated into a crisis owed a great deal to Churchill's abrasive personality and the reaction of others to it.

When he had been at the Board of Trade and the Home Office, Churchill's enthusiasm and energy had led him into radical paths. Now, by a not dissimilar process, his transfer to the Admiralty led him to adopt extreme views; but in this instance they were to lead him into conflict with most of his Party. At his previous offices no call had been made on his interest in military matters, and Grey's habit of keeping foreign policy away from the Cabinet had militated against such subjects being discussed there. But Churchill had arrived at the Admiralty in the middle of a crisis with Germany, and one which could be, and was, plausibly represented as part of a growing German threat to the balance of power in Europe. Churchill accepted, unthinkingly, the 'Whig' history on which he had been brought up, which held that ever since the days of Elizabeth I, Britain's 'traditional foreign policy' had been to act as a regulator on the balance of power in Europe. The only sphere in which Britain could make an effective riposte to this challenge was by responding to the build-up of the German Navy. Naturally enough the Admiralty was permeated with this view, and it was one which not only communicated itself to Churchill, but which he adopted with the energy he brought to all his enthusiasms. A consciousness of the German menace, together with his natural desire to push his own department and its interests, created a major Cabinet crisis.

Churchill had made it clear to Asquith that if the quota of Dreadnoughts for the coming year was reduced below four, 'there is no chance whatever of my being able to go on'.[32] But on 17 December a deputation of Liberals, representing, they said, 100 MPs, protested against the First Lord's earlier foreshadowing of higher naval spending.[33] Sir John Simon, the Attorney-

General, was not the only member of the Cabinet in a 'truculent mood'[34] when Ministers met on 20 December. Churchill's reasons for the increase were many and impressive: improvements in the pay of sailors; the development of the fifteen-inch gun, which, on Fisher's advice and against the resistance of others, Churchill had pushed through; the need to build more Dreadnoughts to meet the Austrian challenge in the Mediterranean; and the necessity of building up large oil stocks now that the Navy was leaving the days of coal and steam behind.[35] It was a formidable list, but not one which Churchill's opponents were disposed to accept without argument. Hobhouse, who had kept a copy of the estimates as they had been fixed the previous February, pointed out, to Churchill's embarrassment, that they were now £5 million higher. 'Eventually, since courage, like fear, is contagious, everyone took up the running, even [Lord] Beauchamp and [Sidney] Buxton joining in'; Hobhouse recorded that, 'as usual', Asquith 'crossed over to the winning side'. Churchill declared that he could not carry out such a policy 'and went off characteristically *banging* the despatch box and door as he went out as loud as he could'.[36]

No political crisis is ever welcome, but this one came on a bad issue and at the wrong time for Asquith. He did not want a general election before the Home Rule Bill went through; to have one would be to hand the Unionists an issue on which the Government was bound to be unpopular in the country. If that could be combined with claims that the Liberals could not be trusted with the country's defences, then defeat was probable. Moreover, if Parliament was dissolved before the Home Rule Bill went through, it would automatically fail, and the Irish would be furious with the Liberals. It was necessary to hold the Government together at all costs. But Churchill's personality created problems. Many Liberals suspected him of wanting to 'sell the pass' over Ulster,[37] and others would have been glad simply to see the back of a First Lord whom they could neither like nor trust.

Lloyd George's position was crucial both to Asquith and Churchill. As the second man in the Government and its leading radical, Lloyd George's interest was in brokering a compromise, as it was hardly in his interests that the Government should split. Churchill, who regarded the obligations of friendship as absolute, expected the Chancellor's support and was correspondingly shocked to find him acting on the aphorism that 'there is no friendship at the top'. If Lloyd George was inclined to try to help Churchill, it was not because of the bonds of friendship, but rather out of political self-interest. The two of them were both moderates on Ulster, and the fact that Churchill's opponents in the Cabinet were led by McKenna, who was an extremist on the subject, inclined Lloyd George against being 'a party to driving Winston out of the Cabinet'.[38] Thus it was that before the Cabinet met to discuss the estimates, he and the First Lord entered into a tacit understanding. But at the Cabinet when Lloyd George saw that McKenna, Simon, Herbert Samuel and Walter Runciman were 'doing their utmost "to down" Winston', he repudiated 'the bargain, which had evidently been come to . . . as soon as he saw others were prepared to fight Churchill'.[39] Lloyd George's only hope now was that Churchill would back down under enough pressure. In a frank interview in the *Daily Chronicle* on New Year's Day 1914, Lloyd George called for a reduction in the estimates and an agreement with Germany. He recalled, with obvious contemporary relevance, what had happened to Lord Randolph Churchill when he had protested against 'bloated and profligate' naval spending.[40] Balfour suspected that Lloyd George would not be averse to splitting the Cabinet on the issue,[41] but his game was a good deal more complicated than that.

Sir Francis Hopwood, whom Churchill had brought from the Colonial Office to the Admiralty, summed up for the King's benefit the political position following Lloyd George's public intervention:

The fact is that the Cabinet is sick of Churchill's perpetually undermining and exploiting its policy and are picking a quarrel with him. As a colleague he is a great trial to them. But their battleground is very ill chosen, as in consequence of their indolence he has probably got chapter and verse for every item of the Naval Programme.[42]

Attempts to secure a compromise by suggesting that next year's estimates might be cut foundered on Churchill's refusal to commit himself to a firm forecast of what those estimates would be. By 19 January he was describing his relations with Lloyd George as 'civil and sombre'.[43]

Churchill was treading upon very thin ice, sustained only by Asquith's masterly handling of his colleagues. Lloyd George was 'hardening to the view that he and Churchill must part',[44] whilst Simon, Samuel and Lord Beauchamp told Asquith on 21 January that the Party would never agree to the estimates 'unless as a guarantee against such future events – Winston Churchill retired, certainly from the Navy, preferably from the Cabinet'. To Asquith's exclamation, 'Oh, this is a personal question,' Simon replied, 'No, a question of temperament.'[45] Lloyd George, still seeking to thwart the group which clearly wanted Churchill out of the Cabinet, sought a compromise and reported to Simon and company on 26 January that Churchill had agreed to reduce the estimates for the following year. When Simon and Hobhouse told Lloyd George that they did not believe Churchill would do it, Lloyd George 'got rather hot' and they parted on bad terms.[46]

However, the following morning Lloyd George received a letter from Churchill which drove him 'to despair'.[47] Churchill warned him that he could not guarantee the figure for the estimates of the following year, which prompted Lloyd George to reply stiffly: 'I now thoroughly appreciate your idea of a bargain; it is an argument which binds the Treasury . . . whilst it does not, in the least, impose any obligations on the Admiralty.' He had, he declared, laboured to rescue 'Liberalism from the greatest tragedy which has yet befallen it', even at the cost of risking 'humiliation' by compromising over the estimates: 'You decreed otherwise, and the responsibility is yours and yours alone.'[48]

Asquith managed to avert a split in the Cabinet by playing on the division between Lloyd George and those who, like McKenna, simply wanted Churchill out. When the Cabinet discussed the estimates on 27 January, McKenna's and Churchill's critics got 'no effective help' from Lloyd George and he, Simon, Hobhouse and Runciman led the attack on the Admiralty by themselves. But Churchill defended himself with 'wonderful fecundity of mind', and Lloyd George's defection left the 'anti-Winston' brigade without an effective means of driving him out.[49]

Churchill's opponents were not persuaded that any promise about the following year's estimates being lower could be trusted, and Beauchamp, Simon, Hobhouse, McKenna and Runciman wrote a collective letter to Asquith on 29 January putting forward their case.[50] Simon urged Asquith that 'the loss of Winston Churchill, though regrettable, is *not* by any means a splitting of Party – indeed large Admiralty estimates may be capable of being carried *only* because W.C. has gone.' The radical element of the Party would, he wrote, be strengthened and the impression created that the 'Cabinet *fights for economy* but pursues Home Rule unflinchingly is just what is wanted'.[51] But that was not necessarily what Asquith wanted, and out of the division between the opponents of the estimates and their united desire to avoid an election, he was able to describe the lineaments of a compromise. Urging Churchill to 'throw a baby or two out of the sledge' in response to his opponents' slackening of 'their pursuit',[52] Asquith secured a solution to the crisis: estimates of £51,580,000 would be agreed to, with a promise that there would be 'substantial reductions' the following year.[53]

After this crisis Churchill turned to Ireland to mend his fences within the Party. In this attempt he was at least partially successful, but the price he paid for this was to besmirch his name still further in Unionist eyes. Churchill had always belonged to that section of the Liberal Party which favoured a moderate solution to the Irish problem, but the intransigence of the Ulstermen and their threats of force led him into public actions which could be (and were) interpreted in an entirely different way. Facing the prospect of Sir Edward Carson and the Ulster Volunteers taking desperate measures in Ireland, and with rumours abounding that the Army might not prove loyal if called upon to take firm action, he made a speech at Bradford on 14 March which 'was widely interpreted as a declaration of war on Ulster'.[54] The official biography describes the speech as 'firm and measured',[55] but stigmatising Bonar Law as 'a public danger seeking to terrorise the Government and to force his way into the Councils of his Sovereign' was neither of these, nor was the ringing declaration: 'Let us go forward together and put these grave matters to the proof!'[56] It was, however, an effective riposte to the threats being made by the Unionists, and at the following morning's Cabinet there was, Asquith told Venetia Stanley, 'great harmony'; Churchill 'preened himself and was stroked by the others – all on account of his Bradford speech'. At the same Cabinet meeting the naval estimates went through 'with hardly a murmur of protest'.[57]

But the Liberals were not the only ones who could act as though they might use force if the Irish situation demanded it. Bonar Law warned Asquith on 19 March that any attempt to arrest Carson or to use force against him would simply divide the Army, whilst Sir Edward himself gave vent to language which, after his dramatic departure, led to rumours that he had fled to Ulster to raise the standard of civil war.[58] Whilst Asquith pondered his next move, Churchill, without consulting him, put into effect a decision sanctioned by the Cabinet a few days earlier, and ordered the Third Battle Fleet to Lamlash, within reach of Belfast, where it was to pick up troops to be landed at Belfast Lough. He was later to argue that this was a sensible precaution,[59] but, according to the Chief of the Imperial General Staff, Sir John French, Churchill declared at the time that 'if Belfast should fight "his fleet would have the town in ruins in twenty-four hours"'.[60] When the news of Churchill's actions broke on 24 March, it raised Unionist ire to new heights, with Leo Amery asking the following day whether Churchill had intended to provoke 'hostilities and bloodshed'. Churchill replied hotly that this was a 'hellish' insinuation.[61] Carson called Churchill 'Lord Randolph's renegade son who wanted to be handed down to posterity as the Belfast butcher'.[62] The price Churchill paid for the privilege of mending fences within his own Party was to be a formidable one.

9

War Lord at Sea

The battle over the naval estimates had tested Churchill's strength in the Cabinet; he had 'shown his fangs' and they were 'pretty big fangs'.[1] The prospect of the First Lord's resignation had not filled his colleagues with the alarm which Churchill might have wished, but he had calculated that most of them were 'a lot of cowards' with 'no stomach for a fight'.[2] He had been hurt at Lloyd George's behaviour, telling the newspaper magnate Lord Riddell, ' "I can't make David out. They can't get anyone to do the job better than me. But perhaps they want to get rid of me." '[3] The events of the next six months, which ought, in theory, to have rescued Churchill's position, did not do so. The Irish question, to which he had turned in an effort to improve his standing with the Party, became increasingly intractable. Churchill switched to a more conciliatory mood, heralding the Government's willingness to seek a compromise in a speech on 28 April.[4] But his initiative bore little fruit. The breakdown of a conference at Buckingham Palace on 24 July drove him to exclaim that it was 'criminal' that Carson was prepared to countenance civil war over something as 'trivial' as Tyrone.[5] This showed how little he appreciated the passions of the Irish. But just as the odds on a civil war had shortened appreciably, events on the Continent overshadowed the Irish question. The outbreak of the war for which Churchill had been preparing should have seen his stock rise, and the fact that he was in charge of the mightiest part of the British war machine ought, in theory, to have allowed him to consolidate his position. He was a 'War Minister'. Why then did these things not happen?

Part of the answer to this question lies in Churchill's character as delineated in the last chapter; the rest of it lies in the events of the first six months of the war. At first it seemed almost an unalloyed gain for the Liberals that the crisis initiated by Austria's reaction to the murder of the Hapsburg heir, Franz Ferdinand, should have assumed the guise of 'the most dangerous situation of the last 40 years'. As Asquith told Venetia Stanley on 26 July, it had 'the good effect of throwing into the background the lurid picture of "civil war" in Ireland'.[6] Miss Stanley replied that the Prime Minister's attitude was rather like cutting off your head to cure a headache, a view with which Asquith concurred; but Churchill 'on the other hand is all for this way of escape from Irish troubles'. Indeed, when it had seemed, the previous evening, as though Grey's appeal for a conference would succeed, Churchill had 'exclaimed moodily that it looked after all as if we were in for a "bloody peace"!'7 But Churchill's fears were groundless, and his hopes that the Irish crisis would be pushed into the background were realised as the 'parishes of Fermanagh and Tyrone faded back into the mists and squalls of Ireland' and a 'strange light began immediately, but by perceptible gradations, to fall and grow upon the map of Europe'.8 On 31 July Bonar Law suggested that they should postpone the Home Rule Bill in view of the European crisis – a suggestion which Asquith agreed to with alacrity.

Despite Churchill's fine prose about 'strange lights' glowing, it was not until rather late in the day that the European crisis became a matter of concern to the British. On 24 July, when news reached London that the Austrians had delivered an ultimatum to Serbia, Asquith could write to Venetia Stanley that, whilst they were in 'measurable distance' of a war between France, Russia, Germany and Austria, 'Happily there seems no reason why we should be more than spectators.'9 The process whereby this confident prediction was falsified has been exhaustively trawled over by historians, and their labours have eradicated any simple image that the Government came into the war because Belgium's neutrality had been infringed. The political balance within the Cabinet, the exigencies of Liberal politics, the influence of the Conservative Party, and the state of mind of Ministers have all been called in aid to account for Britain's entry into the Great War.10 What was Churchill's role in the crisis which led to Britain's entry into the Great War?

In his memoirs Churchill states that his 'part in these events was a very simple one': to make sure that the Fleet was ready if the Cabinet decided for war;11 but he did much more than that. The timing of the crisis was fortuitous for the First Lord. The Fleet had been mobilised for manoeuvres and was due to disperse on 24 July; the First Sea Lord, Prince Louis of Battenberg, now gave orders that it should remain together. On 28 July Churchill secured Asquith's agreement to send the First Fleet into the North Sea, but the Prime Minister would not give him permission to mobilise it, for the same reason that Churchill had brought his request to Asquith and not the whole Cabinet; the Cabinet was divided every which way.

Churchill was the only Minister to feel any sense of exultation at the course of events. 'I am interested, geared up and happy,' he told his wife on 28 July. 'Is it not horrible to be built like that?' But for all his prayers 'to God to forgive me for such fearful moods of levity',12 the First Lord knew what he wanted to do. It was an attitude which marked him out from all his colleagues. Whilst most Ministers consulted their consciences, the newspapers or their girlfriends, Churchill prepared for war, not only in the sense of making sure that the Fleet was ready, but also in trying to influence opinion in that direction within the Cabinet. In case that should fail, he also sent out feelers for the creation of a national coalition. Churchill had always maintained that a 'great war should be carried on by a joint ministry', and as far back as 1911 he had said that if 'such an event took place during the present Liberal administration, Balfour and several more prominent Conservatives should be invited to join the Government';[13] now he acted on that belief. On 26 July he sounded out Lloyd George on the idea, and the following day he asked F. E. Smith to be the intermediary with Bonar Law. But the Conservative leader did not trust a Cabinet stuffed full of 'little Englanders' and preferred to keep his powder dry.[14]

Bonar Law's fears were not unjustified. For all that Cambon and the French believed that the British were under a moral obligation to help them, most of the Cabinet took the view conveyed by Grey to the French Ambassador on 31 July that 'our action must depend upon the course of events – including the Belgian question, and the direction of public opinion'.[15] When the Cabinet met on 1 August, it came 'near to the parting of the ways' on several occasions. Churchill occupied 'more than half the time', and he was 'very bellicose and demanding immediate mobilisation'.[16] Morley, Harcourt, Simon, Beauchamp and Burns were all near the opposite pole, but it was Lloyd George's position which was crucial to the Government's durability. After the Cabinet meeting on 2 August, Asquith was inclined to think that the Cabinet would split. Lloyd George, Morley, Simon, Harcourt and Beauchamp all seemed to be leaning towards following Burns, who had proffered his resignation on hearing that Grey had warned the Germans against using the Channel for military operations. Asquith's own position, like that of Grey, was that if the Germans did this, or seriously threatened Belgium or France with destruction, it would be impossible to keep out of the war.[17] If, however, the Germans simply marched through part of southern Belgium with the permission of the Belgian Government, there would be no *casus belli*.[18] In fact, as at Agadir and the time of the Mediterranean naval agreements, it was the fate of France which crucially influenced Asquith, Grey and Churchill; but that did not necessarily mean that the Cabinet dissentients would agree to go to war on her behalf.[19] The key figure was Lloyd George, and Churchill played a major role in winning his support for a declaration of war.

As the leading radical in the Government, but also as the man whose speech during the Agadir crisis was widely held to have influenced the Germans to back away from a confrontation, Lloyd George's history contained no clear indication of what stand he might take. Asquith found him 'sensible and statesmanlike' on 1 August, but inclined to back Morley the following day.[20] Hobhouse noted that he had initially been 'anti-German', but had 'veered round' in favour of peace as it seemed that Liberal public opinion was moving that way.[21] Churchill got one of his Staff officers to 'lecture Lloyd George on the European military situation' on 1 August, and during the Cabinet passed him a series of notes urging him to 'bring your mighty aid to the discharge of our duty'. Knowing the Chancellor's susceptibility to public opinion, Churchill

urged him to take his stand on the issue of Belgian neutrality, the violation
of which, he reminded Lloyd George, would probably have a profound effect
on the British public. Churchill raised once more the prospect of a coalition
government, in which 'together we can carry a wide social policy'. He
reassured the Chancellor that 'the naval war will be cheap – not more than
25 millions a year'.[22]

Asquith took the view that 'it is against British interests that France shd [*sic*]
be wiped out as a Great Power' – but it was clear that he could not rely on
enough of his colleagues taking the same view; so, as usual, he played it long.
This allowed the differences among his colleagues to cancel each other out,
whilst the march of events took its toll on the waverers. But to the French,
the delay was nerve-wracking. When Cambon was told, after the Cabinet on
1 August, that 'France must take her own decisions' without relying on
Britain, the Ambassador refused to transmit such a message to his Government. 'White and speechless, he staggered into Nicolson's room', exclaiming,
'Ils vont nous lâcher.' Then, as some of Churchill's critics had predicted might
happen back in 1912, Cambon called in aid the naval agreement. France had,
he said, moved her fleet to the Mediterranean 'on our request'. Nicolson
persuaded him not to send a formal note to this effect, but the Frenchman
made it clear that he considered that Britain was morally bound to help
France. When asked by the foreign editor of *The Times*, Henry Wickham
Steed, what he was doing, he replied, cuttingly: 'J'attends de savoir si le mot
honneur doit être rayé du vocabulaire anglais.'[23] However, by his contacts
with the Unionists, Cambon was doing a great deal to ensure that the word
honour remained part of the English language.[24]

Although Grey took the view that the French 'had nothing in writing',[25]
it was clearly necessary to do something to reassure them – hence the decision
on 2 August to warn the Germans off the Channel. But even this limited
clarification of the British position had brought Burns's resignation and the
threat of others following him. As it became clearer where the policy of the
Entente was leading, those who had expressed their doubts about the 1912
naval agreements began to pack their portfolios. Beauchamp, Morley and
Simon wrote to the Prime Minister that evening resigning, despite Lloyd
George's pleas for them to wait. However, the same evening the news broke
that the Germans had demanded unimpeded passage through Belgium, an
event which not only allowed Lloyd George to come out firmly in favour of
intervention, but which prompted Simon and Beauchamp to retract their
resignations.[26] With the loss of only Morley and Burns, the Liberal Cabinet
had finally reached a decision.

That afternoon Grey made a statement in the Commons.[27] He skated with
'wonderful skill' around the exact nature of Britain's obligations to France,
concentrating instead upon his perception that it was in Britain's interests to
maintain her as a Great Power. Britain would, he declared, suffer no more

by participating than she would have suffered had she stayed out. Some of his audience had their doubts about this at the time, but as he and Asquith had fostered the notion that British participation could be limited to the naval sphere, there seemed no reason to doubt him.[28] In any case, Britain, as yet, had no alliance with France, and it remained to be seen how the Cabinet would cope with that question; Ministers never had to consider it. Churchill asked the Prime Minister and the Foreign Secretary for permission to 'put into force the combined Anglo-French dispositions for the defence of the Channel' and, at a stroke, the *Entente* became, in effect, an alliance.[29] It was, somehow, fitting that this should occur in the same manner as the *Entente* had solidified – quietly, between a few Ministers in the know.

The events of the first few months of the war did not work out quite as the First Lord would have wished. The escape of the German cruiser, the *Goeben*, into Turkish waters, the sinking of several British ships at Scapa Flow by German submarines, the defeat at the Coronel Islands in September, all these were unpleasant setbacks for a public reared upon stories of British naval prowess, and the irrepressible First Lord came in for his share of the blame. Even more criticism was aroused by his antics in defence of Antwerp. Public criticism was matched by that made in private, where Churchill's bellicosity soon came to be seen as clouding his judgment. As Lloyd George put it on 10 October: 'Our greatest danger is incompetent English junkers. Winston is becoming a great danger.'[30]

Churchill had told Lord Riddell in 1911 that 'if the country were engaged in a great war he would throw up his position as Home Secretary and go to the front';[31] as First Lord, Churchill acted as though he could remain in the Government and go to the front at the same time. He showed an addiction to *realpolitik* and a propensity to disregard wider strategic considerations, which led his colleagues to feel that he could not be trusted.[32] In his memoirs he made a great fuss about the escape of the *Goeben*, alleging that this helped precipitate the Turkish entry into the war. He devoted a good deal of time to showing that had his orders been obeyed, this could have been avoided, but in doing so he revealed in retrospect as little sense of perspective as he had shown at the time.[33] It was the press which made much of the incident, which actually had no effect on anything very much. The Turks had already signed an alliance with the Germans, and if Churchill's advice to attack the ship in Italian territorial waters had been followed, there might well have been a major diplomatic incident. It is all very well for admirals to behave as though nothing counts more than attacking enemy ships, but First Lords might reasonably be expected to take a wider view. Even had the British ships available attacked the Germans, their armament was not sufficient to have done much damage. The real significance of the episode was to reveal how inadequate and inefficient the Admiralty could be. The signals to the British admirals shadowing the *Goeben* were ambiguous, and they were not made any clearer by Churchill's habit of trying to dictate tactics over the telegraph wires.[34]

By trying to combine political office with a detailed interest in the front, Churchill was to bring upon himself the nemesis traditionally reserved for those afflicted with such hubris.

Criticism of the First Lord came from a number of directions and, as ever, some of it was fair and much of it was ill-informed. Churchill's decision to replace the commander of the First Fleet, Sir George Callaghan, by Sir John Jellicoe was perfectly justifiable, but the manner in which it was done created further animosity towards Churchill within the Admiralty. On 30 July Jellicoe was informed of the decision and immediately sent a telegram declining the appointment. But Churchill remained insistent. Jellicoe and Admiral Beatty kept up a steady bombardment of telegrams to Churchill, the gist of which was that the 'moral effect upon Fleet' of changing the Commander-in-Chief 'would be worse than a defeat at such a moment'.[35] But, despite entreaties from his wife to sweeten the pill for Callaghan, Churchill pushed ahead. Clementine had given him sage advice when she had asked him to offer Callaghan some 'advisory position at the Admiralty'. She did not want Lady Callaghan to join with Lady Bridgeman in a 'league of retired Officers' Cats to abuse you',[36] and she realised how her husband's high-handed behaviour could create enemies.

Clementine offered him equally good advice on another issue which was to damage his reputation. Churchill's longing to be at the front led him to pay frequent trips to the headquarters of the British Commander-in-Chief in France, Sir John French. Such trips irritated his colleagues, who could not see why they were necessary, and they did nothing to soothe the new Secretary of State for War, Field Marshal Lord Kitchener. Churchill took Clementine's advice as far as informing Asquith and Kitchener of his movements was concerned, but he quite missed her wider point which was her wish that 'you didn't crave to go'.[37] Such visits to the front simply confirmed existing views of Churchill's irresponsibility. The fact that he was setting up his own Naval Division at the Admiralty added to the impression that he did not feel that the Admiralty offered enough scope for his strategic genius.

Had the Admiralty been able to deliver some great naval coup, then much of the sniping at Churchill would have been dissipated, but all the First Lord delivered were speeches. His boastful declaration on 21 September that if the German Navy did not come out to fight it would 'be dug out like rats from a hole',[38] was followed by the sinking of three British ships the next day; this did nothing for his public image. Criticism that the Admiralty was negligent was unjust; blockades are, by their nature, undramatic. But Churchill could not and would not rest content with such a situation, and his attempts to impart some drama to the proceedings were not helpful to his reputation.

Once war had been declared Churchill's martial spirit thirsted for action;

in that sense he was at one with public opinion, which wanted some glorious naval victory. Since his colleagues were, with the exception of Lord Kitchener, civilians, it was no use looking to them for inspiration. Nor did Churchill need to, for he had inspiration enough for ten men; too much, it was to transpire, for his own good. On 19 August Asquith recorded that Churchill was in 'quite undefeated' form, and the particular 'swine' at whom he would now 'like to have his fling are his kinsmen in the United States'.[39] A few days later he was all for attacking Turkey (which had not yet declared war). With the aid of 250,000 troops offered by the Greeks, he also 'propounded a Napoleonic plan of forcing the Danish passage with the help of the Greeks, and convoying Russian troops to the coast off Berlin and making a *coup de théâtre*'.[40] Receiving news from the First Lord that the Dutch were refusing to permit the importation of food into Belgium, Churchill told Grey that the Admiralty was capable of keeping the Scheldt open 'at any time you think it necessary'.[41] Churchill had plenty of aggressive spirit, but to direct it at three neutral states with no regard for the political consequences was hardly to inspire confidence in his judgment.

One of the problems with being First Lord was that it simply did not give Churchill enough scope for his aggressive instincts – hence his annoyance with the Imperial German Fleet for skulking in its harbours. What the Germans could not provide, his own ingenuity had to contrive. On 16 August he reorganised the naval reserve to create the Royal Naval Division, or 'Churchill's Pets' as they were known, before things went wrong. Whilst this force was being recruited, Churchill sent marines into operations at Ostend[42] and to assist the Royal Naval Air Service at Dunkirk. This last operation, known as the 'Dunkirk Circus', attracted criticism from regular soldiers, who disapproved of its amateurish antics.[43] It gave Churchill the chance to put troops into action instead of just sitting in the Admiralty waiting for things to happen, but there were those who murmured that the war was not being fought for the First Lord's private satisfaction.

The greatest success for the Admiralty had been the swift transport of the Expeditionary Force to France in early August, but once it was there, all eyes focused upon its fate. The Admiralty made the most of exploits like the raid on the Heligoland Bight off the German coast in late August, but, despite the publicity, what the operation demonstrated, yet again, was that the Admiralty was plagued by inefficient Staff work and lack of co-ordination.[44] Asquith's impression that the 'navy is not doing very well just now',[45] penned in late September, was the result of the sinking of the three British cruisers just after Churchill's 'rats' speech, but this incident, and the freedom with which German cruisers raided British colonial merchantmen, were thrown into the shade by the calamity of the Battle of the Coronel Islands in the South Atlantic in early October. Although this was speedily rectified by the defeat of Graf von Spee's squadron at the Falkand Islands, such incidents

were unpleasant jolts to a nation which took for granted its own naval dominance. Once again there were cries that all was not well at the Admiralty,
and the First Lord's trips to his 'circus' at Dunkirk, and his interference in
'practically everything', came in for criticism. 'If he would either leave matters
entirely alone at the Admiralty . . . or give it his entire and complete attention,
we might go forward, but this flying about and putting his fingers to pies
which do not concern him is bound to lead to disaster.' Beatty's words to his
wife were not simply prophetic; they were an accurate description of current
affairs.[46]

Churchill believed that with 'the special knowledge which I possessed' and
the 'great and flexible authority' which he wielded, in what he called 'this
time of improvisations', he would be able to come up with better solutions
to the problems of war than others. But this 'confidence' in 'my own judgement', which he 'seemed to see confirmed from day to day by many remarkable events', began to look to others like a species of megalomania.[47]

On 2 October, when Churchill was on the way to Dunkirk, he was summoned back to London to be told that Antwerp was about to fall. After a
meeting of Ministers, Churchill set off for Antwerp at 1.30 a.m.[48] In his
memoirs he implies that the decision to send him had been a collective one,
but the very imprecision of his account lends verisimilitude to Grey's version,
which, it must be said, has the ring of authenticity: 'Immediately he entered
the room he said that the abandonment of Antwerp *must* be stopped, and
announced that he was going there at once to stop it.'[49]

The purpose of his self-suggested mission was to see the Belgian Government and to 'try to infuse into their backbones the necessary quantity of
starch', a task which Asquith had every confidence he would do in his own
inimitable way.[50] But the Prime Minister's confidence soon turned to incredulity. The reports that the Belgian Army had decided to evacuate Antwerp
were, it transpired, wrong, and Churchill quickly came to an arrangement
with the Belgians that they would resist the German advance for ten days if
the British could guarantee substantial aid, but for less time if that was not
possible. Churchill asked for both his naval brigades, 'minus recruits', to be
sent to him at once.[51] Churchill's urge to be in action himself could no longer
be contained. Given a choice between commanding the defence of Antwerp
and running the Admiralty, Churchill had no doubt which he preferred:

If it is thought by HM Government that I can be of service here, I am willing to
resign my office and undertake command of relieving forces assigned to Antwerp in
conjunction with Belgian Army, provided that I am given necessary military rank and
authority, and full powers of a commander of a detached force in the field.[52]

When Asquith read out this proposal to the Cabinet, it 'was received with a
Homeric laugh'.[53] Those who thought that Churchill had lost sight of his
political bearings amidst the excitement of war were confirmed in their views,

as were those who merely thought that he was off his head. It is, perhaps, significant that the only Minister who took the proposal seriously was Kitchener, whose military mind readily accepted Churchill's basic premise – that being in the field was more important than being in government. Asquith politely declined Churchill's 'patriotic offer'.

Churchill returned to England on 7 October, surrounded, in the eyes of his civilian colleagues, with the aura of a hero, but all this was to change swiftly following the fall of Antwerp on 10 October, when some fifteen hundred members of the Naval Division were captured, with another thousand of them reported 'missing in action'. Despite Churchill's request that they should be sent 'minus recruits', they had turned up with the rawest reservists, whether through bad Staff work at the Admiralty or the enthusiasm of the new recruits. 'Churchill's pets' now became 'Churchill's innocent victims'. The *Morning Post*, that voice of the Tory right, called the episode 'a costly blunder for which Mr W. Churchill must be held responsible'.[54] Beatty thought that Churchill had made 'such a darned fool of himself over the Antwerp débâcle', telling his wife on 18 October that 'the man must have been mad' to have thought he could relieve Antwerp 'by putting 8000 half-trained troops into it'.[55] Lloyd George confided to McKenna and Riddell that Churchill's 'interference with land operations, or for that matter with naval operations, is all wrong ... Winston is like a torpedo. The first you hear of his doings is when you hear the swish of the torpedo dashing through the water'; he was not the only one to be 'uneasy' at Churchill and his antics.[56]

Some of these criticisms were unjust. It was not Churchill's fault that some of the naval brigade were raw recruits, but he had undoubtedly been too ambitious, and the *Post*'s stricture that Churchill had been using 'the resources of the Admiralty as if he were personally responsible for naval operations' was not wide of the mark.[57] Although, in retrospect, Churchill was able to justify the operation on the grounds that it had helped save the Channel ports, that was not why he had urged its implementation. At the time he had thought that it could help Sir John French's advance north, another over-ambitious scheme which never came off.[58] Nor was that why he had made his famous offer to resign. His sense of proportion, never strong, had quite deserted him. A 'political career', he told an amused Asquith, was 'nothing to him in comparison with military glory', and his mouth 'watered' at the sight of the new armies which Kitchener was raising. Churchill pleaded with the Prime Minister not to take a 'conventional' view of his future; having 'as he says "tasted blood"' these last few days, he is beginning like a tiger to raven for more,' Asquith told Venetia Stanley on 7 October.[59]

Churchill's 'schoolboy simplicity' had not lost its power to fascinate Asquith, who applied to him his favourite definition of genius – 'a zigzag streak of lightning in the brain'. But the Prime Minister's feelings changed as he heard more about the Antwerp operation. By 13 October he was feeling the '*wicked* folly of it all' and inclining to blame Churchill for sending the troops 'like sheep to the shambles'. He hoped that Churchill would 'learn from experience' and 'hand over to the military authorities' his 'little circus at Dunkirk'.[60] With the war at sea going badly and the First Lord leaving the routine work of the Admiralty to him whilst he went off on his little jaunts to the front, Asquith's confidence in Churchill had been dented. Given the public outcry caused by events at Antwerp and the general feeling that Churchill was to blame, as well as the exposed position which he had occupied at the Admiralty for some time, his political situation was not good. The lack of any great naval victory denied him the opportunity to refurbish his reputation. But Asquith was sanguine in thinking that Churchill might have learnt from experience. The First Lord's supreme confidence in his own ability to find some quick and unconventional way to win the war was unimpaired; the search for such a solution was to destroy the Prime Minister's support for his 'genius' at the Admiralty.

10

'Ninepins'

Churchill's search for action led his restless imagination to toy with many ideas before it alighted on the Dardanelles. Because of the importance of that episode it has tended to distract attention from the fact that even before it, Churchill's political position was too weak to stand the impact of any more setbacks. It is more dramatic (and, therefore, in keeping with Churchill's view of history) for the great man to fall because of one cataclysmic event – and it evokes shades of Lord Randolph in 1886, Marlborough in 1713 or Napoleon after Waterloo – but the facts were more prosaic. The Dardanelles episode merely helped precipitate a crisis which deprived the First Lord of the support of his one remaining prop – Asquith.

The general perception of Churchill by late September 1914 was that he was a man whose mind was on every aspect of the war, rather than on that part of it which concerned the Admiralty. As Balfour put it: 'Winston for the moment, unfortunately, is much more anxious to rival Napoleon than Nelson, and thinks more of the Army than the Navy.'[1] His faith in his 'star' seems to have led him to believe that his hour had struck. Hankey, the secretary to the CID, described Churchill as bringing 'an element of youth, energy, vitality and confidence' to a Cabinet of civilians, who were conscious of being out beyond their depth.[2] Churchill's 'unbaffled confidence'[3] was undented by the setbacks of the first few months of the war, and where most of his colleagues worried that the fighting would go on for too long, Churchill's only fear was lest it finish too soon.[4]

But by October confidence in the Admiralty, and its chief, was at a low ebb. The initially favourable reaction of Churchill's colleagues to his exploits at Antwerp turned to 'disgust' in the face of press reaction and reports about the use of untrained troops, and Churchill's habit of blaming everyone else for anything that had gone wrong was no help to his cause.[5] Churchill's statement in Cabinet on 15 October, that the Admiralty could not prevent German submarines from getting into the Channel, was greeted by Asquith with the remark, 'You mean we have lost command of the sea'. Churchill hotly denied this,[6] but these denials were becoming increasingly unconvincing. The failures to prevent the German cruiser, the *Emden*, from causing havoc in the Indian Ocean, or to bring German raiders in East Africa to book,[7] were added to the list of earlier failures, and there was little to set against them. When Riddell went round to the Admiralty on 22 October to discuss with Churchill the 'violent attacks' being made by the press, he found the First Lord 'just pulling on his underclothes (pink silk as before)'. Churchill was in a defiant mood and declared that he had 'no wish to stay if the Cabinet wish me to go. I would rather be at the Front.'[8] A few days later it was reported that even Churchill's normally ebullient spirits were depressed by the load of criticism which his department was having to bear.[9] The sinking of the *Audacious* by a mine on 27 October plunged him even further into gloom. But, as Asquith reported, Churchill was 'resourceful and undismayed', and he had come up with a scheme which would not only, he thought, deflect some of the public criticism, but also materially help in winning the war. He proposed to replace his much-criticised First Sea Lord, Prince Louis of Battenberg, with 'new blood' – in the form of the seventy-four-year-old Fisher.[10]

The scheme aroused much scepticism in naval circles. King George V protested that Fisher did not have the confidence of the entire Navy, and that he was getting senile, whilst the outgoing Battenberg would have preferred to see Sir Arthur Wilson return. But the First Lord was adamant, and with Asquith eulogising Churchill 'to the skies' and saying that he must have the man he wanted, Fisher was appointed, despite the King's grave misgivings.[11] Churchill admired Fisher as a kindred spirit: 'the originality of his mind and the spontaneity of his nature freed him from conventionalities of all kinds';[12] that he was also in his seventies was the sort of pettifogging detail that genius could overlook and override. Churchill had been in touch with Fisher ever since the start of the war, and he had been left 'with the impression of a terrific engine of mental and physical power burning and throbbing in that aged frame'.[13] Fisher was 'in harmony with events',[14] even as Churchill felt himself to be. He was also, as Churchill told Asquith's daughter in May 1915, now 'old and weak', which would allow the First Lord to keep control of operations in his own hands.[15]

Thus, in place of Battenberg, whose weariness and German origins made him a liability to a First Lord under attack himself, Churchill could now shelter behind what he hoped would be the splendid façade of Fisher's public reputation. It was a timely operation. On 4 November the news of Britain's naval defeat at the Battle of the Coronel Islands broke. This could be blamed, as it was, on the failings of the British commander, Admiral Cradock, and on the old regime. As it was swiftly followed up by the victory at the Falkland Islands, this could be set down as the first fruits of the new order. Fisher's dissatisfaction with the manner of the victory and the failure to follow it up were expressed only in private.[16] The Falklands was followed up by a victorious skirmish near the Dogger Bank, and with the news of the sinking of the *Audacious* withheld from the press, and the sacrifice of Battenberg, pressure on Churchill lessened – for the moment. Like Kitchener's appointment, Fisher's was meant to reassure public opinion that the war was being run properly; the Liberals could shelter behind the twin colossi. But in both cases protection did not come cheap. Kitchener's shortcomings were not dissimilar to Fisher's; both men found it difficult to work with a General Staff; they preferred to run their own show and found politicians a tiresome encumbrance. The consequences were administrative disorder and political friction. Public opinion blamed the politicians for any shortcomings, and the reputations of the colossi could not be compromised by revealing the truth, for upon them depended the confidence of the public. Present safety, as Churchill was to discover, had been purchased at a heavy price.

With the advent of Fisher, Churchill at last had someone else at the Admiralty who shared his hankering after action. 'DO SOMETHING!!!!! *We are waiting to be kicked!!!*',[17] was the old Admiral's line; Churchill had no need to be told. His imagination had alighted on so many possible areas for offensive action that Churchill could probably have claimed parentage of almost any operation which the British had pursued. The problem was that he was incapable of realistically assessing the possibility of any particular operation, and the British 'war machine', such as it was, produced no one and no mechanism for imposing a sense of reality on a First Lord who was apt to confuse critical comment on his tribe of brain-children with a lack of intestinal fortitude. Critical of the lack of initiative of others, Churchill never appreciated that the offensive spirit, when carried to excess, simply turned into a frenetic desire to be doing something.

It was out of this situation that the Dardanelles operation emerged; but for all the controversy that has surrounded its inception, it did not hold the field even in Churchill's mind, until late in the day. Churchill can rightly claim that he had been thinking about an operation in the region since August, but as he had been thinking about operations in almost every region since that date, this is not so much a sign of foresight as a symptom of hyperactivity. In July he had put up a host of projects to Asquith, all of which involved operations off Holland, the Heligoland Bight or the Baltic.[18] But even whilst some of these ideas occupied his mind, he came up with others on 19 August which involved linking up with the Russians and landing on the Prussian coast.[19] Soon afterwards Churchill produced the notion of blockading the Scheldt, 'which would have infringed Dutch neutrality'.[20] When he was despondent in late October, he cheered himself up with the idea of sending old battleships up the Elbe – simply, so it seemed, for the sake of doing something.[21]

Convinced as Churchill was that the admirals lacked initiative, he was apt to treat any criticism of any of his ideas as a sign of feebleness. Thus when his advisers pronounced his plan of capturing the Dutch island of Ameland as a 'strategical and tactical futility', he simply looked around for another Dutch island. The one which occupied his imagination the longest was Borkum, although he would settle for Sylt if necessary. His treatment of military operations, both at the time and in retrospect, is marked by its 'extremely theoretical character'.[22] It was almost as though intoxicated by the map and his own ingenuity, all that was needed was the correct offensive spirit. As Admiral Oliver recorded: 'Churchill would often look in on his way to bed to tell me how he would capture Borkum or Sylt. If I did not interrupt or ask questions he could capture Borkum in twenty minutes.'[23]

Churchill's ideas were always bold in conception and promised great results at little cost – and he always underrated the obstacles in the way of their achievement. Fisher had long contemplated a descent on Borkum in the event of a war with Germany, and Churchill, who was attracted by the notion, put its merits to Asquith on 29 December. His advocacy showed all its usual features. 'It alone', Churchill wrote, could 'guarantee' Britain from 'raid or invasion'. The seizure of Borkum would 'in all probability bring about the sea battle' which would decide the war, and within 'a few weeks' all German ships would be 'driven altogether from the North Sea and into their harbours and mined and blockaded therein'. After that Schleswig-Holstein could be 'invaded' from the sea, which would not only threaten the strategically vital Kiel Canal, but also 'enable Denmark to join us'. Then, with the whole Baltic thrown open, Russian armies 'could be landed within 90 miles of Berlin'.[24] It was all magnificent stuff, but Admiral Oliver had clearly understated matters when he said that Churchill needed twenty minutes to capture Borkum – in that time he could take Berlin.

Nowhere did Churchill pause to consider the practicalities of a scheme which promised so much. In the first place the waters around Borkum were mined and within easy reach of submarines and torpedo-boats. Even had the island been captured, how would Churchill have avoided the fate of the Walcheren expedition in 1808? Then, having landed troops, the British found it difficult to supply them – and that was before the advent of the mine and the submarine; how many British cruisers would have been tied down in such an operation? Where were the troops to come from? What made Churchill think that the Danes had any desire to join the war? This, one of his perennial illusions, was to surface again in the Second World War, when he presumed that Pétain's Vichy regime was thirsting to get back into the war and that Roosevelt's America was similarly inclined. Even had all these improbable events occurred, did the Russians have enough trained and well-equipped men to embark upon the enterprise which Churchill envisaged? Moreover, did anyone possess the experience or skill to plan what would have been the largest amphibious operation in history? How would the men get ashore, either on the Baltic coast of Prussia, or, even more crucially, at Borkum, which was defended by forts?[25] The Admiralty had already concluded that an attempt to attack Heligoland was doomed to failure because ships could not fight forts, and what applied there also applied to Borkum; but this would not stop Churchill advocating such an operation elsewhere.[26]

In the face of these considerations, for Churchill to castigate the admirals for their 'lethargy' and 'complete absence of positive effort' in failing to come up with a workable plan[27] is an illustration of his fatal inability to distinguish between what was practicable and what was not. The fact that no one came out straight and told him these things is, in itself, illuminating. Hankey noted in January that Fisher 'frequently disagrees with statements made by the First Lord at our War Cabinet. I wish he would speak up.'[28] The sheer weight of Churchill's presentation of his case, his loquacity and his habit of treating criticism as carping, all prevented or dissuaded his professional advisers from speaking up. His own habit of interfering in operational and planning matters blurred the distinction between the civilian First Lord and his professional advisers, and Churchill was apt, in any case, to give their ideas short shrift unless they happened to coincide with his own. 'No matter what the experts thought, he knew better.'[29] Their main use was to be a retrospective one, namely to allow Churchill to shelter behind the fact that none of them came down decisively against the Dardanelles scheme.[30]

Churchill was not the only person to bombard the Prime Minister with military schemes for the new year. His own frustrated feeling that there must be an alternative to 'sending our armies to chew barbed wire in Flanders' was shared by Lloyd George and Hankey, but their favoured sphere of operations was the Balkans rather than the Baltic. Hankey considered the Baltic option (although how much he knew about Churchill's ideas is uncertain), but dismissed it because he did not think that either Holland or Denmark wanted to join the war; instead, he suggested an operation against Turkey, which would raise the Balkan nations.[31] Lloyd George's conclusions were similar to those of Hankey,[32] and the appearance of the latter's memorandum prompted Churchill to recall to Asquith's mind the fact that he had advocated an operation in the Dardanelles some months before.[33]

Hankey's paper had not, in fact, advocated an assault on the Dardanelles in isolation, but the fact that such a scheme had been one of the many which had surged through Churchill's brain prompted the First Lord to treat it as though it had done so. Churchill's ideas about attacking the Dardanelles had been expressed with the enthusiasm untempered by serious consideration which marked his later designs on Borkum. Back in August the Greeks had suggested that they might join the Allied cause with 250,000 troops; no sooner had they done so than Churchill had them attacking Turkey – oblivious of the fact that the Turks were not in the war. When it looked as though the Turks were about to enter the war on the side of the Central Powers, Churchill decided to get in the first blow. Two days before war was actually declared, he authorised a naval bombardment on the Dardanelles.[34] Much nonsense has been spouted about this alerting the Turks to the dangers of a British attack,[35] but it appears unlikely that the Turks would not, of their own accord, have realised that there was such a possibility.

Churchill had raised the notion of capturing the Dardanelles as a means of defending Egypt back in late November,[36] but it was only one idea among many. Even after he had read Hankey's paper, Churchill continued to favour the idea of an attack on Borkum or Sylt. How and why did the Dardanelles plan come to be considered as peculiarly Churchill's own? The short answer is that the technical objections to the Borkum/Sylt plan were so formidable that finally even Churchill was reduced to lamenting the 'lethargy' of his advisers – being unable to controvert their views. With the demise of that operation, the Dardanelles offered the only other opportunity to a First Lord bent on securing action; the fact that Fisher had scuppered Borkum made it difficult for him to speak out equally strongly over the Dardanelles. Hankey and Lloyd George had drawn attention towards the Balkans, but neither of them had proposed an attack on the Dardanelles in isolation from other offensives; however, that operation offered Churchill the chance he had been looking for – to use naval power by itself to win the war.

In the absence of decisive action on the western front, the idea of mounting an offensive elsewhere had obvious attractions, but Balfour was the only member of the CID to spot the flaw in the Balkan plan. He reminded Hankey that Germany was 'perfectly indifferent to the fate of her allies, except in so far as her own fate is bound up with it', so an attack in the Balkans, 'however successful, must be regarded as merely subsidiary'.[37] That no one else seems to have raised this objection, and that even after it was all over Churchill could seriously argue that 'knocking the props away' from Germany was the way to win the war, illustrates how enthusiasm can override common sense. Anyone who seriously believed that Turkey was a 'prop' to the German war effort deserved a long rest from the strains which had brought him to such a pass.

Part of the difficulty in assessing any scheme which Churchill, Hankey or anyone else came up with was the lack of any forum for considering it. Writing to Balfour on 2 January 1915, Hankey invited him to a meeting of the 'War Council', a body sufficiently new to warrant inverted commas.[38] The first meeting of the War Council had taken place in November, but its relationship to the Cabinet was ill-defined and it was, in effect, an *ad hoc* meeting of parts of the CID. Fisher likened the January meeting of the Council to 'a game of ninepins!', with '"Plans" *ad infinitum*' to be considered. He was willing to 'back my Winston against the field' and urged Balfour to support Hankey's scheme.[39] Here lay the origins of the problems which were to follow. The exact status of members of the War Council was uncertain. Balfour and Fisher, for different reasons, felt themselves precluded from saying much, the one because he was a Unionist and the other because he was only a Service adviser. Of the other members, only Kitchener, Hankey and Churchill knew anything (or sounded as though they did) about military affairs, and the first of these did not want to see troops wasted outside the main theatre of operations. Asquith and Lloyd George were both in favour of trying something fresh, but neither of them knew enough about strategy to be able to distinguish real from fools' gold. There existed no mechanism for securing co-operation between the Services; indeed, because Kitchener and Churchill disagreed on matters, there existed an active impediment to any co-ordination. Asquith, who as Chairman of the War Council might have been expected to have engineered such a state of affairs, was operating in a realm where his previous experience proved no guide. His style of chairmanship, the long leisurely discussions which allowed men to blow off steam and time for a compromise to emerge, whilst suitable for keeping a squabbling Liberal Cabinet together, was not well-suited to deciding upon military operations. Then, beyond this void at the centre, there lay the problems caused by the personalities involved.

Kitchener was loath to use the Army General Staff, which had existed for some years, and Fisher, who had opposed the idea of a naval General Staff, which had come in after his retirement, simply ignored it. Both men, to whom the War Council might have been expected to look for sound strategic advice, proved incapable of giving it, partly because, in Balfour's phrase, they lacked 'strategical genius',[40] and partly because neither of them had an easy relationship with the impulsive and persuasive First Lord.

Churchill's relationship with Kitchener before 1914 had not been a good one, but the two men had co-operated well in August and September. However, Churchill's little 'jaunts' to the front and his frequent confabulations with the British commander, Sir John French, aroused Kitchener's ire. He regarded Churchill's actions as detrimental to his authority as well as unnecessary. In December he had pressed Asquith to stop the trips.[41] Churchill did not respond well to these suggestions, but Asquith, who felt that the First Lord was away from the Admiralty too much 'in what may be critical moments', was 'disposed to agree' with Kitchener.[42] Despite Churchill's efforts to smooth his relations with Kitchener, and his 'affection and admiration' for him, General French thought that his judgment was 'highly erratic' and was equally undisposed to champion the First Lord's cause.[43]

If Churchill's relationship with Kitchener was poor, his relations with Fisher were not much better. During the 'honeymoon' period the two egotists had got on splendidly, with one of them covering business at all times, but Fisher soon began to resent the First Lord's interference in operational matters and his frequent absences at the front. Churchill's refusal to sanction sending out the whole of Jellicoe's fleet in response to the German raids on Hartlepool and Scarborough in December rankled,[44] as did his veto of Fisher's plan to mine the Elbe and Heligoland as a prelude to an attack on the Baltic coast of Prussia.[45] Nor, as he told Churchill on 8 December, did he 'hold with these "outings" of yours'.[46] Fisher told Balfour on 4 January that he had been 'within an ace of leaving', and he did not 'contemplate a long stay where I am!'[47]

It is not often that a successful combined military/naval operation grows out of such soil – and this was to be no exception.

Fisher was not far wrong when he compared the meeting on 7 January to a game of 'ninepins'. The War Council ruled out a plan from Sir John French for an amphibious assault on Ostend–Zeebrugge and listened to Churchill dilate upon his favourite Borkum scheme.[48] Balfour had heard him on the subject a month before, when he had refused 'to recognise even the most obvious difficulties', and he was surprised to hear that such an unthought-out scheme had been under consideration for some time.[49] On this occasion the First Lord was obviously convincing, for authority was given to mount the scheme, which, Churchill said, would not be ready until March. Captain Richmond, the assistant director of operations at the Admiralty, who thought the plan 'quite mad', now had to convince the First Lord that the imprimatur of the War Council did not make it sane.[50]

But even as Richmond and company bent their powers to persuading the First Lord that Borkum was bunkum, another idea had fired his highly combustible imagination. On 2 January Kitchener asked Churchill if there was anything the Admiralty could do by way of attacking the Turks in order to relieve the hard-pressed Russians; he did not think that there was anything they could do to help the Russians in the Caucasus because 'we have no troops to land anywhere', but he did suggest that a 'demonstration' at the Dardanelles might have the effect of stopping reinforcements going east.[51] Churchill asked Vice-Admiral Carden, whose squadron was off the Dardanelles, whether it was a 'practicable operation' to 'force' the Straits 'by the use of ships alone'.[52] Much of the writing on this vexed question assumes that Churchill was already adapting part of Fisher's and Hankey's scheme of a more general Balkan operation for his own use, but there is no evidence to support this; indeed, the scheme he suggested to Carden bore no relation to either of these, nor yet Kitchener's 'demonstration'. The idea of 'forcing' the Dardanelles by 'ships alone' was Churchill's own, and his telling Carden that 'older Battleships would be used', and that the 'importance of results would justify severe loss', suggests that he had already conceived visions of Constantinople falling and was asking for a positive answer.[53]

Fisher, who was far from keen on the Borkum operation, had urged on 4 January that they should adopt 'Hankey's plans' as 'imperative and very pressing',[54] but it was the Borkum scheme which the War Council adopted on 7 January. Two days earlier Carden's reply had been received at the Admiralty. He did not consider that the Dardanelles could be 'rushed', but thought that they might 'be forced by extended operations with large number of ships'.[55] Churchill replied that his view was 'agreed with by high authorities here' and asked him to detail what forces would be needed and what result achieved.[56]

Churchill's comment about 'high authorities' has puzzled many commentators, even as it was to puzzle the Dardanelles Commission of Inquiry. Churchill was to explain that he was referring to Admirals Jackson and Oliver, but this simply elicited further expressions of surprise, as it is by no means clear that Jackson, the chief of the Admiralty War Staff, was in favour.[57] Churchill did not consult Fisher, but then the First Sea Lord was already in favour of 'Hankey's plan', and by not distinguishing between that broad general scenario for a full-scale Balkan war, Kitchener's 'demonstration' and his own 'by ships alone' idea, Churchill fostered the impression that they were all the same thing. Perhaps they were in his mind, for he was still pushing his Borkum scheme and French's Zeebrugge operation; the Dardanelles was just another bee in an overcrowded bonnet. It became a reality when the other schemes did not, because it was less impossible than they were. Any notion that the imprimatur of the War Council meant anything should be dispelled by the recollection that that body had also agreed to the Borkum plan, which was universally denounced at the Admiralty as lunacy. Moreover, as presented by Churchill at the meeting of the Council on 13 January, the Dardanelles seemed an attractive proposition, involving no troops and the expenditure of some old battleships which were no use for anything else.

In his memoirs Churchill attributes his championship of the idea of forcing the Straits to the 'plan' which Carden sent him; it was, he wrote, 'an entirely novel proposition'.[58] But what he received from Carden on 11 January was a 'plan' only in the broad sense that all Churchill's stratagems were 'plans'. Only to a mind like Churchill's, which had been thinking in terms of a few ships 'rushing' the Straits, could Carden's comments have come as an 'entirely novel proposition'.[59] Churchill had asked him how the Straits could be forced; Carden now replied. 'The novelty', Professor Marder remarked sardonically, 'lay in the abandonment of any attempt to rush the Dardanelles, and in the substitution of a scheme to attack the forts methodically.'[60]

The proposal bore all the hallmarks of one of Churchill's ideas.[61] Bold in conception, the First Lord presented it as though it would knock Turkey out of the war and bring aid to Russia. It also bore the second feature of any Churchillian plan – it was fairly cheap. But it ignored many obstacles. No one queried its basic assumption that the Turks would run away at the sight of a British squadron in the Bosphorus, nor did anyone ask what would happen if they did not. Churchill's statement that no one questioned the assertion that guns could fight forts is, to say the least, disingenuous. Admiral Wilson's plans for attacking Heligoland had been ruled out on precisely that ground, and the Borkum scheme was to fall foul of the same fear.[62] It was Churchill himself, because of his experience at Antwerp, who now dismissed Nelson's dictum that ships could not fight forts. Neither he, nor anyone else, appears to have asked how ships could occupy forts, or Constantinople for that matter. It is difficult not to conclude that the force of Churchill's grand conception carried the War Council along, and that its members shared his low view of Turkish capabilities.

There was, however, no suggestion that the Dardanelles operation now had pride of place. One of Fisher's grouses about the way things were being done at the top was that it was 'chaotic', with 'a new plan every week'.[63] Having authorised the Borkum scheme on 7 January, the following day the War Council approved Kitchener's idea for an attack on Alexandretta and Churchill's proposal that they should try to get Holland to join the war.[64] The First Lord wanted the Alexandretta operation to be 'practically simultaneous' with the Dardanelles attack, so that if it failed they could save face by representing it as 'a mere demonstration to cover the seizure of Alexandretta'.[65]

Whilst Churchill argued with Jellicoe over the desirability of the Borkum scheme which Fisher disliked, the old Admiral was beginning to exhibit signs which made the Prime Minister conclude that he was 'unbalanced';[66] the price for the protection Fisher had afforded back in October was about to be paid. On 20 January Hankey reported that Fisher was 'unhappy' about Churchill overruling him on 'purely technical naval matters' and the present and future dispositions of the Fleet. By this stage Balfour and Jellicoe were also aware of Fisher's feelings, the former having been told by Hankey and the latter by Fisher himself, who had said on 19 January that, since he did not 'agree with one single step taken', he was thinking of resigning.[67] The only person who appears to have been unaware of the violence of Fisher's feelings was the First Lord himself.

Perhaps Asquith's suspicion that Fisher was becoming 'unbalanced' was right; his behaviour in May certainly supports such a view; or perhaps it was just, as Captain Richmond thought, that he was 'old and worn out and nervous'.[68] But whether for any of these reasons, or a combination of them allied with his feeling that Churchill always 'out-argues me', Fisher's protests to the First Lord were less than forceful.[69] On 18 January he told him that he much preferred the Dutch scheme; then, on the 25th, announcing that he had 'no desire to continue in a useless resistance in the War Council to plans I cannot concur in', he sent him a long memorandum which, for the most part, consisted of an argument that the Grand Fleet should not be weakened in order to help the Dardanelles operation.[70] Churchill had no trouble countering Fisher's figures, but he did not probe the Admiral further.[71]

On the day of the War Council meeting, 28 January, Fisher pleaded to be allowed to retire and asserted that whether operations took place at the Dardanelles or Zeebrugge, they should be of a combined nature and should not mean taking capital ships from the Grand Fleet.[72] Asquith, increasingly worried by Fisher's behaviour, arranged to meet him with Churchill before the Council met. All parties agreed to drop the Zeebrugge operation but to go ahead with the Dardanelles plan. This makes Fisher's later statement that he did not regard Asquith's judgment as 'completely decisive' sound odd, until it is remembered that operations at Alexandretta and Borkum were still on the table.[73]

When the Dardanelles operation was raised at the War Council meeting, Fisher protested and tried to leave the room, but he was persuaded to stay by

Kitchener. It is easy to see why the Council agreed to the operation as presented by Churchill.[74] Balfour pointed out later to Fisher that if 'the naval views put before the War Council be accepted, the risks do not seem great'. It might be desirable to use troops, but if the forts could be knocked out by gunfire, as Churchill alleged, then it was 'not absolutely necessary'; and the political, military and economic rewards of the operation were 'enormous'.[75] Moreover, as Kitchener pointed out at the meeting, since it involved no troops, the assault on the Dardanelles could be easily 'broken off' if satisfactory progress was not made. Balfour's response to Fisher's complaints shows just how members of the War Council had reacted to Churchill's plan. It was not simply his advocacy which convinced them; there was also nothing in it to cause anyone to worry: it was cheap, approved of by high naval authorities, promised magnificent gains, and could be called off without loss of face if it misfired – what was there to object to?

The fact that Fisher sent his paper to Balfour, despite agreeing with Asquith and Churchill that he would keep it private, is evidence that the old conspirator was still addicted to dark and crooked ways. Hankey hoped that Balfour's response, which reiterated Churchill's optimistic arguments, would 'solve all difficulties'. Hankey told Balfour that if Asquith 'will go to the heart of things himself, he may be able to arrange matters between Churchill and Fisher';[76] he was too sanguine by far. Plans for the operation went ahead, with Fisher fulminating to his intimates, but not to the First Lord; he resembled nothing so much as a mine waiting for something to strike it before exploding – and he did not have to wait long.

11

Dire Straits

The idea that the Dardanelles operation would imperil the Government would have seemed far-fetched in January. The War Council had agreed to a naval operation in the Dardanelles in the confident belief that if it misfired, they could withdraw from it easily; it was only one of a number of operations under consideration. However, the other 'ninepins' were gradually knocked over. Kitchener could not promise a date for the Alexandretta assault, and the Borkum scheme was wrecked on its own impracticability. This left the Dardanelles as the front-runner for approval. Reports that the Austrians were about to mount a major assault on Serbia turned minds towards the sort of campaigns sketched out by Lloyd George and Hankey, but a major land offensive in the Balkans would mean a massive diversion of troops from the western front, unless some of the neutrals could be brought in. On the afternoon of 28 January it was agreed to consult with the French and the Greeks as to the possibility of sending a British brigade to Salonica; this, it was thought, might encourage the latter to enter the war.[1] But apart from this urgent but unfocused desire to 'do something' in the Balkans, Churchill's operation came to hold the field alone.

Despite his later denials, there can be no doubt that the Dardanelles was Churchill's operation. It was Churchill who had thought up the idea of forcing the Straits by ships alone and it was he who had decided that ships could fight forts. Moreover, under Churchill's regime at the Admiralty, the idea of collective responsibility by the Board of Admiralty had atrophied. Even Fisher found that Churchill ignored him, and on this occasion none of the other Sea Lords was taken into the First Lord's confidence. When one of them, Admiral Tudor, told Churchill in January that he would not 'do it with ships alone', he was met with the rejoinder, 'Oh yes we will.'[2] Churchill did not consult either naval or military gunnery experts, and his Chief of Staff, Oliver, was equally negligent. Nor was the Commander-in-Chief of the Fleet, Admiral Jellicoe, consulted. Churchill was so convincing at the War Council because he had first convinced himself; he neither sought nor welcomed advice which ran counter to his own convictions.[3]

One of those convictions, despite Fisher's doubts,[4] was that the operation required no land forces apart from the marine divisions already attached to it. But Fisher was not alone in his belief that the Dardanelles should be a full-scale combined operation. On 10 February Hankey told Balfour that 'every naval officer in the Admiralty who is in on the secret believes that the Navy cannot take the Dardanelles position without troops', and that only Churchill 'still professes to believe that they can do it with ships'; Hankey had already warned Asquith that 'we cannot trust to this'.[5] His argument received powerful support from Admiral Jackson's report on 13 February, which concluded that 'the naval bombardment is not recommended as a sound military operation, unless a strong military force is ready to assist in the operation or, at least, follow it up immediately the forts are silenced'.[6] Asquith, who felt that it was 'of much importance that in the course of the next month we should carry through a *decisive* operation somewhere', was disposed to agree. On 9 February the War Council had decided that the 29th Division should be sent to Lemnos, but since the Greeks had then declined to participate in military operations, it was agreed on 16 February that they should be made available for the Dardanelles.[7]

When the War Council met on 19 February, Haldane raised the question of whether they were now to regard the Dardanelles as being a 'combined' operation. In view of Churchill's later claim that the absence of the 29th Division was the 'decisive factor' in the failure of the operation, the answer to Haldane's question is of more than academic interest. By the time the Council met on 19 February, Kitchener had changed his mind about being able to spare the 29th Division. Russian setbacks in East Prussia inclined him to keep the troops available for the western front and to substitute for them 39,000 colonial troops from Egypt, who could, in any event, get to Lemnos more rapidly.[8] But what did Churchill need troops for when he had always maintained that the operation could be done by ships alone? The answer had been given the day before when he had told Kitchener that he needed at least 50,000 men 'within reach at 3 days' notice, either to seize the Gallipoli Peninsula when it has been evacuated, or to occupy C[onstantin]ople if a revolution takes place'.[9] He had evidently come round, at least partially, to Hankey's view.

The news that the 29th Division might not now be available prompted Churchill to launch into one of his glowing accounts of the possible benefits of the operation, and he reiterated his plea that he should have 65,000 men within reach of the Dardanelles. Evidently his answer to Haldane's question was that the troops would be used after the naval assault. He was still not thinking in terms of a combined operation. The 39,000 troops which Kitchener had offered him would, when combined with the marines and the Naval Division, come to over 50,000 men, which was all he was asking for. It would appear that when, after the event, Churchill realised that a proper combined operation could well have succeeded, he decided to represent himself as having been in favour of one; but he was not. Had the operation been meant as a combined one, he should have insisted that the naval assault be postponed until it had been decided whether to send the 29th Division. The fact that he did not do so, combined with his statements about what he wanted the troops for, all point to the conclusion that Churchill still thought he had found the operation which his mighty war machine could win on its own. As he told the Cabinet on 16 February, there would be a 'military uprising and ultimate revolution on [the] fall of [the] first fort'.[10] Wishful thinking always played a large part in any Churchillian grand design.

Churchill's statement to the Cabinet on 16 February that he would 'take all responsibility' was reflected in his sanguine reaction to the first bombardment of the forts on 19 February, when he issued a press statement announcing both its success and the intention to force the Straits; this, as Lloyd George later commented, made it impossible for the Cabinet to contemplate quietly withdrawing if anything went wrong.[11] But Churchill did not anticipate any such thing. It was regrettable that bad weather hindered speedy progress, but he used the time constructively trying to persuade Kitchener to let him have enough troops to exploit the success of the operation.[12] By this stage, according to Asquith, everyone except Kitchener agreed that 'the naval adventure in the Dardanelles sh[oul]d be backed up by a strong military force';[13] but much hinged upon what was meant by the term 'back up'.

In his memoirs, Churchill makes great play with the failure of his colleagues to send out the 29th Division in time, quoting his own comment on 26 February that 'if a disaster occurred in Turkey owing to insufficiency of troops, he must disclaim all responsibility'.[14] This, it would appear, is conclusive evidence that when the 'disaster' did occur, it was not Churchill's fault. But it is clear, if the course of Churchill's thinking is followed, that he still thought that a naval assault would succeed by itself, and the 'disaster' to which he was referring was not the one which occurred. What Churchill meant was that if there were not enough troops to occupy Constantinople and force the Turks to surrender following the success of the purely naval operation, the fault would not be his. But it was convenient, when he came to mount his own defence later, to be able to quote this passage, for with everyone's mind attuned to the fact that one reason the Gallipoli campaign had failed was the insufficiency of troops at an early stage, it allowed him to give the impression that, as usual, he had been prescient.[15]

But he had not been anticipating his naval operation turning into a combined one. Churchill later made great play with Kitchener's confused state of mind,[16] but the Field Marshal was quite consistent. He wanted most of the British Army concentrated in the west, but was prepared to release a sizeable force of about 50,000 for Churchill's enterprise. In the face of Churchill's pressure for the 29th Division, Kitchener asked him on 24 February whether he 'now contemplated a land attack', to which he received the answer that he 'did not'.[17] When pressed, Churchill said that he needed the troops in case the attack was 'held up by mines, and some local military operation required'. Clearly Churchill contemplated using troops in the initial assault-phase only if landing parties were necessary to take out the forts so that the minesweepers could get close in to do their work. It is hardly surprising that Kitchener remained puzzled as to why Churchill wanted nearly 100,000 men to do this. Churchill's answers showed where the muddled thinking was. He thought that the troops might occupy Constantinople if the assault succeeded, or that they could mount 'local operations' if the assault had almost succeeded. If the assault failed, then the troops could go to Bulgaria or Salonica or somewhere else. When he was asked what they would do if the Turkish armies retreated, Churchill replied that they would be 'required to support our diplomacy'. The idea of one division being able to force the surrender of all Turkish troops in Europe is one to make the mind boggle! Kitchener said that he was quite prepared to send the 29th Division if 'the fleet would not get through the Straits unaided'. If Churchill had been anticipating what he implies in his memoirs, namely just the operation which Kitchener had mentioned, this was his opportunity to say so. He did not; the troops, he said, would have a 'great moral effect' in diplomatic terms.[18] That Churchill was anticipating a purely naval operation with, at the most, some 'local operations by troops' is confirmed by events following the CID meeting on 24 February.

Buoyed up by reports on 25 February of successful operations, Churchill was seized with the fear that, having broken through the Straits, he would be unable to exploit his success through want of troops. At the War Council the following day he pressed Kitchener to release the 29th Division, having previously circulated a paper in which he stated that with 'proper military and naval co-operation, we can make certain of capturing Constantinople by the end of March'. He now had a clear response to Kitchener's questions about what he wanted the troops for: 'to occupy Constantinople and to compel a surrender of all Turkish forces remaining in Europe after the Fleet had obtained command of the Sea of Marmora'. It was at this point that he made the statement he was afterwards to be thankful for, that he must 'disclaim all responsibility' if a 'disaster occurred in Turkey owing to insufficiency of troops'; but he was clearly referring to a 'disaster' after the assault had succeeded, not stating that the assault could not succeed without troops.[19] It was not until late in the day that he finally abandoned the idea of 'by ships alone'.

The anticipation of the great victory and the pressure of events were now clearly telling on the First Lord. At the meeting on 26 February he was 'noisy, tactless and temperless – or – full', and Asquith felt constrained to have a 'quiet word for his soul's sake'.[20] Hobhouse described Churchill as being 'in a hurry to be conspicuous'. Churning out memoranda on anything and everything, Churchill was 'nervous, fretful, voluble, intolerably bumptious and conceited', and he took up an immense amount of everyone's time 'in increasing orations'.[21] Frances Stevenson, Lloyd George's mistress, had recorded earlier that 'people are beginning to get rather dissatisfied with Winston'. There were accusations that the only enquiries he sanctioned into naval mishaps were those where the admiral could be blamed, not those where the Admiralty was at fault, and Fisher's complaints about him were getting out into wider circulation.²² His 'tactless' action in offering Sir John French some of his Naval Divisions and armoured cars aroused Kitchener's ire, and the hard-pressed Prime Minister had to act as conciliator.²³ Margot Asquith felt that 'like all really self-centred people', Churchill 'ends by boring people'.²⁴ His behaviour at the War Council on 26 February, and the fact that he had quarrelled with both the military colossi behind whom the Government had elected to shelter, was having its own effect on a Prime Minister who was, himself, in an emotional state over the likelihood that his epistolary lover, Venetia Stanley, was about to marry his colleague, Edwin Montagu.²⁵

Reports of early success for the strategy of bombarding the forts fired Churchill's confidence. On 27 February Churchill put the Russians on the alert to send ships and troops to the Bosphorus,²⁶ and he told Kitchener that it 'now seems very likely that the passage of the Dardanelles will be completed before the end of March, and perhaps a good deal earlier'.²⁷ The following day he drew up a draft armistice for the surrender of Turkish forces.²⁸ Such confidence was infectious among a group of men who, after six hard months of war, finally saw the horizon lighten. On 3 March the War Council spent its time discussing the terms of the Turkish surrender,²⁹ and the following day, whilst still maintaining to Kitchener that the 29th Division was needed urgently, Churchill stated confidently that the naval operations could not be delayed 'as we must get into the Marmora as soon as possible in the normal course'.³⁰ In an effort to persuade the Greeks to participate, and thus provide troops rather quicker than Kitchener could, Churchill asked Grey to tell them that 'the Admiralty believe it in their power to force the Dardanelles without military assistance'.³¹ This telegram was not sent, as the Russians vetoed any Greek participation so near the great city which they coveted, but it surely helps dispose of the idea that, 'breast-high about the Dardanelles',³² Churchill was fretting because he thought the absence of the 29th Division would make all the difference between success and failure.

But the glittering political prospects which Churchill had foreshadowed did not come about. There was no revolution in Turkey as a result of the first British assaults on the forts, and, far from assisting, the Russians hindered matters because of their unconcealed desire for Constantinople, which helped to keep neutral Bulgaria and Romania on the sidelines. Then, as the operation progressed, doubts were thrown on Churchill's central assumption. On 5 March General Birdwood, commander of the land forces at the Dardanelles, telegraphed to Kitchener that he was 'very doubtful if the Navy can force the passage unassisted'.³³ Even the forts on the outer reaches of the Straits, which had been visible from the ships, had posed problems. Accuracy at the ranges required was, as had been anticipated, only in the region of two–three per cent. Churchill had assured the War Council that sufficient ammunition had been provided, but Carden, who had been ordered to be economical with it, found that his operations were hampered by a shortage of shells. Moreover, although the forts could be hit, with the help of spotter-planes for range-finding, the damage done when they were was minimal. The Turkish howitzers, which could fire from behind the crests of the hills, were not easily accessible to high velocity naval guns with their flat trajectory. It proved necessary to land detachments of marines to destroy the guns, and even then, because some of the howitzers were mobile, this was not easy.[34] On 6 March Carden telegraphed, ominously, that 'experience gained shows that in order to render a fort innocuous, it is absolutely necessary to land and destroy each gun'.[35]

Churchill's bullish statement at the War Council on 10 March, that the 'Admiralty still believed that they could effect the passage of the Straits by naval means alone, but they were glad to know that military support was available, if required', was hardly warranted by the progress of events, but the mood of the Council is shown by the fact that it had been called to 'consider the political, as well as the strategic, questions likely to arise after the fall of Constantinople'; euphoria was obviously infectious.[36] The men on the spot at the Dardanelles had come to the conclusion that a combined operation would be necessary, but this would not solve the problem of how to get the ships through the minefields so that their guns would be close enough to do effective damage to the forts. Attempts on 10 and 12 March to sweep the mines proved unsuccessful in the face of heavy fire from the shore. Churchill was scathing about this,[37] but if the Admiralty would select Grimsby and Hull trawler-men for this operation, then they had no right to be surprised when, in adverse conditions, not all the mines were removed.[38]

Churchill was equally unhappy with the progress, or lack of it, made by Carden. On 11 March, in a thinly veiled effort to infuse some initiative into the Admiral, Churchill, whilst approving his 'caution and deliberate methods', told him that 'the results to be gained are however great enough to justify loss of ships and men if success cannot be gained without'. It was typical of the First Lord in his Napoleonic mood that he suggested how Carden should accomplish a breakthrough. His proposal, that the 'forts at the Narrows' should be overwhelmed 'at decisive range' by 'the fire of the largest number of guns, great and small that can be brought to bear upon them', under cover of which landing parties could destroy the guns and the minefields could be swept, illustrates not only his irritating tendency to tell commanders how to do things, but also his habit of doing so in simplistic terms which took no account of local conditions.[39] It was something Churchill was to repeat in 1940.

'Increasingly apprehensive lest a military breakdown occur', Churchill sought to evade any responsibility for 'action more momentous than any which the Admiralty was taking, but over which I had no control'. Asquith and Kitchener agreed that the latter would assume responsibility for any military action.[40] But at this time Churchill was still confident that the ships could do it alone – with a push from himself. Indeed, when Kitchener told Churchill on 12 March that 'no operations on a large scale should be attempted until the 29th Division has arrived',[41] Churchill ignored him, saying that the naval operations had to continue.[42]

Hankey, who was alarmed at the way in which the operation which had been agreed to was, almost imperceptibly, changing its nature, pointed out to Asquith on 16 March the difference between Churchill's sanguine comments about 'ships alone' at the last War Council meeting, and the reports from the Dardanelles which implied that 'the employment of a considerable land force is indicated'; this was a 'new and possibly very formidable operation'. He urged the Prime Minister to get the War Council to 'ascertain definitely the scope of the operations contemplated', warning him that combined operations were notoriously liable to failure if not accompanied by careful planning. Hankey was worried that having lost the element of surprise that would have been available had they planned a combined operation all along, mounting one at this stage would be difficult.[43] Churchill saw this paper at the War Council on 19 March, but makes no allusion to it in his memoirs. Since it makes plain the distinction which Churchill was at pains to obfuscate between his own original hopes and the operation as it developed at the last minute, this was not surprising. Churchill still believed what he had always maintained, namely that the Straits could be forced by ships alone, which meant that until early March there was no question of a combined operation. Even after that date the First Lord put his faith in the Navy.

Carden fell ill on 16 March, and it was his replacement, Admiral de Roebeck, who, with the newly arrived Army commander, Sir Ian Hamilton, sanctioned the full-scale attack on 18 March. This followed Churchill's advice, taking the form of an attempt by the maximum number of battleships to silence the forts at the Narrows and the batteries protecting the minefields. For much of the day the operation went well, with the forts at the Narrows having been effectively silenced by 2 p.m. But attempts to sweep the Kephez minefield did not work and just after 4 p.m. two British ships, the *Inflexible* and the *Irresistible*, were badly damaged by mines. At 5 p.m. it was decided to withdraw, but just after 6 p.m. the *Ocean*, which was going to the assistance of the *Irresistible*, hit a mine, and both ships foundered that evening. Of the sixteen capital ships involved, three were sunk and three more, including a battle-cruiser, were put out of action for the moment; it was the mines, and not the forts which had proved fatal.[44]

At the very inception of the operation, then again on 11 March, Churchill had stressed, with no one contradicting him, that the importance of the results to be gained justified heavy losses, and he later made much of the folly of the commanders on the spot in deciding to suspend operations until the troops arrived.[45] But again he ignores the fact that, even before the unsuccessful assault on 18 March, the men on the spot had virtually decided that a combined operation would be necessary; no doubt success on 18 March would have changed their minds, but encountering a check encouraged them in their original caution.

Balfour's comment to Lord Sydenham on 23 March cannot be bettered as a verdict on what had happened:

It might well be argued that a simultaneous land and sea attack on the Gallipoli Peninsula made earlier in the day would have had a completer success than we have yet attained. The Navy, however, have all along been confident of their power to deal with the forts and I am still hopeful that they are right.[46]

The last sentence shows to what an extent Churchill's assurances had taken root, as well as a lack of appreciation that it was the mines which had proved the real difficulty; but written as it was, before hindsight was available, it provides useful testimony to the way things were, as well as the way Churchill wanted them to be.

The First Lord was now to be brought up increasingly, and unwillingly, against facts which were not as he would have them. On 19 March Hamilton telegraphed that as it did not look as though the ships would be able to force the Straits, the action required from his troops would not 'take the subsidiary form anticipated'.[47] At the War Council meeting on the same day, although Churchill's desire to tell de Roebeck to press on, if he thought he could get through, was sanctioned, it was accepted that a major combined operation might be necessary – which would take time to organise.[48]

Churchill's optimism in ordering further attacks had been as unjustified as the War Council's in spending time considering the partition of the Turkish Empire. Bad weather conditions made operations between 19 and 26 March impossible,[49] and, at a conference on 23 March, de Roebeck and Hamilton decided to wait until the forces were available for a major land assault – the one available to them if they had decided that the Dardanelles could not be forced. Churchill fulminated, with the advantage of hindsight, that they should have pushed on with a land attack because the Turks were not well-prepared for it,[50] but this is merely a final example of having his cake and eating it. No one was aware of what state the Turkish defences were in, although it was known that they had been strengthened,[51] and, having decided on a major land campaign, it was necessary to draw up plans for one.

No doubt Churchill, the second lieutenant of the Fourth Hussars, would have rushed ashore and won the day, even as he would have done in May 1940 at Narvik, on both of which occasions he implies that more guts on the part of the commanders would have seen victory secured. To be fair to Churchill, he was quite willing to risk his own guts being spilled, but he was over-eager to see caution as indicating cowardice or timidity. He may have believed, as did the French commanders on the western front in 1914, that *élan* would bring victory, but neither Hamilton nor General Mackesy took such a sanguine and potentially sanguinary view. The First Lord was always apt to think that he knew better than the man on the spot what was required; his career provides little evidence for his confidence.

It is a measure of Churchill's aggressive instinct that his reaction to de Roebeck's decision was to urge him to press on, but it is a sufficient comment upon his judgment that he should have urged him to 'dominate the forts at the Narrows and sweep the minefield and then batter the forts at close range'[52] – as though that was not what had already been attempted. For Churchill to go on to say that they should use the 'improved methods of guarding against mines' shows how little he appreciated what was going on. He was, in fact, *still* urging de Roebeck to pursue a purely naval operation. Fisher and the Admiralty Board would not let him send the telegram. The admirals realised, even if he did not, that having committed themselves to a combined operation, it was necessary to wait until one was planned.[53]

Churchill pressed an unwilling Fisher to agree to a telegram on 24 March to de Roebeck urging that the time had not yet come to 'abandon the naval plan of forcing the Dardanelles without the aid of a large Army'. If de Roebeck decided that it had, then Churchill would, he said, abide by the decision, but he then proceeded to enfilade him with fire from a number of directions. The loss of 'a few old surplus ships' would, Churchill argued, be better than losing large numbers of men, and the 'supreme moral effect' of a fleet entering the Sea of Marmora should not be 'underestimated'; nor should the 'incalculable' and possibly 'decisive' 'political effect of the arrival of the Fleet before Constantinople'.[54]

De Roebeck replied on 25 March that to attempt another assault would be to invite the same results as before and might well put in jeopardy the combined operation which they would launch later. For Churchill to allege, as he does, that the Admiral was actuated by a 'sentimental' regard for his old battleships shows how little he had understood events.[55] De Roebeck could not guarantee that the minefields could be swept, and the forts containing the guns which commanded the minefields could not be put out of action by naval guns, so even if the Fleet could, somehow, force its way through the Narrows, it was difficult to see how it could be supplied; 'combined operation essential to gain great result and object of campaign', he telegraphed on 27 March.[56]

Hankey urged that detailed plans be drawn up for what was, in effect, a new operation, and he emphasised the difficulties in mounting an opposed landing.[57] Churchill however did not anticipate 'any difficulty at all'[58] and remained convinced that, with more effort, de Roebeck could force the Narrows by ships alone.[59]

Signs of the strain under which Churchill was now labouring were evident in the strident tone of his despatches to de Roebeck. Lord Esher found him 'very excited' and 'jumpy' about the Dardanelles: 'he says he will be ruined if the attack fails'.[60] Quarrels with Kitchener and Lloyd George in early March brought forth apologetic letters from him.[61] Lloyd George, who thought he was 'looking very ill', was so infuriated by Churchill interrupting him with a grand 'I don't see –', that he broke in sharply and said, 'You will see the point, when you begin to understand that conversation is not a monologue!'[62]

Quarrels with colleagues were accompanied by rumours of political intrigues. A swift naval victory would have brought much-needed relief to both Churchill and the Asquith Government; its failure to materialise put both under pressure. Churchill still saw the military operation as being 'in addition to, and not in substitution for, or derogation from, the naval attack'.[63] By this stage he would have found few military men prepared to agree with him, although his optimism allowed his political colleagues to continue in what were increasingly vain hopes. Fisher and others at the Admiralty were worried that the Dardanelles operation would draw in ships which were needed to combat any attempt by the German Fleet to emerge from its harbours.[64] Churchill deprecated what he considered Fisher's 'unfair' attempts to 'spite this operation by sidewinds and small points when you have accepted it in principle',[65] whilst Fisher was growing increasingly to regret that he had 'sacrificed my conviction . . . to please you!'[66] He told Jellicoe on 20 April, four days prior to the first landings, that the oper-ation was 'a huge gamble, but all the politicians have shoved us into it or rather Winston has shoved all of them!'[67]

Fisher's discontent, and his opinion of who was responsible for the adoption of the operation, were shared by others, and the limited success of the initial landings did nothing to refurbish the First Lord's tarnished laurels or the Government's reputation. Asquith's fondness for Churchill had led him to look for other fields in which his talents might be employed, but the reaction which he got from colleagues to the suggestion that Churchill might go to India as Viceroy suggested that he was widely distrusted. Indeed, Asquith himself was disappointed by rumours that Churchill was involved in various intrigues to replace the Government by a coalition. Lloyd George put this down to the increasingly close contacts between Churchill and Balfour, telling Asquith on 25 March that the First Lord had been 'swallowed whole'. The Prime Minister thought it was 'a pity' that 'Winston hasn't a better sense of proportion and also a larger endowment of the instinct of loyalty'. He thought Churchill would

never get to the top in English politics, with all his wonderful gifts; to speak with the tongues of men and angels, and to spend laborious days and nights in administration, is no good if a man does not inspire trust.[68]

The proof of this was about to be given, but the loss of the Prime Minister's favour was to be the most grievous of all blows to the First Lord's position.

12

Dropping the Albatross

If the Dardanelles operation had succeeded 'by ships alone', then Churchill's career would have moved into 'sun-lit uplands;' once it had failed, his position was precarious. Churchill had risen far and had done so fast. He had alienated the Conservative Party very early in his career and his actions during the 1910 election and over Ireland had ensured that Unionist hostility towards him did not abate. During his time at the Admiralty Churchill had moved away from the mainstream of the Liberal Party; his obvious love of all things military marked him off from the bulk of his colleagues – and made him an object of hostility to the radicals. Churchill's fight over the naval estimates in 1913–14 had added to the animosity with which he was viewed by his Cabinet colleagues, and his behaviour then had helped to cool his relationship with Lloyd George. Churchill had survived because he enjoyed the support of the Prime Minister and because his talents commanded a place in the Government. His manners may have left something to be desired, but no one could doubt Churchill's aptitude for the work he was doing. The experience of the first six months of the war had eroded these last areas of support. His 'jaunts' to the front had exasperated everyone and had created the impression of a man in search of employment – which was thought odd behaviour for one charged with control of the British Fleet. His siren voice had spoken of great gains which could be won at little cost; when they did not materialise, Churchill's political career had no visible means of support. However, none of this meant that his career was over.

It was not the failure of the Dardanelles operation which removed Churchill from the Admiralty, but rather a political crisis which required Asquith to bring the Unionists into a coalition Ministry. It was only then that the weakness of Churchill's political position was fully revealed. In the immediate aftermath of the suspension of the naval attack there was much talk of political intrigue, but no sign that Churchill would be its victim. Asquith had considered moving Churchill from the Admiralty but, given the adverse publicity which he had attracted and the friction which he had caused with the War Office, that was hardly surprising. But far from considering dropping Churchill, the Prime Minister was thinking of making him Viceroy of India; it was a post which would give ample scope for Churchill's tremendous energies. The fact that it would remove him far from the purlieus of Westminster was, of course, no doubt entirely coincidental. It was some indication of the animosity felt towards Churchill within his own Party that the reaction to Asquith's scheme was uniformly unfavourable.[1]

It was with a certain amount of irony that Asquith heard rumours in late March that Churchill was part of an intrigue to replace him. Given Churchill's ineptitude in such matters, Asquith was not disposed to place too much credence in such stories.[2] Churchill vehemently denied such allegations when they were put to him, and he declined an interview with Asquith, saying that he felt 'my case is safe in your hands'; it was. Asquith was perfectly willing to believe that Churchill might have fallen victim to the 'superficial charm' of Balfour through their contact on the War Council, but he was not disposed to put much credence in any nasty stories about Churchill which came from the embittered McKenna. As he told Venetia Stanley on 30 March, 'W[inston] is really loyal to me. I am sure, and have never doubted, that he is.'[3] That the rumours continued to circulate was more a reflection of the lack of trust which many Liberals felt for one who had 'been a guest in our Party for eight and a half years'[4] than it was of anything else.[5]

Churchill's attention was, in fact, still firmly focused on the war at sea. He resurrected his Borkum scheme on 24 March, arguing that the time for it could not be far distant. He still had every faith that the opening of the land offensive would bring the Dardanelles operation to a successful conclusion,[6] but if it did not then perhaps the Borkum project would lure the German Fleet from its lair – with the enticing prospect of a great naval victory to follow.[7] But Fisher, increasingly worried that the latter eventuality might be spoilt by the drain on resources imposed by the Dardanelles, was growing restive. The more restless he became, the more did his own failure to insist upon his objections to the Dardanelles campaign weigh on his mind. He thought of resigning, but feared the consequences of leaving Churchill without any restraint; 'D——n the Dardanelles! They'll be our grave,' he growled on 5 April.[8] Churchill ignored the sulphurous rumblings; he had heard them before. His only anxiety was that Kitchener should not spoil the success of the landings on 26 April by providing insufficient troops.[9]

Most irrationality has some connection, however attenuated, with reality, and the stories which got back to Asquith about Churchill being involved in conspiracies bore such a character. No one could argue that the Asquith Government was proving a perfect instrument for making war. The Prime Minister's gifts were not shown to best advantage when quick decisions were required, and poor Grey at the Foreign Office was increasingly an object of pity; his conscience was troubled by the thought that he might have been able to have done something to have averted the war, and his eyesight was failing rapidly. It was hardly surprising that Churchill should have been heard to advocate his replacement by Balfour.[10] There were tensions within the Government caused by Lloyd George's exasperation with Kitchener's inefficiency at the War Office – in particular, the shortage of munitions was becoming something of a scandal.[11] Moreover, the Government's lack of success was leading to public criticism of its performance, with Haldane and Churchill both singled out for attention. It was clear to those in the know that both Fisher and Kitchener had great limitations, but Asquith was stuck with them; to dismiss the heroes of the popular press was unthinkable. But allowing things to remain as they were was no more inviting a prospect.[12] The Kitchener problem might be solved by leaving him as, in effect, a figure-head. But it was more difficult to know what to do about the Admiralty, especially if the option of moving Churchill to the only important post likely to become vacant, the Viceroyalty, was ruled out. Asquith had never shared Churchill's hankerings after a coalition government, but circumstances were at hand which would force him to change his views.

Churchill and de Roebeck had both looked forward to the Navy helping the land assault, but in practice this had not happened and, in the face of a stalemate on land, the Admiral asked Churchill on 11 May whether it was time for the Navy to play a larger part.[13] The mere idea threw Fisher into paroxysms of articulate fury. He could not, he told Churchill on 11 May, be a party to any such idea.[14] But still the First Lord did not see the danger, telling Fisher that his previous actions meant that he was 'absolutely commit-ted'.[15] The two men quarrelled on 12 May, with Fisher insisting that Churchill abandon the idea of a naval attack and arguing that he should allow the *Queen Elizabeth*, which was in the Dardanelles, to return home. Hankey was able to report to Asquith that evening that the difficulties seemed to have been sorted out.[16] But in Fisher's mind his stay would be 'only for a short time'.[17] The War Council meeting on 14 May was an unhappy affair, and when Fisher received minutes from Churchill on 15 May which apparently sanctioned more reinforcement for the Dardanelles, it was the spark which lit his blue touchpaper – and he duly retired.[18]

Churchill was surprised but not perturbed when he received Fisher's letter of resignation; surprised because he could see no reason for it, but unworried because the old man had talked about resigning before.[19] It was a Saturday morning, and the First Lord carried on with his usual duties, hoping that Fisher would reappear from wherever he had vanished to. If necessary, there would have to be a new First Sea Lord and some public explanation of what had occurred. There seemed to be no reason why Churchill should fear any threat to his own position. Others thought differently.

The King, who had found Churchill's 'jaunts' to the Continent a continual cause of irritation, thought that Fisher's resignation at such a time was 'bound to have a deplorable, if not a disastrous, effect upon the public, not only at home, but abroad'.[20] Bonar Law agreed with him and went further, telling Lloyd George, and then Asquith, on 17 May that if Fisher went and Churchill stayed, there would have to be a debate in the House on the subject.[21] This put Asquith in an awkward situation. Fisher was refusing all blandishments and the previous day the Board of the Admiralty had associated itself with his criticisms of the First Lord.[22] For the opposition to threaten to open a debate on the subject would, indeed, be to open Pandora's box. Asquith could hardly defend Churchill at the expense of a national hero, especially with the Unionists resolved to defend the latter and excoriate the former.

Fisher's resignation came at a bad time for Asquith, who was suffering his own personal crisis over Venetia Stanley, but any idea that this reduced him to a state in which he apathetically agreed to form a coalition is to under-estimate his resilience and resourcefulness.[23] What made Fisher's actions dangerous was that they coincided with a sensational report in *The Times* on 14 May attributing the failure of the Neuve Chapelle offensive to a shortage of shells – when only a week before Asquith had been saying that the Army was well-supplied with munitions.[24] This raised the spectre of the Unionists demanding a debate in the House on the conduct of the war; they might even refuse to postpone the general election which would soon fall due; Fisher's resignation was bound to make this situation worse. Asquith acted quickly to head off the danger to his own position. Lloyd George had proposed a coalition to Bonar Law when the two spoke on the morning of 17 May, and it was a suggestion which had attractions all round. For Bonar Law, it would mean an end to the frustrations of 'patriotic opposition' – without having to take on the whole conduct of the war himself. For Asquith, it would mean keeping control in his own hands.[25] He could, by a judicious selection of men for offices, keep the Unionists away from the levers of power. He could also avoid making a decision over potentially damaging issues such as conscription.[26] It also offered the opportunity to do something about Kit-chener and the War Office under the guise of a general reconstruction of the Government. If there was a price to be paid for all this in terms of other people, then it was one he was willing to pay.

Lloyd George realised at once that Fisher's resignation meant that Churchill 'will be a ruined man',[27] and Bonar Law's attitude confirmed his suspicion. The First Lord failed to realise this dimension of the crisis. He wrote to Asquith on 17 May with his advice about the new Cabinet, stating that he would accept no office 'except a military one'.[28] By the following morning he was beginning to get a clearer picture, and he told Asquith that 'if an office like the Colonies wh[ich] was suggested were open to me I sh[oul]d not be right to refuse it'; but he was vehement in his desire to 'stay here – and complete my work'.[29] Confident that he would receive support from his friend, Lloyd George, Churchill still did not realise the true situation.[30]

Asquith's hopes of keeping Fisher on in some capacity were dashed by a document which he received from the old man on 19 May, which suggested that he was 'off his nut'.[31] In a six-point memorandum which stipulated that 'Mr Winston Churchill is not in the Cabinet to be always circumventing me', Fisher demanded a new Board of the Admiralty and 'complete professional charge of the war at sea', in return for which he would 'guarantee the successful termination of the War and the total abolition of the submarine menace'. It is difficult to quarrel with Asquith's comment to the King that this showed 'signs of mental aberration'.[32] It certainly saved Asquith from having to deal with the Admiral – even his Unionist friends could not argue for his inclusion.

Churchill wrote to Bonar Law on 19 May to 'rejoice' in the prospect that they would soon become colleagues.[33] Given Bonar Law's low view of Churchill's value and Unionist hostility to him, there was little enough chance of this, but any good effect which Churchill's long statement of the background to the crisis might have had was dispelled by Fisher telling Bonar Law that Churchill was 'a bigger danger than the Germans by a long way'.[34] This was not an opinion with which Bonar Law was inclined to disagree. If Churchill's sky was dark, it was with the wings of the chickens coming home to roost.

Any possibility that Asquith might give him the Colonial Office was killed by the hostility of his fellow Liberals. Beauchamp reported that the feeling among Churchill's colleagues was 'that he is the primary cause of trouble and should be first to go instead of others who will lose their seat in Cabinet'.[35] Lord Emmot, another 'mainstream' Liberal, told Asquith on 20 May that there would be a 'revolt' if Churchill was appointed – 'he has neither the temperament nor the manners to fit him for the post'.[36] Another comradely Liberal, Mr Pringle, accused Churchill of helping to inspire the revelations about shell shortages in *The Times*, and declared that many Liberals would 'regard his presence in the Government as a public danger'.[37] This bleak view was shared by the King.

Only a man of Churchill's egotism and naïveté when it came to the feelings of others could still have been blind to this hostility and its implications for his future – but the evidence is that even by 20 May he had not realised these things. On the evening of 19 May he offered Fisher 'any terms he liked, including a seat in the Cabinet, if he would stay with him at the Admiralty'.[38] Churchill's evident distress, and his lack of realism, cut little ice with a Prime Minister fighting for his own political life. When he heard that Churchill wanted to see him on 19 May to 'discuss the situation', Asquith told Lloyd George that this meant 'the situation as it concerns Churchill personally. . . . The situation for Churchill has no other meaning but his own prospects.'[39] He deputed the task to Lloyd George. Churchill came into his room 'with a face like the faces we used to see on old mugs'. He told Lloyd George that he had prepared a resignation statement which he intended to read to the House, only to be told that this would not be possible. Churchill's response was to declare, ' "You forget my reputation is at stake. I am wounded." ' Lloyd George read the statement and 'when I came to the part in which he referred to his own services, I could see his eyes filling with sympathy for himself';

but he persuaded Churchill that any statement on his position would be 'disastrous'.[40] Churchill accused Lloyd George of not caring 'whether I am trampled underfoot by my enemies. You don't care for my personal reputation.' Lloyd George replied, 'No, I don't care for my own at the present moment. The only thing I care about now is that we win the war.'[41]

Churchill's political career had not conditioned him for anything like this, and his optimism refused to give way to reality. Buoyed up by the news that Sir Arthur Wilson had agreed to replace Fisher, but that he was refusing to serve anyone save himself, Churchill was able to day-dream a while longer. Clementine wrote to Asquith on 20 May, pleading with him not to throw 'Winston overboard'.[42] Churchill himself wrote another long screed to Bonar Law on 21 May setting out the reasons why he should remain at the Admiralty,[43] but received in response the polite but firm statement: 'Believe me, what I said to you last night is inevitable.'[44] Beginning to realise the dimensions of the threat to his position, Churchill tried one last urgent letter to the Prime Minister. The situation at the Dardanelles was crucial, Churchill wrote on 21 May, and only he and Admiral Wilson knew 'the whole position'. He was not, he declared, motivated by a desire to cling on to office, or even by 'my own interest or advancement', rather it was a desire to discharge his '*duty*' which lay behind his urgent pleas. With the clear and terrible vision which the imminence of personal disaster confers, Churchill told Asquith that he had not believed that 'it was possible to endure such anxiety'. None of the 'ordinary strains of war' which he had 'borne all these months' had been 'comparable to this feeling'. He was convinced that the Unionists did not really understand his own part in affairs: 'Let me stand or fall by the Dardanelles – but do not take it from my hands.' It was a sign of how little he understood the situation that he could write that the new political combination was one which 'in the nature of things is extremely favourable to me';[45] it was just that 'combination' which demanded his removal.

Asquith replied on the same day, telling Churchill sternly that, 'You must take it as settled that you are not to remain at the Admiralty'; he pleaded with him to 'try to take a large view'.[46] Churchill had already written another letter to Asquith saying that he would 'accept any office – even the lowest' so long as he could continue to take part in the war,[47] and he now replied accepting his fate.[48] It was 'the lowest' post he could have been offered – the Chancellorship of the Duchy of Lancaster. *Punch*, under a picture of Churchill striding forth, had a caption: 'What is a Duchy and where is Lancaster?', which caught the tone just right.

Churchill's bitterness at the way Asquith had treated him was to grow and fester, but the fact remained that in the face of pressure from both Unionists and Liberals, the Prime Minister had kept him in the Government. What had finished Churchill off was the hostility which his career had generated. Asquith had been able to protect him when the going was relatively good, but the crisis which Churchill had helped to generate had required Asquith to protect himself first. As Churchill himself later commented: 'These were the convulsive struggles of a man of action and ambition at death-grips with events.'[49] There were no political advantages to be gained from keeping Churchill at a post where his judgment had been exposed as being suspect; there were many to be reaped from removing him – so he went. For Churchill himself, removal from the Admiralty was a devastating blow; he felt like a deep-sea diver brought suddenly to the surface.[50] If his veins did not burst, then his career and reputation seemed to have done so.

When Riddell called on Churchill at the Admiralty on 20 May, he found him 'very worn out and harassed'. He declared dramatically: 'I have been stung by a viper. I am the victim of a political intrigue. I am finished!' The newspaper magnate tried to provide him with some solace, saying that he was not 'finished at forty, with your remarkable powers!' But Churchill would have none of it, responding that he was 'finished in respect of all I care for – the waging of war; the defeat of the Germans'.[51] He blamed Labour for not defending him and criticised Asquith for being 'supinely weak',[52] but he showed no sign of realising that he had played any part in his own downfall. As Lloyd George told Riddell, he had done his best for Churchill, but when a man in his position could write that only he could bring the Dardanelles operation to a successful conclusion, 'he is on his way to a lunatic asylum'.[53] That acute observer of the affairs of men, Balfour, provided the best comment on the place of the Dardanelles operation in Churchill's downfall:

In the Dardanelles affair the principal actors at home were a soldier without strategical genius, who controlled the military machine, a sailor equally without strategical genius, who ought to have controlled, but did not, the naval machine, and a brilliant amateur who attempted, but failed, to dominate both.[54]

Lack of co-ordination had created a vacuum into which Churchill's exuberant self-confidence had expanded, but, as he later recognised, he had attempted too much with too little power.[55] Having failed to dominate events from the powerful base of the Admiralty, Churchill had not given up hopes of being able to influence them from his room in the Treasury; success in the Dardanelles, would, he thought, revive his reputation.[56]

Churchill nursed his resentments about the 'political intrigue' which had deprived him of power. Lloyd George was excoriated as having 'no sense of honour', and his behaviour was attributed to Welsh baseness; as for Fisher, it was his 'Malay blood' which had caused him to run amok; but it was towards his former political allies rather than the old Admiral that Churchill's bitterness was directed.[57] Clementine thought that he 'would die of grief',[58] but he had not abandoned all hope.

Churchill remained a member of the refashioned War Council (now renamed the Dardanelles Committee) and, through this and his influence with Balfour, strove to make his views felt. For all their conflicts, Churchill had been a 'sincere admirer' of the former Prime Minister. Indeed, when Balfour had resigned as Unionist leader in 1911, Churchill had written him a long letter, regretting their 'antagonistic' political relationship and attributing it to 'my own faults of character and manner';[59] the recipients of acknowledgments of Churchillian frailty were few and far between. The inception of the Dardanelles operation had brought the two men into close contact again, and both Lloyd George and Asquith had suspected that Churchill had fallen victim to Balfour's 'charm'. The decision to make Balfour First Lord of the Admiralty meant, in Churchill's eyes, that there was still a chance to press his ideas. For all his talents, not even his best friend would have described Balfour as dynamic – and Churchill burnt with unexpended energy.

The germ of the plant which broke into efflorescence in the form of the first two volumes of *The World Crisis* can be found in the memoranda which Churchill sent to his new Unionist colleagues in an effort to convince them of the correctness of his actions at Antwerp and over the Dardanelles.[60] He swiftly set about trying to convince the Unionists that Hamilton needed reinforcements in order to press home his attack. On 11 June he urged the Committee to put to Hamilton the suggestion that he should 'place a strong Army astride the Bulair isthmus' in order to cut off the Turkish forces at Kilid Bahr, and urged that reinforcements should be sent.[61] Such themes were the constant burden of his song throughout the summer. On this occasion Hamilton ruled out Churchill's scheme as impracticable, though he welcomed the reinforcements.[62]

Churchill continued to advocate various land offensives, and in his memoirs managed to convince himself that had these been pressed forward, the land phase of the Gallipoli operation would have had a different result. But he nowhere questioned whether these operations were worthwhile. Even had Hamilton been able to capture the Bulair Peninsula, it is by no means clear that it would have had the decisive impact which Churchill's vivid imagination conjured up. The British, as he himself admitted, did not 'possess any of the preponderance necessary for an offensive';[63] yet he refused, even in his memoirs, to draw the obvious conclusion, which was that the assaults he advocated were nothing more than miniature versions of the 'barbed-wire chewing' offensives he so condemned on the western front.

Since Churchill's hopes of political resurrection lay with a success in the Dardanelles, he had persuaded himself by late June that 'most of the important Unionists' were 'fully convinced' not only of the 'obligation' to carry the operation through, 'but of the wisdom of the enterprise in strategy and politics'.[64] This was another example of his remarkable talent for self-deception. Bonar Law disliked the whole business and agreed to the decision to send reinforcements with extreme reluctance.[65] Even Selborne, who favoured going ahead with it, did so largely because he feared the consequences of withdrawal.[66] After the failure in August of the Suvla Bay offensive, Bonar Law grew even more sceptical about meeting Hamilton's requests for yet more troops. 'He was always *nearly* winning,' the Unionist leader said, when the Dardanelles Committee considered the matter on 19 August.[67] But Churchill's faith was undaunted, and he pressed for a renewal of the naval offensive.[68] His optimism about the 'new men', and their support for the Dardanelles operation, enabled him to hope that he would 'regain a fuller measure of control before the end of the year'.[69]

But if the flood of self-exculpatory memoranda did not restore his position, and if success in the Dardanelles was proving elusive, then there was a third route by which Churchill's fortunes might have been revived – the internal tensions which wracked the new coalition. Asquith had used the formation of the new Government as an excuse to avoid dealing with the twin problems of Kitchener and of conscription. But experience of government soon convinced the Unionists that their idol was a hindrance to the effective prosecution of the war. Curzon told Churchill on 14 September that they were reaching the point at which they would demand conscription and Kitchener's removal. This opened up interesting vistas. Many Unionists, particularly those clustered around Milner, wanted someone to take a firm hold of the Government, and Lloyd George, despite his pre-war radicalism, was a figure who appealed to them as a man of 'push-and-go'. His own support for conscription and his performance as Minister for Munitions brought him much Unionist support, but the prospect of joining any revolt against Asquith worried Lloyd George. Tempted as he was to support Curzon, he feared that Churchill might let him down and use the opportunity to curry favour with Asquith.[70]

By the end of August opposition within the Dardanelles Committee to continuing the Gallipoli campaign was growing, but when its members met on 3 September, Churchill, who had felt 'like a man about to be shot', suddenly found that the French had left him 'a large fortune'.[71] Just when it seemed that there were no more troops available, the French offered four divisions. The only problem was that General Joffre, the French Supreme Commander, wanted to keep them in France until late September – and by that time there appeared to be a more pressing need for them elsewhere. Reports that Bulgaria might be about to enter the war on the German side prompted Lloyd George and Bonar Law to suggest that the troops should be despatched to Salonica instead. Despite the impression given by Churchill and the official biographer that he opposed this idea,[72] he actually suggested diverting troops from Gallipoli for it; indeed, he went so far as to advocate that the Allies should seize Serbian Macedonia. It was only when the Greeks, whom he had hoped might thus be persuaded to join the Allied side, declined to do so in early October, that Churchill veered round to opposing Salonica.[73]

Although Churchill wanted to make another attempt to force the Narrows, he was, he told Asquith on 6 October, quite willing to consider other operations, and he advocated the creation of a small War Committee which would consider in detail the various options open to the British in the Balkans.[74] The acrimonious and inconclusive Dardanelles Committee meeting on 6 October decided instead to hear more information from the military, and to send a general out to Gallipoli to report. When the General Staff managed to produce a paper asserting the primacy of the western front whilst arguing that they had committed too much to the Dardanelles to withdraw, Bonar Law and Lloyd George argued that the whole thing was 'insane', and Bonar Law threatened to resign if the Cabinet persevered with the Dardanelles.[75] The problem was that Asquith would not bring the matter to a head because he feared the consequences of trying to deal with Kitchener at the War Office.

Churchill was not alone in thinking that the wooden idol should be removed, and he even contemplated threatening to resign on the issue – but, perhaps bearing in mind the weakness of his own position, he forbore. Asquith, who was well aware of the dangers of a Churchill/Lloyd George/ Unionist combination on the issue of the direction of the war and conscription, once more acted to head off a potential threat to his own position. He announced that he would set up a small policy-making committee to replace the cumbersome Dardanelles Committee. This was in line with Churchill's own ideas, but there was no place on the committee for Churchill himself.[76]

Churchill had hoped that a reconstruction of the Government might work to his advantage, but it was now clear that it would not do so. The Unionists were happy with the decision to do away with the Dardanelles Committee, and Asquith had satisfied them, at least for the moment, on the conscription issue, by announcing that Lord Derby would head an initiative designed to spur recruitment. Lloyd George, although far from happy with Asquith's leadership, was unwilling to conspire against him. Moreover, he was at one with Bonar Law in demanding an end to the Dardanelles expedition; this opinion was reinforced by the report of General Munro, who had been sent out to review the operation. On 30 October Churchill wrote Asquith a letter of resignation. He postponed sending it at Asquith's request, partly in the hope of influencing the Prime Minister's statement in the Commons on 2 November. But Asquith neither used any of the material which Churchill gave him, nor did he defend him from attacks in the House. Churchill's position had become untenable.[77]

Churchill had considered resigning his post and going to the front in early September, when he had asked Asquith to make him a major-general. Whilst Asquith would have been 'glad to get rid' of him, he did not 'wish to embarrass the Army'.[78] Now Churchill came up with the equally embarrassing suggestion that he should be sent as Commander-in-Chief to East Africa to deal with the stubborn German resistance there. He put this idea to Asquith on 6 November, the day of the last meeting of the Dardanelles Committee.[79] On 11 November he formally submitted his resignation to Asquith, placing himself 'unreservedly at the disposal of the military authorities'. His letter, and Asquith's acceptance, were published on 13 November.[80] For the first time in a decade Churchill held no government office.

Back in May, Lloyd George's mistress, Frances Stevenson, had found it 'strange that Churchill should have been in politics all these years, and yet not have won the confidence of a single party in the country, or a single colleague in the Cabinet'.[81] This was the explanation for his fall, and it was further proof of it that Churchill never saw it himself. Asquith had been right when he had written that 'with all his wonderful gifts' Churchill would not 'get to the top' because he 'does not inspire trust'.[82] Much of the comment on his fall recognised his qualities, but most of it bore out Asquith's dictum. His own comment in his resignation speech, that the Dardanelles was a 'legitimate war gamble', illustrates something of what Asquith meant. It was a fair comment, but it was neither a sensible one, nor did it show any sense of understanding for how the families of those who had died at Gallipoli might feel.[83] Churchill expected his own feelings to be respected, but he often failed to do as he would be done by.

Immensely self-absorbed, Churchill appeared to have had no time for the feelings of others. Such egotism is common in children, but it has usually been rubbed away by the time adulthood is reached. Churchill's faith in his star, and the rapidity of his rise, had saved him from having to face too much reality. He had wanted to succeed in politics, and he had done so. He had been led into the belief that his own abilities would protect and promote him, and in the process he had affronted too many of the tribal deities by which political man lives. Party? He had abandoned one and joined another – going on to prosper by his tergiversation; the one would have been bad enough, but the other was insufferable. Consistency? He had, so it appeared, switched from radicalism to navalist overnight, without even trying to claim that he had been consistent. Soundness? Bonar Law was not the only one to think that, along with his 'very unusual intellectual ability', he had 'an entirely unbalanced mind'; he just held that opinion more tenaciously than most because he was immune to the charm which Churchill could exercise when he chose.[84] Character? 'Ill-mannered, boastful and unprincipled' was how he had appeared to Hobhouse, who probably stood as an epitome of the reaction of many ordinary Liberals.[85] Thus, when the crisis came in May, the stories of Churchill's plotting were widely believed; it was also easy to blame him for the Dardanelles operation and Fisher's resignation. He had commented, in 1912, in puzzled fashion: 'I have never joined in any intrigue, everything I have got I have worked for, and have been hated more than anybody.'[86] Now he had paid the price for the feelings he had aroused.

Violet Asquith, writing to condole with him, told Churchill: 'I trust your star';[87] it remained to be seen where it would now lead him.

II

The Lost Leader

1915–39

13

Wilderness Politics

Churchill went to France in November 1915. If his life was like a novel then this was the chapter where the hero, unfairly disgraced at home, goes to the front to redeem his honour and his name. But there was to be no great cathartic event, but rather a slow, steady trickle of disappointment tinged with a bitterness which was new to his experience. He had chosen to leave office; the wind was not tempered to the shorn lamb.[1] Although whilst at the front Churchill showed that the courage which he had possessed as a young lieutenant had not deserted him, he was conscious of the shocking waste (as he and his mother saw it) of his talents; nor could he be treated as though he were just any other officer. Churchill was probably fortunate that he was not granted his wish to run the war in East Africa. The campaign there brought no one on the Allied side any credit, and it is difficult to see how he would have emerged from it with any. Retiring to the trenches was the best thing he could have done, and nothing became his political career like his leaving of it.

Resentful at his treatment by Asquith and Lloyd George, Churchill realised, none the less, that his only chance of recovering his position was by a 'definite and perhaps a prolonged withdrawal';[2] he would become a model soldier. There was naturally some suspicion of him when he joined the second battalion of the Grenadier Guards for training prior to taking command of his own brigade, but, as a young subaltern with the Gordon Highlanders, William Fraser, noted in early January, 'I believe he is going to do all right!' It was felt that Churchill was 'only using the battalion as a stepping-stone to a Brigade', which was true, and there was even some suspicion that 'the whole thing is a political advertisement', but his enthusiasm and 'intelligence' won most people over.[3] Far from shirking action, Churchill thirsted for it, and bravery is a sure passport to the hearts even of suspicious soldiers. But the men found it difficult to forget that he was a politician[4] – and Churchill found it equally impossible to prevent politics from impinging upon his military career. His hopes of becoming a brigadier-general, which flourished in early December, were dashed when Asquith, partly through fear of Parliamentary criticism, vetoed Sir John French's plans to give Churchill his own brigade.[5] Confined thus to the command of a battalion, it would not have been surprising had Churchill's eyes strayed to Westminster.

Churchill saw his share of action and did not shirk the risks of warfare –

no 'château general' he – but being at the front was never an end in itself. It was always meant as part of a strategy of *réculer pour mieux sauter*. Clementine was adjured to keep in touch with powerful newspapermen and with the Government, and to 'show complete confidence in our fortunes'.[6] However, Churchill himself fretted endlessly with dissatisfaction with the 'things that are being left undone' and at his own wasted energies, but he always believed that his time would come again.[7] The fact that the Asquith Government remained unable to bring any vigour to the conduct of the war meant that Churchill's hopes could spring eternal. Churchill's vexation with the Government's inefficiency was matched only by his frustration at 'not having the power which I could use better than any other living Englishman'.[8] But he could not forbear to rush in where others feared to tread – thus proving that adversity had not taught him the virtues of prudence or the necessity of caution.

As part of a campaign of criticism against the Government, Garvin at the *Observer* had been promoting the idea that Fisher should return to the Admiralty, a notion which Churchill originally found unpalatable. But, to the horror of his wife, who regarded the old Admiral as a baleful influence on her husband, Churchill agreed to meet him in early March and was soon convinced that the two of them (helped by the press) could regain lost ground.[9] There was certainly much to criticise the Government for, and Churchill's speech in the House on 7 March 1916 was a powerful indictment, particularly of Balfour's regime at the Admiralty. But any effect it might have had was entirely destroyed when, in his peroration, he called for Fisher's return as First Sea Lord. Balfour was able to quote back at him his own criticisms of the Admiral and thus avoid having to deal with Churchill's criticisms.[10] It was generally assumed that Churchill had been making a bid for personal power. Margot Asquith's comment, that Churchill was 'a hound of the lowest sense of political honour', was not without bias, but her verdict that he was 'a fool of the lowest judgement and contemptible' was widespread.[11]

Lord Selborne, who had been Governor-General in South Africa when Churchill had been at the Colonial Office, and who had served with him in the Cabinet from May to November 1915, had been impressed with his 'vision' and 'power of drive', and thought that 'courage' was his 'great asset'; but these things were vitiated 'because the motive power is always "self", and I don't think he has any principles'. Churchill was written down as 'clever, but quite devoid of judgement'.[12] Whatever small chance he had of regaining a place in domestic political life was gone.

Churchill would have done better to have followed his wife's counsel. She, after all, had been acting as his eyes and ears, and her judgment of the course of events was not only based on closer experience of them, but also on a sounder instinct. She had endeavoured to moderate his resentment against Asquith and to warn him against entering strange cabals – particularly with

Lloyd George, whom she described as the 'direct descendant of Judas Iscariot';[13] but it was to no avail. It was not simply that Churchill felt that Asquith's conduct towards him had reached 'the limits of meanness and ungenerousness',[14] and that he could not face working with him again,[15] for his feelings towards Lloyd George were scarcely less vitriolic,[16] but he realised that 'nothing but a complete change of regime will require me to return or be of any use'.[17] He could not envisage a situation arising where Asquith would need him,[18] but the same was not true with Lloyd George, whose discontent with the Prime Minister might lead him to want to replace him: 'his interests are not divorced from mine and in these circumstances [we] can work together if occasion arises.'[19] This was acute thinking, as far as it went, but it did not go far enough.

For the moment there was nothing to be done except to retire back to Flanders, with his reputation at an even lower ebb than it had been in November. Churchill's slim hopes of commanding a brigade were, once more, dashed and his eyes wandered often to Westminster. But those with his best interests at heart advised him against seeming to leave the front whenever a Parliamentary occasion offered itself – that was not the way to redeem his fortunes. It was not that Churchill found soldiering hard; he actually enjoyed the sensation of being in battle and did not much mind the risk of death. What he did find hard to bear was the sense of being cast aside when, as he saw it, lesser men than he were left in charge of the war. Since leaving childhood he had not tasted failure and now it left him feeling nauseous. Politics was in his blood, it was his life and he could not leave it alone – especially as the chance of military glory was so limited.

Churchill wanted to work with Lloyd George, F. E. Smith, Bonar Law and Carson,[20] but he failed to realise that there was no particular reason why any of these should wish to work with him. Those Unionists who thought that 'Squiff and Squiffery must go'[21] looked towards Carson and Milner from their own ranks, and Lloyd George from outside, as possible saviours,[22] and they had no use for Churchill. Lloyd George, although unhappy with Asquith, would not replace him with Bonar Law,[23] whilst Bonar Law was not applying for the job.[24] F.E., though bound to Churchill by their strong friendship, was happy in office and loyal to both Asquith and Kitchener.[25] Carson, who had come to admire Churchill's dynamism, counselled him against a precipitate return,[26] counsel which Clementine and F.E., who seldom agreed on anything, both supported.[27] But it was all to no avail. Churchill's long-festering sense of grievance and his Chatham complex combined to bring him back to Westminster in May.

'I am so devoured by egoism,' Churchill wrote to his wife in March. He was trying to reassure her about his love for her and to explain why he was not taking her advice, but it was a comment that summarised the reason for his failure – as well as his eventual success.[28] He did not understand why

Lloyd George had let him down in May 1915. When Lloyd George had said that he had not supported the Dardanelles campaign, Churchill had responded characteristically: 'Whatever you thought, I always thought you would stand by me when it came to the point.'[29] In Churchill's eyes Lloyd George was under a 'personal obligation' to him because of the support he had given him during the Marconi affair in 1912, when Lloyd George had been accused of financial corruption, and Churchill looked forward to collecting on that debt. If Lloyd George broke with Asquith, he would need all the Liberal support he could get; 'L.G. is the key to my position.'[30] But the events of the next few months were to demonstrate that Lloyd George abided by his own dictum that there was no friendship at the top.

In April Churchill had encouraged Lloyd George to press his disagreement with the Prime Minister over conscription to the sticking-point,[31] and he was correspondingly disappointed when the crisis failed to materialise.[32] He had, as Clementine had feared, underestimated the resilience of the Government and overestimated the claims which friendship could command. The return to Westminster was a harsh lesson in the penalties of political failure. News of problems within the Government came at second-hand, and as Churchill would not throw himself into the role of Carson's lieutenant, and as the Ulster leader was the main focus for opposition to Asquith, he found himself isolated. Churchill was in the 'wilderness' to an extent which surpassed anything before the late 1930s. His depression was intensified by Asquith's decision to accede to the demand for a commission of enquiry into the Dardanelles and by his refusal to let the full evidence be published. He feared, rightly, that his reputation would be further damaged.[33]

Kitchener's death in June took Lloyd George to the War Office, but Churchill's hopes that he might be offered the Ministry of Munitions came to naught, and his criticisms of the Government in the Commons, although powerfully phrased, cut no ice at all.[34] It was with bitterness that he watched as Asquith continued to reign 'supine, sodden and supreme'.[35] But even when the long-awaited downfall of the Prime Minister came in December, the event, far from bringing Ishmael in from the wilderness, simply emphasised how marginal he had become.

Asquith resigned on 5 December 1916 following a dispute with Lloyd George and Bonar Law over the formation of a new War Committee; they did not want him as Chairman, and he would accept no position but 'the first'. Law declined the opportunity to form a Government, leaving that task to Lloyd George, who thereby split the Liberal Party. Churchill thought that his hour had come, especially when he was invited to dine with Lloyd George at F.E.'s house that evening. Max Aitken, Bonar Law's closest friend, arrived at the house first and the three men discussed the form which the new Government would take. Churchill suggested that Aitken might be made Postmaster-General. But Aitken had been with Lloyd George earlier that evening and knew something which Churchill did not. 'The new Govern-ment', he told Churchill, 'will be very well disposed towards you. All your friends will be there. You will have a great field of common action with them.' The truth now dawned upon Churchill. He always called F. E. Smith by his initials, or else 'Fred', but now, blazing with 'righteous anger', he exclaimed: 'Smith, this man knows that I am not to be included in the new Government', and he stalked out into the street.[36] And so it proved.

Churchill's exclusion came as a dreadful shock, but had he had any inkling of the place he occupied in British politics, it would not have done so. Back in August Lord Derby had told Lloyd George that 'our Party will not work with him'. He added that he personally would refuse to serve in any adminis-tration of which Churchill was a part: 'He is absolutely untrustworthy, as was his father before him, and he has got to learn that just as his father had to disappear from politics so must he.'[37] Lloyd George needed the support of the Conservatives and they 'would not have' Churchill; had he tried to insist on Churchill's inclusion 'he could not have formed the Ministry'. He asked his friend, Lord Riddell, to explain this to Churchill – and to convey with the message a promise that he would do something for him as soon as the report of the Dardanelles Commission had been published.[38] Churchill was not mollified; he had expected better, he told Riddell, and Lloyd George's 'con-science' would 'tell him what he should do'. He warned that Lloyd George's message would not 'fetter his freedom of action'.[39]

Austen Chamberlain, Lord Robert Cecil (brother of Lord Hugh and Lord Salisbury), Curzon and Walter Long had made it a condition of their adhesion to Lloyd George that Churchill should be kept out,[40] and the new Prime Minister was in no position to argue with them, even had he been disposed to do so. Churchill seems to have nursed the illusion that he might be asked to replace Asquith if he retired, but the ex-Premier had as little intention of standing down as he had inclination to lead an effective opposition – so Churchill remained in the position he had occupied since November 1915. In retrospect his decision to leave office for the front seemed to have been the wrong one. Had he remained in office, as he could have done, it would have been much easier for Lloyd George to have offered him something, but Churchill had not understood how he was regarded. Once shorn of power, his enemies had no intention of tempering the wind of their hostility to him.

'His necessities will keep him straight,'[41] Churchill had written to his wife in January 1916, explaining why, despite her doubts, he still looked to Lloyd George for preferment. In the end he was right, but the end was a long time coming. Lloyd George's position as Prime Minister became little more secure as the months passed. The military, armoured in a self-belief that was as invincible as their plans were risible, persisted in pouring the manpower of Britain into 'major' offensives which achieved little save to make Lloyd George doubt their competence. The majority of the Liberal Party had followed

Asquith, and Lloyd George was dependent upon the Unionists for his position. He was fortunate in the fact that the Liberal opposition seemed to stand 'only for the principle that Asquith was divinely appointed to go on being Prime Minister for ever'.[42] Apart from trying to win the war, the new Prime Minister had two desiderata: to win over some prominent Liberals and to prevent his political opponents coalescing. Churchill figured in both calculations.

Churchill's contributions during the debate on the Dardanelles report on 20 March provided a first instalment of what was to become a necessary obsession. Whilst the Dardanelles hung around his neck like an albatross, he was conscious that it would be difficult for him to make any real headway, so even the chance to point out that others had been equally at fault was welcome. But he went further, arguing that the operation had very nearly succeeded, and backing up his statements from the voluminous papers which he had gathered.[43] He followed this up with a series of powerful critiques of aspects of the Government's military policy. The prospect of Churchill possibly linking up with the Asquithians was not one which Lloyd George relished, and he took the view that the Dardanelles report, if it had not absolved Churchill from blame, had at least left him 'grey' rather than 'black'.[44] Indirect approaches from Lloyd George at the end of April were disappointingly vague in terms of what might be on offer, but they were sufficient to raise Churchill's hopes.[45] His intervention in the House on 10 May, in a speech which was considered a 'fine statesmanlike effort',[46] helped push Lloyd George towards making up his mind to find a place for Churchill.

On 19 May Frances Stevenson recorded in her diary that Lloyd George was 'thinking of getting Winston in in some capacity'. Tired of the 'mournful faces' of his colleagues, the Prime Minister wanted 'someone who will cheer him up', and the 'energetic and forceful' Churchill would provide this. She was not sure how serious Lloyd George was, for he knew Churchill's 'limitations and realises he is eaten up with conceit. "He had spoiled himself by reading about Napoleon,"' was one of his comments.[47] After the debate on 10 May Lloyd George had told Churchill that he intended to 'have me at his side',[48] yet it was July before he did anything.

Churchill had said, in early 1917, that he would only come back to office if he was offered a leading position in the Government,[49] but Lloyd George had something rather less than this in mind for him. The obvious post, given Churchill's early interest in the development of air power, was to make him head of the Air Board, but the Ministry of Munitions and even the Chancellorship of the Duchy were mentioned. Churchill, however, wanted a war department or nothing.[50] But the mere rumour that he was going to be offered any post brought coals of wrath down on Lloyd George's head.

Curzon wrote to Bonar Law on 4 June, saying that he hoped the rumours of Churchill's impending appointment were not true: 'As you know some of us myself included only joined Ll[oyd]. G. on the distinct understanding that

W[inston] Ch[urchill] was not to be a member of the Gov[ernmen]t.'[51] The President of the Scottish Unionists, Sir George Younger, was even blunter when writing to Lloyd George on 8 June: 'I am seriously afraid that such an appointment would strain to breaking point the Unionist Party's loyalty to you.'[52] Derby, now Secretary of State for War, doubted his capacity to convince Lloyd George of the unwisdom of appointing Churchill, but insisted that he should not be in the War Cabinet.[53] Derby's leniency was unusual, as most Unionists wanted nothing to do with Churchill.[54] The National Unionist Council passed a motion declaring that Churchill's appointment would be 'an insult to the Navy and the Army'.[55]

For Lloyd George to give way to such protests would have been to weaken his position, so he resolved to call the bluff of the Unionists, gambling that they would not want to incur the odium of upsetting a Government in wartime over a matter of personalities (for there were also objections to his bringing in Edwin Montagu). On 16 July he invited Churchill to join the Government, as Minister of Munitions. The expected storm descended, with Conservative grandees writing in droves to Downing Street.[56] Bonar Law was less than amused at not having been consulted by Lloyd George on the appointment, but he took his revenge, insisting that Churchill should have nothing to do with the central direction of the war or with the Admiralty.[57] The prestige of the Government had been severely shaken, and many Unionists now remembered their former mistrust of Lloyd George; some, indeed, were never again to forget it.[58] By 20 July Unionist backbenchers asked questions of Bonar Law in the House, and it was not until 20 July that *The Times* was able to report that 'feeling on the matter is becoming less intense'.[59]

In 1917 Churchill embarked upon what was, in effect, a second political career. It was different in kind from the first one. Where he had been the rising star and *enfant terrible* of politics, a man whose future was a puzzle to his patron, and whose tremendous energies might take him anywhere, provided his rashness did not prevent it, he was now a man with a past. It was one which he defended passionately in newspaper articles, in a series of books, and in numerous letters to newspapers, friends and former colleagues. By such means Churchill imposed his version of events upon the public mind. But all this took time, and not everyone was convinced. The cry of 'What about the Dardanelles?' was always useful for those opponents who could find no other stick with which to beat him; if that failed, there were always 'Tonypandy' and 'Antwerp' to fall back on. The biggest change, however, was that Churchill had tasted failure. Lloyd George had taken a real risk in appointing him; henceforth, Churchill would be the debtor in their relationship.

14

Master and Servant

Years later, when Churchill was Chancellor of the Exchequer and Lloyd George a little-regarded figure in the wilderness, the two men met and their relationship quickly fell into its old pattern, 'master and servant', with Lloyd George in the role of the former.[1] The relationship was established upon these terms during the period 1917–19. In part this was because Churchill was in a 'chastened mood', shaken by the evident Conservative hostility towards himself, and prepared, for once, to admit that he had been '"a bit above himself" at the Admiralty'.[2] When Lloyd George went over to France shortly after appointing Churchill, the latter warned him: 'Don't get torpedoed for if I am left alone your colleagues will eat me';[3] this was not much of an exaggeration. Walter Long was only mollified by the assurance that Churchill would have no part in the central direction of the war.[4] In August, when Churchill interfered in the affairs of the Admiralty and the War Office in a very minor way, both Secretaries of State talked hotly about resigning unless he was stopped. Lord Derby exclaimed, '"What right has he to express an opinion? He is only an ironmonger."'[5] Such brooding suspicion helped ensure that Churchill was confined to his sphere of 'ironmongery'.

But there was another reason why Churchill's relationship with Lloyd George entered a new phase. Where Asquith had been content to allow discussion of strategy by a large War Council to which Ministers of all sorts and conditions could submit papers, Lloyd George concentrated power in his own hands and those of a small War Cabinet – and Churchill remained well away from the centre of power. As time passed and Churchill's confidence grew again, this was a state of affairs he came to resent.

As Minister of Munitions Churchill was head of the largest employer of labour in the country. His attitude towards the trades union movement was conciliatory and he supported claims for higher wages in return for more productivity. By thus rewarding the forces of labour and appealing to their patriotism, he was able to overcome industrial strife and secure a steady flow of munitions to the front, although he was hindered by a shortage of shipping and other resources.[6] But he proved himself, yet again, a man who possessed more than simply a gift for rhetoric, running his department efficiently and demonstrating his talents as an executive politician.

Churchill had not ceased to have views on wider aspects of the war. As the man charged with responsibility for supplying the Army and Navy, he put forward his views on strategy. These were similar to those of Lloyd George, who held that there should be no great offensive on the western front until the Americans, who had entered the war in April, had arrived in force.[7] But Churchill played no role in the great struggles between Lloyd George and the generals. Given his own estimate of his abilities, and his friendship with Lloyd George, and the success with which he performed his task at the Ministry of Munitions, Churchill expected to receive preferment, and he disliked the War Cabinet system as run by Lloyd George; or, to be more accurate, he disliked his own exclusion from it. He tried to win Bonar Law's support, arguing that the system was wrong in principle. He received the response which might have been expected from that source: 'Mr Churchill, if the Government is doing something wrong in principle, you have your remedy – why don't you resign?'[8] Having experienced the bitter fruits of such an action, and armed now with a better appreciation of his own political position, this was not a course of action which Churchill was inclined to take, and he got on with his own business. But by May 1918, with a victorious conclusion of the war in sight, the question of his future position began to exercise him.

The shape of post-war politics was uncertain. Churchill certainly wanted a coalition government to continue to tackle the tremendous problems of post-war reconstruction, but he was not, he told Lloyd George on 8 May 1918, prepared to 'accept political responsibility without recognised regular power'. He was, he said, prepared to remain in a purely 'administrative capacity' during the war – which left open the implication that he might not be so willing after it had ended.[9] He returned to the same theme on 15 May, arguing that Lloyd George could not hope to succeed unless he welded the elements of his support into a Party. He was quite willing, he wrote, to be left out of the Cabinet, if that helped Lloyd George in his negotiations with the Unionists, and during the war he was content to serve 'without involving myself in political cares or Party bitterness'.[10]

Churchill's willingness to renounce Party politics was not taken at face value by Lloyd George. The timing of Churchill's letters was significant. On 7 May *The Times* had published a letter by General Maurice, which alleged that Lloyd George had lied to the Commons about the strength of the British Army in France and about its future dispositions. Asquith put down a question about this in the House the same afternoon and the matter turned into a full-scale question of confidence in the Government. But Asquith hesitated to press home his attack, and Lloyd George responded brilliantly in a debate on the Maurice affair on 9 May. The final vote was the first test of Lloyd George's Parliamentary support, and it was a resounding success: 293 MPs voted with him and only 106 against him.[11] 'They have gone away saying – we have caught the little beggar out speaking the truth for once,' was Lloyd George's sardonic comment on the affair.[12]

The debate 'marked the final cleavage' between Lloyd George and Asquith, according to Lord Beaverbrook, and if historians no longer hold quite such a clear-cut view, there can be no doubt that it had forced Liberals to take sides.[13] Lloyd George was suspicious of Churchill's contacts with the Asquithians and thought that he was sitting on the fence in order to 'join Asquith' in 'the event of the fall of the Government'. But the Maurice debate made Churchill come off the fence, if, indeed, he had actually been on it. Lloyd George's suspicions are understandable. In February 1918 the Representation of the People Act had become law. This increased the electorate from just over seven and a half million to nearly twenty-one and a half million, a development which would fundamentally alter the structure of British politics.[14] In March negotiations had begun between Unionists and Lloyd George about the terms upon which the coalition might continue. Although the Prime Minister remained an object of suspicion to many Unionists, his abilities as a rabble-rouser, and the reputation which the war would bequeath him, made him a desirable catch. The problem for Lloyd George, as Churchill pointed out, was that he had no clear body of his own supporters.[15]

The questions of when a general election should be fought, and what pro-gramme it should be fought upon, were ones which had a profound bearing on Churchill's future. We have seen that as far back as 1910 he had favoured a national coalition, an idea to which he had returned in 1914. Much as he enjoyed Party politics, he was prone to see them as an unpatriotic distraction in time of national emergency. It had been ironic that Churchill should have been the main victim of the formation of the first coalition, but, as his letters to Lloyd George indicated, he was not willing to remain in the Government in his current position. He wanted to 'rope in the Asquith party', forming a grand coalition which would deal with the major problems facing the country,[16] but Asquith's own refusal to join with Lloyd George left Churchill with little choice other than to stay with the Prime Minister. The coalition won an overwhelming victory at the general election in December. However, the character of Lloyd George's triumph increased, rather than decreased, his need for Churchill's support and presence in the Government.

Out of the 707 MPs in the new Parliament, 382 were Unionists;[17] Bonar Law said of Lloyd George, 'He can be Prime Minister for life, if he likes.'[18] But in reality, as these figures suggested, he could be Prime Minister for as long as the Unionists liked. Selborne spoke for some Unionists when he alleged that their Party was in 'great danger' from the Welsh radical.[19] Lord Robert Cecil and Lord Curzon were 'against touching him because he is such a dirty little rogue'. The 'Welsh Walpole', as others called Lloyd George, was certainly an incongruous leader for a Conservative-dominated majority.[20] Other Unionists, whilst distrusting the men with whom he surrounded him-self, including Churchill, and finding him 'tricky', had been impressed by his wartime leadership[21] and believed with Bonar Law that, in the face of the new democracy, it was essential that Lloyd George remained Prime Minister.[22]

After all, it was nearly twenty years since the Unionists had won an election, and that had been in the middle of the Boer War. If they had not been able to convince the small, middle-class-dominated electorate of 1910, there were many Unionists who did not see how they could convince the new, predominantly working-class electorate. It was, in part, a case of hanging on to nurse for fear of finding something infinitely worse.

Lloyd George had worked hard to ensure that those Liberals who had separated from Asquith during the war remained that way at its end. Conscious of Churchill's resentment at being excluded from the centre of events, Lloyd George acted to make sure that he did not drift back into Asquith's orbit. 'At his best', Lloyd George 'could almost talk a bird out of a tree', and he had 'an intense comprehension of the more amiable weaknesses of human nature';[23] in Churchill's case these were vanity and ambition. On 6 November he invited Churchill and Montagu for lunch and unfolded before them his plans for the election. Churchill poured out his hostility to the current system of government, but Lloyd George 'waved it all aside'. That, he said, had just been for the war; once peace came, then so would a return to the old Cabinet system. Churchill was landed. When Montagu reminded him that he had said he would serve in the coalition only for the duration of the war, he responded that 'once he had joined Lloyd George, he joined him forever, that he had always been Lloyd George's man and that he owed nothing to anybody else'.[24] He tried to extract from Lloyd George a specific pledge that he would be included in the Cabinet, implying, in a letter on 7 November, that he was quite prepared to enter opposition if he was not satisfied.[25] Lloyd George was not having that, and reminded Churchill that if he was dissatisfied with his current post, it was 'better than your position in the Asquith Government'.[26]

Churchill's decision to stick with Lloyd George had not been wholly popular in Dundee, where the local Liberal Association was Asquithian in its loyalties, but Churchill did not intend the fissure opened up by the events of the war to be permanent. Even before the election he had wanted to 'rope in the Asquith party',[27] and the result had not changed his mind. Beaverbrook had tasked him with accepting 'the Coalition compromise as a necessary expedient for carrying on the King's Government but not from the heart',[28] and whilst there was something in this, it was not the whole story. There was certainly a negative aspect to 'coalitionism', but this was most evident amongst the Unionists; it was 'a matter of men as well as measures'.[29]

Churchill was always apt to think in terms of 'men for measures' rather than 'Party', as his previous hankerings after coalition show, and his vision of the Government which Lloyd George should form reflected this tendency. To his mind politics was a 'whole-time job to which men should devote their lives',[30] and he saw the coalition as the focus for such individuals to apply their talents to the massive tasks of making the peace and reconstructing the nation. He wanted to see Asquith back in the Government, perhaps as Lord

Chancellor, which would reunite the Liberal Party and allow Lloyd George to become its leader. Bonar Law, Curzon, Milner and the leading Labour politician, George Barnes, would form a 'limited Cabinet' unburdened by departments, which would be available to guide the Prime Minister. Their old friend and colleague, Rufus Isaacs, now hidden away under the title of Lord Reading, should, Churchill thought, go to the Foreign Office, whilst it was important to include F. E. Smith, who could 'help you v[er]y much with the Tory Democrats'. It was a vision of a professional government with a 'democratic and progressive policy', gathering together 'all forces of strength and influence in the country'.[31]

This version of the future reveals much about Churchill's political thinking. Passionately attached to Parliamentary government, he nevertheless possessed a strong authoritarian instinct. 'His conception of the State consists in a well-paid, well-nurtured people, managed and controlled by a Winston or Winstons.'[32] As Minister of Munitions he had been in charge of a microcosm of the corporate state, where central government combined with employers and trades unions to ensure that both sectional and the national interests were served; he saw no reason why this should not continue into peacetime. For Churchill the Lloyd George coalition was more than a convenient method of governing in an extraordinary situation. It was the model for a form of government which was desirable in its own right – a strong Prime Minister, supported by professional senior colleagues.

The question of where Churchill himself should go was not settled until the end of December. It was clearly necessary for Lloyd George to do something for the most prominent of his Liberal colleagues, but, once again, the question of where to put Churchill aroused various opinions, some of them, no doubt, unprintable. Leo Amery volunteered the view that Churchill should not be sent to the War Office because 'I hear from all sorts of quarters that the Army are terrified of him', and he suggested the new Air Ministry or the Colonial Office as offering him a 'field of adventure and advertisement'.[33] But Lloyd George thought that there would be 'nothing doing' at the Colonial Office and that 'it would be like condemning a man to be head of a mausoleum'.[34] Lloyd George said that he might like either the Admiralty or the War Office. Churchill would have preferred the former, but by the time he had made up his mind, only the latter was on offer.[35] 'What is the use of being War Secretary if there is no war?' Churchill is said to have commented, to which Bonar Law replied cuttingly: 'If we thought there was going to be a war we wouldn't appoint you War Secretary.'[36]

Churchill's administrative expertise and powers of work were, in Lloyd George's mind, to be harnessed to the urgent and complicated task of demobilisation, but even whilst he set about that job, he was doubtful whether it should be as complete as Lloyd George wanted. With the Prime Minister in Paris for the peace conference, Churchill sprang on the Cabinet his idea for retaining compulsory service and an army of 1,700,000, which would eventually be reduced to a million men, on higher rates of pay. Tom Jones, the acting head of the War Cabinet secretariat, tipped off his chief, Sir Maurice Hankey, and Lloyd George, 'much annoyed about Churchill's proposal', wrote to quash the idea.[37] It was characteristic that, as Secretary of State for War and Air, Churchill's vision of Britain's defence forces now comprehended only these two areas. When the Chief of the Imperial General Staff, Sir Henry Wilson, asked him 'where the Admiralty came in', he 'admitted – nowhere!' Churchill was, however, of the opinion that having become a 'military nation' by accident, 'we must endeavour to remain so'.[38] There were urgent tasks which required the maintenance of a strong army, none more so than dealing with the revolutionary situation in Russia, and he was not going to be deterred from his duty by Lloyd George and the demands of domestic politics.

Lloyd George's administration was the first to face a dilemma which was to present itself to every post-war government: 'guns or butter?' Should the demands of domestic politics be met at the cost of Britain's external commitments, or should the former be sacrificed to the latter?[39] One reason for the fate of the Asquithians was that the old Liberal causes, free trade, nonconformity and temperance, seemed to belong to the past; Unionists like Amery welcomed this, but also acknowledged that only a 'really bold and constructive policy of social reform' would enable the Government to beat off the challenge of Labour.[40] Lloyd George saw in such a programme a restatement of a Liberalism which was relevant to the new era, and he proclaimed it in his manifesto; housing, education, wages and conditions of work, all these would be dealt with, and a 'land fit for heroes' would be constructed.[41]

Churchill's priorities were different. Taking the view of the philosopher, Thomas Hobbes, that covenants without swords are but mere words, he wanted to prevent the liquefaction of the Army, warning that 'if we are not careful we shall find ourselves without the strong instrument on which our policy in Europe depends'.[42] His proposal for maintaining a large army was a 'question not of detail but of first-class policy which may involve grave political consequences', and Lloyd George reprimanded him on 18 January for raising the issue whilst he was out of the country.[43] Churchill was unrepentant, pleading that all he had been doing was settling the detail, upon which, of course, the Prime Minister would have to pronounce.[44] Dr Christopher Addison, the Minister for Reconstruction, told Lloyd George that the scheme was 'open to the gravest objection' and that it would raise 'a storm of protest', with some Labour leaders representing it as a threatening move by the Government towards them.[45] Bonar Law was also worried by the political implications of announcing that conscription was to be retained,[46] but for Churchill it was a question of facing 'harsh facts'. The British were committed to maintaining an army of occupation in Germany, a force of 70,000 in India and 100,000 for her new responsibilities in Mesopotamia,

Palestine and Turkey, and it was 'absurd' to think that this could be done on a voluntary basis. Churchill wanted to maintain conscription for a year, which, he thought, would allow him to build up a purely volunteer force. Lloyd George had no alternative other than to give in.[47] But this did not mean that he had changed his mind over 'guns' and 'butter', particularly in the one area which Churchill had avoided mentioning in his letter of 27 January – Russia.

Lloyd George's comment upon Churchill's reaction to the Russian revolution is well-known: 'his ducal blood revolted at the wholesale slaughter of Grand Dukes'. It did, but there was more to it than that. Churchill certainly had a visceral loathing of 'the foul baboonery of Bolshevism', and in that his instincts were perhaps sounder than the legions of the good and the great who imagined that there was necessarily some relationship between Communist rhetoric and practice. For reasons which are obscure, but which perhaps lie in the province of the psychologist, many commentators have taken issue with Churchill's description of Lenin as a 'plague bacillus', sent by the Germans to Russia to undermine the imperial war effort. Churchill's description of the revolutionary leader is certainly a trifle overblown: 'His mind was a remarkable instrument. When its light shone it revealed the whole world, its history, its sorrows, its stupidities, its shams, and above all its wrongs', but it is hard to quarrel with his comment that 'in the cutting off of the lives of men and women, no Asiatic conqueror, not Tamerlane, not Jengiz Khan, can match his fame'.[48] The revolution stirred some of Churchill's deepest instincts: his sense of history was touched by the fall of an ancient empire; the repudiation of treaties by the Bolsheviks and their withdrawal from the war aroused his indignation at treachery, whilst the overthrow of established authority affronted his deeply conservative sense of social order.

Churchill was not unmindful of the influence which the Bolsheviks might bring to bear through fellow-travellers in Britain. As Minister of War he thought he detected its undertones in the Army itself, and he acted swiftly and efficiently to defuse any danger. It took him only days to realise that the existing demobilisation plans, which General Sir Douglas Haig, commander of the British land forces, had criticised as prejudicial to discipline, were just that; it may have made economic sense to release men who were needed for industry at home, but when this meant releasing first those who had been conscripted last, it flew in the face of human nature and destroyed the power of self-restraint. Churchill scrapped the plans, introducing a 'first in, first out' policy, which was economically less defensible, but which calmed the problem.[49]

Lloyd George's attitude towards British intervention in Russia was ambivalent. Intervention had been justifiable whilst the war was still in progress, but once it was over things were different. To avoid creating any dissent within the Cabinet, the Prime Minister favoured the adoption of a formula thought up by the Foreign Office, which was that existing commitments should be honoured, but no further ones taken on.[50] It was a policy dictated by the need for retrenchment and to appease the leaders of the forces of organised labour, who looked upon the new Soviet Union as a 'workers' state'.

Churchill and Sir Henry Wilson both considered that declaring war on the Bolsheviks was out of the question. Wilson pointed out on 19 February that 'the Allies do not dispose of sufficient forces to warrant the attempt being made'.[51] Even if they had, Churchill regretfully concluded that, given the state of morale and discipline in the Army, 'our orders would not be obeyed'.[52] The official biography, countering the view that Churchill wanted a major Allied intervention, quotes much evidence to this effect from Cabinet meetings, but it omits passages which show that Churchill's attitude was a good deal more complex than simply advocating assisting 'White' Russian forces.[53] If Churchill's colleagues believed that he wanted more than this, then both his language and his actions lent some credence to their fears.

In Cabinet on 13 February, where Lloyd George showed himself extremely reluctant to sanction any help at all, Churchill first spoke about Britain simply supporting the 'Russian armies', but he went on to talk about the Allies declaring 'war on the Bolsheviks'. Churchill did not think that the Bolsheviks constituted a very formidable force and he was sure that the 'moral effect' of the Allies declaring war would destabilise them to an extent where the existing 'White' armies and Allied volunteers could finish them off; and he had no doubts that sufficient 'volunteers' would be forthcoming.[54] It was all very reminiscent of the 'Dunkirk circus' and, again, showed the extent to which, once Churchill had an idea fixed in his mind, his obsession could minimise any difficulties in its way whilst at the same time maximising the chances of its success.

In his memoirs Lloyd George, who was always apt to make fun of Churchill's 'Bolshevism on the brain',[55] improves on what was a good story, by having Churchill going off on his own initiative to the peace conference in Paris and taking the opportunity to 'urge his plans in regard to Russia'.[56] But the Prime Minister had sanctioned the visit – even if its results alarmed him. Churchill's own account in his war memoirs selects only the telegrams which present him as arguing for a limited intervention, but although his language was couched in this vein, others doubted if it would stop there. Lloyd George's secretary, Philip Kerr, wrote to him on 15 February: 'Mr Churchill is bent on forcing a campaign against Bolshevik Russia by using Allied volunteers, Polish, Finnish and any other conscripts that can be got hold of, financed and equipped by the Allies.' He acknowledged that Churchill was 'perfectly logical in his policy, because he declares that the Bolsheviks are the enemies of the human race and must be put down at any cost'.[57]

In his account of his meeting with President Woodrow Wilson in Paris, Churchill expressed surprise at the President's support for Allied intervention in Russia;[58] since the official record has Wilson taking precisely the opposite line, this need occasion no surprise. Churchill chose to interpret Wilson's comment that he would go along with whatever the Allies agreed upon as favourable to his own plans, and in doing so he put himself on a collision course with Lloyd George.[59] The Allies had already suggested to the Bolsheviks that they should meet on the Turkish island of Prinkipo to discuss negotiations. Churchill, after conferring with members of the Allied supreme council, suggested to Lloyd George on 16 February that they should now regard the deadline for these talks as having passed and that they should set up an inter-Allied council to co-ordinate military and economic action in Russia.[60]

Lloyd George took alarm at all this, sharing Kerr's view that Churchill 'wants to conduct a war against the Bolsheviks'. He knew his old friend too well, telling Riddell that 'Winston has a very excitable brain. He is able, but may go off on a tangent at any moment.'[61] He sent him a blunt telegram, warning him not to go beyond what the Cabinet had agreed, namely supplying arms to Admiral Kolchak, one of the White Russian leaders, and company 'in the event of every effort at peaceable solution failing'. He wanted to know how much any such assistance would cost, warning starkly that Britain could not afford the burden of 'an expensive war of aggression against Russia'; that would be 'the road to bankruptcy and Bolshevism in these islands'.[62] With the Army estimates running at ten times the figure for 1913–14 (£287 million compared with £28.8 million),[63] the Chancellor of the Exchequer casting around for economies,[64] and with industrial unrest on the Clyde, policemen on strike in Liverpool and threats of widespread social disorder,[65] Lloyd George did not want to 'incense' the forces of 'organised labour' or embark on an expensive foreign adventure.

Churchill protested that he had never intended to go beyond anything which the Cabinet had wanted,[66] but the argument rumbled on after the failure of his mission to Paris. Sir Henry Wilson concluded that the best the Allies could hope to do was to restrict the frontiers of the new Soviet State by supporting those nationalities – Georgians, Estonians and company – who had broken free of Russian domination.[67] But even that raised questions of cost and the exact nature of any British commitment.

Lloyd George was irritated when Churchill did not come up with any figures about cost, whilst Churchill himself was angered by what he saw as the Cabinet's refusal to agree on any 'Russian policy'.[68] He cast around for tools with which to do the job, alarming Lloyd George in April with the idea of employing German troops; 'he is a dangerous man,' Lloyd George told Riddell, 'and he is mad for operations in Russia'. Bonar Law simply regarded Churchill's attitude as another example of his 'bad judgement', and it confirmed him in his belief that he was 'a dangerous fellow'.[69] At one Cabinet meeting, he cut short yet another diatribe by Churchill on the subject with the brutal remark: 'Well, Gentlemen, I think we have discussed Russia long enough – we have heard quite enough of Winston's nonsense; we had better come to a decision.'[70]

But a decision was not easily arrived at. In early March the Cabinet decided that Murmansk and Archangel should be evacuated[71] – something Churchill accepted with a bad grace. He argued that it could be implemented only if more British volunteers were sent there to cover the withdrawal of the troops.[72] Churchill promised that the volunteers would be used only to rescue their colleagues, but he had changed his tune by the end of April. Then he argued that the success of Kolchak's forces advancing from Siberia made it sensible to use the British forces in the Archangel region to force a junction with his armies. This, he assured Lloyd George on 26 April, would make a British withdrawal much easier.[73] On 14 May the Cabinet rejected Churchill's proposal to form additional units of the Slavo-British legion, a move ignored by the official biographer, as it was by his subject; Churchill decided that it was a purely War Office matter.[74]

This, as Rhodes James has commented, was 'rather reminiscent of the prelude to the Dardanelles campaign', with Churchill, from a subordinate position, 'attempting to assist a difficult and controversial military campaign with a sceptical Prime Minister and half-hearted support from the majority of his colleagues'.[75] Churchill's usual optimism magnified the chances of gaining what he wanted and minimised the costs. He was convinced that the Bolsheviks, faced with resolute opposition, would give up the struggle; it was essential for the Allies not to do anything which would encourage them. When the commander of the British forces in Archangel, General Ironside, proposed that he should use his forces to effect a junction with Kolchak's, Churchill pushed Lloyd George to approve, arguing that it was 'not a matter of policy, but purely a military operation'.[76] He explained to some sceptical colleagues on 11 June that although this was the first time they had proposed an 'offensive' operation, it was only necessary as a prelude to withdrawal.[77]

Churchill's faith in the 'White' generals was touching. With military reverses suffered by Kolchak making junction with his forces unlikely, Churchill argued on 18 June that Ironside's campaign should still go ahead because General Denikin's army had done so well in the south that it had recovered more ground than Kolchak had lost.[78] By this time questions were being asked in the Commons and in the press as to the nature of British policy towards Russia, and the discussion of the matter in Cabinet on 4 July showed how dangerous a situation they were drifting into. Lloyd George said 'that actually we were at war with the Bolsheviks, but we had decided not to make war . . . we did not intend to put great armies into Russia'.[79] The Prime Minister wanted to make a 'clean cut', and he used the failure of Kolchak's forces to argue that he had been right all along in discouraging military operations.[80]

Churchill's vision of Bolshevism was cast in a more apocalyptic mode than the one allowed to the Prime Minister by his preoccupation with cost and political calculation. He feared that a Bolshevik victory would lose 'the whole fruits of our victory', with the new League of Nations being impotent and Germany gaining influence over the Soviet state.[81] It was a sombre vision, and as the prospects of victory grew bleaker, so did Churchill's rhetoric grow more strident. Bolshevism meant the war of the 'discontented, criminal and mutinous classes' against the law-abiding; it also meant 'tyranny, pestilence and famine'. This attitude merely drew criticism from the Labour Party,[82] and by the end of July Lloyd George was deprecating any further attempts to help Denikin and his 'reactionary' supporters. On 25 July the Cabinet sanctioned a retreat from north Russia and the Caucasus operations. Churchill could no longer delay, and the future for Denikin looked bleak.[83]

But Churchill still persisted. In Cabinet on 29 July he argued that they should take no firm decision about north Russia before they had decided what to do about Denikin, but now Lloyd George was back from Paris and in no mood to put up with Churchill's equivocations. It was, he said, 'a mistake to treat the present military operations in Russia as though they were a campaign against Bolshevism'; that would take 'great armies'. It was 'true that one member of the Cabinet had always urged this policy, but he himself had always protested against it'. If, as appeared to be the case, the Russian people supported the Bolsheviks, then so be it; it was not Britain's place to intervene.[84] But Churchill held out for support for Denikin for another six months, and in late August he advocated extending support to General Yudenitch's forces in the Baltic states.[85] It was all too much for the Prime Minister.

Lloyd George was anxious to reduce the size of the Army urgently in order to save money, but whenever he talked to Churchill he got 'nothing but Russia'. Russia, he told Churchill in an angry note on 30 August, 'has cost us more than the hundred millions odd we have spent on it', for 'an impression has been left upon my mind that the best thoughts of the War Office have been given to these military adventures in Russia'.[86] In a memorandum to the Cabinet he firmly put all his authority against any further intervention.[87] Churchill protested against the implications in Lloyd George's letter and argued that 'I have made no commitments to Russia of any kind.'[88] Although strictly true, this was irrelevant; without Churchill there would have been no dynamic support for the 'Whites'. He reminded Lloyd George on 20 September that any plans he had for 'fusion' with the Conservative Party might 'miscarry' if it was thought that 'we are not the enemies of Bolshevism in every form and in every land'.[89]

But Churchill had misread the Prime Minister's priorities. Whilst his anti-Bolshevik stance had won Churchill support from the Conservatives, Lloyd George was more interested in winning support from the working classes and old Liberal supporters. He replied to Churchill's letter with one of stinging rebuke, in which, after expatiating upon his strenuous efforts to 'cut down the enormous expenditure,' he blamed Churchill's obsession with Russia for his failure to apply his mind to the pressing problems facing the country. He dismissed Churchill's optimistic prognoses about the chances of Denikin's success by quoting to him his earlier remarks in the same vein about Kolchak. Lloyd George told Churchill that it would cost 'hundreds of millions' to support the regimes which he wanted to uphold, and he warned him, 'you won't find another responsible person in the whole land who will take your view'.[90] Churchill thought Lloyd George's comments 'unkind and unjust',[91] but the Prime Ministerial rebuke was unmistakable and there was no appeal against it.

Churchill continued to hope for a 'White' victory, but by February 1920 the civil war in Russia was effectively over, although it was to be succeeded by a fierce conflict with Poland. Lloyd George's intervention had killed any hopes Churchill had had of sustaining the 'Whites'. The Prime Minister's policy was, in one sense, short-sighted, for it ignored, as Churchill's views did not, the nature of Communism, but Churchill's policy was simply unrealisable. He was wrong in thinking that only a small British force was needed to ensure the defeat of the Bolsheviks. More troops would have been needed, and neither the state of the economy, nor public opinion, would have sanctioned any escalation. Churchill's enemies simply regarded it as another episode in the career of the 'Gambler of the Dardanelles',[92] and the Labour Party long held it against him. It reinforced Lloyd George's doubts about his old friend's judgment, and, if it won Churchill some support in Conservative quarters, it reconfirmed Bonar Law in his opinion that he was 'a dangerous fellow', possessed of no judgment.[93] Once again, Churchill had demonstrated his greatest political gift – that of isolating himself by alienating his supporters without winning over old enemies.

15

Fusion and Fissures

In March 1919 Sir Henry Wilson recorded in his diary that Churchill was 'in a very critical mood about LG & I am sure is watching an opportunity to knife him'.[1] As a great master of political intrigue, at least in his own estimation, Wilson was apt to credit others with intentions he himself might nurse, but whilst there is no indication that Churchill wanted to 'knife' Lloyd George, there is no doubt that by this time any gratitude which he had felt towards him had evaporated. The old resentments for the way he had been treated by one whom he had considered a close friend between 1915 and 1917 were easily brought once more to the surface, and the Bolshevik question was only the chief of the issues which did just that.

Churchill would like to have become Minister of Defence, arguing (as he was to do in 1940) that it was sensible for the three Service departments to be co-ordinated by one head.[2] This would certainly have made sense of his other portfolio, the Air Ministry, where, unable to devote enough time to its affairs, he was only occasionally effective.[3] But although Lloyd George was sympathetic to the idea, he had doubts whether Churchill was the best man for it,[4] and he feared disturbing the balance of the coalition by doing anything to demote the position of the Admiralty, which was held by one of the Conservative leaders, Walter Long.[5] Despite his promises to Churchill in 1918 before the election, Lloyd George had still not restored the old Cabinet system, leaving his War Minister feeling that he had not yet regained his old political position.[6]

The question of a return to Cabinet Government raised a wider one: would the political structure erected in 1918 continue? The Labour Party, which had established itself then as the main opposition force, had built upon this position and, with the growth of class-consciousness fostered by the war and the revolutions on the Continent, it threatened (at least in its rhetoric) to overturn the existing social and political system. The former Secretary of State for War and Lord Chancellor, Haldane, now aligning himself with Labour, declared that he had done so because Liberalism was a spent force. Asquith's return to the Commons after victory in the Paisley by-election in February 1920 seemed to some Liberals a new dawn, but Haldane thought not: 'Parties will have to be re-cast and their scope enlarged before a proper alternative Government can be formed.'[7] It was not only in the Labour Party that such views were held. The Lloyd George coalition had been the offspring of a wartime marriage of convenience; the question of its legitimisation was, by 1920, an urgent one.

Beaverbrook described Lloyd George as a 'Prime Minister without a Party',[8] which, if not strictly accurate (he had the Lloyd George Liberals), conveyed the essence of the matter; his position rested upon his own prestige and upon positive and negative reactions within the ranks of his followers to the postwar situation. For Churchill the coalition served two purposes: it could direct the building of the 'homes fit for heroes'; and it could protect the status quo from the depredations of the Socialists. Such views were also held by Churchill's old friend, F. E. Smith, now ennobled as Lord Birkenhead and translated to the Woolsack, and by Austen Chamberlain and Balfour. It might have seemed that the most natural thing was for these 'glittering birds of paradise' to form the nucleus of a new Party, which would have embodied 'coalitionism' in a more permanent form; but there were two obstacles to this: Lloyd George and the Conservative Party.

Lloyd George's character was not improved by success. Always self-confident and voluble, he had become arrogant. He spent most of the six months after his election victory in France, seldom visited the Commons, and operated with a War Cabinet which he treated as a domineering managing director does his junior executives. Churchill's path to the War Office had been smoothed by Milner's resentment of the way Lloyd George had treated him, and Birkenhead, Curzon, and Churchill himself all had, by mid-1920, reason to share this feeling.[9] The Prime Minister had become 'something of a dictator without having a dictator's apparatus of power and terror';[10] his power depended upon his own prestige and upon the Conservative Party.

The 'glamour' of Lloyd George's 'extraordinary personality' helped bind some Unionists to his side,[11] and Bonar Law, who had begun by distrusting him, became his indispensable lieutenant.[12] But not all Unionists shared their leader's confidence in the Prime Minister, and the spread of industrial unrest at home made some of them sympathise with remarks which Churchill made in a speech in Sunderland on 2 January 1920 in which he warned of the spread of Bolshevik ideas in Britain.[13] The Hampshire division of the National Unionist Association passed a resolution on 26 February which viewed 'with greatest concern the rapid spread of Socialistic and Bolshevist principles'. Selborne, who was the Association's President, told the Party Chairman, Sir George Younger, that whilst 'Our people are very grateful for what the Coalition did in the War', they were 'profoundly unhappy' at the 'dark future' which faced them. They had not forgotten Lloyd George's radical antecedents, and if they and he were 'going to fight shoulder to shoulder against the forces of revolution', they wanted to know 'on what principles' their previous differences were 'going to be composed'.[14] The Hampshire Conservatives were not the only ones who wanted to know upon what principles they were to stand shoulder to shoulder with their old Liberal enemies; nor were they alone in their evident distaste for the idea of doing so.

The defeat of the former Liberal Minister, Sir John Simon, by a Labour candidate at Spen Valley in December 1919, and Asquith's victory at Paisley in February 1920, stimulated talk within the ranks of the coalition about what became known as 'fusion'.[15] Riddell noticed that whilst Unionists like Birkenhead were, despite their personal differences with the Prime Minister, keen on the idea, 'it is obvious that the older section of the Conservatives are not disposed to give up their organisation and place themselves unreservedly in L.G.'s power'.[16] But, faced with a situation in which he saw only three alternatives: to retire from politics before his laurels withered; to resign the Premiership and regroup the Liberal Party; or to opt for fusion, Lloyd George had no hesitation in deciding to go for the last.[17]

The case which Birkenhead put forward for fusion in a series of articles in March was similar to the one which Lloyd George had argued in the coalition talks of 1911: the necessity of rallying all hands to the pumps in a national emergency. But where he was still prepared to argue the case for social reform of the sort which Lloyd George and Churchill had advocated before the war, and which he, as a radical Unionist, had advanced a version of, Birkenhead was now far more concerned with the coalition acting as the locus of resistance to the Socialist menace.[18] F.E.'s reaction to the labour unrest threatening the stability of society was aggressive: 'If the Labour people show signs of revolution, we must shoot.'[19] Balfour formally proposed a fusion of the Parties in a letter to Bonar Law on 10 March, and it was agreed that Lloyd George would broach the matter to the coalition Liberals and that, when the Prime Minister proposed the policy to Bonar Law, he would put it to the Unionist Party.[20]

But the hopes of a great central coalition foundered. The coalition Liberals showed a reluctance to part with their historic name. Lloyd George and Churchill tried to browbeat their colleagues at a meeting on 18 March and their failure was as total as it was fatal to their hopes: 'Even a Coaly Lib was not to be bullied, let alone bought.'[21] Fusion could be, as we have seen, defended on two grounds: the positive and the negative; 'almost incredibly' Lloyd George chose to follow Birkenhead in emphasising the latter reasons. For Birkenhead to do so was understandable; anti-Socialism was a line which appealed to all Conservatives. For Churchill to do so was equally comprehensible given his loathing of Bolshevism. But for Lloyd George, who was still engaged in combating Churchill's attempts to revive the 'White' forces in Russia, to do so was a disastrous miscalculation. There was nothing in his speech about a more progressive policy in India or Ireland, where the Government was facing nationalist disorders, and there was precious little in the way of detailed 'progressive' proposals for dealing with problems at home.[22]

With the Liberals dropping the idea of fusion, and Lloyd George suggesting instead 'closer co-operation' on the lines of that which had existed between the Conservatives and the Liberal Unionists after 1886, the Conservative leaders now felt free to do the same. Bonar Law was not sorry, for he had never favoured 'complete fusion', going along with the idea only because it seemed 'inevitable'.[23] The Unionists continued to support Lloyd George, but on their terms, and, implicitly, as long as his personal prestige survived. For Churchill the chance of realising that central Party, which had long been his dream, had evaporated.

'Winston is the only remaining specimen of a real Tory,' Lloyd George declared in early 1920, to which Churchill riposted that if Lloyd George was going to include all Parties in his coalition, 'you will have to have me in your new National Party'. 'Oh no,' Lloyd George retorted. 'To be a Party you must have at least one follower. *You* have none.'[24] It was a cruel gibe, and one of a number of similarly barbed remarks with which Lloyd George tried to bully his old friend,[25] but it was not without a great element of truth. Lloyd George, who had revived Churchill's career, seemed, by early 1920, to be regretting it. 'He is a wild and dangerous fellow,' he told Riddell, going on to say that 'to secure his own ends he becomes reckless'; 'I have never known any man so self-centred.'[26] 'The worst feature of Winston is his vanity. Everything that he does points to one thing – self.'[27] Without the Prime Minister's patronage, and with the failure of the fusion plan, Churchill was, more than ever, in an anomalous political position. An 'executive' politician, on an almost early-nineteenth-century model, Churchill was not to be compared with those 'experts' like the Geddes brothers and Lord Rhondda, whom Lloyd George was fond of bringing into government to run their departments upon business lines. Such men were purely Lloyd George's creatures and would rise and fall with their master; they had lives outside the political sphere. But Churchill's whole life was devoted to politics, and if he wished to exercise his considerable executive skills, he needed a vehicle in which he could ride.

The convergence of their several views upon Bolshevism was an obvious source of conjunction between Churchill and the Unionists, but the shadow of pre-war days and of the Dardanelles still hung heavily over that relationship. Moreover, as long as Bonar Law was leading the Conservative Party, there would be no place for Churchill in its ranks. Where Lloyd George took the view that however troublesome Churchill was in Government, he would be more so as a critic, Bonar Law 'would rather have him against us every time'.[28]

The different attitude which Churchill and Lloyd George adopted towards events in Russia was symptomatic of a wider gulf between the two men. Sir Henry Wilson wondered why 'the English, who are by far the finest race in the world, should suddenly begin to think that they have lost the art and power of governing', as he surveyed an imperial scene which appeared increasingly gloomy. In the face of nationalist pressure in Ireland, India and Egypt, the reaction of the British Government was to offer 'devolution' or 'self-determination', which, as he recognised, 'means the end of our Empire'.[29]

Under strain abroad and facing unrest at home, Lloyd George wanted to retrench on expenditure and he wanted the Army to be reduced accordingly. But Churchill, like Wilson, thought that this was the wrong way of going about things. He saw a dangerous world, likely to dissolve into chaos, and the notion of disarming in the face of this situation was not one which appealed to him. Britain had an imperial mission, which she should carry out; the essential point was to determine what her responsibilities were and then ascertain what forces were necessary to meet them.[30] It was a habit of mind essentially different from the Prime Minister's. He was 'furious' that 'the English attitude should be one of abdication and fighting a rearguard action'.[31]

To the Whitehall mandarinate such an attitude verged on the irresponsible and Hankey, that doyen of the breed as the Secretary to the War Cabinet, noted during discussions on defence spending in August 1919 that 'Churchill obviously does not care to be War Minister without a war in prospect, and finds the task of curtailing expenditure distasteful'.[32] The Prime Minister simply concluded that Churchill had become a 'Tory' and was 'mad' about Russia,[33] whilst the forces of organised labour wrote him off as a 'class enemy'. But, as the consonance between Churchill's views and those of Wilson shows, there was more to it than was likely to be appreciated by those whose views were from the lofty heights of the Civil Service or the depths of the class-obsessed Labour Party. The Empire was facing the greatest crisis in its history and Churchill wanted to take resolute action.

In May 1919 Churchill circulated a paper by Wilson to the Cabinet, which drew attention to the serious gap which had opened up between Britain's responsibilities and her ability to meet them. Far from the end of the war bringing a cessation of demands for military forces, events in Ireland, India, Egypt and Mesopotamia had increased them:

We must face the fact (and prepare public opinion to face the fact) that we may be called on in the near future to furnish a military effort in defence of vital British interests which is beyond the strength of the forces now available. . . .[34]

To Churchill's mind this necessitated 'some form of remobilisation', but such thoughts were far from the minds of the Prime Minister and the Chancellor. Austen Chamberlain warned of the 'extreme gravity' of the situation in July, forecasting that expenditure on the current scale was 'the road to ruin'; the Army, he observed, was 'the greatest difficulty'.[35] When the Cabinet discussed the question on 5 August, Lloyd George's priorities were clear – and they were not Churchill's. The 'first priority' was to provide for the 'health and labour of the people', and if that meant reducing military expenditure to a level where the Government was taking risks in certain parts of the world, then that would have to be borne.[36]

Churchill, whilst not wanting to 'under-estimate the gravity of the financial situation', was less inclined to gloom than Chamberlain and Lloyd George.

His faith in the 'scientific process' had not been shaken by the war, and he confidently assumed that 'with the return of peace we may count confidently upon its vehement renewal wherever law and order are maintained'. If the Cabinet ruled that the fighting Services 'are not to take into consideration the possibility of another great war occurring in the next five years, and that they are to consider it only remotely possible in the next five years', then they could get on with defining those responsibilities which the Services would have to face. Money could, he thought, be saved on naval expenditure as Britain now no longer had a great naval rival who posed a danger to her – America he discounted.[37]

Out of Churchill's suggestion came the famous, or infamous, 'ten-year rule'. The armed forces were to assume that they would not be involved in a major European conflict for ten years, and therefore the function of the Army would be imperial policing – and keeping law and order at home. This enabled the Chancellor to come up with a figure of £75 million to be spent upon the Army and Air Force. But to Wilson this was to put the equation the wrong way round; 'events' ruled how many troops would be needed in the 'storm centres' of the Empire – and the finance would simply have to be found.[38]

In some areas recourse to 'mechanical contrivances' secured a reduction in expenditure. Churchill, an early enthusiast for air power, saw its potential in Mesopotamia, where the use of aircraft relieved pressure on the Army,[39] but the other regions which caused Churchill such anxiety were not amenable to such short cuts.

Churchill's anxiety for a return to the pre-war Cabinet system was not simply a symptom of his discontent with his personal position; it was a revolt against a situation where the Secretaries of State were 'relieved of all responsibility except for the proper discharge of their departmental duties'.[40] Given his different attitude towards the Empire and Britain's military commitments, it was not surprising that Churchill chafed under the yoke of the policies which Lloyd George seemed to wish to adopt in imperial affairs. The Government of India Act, which was introduced into the House in May 1919 and established the system of 'dyarchy', allowing for the 'gradual development of self-governing institutions', was framed by discussions between the War Cabinet and Montagu, as Secretary of State for India. It was only with the reintroduction of the old Cabinet system in November that Churchill got his chance to comment upon it. Birkenhead, who could not imagine how anyone could think that the Indians were ready to develop a Parliamentary system, opposed the scheme,[41] but despite his friend's influence, and his own misgivings, Churchill went along with it, taking comfort in the fact that it had been decided on long before he had any responsibility for it, and in Montagu's promise that it was not irreversible.[42]

In April 1919 General Dyer ordered his troops to fire on a mob at Amritsar, an action which brought censure from many, but which made him a hero of the Tory right wing, with the *Morning Post* raising a subscription on his behalf. When the matter was debated in the Commons on 8 July, Churchill made a powerful speech defending the Government's action in refusing Dyer further employment. Whilst sympathising with the predicament in which Dyer had found himself, Churchill said that there was 'one general prohibition which we can make ... a prohibition against what is called "frightfulness"'.[43] It was not, he said, permissible to meet terrorism by terrorism: 'such ideas are absolutely foreign to the British way of doing things'. Fortunately for Churchill, no one rose to ask him how he equated this admirable precept with what he was doing in that other 'storm centre', Ireland.

Whatever else had been changed by the war, the 'dreary steeples of Fermanagh and Tyrone', as Churchill called them, still remained to trouble the Government with the Irish problem. In 1919 most of the newly elected Irish MPs refused to take their seats at Westminster and set up a parliament in Dublin. In the Irish context the word 'extremist' must be understood without any vestige of English understatement, and the 'extremist' members of Sinn Fein and the IRA set about demonstrating just that. Whilst the Government fumbled its way towards a new Home Rule bill in 1919, the extremists set about trying to kill anyone who could stand in the way of a bullet or bomb, thus demonstrating their fitness for self-government. In March 1920 the new Home Rule Bill was introduced in the Commons, but by this time it was plain to most people that law and order in Ireland was breaking down. Sir Henry Wilson, one of the most virulent of Unionists, wanted, as we have seen, firm action to be taken; but even he was surprised when he learnt what his Secretary of State had been up to.

In late January 1920 Wilson had noted that 'Winston is realising the state of anarchy and chaos in Ireland' for 'the first time'. He surmised, in his superior way, that 'Winston is losing his nerve'.[44] Whatever else Churchill was guilty of, a lack of nerve was not one of his sins. In the face of disorder in Ireland he reacted as he had done to threats of unrest in England and to the Bolshevik menace abroad – he instinctively resorted to force. In February he pressed the claims of General Sir William Robertson to be General Officer Commanding (GOC) in Ireland as he was 'unquestionably the best man for the job'.[45] Robertson, who had risen from the ranks to command the Army during the war, had fallen foul of Lloyd George and had been shunted sideways to command British forces in Germany. He was a man of courage and tenacity, but he possessed none of the subtlety and political skill necessary to take on the Irish post – but then Churchill was not looking for such skills. He wanted a military man for a military job; the Sinn Feiners would have to be defeated in the way in which other enemies of order were dealt with – by force. In Cabinet on 11 May he proposed that they should raise a 'special force' of '8,000 old soldiers' to supplement the ranks of the Royal Irish Constabulary (RIC), a suggestion unpopular with some professional soldiers, but with which Churchill went ahead.[46]

Wilson characterised the Government's policy as one of 'vacillation and funk': 'we shall have to regularly reconquer the country or lose it,' he warned.[47] This, however, was to ignore the political and financial problems by which the Government was almost overwhelmed. Churchill told the Cabinet in June that military liabilities exceeded capabilities by a dangerous margin.[48] But far from being able to reduce the former, events piled on the pressure. In June a revolt in Mesopotamia demanded more troops, and unrest in Egypt following the publication of Lord Milner's report suggesting that the country should receive conditional independence meant that Wilson's pleas to Field Marshal Allenby to release troops for Persia fell on deaf ears. If an overstretched military machine was incapable of realising Wilson's schemes for the reconquest of Ireland, then the political situation at home made his ideas even more far-fetched. The summer and autumn of 1920 saw the miners, railwaymen and dockers come together in the 'Triple Alliance', raising the spectre of unrest at home.[49] The strike weapon was used to foil Churchill's plan to send aid to the Poles in their struggle against Bolshevism, and the situation made it impossible to denude the mainland of troops in the way that would have been necessary to meet the demands of the Viceroy, Lord French, and the GOC, General Macready, for the declaration of martial law.[50]

Churchill found Wilson's attitude of 'deploring' Government policy in Ireland 'extremely unhelpful', especially as he had no concrete suggestions to make.[51] It was no use simply 'declaring war' on Sinn Fein without a plan of campaign.[52] Wilson had no faith in the scheme put forward by General Tudor, chief of the RIC, for a 'counter-murder association', and was amazed that Lloyd George supported it. He thought such a policy 'insane' and was perturbed to hear that Churchill, whilst in general agreement, 'evidently had some lingering hope of our "rough handling" of the Sinn Feins'.[53] When the Cabinet discussed the matter on 23 July, Churchill advocated a 'trial of strength' with Sinn Fein, wanting to raise an army of 30,000 men in Ulster.[54] This was impossible, but the volunteer force which Churchill had suggested swelled the ranks of the forces available to General Tudor. These 'Black and Tans' as they were known, because their uniforms were a combination of army and police outfits, formed, along with the 'auxiliary force', or the 'auxis', the backbone of the 'counter-murder association'.

For terrorists to call themselves freedom fighters is a licence to behave in the vilest ways, and the activities of the IRA during 1920 bore witness to this fact; but for a government to resort to similar tactics, under the subterfuge that it is endeavouring to maintain law and order, is a dangerous course of action. Wilson first heard of the activities of the Black and Tans in late August and he told Churchill that their 'counter-terror' tactics were 'a scandal'. Churchill bristled, declaring that they were 'honourable and gallant officers'.[55] He resisted pressure from Wilson to call a halt to their activities, taking the view that 'with patience and firmness' the murder-gangs of the IRA could be defeated and Ireland restored to a state in which self-government could be safely conceded – with Ulster being partitioned from the rest of the island.[56]

Churchill's policy towards Ireland was, then, at one with his general attitude towards the problems which beset the Empire – no surrender. But in the War Cabinet system he lacked any control over policy. The first he knew of Milner's proposals for giving Egypt conditional independence was when he read about them in the newspapers on 23 August. He had long protested to Lloyd George about the deficiencies of the War Cabinet, and had even contemplated resigning in 1919 over the issue,[57] but this latest proof of the invidiousness of his position stung him to action. The effect of the proposals on Ireland and India could be most serious, he warned Lloyd George on 24 August.[58]

Churchill's views on these matters brought him even closer to the 'die-hard' wing of the Conservative Party, at least in spirit. In flesh they were kept apart by their long-standing mutual antipathy, and the fact that the latter was highly critical of aspects of the Government's policy, including its treatment of Dyer, which Churchill had defended. Not that Churchill was happy with policy which he was expected to defend without having any say in its formulation. As the situation in Ireland worsened, Churchill wanted to abandon Lloyd George's subterfuges and come out in support of an official policy of reprisals against the IRA; a line which, for political reasons, the Prime Minister refused to sanction.[59] Churchill was even more unhappy about the Cabinet's decision to open trade talks with the Bolsheviks in November,[60] telling Birkenhead that he might resign on the issue. F.E. persuaded him out of such a drastic step, arguing that if he did so, he would 'find yourself the hero of the *Morning Post* and the leader of some thirty Tories in the House of Commons'.[61] With extreme reluctance Churchill acquiesced. But Birkenhead overstated his case when he wrote that the Tories who would have supported Churchill would have disagreed with him on ninety per cent of other matters.

Churchill's dissatisfaction was assuaged to some extent by the reintroduction of the old Cabinet system in November, but Lloyd George's Presidential style of governing prevented any real rapprochement between the two men. The whole thrust of Lloyd George's foreign policy, conciliating the Bolsheviks whilst imposing a harsh peace on Germany, was 'very near the reverse' of what Churchill would like to have done. He was no happier with Lloyd George's policy in Turkey, which consisted of supporting the Greeks in imposing the Treaty of Sèvres, which gave them parts of Asiatic Turkey. It is an indication of their relationship that Churchill felt bound to ask Lloyd George not to take his criticisms in 'ill part' and to protest, 'I am sincerely desirous of continuing to work with you.'[62] A similar mixture of deference and discontent characterised another note to the Prime Minister on the same subject on 4 December. 'No doubt my opinions seem a very unimportant thing,' Churchill began, asking him not to 'be vexed with me' for expressing the view that the Government's policy was plain wrong.[63]

Churchill's remonstrance to Lloyd George showed how adversity had finally taught him valuable political lessons. 'When one had reached the summit of power and surmounted so many obstacles, there is a danger of becoming convinced that one can do anything one likes'; 'no doubt,' Churchill conceded in an untoward burst of humility and real insight, 'I in any time of important affairs was led astray like this.' Using himself as an example, he warned the Prime Minister of the dangers of hubris. But his insight went even deeper. He reminded his old friend that all his 'great success and overwhelming personal power have come from a junction between your Liberal followers and the Conservative party', a union now endangered by pursuing policies which alienated the latter. The Turks ought to be supported and the Bolsheviks opposed. He warned Lloyd George that 'Conservatism is getting stronger all over the world' and that 'in this country you will find a continually stiffer line taken by the Tory Party in its relations to us', just at the time when his old radical supporters were alienated by his policy in Ireland.

Lloyd George would have done well to have heeded Churchill's counsel, for his own discontent had given him an insight into that of others, but the Prime Minister was indeed a victim of hubris. In his letter Churchill had disclaimed any personal ambitions – 'Office has not now the same attraction for me' – but in that he overestimated his own altruism. What Churchill had correctly discerned was that the 'Coaly Libs' were, in the aftermath of the failure of the fusion talks, totally dependent upon Conservative support for Lloyd George – and that this support was, in turn, dependent upon the Prime Minister delivering the goods politically, something which he was now failing to do.

The tone of Churchill's letter suggests, as he later told Wilson, that he felt that his differences with Lloyd George were such that he could not go on for much longer at the War Office.[64] The Prime Minister evidently was of the same opinion. Churchill's name had been canvassed by Montagu as a 'risky' choice for Viceroy: 'It might result in a great failure. It might be a great success. Whichever it was, it would be great.'[65] Lloyd George preferred not to take the risk. The two men were at odds over policy in Turkey, Russia and Mesopotamia, and their differences were not superficial, but stemmed from very different attitudes towards the priorities to be accorded to 'guns' and 'butter'. On New Year's Day, at Philip Sassoon's house near Lympne, Lloyd George suggested to Churchill that he might like to take the Colonial Office. Churchill would have been less flattered if he had known that the Office had recently been offered to, and refused by, Lord Derby.[66] After some thought, he accepted – but only on condition that it became, in effect, an expanded 'Middle Eastern Department' with responsibility for the area between Egypt and India;[67] an 'Asiatic Foreign Office', as the Foreign Secretary, Lord Curzon, called it in alarm.

Churchill's plans for his new office were bound to bring him into conflict with both the India and the Foreign Offices. It was ironic that, having been critical of British involvement in Mesopotamia – 'thankless deserts' into which 'we . . . go on pouring armies and treasure'[68] – he was now charged with the task of making political sense out of Britain's position there; without a 'Middle Eastern Department', Churchill did not see how this could be done.[69] He took up his new office in February 1921 with two battles to fight: a bureaucratic one to establish the extended spheres of influence for himself, and another one to sort out the conflicting claims being made on Britain by the Arab states. The best way to do the latter, Churchill decided, was to take himself off to Cairo to see matters for himself.

Unionists such as the retiring Colonial Secretary, Lord Milner, and his acolyte, Leo Amery, had seen the Middle East as an area for the expansion of British power once the Ottoman Empire had been defeated,[70] and at the end of the war it was the area in which Britain had gained most territory. But the manner of the British acquisitions created problems in itself, quite apart from those inherent in the region. During the war the British had made commitments to the Sherif of Mecca, signed an agreement with the French and put forward the Balfour Declaration promising the Jews a homeland in Palestine. At the war's conclusion they had found that these three were not wholly reconcilable, one with another:[71] 'The British sold the same horse, or at least parts of the same horse, twice, once to the Arabs, once to the French.'[72] Britain had received Palestine and Mesopotamia as 'mandated territories' from the League of Nations, but she still had to face claims from the Sherif for an 'Arab Empire' and deal with the anomalous position of Egypt. These problems now landed in Churchill's in-tray, and he had the chance to try to create a settlement which would preserve British power in the region.

As Secretary of State for War, Churchill had experienced the frustrations of trying to exert military control over 'these thankless deserts' at a time when the Government and the press were clamouring for 'economy', and the Middle Eastern settlement which he planned was based upon the belief that 'no province in the British Empire has ever been acquired by marching in and maintaining a large regular army at the expense of the British Exchequer', but rather by 'careful and skilful improvisations adapted to special needs'. In this time-honoured tradition of imperialism on the cheap, Churchill, influenced in part by his new adviser, T. E. Lawrence ('of Arabia' fame) proposed to set up an 'Arab Government' at Baghdad, which would be 'independent' – under British influence.[73] It was a valiant attempt to make bricks with precious little straw, and Churchill threw himself into the task. In early March he set out for Cairo, where he presided over the settlement, at least for the moment, of his new Empire. But whilst he dwelt in hotels of 'bronze and marble',[74] and parlayed with descendants of the Prophet over lands which had been civilised when the British had lived in wattle-and-daub huts, events in London were depriving the great pasha of what he saw as his own rights.

16

Decline

Churchill's preoccupations with coming to grips with his new responsibilities had not lessened his disagreements with Lloyd George, particularly over the latter's support for the Greeks in Turkey. Churchill took the view, as did other Ministers including Montagu and Curzon, that Britain could not afford to be on bad terms with the Turks and the Russians. Indeed, he felt so strongly that on 24 January 1921 he wrote Lloyd George a letter on the subject, hinting that he might have to resign on the issue; but he decided against sending it.[1] Had he done so he would have added appreciably to Lloyd George's woes.

The Government's lack of success in any of its policies was beginning to take its toll. Events in Ireland had, as Churchill had warned him, alienated many of Lloyd George's natural Liberal supporters, but it had also led to attacks from the right wing of the Conservative Party, in particular from the head of the House of Cecil, Lord Salisbury.[2] The collapse of the brief post-war boom, exemplified in the rise in unemployment to over two million during 1921, placed the coalition under more pressure, and its loss of Dover to an 'anti-waste' candidate run by Rothermere and the popular demagogue, Horatio Bottomley, helped to demonstrate the 'vulnerability' of the coalition.[3] The price for the failure of fusion was now being paid.[4]

Derby's refusal to take the Colonial Office in December was, in itself, a bad sign for the Prime Minister. Under a genial 'bluff John Bull' exterior, Derby was an intriguer[5] and a political weather-vane. Soon after refusing Lloyd George's offer, he made a speech at the Liverpool Conservative Club in which he stated his belief in 'the sound policy of Conservatism' and declared that he would live and die a 'Conservative'.[6] Given the attacks on the coalition, Conservative forces rallied around Lords Salisbury and Selborne for their foreign and Irish policies; this looked suspiciously like a coded attack on the Prime Minister. In late January rumours were rife that Derby intended to set up a new Party, and one variant on them had him becoming Prime Minister with Churchill as his leader in the Commons.[7] Derby denied such stories, but he had been cultivating Churchill since December, sympathising with his views on Turkey, and it is perhaps significant that the stories should have spread at the same time that Churchill was writing his unsent letter of resignation.[8] But Derby's protestations of innocence, whilst not wholly convincing, can be taken as an indication of his realisation that as long as Lloyd George and Bonar Law co-operated closely, the coalition was firmly in place.[9]

Then, on 17 March, Bonar Law decided to retire for reasons of ill-health. Lord Crawford, the former Unionist Chief Whip (now Chancellor of the Duchy of Lancaster), was right to conclude that 'his departure weakens the Coalition as a parliamentary force'.[10] Bonar Law paid more than lip-service to backbench opinion, and he had the respect of his supporters for it; and his importance as a link between the Government and its Parliamentary majority had grown in proportion to Lloyd George's Presidential manner. His replacement was Austen Chamberlain. But where Bonar Law had given ballast to a coalition badly in need of it, Chamberlain brought only a great name: 'Nothing in my head I bring, only to my name I cling.'[11] Chamberlain was a worthy figure, but he was, as Balfour cruelly commented, 'a bore',[12] who lived up to Birkenhead's jibe that 'Austen always played the game, and he always lost it.'[13] Chamberlain was fully committed to the coalition, seeing it as the only hope against the rising tide of Socialism; he sought to nail his colours to the mast – only to find that he had nailed his trousers with them.[14] Although Lloyd George was not to appreciate the fact until it was too late, in losing Bonar Law he had lost the sheet anchor of his coalition.

Lloyd George's loss was Churchill's opportunity. Not only did it remove from the leadership of the Conservative Party a man who was profoundly antipathetic to him, but Chamberlain's elevation left the Exchequer open. That Churchill should have been in Cairo at such a time was 'the joke of the moment', according to Frances Stevenson.[15] He wanted the Exchequer[16] and was correspondingly affronted when Lloyd George gave it to Sir Robert Horne, a political newcomer who was that rarest of things, 'a Scotch cad'. Chamberlain noticed that upon his return Churchill was 'as cross as a bear with a sore head'.[17] Where once he had written to the Prime Minister as 'My dear David' (one of the few to do so), he now began his letters 'Dear Prime Minister';[18] they 'looked out on one another like two distant snow-clad mountain peaks'.[19]

Lloyd George had presumed too far in his hubris. Churchill joined his old friend Birkenhead, the Secretary of State for India, Montagu, and the Foreign Secretary, Curzon, in resenting the Prime Minister's methods and his policies. Birkenhead was piqued at the way Lloyd George had manipulated the recent appointment of the Lord Chief Justice and at his exclusion from real power.[20] Montagu thought, like Churchill, that the Prime Minister's policy towards Turkey was wrong-headed, and he feared that for Britain, as the 'greatest Muslim power in the world', to pursue an anti-Turkish policy would be fatal to her prestige in India.[21] Curzon was simply tired of Lloyd George's domination of foreign policy; 'he wants his For[eig]n Sec[retary] to be a valet, almost a drudge,' he wrote to his wife on 22 April.[22] Constantly vexed by the Prime Minister's treatment, Curzon 'often talked of resignation; but always when he reached the brink of the precipice and looked over, he turned back'.[23] His career had been blighted by his resignation from the Viceroyalty in 1905, and he would not willingly tread that road again. Lloyd George was fortunate that the four men did not combine against him, but such combustible material could not lie about the Cabinet room without attracting sparks; Beaverbrook, who wanted to see a purely Conservative Government under Bonar Law replace the coalition, sought to apply the match.

He tried to interest Bonar Law in returning to public life, telling him of Lloyd George's behaviour and that 'Winston is very-very-very angry and F.E. is as bitter as Winston is angry.' By May he was noting with glee that Birkenhead was intending to challenge Chamberlain's leadership of the Party, a development which would split the coalition.[24] Rumours abounded about 'plots' against the Prime Minister, and Lloyd George, well aware of Beaverbrook's intrigues, told Riddell that he would not be surprised if Winston resigned and coalesced with Birkenhead and those Conservatives who were 'tired of the LG regime because they think it too democratic'.[25] If there was a 'plot' against Lloyd George, as Beaverbrook alleged, then the conspirators so bungled their attempt that Lloyd George had no difficulty dividing and ruling those who would have overthrown him.

On 25 May Churchill's carping came to a head when he told the Prime Minister that he intended to oppose the Government's policy towards Ireland. Lloyd George told him that he could do so at once, as he intended to bring the matter forward immediately; this, he thought, would 'put Winston rather in a fix', as it would require him to commit himself before he had had time 'to work up his Cabal'.[26] He was more than half inclined to let Churchill go as he was 'sick' of constant complaints,[27] but he decided, instead, to 'detach F.E. from Winston'.[28] If Churchill was part of a conspiracy, his actions confirm Asquith's view that he was a 'child' in such matters; if he was not, it illustrates Asquith's dictum that Churchill would never reach the top because he failed to inspire trust.

According to Beaverbrook, the 'plot' centred around the figure of Dr Addison, whose loss of his post as Minister of Health marked the effective end of any efforts to build 'homes' for the 'heroes'.[29] In an attempt to save face and prevent a diminution of the Liberal content of the coalition, Lloyd George had appointed Addison Minister without Portfolio at a salary of £5,000, something which the 'anti-waste' campaigners criticised as a 'reward for incompetence'[30] and Salisbury's Tories attacked as an abuse of power.[31] On 9 June Chamberlain told Lloyd George that 'an undoubted majority of Conservatives is likely to go into the lobby against us' in a vote on Addison's salary.[32] Addison did not help matters when, in a newspaper interview on 15 June, he claimed that he was being driven out by Conservatives who wanted to weaken the Liberal element in the Government; he had, Chamberlain told Lloyd George, 'put in the fire what little fat still remained out of it'.[33] Beaverbrook, who liked to imagine that he had played a great role in bringing down Asquith, and now fondly imagined that he could repeat the trick, later wrote that 'Churchill would be the candidate whom Birkenhead and others would put forward for the Premiership'.[34]

Beaverbrook is the only source for this tale, and if he believed what he wrote, it is clear why the 'plot' failed. Churchill's attitudes towards Russia and the Empire may have been close to those held by many Conservatives, but it was folly to suppose that they would have consented to be led by him; most Conservatives would have agreed with Crawford's remark that, though 'I don't lay much store on Winston's co-operation, Lloyd George has been a pillar of strength to the community.'[35] Those who did not would not have accepted one Liberal in place of another, for they were men like Salisbury and Selborne who wanted a Conservative Government.[36] Nor was there any more chance that they would be attracted to Birkenhead as a leader; his manners, morals and political sensibilities were alien to a man like Salisbury, whose elevation of mind and Anglicanism were exceeded only by a political virtue which, too long-preserved, made him the Parliamentary equivalent of a dried-up spinster. As Crawford put it: 'I don't mind criticism in the least, but I rather resent this kind of thing from one who at a moment of stress was asked to give the Government the benefit of his advice – but refused to take his share of responsibility.'[37] Only a foreigner like Beaverbrook could have imagined that Cecilian Conservatism would consent to be led by two representatives of the 'Tory Democracy' strain; especially when one was a distrusted renegade of notoriously bad judgment, and the other an arrogant drunk, whose temper had not been improved by his temporary abstention from the bottle.

But perhaps there was no 'plot', at least outside of the imaginations of Beaverbrook and the Prime Minister. Lloyd George certainly believed that there were 'intrigues seething everywhere',[38] and, at least in his own mind, did 'something skilful' to crush them.[39] Imagining that Birkenhead was going to 'make a sensational statement off his own bat on fiscal autonomy', Lloyd George asked him what he was going to say, thus, in his own mind, scotching the possibility of F.E. saying something different; it is hard not to concur with the comment of Birkenhead's latest biographer that this vision of Lloyd George 'congratulating himself to Frances for his cunning in preventing F.E. from saying something he was most unlikely to have ever dreamed of saying illustrates the fantasy world Prime Ministers, sometimes inhabit';[40] and, he might have added, in which Beaverbrook habitually dwelt.

To complete the 'Alice in Wonderland' picture, Lloyd George had his press secretary give the *Manchester Guardian* his version of the 'plot', from which it appears that he thought that Churchill's last-minute withdrawal had foiled the conspiracy.[41] When the article appeared on 23 June, Birkenhead wrote to Lloyd George at once, calling it a 'tissue of lies from beginning to end'.[42] But Lloyd George was not convinced, thinking that the new Viscount was 'protesting too much'. If Birkenhead was under suspicion because of his letter, then so was Churchill – because he had not written one: 'D. says that that Winston does not tell actual lies, & that is why he will not deny it. But F.E. does not care what lies he tells';[43] it was hard to win when the Prime Minister was having one of his bouts of paranoia.

However, even paranoiacs have enemies, and Lloyd George realised that he needed to do something to win over the malcontents. But despite its various troubles, the coalition was in no real danger. Selborne disagreed with Salisbury's certainty that 'the Government is toppling to its fall', reminding him that the coalition 'has never been popular with the Unionist Party', but that most Unionists were still of the opinion that 'today there ought to be only two parties in the state, those who are in favour of the Labour Party or Socialists, and those who are opposed to them'; like it or not, this meant co-operating with 'Liberals who are ready to oppose Socialists'. Selborne's grasp of political realities was a good deal firmer than his brother-in-law's, and he warned him that any attempt to withdraw the Unionists from the coalition would merely split the Party, 'which could advantage nobody except ... Labour'. As long as Austen Chamberlain and Horne stayed with Lloyd George, he was safe; or so it seemed.[44]

Lloyd George came to a very similar conclusion. He defused the Addison situation with an adroit appeal for support in the Commons, combined with a proposal to reduce the Minister's salary by more than the £2,000 demanded by his opponents – and then only guaranteed until the end of the session. This saved his skin, but did his reputation little good.[45] The opportunity to bind Churchill and Birkenhead more closely to him came with his decision to open negotiations with Sinn Fein and its leader, Eamon De Valera, in July.

A truce was declared on 11 July and, three days later, Lloyd George had his first talks with De Valera. Opinion was bitterly divided on the merits of opening formal talks with De Valera. Salisbury, characteristically, took the view that the Government had 'asked rebels dripping with the blood of assassinated loyalists to negotiate with them' and wanted to stop them, but could not work out how to do so.[46] Birkenhead, who like Churchill had supported the Black and Tans, and whose pre-war fame as Carson's 'Galloper' had made him a leading opponent of the Nationalists, agreed to the invitation to De Valera only because he did not think anything would come of it; but once the talks had begun, he put his reputation at risk by going along with the Prime Minister's proposals that southern Ireland must be offered the status of a self-governing dominion.[47] Whilst Birkenhead equivocated in the early stages of the negotiations, Churchill, who had 'finally acknowledged the failure of the policy of force', went along with the Prime Minister.[48] Both Churchill and Birkenhead were made members of the nine-man Ministerial team which was set up to deal with the Irish question, and they both formed part of the British negotiating team which opened talks in October.[49]

Lloyd George's adroitness has to be admired. Temperamentally both F.E.

and Churchill had favoured coercion, and had they been left out of the formulation of Irish policy, either of them might have led a revolt against the Prime Minister on the issue. But as it was, they were both deeply embroiled in that policy, something which divided them from many Unionists and, at the same time, tied them closer to the existence of the coalition. The chances of any 'conspiracy' against Lloyd George being mounted were further lessened by the fact that over the summer Curzon became almost as exasperated with Churchill's interference in the affairs of the Foreign Office as he was with that of the Prime Minister.[50] So, although both men continued to be unhappy with Lloyd George's support for the Greeks in Turkey, there was little chance of their coming together – although they could both take some comfort (and alarm) from Turkish successes over the Greeks.[51] Neither man was particularly happy with the fourth discontented Minister, Edwin Montagu; if Curzon and Churchill had their differences over departmental boundaries, they were in agreement in thinking that Montagu was going too fast in fostering Indian self-government.[52]

Ireland was to draw Churchill closer to the centre of the coalition than he had ever been. He continued to disagree with the Prime Minister over the summer – Turkey and the Government's failures at home[53] proving particularly thorny topics; but once Churchill was brought into the team which began negotiations with the Irish on 11 October, he and the Prime Minister, along with Birkenhead and Chamberlain, were all pulled together, not only by the talks, but by a common need for mutual support in the face of growing Unionist hostility.

Churchill's attitude could have been predicted; once it had been decided to negotiate, then, whilst he was prepared to use force as a last resort if the Irish proved intransigent, he urged both sides to make concessions in order to reach an agreement.[54] One of his main concerns was that the Irish should allow the British to keep control of strategic ports and docks; once the Irish had made this concession, he even seemed willing to compromise on the vital question of the position of Ulster.[55] The Irish, for their part, made the expected difficulties over partition and acceptance of any vestige of British sovereignty, and, as Churchill later commented, 'no one could predict the fortunes of a single day'.[56]

One reason why Lloyd George had wanted Birkenhead as part of the negotiating team, apart from the benefits to be derived from his legal skill, was as a sop to Unionist opinion, but in the event the Lord Chancellor simply succeeded in attracting to himself some of the odium which his former associates were wont to lavish on the Prime Minister. Many Unionists went along with the idea of the talks for reasons similar to Selborne's: 'I think the Irish are a wholly irrational, incomprehensible and contemptible race, and I do not regard it as wholly impossible that they may be slobbering the King with loyalty (!) before twelve months are passed';[57] but once they were under way, then opposition grew and, most ominously of all in view of the coalition's dependence upon Unionist support, there were rumours that Bonar Law would lead the 'die-hards'.[58]

Faced with this, and with intransigence from the Irish, Lloyd George was tempted to throw in his hand; his only real help, he complained, came from Birkenhead – 'Winston is contributng nothing – he is just not going over to the other side.'[59] But on the same day that Lloyd George was telling his mistress this, Churchill was writing to urge him not to resign.[60] Churchill wrote that 'most men sink into insignificance when they quit office. Very insignificant men gain it when they obtain it.' Resignation would mean a purely Conservative Government under Bonar Law and an election in which the choice would be between a 'reactionary' government and the Labour Party. In these circumstances it behoved them to go on until, and unless, Parliament refused to accept a final settlement. It is significant that Churchill's arguments were based on domestic English political considerations and not on the merits of the plan being discussed; Ireland had always been an English political problem for Churchill – indeed, his geography of the island was faulty enough for him to imagine that Lough Swilly was in northern Ireland rather than in Donegal.[61]

Churchill's part in the final negotiations was a minor one, but he was in 10 Downing Street when the treaty was signed in the early hours of 6 December. Birkenhead told the Irish leader, Michael Collins: 'I may have signed my political death-warrant tonight', to which he received the sombre reply: 'I may have signed my actual death-warrant'; both men were correct.[62] Hard-line Republicans felt that they had been betrayed, and a few months later Collins was murdered in one of the ambushes which marked the start of the Irish civil war. All Birkenhead faced, by contrast, was character-assassination. Carson, in his maiden speech in the Lords on 14 December, bitterly attacked his former 'Galloper', drawing from him the jibe that Carson's 'constructive attempt at statesmanship would be immature on the lips of an hysterical school-girl'.[63]

Churchill's defence of the treaty in the Commons the following day was one of his most effective speeches, thus proving the truth of his own comment that 'the essence of statesmanship is platitude'.[64] It was an eloquent appeal for all men of goodwill to support the treaty, which, he believed, would mark a new era in Anglo-Irish relations. It was a characteristic utterance which actually said more about Churchill's political philosophy than it did about his understanding of the Irish problem. His belief in the power of rationality and 'progress' is nowhere more apparent than in his belief that Ulstermen would eventually put the past behind them and agree to join an all-Ireland federation, and that the 'main body of Irish and British opinion' could put an end to 'these fanatical quarrels'; and his belief that the 'spirit of Ireland' could be 'reconciled' to 'the Empire' demonstrated both his great heart – and his complete incomprehension of the problem he had been dealing with.[65] Lacking both fanaticism and religion, Churchill was singularly ill-placed to understand those over-endowed with both.

Churchill's speech was impressive, but what convinced most Unionists to go along with the treaty was Bonar Law's declaration that he supported it.[66] The re-emergence of the former Conservative leader was of crucial importance, and Salisbury's comment that 'if Bonar Law comes again into the arena we have at last got a leader in the Commons even if we do not turn the Government out at this moment',[67] showed that his long-preserved political celibacy had not totally dulled his wits. Lloyd George, who practised no form of celibacy and whom no one could have accused of being slow-witted, wondered whether he ought to try to bring Bonar Law back into the Government, or whether he should, perhaps, go for an election on the back of his Irish triumph.[68]

Birkenhead was strongly in favour of an immediate election, which would, he hoped, strengthen the basis of the coalition by forcing its component parts into 'fusion', as they could hardly fight the election under different banners. Lloyd George did not take much convincing that this was the most sensible course to take, and the two of them persuaded Chamberlain and Churchill of its merits over dinner at Birkenhead's 'palace' in Grosvenor Gardens on 20 December.[69] But two Liberals and a drunken Unionist were not the best judges of the likely reaction of the Unionist Party, and Chamberlain's reluctance was founded on the fact that he had a better idea of how it might react; not, as events were to show, a much better idea, just a better one.

Sir George Younger, the Party Chairman, told him bluntly on Christmas Eve that the Party would not tolerate another election and would regard an early dissolution of Parliament as 'unduly cynical'; as for F.E.'s opinion, Younger took the view that he was 'as usual looking after "No. 1"';[70] other soundings told a similar story. Lloyd George's attempt to force the pace by orchestrating a press campaign in favour of an early election backfired, producing 'an avalanche' of letters from Conservative MPs to Chamberlain protesting at the idea. Even worse, from the Prime Minister's point of view, was a letter from Younger to the constituency organisations on 11 January which made future Unionist support conditional upon the coalition dealing with the reform of the House of Lords.[71] Lloyd George thought that Younger had 'behaved disgracefully' in making public advice he had been asked for in private;[72] Birkenhead dismissed him loftily as the 'cabin boy' who was trying to take over the ship;[73] but the damage was done. Lloyd George pondered the relative merits of resignation, leaving Chamberlain to form a government, or of inviting Bonar Law into the Cabinet as Foreign Secretary; the first alternative was rather drastic, so he decided in favour of the second.[74]

Churchill, who was undecided on the merits of an immediate election, did not welcome the prospect of the return of his old enemy; but he need not have worried on either score: Bonar Law refused to join the Government, and Lloyd George and Chamberlain took the view that Younger's intervention made an immediate election impossible.

Churchill was not one of the innermost circle which made the decision, announced on 19 January, that there would be no election.[75] His indecision as to the desirability of an election was understandable. Circumstances were, for the moment, propitious: the Government had just concluded successful naval talks in Washington with America, France and Japan; the Irish treaty, whilst in the bag, might prove difficult to implement, and there were already signs that De Valera was moving away from its acceptance and that there would be difficulty in getting it adopted peacefully; Anglo-Soviet relations were improving, and Lloyd George had suggested an international conference at Genoa, which would convene in March to discuss economic and political relations with the Russians: 'now truly was the time for the Coalition to pull itself together and exploit the peace issue to see[k] a new and wider mandate'.[76] Moreover, as a 'Coaly Lib', Churchill was anxious to be able to take advantage of the superior constituency organisation of the Unionists. He remained firmly of the opinion that the coalition was the only bulwark against Bolshevism and he warned the National Liberal Council in January of the dangers of disunity in the face of the Socialist Labour Party. He could see no good in the Asquithian Liberals, whom he derided as men who had 'stood about with their hands in their pockets' in the face of the problems which the Government was tackling; this was a trifle unfair, but he had never forgiven Asquith for the way he had been treated in 1915.[77]

But a belief in the value of the coalition was not necessarily a vote of confidence in the Prime Minister. Churchill was delighted with the extra responsibility with which Lloyd George loaded him as he went off to sort out the affairs of Europe: Chairman of the Cabinet Committees on Ireland and on the Geddes report on future defence expenditure, Churchill's standing in the Government was greater than it had ever been; but he was not entirely happy. The Geddes report, which recommended swingeing cuts in defence spending, went too far for Churchill, and he successfully managed to protect the armed forces from the worst effects of it; however, he did not feel 'the slightest confidence' in Lloyd George's 'judgement', taking the view that the report was primarily the consequence of his pandering to the 'anti-waste' campaigns of 'ignorant and pliable newspapers'.[78] Such views made him sympathetic to Unionists like Henry Wilson, who regarded Lloyd George as a threat to the Empire.[79]

Wilson, who was about to retire as Chief of the Imperial General Staff and join the Commons as MP for North Down, saw the appeasement of nationalism in Ireland, India and Egypt as all part of the same problem: 'either we govern other people or they will govern us',[80] and at his final official meeting with Churchill he 'rubbed this in'. Churchill admitted 'that he did not know where the devil we had got ourselves to'.[81] He, like Wilson, was 'furious that the English attitude should be one of abdication and fighting a rearguard action'. Victor Cazalet, who lunched with him on 11 April, recorded that he was 'becoming more of a Conservative every day, and is now out to lead the Conservative Party'; but Churchill's own comment on this was that he was 'Conservative in principle but liberal in sympathy'.[82]

Churchill was profoundly opposed to extending economic aid to the 'tyrannic Government' of the 'Jew Commissars',[83] and tried to lay down conditions on which Lloyd George would extend aid to the Soviets at the Genoa Conference.[84] This brought him into fresh conflict with the Prime Minister at a time when relations between the two men were already strained.

Lloyd George's suspicions of Churchill were never far beneath the surface. In late January Churchill pressed him to move Horne from the Exchequer, which Lloyd George took as a sign that Churchill was 'still nursing his ambition'. He saw, in Churchill's opposition to the Geddes proposals, a deep plot to 'defeat' Geddes and then 'blame Horne for not economising'.[85] This probably tells us more about Lloyd George's mental processes than it does about Churchill's motives, which were, as we have seen, tied up with his desire for a strong imperial policy. The two men clashed over the Geddes report in Cabinet on 20 February, when Churchill accused Lloyd George of being 'ungrateful' for the work which he was doing on behalf of the Government; despite an apology, Churchill was not invited to the next meeting of the Finance Committee of the Cabinet.[86]

Churchill's anger is understandable. Not only was he bearing the brunt of newspaper attacks that his opposition to the Geddes proposals was based upon his love of war, but he was also carrying the burden of the Irish treaty. Although probably not meant as such, Churchill's comment to Riddell in early February that 'everyone in Ireland appeared to be unreasonable' showed a distinct advance in understanding the problem confronting him, even if he never quite grasped its inwardness, something revealed by his remark that: 'the Irish will not recognise that they, like every other civilised people, must adopt reasonable methods for settling differences';[87] the optimism and the limitations of Liberalism are here equally exposed.

The Irish declined to adopt the methods which Churchill considered suitable to a 'civilised people', preferring, instead, those which suggested that Salisbury's description of them as 'irrational, incomprehensible and contemptible' was not as wide of the mark as all that. The Irish parliament narrowly approved the treaty, but De Valera refused to accept it and went off into opposition. Within a few months, the Irish were murdering each other instead of the British, something which many Unionists regarded as preferable to the previous situation, but hardly a recommendation for Lloyd George's treaty.[88] Sir James Craig, the Prime Minister of Ulster, rejected the treaty and stalled over the boundary commission which Churchill wanted to set up to delineate the border, and so the IRA carried its murderous thuggery into the north, where it was met in kind.

Churchill's defence of the Irish treaty when he led for the Government on its second reading on 16 February was his third masterly performance in the House in the last eight months. Under the old War Cabinet system and the Lloyd George regime in general, the House of Commons had been treated with scant regard – and Ministers no better – something which had deprived Churchill of the effective use of his most powerful weapon, his oratory. But since the reinstatement of the old Cabinet system, he had thrice dominated the House in debate: in June 1921 over Mesopotamia, when even the estranged Lloyd George could not forbear to cheer;[89] again in December introducing the Irish Bill; and now, once more, he captured most of his audience. He assured Conservatives that no one in southern Ireland wanted a republic and that Britain would 'never' recognise one, adding that there was no question of abandoning Ulster.[90] None of this satisfied the extreme Unionists, but then nothing would; however, most MPs were impressed, with one recording that his 'very clever and unusually good-tempered handling of the problems' enabled him to make a 'great advance' in 'the opinion of the House'.[91]

Churchill regarded the policy which Lloyd George wanted to pursue towards the Soviets at Genoa as just that: 'it is not a national policy but only a purely personal LG affair'.[92] The issue raised in an acute form the dilemma which had confronted him in early January: how to support the coalition, of which he strongly approved, and a prime minister, whose policies he disapproved of. With Lloyd George's failure to win Unionist support for an election, he had cast around him for other expedients; these were not lacking, but it was difficult to see clearly which of them should be taken: he could resign altogether and try to become leader of a reunited Liberal Party; he could remain where he was and try to follow Birkenhead's advice about constructing an anti-Socialist bulwark; or he could resign from the Premiership, leaving Chamberlain to shoulder the blame as and when things went wrong. In characteristic fashion, Lloyd George 'tried to construct a position from which he could move with dignity in whichever direction he chose'.[93] He sought advice from his close colleagues, but more for the purpose of identifying their positions than for taking up one himself.

The position of the 'Coaly Libs' was not enviable. Their political organisation was rudimentary, and if they had to fight an election without the aid of the Unionist organisation outside Westminster, they would be in trouble.[94] They had been no more successful in establishing a philosophy. Some, like Montagu, looked towards Asquith with longing, whilst others, like Churchill, saw the coalition as an 'instrument of Government on the centre and the right'.[95] The two Liberals clashed in February over policy towards the Indian immigrants in Kenya; where Montagu wanted to give them greater equality,

Churchill joined publicly the ranks of those who criticised him for his lack of imperial spirit.[96] Since Montagu, as a Jew and an extreme Liberal, was a favourite hate-figure for the Tory right, this might have been taken as another sign that Churchill wanted an 'evolution to the right';[97] it was certainly a sign of the lack of unity within the ranks of the Lloyd George Liberals.

Churchill's advice to Lloyd George was to go to the country at the head of the coalition in the near future, or, if the Conservatives would not hear of this, then they should be asked to take over, with support from the 'Coaly Libs', provided that they did not pursue 'a deliberately reactionary policy'.[98] Having thus flushed out Churchill's views, which reflected the feeling among coalition Liberals that the Conservative leaders might not persist in their support for the coalition if there was a danger of splitting their Party, Lloyd George then tested this by offering, on 27 February, to step down from the Premiership in favour of Chamberlain.[99] Chamberlain was under a great deal of pressure from Younger, Salisbury and other elements in the Party to break away from the coalition, but, like Birkenhead, he did not believe that a Conservative Party shorn of Lloyd George could successfully fight the Socialists, so he refused the offer – thus becoming the only leader of the Party never to become Prime Minister.

The fluidity of the political situation is attested to by these manoeuvrings, but out of them seemed to come what Churchill wanted, which was a pledge that both wings of the coalition would fight the election 'as a government'.[100] The next few months were to suggest that this confidence was misplaced.

17

The Fall and After

Beaverbrook wrote of Lloyd George at this time: 'He did not seem to care which way he travelled providing he was in the driver's seat.'[1] But he did care, and he grew increasingly suspicious of Churchill as the rumours accumulated that he wanted to 'drive' the coalition vehicle to the right. Because Churchill's vision of the coalition was similar to that of Birkenhead and Chamberlain, stories that 'he means to join the Tories at the earliest possible moment'[2] were bound to circulate. His public rhetoric remained 'coalitionist', in favour of a 'National Government' which would be 'liberal, progressive and pacific' at home, but 'resolute' in upholding the 'traditions of the State' and 'the Empire'. However, all this amounted to little more than a parsonical condemnation of sin. But the cutting edge of his main public speeches, at a by-election in Loughborough, to a coalition meeting in Northampton in March, and to his constituents in Dundee in April was the same: the 'Socialist peril'; Socialists would 'coax and wheedle you into ruin' and Communists would 'ram ruin down your throat with a bayonet on the Russian plan'.[3] On this issue Churchill was sure of Conservative support, and it was here that he chose to challenge Lloyd George just before the Genoa conference.

One of the main criticisms of Lloyd George's admirers (and that even larger group of former admirers) was that under Conservative duress he had moved too far from 'progressivism'; the dismissal of Montagu in early March following his attack on the Prime Minister's Turkish policy seemed yet another surrender in this direction, weakening the coalition Liberals still further and providing a boost for the Asquithians.[4] Lloyd George meant, however, to 'fight' on the question of recognising the Soviet Government. It was, he told Frances Stevenson, 'the real test of whether the Coalition is to be progressive or reactionary', and if he had to resign, then 'I retire on a Liberal issue which I can go on fighting'; if he won, then 'the Coalition is definitely Liberal'.[5] Always suspicious of Churchill's 'Tory' tendencies, Lloyd George's paranoia was fanned by warnings from Beaverbrook about the possibility of an alliance between him and the 'die-hards'; 'at the present moment . . . [he] considers himself the heir to all the Caesars'.[6] His fears about Churchill seemed confirmed when Chamberlain reported on 21 March that he was threatening to resign on the issue of diplomatic recognition of the Soviets.[7] The spectre which haunted Lloyd George of Churchill ousting him and then playing second-in-command to Chamberlain in a right-wing coalition was not entirely fanciful. On 17 March a majority of Conservative MPs had voted against continuing the coalition.[8] Churchill dismissed this as unrepresentative of Tory feelings, but he had warned then that the Soviet question was the only one which could break the Government.[9] Now Chamberlain warned that if Churchill did go on the issue, thus seeming 'more Tory than the Tory Ministers', his situation would become 'impossible'.[10]

Lloyd George's response was, in effect, to tell Churchill to 'resign and be damned'.[11] 'I told you I thought Winston would be a real wrecker,' he told Horne on 22 March. To go to Genoa under Churchill's conditions would, he declared, 'be futile and humiliating in the extreme'.[12] 'The Cabinet', he told Chamberlain, 'must choose between Winston and me.'[13] Through leaks in the press Lloyd George conveyed a similar message, but rumours that Churchill would make the break in a speech at Northampton on 25 March alarmed Lloyd George almost as much as they did Chamberlain and Horne.[14] Birkenhead and Chamberlain both interceded to persuade Churchill not to do anything silly (though there is no sign that he had any intention of doing anything), and a compromise was hammered out in Cabinet, which meant, in effect, that there would be no full diplomatic recognition for Russia.[15]

Thus it was that an episode which had been meant by Lloyd George to demonstrate his Liberal credentials had, in fact, underlined Churchill's importance in the fluid politics of early 1922. Lloyd George had feared that his defection, coming as it did after that of Montagu and the eclipse of Addison, could wreck the 'Coaly Libs', whilst he, Chamberlain and Horne had all feared that he could wreck the whole coalition by an alliance with the right of the Conservative Party. As one commentator has put it, early 1922 marked the emergence of 'a Churchill who could not be easily distinguished from a Tory'.[16] But such a comment misses the essential point, that what made Churchill central to everyone's political calculations was precisely the fact that he could be 'distinguished from a Tory': a magnet for right-wing Liberals and an ally to right-wing Conservatives, he was the fugleman of coalitionism. The rumours which had him about to join the Conservatives were wide of the mark, because he considered the old Party labels irrelevant: 'the line of division is not on . . . old quarrels'; both Liberals and Conservatives had to unite in the face of the great new threat – Socialism. He was prepared to argue that 'Liberalism is the greatest form of Conservatism' and wanted the Party disputations of the past 'terminated'.[17]

But Churchill's position was only central as long as the Unionists placed more confidence in Lloyd George's ability to defeat the Socialists than they did in their own; the events of January had shown that this state of affairs was changing, and by the summer it had all but vanished.[18] Civil war in Ireland and the spread of terrorism to the mainland, with the assassination of Henry Wilson outside his home in Eaton Place, outraged Unionist opinion[19] and brought Bonar Law back into the political arena with scarcely veiled criticisms of the Government's policy.[20] Churchill won Conservative applause for his announcement on 26 June that the Government might have to regard the treaty as at an end if the terrorist campaign did not cease,[21] but the coalition's prestige was lowered. The problem was that Lloyd George appeared incapable of doing anything to revive it. All the great hopes that the Genoa conference would settle the outstanding issues in Europe came to naught, and the Prime Minister's habit of spending a great deal of his time at such conferences, which had once established him as a statesman, now showed that he was 'out of touch'.[22] To add to the Government's embarrassments, revelations about the sale of honours led to criticisms in the House in mid-July, and Lloyd George's halting response did nothing to clear the Government's name from the allegations, which were quite correct, that it had been trafficking in honours.[23]

Perhaps none of these blows was, in itself, fatal, but the cumulative effect was to raise considerable doubts within the Unionist ranks as to whether it was worthwhile maintaining a coalition so badly tarnished in reputation.[24] In response to complaints from junior Ministers, Chamberlain called a meeting on 3 August to listen to their arguments and, ostensibly, to put the case for the coalition. Unfortunately Birkenhead 'began by rating them for their impertinence' and 'went on to lecture them for their silliness and want of loyalty';[25] the 'vigour and virulence' of his arrogant attack 'caused desperate umbrage', and Crawford learnt afterwards that some junior Ministers 'considered his speech had gone further to smashing up the coalition government than any shortcomings of the Prime Minister'.[26] F.E.'s drunken outburst certainly ended whatever hopes he had had of becoming Conservative leader,[27] but it did not mean that the coalition was at an end; those who disliked it still had to find some issue of 'policy' upon which a break could be made.[28] What Lloyd George had to prove was that the Unionists still needed the 'coalition' label to sell themselves to the new democracy; what he provided, instead, was proof that the package he represented had passed its 'sell-by' date.

The question of just when to hold the general election was one which exercised the coalition's leaders during the late summer when they met at Beaverbrook's home at Cherkley on 26 August. Lloyd George accused Churchill of having opposed a January election because he had not wanted him to have a great personal triumph, a charge which 'was met with great resentment, but not with a denial'; the two men quarrelled so violently that Beaverbrook wondered whether they could 'ever work together again'.[29] His Lordship's fears ignored the necessities of political reality. In the aftermath of the Conservative débâcle of 3 August, rumour had it that the opponents of the coalition would take their case to the meeting of the Unionist National Association in November, where they could expect a sympathetic hearing. Birkenhead wanted an election in October to avoid this eventuality, and Lloyd George, who dined with Churchill on 11 September, was inclined to go in the same direction. Churchill would have preferred to stick things out until the summer, but was persuaded that an earlier appeal to the country was necessary. It was settled that there should be a meeting on 16 September at Chequers to discuss what should go into the manifesto.[30] During the meeting at Cherkley Beaverbrook had wanted to discuss the situation in Turkey, but had found Lloyd George's mind was focused on the election; by 16 September the Prime Minister had to give it a higher priority.

At the Treaty of Sèvres in 1920 the punitive policy towards Turkey sponsored by Lloyd George and Curzon had triumphed, with the Greeks being given huge slices of Turkish territory. But this victory for neo-Gladstonianism and Curzonian imperialism was short-lived.[31] Churchill had always opposed this policy, partly because as 'the greatest Mohammedan Power in the world' it behoved Britain to be on good terms with the Turks for the sake of Moslem opinion in India and the Middle East, and partly because he saw a nationalist Turkey as a barrier to the spread of Communism.[32] He had never been convinced that the Greeks possessed the military ability to prevail, and on 26 August a crushing Turkish victory proved him correct; as the Turks advanced on Constantinople the name of the Dardanelles returned to haunt Churchill's career. Despite his previous opposition to their policy, Churchill now agreed with Lloyd George and Curzon that there must be 'force behind our diplomacy' and that, if possible, a league of Balkan states must be gathered together to help Britain resist the Turks.[33]

There was no inconsistency here, in Churchill's eyes; 'in victory, magnanimity', but 'in defeat, defiance'.[34] He had just been arguing with Lloyd George and the War Office that Britain must reduce her armed forces in Mesopotamia (or Iraq as it was now being called) and rely upon air power,[35] but a commitment to war in Turkey was not inconsistent with this in his eyes. Although the Government should 'in future confine themselves to British interests', he believed that 'the Empire would put up some force to preserve Gallipoli, with the graves of so many of its soldiers';[36] in this he and the Cabinet were profoundly wrong. A long and rambling discussion left the Cabinet secretariat in some doubt as to what had been decided upon,[37] but Churchill had no doubts; he drafted a 'manifesto' of appeal to the Dominion's Premiers, from which it was obvious that the Cabinet was contemplating the 'prospect of renewed warfare on a grand scale'.[38]

At one level there was nothing wrong with the Cabinet's decision; indeed, it was even praiseworthy, for Ministers were expressing their willingness to use force to defend one of the peace treaties. Churchill thought that a combination of Liberal outrage at Turkish atrocities, and Conservative unwillingness to 'see the British flag fired on', would rally opinion behind the Government;[39] but he had miscalculated. With the exception of New Zealand, all the Dominions refused the request for aid, and public opinion at home was no more eager to embark on another war.[40] The *Daily Mail's* headline on 18

September: 'STOP THIS NEW WAR!', captured the public mood, as it did when it thundered that no Dominion soldier should be allowed to lose his life 'in order that Mr Winston Churchill may make a new Gallipoli'.[41] Amery summed up the opinion of many Unionists when he described the Government's '*pronunciamento*' as 'unfortunate' because 'we are bound to hand over Constantinople and Eastern Thrace to the Kemalists'; this 'final collapse of L.G.'s Near Eastern policy' would, he thought, weaken him greatly and 'may strengthen the movement for independence in the Unionist Party'.[42] Amery was correct. The crisis 'queer[ed] the pitch' for an election before the Unionist conference, with Younger insisting that Chamberlain should call a meeting of all Unionist Ministers in the near future to discuss the election issue.[43]

The assumption that Churchill was behind much of the Cabinet's bellicosity was not confined to public opinion and a partial view of Churchill's record. Arthur Lee, now First Lord of the Admiralty, recorded Churchill as telling him enviously on 23 September: 'Aren't you in luck to be at the Admiralty when there's a show on.'[44] Churchill could not understand why anyone should make a fuss about his 'manifesto' of 16 September, and when the Turks agreed to listen to Allied peace proposals on 23 September, he put their attitude down to the success of the hard line he was advocating.[45] He did not think that they would accept Curzon's 'Angora Note', which held out the offer of Constantinople and Eastern Thrace, if the Turks would settle the crisis peacefully – and he thought he discerned the sinister figure of Bolshevism egging them on.[46] When a Liberal revolt in Athens on 26 September overthrew the pro-German King Constantine, who had been responsible for the plight of the Greek armies, Churchill saw in prospect a war in which Britain would help the Liberal Prime Minister, Eleutherios Venizelos, defend the Greek homeland against the marauding Turks, who had already violated the neutral zone and were threatening General Harington and the British troops in Chanak. Hankey, who attended a meeting with him and Lloyd George on the evening of 27 September, recorded that he was 'violently Turko-phobe and even Phil-Hellene' and that 'all the talk was of war'.[47] Harington, who was heavily outnumbered, was told that there was no question of holding Chanak 'at all costs', and that he had to make his own mind up whether or not to withdraw; but it was made clear to him that 'we intend to support you with our full power', if it came to war.[48]

There then followed what Hankey characterised as a 'curious struggle'.[49] Compromises put forward by the British representative in Constantinople, Sir Horace Rumbold, and by the French were rejected at Cabinet on 29 September, and Harington was told to present the Turks with an ultimatum that unless they withdrew their forces, by a date to be fixed by him, there would be war. Churchill took the view that 'when Mustapha Kemal found he was up against people who would stand up to him, he might change his attitude'.[50] This was dangerous 'brinkmanship' and too much for the nervous

Curzon, who thought nothing of the 'worthless alliance' which Churchill and Lloyd George wanted with Greece.[51] Hankey thought that both men, along with Birkenhead, seemed to 'dread' Kemal accepting the Angora Note, which would mean 'losing our credit with the Greeks'.[52]

Tension grew on 30 September: on the one hand came indications that Kemal might be prepared to negotiate; on the other, there was no news as to whether the ultimatum had actually been delivered. The Cabinet met at five and waited an hour, hoping news would come through from Harington. Curzon, who saw the chance for a peaceful settlement, was worried by the attitude of the Prime Minister, Churchill and Birkenhead, who were 'bellicose – [they] almost demand war'.[53] Crawford, who had just joined the Cabinet, was warned by Churchill's successor at the War Office, Sir Laming Worthington-Evans, to expect a 'strong war-like tendency' when the Cabinet reassembled – so he was not surprised when 'there was';[54] nor was Hankey, who later overheard the Lord Chancellor, much the worse for drink, telling Chamberlain all about the 'manoeuvring' which he, Churchill and the Prime Minister had been doing earlier over dinner.

Crawford noticed that Birkenhead was 'very much flushed and excited' when the Cabinet reconvened at 10.30, and that Churchill was 'in a nervous condition'. The three men attacked 'Harington with varying violence'. A long telegram from the General was being decyphered as the Cabinet met, and from what was becoming known, it seemed that Harington had not handed over the ultimatum and was, instead, suggesting that they should respond to Kemal's willingness to have talks – which led F.E. and Lloyd George to berate 'political Generals'. Churchill thought that they should forthwith reject any meeting, but he got little support. Lloyd George also protested against 'whittling down' the Treaty of Sèvres, but when, by midnight, no intelligible decrypts of Harington's despatch had arrived, the Cabinet adjourned until the following morning.[55]

Crawford's account of the Cabinet meeting, which was not used by the official biographer, confirms Lee's suspicions as he left the meeting that 'L.G., Winston, Birkenhead, Horne, and even Austen, positively *want* hostilities to break out',[56] at least as far as the first three are concerned. Curzon had no doubt about their motives – they hoped, he thought, to force him into a position where he would have to resign, and his place could then be taken by Birkenhead.[57] Lloyd George's reasons might be many and varied, but his philhellene sentiments and Gladstonian distaste for the Turks disposed him, Crawford thought, in the direction he evidently wished to take. It seemed difficult to account for Churchill's actions in the same way, given his previous views, but perhaps he 'wants to recover a strategic prestige already lost at Gallipoli'.[58] 'The evidence amounts to a serious charge', F.E.'s latest biographer concludes, 'that the leading personalities of the Coalition really did want to involve Britain in renewed war with Turkey'.[59]

Churchill's attitude when the Cabinet reconvened the following morning certainly suggests that he was not best pleased with Harington. When the General's long telegram had finally been deciphered at 1.30 that morning, it revealed that he had not sent the ultimatum to Kemal, taking the view that, as the Turks had already begun a partial withdrawal, there was no point in doing so. Churchill had drafted a reply, which Crawford characterised as 'the most extraordinary tirade one had ever heard'. Harington was criticised for 'mixing himself up in political problems' and misleading Ministers about the military situation. It was 'a long polemical speech utterly unsuited to the occasion', and even by the time Churchill had finished, everyone 'perhaps including himself, saw that the thing was impossible'. The telegram was not sent, but Crawford thought it 'worth recording that it contained no syllable of relief at our escape from warfare'. Instead, Churchill pressed that 'in self-defence', it should be made clear that the Cabinet had only acted on the misleading advice of the men on the spot; but 'instead of welcoming the change Churchill (and the PM too) wanted to give Harington a good scolding'.[60]

Churchill did not believe that anything would come of the conference between the Turkish and Allied generals at Mudania on 3 October,[61] but he was wrong. War had been averted and public opinion was relieved – and not a little alarmed.

By 6 October Lloyd George, Birkenhead and Churchill had all acknowledged that, if necessary, they would have to stand by and let the Turks chase the Greeks into Eastern Thrace: 'Churchill who has been a fire-eater contented himself with a few grumbles about humiliation.'[62] But the prospect of going to war had made Unionists inside and outside the Cabinet grumble more than a little. Before the Cabinet meeting at which Churchill and company were so unexpectedly pacific, some of the second-ranking Ministers had had a private meeting at Curzon's house, among them Stanley Baldwin, the Financial Secretary to the Treasury, at which the subject of resignations had been aired.[63] Unionist dissatisfaction was most dramatically expressed in a letter from Bonar Law to *The Times*, in which the former Conservative leader voiced what many felt when he said that Britain could not 'act alone as the policeman of the world'.[64]

Bonar Law's intervention raised the hopes of the Unionist critics of the Government. One of their problems, even as the Chanak crisis seemed to be getting worse, was that an exit from the coalition seemed to mean the 'break-up of the Conservative Party', with the leadership sticking with Lloyd George. Bonar Law, when sounded out on the prospects by Salisbury on 21 September, expressed gloom at the idea, but said that he 'could and would do nothing';[65] but the narrowness with which war had been averted allowed Bonar Law's supporters to urge that it was his duty to save both the Party and the country from the dangerous adventurers who were running the Government.[66]

At this stage there were relatively few Conservatives who wanted to see an end to the coalition; indications are that most of them would have been willing to go along with it, without Lloyd George as leader.[67] What precipitated the end of the coalition was the decision of its leaders on 10 October to hold an election, which Birkenhead and Chamberlain thought would force the dissidents into line; the latter thought that there would be advantage in calling a Party meeting 'and to tell them bluntly that they must either follow our advice or do without us in which case they must find their own Chief and form a Government *at once*. They would be in a d——d fix.'[68] In this both men were mistaken, and their efforts at driving the rebels into submission simply drove them into a corner and, by nailing their colours to Lloyd George's mast, the two leaders were unable to escape when, at the Party meeting at the Carlton Club on 19 October, 187 Conservative MPs voted against a continuation of the coalition. Having elected to stand or fall by Lloyd George, they fell by him, when Bonar Law's speech at the meeting made it clear that there was an alternative Unionist Prime Minister.[69]

These developments, which lay outside his control, had, nevertheless, profound significance for Churchill. Had Chamberlain and Birkenhead accepted the advice which they were getting from many quarters to abandon Lloyd George, the coalition would have remained intact and Churchill, as the leading Liberal left in it, would have been in the position of centrality which he had enjoyed earlier in the year; if they had had to call an election, he would have received Unionist support. Now, with the Government's resignation on 19 March and the refusal of Birkenhead and company to form a 'centre Party' with him,[70] Churchill had to fight the election as an independent Liberal supporter of Lloyd George; ranged against him was a Unionist Government led by his old enemy, Bonar Law. As if this prospect was not chilling enough, Churchill also had to contend with the fact that he had gone down with appendicitis and would be out of action for most of the election campaign.

Churchill's attitude towards the new Government was not much different from that expressed by Birkenhead when he contemptuously called it a government of 'the second eleven'.[71] It was 'absurd' to suppose that Bonar Law had Lloyd George's 'vital resourcefulness or constructive capacity', and he marvelled at the 'temerity and presumption' with which a Cabinet, which had to have four out of the five Secretaries of State in the Lords, had 'stripped the State of so much experience and power'. He defended his own record, attacked the Socialists vigorously and expressed his willingness to work with moderate Unionists.[72]

Most Unionists were still in favour of some sort of coalition after the election, few thinking that they could win a majority of the new democratic electorate[73] – a point which Churchill and Birkenhead rubbed home with their emphasis upon the aristocratic character of the Cabinet. The election was the most confused of modern times, with a whole variety of Liberals standing under various prefixes, or none, some owning allegiance to Lloyd George, others to Asquith and some to no one. The Conservatives were without their most experienced leaders, who, in the event of a 'hung Parliament', would have, somehow, to be conciliated; whilst even the Labour Party, which had prospered at by-elections, had no settled leader.[74] Churchill's campaign, with its emphasis on the dangers of Socialism and the need for national unity, could have been that of one of the 'moderate Unionists' with whom he was willing to coalesce, but his attempt to rally the electors of Dundee for the fifth time was hampered by his own fragility and Liberal divisions.

The Unionists agreed not to oppose him, but the presence of another National Liberal and an Asquithian meant that, even though Dundee was a two-member constituency, the Liberal vote was being split three ways, which worked to the benefit of the single Labour candidate, E. D. Morel, who was a notable figure in pacifist circles, and to that of Churchill's old foe, Mr Scrymgeour, who was standing as a Nationalist and prohibitionist.[75] Although she was still recovering from the birth of their final child, Mary, Clementine agreed to plunge into battle on her husband's behalf, and received rough treatment from supporters of the Communist candidate, Gallagher.[76] Churchill was forced to reply through the medium of his election addresses, which, although, as ever, brilliantly pungent in their attacks on his enemies, did not carry the same force as his own orations might have done. Birkenhead came up to speak for his old friend, but Clementine lamented that 'he was no use at all, he was drunk'.[77] Even drunk, F.E. was usually a better speaker than many another sober, but neither he, nor a last-minute personal appearance by a wan and stricken Churchill, could avert the damage done by the Liberal split and the Labour attacks on Churchill's past record; and the cry 'What about the Dardanelles?' did service, when real argument was lacking.[78]

Churchill's hopes, like those of Lloyd George, lay in their group of Liberals winning seventy to eighty seats in a Parliament where the Unionist Government would need their support, which would only be given if some form of proportional representation were conceded, which would mean two things: that the Liberals could, even in the new Parliament, influence the Conservatives in a 'progressive' direction, and that, thereafter, they would not even be dependent upon the Conservatives for support during election campaigns.[79] Churchill's sense that the election would be close was correct: more seats were won on small majorities than ever before, or since; each of the three main Parties received about a third of the vote, and a sixth of MPs were elected with majorities of under a thousand. The Liberal split in seats like Churchill's severely damaged Liberal chances, to the advantage, usually, of the Unionist candidate – and so it proved in Dundee.[80] Nationally, to everyone's surprise, Bonar Law had a majority of seventy-seven, whilst Churchill went down at Dundee by over ten thousand votes, with Scrymgeour and Morel being elected: in a month he had lost his office, his appendix, and now his seat.

For the first time in twenty-two years Churchill was without a seat in Parliament. He received many condolences and, more usefully, offers from Liberal associations asking him to contest their seat next time; his old Army friend, Louis Spears, even offered to stand down in his favour at Carlisle.[81] But all these offers were turned down. In retrospect, like his defeat on another occasion, this was to prove a blessing in disguise. Bonar Law's victory had ended any hope of reviving the coalition. The Unionist leaders who had excluded themselves in October adopted a variety of attitudes towards the new Government: Birkenhead was contemptuous;[82] Chamberlain was unhappy and indecisive, whilst Balfour held aloof;[83] some of the smaller fry sought salvation in making their peace with Bonar Law – one of them, Worthington-Evans, known as 'Worthy', adding a new meaning to the phrase 'for Worthy reasons', thereby. Lloyd George himself was left in the wilderness with a small following, eyeing the Asquithians who returned the compliment with suspicion: they wanted the money accumulated in his political fund, whilst he wanted their organisation and the leadership of a united Party: neither side obtained what they wanted.[84] It would have been difficult for Churchill to have found a Party label here which would have suited him. He was, he told Riddell in May, 'what I have always been – a Tory Democrat'; he had changed his Party because of force of circumstances, 'but my views have never changed, and I should be glad to give effect to them by rejoining the Conservatives'.[85]

But the search for a moment at which Churchill became a 'Conservative' would be as futile here as it was when applied to his earlier change of Party. On both occasions the fluid nature of the political situation encouraged his hopes of finding a home in a centre Party which put aside the old labels. The few speeches he made in early 1923 left him with all his options open: Lloyd George and Cabinet were praised, but not excessively; moves towards Liberal reunion were welcomed, but not too warmly; the Government was criticised, but not too harshly; the anti-Socialist drum was banged vigorously; and, above all, the need for unity in the face of the Socialist menace was stressed; he was even willing to accept compromises on the one thing upon which he had declared himself a 'Liberal' – free trade.[86]

Churchill was wise to keep his options open. A Conservative Government led by Bonar Law held little prospect for him, and had the Parliament continued to its appointed end in 1926 or 1927, the pattern of his career would have been very different. The possibility of a reunited Liberal Party was not, in these circumstances, to be ignored. Then came events which proved the wisdom of his cautious approach. In April Bonar Law was removed from the scene by a fatal illness, and with the wounds of the last election still unhealed and Chamberlain out of the running, the Conservatives were forced to choose between Curzon and Baldwin.[87] The first was considered altogether too pompous and grand, charges which could not be levelled against his rival, whom he described as a 'man of the utmost insignificance'.[88] However, after the flamboyant antics of Birkenhead and company, the Conservative Party was in the mood for 'insignificance'. Baldwin's accession to the leadership removed one obstacle in the way of Churchill's hopes of preferment in the Conservative Party, but it soon raised another. In May Churchill had declared that the old political issues were dead, including the free-trade/protection controversy; that this was wishful thinking was shown in November when Baldwin, to everyone's surprise, went for an election on the issue.

If Baldwin was looking for an issue on which to bring his own Party together and to banish the spectre of the former coalitionists reuniting, he could not have chosen better. 'I expect your course is simplified,' Chamberlain wrote to Churchill on 31 October, 'tho' not in the way or on the lines we both hoped'; he would have to be on Baldwin's side and 'I fear that you must be on the other.'[89] The issue which had divided Churchill from the Conservatives twenty years earlier kept him parted from them now. Churchill bitterly condemned Baldwin's decision as an attempt by 'party politicians' to obtain a 'party verdict',[90] and he accepted an invitation to stand at Leicester West as a Liberal Free Trader. Baldwin may have divided the coalitionists, but he had reunited the Liberals, and his achievement was at the price of the Conservative majority. Churchill himself went down to defeat by over four thousand votes, the victim of the phenomenon he had earlier deplored: a split Liberal and Conservative vote let the Labour candidate, Pethick-Lawrence, in on a minority vote.[91]

Churchill's wife had hoped that the campaign might see him reinstated into the bosom of the Liberal Party, and the recovery of his portrait, along with Lloyd George's, from the cellars of the National Liberal Club seemed a good omen; but the prospects of any such development were to be scuppered by Asquith's reaction to the hung Parliament which the election had produced. The Conservatives had 258 seats compared to 191 for Labour, 158 Liberals and 26 Lloyd Georgeans. Churchill argued hotly against supporting Labour in its bid to oust the Conservatives. The idea of a Labour Government appalled him; it would be, he declared, 'a serious national misfortune such as has usually befallen great States only on the morrow of defeat in war'.[92] The letter to *The Times* in which he announced his views marked, in effect, his final breach with the Asquithian Liberal Party and identified him as the fugleman for those Liberals who were similarly disenchanted with the vote on 21 January by which Asquith helped Ramsay MacDonald become the first Labour Prime Minister.[93]

It was clear that the minority Labour Government could not last for long, especially if it tried to introduce anything in the way of Socialist legislation; the question for Churchill was what label would he stand under at the next general election?

18

Reforging a Reputation

'I have not done one scrap of work or thought about anything. This is the first time such a thing has happened to me. I am evidently "growing up" at last,' thus wrote Churchill to his wife in March 1920;[1] over the next two years he was to do even more 'growing up'. The death of his mother in June 1921 cut a last, lingering link with childhood, whilst the death of his daughter, Marigold, at the age of three and a half, in November, was a reminder of how capricious fate can be. These 'rites of passage' were accompanied by other signs of 'growing up', and it was during this period, 1921–3, that the pattern for much of the rest of Churchill's life was set. In 1922, using the proceeds of a legacy, which for the first time gave him a substantial amount of capital, Churchill bought a small country house called Chartwell, at Westerham, which he immediately set about knocking down and rebuilding according to his own ideas of comfort. At the same time he was devoting himself to one of the activities which, along with Chartwell and his family, was to occupy much of his time – the writing of his war memoirs. This served two purposes: it brought in money, which Churchill always needed; but even more than that, telling his own story would allow him to put his own case before the public and so refute the charges of those who cried, 'What about the Dardanelles?'

The first volume was published in 1923 and prompted, so it is said, Balfour to comment: 'I hear that Winston has written a big book about himself and called it *The World Crisis*.' The second volume also came out in 1923 and caused a great deal of controversy. Churchill's handling of his days at the Admiralty was, as we have seen, partial and, at times, positively misleading, but he backed it up with such a wealth of documents and with such force of argument that historians have been arguing over his account ever since; so it is no wonder that many contemporaries found it convincing. If *The World Crisis* did not exonerate Churchill's name in the eyes of the great British public, it did at least cast doubt about his sole responsibility for Gallipoli – which was enough to lift some of the shadows from his reputation. The money which the volumes brought in, £5,000 for volume two, was also useful to a man suddenly deprived of not only his main occupation, but also his income.

The *enfant terrible* of 1914, the ambitious young man of 1914 who had, so it seemed to those who did not know him closely, risen without effort, had since received more than his fair share of rough treatment from the 'march of events', and the 'glad confident morning' had faded into an overcast day. He now faced the grey light of middle age battered and bloodied, but his spirit had not broken. His enthusiasm and energy were not perceptibly dimmed, and it was not until 1920, when he was forty-five, that he was able to go on holiday and simply relax; it was not a habit he was to acquire.

With the acquisition of Chartwell on 14 September 1922 and the birth of his final child, Mary, the following day, two of the last figures were added to the picture of his life. He would describe the house as a 'citadel' into which he could retreat, surrounded by his family; his wife would have other descriptions of a house which she never liked and which she thought, correctly, engulfed too much of their capital as her husband expanded it, installed a swimming-pool and, most famously of all, practised his brick-laying.[2] The inwardness of any marriage is known, if at all, only by the two partners concerned. Their marriage had weathered the storms of 1915–16 when Clementine had been profoundly upset at the depth of her husband's depression.[3] She had not offered merely sympathy, but had thrown herself into a last effort to save him in an anguished letter to Asquith, and even though she had failed, she ever sought to moderate the venom of her husband's attacks upon Asquith and his former Liberal colleagues;[4] she had seen with satisfaction his move back towards mainstream Liberalism in 1923 and, after the advent of the Labour Government cut off this development, begged him not to sell himself too cheaply to the Tories.[5]

If his enthusiasm remained undimmed and his energy enormous, this did not mean that the events of the previous ten years had left no mark on the Churchill of 1924. The revelation of the truth of Lloyd George's dictum that there was 'no friendship at the top' had shocked him; he had expected Lloyd George and Asquith, as friends, to help him in 1915, and he had been bitterly disappointed that they had abandoned him.[6] But the iron did not enter his soul, except perhaps in Asquith's case; he did 'not harbour malice', although he wondered whether 'I w[oul]d be a stronger character if I did'; life was too 'full of interesting work and movement & so happy & comfortable' to take the 'trouble' to indulge in mean-spirited vendettas.[7] None of this, of course, stopped him from indulging his Macaulayesque taste for sitting in judgment when he wrote his historical works, nor did it prevent him hitting his opponents with the full armoury of his verbal arsenal; he was curiously blind to the effect which this had on those who were attacked, and, as Neville Chamberlain once commented, he was 'singularly sensitive for a man who constantly attacks others'.[8]

But there was another sense in which the events of the previous decade had made the Churchill of 1924 a more sombre figure than the rising young politician of 1914 had been; his faith in 'progress' had received a severe jolt. Churchill, for all his personal idiosyncrasies, was, as we have seen, a child of his age, absorbing the Social Darwinism of the time and adapting it to his Whiggish view of history. To him Waterloo and Trafalgar had been the 'fit & predestined ending to the long drama of our island race';[9] but this faith had perished amidst the slaughter of the trenches and the barbarity of modern war. Churchill's experiences of war had been forged on the frontiers of Empire; they had involved some barbarity, but it had been possible to portray them as 'gentlemen's wars'; after 1914–18, after the horrors of submarine warfare and mustard-gas, this was no longer possible.[10] It is fashionable for historians to disparage the impact of the Great War, but such a view would have been received sceptically by those who, like Churchill, had seen the sun set on a world which they were coming to realise had vanished for ever. That *'douceur de vivre'*, which Harold Macmillan was to lament would never be known by those who had not experienced Edwardian Society in its heyday, may have been the preserve of an elite, but Churchill had been part of that elite, and lamented accordingly. As he surveyed the world which emerged from the ruin of war, with civil disorder, famine, conflict and Bolshevism taking the place of the ordered civilisation which he had known, he could only conclude: 'What a disappointment the Twentieth Century has been.' The forces of civilisation were under siege, the prospects of success grim, and only 'intense, concentrated & prolonged efforts' could avert total catastrophe.[11]

This new, grim mood carried Churchill far from the optimistic shores of Edwardian Liberalism. He had hoped that what was clear to him would be equally so to others and that all men of goodwill could combine against the disasters which loomed ahead, but 'Party spirit', which he excoriated accordingly, wrecked Churchill's hopes, leaving him, as two decades and a whole world earlier, looking for a berth in the Party whose objectives were closest to his own; it meant, as then, trying to fit a centrist frame of mind into the requirements of Party politics. This operation had already been attempted once, and it had not been attended with total success; there was no reason to suppose that it would be more successful a second time. But if Churchill wanted to fight the enemies of civilisation, he needed a seat in the Commons – and that was hard to obtain without Party backing.

The prospect of winning a seat without Conservative backing was slim, but as a Liberal who wanted a 'Conservative and Liberal union',[12] he might hope for that support without having to adopt a Party label, as Baldwin was particularly anxious to win over disillusioned Liberals.[13] The announcement of a by-election in the Abbey Division of Westminster gave Churchill a chance to test this theory, as he put himself forward as an Independent. Baldwin's reaction might have been expected to have been one of anger, but when Austen Chamberlain lunched with him on 24 February he was 'surprised' by 'the friendly way in which he talked of Winston and by the sense which he expressed of the advantage of getting Winston over'; Chamberlain promised to 'make enquiries'. He found, as he told Birkenhead on 26 February, that the general feeling was 'that it is too early for Winston to come out as a Conservative with credit to himself'. The local association would not back him under any other label, and so, Chamberlain concluded, he should wait. Baldwin would see him and explain that 'we want to get him and his friends over, and though we cannot give him the Abbey seat, Baldwin will undertake to find him a good seat later on', when he had been able to 'develop naturally his new line and make his entry into our Party much easier than it would be today'; he hoped that Birkenhead would persuade him not to 'rush the fence'.[14]

Chamberlain's letter illustrates the caution which had already twice deprived him of the highest office; Churchill was of an altogether different mettle. He did not want to enter the Conservative Party in a white sheet; he wanted to do what Chamberlain's father had done in 1886, lead a group of Liberals into alliance with the Conservatives. Chamberlain was, none the less, correct in anticipating opposition from within the Party to Churchill, particularly from some of those junior coalition Ministers who had profited by the 'Peasants' revolt' of October 1922. Bridgeman, who had been Home Secretary in Baldwin's Government, lamented the possibility that 'that turbulent, pushing busybody Winston is going to split our Party'; and, like many Conservatives, he failed to 'understand how anyone can want him or put any faith in a man who changes sides just when he thinks it is to his personal advantage to do so'.[15] He was right to anticipate divisions within the Party.

When the local association nominated Otho Nicholson as their candidate on 28 February and Churchill refused to stand down, Conservatives split in their attitude. Churchill hoped that Baldwin would not 'fire upon the reinforcements I am bringing to y[ou]r aid', and that purported 'irregularities' in Nicholson's selection would allow Baldwin either to repudiate him, or at least to deny him the aid of Conservative Central Office.[16] However much Baldwin was attracted by Churchill's promise that his victory could 'lead directly to the creation of a Liberal wing' working with the Conservatives 'in the coming struggle', he had to reckon with those Conservatives who took Bridgeman's view.

Leo Amery, who had been slightly senior to Churchill at Harrow, had never much cared for his old school-fellow. It was not simply that the dwarfish Amery had been precipitated into the pond by Churchill, who had mistaken him for a younger boy.[17] Amery, who was a fanatical tariff reformer, regarded him as a traitor to his Party on the issue. Mindful of the rumours about his conduct when escaping from the Boers, Amery concluded: 'It is a case of true to type and Winston will desert his Liberal colleagues with the same swift decision that led him to climb over the railing at Pretoria and escape without Haldane and Le Mesurier 25 years ago.'[18] Austen Chamberlain's long association with Churchill made his opposition more genteel,[19] but his half-brother

Neville, who had been another of the beneficiaries of the events of October 1922, was at one with Amery.[20]

It was Amery's determination to 'resist Churchill's attempt to force our hand to create disruption in our Party for his own end'[21] which frustrated Baldwin's efforts to play down the issue. Baldwin was 'very angry and excited' when Amery and Neville Chamberlain announced that they were going to speak for Nicholson, and he threatened that in that case he would speak for Churchill.[22] He told Amery gloomily that 'if I insisted on speaking in Westminster it would bust the whole Party up'.[23]

The determination with which Amery and Neville Chamberlain pursued Churchill was partly to do with their fear that he might help create another coalition. The Conservative coalitionists were in the process of being welcomed back into the Party. This was a delicate process, as Birkenhead still despised Baldwin and company, whilst they wanted Austen Chamberlain and rather resented the fact that they had to buy F.E. as part of the bargain.[24] Bridgeman, Amery and Neville Chamberlain had been the leading opponents of any attempt to ally with the Liberals after the 1923 election defeat, and the three men still opposed any accommodation with what Amery regarded as a discredited and outdated creed whose opposition to Protection would stand in the way of his dream.[25] The right course was for the Liberal Party 'to disappear' by 'one section of it gradually joining with and diluting the Labour Party and the other section coming into line with us'; he was not prepared to see the pure milk of the Protectionist doctrine watered down to achieve an end which he thought inevitable.[26]

Amery, Neville Chamberlain and Bridgeman were, by this stage, the only three leading Conservatives who 'continued to believe that an effective anti-socialist platform must combine Protection and Imperial Preference with a constructive programme of social reform',[27] and Amery, at least, could not sit still whilst, in his eyes, Baldwin committed 'suicide'.[28] On 14 March, five days before polling, he sent Nicholson an official letter of support.[29]

But if the hardline Protectionists distrusted Churchill as a traitor and an ex-coalitionist Lloyd George free-trader, there were others who discounted the first of these objections to him, and who regarded the last two as positive recommendations. It was by no means out of the question that Churchill might bring figures like Viscount Grey of Falloden (as the former Sir Edward Grey now was) across with him, and other right-wing Liberals.[30] The very prospect of a kind of renewal of coalitionism, which so appalled Amery, came like manna in the wilderness to those who had condemned Baldwin's sudden adherence to Protection in 1923; for men like Balfour, Birkenhead and Austen Chamberlain, such a fusion was a guarantee against the adoption of policies which seemed to have little chance of winning over the electorate.[31] The publication of Amery's letter freed Balfour from the Baldwinian edict that former Ministers should not be seen to take sides, and on 15 March his letter of support for Churchill was published.[32]

These cross-currents within the Conservative Party are worth delineating, for they do much to explain the course which Churchill was to chart over the next five years; those who had opposed him so strongly over the Abbey by-election were not to change their minds about him once he had joined a Cabinet in which they all sat.

The by-election created tremendous publicity, and Churchill campaigned with his usual vigour. There was nothing new in his message: anti-Socialism seasoned by appeals for national unity; but what was new was that he was saying these things as a candidate standing with the backing of many prominent Conservatives. Baldwin, he stressed, had asked for the co-operation of Liberals, and now that he was getting it, he should put 'country before Party'.[33]

Amery duly voted for Nicholson, and Bridgeman hoped that Churchill would 'get a thorough licking', or, failing that, split the vote and let the Socialist in, which, he thought, would be 'fatal to him'.[34] Churchill was certainly playing for high stakes, but his determination was essential if his hopes of forging an anti-Socialist coalition were to be achieved; contrary to Amery's cynical view, Churchill was not only seeking salvation for himself. Lord Derby, who wanted to see Churchill elected, feared that he would be 'done for' if a split vote let the Socialist in,[35] but his Lordship's fears were no more realised than were Bridgeman's hopes: Nicholson beat Churchill to win the seat, but by a bare forty-three votes. It was a magnificent effort. Had he won, Churchill would have incurred further wrath from many Conservatives for losing them a seat; as it was he gained great kudos from an honourable defeat – and established himself as a central figure in any struggle to win over former Liberals to vote Conservative.

The 'urgent need' after the election was, Churchill told Derby, 'to afford a broad rallying ground for those forces which work for the greatness of Britain, and the Conservative Party have an imperial duty to perform in this respect far superior to ordinary Party lobbies'.[36] With assurances from the Conservatives that their seats would be uncontested, Churchill reckoned that about thirty Liberal MPs would follow him; moreover, there were about twenty other seats where, in the absence of a Conservative challenge, the Liberals could win. This would give him about fifty seats, which, as he told Balfour on 2 April, would enable him to play a crucial role 'in maintaining a stable Government in the next House of Commons'.[37] As so often happened when he confronted a military campaign, optimism had taken over from common sense; starting out with hints and half-promises from men like Grey, Churchill worked on the same principle as Falstaff with his men in 'buckram', and before long a whole stage army was in being. But in the uncertain politics of 1924, it might be that such an army would materialise.

Birkenhead wanted the Shadow Cabinet to accept an arrangement with Churchill similar to that which Salisbury had come to with Chamberlain in 1886, where the Liberal Unionists had kept their name but supported the Conservatives.[38] In this respect it was significant that when Churchill appeared on 7 May on a Conservative platform for the first time in twenty years, he did so in Liverpool to a joint meeting of the Working Men's Conservative Association and Women's Unionist Federation. Liverpool was a bastion of 'Tory Democracy', and the chairman of the meeting, Sir Archibald Salvidge, had organised Lord Randolph's last meeting in the city. Salvidge was a close associate of Birkenhead, who had recently published a 'profile' of Churchill, emphasising, *inter alia*, his innate Toryism.[39] In his speech Churchill spoke with regret of the breach in the coalition in October 1922 and looked forward to an end to the 'artificially fomented jealousies of Conservatives and Liberals', which simply played 'into the hands of the Socialists'. Calling the Government 'one vast monument of sham and humbug', which was 'deliberately and wantonly corrupting the character of the British nation', he advocated a return to 1922, or 1886, where a 'strong and active Conservative Party' would receive support from a 'Liberal wing' in pursuing policies for the 'national and common interest'.[40] The place, the organiser, the build-up and now the resonances of the speech all proclaimed the same message – 'Tory Democracy' was come again.

During 1924 it was 'difficult to determine exactly what the Liberal Party stood for',[41] but Churchill's speech made it absolutely clear what he thought. The Liberals were no longer strong enough to prevail against Labour on their own; they needed an alliance with the Conservatives. It was now up to the Conservatives to respond in the way Balfour's uncle, Lord Salisbury, had after 1886 – by not challenging the seats of those Liberals who supported the common cause. Baldwin, having helped destroy one coalition, had no desire to enter another one, but Churchill's strategy suited his purpose, which was to provide a home for stray Liberals when their Party was destroyed.[42] Thus it was that he cultivated Churchill as a means of encouraging the break-up of the Liberal Party. When Churchill enquired at the end of May about standing again for the Abbey division, Baldwin dissuaded him, but with the clear indication that a seat would be found for him.[43]

Nor was Central Office slow to fulfil the promise. On 5 August the Chairman of the West Essex Conservatives, Sir Harry Goschen, wrote to ask Churchill if he would be willing to stand with Conservative support at the next election 'as a supporter of the Conservative Party, their leaders and Policy'.[44] Churchill, in reply, anticipated no difficulty 'so far as policy is concerned'.[45] His main difficulty with the Epping seat was that there would be a Liberal candidate opposing him, which made it 'not exactly the kind of seat' which the Conservatives wished to offer him;[46] but no other materialised, and, in view of the fact that an election might be called at any time, Churchill and Central Office agreed that he should take it. Churchill accepted the nomination on 11 September.[47] When the general election came in October, he stood as a 'Constitutionalist', beating the Liberal by nearly ten thousand votes; but he was swept in on a tide of Conservative success which was fatal for his hopes of coalition.

The election was fought on congenial territory from Churchill's point of view. The Labour Government resigned because of allegations about its handling of the proposed prosecution of the editor of a Communist newspaper, who was charged with inciting troops to disaffection, and during its course the famous 'Zinoviev letter' was published, which seemed to show that the Labour Party was tarred with the brush of Bolshevism. With Baldwin having dropped the tariff issue, it was an election which polarised opinion between Labour and Conservatives, with the Liberals being squeezed out. Labour won 151 seats, the Conservatives 419 – whilst the Liberals were reduced to a paltry 40 MPs, with Asquith losing his seat at Paisley.[48] If the election was fatal to the Liberal Party, it did nothing for Churchill's hopes of leading a 'Liberal wing'; there was hardly a Liberal 'parson's nose', and the Conservatives had no need of any support from elsewhere.

Those Conservatives who had opposed any alliance with Churchill and the Liberals were relieved by the result, but the question of what should be done with Churchill himself was not easily shelved. Even Neville Chamberlain, who had thought that his support would 'only handicap us in the country', acknowledged that he 'would be a power in the House'.[49] Now that he was in the House he could not, Austen told Baldwin, be ignored: 'If you leave him out, he will be leading a Tory rump in six months' time.'[50] Baldwin received similar advice from his confidant in the Cabinet Secretariat, Tom Jones, who told him on 4 November that 'I would certainly have him inside, not out.' But he scouted Baldwin's suggestion of sending him to the India Office and suggested the Board of Trade or the Colonial Office.[51]

When Baldwin saw Neville Chamberlain the following day, he told him that he had decided to 'take Winston in at once' as he would be 'much more under control inside than out'; he would be offered the Ministry of Health.[52] But this conflicted with Chamberlain's own desire for a post where he was convinced that he could be a 'great' Minister.[53] Baldwin had wanted Chamberlain to go to the Exchequer, and he rejected the idea of putting Sir Samuel Hoare there; 'he suggested Winston but said he supposed there would be a howl from the Party'. Chamberlain agreed that there would be, but thought that there would be one if he came in at all 'and I didn't know that it would be much louder if he went to the Treasury than to the Admiralty'. Going downstairs, Chamberlain met Churchill and, in retrospect, concluded that his conversation with Baldwin had been something of a sham, and that the Prime Minister, knowing he would refuse the Exchequer, had already decided to give it to Churchill.[54]

Churchill had no idea what Baldwin would offer him, or even if he would be offered anything at all. With the collapse of the Liberal Party there was no reason for Baldwin to offer jobs to anyone outside the Conservative Party.[55] But this was to underrate Baldwin's political nous, something Churchill was to do again and again, usually to his own detriment. Baldwin still wanted to win over those Liberals who were now homeless; moreover, after the débâcle of 1923, he had to calm fears that despite seeming to have dropped Protection as a policy, it would nevertheless be introduced; there was no better way to calm such fears than to appoint a prominent free-trader to the Exchequer. Baldwin asked him if he would be willing to become Chancellor of the Exchequer. Churchill was 'astonished. I had never dreamed my credit with him stood so high.' Churchill knew that Austen Chamberlain and Birkenhead wanted Horne brought back to the Exchequer, but when he mentioned his name to Baldwin, it was clear that the Prime Minister did not want him. When Baldwin pressed him, 'Will you go to the Treasury?', Churchill would 'have liked to have answered, "Will the bloody duck swim?"', but since it was a formal occasion he contented himself with saying: 'This fulfils my ambition. I still have my father's robes as Chancellor. I shall be proud to serve you in this splendid office.'[56]

According to the account which Baldwin later gave to Tom Jones, Churchill pledged his loyalty and said, 'You have done more for me than Lloyd George ever did.' Amongst those stupefied by the news was Austen Chamberlain. He told his half-brother Neville that Baldwin was a 'maddening person' and that Churchill's appointment would cause 'consternation and indignation in the Party',[57] and repeated the latter sentiment to Baldwin by letter on 6 November;[58] but Horne stayed out and, to the 'surprise' and 'annoyance' of Amery and other Conservatives, Churchill stayed in.[59] But the appointment was, as Neville Chamberlain recorded a few weeks later, 'well-received'.[60]

Baldwin's actions were not as surprising as some commentators have made them appear. For the best part of a year Baldwin and Churchill had, each for his own reason, been cultivating each other, and if the election results meant that Baldwin did not need the support of a 'Liberal wing', which, in any case, no longer existed, he still wanted to subsume what could be salvaged of the old Liberal Party into his own Party. Churchill's appointment was one way of encouraging this process of establishing the Conservatives as the natural Party of resistance to Socialism.[61] With a free-trader at the Exchequer, there could be no grounds for anyone fearing an imminent revival of Protectionism.

Moreover, it is easy to overlook the advantages which Baldwin gained by making Churchill Chancellor. He was by far the most experienced and able executive politician available to Baldwin; indeed, he was probably the ablest in British politics. Lloyd George, who was not wanted, had more experience, but had not been a good departmental Minister, and the only other politicians with more experience were now in the senescence of their careers, men like

Haldane (recently a Labour Lord Chancellor), Grey (who was nearly blind) and Asquith (who had lost his seat and would soon try to become the Earl of Oxford by way of compensation). Most of Baldwin's Cabinet, like the Prime Minister himself, were victims of the long exclusion of their Party from office: Baldwin had briefly held the Exchequer and had had a longer period as Financial Secretary; Birkenhead had served in purely legal posts and then not before 1915; of the other Cabinet Ministers, Amery, Bridgeman, Hoare, Edward Wood and Neville Chamberlain had all owed their elevation to the revolt of October 1922 and were, when compared to Churchill, political virgins; only Austen Chamberlain, who had entered politics as long ago as 1893 and had served as Balfour's Chancellor before 1905, had any experience of holding high office for any period of time. So the gain was not all on Churchill's side.

By placing Churchill at the Exchequer, Baldwin made a number of calculations. Unlike Bonar Law, he held firmly to the view that Churchill would do less harm inside than outside a government. He wanted to deprive Lloyd George of allies, and by offering Austen Chamberlain the Foreign Office, Birkenhead the India Office and Churchill the Exchequer, he ensured that none of them had any motive to cast any lingering glances towards the Welsh wizard as he sat in splendid isolation. By depriving Churchill of 'every possible personal grievance', Baldwin hoped to win his loyalty – 'if he is capable of loyalty'. By placing him at the Exchequer, which was a demanding office, Baldwin would achieve two things: he would acquire a Chancellor who would immerse himself in the business of his department; and, with any luck, this would prevent him interfering elsewhere in the Government. It would also keep him away from 'direct contact with Labour'.[62]

Baldwin's desire to keep Churchill away from 'direct contact with Labour' was rooted in his conception of the function of the Conservative Party.[63] He wanted to ameliorate the climate of relations between 'labour' and 'capital', and, by softening the edges of class conflict, to avert the danger of any revolution. Baldwin wanted to bring the Labour Party within the pale of the constitution; one of his reasons for refusing to coalesce with the Liberals after his defeat in 1923 was that he did not wish to give the impression that the old Parties were 'ganging up' on Labour; that might have driven them to extra-Parliamentary action. As it was, by letting them into office when they were in a minority, Baldwin ensured that Labour could do no harm whilst, at the same time, assuring them that they could hope to form a government. The intention was not simply to be a Party of resistance on the model that Birkenhead or Churchill wanted, but to show genuine sensitivity to the problems and aspirations of the new democracy created in 1918. Like a former Conservative leader, Disraeli, Baldwin sought to play the 'One Nation' card – a rhetorical device whose very lack of content was an advantage as it allowed 'its proponents to be as pragmatic as they wished or the situation demanded'.[64]

Baldwin's conservatism was, in one perceptive summary: 'self-consciously ordinary, moral, unprovocative, English and professional'.[65]

The 'moral' tone which Baldwin brought into political life was not simply a reaction to what were perceived as the excesses of Lloyd George, it was a function of his own decency and the religiosity of some of his closest adherents. Edward Wood, who had been Churchill's Under-Secretary at the Colonial Office and was now appointed Minister of Agriculture, was described in a popular contemporary work as a representative of 'the highest kind of Englishman now in politics ... whose life and doctrine were in complete harmony with a very lofty moral principle';[66] a devout Anglo-Catholic, he had been the co-author of a small book called *The Great Opportunity*, which became 'a bible to many of the young men of the immediate post-war era'. Its message, that Britain should be strong abroad whilst eschewing adventurism, and that 'progressive' social legislation should be enacted at home, was the same as Baldwin's.[67] Sir Samuel Hoare, who was made Minister of Air, was another High-Anglican with a social conscience; his prim and precise manner prompted Birkenhead to quip that he looked like he had come from a long line of maiden aunts. At the opposite end of the Anglican spectrum was the new Home Secretary, Sir William Joynson-Hicks, a leading Evangelical, who believed that closing down night-clubs and other such dens of vice was next to godliness; 'Jix', as he was known, was a vaguely ridiculous figure, but as an earnest, middle-class, Evangelical solicitor, he added to the Government's appeal to his ilk. Completing the picture was Baldwin's close friend, William Bridgeman, who went to the Admiralty; 'thoroughly sound and straight',[68] he was the quintessence of the 'English country gentleman', who served his country honestly and without fuss.[69]

These men, sound, religious and unspectacular, all fitted into and helped create the mood of Baldwinian Conservatism. It was safe, honest and English, which, after the dangerous (Chanak), dishonest (honours scandals) rule of the Welsh Lloyd George, was all the more welcome. Baldwin and company brought to politics a 'Gladstonian admiration for the judgement and cultural values of the common man'.[70] As a Midlands iron-master, Baldwin conceived of himself as a better judge of what the mass of the electorate wanted than those who, like Salisbury, were 'born to the purple',[71] even if he did only leave Balfour out of his Cabinet because of his own sense of '*gaucherie* and inferiority'.[72] But where did Churchill fit in?

19

'A Cabinet of Faithful Husbands'

It is said that when Baldwin formed his first Cabinet in May 1923 and decided to leave Birkenhead out of it, he commented, 'so, gentlemen, we will remain a Cabinet of faithful husbands'; the point being made here went beyond F.E.'s marital infidelities and, as an understanding of it is crucial to Churchill's career over the next decade, it is worth lingering over it. Baldwin's confidant, J. C. C. Davidson, reported back to Central Office in 1923 that at the meeting of his local constituency at which he had been adopted as their candidate, 'several of the delegates asked me specifically to say a word about Birkenhead'; when he had demurred, they had indicated that 'feeling throughout the constituency' was so strong that 'a large number of the electors would find it difficult to support me'. The Conservatives of Hemel Hempstead did not want Birkenhead back in the Cabinet, and Davidson drew from the episode the conclusion that 'We have underrated the latent Puritan spirit of the British people, which is not confined to the Free Church nor in fact to Church and Chapel goers, but it is in the blood.'[1] Baldwin had never 'underrated' the 'Puritan spirit', not least because it was in his own blood.

It was not just the respectable middle and lower-middle classes who felt this way about the ex-Lord Chancellor. Salisbury's objections to having him back in the Shadow Cabinet illustrates another strand of the feeling against him: 'F.E. is disreputable. . . . I do not imagine he has got many political principles and most of what he has got are wrong. . . . Poor devil, he will probably drink himself to death.' If his character would give the wrong tone to Baldwin's conservatism, then the nature of his political beliefs would do even more harm. Salisbury argued that the 'leaders of thought in the democracy' had 'no sympathy with the hard-shelled defence of the Haves against the Have-nots', and he thought that F.E.'s 'crude attachment to the interests of wealth' would lose them more votes than Austen Chamberlain's name would win.[2] Neville Chamberlain, although without much in the way of religious beliefs, was a pillar of middle-class moral rectitude,[3] and took the view that Birkenhead had 'so often and so deeply shocked the moral sense of the country by his drunkenness and loose living character that our Gov[ern-men]t which rests largely on public confidence in our character would be seriously tarnished by association with such a man'.[4]

Whilst the worst of the allegations about Birkenhead's character could not be applied to Churchill, some of them could be, and their friendship and political views were sufficiently similar for Churchill to be tarred with the same brush. Churchill's personality certainly fitted in uneasily with the puritanical spirit of the new Government. Neville Chamberlain quickly noticed that although he was 'a man of tremendous drive and vivid imagination', he was obsessed with the glory of doing something spectacular which should 'erect monuments to him'.[5] One reason for the surge of outrage against Birkenhead in 1923–4 was that he had just given a cogent statement of his beliefs in a rectorial address in Glasgow University, which became known, after its most striking phrase, as the 'Glittering Prizes' speech.

The views which F.E. addressed to the youth of Scotland were those which guided his own career and Churchill's. The world, he declared, 'continues to offer glittering prizes to those who have stout hearts and sharp swords'.[6] The impression thus created, that politics was about winning fame and glory, was a fairly exact definition of part of the credo which both Birkenhead and Churchill shared; they would both have said with Disraeli that 'we are here for fame', and neither disdained the honourable sense of the title of 'adventurer'.[7] This attitude contrasted sharply with that held by men like Neville Chamberlain, who, when praised by Baldwin for being willing to take the less prestigious post of Minister of Health, replied that he had sacrificed nothing he cared about: 'I believe I may do something to improve the conditions for the less fortunate classes – and that's after all what one is in politics for.'[8] This was not what Birkenhead and Churchill 'were in politics for'.

F.E.'s speech had shocked the staid burghers of Hemel Hempstead and the lofty aristocrats of Hatfield House, because, before an audience of young men, he had rubbished the notion of 'idealism in international relations' and, by implication, the role of idealism in political life. F.E. told his audience that 'self-interest not only is, but must be, and ought to be the mainspring of human conduct'. Idealists, he maintained, made better 'preachers' and 'teachers' than they did practical men. His was a Hobbesian vision of a state of nature where each man's hand was, potentially, raised against his brother's. F.E. had little time for the League of Nations and the international peace and goodwill preached by 'sentimentalists'. He had heard the siren voices of Liberal idealism before the war, when they had, momentarily, overcome even Churchill's 'robust patriotism'. War could not be abolished; it was inherent in human nature: 'nations wax and wane' and imperial Spain should serve as a grim lesson of the fate which awaited great empires which rested upon their laurels. Civilisation could not be defended by pious hopes, but by strong arms and stout hearts. If there were fairies at the bottom of the garden, the chance was that they were heavily armed and had designs on next door.

All this fitted into the sombre vision which Churchill had of the 'failed' twentieth century. For both men the job of the Conservative Party was to conserve. Where Baldwin looked to adapt the old order to the new and to slow down the pace of change, adopting thus a Peelite approach to the perennial question posed of Conservatism – 'What should be preserved and how?' – Birkenhead and Churchill gave a very different answer. Both men belonged to the 'aggressive, late-Victorian, Social Darwinian, free-thinking elite; both believed in individual expression',[9] and neither had much time for the values of 'middle England' which Baldwin cultivated so assiduously.

How then did either of them fit into Baldwin's Party? To this there are three answers. The first is that the Party as constituted in 1924 was not 'Baldwin's'; he still had to prove himself and to show that he could successfully govern the 'millions of hard hands' by a mixture of concession, resistance and evocations of 'Englishness'. The second answer is that Baldwin had to take the ex-coalitionists in for political reasons. From this follows the third answer – which is that Birkenhead and Churchill never really did 'fit in', and that there was, during the life of the Government, a tension between the 'faithful' husbands and the 'adventurers'.

At one level co-operation was obviously possible, at the lowest common denominator of 'Tory Democracy'. Baldwin wanted to ameliorate and thus avert the class war, but that could not be done by soothing words alone; his Disraelian rhetoric would have counted for little had it not been supplemented by the Peelite practice of Neville Chamberlain. Chamberlain's radical, Unitarian background made him uncomfortable with the title 'Conservative'; he had no reverence for established institutions and lacked the high Tory mistrust of 'tidy solutions'. He had entered national politics late in life and had, on his shoulders, the chip which came from knowing that it was his brother Austen who was intended for political life and had received the education appropriate to that objective; Owen's College, Birmingham, and a spell trying and failing to grow sisal in the West Indies, had been partially redeemed by a successful career in business and local politics, but the feelings of resentment had surfaced again after an unsuccessful few months as Lloyd George's controller of boots. Neville, the 'least of the Chamberlains' as he thought of himself, had two missions in life: to better the lot of the 'less fortunate classes', and to prove that his revered father had been wrong to dismiss him as a potential politician.[10] This desire to 'do something' for the 'poor' fitted in easily enough with F.E.'s pre-war advocacy of 'Unionist social reform' and with Churchill's legislative achievements as a Liberal.

The Disraelian Baldwin, Peelite/Liberal Unionist Chamberlain and the heirs of Lord Randolph Churchill could all co-operate on measures which 'would sweeten and enrich the lives of people without resort to socialism'.[11] Churchill knew as well as anyone, and had repeatedly said so between 1922 and 1924, that a policy of pure 'reaction' at home was of no use; 'progressive' legislation was essential if Labour was to be kept at bay. Baldwin provided an atmosphere, Chamberlain provided the ideas and the drive, and Churchill provided the money and his own initiative; that F.E. provided little is partly explained by the fact that he took the India Office, and partly by the fact that by this stage he was 'played out, backward-looking' and 'his mental arteries had hardened'.[12]

However, such a view, which comes perhaps naturally to the 'maiden aunt' frame of mind which, as F.E. feared, has come to dominate British political and intellectual life,[13] tells us little about Birkenhead's Conservatism. In an essay first published in the *Weekly Despatch* on 31 August 1924, and later expanded for the *News of the World Weekly*, Churchill praised his old friend's 'sombre' Conservatism.[14] In *Great Contemporaries* Churchill wrote: 'He had reached settled and somewhat sombre conclusions upon a large number of questions, about which many people are content to remain in placid suspense.'[15] Both men anticipated danger from Bolshevism and other external threats; the lowest common denominator which operated in domestic politics was absent when it came to imperial affairs.

Birkenhead, writing to the Viceroy, Lord Reading, on 21 January 1925, told him that it was 'most important' for him to understand that the 'general atmosphere' of the Cabinet was 'one of reaction against weakness and surrender'; the 'influence in it of Austen, Winston and myself is very great'.[16] F.E. was too sanguine in assuming that Austen Chamberlain shared the views which he and Churchill had about the need to save the Empire by resolute action – his attention was concentrated on Europe, and he was content to adopt the Foreign Office's 'hand to mouth' policy of trying to buy off nationalist movements in places like Egypt with concessions.[17] It was here, in the field of imperial affairs, that the fault-line between the Conservatism of Baldwin and that of Birkenhead and Churchill was to become most apparent.

Baldwin was willing to come to terms with change; F.E. and Churchill saw it as a fundamental threat to their world and wanted to resist it. This was not an intellectual attitude which was amenable to argument; it was a visceral reaction. In this sense, whatever label he wore, Churchill was a deeper Conservative than either Baldwin or Neville Chamberlain. He could co-operate in measures of social reform, but when it came to a major threat to the social order, like the general strike in 1926, Churchill instinctively wanted to take a harder line than the other two. Emotionally, there was much common ground between Churchill and the extreme right of the Tory Party, which still, in 1924, distrusted him; but whilst Baldwin held his team together, the full significance of this was not apparent.

It was, therefore, ironic that it should have been mainly on the right wing of the Conservative Party that voices were raised in hostility to Churchill's appointment; but the flurry of surprise and indignation soon died down. In 1925 Churchill was formally re-elected to the Carlton Club, and the label of 'Constitutionalist' joined the dreams of a 'Conservative–Liberal Union' in that limbo reserved for political ideas which never come off but looked at the time as though they might. But that did not mean that Churchill had done with Liberalism – as he told the aged Lord Rosebery in reply to a letter of congratulation: 'Five years of steady sensible liberal (with a small 'l' of course) Government will improve our affairs appreciably.'[18] He did not want the Government to 'fritter away its energies on all sorts of small schemes'.[19] In part this reflected the desire to 'erect monuments to him', which Chamberlain soon noticed and which was such a part of Churchill's character. He wanted the Government to 'concentrate on one or two things which will be big landmarks in the history of this Parliament' – housing and pensions stood out in his mind. He had been, he reminded Tom Jones, 'all for the Liberal measures of social reform in the old days' and he 'wanted to push the same measures now'. Whether measures which had been appropriate in 1909 were still applicable in 1924 was not something which seems to have troubled Churchill.

The new Chancellor also wanted to try to reduce the burden which fell on the taxpayer in a manner which would 'stimulate enterprise', but he recognised that 'social and political justice' meant that this could not be done unless the rest of the public benefited from a reduction in indirect taxes.[20] The success, or otherwise, of his measures would depend, in main part, upon the general performance of the economy, but the Chancellor looked towards the armed services, particularly the Navy, for a reduction in expenditure which would allow him to spend money on social reform at home.[21] That the man who had been lamenting Britain's retreat from power should have chosen to attack expenditure on the Navy is, at first sight, surprising, but it is consistent with the line Churchill had taken as Secretary of State for War, which was that of all the Services, the Navy was the one which could most bear cuts because it had lost its main rival, the Imperial German Fleet; but there was more to Churchill's attitude than this suggests.

Churchill had a tendency, which we have already noticed, to absorb himself in the work of his department, and at the Exchequer he was more in the hands of his officials than he had ever been before. He was not conversant with the intricacies of finance in the way he was with those of the Army and the Navy. There he felt that he could argue with his experts from a position of knowledge and strength, but at the Exchequer he felt the need 'to be considered orthodox'.[22] Robert Boothby, who was to become his Parliamentary Private Secretary (PPS) in 1926, recalled Churchill saying of his officials: 'I wish they were admirals or generals. I speak their language. But after a while these fellows start talking Persian. And then I am sunk.'[23] But whilst these things predisposed him to follow the official line on measures such as the return to the Gold Standard, too much should not be made of them; only a few weeks after Churchill's appointment, P. J. Grigg, Churchill's new Secretary at the Treasury, was lamenting to Tom Jones that 'he has not found Winston so malleable as Horne or [Philip] Snowden [the former Labour Chancellor]'.[24] When it came to the Navy, filial piety and political habit drove the new Chancellor to press for economies.

On the day Churchill arrived at the Treasury he brought with him 'the one-sheet summary in his father's writing of the Budget which Lord Randolph never introduced'.[25] By itself that should have been ominous news for the Navy; it was over the issue of increasing spending on the Navy that Lord Randolph had resigned. Churchill's experience of the Asquith Governments had predisposed him, perhaps, to see naval expenditure and that on social reform as a natural field of antagonism, so when Bridgeman and the Admiralty came up with plans for increasing the naval estimates, the Chancellor struck: tax cuts, increases in pensions and the housing programme were the priorities which he had agreed with Baldwin and Neville Chamberlain, and an increase in spending of £10 million on the Navy would swallow up the whole of the savings which he had planned to make: 'this . . . renders impossible any relief of taxations and blots out many social schemes'.[26]

Over the next six months a major conflict developed between Churchill and Bridgeman, one complicated by the conviction of the latter's junior Minister, Davidson, that the whole episode was part of plot by the 'old gang' to eliminate Baldwin.[27] Bridgeman was not unwilling to make some compromises, but as an inexperienced First Lord, with the formidable presence of the First Sea Lord, Beatty, behind him, he could not and would not go as far as Churchill wanted.[28] Bridgeman, the Board of the Admiralty and Amery all threatened to resign if, in Bridgeman's words, Churchill was allowed to 'ruin the Navy'.[29] At Cabinet on 12 February it was decided, in an attempt to defuse the situation, that the estimates would be divided into two: Churchill and Bridgeman, under Baldwin's chairmanship, would decide on the running costs, whilst a Cabinet committee, chaired by Birkenhead, would look at the construction programme which the Admiralty claimed to need.[30]

It was, of course, pointed out by the press that Churchill's attitude towards the Navy appeared somewhat inconsistent with the one he had adopted before the war. Under the 'ten-year rule' which had been agreed when Churchill was at the War Office, the Chancellor certainly had a case for protesting about estimates which were based on the need for Britain to increase her forces in the Far East to guard against a possible war with Japan, but by his own standards he was being short-sighted. As we have seen, he had been on the 'guns' side of the 'guns versus butter' debate which had marked the 'crisis of Empire' between 1919 and 1922, and, in general, he wanted a 'firm' imperial policy; now, he poured scorn on the Admiralty's figures in a way almost reminiscent of the way in which Lloyd George had queried his own figures in 1914. His apprehensions that the Government would be 'branded as a Jingo Armaments Administration'[31] and that this would open the way to a Socialist triumph whilst ruining his own spending plans,[32] although perfectly understandable, come oddly from a man whose admirers have claimed for him the status of a far-seeing statesman.

Indeed, far from showing any signs of vision, Churchill's arguments suggest that, once again, he had allowed his departmental preoccupations to blind him to considerations which, in another context, he would have stressed. Churchill was not content simply to argue against Bridgeman's estimates, he wanted the Cabinet to rule that 'no naval war against a first class Navy is likely to take place in the next twenty years', and privately he did 'not believe there is the slightest chance' of war against Japan 'in our lifetime'.[33] This was to ignore every lesson which the previous decade had taught about the unpredictability of the world, and one can imagine what Churchill's response would have been had he been at the Admiralty and not the Treasury. Not only was it, as Bridgeman put it, 'too comfortable an attitude', but it also ignored the arguments put forward by Hankey about the devastating effects which cuts in expenditure were having on Britain's heavy industries[34] – something which Churchill had written much about in 1913–14.

Churchill was swift enough in *The Gathering Storm* to regard as 'deeply blameworthy' the 'delight in smooth-sounding platitudes, refusal to face unpleasant facts, desire for popularity and electoral success irrespective of the vital interests of the State' of British Governments in the 1930s,[35] but he ignored his own part in these things. Indeed, he gives a positively misleading account of that part in three short paragraphs in *The Gathering Storm*; he states that he asked the CID 'to review this rule', which, in the context of Churchill's argument, might have been read by some as implying that he had asked for it to be lifted.[36] It is hard to avoid the conclusion that Churchill was relying upon his reputation as a far-sighted statesman to mislead the reader, or to dissent from Davidson's estimate that 'Winston Churchill must share the collective responsibility of the 1924–9 Cabinet for many of the delays in rearmament against which he protested so vehemently in the 1930s'; it was no wonder that such things were remembered against him in the 1930s and that those who knew his record should have thought that it did 'not lie in the mouth of the former Chancellor of the 1920s to arraign the 1931–5 Government – which repealed the "ten-year rule" in 1923 – for neglecting the nation's defence'.[37]

That the Cabinet did not ratify the 'ten-year rule' until 1928 was no thanks to Churchill, and to judge from his letters and memoranda at this time, he would have been quite happy to assume that there would be no war in the Far East before at least 1940, and was content to think that Japan had no intention of making war on China – attitudes as 'deeply blameworthy before history' as any of those he was to condemn in Baldwin, and all the more surprising coming from a man who, when he surveyed the British position in Egypt and India, urged the necessity of standing firm. The conclusion of the Treaty of Locarno in March 1925, which seemed to mark the beginning of a new era of peace in Europe, certainly contributed to a general atmosphere in which spending on defence was criticised, but it cannot be held responsible for Churchill's views in December 1924, nor can his statements that there was no 'immediate' danger in the Far East excuse him from the folly of prophesying twenty years hence.

The determination of Beatty and company to resign rather than accept Churchill's figures, and Davidson's conviction (doubtless born of his own conspiratorial nature) that what was going on was the 'old gang' trying to get rid of Baldwin, helped the Admiralty to resist Churchill. Davidson convinced Baldwin that F.E. and Churchill were 'prepared to go to any lengths to down him' and that he would 'lose the support of his own Party' if he 'sacrificed the Navy'.[38] Bridgeman had been defeated at the Cabinet on 11 and 12 February because he had failed to rally support beforehand, which allowed Churchill's superiority in argument to prevail, but Davidson's attempt to play on fears that the old coalitionists were out for Baldwin's scalp helped his chief out. By July the Admiralty and the Treasury were deadlocked. Bridgeman had moderated his demands, but both he and Beatty took exception to the idea that the Foreign Office 'or anyone else could predict the next war'. They came up with proposals which would see four cruisers laid down in the next year and three in each of the following years, but Churchill refused to accept even this, demanding a complete suspension of the building programme for a year. F.E.'s committee reported in his favour, and when the Cabinet discussed the report on 15 July, it came down against the Admiralty.[39]

Churchill helpfully sent the First Lord the draft of a statement which he might make to the Commons on the issue, but Bridgeman made it clear to Baldwin that the only statement he would be making to the Commons was from the fourteen pages of notes which he had prepared as his resignation speech; he would, he told the Prime Minister, be followed by Beatty and most of the Board of the Admiralty. Baldwin, who hated argument almost as much as he disliked making decisions, was forced into making one. He told Bridgeman that he could not go against most of the Cabinet, but the thought of the reaction of the Party to a mass resignation at the Admiralty appalled him, it transpired, even more.[40] Perhaps, as Bridgeman suspected, it was reports from the Whips telling Ministers that 'the most loyal part of the Conservative Party' supported the Admiralty, which turned the tide when the Cabinet met on 22 July; at any rate most Ministers, followed by Baldwin, agreed that Churchill should accept the compromise offered by Bridgeman – which Churchill, outflanked and outnumbered, had to agree with.[41]

The 'cruiser crisis' had demonstrated something which Churchill was not to forget, namely that on imperial questions a determined Minister could rely upon support from much of the Tory press and backbench goodwill; Bridgeman was too straight and loyal to Baldwin to have exploited these advantages to the full, but even so, he had won the day against a Cabinet which was so concerned with the 'appeasement of England'[42] that it did not much care who else it appeased in the process. On other issues, particularly Egypt, Churchill was to be found numbered with those who wanted to pursue a more robust policy than the Foreign Office wished, and here he was to find, as Bridgeman had, that the prospect of a public appeal being made to the imperial instincts of the Conservative Party could force Baldwin into decisions he would not have come to of his own accord.

Baldwin was also influenced by the fact that Bridgeman would have resigned over the issue of the cruisers, whereas Churchill would not have done so. The new Chancellor was 'absorbed in his work', still grateful to Baldwin for the chance he had been given,[43] and eager to make his mark on the Government. As Chancellor, and one of the leading figures on the front bench, he now had the opportunity to do something which he had not been in a position to do since 1914 – to dominate the House by his oratory. The Prime Minister's style in the House was conversational and effective in an intimate way; he could rise to the great occasion, but no one would have called him a dominating personality. Neville Chamberlain, who was drawn into close co-operation with the new Chancellor, disliked the way in which he thought Churchill claimed the credit for a new pensions scheme which belonged to his department, but he recognised that his own dry, staccato performances, which relied for their effect upon his own mastery of detail, were no match for the pyrotechnics which Churchill could produce.[44] The only superior whom Churchill acknowledged when it came to speaking was F.E., and he was immured in the Lords.[45] Thus it was that surrounded by able colleagues who were, on the floor of the House, pedestrian, Churchill's brilliance shone all the more. These, and his plans for social reform, were not to be sacrificed easily; he had resigned once and would think hard before doing so again.

From the very start of the Government Churchill's prowess in the Chamber was obvious. Writing to the King with a report of the debate on the Safe-guarding of Industries Act on 18 December, Baldwin described, not without some awe, the way in which the Chancellor had held the House, alternately reducing his audience to laughter by his sallies at Lloyd George and Philip Snowden, and then to silence by the cogency of his argument: the 'whole House', he concluded, 'was enthralled by his speech'; 'full of confidence and fight, crushing yet good humoured', it was Churchill 'at his best' – and that meant 'full of eloquence and power which cannot be surpassed by any Member sitting in the House of Commons'.[46] Budget speeches which, at least since the days when Gladstone used to deliver them, had been looked forward to for their content rather than their manner of delivery, found a new champion of a lost art in Churchill. After his first budget on 28 April, Baldwin wrote that the 'general impression was that Mr Churchill rose magnificently to the occasion'. In a bravura performance of two hours and forty minutes he managed to infuse into the 'dry atmosphere of a budget speech' elements of 'witty levity and humour', and, when introducing the scheme for pensions for widows and mothers, he 'soared into emotional flights of rhetoric in which he has few equals'. Churchill showed, Baldwin told the King, 'that he is not only possessed of a consummate ability as a parliamentarian, but also all the versatility of an actor'.[47]

It might be that, as Baldwin thought, Churchill had gone on rather too long – brevity was a word of which he never did master the meaning – but no one in the House had ever heard a budget speech like it; and if repetition was to temper the treat by 1929, Churchill's budget speeches remained a perennial favourite. Moreover, this first budget held all the interest which came from watching a virtuoso pianist attempt the violin; Churchill was not known for financial expertise, and members wondered how he would acquit himself. The answer was that he set out measures which were, along with Chamberlain's proposals at the Ministry of Health, the foundation of the Government's claims to be addressing the social problems of the country without recourse to Socialism: tax cuts, pensions, the promise of major house-building programmes. The content as well as the presentation of the budget were designed to lift Conservative spirits. It was a sound, orthodox budget, presented with great panache. What more could the Conservative Party have asked of its new Chancellor?

P. J. Grigg had predicted that 'within a year Winston will have committed some irretrievable blunder which, if he does not imperil the Government, will bring Winston down'.[48] In the eyes of many economic historians Churchill had already committed that error in the budget, for one of the orthodox measures announced in it was a return to the Gold Standard. During the period when Keynesian economics reigned supreme, the view put forward by its founding father in *The Economic Consequences of Mr Churchill* came to hold the day. On this argument, by restoring sterling to the Gold Standard the Government over-valued it in relation to the dollar, which meant raising the cost of British exports and, by restricting the money supply, forcing down wages at home. By overrating the strength of the British economy, so the charge went, the Treasury had weakened it.[49]

Churchill had always had doubts about the Treasury advice on the subject,[50] but he lacked the expert knowledge needed to challenge it successfully.[51] But that did not mean that he rolled over and played dead. He sought advice from as many economists as he could, with a result which confirms the popular prejudice that if you put three economists in a room, you will get at least four sets of advice (the Treasury man wishing to cover himself both ways).[52] The predominance of heavyweight opinion, that is the Governor of the Bank of England and the head of the Treasury, came out in favour of a return to the Gold Standard. But as the tide of Keynesian orthodoxy receded, the view, advanced by some at the time, that the real mistake was the level at which the pound was valued, became more fashionable.[53] But here again Churchill was at the mercy of 'expert' advice. The chief cashier of the Bank of England, Lord Bradbury, said that it was not worth endangering 'our international reputation' by returning to the Gold Standard at anything less than the old rate.[54]

But the caveats and criticisms of later historians and some contemporary economists only cast a blight over Churchill's decision in later years; at the time it seemed another mark of the orthodoxy of his financial management and detracted not at all from his burgeoning reputation. Success at a conference on inter-Allied debts in January had boosted his standing in the Party and the country,[55] and his performances in the House and his budget all confirmed that Baldwin had made no mistake in bringing Churchill into his Government. If Churchill owed the Prime Minister a debt of gratitude, he was paying it off handsomely. The only cloud came, as Baldwin had feared it might, when Churchill came into 'direct contact with Labour'.

20

Staking Out a Claim

It would have been too much to have expected the 'ranks of Tuscany' to have joined in the cheers for Churchill's first budget. The former Labour Chancellor, Philip Snowden, called it 'the worst rich man's budget ever presented'.[1] A crippled Yorkshireman, whose withering contempt embraced most of mankind, Snowden spoke for most of his Party in his attitude towards the new Chancellor. Churchill was an object of distrust to Labour; indeed, he would probably have been offended if that was not the case, and, unlike Baldwin, Churchill went out of his way to be offensive to the 'Socialists' as he was always careful to call them.

One of the earliest questions which Baldwin was called to decide upon was whether trades unionists should 'contract in' or 'out' of the levy which unions paid to the Labour Party. Labour, which received much of its finance from this source, naturally took the view that they should; equally, Tory backbenchers thought it monstrous that men should have to pay towards an organisation which they may not have supported. Labour could point out that the workers could always opt out, but that was beside the point: in the workplace most men would not care to do so – even if they could find the shop-steward and even if he could find the relevant forms. The Conservatives kept silent on a more cogent point, which was that company directors never consulted their shareholders before paying large sums to the Tory Party.

Baldwin, with the need to conciliate Labour in mind, would have preferred not to have had to deal with the question, but the Conservative backbenchers in triumphalist mood had no intention of obliging him. Attempts to reform trades union law had been made in 1922 and 1923, and on the first occasion Baldwin had committed himself to support a bill which did away with the political levy, which put him in a difficult position when F. A. Macquisten introduced his own bill along the same lines in March 1925.[2] Churchill suggested that the issue might be defused by subsidising the expenses of serious Parliamentary candidates, at the same time as abolishing the levy – which was ingenious, but revealed how little he understood of the importance of the issue to the trades union movement.[3] Those who, like Birkenhead, took the view that it was a pity that such a 'good army' was led by such a 'bad general', were taken aback by Baldwin's response.

It was said of Baldwin that his spiritual home was in the last ditch. He was essentially a lazy, good-natured man, who, despite the phlegmatic demeanour he carefully cultivated, lived much on his nerves; his habit of sniffing blotting-paper and his order papers in the Commons gave away something of this part of his character. The fortuitous way in which he had become leader, allied with his mistake in 1923 in calling an election and then losing it, made him an easy man to underrate; and Churchill was among those who, despite liking him, fell into what was to prove for most of those who did it an expensive mistake. When pushed, but only then, Baldwin could rise to heights which few could match. He spoke on Macquisten's Bill on 6 March and said that, whilst he supported it, he did not think that something of such importance should be decided by a private member's bill. Then, in his most intimate and conversational style, he appealed to his own Party's sense of British fair-play; they should not, he said, push home their advantage at a 'time like this'. Stability at home and abroad was what was needed, Baldwin told the House, and he would not fire the first shot; he concluded with an appeal from the Book of Common Prayer – 'Give peace in our time, O Lord.'[4]

It was probably Baldwin's greatest speech, and it drew praise from all sides of the House, with even the bitterest of the usual class warriors writing to congratulate him. It astounded Churchill, who 'had no idea he could have such power'. It brought to mind, he told his wife, Abbé Sieyès comment about Napoleon after the eighteenth Brumaire: 'Nous avons un maitre.' 'I cease', he declared, 'to be astonished at anything.'[5] If Baldwin could soothe Labour's ruffled feathers, then Churchill's own propensity to 'walk through the Lobbies of the House of Commons with an air appropriate to Napoleon Bonaparte on the morning of the crisis of the 18th Brumaire' contrived to give the Socialists the impression that he was their enemy, even if he did not mean 'to be either rude or reserved'.[6] The end of the budget debate provided an example of what could happen on such occasions.

Having listened to Labour's attacks on the budget, Churchill hit back and, as part of his speech, mentioned how odd it was that unemployment was continuing to rise despite the increase in exports – he hoped, he said, that both employers and trades unions would make sure that there was not 'growing up a certain habit of learning how to qualify for unemployment assurance'. For reasons which probably have more to do with psychology than strict regard for veracity, Labour politicians have always been easily stung by allegations of 'malingering' or, as the contemporary phrase is, 'scrounging', and, in reaction to Conservative myths that there are vast numbers of idle layabouts content to sponge off the state, Labour has constructed its own mythology in which no 'worker' would dream of doing so; both positions are essentially political fictions. Labour responded to what it took to be Churchill's allegations with 'an unwarranted display of resentment which found expression in a noisy demand' that Churchill withdraw his statement. Baldwin, who did not think that Churchill had meant to be provocative, thought it unfortunate that he did not 'adopt a more conciliatory attitude'; but that was the essential difference between himself and Churchill: in the face of Labour outrage, Baldwin was prepared to 'go out of his way in the direction of conciliation', whilst Churchill's 'bold and defiant attitude, added fuel to the flames'.[7] Nowhere was this to be more apparent than during the general strike.

In general and in principle Churchill went along with Baldwin's conciliatory policy towards the labour movement. One of the reasons why the Prime Minister had been so anxious to resolve the 'cruiser crisis' was that he was faced with one in the coal industry. With mine-owners and workers at logger-heads and the threat of industrial action from the 'Triple Alliance' of miners, dockers and railwaymen, July 1925 was no time to have resignations from the Government. Conservative backbenchers, who had not liked Baldwin's stance on the Macquisten Bill, wanted the Government to back the owners, and they certainly wanted the Government to confirm that its subsidy to the coal industry would end, as planned, that year. Churchill, however, supported Chamberlain and the Prime Minister in arguing that the subsidy should continue for another nine months – this in an effort to ensure that every avenue for compromise was explored. The Cabinet announced its decision on 30 July – 'Red Friday', as the union movement called it.[8]

Not only had Churchill supported the idea of extending the subsidy, but as Chairman of a Cabinet committee on mining royalties, he suggested that the state should, in effect, nationalise them, and he supported the idea of setting up a Royal Commission on the Mining Industry;[9] but all his benevol-ence turned to bile in May 1926 when, after the subsidy expired, the miners and the TUC called a general strike. Individual working men wanting better pay and conditions after having shown that they deserved them aroused Churchill's compassion; organised Labour challenging the authority of the state brought out in him the same spirit which the Russian revolution had aroused: once the barricades were erected, Churchill knew which side of them he was on. If there was a fight, it was one which the Government had to win; afterwards, of course, there would be room once more for magnanimity – but 'in war, resolution'.

After 'Red Friday' the Government had set up a commission under Herbert Samuel to enquire into the coal industry, and its report, on 11 March 1926, recommended a number of reorganisations, but also an immediate cut in wages for the miners. The Government accepted its recommendations and hoped that the owners and miners would be able to sort things out among themselves; they could not. A government team, in which Birkenhead played a leading role, tried to bring the two sides to terms, but on 1 May the talks broke down with a lock-out on the part of the employers. The TUC, which had earlier declared its willingness to call a general strike, hoping thereby to persuade the Government to repeat the events of 'Red Friday', was now caught by the miners' intransigence and announced that unless there was a settlement, the strike would start on 3 May.[10]

If the TUC was kept to the sticking-point by the miners, then the Cabinet was well aware that the Conservative Party would hardly tolerate another climb-down. Some Ministers, including the Home Secretary, Joynson-Hicks, were convinced that there was a deep-laid Communist plot afoot,[11] which was matched, on the other side, by those who believed that the Government wanted a confrontation; in fact, both beliefs were equally barmy. Baldwin was 'paralysed' by the failure of the talks in a way which Chamberlain found 'painful to witness'.[12] Birkenhead warned Chamberlain that Churchill was becoming restive at being left out of the last-minute talks with the TUC, something which became apparent on 2 May when Ministers meeting in Churchill's room were informed that the printing of the *Daily Mail* had been stopped by the print-workers because they considered its leading article inflammatory. F.E. exclaimed jokingly 'Thank God!', and was 'immediately and hotly attacked by Winston', who said: 'A great organ of the press is muzzled by strikers & you say "Thank God".'[13]

The Ministers had gathered at Churchill's house to hear the results of eleventh-hour talks with the TUC leaders. Some Ministers were 'uneasy' at such conversations taking place after it seemed as though the TUC was organised for a general strike. The formula which emerged from the talks was stigmatised by Bridgeman as 'very feeble & unsatisfactory'[14] and Churchill, who had been 'getting frantic with excitement and eagerness to begin the battle',[15] joined with the Attorney-General, Douglas Hogg, and 'Jix' in hotly denouncing it as weakening the Government's position.[16] But, as Bridgeman recorded, the news about the *Daily Mail* 'arrived at that moment, rather fortunately, as it brought the doubtful people right up against the situation that the general strike had actually begun'.[17] At this point even Birkenhead agreed that there could be no more negotiations until the threat of the general strike was lifted; the TUC was so informed and, on 3 May, the strike began.

The official biographer acquits Churchill of Labour charges that he was part of a 'war party' in the Cabinet,[18] but as the account in Chamberlain's diary makes clear, this cannot be sustained without qualification: by the evening of 2 May, Churchill was one of a number of Ministers who were against making any further concessions. Moreover, his behaviour after 3 May was to give Labour ample grounds for believing the more lurid accounts of the part which Churchill had played in the breakdown of negotiations.

Churchill was made a member of the Supply and Transport Committee, and, from the start, there was a 'distinct cleavage of view' with 'Winston and F.E.' regarding the strike as 'an enemy to be destroyed', whilst 'Jix', who had been known as 'Mussolini Minor' before the strike, took the moderate line favoured by Baldwin.[19] An initial decision by the Committee to produce a news-sheet for distribution was turned by Churchill into a decision to have a newspaper, and he took it on himself to tell the press barons that if they were not prepared to produce it, then the Government would commandeer their presses to do so and would 'take responsibility' for what was produced.[20] The first edition came out on 5 May, and it was known as the *British Gazette*. According to Davidson, it was he who suggested to Baldwin that Churchill should be allowed to edit it. The Prime Minister agreed: 'Well, it will keep him busy, stop him doing worse things'; he was, he confessed 'terrified of what Winston is going to be like'.[21] Nor were Baldwin's fears without foundation.

In Churchill's mind there was a clear division between the dispute in the coal industry, on which he was prepared to be 'conciliatory', and the general strike, 'which is a challenge to the Government and with which we cannot compromise'.[22] The firmness of his resolve that the TUC must surrender unconditionally won him no friends in that quarter, and the high-handedness he exhibited towards the press angered his old friend Beaverbrook. When the latter proposed to bring out an edition of the *Daily Express*, Churchill forbade him to do so, threatening to requisition his presses and paper. Beaverbrook described him as being full of the 'old Gallipoli spirit' and in 'one of his fits of vainglory and excessive excitement'; the two men quarrelled and it was years before they co-operated again.[23]

Most of Churchill's energies were poured into the *British Gazette*, where his articles appealed to the patriotism of the working man against the threat which the TUC had posed to the country. Davidson had to 'spike' some pieces which he considered too provocative, but took the view that at least it kept the Chancellor away from doing more serious harm.[24] However even-handed Churchill tried to be, the fact that he was identified as the Government's mouthpiece was bound to win him the enmity of organised Labour. His determination to treat the TUC as though they were the Germans during the war caused Churchill to cavil at any attempts to conclude a negotiated settlement. When Tom Jones came up with such a plan, he had 'one of the fiercest and hottest interviews in my life'. He put his ideas to Churchill on 7 May and was met with a 'cataract of boiling eloquence': 'We are at war,' the Chancellor exclaimed, and matters had now changed to such an extent that what might have been acceptable before 3 May was no longer so. 'We must go through with it. You must have the nerve.' Grigg told Jones later that he had persuaded Churchill not to print an article advocating the use of the Territorial Army.[25]

The attitudes which Churchill adopted in the *British Gazette* may have struck those close to the Prime Minister, and thus imbued with his desire for compromise, as rather excessive, but they represented the normative reaction of most Tory backbenchers and many Conservative voters. Whatever harm Churchill did himself with Labour, who would have been his enemy in any event, he did himself none with most of the Conservative Party. Jones was right to conclude that it was 'a paper for suburbia not for the working man'.[26] Churchill had a sentimentalist upper-class view of grateful workers co-operating with their *bien-pensant* betters for the good of the nation; he neither understood, nor realised that he did not understand, the Labour movement. To have written about the TUC leaders as though they were potential Lenins and Trotskys said more about the state of Churchill's imagination than it did about his judgment. Proposals that the Government should seize union funds may have been appropriate to the situation which Churchill imagined he was in, but Grigg and calmer souls deplored his 'wild ways'.[27]

The announcement in the *Gazette* on 8 May that any member of the armed forces who wanted to 'aid the Civil Power' would receive the support of the Government angered the King,[28] and Chamberlain recorded, before a meeting of the Supply and Transport Committee on 9 May, that 'some of us are going to make a concerted attack on Winston. He simply revels in this affair, which he *will* continually treat and talk of as if it were 1914.'[29] His attitude had alienated the Government's allies in the press, with H. E. ('Taffy') Gwynne of the *Morning Post* having begged Davidson to keep Churchill away from the presses because he was interfering with production.[30] This was a little unfair, for there could be no doubt that it was Churchill's drive and energy which made the *Gazette* the success which it was in terms of circulation; but whether that energy and determination were well-applied is another matter. Perhaps Davidson had it right when he commented that Churchill was 'the sort of man whom, if I wanted a mountain to be moved, I should send for at once. I think, however, that I should not consult him after he had moved the mountain if I wanted to know where to put it.'[31] In his determination to control the press, and his efforts to manipulate the infant BBC, Churchill demonstrated the truth of Beaverbrook's comment that when on the 'top of the wave' he had in him 'the stuff of which tyrants are made'.

Of course, once it was all over and the strike, at least outside the coalfields, collapsed on 12 May, Churchill became once more sweetness and light and pressed for a conciliatory settlement for the miners. He never would understand why his defeated opponents would not 'live and let live', but then he was not on the losing side and no one had made him feel as though he were a traitor.

It was typical of Churchill that, when he was placed in charge of the Cabinet Coal Committee in late August when an exhausted Baldwin went off on holiday, he should have aroused the anxieties of his colleagues through appearing too eager to compromise with the unions.[32] But he was to discover that F.E. had been right when he had concluded that the miners' leaders had been the most stupid men he had ever met, until he met the leaders of the owners. So the miners had to straggle back, in October, defeated, whilst the Conservative Party, much against Baldwin's instincts, proceeded to pass a new version of Macquisten's Bill making the political levy optional. It was an unworthy attack on opponents who were down and all but out, and for the damage which it was to do to the climate of relations between 'capital' and 'labour', it was not worth it; to his credit, Churchill opposed it.

For most of the Cabinet it had been their first personal experience of Churchill's almost legendary tendency to be overtaken by his own exuberance, but for all the private head-shaking over some of his antics, when it came to making criticisms in public, Amery found that hardly anybody had the 'courage to say anything' when he raised his voice in Cabinet on 11 May.[33] Churchill's defence of his actions in the Commons on 8 July was 'dazzling and brilliant'; he declined, he said, 'to be impartial as between the fire brigade and the fire'. In his peroration Churchill turned to the revolutionary threats uttered by some Labour MPs and, adopting his most 'dramatic tones' and 'shaking his finger' at the opposition, he declared, menacingly, that if they 'let loose' another general strike, 'we will loose upon you another' – and then he paused as Labour MPs prepared to howl him down – '*British Gazette*'. The 'anti-climax', Baldwin wrote, 'was perfect', and the House, having been led to expect a tremendous threat to use the Army, collapsed into laughter.[34] With the Prime Minister evidently worn out, Chamberlain thought that Churchill 'has decidedly improved his position' and was 'very popular . . . with our side', as he was 'with the whole House for the wonderful entertainment he gives them'.[35] He seemed, to others, to be 'playing the game very well', and fears of the 'old gang' attacking 'S.B.' receded,[36] except in inveterate conspiracy theorists like Davidson.[37]

For the first time in his life Churchill was attracting followers. In part this was a generational phenomenon, for most of those who sought his advice and company were young men just entering politics; to them he was a figure to look up to and admire. Of the race of giants which, it seemed in retrospect, had populated Westminster before the deluge of the Great War, Churchill was the only one who patently obviously had a future before him. The Earl of Oxford and Asquith, as the College of Arms had forced the would-be Lord Oxford to become, and Viscount Grey were both worn-out emblems of a broken Party, whilst Lloyd George, although far from worn out, was not a 'safe' figure for young Conservatives to cultivate.

Birkenhead was, at least, a Conservative, but, although attractive, his company was 'unsafe' for other reasons. He could be 'very rude' and, whilst being 'staggered by his genius', it was possible to see 'why it is that some people dislike him so'.[38] He could be such a formidable verbal antagonist that even Churchill, 'who knew him so well, refrained from pushing ding-dong talk too far when others were present lest friendship should be endangered'.[39] F.E.'s example, whilst seductive, was not one which those who sought to follow it found profitable – and one of the most notable casualties was Churchill's own son Randolph. As an undergraduate at Christ Church, Randolph was a frequent visitor to F.E.'s 'court' at Charlton and was, indeed, dazzled by his brilliance.[40] But without 'his style or his majestic command of language, I sought to emulate his style of polished repartee. It didn't work in my case,' Randolph later admitted;[41] he might also have added that his attempt to emulate F.E.'s consumption of alcohol was not much help to him either. Birkenhead's drinking was part of his 'cult of masculinity', which, along with his tennis-playing, yachting and brilliant powers of speech, all made him an attractive but dangerous personality; but he drank a lot 'even by the standard of an age whose normal consumption makes strong drinkers blench today';[42] and by 1926, the drink was beginning to take its toll.

If F.E. was strong meat and stronger drink, then Churchill, in contrast to his public reputation as a 'domineering', even 'rude', figure, had 'in the intimacy of personal friendship a quality which is almost feminine in its caressing charm'; as F.E. wrote of him, he had a 'simplicity which no other public man of the highest distinction possesses'.[43] One of the younger men who fell under this charm was Victor Cazalet, the new MP for Chippenham, who had first met Churchill during the war. He had been captivated by the 'consideration' which Churchill had shown him at their first meeting. It was not simply that this older and immensely distinguished man had taken the trouble to tell him about trench warfare and the duties of a platoon commander; he had then, quite unconscious of making any impact on the young man, told him the 'inside story' of the Dardanelles, before insisting that Cazalet should come to dine with him again.[44] Cazalet came again, many times. He told Churchill that he could 'win over any young man' if he cared to try; the only problem, Churchill confessed, was that 'I don't like new people.'[45] But his 'inspiration, courage, affection, vitality and ability'[46] attracted 'new people' to him.

Cazalet saw himself as a 'liberal' Conservative on the 'Tory Democrat' model, and it was natural that he, and others who saw themselves in the same light, should look towards the 'great man' for inspiration and, after they had entered the House, for advice. Those who possessed a good war record started off with a decided advantage in breaking down Churchill's dislike of new faces. Amongst those who sought his advice and assistance was the new MP for his old seat at Oldham, Duff Cooper DSO. The son of a doctor and a *déclassé* daughter of an earl, Cooper's career as an Oxford 'blood' combined F.E.'s taste for drink and Society with an insatiable appetite for women which was all his own. In so far as he created himself, it was in the image of Charles James Fox, and his fiery personality and literary bent naturally inclined him towards Churchill. Upon his election to the House, he asked Churchill if he could become his PPS. Churchill advised him to keep his freedom to speak whenever he wanted, sage advice which Cooper heeded. That Churchill should then have replied in a long letter in his own hand was the sort of personal touch which won men over: 'You can certainly rely on any help that I can give you,' he told Cooper, promising that he would use his position to help ensure that the Speaker called him.[47]

Churchill's habit of treating the young men who did seek him out without condescension added to his attraction. He might talk to them at length, but it was flattering to be on the receiving end of so much brilliant conversation, and to hear about Asquith, or 'old Fisher', and events which were already passing into history from one of the participants was something which it was well worth keeping silent to hear. When the young MP for East Aberdeenshire, Robert Boothby, wrote to him in the aftermath of the general strike, telling him of his worries that the Government was becoming one of 'reaction' and appealing to him as a 'liberal' to do something about it, Churchill did not toss the letter away. Instead, he wrote a long screed in his own hand, putting a more balanced view, and asked Boothby to come and see him; when he did, Churchill offered him the post of his PPS.[48]

Churchill always had a taste for the rebel, the unconventional and those who believed in living life to the full, which is perhaps why Duff Cooper and Bob Boothby remained in his circle for many years; but neither of them was quite as unconventional as the young man who attached himself to Churchill during his campaign in the West Leicester by-election; Cooper and Boothby were both Old Etonians of good family, but no one knew where Brendan Bracken had come from – and he was careful to keep it that way.

Of course, in addition to the personal attraction, Cazalet, Boothby and Cooper also looked towards the Chancellor for political preferment, but it says much about Churchill that their relationship was always based on more than ambition. But for Bracken, Churchill was his entrée to English political life. With his gig-lamp spectacles and unruly mop of carrot-coloured hair, the tall, gangling Bracken was in every sense an incongruous figure in Churchill's life. He seems to have first met him at J. L. Garvin's house in 1923, and Churchill's wife recalled coming home from the seaside one day and finding 'this "red-haired freak" established and making himself at home as if he were one of the family's oldest friends'.[49] His self-assurance would have made him a marvellous con-man, and indeed there were those, including Mrs Churchill, who suspected that that was what he was. But he was an odd sort of con-man, making himself useful to Churchill in the West Leicester and Abbey by-elections, and then fighting hard for him at Epping. His 'cavalier familiarity' with the great man, and his sudden and mysterious appearance as from nowhere, gave rise to rumours that he was really Churchill's bastard son, and Bracken was careful never to deny them – although he did not confirm them either. Neither this, nor his habit of calling her 'Clemmie', recommended him to Mrs Churchill, and she was not sorry when he fell out of favour in 1925 or 1926.[50]

But if he had become a figure whom the liberal-minded, younger Tories with a taste for adventure could admire, Churchill had also managed to improve his standing with the right wing of the Party. His firm stance at the time of the general strike helped, as did his advocacy of breaking off diplomatic relations with the Soviets, but it was his attitude on imperial matters which drew most support. One of those who came to look to him for help was the

High Commissioner in Egypt from 1925, Lord Lloyd. Lloyd had first entered Parliament in 1910 and had fiercely opposed Churchill during the elections of that year; an ardent tariff reformer and close acquaintance of Leo Amery, he might have been expected to have shared the latter's frustration with Churchill's opposition to any further measures of Protection, but a common cause brought them together.[51]

As one who shared Churchill's views about the undesirability of imperial retreat and the folly of the 1922 Milner declaration of independence for Egypt on conditions, Lloyd was determined to use his post to strengthen British prestige in the country. In this he was soon to find himself at odds with the Foreign Office, who wanted a quiet life and a treaty with the nationalists. When elections in 1926 produced a majority for the leader of the Wafd Party, Saad Zaghloul, Lloyd was faced with a crisis. Zaghloul had been implicated in the murder of Sir Lee Stack, who had been the British commander of the Egyptian Army in 1924, and Lloyd thought that it would undermine Britain's prestige if he became Prime Minister; the Foreign Office, preoccupied with troubles elsewhere, told him that they could not afford to allow him to 'embark upon a big statesmanlike policy in Egypt'.[52]

Lloyd told Zaghloul that he would not allow him to become Prime Minister and asked London for permission to have a gun-boat despatched to Alexandria to back up his words with the threat of force. Austen Chamberlain was hesitant, but Lloyd's advocacy of a strong line received support from Churchill, who wrote to Chamberlain at the end of May 1926.[53] Over the next two years, as the dispute between Lloyd and the Foreign Office developed, the former came to look upon Churchill as one of his main sympathisers in the Cabinet.

An advocate of a firm policy in Egypt, Churchill, along with Birkenhead, was also one of the few Ministers who advocated breaking diplomatic relations with Soviet Russia.[54] Thus it was that, within a year of his rejoining the Conservative Party, and within two of being appointed Chancellor, Churchill had established for himself a formidable position. But support from imperial proconsuls, die-hards and ambitious young men, whilst welcome, and a sign of progress, was not the same as carrying the support of the weighty men in the Cabinet – the 'faithful husbands'.

To Bridgeman he was the 'most indescribable & amazing character', whose 'fertile brain turned out ideas by the score on all subjects', most of which were 'eggs' which failed to 'come to maturity'. In a good mood he could be 'alluring', and even in a bad one he was seldom vindictive; but his main fault was his 'inconsistency': 'He lives entirely in the present & takes his colour from the particular office he is holding at the time.'[55] This last was a view clearly formed by the 'cruiser crisis'. Churchill himself would have concurred with the view that consistency is the hobgoblin of small minds: 'The only way a man can remain consistent amid changing circumstances is to change with them while preserving the same dominating purpose.'[56] But such a defence was not likely to appeal to many of his fellow politicians, who, in any case, doubted his judgment. Even F.E., who maintained that Churchill was often right, had to admit, 'but my God, when he's wrong!!'[57]

The Minister with whom Churchill came into closest co-operation was Neville Chamberlain. Despite early doubts about Churchill's appointment, Chamberlain felt as early as August 1925 that 'he has been a source of increased influence and prestige to the Government as a whole'. He described him to Baldwin as a 'brilliant creature', but he felt that 'there is somehow a great gulf fixed between him and me which I don't think I shall ever cross'.[58] He had a strong sense that his world and Churchill's 'are totally different in that he is incapable of understanding how my mind works'.[59] Whilst acknowledging the position which Churchill had built up for himself by August 1926, Chamberlain was uneasy about it. He was one of those who was disarmed by Churchill's personality – 'I can't help liking and admiring him,' he wrote; but that 'liking' was accompanied as time went on by 'a diminution of my intellectual respect for him'. Chamberlain noticed that 'in all disputes of a departmental character that I have had with him he has had to give way because his case is not really well-founded'.[60]

In part Chamberlain's attitude derived from the temperamental differences between him and Churchill. A 'first-rate' administrator, if a 'little too bureaucratic',[61] Chamberlain was always inclined to adopt a cautious, piecemeal approach to the problems confronting the Government in the field of social reform and local government; Churchill, by contrast, favoured broad, sweeping reforms. But there was more to it than this; Chamberlain's caution was founded upon long experience and detailed knowledge of local government and the Poor Law, and he was naturally contemptuous of Churchill's schemes, which were not.[62] Churchill's first budget may have been a political success, but Chamberlain, who knew what had gone on behind the scenes, was less impressed. The Treasury had told Churchill that a prudent budget was needed, but he had gone ahead with his planned tax cuts, optimistically assuming that with no further expenditure, the figures would come out right – but the coal subsidy had falsified these expectations.[63]

Sir Warren Fisher, the Permanent Secretary at the Treasury, told Chamberlain that the predicted deficit of £36 million for the year 1926–7 was 'entirely the fault of Churchill', whom he described as 'an irresponsible child'; it was no use trying to argue with him: 'If you don't have him out, he will bring you down, and indeed I am not sure that he won't bring you down anyhow whether out or in.' But Chamberlain had not seen then, in November 1925, how he could be 'got out' safely, and a year later the task would have been even more difficult.[64]

Churchill's bravura performances at the despatch box were, for most MPs, the closest they got to seeing his work at the Treasury, and they contrasted so well with the generally uninspiring utterances of most Ministers that few enquired further. For Leo Amery, with his firm desire to introduce Protection-ist measures, Churchill was an obstacle to progress, and his budgets mere ingenious tinkering, but Amery counted for little in the Cabinet, where his long-windedness and obtuseness made him ineffective.[65] By the end of 1926 Baldwin was clearly exhausted, whilst Austen Chamberlain was so absorbed in the Foreign Office and its affairs that he had ceased to play any part in the general business of the Government;[66] of other senior Ministers, Birken-head was beginning to buckle under the strain which he had for long put upon his superb constitution;[67] Joynson-Hicks suffered from the fact that his own verbosity and self-importance made it difficult to 'take him as seriously as one ought';[68] and most of the rest were fustian figures. Only Neville Chamberlain and Douglas Hogg had substantially improved their positions, but the first was too cold and too austere in his public performances to win any hearts, though the cogency of his argument might command their minds, and the latter was a political newcomer who was caviare to the general.

The fact was that surveying the front bench at the end of 1926, it was hard to dissent from the Earl of Oxford and Asquith that Churchill was 'a Chimborazo or Everest among the sandhills of the Baldwin Cabinet'.[69]

21

Bidding for the Leadership

Churchill's orthodoxy as Chancellor, which led later historians and some contemporary economists to criticise him, did him no harm in the eyes of most Conservatives; indeed, given his reputation for lacking judgment, it probably did him some good. His 1926 budget was overshadowed by the crisis leading up to the general strike, which, as Sir Samuel Hoare observed, was 'not a bad thing' because, although 'ingenious', it was not calculated to 'excite much enthusiasm'.[1] 'Ingenious' was a word which commentators had much recourse to when describing Churchill's budgets. In 1926, facing the deficit of over £36 million which his own actions the previous year had helped to create, he resorted to short-term expedients to balance the books: the brewers were asked to pay their duty to the Treasury a month earlier than usual, which brought in about £5 million; the Road Fund was raided for £7 million; and a tax on betting was introduced, which Churchill expected to bring in £6 million. This would have produced a small surplus had it not been for the general strike, but by April 1927 the Chancellor found himself facing a deficit of £36½ million, which he tackled in the same way. This time the brewers lost another month's credit, the Road Fund was emptied of its remaining surplus of £12 million, and by making income tax on property payable in one instalment, he brought in another £15 million.[2]

This certainly demonstrated a tremendous ingenuity, but there were those who doubted that it showed anything more than the fact that Churchill was in the wrong post. Amery, who had found Churchill a drag on all his plans to introduce greater tariff protection for British industry, and who wanted a radical overhaul of the British financial system, found his budgets lamentable – a 'few hand to mouth dodges for picking up odd windfalls' and a hope that trade would improve, accompanied by 'cheese-paring here and there' would do nothing to solve the fundamental problems facing the country.[3] In retrospect it is clear that Amery was right in condemning Churchill as essentially a fiscal opportunist, but it is by no means clear that his own favoured remedies, Protection and imperial economic union, would have done the job which he wanted; both men were equally prisoners of the particular form of financial faith which they adopted. In any event, Churchill's speech was the usual great public occasion, showing his power of attraction as a 'star turn', and his performance was as brilliant as ever, turning the 'trepidation' of Conservatives into 'intense rejoicing and intense admiration' for his 'cleverness'.[4] The newspapers may have spoken of 'trickery', and Montagu Norman, the Governor of the Bank of England, may have compared Churchill to the tight-rope walker, Blondin,[5] but Churchill had achieved his usual feat of making Conservative MPs feel good about themselves and their Government.

'The smiling Chancellor', as Churchill was dubbed by one cartoonist, certainly had much to be happy about. Three years had brought an astonishing revival in his fortunes, and, on good relations with Baldwin, to whom he was grateful for the chance he had taken so well, he flourished. Cazalet, who visited Chartwell on 2 January 1927, had never known him 'in better form', 'full of fun and talk, charming, affectionate and vivacious'.[6] Nor was it only in private that Churchill's new mellowness was demonstrated. Lord Winterton, who was F.E.'s Under-Secretary, writing to the Viceroy, Lord Irwin, in June, commented on his 'remarkable good humour' and 'patience' in the House, and his accessibility in the lobbies and the smoking room; he had become 'what he never was before the war, very popular in the House generally'.[7] With the publication in 1927 of the third volume of the *The World Crisis* going far towards dispelling the clouds which had sullied his reputation, and his political position firmly established, there seemed no limit to the heights which Churchill might not now ascend.

But those colleagues who were closest to him in the Government harboured more doubts than those who saw Churchill from further away. He could be difficult to handle, and only the authority of the Prime Minister could 'control him', whilst his 'impulsiveness and combativeness' were 'an awful danger in negotiations'.[8] On the other hand, such opinions could often be, as they were in this instance, an expression of 'sour grapes'. Sir Arthur Steel-Maitland, the Minister of Labour, was writing to Davidson during the ultimately unsuccessful attempts to negotiate a settlement with the miners, and his 'nose [was] put out of joint by Winston's predominance' – and by the fact that whereas his own speech on the subject in the House had been 'very poor', Churchill's had 'achieved a remarkable success'.[9] But it remained true that, at the centre of the Party, not even Churchill's successes could erase a lingering distrust that such brilliance could not be compatible with 'soundness'; those political deities whom Churchill had so often affronted were not so easily propitiated.

In July 1927 Baldwin, who had been slow to recover from his exhaustion in 1926, speculated with Neville Chamberlain as to what would happen to the leadership if he were to retire. He 'wondered if Winston would jump for the Premiership', but did not 'think the Party would take him ... His candidature would split the Party from top to bottom.' Baldwin hoped that either Chamberlain himself, or Douglas Hogg, would succeed him, but that rather depended upon when he went.[10] At this stage neither man could match Churchill's claims, but then they were both free of the great flaw in those claims, which was Churchill's past reputation.

The Conservative Party had no mechanism for electing a leader. If the leadership fell vacant whilst the Party was in power, as it had in 1901 and 1923, then in theory it was up to the King to select the figure who could command most support, but, in practice, that meant taking the advice of the Party grandees: in 1901 'Prince Arthur' Balfour had succeeded his uncle Salisbury *nem. con.*; in 1923 Curzon had not succeeded because Balfour, amongst others, had made sure that he did not do so. Given the attitude expressed by Baldwin, it is clear that Churchill's chances of joining Curzon in being given the black spot rather than the imperial purple were very large. Baldwin told Chamberlain in October that he would like to go on for one more Parliament, which should ensure that the succession went either to himself or to Hogg.[11] Hogg spoke for many 'insiders' when he told Chamberlain in March 1928 that, whilst he had 'no particular ambition' to be Prime Minister, he did not want to see Churchill in the job because despite having 'the greatest respect for his brilliant abilities', he had 'none for his judgement'.[12] As Baldwin put it: 'Our people like him . . . love listening to him in the House, look on his as star turn and settle down in the stalls with anticipatory grins. But for the leadership, they would turn him down every time.'[13]

Churchill's chances of the leadership depended then, at least whilst the Party was in office, upon the opinions of his peers, and his standing in Chamberlain's eyes was not improved by the dispute which the two men entered into between 1928 and 1929 on plans to reform the rating system. The subject of reform of the rating system, and with it the whole of local government finance, illustrated better than anything else the difference between Churchill's love of grandiose schemes and Chamberlain's preference for cautious, less dramatic reform. Chamberlain saw an opportunity to clear up an administrative muddle. Outside of London it had been thirty or even forty years since rates had been reassessed in some areas, and now that the Government provided, through grants in aid of local rates, some £82 million, or a third of the cost of local expenditure, it was, Chamberlain thought, high time the whole matter was sorted out.[14]

Churchill, on the other hand, searching for a 'large issue or measure' which the Government could 'place before the country' and thus 'hold the public mind', and worried by the lack of effect of his policy on the economy, saw, as he told Baldwin on 6 June, rating reform as the 'large issue' of 1927–8. Perhaps only Churchill's vivid imagination would have found, in the dreary subject of local government reform, a measure which would restore national prosperity, but he did.[15] The only trouble was that his scheme involved interfering in the Bill which Chamberlain had been preparing for the past two years.

Chamberlain was proposing to reduce the number of rating authorities by a half; then he wanted to simplify procedures for valuation by introducing a uniformity of practice between authorities. This, in turn, would mean conflict with the Poor Law Authorities and a reform of that institution. But, at the end of the road, Chamberlain hoped to be able to increase the strength of properly organised local authorities, who could then be given block grants from the Treasury, which would settle the relationship between national and local authorities, with the former knowing, in advance, what sums would be needed for the latter. However, he was far from convinced that all this could be achieved in the lifetime of the current Parliament; by the time his legislation was ready in early 1927, Baldwin was only one of a number of Ministers who wondered whether it was wise to court public unpopularity by tackling such a controversial subject so late in the day.[16] Now along came Churchill with plans to raise £30 million by cutting spending on defence and raising taxes on petrol, which could then be applied to a reduction in the rates, thus helping 'every class' as well as businesses and industry: 'Rates', Churchill told him on 7 June, 'are the key which will unlock our difficulties.'[17]

Chamberlain replied cautiously, asking why so much money needed to be saved;[18] in private, whilst admiring the Chancellor's 'fertile mind', he feared that 'in pursuing these imaginative flights he will lose all interest in really practical proposals'.[19] To put Churchill's proposals into context, total government expenditure in 1927 was £800 million, of which more than half was taken up by servicing the National Debt and pensions. Education, housing and other social expenditure came to about £100 million, most of which was an irreducible minimum; thus Churchill was proposing to save £30 million out of the remaining £200 million or so of government expenditure, which meant, in effect, defence.[20] Chamberlain was right to think of the Chancellor's scheme as grandiose, and after his officials had studied the matter, he replied to Churchill on 14 October telling him that a 'scheme of such magnitude' would need careful examination; in the meantime, he thought that they should proceed with his more modest reforms of the Poor Law system.[21] This was too pettifogging and cautious for Churchill, who did not see why 'your plans and mine should not be interwoven'.[22]

Churchill's proposed cuts in expenditure meant another row with Bridgeman at the Admiralty, who was 'amazed' at the notion that, having postponed his cruiser programme the previous year, he should now abolish it.[23] He had similar quarrels with the Board of Education and with Chamberlain's own department, both of which wanted increases of £2 million in the coming year, and was forced for a while to put his grand schemes 'in the background'.[24] But he did not drop them and, after many revisions and arguments, he presented his plans to the Cabinet on 20 January 1928.[25] Chamberlain's reaction to the first drafts of the scheme was that it was 'like Gallipoli again'[26] – a masterplan, to which any opposition was to be treated as fractious and of which the advantages were to be overestimated, just as the difficulties in the way were underestimated.

But it was not just Churchill's behaviour which had created the Dardanelles fiasco, and now, as then, the attitudes struck by colleagues created the potential for trouble. The Prime Minister, who liked neither Chamberlain's Poor Law proposals nor Churchill's rating reforms because he thought 'we have tired our people with over-legislating', would not come out and say so directly.[27] Chamberlain liked the idea in principle, but he feared that the legislation needed would be so complicated that it could not be carried out in the present Parliament; moreover, he was concerned about the increases in petrol tax which would be required. He foresaw the Government placing itself in a situation where the electors, having already received their benefits on rating, would vote against the Conservatives because of tax increases: 'Past experience shows that political gratitude is confined to the anticipation of favours to come.'[28] Chamberlain thought the scheme 'impracticable',[29] but did nothing to veto it. In part this was because he hoped that the more it was investigated the more obvious the objections to it would become, but there was also the fact that, as Churchill put it in an unsent letter, without some great piece of legislation, the Government would be going into the election with the 'Flapper vote' and 'an emasculated Factory Bill' to provide momentum.[30]

But Churchill was not to be deflected, either by the coolness of his colleagues or the scepticism of the Treasury.[31] Much of the work of responding to technical and other criticisms was done for Churchill by another of the liberal-minded young MPs attracted into his orbit, the 'unprepossessing, bookish, eccentric'[32] son-in-law of the Duke of Devonshire, Harold Macmillan.[33] Macmillan sat for Stockton, one of the areas worst hit by the deflationary policies which the Government was pursuing, and his developing social conscience was eventually to lead him to question the whole of the orthodoxy to which Churchill was still wedded and to advocate unbalanced budgets and deficit financing.[34] All this lay in the future, but it had been his remarks to Churchill about the way in which the burden of the rates was hitting industry and business in his constituency which had planted in Churchill's mind the seeds of the rating reform plan,[35] which was eventually circulated to the Cabinet on 20 January.[36]

But Chamberlain was not the only one who had noticed a generic resemblance between the current situation and that leading up to the Dardanelles. Churchill told him at Christmas that he 'doesn't want another Gallipoli',[37] and Grigg warned his chief that 'the Dardanelles situation seems to be recreating itself. Everybody loves the idea, everybody but you is frightened by its boldness & magnitude.'[38] There was some truth in this, but even more flannel. Macmillan was inclined to dismiss arguments about administrative difficulties as a sign of departmental jealousy by the Ministry of Health, and he did not think that Chamberlain would want to endanger his reputation as a 'constructive and progressive politician' by listening unduly to the 'obscurantist' 'Tory squirearchy', whose only desire was to see a 'policy of drift erected into a system'.[39] Whilst there was something in this, there was not as much as Macmillan thought there was.

Chamberlain's fundamental objection was that by removing industry and agriculture from local rates, directors and farmers were deprived of any interest in good, efficient local government; nor did he like the extra burdens which would be placed on the Exchequer by a system of block grants to local authorities. Perhaps, as Churchill hoped, increasing prosperity would enable the projected deficit of £12–13 million for 1931 to be met without extra taxation; but then again, it might not. Moreover, local authorities would require guarantees from the Government that the cost of providing services to any new industries would be met in the new block grants. On closer examination his fears grew. He did not think that the amount Churchill proposed to give the local authorities would recompense them for the loss of rates.[40] His confidence in the measure was not increased by the Chancellor's performance in the Policy Committee when the detail was examined: 'it is comic how he flounders directly we get to the difficult details. His part is to brush in broad splashes of paint with highlights and deep shadows. Accuracy of drawing is beyond his ken.'[41]

Of course, such comments were a little unfair. It was not, it might be argued, Churchill's business to be conversant with every detail, but to a man like Chamberlain, who was an expert in the field, it was frustrating to be told by a man who did not appear to know what he was talking about that the detailed objections which he was making were irrelevant. Chamberlain's respect for Churchill's intellectual equipment was not increased by the episode. He was also doubtful about a proposal from Churchill that a fixed rate of five shillings in the pound of assessable value should be levied on the properties which were to be derated, and he insisted that this money should go to the local authorities to help defray their other expenses. On 9 March, a Saturday, with the Policy Committee due to meet on the Monday, Churchill circulated a paper arguing his case.[42] It was not often that Chamberlain showed anger in public, but what he regarded as an attempt to 'bounce' him provoked him to 'hit back as hard as he could'.[43]

Churchill was 'not only concerned but startled' by Chamberlain's 'air of antagonism'. He said that he had 'no wish to overbear you in the matter' and offered to withdraw it. He could not, he said, make any progress in the face of a 'veto' from Chamberlain, which meant that he was 'the master'.[44] Chamberlain replied that unless they worked together, there could be no progress: 'Up to now I have done all the giving but very little weight has been attached to any views if they have differed from yours.' He reminded Churchill that he had dropped his own scheme of Poor Law reform to fit in with Churchill's plans (something which was not strictly true: he had dropped them because Baldwin was not keen on them).[45]

In the face of well-founded criticism from a senior colleague whose help was vital, Churchill knew when to be gracious. When the two men met at the Treasury on 15 March, Churchill told Chamberlain that he recognised that he should not have circulated the memorandum, and he promised in future to co-operate closely.[46] None of this altered the fact that Chamberlain did not like the scheme as it had been agreed by the end of March, nor that, despite this, he felt that he must go along with it. Baldwin would give no guidance, and Chamberlain felt that, with the scheme still changing at every point in its progress, he had no firm ground on which to reject it.[47] Argument continued into late March, much of it centring around whether railways should be excluded from paying rates (which was Churchill's position), and where the money raised from the one-off valuation of derated businesses should go.[48]

Chamberlain told Baldwin that he was 'determined to go rather than assent to a scheme which I believed to be dangerous to the future of local Government'. To the Prime Minister's response that 'the Cabinet' would 'never' let him go and enquiry as to a possible compromise, Chamberlain suggested that if Churchill were to be given his way over railways and public utilities, and if he gave way over the five-shilling fixed rate, 'I will work enthusiastically for the plan.'[49] But Churchill was not willing to compromise when the Cabinet met to discuss the issue on 2 April, and it took another day's heated debate before a final compromise was hammered out.[50] Chamberlain benefited from this process. Most Ministers looked upon Chamberlain as the expert in a field in which they were novices,[51] and his clear exposition of the nature of the problems at issue naturally inclined towards his own case. Churchill argued forcefully, but clarity on the details was not his forte. Thus it was that most Ministers leant towards Chamberlain and Churchill 'began to trim his sails according to the wind'.[52] With Chamberlain agreeing that in place of the fixed rate of five shillings there could be a variable one, the argument switched to what fraction of the local rate should be levied; Churchill wanted a fifth, Chamberlain a third, coming down, finally, to a quarter. With that he and Churchill 'shook hands and vowed eternal friendship'. Churchill had got his legislation and Chamberlain felt that he had modified its most objectionable features – so they were both happy.

The derating episode was important for two reasons: it was, as Churchill had predicted, the great piece of legislation which dominated the 1928–9 session; and it strengthened Chamberlain's doubts about Churchill's suitability for the Premiership. Towards the end of the long debate an event had occurred which rather disturbed Chamberlain's calculations for the leadership 'stakes'.

On 26 March the Lord Chancellor, Viscount Cave, had told Baldwin that he was going to resign through ill-health. This raised the question of who would succeed him. The obvious candidate was Birkenhead, who, as a former Lord Chancellor, had a 'practically irrefutable claim' to the position, if he wanted it.[53] However, not only did he not want it, but Baldwin did not want him to have it: 'He might be seen drunk in the street.'[54] This meant that the obvious alternative was Douglas Hogg, the Attorney-General, Chamberlain's favourite in the leadership 'stakes'.

Hogg, realising that 'it barred any chance of the premiership', sought Chamberlain's help. 'I don't know that I have much ambition that way,' he told him on 26 March, 'but I don't want to see W. Churchill Prime Minister.' Chamberlain was equally alarmed. He knew from his brother Austen that F.E. and Churchill would serve under Hogg, but 'was not sure that either would serve under me'; nor, Chamberlain added, did he want the job.[55] These noble (and slightly unconvincing) protestations of lack of desire for the Premiership may have concealed personal ambitions, but they revealed how set both men were on denying the job to Churchill – why, they were even willing to take it themselves. It was to no avail. Baldwin wanted Hogg, and so Sir Douglas became the first Viscount Hailsham – and was scratched from the race.

This was a fact of some significance. The last date an election could be held was May 1929, and with Hogg out of the way and Churchill's derating bill and budgets still to come, the road was clear for the Chancellor to consolidate the position he had now built up.

Churchill thought that Chamberlain had been 'unreasonable' at the Cabinet meetings on 3 April,[56] and a weekend spent building a concrete dam and supervising pregnant sheep at Chartwell put him in a more 'robust' mood. He told Baldwin on 7 April that he wanted the railways exempted from rates; 'half-measures' and 'caution' would, he wrote, be 'to run the greatest risks and lose the prize' – 'let us be audacious. One does not want to live forever. We have the power: let us take the best measures.'[57] Baldwin did rather want to 'live forever', at least politically, and he was not at all disposed to risk that for an idea which Chamberlain, other Ministers and some Treasury officials condemned.[58] So Churchill 'bow[ed] to the storm',[59] although he resented Chamberlain's 'tyrannical' letter, which scotched his plans; 'but let him strut,' he wrote to his wife on 15 April.[60]

But the Chancellor had still not given up. In a long session with Baldwin on 18 April he marched about the Prime Minister's room, 'shouting, shaking his fist', and generally inveighed against Chamberlain for 'always pouring cold water on his schemes' and for being 'evidently . . . jealous of him'. Baldwin told Churchill that he had only himself to blame for chopping and changing, adding that he 'did not understand' Chamberlain. Telling Chamberlain all this on 19 April, Baldwin said that he hoped 'it wouldn't worry me too much to know of W[inston]'s attitude but he thought I ought to know where I stood.' If Chamberlain had been in any doubt, he now knew exactly where he stood – in Churchill's way, and firmly so. He told Baldwin that Churchill's behaviour was 'too childish & contemptible for me to be upset over it'.[61]

There is no reason to doubt that Chamberlain was describing his own attitude exactly, and he gave in to Baldwin's desire to give the railways relief from rates.[62] But Chamberlain was not a man much possessed by the notion that one's enemies should be forgiven; smiting them hip and thigh was more his style. Churchill, Baldwin said, was appalled at the idea that a man like Chamberlain, so much less eloquent than himself, should have the influence which he had in the Cabinet;[63] Chamberlain did not forget these things.

The derating scheme was the jewel in the crown of Churchill's 1928 budget and made the tremendous impact which he had hoped, but electorally it was to be a liability. Chamberlain's instincts were to prove correct, although the measure did prove beneficial; by May 1929 the electors had had the benefits and were feeling the impact of higher taxes on fuel. Moreover, as the new rating levels were only announced at the same time as the election, many rate-payers found that their bills had risen. The episode was to stand as a warning to successive Conservative Governments never to interfere with local government finance; one they heeded until recently.[64]

Generally Churchill enjoyed robust good health, but a bad attack of influenza soon after his budget speech in April put him out of action for the best part of three months – which meant that he joined a long list of Ministers who were incapacitated by ill-health; but unlike his fellow invalids, Churchill's political future looked healthy. There was much discussion over the next year as to the Government's prospects at the election, and much speculation about the future Conservative Cabinet. Baldwin had been notably reluctant to 'reshuffle' his Cabinet, and the only changes since 1924 had been those occasioned by necessity.

Edward Wood had become Baron Irwin of Kirby Underdale and Viceroy of India in 1925; Lord Robert Cecil had resigned in 1927 over Government policy in China to become, initially, Baron Cecil, but on the insistence of his brother, Lord Salisbury, he had been made a viscount; Cave had died, but had been replaced by another member of the Cabinet; and in October F.E. finally left office to try to recoup his fortunes, but his replacement was another old-stager, Lord Peel. The younger Conservatives got barely a look in and felt correspondingly disappointed.[65] Only Walter Elliot at the Scottish Office, Duff Cooper at the War Office and Anthony Eden at the Foreign Office received anything, and then only the most junior of posts. With Austen Chamberlain invalided from the Foreign Office for most of 1928–9 and the aged Lord Balfour now so infirm that it was an occasion for remark when he could actually attend Cabinet,[66] and with Bridgeman having decided not to stand at the election, the opportunity existed for Baldwin to restructure his Government before the election. Churchill advised him to bring in some of the 'wealth of young talent': 'We don't want to be left alone with Jix and Amery.'[67] But despite this, and similar urgings from Chamberlain, Baldwin procrastinated and did nothing.

The vicissitudes of politics are, of course, endless, but on the assumption that the Conservatives won the election and stayed the full term, time alone would force Baldwin to make changes. 'Most of us', Chamberlain wrote, 'will be a good deal older and a good deal the worse for wear.' If they proceeded to lose the following election then Chamberlain thought that Churchill's chances of the leadership would be strong, for his 'wonderful debating and oratorical gifts would have full play', whilst his 'half-baked ideas' would 'not matter'.[68] What Chamberlain neglected to consider was that such a situation might arise a good deal more quickly if the Government lost the 1929 election.

The question on the mind of the Minister of Health was what should be done with Churchill after a successful election in 1929; it was not an easy one to answer. His triumphs had been such that he could not be denied a place, but what place? To Amery and the Protectionist wing of the Party Churchill was 'the old man of the sea', and it was even worth being beaten if it would remove him from the Treasury.[69] Churchill's defence of free trade in two speeches in July almost brought Amery's resignation,[70] and he pressed Baldwin strongly to send him anywhere but the Treasury. But when he suggested to Neville Chamberlain that Churchill might go to the Foreign Office, he received the response that the Prime Minister 'would not run such a risk' and would 'dread to find himself waking up at nights with a cold sweat at the thought of Winston's indiscretions'.[71]

The free-trade issue was an outward and visible sign of Churchill's Liberal past, and he appreciated its seriousness as a 'handicap'.[72] There were other indications that he did not always 'understand the psychology of our Party', as Amery put it, in a distinction which is all the more telling for being unconscious. On 19 February during a debate on supplementary estimates to compensate the Irish Loyalists who had lost property and possessions after partition in 1922, backbenchers, led by Churchill's old colleague, Lord Hugh Cecil, revolted against the Government's attempt to cut the amount to be paid. Lord Hugh, and others, took the opportunity to attack the whole 1922 settlement – and Churchill's part in it.[73] Cecil's political career had long ago failed to live up to the hopes of those far-off Edwardian days, and Churchill's epigram, that he 'began by being a monk without vows and now he is a sybarite without vices',[74] summed him up well. But the Chancellor's desire to stand fast on the Government's proposals illustrated his own inability to appreciate how strongly many Conservatives felt on the issue; Baldwin and Chamberlain knew, and climbed down accordingly.

If Amery thought that Churchill influenced the Cabinet in a 'little England' and even 'anti-imperial' direction,[75] others thought the opposite. Churchill had supported Lord Lloyd in 1927 against Foreign Office plans to conclude a treaty with the Egyptians behind his back, which would, in effect, concede nationalist demands for more control over the Suez canal and Egyptian finances,[76] and the diplomats, foiled of their treaty, inveighed against the

'W[inston] C[hurchill] section of the Cabinet'.[77] Viscount Cecil thought that it was not so much that Churchill was against 'this or that proposal' for disarmament in negotiations at Geneva, or in talks with the Americans about reductions in naval construction, as that he 'is out of tune' with the whole idea represented by the League of Nations: 'War is the only thing that really interests him in politics.'[78] He went even further when writing to Irwin: 'I don't believe Winston takes any interest in public affairs unless they involve the possibility of bloodshed. Preferably he likes to kill foreigners, but if that cannot be done I believe he would be satisfied with a few native Communists.'[79] Whilst showing signs of Cecilian exaggeration, such a verdict cannot be dismissed out of hand.

The fault-line in the Baldwin Cabinet between those who shared Irwin's views on the need to appease threats to Britain's world position, and those who took Birkenhead's altogether more robust view, ran deep. Despite his attacks on naval spending and his part in reaffirming the ten-year rule in 1928, Churchill clearly belonged, as Cecil recognised, to the latter group. He was firmly sceptical of the claims of Cecil and company that the League could maintain world peace – Churchill preferred the older and then unfashionable method of 'understandings between groups of Powers'.[80] His opposition to the idea that Britain should settle for 'parity' with America in cruisers, despite the far-flung nature of the Empire, was pressed hard in 1927 and 1928. 'No doubt', he wrote in July 1927, 'it is quite right in the interests of peace to go on talking about war with the United States being "unthinkable". Everyone knows this is not true'; such a war might be 'foolish and disastrous', but it was not impossible. 'We do not', he argued, in a phrase which the years were to invest with an irony unintended at the time, 'wish to put ourselves in the power of the United States.'[81]

Such views would have made him an uncomfortable Foreign Secretary, but Baldwin wondered whether he might not give Churchill the India Office.[82] But when he put the idea to Irwin, the Viceroy was far from keen on it. India, he told Baldwin on 28 March 1929, was at a 'cross ways', and she needed not only someone with 'courage', but also someone with the 'vision' and 'sympathy' to help her get over her 'inferiority complex'. He did not think that Churchill fitted the bill; he was too like F.E. in his attitudes towards Indians, and he had become, Irwin thought, 'or perhaps it is more true to say – has always been, a much more vigorous Imperialist in the 1890–1900 sense of the word than you & me'.[83]

Irwin's reply gave Baldwin pause for thought. By the time of the election in May nothing had been decided; it was not even certain that Churchill would leave the Treasury afterwards. In the uncertainty engendered by the prospect of an election, that old ghost from 1924 walked again: what would happen if the Liberals held the balance of power? Baldwin and Chamberlain were both determined that they would not serve with Lloyd George, in which case Baldwin thought the leadership would go to Churchill.[84] Having decided against reconstructing his Cabinet, Baldwin went into the election on the uninspiring slogan of 'safety first'. The election was called because it had to be, and there were no great burning issues for the Government to exploit; those that existed, the economy and unemployment, hardly worked in its favour.

Churchill had thought that the Conservatives would win the election,[85] but he had been intrigued by the possibilities which opposition might open up. He had spent less time in opposition than any other leading politician, and there were moments when he rather wished that 'Labour could be in for a short spell to allow him to display his powers in opposition'.[86] As the Conservatives lost the election on 30 May, by 1 June he was in a position to find out whether Chamberlain's guess that his oratorical prowess would propel him to the fore had been correct.

22

Shooting at Santa Claus

Beaverbrook once commented of Sir William Robertson's failure to be awarded anything more than a baronetcy and £10,000 at the end of the war when others had done so much better: 'after all Robertson had taken a pot-shot at Santa Claus, and missed'.[1] Contrary to what is often written about the timing and the reasons for Churchill's entry into the famous 'wilderness', it was his 'pot-shot' at 'Santa' Baldwin in 1929 which began the process, and it was his repeated missed attempts between then and 1931 which ensured his eventual consignment there. Within two years of the election defeat Churchill had destroyed the position which it had taken him five years to build up; but then he had begun the process within a month.

The election had left Labour with 288 seats, the Conservatives with 261. The Liberals, with only 59 MPs, had to take what comfort they could from the fact that their success in splitting the anti-Socialist vote had kept the Conservatives out even though they had won more votes than MacDonald's Labour Party. The short Parliamentary session of June–July 1929 would provide Baldwin and company with a 'dry-run' for what might be a considerable period of opposition. It was a situation which might have been tailor-made for Churchill. Baldwin's stock in trade, emollience, would be no use in opposition, and his inability to hit Labour hard would tell against him. Moreover, now that he was deprived of the quasi-divinity which hedges a Prime Minister, he would find it difficult to prevent the splits which had been present even in Government between Protectionists and anti-Protectionists, and imperialists and appeasers, from breaking out with greater virulence. Neville Chamberlain could certainly treat Labour with the contempt he believed it deserved, but he was not a great Commons speaker and lacked the 'star quality' which everyone agreed was possessed by Churchill. All the latter needed was a cause to fight for – and *mirabile dictu* one came along before the summer recess.

The Foreign Office had seen the change of Government as an opportunity to rid itself of Lord Lloyd.[2] The new Foreign Secretary, Arthur Henderson, was disposed to wait and see whether Lloyd was willing to co-operate with him, but the Permanent Under-Secretary, Sir Ronald Lindsay, was having none of that: 'I did not hide my desire to see Lord Lloyd replaced by some other High Commissioner.'[3] Henderson's caution was natural: for a Labour Government to replace a Conservative High Commissioner was bound to provoke storms in the Commons, and it might be interpreted as a sign that

Labour wished to pursue a weaker policy in Egypt. However, these fears were overcome by the diplomats, who provided him with full details of the many disputes which Lloyd's policy had created within the Baldwin Cabinet. Henderson was thus in clover. If he made Lloyd 'resign' now on the grounds of his disagreements with the previous Government, the Conservatives would be thrown into disarray.[4] This was what he did.

'*The main point*', Lindsay had stressed, '*is that Lord Lloyd shall be removed from his post the moment he arrives in England*';[5] he was. Lloyd had been aware that the diplomats were trying to dish him, but with the naïve confidence of a perfectly honest man, he could not believe that his friends, especially 'Baldwin or Winston', would let him down.[6] Therefore, when Henderson forced his resignation on 20 July, Lloyd appealed to his friends for help. The evening before Henderson announced the news to the Commons on 24 July, Lloyd went to Churchill and 'appealed to me to do him justice'.[7] Thus it was that after Henderson's announcement Churchill rose and demanded to know whether the 'resignation' had been 'extorted'. Baldwin sat 'silent and disapproving', but Churchill's pertinacity secured the promise of a debate on the issue.[8]

Hugh Dalton, Henderson's Old Etonian junior at the Foreign Office, noticed with interest the silence of Baldwin and other former Ministers; only 'Winston and certain Tory backbenchers' were 'howling with fury', and he thought that Churchill 'was half-drunk'.[9] Others had different explanations for Churchill's behaviour which were equally uncharitable. Neville Chamberlain noted that: 'All through this short session he has been trying to take the lead away from S[tanley] B[aldwin] and he thought he saw his way to make a real splash in the Adjournment and leave the House the hero of the day.'[10] Neither Baldwin nor Chamberlain had any intention of letting Churchill do such a thing.

Henderson had given the Conservative leaders 'warnings of the most definite character as to the case which the Government could put up'; these were passed on by the Whips to the backbenchers. Thus it was that when the debate was held on 26 July, Lloyd was left to the wolves. Baldwin's contribution was a moderate criticism of the Government, but he said nothing in praise of Lloyd. The key figure on the Conservative side was Austen Chamberlain, but he was conveniently absent in Norway. Henderson's fighting speech revealed why it was a good idea that Chamberlain was not present. He gave a detailed account of Lloyd's disagreements with the Conservative Government and he made it plain that any attempt to press the issue further must lead to a close examination of relations between Lloyd and Chamberlain. Therefore, when Churchill rose to defend Lloyd, it was 'without a Tory cheer'. As he wrote gloomily to Lloyd afterwards, 'the wind was very bleak in the House of Commons'. With the Government enjoying the support of 'a vindictive Foreign Office', the Liberals 'sourly impartial' and the Conservatives filled with political bromide handed out by the Whips, Churchill 'felt the current running so strongly that I did not push matters beyond a certain point, and even going so far, I encountered censure'.[11]

For a man who had grown used to basking in the warmth of the cheers from behind him, the experience of a chill wind of disapproval came as a shock, and, correspondingly, it was not one of Churchill's best performances. Churchill liked to prepare his speeches well in advance and then deliver them; this made them polished orations, but it left him vulnerable when, as on this occasion, the mood of the House was not what he had thought it would be. He attacked Henderson's actions and defended Lloyd, but when his own leader had said little and the former Foreign Secretary was absent, Churchill made little impact. He was correct to say that there had been a conspiracy by the diplomats against Lloyd, but it was unwise to say so as it affronted the House's sense of fair-play. Dalton noted with delight that Churchill 'got the worst of it' in his exchanges with Henderson and that he 'even began to lose the House'.[12] Neville Chamberlain noticed with satisfaction Churchill's 'discomfiture'; 'I must say he deserved it . . . he insisted on rushing in to his fate.' Thus, whilst Baldwin's speech was 'applauded as equally dignified and proper, Winston was made to look exceedingly foolish'.[13] Even Lady Lloyd, who was grateful for Churchill's gallant effort, thought his speech 'unwise and unhelpful'.[14]

The satisfaction with which Churchill's discomfiture was observed by many of his former colleagues is an index of the fear which they felt of his seizing the lead because of his talents in the House, and their relief at his failure was almost palpable. Austen Chamberlain, from his Norwegian hide-out, told his brother that he had been tempted to send Churchill the transcription of a message which Lord Melbourne had once sent to Lord John Russell: 'I hope you did not say anything damned foolish. I thought you were rather teeming with imprudence when I left you yesterday.'[15] But, of course, he had not done so; none of his former colleagues had, and not one of them seemed sorry.

Churchill would not forget that they had left him to support Lloyd alone, and he drew a gloomy moral from the episode, as he told the former High Commissioner: 'the march of events will vindicate your administration; and your reputation will grow step by step with the melancholy decline in British and Egyptian affairs'. There was, he told Lloyd, 'nothing for it but to await developments, which I am sure will be swift and evil'. Henceforth, this would be the burden of Churchill's song: 'Never mind, you have done your best, and if Britain alone among modern States chooses to cast away her rights, her interests and her strength, she must learn by bitter experience.'[16] 'Here', Churchill wrote later, 'began my differences with Mr Baldwin.'[17]

The main difference between them was the one which Irwin had foreshadowed when he had told Baldwin that Churchill was more of an 'imperialist' on the 1890–1900 model than either of them was, but there was also a difference in temperament, of which this was a reflection. Churchill was by nature an activist; he liked to do things and possessed abundant stores of energy. Baldwin's scant stores of the latter had been depleted by the election, and the lethargy which overcame him after any effort compounded with his own temperament to make him an ineffectual leader of the opposition.[18] Churchill wanted the Conservatives to 'confront' Labour on 'all great imperial and national issues', but Baldwin was not keen.[19]

Churchill was not the only Conservative to take a pot-shot at Baldwin between 1929 and 1931; indeed, there were times when it seemed as though it was open season of the Conservative leader. Nor was Churchill the only one to feel the need for a 'robust assertion of Britain's imperial greatness'. The fault-lines apparent in government now opened into fissures once the Conservatives were in opposition.[20]

Because the ensuing crisis failed to bring Baldwin down, it is easy to ignore how close it came to doing so. Indeed, a more sensitive, less stubborn man might well have chosen to retire in the face of humiliations far greater than those which had driven Balfour out of the leadership in 1911.[21] Churchill took his 'pot-shots' during a unique 'window of opportunity', and the fact that he failed to finish Baldwin off owed more to bad luck and circumstance than it did to any defects on Churchill's part. The unease felt by many Conservatives after the election defeat was widespread. Sir Henry Page-Croft, a long-time tariff reformer whose right-wing views on just about everything made him the ideal MP for Bournemouth, one of the few places where he could appear as a moderate, spoke for many others when he wrote to Lloyd on 1 August: 'much exercised about the Party – all is not well with us'. There was, he complained, no cause or leader to inspire Conservatives, and 'we have no Empire policy and no industrial policy'.[22] The post-election period was a good time to do something about this situation.

It was not simply that Baldwin's prestige as leader was dimmed because of his defeat, or that the fitful flame of his energy was burning low, but that the nature of the defeat had weakened his position. Those progressive young Conservatives who had admired Churchill for his liberal-Toryism had also admired Baldwin, but most of them sat for marginal seats, which, in 1929, they had lost: Duff Cooper, Harold Macmillan and Baldwin's former private secretary, Geoffrey Lloyd, were the most notable casualties. The imperialist wing of the Party had suffered much less – seats like Bournemouth would elect a donkey with a blue rosette; indeed, there were those who alleged that it had been doing so for years. Moreover, many 'die-hards' were, like Lloyd, peers and thus impervious to what the electorate thought. The balance of the Parliamentary Party thus shifted towards the right. On one estimate, where the 'die-hards' had held about 60 of the 400 seats which the Conservatives had in 1924–9, after the election they had 'at least 50 out of 261'.[23]

Deprived of a Liberal leaven, Baldwin also lacked the support which he had once received from senior colleagues. Bridgeman had retired to the Lords with a peerage, Neville Chamberlain grew increasingly impatient with his leader's shortcomings, whilst Amery and Churchill expressed in their different ways both strands of the Party's imperial angst. From the moment the Party lost the election Amery was determined that it should commit itself to a policy of full-scale tariff reform, in which he had the support (even if he did not always welcome it) of the press barons, Beaverbrook and Rothermere, who opened their 'Empire Crusade' policy in July 1929.[24] Churchill stood opposed to any such policy. He feared that Amery's line would result in a 'Lib–Lab block in some form or another and a Conservative Right hopelessly excluded from power'.[25]

But Churchill's desire to conciliate the Liberals and opposition to tariffs ran foul of two streams of thought within the Party: the Protectionist lobby and anti-coalitionism, thus providing another example to set alongside the Irish Loyalist debate of his lack of instinctive understanding of Conservative activists. For men like Amery, who had been committed to tariffs since Joe Chamberlain's great crusade, the issue transcended economics and became one of faith in the future of the Empire. He doubted whether Churchill even understood the economic arguments. The two men crossed the Atlantic in each other's company in August, and, after talking with Churchill every evening, Amery concluded: 'He just repeats the old phrases of 1903 and no argument seems to make any difference on him. He can only think in phrases and close argument is lost on him.' Churchill said that if Amery had his way and the Conservatives adopted a tariff policy, he would 'retire from politics and concentrate on making money'. Amery thought that the 'key' to understanding Churchill 'is to realise that he is mid-Victorian, steeped in the politics of his father's period, and unable ever to get the modern point of view'.[26] There was a good deal in this, and there would have been more if the prefix 'late' were substituted for 'mid'.

Baldwin managed to postpone coming to any decision about Protection during the summer of 1929, but by the time the new Parliament met pressure was building up from local constituencies and national figures as diverse as Amery, Lloyd and Beaverbrook for a commitment to introduce protective tariffs.[27] In the face of this pressure, which had support from Neville Chamberlain, Churchill's resistance came to count for less in Baldwin's eyes, especially now that the Liberals and Labour had failed to come to any alliance. But it was on India, not tariffs, that the new season of shooting at Santa was to start, and for that Santa had only himself to blame.

On 31 October Irwin declared that the ultimate aim of British rule in India was to grant the country Dominion Status. In doing this Irwin and the Labour Government were acting, at least in part, to pacify nationalist opinion, but they also anticipated the report of the 1928 commission chaired by Sir John Simon into the future constitutional development of India. It was a declaration which outraged many Conservatives; but when it was reported that

Baldwin had stated that he and the Party agreed with it, the leader found himself under fire.

It was not simply 'die-hards' who were enraged, but also many moderate backbenchers. To those Conservatives like Davidson, in whose mental processes the coalition assumed the proportions which King Charles's head did in that of Mr Dick, the assault which was called forth on Baldwin was, as he told Irwin, evidence of a coalitionist plot.[28] It might be thought that to see in Churchill's opposition to a liberal policy on India evidence of the hairy paw of Lloyd George was taking paranoia too far, but other Conservatives held similar views. Baldwin also believed it, telling Bridgeman that 'all this fuss about India had been organised by L.G. and some of . . . [his] disloyal colleagues to try & drive him out of the leadership';[29] if it was paranoia, then it was widespread, and reflected a continuing anxiety about a revival of the coalition.

If Churchill was involved, as some of the latest commentators on the subject are inclined to think, in an 'ex-coalitionist' plot to get rid of Baldwin on the issue, then clearly those who were apt to attribute his activities on India to motives of personal ambition would find extra arguments to commend their position. But the fact that Davidson thought this was so, and told Baldwin and Irwin,[30] does not mean that it was necessarily so. Hoare, who was one of the few to support Baldwin, certainly described the 'old coalition element' and the 'die-hards' as being against Baldwin's stance, but then, as he pointed out, 'scarcely anyone in the Party liked it'.[31] Lloyd George was certainly playing for allies and naturally looked towards Churchill and other former colleagues, but that did not mean that they reciprocated. It may be that, as Davidson thought, Lloyd George planned to destroy the Government by putting down a question in the House asking whether Irwin's declaration portended a new policy, and that he hoped this would also break the Conservatives by forcing Baldwin to side with MacDonald; but it may also have been a sign of Davidson's phobia about the coalition. 'The fools never saw it,' he lamented, but maybe there was nothing to see.

When the matter was debated on 7 November, Baldwin saved the day by adroit tactics and oratory. He refused to allow the question to be put to the vote, which prevented the Party dividing on the issue. Then, in a high-minded oration of the sort which only a crisis seemed to drag out of him, Baldwin explained that his statement of approval had been made on the understanding that the members of the Simon Commission had all concurred in the declaration. After moralising upon the theme that the British and Indians were from the same Aryan racial stock, he sat down, having been studiously vague about his own position on India's future constitutional status.

The whole incident raises the question of Churchill's motives on India. Hoare described him as 'almost demented with fury' during the debate and, as we have seen, others thought that he was engaged in a coalitionist plot. The evidence in favour of the view that he was trying to remove Baldwin is fragmentary and not very convincing. Chamberlain *thought* that Churchill's intervention in the Lloyd debate was designed to 'take the lead' during that session; Baldwin certainly *thought* that he was involved in some way in the 'Beaverbrook–Rothermere game', but only because Duff Cooper told him so;[32] whilst Beaverbrook *thought*, in October, that Churchill ought to be leading the Conservative Party[33] and hoped that he would modify his opposition to tariffs in order to do so. Churchill did so over the next year, but he would have found himself even more at odds with his Party had he not adapted himself to the strong pressure in favour of tariff reform.[34] All this, then, amounts to ill-natured gossip and wishful thinking. It might be commented that politicians seldom act from one motive, and that they are not always aware of the complexity of their own motivation, but this would hardly be helpful.

Self-interest or patriotism? Contemporaries tended to divide into one of these camps when assessing Churchill's motives, but modern historians have generally been more cautious. This approach is exemplified by one of the most recent commentators, Dr Ball. Having asserted that between the Irwin declaration and the opening of the first Round Table conference in November 1930 Churchill was 'a politician in decline, looking for an issue with which to revive his career',[35] Dr Ball qualifies this by commenting that Churchill was 'a curious and complex political character' and that it would be 'too simple' to say that 'he took up the India question in order to restore his political fortunes, or that he did so only out of concern for the future of the British people'. It is no surprise to learn that 'both factors influenced his actions, and the truth lies in between'.[36] So judicious an assertion, worthy of a Foreign Office document in its studied covering of all the options, is followed by a definite conclusion: 'this does not mean that he plotted to oust Baldwin as leader – his position was far too weak for such pretensions'.[37] But this is to choose the wrong point upon which to rest.

Churchill's position had been strong in early 1929. He may have made a fool of himself, or have been made to look one, over the Lloyd debate, and the revival of the agitation for Protection did him no favours, but in a Parliamentary situation where the Liberals held a balance of power, and where his oratorical powers could command the day, Churchill's position remained, potentially, very strong. This is not to say that he was actively plotting to get rid of Baldwin in 1929, but he was determined to prevent the Conservative Party from being committed to a policy in India of which he disapproved. This was to bring him into conflict with Baldwin but it also brought him support from sections of the Conservative Party which had traditionally been hostile to him. Churchill was an ambitious man, and if the leadership had come his way he would have taken it; but it was not his main motive.

What Churchill was fighting was the phenomenon to which he had referred in his letter to Lloyd of 28 July – that malaise against which he had protested as far back as 1921–2: Britain's loss of grip in imperial affairs. Writing to

Irwin on 1 January 1930, Churchill commented that 'after what occurred in Ireland . . . and what is being done in Egypt', he could not blame any imperial governor 'in distant lands for feeling that they have no strong nation behind them'; but henceforth things would be different. 'On the supreme issue of India,' Churchill declared, the 'British Empire will arise in its old strength.'[38] This was Churchill's motivation: he wanted to put a stop to the rot which was undermining the Empire, and he would take his stand on the greatest imperial possession, British India. It was an impulsive, romantic reaction at one level: he could not bear to see the jewel in the Crown go; but at another level he knew that if it did go, then the Empire was finished and with it 'the continuance of British fame and power'.[39]

When discussing Churchill's motives it is essential to make a distinction between the period 1929–31 and that which followed. During the first period, Churchill led Conservative opposition to what he and many Conservatives saw as a feeble Socialist policy, something which was perfectly within the ambit of normal Party politics; it was only after 1931, when the Conservative leadership seemed to adopt that policy and then pursued it under cover of the 'National Government' label, that Churchill turned his sights on them.

The Irwin declaration and reactions to it had revealed not a coalitionist plot, but something more important – a major fault-line in the Conservative Party along which tremors were to pass for the next decade and beyond. 'The Peril in India', published in the *Daily Mail* on 16 November, was the first of what was to become a flood of articles by Churchill which argued that India was unfit for Dominion Status.[40] F.E. was roused to a final political campaign by what his articles called 'the peril to India'. Describing the Indian nationalists such as Nehru as 'a collection . . . of very inferior Kerenskis', F.E. declared that it was 'a commonplace that if Great Britain left India tomorrow India would dissolve into anarchy'.[41] With an acuteness which showed that his collapsing health had not dimmed his lawyer's eye for the weak point in an opponent's case, F.E. pointed out that Irwin's statement was 'so ambiguous that it is almost impossible to select from it any clear and unambiguous proposal'.[42] Lloyd took a similar line in a series of articles in the *Daily Telegraph* in March 1930, that most Indians would be much worse off if 'abandoned' to the 'domination' of the 'Brahmin'.[43]

India was the first issue upon which the differences of opinion which had been apparent in the 1924–9 Government on imperial policy became a divide. Conservative reaction to the Irwin declaration made Baldwin 'feel the hopelessness of trying to liberalise the Tory Party'.[44] During his speech in the House on 7 November, Baldwin had declared that: 'If ever the day comes when the Party I lead ceases to attract men of the calibre of Edward Wood, then I am finished with my Party.'[45] Irwin's attitude demonstrated the same mixture of high-minded superiority and pragmatic virtue. The question for him was whether Indian nationalism could be guided along 'imperial' lines or whether it would be 'deflected on to separatist lines'; the problem would 'never be solved by F.E. or Winston'.[46]

Irwin and Baldwin did not want to 'throw away' India any more than did Churchill, Birkenhead and Lloyd. Their policy was, as later historians have recognised, to concede where necessary but to retain control over the essentials of power for as long as possible;[47] and it is one which, given the modern aversion to imperialism, has come in for a good deal of praise.[48] But it is arguable that it was as unrealistic and confused as Birkenhead and Churchill alleged. In Egypt and in India, Baldwin, Irwin and company pursued a chimera. They sought to channel nationalism along 'imperial lines', which was to mistake the essential nature of the phenomenon; they thought that they could find, somewhere, the nationalist who would sign a treaty which would give them what they wanted; but such a creature did not exist outside their imaginations. Had he done so, his fellow nationalists would have condemned him for 'selling out'.

Churchill, Birkenhead, Lloyd and the imperialist wing of the Conservative Party knew what they wanted: to hold on to the Empire. Over the year following the Irwin declaration it was to become apparent that there was a fundamental divide between their way of thinking on how this could be done and that of the official leadership. Historians have tended to dismiss the case which Churchill advanced, but it contained in it more realism than that of his opponents; he knew that the moment the British began to talk in terms of making concessions to nationalist demands, they had embarked upon a road which had no turnings. This was more than his opponents realised. They sincerely believed that they could make concessions on inessentials and hold on to the levers of power; they were wrong. They were also, it might be noted, the men who thought that Hitler's greater-German nationalism could be appeased by throwing him sops without having to give him anything important.

During 1930–1 these two very different approaches to imperial affairs were to be uncovered by the course of events; but those historians who have praised Churchill's stance against appeasement would do well to recall that it was part and parcel of a general attitude which influenced his policy on India too: Churchill fought to preserve British power. He may have been wrong to have thought that he could conserve it, but over India and appeasement, and in 1940, he acted on the assumption that he was right: the road to 'their finest hour' was begun in 1929. The determination not to surrender in 1940 was founded upon the same sense of Britain's duty to her high destiny which prompted his campaign on India; the one depended upon the other. As we shall see, all the 'sound', 'realistic' men who advocated compromise over India: Irwin (in a new guise as Lord Halifax), Hoare and his Under-Secretary, 'Rab' Butler, Sir John Simon and Baldwin, went on to apply the same mind-set to Hitler, both before 1939 and in 1940. These men saw the limitations of British power and wanted to make realistic adjustments which would preserve what could be preserved; Churchill did not see the limitations. Lord Melbourne's comment about the 'bloody fools' turning out to be better prophets than 'all the wise men' comes irresistibly to mind in this context.

Baldwin's speech in November helped to create the appearance of Conservative unity on India; everyone could agree that Britain was not retreating, it was only a matter of 'safeguards' and preserving 'vital interests'. It was only with the advent of the Round Table talks in November 1930 that this illusion became difficult to maintain. Before that the main line of attack on Baldwin came from the tariff reformers – or the 'Empire Free Trade' campaign, as Beaverbrook rechristened the Protection movement. This was not territory which Churchill found conducive. Harold Nicolson, who had just left the Foreign Office to join the Beaverbrook press (before realising his mistake and making another one by entering politics), met Churchill at his new chief's London house, Stornoway, and found him 'very changed' with a 'great white face like a blister. Incredibly aged.' Given Churchill's reputation for pugnacity, Nicolson was disappointed to see that his 'spirits have also declined and he sighs that he has lost his old fighting power'.[49]

In view of the campaign which Churchill was to put up later in the year, and the vigour with which he was to sustain it, Nicolson's verdict might seem surprising, but as Beaverbrook had asked him to Stornoway to convince him of the merits of 'Empire Free Trade', it was hardly surprising if, as another of Beaverbrook's guests, Robert Bruce Lockhart, recorded: 'Winston is very depressed about his position.'[50] According to Nicolson, Churchill told Beaverbrook that he was 'too old to fight' his new campaign: 'But Max, Max, you are destroying my Party.' It all sounds very dramatic, even if Churchill was, as Lockhart thought, 'drunk'. Had Beaverbrook been able to win over Churchill, or had he been willing to swallow his free-trade principles, then there could indeed have been a united campaign against Baldwin. But this did not happen, and the fact that it did not must be counted as evidence against any theory that Churchill's main desire was to topple Baldwin.

In November 1929 Churchill told Amery that, if necessary, he would become 'the super turncoat of British politics to maintain consistency',[51] and whilst, under pressure from Beaverbrook and from the fact that opinion in the Conservative Party seemed set in a Protectionist direction, Churchill wavered so far as to agree to 'exploitation of the crown colonies and to "tariffs for negotiation"', he would not agree to 'taxes on food';[52] by February 1930 he had even decided that he could accept 'industrial protection', consoling himself with the thought that 'mass production' was an entirely new phenomenon. But he would still not accept taxes on food, even under the threat of Rothermere standing an 'Empire Free Trade' candidate against him at Epping in the next election.[53]

Churchill had accepted Baldwin's announcement on 5 February that Protection should be extended to the iron and steel industries, but this did not satisfy the press lords for long, and the proposal to stand a candidate against him at Epping was part of their decision in late February to turn their 'Crusade' into a 'United Empire Party'. Churchill would have liked Baldwin to challenge Beaverbrook and Rothermere outright by calling a series of by-elections, but he was too concerned for Party unity to do that. However, reaction within the Conservative Party to Beaverbrook's decision was so hostile that his Lordship, whose main desire was probably to capture the Party for his cause, backed down and, to Churchill's pleasure, came to an agreement on 3 March with Baldwin that the Conservatives would pledge themselves to hold a referendum on Protection.[54]

But the truce could not last. Baldwin saw the referendum pledge as a shield with which to ward off further demands, whilst Beaverbrook saw it as a sword with which to make further advances. In May Davidson, who had been blamed by some for the Party's failure in 1929, and who was thought to be insufficiently enthusiastic about Protection, resigned as Party Chairman and was replaced by Neville Chamberlain.[55] However, although it had been Davidson who had received the bullet, there was little doubt that, as Sir Joseph Ball put it in a letter to Davidson on 14 August: 'The attacks on you were really aimed at SB.'[56]

Seeking to elevate vagueness into a political style, and apathy into an art form, Baldwin simply succeeded in eventually infuriating everyone. It was fortunate for him that those Conservatives who, by June, wanted him to go, feared to remove him during the summer because of the press campaign against him following the breakdown of the 'truce' in June: no one wished to seem to be bowing to the power of the 'gutter press'.[57] It was easy to criticise Baldwin's leadership – it must have been, everyone did so. Even the loyal Bridgeman thought it would improve matters if Baldwin did not 'cultivate the attitude of being on a transcendental plane above the sordid turmoil of political life'; doing *The Times* crossword on a long train journey instead of reading the news was not, Bridgeman thought, quite the attitude which the public expected: 'nobody saw him, fortunately,' he told Chamberlain.[58] But it was difficult to know which way he could have led the Party.

Baldwin gave his colleagues in the Business Committee (as what is now the 'Shadow Cabinet' was then known) a good deal of leeway, balancing the concessions to the Protectionists with letting Salisbury and Churchill speak out for their side of the case. But there was a good deal more calculation in this than Churchill realised. Baldwin told Amery on 26 May that he was 'proceeding on the policy of giving Winston as much rope as possible to hang himself': 'After the election Winston had thought he was going to command the whole situation in the Commons by virtue of his debating powers, and had only made one blunder after another.'[59] In fact, having taken a few pot-shots at Baldwin, Churchill was now to find himself under fire.

23

Birkenhead's Legatee

The move into opposition had not only provided Churchill with an opportunity to take pot-shots at his leader, it had given him the leisure – and a reason – to step up his literary activities. Chartwell provided him with an idyllic rural base where he could indulge in bucolic pursuits and play the amateur builder, but it was a drain on his financial resources; and those resources diminished with the loss of office. Chartwell, a London home, Randolph at Christ Church and three daughters all remained a charge upon his purse, and Churchill was not a rich man. The royalties from his books had gone into a trust fund for his children, and little Mary, who had come along too late to be provided for as the others were, was assigned royalties from books published after 1925.[1] The fourth volume of *The World Crisis*, *The Aftermath*, was published in March 1929. The reaction of his colleagues can be glimpsed from Irwin's Janus-faced comments. Writing to the Archbishop of Canterbury, he said: 'What an astounding thing it is that any man should be able to combine authorship on that scale with being Chancellor of the Exchequer';[2] but he lapsed into a less charitable tone to Neville Chamberlain, supposing that 'the first comes easily to him and the second no doubt sits lightly on his shoulders'.[3]

The author of an arid little volume on John Keble could be forgiven his 'sour grapes'. What was astonishing, as men like John Buchan and T. E. Lawrence, who had written best-sellers, recognised, was the 'architectural power of the book'.[4] In his marshalling of his material, as in its presentation, Churchill had produced, as Buchan told him, 'the best thing anyone has done in contemporary history since Clarendon'. Balfour, whose good opinion Churchill valued most amongst the diminishing band of his elders[5] (praise from that source was, he thought, 'like being "mentioned in despatches"'),[6] simply told him that: 'Five volumes of immortal history is a wonderful addition to this great period of administrative activity.'[7] Balfour was right.

It was to his pen that Churchill turned once in opposition to supply the place of his Ministerial income. For some time he had contemplated writing a life of the first Duke of Marlborough, but until Rosebery lent him a copy of Paget's *Examen*, which refuted some of the charges which Macaulay had made against 'Duke John', he had hesitated to do so.[8] Now, with his magazine primed with this ammunition, and with exclusive access to Marlborough's papers at Blenheim, he signed a contract for £10,000 in July 1929 to complete the work in five years; this brought him £6,000 immediately.[9] This was supplemented by what he called 'the Reminiscence',[10] a volume on his early life which was planned to bring in some money quickly; but if it originated as a 'pot-boiler', the only appropriate comment is Baldwin's upon reading the proofs of what became *My Early Life*: 'It is a remarkable production and I have read it with real delight. I kept saying "My wig," or words to that effect, "that is GOOD."'[11] Churchill's hope that it would 'do more than it was originally meant to do, namely, to pay the Tax collector', was amply realised when it was published in the autumn.[12] The initial run of 5,750 copies was followed up within the month by a second impression of 2,500, with two more of 1,500 each in the next two months. Published in October 1930, by the end of the year it had sold 9,346 copies; and it has not been out of print since.[13] By such means, and a prodigious output of articles, Churchill lived from 'mouth to hand' – as he dictated his works. His trip to America in the summer of 1929 resulted in some useful contacts on Wall Street and produced a profit of £21,825 from speculation on his behalf.[14]

But despite such financial success, Churchill's mood by the autumn of 1930 was not an optimistic one. Part of this is to be explained by the events retailed in the last chapter, but another part of the explanation lies elsewhere. T. E. Lawrence had noted about *The Aftermath*, 'your sense of decaying comes uppermost';[15] and the process of writing about his past life seems to have stimulated the process. Lawrence caught the book's tone when he told Churchill that: 'I felt as I read it . . . how past is the epoch of your youth. Nothing of the world, or attitude or society you lived in remains.'[16] Examples abound of Churchill reversing Macaulay's habit of comparing the present with the past to the advantage of the former; for him the present always marked a falling away from the security and prosperity of yesteryear. The Whig historian had given way to the Tory one.

Churchill was only fifty-five when he wrote *My Early Life*, but the predominant tone of the book is of a much older man looking back to a world which had vanished; one who could no longer share Macaulay's impatience with those who believed that there had been some 'golden age' in the past. The period of his youth was, for Churchill, what the Age of the Antonines had been for Gibbon. Thus, when writing of his first election campaign in Oldham in 1899, Churchill felt that he had to explain to his readers that the town was 'in those days an extremely prosperous community', where 'for more than half a century things had been getting slowly and surely better'; 'I have lived to see them falling back in the world's affairs.' It was a comment which the present author's mother and grandmother, who lived there at the time Churchill was writing, would have endorsed. My grandmother would have agreed that, even in 1930, the standard of living was superior to what it had been when she had campaigned for Churchill in 1899, but she would not have disagreed with him that Oldham was 'gripped in the ever-narrowing funnel of declining trade and vanished ascendancy'.[17]

One of the things which gives *My Early Life* its power is that it is an elegaic evocation of a lost golden age. Churchill contrasts, for example, the 'wise and prudent law' which 'in those days' had spread a general election over 'nearly six weeks' with the current system of 'all the electors voting blindly on one day, and only learning next morning what they had done'. In those days, he tells his readers, 'national issues were really fought out', and the 'electorate of a constituency was not unmanageable'. 'Great speeches by an eminent personage would often turn a constituency or even a city,' Churchill comments with nostalgia for an age when such speeches were 'fully reported in all the newspapers and studied by wide political classes'.[18] In 'those days we had a real political democracy led by a hierarchy of statesmen, and not a fluid mass distracted by newspapers'.[19] As Robert Rhodes James has commented, this 'real democracy' consisted of only twenty-seven per cent of the population,[20] but for Churchill it was preferable to what had replaced it.

If the contemplation of his own early life produced in Churchill a conservative mood and a reactionary distaste for the current age when compared with the glorious past, these tendencies were strengthened by another of his literary activities – the writing of obituaries. The sense of a vanishing age could not but be strengthened by the deaths of Asquith in 1928, Rosebery and Morley in 1929, and Balfour in 1930; as the giants of the past died, they were not replaced. 'Nowadays,' Churchill wrote, when '"one man is as good as another – or even better"', 'such men are not found'. There were no successors to the 'Liberal Statesmen' of the 'Victorian Epoch'; 'democracy' and 'the war' had swept 'the shores bare'. Churchill lamented that the 'leadership of the privileged has passed; but it has not been succeeded by that of the eminent': the 'pedestals have for some years been vacant, have now been demolished'.[21] The modern tragedy was that where men like Rosebery 'flourished in an age of great men and small events',[22] now, when Britain faced the 'possibility of national ruin' and the 'main foundations' of civilisation were threatened, there were only small men to meet them. Balfour was a 'Statesman'; now there were none.[23] In an essay on Joseph Chamberlain, first published in February 1930, Churchill wrote that the 'mark' of a 'great man' was not simply that he had 'the power of making lasting impressions on people he meets', but also 'so to have handled matters in his life that the course of after-events is continuously affected by what he did';[24] the breed was now almost extinct.

Contemplation of the glories of the past stimulated in Churchill the desire, already noted, to ensure that Britain's imperial heritage, garnered by the 'great men' of history, was not thrown away by the 'small men' of the present. Some 'great men' still existed. Churchill clearly placed himself in this category, but of all his exact contemporaries in British politics, only F.E. was accorded a place in *Great Contemporaries*. It was, therefore, a tragic irony that his should have been the next obituary which Churchill had to write; where Asquith,

Rosebery and Morley had all died full of years and with their political campaigns long-ago put to rest, F.E. died just when Churchill was looking forward to his aid in helping to combat the deliquescence of Britain's imperial heritage: 'F.E. has gone,' he lamented in the foreword to the second Earl's life of his father, published in 1933, 'and gone when sorely needed.'[25]

Birkenhead died on 30 September 1930 at the age of fifty-eight. Comforting his son, Freddie, Churchill told him: 'Think of the great Duke of Marlborough – how he lingered on in surly decrepitude. How much better it would have been had he been cut off in his brilliant prime – a cannon ball at Malplaquet.'[26] 'Between the setting of the sun and night there was only the briefest twilight. It was better so.' Thus he comforted himself for the loss of his closest friend. It may be, as F.E.'s most recent (and excellent) biography implies, that he was 'burnt out',[27] but that was not how it seemed to Churchill. At a meeting of the dining club which he and F.E. had founded in 1911, 'The Other Club', Churchill lamented: 'Just at the time when we felt that our public men are lacking in the power to dominate events, he has been taken.'[28]

After his father died, Churchill had described himself as picking up the flag from the 'stricken field'; this was very much what he proceeded to do after F.E.'s untimely death. Just before Birkenhead died, Churchill sent a letter to Beaverbrook which is redolent of the air that he had been breathing over the previous twelve months. Congratulating him on the rapid 'growth of your influence' in the Conservative Party, he naturally regretted that it should 'have been almost exactly proportionate to the diminution of mine'. But he was, he said, 'old enough to take a philosophical view of these things'. He asked Beaverbrook to use his power in the wider cause which he now discerned as his 'only interest in politics' – namely 'to help our Island out of the rotten state into which it has now fallen'. Contemplating the sacrifices of the Great War, Churchill could not 'understand why it is we should now throw away our conquests and our inheritance, through sheer helplessness and pusillanimity'. Beaverbrook should 'broaden' his policy to 'make it represent a new and strong assertion of Britain's right to live and right to reign with her Empire splendid and united'.[29] Beaverbrook could, and did, play the deaf adder; but Churchill would fight on – alone, if necessary.

However, Churchill's attachment to the things of the past was not shared by everyone in the Conservative Party; indeed, to those who wanted to revamp the Party before the next election, he was one of the 'old gang' who ought to go. Neville Chamberlain, as the new Conservative Chairman, heard many complaints about the 'old gang' and commented to Bridgeman that it was 'remarkable' how the 'notion' had 'bitten into the minds of the younger members of the Party'.[30] Membership of this group was usually the same: 'Jix easily heads the list, then comes Winston, and finally, I regret to say, Austen.' It was a matter of even more regret that Baldwin had not used Churchill's opposition to tariffs 'to get rid of him'.[31]

With the Conservative leadership under increasing pressure from Beaver-brook and the 'Empire Free Trade' campaign, sacrificing one of the 'old gang' was a tempting alternative to sacrificing the leader. So bad had the pressure become by the end of September that Conservative Central Office felt obliged to issue a statement denying that Baldwin was about to resign. In an attempt to stem the tide Chamberlain released to the press his own 'unauthorised programme' (an echo of his father's famous campaign of 1885), which advocated an emergency tariff and a ten per cent import duty across the board.[32] As he commented later to Bridgeman, 'hardly any' of the Party 'know what they mean by "Empire Free Trade"', so if the leadership could come up with a coherent definition, along the lines of the 'free hand' (to impose retaliatory tariffs) which had been mentioned early in the year, they could seize the initiative.[33]

This step almost drove Churchill from the Business Committee. Having succeeded, on 7 October, in delaying consideration of the plan, he was faced a week later with a united phalanx of his colleagues who wanted to accept it. At this point Churchill 'suddenly declared that he could not accept it and must publicly state his disagreement'. He then thanked all those present 'for our consideration during the time we had worked together', declaring that whilst he would continue to speak on India and against Socialism, he could not support 'the new policy'. Neville Chamberlain thought that this was just a 'pretext for running out', but his half-brother Austen pleaded with Churchill to reconsider his decision.[34]

Churchill drafted a letter of resignation,[35] but after Austen Chamberlain's plea was followed up with an emollient letter from Baldwin,[36] and the morning newspapers treated the announcement of Conservative policy as nothing new, he felt that he should not send it.[37] But Baldwin felt that it was only a matter of time until he did so.[38] Neville Chamberlain regretted that Baldwin had 'missed' the 'opportunity of ridding himself of a dangerous liability', especially since it seemed 'pretty clear that Winston does not intend to run out'.[39] The Party Chairman was right and wrong at the same time. He was wrong in so far as he thought that Churchill would stay in the Business Committee and swallow anything to do so. 'Empire Free Trade' was something upon which Churchill compromised, and he did so because it was not important compared with the 'supreme issue' of India. He took the meaning of Austen Chamberlain's comment that because 'everything about us has changed so much since you & I formed our political creeds' the only true consistency was 'not of means & methods but of purpose',[40] but he took it further. It was here that Neville Chamberlain was right without knowing it. Where the Chamberlains' 'purpose' was inextricably linked to the fate and unity of the Conservative Party, Churchill's was not; it went deeper. On 24 September he had told Baldwin that he hoped he would 'not allow your friendship for Irwin, to affect your judgement or the actions of your Party' on what was, since the war, 'probably the greatest question Englishmen have to settle'. Churchill would not let any such ties hold him back: 'I must confess myself to care more about this business than anything else in public life.'[41]

With F.E. 'taken from us at this period when he would have been of decisive importance',[42] a double burden of responsibility fell upon Churchill's shoulders. Irwin's 'policy of appeasement' had to be stopped. As long as there was a chance that the Conservative leadership would prove serviceable in that cause, then Churchill could stay with them; but once it was clear that Baldwin did allow his 'friendship for Irwin' to run counter to Churchill's conception of where the Conservative Party's duty lay, he could do so no longer. India was not another 'Party political' issue; it was not really even a political issue at all; it was a symbol of the world which Churchill had depicted so lovingly in *My Early Life*, and of his deepest friendship: that is why it moved him so much – it touched the deepest chords of his being. In one sense all this equipped him but ill for the struggle he had undertaken, for he was unable to see when compromise would be possible.

The Round Table conference to discuss the future constitutional status of India opened in London on 13 November. The Indian delegates, led by the Maharaja of Bikaner, put forward not a demand for immediate Dominion Status, but, to the delight of the British delegation, one for all-India federation, which would provide a constitutional settlement which would give 'dominion status with safeguards'. Such an agreement would have given the princely states a privileged position, which would have saved their autocratic rulers from being swamped by the 'communalist and nationalist agitation'; henceforth they would have been co-partners with the Raj.[43] This gave Hoare, who was leading the Conservative delegation, a great deal more room to play with than he had imagined, particularly as the various Indian delegates had not agreed amongst themselves what the phrase 'all-India federation' meant in detail.[44] Sir John Simon, whose *amour-propre* had been bruised by the way in which the Irwin declaration seemed to disregard the report of his Commission, found that he could agree to negotiate along such vague lines, even as he was also finding that his old opposition to tariffs was weakening; the road to co-operation with the Conservatives was opening up.[45]

But if Churchill's old Liberal Cabinet colleague from pre-war days was moving closer towards the Conservative leadership, Churchill himself was moving the other way. Although he had not resigned from the Business Committee, he was still, according to his cousin, Freddie Guest, 'in doubt whether to "lay an egg or not"', and the opening of the conference disinclined him to take Guest's advice that 'when in doubt . . . don't lay it!'[46] On the day the conference was opened Baldwin described Churchill as being 'in the depths of gloom', and he thought that he wanted it 'to bust up quickly and the Tory Party to go back to pre-war and govern with a strong hand. He has become once more the subaltern of Hussars of '96.'[47]

This was a tempting shorthand description of the state of mind described above and had, as a result, just enough truth in it not to require further reflection on the part of those who had always nourished suspicions of Churchill. That India would do what tariffs had not, namely to part Churchill from his colleagues on the Business Committee, became apparent as the Round Table conference proceeded. On 14 October, the day he had almost resigned, Churchill had taken a step which presaged what was to come; he had joined the Indian Empire Society. The Society had been set up a few months earlier, and its function was to draw together those groups within the Conservative Party (and without) worried about the Labour Government's policy towards India. This is an important point to stress. At this stage the most forceful criticism was directed at Ramsay MacDonald and his Secretary of State, William Wedgwood Benn; criticism of the official Conservative leadership was implied and understated.

Enthusiasm within the Conservative Party for the Irwin declaration was, to say the least, noticeable mainly by its absence, but publication of the report of the Simon Commission in June, and the acceptance of its recommendations by even the most 'die-hard' members of the Indian Empire Society, gave the leadership a position of some strength to which they could fall back. It had been Birkenhead who, as Secretary of State for India, had set up the Simon Commission, and when it did not go as far as Irwin in recommending Dominion Status, F.E. and Churchill had both welcomed it. This was to sacrifice a strategic position for tactical advantage. On the one hand, it gave Churchill a stick with which to beat Labour and Irwin, but Baldwin and company were able to claim that at local level the report gave far more power to the Indians than had been envisaged by the Montagu–Chelmsford reforms of 1919, whilst its provisions to ensure a 'grip on the centre' failed to do that. Simon proposed a central assembly which would have a far larger proportion of elected representatives than the old one, and, by removing the large 'official bloc' which was composed of nominees of the Executive, he could actually be said to be weakening British control.[48]

Tariff reform was an issue which had captured the imagination of many Conservatives, but which left large sections of opinion elsewhere in the country actively hostile; India was analogous in that it stirred deep feelings in sections of the Conservative Party, but it differed in leaving opinion elsewhere cold. At a time of growing economic crisis, India was not a cause which rallied much support outside the *Morning Post*-reading classes. This was a measure of how little direct impact the existence of the Empire made on the lives of most people. For the members of the Indian Empire Society, with its former State Governors like Lloyd and Lord Sydenham, and for Page-Croft's Bournemouth 'old India hands', ex-members of the Indian Army or the Indian Civil Service, who turned naturally to the 'Indian news' section of the *Morning Post* to see how the regimental polo team was doing, or who was marrying whom, India was part of the fabric of their lives; they read Kipling with deep empathy and nostalgia. But for most of the people of Great Britain India was a far-away country about which they knew only what their elementary history books had told them: it was a great imperial possession and it made the King an Emperor – which was not a very English-sounding title.

Because Churchill himself felt so very deeply on the subject he failed, as he so often did once self-absorbed, to realise that for most people India was a subject of minor importance. Where his rhetoric had more impact, however, was within the Conservative Party. But here again, most MPs were uncertain where they stood; few of them liked the Irwin declaration, but few of them liked the idea of rebelling against a leader whom they trusted at the behest of a man whom many of them regarded with suspicion. As the struggle for the heart of the Conservative Party gathered momentum in December and January 1931, this was where the question came to settle: who did Tory MP's trust? Churchill's cause was not helped by the simultaneous attacks on Baldwin from the Empire free traders. Conservative MPs, who were alarmed by what Churchill told them about the situation in India, were going to be even more chary of throwing over a leader when this might be represented as truckling to the insolent demands of the gutter press. Baldwin was, once more, to be saved by disunion among his enemies – and by his own ability to rise to a crisis.

Churchill's first speech to the Indian Empire Society on 11 December, where he shared the platform with Lord Lloyd, was couched in the authentic tones of the 'die-hard' – a group to which Lloyd had always belonged, but which could now welcome Churchill. His portrayal of an independent India in which 'white people' would exist 'only upon sufferance', in which 'debts and obligations of all kinds will be repudiated' and where 'an army of white janissaries, officered if necessary from Germany, will be hired to secure the armed ascendancy of the Hindu', certainly made the flesh creep. The key point in his speech, as it was in Lloyd's, was one which both men were to make a thousand times: 'The withdrawal or suspension of British control means either a Hindu despotism . . . or a renewal of those ferocious internal wars which tortured the Indian masses for thousands of years before the British flag was hoisted in Calcutta.' Demands from within India were dismissed as the product of two phenomena: one was the tiny, westernised Hindu elite who wanted to establish their despotism; the other was the 'apparent lack of will-power and self-confidence exhibited by the representatives of Great Britain'. These themes: the artificial nature of Indian 'nationalism'; the danger of 'Hindu despotism' and of communal strife; India falling into the sort of chaos which marked contemporary China; and finally, the weakness of the official British attitude, were the staples of the campaign upon which Churchill had now embarked.[49]

The expression of such views naturally led Baldwin to conclude that

Churchill had 'gone quite mad about India'.[50] *The Times* loftily dismissed his 'extremism' as that of the 'omniscient subaltern of 1896',[51] whilst others assured Irwin that the 'general block of Conservatives' would prefer to follow Hoare and Viscount Peel, rather than Churchill and the Marquess of Salisbury.[52] This last opinion was accurate in so far as many Conservative MPs were perturbed, but willing to be calmed if suitably soothing noises could be made; after all, it was the Labour Government's policy which was under attack.[53] Hoare advised Baldwin to use the considerable scope for such noises provided by the Round Table conference, but Baldwin chose, instead, to stand by Irwin. It was this decision which made Churchill's severance from his colleagues inevitable.

The Commons debate on the results of the conference opened on 26 January, and Hoare's cautious line showed just what syrup could be provided as an aid to swallowing pills which might prove bitter to the taste. The fact of the conference was welcomed, as was the constructive atmosphere which it had helped to create. Hoare expressed the approval of the front bench for the federal scheme, but stressed that this was subject to satisfactory safeguards on defence, trade, finance, pensions and minority rights; these provided enough elasticity to enable the Conservatives to move in any direction for the future.[54] But Churchill was not in the mood to be soothed. He was booked to speak at a major Indian Empire Society meeting at the Manchester Free Trade Hall at the end of January, and from the start of the new year had described India as a question 'one cares about far more than office, or party or friendships'.[55] The fears of Irwin's friends that Churchill was 'out to make serious trouble' were borne out by his contribution to the debate.

The previous day, 25 January, Irwin had released Mahatma Gandhi from prison and legalised the Congress Party as a means of facilitating, it was hoped, further progress in the next Round Table talks. This was too much for Churchill. Taking his stand on the Simon report, which should, he said, have formed the basis for a further Act of Parliament, he condemned the Irwin declaration as a reckless departure from moderation, inspired by weakness and defeatism. By 'dangl[ing]' the 'orb of power' before millions of Indians, the Government had stirred up political unrest in the sub-continent, and the 'well-meaning and high-minded Viceroy' had made things worse. This was strong stuff, but Baldwin could have elected to have ignored it, as Churchill had not condemned Hoare and the Conservative delegates at the Round Table conference. Instead, he described Churchill's speech as one which might have been given by 'George III' had he been 'endowed with the tongue of Edmund Burke'. Commending the Irwin–MacDonald policy of conciliating Congress, Baldwin stunned many of his own followers into a silence made the more ominous for being accompanied by Labour cheers, when he declared that if he were returned to power he would 'implement' the resolutions of the conference, subject to Hoare's caveat.[56]

Baldwin had thrown down a challenge. Churchill could have elected to ignore it, for it was not unknown in the history of the Conservative Party for leaders and followers to exchange harsh words in Parliament; Disraeli had described Salisbury in 1875 as a 'master of jibes and flouts and jeers', yet the two men had remained in the same Cabinet. Baldwin could not but have been aware of the likely reaction to his speech, and Churchill's letter, written the following morning, resigning from the Business Committee, came as no surprise.[57] His reply was couched, as was Churchill's, in moderate tones, and both left room for co-operation on other issues, most especially the defeat of the Socialist Government; but Baldwin was not discontented that Churchill had severed himself 'from the Party'.[58] Neither man was ignorant of the stakes which were now on the table.

The silence of Conservative MPs during Baldwin's speech, which had been noticed by both the Chamberlains and by Irwin's brother-in-law, George Lane-Fox, betokened, as the latter commented, a feeling that he was 'weak and woolly', as well as a regret that he had not chosen to attack the Socialists. In committing the Party to the Round Table conference Baldwin had gone much further than had been agreed beforehand, and his position, in consequence, was weakened.[59] Hoare's 'syrup' had been rendered ineffective. If Churchill and the Indian Empire Society could rally enough support in the Party, which they might do by attacking the Socialists with gusto, then Churchill's prowess as an opposition leader might yet lead to Baldwin's downfall.

On paper the forces at Churchill's disposal for the task of capturing the Conservative Party were far from contemptible. Rothermere and the power of his newspaper empire were behind Churchill,[60] and he could count on a core of about fifty MPs to back him.[61] The power of his own oratory was a formidable weapon. The meeting at the Manchester Free Trade Hall on 30 January was packed out and cheered his caustic criticisms of Gandhi.[62] Manchester had not been chosen as a venue by accident; Lancashire Conservatives were particularly concerned about the future of India because it was tied up so closely with their own main industry of cotton, and the Indian Empire Society looked forward to being able to rally support here and in other specific regions.[63] When the Unionist India Committee met on 9 February, Lloyd made a 'forcible, very Die-hard speech', and was followed in this line by a clear 'majority'. Baldwin's reply was in his worst vein; he 'ambled along' telling the story of 'all that had happened, and rather evaded definite replies to definite questions'. Even Amery, who was one of the few who supported him, thought that he had done no more than partially to convince his audience;[64] those who disagreed with both Amery and Baldwin were less sanguine.[65]

Rothermere was not only backing Churchill's assault on Baldwin, he was also supporting that of Beaverbrook. Churchill described the latter as 'running amok in all directions'.[66] His decision to run a candidate at East Islington in

February marked a direct challenge to Baldwin. Brendan Bracken's reading of the situation, that 'if this parliament lasts until winter Baldwin will depart ignominiously' and that he would be succeeded by Churchill, might be thought biased, particularly as he was writing to Randolph Churchill;[67] but it was backed by solid evidence from elsewhere.

On 23 February Neville Chamberlain noted in his diary that Hoare 'reports that feeling in the House could not be worse'.[68] The Party's Principal Agent, Sir Robert Topping, reported 'growing concern in the ranks of the Party with regard to the position of the leader'. Most MPs thought that Baldwin was simply 'too weak' to lead them to victory. On India, 'many of our supporters' leant 'much more towards' Churchill's views than those expressed by Baldwin in the Commons. Topping did not think that anyone wanted to replace Baldwin simply on this one issue, but when considering the whole picture, he thought that it might be in 'the interests of the Party that the leader should reconsider his position'.[69] Neville Chamberlain, who had now emerged as the most likely successor, felt himself in an invidious position, but Austen, who had never forgiven Baldwin for the way he had been treated in 1923, felt that 'poor Neville' would simply have to tell him, in the interests of the Party, that 'he is not a leader and nothing will ever make him one'.[70] Austen was joined by Hailsham and Philip Cunliffe-Lister in urging Neville to show Topping's memorandum to Baldwin. None of them was favourable to Churchill's policy on India, and it was beginning to look as though the longer Baldwin held on, the better were the chances that he would be replaced by Churchill.[71]

Making sure that his constituency base was secure, Churchill demanded a meeting of the Council of the West Essex Conservative Association. It met on 23 February and heard a slashing speech from its MP. Churchill calmed the Party loyalists by pointing out that he would remain Chairman of the Conservative Finance Committee and lead the assault on the next Labour budget. Only on India was there a difference between himself and Baldwin. Churchill made great capital of Baldwin's own shilly-shallying, first giving the impression that he supported Irwin, then stating that he was committed to nothing more than giving 'fair consideration' to the Round Table proposals for all-India federation. Then, in what was to become one of his most famous passages, he described Irwin's recent decision to have talks with Gandhi. It was, he said, 'alarming and also nauseating' to see a 'seditious Middle Temple Lawyer, now posing as a fakir of a type well-known in the East, striding half-naked up the steps of the Vice-regal palace' to 'parley on equal terms with the representative of the King-Emperor' at the same time as he was stirring up sedition. Calling for a concerted assault upon the policy of the 'Socialist Government', Churchill won a unanimous vote of confidence. How could he have failed? It was just the sort of stirring stuff which Baldwin never gave the troops.[72]

The following day, 24 February, Churchill attended a meeting of the National Union of the Conservative Party. It says something for his exalted view of how politics should be conducted, as well as something about his relationship with the Party six years after rejoining it, that he had never before 'ventured onto this highly orthodox Central Office ground'; it said even more about the opinions which Topping had expressed that he was received with 'unequalled acclamation'. An emergency motion was passed calling for 'firm Government in India'.[73] Churchill hoped that if Lloyd George could be squared to ensure that Labour remained in power a little longer, his line could prevail.

The death of Sir Laming Worthington-Evans on 15 February had left vacant the safest Conservative seat in the country, St George's in Mayfair. The official candidate should have had a walk-over; instead, he walked out when on 28 February it was announced that the Empire Free Traders were going to put up a candidate, Sir Ernest Petter; no replacement stepped forward. Neville Chamberlain felt that he could delay no longer – Baldwin must be shown Topping's memorandum.[74] Cunliffe-Lister showed him an abbreviated version of the memo on 1 March and confirmed that only Bridgeman doubted whether he should follow Topping's advice. When Bridgeman and Davidson saw Baldwin that evening, he was 'contemplating immediate resignation'. Mrs Baldwin greeted them with the salutation that, as they had been together at the start of her husband's leadership, it was appropriate that they should be there at its end. But Bridgeman and Davidson had not turned up to mourn: 'Farewell be damned,' Bridgeman exclaimed. He and Davidson had come up with the idea that Baldwin should fight the St George's by-election, if necessary himself, and do so as a direct challenge to the power of the press barons. The immediate effect would be to give Baldwin 'great credit for such a courageous move': if he won, it would strike a 'damaging blow at the vile press'; if he lost, 'he could retire with honour & dignity as the champion of a cause which 99% of people knew in their hearts was right'.[75] Lucy Baldwin's nick-name for her husband was 'Tiger', a sobriquet whose suitability, at least to the public sphere of his life, may be doubted; but on this occasion, roused by her and his friends, he proved its applicability. Had he stood down Churchill might, at least, have vindicated Birkenhead's legacy – and, at best, even if Chamberlain had taken the leadership, his own position in the Party would have been strengthened; but Baldwin decided to fight.

24

Scalped by Baldwin

On the evening of 1 March *The Times* leader was set up in type – 'Mr Baldwin withdraws'; but not for the first time, the 'Thunderer' was wrong. The headline was withdrawn. On paper the challenges facing Baldwin were formidable, but once the resolution had been summoned up to make him fight, so it transpired were his forces. It has been said that loyalty is the Conservatives' secret weapon, and on this occasion it proved its value. As Bridgeman had astutely observed, election agents were apt to get things wrong as they 'are always affected by the loud-voiced malcontents, & never consider the great volume of quietly loyal supporters'.[1] Neville Chamberlain had always been uneasy at the notion that he might be suspected of wanting to supplant his leader, and when Baldwin told him on 2 March that he intended to fight, Chamberlain rallied to him; so did the other leading Conservatives.[2] They had little choice: if Baldwin failed, then they would be adjudged to have stood by their leader, which would redound to their credit should he fall.

The real crisis in early 1931 was in Baldwin's leadership; the moment he showed that he could lead the Party, the crisis began to evaporate. By turning the St George's by-election into a contest to decide whether the 'press or party is to rule', Baldwin tapped once more the reservoir upon which he had drawn as Prime Minister: the fundamental 'decency' of the English people.[3] Beaverbrook's intervention at Islington had delivered the seat to the Socialists, and the increasingly insolent tone which he and Rothermere adopted, with the latter demanding guarantees from Baldwin about the composition of a future Conservative Cabinet, played straight into Baldwin's hands, enabling him to exploit the resentment caused by their behaviour. Baldwin was relieved of the necessity of standing for the seat himself by Duff Cooper. An essentially metropolitan figure, Duff and his wife, the Society beauty, Lady Diana Cooper, proved formidable campaigners; and they enjoyed Baldwin's full support.

On the very day Cooper offered himself for St George's, Baldwin met Lloyd, who had begged him to avert a split in the Party by withdrawing from a commitment to immediate federation.[4] Lloyd warned him not to be 'surprised if there was a grave split in the Party in the next two or three days'. Baldwin wondered aloud whether he ought to resign, leaving Lloyd to try to sound reluctant as he said 'yes'.[5] The announcement of the agreement reached between Irwin and Gandhi on 5 March, which meant the latter accepting the results of the Round Table conference, certainly improved Baldwin's position,[6] but it was a close-run thing for a few days. He did not resign, but his first attempts at providing some leadership were, to say the least of it, proof that his opponents had a point.

In a speech at Newton Abbot on 6 March, Baldwin's 'contempt' for the 'die-hards' showed in a lack-lustre performance which may have undone some of the damage he had inflicted upon himself by his unscripted speech on 26 January, by laying greater stress upon the 'safeguards' which would be required of any new Indian constitution, but did little else. His performance at the Party's India Committee on 9 March was as lamentable as all his meetings with those fundamentally antipathetic to him tended to be. Churchill 'worked himself into a fine state of rhetorical eloquence about our being pushed out of India', and Baldwin's response was, by contrast, perfunctory. Amery, at least in his own estimation, made a speech which countered Churchill, but its success (if real) was vitiated by Baldwin agreeing to the publication of a motion passed at the meeting welcoming his own decision not to take part in the conference which the Government was proposing to hold on India; this had actually been agreed to before the meeting, but its publication made it appear as though Baldwin had been forced to back down. 'He really is pretty hopeless,' Amery concluded.[7]

Amery was not alone. Neville Chamberlain had told him on 5 March that he feared that any assistance afforded to Baldwin by Irwin's agreement with Gandhi 'was only temporary',[8] and the following day Hoare agreed that Baldwin's position was 'irretrievable'. But as Hailsham, who agreed with everyone else, pointed out, it was impossible to get rid of Baldwin before St George's.[9] Neville Chamberlain felt the delicacy of his own situation too much to give Baldwin a shove, and there was consensus only upon who should not succeed him – Churchill.[10] Thus, as he was backed into the last ditch, Baldwin reached, at last, a position where he felt comfortable.

Baldwin was a creature of intuitions and hesitations. Davidson and Bridgeman had screwed him up to the sticking-point, and a third confidant, Tom Jones, encouraged him to be 'absolutely frank' when he spoke in the big Commons debate on India on 12 March: 'He might lose his Party and his place, but he would go down with the great mass of the country on his side.' Jones pointed out, as others had, the essentially artificial nature of the alliance between Churchill and 'the Diehards who for the last six years had loathed Winston'.[11] Baldwin responded well to such encouragement; he needed to be told that what he wanted to do was popular with the wider constituency upon which he always kept an eye fixed. The result was an 'amazingly good' speech in the Commons on 12 March,[12] and an equally astonishing one two days later.

In the Commons he expounded a moderate policy on India, which reassured those Conservatives (the vast majority) who were looking for reassurance. Amery thought that it was a little too much like a 'lecture to his own side', but Baldwin felt that they needed it and he gave it to them. He criticised Churchill for the negativity of his response and showed, beyond peradventure, that he was not going to surrender. Churchill's speech, by contrast, sounded sarcastic and 'fell very flat'.[13]

St George's contained a larger number of MPs and peers than any other constituency in England, and it allowed the voice of what would later be called 'the Establishment' to express its protest at the antics of Beaverbrook and company. Lords Grey, Crewe and Reading spoke for many when they issued a statement that 'with the bulk of the electorate . . . still in the elementary stages of its political education', the power of the press barons as 'irresponsible amateur politicians to mislead their readers' by 'distortion' was a 'menace to our treasured political institutions'.[14] Asquith's widow, Margot, wrote to support Duff Cooper, telling him that Harold Macmillan 'reproaches himself bitterly for going on Winston's platform'. She could not, she wrote, trust herself to comment on Churchill, but did so all the same, castigating him for his 'fundamental disloyalty and lack of character (another word for lack of judgement). He is the falsest of political gods to worship and has done for himself now.' Lady Oxford and Asquith had a point.[15] On 17 March, in an electrifying passage in a good fighting speech, Baldwin rubbed home the message of the campaign by accusing the press lords of wanting 'power without responsibility – the prerogative of the harlot throughout the ages'. Two days later Duff Cooper came home comfortably with a majority of over five thousand. Churchill wrote magnanimously, but with a touch of resentment: 'On every personal and several public grounds I am very glad indeed that D. is safe in Parliament, and with so many feathers in his cap or tail, and such good marks in Mr B.'s book.'[16]

Having taken a very clear pot-shot at Santa Claus, Churchill now had to pay the penalty. Part of the problem was one which was to dog him for the next four years, which was that Baldwin and those who supported him did not really believe in Churchill's sincerity. 'Winston's game, of course, has been very obvious, as it always is. He is not the son of Randolph for nothing,' Davidson wrote to Irwin on 6 March; his contact with the 'die-hards' was thought to be 'transient' and for the purpose of removing Baldwin.[17] The whole business had simply confirmed men like Chamberlain and Hailsham in their low opinion of Churchill's judgment, and redoubled their determination that he should never be leader of the Party; moreover, by aligning himself with the 'die-hards', Churchill ensured that they would have their way.

Beaverbrook's diarist on the *Evening Standard*, Robert Bruce Lockhart, recorded a group of the younger Tories at one of Duff Cooper's campaign dinners saying that the only people who wanted Baldwin 'to go are the old men in the party and that the young men are on his side'.[18] They had been on Churchill's side once, because he too had been a liberal-Conservative, but they could not be expected to follow him in his deeply felt personal crusade to rescue the lingering embers of his youth; nor did they. Moreover, those cynics, who, like Davidson, dismissed the alliance between Churchill and the 'die-hards' as mere opportunism, knew whereof they spoke – at least most of the time.

Some 'die-hards' shared Churchill's elegiac vision. Lloyd, for example, compared what was happening in India with the Romans withdrawing their legions from Britain; that, he said, was the point at which 'they lost faith in themselves' and began to lose their Empire: 'Had we better not be careful that we don't withdraw our legions?'[19] It is not surprising that his vision drew him along the same road as Churchill with regard to other threats to Britain's external position.[20] But it was a road along which few followed them. The 'old India hands' were not interested in events on the Continent of Europe.

For the moment, however, Baldwin was safe. Twice in the previous twelve months he had had to pull out of his repertoire speeches to save the day, and there was no certainty that he would not have to do so again. Although relations between Baldwin and his Business Committee colleagues were patched up, Austen Chamberlain told him bluntly on 26 March that 'he would have to bestir himself and put a more fighting and less negative spirit into his speeches if the situation was to be restored'.[21] What really saved him, however, was not the sort of personality transplant which would have been necessary if Chamberlain's advice had been followed, but rather the evident failure of the Labour Government. With unemployment standing at nearly three million by the end of 1930, and the Government borrowing heavily to maintain public spending, all Conservatives could agree on two points: that MacDonald's Government was a national disaster; and that it ought to be replaced by a Conservative one as soon as possible. Churchill summed up this mood when he wrote to Neville Chamberlain on 9 April offering to help him criticise Snowden's budget, even though he had resigned from the Unionist finance committee the previous week: 'I certainly do not think that our differences over India, grave as they are, should be any bar to friendly relations or opposition to the common enemy.'[22] There is no doubt that Churchill sincerely meant what he wrote, but he was aware that after the resentment he had stirred up, it was 'a very good line for me to take generally'.[23]

The Indian Empire Society continued to hold meetings, but the hope now was to influence Baldwin's policy on India if and when he became Prime Minister. Churchill's main contribution to the cause was the publication in the summer of a volume of his speeches on India.[24] But most of his time was taken up with his own affairs: a little work on *Marlborough*, the final volume in *The World Crisis*, published as *The Eastern Front* in November, and, most lucratively of all, a lecture tour of America arranged for the autumn, which would bring him £10,000.[25] But any expectations of a quiet summer were spoilt, not only for Churchill, but for everyone else.

By the middle of the summer it was evident that the Government was in serious trouble; the cuts in public spending which the May Commission recommended at the end of July plunged the Cabinet into a fatal crisis. Meetings on 19 and 21 August revealed that the Government was at the end of its tether. Most of its members acknowledged that there would have to be a cut of ten per cent in unemployment benefit as part of the economy measures needed to restore confidence in sterling, but they could not bring themselves to act on this conviction. The crisis of capitalism, which Labour had long expected, had arrived. The Party's response was best summed up by the ex-Labour Minister, Sir Oswald Mosley: 'It was as though the Salvation Army had taken to its heels on the day of Judgement.' Cruel though this may have been, it was deadly in its accuracy.

On 23 August MacDonald took himself off to Buckingham Palace to throw in the towel. The King asked him to stay on as Prime Minister and see whether he could form a National Government. Baldwin, who was on holiday, reluctantly came back from Aix-les-Bains, and, even more reluctantly, agreed to Neville Chamberlain negotiating the Conservatives into a National Government headed by MacDonald. Thus it was that the man who had helped lead the Conservatives from the bondage of one coalition, led them into another. To those Conservatives who were disconcerted by this turn of events, the answer was that it was a temporary measure; the Government would keep Britain on the Gold Standard and then go its way. But in the best tradition of 'make do and mend', the Government, after taking Britain off the Gold Standard, went to the country in October and won an overwhelming popular mandate.

These events dramatically altered Churchill's prospects. When the idea of a National Government had been bruited to him in late July, Churchill had met with Lloyd George and Sir Oswald Mosley to discuss what they might do. Lloyd George had thought that they might form a 'National Opposition', but he did not expect them to be in that position for long.[26] His reasoning is plain to see. Gathered at the house of Sir Archie Sinclair, a leading Liberal whom Churchill had first got to know in the trenches, was what was probably the greatest assemblage of political talent in the country – not least in their own estimation.

In addition to his great services during the war, Lloyd George had, in his 'Yellow Book' of 1929, been the only major political leader to have come up with radical schemes for reviving the British economy. In this, as in other things, he had a good deal in common with Sir Oswald ('Tom') Mosley. 'Lord Oswald', as another Old Etonian 'comrade', Hugh Dalton, dubbed him, had resigned from the Labour Cabinet in May 1930 over its refusal to adopt his proto-Keynesian proposals to revive the economy through a programme of planned deficits and public spending. Of all the young men to enter politics since the war, Mosley was indubitably the most able. Starting as a Conservative, he had moved to the Labour Party and was, as his 'Mosley Memorandum' showed, the only Minister in MacDonald's Cabinet with any constructive ideas for dealing with unemployment. But the proletarians in the Party had always distrusted Mosley as too 'flashy' and clever by half. A baronet, married to Curzon's daughter and with an affluent life-style, what could such a one know of the condition of the 'workers'? The fact that he knew how to go about bettering that condition counted for little set against the inverted snobbery and envy of his colleagues. After his resignation he had founded the New Party, and such was his charisma and reputation that he attracted to him young men from all Parties who were fed up with waiting for their own particular 'old gang' to do anything save occupy office space.

Churchill and Lloyd George both looked towards Mosley for help because he could bring with him what they could not – the 'youth' vote.[27] Harold Macmillan and Bob Boothby flirted with the idea of joining Mosley, as did the young radical Welsh Labour MP, Aneurin Bevan, but only Harold Nicolson, seeking an escape from working for Beaverbrook, actually did so. Mosley was far from unwilling to adopt the pose of Saviour. Egotistical to a degree which made Churchill appear modest, Mosley was a womaniser on a scale which made Lloyd George appear celibate. Three brilliant and talented leaders would offer themselves to the British people as the crisis worsened. It was an alluring prospect, but, as Boothby had warned Mosley a year earlier, public reaction to such a combination was equally likely to be: 'By God, now all the shits have climbed into the same basket, so we know where we are.'[28] There was a sense in which the MacDonald–Baldwin coalition achieved just this result by leaving all the 'shits' in one basket – the one out in the cold.

This is not to say that the National Government was designed to exclude Churchill and company, merely that it achieved that result. By establishing its credentials as sole occupant of the 'middle ground', the new Government was able to pin the label of 'extremist' on those of its opponents who could not be dismissed as 'duds'. This, as Hoare reminded Chamberlain, was not achieved without the 'great good luck' that Churchill was out of the country and Lloyd George was ill during the crucial days at the end of August when the coalition was forged.[29] But the real 'luck' for Hoare and Baldwin was Churchill's resignation from the Business Committee. Had he not thus ruled himself out, he would have had to have been consulted; as it was, he was effectively marginalised. This pattern was to last for most of the next decade.

The new politics changed the significance of Churchill's campaign on India. Hoare, who became Secretary of State for India, recognised, as he told Irwin's successor, Lord Willingdon, that 'Conservative opinion' was 'very nervous' about the Government's policy towards India: 'They are horrified at the suggestion that we are engaged in shuffling out of difficulties and liquidating a bankrupt state';[30] it became his objective to calm such fears. Equally, Churchill aimed at stimulating them. Churchill and Lloyd were placed in an unenviable position by the announcement that the new Government accepted both the Irwin declaration and the results of the second Round Table conference, which met from September to December. Formerly they had been fighting the Socialists and Baldwin had come under fire only incidentally, and then only for seeming to support Labour. Now the position was very different. They were fighting a Government with a majority of more than five hundred seats where, to allegations that he was truckling to MacDonald, Baldwin could reply that it was the price he had to pay to maintain the National Government. It was all very well for Lloyd to declare that Baldwin could not 'expect that we should subordinate the future of the Empire to considerations of Party harmony',[31] but that was just what he expected – and got.

Churchill had hoped that alarm about the implications of the Statute of Westminster, which gave the Dominions, in effect, full control over their own foreign as well as domestic policies, would rally support against the Government's commitment to make India a Dominion, but when he spoke against that policy in the House on 3 December and insisted on forcing an amendment, Churchill ran up straight against Baldwin's 'national unity' card; he received only 43 votes to the Government's 369. Lloyd enjoyed better fortune in the Lords, rustling up 58 votes to the Government's 106. Hoare could take satisfaction from 'collapse of the Churchill movement' in the Commons,[32] but the vote in the Lords showed the 'need for caution'.[33]

The 1931 crisis had two unfortunate results for Churchill. He lost, as his wife put it, 'his position in the Party'; and he also lost a good deal of money in the economic crash which had accompanied the crisis.[34] With *Marlborough* proving a longer work in the gestation than he had contemplated, Churchill turned to journalism and the republication of collections of old articles to recoup his finances. In August Bracken negotiated him a contract with the *Daily Mail*, which would bring in £7,800 for an article a week.[35] This, with the fees which he was to earn from other pieces and from his American lecture tour, served to bring him in an income which was comfortably twice what the Prime Minister, at £5,000 a year, received. The last article he completed for his American publishers before leaving for the United States was entitled, with unconscious autobiographical reference, 'Great Fighters in a Lost Cause'. It was typical of Churchill's spirit that when he was knocked down in a motor accident on 13 December, he should have converted the experience into an article which earned him £600. Loss of money, political position and health made 1931 a bad year for Churchill. But he did not repine. Journalism brought in cash, whilst his own robust constitution overcame the effects of the accident. As for the political situation, he could not see it lasting.

Following its victory in the December debates, the Government had set up commissions of enquiry into Indian affairs which would be the prelude to further legislation towards the end of 1932. Whilst Churchill awaited their reports and the proposals which would follow, it seemed to him that events in

India were proving his grim prophecies correct. Willingdon, the new Viceroy, although officially a Liberal, lacked Irwin's instincts for appeasement and in January 1932 ordered the arrest of Gandhi and company following outbreaks of unrest. Churchill welcomed such firm action: 'there seems to be nothing to quarrel with them over now,' he told his son, Randolph, on 5 January 1932. Recalling the great Lord Salisbury's dictum that there were only two ways of governing man, 'Bamboozle or Bamboo', he thought it ironic that MacDonald should have chosen to apply them both at the same time in India.[36] His opinion of the Government remained low, but he expected it to 'last for some time in a sort of amorphous and gelatinous condition', before the need for 'more clear-cut solutions' came 'home to the public'.[37] As the Government moved slowly towards the adoption of a tariff-reform policy at the Ottawa conference with the other Dominions, Churchill was, he told Boothby, thankful 'not to be mixed up in this slatternly show!' The 'Two Tired Tims of the Commons' had, he declared, 'ceased to command my allegiance'.[38] Speaking at the Royal Academy dinner on 30 April, soon after his return to England, Churchill poked mild fun at the 'Tired Tims', but announced firmly that he was 'not exhibiting this year'.[39]

Churchill supported any signs of a tougher policy towards Gandhi, and he was not slow to claim publicly the credit for pushing it in that direction. But when the committee on the Indian franchise recommended increasing the electorate from seven million to thirty-six million, Churchill called it 'almost a farce'. Echoing Birkenhead, he declared that 'democracy is totally unsuited to India'.[40] But Hoare, who resented Churchill's allegations, and was concerned about the possibility of his attracting backbench support, did his best to calm Conservative nerves. In June he announced that the Round Table proposals would be studied by a Joint Select Committee, which would then report to the House on the future constitution of India. Churchill, as Baldwin told MacDonald, was 'completely knocked out' to find that the Government had, in effect, shot one of his foxes; it was difficult now to claim that India was being dealt with behind the back of the House. He reported happily to MacDonald that he was sure that Churchill's 'bitter' attack had 'gone down badly' with everyone 'except his own crowd'.[41]

The difficulty of making any headway in the Commons would, in the end, defeat Churchill's efforts. Everyone was well aware that the Government's policy created a good deal of unease within the Conservative Party, and at that level Churchill and company enjoyed a great deal of success. Churchill was ill with paratyphoid when the Party conference met at Blackpool in October, but Lloyd moved a resolution tabled by the Epping Conservatives condemning the franchise proposals. His appearance on the platform produced 'an ovation so prolonged and enthusiastic as clearly to indicate that he and his convictions had the support of the great majority'.[42] Lloyd delivered an effective condemnation of the franchise committee's proposals and criticised the Government for moving too hastily; by the time he sat down, Hoare was convinced that his resolution would be carried. However, appeals to loyalty to the Government rallied the faithful and managed to produce a majority for an amendment to the resolution which expressed confidence in the Government's India policy. Neither Hoare nor anyone else was fooled by the figures. He knew that 'the sentiment apart from the reasoning of the meeting was on the other side';[43] whilst the *Morning Post* declared that only the 'discipline of the Conservative Party' had secured a 'paper victory' and that the 'Party in the country is nearing the limit of its patience'.[44]

The question of which way the Conservative Party would jump on India exercised minds on both sides of it before the Government's Bill was published in March 1933. Churchill's view was sombre and, as it transpired, accurate: 'Irwinism has rotted the soul of the Tory Party and I have no doubt they will vote for any measure, however disastrous, when the Whips are put on.'[45] Even so, he believed that it was the duty of those who thought like him to 'fight with every scrap of strength we can command'. But the results were always the same. In the Commons defeat was constant. When Page-Croft put down a motion in the House on 22 February calling for a return to the proposals of the Simon Commission, it was defeated by 297 votes to 42 – thanks to the efforts of the Whips.[46] However, when the Central Council of the National Union, a purely Conservative body, met at the end of the month, Hoare's policy was approved by only 189 to 165 votes, and he warned Willingdon that there was 'the making of a first-class crisis here and a break-away of three-quarters of the Conservative Party'.[47]

Hoare had always anticipated 'an extensive attack from the extreme right wing',[48] and his description of the Conservative Party as 'jumpy' applied equally to himself.[49] But he did not think that Churchill and Lloyd would 'sink the ship', for if his own 'guns' were 'light', those which Baldwin commanded were 'very formidable'.[50] The size of the forces at Churchill's disposal were shown on 14 March when he, Lloyd and others met to form the India Defence Committee (IDC), which was committed to reject the Government's policy whatever the White Paper contained.[51] Given such an attitude it was not difficult for the Government Whips to portray the IDC as a bunch of 'die-hard' extremists who were intent on bringing down the Government. This was not just a matter of tactics. Hoare, at least, genuinely thought that 'Winston ... is determined to smash the National Government and believes that India is a good battering ram as he has a large section of the Conservative Party behind him.'[52] Accordingly, the Government left nothing to chance in the debate on 25 March.

The White Paper on India took the form of suggested terms of reference to the Joint Select Committee, which allowed the Government to centre the debate around a motion approving the setting up of that Committee. This made it difficult for the Government's opponents to rally their forces, as no one was against such a committee, and in the end Churchill did not press for a division; with a three-line Whip operating, it was just as well. There were holes in the Government's scheme for all-India federation, most particularly in the fact that many of the princely states were not keen on the idea. But the Government was able to say that it would bring in provincial autonomy at once whilst leaving federation until the princes came to an agreement. This had the advantage for the Government that nothing would change for some years as regards control at the centre, which made the task of alarming backbenchers even more difficult.

It is an indication of how strong the feeling inside the Party was felt to be that all these precautions were thought necessary, and that, even so, Hoare should have been nervous as to the course which the debate would take; his nerves were not calmed by hearing that Churchill was going around talking about 'the blow that he was going to strike'.[53] Hoare's opening speech was 'dull but competent', which was 'perhaps the right note' on which to introduce such a measure.[54] The second day of the debate, 26 March, went very much Churchill's way, and by the end of it he was, according to Hoare, 'going about . . . saying that he had not only smashed the scheme but that he had smashed the Government as well'.[55] Whether it was, as Hoare thought, through over-confidence, or, as Neville Chamberlain surmised, the effect of the three whisky-and-sodas which he downed before speaking,[56] Churchill's 'much advertised speech was one of the greatest failures of his life'.[57] He made the same mistake which he had in the Lloyd debate in 1929, which was to attack the civil servants concerned. His allegation that the Government was appointing only its own supporters to senior positions in the Indian Civil Service brought the Chairman of the India Committee, Sir John Wardlaw-Milne, to his feet. Nine years later the two men would again clash on the floor of the House, but on this occasion it was Wardlaw-Milne who came off best. Churchill went on for too long and lost the ear of the House. It was, to Hoare's unconcealed delight, a 'most surprising crash', which, he hoped, would give 'heart to the undecided' and convince some of the newspapers that Churchill was not 'the divine leader they had assumed'.

The Commons debate only revealed what was already apparent, that if Churchill was going to get anywhere on India, it would be through the medium of the Conservative Party. But Hoare was equally aware of this, and he thought that however 'effective Winston's attack may be, there is a great body of opinion in the country what [sic] will never trust him'; and he doubted whether even the 'extreme right of the Conservative Party', whilst they would 'use him for their own ends', would 'take him as their leader'.[58] This proved to be the case. Churchill's refusal to serve on the Joint Select Committee, although supported by Lloyd,[59] was deplored by Salisbury, whilst many of those who opposed Baldwin over India, such as Page-Croft, supported him over a wide range of other issues.[60] The refusal to serve on the Committee was a tactical error. Churchill was probably right to feel that he and Lloyd would be in a minority, but they could still, as Gwynne, the editor of the *Morning Post*, pointed out, 'produce a minority report that would run up and down the country like a flame in dry grass'.[61] Churchill's refusal to serve made it easy for the Government to suggest, in private, that his real aim was 'to smash the Government', and perhaps even more than that. Hoare told Willingdon that Churchill thought that 'England is going Fascist, and that he, or someone like him, will eventually be able to rule India as Mussolini governs North Africa'.[62]

'Fascism' was much in the air. In March 1933 Hitler's Nazi Party forced the 'enabling law' through the Reichstag, which was the prelude to the establishment of a full dictatorship, whilst in Britain, on a more modest scale, Mosley's 'British Union of Fascists' was claiming that Parliamentary democracy had failed and must be replaced by a more 'virile' system. There were signs which suggested that Hoare's fears about Churchill's political orientation might not be wholly fanciful.

This is not to say that Churchill had much time for what was going on in Germany. As early as 13 April 1933 he was warning of the dangers which might be apprehended from the 'grim dictatorship' of Hitler, and his awareness of the militaristic nature of German nationalism made him conscious of the challenge which it might present to the Versailles system.[63] That would not stop him, over the next few years, from admiring the way in which Hitler restored the self-respect of many Germans; as he put it in an article first published in November 1935:

We cannot tell whether Hitler will be the man who will once again let loose upon the world another war in which civilization will irretrievably succumb, or whether he will go down in history as the man who restored honour and peace of mind to the great Germanic nation. . . .[64]

Looking at Britain since the advent of democracy, Churchill, as we shall see, was drawing some fairly sombre conclusions about the success of the experiment, but most of these came, at least in part, from the demoralising experience of trying to make some impact on a Government with 556 seats in the House.

Frustration came from the fact that despite the existence in the constituencies of dissatisfaction with the Government's India policy, there seemed no effective way to vent it in Parliament. J. C. C. Davidson, who was on the Joint Select Commitee, suffered the embarrassment of having his local association refusing to endorse his position on India, as did Lord Winterton. On 20 April Lloyd suggested to Churchill that all the opponents of the White Paper, the IDC and the Indian Empire Society should combine to form an India Defence League. With Kipling and Lord Carson as Vice-Presidents, and Churchill, Lloyd and Page-Croft all in senior positions, the IDL acted as a focus for grass-roots feeling in the Conservative Party. Now historians are ill at ease with grass roots which are not of radical origin, whilst the Conservative Party has never welcomed opinions which differ from those expressed by the leader, so the IDL has generally received a bad press. But with support from over fifty MPs and local associations such as Eastbourne, Camberley, Bexhill, Chichester, Bournemouth, Guernsey, Newport, Scarborough and Bristol, the IDL was, and remains, the nearest thing which the Conservative Party has had to a genuine grass-roots revolt than at any time since the 1840s. The seaside resorts of England resounded with the growls of red-faced colonels, who were easily mocked by smart-alecs like David Low, as 'Colonel Blimps' with their fat stomachs and their crimson-mottled complexions; but the fictional 'Blimp' had the answer to such jibes, when he asked his cocksure young critic whether he had considered that he had acquired his complexion from years of serving his country in the heat of the Indian summer, and his stomach from muscle turning to fat.

The conservative denizens of the genteel watering-places of England have not yet attracted their historian, and with their rigid moral codes, their quiet, persistent snobberies, and their worship of the great god, Respectability, they have proved easy targets for satirists from George Orwell and John Betjeman to John Osborne. But it was these people, and they tended to be active in local Conservative associations,[65] who provided the backbone of the Empire, who served their country without question, and who now saw all that they had worked for and loved threatened. Their fears responded easily to Churchill's rhetoric about lack of willpower in high places; their lives had been built on self-sacrifice and the exercise of willpower and they could spot its absence at twenty paces. 'MacStanleyism', as Lloyd called it, was rotting the fabric and the vitals of the Empire, and it had to be stopped. The Central Council of the National Union of Conservative and Unionist Associations, which met in June, and the Party conference in Birmingham in October, were the forums at which the growl from the seaside could be heard and, it was hoped, turn the tide.

25

Colonel Blimp's Last Stand

'In opposition to the Government of India Bill there were really two groups; there was the Tory Opposition and the Churchill Opposition, and although they synchronized up to a point, it was only up to a point.'[1] This charge by Davidson, with its implication that Churchill was out to wreck the National Government, was, as we have seen, believed by Hoare, and its contemporary character has led historians to ponder the purity or otherwise of Churchill's motives. But the implication in Davidson's charge, which was repeated publicly in a speech by him in July 1933, and which prompted Baldwin to respond to the formation of the IDL by commenting that it was the 'time of year when midges come out of dirty ditches', was hardly the product of disinterested by-standers. Not only was it in the Government's interest to foster such an impression, but Hoare made it the Government's business to do so. There was a difference between Churchill and some of the Tory opposition; the latter were, at heart, loyalists, and they found it difficult to break the habits of a lifetime. Churchill was a former Liberal who had been a Conservative, and it was the business of a minute to suggest to staunch Tories like Colonel Gretton, Chairman of the Bass brewing conglomerate which dominated the town of Burton in Staffordshire for which he had sat since 1895, that pure as his motives were, could he trust those of his self-appointed leader? As Derby told Lloyd, 'While Winston is out to break up the Government that is far from being your wish.'[2]

Such tactics worked well with men whose whole political careers had been devoted to the Conservative Party, and who, but for the disappointment they felt over India, would be only too happy to resume the habits of a lifetime. Lloyd was deeply hurt at Baldwin's 'dirty ditches' speech and the charge that he was trying to split the Conservative Party. He asked Baldwin to 'indicate to me what Conservative cause I have ever abandoned since I entered public life'; and like many 'die-hards', he saw himself as being *plus royaliste que le roi*: 'Some of us, indeed, have suffered not a little in our attempts to conserve what "Conservative" leaders have sometimes been ready to abandon.'[3] Men of this spirit were easy targets for barbed comments about the fact that they were working with a renegade Tory against their Party's leadership; and nothing save the strength of their despair over India would have enabled them to bear such charges.

The Government did not rely merely upon innuendo and gossip in the smoking room to do its work of driving wedges into the opposition to the India Bill. Stoutly though it was denied at the time, an organisation called the 'Union of Britain and India' (UBI), which was formed in April 1933, was sponsored by Conservative Central Office, which supplied its funding and publicity material. A pale, *ersatz* version of the IDL, it nevertheless provided a forum through which Davidson, now Chancellor of the Duchy of Lancaster and a leading light in the UBI, could spread his anti-Churchill poison. Even sixty years later the sour dregs of his propaganda pollute the stream of history, by encouraging doubt over Churchill's motives.

But it must be admitted that some of Churchill's actions gave the UBI a helping hand. Churchill always gave the impression of being bitter and out for a fight. His refusal to join the Joint Select Committee was not understood even by Gwynne of the *Morning Post*. Lords Salisbury and Burnham, who usually supported Churchill's line, none the less agreed to serve on the Select Committee.[4] Eddie Cadogan, the MP for Finchley who had served on the Indian finance committee, had no great love of the India Bill, but he agreed to serve on the Select Committee on the grounds that, important as India was, it was even more important to ensure that the Government remained in power and kept the Socialists out.[5] His attitude was one shared by many Conservatives. As Bridgeman put it: 'I doubt if the ordinary Conservative has any sympathy with their exaggerated statements as to the danger of the White Paper policy, when the risks of any other course are brought to his notice.'[6]

The Government's tactics were simple enough: Conservatives were reminded of Churchill's association with men like Lloyd George and Beaverbrook.[7] He was accused of exaggeration and of desiring to split the Conservative Party;[8] and rumours abounded in the period before the National Union conference that he was so sure of victory that he had sketched out an alternative Cabinet; although with Page-Croft at the Dominions Office, Lloyd George at Agriculture and Beaverbrook at the Colonial Office, the 'Shadow Cabinet' had about it the air of a body dreamed up at Central Office rather than Chartwell.[9] It would hardly be a misnomer to call this a 'campaign', for it followed so closely the lines of one laid down by Davidson, when he had been Party Chairman, that it beggars belief that the Government's counter-attack was not based upon it.[10] If the Party managers were relying upon what they considered Churchill's notorious lack of judgment to give verisimilitude to their campaign, they did not hope in vain.

There was, of course, a scintilla of truth in some of what the UBI, Hoare and others were saying about Churchill – just enough, given the view which many Conservatives held of his career, to allow doubt to enter into the relationship between Churchill and those who looked, unwillingly, towards his oratorical talents to utter the sentiments which their own inarticulacy prevented them from giving vent to. He was not bound by any lifelong loyalty to the Party from assaulting it; and for Churchill, once war had been declared, then it was essential to smite his foe hip and thigh. Cazalet, who visited him on 19 April, found him in sombre mood: 'He said he felt like cutting people and hating them as he had never hated before in his life.' It was not, as Cazalet remarked, the way to win over the uncommitted.[11] That was the heart of the problem. Lord Linlithgow, Chairman of the Joint Select Committee, offered Churchill equally good advice when he pointed out that 'you are in the process of working yourself into a very poor tactical position. The Indian problem does *not* interest the mass of voters in this country.' He would, Linlithgow thought, do better to concentrate his fire on the issue of Protection.[12] But, like Cazalet, Linlithgow was met with a reply which revealed the depths from which Churchill's own concern sprang: 'I do not think I should remain in politics, certainly I should take no active part in them, were it not for India.' As usual, Churchill found it impossible to believe that what obsessed him was not of equal concern to others: 'You are greatly mistaken in supposing that India does not interest the mass of voters. It interests profoundly all those loyal, strong faithful forces upon which the might of Britain depends.'[13]

Churchill's concern over India sprang from sources deep in his psyche. For him the Empire represented the world of his vanished youth, and he wanted to preserve it. The Empire was the heritage left by the great men of British history, and he could not bear to see it dismantled by their unworthy successors; nor could he, as their worthy successor, stand by and see it happen. The contemporary world was one in which the 'mild and vague Liberalism of the early years of the twentieth century' had no place. The triumph of nationalism, especially in its most militaristic form of Fascism, hardly suggested that Britain ought to divest herself of her Empire. As he told Linlithgow: 'You assume the future is a mere extension of the past whereas I find history full of unexpected turns and retrogressions.' For Baldwin and company to go on 'mouthing the bland platitudes of an easy safe triumphant age which has passed away' in an age dominated by the aggressive nationalism of Fascism, was folly: 'the tide has turned and you will be engulfed by it'.[14]

This was what really divided Churchill from Hoare and Baldwin. On the details of the White Paper policy, compromise would have been possible; no one was proposing that federation would come into operation at once, or without safeguards. But underlying India was a deeper difference. Churchill thought that Baldwin and company were hopelessly in thrall to an outmoded philosophy, whilst they were equally convinced that he was. Their Edwardian liberalism saw him as holding the views of a subaltern of 1896, on India, in which they were not wholly wrong; but what they failed to perceive was the inadequacies of their own philosophy when confronted with a world made dangerous by economic crisis and militaristic nationalism. This is why there was no compromise between Churchill and his opponents; each was convinced that the other was addicted to outmoded shibboleths. But, as Clemenceau had it at Versailles, commenting upon President Wilson's Utopian schemes for 'open diplomacy' and world peace and co-operation: 'Wilson has his fourteen points, God has his ten commandments: we shall see.'

Given the sombre nature of this vision, Churchill's bitterness against the machinations of Party politics is understandable; but in Great Britain, Parliamentary democracy still survived, and Churchill had to work within its limitations, however irksome he found them. The fact was that whilst there were enough 'die-hards' to cause trouble for Baldwin and Hoare, there were not sufficient to cause a real crisis without aid from external events. In some areas, like Hitchin, where Salisbury exercised great influence, then it could be used to select candidates like Sir Arnold Wilson, who were sympathetic to the IDL. But for every success there were failures, such as the attempt at Altrincham in Cheshire to overturn the selection of Sir Edward Grigg; there Lord Derby's influence and that of Central Office was decisive.[15] Although Hoare worried about the effect of Churchill's activities, he thought that he was 'overbidding his market'.[16]

At the meeting of the Central Council on 28 June, Baldwin successfully lavished oil upon troubled waters. The White Paper, he explained, could not be discussed because it was *sub judice*, but there would be a special meeting of the Council once the Joint Select Committee had reported. He was 'clear, persuasive and impressive', and by avoiding committing anyone to anything, he was able to use his position as leader to do what he did best – appeal for loyalty on the ground that he was a man everyone could trust.[17] Lloyd did not speak well, whilst Churchill's bitterness again got the better of him, as he accused the leadership of mounting a campaign against him.[18] It was, therefore, a disappointment to Hoare, as well as a sign of the strength which the IDL had in the councils of the Party, that Lloyd's resolution expressing 'anxiety' over the Government's India policy was only defeated by 838 votes to 356.[19] This was, as Hoare hoped, 'the high water mark of Winston's influence'.

The personal hostility shown towards Churchill at the meeting had been remarkable enough to unsettle him during his speech, and the propaganda put out by the UBI over the next few months was able to capitalise on it. It could have been said of Churchill, as it was of Disraeli on one occasion, that he was both a 'necessity' and a 'curse' to the cause he served.

Churchill's refusal to join the Joint Select Committee allowed Hoare, in effect, to divide and rule. Although it took an immense amount of his time and energy, he was able to deal with Salisbury's nervous querulousness without much difficulty, and Hoare's arguments gradually won over the uncommitted members of the Committee like Sir Austen Chamberlain and the former Governor of Bengal, Lord Zetland. He was quite willing to accede to their demands for 'safeguards' on policing and other matters, not only because he thought them justified, but also because it would allow Chamberlain and

Zetland to calm Conservative nerves by claiming that Hoare had given in to their demands. Churchill's own evidence before the Select Committee in late October showed up the limitations of his detailed understanding of what the White Paper was proposing.[20]

Both sides geared themselves up for the Party conference in Birmingham in early October. The IDL canvassed all 2,000 delegates with leaflets and other propaganda material; one of its circulars has been characterised by an impartial historian as 'a ruthless compilation of deception and lies'.[21] The Government's problem, as Hoare had always recognised, was that 'our case is a complicated case of detail, whilst the attack is an attack of headlines and platform slogans'.[22] Given the nature of the Conservative Party conference, this gave the IDL a certain advantage. But the Party leadership possessed much greater ones: the threat of the National Government breaking up if the conference disowned its India policy was a very effective weapon in its armoury. Amery may have found Neville Chamberlain's emphasis upon this point 'not too tactful', but it worked.[23] In public, Chamberlain stressed that the delegates 'were not competent to express an opinion on such a difficult subject'; in private, he resented having to waste time talking to 'all these very foolish people'.[24] But it proved worth it. The Government easily defeated the 'die-hard' resolution of criticism by 737 to 344 votes.

Baldwin's soothing syrup had done its job, but it had had to work on another issue which Lloyd had brought up at the conference. During his speech, Baldwin had acknowledged that Britain could no longer rely upon her insular position for protection from events on the Continent. In this he was responding to a motion from Lloyd on 4 October expressing 'grave anxiety as regard to the inadequacy of the provision made for imperial defence'. Accompanied by an amendment from Chamberlain which made reference to the heaviness of the burden of defence costs, the motion had been approved.[25] In retrospect, this could be, and was, presented as a prescient move, designed to show that those who supported it had anticipated the course of events to 1939. In fact, it was nothing of the kind. It was an expression of general anxiety by many Conservatives of the effects of a decade of defence cuts upon British power. Some Conservatives were becoming aware of the dangers which might be apprehended from Hitler's Germany, but they were in a minority, and their fears were, in any case, an expression of their distrust of the whole 'League of Nations' mentality expressed in things like the disarmament conference which was then meeting in Geneva. Duff Cooper, who disagreed with Churchill on India, shared his more general outlook. He had spent part of the summer in Germany and had been shaken by the 'astounding and terrible' 'enthusiasm' which the Germans were showing in 'preparing for war'. He warned Churchill of this in a letter on 8 September, which noted the incongruity of the fact that the morning paper carried a report of the Cabinet discussing 'disarmament'.[26]

The darker tone with which Churchill portrayed the contemporary world was to be evident from 1933 onwards, but the very bitterness with which he pursued Baldwin over India prevented his message from being effective. It was regarded by many as part of a 'die-hard' view of the world, which it was; but many liberal-Conservatives, like Cooper, felt themselves cut off from Churchill by the fact that those who supported him on India were the sort of antique right-wingers whose influence upon Conservative counsels was deplored by liberal opinion. Churchill was in a vicious circle: he could not fight India without the 'Blimps', but many of these did not share his views on the dangers to be apprehended from the Continent; whilst those who shared his view on the latter deplored his associates and actions over India. As long as Churchill could be portrayed as being more interested in wrecking the Government than he was in India, then his position would be a difficult one and his word would be at a discount.

Churchill's bitterness against the Government was partly the result of natural frustration: he *knew* that many Conservatives agreed with him on India, but he simply could not make this opinion count thanks to what he regarded as illegitimate government influence. It was not simply that Chamberlain and Baldwin would always call in domestic political consider-ations to frighten Conservatives; it was the misrepresentations in which the UBI indulged, the fact that he was denied access to the BBC to propagate his views,[27] and the feeling that the Government was behaving in a generally underhand way, which aroused his ire. The 'influence' which Hoare used to 'square' some of the Indian princes by judicious use of carrot and stick made him particularly sick: 'It is a very dirty business, from beginning to end, done by our own people to tear down their own strength.'[28] Churchill was not content to put down his defeats to the difficulty of translating latent support in the country into votes in the Commons, and when, in early 1934, proof fell into his hands that Hoare had manipulated evidence given by the Manchester Chamber of Commerce (MCC) to the Joint Select Committee, Churchill thought that he had the opportunity of exposing the Government and its misdeed to the country; he therefore pressed for the Select Committee of Privileges to investigate his allegations.[29]

The charges could hardly have come at a worse time for the Government. The uncommitted members of the Joint Select Committee had, in October 1933, submitted a detailed critique of the White Paper's proposals, and it had taken Hoare until April 1934 to come up with a compromise which satisfied Austen Chamberlain; but, having done so, he was looking forward with confidence to the India Bill going forward smoothly. But Churchill's allega-tions threatened to change all that.[30]

Churchill had first become aware that there were signs of undue govern-ment interference in the evidence submitted by the MCC at the end of March, when the Managing Director of Rothermere's newspapers sent him the text of an article which the *Daily Mail* was going to publish on the subject on 1 April. Once Churchill had seen the documents, and talked with two members of the MCC who showed him further documentation, he was convinced that he had the Government cold.[31] He raised the issue in the House on 16 April and the Speaker, cutting across what might have been a damaging debate for the Government, ruled that there was a case for the Committee of Privileges to investigate.[32]

Churchill circulated his evidence to various friends, who were all duly impressed by it.[33] But in private Lloyd George, who thought he had a 'strong case', did not think that he would succeed in establishing it as 'the forces against him are very powerful'.[34] Lloyd George was right on both counts. One of Churchill's problems was that the documents which he had access to were merely the tip of the iceberg. Derby's papers,[35] and more recent research, reveal the lineaments of the iceberg and leave no doubt that, in substance, Churchill was correct. According to Churchill, Hoare, having tried in May 1933 to induce the MCC President, Richard Bond, to modify the evidence he was going to submit to the Joint Select Committee, had then arranged, through Derby, to meet him at a dinner in June, which had resulted in his statements not being heard until October, when, after further pressure from Derby, one much more favourable to the Government was presented.[36] But the evidence available to Churchill did not prove this beyond doubt. His other problem was the nature of the tribunal by which his incomplete evidence was to be judged. The Committee of Privileges reflected the composition of the House of Commons, and of its members, only Lord Hugh Cecil could be relied upon to decide without any thought of the wider implications of Churchill's allegations.[37]

Others were not so unworldly. The Speaker told Lloyd George on 6 May that the whole business might 'work up into a serious crisis',[38] whilst Hoare knew that if Churchill 'got away with' his charge, even on a technicality, his position would 'immediately become impossible'.[39] If Hoare resigned then even if the Government did not fall, the India Bill would. In these circumstances the Government mobilised all its forces. As Churchill's evidence was suggestive, rather than conclusive, and as the procedure adopted by the Committee of Privileges did not allow him to examine or cross-examine witnesses, it was impossible to refute the defence mounted by Hoare.

Hoare claimed that his letter of 5 May to the MCC, and the subsequent dinner, were entirely at the request of the MCC, and that what he had told them was legitimate advice, not illegitimate pressure. The MCC desire to have the Viceroy, in effect, fix a tariff and ensure that the Indians played fair was, Hoare said, likely to cause friction between representatives of the MCC in India and the Indian mill-owners, with whom they were trying to negotiate a reduction in tariffs, so it was entirely appropriate for him to advise them against such demands. No one denied that the MCC had subsequently changed its mind and its report, but this, Hoare argued, was the result of cables from its own representatives in India, whose advice coincided with his own. There was, he piously asserted, no illegitimate influence.[40]

This was not simply being 'economical with the truth', it was being downright stingy with it. It had been Derby and Hoare who had arranged for the dinner with the MCC in June, and beforehand Derby had committed a breach of confidentiality in first receiving, then letting Hoare see, a copy of the evidence which the MCC was going to submit to the Joint Select Committee. From this it was clear that its members considered further weakening of British control in India would be fatal to their trade prospects, and that they thought they needed the sort of Vice-regal powers which the Indians had not had to accept since the grant of financial autonomy in 1919.[41] Hoare had used Derby's influence to postpone the submission of this evidence, and then Derby, with the help of the India Office, had suggested amendments. The prospect of revealing the minutes on this subject was not one which appealed to the Government, and Derby was warned that if the papers were called for, he would have to account for the discrepancy between his earlier opinion that the evidence was satisfactory and his subsequent actions; but it was hoped that a claim of 'departmental privilege might be used to protect these minutes'.[42] Churchill was not aware of Hoare's letter to Willingdon in late October 1933 claiming that he had been 'doing my best to stave off the evidence of the Manchester Chamber of Commerce' as it was 'likely to be of a threatening and embarrassing character',[43] or of his later comment that 'Derby has been exceedingly good' with the MCC and had 'induced them to withdraw' their 'dangerous and aggressive memorandum'.[44] Nor was Churchill aware of the 'confidential' discussions between Thomas Barlow, Chairman of the MCC, and Derby, which, in November, had resulted in the substitution of a report based upon the India Office suggestions for the original one.[45] Without this mass of material, Churchill could only make allegations, and Hoare had no trouble in explaining away the 'tip of the iceberg' which was all that Churchill had seen.

The result was inevitable. Hoare protested his innocence and bemoaned, as did other members of the Government, that they were having to waste so much time answering allegations which were founded on malice and a desire to upset the Government.[46] On 7 May, when Churchill saw Ramsay Mac-Donald, the Prime Minister tried to persuade him not to submit a further lengthy memorandum to the Committee; he also let drop a suggestion that the Government wanted someone 'of good standing and a knowledge of the Dominions' to 'go and talk to them' about the deteriorating international situation. 'Scenting a trap', Churchill said that he would not suppress the results of his enquiry.[47] But those enquiries failed to turn up the important documents to which historians now have access. Hoare regarded Churchill's attack on him as a 'completely unscrupulous' affair,[48] and he was determined to smash him on the issue.[49] The debate upon the Committee of Privileges report in June did just that.

The report was published on 9 June, and it cleared Hoare and Derby. Churchill had received sage advice from a fellow MP, Sir Terence O'Connor, on how he should react to such a report: he should avoid casting aspersions on the membership of the Committee and concentrate instead upon the fact that the detailed evidence (which the report did not contain) was capable of more than one interpretation, which was why an investigation had been necessary.[50] Such a conciliatory tone would have been wise, and was dreaded by Hoare, who thought that it would allow Churchill to escape the retribution which he so richly wished would fall upon him.[51] Hoare need not have worried. When the debate took place on 13 June, Churchill launched into a direct attack on the Committee and accused it of suppressing essential evidence. His quotation from some of the evidence (none of which had been published) alarmed the Prime Minister, who attempted to get a ruling that it was out of order for him to do so; but the Attorney-General ruled that there was no legal bar to Churchill quoting from documents in his possession. But Churchill's speech was too long, too detailed and too bitter in tone to carry weight, and it created the impression that he was a 'bad loser'.[52]

Amery, who spoke immediately after him, congratulated Churchill on discovering 'a mare's nest within a mare's nest', and criticised him for his attitude. Chaffing Churchill for the portentous tone of his own contribution, Amery declared that he had tried to force Hoare's resignation, had delayed the report of the Joint Select Committee and tried to break the Conservative Party, all so that he could live up to 'his chosen motto, *Fiat justitia ruat caelum* [Let justice be done though the heavens fall]'. Unwisely Churchill interrupted with the cry 'Translate'. Scarcely able to believe his luck, Amery obliged: 'If I can trip up Sam, the Government's bust.'[53] The House dissolved into fits of laughter. Churchill was routed. Amery was not renowned for his wit, which made his sally all the more effective, and there was enough verisimilitude in his allegation, at least in the view held by many MPs, to make it plausible. As the *Manchester Guardian* commented, the impression left was not simply that Churchill had failed, but that 'he has failed so disastrously that the Government may now feel secure in their policy'.

Amery, like most other speakers on the Government side, was heavily critical of Churchill personally, and it is clear that one reason why the relative flimsiness of the Government's case was not revealed was that it could rely upon hostility to Churchill to blunt his sallies. It is noticeable that none of Churchill's great orations upon India in the House were particularly effective. Commentators noted the bitter tone he adopted, but there was more to it than that. Churchill had been speaking in the House for a very long time and if his listeners were not exactly bored, they had the feeling that they had heard it all before.[54] Churchill's grand rhetorical style was ill-suited to an age when 'rhetoric and, indeed, eloquence were held up to obloquy as camouflage for literary and moral Pecksniffs';[55] his rolling Augustan periods came to seem 'so much tinsel and hollow pasteboard' to many of the younger generation.[56] Even Duff Cooper, whose own rhetorical tastes were not dissimilar to Churchill's, could wonder, in March 1934, why his former patron remained in politics: 'Odd that he should not realize that the game is up. I suppose that he goes on intriguing and making speeches in the same spirit that my mother-in-law goes on painting her face and wearing a wig'; he thought that Churchill was growing 'more foolish and fractious'.[57] After the Hoare–Derby fiasco, many Conservative MPs seemed disposed to agree.

When Churchill addressed the Manchester IDL on 26 June, not a single Conservative MP turned out to meet him. The *Manchester Guardian* had the explanation for this phenomenon: 'Any Tory who now associates himself with Mr Churchill in his activities must inevitably be regarded as guilty of an unfriendly act towards the Government, and especially to Mr Baldwin.'[58] With rumours of possible Cabinet reshuffles in the offing,[59] few ambitious Conservatives wished to prejudice their chances of promotion by association with Churchill.

If the episode badly damaged Churchill's reputation at Westminster, it did nothing to endear Westminster to Churchill. His frustrations over the India Bill served to reinforce his doubts about the success of the system of universal suffrage which had been introduced in 1918. For 'three or four hundred years' some 'three or four hundred families' had guided England from being a 'small struggling community to the headship of a vast and still unconquered Empire', but within his own lifetime that aristocracy had 'lost their authority and control'. What Churchill wrote in the obituary of his cousin, 'Sunny' Marlborough, in July 1934 applied equally to himself: 'He was always conscious that he belonged to a system which had been destroyed, to a society which had passed away.'[60] But where this had 'cast a depressing shadow' over Marlborough's life, it inspired in Churchill a stout resistance.

Churchill's doubts about universal democracy derived from this source, rather than, as his enemies alleged, a desire for dictatorship. What he wanted was not to replace the Parliamentary system, but to reform it. Being a romantic reactionary Churchill imagined that this could be done by bringing it more into line with the system which had obtained in his youth. In an article in the *Evening Standard* on 24 January 1934 on how to 'restore the lost glory to democracy', Churchill told his readers that 'the proceedings of the House of Commons have sunk to the lowest ebb'. In real 'die-hard' spirit, he deplored the 'lack of any continuity of political thought or direction'. The 'old life of the House of Commons is rapidly passing away' and it was being replaced by 'a timid Caesarism refreshing itself by occasional plebiscites'; he feared that within a decade 'we may well see the end of the English parliamentary system'. Much of this he put down to the failure of universal democracy, and his own solution was to give all householders a second vote and to have a system of proportional representation which would allow the large cities, 'the pulling and driving power of the country', greater weight than other areas.[61] Only by recreating a system which had produced 'statesmen' and a responsible electorate could England be saved from the menace of 'dictatorship real or veiled' that was threatening 'almost every country'.[62]

In part this was a feeling that any system which could allow the failing and semi-senile MacDonald to be Prime Minister, and the supine Baldwin to be his Mayor of the Palace, whilst Churchill himself was in the wilderness, had self-evidently failed; but it was also part of Churchill's threnody on a lost golden age. As Churchill became more alarmed by events in Germany and the Government did not, he was to add that to his indictment. India, Germany, southern Ireland, Palestine – wherever he looked he could see the accumulated heritage of generations being squandered by lesser men. Britain's difficulties, he had declared in a speech on St George's Day 1933, arose from 'the mood of unwarrantable self-abasement into which we have been cast by a powerful section of our own intellectuals' and the 'defeatist doctrines' which had been accepted by most politicians.[63] This, indeed, was the authentic voice of the 'die-hard', which was one reason why Churchill's warnings about Germany had as little impact as his warnings about the dangers of allowing all-India federation; it was not simply, as has been asserted, that he 'debased the coinage of alarmism',[64] but rather that both warnings derived from the same world-view, which was not shared by many of his fellow countrymen.

In 1933 Churchill had called for the scrapping of the 'ten-year rule', a cry he reiterated in February 1933, when he criticised government policy for wanting to continue with restrictions upon armaments. He had called, in particular, for Britain to have the largest air force in the world, a cry which was to become increasingly familiar over the next few years.[65] In criticising the Government's White Paper on defence in March, he had derided Baldwin's comment that 'public opinion' needed 'working up' to accept the need for rearmament: 'You must not go and ask the public what they think about this. Parliament and the Cabinet have to decide,' Churchill declared grandly[66] – as though forgetting, or impatient of, the source whence they derived their power.

Churchill's criticisms of the pace of the Government's rearmament policy habitually ignored two considerations which, perforce, bulked large in Baldwin's mind: finance and public opinion. But, as over India, the Government's case was one of detail whilst Churchill's was one of headline-grabbing simplicity. The Defence Requirements Committee of the Cabinet, set up in late 1933 and responsible for the White Paper of February, had recommended spending £71.3 million over the next five years, exclusive of spending on the Navy, but, unlike Churchill, the Cabinet had had to struggle with the question of where the money was to come from. An increase in taxation was ruled out, and no one much liked Baldwin's suggestion of a defence loan. There was, moreover, the question of who Britain was preparing for a war against. This was a vital question. If it was just Germany, there would still be arguments about *what sort* of war was being prepared for; but if it was Germany and Japan, the naval costs would become crippling. Chamberlain, as Chancellor of the Exchequer, declared that Britain could not afford to do the latter, and that spending on the Army should be cut to allow for increased spending on the Air Force; the question of naval construction was deferred.[67]

The implications of the Cabinet's decisions in July 1934 will be further explored in the next chapter, but here it is sufficient to notice that Churchill was able to use the debate on defence at the end of July partially to redeem the failure of the Hoare–Derby fiasco.[68]

If Churchill's reputation had been damaged by the events of April to June, that did not mean, as Hoare imagined, that the IDL campaign had been crushed. Churchill did not attend the Party conference at Bristol on 4 and 5 October, and Hoare felt safe enough to dispense with speeches from either Baldwin or Chamberlain. This was a mistake. The vote, which took place on Page-Croft's motion condemning the Government for 'muzzling' the conference by asking it to postpone its decision until after the Joint Select Committee reported, was only 543 to 530 in the Government's favour.[69]

The fact that the IDL should have enjoyed its greatest success at the Conservative Party conference in the absence of its most famous speaker was not lost on some of its members. Party loyalists such as Salisbury were not happy with the lengths to which Churchill appeared to be willing to go in order to defeat the Government. The Hoare–Derby affair had delayed the report of the Joint Select Committee by two months, but when it was published in October nineteen members of the Committee were in its favour as opposed to nine (including four Labour MPs) against it. The concessions which had been made to satisfy Austen Chamberlain and Zetland had a similar effect upon many Conservatives; few of them liked the India Bill, but Hoare's promises of adequate safeguards for British interests and for the interests of the minority communities deprived Churchill of any swell of backbench support.[70] Many Conservatives now rallied to the Party leadership, and the divide which had always existed between Churchill and the loyalist members of the IDL began to open up.

Where men like Page-Croft and Salisbury objected to the India Bill, they did not have Churchill's deep-rooted aversion to the Government as such, and it began to seem as though his main motive was the one attributed to him by Amery. Over a bill to prevent betting on the Irish sweepstake, Churchill led opposition to the Government,[71] whilst his attacks on the Government's rearmament programme on 28 November appeared to be exaggerated in the light of Baldwin's reassuring replies to his statements that the German Air Force was 'rapidly approaching parity with our own'.[72]

When the Conservative Central Council met on 4 December, Baldwin successfully soothed away the fears of most Conservatives, and Salisbury's amendment, favouring provincial self-government in India but opposing central self-government, was defeated by 1,102 to 390 votes. Churchill's 'highly rhetorical' speech took what was now his usual line: the dangers of giving away the Empire when everyone else was bent on acquiring one.[73] At the end of the Bill's report stage in the Commons on 12 December, an anti-Government amendment was defeated by 410 to 127 votes, with nine members of the IDL either abstaining or voting with the Government. In the Lords, Lloyd and Salisbury were defeated by 239 to 62 votes.[74]

Yet again the Government's massive Commons majority had prevailed, and whilst seventy-five Conservatives had voted against the Joint Select Committee report, it had been approved, and it was unlikely that anything could stop it from becoming law. Churchill was not daunted, and when his son Randolph decided to stand as an Independent candidate in the Wavertree by-election in January 1935 on the question of India, he supported him.[75] But many members of the IDL were unhappy about actually opposing a Conservative candidate, and their unhappiness increased when, thanks to a split Conservative vote, a Socialist was elected. The Executive Committee of the IDL decided that it would not support any candidates at by-elections, a decision which Lloyd stigmatised as 'the turning-point in our campaign' and the acceptance of eventual defeat.[76]

That Parliamentary arithmetic which had always made Churchill's defeat likely now had allied to it the feeling of many loyalists that Churchill's support for their cause was becoming a liability. On 11 February the Bill received its second reading by 404 to 133 votes, and, after Churchill had been defeated by 283 votes to 89 at the end of the committee stage of the Bill on 26 February, Salisbury told Lord Wolmer that he had 'entirely lost parliamentary touch'. He refused to take the chair for Churchill at an IDL meeting in the Albert Hall, and his reason for doing so illustrates how wide the gap now was between Churchill and the 'Blimps':

I am afraid I am not prepared to identify myself with Winston and the kind of speech which he will wish to make on that occasion ... my impression is that the bill is becoming more and more discredited and I really believe that if Winston were to have a long spell of influenza a great deal more might be done. But if it comes to be believed that our object is to break up the party, the House of Commons may stick its toes in and vote black is white to save the Government....[77]

In June 1935 the India Act was passed by 382 votes to 122, with 84 Conservatives in the minority. It was Colonel Blimp's last stand, but it was not good enough.

26

The Prophet Jeremiah?

'Here endeth the last chapter of the Book of the Prophet Jeremiah';[1] thus wrote Amery on Churchill's final speech on the India Bill in June 1935. Duff Cooper called Churchill's campaign against the Bill 'the most unfortunate event that occurred between the two wars', because, in his view, it isolated Churchill from those like himself, who on 'appeasement' were his natural supporters.[2] Most commentators have drawn a similar distinction between Churchill as 'Jeremiah' and Churchill as 'Cassandra'. The argument pursued so far here is that this is a false distinction, a product, like so much of the writing about the period after 1933, of the rich mythology of what Churchill called 'the years which the locusts have eaten'.[3] The myths are legion, and because they all have a bearing on Churchill's reputation, they must be dealt with.

In the first place, despite the fact that commentators have tended to put them in separate compartments, there was a direct connection between Churchill's campaign on India and his call for rearmament; indeed, for the last year, and especially the last six months of his fight against the India Bill, he was deeply embroiled in warning about the dangers to be apprehended from the growth in the size of the German Air Force. Secondly, far from the latter campaign constituting part of the long war which Churchill waged from 'the wilderness' against the Government, it actually provided the means for a rapprochement between him and the Party leaders; so much so that after the India Act was done with, Churchill made his peace with Baldwin,[4] congratulated him on his achievements as leader[5] and campaigned for the Conservatives in the 1935 election[6] – thus doing his utmost to make sure that the frequent rumours that he was going to be taken into the Government came true.[7] From this a third part of the myth comes into question. Such a rapprochement calls into question the notion that there was some great gulf between Churchill and Baldwin on rearmament. Churchill himself said in December 1935 that there was 'no difference of principle' between him and the Government; nor was there. What divided Churchill from most Ministers was what had divided them on India – a view on how to preserve British power and the Empire. The notion that Britain rearmed too little and too late has little support amongst historians,[8] and it is time that it was laid to rest.

In writing *The History of the English-Speaking Peoples*, one of Churchill's research assistants queried his use of the story of King Alfred burning the cakes, but Churchill insisted that it should be left in because it was part of English history; even if it had not happened, most people 'knew' about it, so it should be there.[9] Something similar might be said about the story of Churchill's lone stance in 'the wilderness'. The notion of him as 'Cassandra', whose prophecies proved true but were ignored by her fellow-Trojans, has entered the popular consciousness, thanks in large part to the propaganda of 1940 and to Churchill's *The Gathering Storm*. But the Government was neither 'foolish' nor 'fatuous', nor did it neglect rearmament, nor did 'Baldwin . . . put Party before country'.[10]

By 1950 nearly half a million copies of *The Gathering Storm* had been sold in Britain and the United States.[11] If it had only been on the strength of Churchill's wartime reputation, the book would have made an impact, but buttressed as it was, in Churchill's usual style, with copious documentation, it soon established itself in the popular domain as *the* interpretation of the 1930s. However much specialist historians have laboured since the 1970s to show that Britain was rearming as fast as she could within the constraints imposed by the economy and public opinion,[12] however much doubt they may cast on the notion that Hitler should somehow have been 'stopped' before 1939, theirs is a case which depends on the fine detail, and they lack the power and the prestige (not to mention the sales) which have implanted the Churchill version of the age of 'appeasement' as firmly in the public mind as the story of King Alfred and his cakes. Still, Churchill did admit that the 'cakes' should be placed in context, and so must the mythology of appeasement.

What divided Churchill from Baldwin and company over 'appeasement' was what divided them over India – an attitude of mind. 'The day is . . . past in my humble opinion when Winston's possessive instinct can be applied to Empires and the like. That conception of Imperialism is finished,' Irwin had told Davidson in March 1931.[13] What one historian has called 'the new humdrum imperial style'[14] was the product of high morality out of low cost and democratic necessity. As we have seen, even by the end of the Lloyd George coalition it was clear that the British people would tolerate easily neither the moral cost of the use of force – as the reaction to Amritsar and the Black and Tans had shown – nor yet the financial cost. Balanced budgets and democracy demanded imperialism on the cheap. Despite Churchill's allegations to the contrary, Baldwin and Irwin were not trying to give away the Empire; they were trying to preserve it as best they could given these constraints. The same could be said of their policy towards Germany.

The belief that by defining British interests and then hedging them about with safeguards, it would be possible to come to power-sharing agreements with nationalist movements, was the hallmark of British imperial policy under Baldwin. It was cheap, moral and liberal in tone; not for the British the methods used by the French in Syria in 1923, when thousands died as nationalists were taught a lesson in who was in charge. The victory of Hoare and Baldwin over the India Bill ensured that it would continue. The future lay with that style, and it is easy, to quote only the most recent of the many commentators who have taken a similar view, to dismiss Churchill, Lloyd and company as 'the men of yesterday'.[15] This was certainly the view of Churchill's opponents at the time. Linlithgow described him as 'hanging, hairy from a branch, while you splutter the atavistic shibboleths of an age destined very soon to retreat into the forgotten past'.[16] What Amery called 'the modern point of view' could, it thought, afford to be condescendingly triumphalist in its attitude to yesterday's men.

As a strategy for managing the decline in British power and yet holding on to as much as possible, this same technique of 'power-sharing' could be adapted to use nearer home. Irwin (or Viscount Halifax as he was after 1934), Hoare and the man who was Under-Secretary to them both, R. A. Butler, brought to bear upon the affairs of Europe the same pragmatic realism which they had applied to India. Halifax heard the thunder from Churchill and from the left about 'morality', but although a devout High-Churchman himself, he took the view that 'we go badly wrong if we allow our judgement of practical steps to be taken' to be 'perpetually deflected by our moral reactions against wrong that we can in no circumstances immediately redress'.[17] The natural arrogance of liberal pragmatism was further strengthened by what might be called the 'mandarin' frame of mind; 'perhaps the greatest difficulty in the conduct of foreign affairs, and the one least appreciated by those not engaged in it, is the fact that the ideal policy is scarcely ever practicable'; compromises had to be hammered out in the face of 'harsh and obstinate realities'.[18] Butler heard fulminations about the 'traditional British foreign policy' of trying to hold the balance of power, but he dismissed this as the product of an Edwardian frame of mind; a world-wide Empire could have no simple foreign policy.[19] As in India or Egypt, so it would be with Hitler. Gandhi and Nehru were reasonable fellows. Their rhetoric and some of their actions might have been rather extreme, but, at bottom, politics was 'the art of the possible'. It was necessary to find out what they *really* wanted, and then to give them as little of it as possible – just enough to keep them happy.[20]

Of all the ironies which history affords examples, one of the better ones is that the attitude which was to bring so much praise to its protagonists from liberal-minded historians should have brought coals of wrath upon the same heads when it was applied to Europe. It is no wonder that 'India' and 'appease-ment' have tended to be separated by those writing about Churchill. If it were not so, it would involve historians in a pretty dilemma: how could the illiberal and reactionary attitudes which call for condemnation when they were applied to defend 'imperialism' suddenly become an object for praise when they were applied to Germany? Yet it was the same set of attitudes which Churchill brought to bear on both questions, because to him they were part of the same larger problem – how was Britain to hold on to the great position which his generation had inherited and which it should bequeath to its children?

Churchill's scepticism about the results of universal suffrage in Great Britain made him even more dubious about the application of democracy in places like India, and he shared Lloyd's view about the 'fundamental unsuitability of modern western democratic methods of government to any oriental people'.[21] He had ceased to believe the Whig version of history and preferred a more Tory one, where history was 'full of unexpected turns and retrogressions'.[22] This gave him some purchase on the liberal assumptions which informed the imperial and foreign policy preferred by Halifax and Baldwin. Where they thought he was out of date, he knew that they were. The world was a dangerous place, and because of that Britain should neither divest herself of India nor should she ignore the need to rearm.

Churchill and Lloyd were correct in assuming that 'power-sharing' would not work: it did not in Egypt, and even if the outbreak of war had not prevented the 1935 Act from being implemented, it would not have worked in India. It was the 1930s' equivalent of those beautifully drawn-up constitutions which Churchill's son-in-law (and, ironically, Lloyd's adjutant during the India debates), Duncan Sandys, was to present to the newly independent Commonwealth countries in the late 1950s and early 1960s; it ignored the nature of colonial nationalism. Zaghloul, Gandhi, Nehru and company were no more interested in sharing power with the British than were Nkrumah and Kaunda in sharing it with their own people. It was all very well for Britain to give provincial autonomy to India, but real power could not be shared.

Exactly the same view informed Churchill's vision of Europe. He told Rothermere in May 1935 that the idea of coming to 'an understanding with Germany to dominate Europe' was 'contrary to the whole of our history'. Britain had 'traditionally' aligned herself with the 'second strongest power in Europe' and had thus foiled the machinations of Philip II of Spain, Louis XIV and Napoleon of France, and the Kaiser's Germany.[23] Earlier that year Churchill had told Sir Edward Grey's biographer, G. M. Trevelyan, that 'his life's justification depends upon whether England ought to have done in 1914 what she did against Philip II of Spain, against Louis XIV and against Napoleon'. Churchill had 'no doubt what the answer should be'.[24] Whether it was in India or Europe, he resolved to stand on the old ways. The new democracy at home had seen a recension from the glories of old, and he had no doubt that the new style which it seemed to have brought to the pursuit of British imperial and foreign policy would have similar results.

But if Churchill's 'Tory history' enabled him to see the 'mote' in the eye of Baldwin's liberalism, he was blind to the 'beam' in his own. It may have been true, as Davidson concluded on a visit to India in 1932, that the Viceroy had been 'bounced by Gandhi into believing that a few half-baked semi-educated urban agitators represent the views of 365 million hard-working and comparatively contented cultivators',[25] and Churchill may have been right that the nationalists had no intention of sharing power, but he had little knowledge of contemporary India, and no answer to the question of how Gandhi and company should be handled. He did not want repression, but he had no solution to the question which afflicted the Government, which was how to deal with the nationalists.[26] On several occasions in early 1935 Hoare's Bill was almost scuppered when the Indian princes were revealed to be less in favour of federation than he and the Viceroy had liked to pretend.[27] But they were at least attempting to come to terms with nationalism, whilst Churchill seemed to think that it could be ignored. In this, he enjoyed the support of most Conservatives, for many of those who voted for the Bill did so only because their leaders assured them that its 'safeguards' were adequate.[28]

The IDL stood for the glories of the Raj, for the fair treatment of the 'Untouchables' and against what they saw as the dangers of a Hindu despotism. Churchill and Lloyd warned that federation would not work, that there would be communal violence and that it would all end with Britain losing her Empire. In all of these things their prophecies were as true as they were to be when they spoke of Europe. But in both cases the prophets rested upon a foundation which was unstable. They assumed that Britain still possessed in the 1930s the power which had made the Empire, and they dismissed those who thought otherwise as 'defeatists'.[29] Yet by 1934 the 'balance of merchandise trade had tipped in India's favour', whilst the Indian Army, far from being a source of strength to the imperial power, was a drain on resources; the Chatfield report of 1939 revealed that it would cost £34.33 million to upgrade its equipment.[30] The considerations of economy, of public opinion and of the strategic weakness of the Empire which informed imperial policy also informed British foreign policy; in both cases Churchill ignored the limitations on power.

Churchill was scornful of arguments that rearmament could not proceed apace because of public opinion. The Government had a massive majority; let it use it, was the line he took in the defence debate in May 1935 and subsequently.[31] As early as March 1934 he had pointed out the need for rearmament in the air, and from November onwards made this one of his main causes.[32] Yet he did not stop to ask whether putting massive resources into a particular type of air force was the best policy, nor did he wrestle, as the Government had to, with the question of how to divide a limited budget between apparently unlimited calls upon it. At times Churchill spoke as though Britain could afford a large air force, army and navy simultaneously, and as though she could act in Europe and in Asia in similar fashion. He assumed, too easily, that any deficiencies in British power could be made up by alliance with France. But most of all he assumed too much of public opinion.

During the air defence debate in May 1935, he said that 'Nothing that has ever happened in this country could lead Ministers of the Crown to suppose that when a serious case of public danger is put to them [the people] they will not respond in overwhelming strength to any request.'[33] This sounds better in retrospect than viewed in context. At the time no one, including Churchill, had made out anything like an overwhelming case that vital British interests were threatened by Hitler. His perception that this was so was founded upon his view of Britain's role as regulator on the balance of power, but the idea of 'sharing' power in Europe with a revived Germany was not, for most of the electorate, 'a serious case of public danger'. As for evidence that the people would back a strong rearmament programme, neither by-election results, nor the 'peace ballot' of the summer of 1935 when nine million people voted against using military sanctions even in support of the League of Nations,[34] suggested to 'Ministers of the Crown' that Churchill was right. He could ignore public opinion, and the economic and industrial limitations on rearmament, but they could not. Yet, because Ministers shared some of Churchill's fears, his campaign on air defence did not act, as the India Bill had, to divide him from Baldwin.

The fundamental differences thus far outlined were not to be fully apparent before 1938, when Churchill's conviction that coming to a deal with Hitler over the future of eastern Europe was contrary to the traditions of British foreign policy, clashed with Neville Chamberlain's belief that it was no such thing.[35] But on rearmament, the one issue which divided Churchill from the Government in 1935 was an argument about the pace at which it should proceed and where the effort should be concentrated.

The much-derided Neville Chamberlain was not unwilling to go to the country in 1935 on a cry of rearmament.[36] Ever since the Defence Requirements Committee of the Cabinet had reported in March 1934, the Cabinet had wrestled with the problems posed by a decade of disarmament. It was all very well for Churchill to call for the scrapping of the 'ten-year rule' in 1933, but when the Cabinet did that they found themselves faced with a fearsome dilemma.[37] To have remedied deficiencies in all branches of home and imperial defence would have demanded expenditure far beyond what the economy, still weak from the slump, could have afforded – even assuming that industry had possessed the skilled manpower and material necessary. Neville Chamberlain did not see how bankrupting the country would discourage potential aggressors, and by the end of July the Cabinet had accepted his view that they should not bargain on a war against Germany, Japan and Italy at the same time. If Germany was taken as the main potential enemy, that simplified matters – a little. The question still remained as to what sort of war it was they were planning for.[38]

The War Office wanted a large army because it planned on the basis of the last war, but Chamberlain, who was familiar with the military theories of

Basil Liddell-Hart, begged to doubt whether the next war would be like the Great War. Would it not rather be a war of movement, of mechanisation and aerial warfare? If so, why spend vast sums on a large expeditionary force? The War Office argued its corner through 1934 into 1935, but in the summer of 1935 the Cabinet accepted Chamberlain's order of priorities.[39] Money would be spent firstly on the Air Force, secondly on the Navy, and lastly on the Army, whilst imperial defence could, so to speak, be left to look after itself.

Thus it was that Churchill's calls in 1934–5 for large increases in spending on the Air Force did not come as a totally unwelcome development to a Government conscious of the need to awaken a pacifistic public opinion to the dangers that were abroad. Churchill, as a non-official figure, could point out that the dangers came from Germany, at a time when, before Hitler's admission in March 1935 that Germany had an air force, Ministers could not do so for fear of being accused of provoking the German dictator. The figures which Churchill used on 28 November 1934 to claim that Germany would soon enjoy air 'parity' with Britain came to him from a source which was also available to the Government – the head of its Industrial Intelligence Centre, Desmond Morton.[40] If the Government did not actually authorise Morton to give Churchill the figures, Ministers were not sorry that he had them, even if it was necessary to qualify his highly coloured claims that all German civil air production could be converted easily to military use, by getting Baldwin to err too far in the opposite direction by giving the impression that Britain would enjoy air superiority throughout 1935–6.[41]

Churchill's claims, and fresh evidence about Germany's rate of aircraft production, stimulated the Government in early 1935 to increase the programme upon which it had agreed in 1934; but this was not necessarily a good thing.[42] The Defence Requirements Committee report of March 1934 pointed out that in order to meet all its possible commitments, the Air Force would need another twenty-five squadrons. The Permanent Under-Secretary at the Foreign Office, Sir Robert Vansittart, was later to regret that he, and the chief of the Air Staff, Sir Edward Ellington, did not press for this, but even had they done so, and even had the factories existed to make these machines, what they would have turned out would have been aircraft which were already obsolete.[43] The Minister for Air, Lord Londonderry, who was Churchill's cousin, had doubted whether this 'Scheme A' was not 'better designed for public consumption rather than real utility'.[44] Speeding it up, as the Government did in November, by promising that twenty-two of the new squadrons would be ready by the end of 1936, was to compound the problem.[45]

If the Government had followed Churchill's advice to the letter, it would simply have wasted scarce resources on obsolescent air frames – a problem which it was conscious of having even with the increases sanctioned under the White Paper of March 1935. Rolls-Royce had only just come up with the

PV-12 (Merlin) engine, and it was not until November 1934 that Specification F.5/34, the design for the prototype of the Hurricane, was produced. The first prototypes were tested in May 1935 and the first Hurricane fighter only took to the air on 6 November 1935.[46] If the Government had spent its budget on following Churchill's advice, it would have built out-of-date bombers instead, which would have been no use in the summer of 1940. Churchill owed his 'finest hour' to the fact that his advice had not been taken in 1934–5.

There is, of course, the danger of developing a circular argument, and it is possible that by adopting the defence plan it did after 1937 in particular, the Government made 1940 more rather than less likely. By spending more on the development of radar and fighters, and less on the Army, the British not only prepared themselves for Churchill's 'finest hour', but they also made it inevitable. Had they had a large army with which to support the French, then perhaps the French would not have collapsed in May 1940? But given the existing superiority in arms which the Allies enjoyed in the summer of 1940, it is equally arguable that all the Government would have done would have been to leave more equipment behind at Dunkirk, only to have found that it lacked the capacity to defend the home islands. But the fact remains that if it had built the air force which Churchill was demanding in 1935–6, then the Hurricanes and Spitfires would not only have been starved of the funds needed to produce them in any quantities, but their very development might have fallen victim to economies imposed by the need to produce the bombers which Churchill wanted.

But the differences between Churchill and the Government in 1934–5 seemed rather ones of degree than fundamental principle; both favoured rearming, both laid emphasis upon the Air Force and both worried about the darkening international situation. The dangers apparent in overtly pursuing an accelerated rearmament programme, which looked as though it was directed against Germany, were made plain in March 1935 when Hitler used the British White Paper as an excuse to declare that not only did Germany have an air force, but she also had air parity with Britain. Churchill, who believed the claim because it matched what he had been saying since November, used it as a stick with which to prod the Government.[47] But it is doubtful whether Hitler's claims were any more truthful than his protestations that all he wanted was peace.[48] Still, it did the Government no harm to have Churchill berating it for going too slow, for there were many critics who alleged that it was doing too much, and in the circumstances of electoral dilapidation in which it found itself in early 1935, it could ill afford to add to its problems.

Early 1935 was not a good period for the Government to presume on public opinion. The India Bill remained vulnerable to attack until May, and there were rumours that it might have to be dropped altogether in March when the opposition of some of the princes to federation became known.[49] The new Unemployment Act of 1934, which came into force in early 1935, was

universally condemned for the low rates of benefit which it helped to produce,[50] and with little sign of economic recovery, or any prospect of one
outside of the Chancellor's speeches, there were continual rumours that the
Government might be reconstructed to bring in Lloyd George and Churchill.[51]
The launch by the former of his 'British New Deal' in January, with its plans
for stimulating the economy by government spending, made him an attractive
figure to younger Conservatives like Macmillan and Boothby, who were
becoming increasingly frustrated with the economics of Chamberlain.[52] The
Defence White Paper, which Churchill thought inadequate, was criticised by
liberal opinion as excessive, whilst in the House the Labour Party put down
a motion condemning it.[53]

It was not simply that defence, economic problems and disputes within the
Conservative Party made the Government vulnerable to attack; what made
the situation potentially serious, and lent credibility to the rumours that it
might reinforce itself by bringing in major figures like Churchill and Lloyd
George, was the evident incapacity of its own leadership. It may have been
cruel of Churchill to have called MacDonald 'almost a mental case', but he
was telling little more than the truth, and he was certainly correct in assuming
that a government without any discernible leadership would not long survive
unchanged.[54] MacDonald, whether through the effects of age and over-work,
or whether through the exacerbation of these things by the blackmail to
which he was subject thanks to the letters which he had written to a foreign
tart, was universally held to scorn.[55] That leading light of London Society,
who burnt with a somewhat reduced flame on the Conservative backbenches,
Henry 'Chips' Channon, was not the only one to assume that if the Prime
Minister stayed, the Government would probably go.[56] The performance of
Sir John Simon as Foreign Secretary was not regarded with any great appro-
bation by the Conservatives either, and many of them could not see why the
smaller parties, which made up the 'National' element of the Government,
should have so many plum posts; the mood was getting to be reminiscent of
the end of the Lloyd George coalition.[57]

Had the India Bill fallen, the Government would have had to renew itself
in a Churchillian direction; and, for as long as it remained in trouble, rumours
of such a realignment persisted, with Baldwin doing nothing to discourage
them – he was not noted for prematurely closing his options. Londonderry
was right when he told Churchill that over rearmament 'there is very little
difference between us in our aims and objects',[58] and MacDonald responded
to pressure from Sir Austen Chamberlain and Churchill by telling them in
early January that a special sub-committee of the CID had been set up to
consider the problem of air defence.[59] This was not what Churchill's scientific
guru, Professor Lindemann, wanted, but the invitation to join the Tizard
Committee (as it was known after its Chairman, Sir Henry Tizard) was a sign
that the Government was prepared to make friendly gestures to those associ-

ated with Churchill, whilst the setting up of the Air Research Defence Committee in March was another sign that the Government took rearmament in the air seriously.[60] Churchill launched another attack on the Government in debate on 2 May, in which he not only stated (incorrectly) that the Germans had air parity with Britain, but added (even more incorrectly) that by the end of the year they might have three or four times 'our strength'. The Government's response was to announce that it had once more increased the rate of aircraft production.[61]

Whilst the India Bill remained an active issue, one way or the other, there could be no rapprochement between Churchill and the Government, but once it was out of the way in June, with the Government victorious, Churchill declared that he had no hard feelings,[62] and nothing which had happened in the various debates over rearmament had done anything to create another feud between him and the Government. Whilst the prospect of defeating the Bill had remained, Churchill had been far from enthusiastic about joining the Government; he did not see why he should lend a failing Cabinet any credit.[63] Lloyd George felt the same. He did not want to join any Government which had MacDonald at its head, Simon at the Foreign Office and Chamberlain at the Exchequer.[64] As Chamberlain was no more anxious to work with him, Lloyd George need not have worried. The Chancellor regarded the man who had sacked him in 1918 as 'treacherous and unscrupulous' without 'the rudiments of the instincts of a gentleman'.[65] Thus it was that when the long-awaited reshuffle came in June, Lloyd George got nothing; but no such bar existed against Churchill.

The reshuffle, in which Baldwin swapped offices with MacDonald and became Prime Minister, also saw Hoare receive his reward for India by going to the Foreign Office. With the Conservative element in the Government thus strengthened, Baldwin was anxious to heal the rifts within his Party which the India Act had inflicted, but he kept an 'open mind' upon whether to do so by inviting Churchill into the Government. There would be an election in the near future and he could decide after that.[66]

Baldwin's concern for public opinion was to lay him open to the charge made by Churchill in his memoirs that he had put his Party before his country. Churchill once called the Committee of Privileges report a 'masterpiece of *suppressio veri* and *suggestio falsi*',[67] and his treatment of Baldwin on the question of public opinion and rearmament shows that he knew whereof he spoke. The idea, which Churchill canvasses (if he did not invent it), that events such as the loss of the East Fulham by-election in October 1933 influenced the pace of the Government's rearmament programme,[68] has little evidence to support it; economic considerations played a far more important role.[69] That is not to say that Baldwin did not bear in mind the possibility that he might lose the election, which was why he rejected Chamberlain's suggestion in August that the Government should fight it on the rearmament issue;[70] but only Churchill, in the disenchanted mood he was in with the results of democracy, could have supposed that Baldwin could have ignored the evidence which June 1935 provided of the pacific mood of the people. The 'peace ballot', organised by the League of Nations Union, revealed nearly ten and a half million people in favour of further disarmament, with ten million favouring the use of economic sanctions only against an aggressor – and then only with the approval of the League.[71]

Churchill later claimed that 'the Peace Ballot was misunderstood by Ministers' and that 'events soon showed' that men like Lord Cecil, who helped organise it, were in fact willing to go to war; but how the Government was supposed to draw this comforting conclusion, which was available only with hindsight, from the circumstances of 1935, Churchill wisely declined to explain. He sought refuge in the somewhat banal conclusion that 'the British people in the ebb and flow of their party politics and public opinion are often too capricious, changeable and inconsequent for foreigners to understand';[72] he might have added that it was not too easy for the British Government to understand them either. Chamberlain accepted Baldwin's verdict that they should not fight the election on the rearmament issue because he respected his leader's judgment of the 'floating vote';[73] there is nothing to suggest that Churchill's instinct for what the voters wanted was sounder than Baldwin's.

The threat of Mussolini invading Abyssinia raised the question of how Britain should respond to such a move. Churchill's instincts were all in favour of a bit of 'blood and thunder',[74] but Baldwin judged it more advisable to get Hoare to make pleasant-sounding noises about the uses of the League of Nations in a speech at Geneva in September.[75] As ever with Baldwin, it was all a matter of fine judgments. Churchill's noises in April and May had served to alert public opinion to dangers which might (or might not) lie ahead, but it would hardly do to insult Hitler in the way he did. The same 'humdrum imperial style', which meant that one searched behind Gandhi's rhetoric to find what he wanted, suggested itself as a way of dealing with Hitler. After all he did claim, after saying Germany had air parity, that he wanted an agreement with Britain, and the conclusion of an Anglo-German naval treaty in June supported the idea that he could be dealt with. The Versailles treaty had few defenders, and a revived Germany was bound to want to expand her sphere of influence; everything depended on how Hitler went about it.

Not even Churchill suggested that war should have been waged upon Hitler in 1935. His firm grasp of what he considered to be the central theme of British foreign policy enabled him to see dangers ahead which others thought illusory, but no one has ever suggested that the electorate was in the mood to take such a view in 1935. For all his scorn at the idea of being influenced by such considerations, Churchill himself wrote at election time: 'it is a fearsome thing to cast the whole future of the Empire on the franchise of so many simple folk'.[76] So it was, but Baldwin was stuck with it – and, unlike Churchill, he had to try to win the election.

As the election drew closer, so did relations between Churchill and Baldwin. In July he agreed to Baldwin's request to serve on the Air Defence Research Sub-Committee, which was the first time since 1929 that he had any official connection with a government committee.[77] Baldwin had no objection to Churchill's insisting that membership would not gag him; that was not why he was being asked to join. If Baldwin was leaving his options open to take Churchill into the Government, Churchill was doing his best to make himself *papabile*. A kindly reference to Sir John Simon in the House on 11 July might have been thought a little excessive,[78] but making up his quarrel with Derby in September was a sensible mending of fences.[79] Praise of Baldwin at the Conservative Party conference in early October was a fairly obvious reminder to the Prime Minister that, if he was going to call the election which everyone predicted, he was ready and willing to serve under him. Baldwin responded generously by saying that 'whatever differences have existed among us during the past two years' were at an end – although the pronoun left it open as to whether he meant Churchill or the Conservative Party as a whole.[80]

When the election was announced on 14 October, Churchill offered his services to Central Office for campaigning elsewhere, an offer which it was not felt politic to refuse.[81] One of the beneficiaries of this generosity was the only surviving son of his old enemy, Bonar Law, Richard, who was standing at Hull West.[82] The Government, still under its 'National' banner, won a resounding victory, with 429 seats to the Labour Party's 154. Although this compared with 554 to 52, respectively, in 1931, the circumstances in which that election had taken place were sufficiently unusual for the loss of seats to be discounted. The Conservatives had 388 seats. Beaverbrook's comment to Churchill on election night was 'Well, you're finished now.' With such a good majority, he told Churchill, Baldwin 'will be able to do without you'. To Churchill's deep disappointment, Beaverbrook was right.[83] Churchill's attacks on Germany, and on Hitler in particular, in October, had raised a good deal of diplomatic dust, and taking him straight into the Government would have been regarded as an unfriendly act by the Germans.

According to one account Baldwin did not offer Churchill a post because he wanted to 'keep him fresh to be our War Prime Minister', but this has the smell of retrospection about it.[84] Certainly at the time speculation continued that Churchill would be offered a post in any government reshuffle, and as he departed for a holiday in the Mediterranean in early December, Churchill had not despaired of getting a job. There were, he declared in a letter to *The Times*, no 'differences of principle' between him and the Government on rearmament – and only the next session would show whether there were ones of 'method and degree'.[85]

27

Fortune's Vicissitudes

The Mediterranean holiday was a much-needed rest; that it got Churchill out of harm's way whilst the rumours that Baldwin might yet take him into the Cabinet still circulated was an additional advantage.[1] Churchill had reached his sixtieth birthday on 30 November 1934, and the year which had passed since then had witnessed vicissitudes in more than his political life. He was wont to describe Chartwell as his citadel from the storms, where he dwelt at peace, surrounded by his family; but as was so often the case, a perception strongly held by Churchill was not necessarily shared by others.

Clementine Churchill had never liked Chartwell. She had not wanted to buy the house in 1922, and she regarded it, not without justice, as an enormous drain on their finances.[2] Winston loved the house, its setting with a magnificent view across the Weald of Kent, and the opportunities which it gave him to indulge a taste for landscape gardening and brick-laying. If it was expensive, well, what of that; he earned a fortune through his pen, so was he not entitled to his luxury? The problem was that he also spent a fortune. In 1934 he earned over £12,000 from his literary endeavours.[3] Nothing that came from his pen, or rather his lips (for he loved to dictate) was wasted, and material would be recycled; parts of *My Early Life* would be recast into more popular form for serialisation in the *News of the World*, which would bring in another £3,500 for little extra work.[4] When other resources failed, Churchill could always use the selling-power of his name to secure lucrative contracts retelling famous stories, Shakespeare's *Julius Caesar* or *Anna Karenina*; he was not too enamoured of the latter, telling Eddie Marsh that he was 'not attracted by these thin-skinned, self-disturbing Russian boobs'.[5] Introspective despair was not calculated to appeal to Churchill, but as he was being paid over £300 an article to summarise it and other works, such as *Uncle Tom's Cabin*,[6] and as he was only paying Eddie Marsh £25 a time to actually do the work,[7] he could afford not to mind.

If Churchill was not the best-paid journalist in the country, someone else must have been earning vast amounts from the profession.[8] In 1932 *Colliers* magazine in America was paying him $1,500 for six articles on topics such as 'Defense in the Pacific' and 'Who'll pay the Jobless?',[9] some of which he managed to re-sell to British newspapers; he had the *Daily Mail*'s contract of £7,800 for a weekly article,[10] and he added to that the money from Riddell, for the rehashes of classic novels. He was also highly paid as an author. As well as his income from journalism in 1932, there was the prospect of a contract for £20,000 to write a book on the *History of the English-Speaking Peoples*.[11] The contract for this was not signed until 1934, but it gave Churchill £500 immediately;[12] this was in addition to his journalism for that year (which brought in over £7,000) and the £3,500 which he received upon the publication of the first volume of *Marlborough*.[13] Churchill added script-writing to his quiver of lucrative activities, signing a contract with Alexander Korda to write, amongst other things, the 'treatment' for a film on the reign of George V to coincide with the Silver Jubilee; for this he was promised £2,500 at the beginning of 1935, another £2,500 when the film was finished, and £5,000 when it was shown.[14] It was this which had taken him out of the country at the time of the Conservative Party conference in 1934.

But if Churchill earned a salary twice that of the Prime Minister, he spent it with almost regal prodigality. Despite his earnings in 1934, he calculated at the beginning of the following year that he was still £1,500 in debt – but, of course, he hoped this would improve.[15] It did not. Chartwell was expensive to maintain, and if he did not pay Eddie Marsh well for all his devilling, then an eminent historian like Keith Feiling of Christ Church might receive £500 a time for his assistance on parts of *Marlborough*.[16] It was *Marlborough* which was at the root of Churchill's growing financial problems. The book should have been completed in two volumes by 1935, but at that date he had finished only half of it.[17] Churchill was proud of the fact that no publisher had ever suffered by collaboration with him, so he was not pleased to hear that the first two volumes of *Marlborough* had sold badly.[18] He was, he told his publishers (in the sort of letter which they must have been used to receiving from many authors) in October 1935, determined to complete the book in three volumes, and he hoped that despite the 'course of public events', he would be able to have it done by late 1936.[19] Political activities slowed him down, but not as much as his methods of composition, for although a volume was ready for 1936, it proved to be the penultimate one. A book that had started out as a 200,000-word project to be completed by 1935, ballooned into one of over a million words which was not completed until 1938;[20] and by the time of the last volume, Churchill was writing for nothing, which he could not afford to do.[21] His life-style depended upon the literary machine producing large quantities of material on time, and the delays and distractions which the later volumes of *Marlborough* provided acted as grit in the works.

By the time of Churchill's holiday at the end of 1935, the problems which this was to cause were no bigger than a small cloud on the horizon, but there were other dark clouds cluttering up that prospect, not the least of which were those to do with his marriage. From Rabat, on Boxing Day, he wrote to Clementine telling her that he had felt a 'little sad and lonely' two days earlier when he had realised that it was Christmas Eve and he was without her; he wished 'you were here so that you could pet me – for I do love that'.[22] But she was not there, and it was not, as the tone of the letter indicates, the first time that he had had occasion to feel 'disconsolate' at her absence.

Churchill had concluded *My Early Life* with his marriage and the words 'and I lived happily ever after'. But it is only in fairy stories that such things happen, and Churchill's life bore more resemblance to some great romantic epic. The Churchill children, as they grew up, provided worry for their parents. Randolph, handsome as a Greek god and twice as arrogant, had decided to leave Christ Church without taking a degree. The chance of being paid to do a lecture tour in America was too good to miss, and he preferred the delights of being paid to lecture to those of listening to lectures on an allowance of £400 a year.[23] On 28 May 1932, Randolph's twenty-first birthday, Churchill had given a grand dinner party at Claridge's, the theme of which was 'Great Men and their Sons': as well as the two Churchills, the second Earl of Birkenhead was present, along with Lord Hailsham and his son, Quintin Hogg, as were Lord Reading and his son, Viscount Earleigh. It was a splendid occasion, meant to mark the start of what Randolph certainly took to be his inevitable rise in the world of politics.[24]

Randolph's problem, as he later acknowledged, was that whilst he possessed 'fine natural abilities', he lacked application. 'Clever and facile', he imitated his godfather, F.E., without his industry and intellect.[25] Winston, envying his son's natural facility with words, likened him to a machine-gun, but Beaverbrook's comment on this proved to be apt: 'it was to be hoped he would accumulate a big dump of ammunition and learn to hit the target';[26] he never did. Perhaps it was the very fact that he was so prodigally showered with advantages which his father had either never possessed, such as good looks and a fine-speaking voice, or had had to struggle to acquire, such as the power of oratory and writing, which encouraged Randolph in his two fatal vices: arrogance and indolence. Because things came naturally to him, he could not be bothered to work hard. Lord Londonderry got to the root of the matter when he told Churchill that whilst Randolph was 'so like you' in his 'enterprise, courage and forcefulness', he was 'unlike you because he does not seem to recognize what you always recognize that knowledge is the secret of power'.[27] He was prepared to coach his father in a more conversational speaking style,[28] but Randolph never worked to acquire the authority without which fluency becomes glibness. Journalism was his natural career. His intervention at Wavertree, and then at Norwood in March 1935, were not easily forgiven by the establishment in the Conservative Party. His hedonistic lifestyle was almost as expensive as his father's – and it was his father who was expected to pay his debts.[29] By the end of 1935 these too were problems which appeared only in the middle distance.

Churchill's devotion to his eldest son, who was the repository of all his dynastic hopes, was not shared by Clementine, who thought that he was only encouraging him in traits which would ruin him.[30] Churchill was certainly a

more indulgent parent than Clementine; and there was much about which
to be indulgent. Only little Mary presented no problems. Diana had married
and just divorced John Bailey, the son of one of her father's oldest associates,
the mining magnate, Sir Abe Bailey; but her involvement in Randolph's
campaign in Norwood had an unexpected bonus – she fell in love with his
opponent, Duncan Sandys, and their engagement was announced in August.[31]
Sarah's ambitions to go on the stage as a dancer would have strained the
indulgence of any upper-class Victorian parent; whilst some chorus girls might
become ladies (through marriage), 'ladies simply did not become chorus
girls'.[32] But here, too, Churchill proved an indulgent father.

A visitor to Chartwell in August 1935 noted that 'Mrs Churchill is also
very interesting, but when her husband talks she simply listens.'[33] After a
quarter of a century of listening, and of shaping her life to his requirements,
and those of the children, by the end of 1934 Clementine wanted some time
for herself. In December she went with Walter Guinness (now Lord Moyne)
on a cruise to Indonesia to capture one of the famous komodo dragons.
Winston had been invited, but he could not spare the time, and it was with
sadness and reluctance he saw her go. He felt 'v[er]y unprotected', but did
not feel he could deprive her of something upon which she had set her heart.[34]

Clementine was away for five months, and during that time Winston
wrote to her regularly, keeping her informed of events at Chartwell and of
Randolph's progress at Wavertree and Norwood, but behind his letters was
a sadness at her absence, and at the thought that he had not always cherished
her as she deserved.[35] Perhaps it was inevitable that 'in a dream world of
beauty and adventure' Clementine should have fallen 'romantically in love'
with Terence Philip, a handsome, younger, art dealer, who was her 'constant
companion'. Those with a taste for such things can speculate upon the nature
of their relationship, but the exquisite description in Clementine's official
biography, '*C'était une vraie connaissance de ville d'eau*', is impossible to improve
upon.[36] It is unclear how much Churchill knew of this relationship, but that
he was unaware that something more than a matter of thousands of miles
was parting him from his 'darling one' is unlikely; it might help explain part
of the disconsolate tone which his own letters took on at times.

Certainly their parting at the end of 1935, as Churchill took himself off
to the Mediterranean and Clementine went to Switzerland, brought back
melancholy echoes for him; but politics provided him with a distraction. In
Churchill's absence a crisis had blown up which threatened to overturn a
government elected only the month before with an overwhelming majority.
Mussolini's invasion of Abyssinia in October had outraged liberal opinion in
Britain. A direct breach of the covenant of the League of Nations, it seemed
to call for stern action on the part of that august body. Hoare's speech at
Geneva in September had seemed to align the Government firmly with the
League, and the appointment of the dashing young Anthony Eden, with his

impeccable liberal credentials and his appeal to the 'youth vote' as Hoare's deputy, further strengthened the Government's appeal to the floating voter.

The fact that handsome, young Captain Eden had not been appointed to the Foreign Office, but had been given the oddly named and hitherto unknown post of Minister without Portfolio for League of Nations Affairs, might have given pause for thought about the Government's 'League credentials'. Any suspicions thus aroused were more than confirmed by the morning papers on 9 December, which revealed that during a visit to Paris Hoare had signed a pact with his French opposite number, Pierre Laval, which proposed to settle the Abyssinian dispute by the simple expedient of giving most of the country to Mussolini. It is sufficient evidence in favour of Churchill's view that in a crisis the British people could be relied upon to take a sensible line, that the Hoare–Laval pact should have been greeted by such a popular outcry. George V may have given vent to one of his few recorded witticisms, 'No more coals to Newcastle, no more Hoares to Paris', but vast numbers of his subjects deluged their MPs with letters demanding that Hoare should go – with many of them suggesting that the Government might care to follow him. Duff Cooper, who had just been made Secretary of State for War, had never seen a post-bag like the one he now received.[37] In the press and the Commons the mood was one of indignation.[38] It was, Bracken told Churchill on 11 December, 'a political earthquake'.[39]

Baldwin extracted himself from the political guano by persuading Hoare that it was up to him to shoulder all the blame – with the implied promise that if he did the decent thing, then, when all the fuss had died down, he would be brought back. Hoare, under pressure, obliged. On 19 December, with his nose still in a splint from a skating accident, the unfortunate Foreign Secretary said his 'mea culpa' and, to the relief of his colleagues, departed.[40]

Wisely, Churchill did not rush home. Randolph's feeling that 'Baldwin will get away with it' proved accurate.[41] By giving Sir Austen Chamberlain the impression that he might secure the reversion of Hoare's job, Baldwin obtained his support in the important debate on 19 December, when the ex-Foreign Secretary made his apologies. As a respected elder statesman, Austen's backing helped steady the boat, but when he went for his reward, he was told that, in effect, he was too old and gaga to be Foreign Secretary.[42] Baldwin had needed his support, but now it was more important to conciliate the League-minded folk of the country, which could best be done by offering Eden the Foreign Office. Once more Baldwin had shown that in a crisis he had more lives than the average cat.

By not hurrying back to England, Churchill avoided giving any impression that he was anxious to take advantage of the Government's embarrassment. His relationship with it, and his hopes of office, were both sufficiently good for him not to want to spoil things. In the June Cabinet changes his cousin, Londonderry, had been replaced by Sir Philip Cunliffe-Lister at the Air Ministry. Londonderry, whom Churchill had been heard to dismiss as a 'half-wit',[43] was said to have owed his position to the fact that MacDonald 'greatly enjoyed standing at the top of the grand staircase in Londonderry House . . . in full evening dress',[44] and he had lacked the capacity to get a grip on his department. The successive air rearmament plans over which he had presided had been haphazard affairs, seemingly more concerned to respond with large targets for public consumption than to develop a policy. Churchill's allegations had simply served to make a bad situation worse. But his successor, Cunliffe-Lister, or Lord Swinton as he became, was a man of quite different calibre. An acerbic and efficient Yorkshireman, he had been an ever-present figure in Conservative administrations since the overthrow of Lloyd George, but he lacked anything approaching the popular touch. At the Air Ministry he showed a grasp which far exceeded that of his predecessor, and as the appointment of Churchill to the Air Defence Research Committee (ADRC) showed, he was prepared to utilise the energies even of his critics.[45]

It was Swinton who had asked for Churchill to be put on the ADRC, and he would have liked to have Lloyd George there too, but was not sure whether he would accept.[46] With Lord Weir as his adviser on industrial matters, Swinton set about collecting information that would allow him to develop a coherent plan for the Air Force. Churchill's opinions were taken into account in this process,[47] and this partly explains his quietness at the time of the Hoare–Laval business. The results of Swinton's labours were expected in February as part of the new White Paper, and if, as was being widely canvassed, that document recommended the appointment of a Minister to co-ordinate defence planning, then Churchill, at least, had someone in mind who could fill the post perfectly.

There was considerable room for collaboration between Swinton and Churchill. If Churchill's figures about German air power were exaggerated, it was, as everyone confessed, difficult to calculate exact strengths. Not only did the Germans not release figures, but 'parity' rather depended upon what was meant by 'front-line strength'. Churchill's claims in November and May had been based upon figures from Desmond Morton, but he and the Air Staff disagreed upon whether simply measuring this figure (whatever it was) was actually an adequate way of summing up comparative air strengths;[48] because Churchill relied upon Morton, he became entangled in his exaggerated fears and, as a result, he was to get caught up in Morton's own private war. This was not to damage his position until late 1936, by which time his own hopes of office had evaporated.

Whilst the honeymoon created by the advent of Swinton and his hopes of office lasted, Churchill was a valuable member of the ADRC. As always he was brimming with ideas, many of them Lindemann's, some slightly barmy (a projectile discharging 'coils of piano wire' in which enemy aircraft would become entangled was ingenious, but definitely daft); others, like an 'aerial mine curtain', were worth further investigation.[49] Here again, his reliance upon others was to bring him into conflict with Swinton. Bracken once said of Churchill that he was 'very credulous, he has always been easily taken in'. His presence in Churchill's entourage was evidence enough of the accuracy of his comment.[50] There were those who thought Lindemann's presence there amounted to further proof. Half-Alsatian, half-American, Lindemann had been Professor of Experimental Philosophy at Oxford since 1919. Based at Christ Church, he had first cultivated Churchill in the 1920s through Randolph. A snob of tremendous proportions,[51] Lindemann was fiercely anti-German. A vegetarian teetotaller, the 'Prof.', as Churchill called him, was hardly the most obvious boon-companion; but he possessed two things which Churchill valued: total, unconditional loyalty to his few friends, and scientific expertise. When he accepted a place on the ADRC, Churchill asked Baldwin to put Lindemann on the Tizard Committee.[52] Lindemann supplied Churchill with ideas, Morton with figures. Unfortunately for Churchill, both men had their own axes to grind and he ended up grinding them.

From July 1935 to February 1936 Churchill and Swinton worked in harness. The Minister may have been slightly irritated at times by Churchill's attitude that not enough was being done, but he respected the source of Churchill's anxiety and tried to use his ideas whilst attempting to impress on him the hard realities of life. It was no use Churchill declaring (with figures plucked from the blue) that the Germans were 'spending £1000 millions this year on military preparations'.[53] Even on Churchill's own admission, the Germans could not be ready for war until 1937–8 at the earliest, and if they were spending at that rate, they might well go bankrupt before then. British rearmament had to be done in a manner that ensured that the economy did not collapse under the strain; this was something which, given his own Whiggish attitude towards finance, Churchill never really appreciated. The original defence estimates for 1935 were £124 million; completing the full White Paper programme added £50 million to the cost, and by 1938 this was set to rise to £132 million. The new report by the Defence Requirements Committee, which came before the Cabinet in November 1936, planned for an increase in spending of £49,650 million in the current year and £86,750 million the following year, rising by £102,400 million for 1938.[54] This was an enormous burden for a peacetime economy to carry whilst trying to provide the wherewithal for normal economic activity.

Churchill's ideas on how to rearm were really based upon his experiences as Minister of Munitions during the last war, and as Swinton tried to point out, there was all the difference in the world between getting existing industrial capacity to switch to a war-footing during a major conflict, and the current situation.[55] Lord Weir, who as the Government's industrial adviser was intimately involved with Swinton in developing new 'shadow factories' to take on the new production, told Ministers in early 1936 that the rearmament programme contained in the new Defence Requirements Committee report could not be carried out in the specified five years without seriously damaging British exports. Churchill's Ministry of Munitions solution could only work if the Government took powers to control industry, and that no Ministers were willing to do.[56] On top of that, even if Weir's schemes for building new factories in co-operation with industry worked, it would be at least a year before 'green field' sites produced anything.[57] There was also the problem of getting enough skilled labour to produce the high-technology materials which arms production required, particularly in aircraft production. Weir reported that this was a major problem. It could be solved, in part, by allowing semi-skilled men to do skilled work, but that brought the Government up against the trades unions. Their experience of the Great War suggested that if they allowed 'dilution' of skilled labour, employers would, when peace came, reduce wages.[58] In the meantime, they were using the shortage of such labour to demand wage increases, which were, by early 1936, having an inflationary effect upon the economy.[59]

These were matters which Churchill's great public calls for rearmament simply ignored; no one, not even him, suggested that the Government should take upon itself powers which had only been allowed during the darkest days of the war – and even under Churchill's regime at the Ministry of Munitions, industrial conscription had been ruled out. The White Paper of March 1936 was produced within these limitations; but it was not this which caused Churchill to move away from Swinton and company.

The Defence White Paper of March 1936 had to wrestle with these complex industrial and financial problems, as well as with the military question of what sort of war it was that was being prepared for. The nature of its brief had had to be changed to allow for the possibility, opened up by the Abyssinian crisis, that Italy must now be considered an enemy.[60] The amount of money allocated to the Air Force was increased from the £20 million in the 1935 White Paper to £45 million for the year 1936; for the following year the increase was even greater, with spending up to £60 million. Total spending on defence by 1938 was forecast to rise from the £124 million in the first Defence Requirements Committee report of 1934 to £239 million; by 1940 another £178,500 million would have been added – a total of £417,500 million over the five years. Not only had the Air Force been well-treated, but the emphasis upon the development of bombers for a counter-strike against Germany, which had been present in both previous White Papers, was actually increased.[61]

During the period from November to March when the White Paper was in gestation, a fierce skirmish was fought out in Whitehall and in the press between those, like Hankey, who thought that the existing government machine would be sufficient to see the new programme implemented, and those, like Churchill, who thought it necessary to have a Minister to co-ordinate defence. Hankey lost.[62]

Churchill had expected to get such a post. He had been horrified in January when Randolph had stood against Ramsay MacDonald's son, Malcolm, in Ross and Cromarty, stigmatising his action as both 'unfortunate and inconvenient' from his own point of view.[63] He need not have worried that this reminder of Wavertree would rule him out, for there is no sign that Baldwin seriously considered him. The press canvassed names as diverse as Hoare's and Ramsay MacDonald's, but on 13 March Sir Thomas Inskip, the Attorney-General, was appointed Minister for the Co-ordination of Defence; the 'Prof.' called it 'the most cynical thing that has been done since Caligula appointed his horse a Consul'.[64] But whilst it was only rumour which stated that Caligula had acted in such a fashion, it was a fact that Churchill had been passed over for a post he felt eminently qualified for – and in favour of a man who, whatever his excellent qualities, was a tyro in defence matters.

It was only with some reluctance that Baldwin had been converted to the idea of appointing a Minister at all, and both the senior civil servants most concerned with the new post, the heads of the Treasury and Home Civil Service, Sir Warren Fisher and Sir Maurice Hankey, actively disliked the notion and pressed for the appointment of a man who would not rock the Whitehall boat.[65] Given Hankey's view of the figures which Churchill used to back his campaign for air rearmament, and the general Whitehall view of Churchill as a rogue elephant, his appointment was never likely. Duff Cooper, who admired Churchill and shared his fears about the threat which Germany posed to the balance of power,[66] doubted whether he would be suitable for the job: 'he would be all for the Navy at one time and all for the Air at another. His enthusiasms carried him away.' Cooper had never served in a Cabinet with Churchill, but his words have the ring of coming from listening to his old boss at the Treasury, Neville Chamberlain. He thought that 'at Winston's present age and after holding so many high offices, he would have been content to settle down philosophically to become an elder statesman and to devote himself to letters'.[67] Although he had long been a member of 'The Other Club', Cooper had evidently not profited by the opportunity thus afforded to study his former patron at close quarters. The last thing Churchill was thinking about was retirement.

On 7 March Hitler's troops had invaded those areas of the Rhineland which had been demilitarised since 1919. It was the first direct breach of the territorial principles of Versailles. Churchill had feared that such an action was imminent, and when the Commons debated the issue on 26 March he was unsparing in his warnings. Hitler, to whom he gave 'honour' for having 'raised his country so high', was, Churchill said, using his foreign policy triumphs to unite the country behind him. Would 'Austria, Memel' and 'other territories and disturbed areas' follow where the Rhineland had led? The League of Nations and the 'principle of the reign of law' had suffered 'an immense blow'. The real danger, however, was that the rearmament of

Germany portended another war. Against this two barriers could be erected: the first an Anglo-French alliance; the second, and the one he hoped would attract most approval, 'the establishment of real collective security under the League of Nations'.[68]

The emergence of Churchill as a champion of 'collective security' and the League, at a time when whatever authority it had ever had had been blasted by the Abyssinian war, was not without its ironies. Espousal of the League was a flimsy cover for his balance-of-power conception of foreign policy; but where the political left would excoriate the latter view, they were more likely to support Churchill if he covered the nakedness of his *realpolitik* with the veil of the League. Yet Churchill, like most Conservatives, had opposed the idea of imposing harsh sanctions on Mussolini in 1935, and he had done so because he feared that such an action would drive the Italians away from the Stresa Front, which they had joined with Britain and France in January 1935.[69] Such a view was, of course, anathema to the 'born-again' enthusiasts for the League – but in the face of danger, Churchill was not going to let that stop him. On 9 April he wrote to the President of the League of Nations Association, Lord Cecil (his former Cabinet colleague, Lord Robert Cecil), telling him that he had postponed a public meeting 'against the dangers of the German dictatorship' because of its proximity to Cecil's meeting 'against the *Italian* dictatorship'. Obscuring their very different views on Abyssinia, Churchill told Cecil, 'we are in pretty good agreement on several big things', including the danger to democracy and the need to organise to preserve peace. The League, Churchill thought, might formulate principles, but they would still need 'ways and means', which was where he came in. 'You need a secular arm. I might help in this.'[70] 'Arms and the Covenant' would be his slogan henceforth – at least for a while.

28

Searching for Allies

Although the relationship between Churchill and the Government deteriorated after Inskip's appointment, the main points at issue remained what they had been hitherto: the rate of rearmament and the traditions of British foreign policy. Churchill criticised the Government for the slowness of its policy, whilst the Government thought that he underestimated both what had been achieved and the obstacles in the way of achieving more. Moreover, the Government thought Churchill's ideas about 'collective security' were simplistic and unworkable, whilst he regarded Baldwin and MacDonald as falling well below the level required by events.

Speaking on 10 March, Churchill said that the 'gravamen' of his charge against the Government was that 'they did not realize effectively, or at any rate that they did not act in accordance with, the marked deterioration in world affairs which occurred in 1932 and 1933.' If the Government had taken in 1933 the steps which the 1936 White Paper was proposing, there would have been no need for anxiety. He blamed the Government for spending a 'modest sum' on defence when the Germans were expending a vast fortune, which he estimated at over £800 million in the current year. Referring to the Weir programme for the creation of 'Shadow industries', Churchill called for the creation of a 'skeleton Ministry of Munitions' and the organisation of industry so that it was ready to supply the Government's needs.[1] The Government's counter-argument was that it could not take any compulsory powers without evidence of an overwhelming national emergency, because to do so would be to interfere with the normal processes of trade upon which the whole economy rested.[2] Churchill took the view that the situation was serious enough to take measures which would 'impinge upon the ordinary daily life and business of this country'.[3]

It was around this point which Churchill's main argument with the Government revolved during the year. As long as the Government took the view that it could not interfere with the normal economic life of the country, then even the sums voted for rearmament could not be spent. To Churchill this was proof that the Government was negligent; to Chamberlain it was proof that it did not neglect the essential 'fourth arm' of defence – sound finance. Lord Weir, who sympathised with Churchill's speech on 23 April, did not, he told Churchill, have 'your confidence' that the 'pros and cons' of interfering with British industry were as clear-cut as he had made out.[4]

Churchill's ideas on how to contain Germany did not inspire members of the Government with confidence about his judgment. He wanted to gather together, under the aegis of the League, the Baltic states, Holland, Belgium, France, Italy, Switzerland, Austria, Russia and Poland, in an effort to 'deter' Germany from further aggression. As part of this idea, he thought that part of the British Fleet might be sent to the Baltic to ensure that the balance of power there was firmly turned against Germany. Hankey, to whom he entrusted these notions, stigmatised the latter idea as 'fantastic'. Churchill was a little uncertain as to whether Russia would be of any use as an ally, but thought that the Prime Minister might ask the French, who had recently signed an alliance with the Soviets, for any information.[5]

This idea, which by 1938 was being dignified by the title 'the Grand Alliance', remained a feature of Churchill's thinking right up to the outbreak of war – and beyond – but, attractive as it sounded, it ignored two questions: whether the other powers mentioned would collaborate; and whether such a league was not likely to drive Germany in the direction of a war with Britain? It was not simply that most opinion in Britain about the occupation of the Rhineland agreed with the comment of Eden's taxi-driver, 'I suppose that Jerry can do what he likes in his own back garden, can't he?'[6] – although the evidence suggests that it did,[7] but there was little consensus on the view that Germany posed a direct threat to British interests.

Some of this latter feeling was undoubtedly due to pro-German sentiment in sections of British society, but it also suggested, as Baldwin told Churchill and a deputation of senior Conservatives in July, the view that German ambitions might be directed elsewhere. Baldwin told them that he was not convinced that Hitler did not want to 'move east', and if he did, 'I should not break my heart.' If there was any 'fighting in Europe to be done', Baldwin would 'like to see the Bolshies and the Nazis doing it'.[8] This did not mean that the Government was actually doing anything to foment such a prospect, but it did mean that it was not yet convinced that the dangers to be apprehended from Germany warranted dislocating the national economy in the way Churchill and his supporters contemplated.

Here again the fundamental difference between two ways of looking at British foreign policy is apparent. Churchill's cousin, Londonderry, accused him of being convinced that 'an Anglo-German war is inevitable',[9] but as Churchill told him on 6 May, his views were not the result of 'an anti-German obsession'. 'For four hundred years', he said, 'British policy ... has been to oppose the strongest power in Europe by weaving together a combination of other countries strong enough to face the bully.'[10] But Churchill's most immediate problem was not how to weave together a Continental combination of the sort which his study of Marlborough's life made familiar to him, but rather how to put together a Parliamentary combination to put pressure upon the Government.

Churchill's views upon the League and Italy may have made him an odd ally for the League of Nations folk, but he was aware of the sentimental attachment which many Britons had for the League, and correctly took the view that his own ideas for a grand alliance would be much more attractive if it flew under League colours. His friendly overtures to Lord Cecil met with a cautious response, and the latter's reminder to him not to 'underrate the very strong anti-French feeling that is raging in this country' illustrated the difference between the League 'mind' and Churchill's.[11] Churchill's efforts in this direction were assisted by his pro-Zionist tendencies, and the close links between the League of Nations Union and the Zionist lobby gave him one set of allies.[12] Although Churchill's main objection to Hitler was that he would upset the balance of power in Europe, he was well aware that his anti-Semitic policies created obvious support from the Zionists, whilst his anti-trades union policies meant, as Churchill was not slow to remind Labour, that it should speak out against the Führer.[13]

Londonderry was hardly alone in taking what one of the leading English Zionists, Balfour's niece, 'Baffy' Dugdale, called a 'pro-German view'.[14] Harold Nicolson, who had entered the House in 1935 as the National MP for Leicester West, defined 'pro-German' as 'afraid of war',[15] and there was certainly a great deal in that. But there was also a good deal of sympathy in certain circles for a strongly nationalist regime which took no nonsense from Communists and trades unions.[16] Conservatives who held this view were generally hostile to French 'decadence' and shared Baldwin's opinion that as long as Hitler's aims were anti-Bolshevik, then there was no real harm in him. Churchill challenged this view directly when talking to the Government's foreign affairs committee on 16 July. He told MPs that if they allowed Hitler a free hand in the east, 'within the course of a single year' Germany would 'become dominant from Hamburg to the Black Sea, and we should be faced by a confederacy such as had never been seen since Napoleon'. But most of his audience were 'at heart anti-League and anti-Russian', Nicolson thought, who really wanted 'a firm agreement with Germany and possibly Italy by which we could purchase peace at the expense of the smaller states'.[17] He did not think that 'this mood will last', but whilst it did, Churchill's main allies would have to come from quarters which could only increase the distance between himself and the Conservative Party.

Existing organisations such as the Jewish 'Anti-Nazi League' were obvious allies for Churchill, and at the first of a series of private luncheons given by this shadowy organisation on 19 May,[18] Churchill appealed to those Labour figures present, especially Walter Citrine, the former TUC President, and Hugh Dalton, to subscribe to some common manifesto. But when it came to defining what should be in it, problems became apparent. Asquith's daughter, Lady Violet Bonham-Carter, a leading Liberal, pointed out that a policy of 'encirclement' of Germany would have little popular appeal.[19] 'The Focus', as this group became known, gave Churchill allies, but they were not such as would serve to recommend him or his case to the constituency which he really needed to convince – the Conservative Party. Nor did Churchill's contacts with the Russian Ambassador, Ivan Maisky, help his cause in this respect. It was not only in France that many, if pushed, preferred Hitler to a figure like Leon Blum, the Socialist leader of the Popular Front Government. Chips Channon spoke for many Conservatives when he told Nicolson that 'we should let gallant little Germany glut her fill of the reds in the East and keep decadent France quiet while she does so'. Nicolson's view, that 'We represent a certain type of civilised mind, and that we are sinning against the light if we betray that type', was not so widely held.[20] And even he admitted that whilst it was wrong to buy Germany off in such a fashion, as well as being short-sighted, 'in practice it would be quite impossible for us to get the British people to fight Germany for the sake of the Czechs'.[21]

Even those who did share Nicolson's views about 'civilisation' were not necessarily convinced that its cause was much advanced by allying with the butcher of Abyssinia, Mussolini, or with Stalin. To Lord Hugh Cecil, Churchill advocated putting down his 'censures' in order of priority.[22] But not everyone shared Churchill's view of where the 'light and shade' were to be distributed. When the Spanish Civil War broke out in June, Churchill's support for Franco and the Nationalists put him in opposition to many of his potential followers on the left, for whom the cause of the Spanish Government became a veritable crusade. Although Churchill and the idealogues on the left could speak the same rhetoric when it came to Germany, this disguised differences in thinking on foreign policy which were at least as large as those which existed between him and the Government. Indeed, on Spain, Churchill's own favoured policy of neutrality won the warm approval of the Foreign Secretary, Anthony Eden.

But not all Churchill's supporters came from the left. The deputation which he formed part of which saw Baldwin in late July was an entirely Conservative body. Churchill may have been one of the noisiest of those who criticised the pace of the Government's rearmament policy, but he was not the only one, and within the Party the voice of Sir Austen Chamberlain was one which counted for more. Chamberlain, who as doyen of Conservative backbenchers, now commanded more support and certainly more affection than he ever had as leader of the Party, was one of a number of senior figures in the Party who associated themselves with Churchill. When the two of them, along with Sir Robert Horne and Sir Edward Grigg, met at Lord Winterton's home, Shillinglee Park, in late May, it was represented in some parts of the press as an 'Anti-Baldwin "Shadow Cabinet"', but Austen reassured his brother Neville that they did not 'wish to embarrass the Government' – they merely wanted to press it on the pace of rearmament.[23]

Such assurances were all very well, but since the Government had just suffered the enforced resignation and disgrace of the Colonial Secretary, J. H. Thomas, because he had 'leaked' budget secrets, the malcontents had chosen a sensitive time at which to advertise their existence as a group. Baldwin referred to the meeting by commenting that it was 'the time of the year when midges emerged from dirty ditches'.[24] Half-hearted rumours that Churchill would be offered something in the Cabinet reshuffle necessitated by Thomas's retirement and that of the First Lord of the Admiralty, Lord Monsell, were dissipated by the return to the Government of Hoare, who went to the Admiralty and soon recovered much of his lost position.[25] Channon had never thought that Churchill's attacks on the pace of rearmament would win him the post he seemed to crave, of Minister of Munitions, if only because 'Baldwin hates him so much'.[26]

In this there was much exaggeration. It was hardly in Baldwin's nature to 'hate' anyone; charity and indolence militated against the possession of such a restless, bitter emotion. His feelings towards Churchill remained what they had been at the time when he made the Inskip appointment: 'if brought back, he would have tried to do too much, would have attempted to do the work of everyone else, and would have alienated his colleagues'.[27] By mid-summer Baldwin was tired out, indeed, on the edge of a nervous breakdown.[28] His own instincts suggested that as long as Hitler's aims remained uncertain, it would be irresponsible to risk wrecking the economy by taking the sort of measures which would be needed if the rearmament programme was to be speeded up.[29] Moreover, as the famous 'confession' which he made in June and which Churchill so misrepresented in his memoirs showed, Baldwin was ever mindful that in a democracy the Government should not get too far ahead of the people.[30] Increasingly power was devolving on to the Mayor of the Palace, Neville Chamberlain. He found Baldwin's inability or unwillingness to impose priorities on the rearmament programme as exasperating as he found his general idleness. As Chancellor he was involved in a major argument with the War Office under Duff Cooper. Taking the view, as he did, that the next war would be one of movement and mechanisation, he did not see the point of Cooper's argument for a large expeditionary force; he wanted the money spent upon the Air Force.[31] However, with Baldwin's retirement likely to coincide with the coronation of the new King, Edward VIII, the Chancellor could afford to bide his time. But he was no more inclined than Baldwin to welcome Churchill back.[32] With memories of their time in the Government together, Neville might have said of Churchill what Salisbury had said when asked whether he would take Lord Randolph back: 'Whoever heard of a man, once having removed a carbuncle from his neck, welcoming it back?'

Old memories were stirred up by the way in which Churchill himself behaved. His quoting of what seemed alarmist figures for the strength of the German Air Force was bad enough, but perhaps he had access to figures which the Government did not? But when Hankey had quizzed him in January,[33] Churchill had admitted that he had no 'special sources of intelligence'. However, he had also defended his figures and replied that 'the real position is probably far more serious'.[34] Despite official contradictions,[35] Churchill persisted in his claims that the German Air Force was very much larger than the Air Ministry believed,[36] but Swinton and Hankey continued to think that he was inflating the figures by including in them reserves which were not 'front-line' forces.[37] This did not endear him, however, to the Government. Nor did his criticisms of the 'slow progress' of the ADRC.[38] When, in May, he used his position on the Committee to launch an attack on the Tizard Committee, obviously inspired by Lindemann, he created a major bureaucratic furore.[39]

Tizard thought that Lindemann was not only lobbying outside the Committee for the 'aerial mines' project which Churchill was sponsoring, but that he was also playing down the importance of the development of radar in favour of his own schemes. On 12 June he told Hankey that either Lindemann went or he would.[40] Swinton, much as he had wanted Churchill to have access to reliable information, was becoming increasingly irritated by the way in which he preferred to use his own figures instead. He deprecated Churchill's attempts to use the ADRC as a forum to open the whole question of comparative air strengths and began to wonder whether it was worth the trouble it was causing to keep Churchill there.[41] Hankey thought that the question of whether Churchill should continue to be supplied with confidential material depended upon whether he was willing to accept the latest, and 'very convincing', figures from the Air Staff. The problem, he told Inskip on 29 June, was that 'Mr Churchill does not want to be convinced.'[42] On the immediate issue of Tizard versus Lindemann, the old Committee was closed down and then reassembled, without Lindemann – but that turned out only to be the first round in a long battle.

Churchill's 'confidential' information did not only come, as has been seen, from the papers to which he had access through the ADRC. Morton continued to supply him with critiques of the Government's own figures, whilst additional information came from an assistant Under-Secretary at the Foreign Office, Ralph Wigram, and Wing-Commander Torr Anderson, who gave him figures on current British air strength, which revealed that the rearmament programme was not proceeding even as fast as the Government wanted.[43] Churchill, who retained an almost child-like love of 'secret' information, added all these things as grist to his mill. Even if, as the Air Ministry alleged, he was exaggerating the size of the German Air Force, he was convinced that he was not exaggerating the danger to be apprehended from Germany. The Government was only too well aware of the difficulties which dogged its rearmament programme,[44] but it was easier to criticise than to suggest how the bottle-necks in production and the lack of skilled labour could be dealt with.

The Government was not, by July, in a position from which it could simply repulse assaults on itself with impunity. Had Churchill been a lone voice, it would have been different, but he was not. Sir Austen Chamberlain, Sir Robert Horne and the other 'midges' from the Shillinglee Park meeting were not men who could simply be ignored. Moreover, they were joined in their anxieties by men such as Amery and Lloyd, who were anxious not only about the rate of rearmament, but also about rumours that the Government was contemplating returning some of the former German colonies in Africa to the Nazi Reich.[45] If influential figures in the centre and on the right of the Party were showing signs of unrest, Neville Chamberlain's statement on 10 June that continuing sanctions against Italy over Abyssinia was the 'very midsummer of madness', did little to reassure 'League-minded' folk who had hardly recovered from the Hoare–Laval pact.[46] With Neville Chamberlain giving a lead which the group around his half-brother applauded, it was time for the Government to do something to calm down feeling in that section of the Party.

The idea, propounded by Sir Austen, that the House might go into secret session, where the facts about rearmament and the German danger could be revealed, did not commend itself to his brother or to Baldwin. Neville did not much like the idea of a series of defence 'deputations', seeing in it the spectre of that old nightmare, a Lloyd George–Churchill alliance. He put forward the notion of an all-Party deputation, which would show that the Government was taking the concerns of the House seriously – but would, of course, dilute the impact of Churchill and Lloyd George. Neither Baldwin nor MacDonald relished the notion, which Baldwin said was afoot, of Churchill delivering a four-hour philippic on the Consolidated Fund Bill, so it was decided that a deputation should be received.[47] Despite a tremendous onslaught from Churchill in the Commons on 20 July, the Government stuck to its refusal to have a secret session, and when the opposition Parties declined to join in the defence deputation, it was a purely Conservative group which met Ministers on 28 and 29 July.[48]

The deputation achieved little, with Ministers putting the case for their policy, stressing both the economic restraints and the uncertainty over Hitler's aims, while the members of the deputation emphasised severally their fears. Churchill repeated his exaggerated claims for Germany's air strength and his equally exaggerated fears of the effects of aerial bombing on London and other British cities. He met the Government's claims about being unable to turn industry over to 'war conditions' with the suggestion that, say, '25 per cent, 30 per cent' of industry ought to be so controlled.[49] It was an ingenious suggestion, but no one could figure out exactly how only thirty per cent of which industries should be so dealt with. The Air Ministry's reply emphasised that it was 'essential to do everything possible to allow the firms concerned to carry on with their export and civil work, and so create revenue for the country and themselves'.[50] Even Churchill, however, had to admit that war with Germany could not be regarded as 'inevitable'.

By the end of July Churchill's search for allies was enjoying a great measure of success. The members of the defence deputation were senior Conservatives, and if the leaders of the opposition Parties refused to join it, then 'The Focus' group provided an alternative forum where Churchill could garner support from the left. On 24 July Churchill had invited some of its members to luncheon at his flat in Morpeth Mansions. With funding of £25,000 courtesy of Sir Robert Waley-Cohen, the Chairman of British Shell and an ardent Zionist, already promised, and with more in the pipe-line,[51] 'The Focus' was to act as its name suggested; by producing research papers and holding large meetings, it was to bring the German menace before the British people. It was decided to hold a large meeting at the Queen's Hall in October.[52] With Churchill having accepted the Presidency of the British section of the New Commonwealth Society in June, he had indeed provided himself with allies of all shapes and sizes.[53]

The membership of 'Focus' and the New Commonwealth Society was not such as was likely to recommend Churchill to most members of his own Party. Sir Austen, who had tried to deal with the League of Nations people involved in both groups, had described them as 'some of the worst cranks I have ever known'.[54] A leading trades unionist, Sir Walter Citrine, noted pacifists with leftist inclinations, such as the author, Sir Norman Angell; and the feminists, Sylvia Pankhurst and Eleanor Rathbone, were hardly people with whom most Conservatives would have chosen to consort. Churchill's habit of hunting with packs other than his own was liable to misinterpretation. Churchill's bitterness against Baldwin failed to attract younger MPs like Caza-let,[55] and it looked to many like simple resentment at being excluded. As Tony Muirhead, the Conservative MP for Wells, told Mrs Dugdale, 'It's a pity Winston's swimming bath has no shallow end.'[56] By late 1936 he could have added that it was also a pity that the 'swimming bath' was filled with such strange objects.

Churchill's balance-of-power ideas consorted but ill with the ideas of some of his new collaborators, but by linking any regional alliances to the Covenant of the League, Churchill could obfuscate this difference.[57] When 'The Focus' group met again in early October, it was decided to set up a new public movement, 'Defence of Freedom and Peace', under the auspices of the League. As Churchill put it, 'Our policy is that we adhere to the Covenant of the League of Nations; that is our rock.'[58] By using the slogan 'Arms and the Covenant', Churchill hoped to gather as much support as he could – but the question of what this support was for was not easily answered. As he moved towards a great meeting at the Albert Hall in November, Churchill exulted to Randolph that 'All the left-wing intelligencia [*sic*] are coming to look to me for the protection of their ideas',[59] and the *New Statesman* could proclaim on 21 November that 'The logic of present politics is surely the formation of a Centre front with Winston Churchill as the effective leader.' His Presidential address to the New Commonwealth Society on 25 November, followed by a speech at the Albert Hall on 3 December for 'The Focus' front, were all part of Churchill's search for allies, but those he was finding were hardly likely to endear him to the majority group in the Commons – the Conservative Party. His attempts to get Sir Austen Chamberlain to come along to some of these events failed, whilst his wanting to have Lord Lloyd turn up was frustrated by the fact that the secretary of the Anti-Nazi League thought that the presence of such a notable figure of the right would make difficulties for men like Citrine.[60] It may not have been without significance that Lloyd was also well-known as a supporter of the Arab cause in Palestine, something which would not have endeared him to some of Churchill's new friends.

It was little wonder that men who compared the company which Churchill had kept in the early 1930s with that he was now keeping should have come to the conclusion that his campaign was little more than another round in his war against the Government. Lady Houston, a figure much further to the right than even Genghis Khan is reputed to have been, and who had provided funds for both Lloyd and Randolph Churchill during the battle over the India Bill,[61] told him that he was 'backing the wrong horse' and begged him not to try to resuscitate the League.[62] The presence of the Russian Ambassador, Maisky, at the New Commonwealth Society lunch would have been, for many Conservatives, simply another sign that, whatever grounds there might be for Churchill's charges and suspicions, his motives were of the lowest. Speaking in the Commons on 5 November, he admitted that Russia was still 'a very great peril', but, letting the wish become father to the thought, he affected to discern 'another Russia' emerging, which wanted to 'be left alone in peace'.[63] Quite how an isolationist Soviet Union would be of any use as part of a 'grand alliance', he wisely did not attempt to explain.

Churchill denied that he was 'in favour of the encirclement and oppression of Germany',[64] yet he had told Lady Violet Bonham-Carter back in May that he wanted 'under the authority of the League of Nations and by means of regional pacts linked together to make the strongest and closest encirclement of Nazidom which is possible'.[65] Both statements could not be true. Churchill believed that his idea would either 'secure the peace of the world' by persuading Germany that she had to join a regional pact, or else it would provide 'an overwhelming deterrent against aggression'. But as so often, Churchill paid little heed to the time that would elapse between the thought and its execution. Was it likely that Germany would, after the experience of 1914, simply sit still and let herself become encircled? If she were not bent on a campaign against the west before, she would swiftly become so after such a scheme commenced. For all his protestations that he did not regard a war against Germany as inevitable, his course of action was likely to make it just that. Moreover, he had not stopped to weigh up either the probability of his 'grand alliance' being formed, or its likely military effectiveness.

Churchill might argue that he had to acquire allies where he could for his cause, which transcended the bonds of Party loyalty, but this would have been more impressive coming from someone who had shown a scintilla of such loyalty, and who did not plunge the whole cause into jeopardy by mounting his own crusade to save Edward VIII from abdicating. The issue became public knowledge on 3 December, and Churchill wanted to speak on it at the Albert Hall meeting which took place the same evening – only to be dissuaded by Citrine and others. Churchill gave his speech as scheduled on 'Arms and the Covenant', but he then immediately plunged into the fray.[66]

Churchill's reaction to the abdication crisis was to bring his carefully constructed alliance collapsing about him. When Duff Cooper had told him on 16 November that the King was thinking of abdicating, Churchill had been most indignant: 'just as men had given arms and legs and indeed their lives, for the sake of the country, so the King must be prepared to give up a woman'.[67] But by the end of the month Churchill's view had changed, and he was arguing that the King had to be defended. Duff Cooper put this down to the malign influence of Beaverbrook, who had just returned from America. When Baldwin consulted him on 25 November, along with the Labour leader, Clement Attlee, and his Liberal counterpart, Archie Sinclair, both the latter said that they would not form an administration in the event of the King asking them; Churchill was more ambiguous, stating that he 'thought his attitude was a little different, [and] he would certainly support the Government'.[68] In his own account of his meeting with Churchill on 4 December, the King recalled him being 'particularly outraged' by Baldwin's actions vis-à-vis the opposition leaders'.[69] At the meeting Churchill told the King that he would try to ensure that he was given more time to make his decision.[70]

The mood inside the Government was not one in which Churchill's pleas for more time were likely to be welcome. Some of the more excitable Ministers, William ('Shakes') Morrison, the Minister for Agriculture, and the flamboyant Transport Minister, Leslie Hore-Belisha, feared a '*coup d'état*' with Churchill being asked by the King to lead a Government of his 'friends', and then calling an election on the issue of the King's marriage.[71] Such ideas, slightly potty though they now appear, give some notion of why it was that Churchill's attempts on the King's behalf were to bring him into such disrepute. He was not helped by his close association during the crisis with Beaverbrook, who was out to use 'the King issue to beat Baldwin with'.[72] Churchill's statement, published on 6 December, maintained that 'No Ministry has the right to advise the abdication of the Sovereign.' At the very least the Government ought to obtain the opinion of the Commons. He criticised the Government for putting 'pressure upon him' by the arrangement which had been reached with the leaders of the opposition, and pleaded for more time to be given to the King.[73]

The idea that the crisis should be perpetuated for months to come was not one which was likely to have any widespread appeal, and the terms of Churchill's statement hardly suggested a desire to help the Government. When the matter was discussed in the House on 7 December and Baldwin announced that the King had been given a few more days, it was evident to observers that Baldwin had the 'deep sympathy' of the House, whilst Churchill, who attempted to intervene with a supplementary question, was twice called to order by the Speaker, before subsiding: 'he almost lost his head, and he certainly lost his command of the House,' Harold Nicolson told his wife.[74] Amery, who had started with the view that 'Winston is never so excited as when he [is] doing a ramp of his own', and had thought that his attitude was influenced by his desire to work up a 'big intrigue' in the press against the Prime Minister,[75] was now inclined to think that he had been a little unfair. Churchill was 'very fond' of the King, after all. But he was not sad that he had received a 'very bad facer' in the House, where opinion was 'unanimously hostile' to him.[76]

Churchill's interventions had been greeted with cries of 'Drop it' and 'Twister', and he had sat down white-faced and shaken. To Boothby, who had been co-operating with him in trying to find a formula which would allow the King to remain on the throne, 'what happened this afternoon makes me feel that it is almost impossible for those who are most devoted to you personally to follow you blindly. . . . Because they cannot be sure where the hell they are going to be landed next.' Boothby told him angrily that he had 'reduced the number of potential supporters to the minimum possible – I sh[oul]d think about seven in all'.[77] *The Times* simply called it 'the most striking rebuff of modern parliamentary history'.[78]

Boothby told Nicolson that he had known Churchill was 'going to do something dreadful'. During the week-end, which Boothby had spent at Chartwell, Churchill 'was silent, restless and glancing into corners. Now when a dog does that, you know he is about to be sick on the carpet. It is the same with Winston'; he had, Boothby said, been sick right across the floor of the House. 'He has undone in five minutes the patient reconstruction work of two years.'[79] Mrs Dugdale thought that the damage had been done in an even shorter time: 'In three minutes his hopes of return to power and influence are shattered. But God is once more behind his servant Stanley Baldwin.'[80]

29

Churchill and Chamberlain: 1

Churchill did not feel that his own 'political position' was 'much affected by the line I took',[1] an opinion shared by his official biographer,[2] but few others. The Albert Hall meeting of 3 December was supposed to be the start of a campaign by Churchill's rag-tag army, but 1937 saw no such campaign; indeed nothing much was heard of the 'Defence of Freedom and Peace' front, whilst 'Focus' retreated into the shadows; as in the Sherlock Holmes story, *Silver Blaise*, what was significant was the fact that the dog did not bark in the night. Baldwin had not only made up the ground lost by what Amery called his 'fatuous confession that he had done nothing about defence because public opinion was pacifist',[3] but he had achieved a mastery over the House which is given to few. His position was secure for as long as he wanted – and all the more so as it was known he intended to go after the coronation in the summer.[4]

Men's eyes turned, as they are apt to do in such situations, towards the rising sun. There was no doubt that Neville Chamberlain would succeed Baldwin when the time came. Chamberlain has received more abuse than any other twentieth-century British Prime Minister, most of it based upon the *parti pris* allegations of his opponents. In *The Gathering Storm* Churchill paints a portrait of Chamberlain as a man who was unfit to deal with a cunning dictator like Hitler; a Birmingham businessman who, in Lloyd George's words, would have made a good Lord Mayor of Birmingham in a lean year. The architect of 'appeasement', Chamberlain thought that he could bargain with Hitler by giving him what he wanted, only to find that Hitler wanted everything. The fact that Chamberlain's foreign policy ended in failure lent verisimilitude to this portrait from the start of its composition. At this late stage it is perhaps unlikely that anything will controvert this picture in the public mind. But Chamberlain was neither a fool nor a knave.

In a letter to the Liberal peer and prominent 'appeaser', Lord Lothian, written in June 1936, Chamberlain had said:

I am afraid I have a lurking suspicion that there is no real *bona fides* in Germany, and that she is merely playing for time until she feels herself strong enough to make her next spring. At the same time one must not let any opportunity slip by, and I am prepared to deal with her on the basis that she means what she says; and if I could see a prospect of a real settlement, I would be prepared to go a long way to get it.[5]

This is the best summary of Chamberlain's foreign policy. But whilst he was prepared to look for a settlement, he was not prepared to trust to luck if one was not available. The rearmament programme would, by the time it was completed in 1939, make Britain fit for war against Germany. Chamberlain had very firm views upon what type of war the country needed to prepare for. During the winter of 1936–7 he finally won his argument with Duff Cooper and the War Office over the question of a large expeditionary force. The very notion of such a thing raised images of 1914–18, which would not, Chamberlain thought, be helpful in obtaining public confidence.[6] He was convinced that the War Office, ignoring the latest military thinking, was busy (as usual) planning for the last war. He wanted to plan for a war of mechanisation and movement, and it was in this connection that he began to have doubts about the Air Ministry's policy.

Churchill continued to question the Air Ministry's figures about the 'front-line strength' of the German Air Force, but both he and Swinton were arguing over respective bomber strengths. In November 1936 Swinton submitted a new expansion scheme, Scheme H, to the Cabinet. The Air Staff believed that Germany would have 1,700 bombers by 1939. Under the existing Scheme F, the British were due to have 1,000 bombers by that date, but production was already behind schedule.[7] When Churchill spoke to the 1922 Committee on 8 December 1936, he told its members that Britain was not only 'incapable of defending ourselves against aerial attack from without', but she also lacked a 'striking force of such power and dimensions' as would act as a 'deterrent' to others. His estimate of 'front-line strength' included not only the aeroplane and its crew, but also spare parts for it and a 'reserve' of '75%–100% of the first-line strength'. Counting a squadron as twelve aeroplanes ('9 in front and 3 in reserve'), Churchill thought that by 1 January 1937 the German Air Force would have 150 squadrons – 'at least *1,750 first-line machines*'. To this he added 250 civil aircraft, which could be 'transformed almost immediately into bombing machines'. Behind these was a reserve of 1,500 machines, plus the forty-five squadrons which made up the training schools – 'nearly 4,000 machines'. Against a 'front-line strength' of 2,000 machines the British had, at best, 2,000, many of which were obsolete and none of which could bomb Berlin. It is unsurprising that such revelations should have caused 'anxieties' amongst Churchill's hearers.[8]

Churchill put a version of these figures to Hankey in a memorandum which was circulated to the Committee of Imperial Defence on 11 January 1937. He admitted that he based himself upon the French estimate that there were twelve machines in a squadron, but even if he accepted the British figure of nine, he reckoned that Germany still had just over 1,500 machines ready for immediate use, with another 405 available from the training squadrons. If the three reserve aircraft which the Air Ministry 'prefer to ignore' were included, the Germans had 2,369 machines available for immediate use – and the figure was rising.[9]

The Air Ministry did not disagree with Churchill's totals, but its staff were critical of the way he handled them. They did not believe that there was much utility in trying to compare reserves, but if this was to be done, it seemed perverse to include the German reserve and exclude the British one – that way alarmism lay. Alarmism became something close to scaremongering when civil aircraft and the forty-five training squadrons were added.[10] But if Churchill's figures about the German Air Force were alarmist, he was right to be alarmed about the Air Ministry's complacency over the rate of British aircraft production. His fears were shared by Chamberlain, who, after studying the figures for production under Scheme H, decided that there was little use in increasing a programme which was already falling badly behind in production.[11] Whilst Churchill, in February, quizzed Hankey as to what had happened to his memorandum and threatened to circulate it to his friends,[12] Chamberlain was cutting through the sterile argument about figures and getting to the heart of the matter.

Churchill's fears about 'parity' were shared by Chamberlain. It certainly meant that Britain should have what she did not at that moment, a bomber force which was not inferior to Germany's, but Chamberlain thought that it ought also to include not simply a fighter force strong enough to meet any 'probable' attack, but any 'anticipated attack'.[13] His scepticism over Scheme H prevented it from coming fully into effect, and the defence review which he ordered when he became Prime Minister was to give more emphasis to the development of fighters.[14] Far from Chamberlain being a silly old fool with an umbrella who underrated Hitler, he was a man who, whilst wanting peace, prepared for war – and did so by trying to maintain as strong an economy as possible. Inskip and Swinton had both pressed in June for the Government to take 'emergency powers' to allow them, for example, to order Austin's to turn its factories over to war production. But Chamberlain had opposed the idea: 'The disturbance of industry produced by acceleration might result in grave consequences, financial, economic etc.,' which could only be justified when and if the situation deteriorated further.[15] This was to remain his position until early 1938. Economics had never been Churchill's strong point, and one of the problems facing Swinton was that it took time to develop new aircraft types. He could, of course, have spent all the money he had been given on obsolete types, but he preferred to wait – and thanks to the delays incumbent upon a normal peacetime economy, he had to wait too long for his own political good.[16]

If Churchill's criticisms tended to ignore considerations of economy, he could not afford to take such a line when it came to his own domestic economy; it was now that the chickens hatched by the problems with *Marlborough* were coming home to roost. If the news that the book was going to expand to four volumes was unwelcome to Churchill's American publishers,[17] it was no more welcome to Churchill's bank. He had earned £12,914 during 1936–7 from his literary works[18] and had contracts worth £12,191 for the forthcoming year, but the money for the last volume of *Marlborough* and for articles in the *News of the World* on 'great contemporaries' would not fall due until the end of the next financial year, which left him having to ask his bank to allow his current overdraft of £2,600 to rise as far as £7,000, on the understanding that he reduced it to £5,000 by the end of 1937.[19] Expenditure for 1937–8 would, he told Clementine in April 1937, have to be reduced by £6,000 a year or the consequences would be dire.[20] Keeping up Chartwell and 11 Morpeth Mansions had cost £10,000, and he would not, as he told his wife on 2 February, refuse a 'good offer' for Chartwell – 'having regard to the fact that our children are almost all flown, and my life is probably in its closing decade'.[21] The question of whether he would be taken into the Government when Chamberlain succeeded Baldwin in May would have a bearing upon not only his political future, but also his financial one; it was by no means certain that he could afford to take office.[22]

In contrast to 1936, the first months of 1937 saw a marked decline in both the quantity and the volume of Churchill's criticisms of the Government. The main difference between it and him had concerned the rate of rearmament, and as he recognised in his contribution to the debate on the Defence Loan Bill on 4 March, the new Government White Paper published on 16 March, which envisaged £1,500 million being spent on defence over the next five years, made most MPs feel that it was 'doing everything that the situation demands, or at any rate, everything that could be reasonably asked for'. Although he disagreed with the refusal to take emergency powers, and whilst he would have liked to see the creation of a Ministry of Supply, he could not criticise the Government's foreign or defence policy. He hoped that it would be given the time to carry out the latter, but he explicitly declared that the time to 'sound the alarm' had passed: 'once everybody can see that we are marching though that long, dark valley of which I spoke to the House two years ago, then a mood of coolness and calmness is enjoined'. As Churchill recognised, the 'Parliamentary position of the Government is, therefore, as strong as it could possibly be'.[23]

This was a mood far removed from that which had marked his speeches the previous year, and if the tone had changed, then so had the frequency of the attacks. Churchill's words during the defence loans debate could easily be read, by the Government's business managers, as a coded declaration that he was ready to take office under the new Prime Minister; but would it be offered?

The arguments against including him in the new administration were, the Chief Whip, David Margesson, told Chamberlain, 'obvious'. 'Alarm', he wrote, would be occasioned 'in some quarters'. Obviously the German Government would interpret his inclusion as no friendly gesture, but Margesson thought that if he were included, he might be sent to the Board of Trade, which needed a '1st class man ... of proved ability'. It would keep him 'well away from defence departments, where he would be a great nuisance', and there was 'so much to do in that Department' that 'he would be kept thoroughly busy and out of mischief'.[24] As the time for Chamberlain's succession approached, Hoare wrote to him on 6 May: 'I imagine that you have finally excluded the possibility of Winston. If you have not, the Admiralty would give him scope and employment.'[25]

Churchill had a great deal more respect for Neville Chamberlain than he had for Baldwin, and he looked forward to 'some real and straightforward politics now he is out of the way'.[26] With the death in March of Sir Austen Chamberlain, Churchill was now the most senior Privy Councillor in the Commons, and as such he was asked to second the formal motion which would make Neville Chamberlain leader of the Conservative Party on 31 May. Lord Derby, who was moving the resolution, wrote to express his pleasure that Churchill would 'make up for any of my deficiencies'.[27] Channon described Churchill's speech as 'able' and 'fiery', but 'not untouched by bitterness'.[28] After the compliments to the new Prime Minister, Churchill, reminding MPs that the Party leadership had never been interpreted in a 'dictatorial or despotic sense', appealed for the rights of those who dissented from Party policy; he felt sure, he said, that Chamberlain would not 'resent honest differences of opinion arising between those who mean the same thing, and that party opinion will not be denied its subordinate but still rightful place in his mind'.[29] If Churchill meant this, he had mistaken his man; but perhaps he mentioned it because he had not mistaken the new leader.

Chamberlain reminded Rab Butler of 'the Stuart Kings, he is clear and upright but inelastic';[30] leaving aside the intriguing question of which of the Stuart monarchs fitted such a description, there was much to recommend this view of Chamberlain's character. Churchill's expectations of some 'clear and straightforward politics' under the new regime were to be justified. Those whom Butler classed as the 'weak-kneed Liberals who felt safe with S.B.' were to find that Chamberlain was 'leading us back to Party politics'.[31] Determined to bring order where Baldwin had allowed drift, Chamberlain asked for a review of defence spending with a view to establishing priorities. He was aware of the strains under which the economy was already labouring and did not think that a repetition of 1931 would discourage the dictators.[32] His attempt to raise some of the extra money required in his last budget by a tax on business profits, euphemistically called a 'National Defence Contribution', had been defeated, and it showed the political limits upon defence spending; the economic ones he was more than aware of.[33]

If Chamberlain wanted to bring some order into defence policy, he also wanted to do something similar with regard to British foreign policy, which must, he thought, cut its coat according to the cloth available to cover it. The job of British foreign policy was to reduce the number of Britain's potential adversaries. He would like to have secured better relations with Germany, but failing that he was quite prepared to begin with the Italians.[34] In one sense his thinking on foreign policy did not differ radically from Churchill's views in 1936; he too had wanted to 'reform the League and develop a series of pacts', but unlike Churchill, who appeared to be willing to take on limitless responsibilities under the Covenant, Chamberlain thought that 'we should enter such [pacts] as directly concern our interests, e.g. Locarno or Far East, but should leave Eastern Europe to others'.[35]

The two crucial differences between Chamberlain and Churchill were over their willingness to take compulsory powers to switch sections of the economy over to war production at once, and over their respective attitudes towards eastern Europe. Chamberlain thought that adopting a Churchillian policy would simply lead the country to ruin very quickly, and he was not convinced that eastern Europe was, of necessity, such a vital British interest that she should go to war over it. He was not insensible to the argument that the rule of international law should be maintained, and he was not willing to let Hitler simply seize areas which he wanted – the rearmament programme was there as an ultimate safeguard against that. But if Hitler could be persuaded to negotiate, and if his demands were reasonable, then they might be satisfied and peace preserved.[36] It was the 'humdrum imperial style' applied to Europe with a clear eye and a firm hand.

It was precisely because Chamberlain was determined to replace Baldwinian fuzziness with clear thinking that the differences which underlay his attitude to foreign policy and Churchill's were to become more apparent when the march of events provided cases where these differences were necessarily exposed.

Sir Norman Angell, a fellow member of 'Focus', wrote to Churchill in March 1937 to express his fear that 'there is growing up among sections of the Conservative Party, support of a policy which is, in fact, a reversal of the purpose of the Great War – a surrender to the German hegemony which would place the British Empire at the mercy of an all-powerful *Mittel-Europa*'. Like Churchill, Angell unquestioningly accepted the view that German expansion in eastern Europe was so fundamentally opposed to British interests that it was worth a war to stop it.[37] This was not Chamberlain's view. He did not doubt that Germany might be a menace to Britain, but he was not prepared simply to apply a *nolli possumus* to any German ambitions in a sphere which was one in which she naturally had an interest; everything would depend upon how she tried to exert that influence.[38]

The differences between Churchill and Chamberlain were of long standing. At one level they did not seem to be fundamental, but rather arguments over tactics, but at the deeper level just described, they were more fundamental. In the preface to the third volume of *Marlborough*, which was published in October 1936, Churchill had drawn a parallel between his own times and those he was writing about: 'We see a world war of a League of Nations against a mighty, central military monarchy.'[39] Writing about the start of Britain's rise to imperial greatness, it did not occur to Churchill that he might be living in the age which was to see the end of that grandeur. The feelings, impulses and convictions which had made him fight Baldwin over India would, as events progressed, lead him to fight Chamberlain over policy towards Germany. Churchill still saw Britain as a Great Power, able to weld together a grand coalition in defence of civilisation. Chamberlain saw the weaknesses of the foundations upon which British power rested. He did not suppose that even a 'successful' war would leave that power intact, so in that sense Britain could not gain anything from a war; that this was the case was something only borne in on Churchill during 1940.

Churchill continued to be the repository of information from every figure who had an axe to grind against the various strands of the Government's rearmament policy,[40] but his public utterances were muted compared to those of the previous year. Some put this down to a desire for office on his part,[41] but it is just as likely to have been due to two other facts: firstly, that there was no real grist in foreign affairs to feed his mill; and secondly, that the new Prime Minister seemed to be getting such a grip on affairs that there really was very little leverage for public criticism. Churchill confessed to the new Secretary of State for War, Hore-Belisha, that he was willing to serve under Chamberlain. The Prime Minister's reaction was what it was to be until September 1939: 'If I take him into the Cabinet, he will dominate it. He won't give others a chance of even talking.'[42]

Chamberlain did not think that war was 'imminent'; indeed, he hoped that by 'careful diplomacy . . . we can stave it off for ever'. In pursuit of this aim he sought to improve relations with Italy and Germany. But he did not neglect defence. The policy review presided over by Inskip was completed before the end of the year. Underlying it were Chamberlain's strategic priorities – the Air Force first, followed by the Navy and finally the Army – and its cost was shaped by Chamberlain's belief that 'if we were to follow Winston's advice and sacrifice our commerce to the manufacturers of arms we should inflict a certain injury upon our trade from which it would take generations to recover'.[43] The attempt to raise extra money by the National Defence Contribution had caused a slump on the Stock Exchange, and the issue of £100 million of two and half per cent defence bonds in April was 'a complete fiasco as far as subscriptions from the general public were concerned'.[44] The Inskip report also attempted to tackle the other question which Churchill could afford to ignore. Built into Churchill's line of policy was the assumption that war would come sooner rather than later, but the Government could not even be sure that it would come at all; if it did not, how long could it afford to spend the enormous amounts currently being planned for? It was true that the Germans faced a similar dilemma, but Hitler could always escape from it by deciding to go to war – an option which the British Government did not have – at least before late 1939. Chamberlain was planning for the future, Churchill for Armageddon. It was a nice irony which landed Churchill with the bill for Armageddon.

In February 1938 the Cabinet agreed that over the next five years total defence spending should be £1,570 million; this was the limit that could be afforded 'unless we turned ourselves into a different kind of nation'.[45] Here was another crucial difference which Churchill ignored. Perhaps because he thought that his life was in its 'last decade', and perhaps partly because he was prone to obsessions, Churchill's view was a strictly short-term one. He not only had no answer to the question of what would happen if war did not come, but he had no answer to the question of how to manage the period beyond the end of high defence spending. The state could exert more control over the economy and could raise income tax, but to do so would be to change the existing political system fundamentally – which was not what Churchill wanted to do. If Churchill thought that the trades unions could be brought into the counsels of the nation, only to be told at the end of a period of time that they were no longer required, and if he thought that spending massive amounts of money and disrupting the economic life of the nation would have no long-term effects, then he was wrong. He was wrong because he gave no thought for the morrow. In the period 1937–9, as in the period 1941–5, this was a grave defect in his political thinking; but, *mutatis mutandis*, it was to be the source of his greatest strength in 1940.

The Inskip review provided a defence policy which the country could (just) afford for five years, and the prospect of the economy still being intact in five years' time.[46] But it also provided a coherent defence policy. Hore-Belisha accepted willingly what Duff Cooper had sullenly acquiesced in – that the Army's main function was to be in the field of imperial policing.[47] The question of whether 'air parity' should have priority over increases in naval spending was less easily decided, particularly since Swinton admitted in October that bomber command would not be ready for war by the start of 1938.[48] Fortunately this bad news was counter-balanced by signs that the technology of defence – radar, searchlights and anti-aircraft guns – was improving rapidly.[49] Out of the debate came, in the final report, an increased emphasis, for the first time, on air defence in the form of fighter aircraft, although it was not until the autumn of 1938 that fighters were given priority.[50]

But if the Inskip report attempted to provide an affordable and coherent defence policy, it also emphasised, as Halifax (now Lord President of the Council) pointed out when it was discussed by the Cabinet on 22 December, 'how the limitation imposed on defence by finance threw a heavy burden on diplomacy'. The situation which back in 1934 it had been thought essential to avoid, being 'faced with the possibilities of three enemies at once', had now happened, and it was clear that Britain simply could not afford to be in that position; diplomacy would have to bear the strain, and 'we ought to make every possible effort to get on good terms with Germany'.[51] This had been the motive behind Chamberlain's sponsorship of a visit by Halifax to meet Hitler in November, and it also lay behind his policy of trying to improve relations with Italy.[52]

Apart from a spat with Hankey over their usual topic of air defence, Churchill was relatively silent during this period; indeed, by January 1938 the Government's chief industrial adviser, Sir Horace Wilson, could write to his old secretary, P. J. Grigg, that 'WSC has been very quiet for 8 months, which is rather a long time for him.'[53] With Chamberlain firmly ensconced and a defence programme about which it was impossible to raise a public storm, there was indeed little scope for Churchill's pyrotechnics, and apart from a few speeches in the Commons, and inviting Eden and Derby to 'Focus' luncheons, there was little sign that the underlying differences between him and Chamberlain would have any public expression. But early 1938 was to provide an opportunity for differences to be aired. First of all Eden resigned from the Cabinet on 20 February; then, on 12 March, Hitler announced the *Anschluss*, the union of Austria with Germany. Once more the game was afoot.

Much nonsense, most of it by Churchill and Eden, has been written about the resignation of the latter. It had nothing to do with the appeasement of Germany and not really that much to do with its ostensible cause, the appease- ment of Italy. Eden had long accepted, at least in writing, the need to improve relations with Italy, which meant recognising her conquest of Abyssinia. However, he could not bring himself to do the latter and he covered the confusion of his position with the doctrine of 'ripe time'. Recognition would be given, but not yet.[54] By early 1938 the Prime Minister was tired of his procrastinating. Chamberlain's sister-in-law, Sir Austen's widow, Lady Ivy, was telling him, as was the British Ambassador in Rome, that Mussolini would welcome an overture from the British, and he did not intend to lose the chance of detaching him from Hitler just because his Foreign Secretary could not bring himself to talk to the Italians.[55] Halifax felt that the problem owed its genesis to Eden's 'dual personality': 'Anthony Eden', the 'generous idealist' who was 'intolerant of baseness' and hated dictators 'with every fibre in his body', could not get along with the 'Foreign Secretary', who had to do things which were not 'idealistic'; so at the moment when he was confronted by Chamberlain with a firm choice, 'Anthony Eden stepped in and told him it was all too beastly for words.'[56] Contrary to the story purveyed by Churchill and Eden, Chamberlain was not trying to get rid of Eden; he was trying to get a decision. If Eden would not follow the logic of the policy of appeasement, it was best he went. But it was not until 18 February that he reached the decision that 'Anthony must yield or go'.[57]

Eden's resignation occasioned one of the oddest passages in *The Gathering Storm*. By the time the book came to be written, Eden and Churchill had been colleagues through the war, and they were respectively leader and deputy leader of the Conservative Party, all of which may have more to do with the story which Churchill told of passing a sleepless night. He was, he wrote, 'consumed by emotions of sorrow and fear', as the 'one strong young figure' who stood up against 'long, dismal, drawling tides of drift and surrender', the man who at that moment 'seemed to embody the life-hope of the British nation', now went from the scene; as the day dawned he saw before him 'the vision of death'.[58] This reads like another example of King Alfred and the cakes. There is no contemporary evidence that Churchill regarded Eden in such a light; indeed, the portrait which Churchill paints of his whole relation-ship with Eden (and with which Eden colluded) reeks of afterthought. Who, to read it, would have imagined that Churchill's had been the fourth signature on a 'round-robin' expressing confidence in the Prime Minister's policy, only a few days after Eden's resignation?[59] What is clear is that Churchill saw the opportunity for gathering a fresh ally – and he urged Eden not to spare his former colleagues in his resignation speech.[60]

The 'vision of death' passage allowed Churchill not only to compliment his lieutenant, but also to give the impression that thenceforth there was a group of anti-appeasement Tory MPs of whom he was the leading light. But the truth was far from that and more complex. Eden resigned, but he did not inveigh against the Government; indeed, far from doing so, he kept one eye on the possibility of returning to the Cabinet at some time in the future.[61] In his isolation Churchill could be forgiven for welcoming the prospect of an ally. But as Harold Nicolson, who supported and admired Eden, told his wife: 'Don't be worried my darling. I am not going to become one of the Winston brigade.'[62] The liberal Nicolson was shocked by the way in which 'all the Tories and diehards are hugging themselves at having got rid of all the nonsensical notions of the past and having got back the good old Tory doctrines'.[63] Certainly those Conservatives who had had little time for the League and its works, men as different as Channon and Amery, rejoiced to see the end of a man tarred with its brush, with the latter describing Chamber-lain's speech in the debate which followed as 'the first breath of fresh air on the Government bench for many long years'.[64]

This was all very well, but it did little for the Government's 'National' credentials, a fact upon which Churchill seized. 'The Liberal, Labour and non-party voters whom Mr Baldwin had painstakingly gathered have been summarily dismissed', he said on 4 March, 'and will not be easy to recall.'[65] Those who expected that Churchill would 'exploit the situation to the full' were not disappointed.[66] But there were problems in doing this. Eden's resig-nation had come so suddenly and on such an arcane issue that all his Cabinet colleagues were taken by surprise, and the two-day debate in Cabinet before he went had brought him no support; indeed, his behaviour had seemed to confirm rumours (put round by Simon) that he was 'cracking up'.[67] His resignation speech was such a mild affair that no one who was not in the Cabinet (and even some who were) was any the wiser as to why he had gone.[68] Chamberlain's forthright statement that collective security was nothing more than a sham delighted his own backbenchers, who were also soothed by the news that Halifax would be replacing Eden at the Foreign Office.[69] Churchill 'spoke with pretty hostile intent but great restraint of diction, evidently sensing the feeling of the House and realising that there was no hope of any cave worth mentioning'.[70]

Churchill spoke of a 'good week for dictators' and said that he could no longer maintain the silence he had imposed upon himself – and by implication he gave the impression that his 'disinterested and independent support' was also in danger. But it was Lloyd George who really tried to launch into the Government, only to come a cropper because he had not properly understood the sequence of events.[71] The prospect of a Churchill–Lloyd George 'cave' raised old spectres in the minds of some Conservatives, and Churchill's 'unnecessary' 'eulogy' of Eden at a meeting of the Government's Foreign Affairs Committee on 24 February did nothing to soothe such anxieties; but as Cazalet told Baldwin, 'the only thing that relieved my anxiety was the conviction that a combination of Lloyd George and Winston was fatal to any attack on the Government and as good as a combination of Beaverbrook and Rothermere against you'.[72]

But where the march of events had helped to save Baldwin from the press barons, it was now to foster the faint and flickering revolt against Chamberlain. Eden's resignation was followed on 12 March by the *Anschluss*, which, in turn, was followed by the crisis over Czechoslovakia. The first eight months of Chamberlain's Government had been ones of comparative calm, but they had proved to be the ones which preceded the storm. It was not merely that it would never be 'glad confident morning again', but there would hardly be another period of calm and stability for the rest of the life of the Government – and its leader. As evidence seemed to accumulate that Hitler was bent on a sinister career of conquest, so would Chamberlain's foreign policy be shaken and, with it, confidence in the Prime Minister. He maintained his hold on the Conservative Party to the end, but the events of the next thirteen months were first to reassert, then fatally to shatter, his hold on the country. When his fortunes waxed, those of Churchill waned, but as they waned, so 'Jeshun waxed fat and kicked'.

30

'Cads Like the Apostles' or 'Cavemen'?

Speaking in the debate which was to bring down the Chamberlain administration in May 1940, one MP, recalling that his local vicar had said in a
sermon that what the Church needed was 'some more cads like the Apostles',
commented that the Government could do with 'a few more cads'.[1] Within
a few days he had his wish. Once the 'cads' had won the war, they set about,
in their memoirs, winning the debate too. It was, the argument went, clear
that Hitler was bent on world conquest, and it was only Chamberlain's
stubborn folly which prevented Britain from moving against him sooner.
There should have been a firm reaction to the Rhineland, to the *Anschluss*, to
the crisis over Czechoslovakia and to the occupation of Prague in March
1939; thus the story went. A gallant band of 'cads' had advocated such action,
but they had been ignored. But as they came to write their memoirs, it is
evident that some of them had difficulty recalling exactly who had been in
this gallant band. Leo Amery wrote to the former Vice-Chairman of the old
Foreign Affairs Committee, Paul Emrys-Evans, in 1954 to try to refresh his
memory. Emrys-Evans reminded him that 'our group', which was gathered
around Eden, would have 'nothing to do' with Churchill. This was partly
because 'he would have dominated our proceedings and would associate us
with causes we did not want to follow', and partly because 'he would bring
in Bob Boothby who, it was felt, was not to be trusted'. As the post-war
myth dissolved in the solvent of memory, Emrys-Evans reminded Amery that
'Winston greatly resented his exclusion . . . and has never forgotten it.'[2]

Far from Eden's resignation being the first stone in what was to become
an avalanche of support for Churchill, what it actually provided was a more
respectable alternative to him. It was the failure of Eden to provide the
leadership which was expected which gave Churchill his opportunity. In early
1938 Eden was the great white hope of those who opposed Chamberlain, but
he was too much of a Conservative loyalist ever to rock the boat effectively. It
was a sign of what was to come that he not only did not concert action with
Churchill following the *Anschluss*, but that he was not even in the House for
the debates on it. Like all 'respectable' opinion, he did not want to push his
differences with a powerful Prime Minister too far – Churchill's career provided an example of where such a road could lead. Churchill gave the impression of being bitter and out for a fight. The idea of a Churchill–Eden coalition
may have warmed the cockles of the cold heart of Labour's Hugh Dalton and

other members of the opposition who faced the daunting task of displacing a Prime Minister with a massive Parliamentary majority, but it was a pipe-dream.[3] If Churchill was 'a cad', he had few 'Apostles'. A better description would be to adopt Amery's phrase about looking for 'a cave', and to call Churchill a 'caveman'.

In the Old Testament the Cave of Adullam was where the future King David fled when Saul tried to murder him. When the news got around that he was holed up there, he was joined by 'everyone who was in distress, and everyone who was in debt, and everyone who was discontented'; he soon gathered around him 400 supporters, a task in which he was no doubt aided by his remarkable ability to collect the foreskins of 200 Philistines. Unfortunately for Churchill, his supporters were fewer in number, and the 'Philistines' remained quite unscathed. But the *Anschluss* gave him an opportunity to proclaim that he had been right all along in fearing that Germany had fell designs.

Churchill spoke in the House on 14 March, giving what one observer called 'the speech of his life'. It was the classic statement of his desire for a 'Grand Alliance'. Britain and France should, he said, concert their 'Staff arrangements' and gather together, under the Covenant of the League, a great alliance which could 'even now, arrest this approaching war'.[4] Contrary to the belief of some commentators, Chamberlain did not simply ignore Churchill's idea.[5] He had been 'bitterly disappointed' by Germany's action, and the balance of doubt in his mind moved against Hitler.[6] Like everyone else, the Prime Minister recognised that the *Anschluss* had put Czechoslovakia in a dangerous position, and he asked both the Foreign Office and the Chiefs of Staff to look at how a 'Grand Alliance' would help matters.

The results of Chamberlain's enquiries were instructive. 'There was', he told his sister Hilda on 27 March, 'almost everything to be said for it until you come to examine its practicability. From that moment its attraction vanishes.' Simply by looking at a map of Europe, Chamberlain wrote, one could see 'that nothing we or France could do could possibly save Czechoslovakia from being overrun by the Germans if they wanted to do it.'[7] The British Minister in Prague, Basil Newton, confirmed this, pointing out that the most that could be done was to 'restore after a lengthy struggle a *status quo* which had already proved unacceptable and which, even if restored, would probably again prove unworkable'.[8] William Strang, one of the senior Foreign Office men dealing with the affairs of central Europe, took the view, shared by Chamberlain, that even if the 'Grand Alliance' was practicable, it was not to be had overnight – and it was hardly likely that Germany would sit around waiting for a coalition to form. The idea, canvassed by some, that Britain should give France a guarantee if she became involved in a war because of her alliance with Czechoslovakia, did not appeal to Strang. To those who argued that war with Germany was better now than in two years' time, Strang riposted that this was 'not a good argument for risking disaster now'.[9] Military and diplomatic advice coincided with what Chamberlain's instincts told him. Until the rearmament programme was further advanced, it was not a good idea to get involved in a war – and to get involved in one over Czechoslovakia, which could not be helped anyway, was simply to compound one folly with another.

The 'Grand Alliance' was a wonderful slogan, but it was not practical politics. Of its various components, Britain was not ready for war, nor were the French; in any case, neither of them were preparing for an offensive war, and the British had no plans ready to cover the eventuality of a war over Czechoslovakia. Russia, whom Churchill now called in aid, had recently purged her armed forces, and, according to reports from Moscow, her Army was only about seventy per cent effective – and then only in defence.[10] Moreover, Russia caused more problems than she solved as a member of a potential alliance. The Czech Government, the Poles, the Romanians and other members of a possible alliance all distrusted the Russians at least as much, and in some cases more, than they distrusted the Nazis.[11] Then there remained the Americans.

Because the war was won by the Americans and the Russians, with the British hanging on and doing most of the fighting in the west for five years, there is an understandable tendency to suppose that if the 'Grand Alliance' of 1941–5 could have been constructed in 1938, the war could have been avoided. But that is to ignore the contingent nature of the circumstances in which Russia and America entered the war. Neither of them did so willingly; both had to be attacked before they entered the war. There is no reason to suppose that either country would have acted from altruism in 1938. Churchill's hopes were founded on a combination of wishful-thinking and talks with the Russian Ambassador, Maisky, but they ignored Stalin's deep suspicion of the west – just as they ignored the large section of opinion in Britain which suspected the Soviets. To go on a crusade against evil was one thing; to do so with evil at your side was another. But what about America?

In his memoirs Churchill, like Eden, made a great deal of fuss about the offer by President Roosevelt of a conference in early 1938 to discuss international affairs; indeed, he went so far as to call Chamberlain's rejection of the offer 'the loss of the last frail chance to save the world from tyranny otherwise than by war'.[12] If Churchill really believed this at the time, he was showing the first signs of what was to become an overwhelming tendency to assume that the Americans were just straining at the leash to get into the war. Of this there is no sign.[13] In October 1937, when the war which had been sporadically going on since 1931 between Japan and China flared up, Roosevelt had made a speech in Chicago about putting aggressor nations in 'quarantine'. Great hopes were aroused by this in Britain; indeed, Chamberlain's oft-quoted remark that it is 'best and safest to count on *nothing* from the Americans except words' actually comes from a letter in which he went on to say that 'at this moment they are nearer to "doing something" than I have ever known them and I cannot altogether repress hopes'.[14] The Prime Minister might as well not have bothered. Roosevelt's words, as so often, came to nothing. His idea for a conference was just that, an idea with little content, and when Chamberlain did not respond enthusiastically at first, but under pressure from Eden expressed some interest later, Roosevelt does not seem to have minded either way.[15]

This then was Churchill's 'Grand Alliance'. He was always apt to become the slave of his own ideas and to assume that to enunciate a brilliant phrase was to solve a problem, but the road to the 'Grand Alliance' was a long and hard one. Only when dire necessity convinced its putative members that if they did not hang together they would hang separately did it come about.

The new Foreign Secretary, Halifax, applied to foreign policy the same instincts which he had brought to imperial policy. The 'world is a strangely mixed grill of good and evil', and 'for good or ill we have got to do our best to live in it and not withdraw into the desert because of the evil, like the ancient anchorites'.[16] He and Chamberlain were willing to recognise Germany's special interest in Austria, and they did not object to her having 'economic hegemony in Central Europe'. Both men recognised that the status quo of Versailles could not be 'maintained for all time'. What mattered was the way in which Hitler went about getting these things, if that was what he wanted.[17] As Halifax told the Foreign Affairs Committee of the Cabinet on 18 March, the idea of the 'Grand Alliance' was impracticable: 'the long and difficult negotiations which would be necessary ... would afford both a provocation and an opportunity to Germany to dispose of Czechoslovakia before the Grand Alliance had been organised'.[18] Halifax also had in mind one of the 'lessons' of pre-1914 diplomacy: 'The more we produced in German minds the impression we were plotting to encircle Germany the more difficult it would be to make any real settlement with Germany.'[19]

Instead of following Churchill's advice, Chamberlain and his Foreign Secretary embarked upon a two-pronged strategy: in the first place, Germany would be given a warning about the solidarity of Britain and France, which would act as a warning shot, as well as calming British opinion; but in the second place, the Czechs and Germans would be encouraged to enter a dialogue to discover what it was the latter wanted and how far the former could go towards giving it to them.[20]

But if Churchill's 'Grand Alliance' speech had failed to win over the Government, it did attract those who were furious with Chamberlain's remarks about the futility of 'collective security'. What to Amery was a welcome 'breath of fresh air' was to others blasphemy uttered by 'that miserable middle-class businessman with no scrap of imagination', as Irene Noel-Baker (wife of the Labour MP, Philip) called Chamberlain. But then the

'Grand Alliance' was a small pill to swallow for one who could see her pacifist husband, Eden, Archie Sinclair, Attlee, Lloyd George, Baldwin and Churchill all uniting together as 'a band of warriors in the House'.[21] The rag, tag and bob-tail nature of the following he was likely to attract seems to have been one of the reasons for Churchill's cautious approach towards outright opposition to Chamberlain. He had abstained in the vote which followed the debate over Eden's resignation, but, even leaving aside the fact that most of the other twenty National MPs who went into the same lobby had been 'Eden' men, most of them were hardly names to conjure with.

With the exception of Eden and his deputy, the eldest son of the Marquess of Salisbury, Lord ('Bobbety') Cranborne, the other abstainers were a motley crew. J. P. L. (Jim) Thomas was Eden's PPS, Harold Nicolson was not even a Conservative, whilst Harold Macmillan was a notoriously bad Conservative. Of the non-Churchillians, there was a long tail: Mark Patrick, Anthony Crossley, J. W. Hills, J. R. J. Macnamara, R. H. Turton, R. A. Cary, H. J. Duggan, R. Pilkington, L. Ropner, R. L. Briscoe, Ronald Cartland, Duff Cooper's PPS, Hamilton Kerr, and Paul Emrys-Evans; the two others were Bracken and General Louis Spears, the man who, as a National Liberal, had offered Churchill his seat at Leicester back in 1922. These were hardly names to put before the monarch as a Cabinet-in-waiting; indeed, if they are compared with the list which Emrys-Evans gave to Amery in 1954 as comprising the 'Eden group', only ten of the same names appear.[22]

Thus it was that Churchill moved cautiously. As he told Nicolson on 16 March, he did not put the blame on Chamberlain, but rather on Baldwin. He would wait to see whether the negotiations going on between Chamberlain and the opposition leaders for a formula on a policy which would unite the House succeeded. This was not so much a concession as a necessity, for, if the talks did succeed, then it would be difficult to see who would follow Churchill. But he was confident that if they did not, and if he then refused the Whip, 'some fifty people' would go with him.[23] But this was akin to whistling in the dark. It was true that at a meeting of the Foreign Affairs Committee on 17 February most of the 100 MPs present had seemed to approve the firm line which Churchill and Nicolson advocated towards further German expansion in eastern Europe,[24] but when it came to putting their 'hear, hears' to practical use, they melted away.

In statements in the Commons and the Lords on 24 March, Chamberlain and Halifax rallied the faithful. A deliberate ambiguity was maintained about how Britain would respond to further German aggression. This was to bluff the Germans whilst keeping the French from doing anything silly. Those commitments which involved a *casus belli*, including the Locarno pact (which covered France and Belgium if they were attacked), and the Covenant of the League (where vital British interests were touched), were reiterated, but it was stated that Britain had other interests too. At the same time the increases in spending on armaments as a result of the Inskip review were announced. 'By reason if possible – by force if not' was the message which the Government sent out.[25]

Chamberlain regarded the statement as an *'éclatant* success,'[26] and it certainly went down well in the House. Churchill's criticisms were circumspect. He would have liked a definite alliance with France, but neither he, nor Amery, nor any other Conservative advocated either trying to reverse the *Anschluss* or extending a guarantee to Czechoslovakia.[27] Chamberlain saw Churchill privately and impressed upon him the reasons why the otherwise attractive option of the 'Grand Alliance' had been rejected. Churchill assured him that 'he would not intrigue against me', and that even when his attitude towards the Government was 'critical', it would remain 'avuncular' – an echo of a phrase which Churchill had used in his first Commons speech following Chamberlain's election. Chamberlain assured his sisters that whilst 'everyone in the House enjoys listening to him and enjoys his sallies', Churchill had 'no following of any importance'.[28]

The outward differences between Chamberlain and Churchill were once more minimal. The Prime Minister did not regard the Soviets as likely or desirable allies, and he rejected their request at the end of March for a conference.[29] But, despite his later advocacy of a Soviet alliance, Churchill had not mentioned it in his 'Grand Alliance' speech. Indeed, as late as 9 May he was saying that Britain should not go 'cap in hand' to the Soviets.[30] Churchill did not support the idea of an automatic guarantee to Czechoslovakia, and he shared the common belief that the leader of the Germans in Czechoslovakia's Sudetenland, Konrad Henlein, was not Hitler's puppet, but a man with whom the Czech Government could have a dialogue. He saw him during his visit to Britain in May and listened with interest to his seemingly moderate demands.[31] So he had no choice but to support the Government's attempts to get the Czech President, Eduard Beneš, to negotiate with Henlein over the grievances of the Sudeten Germans.

But underlying this lay what had always been there. When Halifax was discussing the options facing the Government at the Cabinet's Foreign Affairs Committee on 18 March, after he had pointed out the dangers which might follow if Germany became convinced that she was being 'encircled', he had gone on to say that he drew a distinction between 'Germany's racial efforts', which 'no one could question', and her 'lust for conquest on a Napoleonic scale which he himself did not credit'.[32] This was where the difference lay. Churchill, who habitually thought on a Napoleonic scale, could envision such a 'lust for conquest'. But again, for the moment, the gap between him and Chamberlain was largely hidden from view. Once the Government committed itself to Staff talks with the French in April, there was, it seemed, little to divide the two men save Churchill's desire for an Anglo-French alliance.

Churchill certainly counted as 'discontented' enough to be an inhabitant of the Cave of Adullam, and by March he was both 'in debt' and 'in distress'. The resolve to limit his expenses for 1937–8 to £6,000 was always going to be difficult. Churchill turned down requests from the New Commonwealth Society in February 1938 because he had to finish *Marlborough* in order to get down to work on the potentially highly lucrative *History of the English-Speaking Peoples*.[33] But suddenly the £15,000 which he could expect from this was placed in jeopardy. A slump in the American stock market in the second week in March left Churchill's account with his brokers £18,000 in the red; with super-tax and income-tax demands to meet, Churchill was in deep financial trouble.[34] Even if he devoted all his time to writing, he could scarcely hope to balance his accounts before the end of 1939 – if then. He turned to Bracken for advice and to the estate agents to put Chartwell on the market.[35] As though this news were not bad enough, Pelion was heaped upon Ossa when Beaverbrook cancelled Churchill's profitable contract with his newspapers, which syndicated his articles throughout the country. Beaverbrook did not like the direction which Churchill's articles on foreign policy were taking and had resolved to carry them no more.[36]

It is often said that what distinguishes real life from fairy tales is that the former lacks those fairy godmothers with which the latter is so prodigally endowed, but those who hold that real life is stranger by far than fiction will hardly be surprised at the sudden appearance of a fairy godfather. Sir Henry Strakosch was a South African financier of great wealth and influence, and as such it was hardly surprising that he was an acquaintance of the ubiquitous Bracken. What might be considered more surprising was his agreeing to take over Churchill's losses for three years.[37] It was an act of tremendous generosity, which enabled Chartwell to be taken off the market; but was it more than that?

On 7 April the Government's Foreign Affairs Committee met to discuss Czechoslovakia. Determined to root out dissent, the Whips had put on pressure to get Nicolson removed from the Vice-Chairmanship of the Committee and had quizzed Emrys-Evans as to whether he was 'pro-Chamberlain' or 'pro-Eden'.[38] During the discussions at the meeting, Lady Astor, the American-born MP for Plymouth and a devoted Chamberlainite, said to one MP who was clearly advocating a British commitment to Czechoslovakia which might involve Britain in war, 'You must be a bloody Jew to say a thing like that.' Churchill replied, 'I have never before heard such an insult to a Member of Parliament as the words just used by that bitch.'[39] Yet precisely the same charge has, at least by innuendo, been levelled against Churchill himself. Strakosch, we are told as though it were significant, was a Moravian Jew,[40] and 'Focus' was certainly bank-rolled by wealthy Jews who were, not unnaturally, concerned at the fate of their co-religionists in Germany. So was Churchill a 'hired help'[41] for a Jewish lobby, which, regarding Jewish interests as superior to those of the British Empire, was determined to embroil that Empire in a war on their behalf?

Such is the sensitivity about anti-Semitism since the revelations from the Nazi death camps that even to ask such a question is to risk the grave imputation of racial prejudice. But people have such prejudices and they were a great deal more willing to express them openly before 1945. Beaverbrook certainly believed that 'the Jews may drive us into war',[42] and he was far from the only one; it was, and has remained, a central tenet of the argument of Sir Oswald Mosley and his fascists that it was the Jews who, through their influence in the British press and elsewhere, pushed against Chamberlain's attempts for a *rapprochement* with Germany, thus making war more, rather than less, likely.[43]

Churchill was certainly involved with the Zionist movement, but only on the periphery (indeed he refused to lead a delegation on the Palestine issue to Chamberlain in early 1938)[44], and he was certainly associated with Jewish organisations which did take the view that the British Empire and its resources would serve their purposes well. But Churchill's search for allies had also brought in the Russian ambassador, Maisky, pacifists and crypto-Communists from the left of the British political spectrum, trades unionists, feminists, and the weird and wonderful of all descriptions, as well as many ordinary men and women who, for reasons similar and dissimilar to his own, felt that Britain ought to pursue a stronger line in Europe. But unless we take the view that the communists, pacifists, etc., etc., were all part of this great Jewish conspiracy, then this line of argument begins to look threadbare, for we should have to allege that Churchill was a Communist sympathiser, or maybe a closet pacifist – and at the latter the mind will take no more.

Churchill's association with the Jewish lobby was on the same terms as his association with Citrine, Dalton or Philip Noel-Baker – those who were against Hitler were his allies, and he was not going to ask too many questions about their motives or ultimate objectives. It was a line he was to pursue until February 1945, when he finally began to realise that a mutual hatred of Hitler did not amount to a community of views on anything else; but by then it was all a little late. Strakosch had been feeding Churchill masses of information about German rearmament since 1935,[45] and he shared with him a view that Hitler's ambitions were of the Napoleonic kind. He had looked to Churchill to champion his ideas, and he was only too willing to bail him out financially to enable him to continue to do so. Those with a taste for more sinister and lurid interpretations may indulge it, but no one would argue that Churchill only opposed Hitler because he was receiving cash for it; that opposition was, as we have seen, part of his general vision of British history.

Churchill's main difference with the Government, apart from his desire for an alliance with the French, remained the one over 'air parity' and the rate of rearmament in the air. Churchill's fears were shared by the head of the

Treasury, Sir Warren Fisher, who told Chamberlain on 2 April that all they had received from the Air Ministry was 'soothing syrup and incompetence in equal measure'.[46] During the defence debates in March the Government had announced that 'parity' was no longer to be counted in terms of 'equal first-line strength', for which they had been much criticised by Churchill.[47] Fisher's allegations were even more alarming. According to his figures, current German production was 6,100 aircraft for 1938, compared to Britain's 2,100–2,250, many of which were obsolete. He estimated that where the Germans would produce 7,250 aircraft in 1939, the British would produce only 5,000 – and that relied upon an acceleration of production. Fisher's figures, like Churchill's, were, it is now clear, exaggerated. The German figure was 5,235 for 1938, but thanks to expansion in 1938–9, that became 8,295 for 1939.[48] It was decided to set up a Supply Committee to remedy deficiencies. In March the Cabinet had finally agreed to relax the assumption that rearmament should not interfere with the normal course of trade, and in late April the Air Ministry was authorised to accept as many aircraft as it could get from the British aircraft industry upto a maximum of 1,200 machines over the next two years.[49] In the next two months orders worth £43 million were placed for new aircraft, but less than £7 million was devoted to building new plant. As far as Churchill was concerned, this was too little, and as far as Swinton was concerned, it was too late.

It was unfortunate for Swinton that the expansion of the Air Force coincided with a revolution in aircraft design. He may have been correct to wait for the Hurricanes and Spitfires, but the delays in their delivery were even greater than those for existing aircraft types, which left him vulnerable to political criticism – not least from Churchill.[50] Churchill wrote to Chamberlain on 18 April, the week before the Cabinet authorised the new expansion scheme, reminding him of the defects in the Government's programme. Chamberlain hoped that the new plans would lessen his criticism, but they did not.[51] In the second of a new series of articles for the *Daily Telegraph* (which replaced those which Beaverbrook no longer wanted), he severely criticised the pace of the air rearmament programme.[52] He followed his article on 28 April with a similar one on 1 May, on 'Future safeguards of national defence', in which he called for a strong force of fighters and bombers – during the course of which he stated that he did not believe in 'reprisals upon the enemy civilian population'.[53] On 12 May the Commons debated a motion to reduce Swinton's salary – the traditional means of censuring a Minister. His Under-Secretary, Earl Winterton, an Irish peer who was one of the 'lightest weights in the Cabinet',[54] lived up to Duff Cooper's estimate of him in a lamentable performance, where Churchill had him stumped several times.[55] Although the Government won the vote, it was clear that there was widespread dissatisfaction in the House, and Chamberlain thought that Swinton would have to be sacrificed to appease it. He went on 16 May.[56]

Any enforced resignation is awkward for a Prime Minister, but Chamberlain was able to muffle the impact by combining it with a reshuffle (it was too perfunctory to warrant the term reconstruction) forced on him by the fathers of Lord Harlech and the Duke of Devonshire. As the new Lord Harlech, William Ormsby-Gore, was Secretary of State for the Dominions, this meant Chamberlain now had more than the permitted number of peers occupying Secretary of Stateships so a reshuffle was necessary.[57] There were rumours that Churchill might be brought in, and perhaps even appointed to the Ministry of Supply which he was demanding. But there was no job for Churchill.

The rhetoric of Churchill's attack exaggerated the differences between himself and the Government. His criticisms about the size of the Air Force were justified, but ignored the formidable problems which had been in Swinton's way, whilst his allegation about Britain being defenceless against attack from the air could only have been disproved by the Government revealing the secret of radar.[58] When the Government examined the detail of his proposals for a Ministry of Supply, the lack of which he alleged was so crucial, it was discovered that what Churchill actually proposed was not 'State interference in the actual functions of industry', but something more ambiguous: 'a definite chain of responsible authority' descending 'through the whole of British industry'. It was hard to deduce from the detail of Churchill's proposals, as opposed to the rhetoric, that there was a great degree of difference between him and the Government.

One of the subjects upon which Churchill had come out as a full opponent of the Government was over the signing of a treaty which renounced British naval rights at various Irish ports which had been retained in 1922. Churchill wanted to try to divide the House on the issue, but his old India Defence League colleague, Sir Henry Page-Croft, told him at the end of April that he did not think there was enough support for such a motion.[59] This did not stop Churchill from intervening when the issue came before the House on 5 May. In his best declamatory style, he condemned the new Irish treaty as 'an improvident example of appeasement' and compared it to the abandonment of Gibraltar or Malta.[60] The speech was not well-received, and Channon, now PPS to Rab Butler at the Foreign Office, noted with incredulity 'Winston Churchill is even against the Irish Treaty', and wondered whether that 'fat, brilliant, unbalanced, illogical orator is more than just that?'[61]

There are signs that Churchill's rhetoric, even when it was as splendid as his speech on 24 March, which spoke of 'this famous island descending incontinently, fecklessly, the stairway which leads to a dark gulf' and the 'moral catastrophe' which might be about to engulf it, was having less than the desired effect.[62] Randolph's efforts to coach his father in a new, more conversational style of speaking appear to have borne no fruit, for the old rhetorical flourishes still predominated. After the speech on 24 March an observer asked one MP what he had thought of it, only to receive the response: 'Oh the usual Churchillian filibuster; he likes to rattle the sabre and does it jolly well, but you always have to take it with a pinch of salt.'[63] If Churchill's intervention over the Irish treaty failed to help his search for allies or to advance his reputation, then the next episode upon which he clashed with the Government did, if possible, even less to advance these causes.

Churchill wrote to the new War Minister, Hore-Belisha, on 4 June about deficiencies in the Army and the anti-aircraft defences of the country.[64] He was joined in this by his son-in-law, Duncan Sandys, who sent the Minister the draft of a question which he proposed to ask about the capital's defences. The material in Sandys's question revealed that he was in possession of information which contravened the Official Secrets Act, and when he saw the Attorney-General on 23 and 24 June, Sir David Somervell told him that unless he revealed the name of his informant, he might be liable to prosecution. Sandys told the story to the House on 27 June, when he asked for a select committee to be set up to investigate whether the Act applied to MPs in performance of their duties.[65] Before the House could debate the issue, Sandys found himself summoned to attend a War Office court of enquiry, something which he reported to the Commons on 29 June, calling it a 'gross breach' of the privileges of the House. A Committee of Privileges was set up to investigate this, one of whose members was Churchill. The following day the House voted, in a motion supported by Sinclair and Attlee, to investigate Sandys's original complaints.[66] Churchill was reported to be 'in the brightest spirits'.[67]

This was not surprising. Swinton's resignation had set the dovecotes of Chamberlain's opponents fluttering. There were rumours that Baldwin, worried that 'the country will not stand Neville's Government much longer', was in touch with Eden,[68] whilst Nicolson thought that there was a 'real impression that the whole show is going to crack up'.[69] Other rumours had it that the reshuffle of May was simply the prelude to widening the base of the Government in order to embark upon a more vigorous rearmament programme.[70] Even the new King, George VI, got in on the act, telling Butler that the Government's policy was 'without morality' and suggesting that 'the Prime Minister tended to break the basis of the National Government by being rude to the Opposition'.[71] Halifax, who could be regarded as a bell-wether for Tory feeling, was also beginning to speculate upon whether it might be necessary to broaden the base of the Government – perhaps by bringing back Eden.[72] A sudden crisis towards the end of May, caused by reports that the Germans were about to present Beneš and the Czechs with an ultimatum, had threatened to cut across Chamberlain's policy to persuade the Czechs to negotiate with Henlein. Chamberlain believed that his warning to the Germans had prevented a coup, but it made him warier of the 'utterly untrustworthy and dishonest' regime of Hitler,[73] and did nothing to help his foreign policy.

The findings by the Committee of Privileges that there had been a breach of privilege in Sandys being summoned to appear before a court of enquiry was, however, swiftly invalidated when it was revealed that it was not the court, but the Eastern Command, under whose authority Sandys, as a member of the Territorials, came, which had summoned him.[74] The Select Committee, which was enquiring into the initial allegations, reported in mid-July after sitting for seventeen days. The longer the sitting went on, the more apparent did it become that the Government had done nothing to warrant censure, and by 14 July Sir John Simon, now Chancellor of the Exchequer, was writing with confidence to Chamberlain that 'Winston and Co. are getting thoroughly sick of this business and would not be sorry to see it dropped, provided, of course, they escape the discredit which may come to them.'[75] They did not.

The Independent MP for Oxford, the humorist, A. P. Herbert, made play of Churchill's portentous allegation that the Committee's report 'will be read with the greatest interest abroad'; in a manner which recalled Chesterton's mockery of F. E. Smith's claim that the second reading of the Welsh Disestablishment Bill would be followed with great interest abroad – 'Are they clinging to their crosses, F. E. Smith, where the Breton boat-fleet tosses, are they, Smith?' – Herbert expressed the hope that when Churchill went to Paris the following week, he would send them all a telegram 'to report on how many envious and admiring eyes are turning on that report which he now assures us is absurd and wrong'. He also pointed out how odd it was that Churchill should have thought it was appropriate for him to sit on the Committee in the first place: 'He seems to be attempting to combine the incompatible and separate functions of the centre-forward and the referee.' The House was reduced to laughter as Herbert went on: 'One minute he is bounding forward to the attack, shooting goals in all directions, and the next moment, with dignity but still bounding, he is blowing the whistle.'[76]

Chamberlain was happy to see the affair rebound on to its prime mover. He thought that Churchill had seen 'an opportunity of giving the Government a good shake' and tried to take it, but he had ended up by increasing his own isolation.[77] The Edenites had little contact with Churchill; they had not even responded to his attempts to concert forces over the Anglo-Italian treaty, which had been signed on 16 April, and which had been, in a way, the proximate cause of Eden's resignation.[78] The number of 'insurgents' was, in any case, pitifully small; Channon estimated it at seventeen, which included Amery,[79] who was far from agreeing to Churchill's 'Grand Alliance' and League-based ideas,[80] and Boothby, who had actually spoken in favour of the Prime Minister in the debate on Eden's resignation.[81]

It was 'during the summer of 1938', as Eden put it, that a 'number of Conservative Members of Parliament who shared the same opinions about the threatening international dangers' began to meet together. Given the vagueness of this, it is no wonder that, far from quaking in their boots, the

Whips gave the group the derisive name of 'the Glamour boys'.[82] But according to Nicolson, it was not until the very different circumstances of November that the group really got together – and even then 'we decided that we should not advertise ourselves as a group or even call ourselves a group'.[83] It is not by such rose-water methods that a Government with a majority of nearly three hundred is overthrown. What the 'Glamour boys' needed was a 'few more cads like the Apostles'.

But they would not touch the nearest thing to it which was available – Churchill, and even he was expressing his views with moderation. Churchill knew full well, none better, the consequences of trying to lead a Parliamentary revolt against the National Government. Encouraged by the Liberal MP, Richard Acland, to form an all-Party group, with Attlee, Sinclair and Eden,[84] he excused himself from any such attempt: 'The Government have a solid majority, and Chamberlain will certainly not wish to work with me.' Only if the 'foreign situation darkened' would this situation change, 'but events, and great events alone will rule'.[85]

31

The Myths of Munich

The differences between Chamberlain and Churchill over the Czech crisis, which led to the Munich settlement, have usually been overstated. During August and early September the Government pursued a policy of putting pressure upon the Czechs to cede territory peacefully to the Sudeten Germans. The mission under Churchill's old colleague from the Asquith Cabinet, Lord Runciman, which went to Czechoslovakia in August, was part of this policy. Churchill did not oppose it; indeed, in an article in the *Daily Telegraph* on 26 July, the day the news of the mission leaked to the press, Churchill urged that the Czechs 'owe it to to the Western Powers that every concession compatible with the sovereignty and integrity of their State shall be made'. This was exactly what the Government was telling the Czechs, and Halifax would not have dissented with Churchill's comment that 'I am sure that all the elements of a good and lasting settlement are present, unless it is wrecked.'[1] Indeed, when Churchill met Albert Foerster, the Nazi leader in Danzig, in July, the language which he held might almost have been that of the greatly excoriated British Ambassador in Berlin, Sir Nevile Henderson. Churchill told him that 'most people ... would not resent gradual peaceful increase of German commercial influence in the Danube basin but that any violent move would almost immediately lead to a world war'.[2]

Until late September the only real difference between Churchill and Chamberlain was that the former was more willing than the latter to risk the arbitrament of war. Churchill held no brief for the territorial integrity of Czechoslovakia; like many of his fellow countrymen, he was susceptible to the cry of 'self-determination' for the Sudetens, and he did not urge the Government to guarantee Czechoslovakia even when by early September it was clear that Runciman's mission would produce no results, and that Hitler was threatening to use force.[3] Then he urged once more his scheme of the 'Grand Alliance'.[4] But the passage of six months had not rendered what was impracticable in March practicable in September. Churchill, listening to Maisky and his own beliefs, held that the Russians and the French would stand firm; but the Government had its own reasons for believing that the truth was far from that.[5]

Reports from Paris indicated that the French Government was, whatever Churchill's French friends held, in a state approaching panic. Anxious neither to abandon publicly the Czechs, nor yet to be dragged into a war on their behalf, they were known to be urging concessions upon Prague with an urgency born of fear.[6] As for the Russians, their military potential was no greater than it had been before, and their impact upon the diplomatic situation was as negative as ever. The Russians could only help the Czechs if the Poles would allow their army to pass through Poland – and this they were unwilling to do.[7] Moreover, there was another objection which could be offered to Churchill's grand vision. If Hitler did have Napoleonic ambitions, was he likely to be deterred from action by an 'alliance' which his own diplomats could tell him was a paper tiger? Churchill thought so, especially if Roosevelt somehow associated himself with the scheme. In an article on 15 September Churchill urged this scheme, at the same time as he expressed his confidence that the Czechs could stand up for a long period to Nazi bombardment.[8] But Chamberlain was not convinced that things need come to such a pass.

On the same day as Churchill's article, Chamberlain seized the political and diplomatic initiative by a dramatic flight to meet Hitler at Berchtesgaden; his action revealed how divided and hollow was the opposition to him at home.

Randolph Churchill, whose edition of his father's speeches, *Arms and the Covenant*, had been published in June, saw in this a 'surrender' and a justification for his own hostility to the Government. The editorial comment in the book had given to Churchill's speeches a far more consistent note of hostility towards the Government than was actually warranted, and Randolph had not been pleased at the extent to which his father had thus far gone along with Chamberlain's policy – it would, after all, render the task of editing the next volume more difficult. He did not lose the opportunity to chide his father: 'Please in future emulate my deep-seated distrust of Chamberlain & all his works & colleagues ... now we have the submission you have so often predicted. Bless you & please in future steer your own course uncontaminated by contact with these disreputable men.'[9] But political life was not so easily conducted in the shades of black and white which Randolph preferred.

Churchill had called Chamberlain's flight to meet Hitler 'the stupidest thing which has ever been done',[10] but this was not a view widely shared outside his own immediate circle and the Labour Party. Nicolson, who was no friend of the Prime Minister, felt a sense of 'enormous relief' at the news,[11] whilst Amery, who was inclined to be sceptical, nevertheless thought that there might be an 'off chance' that his 'courageous action' had averted war.[12] Whatever else Chamberlain's action had done, it had given him the initiative and left his putative opponents divided. Eden was in a particularly cruel dilemma. He shared Churchill's hankering after a 'Grand Alliance',[13] but he was aware that 'if he had been in Halifax's place, he might have done the same', and he did not want to 'lead a revolt or to secure any resignations from the Cabinet'.[14]

The reaction of those in the Cabinet who disliked the plan which Chamberlain brought back from Berchtesgaden suggested that Eden would have had little hope of effecting any other course of action. Runciman told the Cabinet on 17 September that 'Czechoslovakia could not continue to exist as she is today', and Chamberlain unfolded a scheme by which the British and French would encourage the Czechs to cede those areas which Hitler had told him that he wanted. This was all rather like negotiating under duress, and many stomachs revolted at the prospect. But when pressed for an alternative policy, the would-be rebels had none.

Even before Chamberlain had gone to Germany, Duff Cooper and Oliver Stanley, the President of the Board of Education and younger son of the Earl of Derby, had agreed that they would 'not form any group of those who shared our opinion',[15] and whilst they demurred in Cabinet, they were stuck when asked for an alternative policy. Cooper appealed, in a Churchillian fashion, for the 'traditional' policy of 'the balance of power', but when it was urged upon him that Britain did not actually possess the power to prevent a German attack on Czechoslovakia, he had no answer other than to hope that something would happen to remove Hitler.[16] Another would-be dissentient, the Minister of Health, Walter Elliot, was 'depressed and bewildered' and had little idea of 'what we should do'.[17] Elliot thought vaguely about resigning, perhaps with the leader of the National Labour group, the Lord Privy Seal, 'Buck' de la Warr,[18] and trailed his conscience round his friends, hoping that someone would tell him what to do with it. The problem for those who thought like Cooper and Churchill was that they were relying upon the French, and the Anglo-French meetings on 18 and 19 September revealed, as Halifax was not slow to tell Churchill, that France was a broken reed.[19]

Chamberlain's policy had entangled Britain in the toils of France's 'eastern policy' and the fate of Czechoslovakia; now his efforts were addressed to cutting through the web. The Czechs, he and Edouard Daladier, the French Prime Minister, agreed, would be advised not to mobilise their forces, and they would be asked to suggest concessions of territory – as though this was their own idea, which would dispose 'of any idea that we were ourselves carving up Czech territory'. Thus far so good, especially in view of the fact (unknown to Chamberlain) that Beneš was already willing to give up territory. But Daladier needed to save face, and he insisted that he could not recommend the Czechs to cede territory without the British and the French giving a guarantee to what remained of Czechoslovakia. This Chamberlain agreed to.[20] He left for Bad Godesberg on 22 September, where he put the Anglo-French proposals to Hitler.

Churchill had enjoyed little success in rallying support during the interval between Chamberlain's two visits. In part this was because some of 'the Glamour Boys' advised Eden against embroiling himself with Churchill and his 'cabal', who 'were notorious for plots against the Government',[21] advice he was willing to heed. But in part too it was because no one wanted to go to war for Czechoslovakia's current frontiers, and few even wanted to extend a guarantee to that country – including Churchill.[22] There was a widely held view that Czechoslovakia was an artificial creation and that the dominion which the long-subjugated Czechs had held over their former German over-lords had not been wisely exercised. Nicolson, who as a young diplomat had been at the peace conference which had created Czechoslovakia, tried to combat his wife's argument that the Germans were justified in wanting self-determination for the Sudetens, but found himself at a loss. After all, it had been the great liberal principle of self-determination which had triumphed in the Treaty of St Germain; how could it now be disclaimed? 'Hitler', Nicolson reflected with impotent anger, 'has all the arguments on his side, but essentially they are false arguments. And we, who have right on our side, cannot say that our real right is to resist German hegemony. That is "imperialistic".'[23]

Boothby supported the idea of an announcement of Anglo-French-Russian talks because he believed it would deter the Germans, not because he wanted to resort to force.[24] Amery, whose earlier willingness to suspend disbelief about Nazi ambitions in favour of his imperial preoccupations had been dissipated by the *Anschluss*, nevertheless shared the belief that a war for the territorial integrity of Czechoslovakia would not be justified: 'Nothing short of a victorious war, with Germany crushed and Nazidom discredited, would have made it possible for the Sudetens to sit down quietly as good citizens of Czechoslovakia.'[25] He resolved to remain undecided in his view of Chamberlain's initiative until he had seen its results.[26]

It was, thus, a small group of Adullamites which foregathered at Churchill's flat in Morpeth Mansions on the day Chamberlain left for Godesberg. The mood was dramatic, with Nicolson telling Churchill, 'This is Hell,' and receiving the reply: 'It is the end of the British Empire.' But the conclusions reached were less dramatic. They decided that they would support Chamberlain if he 'comes back with peace with honour or he breaks off', but that they would 'go against him' if he 'comes back with peace with dishonour'. They were prepared to agree to a peaceful transfer of Czech territory under international supervision; their objections to Chamberlain's policy were visceral rather than intellectual.[27] Churchill took comfort from the hope that the Czechs would refuse to make the concessions required (despite his earlier attitude), in which case there would be a war. He did not think that the Czechs would be defeated swiftly, and he had every confidence that Britain, France and Russia would be dragged into the ensuing conflict.[28] His optimism about the result belied his criticisms of the Government's rearmament policy.

After the crisis was over, Sir Henry Page-Croft told Churchill that this had been the point of 'fundamental disagreement' between the two of them. He was surprised that Churchill should have been willing to risk the 'arbitrament of war rather than make the Munich settlement, when you had convinced me that we were in a hopeless disparity in the Air arm'.[29] Nicolson seems to have imagined that saying that the state of Britain's defences proved that Churchill had been right to criticise the Government was a sufficient answer to this point.[30] Leaving aside the immense problems which the Government had had with the rearmament programme and the fact that it was not due to peak until 1939, this was still a jejune line of argument. Whether it was the fault of the Government or not, Britain was not ready to fight a war, and being able to blame the Government would be little solace in the event of defeat. But Nicolson, like Churchill, looked towards the French and the Russians for salvation.

However, Churchill and company were not the only ones who contrived a misleading impression of their contemporary reaction when they came to write about the crisis. It became the classic defence of the Chamberlainites to claim that Munich 'bought' another year of rearmament, which was crucial to Britain's survival in 1940.[31] As with the Churchillian version, there is enough truth in this to make it seem plausible to anyone who does not look below the surface. That Chamberlain's policy had such a result is undeniable, but it is a far more dubious proposition to assert that this was its desired result. Chamberlain's main objective was to avert war, and he was prepared to go a very long way down the road of national dishonour to get his way – and it was this which eventually rallied forces to Churchill.

At Godesberg Chamberlain was shocked by the way in which Hitler brushed aside the Anglo-French plan. He wanted the Czechs to cede large areas of territory, and if they did not do so within a limited time-span he would attack.[32] When Churchill heard that Chamberlain was coming straight back to England, he assumed that war was imminent.[33] In fact, as the Cabinet discovered on 24 September, Chamberlain wanted to capitulate. Hitler wanted the British and the French to put his proposals to the Czechs and to sponsor them, and that was what the Prime Minister suggested they should do. The Permanent Under-Secretary at the Foreign Office, Sir Alexander Cadogan was 'completely horrified' at what he called 'total surrender'.[34] Cooper's notoriously short temper began to fray, as he said that, where he had once taken the view that there were only two alternatives, 'war or dishonour', he now espied a third: 'namely war with dishonour, by which I mean being kicked into war by the boot of public opinion'.[35] But, after a night's sleep, Halifax retracted his earlier support for the Godesberg proposals and, on 25 September, led what was, in effect, a Cabinet revolt against the Prime Minister. Despite Chamberlain's protests, Halifax's decision that he could not countenance telling the Czechs that, unless they supported the Godesberg terms, they would receive no help, tipped the balance. Much emboldened, Cooper, Elliot and company now gave voice to their views.

The Cabinet met thrice that Sunday, and there was an agitated meeting between British and French Ministers in the evening, in which Daladier avoided attempts to pin him down to definitions of what he would actually do if Czechoslovakia were attacked. He was full of moving rhetoric about the rights of small nations but short on proposals for action. It was decided to send the head of the Civil Service, Sir Horace Wilson, to Hitler with a warning that if he attacked Czechoslovakia, the consequences would be grave.[36]

Opinion as to what this decision meant varied. For Chamberlain it clearly gave Hitler another chance to pull back from the brink; to Halifax it represented something similar, but it was also a sign that there were limits beyond which it was not safe to go. The Foreign Secretary had become profoundly impressed whilst Chamberlain was in Godesberg by what he discerned to be a shift in the popular mood against seeming to hand over Czechoslovakia for dismemberment.[37] He had once said that if he thought Hitler possessed of Napoleonic ambitions, then his attitude would change; Hitler's behaviour at Godesberg helped effect that change, aided by signs that, in the face of national dishonour, sections of the Conservative Party were beginning to revolt. Amery had written him an anguished letter on 24 September saying that he did not think the Commons would 'stand any more surrender to Hitler'.[38] Louis Spears organised a letter of protest from Conservative MPs expressing 'strong feelings' that the Czechs 'ought not to be pressed any further'.[39] He was aware of Eden's growing unhappiness,[40] and it was doubtful how much longer the Prime Minister could call upon Party loyalty. Halifax's firmness had preserved the unity of the Government and his own Party.

Some indication of the soundness of Halifax's view about the state of the Party can be gauged from attendance at the next of Churchill's Morpeth Mansions meetings on 26 September. Amery, a fellow Birmingham MP, had heard that the whole city was 'getting fed up of Neville', and whilst he thought this an exaggeration, he joined with Louis Spears and others in going to Churchill's flat. The fact that he called the assembled Adullamites 'a queer collection' is some indication both of the way in which orthodox Conservatives regarded the company Churchill kept and of the strength of the feeling which was needed to overcome it.[41] They decided that 'If Chamberlain rats again we shall form a united block against him', but they did not think that he would 'rat'. In that event, they agreed to rally behind him in the war effort.[42] There was considerable enthusiasm for pressing the Government to announce that it was in direct touch with the Russians, but at this point Amery, who 'strongly objected' to the idea, reminded the 'queer collection' that most Conservatives shared his view; there were limits – at least until war was declared.[43]

Churchill and company were assuming that Hitler would never climb down far enough to agree to a conference, and the vicious speech which the Führer delivered that evening gave no hope of a reprieve; it was generally assumed that war was imminent.[44] The Fleet was mobilised on 27 September, and that evening Chamberlain gave what was to become a famous broadcast in which he spoke, in a broken voice, of how 'horrible, fantastic, incredible' it was that 'we should be digging ditches and trying on gas masks here because of a quarrel in a far-away country between people of whom we know nothing'.[45] The 'general impression', according to Amery, was that Chamberlain was 'a broken man'.[46] Perhaps there was something to this. He certainly caused Cooper's temper to flare when, at the Cabinet meeting afterwards, he suggested giving effect to the Godesberg terms on the grounds that it was not worth risking war over an issue as small as when and how Czech territory should be transferred. But with Cabinet unity stretched to the limit, it was Halifax who once more pulled things together. Hitler would be told that he could have some of the areas he wanted by 1 October, with the rest following by the end of the month, if an international commission agreed. A final appeal for a conference was despatched to Hitler and Mussolini.[47]

The House was crowded the following afternoon, 28 September, as MPs assembled to hear what those who had been there in 1914 assumed would be a repetition of events. Indeed, as Chamberlain recapitulated events since August, it seemed to Amery that a declaration of war was imminent. As Nicolson looked along his row, he saw Churchill receiving a host of telegrams. As Chamberlain reached the point at which he was describing current events and how an appeal had been addressed to Mussolini and Hitler to attend a conference, Chamberlain paused as a telegram was handed to him. Less bulky than the mass which Churchill had received, it was nevertheless far more crucial. With a relief which was visible, and which soon communicated itself to the whole House, Chamberlain announced that Hitler had agreed to postpone German mobilisation and to hold a conference on the morrow at Munich. Channon was not the only one who 'felt sick with enthusiasm', for the whole House 'rose, and in a scene of riotous delight, cheered' and 'bellowed their approval'.[48] Amery recorded a similar sense of relief, with 'all our people ... on their feet' cheering 'vociferously'.[49] Nicolson too thought that the 'whole House' rose in acclamation of the man who had averted war.[50]

Did Churchill join in? His official biographer says that he did not, nor did Eden, Amery and Nicolson.[51] Although no source is given for this, Eden's memoirs confirm that he, Churchill and Amery did not join in the demonstration,[52] and Amery's memoirs do the same, as do those of Macmillan.[53] Thus historians have repeated the tale of Churchill's not joining the demonstration, supporting the image of his lonely stand against Chamberlain. But the answer to the question, 'When is an historical fact not a fact?', would appear to be, 'When it concerns the Munich crisis!' No contemporary account mentions Churchill remaining seated or looking grim. Eden does not give his own recollection as evidence, but cites a book by R. W. Seton-Watson, which, oddly enough, is what Amery does. By the time they came to write their memoirs, both men had good reason to cite Seton-Watson. 'Munich' had become the moment of truth – the test of anyone's 'anti-appeasement' credentials. For Eden in particular, whose actions between his resignation and September 1939 were so unheroic that he was the despair of some of his supporters, an action such as the one described in his memoirs was an important demonstration of his political virility. But did it happen?

In his contemporary diary Amery does not mention that he remained seated, nor does he say anyone else did.[54] Channon, who disliked Eden and Churchill and would have been happy to have recorded an event which he would have thought to their discredit, mentions nothing.[55] The only contemporary account which does mention anyone remaining seated is Nicolson's diary on 29 September, which records that his action had created a considerable stir.[56] Nicolson was sitting further along the same bench as Churchill, and he was a great admirer who had every reason to note such an action by his hero; with everyone else on their hind legs, Nicolson would have seen whether or not Churchill remained seated, but no such act is mentioned. Indeed, what Nicolson did record was Churchill getting to his feet to talk to Chamberlain.[57] *The Times* described him as receiving a loud cheer as he shook Chamberlain's hand.[58] The official biography has this action taking place as Chamberlain 'rose to leave the Chamber',[59] but Amery's contemporary account recorded that whilst Churchill 'looked very much upset', he was 'among the first to go forward and congratulate Neville'.[60] What neither Amery nor *The Times* was in a position to do was to hear what Churchill said; Nicolson was: 'I congratulate you on your good fortune. You were very lucky.'[61]

In one sense it does not matter whether Churchill did or did not remain seated as the rest of the House rose to salute Chamberlain on 28 September, but in another sense it does. A cumulation of small incidents can make up a larger picture, and there is a symbolic importance about this one. Significantly perhaps, Churchill says nothing about it in his memoirs.[62] Unlike Eden, who did resort to lies in his memoirs to conceal the extent of his collusion with the Israelis at the time of the Suez crisis in 1956, Churchill usually adopted subtler tactics when the truth was inconvenient for his version of history – he preferred to maintain a decorous silence. That he chose to do so on this topic is perhaps significant. So too is the fact that the MP who only a few days previously had warned Eden against associating with Churchill, Anthony Crossley, should have written to Churchill on 29 September offering to state in the House that, contrary to popular rumour, 'it is not true that you were party to intrigues',[63] an action he would hardly have taken if Churchill had remained seated and thus incurred the wrath of most Conservatives. Moreover, Churchill's own press statement wishing Chamberlain 'God-speed', whilst it breathed an air of still expecting war, was warm in praise of the Prime Minister.[64]

That Eden, Amery and Macmillan should have presented the accounts which they do in their memoirs is not evidence of what happened, but rather of how the myths of Munich were manufactured. Perhaps by the time they came to write their memoirs they really believed that because, symbolically, Churchill ought to have remained seated, he had in fact done so. But his behaviour was at one, not with the symbolic truth, but rather with his attitude throughout the crisis. He had supported the idea that the Czechs should be put under pressure to cede territory to the Germans. His main difference with Chamberlain was over the practicability of the 'Grand Alliance'. Of course he did not get up and dance about and cheer, but by shaking Chamberlain's hand he allowed an impression to be created that he shared the joy of the rest of the Conservative Party. Powerlessness had the advantage of letting Churchill have his cake and eat it; the memoir writers obligingly iced it for him.

Churchill's press statement on 28 September contributed a little to another myth of Munich, when he credited Duff Cooper with giving the order to mobilise the Fleet on 27 September. It is certainly true that Cooper telephoned the news to the press, but that is not quite the same thing. The order had actually been given by Chamberlain that afternoon, but he had preferred to keep it secret for fear of worsening the diplomatic situation. After the Cabinet meeting that evening, there was no point in keeping it secret any longer, so when Cooper asked if he could make it public, Chamberlain said yes. But Churchill's version, repeated with more emphasis in his memoirs, creates an impression of Chamberlain as a weak figure, with Cooper, who was to resign from the Cabinet, cutting a figure somewhat more bellicose than he struck at the time.[65] That is not to say that Cooper was not opposed to what Chamberlain was doing, but it is to say that he did not push that opposition to the limit until the end – and even then could suggest no other policy which could actually have been followed.

Cooper met Churchill at 'The Other Club' on the evening of 29 September and ended up in a furious argument with him over what Chamberlain was doing at Munich.[66] That Churchill should have been in a 'towering rage' and in 'deepening gloom' is hardly to be wondered at. A small group of Adullamites had gathered that lunchtime at the Savoy. Lord Lloyd, who, unlike Churchill, had always opposed giving territory to the Germans, and whose dislike of the Government's policy was equal to Randolph Churchill's, opened with a forthright declaration that Chamberlain was going to rat again and must be stopped. Churchill had brought with him a telegram which told Chamberlain that if he imposed further 'onerous terms' on the Czechs, he would find himself opposed in the House. But attempts during the day to get anyone of importance to sign it failed dismally. Eden would not do so because 'it would be interpreted as a vendetta against Chamberlain' (little wonder that he wished in his memoirs to give the impression that he had remained seated on 28 September – at least that had him *doing* something). Attlee refused to sign it without his Party's approval.[67] Amery said that whilst he sympathised, he proposed to take a different line, not one of 'protest' but rather one of stressing that they must all learn from experience.[68] Boothby took a similar line for similar reasons, telling Mrs Dugdale: 'Nobody could oppose Neville just now, but the Government must learn that, if they stay in power a few months more, these must not be wasted like the last three years.'[69] With Chamberlain 'by way of becoming, not only a national, but a world hero',[70] it was a sensible line to take.

At 'The Other Club', Churchill's temper broke. He asked Cooper and Walter Elliot how they could condone a policy 'so cowardly? It was sordid, squalid, sub-human and suicidal.'[71] Duff Cooper's 'veiners' were notorious among his friends. When angry a large vein in the centre of his forehead would pulsate and his face would suffuse with blood until onlookers feared for his health.[72] Now his fury was turned on Lindemann, Boothby and the editor of the *Observer*, J. L. Garvin. As the argument raged 'everybody insulted everybody else and Winston ended by saying that at the next general election he would speak on every socialist platform in the country against the Government'.[73] But would he feel the same in the cool light of morning?

As it transpired the following morning was anything but cool. Chamberlain arrived back at Heston waving his famous piece of paper 'signed by Herr Hitler and myself', declaring from the balcony at No. 10 that it was 'peace with honour'. The crowds went delirious with relief, forgetting, those who felt it, at what a price peace had been purchased.[74] Duff Cooper read the terms of the agreement, which were actually an improvement on those at Godesberg, so intellectually there was no reason to resign. Most of those who had shown dissent, like Elliot and Oliver Stanley, took this way out of the dilemma of whether to resign or not; as Mrs Dugdale recorded: 'I did not realize quite what courage it requires for a Conservative MP to go against the tide *tonight*.'[75] But Cooper simply could not stomach the whole notion of handing over territory to the Germans in such a manner and resigned. It took courage to do it on that afternoon when Chamberlain was the world's hero.

Cooper's role in the debate on the Munich settlement was cast, but what would others do? Amery went along to a meeting of Churchill's 'queer mixed group', where there were two burning topics: whether the Government would call an election, and, if it did, what would be the attitude towards MPs who refused to support it in the debate?[76] On the question of the tactics to be followed in the debate, it was decided to try to get the Labour Party to put down an amendment to any Government resolution, which would allow them to vote against the Government without actually opposing its motion; it was hoped that if thirty or so MPs voted this way, including Cooper and Eden, the Government would not be able to threaten to withdraw the Whip from dissentients.[77] But the Government was determined to play rough.

Cooper's resignation speech opened the debate,[78] and Churchill's description of it as 'admirable in form, massive in argument' and shining with 'courage and public spirit'[79] did it justice. That evening there was another meeting at Churchill's flat, in which the main worry expressed was that Chamberlain would call an election. Churchill felt that the dissentients should form themselves into a group, but that was too much for Amery, who demurred and thought that they should take things more cautiously.[80] His fears were understandable. Following the debate on 4 October, Boothby found himself threatened with deselection if he voted against the Government. Making the issue a vote of confidence, the Government threatened not only to withdraw the Whip from dissentients, but to run candidates against them at the next election.[81]

When the Adullamites foregathered at Bracken's house in Lord North Street on the morning of 5 October, Churchill wanted to take the extreme course of voting against the Government, but Amery advised against it – 'unless they were ready to say that they had an alternative Government in sight'. It may not have been very heroic, but it 'can be defended in one's constituency'.[82] Churchill could not concur, and it was decided to let members vote as they wished.[83] In his speech Churchill came out, for the first time, as an opponent of the Government's policy: 'we have sustained a total and un-mitigated defeat,' he told the House, to cries of 'nonsense' from Lady Astor. His assertion that the 'Grand Alliance' would have saved Czechoslovakia was more dubious than his condemnation of the guarantee which the Government had now seen fit to extend to the country: 'Silent, mournful, abandoned, broken, Czechoslovakia recedes into the darkness'; he predicted that the 'mutilated' state would not long survive. He blamed the affair upon the weakness of British Governments in neglecting Britain's defence; it was, he said, 'a disaster of the first magnitude'. The French system of alliances in the east was swept away and German influence would now be dominant in that area. The 'enormous popular movement' which Churchill (perhaps uniquely) discerned in Poland, Romania, Bulgaria and Yugoslavia, which had looked to the west, would do so no longer. The day would come, he predicted, when Hitler would turn on the western powers.[84]

It was an eloquent statement which at last laid bare the roots of the differences between Churchill and the Government. Beneath the tactical compromises, Churchill did not believe that the democracies and the Fascist dictatorships could live together, and he believed that the balance of power was being destroyed. But when the vote came on 6 October, despite his earlier belligerence, Churchill abstained; he did not vote against the Government, but, as an extra mark of protest, he remained in his seat whilst the vote was taken.[85] Eden and Amery were so impressed by Chamberlain's final speech on 6 October that they told him that, had it not been for their supporters, they would actually have voted for him.[86] The Government won the vote with ease.

Counting the tactical abstentions of Eden and Amery, there were twenty-two abstentions on both the Government motions and the Labour amendment – Boothby voted against the latter but abstained on the former. 'That', Nicolson recorded, with more immodesty than may have been warranted, 'looks none too well in any list.'[87] But with Eden and Amery privately assuring Chamberlain of their sympathy, it was more or less the usual mixture of 'cavemen' and 'Glamour boys', with the addition of Cooper, who could hardly have been expected to vote any other way.

But the debate had revealed deeper rifts within the Conservative Party than the division lists bore witness to. Both Hoare and Halifax urged Chamberlain to make some gesture towards national unity by rewarding Eden for his moderation by bringing him back into the Government.[88] But Chamberlain wanted 'support for my policy', not arguments over it, so Eden remained excluded.[89] The Prime Minister was particularly angry with Churchill, whose contacts with Maisky and the Czech Ambassador, Jan Masaryk, were known to him through the Intelligence Services. His actions, Chamberlain thought, 'demonstrated for the nth time how completely Winston can deceive himself when he wants to'.[90] Resolved to stand on old ways, the Prime Minister left Churchill in the cold – and the political winds that winter were as bitter as the fruit which the harvest of Munich was to yield.

32

The Winter of Discontent

Those who had dared to dissent from the Government faced a bleak winter. Duff Cooper, whose seat at St George's had been won in such spectacular fashion in 1931, and which was probably the safest Tory seat in the country, was hauled over the coals by his local executive and warned that he was, in effect, on probation.[1] Of the Edenites, Jim Thomas, Anthony Crossley,[2] Lord Cranborne, Dick Law and Emrys-Evans all faced similar pressure. Cranborne told his uncle, Lord Cecil, that he had managed to get a 'free hand to say what I like about the Government's foreign policy' despite his 'local blimps', but at the cost of being considered 'a socialist ... a war-monger and ... a poison-pen about the PM'.[3] Even Viscount Wolmer, in South Hampshire, whom Chamberlain classed as one of those who, although 'troubled in mind', would 'come home and bring their tails behind them' if left alone,[4] faced a 'shaking up from his Committee'.[5] Boothby was told by his executive that if he voted against the Government, he would never again receive the Unionist nomination.[6] Religious sects may thrive under persecution, political ones rarely do.

The great dissident who dwelt in Morpeth Mansions had had more experience than anyone of being at odds with the National Government, and he had always taken care to carry his local association with him; as he told Boothby, in the final resort he should threaten to resign his seat.[7] But Churchill himself was neither unscathed nor calm in spirit. During the Munich debate he had protested at the Prime Minister's proposal that the House should adjourn until November, only to be criticised by Chamberlain for the tone of his comments. He sent what Chamberlain characterised as a 'ridiculously pompous note of protest'.[8] Chamberlain responded by telling him that he was 'singularly sensitive for a man who so constantly attacks others'. He told Churchill that he considered his remarks 'highly offensive', adding, 'You cannot expect me to allow you to do all the hitting and never hit back.'[9] And, despite his confident tone to Boothby, Churchill too faced trouble in his own constituency, so much so that he began to ponder whether, in the event of a snap election, he would be able to fight it as a Conservative.[10]

The Munich debates had seen Churchill open secret contacts with the Labour Party, using Harold Macmillan as his intermediary with Hugh Dalton. With the unpleasing prospect of another 'Coupon' election on the pattern of 1918, he wanted to find a common platform with Labour, based on collective security and 'national unity and strength'. When Macmillan had protested, 'That is not our jargon,' he had been met with the cry: 'It is a jargon we may all have to learn.'[11] But the Edenites were no more willing to collaborate with Churchill than they had been before the crisis, and Churchill by himself was not much use to the Labour Party. Worried at the prospect of an early election, the Edenites decided to band together, but not to call themselves a 'group' or to advertise their existence. Nicolson was happy to be associated with men such as Eden and Amery, who did not give the impression, as Churchill did, of being 'more bitter and determined, and more out for a fight than for reform'.[12]

In the first tests of Parliamentary strength after Munich, the vote on a Liberal motion for the creation of a Ministry of Supply on 17 November when Churchill appealed for fifty Conservatives to join him, only Macmillan and Bracken did so. To make matters worse, Duff Cooper criticised him for attacking the Prime Minister.[13] It was, he told Cooper bitterly, necessary for their 'small band of friends' to 'stick together'. But there was no 'band', as Churchill tacitly admitted when he told Cooper that 'some of my friends' had wondered whether there was not, behind the attack, 'the desire to isolate me as much as possible from the other Conservatives who disagree with the Government'.[14] But there was no need to do any such thing. Even his son-in-law, Duncan Sandys, when he was thinking of forming a 'nucleus of abstentionists' in October and November, agreed with Nicolson that association with Churchill would 'kill them' and looked instead to Amery for leadership.[15] Chamberlain's pointed remark during the debate on the Ministry of Supply had rubbed salt into an open wound: 'If I were asked whether judgement is the first of my Rt Hon. friend's many admirable qualities I should have to ask the House of Commons not to press the point.'[16] The shaft went home because it corresponded so closely with the view which many Conservatives held of Churchill.

This perception of Churchill was not to be wholly changed even by the events of the next five years, but what brought a revival of his fortunes was the decline in those of the Prime Minister.

In his weekly article for the *Daily Telegraph* on 17 November Churchill surveyed the 'nation's hopes and misgivings since Munich'. In keeping with the need for circumspection, it was far from being simply critical of Chamberlain. 'Everyone', he wrote, 'must recognise that the Prime Minister is pursuing a policy of a most decided character and of capital importance.' He impugned neither Chamberlain's 'convictions nor his courage'. The Prime Minister believed that he could 'make a good settlement for Europe and the British Empire' by coming to terms with Hitler and Mussolini. Those who differed from him, both in their estimate of 'the principles of our foreign policy' and of the 'facts and probabilities with which our country has to deal', were 'bound to recognise that we have no power at all to prevent him ... from taking the course in which he sincerely believes'. If Chamberlain was right in believing that Hitler had no further territorial demands and that his friendship could be won, then so be it – but 'a whole set of contrary possibilities must be held in mind'. Only the 'march of events' would show.[17]

This was Chamberlain's problem. Having rejected the option of broadening his Government by including Eden, he depended for success on Munich actually delivering some tangible goods – and this it did not do. It was Chamberlain's misfortune to have embarked upon his policy just at the time that Hitler was beginning to wonder whether he might not, after all, have to deal with the western powers before he could fulfil his real ambitions in the east. Chamberlain's interference in the affairs of Czechoslovakia had done nothing to convince him that he should not do so; indeed, his annoyance at having climbed down at Munich increased the possibility that he would have to strike at the western powers first.[18] Certainly nothing in the months which followed Munich did anything to suggest that Chamberlain's hopes were going to be realised.

The terms of the Munich settlement may have been more favourable to the Czechs than the Godesberg ultimatum, but Chamberlain's hopes rested upon Hitler standing by his promises, including the one that any frontier rectifications after occupation would be decided in favour of the Czechs. But as one of the British members of the commission, Roger Makins, told Rab Butler, 'negotiation . . . is not the Nazis' strong suit', and the ambassadors of the Great Powers were 'soon presented with a twelve-hour ultimatum, to which they had no choice but to agree'. After the Germans had 'obtained all (and more) to which in the most generous assumption they were entitled, plebiscites became . . . unnecessary'.[19] This did not stop the Germans from suggesting them in areas where they thought they might benefit. This produced a howl of outrage from Nevile Henderson, who said that if Hitler went back on all his assurances, 'the Prime Minister's confidence in his good faith would be completely destroyed' and there would be 'no possibility of any talk of an Anglo-German understanding'.[20]

One of the reasons why Chamberlain had opposed the idea of the creation of a Ministry of Supply was that he was still hoping that diplomacy would 'allow us to stop arming and get back to the work of making the world a better place'.[21] By the time such a Ministry was set up, 'we might find that the need was slowing off'.[22] But the Nazis seemed determined to thwart Chamberlain's hopes. The anti-Semitic excesses of *Kristallnacht* revolted large sections of British opinion, and Hitler's speech on 10 November in which he spoke with great harshness of Britain and of his determination to expand in eastern Europe hardly augured well.[23] It seemed to Chamberlain that there was 'some fatality about Anglo-German relations which invariably blocks efforts to improve them'.[24] The Cabinet's Foreign Policy Committee, meeting on 14 November, accepted Halifax's view that further diplomatic appeasement was, for the moment, impossible, and that priority should be given to 'the correction of the false impression that we were decadent, spineless and could with impunity be kicked about'.[25] Although Chamberlain took the signs and auguries less tragically than did Halifax, by December even he was lamenting that, 'a section of opinion in this country holds that it is impossible to get on terms with the "Dictators". The latter certainly seem to do their best to justify this point of view.'[26]

As rumours circulated during the winter that Hitler intended to launch a strike westwards, so did the Government tighten up their defence plans – and so did Churchill's credit rise. A lack-lustre reshuffle of the Cabinet in late November, bringing in such young blood as the sixty-eight-year-old Runciman and the ex-Governor of Bengal, Sir John Anderson, did nothing to improve the morale of the Conservative Party, and by early December Randolph Churchill was busy disseminating rumours of an 'Under-Secretaries' Revolt', aimed at getting rid of Hore-Belisha and speeding up rearmament.[27] Moreover, there were signs that Halifax's objective of preserving 'national unity' was becoming incompatible with Chamberlain's 'major objective' of bringing British policy 'back to saner and more realistic grounds'.[28] Munich had seen Halifax emerge as a major figure in the Government, and one whom the Prime Minister, with one Foreign Secretary under his belt, could not afford to ignore. But if Chamberlain was at times inclined towards self-pity, he could always take some comfort by looking at his opponents.

The expectations of some of Eden's more ardent supporters that he would 'break away from the Prime Minister and lead a crusade in the country'[29] were still-born. With his 'group' that feared to call itself that, he struck out along the line of presenting himself as an alternative 'national' leader to Chamberlain, but the problem was that he was so decorous that few could distinguish between him and Halifax.[30] By the following summer Nicolson was still lamenting that Eden did not 'wish to defy the Tory Party and is in fact missing every boat with exquisite elegance'.[31] Eden continued to miss every available boat. He did not want to lead a revolt, he was not by nature a *frondeur*, and he knew the Conservative Party well enough to know what rewards usually awaited those accused of the dread crime of disloyalty to any leader not already stricken.

With Eden sinking quietly into the role of a younger Lord Halifax, the isolation into which he had helped place Churchill had an unexpected result. If Chamberlain's policies should fail, then only one figure seemed to be peddling an alternative one – Winston Churchill, who thus began along the road which would lead him to power.

In November Hitler had spoken in venomous terms about Churchill, Eden and Duff Cooper, but it was only the former who hit back – and it was only Churchill who, partly thanks to the way in which the Edenites treated him, appeared to be prepared to fight the Government. The nature and speed of the change in his position must not be overstated, for it was not until the spring that Chamberlain lost ground which he could never recover.

The Prime Minister was a tough old man, and, unlike some of his Ministers, he was aware that there was an element of 'scaremongering' in the stories which spread in early 1939 about Hitler's intentions. But when Chamberlain was urged in early 1939 to adopt Churchill's policy, he declared that he was not ready to do that: 'Fortunately my nature is, as Lloyd George says, extremely "obstinate" and I refuse to change.'[32] By early spring, with a successful visit to Mussolini behind him, and no sign of the much prophesied Nazi aggression, the Prime Minister was in a more optimistic mood. Growing more doubtful about Halifax's soundness,[33] he remained resolute against admitting any of his opponents into the Government – even the well-behaved Eden: 'Our Anthony is in a dilemma from which he would very much like me to extract him,' he told his sisters in February; but Eden would have to wait and 'proclaim his repentance'.[34] By early February he was beginning to feel 'that at last we are getting on top of the dictators'; Hitler had, he thought, 'missed the bus last September'.[35] In a 'counter campaign' against the doom and gloom merchants, Chamberlain encouraged Ministers to wax optimistic about the future.[36] Hoare went embarrassingly far in a speech on 10 March in which he spoke of the dawn of a new 'golden age'.[37] On 12 March a highly satisfied Prime Minister told his sisters that 'all the prodigal sons are fairly besieging the parental door', with even Churchill making favourable references to him.[38] Three days later German troops entered Prague.

The old view that Chamberlain abandoned appeasement after Prague cannot be sustained. The Prime Minister certainly talked more toughly and entered into negotiations with the Poles, but these were tactical moves, designed to outflank his opponents, rather than an abandonment of his basic policy.[39] The real effect of the German occupation of Prague was on the position of Churchill.

In the concentration upon the fate of Chamberlain's hopes, sight of Churchill has been somewhat lost – which is a fair representation of the state of affairs at the time. As he had done in 1935 when hoping for office, and in late 1937 when there was no alternative to seeing whether Chamberlain's policy was going to work, Churchill had, since his failures in November to organise an effective 'cave', adopted what would now be called a lower profile. An echo of the Sandys case in early December, when Churchill accused Hore-Belisha of being complacent about anti-aircraft defences, turned into a fiasco when, challenged to substantiate his charges, Churchill read from a series of press extracts which proved irrelevant. One Conservative MP told Nicolson that Churchill was 'becoming an old man'; he preferred the kindlier verdict that Churchill was 'certainly a tiger who, if he misses his spring, is lost'.[40] The problem for the 'tiger' was that there was not much prey.

Churchill supported the Duchess of Atholl in her by-election, but she lost, and he made it plain from the start that his support for her did not mean that he was a disloyal Conservative.[41] One of the Government Whips told him that he really ought to resign the Whip, but Churchill told him 'to go to Hell or Epping'.[42] If Churchill was relatively quiet, it was not only because he did not want to stir up trouble for himself in Epping. His financial situation demanded that he work 'double shifts' at his *History of the English-Speaking Peoples*, which took up much of his time.[43] He watched the Government go through its gloomy moods and witnessed its reviving optimism with scepticism from his Chartwell fastness. He had expected Hitler to move against Poland in February and March,[44] and was not displeased to be proved wrong when he marched into Prague instead. Not the least of the reasons for his pleasure was that he was due to face his executive on 15 March to talk about his attitude towards the Government's foreign policy.

Discontent with their MP's lack of support for the Prime Minister had led some Epping Conservatives to harass Churchill ever since Munich, and by early March there were moves afoot to replace him.[45] He had taken good care to speak in the constituency frequently over the winter, and in a speech in Chigwell on 10 March he had been careful to pay tribute to the 'good effect' produced by Chamberlain's sincere work 'for peace'.[46] Now he was able, triumphantly, to tell his auditors at Waltham Abbey on 14 March that, with Czechoslovakia being 'broken up before our eyes', he had been proved correct when he had prophesied that Munich sealed 'the ruin of Czechoslovakia'. Churchill was prepared to stand as an independent Conservative if he were disowned, but after Prague there was little chance that he would be.[47] Whilst Chamberlain trimmed his sails to the new wind, Churchill's, which were already set in that direction, were filled.

Adversity had taught Churchill not to snatch. Within the Government the influence of Halifax, already large, had been augmented. Chamberlain's initial acceptance of the Nazi action as a *fait accompli* on 15 March in the Commons was superseded by a tougher approach in a speech in Birmingham. Posing (but carefully declining to answer) the rhetorical question of whether Hitler's action was 'a step in a direction to dominate the world by force', Chamberlain announced that he was conferring with France and other powers who knew that 'we are not disinterested in what goes on in South-Eastern Europe'.[48] Now convinced of Hitler's Napoleonic ambitions, Halifax led the Government towards the guarantee which was extended to Poland at the end of the month. It was, for him, a moral stand. For the Prime Minister it was a line in the sand over which he did not think Hitler would tread.[49] For Churchill it was a sign that things were going his way.

Harold Macmillan may have written to *The Times* demanding the creation of a broad-based National Government[50] and have thought Eden 'too soft and gentlemanlike' for not trying to get rid of the 'boneheaded' Chamberlain,[51] but Churchill played an altogether cannier game. With events proving his case for him, he did nothing which could have erected a barrier between him and a place in the Government. At a meeting of the 1922 Committee on 21 March he remained silent whilst others pressed the case for conscription: 'v[ery] much of a politician,' Amery noted, with disapproval.[52] Although he supported a Parliamentary motion on 28 March calling for a National Government,[53] the Polish guarantee reconciled him to Chamberlain's foreign policy.[54] As fresh crises arose in April he kept in close touch with Chamberlain and Halifax,[55] and let his 'strong desire' to enter the Government be known.[56] Following the Italian invasion of Albania on Good Friday, he deluged the Government with advice about the dispositions of the British Fleet and diplomatic action. It was all well meant, but Chamberlain found telephone calls from him at 'almost every hour of the day' rather wearing.[57] The Prime Minister's tough public stance contained ambiguities which he thought useful for dealing with the dictators; taking Churchill into his Cabinet would give out signals which could not be mistaken. Until and unless war became unavoidable, Churchill would remain outside the Government. As Chamberlain told his sisters on 23 April: 'the fact is that the nearer we get to war the more his chances improve and vice versa'.[58]

Thus subsisted the relationship between Churchill and Chamberlain until the eve of war. Churchill's 'confidence that he could work amicably under the PM who had many admirable qualities, some of which he did not possess himself,'[59] was not put to the test. Despite an unprecedented publicity campaign in his favour, with the *Sunday Pictorial* asking on 23 April, 'Why isn't Winston Churchill in the Cabinet?', he remained excluded as long as the Premier thought that war could be avoided. Under pressure from the French and events in the Mediterranean, guarantees were extended to Greece and Romania in mid-April; a few days later Chamberlain announced that a Ministry of Supply would be set up. But, deciding that Churchill would probably 'wear me out ... [with] rash suggestions', Chamberlain appointed Leslie Burgin to the post.[60] The march of events, the logic of the Polish guarantee and the urgings of Halifax forced Chamberlain to open talks with the Russians. The same malevolent 'star' which had juxtaposed Chamberlain's attempts to come to an agreement with Hitler and the Führer's growing conviction that he would need to deal with the British and the French now shone on his attempts to deal with Stalin.

Churchill had long trumpeted the necessity for a Russian alliance, but, lulled by the siren voice of Ivan Maisky and the grandeur of his own vision, he had never stopped to ask what might be the price which Stalin would demand. The Polish Premier, Colonel Beck, told Chamberlain in April that it would be 'dangerous to bring Russia into any discussions',[61] a view shared by the newly guaranteed Romanians.[62] It soon transpired that Churchill's view that geographical propinquity and ideological necessity would suffice to persuade the Soviets to enter an alliance had been wide of the mark. The mainsprings of Soviet policy remain in some obscurity, but Stalin was aware of the dangers which would threaten him if the wicked imperialists directed the Nazis towards the east.[63] His mind was open to the possibility of a pact with the Nazis even as Chamberlain's first, hesitant overtures began in late April. What Stalin wanted could, in truth, be more easily delivered by another robber baron than by the Prime Minister of a democratic state. For all Churchill's criticisms of the slow progress of the Anglo-Russian talks, what they foundered on were demands from Stalin which raised suspicions (already abundantly present in any case) about his motives. Why did he insist that the guarantee to Poland should only operate against Germany? Colonel Beck could have provided an answer, which would have wrecked any chance of Anglo-Polish co-operation and perhaps pushed him towards an accommodation with the Nazis.[64]

The problem for Chamberlain was that although he had not thought so at the time, the Polish guarantee had, in effect, nailed his trousers firmly to the mast. Originally the guarantee had not been meant to include areas such as the free city of Danzig, which was under League of Nations supervision,[65] and it certainly had not been meant to give the Poles a free hand, but rather to reassure Beck that he would not be served as Beneš had been and to warn the Germans that this was the case. The hope still was that Hitler would be deterred by the simulacrum of an alliance.[66] An unequivocal commitment to a Soviet alliance would have dispelled the necessary element of ambiguity, and it might have wrecked the diplomatic front formed with Poland and Romania. It was only in the summer that the Cabinet overcame its collective mistrust of the Russian proposals, but by then it was too late.

Their different reactions to the prospect of a Russian alliance indicated the differences which still divided the Prime Minister from Churchill. The former approached it hesitantly and with many misgivings, fearful of its effects upon both the Poles and the Germans, and anxious lest it make war more rather than less likely. Churchill embraced it with a will, ignoring the objections of both the Poles and many Conservatives, convinced that it would make war less rather than more likely. In a broadcast to America on 28 April, he attributed any recent improvements in Hitler's behaviour to the deterrent effect of the Government's new foreign policy and to Anglo-French solidarity.[67] In the preface to the latest collection of his articles, *Step by Step*, Churchill wrote on 21 May of his 'gratification' that the Government 'have at length by leisurely progress along their own paths of thought, adopted even in detail the policy and theme set forth'.[68] In this he was over-sanguine, for the Prime Minister continued to hope that there could be 'permanent peace between this country and Germany'.[69] Churchill picked up such intimations with alarm, taking the view that there could be no further negotiations with the Germans until the 'character of the present Nazi Regime shall have undergone a fundamental change'.[70]

The fact that Churchill was more willing to contemplate war than Chamberlain was does not necessarily imply, as one account has it, that he actually wanted a war;[71] although his conviction that a war to preserve the balance of power did come, at times, perilously close to being a self-fulfilling prophecy. His conviction that Britain would emerge victorious from any such conflict was, according to the taste of the auditor, frightening or awesome. At a dinner with the noted American political correspondent, Walter Lippmann, Churchill chided him for the defeatist precepts held by the American Ambassador, Joseph Kennedy, father of the future President. There would, he declared, waving his drink in one hand and his cigar in the other, be 'dire perils and fierce ordeals', but 'trials and disasters' would serve only to 'steel the resolution of the British people and to enhance our will for victory'.[72] Churchill could not imagine that the German Army could 'pierce' the 'French carapace' of the Maginot Line, and he could not see how, with a hostile central Europe and Russia at his back, Hitler could successfully prosecute a war.[73] Should the worst happen, and should Britain fall, then he looked to the Americans 'to preserve and to maintain the great heritage of the English-speaking peoples'.

In these phrases can be traced the whole of Churchill's grand design and vision. The events of the next year would shake it, but it was too deeply a part of him to be uprooted. If the 'French carapace' was pierced, then the will of the English people would stand any ordeal, until the Americans entered the war – the advent to which would be short. This vision sustained him, and through him created the steely resolution which, along with the want of any German invasion plans, sustained the nation until, at length, there was a glimmer of light in the west. That that light was long in coming, and that the day it beckoned was different to the one Churchill had envisioned, was another chapter to a story which had an ending he had not expected. But without faith in it and without the inner vision here revealed, there would have been no 'finest hour'.[74]

With the rumour factory pouring forth its products and the growth of a conviction that there might be a 'crisis' over Poland in the late summer, Chamberlain was not lacking advice to fire a warning shot across Hitler's bows by taking Churchill into the Cabinet. Posters asking 'What price Churchill?' appeared in July, and support for the idea, at least in the popular press, was strong.[75] But Chamberlain held to the old (if cruel) adage that 'there are more ways of killing a cat than strangling it', and if he refused 'to take Winston into the Cabinet to please those who say it will frighten Hitler', it did not follow that 'the idea of frightening Hitler, or rather of convincing him that it would not pay him to use force, need be abandoned'. Chamberlain thought Hitler was aware that 'we mean business' and that the only question in his mind was whether the British would 'attack him as soon as we are strong enough'. Mussolini had been warned that if Hitler attacked Danzig, 'it will mean starting the European war'.

Chamberlain himself now doubted whether 'any solution short of war' was 'practicable at present', but if the dictators would 'have a modicum of patience', he could 'imagine that a way could be found of meeting German claims while safeguarding Poland's independence'.[76]

If Chamberlain remained unwilling to bring Churchill back for fear of tipping the delicate balance between war and peace in the direction of the former, the very existence of that balance helped to restore Churchill's fortunes elsewhere. The willingness of Halifax to address a meeting of 'The Focus' in the spring had been a sign that the Foreign Secretary was not unconscious of the need to make the contacts which might yet be required to restore to the Government those 'national credentials' which Chamberlain's conduct of foreign policy had eroded.[77] The speech with which Churchill introduced Halifax at a meeting of the 1900 Club on 21 June was a clear indication to the Foreign Secretary that there was now more common ground between them than ever before. Not even in his comments about India did Churchill venture a criticism of Halifax. As to foreign policy: 'If differences remain, they will only be upon emphasis and method, upon timing and degree.'[78] The rapprochement with Halifax was accompanied by one with Eden,[79] and with sections of the Labour Party, as they came together over the necessity of a Russian alliance.[80] Chamberlain rejected suggestions that either Churchill or Eden might be sent to Moscow to expedite the long-drawn-out negotiations. This he saw as the first step towards the duo being restored to the Cabinet and 'perhaps later on the substitution of a more amenable Prime Minister'.[81]

Despite the growing press campaign for Churchill's recall, with the *Daily Telegraph* joining in the cry in a leading article on 3 July, Chamberlain remained unwilling to take Churchill into his Cabinet until the crisis which both men had feared would arise over Danzig actually did so; indeed, it was not until that crisis entered its acute stage that overtures were made to Churchill. Chamberlain's attitude was the result not only of worry about the reaction of Hitler to such a move, but also of Churchill's tendency to 'monopolise the time of the whole Ministry', and he did not feel that, at present, he would 'gain sufficiently from Winston's ideas and advice to counterbalance the irritation and disturbance which would necessarily be caused'.[82] But the Prime Minister's comments left no doubt that Churchill had eclipsed in importance any other dissident, including, to the evident displeasure of some of his acolytes, Eden.[83]

But popularity with the press and the general public was not the same as popularity inside the Conservative Party, and despite the great press campaign of June and July, Hoare still reckoned that 'four out of five' Conservative backbenchers would vote against Churchill's inclusion in the Cabinet.[84] Churchill, convinced that the final crisis was coming, bided his time.[85] He and the Prime Minister exchanged sharp words at the end of the Parliamentary session when Churchill supported a Labour motion calling for the Commons to reassemble on 21 August. This was prompted by the fear amongst some dissidents that Chamberlain would 'do another Munich'[86] over Danzig, once the House was in recess. Churchill stated that he could not trust the Prime Minister's judgment, to which Chamberlain delivered the obvious '*tu quoque*' retort. According to the Prime Minister, this annoyed Churchill so much that he 'actually went out of his way to associate himself with Sinclair's fatuous & imbecile proposition that if Parliament had met earlier last September', Czechoslovakia could have been saved. Chamberlain disputed this, which left Churchill in a state of 'red fury'. The fact that by the morrow Churchill was saying words in support of the Prime Minister's appeasement of Japan did not reassure Chamberlain: 'That is Winston all over. His are summer storms, violent but of short duration and usually followed by sunshine. But they make him uncommonly difficult to deal with.'[87]

Eden had not supported Churchill's line on 2 August. He and 'the Glamour boys' were, like others, increasingly worried by the prospect of an autumn election. If the summer passed with only the usual alarums and excursions, Chamberlain's critics faced the unpleasant prospect of an autumn general election. Few expected Chamberlain to follow Baldwin's precedent of 1929 by going to the end of the Parliament, which would mean a 1940 election. Whilst Eden and company pondered about what they should do in such an eventuality and what their relations with Churchill should be, Churchill took himself off to see the Maginot Line.[88] But news of the Nazi–Soviet pact, announced on 21 August, brought him back to London in time for the emergency debate called by Chamberlain for 24 August.

Churchill's main concern was that the Government did not try to back away from the commitment to the Poles.[89] Chamberlain, whilst hoping Hitler would back down, had no intention of 'doing a Munich'; indeed, any doubts about his resolution to support Beck would have vitiated this hope. On 1 September the Germans invaded Poland. The Commons was summoned to meet that evening, but, in accordance with the view that the nearer the country approached war the more Churchill's chances of entering the Cabinet improved, Chamberlain asked him to join a small War Cabinet.[90]

The news of Churchill's appointment helped to still fears that the Government intended to desert the Poles, and gave Chamberlain breathing-space, which was much needed in view of the reluctance of the French to take any action. Expectations were high on 2 September that there would be an announcement of an ultimatum to the Germans; instead, that evening Chamberlain told the House that he and the French were still considering what time-limit to attach to any ultimatum in view of the fact that Mussolini had suggested holding a conference on Poland. With the House in uproar, Amery cried 'speak for England', when Labour's deputy leader, Arthur Greenwood, rose.[91] Faced with the choice between browbeating the French and facing the Commons in such a mood on the morrow, the Cabinet, in effect, staged a revolt, demanding that 'in no circumstance should the expiry of the ultimatum go beyond noon tomorrow'. Faced with the choice between browbeating the French and a Cabinet revolt, Chamberlain chose the same option which his colleagues had: the French were told that if, by noon on 3 September, the Germans had not begun to withdraw from Poland, a state of war would be deemed to exist.[92]

Unlike some of Chamberlain's opponents, Churchill kept his head amidst the tensions. He asked Chamberlain for more information, but sympathised with the difficult position in which he found himself. Churchill's main concern was that Chamberlain would make no announcement about the War Cabinet's composition until the two men had talked. He wanted Eden and other 'national' elements included in the Government, but acknowledged that if Labour and the Liberals refused to come in, it would have to be a largely Conservative administration.[93] The fact that the Liberals and Labour would not come in with Chamberlain greatly restricted Churchill's freedom of manoeuvre. Boothby wanted Churchill to 'break' Chamberlain, whilst Eden was unhappy that his decorous opposition had been rewarded with a lesser prize than Churchill had received, but the news of the Cabinet revolt quieted some of the anxieties.[94]

At eleven o'clock on the morning of 3 September Chamberlain announced that Britain was at war. As the House convened Churchill felt 'a very strong sense of calm' come over him.[95] He spoke with sympathy of the Prime Minister's efforts to preserve the peace, and stirringly of the task which lay ahead. Giving rein to the vision which had sustained him throughout the 1930s, he said that they were not fighting for Poland or Danzig, but 'to save the whole world from the pestilence of Nazi tyranny'.[96] It was a stronger speech than that given by the Prime Minister, who did not sound, according to Boothby, as though he meant to lead the country through the war.[97] Amery thought that he would probably yield the lead to Churchill within the year.[98] After the debate Churchill went to see Chamberlain, who offered him a place in the War Cabinet as First Lord of the Admiralty. The message went out to the Fleet: 'Winston is back.'[99] And so he was.

From the days of the Lloyd George coalition Churchill had come to nurse a distrust of what he once termed the 'failed twentieth century'. It had come to seem to him that the age in which he was living was one in which the great heritage bequeathed by generations of British heroes was being dissipated. He sought around for the causes and found them variously in universal democracy and the sort of leaders which it fostered. Baldwin and Chamberlain were, he came to hold, small men, unfit to wear the mantle of Elizabeth I, Cromwell, Marlborough, Chatham, the Younger Pitt and the other heroes of his long chronicle of English history. His feeling that the heritage of the past was slipping away was correct, but his diagnosis of why was too simple by half.

The imperial and foreign policies pursued by successive Governments had been inspired by a desire to hold on to what could be held on to with limited resources. As Churchill had found when Chancellor, the demands of social reform at home were urgent and the temptations to save money on defence policy were great. The British Empire was, as Chamberlain realised, in a precarious position.

To fight a war was, in a sense, already to have lost it. The British rearmament effort peaked in 1939, and the country could not easily have sustained the current burden of spending for much longer. This made it both easier and imperative for Chamberlain to be 'tough' in September. But Britain faced a grave problem. Militarily she and France were planning for a long war. They would remain on the defensive and use the Maginot Line and the blockade to strangle the German economy. Perhaps Hitler would be brought down when the Germans realised that they could not win a long war. But could the Allies? One reason for Chamberlain's hesitancy in spending too much money on armaments too soon was the fear that the 'fourth arm' of defence, the economy, would be unduly weakened thereby. Economically the Allies were not well-equipped to win the long war for which they were militarily prepared.

Unable to win a short war, unable to sustain a long one, here was the dilemma of an Empire whose resources and home-base failed to provide an adequate support. Churchill had long excoriated lesser men for lack of willpower, convinced that this was at the basis of British weakness. But was the lack of willpower a cause or effect? Had men come to lack the will to power because they lacked the means to it? What were the limits of willpower when faced with the economic 'realities behind diplomacy'? Could the force of the human will prevail against the tides of history – or was the man who made the effort doomed to a Canute-like impotence? With 'Winston . . . back', the question which Churchill had posed throughout the 1930s was to be answered.

III

'The Trumpet's Silver Sound'

1939–45

33

Churchill and Chamberlain: II

To one of his former opponents who wrote to apologise and congratulate him Churchill replied, 'so far as I am concerned the past is dead'.[1] What Baldwin once called Churchill's 'sentimental side',[2] allied with the dictates of political necessity, imposed, for the moment, a statute of limitations on the deeds of the past. But if Churchill wanted to forget about the past and get on with the war, that was not so easily done for others. Hankey, who was brought into the Cabinet as Minister without Portfolio, found that his 'main job is to keep an eye on Winston!'[3] The 'carbuncle' factor was to loom large throughout the next eight months. At a personal level the Prime Minister and his new First Lord got on well enough, but their methods of working, their personalities and their very different conceptions of what the next stage of the war involved made friction inevitable.

For Chamberlain, 'life' was 'just one long nightmare'.[4] In his element striving to save peace, he was out of it fighting a war – and he knew it: 'How I hate and loathe this war. I was never meant to be a War Minister.'[5] Churchill, by contrast, knew that if there was one thing which he had been meant to be it was 'a War Minister'. If he did not coin the phrase 'the phoney war', it certainly summed up his attitude to the first phase of the war against Germany. As he galvanised the staff at the Admiralty in search of plans which would allow the British to dominate the Baltic and looked for the most expeditious way of striking at the 'Hun', Churchill revealed not only the same bellicose spirit and over-optimism which had marked his behaviour in 1914,[6] but he also demonstrated a profound misunderstanding of the Prime Minister's strategy.

Chamberlain was not looking for a 'shooting war'. It was not simply that he regarded the possibility with dread, he did not think that it would be necessary. 'Time', he believed, 'is with us.'[7] His plan was to 'hold on tight, keep up the economic pressure, push on with munitions production and military preparations with the utmost energy', but to take 'no offensive unless Hitler begins it'.[8] The main offensive to be resisted was the 'peace offensive', by which Chamberlain expected Hitler to try to escape from a position fraught with peril for Germany.[9] After all, that diplomacy which had failed to avert war had prevailed at least far enough to lessen the number of enemies faced by the Allies. The French had always been concerned with the possibility of the Italian front, and Allied war plans contained provisions for taking the

offensive in North Africa whilst lying on the defensive in Europe; but Mussolini had not entered the war. With Allied military strength nearing its peak,
the only comfort which Hitler could take was from the speed of his conquest
of western Poland and his pact with Stalin; but whether that would hold now
that the fourth partition of Poland had given the two dictators a common
frontier was a matter for speculation. The German economy was known to
be weakened by the scale of the rearmament effort and, whilst the Polish
campaign had been swift, it had placed an extra strain on the 'fourth arm' of
warfare. To win the war Hitler would have to launch an assault in the
west, where he would be greeted by the impregnable Maginot Line and an
Anglo-French army, which was larger than his and which had at its disposal
more tanks and aircraft than the Germans could command. This was not a
position which Chamberlain wished to put at hazard by any wild scheme
emanating from the Churchillian stable of mares' nests.

When Chamberlain had been considering whether to invite Churchill into
the Cabinet in April, one of his reasons for hesitating had been the fear that
he would 'wear me out resisting rash suggestions'.[10] His previous experience
of working with Churchill had not led him to the conclusion that including
him in the Cabinet 'would make his own task any easier'. It was true that he
liked to run his Cabinet on a tighter rein than Baldwin had ever done, but
that in itself posed a problem.[11] In his Cabinet reshuffles Chamberlain had
shown two kinds of preference: for 'experts' and for what the unkind might
have termed 'yes men'. The appointment of a skilled civil servant and former
Governor of Bengal, Sir John Anderson, as Lord Privy Seal after Munich, and
of Admiral Lord Chatfield to co-ordinate defence and Sir Reginald Dorman-
Smith to Agriculture in January 1939, all fell into the first category; those of
Runciman and Lord Stanhope after Munich, and Winterton, Burgin and
Shakes Morrison in January, might all be assigned to the latter category. The
Cabinet contained no powerful figure in the Commons who might be a rival
to Chamberlain. Hoare was damaged political goods, whilst Sir John Simon
was a National Liberal, whose political antecedents and personality ruled him
out for the succession quite as effectively as did the character and the peerage
of the only senior Minister with real stature of his own, Viscount Halifax.
This comfortable situation was disturbed by Churchill's advent to the Cabinet.

That Chamberlain was not unmindful of the political balance of power is
demonstrated by his reaction to the imminent outbreak of war. His offer to
Churchill had skilfully denied his opponents their most powerful weapon at
a time when his Government was at its most vulnerable. Once the hurdle
had been negotiated, Churchill was offered a post which was prestigious
enough to accept but which would, it was hoped, keep him fully occupied.
The rest of his opponents Chamberlain treated, frankly, with contempt. Eden
was not sent for until 3 September, when he was offered the post of Dominions
Secretary, outside the War Cabinet. By accepting this 'humiliating offer',

Eden took the path which Austen Chamberlain had taken in 1924, thus acknowledging that he did not have in him the stuff of which leaders are made.[12] Cut off at once from his 'Glamour boys' and influence on policy, Eden sank with little trace. For the rest, to his evident dismay, Amery remained in the wilderness, where he proved a fustian leader for the erstwhile 'Glamour boys', and Duff Cooper was left to cool his heels.[13]

Chamberlain had managed to divide his opponents and he continued to rule; if his strategy proved successful, there was no reason why he should not continue in this felicitous situation. The War Cabinet was, with the exception of Churchill, a body which well-reflected Chamberlain's preferences when reshuffling Cabinets: apart from the other members of the 'big four' (Halifax, Hoare and Simon), Chatfield, co-ordinating defence, and Hankey as Minister without Portfolio were 'experts', whilst Sir Kingsley Wood at the Air Ministry seemed to embody, in his own Pickwickian person, the very model of the 'yes man'. Hore-Belisha at the War Office fitted comfortably into neither category, which was perhaps one of the reasons he was the first member to go. But Chamberlain had had no choice other than to take Churchill into the Cabinet in a senior post. Stanhope, who had been unceremoniously ejected from the Admiralty to make way for Churchill, nursed a not uncommon hope that Churchill might not 'stay the course of administrative work after years of soft living' – a hope stimulated by the story that his first action on arriving at Admiralty House had been to order a bottle of whisky. But Amery was right in thinking that this underrated Churchill's 'power of nervous output and will power'.[14]

It could be said of Churchill, as Macaulay said of Lord Mordaunt, that 'the age had produced no more inventive genius, and no more daring spirit. But, if a design was splendid, Mordaunt seldom inquired whether it were practicable.'[15] It would be unfair to say that Churchill did not enquire whether his ideas were practicable – he spent a good deal of his staff's time doing precisely that – but he had not lost his old ability to magnify the chances of success whilst minimising the possibility of failure of any scheme upon which his favour fell. It was at this point that the quality of his staff and the nature of his relationship with them became important. During the Great War he had dominated his staff, and even the extrovert Fisher had felt in awe of his tongue and quick wits. This situation had contributed materially to what had happened at the Dardanelles. There is some dispute amongst historians as to whether Churchill once more dominated his advisers, with some holding that he more or less 'rode roughshod' over the First Sea Lord, Sir Dudley Pound, and others arguing for a more coeval relationship.[16]

The truth is not found in 'the middle' quite as often as historians are fond of believing, and during Churchill's nine months at the Admiralty the evidence suggests that if the pejorative implications of 'rode roughshod' are replaced by 'dominated', then the new First Lord did dominate the Admiralty. The style had changed. The abrasive and bumptious young man of 1914, whose self-confidence in his own expertise was not shared by older admirals, had given way to an elder statesman whose experience of the last war and prestige were unquestioned. He was 'far more mellow, far less abusive and over-bearing' than he had been.[17] He made it clear from the start that his 'ideas' were submitted for 'criticism and correction',[18] but it still took a brave man to offer either. This was not necessarily because Churchill overbore criticism; it was simply a function of the difference between him and his staff. Churchill would not, as the official historian puts it, 'readily take no for an answer. Using his great powers of argument he could bring extreme pressure to bear on his advisers.' He was loath to overrule advisers who stood firmly by their position with reasoned arguments: 'But it was important that they should stand firm.'[19] This was not easy in the face of the torrent of eloquence with which the First Lord would defend what some of his staff came to call his 'notions'.[20]

The first of these 'notions' was mentioned by Churchill to Admiral Pound on 6 September and outlined by him in a paper of 12 September. The attitude of the Cabinet towards the war was cruelly caricatured by Louis Spears in his memoirs, when he recorded Sir Kingsley Wood replying to Amery's suggestion of bombing the Black Forest with the immortal words: 'Are you aware it is private property?'[21] In fact, Sir Kingsley actually told Amery that the Government would not bomb civilian areas for fear of alienating American opinion,[22] which was a perfectly sensible answer; but any stick would do to beat the appeasers. The Government's reluctance to take any action was all part of the Allied strategy of sitting it out and waiting for Hitler either to collapse or to bang his head on the Maginot Line. But this was not how Churchill waged war. His paper of 12 September was an echo of Fisher's old King Charles's head – an invasion of the Baltic. 'Operation Catherine' provided for a naval attack in the Baltic, which would cut Germany's communications with Norway and Sweden, thus depriving her of essential iron-ore supplies. It was an imaginative conception, but it ignored the advent of air power. Churchill's confident assertion that the mere arrival of the force in the Baltic would 'probably determine' the entry of Denmark, Sweden and Norway into the war on the Allied side,[23] was rather too reminiscent for comfort of his belief in 1915 that the sight of a British squadron in the Sea of Marmora would cause the Turkish Government to collapse.

This attitude lay at the base of many of Churchill's miscalculations during the war. Bellicose and courageous himself, he was apt to attribute these same qualities to others without regard to their circumstances or to the interests of other powers. It was this attitude which was to lead him to sanction de Gaulle's 'Operation Menace', with its assumption that the mere appearance of British ships off the coast of Freetown would persuade French West Africa to rally to the Allied side. It was this same optimism which, *mutatis mutandis*,

A misleadingly sober-looking Lord Randolph

An equally unusually stern-looking Lady Randolph

The young lieutenant of the 4th Hussars, hoping to steer clear of financial ruin and on to glory, 1895

The war correspondent who finally made the news, 1899

The two War Lords: Kitchener and Fisher

The fallen Minister with his successor, the languid Arthur Balfour,
1915

On the way out, 1915: Winston and Clementine

A sombre-looking Churchill at the front
with Sir Archibald Sinclair, 1916

WINSTON'S BAG

HE HUNTS LIONS AND BRINGS HOME DECAYED CATS

Recovering office if not reputation:
a contemporary view of Churchill, 1920

THE FIGHT FOR THE FAVOURITE.

Mr. Lloyd George. "HERE, I SAY, THIS IS MY MOUNT."
Mr. Winston Churchill. "NO, IT ISN'T. I THOUGHT OF IT FIRST."

Scrambling back into the saddle: Lloyd George and
Churchill vie for the anti-socialist ticket, 1924

Back in favour, 1929. Churchill (with Bob Boothby behind him) links arms with Clementine on Budget Day. They are accompanied by Sarah and Randolph.

Living from mouth to hand: Churchill checking his proofs, February 1939

Friends and enemies in the Wilderness Years: Duff Cooper and Baldwin

The long and short of it: Churchill badgers Halifax
at the time of the *Anschluss*, March 1938

Winston is back at the door of Admiralty House, 1939

In the War Cabinet, 1939. Left to right, back row: Sir Kingsley Wood, Churchill,
Leslie Hore-Belisha, Sir Maurice Hankey (Cabinet Secretary); front row: Lord Halifax,
Sir John Simon, Neville Chamberlain (Prime Minister), Sir Samuel Hoare, Lord Chatfield,
with the 3rd Marquess of Salisbury looking down disapprovingly, as well he might.

THE EMBLEMATIC WAR LEADER, Churchill mythologised: the legendary war leader looking imposing for both contemporaries and posterity, in the famous photograph by Karsh of Ottawa, 1941

His own War Cabinet, 1940. Left to right, back row: Arthur Greenwood, Ernest Bevin, Lord Beaverbrook, Sir Kingsley Wood; front row: Sir John Anderson, Churchill, Clement Attlee, Anthony Eden.

'Getting mixed up together': the first Churchill and Roosevelt wartime meeting, October 1941.

Prime Minister at work and play, 1941. Left to right: Novikouv (Soviet Counsellor), Soubbotitch (Yugoslav Minister), Masaryk (Czechoslovak Foreign Minister), Lisicky (Czechoslovak Chargé d'Affaires), Nincic (Yugoslav Foreign Minister), Raczinski (Polish Foreign Minister), Eden, Spaak (Belgian Foreign Minister), General Sikorski (Polish Premier), Simopoulos (Greek Minister), Churchill, Pierlot (Belgian Premier), Winant (US Ambassador), Nygaardsvold (Norwegian Premier), Maisky (Soviet Ambassador), General Simovitch (Yugoslav Premier), Dr Wellington Koo.

FOR AULD LANG SYNE: Churchill and his old chief Lloyd George in December 1942 with Megan Lloyd George and Oliver Lyttelton looking on

Becoming marginalised: Churchill looks on as Roosevelt and Chiang Kai-shek contemplate the Pacific War, Cairo 1943

Warlords at play: Roosevelt, Churchill and Stalin at the Tehran conference, 1943

Paris liberated: Churchill with the 'Cross of Lorraine', General de Gaulle, November 1944. Bringing up the rear: Anthony Eden and the Ambassador to France, Duff Cooper.

Squeezed out: Churchill wearily watches the ailing Roosevelt and the enigmatic Stalin. Behind them are Sir Andrew Cunningham (First Sea Lord), Lord Portal (Chief of the Air Staff), and Roosevelt's Chief of Staff, Admiral Leahy, February 1945.

To the victors the triumph. Left to right: Major-General McLain, Field Marshal Montgomery, Churchill, Major-General Gillom, Field Marshal Sir Alan Brooke, and General Simpson at the Citadel Fortress of Julich, 1945.

By popular acclamation: the victorious leader receives the plaudits of the crowds, 8 May 1945. Left to right: Oliver Lyttelton, Ernest Bevin, Churchill, Sir John Anderson, Lord Woolton and Herbert Morrison.

OUR SKIPPER: a Conservative Party pin-up poster from 1950

led him to think that the German bombing of England's heritage would bring America into the war, and that Marshal Pétain and General Weygand were just waiting to join the Allied side in 1942. It was this short-term obsession with doing anything which might help the immediate war effort which led Churchill to believe that America and Russia shared his war aims.

On this occasion, when it came to helping Finland, Churchill's ingenious optimism led Pound and the naval Staff a merry dance for some months. Doubting the practicability of 'Catherine', Pound did not like to say 'No'. Instead, he told Churchill that the operation would only be practicable if Russia did not join the Germans, and if Britain had the '*active* co-operation of Sweden' for the 'supply of oil and the use of a base and her repair facilities'; any plan must also deal with the air menace.[24] Churchill agreed, stressing that it was all 'only for exploration', 'but the search for a naval offensive must be incessant'.[25] This obsession with using 'ships alone' showed how little Churchill had taken on board either the lessons of 1915, or the development of air power. In pursuit of his objective, Churchill appointed Admiral of the Fleet the Earl of Cork and Orrery, as Commander-in-Chief designate and put him in charge of planning for 'Catherine'. His plan required a larger force than that envisaged by Churchill, but the date of 15 February was set for 'Catherine' to begin. But the modifications which needed to be made to the ships which were available, and the unavailability of others, meant pushing the date back to the end of March.[26] The more the plan was studied, the more sceptical did the Admiralty become. Pound doubted whether the Nazi–Soviet pact made the scheme at all feasible and, in early December, advocated halting all work on it.[27]

In view of developments in the war, particularly the Soviet attack on eastern Poland and the invasion of Finland in November, it might have appeared that there was much to recommend Pound's advice. But Churchill would have none of it: 'An absolute defensive is for weaker forces,' he told Pound on 5 December.[28] Indeed, the situation of Russia, which so worried Pound, was so far from worrying Churchill that he regarded the possible recruitment of the Scandinavian states into a conflict against the Soviets as a positive advantage, as he told the Cabinet on 11 December.[29] Writing to Pound the same day Churchill waxed optimistic: 'It may be that we may find ourselves at war with Russia, and Allies of Sweden, Norway, Finland and Italy,' in which case the Baltic would be 'of capital importance' and Britain would need to have plans. Even if, as he admitted was more likely, the situation 'remained obscure', and even if, as Pound stated, shipping losses and other commitments made 'Catherine' unlikely, Churchill could 'never become responsible for a naval strategy which excluded the offensive principle'.[30] So the planning went on, and it was not until 15 January that Churchill finally accepted that the operation was unlikely ever to occur, by which time its cost 'in wasted hours had been prodigious'.[31]

Churchill's desire to take the offensive, and his habit of quoting in aid of his 'notions' his previous experience in long memoranda, all took a toll upon the patience of both the Prime Minister and his colleagues. Hoare told Beaverbrook on 1 October that Churchill had been 'Much as you expected he would be, very rhetorical, very emotional and, most of all, very reminiscent. He strikes me as an old man who easily gets tired.' But all this was seen only by his colleagues, and, as Hoare acknowledged, he had a 'very big position' in 'the Country'.[32] His speech in the House on 28 September had gone down markedly better than had Chamberlain's uninspiring effort,[33] and he was, as Hoare told Beaverbrook, 'the one popular figure in the Cabinet'. But not necessarily with his colleagues. John (Jock) Colville, Chamberlain's private secretary, noted that he seemed 'too old' to provide the 'younger, forceful successor' to Chamberlain which would be required if the war was to be won.[34] Colville considered him 'too unstable' to be a possible Prime Minister,[35] a view with which others were inclined to concur.

The oratory which had for long been almost Churchill's only weapon was now to be mobilised in the service of the war. The problem here was that his ideas were somewhat more robust than the Government – which was still looking for a peaceful end to the war – cared for. On 12 November he gave a talk on the radio which was broadcast to a world audience. Setting aside his past differences with the Prime Minister, Churchill declared:

I can tell you that he is going to fight as obstinately for victory as he did for peace. You may take it absolutely for certain that either all that Britain and France stand for in the modern world will go down, or that Hitler, the Nazi regime and the recurring German or Prussian menace will be broken and destroyed.

Now to a Government which was still hoping to divide Hitler from the German people and even other Nazis, such a message was not at all what was wanted. 'Time', he declared, in a sentence which might have been lifted from one of Chamberlain's letters, 'is on our side', and he was bold enough to assert that 'if we come through the winter without any large or important event occurring we shall in fact have gained the first campaign of the war'. With 'Nazi Germany barred off from the east', she had to 'conquer the British Empire and the French Republic or perish in the attempt'; and as the Nazis looked out from their 'blatant, panoplied, clattering' Germany, they could not discern 'one single friendly eye in the whole circumference of the globe': 'the whole world is against Hitler and Hitlerism'.[36]

It was all good stirring stuff, showing in the final section that optimism which was so often to lead Churchill astray, but without which he would have been unable to lead the nation anywhere. But to Rab Butler it was 'beyond words vulgar',[37] and Chamberlain thought that it had done 'incalculable harm' in offending neutral powers like Holland and Belgium, who, Churchill had implied, were next on Hitler's shopping list.[38] But there was no question of doing anything more than trying to persuade Churchill to tone down his speeches. Churchill's position was not unlike that which Kitchener had occupied in the last war. He was taken by the nation as a symbol of the determination to win the war, and if he was damaged in the eyes of the public, then the war effort and the reputation of the Government would suffer accordingly. Just as Asquith had had to hang on to Kitchener once he had elected to shelter behind him, so too did the Prime Minister have to hang on to Churchill once he had chosen to take him into the Government. And, unlike Kitchener, Churchill could be a very formidable Parliamentary opponent if crossed.

With one or two exceptions, Chamberlain and Churchill rubbed along well enough as colleagues. Both of them were agreed in rejecting Hitler's offer on 6 October of a negotiated peace, and both men agreed to keep up the diplomatic offensive to persuade Mussolini to stay out of the war.[39] It says something about their relationship that they should have dined together, with their respective wives, at Admiralty House on 13 November; but it says even more that this should have been the first such occasion in their long acquaintance-ship. Churchill had his 'only intimate social conversation' with Chamberlain, and learnt with some surprise the story of how, in his youth, he had spent five years of his life trying to grow sisal in the West Indies. As he listened, Churchill thought to himself: 'What a pity Hitler did not know when he met this sober English politician with his umbrella . . . that he was actually talking to a hard-bitten politician from the outer marches of the British Empire!'[40]

There were times when Churchill's belligerency could become a positive nuisance, and ironically it was Eden who was one of the first Ministers to suffer from this. Of all the British Dominions, only Eire, under the leadership of De Valera, declined to enter the war. Between the Fascist fire and the British fire-brigade, De Valera proclaimed that he was neutral, an attitude which he was to push to the extent of being one of the few heads of state to extend condolences to Admiral Doenitz on the sad occasion of Hitler's untimely demise. Churchill had denounced the 1938 treaty which had relinquished control of Irish naval bases, and he rejected angrily Eden's suggestion that there was nothing which the Government could do if the Irish declined to let the British use the bases. Legally, he told Halifax on 22 October, 'I believe they are at war but skulking.'[41] At Cabinet on 24 October he advocated challenging the 'constitutional position' of the neutrality of the 'so-called Eire'. He even suggested that Britain might have to 'insist' on using the bases. Eden was horrified at the idea, and there was no opposition to Chamberlain's summing up in his favour of leaving the Irish alone.[42] Eden thought that Churchill's attitude over Eire and any constitutional changes in India both showed such 'bad judgement' that he was 'beginning to doubt whether Churchill could ever be PM'.[43]

Churchill's eyes were too firmly fixed on the war for him to worry about

377

becoming Prime Minister. As a member of the War Cabinet, he did not consider that his attention had to be confined to his own department, and he took upon himself a watching brief with regard to other matters – something which caused some irritation to his colleagues, and especially to a Prime Minister who had been a great advocate of confining his Ministers to their own kennels. He made this intention plain from the start, politely telling Halifax on 10 September that he hoped he would not 'mind my drawing your attention from time to time to points which strike me in the Foreign Office telegrams'; it was, he said in a pointed postscript, 'so much better than that I should raise them in Cabinet'.[44] But his willingness to offer his colleagues the benefit of 'experience and knowledge, which were bought, not taught,' could become irritating. 'He is writing his new memoirs,' one colleague told Hoare, after listening to a long monologue from Churchill,[45] and the Prime Minister felt that some of Churchill's long minutes were written more for 'quotation in the Book that he will write hereafter' than for any other purpose.[46]

In his memoirs Churchill quotes a long memorandum written to Chamberlain on 1 October which shows his concern about the size of both the Army and the Air Force as well as his worries about defence against air raids.[47] Chamberlain, suspecting that this would indeed be where the memo ended up, sent for Churchill. The two men had a 'very frank talk', and Chamberlain referred to the similarity between what was in the memorandum and what was in the newspapers. Churchill 'withdrew his letter and promised to write no more'. He disclaimed any desire to intrigue against the Prime Minister and said that 'his sole desire was to help me win the war'.[48] There could be no doubt about the last point, but the long memoranda, destined for the war memoirs, did not cease; nor did the thirst to take the offensive. 'Operation Catherine' may have been a dead letter by the middle of January, but Churchill's restless imagination had been fixed upon Scandinavia as a theatre of operations where a decisive blow might be struck by the Allies against the Nazis; the fact that Norway, Sweden and Denmark were neutral was no bar, in his eyes, against taking action there.

At the same time as 'Operation Catherine' was under consideration, Churchill was also considering plans to mine the Leads. These were ice-free Norwegian territorial waters within a chain of outlying islands along which German iron-ore traffic travelled. If they could be mined, the transport of iron-ore from Narvik to Germany could be disrupted. This would, of course, infringe Norwegian neutrality, but Churchill brushed aside such considerations by pointing out that by using this route the Germans themselves were abusing Norwegian neutrality. However, his colleagues were a good deal more scrupulous than he was, and it was not until the Russian attack on Finland in November that a climate existed in which he could press his demands. There was considerable support inside the Cabinet for urging Norway and

Sweden to allow men and equipment across their territory to help the gallant Finns, and if Narvik were used as a base for this, it would be easy to prevent the Germans using it as an *entrepôt* for their iron-ore supplies from Gällivare in Sweden.[49] 'Small nations', he told his colleagues on 16 December, 'must not tie our hands when we are fighting for their rights and freedom.'[50] Four days later, at a meeting of the Military Co-ordination Committee presided over by Chatfield, Churchill seized upon a plan of French origin to further his cause.[51]

At the Supreme War Council, of which Churchill was not a member, the French consistently favoured taking action in Scandinavia, even at the risk of embroiling the Allies in war with Russia as well as Germany. This had two advantages. Militarily it shifted the scene of the war from France's frontier, and politically it allowed the anti-Communist right to unite behind a war effort about which they were never more than luke-warm. Unencumbered by such considerations, Chamberlain found this prospect a good deal less appealing than did his opposite number, Daladier. A French plan to send an expeditionary force to take Narvik and then advance into Sweden to capture the ore-fields at Gällivare was put to the War Cabinet, and Churchill found it even more attractive than the idea of mining the Leads. Churchill acknowledged that in helping the Finns 'we might ultimately be drawn into a general war with Russia, but this was a risk which we should have to run'.[52] The more his mind dwelt on the prospects, the more striking did its virtues become. In accordance with the usual Churchillian pattern, by the time he reached the War Cabinet on 22 December, the new plan was 'worth all the rest of the blockade', as well as offering a 'great chance of shortening the war and possibly saving immeasurable bloodshed on the Western Front'.[53]

Chamberlain was more impressed by the difficulties than his First Lord. The operation might drag the Allies into a war with Russia and outrage American opinion by violating the neutrality of two peaceful nations. There was also the fact that, by April, the Gulf of Bothnia and the Baltic would be ice-free, and the iron-ore supplies could proceed by sea in a different direction. Churchill's answer to the last point was that the Allies could, by then, take 'military or naval' measures which would deprive the Russians and Germans of the use of the ore. But this failed to soothe Halifax's deep fears about the diplomatic repercussions of action such as Churchill was proposing, and the most that was allowed was for the Chiefs of Staff to consider the implications of any such operations.[54] Unfavourable reaction from Norway and Sweden to such Allied 'aid', fears of the diplomatic consequences in America and elsewhere, and doubts about whether depriving the Germans of their Swedish iron-ore would actually win the war quickly, all contributed to the Cabinet deciding against the plan in early January 1940.[55]

Churchill's frustrations poured themselves into a letter to Halifax on 13 January. His criticism came down to two points: the current 'machinery of war-conduct' might almost have been designed to prevent 'positive action'; and unless the Allies took such action, they would lose the war.[56] The first point certainly had much to commend it: wars are seldom waged with expedition by committees. But conscious though Chamberlain was of Churchill's desire to become defence supremo, with oversight of the War Office and the Admiralty, he thought 'that just won't do'.[57] But the pressure remained, and when Chatfield resigned in April, Chamberlain let Churchill preside over the Military Co-ordination Committee. In his own eyes this was a victory for his handling of the First Lord, whom he described as 'in the seventh heaven' and profuse in gratitude for 'the confidence I have given him'.[58] Churchill, Chamberlain thought, had been given the appearance but not the substance of power. As to Churchill's second point, about the war being lost for want of an offensive operation, that was not the Prime Minister's view, and he was not sorry to see the French-inspired plans for operations in Narvik suffer a setback with the collapse of Finnish resistance in March.[59] Churchill, by contrast, was driven once more to press that an opportunity for action should not be lost through fear of violating the sensibilities of neutral states.

Churchill's somewhat cavalier attitude towards the neutrals caused Chamberlain and Halifax a good deal of concern. The seizure of the German ship, the *Altmark*, in Norwegian territorial waters in mid-February, and the consequent release of British prisoners which it had been carrying, was trumpeted forth as a great British triumph, and Churchill certainly played it up as an example of the old Nelsonian spirit in a speech at the Guildhall on 23 February.[60] But the Norwegians did not appreciate the episode any more than they and other neutrals had appreciated his comments about them in a broadcast on 20 January. In this speech (which was not reproduced in his collected wartime orations) he had praised the Finns for their bravery in fighting against the threat of a return of 'the Dark Ages' and contrasted them with the neutrals, whose policy was characterised as to 'bow humbly and in fear to German threats of violence'. They were all hoping, he said scornfully, to be the last one to be eaten by the 'crocodile', but salvation was only to be found in unity with the Allied cause.[61] Halifax, who received numerous complaints about the speech, chided the First Lord and asked him to clear any future speeches with him.[62] How little Churchill understood the perhaps over-subtle foreign policy of the Government of which he was a part was revealed in his reply. He wrote that he had thought that 'the statement of these truths w[oul]d be beneficial in neutral opinion'.[63] Churchill simply failed to comprehend that other nations could be so blind as to what he conceived to be their interests as to take a view different from his own.

The news of the Finnish armistice did not seem to Churchill reason enough to abandon the plan to attack Narvik upon which the Supreme War Council had agreed in February. After all, the 'real object', he told his colleagues on

12 March, had been to 'secure possession of the Gällivare ore fields'. But his colleagues, once more, put the damper on his enthusiasms.[64] Again, his response was to write an anguished letter to Halifax stressing the dangers consequent upon delay and the futility of having no 'positive project to gain the initiative'.[65]

The decision by the Supreme War Council on 28 March to go ahead with a plan for mining the Leads provided Churchill with some cheer, as did his appointment as Chairman of the Military Co-ordination Committee, but the lack of identity between his views on how the war should be conducted and those of some of his colleagues was bound to lead to conflicts within the Government.

One of the fiercest opponents of Churchill's cavalier attitude towards the neutrals was Halifax's Under-Secretary, Rab Butler, who added this to the long list of their disagreements. He had told Cadogan and Halifax on 11 January that the proposed Narvik operation might well come to 'rank in history with Walcheren and the Dardanelles'.[66] One reason for Butler's hostility was that he still hoped that there would be a peaceful resolution to the war which had been declared in September. As late as July 1939 he had still been looking towards concessions, which he hoped might avert an Anglo-German conflict from which, like Chamberlain, he could see no good emerging.[67] He saw in the collapse of Finnish resistance an opportunity to respond to the attempts of the American Government to secure a negotiated peace.[68] Chamberlain and Halifax were more circumspect, but neither of them ruled out such a peace, provided Hitler could be removed and his Polish conquests reversed – an unlikely contingency. Churchill, by contrast, told Sumner Welles, Roosevelt's envoy, that 'Now we had entered the war we must fight it to a finish.'[69] Differences there were, but to assert, as one commentator has recently done, that Churchill did not know of Chamberlain's views and would have been 'extremely provoked' if he had,[70] is to take the myths of the Munich period into the 'phoney war'. Churchill was at the War Cabinet meeting at which Chamberlain declared the views he had put to Welles. He and the Prime Minister differed in their devotion to the offensive spirit, but both men agreed that the war was going well for the Allies. Churchill wished to press this home with an assault on the German ore supplies, whilst Chamberlain was convinced that simply by sitting and waiting he was sealing Hitler's fate.

Contrary to the view implied by statements that Churchill was not aware of Chamberlain's attitude, the Prime Minister and his First Lord were, by the end of March, getting on well and, following his appointment to the Chairmanship of the Military Co-ordination Committee, Churchill wrote to Chamberlain telling him: 'I value highly the confidence which you are showing in me and will do my best to deserve it.'[71] Chamberlain had heard from several sources of the 'admiration' which Churchill had expressed for him, and the care he took to consult with him before making Cabinet changes at the end of March shows the trouble he was willing to go to with him; the fact that he ignored all Churchill's suggestions shows the limits of their relationship. The press reaction to the news of Churchill's appointment showed, once again, that the Prime Minister had saddled himself with a problem analogous to the one Asquith had acquired in 1914 by the appointment of Kitchener. Whilst welcoming the news as a sign that the Government was in earnest, many newspapers pressed for Churchill to be given more power[72] – a notion which was viewed with some alarm within Whitehall.

In the eyes of the public Churchill was the great strong man in the Government, a guarantee of the Government's will to victory. It was in the Government's interests that this image should be fostered, particularly as nothing very much was happening in the war. But as the press reaction in early April showed, this could be a double-edged sword. Within Whitehall the idea of giving the already heavily burdened Churchill extra work was received with little pleasure. If his 'personality and popularity' were a great 'asset' to the Government, there were times when the Prime Minister wished he could have the latter without the former. Over the next month the Prime Minister was to discover not only that this was impossible, but that Churchill's 'popularity' was proof against military failure. Asquith had paid a high price for the popularity which Kitchener brought to an administration lacking in public confidence; the price which Chamberlain was to pay for his 'Kitchener' was to be even higher.

34

Failure and Apotheosis: I

The irony that it should have been a campaign of which Churchill had been such an ardent proponent that brought Chamberlain down has frequently been remarked upon; it has less often been noticed that it was the 'Kitchener' factor which contributed materially to this result. Indeed, Chamberlain's own tactical success in appointing Churchill to chair the Military Co-ordination Committee aided the process by which the Prime Minister was undone. With a campaign in Norway about to begin, Churchill's iconic position was strengthened. Should the operations go well, then no one would attribute credit to the Prime Minister; whereas if they went badly, then it would be upon the Prime Minister's head that the coals of wrath would fall. It would be asked why he had hamstrung the only man of war in the Government. Making war by committee is a project seldom attended with success; by confining Churchill to an ill-defined role, Chamberlain provided both a rod for his own back and an alibi for Churchill should the campaign misfire.

At the Supreme War Council on 28 March, at which the new French Premier, Paul Reynaud, was present, Chamberlain had put forward a number of plans for offensive operations. These included a scheme of Churchill's called 'Operation Royal Marine', which involved floating mines down the Rhine, and a plan for attacking the Baku oilfields in Russia from which Germany obtained much of her oil. Aerial mines dropped into the Rhine seemed to Reynaud to be bringing the war rather closer to France's frontiers than was comfortable, whilst attacking the Baku fields, although a more attractive prospect, involved the risk of war with Russia. But everyone could agree upon the utility of mining the Norwegian Leads; indeed, if the British agreed to it, Reynaud would agree to 'Operation Royal Marine'.[1] The die was cast.

The plan received the code name 'Wilfred' because, although 'small and innocent', it concealed a greater design.[2] Since January the Allies had been aware that a descent on Narvik might inspire a pre-emptive German strike. In the week before the operation was launched, the trickle of rumours became a flood, with the British Embassy in Sweden reporting a concentration of German troops and shipping in the Baltic.[3] The planned date of 5 April for the launch of the Allied landing had to be put back three days because of disputes with the French over their lack of enthusiasm for 'Royal Marine'. This was unfortunate. Addressing the National Union of Conservative Associations on 4 April

Chamberlain gave vent to the view which was prevalent within the Government: the events of the first phase of the war had strengthened the Allied cause and Hitler had 'missed the bus'. In his memoirs Churchill is suitably censorious about Chamberlain's 'ill-judged utterance'.[4] But once more, this is to allow hindsight to endow him with a prescience he lacked. Churchill's own broadcasts had shown that he too took a generally optimistic view of the events of the previous seven months.

It was, however, the Allies who had 'missed the bus'. So loud had been the broadcast of their intentions in Norway that the Germans could have been forgiven for supposing that they were in the presence of a peculiarly clumsy campaign of disinformation. But the head of the German Navy, Admiral Raeder, advised Hitler that the Allied scheme was what it appeared to be – a genuine plan – and on 9 April, even as the Allied Fleets sailed towards Norway, the news came through that the Germans had reached Narvik first.[5] Far from being downcast at the news, Churchill welcomed the prospect of at last encountering the Germans in combat. His first reaction had been to disbelieve the reports that the Germans were invading Norway, but when it was clear that they were, he did not repine. He told his colleagues on the morning of 8 April that the German ships might well be intercepted before they reached Narvik by the forces which had laid the minefield: 'It was impossible to foretell the risks of war, but such an action should not be on terms unfavourable to us.'[6] Seeing 'a chance for action' at last, Churchill was disappointed when this action did not come off on 9 April. Colville described him as 'jubilant',[7] a view certainly borne out by Churchill's attitude in Cabinet. 'We were', he told colleagues, 'in a far better position than we had been up to date. Our hands were now free, and we could apply our overwhelming sea-power on the Norwegian coast. The German forces which had landed were commitments for them, but potential prizes for us.'[8] By comparison with this, Chamberlain's remark about Hitler having 'missed the bus' appears almost sensible.

At this stage of the war, and for years to come, Churchill grossly overestimated what could be achieved by sea-power. As a 'navalist' he was, as one historian has it, in thrall to Francis Bacon's aphorism: 'He that commands the sea is at great liberty, and may take as much or as little of the war as he will.'[9] This was evident not only from his comments in the Cabinet on 9 April, but from his whole conduct of the operation; that ships could fight forts (or at least a defended shore-line) was still the kernel of his doctrine. It led to the Fleet being ordered to recapture Trondheim and Bergen, and it persuaded Churchill that if Narvik could be seized, the Germans would suffer a material defeat. It led to the belief that eight British battalions, without proper equipment for operating in the climatic conditions and terrain they were to encounter, could deal with fifty-one German battalions. It omitted considerations of air-power and it led to fiasco. For this Churchill was not wholly to blame, but his share was larger than he was to make out – and his attempt to shift some of it on to the British land commander at Narvik, Major-General Mackesy, revealed him at his worst.

It was Churchill who fixed upon Narvik as the object of the Allied campaign, despite objections from the Secretary of State for War, Oliver Stanley, that it would be a mistake to let the other areas remain in German hands.[10] The whole operation was spatch-cocked together in the most amateurish fashion. Mackesy, who had been appointed some weeks earlier to plan the operation for the seizure of neutral Narvik, was suddenly told that he was in command of one designed to capture it from the Germans. Mackesy had expressed doubts about the first operation, especially in the face of a German riposte; he was also worried about the lack of anti-aircraft equipment. These worries paled beside the fact that the force which Mackesy had originally been allocated was broken up, so that he was sent off to Narvik with only part of it. He was told that his objective was to 'eject the Germans from the Narvik area and establish control of Narvik itself'. The Chief of the Imperial General Staff, General Ironside, told him that he might be able to take advantage of naval action: 'Boldness is required.'[11] But at that stage the Cabinet and Chiefs of Staff were only just beginning to appreciate how completely the Germans had succeeded in their objectives.

An attempt to enter the Ofotfjord on which Narvik lay succeeded in sinking two German destroyers and damaging two more, with only two smaller British destroyers being sunk. The British press magnified this into a great triumph, and to Chamberlain's annoyance there were even reports that Trondheim and Bergen had been recaptured. Churchill put forward the correct position in the House on 11 April, but the damage had been done. Although blame was placed upon the hapless Ministry of Information, Chamberlain thought it more properly belonged to the Admiralty's hesitation in denying the rumours, which, in turn, he attributed to the fact that 'Winston has got everyone so terrified there that none of them dare take any responsibility for anything.'[12] Although he recognised that Churchill 'only means to be helpful', the Prime Minister was finding, now that the war had started, that he gave him 'more trouble than all the rest of my colleagues put together'.

The experiment of having Churchill as Chairman of the Military Co-ordination Committee coincided with the opening phase of the fighting war, and it was not a success. This Churchill attributed to the failure to define proper areas of responsibility and mechanisms for ensuring that decisions were carried out.[13] There was something in this, but Churchill's own working habits did not help. They were depicted by Chamberlain in a letter to his sisters on 13 April:

His methods of work are most wearing to others. He goes to bed after lunch for a couple of hours or so and holds conferences up to 1 in the morning at which he goes into every detail, so I am informed, that could quite well be settled by subordinates. Officers and officials in his own and other departments are sent for and kept up until they are dropping with fatigue and service Ministers are worn out in arguing with him.[14]

It was the price, as Chamberlain acknowledged, which he had to pay for Churchill's 'popularity'; but the time for payment had come.

The Norwegian campaign was flawed in concept and muddled in execution. As a study in how 'order, counter-order' can produce 'disorder', it is almost unsurpassed. The forces which, until the last minute, had been intended to land at Narvik against token opposition from the Norwegians, were now hurriedly embarked and despatched. The 24th Guards brigade was sent without artillery, engineers or transport; nor were they supplied with craft which would have safely ferried the lightly armed troops ashore against a fortified beach; and once there the soldiers would find themselves lacking equipment which would enable them to move through snow and ice. The four battalions of the 146th and 148th brigades were embarked with their stores and equipment in disorder, a state of affairs made worse by changes of plan once the forces had been embarked; swiftness of despatch had been purchased at the price of efficiency.[15]

The command structure might have been designed to produce the result it did – chaos. Mackesy had been co-ordinating his plans with Admiral Sir Roger Evans, but Churchill now replaced him with his own man. Admiral of the Fleet the Lord Cork and Orrery was the sort of war hero for whom Churchill always had a weakness, but as a 'dug-out' from the last war, whose seniority meant that he outranked every other military man involved, he was not the best choice for the job. Moreover, having appointed Cork, Churchill gave him neither a verbal nor a written brief. Cork attended a meeting of the Military Co-ordination Committee and had a desultory discussion with Churchill; he also had a few minutes with the First Lord as he drove to the Commons, but Churchill was too busy responding to the crowds to say very much. Cork was not asked to, nor did he, consult with Mackesy, who was already on his way to Narvik. Neither did he see Mackesy's written instructions from Ironside, but then the Chiefs of Staff and the Military Co-ordination Committee never saw them either. Mackesy had embarked for Norway from Scapa Flow on the *Southampton* whilst Cork departed from Rosyth in the *Aurora*.[16] To divided commanders with different instructions was added the burden of divided counsel. Churchill was unhappy when, on 13 April, his colleagues pressed for action to be taken at other places. But following the destruction of seven German destroyers in the Ofotfjord that day, he changed his mind and, in an episode left unreported by the official biographer, he went to see Ironside at 2 a.m. on 14 April and, to his fury, told him that 'we should go for Trondheim'. Ironside's efforts to explain that this would fatally weaken the forces available at Narvik were unavailing.[17]

Churchill's nocturnal habits were not only unconducive to efficiency in others, they were not always good for him. Nicolson had noticed how 'very tired' he seemed during his 'feeble, tired speech' to the House on 11 April.[18] If the speech seemed 'less polished than usual',[19] that was because it had been completed only fifteen minutes before it was due to be delivered.[20] Following that, Churchill went to the Admiralty before, at 6.30 p.m., chairing a meeting of the Military Co-ordination Committee. Afterwards he chaired a meeting at the Admiralty, which did not finish until nearly midnight. At this meeting he managed to annoy some of his staff by trying to be a 'naval strategist if not an actual tactician'.[21] Churchill simply would not believe what every available piece of evidence suggested, which was that he had inherited little of 'Duke John's' military genius – or that if he had, he was some two hundred years out of date. There was certainly much activity, but to what effect? Kingsley Wood described the Military Co-ordination Committee as a 'farce' with Churchill having 'gotten himself and everybody else' into a 'dreadful state', whilst the Minister of Information, Sir John Reith, who attended a meeting with Churchill on 14 April, thought that he 'looked as if he had been drinking too much'.[22] The 'Kitchener' factor saved Churchill from the opprobrium visited upon the 'tired' Ministers in a *Times* leader on 16 April.

Chamberlain's resentment at such strictures was as little surprising as the strictures themselves. The Norwegian campaign was evidently not going smoothly and the lethargy of the Government was to blame; that was fair enough. But when Chamberlain was going to have to chair the Military Co-ordination Committee that morning because of the 'strained feelings' to which Churchill's handling of it had given rise,[23] the Prime Minister could have been forgiven a wry grimace as he read his morning newspaper. The Committee, he told his sisters, was 'getting into a sad mess, with everyone feeling irritable and strained and with a general conviction that Winston had smashed the machine we had so carefully built up'. The problem, Chamberlain thought, was that 'he does enjoy planning a campaign or an operation himself so much' and believed 'so entirely in all his own ideas (for the moment) that he puts intenser pressure on the staff than he realises'. Here Chamberlain touched upon the root of the matter. The result of this was that Churchill's staff were 'bullied into a sulky silence – a most dangerous position in war'. It was Churchill himself who had asked Chamberlain to chair the Committee, telling him, 'They'll take from you what they won't take from me.'[24] Conscious of discontent amongst the military and his own colleagues, who felt that the Committee was bypassing the War Cabinet itself, Chamberlain was only too happy to take control.[25]

The Prime Minister was able to report that business was, henceforth, conducted with greater expedition, but excellent chairmanship was not the same as ability to conduct a combined operation in Scandinavia – and it was becoming distressingly clear that what was really wrong was that the Chamberlain Government was not an effective instrument for the conduct of a war.

Churchill's desire to take the offensive led him, as usual, to underrate any difficulties in the way of the fulfilment of his plans. When Cork reported on 15 April that Mackesy 'did not consider an immediate attack practicable',

Churchill wanted to sack the General, but Cork ignored the implications in Churchill's response.[26] Churchill's enthusiasm for the assault on Trondheim, which he had originally opposed, became such that when the Commander-in-Chief of the Home Fleet advised against the operation because of the likelihood of heavy losses, he, like Mackesy at Narvik, was urged to think again. The Admiral agreed that the operation might be possible with numerous landing-craft, but there were only ten available.[27] Here, in short compass, was the central problem: a lack of equipment, preparation, co-ordination and leadership. Churchill's constant harping on about the need for boldness and the offensive spirit resembled nothing so much as the sort of harangue which French generals used to deliver before 1914.

One result of Chamberlain taking over the Military Co-ordination Committee was that the Trondheim plan was finally submitted to the Chiefs of Staff for consideration. This was partly due to Hankey, who reminded the Prime Minister that it was for not doing such things that the Asquith Government had been censured by the Dardanelles Committee.[28] The Chiefs of Staff agreed, but as with so much else during the campaign, they did so on false premises. It had been assumed that Mackesy would take Narvik and that some of his forces could be used in the assault, but on 17 April he reported that he could not make a direct assault on Narvik until the snows had melted. Nothing was better calculated to bring out the impetuous subaltern in Churchill. The idea of one of the best brigades in the Army 'wasting away' horrified him, and he telegraphed Mackesy and Cork urging them to action.[29] In his memoirs Churchill was particularly severe on Mackesy's negative response to these suggestions.

To the General's argument that he would be sending his men, in open boats, against a shore commanded by German fire, Churchill had two ripostes. In the first place, his orders 'so evidently contemplated heavy losses that they should have been obeyed'.[30] But Mackesy's argument was that heavy losses by themselves were useless; they could be justified only by a successful outcome, and the General on the spot did not consider the chances of success high enough to warrant a real 'waste' of lives. Churchill's other reason for censuring Mackesy was that a naval bombardment of Narvik would provide sufficient cover for the British forces to reach the shore. Cork agreed with this classic example of Churchill's conviction that ships could 'fight forts', but Mackesy did not. Churchill grossly overestimated the effectiveness of a naval bombardment against shore targets. He was correct to think that the Germans had no real response to such a bombardment, but he ignored the inaccuracy of naval fire at this period of the war. Moreover, with their high velocity and flat trajectory, naval guns could not search 'dead ground' behind the crest of the bluffs fronting the sea; so machine-guns could still have enfiladed any landing forces from the flank. The small quantity of high-explosive ammunition available meant that there was no possibility of blanketing the whole area with fire. There was also another consideration to be taken into account: the Norwegians. Mackesy's orders were not to endanger the lives of the civilian population; after all, the British were hoping to rally the Norwegians, not to kill them. For Churchill to respond to this by contrasting Mackesy unfavourably with the 'absolutely reckless gambling in lives and ships' of the Germans, is not only chilling in itself, but an early indication of the spirit which was to lead to Dresden. Adopting the Nazi spirit was hardly likely to win the minds and hearts of the neutral Americans, the moral high ground or, even more importantly in Mackesy's eyes, the campaign itself.[31]

Churchill, however, insisted upon trying to run the Narvik campaign from an office in Whitehall several hundred miles away from the scene of the action, a course fraught with dangers for anyone, let alone an amateur tactician with Marlborough antecedents. If Churchill was ignorant of conditions at Narvik, he had, in large part, only himself to blame. Since Cork had been placed in supreme command of the operation, Mackesy could only communicate with Whitehall through the Admiral; but Cork suppressed some of his communications and summarised others in an unfriendly spirit. Churchill sent a telegram to Cork shortly before midnight telling him that if he considered that the situation was 'being mishandled', he should report to the Admiralty with alternative proposals.[32] This was, in effect, an invitation to override the opinion of the army commander on an operation involving his troops – and it was declined by Cork.[33] With no possibility of reinforcements, no field guns, no anti-aircraft guns, almost no ammunition for his mortars and a force which was probably inferior to the enemy, and which was not equipped to operate in snow and ice, Mackesy too refused to reconsider his views.[34] Upon his appointment to the Admiralty, Churchill had stressed that the staff were not to be overawed by his views, and he was sometimes inclined to wonder, as he had at the time of the Dardanelles, why, if his advisers disagreed with him, they did not say so. What he failed to appreciate was that a style which he thought of as robust, appeared to subordinates (and others) perilously close to bullying. Indeed, as his treatment of Mackesy showed, it came so close at times that it was indistinguishable from it.

On 19 April the Chiefs of Staff recommended abandoning a direct assault on Trondheim, preferring instead to pursue the chimera of a pincer movement on the town from the north and south – although how the Allied troops were going to advance as quickly as necessary over several hundred miles of snow down a single-track road was not stated.[35] Churchill urged Cork and Mackesy to action at Narvik, but it was evident that there would be no swift victory – and increasingly doubtful that there would be one at all. The Germans were by this stage in control of most of Norway, and intelligence reports indicated that a fresh offensive would be launched somewhere in the near future. Churchill thought an attack on Sweden was imminent, but Chamberlain doubted this. On 26 April the Allies abandoned the whole idea of any attack on Trondheim, and Narvik now remained the single prize available – although quite what would be done with it, with the rest of Norway in German hands, was a question which got lost in the momentum of planning. It was not until 12–13 May, after Churchill had left the Admiralty, that landings finally took place – and by that time they were hardly noticed.

Churchill was far from holding sole responsibility for all that went wrong. The roots of the Allied failure lay in the conceptions which underlay it: an overestimate of what sea-power could achieve; an underestimate of what the Germans could do; and an ignorance of the possibilities of air-power. These were compounded by poor lines of management and all the defects which follow from trying to run a war by committee. Charges that Churchill interfered in specific details of naval strategy cannot be substantiated on any scale, but what is clear is that his chairing of the Military Co-ordination Committee produced disorder where there was already too much of it. By 24 April Churchill was wanting greater control over the Committee.[36] This placed Chamberlain in a dilemma which brought home the cost of the 'Kitchener' factor. If he did not give in to Churchill, rumour had it that the First Lord intended to 'go down to the House and say he can take no responsibility for what is happening'.[37] With Churchill behaving 'like a spoiled sulky child' at the Committee on 23 April, Chamberlain thought that the time had come to act.[38]

At a late-night meeting on 24 April Churchill was 'profuse' in his protestations of 'complete loyalty' and his desire 'to help'. Chamberlain accepted this, but had severe doubts about his demand to become, in effect, Minister of Defence. No decision over Norway had been taken against Churchill's advice, and 'although he puts out many nonsensical proposals he very rarely maintains them against reasoned argument'. But the idea of making Churchill military supremo had little appeal.[39] On the other hand, if Churchill disclaimed responsibility for operations, there would be, as Colville noted, 'a first-class political crisis, because the country believes that Winston is the man of action who is winning the war and little realise how ineffective, and indeed harmful, much of his energy is proving itself to be'.[40] It was little wonder that the harassed Prime Minister, painfully conscious of his shortcomings as a war leader, felt a 'strong inclination to take my head out of the collar and let someone else do the donkey work'.[41] However, he could not see who else could be trusted with the job. But the popular perception, wrong though it was, was to solve for him the problem he could not – which was what to do with Churchill. On 1 May Chamberlain announced that Churchill was to be responsible, on behalf of the Military Co-ordination Committee, for 'giving guidance and directions to the Chiefs of Staff.[42] It was the last despairing tactical manoeuvre of a Prime Minister who was running out of options, but he was also running out of time.

The House was due to debate the Norway campaign on 7 May, and from the start of the month there were rumours of a 'cabal' against Chamberlain. Channon, a Chamberlainite of the deepest hue, picked up gossip to the effect that '"They" are saying that it is 1915 over again, that Winston should be Prime Minister as he has more vigour and the country behind him.'[43] If the atmosphere was reminiscent of anything, it was of December 1916, just before Lloyd George replaced Asquith. The idea of Churchill as the supremo who would win the war was, to 'insiders', little more than risible. To Churchill's comment on the filthy weather on May Day, 'If I were the first of May, I should be ashamed of myself,' Colville's mental riposte was: 'I think he ought to be ashamed of himself in any case.'[44] Ironside, who thought that Churchill had 'genius', also believed that he was too 'unstable'[45] to run the war – and noticed how tired Churchill was becoming under the strain of operations.[46] But whatever Whitehall thought, it was Westminster which would count – and there Churchill's name stood high.

Churchill's actions during the period leading to the debate were the subject of much scrutiny. There were rumours that he was being egged on by the Socialists and Liberals to 'lead a revolt against the PM'.[47] Colville heard that he was 'being loyal' but that his 'satellites', such as Duff Cooper and Amery, were doing 'all in their power to create mischief and ill-feeling'.[48] Chamberlain was 'extremely anxious not to have any break' with Churchill, 'for that would be disastrous to the Allied cause'. He did not think Churchill wanted a break, although he suspected that his 'friends', exalting him as 'the war genius', were stirring him up. The Prime Minister found himself in the strange position of being 'thankful' that 'the good British public does not know the truth and persists in ideas which recall the Kitchener legend'. It might well have damaged Churchill had they known that he had changed his mind four times about the Trondheim campaign, or that he had opposed strengthening the Mediterranean Fleet, but even if it did, the Government would be damaged more. As the debate approached, the question which began to worry some of Churchill's friends was whether 'the Norwegian fiasco had diminished his chances of assuming the leadership by weakening his position in the House and in the country'.[49]

Whatever the 'tadpoles and tapers',[50] those wire-pullers and maggots of the Westminster commonwealth, did or said about him, self-interest allied with loyalty and prudence combined to ensure that Churchill's actions before and during the debate were above reproach – even if they could never be above suspicion.[51] He had, after all, been heavily involved in the Norway campaign, and to criticise it would be akin to self-immolation. In any event, he was still, to many MPs and the public, the 'Kitchener' figure, and a display of loyalty could only do him good.[52] If the Prime Minister did fall, there would still be plenty of Conservatives whose support he would need. Moreover, it was by no means clear that Churchill would be able to form a Government without Chamberlain's support. It would also be unduly cynical to discount all those protestations of loyalty which he had made to Chamberlain. As Baldwin had once commented, Churchill 'cannot really tell lies. That is what makes him so bad a conspirator.'[53]

With the Whips out in force before the debate, Chamberlain tried to rally the Tory Party by appealing to one of its most powerful instincts – loyalty to the leader. But despite a warm welcome from his backbenchers,[54] his speech was a 'terrible failure' and neither held the House nor helped his cause.[55] The 'yes men' applauded him, but what was that compared to the sight of Admiral Sir Roger Keyes in full-dress uniform making an 'absolutely devastating attack upon the naval conduct of the Narvik episode' and taking his seat to 'thunderous applause'?[56] It 'knocked the House in the pit of its stomach',[57] and the men who the Whips put up against him made little impact. Amery damned them, in Cromwell's words, as 'old decayed serving men and tapsters, and such kind of fellows', before levelling with deadly effect at his old friend, the Prime Minister, the words which the Lord Protector had addressed to the Long Parliament: 'You have sat too long for any good you have been doing. Depart, I say, and let us have done with you. In the name of God, go!'[58] The Whips could try to steady the troops against such devastating broadsides, but with Lloyd George still to speak, the only weapon of comparable calibre available to them was Churchill himself. That night the question on everyone's lips was that posed by Channon: 'What will Winston do?'[59]

Any satisfaction which Churchill's friends felt at what they took to be the approaching demise of the 'old gang' was tempered by the thought that their man might go down with the wreck.[60] Thus it was that on the morrow when the debate resumed, Lloyd George appealed to Churchill not to 'allow himself to be converted into an air-raid shelter to keep the splinters from hitting his colleagues'.[61] The pent-up bitterness of two decades found expression in a 'violent attack' on the Government and upon Chamberlain in particular;[62] referring to the latter's appeal for 'sacrifices', he concluded by saying that 'the Prime Minister should give an example of sacrifice, because there is nothing which can contribute to victory in the war than that he should sacrifice the seals of office'.[63] The 'decayed serving men' who attempted to respond to this onslaught only emphasised its power, and when Duff Cooper joined in with a 'damaging speech',[64] it was evident that the Government was not only holed but sinking. In a last attempt to keep it afloat, the Whips were busy in the corridors and the smoking room, and the rumour had it that if only the Prime Minister could be given 'one last chance', there would be a major reconstruction of the Government.[65] It was in this 'context' that the Prime Minister appealed to his 'friends', and no one save an academic could have been in any doubt as to what he meant.[66] But the speech which everyone awaited with interest was that of the Rt Hon. member for Epping.

Nicolson thought that Churchill had an 'almost impossible task', having, on the one hand, to 'defend the Services' and, on the other, to remain loyal to the Prime Minister – and to do all this without damaging his reputation.[67] In fact, although his position was delicate, it was not that difficult. Most of Chamberlain's critics were disposed to discount any defence of the Government as something which the position he occupied obliged Churchill to do, and they were certainly disposed to exonerate him from blame, if only because he was their 'Kitchener', and because it allowed it all to be heaped on Chamberlain's head. Churchill gave them every assistance in acquitting him. Out of a fifty-minute speech, forty-eight minutes were spent in what Amery described as 'a quite incomprehensible account' of why the Allies had not pushed into Trondheim in the first place.[68] Channon, who was always disposed to suspect Churchill, could not complain at the loyalty which he showed to the Government, and the very fact that he was the only front-bench speaker who 'amused and dazzled everyone with his virtuosity' simply underlined how essential he was to any new Government. Towards the end of his speech he criticised Labour for converting the debate into one of confidence in the Government, and accused the Labour MP, Emmanuel Shinwell, of 'skulking' in a corner. One Labour MP, 'rather the worse for drink', misheard and thought Churchill had said 'skunking', which caused nervous laughter.[69] The tension as the House voted was palpable.

All the blandishments of the Chief Whip, David Margesson, who pointed out that Churchill was voting with the Government and promised a major reconstruction of the Government on the morrow, managed to produce a Government majority of eighty-one votes – 281 to 200. They had won the vote but lost the debate, which had revealed that the Government had exhausted its credit. It was true that only thirty-three Conservatives and eight other National Government supporters had gone into the lobby with the Labour Party and the Liberals, but these included men of the calibre of Amery, Duff Cooper, Eden, Hore-Belisha, Boothby, Spears and Macmillan. Even more damaging was the fact that sixty other Conservatives had chosen to abstain; a Government which could drive men like the member for Oldham, Roy Wise, or Charles Taylor, the MP for Eastbourne, to adopt a stance of defiance, had indeed run its course. But the main question now was what would Chamberlain do next?

The Prime Minister had three options: he could stay on and try to reconstruct his Government; he could resign and have done with it; or he could try to soldier on. But the last was clearly impossible in view of the promises which Margesson had been making, and the second was contrary to every instinct in his body, so it had to be the first. What did for Chamberlain was that when he consulted Labour the next day, Attlee and company were quite explicit – they would not serve under him.[70] Not only that, but they wanted Simon, Hoare and possibly Kingsley Wood out too.[71] Any hopes of getting away with a minor reconstruction seemed to be dashed. But, as Dalton put it in a characteristically unpleasant simile, Chamberlain seemed 'determined to stick on – like a dirty piece of chewing gum on the leg of a chair'.[72] But the proverbial knack of rats for deserting sinking ships was about to exhibit itself.

Whilst Chamberlain was telephoning the Labour leaders and getting nowhere fast, Churchill was lunching with Eden and Kingsley Wood. The latter was considered a loyal Chamberlainite, so it was something of a shock to Eden's delicate sensibilities to hear him telling Churchill that as Chamberlain had to go, he must succeed to his place.[73] He was not the only one to do so. According to an account which Bracken detailed much later to Churchill's physician, Lord Moran, he had remonstrated with Churchill after the vote, when he had heard the rumour that Churchill intended to serve under Halifax in a new Government. Bracken's account has him telling Churchill that he could not do such a thing, Churchill responding that he would do his duty, and Bracken finally eliciting from him a promise that in any interview with Chamberlain and Halifax, he would not be the first to speak.[74] It is a nice story, and certainly at least another candidate for the 'King Alfred's cakes' stakes, in that it expresses some essential truths; but it may, alas, be akin to that tale in being apocryphal.

There is no contemporary evidence for it. Spears repeats a version of it, but, as he gives Bracken as his source, this cannot be accounted as supporting evidence.[75] Churchill does not mention it, nor does any other contemporary source, and the account as recorded by Moran has about it the familiar smell of afterthought. How could Bracken make Churchill promise that he would not speak first when he was invited to No. 10 Downing Street on the morrow, when no such invitation had yet been issued? Beaverbrook told a similar story, but attributed some of the credit to himself, and placed the conversations with Churchill, both his own and Bracken's, later on the morning of 9 May.[76] But both he and Bracken were notorious for their love of fantasy and the skill with which they would embellish a good story – and this one, alas, appears to have no other foundation. With reluctance the historian must discard the pretty bauble and adopt, instead, the Pickwickian figure of Kingsley Wood as the author of the advice to Churchill to hold his tongue; Eden's account is contemporary, and by lunchtime Churchill knew that he and Halifax were going to meet the Prime Minister.

It is ironic that Churchill should have misdated this vital meeting in his memoirs, assigning it to 10 rather than 9 May. Chamberlain told both men that the essential thing was to ensure national unity. He asked Attlee and Greenwood to join them and formally asked 'the definite question whether the Labour Party would serve under me or if not under someone else'. He did not name that 'someone else', but he 'had understood that they favoured Halifax, and I had him in mind'.[77] After the Labour men had departed, Chamberlain turned to Churchill and Halifax and told them that he had no doubt that he would have to resign – the only question to be decided was whose name should he put before the King as his successor? Churchill described the ensuing pause as 'longer than the two minutes' silence on Armistice Day'.[78] Halifax spoke first, dilating upon the difficulties which he, as a peer, would have in trying to run the Government from the Lords. In conversation with Chamberlain that morning, the idea of being Prime Minister had given him 'a bad stomach ache',[79] and his comments now showed that he lacked the stomach for the job. He would, he thought, be in an invidious position as Prime Minister, for Churchill would undoubtedly run the war whilst he became a 'more or less honorary Prime Minister, living in a kind of twilight just outside the things that really mattered'.[80] According to Halifax's account, it was only after this that the Labour leaders came to Downing Street. According to Chamberlain's record, he later heard that Labour were 'moving towards Winston' and he agreed with Churchill and Halifax 'that I would put Winston's name to the King'.[81] He resigned that evening, but the morrow made him reconsider his action.

In the early hours of 10 May the Nazi *blitzkrieg* on Holland and Belgium began. In view of this Chamberlain felt that he ought to stay on as Prime Minister, but once more it was Kingsley Wood who played the role of Churchill's advocate, telling Chamberlain bluntly that the crisis made it all the more imperative that he should go.[82] Chamberlain's actions did more credit to his patriotism than to his political instinct; it was plain that the initiative no longer lay in his hands. At the War Cabinet that afternoon Chamberlain told his colleagues that, in view of the Labour refusal to serve under him and the necessity of forming a national coalition, he intended to resign.[83]

Nothing was said about the name of his successor, and when Chamberlain saw the King, the latter was keen to appoint Halifax, but agreed in the face of Chamberlain's arguments and Halifax's reluctance that Churchill was the only man for the post.[84] Churchill was summoned to the Palace and, after the opening pleasantries – 'I suppose you don't know why I have sent for you?', 'Sir, I simply could not imagine' – Churchill was asked to form a Government.[85] His first action upon returning to the Admiralty reflected his sense of political reality – he wrote to Chamberlain to ask if he would be willing to serve in his Government, and then telephoned him to ensure that he would do so; he then wrote to Halifax asking him to stay as Foreign Secretary. It was only when he had ensured that the Conservative Party would support him that Churchill set about enlisting Labour's backing.[86] It was not until 3 a.m. on 11 May that Churchill finally retired to bed, but as he did so he was 'conscious of a profound sense of relief': it was as if he 'were walking with destiny, and all my past life had been but a preparation for this hour and for this trial'. At last the dreams had become facts – and 'Facts', as he was later to record, 'are better than dreams.'[87]

35

Walking with Destiny

If Destiny was walking with Churchill, it had brought him into something which resembled a trap. On the one hand, he was faced with clearing up the remnants of the Norway fiasco and tackling the Nazi onslaught in the west; on the other, his political position hardly gave him that control over events which he would like to have had. Chamberlain may have been replaced as Prime Minister, but he was still leader of the Conservative Party, and anyone who was expecting a clean sweep of the 'men of Munich' was doomed to disappointment – as the shape of Churchill's first administration showed.

The need for caution was apparent on 13 May when the House met for the first time following the change in Prime Minister. When Chamberlain entered the Chamber, Conservative MPs 'lost their heads', shouting and cheering him to the echo; Churchill by contrast received a muted welcome.[1] Churchill's ally from the India Defence League days, Patrick Donner, wrote to tell Chamberlain that it was 'only by the negation of democracy' that the 'Ministry has forced its temporary will, as the loud cheers which greeted you today clearly indicate'.[2] The former Prime Minister received many such letters from loyalists, all of whom would have agreed with the comment that it was only 'the fact that you are prepared to serve under the new Prime Minister' which 'resolves the doubts of a good many of us who had been doubtful of whether we should take the Whip under these circumstances': if Churchill was good enough for Chamberlain, 'he must be good enough for us'.[3] Churchill's kindness and consideration touched Chamberlain's heart,[4] but they were not entirely prompted by altruism; without Chamberlain Churchill might not have a Government. The Labour Party objected to his presence and ensured that he did not take the Exchequer, but Chamberlain remained Lord President of the Council, Chairman of all important Cabinet committees on domestic matters and leader of the Conservative Party.

The notion that the new administration might prove to be only a temporary expedient was not confined to Chamberlain loyalists. Looking at its composition and at Churchill taking on the roles of Leader of the House and Minister of Defence, Amery was strengthened in his feeling that 'he really means the present arrangement to be temporary'.[5] The constraints upon Churchill's freedom were apparent from the shape of his administration. Of the 'Municheers', only Hoare, who had, of course, also fought Churchill over India, actually lost his place in the Cabinet; Chamberlain and Halifax remained, and Simon was kicked upstairs to become Lord Chancellor. The best-rewarded of all the 'rebels' was, appropriately enough, Sir Kingsley Wood, who went to the Exchequer in Simon's stead. Of the long-time dissentients, Amery was fobbed off with the India Office, Duff Cooper with the Ministry of Information (which had already proved a graveyard of reputations) and Eden received the War Office; none of them joined the War Cabinet. The only dissident who was entirely happy with his post was Lord Lloyd, who, to his delight, now sat in Joseph Chamberlain's old chair at the Colonial Office.

If the dissident Conservatives received a meagre ration of the loaves and fishes, the portion allotted to the Labour Party was not much better. It was true that Attlee joined the War Cabinet as Lord Privy Seal, and that he was joined by Greenwood as Minister without Portfolio, but anything less would have been unacceptable to the Labour Party. Even so, some Labour MPs, such as the former leader of the London County Council, Herbert Morrison, were inclined to stay out of a Government which sounded little better than its predecessor.[6] But Morrison did come in, accepting the Ministry of Supply on 12 May. The only two other Labour MPs to be offered posts of Cabinet rank were Hugh Dalton, who became Minister for Economic Warfare, and Sir William Jowitt who was made Solicitor-General. The most significant of the 'Labour' appointments was Churchill's own idea: he asked the former TUC leader, Ernest Bevin, to become Minister of Labour; Bevin, who was not even an MP, had to be found a safe seat with alacrity.

If Churchill was justified in saying that his was one of the broadest-bottomed administrations in English history because it stretched from Lloyd on the right to Ellen Wilkinson (in a junior post at Pensions) on the left, then that was only a tithe of the story. Including Churchill, of the thirty-four Ministers, twenty-one had been members of the Chamberlain administration, and there were eighteen Conservatives to seven Labour MPs. Of the old 'National elements', only Simon and Ernest Brown remained to represent those Liberals who had adhered to MacDonald and Baldwin after 1932, whilst poor Malcolm MacDonald, as Minister of Health, was the sole surviving remnant of 'National Labour'. There were three 'non-Party' appointments (if Bevin is discounted), all of whom had been members of the last Government: Hankey moved to the Duchy of Lancaster *en route* to the wilderness; Reith, travelling a similar road, went from Information to Transport; whilst Sir John Anderson, who was treading the opposite path, became Home Secretary. Churchill's interest really only extended to the senior posts, and he was content to leave the tadpoles and tapers to sort out, with the help of the Whips and Party managers, who should get which Under-Secretaryship – but it might be noted that Butler remained at the Foreign Office, as did Channon. It was a Government with Churchill as Prime Minister, but it was not Churchill's Government.[7]

It was to take another six months before Churchill could really claim to be in total command of his administration; in this process he was aided by three events, two fortuitous (at least for him), and one so momentous that it threatened the survival of far more than an administration. The fortuitous events were the deaths of Chamberlain in November and of the Ambassador in Washington, Lord Lothian, in December: the first allowed Churchill to become leader of the Conservative Party; the second enabled him to ship his main rival for that post, Halifax, off to America on a slow boat to political extinction. But everything was overshadowed by the third event, which was the totally unexpected collapse of the Allied front in France and a sweeping German victory. This turn of events forced a trial of strength between Churchill and the 'old guard' far sooner than he would have wished; but it did so in circumstances which allowed him to use his greatest weapon – his oratory – to appeal over their heads to the British people.

Instances of Churchillian modesty are not so frequent that the historian can dismiss even one of them without some regret. But this must be the case with his utterance that in 1940 'it was the nation and the race dwelling all round the globe that had the lion's heart. I had the luck to be called upon to give the roar.'[8] Churchill did not simply 'give the roar', he created it, and he did so out of the materials which had fashioned his own vision of Britain – and by communicating that vision to the nation. Having been brought to power because of a popular conviction that he was this war's version of the 'man of push and go', the latest in a line of heroes stretching back through Lloyd George, Palmerston and the Younger Pitt to the great Chatham, Churchill and the nation suddenly found themselves facing disaster. Churchill had come to power to prosecute the war more forcefully, but so forcefully did Hitler prosecute it that by the end of May the Allied armies in France had been divided and were facing total defeat. Not only had the old Chamberlainite strategy failed, but it was hard to see what could replace it. In the eyes of many sensible folk, the time had come to think about coming to terms with Herr Hitler.

There had always been sections of the nation which had opposed the war. At one extreme were Harry Pollitt's Communists, in thrall to one of the most sterile ideologies and evil dictators in a century overburdened with both. They held that this was a capitalist war, nothing to do with the working classes; a view clung to with all the tenacity a barnacle displays towards a rock – until their master's voice barked other instructions, at which they stood upon their heads. It is not easy to understand how men can allow their understanding to be so readily imposed upon. Those disposed to place the British Union of Fascists in the same boat mistook their target. Despite the ban it was to come under, actuated by an excess of patriotic spirit, it encouraged its members to go off and die for the country which was soon to imprison its leaders. But it was widely supposed that, being Fascists, they had more than a little sympathy with Hitler and would not be averse to his victory; in this there was little truth. Ironically it was the British Union of Fascists which was banned, whilst the Communists remained free to campaign against the 'imperialist' war.

Away from the very margins of political life, but still on its wilder shores, were a variety of folk opposed to the war, ranging from the 'fellow-travellers of the right', to thespians with heads as soft as their hearts. Such pre-war admirers of Hitler as Rab Butler's friend and neighbour, Lord Brocket, and the Duke of Buccleuch had seldom ceased from writing to Chamberlain and Halifax emphasising that Germany had a case.[9] Chamberlain and Halifax knew this perfectly well, but they also knew how much value to attach to Hitler's word. Both men had shown, back in October, that they would be prepared to deal with some other German leader, but Hitler was beyond the pale.[10] From the theatre, luminaries with the political penetration of John Gielgud, Sybil Thorndike and George Bernard Shaw had urged the Government in March to 'give sympathetic consideration' to any proposals for peace sponsored by the neutrals.[11] As might have been expected, some Churchmen were also prominent amongst what one old Tory called this 'little group of defeatists'.[12] Such a description may have been a little unkind, but war distorts charitable perceptions, and heated blood boils easily. Lord Beaverbrook, whom Churchill was to bring in from the wilderness, was, before his sudden conversion to the man who won the Battle of Britain, all in favour of a negotiated peace.

Because 'their finest hour' has entered the national mythology, any action which can be represented as contrary to its spirit has been easily dismissed in an excess of *realpolitik* and patriotic fervour. Even now questions as to whether or not the British Union of Fascists should have been banned and its leaders imprisoned are met with the response, 'Why not? We were at war,' as though that were a full and sufficient answer. In order to understand Churchill's contribution in its proper light, it is necessary, once more, to go behind the myths.

Beaverbrook was neither a coward nor a traitor, and his advocacy of a negotiated peace was based upon considerations that made a good deal of sense to many people. Indeed, at the time he abandoned them, his ideas made more sense than ever before. He encouraged Labour MPs such as Richard Stokes and James Maxton to persevere with their campaign for a negotiated peace: 'He could not see any alternative at that time but to negotiate an honourable settlement, retire behind our Empire frontiers, arm ourselves to the teeth, leave the Continent to work out its own destiny and defend the Empire with all our strength.'[13] Whatever merits such an idea had were trebled by the sudden collapse of France. After all, what could Britain hope to do without a Continental ally? Beaverbrook abandoned this position after Churchill made him Minister for Aircraft Production, but it was held by many – and it seemed to have much to commend it. The fact that during the

Commons debates on Norway, Lloyd George had reminded the House that Britain had first broken faith with Germany, was taken by Chamberlain and others as deliberately distancing himself from the Government to 'stake a position from which ultimately he might be called to make the peace'. What may have seemed improbable on 11 May, when Chamberlain wrote, was, by the end of the month, far from it. With the collapse of the Allied war effort in France, the only comfort which Chamberlain could find was the fact that the 'public don't in the least realise the gravity of the situation'.[14] But there were those in the War Cabinet who thought that the art of leadership lay not in exploiting that ignorance, but rather in trying to save what could be saved from the wreckage. Prominent amongst these was Halifax, and it was on this point that he and Churchill came close to a parting of the ways that would have wrecked the Government.

The decision to appoint Churchill Prime Minister instead of Halifax had consequences of the most wide-ranging character. Despite Churchill's rhetorical declarations that he would have been 'torn from his place'[15] if he had tried to make peace in May/June 1940, there was, as we have seen, a plentiful supply of opinion which would have applauded the idea, albeit with reluctance and the proviso that any terms of peace must be honourable. The hungry sheep looked up for sustenance. What they got was Churchill's deeply felt and brightly caparisoned vision of the destiny of a Great Nation. Ignorant of the real situation, the public fed gratefully upon a substance which gave to them a place more glorious than that which, in their hearts, they felt they deserved. But had the hungry sheep looked up and received, instead, in the manly and soothing tones of Viscount Halifax, the verdict that the British could not hope to win the war by themselves and that, in the absence of anything from the Americans save the usual kind words, and with nary an ally in sight, the time had come to talk with Herr Hitler, then it is likely that the hungry sheep would have eaten that gruel instead – with less relish perhaps, but knowing that there was no alternative. With Lloyd George coming out in favour of such a line, and no one of stature to oppose it, the 'realists' would surely have had their way. What would then have transpired lies in the realm of conjecture, but it would have been no one's 'finest hour'. At his trial, the French collaborationist leader, Pierre Laval, excused his actions in June 1940 by asking who, in their right minds, could then have believed in anything save a German victory? The answer was Churchill.

It was by this margin that Britain stayed in the war; and despite the later mythology, it is plain that there was a good deal of support for the idea of at least opening talks to find out what Hitler's peace terms might be. Of Churchill's determination to continue the war there was never any doubt, and from the start of his Premiership he looked across the Atlantic for the sustenance which the French alliance was failing to provide. Since entering the Government Churchill had corresponded sporadically with President Roosevelt, with the full knowledge and support of the Prime Minister; now that he was Prime Minister, Churchill used this channel to impress upon the American President that, whatever rumour said to the contrary, 'if necessary, we shall continue the war alone'. 'We are determined', he told Roosevelt on 18 May, 'to persevere to the very end whatever the result of the great battle raging in France might be.'[16] Two days later he made it plain that his Government would never 'parley' with Hitler – although he warned Roosevelt that 'if members of the present administration were finished' others 'might come in to parley amidst the ruins'.[17] The sombre message was that if America did not help, she might one day have to face the might of Germany alone.

But the telegrams served another purpose. Certainly at one level they were an appeal for aid and a warning of what might happen if that aid was not forthcoming; but there was more to them. They set a policy which had not been discussed in the Cabinet. Churchill was committing his Government to a policy of 'no surrender' without asking its members if they agreed with him. But he was not doing so behind their backs. His telegrams were circulated to the Cabinet, which left it open to Ministers to challenge him; so, as one historian has put it, 'Churchill was placing the onus on his colleagues to challenge his prejudgement of the issue, while at the same time directing their attention away from any balanced consideration of the pros and cons.'[18] Churchill laboured unceasingly to create a climate in which the very idea of 'parleying' with Hitler was unthinkable – or at least ought to be so.

By opening out the possibility of American aid, Churchill provided his colleagues with some hope for the future. But emphasising the American dimension was only one of the ways in which Churchill sought to create the mood which he later claimed merely to have represented. In his first speech to the House on 13 May, before the full seriousness of the situation he had inherited was plain, he threw down the gauntlet: 'I have nothing to offer but blood, toil, tears and sweat.' He stated his policy with simple grandeur: 'It is to wage war, by sea, land and air, with all our might and with all the strength that God can give us.' His aim? 'Victory – victory at all costs.' Without victory, he warned, 'there is no survival'. This was not simply a war in which the country was engaged, it was a crusade, and Churchill's rhetoric was the perfect instrument for expressing this. Britain was fighting against a 'monstrous tyranny, never surpassed in the dark, lamentable catalogue of human crime'. It was not just the British Empire and Britain herself which were at stake, but the 'urge and impulse of the ages, that mankind will move forward towards its goal'. The whole Churchillian vision was laid out in its magnificent splendour: what was at stake was civilisation itself, the whole future of mankind. It was to be Britain's destiny to fight the crusade against the Evil One: 'At this time I feel entitled to claim the aid of all, and I say "Come, then, let us go forward together with our united strength."'[19]

What Isaiah Berlin called the 'strength and coherence of his central, lifelong beliefs'[20] are displayed clearly in this first speech. Those beliefs which, for the last decade and more, had seemed increasingly archaic, had now come into their own. The new imperial style had demanded administrators and bureaucrats, men of cautious mind and circumscribed action. The virtues of the new age were not the heroic ones; there were no gods and precious few heroes. Men could not live on a high plane of intensity. This was not Churchill's vision. He took the side of Marlborough against Harley and those who would palter glory for political advantage. Life was an epic poem; men must not fall below the level demanded by events. The very language in which he was wont to clothe his thoughts was cast in an archaic mode, which heightened the tone of what he said; the style had not always been equal to the demands which history made upon the orator – now it was. In an hour of peril such as none had ever known, Churchill's vision of the destiny of England began to fill the stage.

But was it not all rather like the Charge of the Light Brigade? – '*C'est magnifique, mais ce n'est pas la guerre.*' 'Victory at all costs' sounded magnificent, and, when cast in the vision which Churchill proclaimed, the heart was uplifted – but was the mind eclipsed? There were some who wondered whether the Prime Minister was not a slave to his own language. After all, as Belgium surrendered and France began to collapse, what hope was there of victory – at any cost? All the Prime Minister's fine words to Roosevelt failed to produce anything other than fine words – and enquiries as to whether the British might not consider sending their Fleet out of Hitler's reach in case they did lose the war. Not much comfort here for those whose minds dwelt on a less exalted plane than did the Prime Minister. Viscount Halifax had not dreamed dreams when he was a young man, and he did not see visions now. What he saw was an Empire beset on all sides, with her one ally vanishing and the Continent of Europe falling under the dominion of the greatest military power which the world had ever seen. In six short weeks the whole war strategy of the Allies had been destroyed: Denmark, Holland, Belgium and now, but for a miracle, France, were all under the sway of an army which had won victories which had been pronounced impossible. Facing this might was an island empire, whose financial resources were already near collapse and whose army, tiny as it was, was in retreat. What sense did it make to talk of 'victory' in such circumstances? Churchill could declare, as he did in the War Cabinet on 21 May, that the situation in France 'was more favourable than certain of the more obvious symptoms could indicate',[21] but his confidence that the plan prepared by General Weygand could snatch victory from defeat proved vain. By 26 May, when he finally accepted that France would be defeated, the British Expeditionary Force was already preparing to try to get out of France as best it could. In these circumstances the visions of Churchill and the fears of Halifax came into conflict.

Churchill's vision of what might happen in the event of Britain failing to win can be seen from the terms of reference which he gave the Chiefs of Staff on 26 May, when he asked them to say what situation would arise in the event of 'terms being offered to Britain which would place her entirely at the mercy of Germany through disarmament, cession of naval bases in the Orkneys, etc.' The alternative scenario which they were asked to outline was equally cast in Churchillian mode: 'Can the Navy and the Air Force hold out reasonable hopes of preventing serious invasion, and could the forces gathered in this island cope with raids from the air involving detachments not greater than 10,000 men?'[22] The very act of posing the alternatives in such a stark form helped predetermine the answer; but what grounds were there for supposing that Germany's terms would necessarily be so Carthaginian? Were there not grounds for supposing that Hitler might be disposed to pay handsomely to avoid the perilous task of a sea and air-borne invasion? Viscount Halifax thought so.

When the War Cabinet met on the morning of 26 May, it heard from Churchill that Reynaud and the French were in favour of making concessions to Italy in the hope of keeping Mussolini out of the war. Churchill told his colleagues that he had told Reynaud that 'we would rather go down fighting than be enslaved to Germany'. But when the discussion moved on, it became plain that not everyone was of his view. Halifax stated that 'we had to face the fact that it was not so much now a question of imposing a complete defeat upon Germany, but of safeguarding the independence of our own Empire and if possible that of France'. He told his colleagues that the previous evening the Italian Ambassador had clearly indicated that Mussolini would be willing to propose a conference; he had replied that Britain would 'naturally be prepared to consider any proposals' which would secure 'peace' in Europe and which would guarantee Britain's safety and independence. If France collapsed, he reminded his fellow-countrymen later, that would mean that the Germans could switch all their aircraft production to the manufacture of aeroplanes, which would ensure them mastery of the skies; people could work out for themselves the implications of such a situation. Only Churchill spoke against the sense of Halifax's remarks. He did not, he said, object to approaches to Mussolini which 'did not postulate the destruction of our independence', but he was not willing to make concessions to Germany to do so. 'Security and independence' could, he stated, be achieved 'under a German domination of Europe'. It was essential to 'secure our complete liberty and independence', and he could not see Germany allowing that. Halifax disagreed and doubted whether it was in Hitler's 'interest to insist on outrageous terms. After all, he knew his own internal weaknesses.' This was a fundamental challenge to Churchill's basic assumption; although he did not meet it at once, he did stress that he did not think that Germany's terms would allow Britain to completely rearm – so they were, *ipso facto*, unacceptable. Cadogan described Churchill as being 'too rambling and romantic and sentimental and temperamental', a view shared by Lord Halifax.[23]

The possibility of 'buying off' Mussolini with concessions was, for Halifax, only the beginning of a policy which offered an escape from the supreme danger of defeat. Churchill was well aware of the dangers which might be apprehended from even the thought that the war might not be carried on to the end; the moment the sinews relaxed, even if only for an instant, it would be difficult to summon up the willpower to brace them once more. When Chamberlain reported on the morning of 27 May that the Australian High Commissioner was urging the advantages of seeking mediation by Mussolini and Roosevelt, Churchill said that it would be as well to 'issue a general injunction to Ministers to use confident language'. He was convinced that 'the bulk of the people of this country would refuse to accept the possibility of defeat'.[24] But could such an act of will by itself avert 'the possibility of defeat'? Halifax thought not.

When the Cabinet met again on the afternoon of 27 May, he and Churchill clashed – ostensibly over the French proposal to involve the Italians, but 'also largely about the general policy in the event of things going really badly in France'.[25] Halifax expressed little optimism about an approach to Mussolini being successful, but it was, he said, what the French wanted, and he did not want to give them anything to complain about. Churchill thought that any approach to Mussolini would 'ruin the integrity of our fighting position in this country'. Let the French 'give up' if that was what they wanted, though he did not think they would; Britain would 'fight it out to the end'.[26] Chamberlain, who took the view that 'there could be no harm in trying Musso & seeing what the result was. If the terms were impossible we could still reject them',[27] was inclined to go along with the Foreign Secretary. Halifax said that if it were possible to obtain a 'settlement' which did not conflict with 'fundamental conditions which were essential to us', he could not accept Churchill's view. It was better to 'accept an offer which would save the country from avoidable disaster' than to take the risk of 'two or three months of air attack'. But Churchill was only prepared to listen to a peace offer, not make one – and then only if Hitler would agree to relinquish his conquests.[28] Halifax had listened long enough: 'I thought Winston talked the most frightful rot ... and after bearing it for some time I said exactly what I thought of them, adding that if that was really their view, and it came to the point, our ways must separate.'[29]

The implications of Halifax's resignation at such a juncture were enormous, and not to be borne. Taken aback, Churchill retired with Halifax into the garden. Halifax repeated his point of view and found Churchill 'full of apologies and affection'. Halifax was very close to resigning. He told Cadogan: 'I can't work with Winston any longer,' but allowed himself to be persuaded not to 'do anything silly'.[30] But he was tempted to despair when Churchill 'works himself up into a passion of emotion when he ought to make his brain think and reason'.[31] Finding the War Cabinet an unserviceable instrument for the projection of his vision, Churchill summoned a meeting of all Ministers of Cabinet rank for the following afternoon.

The military situation on 28 May was as bad as at any period of British history since the collapse of the third coalition against Napoleon. At midnight the King of the Belgians had ordered his Commander-in-Chief to ask for an armistice; most of the British Army was still on beaches at Dunkirk, and Britain's fighter defences were almost at 'cracking point'.[32] In the Commons that afternoon Churchill made plain his determination to carry on the fight. But at a meeting of the War Cabinet in his room afterwards, he found himself once more faced by opposition from Halifax. The Foreign Secretary thought that there were advantages in making concessions to Italy, as the French wanted, in order to get Mussolini to propose a conference which would bring an end to the war. Churchill would not hear of it, dilating at length about the dangers of the 'slippery slope'. As he had the previous day, Churchill refused to acknowledge that a middle position was, at that time, possible. After the Germans had tried, and failed, to invade Britain, the situation might be different – but he did not want to open talks now. Halifax, who thought that they might get better terms now than in a few months when France had dropped out of the war, disagreed. Churchill's response was to stress, once more, the harshness of any peace terms which the Germans were bound to offer, but both Halifax and Chamberlain pointed out that there was no guarantee that Hitler's terms would be intolerable; might it not, they asked, be a good idea to find out? Churchill dismissed the chances of the 'terms' being 'decent' as 'a thousand and one against': 'nations which went down fighting rose again, but those which surrendered tamely were finished'. On that note the meeting adjourned.[33]

There followed perhaps the most crucial meeting of 1940. Churchill had failed to impose his vision on the War Cabinet; indeed, in order to keep Halifax he had had to make noises which sounded as though he would, in some circumstances, countenance the idea of a compromise peace. That these hesitations, which have led some historians to conclude that Churchill's attitude was less resolute than it appeared to be,[34] reflected nothing more than momentary concessions to Halifax can hardly be doubted. His real view, the one he had put forward on 13 May and which had encountered opposition in the War Cabinet, he now expounded to an audience containing men such as Lloyd, Amery and Dalton, who shared it. In this company Churchill felt free to start by saying that 'we must decline' mediation 'and fight on'.[35] Dalton described him as 'quite magnificent. The man, and the only man we have, for this hour.' Churchill's approach was one with which the whole nation was soon to become familiar. Yes, there were grave dangers ahead. The Germans would try to invade, but they would find it difficult given the

Navy, the Air Force and the Dominions, whose support Britain had. He then adverted to the question of talking peace terms – or, as he put it in a tone and manner which, given his audience, prejudged the issue beyond peradventure:

I have thought carefully in these last days whether it was part of my duty to consider entering into negotiations with That Man. But it was idle to think that, if we tried to make peace now, we should get better terms than if we fought it out. The Germans would demand our Fleet – that would be called 'disarmament' – our naval bases, and much else. We should become a slave state, though a British Government which would be Hitler's puppet would be set up – 'under Mosley or some such person'. And where should we be at the end of all that? On the other side we had immense reserves and advantages.[36]

Having thus polarised the issue in a way which made Halifax's suggestions for exploring the possibilities of a negotiated peace look defeatist, Churchill then proceeded in his most magnificent vein to make those views appear both immoral and unworthy of the destiny of a great nation:

'And I am convinced', he concluded, 'that every man of you would rise up and tear me down from my place if I were for one moment to contemplate parley and surrender. If this long island story of ours is to end at last, let it end only when each one of us lies choking in his own blood upon the ground.'[37]

When he finished there were, Dalton noted, 'loud cries of approval all round the table, in which, I think, Amery, Lord Lloyd and I were loudest'. It was clear to him that there was a difference between Churchill and the old appeasers, and Dalton knew who he was supporting.[38]

Churchill had succeeded in doing a number of things at this meeting. He had not simply appealed over the heads of the War Cabinet to the wider Cabinet, he had made an implicit distinction, which Dalton picked up, between the old appeasers and his own Government. It was a slightly unfair distinction, for, contrary to Dalton's suspicions, it was not Chamberlain who was taking the lead in wanting to consider negotiations, and Attlee and Henderson were no more certain than he was about whether or not they ought to negotiate.[39] But it was a distinction which succeeded not only in appropriating the moral high ground, but in conveying a vision and a sense of leadership and history which Halifax simply could not command. Where the Foreign Secretary was hesitant and intellectual in his approach, Churchill was forceful and visceral. He imposed his vision on Ministers by the very power with which he expressed it. No one wanted to believe that the war was lost. Churchill gave them assurances that it was not lost. Every Minister in that room had been brought up on a version of English history where, if 'we' lost the early battle, 'we' always won the war in the end; it was to this that Churchill appealed – and he did not do so in vain. Amery was not alone in leaving Churchill's room feeling 'tremendously heartened by Winston's resolution and grip of things. He is a real war leader and one whom it is worthwhile serving under.'[40]

When the War Cabinet reassembled at seven o'clock, Churchill's position vis-à-vis Halifax had been immensely strengthened. He had never, he told his colleagues, 'heard a gathering of persons occupying high places in political life express themselves so emphatically'. Chamberlain, who had been wavering, now lined up behind Churchill, saying that they should try to persuade Reynaud that it was worthwhile fighting on. Halifax's suggestion that they should appeal to America to enter the war at once won no favour from Churchill. Such an appeal was bound to be turned down, and that would destroy the whole psychological effect which his own appeals for her aid had had. No, said Churchill, that would be 'premature': 'If we made a bold stand against Germany, that would command their admiration and respect, but a grovelling appeal, if made now, would have the worst possible effect.'[41] Britain would fight on, if necessary alone. In his memoirs, Churchill wrote that he was convinced that the Ministers at the meeting 'represented the House of Commons and almost all the people', and he referred to the 'white glow, overpowering, sublime, which ran through our island from end to end';[42] but that was not quite how it was. In his telegram to Reynaud after the War Cabinet meeting had finished, Churchill rejected an appeal to Mussolini, saying that this was not the 'right moment'. He feared that 'the effect on the morale of our people, which is now firm and resolute, would be extremely dangerous'.[43] If there was a 'white glow', it emanated from Admiralty House and its chief occupant – Winston Churchill. As his new private secretary, John Martin, recorded in his diary on 30 May: 'The PM's confidence and energy are amazing. "Nobody left his presence without feeling a braver man" was said of Pitt; but it is no less true of him.'[44]

There were those to whom Churchill's 'theatricality' was rather distasteful.[45] Reith, who admitted to himself that he was frankly 'jealous' of Churchill's orations,[46] found his speech on 28 May 'dramatic; unreal; insincere',[47] whilst Halifax had never seen 'so disorderly a mind. I am coming to the conclusion that his process of thought is one that has to operate through speech. As this is exactly the reverse of my own it is irritating.'[48] There was something in this, but not much. Churchill's oratory was not the product, perhaps, of conscious calculation, but it was the product of his most deeply held beliefs. During the 1930s, when the times had seemed to demand smaller men for smaller measures, these same beliefs had left him stranded, like a great whale, on the beach of history. The tide had gone out, but it had now returned. Those who had been comfortable with the 1930s were correspondingly uncomfortable with Churchill. On the evening of Churchill's appointment, that quintessential Baldwinian Conservative, Rab Butler, had given vent to the opinion that,

The good clean tradition of English politics, that of Pitt as opposed to Fox, had been sold to the greatest adventurer of modern political history ... this sudden coup of Winston and his rabble was a serious disaster and an unnecessary one.

The 'pass' had been 'sold' to a 'half-breed American'.[49] He, Channon and Chamberlain's PPS, Lord Dunglass (the future Lord Home), had raised their glasses of champagne to toast Chamberlain as 'the King over the water', and by the end of May Channon feared that there was a 'definite plot to oust Halifax, and all the gentlemen of England, from the Government'.[50] Baldwinian Conservatives and civil servants like Colville and Cadogan could all agree with that epitome of bureaucratic 'soundness', Lord Hankey, that Churchill's judgment was 'unreliable' and doubt with him whether 'the wise old elephants will be able to hold the Rogue elephant'.[51]

Churchill had seldom burned offerings on the altars of the deities worshipped by the pin-striped civil servants and the tadpoles and tapers, and in an age when their gods held sway, his fortunes had been requited accordingly. But their day was, for the moment, past; they had no power equal to an occasion which their devotees had never imagined. But for Churchill, whose imagination had long dwelt in regions unknown to sensible men like Halifax and Cadogan, and whose faith in his 'star' had been tested for so long, it was as though the hour of destiny had struck. Having through an effort of his own will imposed his vision upon the Cabinet, Churchill had now to set about inspiring the French and his fellow-countrymen with it.

36

Giving Destiny a Helping Hand

On 29 May all Ministers and senior civil servants received a personal message from the Prime Minister telling them that he would be grateful if they would 'maintain a high morale in their circles' and that 'no tolerance should be given to the idea that France will make a separate peace' and that 'whatever may happen on the Continent, we cannot doubt our duty'. Two days later the Prime Minister departed for France to convince the French.[1] Over the next two weeks France was to demonstrate the limitations of what could be achieved by willpower alone. The contrast between Churchill's spirits and resolution and that of the French Government was apparent from the start – twenty miles of sea made a tremendous pyschological difference, and not all Churchill's urgings could change what geography and German military efficiency combined to dictate. Weygand, the French Commander-in-Chief, was 'querulous and aggressive', pointing out that more British than French soldiers had left Dunkirk.[2] Marshal Pétain, the great hero of Verdun in the last war, now Vice-President of the Council, cut a sad and dejected figure in civilian clothes; the Military Secretary to the Cabinet, General Ismay, thought he looked 'senile, uninspiring and defeatist'.[3] Even Reynaud, from whom so much was hoped, was tired and emotionally drained. The great French Army, upon which so many hopes were pinned, had broken in their grasp; not all the planning in the world could have provided for such a moment. The French were shattered by a terrible mixture of shock, sorrow and fear. The French wanted more troops; Churchill could offer them only rhetoric.

He promised them that British and French soldiers would leave Dunkirk *'bras dessus, bras dessus'*, and dilated upon the advantages which would accrue to the Allied cause if they could only hold out. The Germans had suffered heavier losses than the Allies, their second-line troops were of inferior quality, and the Empire would soon provide even more troops for the Allied cause than were already being raised in Britain; in the meantime, the RAF was shooting down four German aircraft for each of its own losses. By the end of the summer Britain would emerge, militarily, as a 'most important factor'. Britain and France must stand together. What did it matter if they could not pay for the vast amounts of equipment which they needed? 'America would nevertheless continue to deliver.' Churchill was, he declared, 'absolutely convinced that they only had to carry on the fight to conquer'. If Britain was invaded, it would have a 'still profounder effect' on American opinion.

Whatever happened, he emphasised, there would be no surrender. He repeated to them what he had said to the Cabinet: 'Germany ... would give no quarter: they would be reduced to the status of vassals and slaves for ever.' Churchill clearly meant to galvanise his listeners, but whether his words had that effect on men facing just the fate he had outlined is another matter. He emphasised that, if necessary, the British would retreat to the 'New World' to carry on the conflict.[4] With 'emotion' surging from him in 'great torrents' which carried even over the language barrier, Churchill declared: 'The British people will fight on until the New World conquers the Old. Better far that the last of the English should fall fighting and *finis* be written to our history than to linger on as vassals and slaves.'[5] It simply never occurred to Churchill that many, perhaps most, men and women would rather hang on to life, of whatever quality, than die.

Certainly many of the men in the room with him on that day were unwilling that they, or their countrymen, should make the final sacrifice in a vain cause. It was plain even then to Churchill that the venerable Pétain was not thinking in terms of a final redoubt in Brittany, or a retreat to North Africa.[6] Yet it was options such as these that Churchill was to press on the French during his frequent visits over the next two weeks. It was, to use a simile later used by the American Ambassador to Pétain's Vichy regime, like trying to put backbone into an eel. And yet the simile is unfair. Churchill's rhetoric and willpower could not, in Pétain's eyes, provide sufficient motive for sacrificing the French people. Only one French Minister shared Churchill's vision and willingness to sacrifice everything and everyone rather than surrender – which is why Churchill's spirit went out to the man he called, on his final visit to France on 13 June, '*l'homme du destin*', General Charles de Gaulle; it is also why the two men were fated to clash – they resembled each other too closely.[7]

If France demonstrated the limitations of willpower (with the exception of de Gaulle, who, like Churchill, believed that it could conquer everything), Churchill's response to the approaching disaster there demonstrated what it could achieve in terms of rallying the nation. Halifax, and others who thought like him, had not abandoned the hope of a successful mediation, but what Churchill now proceeded to do was to appeal over their heads to the people – and in so doing create a climate in which defeat became unthinkable and to think of it became, itself, unspeakable. On 4 June, following the unexpected success of the Dunkirk evacuation in bringing away four-fifths of the British Army, Churchill spoke to the House. He did not try to turn a defeat into a victory – 'wars are not won by evacuations' – but he did emphasise the heroism of the Allied forces, in particular the role to be played by the RAF, whom he likened to 'the Knights of the Round Table' and 'the Crusaders'; these had not parleyed with the enemy or surrendered – at least not in the history which Churchill read and wrote. It was to that history, and especially to the failures of Napoleon, that he referred his auditors for some comfort when considering Hitler's prospects of invading Britain. He had every confidence, he said, that 'if all do their duty ... we shall prove ourselves once again able to defend our island ... if necessary for years, if necessary alone'. That, he told the House (with Churchillian exaggeration) was 'the resolve of His Majesty's Government – every man of them'. His peroration will live as long as the English language:

We shall go on to the end, we shall fight in France, we shall fight on the seas and the oceans, we shall fight with growing confidence and growing strength in the air, we shall defend our island, whatever the cost may be, we shall fight on the beaches, we shall fight on the landing grounds, we shall fight in the fields and in the streets, we shall fight in the hills; we shall never surrender, and even if, which I do not for a moment believe, this island or a large part of it were subjugated and starving, then our Empire beyond the seas, armed and guarded by the British Fleet, would carry on the struggle, until, in God's good time, the new world, with all its power and might, step forth to the rescue and liberation of the old.[8]

It was sublime – nonsense – but sublime nonsense.

Quite where the 'growing confidence' was to come from, except from the reservoir of Churchill's own spirit, he wisely did not say, nor did he expand on the chances of America joining the war, or of offering the British Government a refuge from which it could carry on the struggle. But that optimism, which in the past had contributed to ruin at the Dardanelles and Narvik, now provided the eloquence to preach victory on the verge of defeat. Amery thought its implication that France was ready to drop out of the war would wound French susceptibilities, but found the speech 'very fine and really inspiring' for all that.[9] For Nicolson it was simply 'the finest speech that I have ever heard. The House was deeply moved.'[10] Dalton too found it magnificent, 'very grim and determined' and designed, he thought, 'to pull ostrich heads out of the sand both here and in the USA'.[11] Even the sophisticated and cynical Channon was won over, describing the speech as 'important and moving' and its author as 'a mountain of energy and good nature'. It even moved Reith, whose egotism was so vast that it left no room for anything else, to the reflection that 'I wish I had had to make the sort of speech Churchill did.'[12]

It was certainly a 'magnificent oration which obviously moved the House',[13] but only Dalton had spotted its wider significance. It almost dared anyone to rise and propose peace; and it sent clear signals to the Americans that Britain, under Churchill's leadership, would fight on. For it was here that the heart of Churchill's policy now lay – in the hope of American aid and in the necessity of convincing America that that aid would not be wasted by the country surrendering in the near future.[14]

Churchill's great speech was broadcast (with an actor delivering the lines) over the radio the same evening. To Spears, listening to it in France, it established Churchill as 'the supreme leader who would give each and all of us the impulse we expected and awaited'; it was as though, he wrote, the British people had been given a 'password, the significance of which only we could grasp, it bound us in a great secret understanding'. It was as if the British were passing through 'an intense fire and light that burnt out everything mean and selfish in us, leaving only a common purpose and a common unity, fusing us into the single soul of the British people'.[15] Which was what its author had intended. From Sissinghurst Castle in the Kent countryside, another Romantic with the same historical imagination, Vita Sackville-West, wrote to her husband, Harold Nicolson, that, 'even repeated by the announcer' the speech had 'sent shivers (not of fear) down my spine'. She thought that one of the reasons she had been so stirred by 'his Elizabethan phrases is that one feels the whole massive backing of power and resolve behind them, like a great fortress: they are never words for words' sake'.[16] This, again, was the message which Churchill had wished to convey. To the severe rationalist, to the dull grey men who distrusted him as a swashbuckling adventurer, it may have sounded grandiloquent, and they may have been tempted to ask what 'power' lay behind the 'resolve'; but to the majority of a nation shaken by the sudden cataclysm which had overtaken France, the words carried their own power. Like Spears and Miss Sackville-West they felt themselves bound together in a high and solemn undertaking. Had they been told that all was hopeless, then they would have submitted, resignedly, to their fate; but when Churchill told them that if they all stood together they would win, when he told them that theirs was the cause of civilisation against barbarism, and when he called upon the aid of the Lord God of Hosts, mighty in battle, they heard ancestral voices, coming down from their history-book memories of the Armada and of the Napoleonic wars, and in them stirred the blood of the people of Crécy, of Agincourt and a thousand forlorn stands in every corner of the world, and they resolved that they would not be the first generation of Britons to live as slaves. If they had known what Churchill knew, they might not have been so sure, but they knew only that Churchill said that they would win – and that Right usually prevailed – so they stiffened their sinews and waited for the onslaught which their leader had told them would come.

There were many who felt otherwise, but Churchill's rhetoric was creating a climate in which, unless the final disaster overtook the nation, the expression of the contrary point of view looked not only treasonable, which was bad enough – but cowardly, which was worse.

If Churchill's vision of British history provided the foundations for his belief in ultimate victory, it also contributed largely to his faith that the Americans would save the day for the Allied cause. He could not conceive that the Americans might have no intention of getting involved in the war, and this was one of his principal arguments in bolstering the waverers in

Britain and France. His implicit faith in the land of his mother's birth was made explicit on a host of occasions. He told the French on 31 May that if the Germans began to bomb historic English towns and cities, their American namesakes would be profoundly moved. It was the hope of American aid which Churchill held out to the French as their resistance began to collapse. When Roosevelt made a speech at Charlottesville on 10 June, in which he spoke movingly of extending aid 'full speed ahead' to the Allied cause,[17] Churchill responded eagerly, grateful for his 'strong encouragement in this dark, but not unhopeful hour'. He hoped that it would give the French the resolve to fight on, and he made plain, once more, Britain's determination to do so, asking for some destroyers.[18] He told Roosevelt on 12 June that it was up to him to try to stiffen the French in their time of trial,[19] and the President duly sent encouraging words to Reynaud.[20] But that was all the French got, and it was what the British got too. It was enough for Churchill.

Despite his own private frustrations at getting 'no practical help' from the Americans,[21] buoyed up by Roosevelt's rhetorical flourishes, which he took far more seriously than did their author,[22] Churchill resolved to make one more effort to revive the French; the only trouble was that no one could tell him, on 10 June, where the French Government was. It had left Paris, but even the Foreign Office was not quite sure where it had got to. Spears, who dined with Churchill that evening, watched him with amazement. The news as it came in was all of the worst variety: the French were in retreat; the Germans were advancing; the means for tackling an invasion were almost certainly inadequate; and, worst of all, Italy had entered the war. It was not that Italian military power was feared. As Duff Cooper implied in a broadcast, the advent of the Italians gave the British an enemy they were sure of beating. But if the jackal felt it was safe to enter the fray, then it must be almost over. Churchill quizzed Spears as to the state of morale and efficiency of the French forces, and all his verdicts were gloom-laden. As they spoke into the early hours of the morning, Spears

did not take my eyes off the heavy hunched figure in black. The strong light under the green shade caused the pale face to look paler than usual. For the first time in my life I understood the Agony of Gethsemane, what it meant to carry absolutely alone an immeasurable burden. Churchill was profoundly unhappy. For the first and only time in my experience I heard words akin to despair pass his lips.[23]

There were plenty of words of despair later that day when the two men went to France. At Briare, where the French Government had foregathered, the mood was one of hopeless resignation. Weygand appeared to have 'abandoned all hope', whilst Pétain 'looked more woe-begone than ever'.[24] Churchill still expected the Germans to establish a front in France and then attack Britain, so it was, he said, essential to discuss how to 'carry on with the struggle which nothing could prevent the British from pursuing'.[25] Weygand

and company responded with a litany of woe, with the former unable to guarantee 'that our troops will hold out for another hour'. Only one Frenchman, chain-smoking cigarettes, appeared imperturbable – and Churchill, Spears noticed, kept glancing towards him. When Churchill tried to revive memories of the German 'breakthrough' in the 1918 'Hindenburg' offensive, it simply drew from Pétain the unanswerable retort that 'in those days there were 60 British divisions in the line'. The French appealed for every British aircraft to aid them. Spears feared that Churchill's 'generous, warm-hearted, courageous' nature would respond to the appeal – but he did not. With the breach now opening, he declared that the current battle was not the 'decisive' one – that would come when 'Hitler hurls his Luftwaffe against Britain' – and for that battle the aircraft would have to remain where they were. Reynaud's response was to remind Churchill that if France fell, all Germany's might would be concentrated against Britain. 'And then what will you do?' Churchill replied that he had not thought that out very carefully, 'but that broadly speaking he would propose to drown as many of them as possible on the way over, and then to "*frapper sur la tête*" anyone who managed to crawl ashore'. French reaction to his suggestions for a Breton redoubt suggested that – save for de Gaulle – there was no will to fight on.

The morrow brought no relief. Spears found Churchill in a grumpy mood on the morning of 12 June. This was not so much because of French defeatism, but rather the result of being deprived of the personal service upon which his private life depended. The Prime Minister was used neither to dressing himself nor to finding his own breakfast in the morning. Two French officers on guard had been astonished at the sight of Churchill, resembling 'an angry Japanese genie, in a long, flowing red silk kimono over other similar, but white garments, girdled with a white belt of like material', standing there, 'sparse hair on end', growling 'Uh ay ma bain?'[26] He eventually got his bath, but with breakfast consisting of a pot of coffee and a roll, his fleshly wants could hardly be said to have been satisfied. Further talk with the French high command and Ministers did nothing to feed his spiritual and military ones.[27] As he flew back to London, he knew that the Anglo-French alliance was at an end.

There remained to be seen only whether American help would materialise and whether anything of utility could be saved from the wreck. At the War Cabinet that evening at which Churchill outlined the seriousness of the French position to his colleagues, he seized upon the 'young and energetic' de Gaulle as a last hope, and upon American aid as a *deus ex machina*.[28] A further trip to France, his last for four years, on 13 June, simply confirmed the feeling which he had come away with before: the French were finished and de Gaulle, with his talk of a Breton redoubt, was the only one of them who offered anything save despair.[29] Roosevelt's promise of support to Reynaud, which was in fact little more than a polite bromide, was converted by

Churchill's willing imagination into almost an imminent entry into the war by the Americans. He told the War Cabinet that evening that it came 'as near as possible to a declaration of war' and was 'probably as much as the President could do without Congress'; after all, he argued plausibly, Roosevelt could 'hardly urge the French to undergo further torture if he did not intend to enter the war to support them'. Churchill's colleagues agreed – it must be true – no one would have encouraged the French to carry on fighting unless he intended to do something to help them. But they did not know Roosevelt. It was, it was true, disturbing to learn that the Secretary of State, Cordell Hull, did not want Roosevelt's message published, and the news that the President 'did not realise how critical the situation was' was hardly more reassuring. But surely, the reasoning went, these things could be solved by an impassioned appeal.[30]

Thus it was that at 3 a.m. on 14 June Churchill told Roosevelt that the publication of his message was 'absolutely vital' if the French were to carry on the fight.[31] The response was that only Congress could commit America to the war.[32] Churchill declined to become the conduit for this discouraging information. If Roosevelt wished Reynaud to know what lay behind his words, then that was a job for the American Ambassador.[33] That afternoon came news that organised French resistance had ceased. There would be no Breton redoubt; there would be no gallant last stand; and there would be no God emerging from any machine. The Germans entered Paris that afternoon. Where, on 13/14 June, Churchill had been able to use Roosevelt's telegrams to bring hope where there seemed none, the news that they contained no hope came through to Reynaud on 15 June just in time to give those members of his Cabinet who wished to sue for peace their opportunity.[34] That afternoon the French asked to be released from their promise not to conclude a separate peace.[35] A desperate situation called for no common remedy.

The British response to Reynaud's anguished telegram was to give permission, provided the Fleet and as many aircraft as possible were sent to Britain, but no sooner had the telegram conveying this arrived in Bordeaux than it was superseded.[36] A telephone call came through from de Gaulle, who was in London, to Reynaud whilst Spears was with him; he was offering, with Churchill's approval, a plan whereby Britain and France would become one nation. For a moment this conception, which had originated with two members of the French mission in Britain, Jean Monnet and René Pleven, rallied Reynaud, but his colleagues saw it as a perfidious British plot to snap up French colonies – and it came to naught.[37] Reynaud resigned and was replaced by Pétain, who asked the Spanish to mediate with Hitler. On 22 June an armistice was signed and France left the war of which she had become the most prominent casualty. De Gaulle, who had come back to France to help organise a last stand, found himself under the necessity of hitching a lift back to London with Spears on 17 June: 'His martyrdom had begun.'[38]

Disappointed at Roosevelt's refusal to allow his message to Reynaud to be published, and with American tardiness, Churchill had delivered a solemn warning to Roosevelt on the evening of 15 June. Failing an American declaration of war, he told the President, France would collapse and Britain would be left alone. Seizing on the one point which he knew would alarm Roosevelt, Churchill warned him that, whilst his Government would never refuse to send the British Fleet across the Atlantic, 'if resistance was beaten down here a point may be reached in the struggle where the present Ministers no longer have control of affairs and when very easy terms could be obtained for the British Isles by their becoming a vassal state of the Hitler Empire'. This, which ran totally counter to the assumptions deployed at the Cabinets of 26–28 May, when Churchill had consistently assumed that Germany's terms would be the harshest possible, was in part designed to scare Roosevelt into action, but his warning was not wholly tactical in nature.[39]

Churchill's seizure of the initiative since the end of May, and his victory in the War Cabinet over mediation, had enabled him to carry out his own policy. But one of the main supports of that policy was now crumbling as France fell, and the other, American support, appeared not to be materialising. Churchill was convinced, as were many other observers, that the German economy was already at breaking-point. As he stressed to Roosevelt on 15 June, he was not expecting the Americans to send an expeditionary force; rather he was relying upon the 'tremendous moral effect' which an American declaration of war would have on the Germans. If their economy and war effort was on the verge of collapse, it was only a matter of hanging on, as he had told the French, for a few more months.[40] The assumptions behind his strategy were still recognisably those which had informed Chamberlain's; and if he failed, he could expect to suffer Chamberlain's fate. One of the things which had sealed this was the existence of an alternative leader of stature, with what was thought to be a different policy: the cry had been to press the war with greater vigour, and so all eyes had turned to Churchill. But should it turn, as French opinion had, to talk of peace, then there existed alternatives to Churchill.

Halifax, his main rival only a month before, was already, like Chamberlain, suffering from the 'Guilty Men' myth which was manufactured by left-wing publicists in the aftermath of Dunkirk. Books such as the famous *Guilty Men* by 'Cato' cast the blame for Britain's plight on the 'appeasers', and there were calls for Churchill to get rid of Halifax, Chamberlain and the other 'men of Munich'. This was a convenient escape from the realities of the situation. 'Cato', one of whose constituent parts was the future Labour Party leader, Michael Foot, was able to lay the blame for everything which went wrong on to the old regime, which left Churchill as the hero of the hour.[41] What it ignored was the fact that a numerically larger force, with more aircraft and tanks, had been overwhelmed, not by lack of material, but by a better army;

but that would never have done. Much though Churchill was later to contribute to the myth, at the time it was most inconvenient to him. At Chamberlain's request he reminded some of his press contacts that Chamberlain and company still enjoyed the overwhelming support of the Conservative Party, upon which his own position depended, and asked them to call off their hounds.[42]

Chamberlain himself, sadly, still nursed hopes that he might once more become Prime Minister, but his day was long past.[43] If an alternative to Churchill was needed, if a policy of peace was called for, then the obvious man was Lloyd George. Chamberlain had thought that Lloyd George was angling for just such a position at the time of the Norway debates by the way in which he had emphasised that it was the Allies who had first broken faith with Germany. But Chamberlain detested Lloyd George and there was no crime, however base, of which he did not think him capable.[44] On 28 May, at the height of the debate within the War Cabinet on possible Italian mediation, Churchill had raised with Chamberlain the question of Lloyd George joining the Cabinet. Given that Churchill too suspected Lloyd George of 'defeatist' tendencies, this might appear somewhat surprising; but he would, of course, be safer inside the Government than outside it. But Chamberlain did not want Lloyd George, and Churchill was not willing to lose the leader of the Conservative Party in order to accommodate his old chief.[45] With the growth of the 'Guilty Men' outcry, Chamberlain agreed to drop his opposition, provided Lloyd George would give assurances that he would end his feud against the 'appeasers'.[46] Lloyd George responded by asking for time to think the matter over, but had still sent no reply by 18 June.

By this time Churchill had been made aware that there were mutterings about his conduct of the war within his own Cabinet. On 17 June Amery, Boothby, Macmillan and Lloyd had met to discuss what 'practical changes' were needed in 'our system of Government'. Amery typed out a memorandum containing their suggestions, but Lloyd advised against showing it to Churchill that evening. The following morning Chamberlain told Churchill that Lloyd and Amery were involved in a plot to change the Cabinet. This, as Amery put it, 'aroused Winston's authoritarian instincts'.[47] He told Chamberlain: 'I shall dismiss them. I shall tell them that if there is any more of this nonsense they will go', and he did tell Amery just that. In conversation with Chamberlain he referred to the lack of any response from Lloyd George to the offer of a Cabinet post. With events in France in mind, Chamberlain wondered whether the old man was 'waiting to be the Marshal Pétain of Britain'. Churchill responded: 'Yes, he might, but there won't be any opportunity.'[48] In his speech to the House that afternoon, Churchill did his best to make sure that came true.

With discontent in his own ranks, the French alliance in ruins and no sign that America was about to do anything even mildly dramatic, let alone heroic, and with an alternative leader of charisma and great reputation in the wings, Churchill's position was delicately poised. But he responded, as he did throughout the crisis, by appealing to the Commons and to the nation at large. His appeal was through the emotions, to the vision which he had of Britain's destiny.

Churchill began by recapitulating the events in France, not trying to hide the magnitude of the disaster, but appealing for national unity. With an obvious swipe at those who had nothing better to do with their time at this crisis in the nation's affairs than to write scurrilous pamphlets which threatened that unity, he referred to the futility of opening 'a quarrel between the past and the present' and made it clear that he stood by all his Ministers. On the pressing subject of the hour – the threat of a German invasion – Churchill declared that by land, and sea and air, the British were ready to repel anything which the Nazis might seek to throw at them. It was not, he said reassuringly, simply a question of 'death' or 'tyranny' – there was a good chance of most people avoiding both. Germany would, he said, struggle to keep her dominion over her conquests, and time was not on her side. He reminded his auditors that during the last war they had suffered 'disaster and disappointment', but still they had prevailed. 'What General Weygand called the Battle for France is over. I expect that the Battle of Britain is about to begin.' Then he drew deep upon his vision in a peroration which had echoes of every heroic moment in the long history of the Island Race: 'Upon this battle depends the survival of Christian civilisation. Upon it depends our own British life, and the long continuity of our institutions and our Empire. Hitler knows that he will have to break us in this island or lose the war.' It was no ordinary destiny which called them. If they could prevail, then 'all Europe may be free, and the life of the world may move forward into broad, sun-lit uplands'. The price of failure was almost unthinkable, for in that event 'the whole world' would 'fall into the abyss of a new dark age'. But this one, unlike that which had followed the end of the Roman Empire, would be 'made more sinister, and perhaps more protracted by the lights of perverted science'. There was only one thing to do: 'Let us therefore brace ourselves to our duties, and so bear ourselves that, if the British Empire and its Commonwealth last for a thousand years, men will still say, "This was their finest hour."'[49]

Reaction in the House was less rapturous than for his previous oration. Colville, who thought Churchill had spoken 'less well', recorded that he had 'ended magnificently'.[50] Channon, by this time recovered from the vapours, and beginning to suspect that Churchill 'loves war',[51] was 'not impressed', but supposed that 'the nation will be'.[52] In the latter assumption Channon was not necessarily correct. John Martin noted that Churchill's 'halting delivery at the start' of the broadcast that evening 'seems to have struck people',[53] whilst Nicolson, who had felt that it was 'magnificent' in the House, thought that it sounded 'ghastly on the wireless. All the great vigour he put into it seemed to evaporate.' He wished that Churchill 'would not talk on the wireless unless he is feeling in good form'.[54] Dalton noted that whilst the speech had gone down well enough in the House, Churchill had been 'much more loudly cheered by the Labour Party than by the general body of Tory supporters', and drew from it the conclusion that Chamberlain should not be driven from the Government, where he would become a 'rallying-point' for those many Conservatives who were still loyal to him: 'Leave him where he is as a decaying hostage.'[55]

Churchill had, once more, staked his own survival as Prime Minister upon a strategy of 'no surrender'. That was the badge of his administration, that was his contract with the nation. But, as he had warned Roosevelt, his was neither the only road nor yet the only possible Government. With Lloyd George still refusing to join the Government, there remained a possible British Pétain, if the hour for one should strike. Churchill had imposed his policy upon the War Cabinet and his will upon the nation, but it was to take a continuous effort to keep both where he had established them by 18 June 1940.

37

The Struggle for Survival

The 'finest hour' speech was only the first of a number of actions by which Churchill sought to consolidate his position over the next two months. It was not the only speech, either, made that day which would achieve legendary status. On the same evening de Gaulle broadcast to France, very much in Churchillian vein. France, he told his fellow countrymen, had lost a battle, but not the war. Had it been left to the Foreign Office that broadcast would not have taken place. With the Pétain Government still an uncertain quantity in the eyes of the diplomats, the Foreign Secretary was anxious to do nothing to upset it – and asking a former junior Minister to make an appeal for volunteers to carry on the war, particularly one who was known to have quarrelled with Pétain in the past, was hardly the way to do this. It took Spears's influence with Churchill to ensure that the tall General made what was to become the most famous French broadcast in history.[1] De Gaulle's motives were only gradually to become clear. Churchill's motives in backing him were plain from the start. Here was a courageous fighting-man, who could rally French forces and, after the armistice, perhaps French colonies to the Allied side. Churchill accepted the need to be nice to Pétain's Vichy regime, but only because he nursed fantasies that the aged Marshal or some of his colonial satraps might be persuaded back into the war. De Gaulle seemed to Churchill to embody the same sort of fighting spirit which he himself represented, and with Spears as his liaison officer to the Free French, Churchill looked forward to the rallying of substantial forces to the side of the fighting de Gaulle.[2]

It was only gradually that it became clear that both Churchill and de Gaulle had made the same mistake. Both had imagined that many Frenchmen possessed their vision and willingness to fight. Most of them preferred to get on with their lives as best they could. Churchill's action on 4 July in ordering an attack upon the French Fleet at Oran, partly in order to impress the Americans with Britain's determination to fight on, did nothing to help de Gaulle's cause. But even without it, few rallied to him. But Churchill had made a mistake which only slowly became apparent. De Gaulle was a political general; he was not content to organise a sort of foreign legion. He was also a dreamer of dreams and an egotist on a Churchillian scale. If Louis XIV had said '*l'état, c'est moi*,' de Gaulle believed it. His dream of France did not encompass her defeated and grovelling before the enemy; when France was not great she was not France, so the Pétain regime could not represent her: '*Le Gouvernement de la France ayant capitulé est au pouvoir de l'ennemi. Il ne représent donc plus la Nation française.*'[3] In that case, he, de Gaulle, must take on the burden. It was not until the abortive operation to seize Dakar, 'Operation Menace', in October, that it became plain that most of the French colonies would stay with Vichy. By then, however, as relations with Vichy cooled, the Foreign Office became rather keener on the General than it had been before. It was not until 1941, and the campaign to take Syria, that it became clear to Churchill that de Gaulle's motives were not what he would have them be; but by then the General was too firmly established, and in too good an odour with the Foreign Office, to be dumped as precipitately as Churchill might have liked.[4]

If backing de Gaulle because it was one way of carrying on the war turned out to be a decision pregnant with future trouble, the rest of the Churchillian strategy turned out to have unexpected flaws too. Churchill followed up his speech on 18 June with a secret session of the House two days later. This expedient, which he adopted only at moments of crisis, was designed to give MPs the chance to voice their views in private – and for him to tell them things which he did not want to make public knowledge. From the fragmentary notes which survive for the speech he delivered on that occasion, and from the recorded remarks of MPs who were present, it is clear that Churchill outlined to them the strategy which he had formulated and put to the War Cabinet. This had three parts: in the first place would come the task of repelling the expected invasion. If that failed, Hitler 'has lost the war'. But it was not enough for Hitler to 'lose'. How was Britain going to win? This was where the other two parts of his strategy came in: 'I look to superiority in air power in the future', and to 'transatlantic reinforcements'. The timescale for victory was uncertain, but if they could get through the 'next 3 months' they could get 'through the next 3 years'. In addition, Britain enjoyed what Churchill always took to be the advantage traditionally enjoyed by a sea power – the ability to attack the enemy's long and vulnerable coastline at a point of her choosing. He had already told the French and the War Cabinet that he expected German bombing of England to have a powerful effect upon the Americans, and now he told the House that 'nothing will stir them like fighting in England'. It might be, he told them, that they would have to wait until the American election was over in November, but even before then they could rely upon the Americans for 'aid'. If the British held out until then, 'I cannot doubt the whole English-speaking world will be in line together.' But the Americans could only be impressed if the British stood firm and united and resolute.[5]

It was in pursuit of this objective that the French Fleet was attacked; it was also in pursuit of it that Churchill wooed Roosevelt and that Churchill assumed an identity of views between Britain and America. Part of this strategy was successful. Roosevelt, who throughout June and early July was chary about both Britain's will and her ability to carry on the fight, gradually came round to the view that he ought to extend to her enough aid to keep her going.[6] But Churchill was wrong in supposing that either he, or his country, were just awaiting the opportunity to enter the war. Indeed, despite his great hopes that November would bring succour, he had to wait another thirteen months, and even then America only entered the war when booted into it. The famous 'bases for destroyers' deal of August 1940 was, or ought to have been, a warning that British and American interests were not always identical. For fifty clapped-out ships, which were, for the most part, of little practical use, the British had to hand over leases on valuable bases in the Caribbean. Empire enthusiasts within the Cabinet like Lloyd and Amery viewed the whole episode with both distaste and alarm.

The second part of Churchill's strategy for victory, the strategic bombing of Germany, was equally over-optimistic in its basic assumption. The Blitz was to show that a nation could carry on the fight even under heavy bombing, which was not, when it came, the Armageddon which everyone had thought it would be. The German economy was not, as Churchill had thought, at breaking-point; indeed, flush with the gold of looted chancelleries, it was not until late in the war that the economy was fully mobilised for war. Relying on strategic bombing and German economic collapse were even dicier prospects than gambling upon a quick American entry into the war.[7] One historian has even gone so far as to conclude that although Churchill made the 'right decision', he did so 'for the wrong reasons'.[8] Others have gone even further. After all, if the reasons were 'wrong', how could the decisions be 'right'?[9]

Churchill's view of what a German armistice would involve changed according to the audience he wished to address. To the War Cabinet and to the French, German terms would involve being turned into a 'vassal state'; but when he wished to alarm Roosevelt, then German terms might well be temptingly acceptable to someone other than himself. The armistice imposed upon the French gave an idea of how the Germans treated defeated foes – two-thirds of the country occupied, the Fleet and Army neutralised, and massive 'reparations'. But Churchill had never doubted that the nature of the Nazi regime would mean just that sort of thing. But what terms might await an undefeated Britain? Churchill's own comments in the debate in May had indicated that he might be willing to listen to the answer, but not before Britain had demonstrated her power to resist. And long before that happened Churchill expected America to have entered the war. But there were some who thought that there were advantages in getting an answer to this question before the bombing started, if only because they remained unconvinced by Churchill.

The 'finest hour' myth has such a hold on the British national consciousness that even to suggest, fifty years later, that a compromise peace might have been had is enough to prompt letters to the press denouncing such an idea as 'shameful' and the product of 'dubious hindsight'. But it was not only with hindsight that peace was considered, and to label those who wanted it as 'candidates for the role of the British Pétain and Laval' is to employ as an instrument of historical criticism a pole-axe originally designed as an offensive weapon against those people in 1940.[10] The best of the accounts of the Second World War written to mark the fiftieth anniversary of 1939 declared grandly that, after the fall of France, 'German peace feelers were brushed aside with scant evidence of interest in them from anyone other than R. A. Butler and the Duke of Windsor, who counted for little';[11] but such a statement ignores the fact that one reason why the 'evidence' is 'scant' is that much of it is still concealed. It also ignores the continued existence of the theme which had surfaced in Cabinet on 26–28 May. Contrary to the myth and its makers, there was a continued interest in 'peace'. The fact that Halifax's deputy at the Foreign Office should have contacted the Swedish Minister in London, Bjorn Prytz, at the same time that Churchill was making his great speech, is a truer reflection of the ambiguous realities of the time, and of Churchill's achievement, than memories of a golden summer of glory fifty years before.

No British record was kept of the conversation between Butler and Prytz on 17 June, and the British Government intervened on two occasions to prevent publication of Prytz's version.[12] But Prytz's account is not only in line with what Butler had been saying since before the war, it is entirely in accord with what Halifax had been saying in May. According to Prytz, Butler said that the 'official attitude' would 'for the present be that the war should continue, but he must be certain that no opportunity should be missed of compromise' on 'reasonable conditions'; 'no die-hards' would be 'allowed to stand in the way'. After interrupting the meeting to see Halifax, Butler assured Prytz that 'common sense and not bravado would dictate the British Government's policy'.[13] A telegram from the Foreign Office to Sweden, which was despatched that evening, is still 'withheld from public inspection', so is an item on the agenda of the War Cabinet on the afternoon of 18 June.[14] Whether the 'closed' item 5 on the agenda relates, as Clive Ponting speculates, to the Butler/Prytz conversations can only be known to officialdom, but the silence is suggestive. Cadogan's diary refers to the meeting, at which Churchill was not present, in cryptic terms: 'No reply from Germans.'[15]

Whether Cadogan's remark and the censored item on the Cabinet's agenda were part of a Foreign Office-sponsored 'peace initiative' is unclear. If it was not, successive British Governments have only their own addiction to secrecy to thank for fostering any suspicions otherwise. If it was, and if there was more than a contingent connection between Butler's remarks and the Italian conviction that there had been an 'official' British peace overture, then it is remarkable that there are no other references to it. That does not mean it was not so, but for Halifax to have taken such a bold initiative would have been out of character, and for the War Cabinet to have sanctioned it in Churchill's absence would have been even more remarkable. The only 'intrigue' which Halifax was interested in on 19 June was the one 'going on in the House of Commons against Neville and no doubt also against me'.

But he did not know 'of what importance it may be & it leaves my withers quite unwrung. If anybody thinks they can run the job better I shan't grumble!'[16] Chamberlain referred to 'rumours' emanating from American journalists that he and Halifax were 'intriguing to oust Winston in order to negotiate with Hitler on peace terms',[17] but he was, in fact, behaving towards Churchill with the same 'unimpeachable loyalty' which the Prime Minister was showing towards him.[18] But there is no sign, in any private correspondence or diary, that anything as momentous as an 'official' offer was made. When Butler's language came to Churchill's attention, he condemned it as 'odd and defeatist'.[19] Butler denied that he had held the language reported: 'Had I not been ready to subscribe to the Prime Minister's courageous lead in the House ... I should have felt bound to inform you and to leave the administration,' he told Halifax on 26 June, when he also offered to resign.[20] Halifax refused Butler's offer and told Churchill on 27 June that he was 'satisfied that there is no divergence of view' or doubt about Butler's 'complete loyalty to Government policy'.[21]

But lest this should be thought to dispose of the matter, it might be noted that a week later 'silly old Halifax' was 'hankering' after Papal suggestions for a negotiated peace.[22] These too were hit on the head by Churchill: 'I hope it will be made clear to the Nuncio that we do not desire any inquiries to be made as to terms of peace with Hitler.'[23] There could be few doubts as to this after the attack on the French Fleet at Oran, which also provided the occasion for the Chief Whip, Margesson, to organise a demonstration of support for Churchill in the House of Commons.[24] Whatever individual Ministers now thought, in public they could not be seen to be giving vent to a view different to the one which Churchill espoused.

Macaulay believed that it was one of the marks of an 'imperial race' that whilst it was inclined to look with 'imperious' disdain upon lesser races, 'the thought of submitting to a foreign master, or of turning his back before an enemy, never, even in the last extremity,' crossed its mind;[25] what Churchill succeeded in doing was in tapping and nourishing that 'peculiar virtue'. It is one of the more remarkable of the phenomena of that summer that far from the fall of France making the English down-hearted, it might almost have been said to have cheered them up. Chamberlain, despite regarding the collapse of France as a 'blow',[26] took comfort in being 'alone' from the fact that 'we are at any rate free of our obligations towards the French who have been nothing but a liability. It would have been far better if they'd been neutral from the beginning.'[27] The King was glad that we had 'no more allies to pamper', whilst Hankey spoke for many when he wrote that it was 'almost a relief to be thrown back on the resources of the Empire and of America'.[28] As the French failed to rally to de Gaulle, Dalton took the characteristically British francophobic view that 'Their insularity and non-travelling habit are coming out with a rush. They are too much attached to their mistresses, and their soup, and their little properties!'[29] They could compare their own resolution with the lack of it shown by the rest of Europe. This deep vein of the xenophobia characteristic of an imperial race was successfully mined by Churchill during that summer. The French Fleet was attacked and peace overtures rejected with scorn. In the face of an invasion, even Lloyd George thought it wise tactics to hold his tongue until it was clear whether or not Churchill's policy would succeed;[30] he did not see how it could, but although he had come to the secret session on 20 June, he had 'put his notes in his pocket'.[31] By 12 August even Butler could write to the new British Ambassador in Moscow, the Labour politician, Sir Stafford Cripps:

There is very little tired spirit here, and very few advocates of any policy other than that we are pursuing. There is a dying down of criticism of the Government, and a very considerable unanimity in the support of Churchill, who, with his warm oratory and stout leadership, is swinging us along.[32]

Thus it was that whilst the threat of invasion was imminent, the policy which Churchill had impressed upon the Cabinet and the nation by force of will, oratory and the exercise of a good deal of political skill would remain dominant. Warning of what could happen to opponents was provided by the operation of section 18B of the Defence of the Realm Act, under which Mosley and other suspected 'defeatists' were rounded up and bundled into gaol. They were no real threat to anyone, as Churchill knew, but the nation had to speak with one voice – and if that meant *habeas corpus* going west for a while, *tant pis*.

If Churchill had impressed his vision upon the country and encouraged it to adopt it for itself, his impact upon the Whitehall machine and his colleagues had been equally dramatic. When Churchill had been appointed Prime Minister, there had been a general fear in Whitehall that he and his minions, Bracken, Desmond Morton and 'the Prof.', would be inserted into positions of responsibility, thus leading to a situation even worse than that which had obtained during Lloyd George's Premiership; Churchill's love of unorthodox men and methods was well-known.[33] The thought of Bracken replacing the 'charming, inoffensive and extremely sensible' Alec Dunglass made Jock Colville 'shudder'.[34] But these fears turned out to be exaggerated. Bracken certainly replaced Dunglass, but men like Morton and Spears, whilst they could be usefully put to work helping de Gaulle, were unable to secure any real hold on power. Churchill backed them, for a while, in their attempts to support the Free French, but, on the whole, he preferred to work with the Whitehall machine. This should have occasioned no surprise. It is a sign of how long it was since Churchill had held office that none of the civil servants could remember just how well Churchill had always managed to work with the Civil Service. The problem was whether the Civil Service could work with him. Churchill had always been a demanding and imperious Minister, and under the strains of the summer of 1940, and lacking the restraint of a Prime Minister above him, he became even more difficult to handle.

Hankey had described Churchill as a 'Rogue elephant' and had doubted whether Chamberlain and Halifax, 'the wise old elephants', would be 'able to hold' him;[35] this proved an accurate premonition. Chamberlain remained a force in the Government by virtue of his position as leader of the Conservative Party, but his position was damaged by the 'Guilty Men' campaign. He remained, however, an essential prop for Churchill. Chamberlain, in turn, felt that Churchill was 'the right man for the head in view of his experience and study of war', whilst Churchill was heard to give expression to the view that: 'I can't tell you what a help Neville is to me. I don't know what I should do without him.'[36] He certainly provided Churchill with an efficient chairman of Cabinet committees and took on the role of an experienced Chief Executive;[37] but except when it came to Lloyd George or Labour attacks on the 'Guilty Men', he no longer asserted his will as once he had. His self-confidence, which had always been one of his main assets (and which his enemies saw as arrogance), had been badly damaged by the events of 8–10 May. He felt happy with the new role he had taken on and was content to leave the major responsibility to Churchill. Although Churchill assured him of his indispensability, and stood by him during the 'Guilty Men' campaign, Chamberlain could not 'settle my mind to the idea that my stay here will be other than temporary'.[38]

Chamberlain found Halifax a 'great comfort because he remains so steady and seems always to keep his sense of humour even on the worst days'.[39] But, as the debate over policy at the end of May had shown, the one thing which could wring the Foreign Secretary's 'withers' was Churchill's highly emotional attitude to problems which he thought required the use of the brain rather than the mouth. On 19 June he told Hoare that 'Winston remains in good heart, exceedingly diffuse and irrelevant at Cabinets, which consequently wander over the whole field discursively.'[40] Such criticisms, which mirrored those of civil servants like Cadogan,[41] were, however, as far as Halifax could, or would, go. The fact that Churchill had imposed his own policy over Halifax's wishes had settled, at least for the moment, whose will would dominate the Cabinet; but then Halifax's refusal to take the Premiership when it was his for the asking had really settled that issue long before. Halifax lacked the personality to impose his will; Churchill did not.

By creating for himself the new post of Minister of Defence, Churchill secured a dominant position in the direction of the war. The Chiefs of Staff and the various Service Ministers now all came under his direct control; as ever, it took a great deal of strength of character to stand up to Churchill – and now that he was armed with the full panoply of powers of a Prime Minister in wartime, it took more courage than ever to do so. His first Chief of the Imperial General Staff, Sir John Dill, lacked the ability to stand up to him effectively,[42] as did

Sir Dudley Pound at the Admiralty.[43] Of the Service Ministers, A. V. Alexander at the Admiralty was either in the hands of his admirals, or in awe of Churchill; not even the most daring of revisionists has dared to claim great abilities or force of character for this hitherto and hereafter obscure Labour MP.[44] Churchill's old friend Archie Sinclair, who went to the Air Ministry, did his job well, but, like Alexander, existed in Churchill's shadow. The Secretary of State for War, Anthony Eden, kept up 'his popular position', according to Butler,[45] which gave him a better power-base than either Alexander or Sinclair, but having lacked the willpower to impose himself on Chamberlain, it was hardly to be expected that he would suddenly find the strength to do this to Churchill. There were times when he thought Churchill would be 'a better PM if he did not argue the details of war himself',[46] and he was inclined to be wary of some of his cronies such as Beaverbrook, but he was hamstrung in making criticism by his own admiration for Churchill and the feeling, shared by Halifax, that 'a Prime Minister, in times like this, must be allowed to choose whom he wants to help him with his burden'.[47] Moreover, by complimenting him, and by flattering him that 'he, I and Max [Beaverbrook] had to carry the Government', Churchill kept him sweet.[48]

In receiving compliments from the Prime Minister, Eden, like Beaverbrook, was in a small select company. The latter had written in his own memoirs of the Great War that Churchill had in him the 'stuff of tyrants' when he was on the crest of the wave; Clementine Churchill was, by the summer of 1940, inclined to agree with this verdict from a man with whom she was more usually inclined to disagree. On 27 July she put pen to paper to tell Churchill 'something I feel you ought to know'. This was what many others were thinking but no one else dared say – which was that Churchill's 'rough sarcastic & overbearing manner' was breeding 'either dislike or a slave mentality'; colleagues and civil servants either disliked the Prime Minister intensely, or else concealed their real feelings and any objections which they had to his ideas because of his attitude: 'My Darling Winston. I must confess that I have noticed a deterioration in your manner; & you are not as kind as you used to be.' It was, perhaps, a sign of his mood at that time that even Clementine doubted whether she should give him this letter, and delayed before doing so.[49]

Certainly some of Churchill's odder ideas did not find the opposition for which, perhaps, their nature seemed to destine them. The day after Clementine wrote her letter, the Chiefs of Staff agreed to Churchill's plan to meet any German invasion by the use of 'Leopard Groups'. This idea, for a force of '20,000 British Storm Troops', drawn from existing units, which would be held no more than four miles from the coast, 'ready to spring at the throat of any small landings or descents',[50] was typically Churchillian. In conception it was bold, and it drew its inspiration from a desire to be seen to be doing something, but in practice it created 'chaos' by 'completely disregarding the accepted service view that the best chance of fending off an invasion was by meeting it on the beaches'.[51]

Lloyd George was apt to claim that there were two main differences between himself and Churchill as war leaders: the first was that where he had surrounded himself with men of the stature of Milner, Balfour, Austen Chamberlain and Curzon, Churchill surrounded himself with 'yes men'; secondly, that where he had been willing to split the Liberal Party, Churchill would not do the same to the Conservative Party. There was a little truth in both, but not as much as Lloyd George liked to claim. Indeed, Lloyd George had only himself to thank for his not being in the Government. Beaverbrook thought that Lloyd George's attitude would depend on 'whether the Americans will come in or not' – 'in other words, if there is a good chance of our winning he will come in and get his share of the glory'; but if not, then he would remain outside 'ready to form another Government & make the peace for the terms of which he would be able to blame the maladministration of his predecessors'.[52] Churchill's seizure of the initiative following the fall of France did not, of course, rule out such a move by Lloyd George at some later date.

Although Chamberlain had gone along with Churchill's optimistic remarks about the likelihood of American aid, he had privately taken his usual view that not much could be expected from them except for words: 'unfortunately they are so unready themselves that they can do little to help us *now* while preaching at Hitler is not likely to be effective'.[53] The French had discovered the terrible truth of this, and it was now to be Britain's turn. On 17 June Churchill had told Lothian, the British Ambassador in Washington, that he was 'deeply sensible' of Roosevelt's 'desire to help us' and that the 'most effective thing he can do is to let us have destroyers immediately'.[54] But nothing came. Instead, as Lothian reported on 27 June, a 'wave of pessimism' swept America as to Britain's chances of winning the war; there were even signs that 'it is beginning to affect the President'.[55] If the reality of 'their finest hour' was a great deal more complicated and ambiguous than Churchill's myth-making made it appear, so too was the nature of the relationship between Churchill and Roosevelt. Because Churchill placed all of his eggs in the American basket, so to speak, it was essential for his purpose, both as historian, but also as the great proponent of Anglo-American co-operation, that nothing should appear which would mar the image of perfect harmony. As one commentator has put it, there is a sense in which Churchill's *The Second World War* is a 'political speech – in a direct line from his famous 1943 address at Harvard and his more famous 1946 speech at Fulton, Missouri', and he did not scruple; indeed, he thought it was his 'patriotic duty' to 'rewrite world history to serve his country'.[56] Nowhere is this more apparent than in his treatment of his relationship with Roosevelt.

Churchill was fond of recalling that he and Roosevelt had met before the war, but the President had no memory of the event.[57] In fact, he formed his opinion of Churchill from the reports sent back by his emissaries. The American Ambassador in London, Joseph Kennedy, was downright defeatist about Britain's possibilities of survival and positively insulting about Churchill, whom he described on 15 July as 'a fine two-handed drinker' whose 'judgement has never proven to be good'. Another of Roosevelt's aides described the President as having heard that Churchill was 'drunk half of his time'.[58] Despite the Churchillian legend, to which American participants in the war were only too happy to pay lip-service later, there was no widespread desire in June or July 1940 to help the British; instead, there was considerable scepticism about whether it was worth sending them any more war materials.[59]

If the Americans were divided on this issue, Churchill was in two minds on the utility of any further appeal to Roosevelt. On 28 June, despite advice from Lothian, and the Government's Chief Diplomatic Adviser, Sir Robert Vansittart, Churchill rejected the idea of a propaganda campaign to 'pander to American opinion', telling them both that it was 'events which move the world. If we smash the Huns here we shall need no propaganda in the United States.'[60] It was exactly this message which he conveyed to Lothian the same day. Up until April, he wrote, the Americans had been 'so sure the Allies would win that they did not think help necessary. Now they are so sure we shall lose that they do not think it possible.' The best method of frightening Roosevelt into giving help was to warn him of the dangers of the British Fleet falling into the hands of the Germans if the British had to make an armistice: 'Feeling in England against the United States would be similar to French bitterness against us now. We have not really had any help worth speaking of from the United States so far.'[61] He was reluctant to take up the American offer, on 17 June, of secret Anglo-American Staff talks, fearing that they would 'turn almost entirely on the American side upon the transfer of the British Fleet to transatlantic bases', which would 'weaken confidence' in Britain. It was only under pressure from Halifax and Lothian that he agreed to do so.[62]

Churchill's warnings in May and June about the possibility of the British Fleet being used by some 'Pétainist' Government as a bargaining counter with Hitler were, in fact, too effective and aided the process of inhibition in Washington.[63] When Churchill wanted to send another telegram asking, once more, for destroyers, and stressing the danger that the Irish might be about to throw their lot in with Hitler, Kennedy advised against sending it on the grounds that it was too pessimistic in tone; reluctantly Churchill agreed with Halifax that his message should be postponed.[64] Churchill was, however, correct in his assumption that the fact of survival and the evidence of his own words, along with actions such as the attack on the French Fleet, would persuade the Americans to give the British some support. But the expectations which he held, both of the amount of support and of the speed with which it would arrive – and the price that would be exacted for it – were all to be cruelly disappointed.

Churchill may have seen the Americans as a branch of the 'English-

Speaking Peoples', but they were, in fact, foreigners who disliked the British Empire even more than did Hitler. The Americans had never forgotten that they had once been a British colony, and their image of the British was influenced by that fact.[65] Neither Roosevelt nor his advisers were impressed by British cries of poverty. By August they had decided that the British probably would fight, and they, in turn, were prepared to fight – to the last Briton.[66] When Churchill renewed his appeal for destroyers at the end of July,[67] Roosevelt felt that he could respond. The assumption which underlay the British offer of an exchange of bases for destroyers was one which came to dominate British policy towards America, namely that 'the future of our widely scattered Empire is likely to depend on the evolution of an effective and enduring collaboration between ourselves and the United States'.[68] The question of whether the United States would be willing to underwrite the British Empire was not one which much troubled the Foreign Office. Old imperial hands like Lord Lloyd, who as Colonial Secretary would actually be handing over the Caribbean bases, were less sanguine. Lloyd thought that it was the thin end of a particularly nasty wedge: 'All this is the doing of Philip Lothian. He always wanted to give away the Empire and he now has a perfect opportunity for doing so.'[69] But the logic was inescapable. If the British wanted to fight the war, they needed American help; if they intended to fight Hitler to the finish, as Churchill realised, they needed more than simply 'aid', they needed American participation.

In order to gain the latter, it was, the Foreign Office held, worth making considerable sacrifices to win American 'goodwill'. Ironically, the posture of stern, heroic defiance of Germany could be purchased only by the most servile grovelling to the Americans. The pill could be sweetened, and none could do it better than Churchill. When he surveyed the 'first year' of the war in the Commons on 20 August 1940, he referred to the 'bases for destroyers' deal in the context of being able to 'see a little more clearly ahead' in at least 'one direction'. The Government had, he said, with strict veracity which was, nevertheless, disingenuous, offered the bases to the Americans of its own free will and without asking or offering 'any inducement'. He portrayed it as part of what would be a continuing process: 'these two great organizations of the English-Speaking democracies ... will have to be somewhat mixed up together in some of their affairs for mutual and general advantage'. He did not look upon the future with 'misgivings'. The process of 'mixing up' was unstoppable: 'Like the Mississippi, it just keeps rolling along. Let it roll. Let it roll on full flood, inexorable, irresistible, benignant, to broader lands and better days.'[70] He might have interpolated the words 'Let it roll away the British Empire.' In private he was worried about how little aid the Americans were giving, and the price which had to be paid for it, but in public he had to remain cheerful. It was his policy to rely upon American goodwill, but it seemed in ominously short supply.[71]

38

The Liquidation of the British Empire

At the Guildhall on 10 November 1942, in one of his most famous speeches, Churchill marked what he called 'the end of the beginning' by a ringing declaration that: 'I have not become the King's First Minister in order to preside over the liquidation of the British Empire.'[1] This certainly reflected his feelings, and the policy which he had pursued since at least 1929; unfortunately, it did not represent the reality of the situation. By that stage of the war the Empire was already on the way to liquidation, with the Americans taking the role of receiver to the bankrupt concern. It had been the necessary price which Churchill had had to pay for her 'finest hour' – or had it?

Churchill had been unhappy at the American insistence upon publicly connecting the exchange of bases with the destroyers deal, and he was even more unhappy at the American demand that the whole thing should be linked with a guarantee about the future of the British Fleet in the event of a successful German invasion; but the Americans insisted, and what Roosevelt wanted he got. The RAF could maintain Britain's independence from Germany, but there was not much anyone could do to preserve it vis-à-vis America. If the Chamberlain policy of building fighters rather than bombers had helped place Britain in a position to survive the Battle of Britain, his prudent housekeeping had enabled the economy to stagger on through the same period, but by the autumn the British Government was approaching the end of its reserves of dollars. There was still about £4,000 million in overseas assets, but these were not readily realisable at a decent price.[2] But, so the assumption went, once Roosevelt had won his Presidential election in November, things would look up. At the least he would underwrite essential British purchases in America; at the best he would actually bring America into the war.[3]

The question of what would happen if these optimistic assumptions proved false was not one which Churchill cared to ask; others were not so reticent. In an article on 28 July, Lloyd George, who struck a resolutely patriotic note throughout the period of the Battle of Britain, stated that once it had been proved to Hitler that Britain could not be defeated with ease, the time would come to 'discuss terms with him'.[4] He told the Duke of Bedford, who wanted an immediate peace, that the time would come only when Britain had faced down an invasion attempt: 'our prestige will be higher than ever, and we should enter a Conference with our heads held high'.[5] In a memorandum written two days earlier, Lloyd George outlined a compelling case for his policy. Britain was isolated on the Continent, in a way she had never been before. In order to defeat Germany, she would need to equip, raise and land a massive army on the Continent and wage war for years; by that time she would be bankrupt and most of her Empire would be in other hands, including that of the Americans. Lloyd George's expectations of America were guarded: 'She will', he wrote, 'no doubt help us in all ways short of War', but he could not see her sending another 'huge Army' to Europe; even if she did, it would take at least two years for it to become anything like an effective fighting force. That compared well, in the prophecy stakes, with Churchill's views, but although the Government did not have access to Lloyd George's memoranda, it was reading his correspondence to America. Knowing that he saw himself as an 'honest broker' after the Battle of Britain, Churchill was unlikely to give him the opportunity to adopt that role.[6]

Churchill established a unique place for himself as an emblematic Prime Minister, but being a symbol of resistance and defiance did not provide political security against the buffets which Fate surely had in store; symbols could outlive their symbolism – as the fate of Lloyd George after the Great War had shown. The prospect of greater security was provided by Chamberlain's worsening health. Churchill showed exquisite courtesy towards the former Prime Minister in his distress. Chamberlain recorded that Churchill had told him 'with great vehemence that whether it were 3 weeks or 3 months made no difference, I must stop on'.[7] He sent him Cabinet papers and kept him informed of the progress of the war, but by late August Chamberlain was 'frail' and weighed under nine stone. When he asked Churchill for more time to recover before deciding whether to resign, Churchill granted his request; but he told Eden privately that 'in his place . . . he would resign'.[8] Churchill's sympathy was perhaps a little strained by the burden which had fallen on him in Chamberlain's absence. He felt that he was getting little help from Attlee or Greenwood; and Halifax remained as unsympathetic a figure as ever. But where, as he asked Eden on 21 August, 'were the other men he could bring in? He did not know. Did I?' Churchill sometimes felt 'tired' and had never 'felt so lonely'.[9] He sounded Eden out about taking the Foreign Office, but he was as reluctant to take it as Chamberlain and Halifax were to let him have it.[10]

Churchill's problems in trying to get a War Cabinet more to his taste were complicated by a number of considerations. Margesson, as Chief Whip, insisted that the Conservatives received proper representation in the Government; but given Churchill's pre-war isolation, there were few Conservatives whose promotion would please both him and the Party.[11] Those whose pre-war attitudes made them acceptable to Churchill were not only unpopular with the Party, but most of them were hardly proving an unqualified success in office. Men such as Boothby and Macmillan were too junior for promotion to Cabinet rank and had, in any case, done themselves no good by their attempt to coerce Churchill in mid-June.[12] Amery, who was in the Cabinet, was tarred by that same brush, and his liberal attitudes towards India did nothing to commend him to his leader.[13] If Amery was sinking into the obscurity of the India Office, Duff Cooper, as Minister of Information, would have welcomed such a fate. The newspapers disliked his attempts to control them, and they played up, for even more than it was worth, the fact that he had allowed his only son, John Julius, to be evacuated to Canada.[14] As Butler told Hoare, the 'political stockbrokers' were 'selling Duff Coopers'.[15] Lloyd, who was proving a great success at the Colonial Office, was happy with his berth, and his imperial ardour would not only render him unpalatable to Labour, but made him an uncomfortable bedfellow when concessions to the Americans were being discussed. Beaverbrook, who was doing a splendid job at Aircraft Production, was brought into the War Cabinet on 2 August, but that was a recognition of his relationship with Churchill, not a sign of his political acceptability to the Tory Party; indeed, there his appointment aroused fresh suspicions about Churchill's 'judgement'.[16] Eden was the one Conservative Minister who enjoyed both popular support and the approval of Churchill and most Conservatives.

Churchill praised Eden's work at the War Office, but the two men disagreed about the relative need to reinforce the British position in the Middle East. Churchill wanted all available troops in the home islands to meet the expected invasion, whilst Eden wanted to reinforce the British position in Egypt ready for the only land campaign in which Britain could take the offensive – against Italy in North Africa. Eden found Churchill's refusal to allow colonial troops to be sent to Egypt 'maddening'; 'the Australians', he wrote in his diary on 19 September, 'cannot decide the battle of Britain; they might decide the battle of Egypt'.[17] On this occasion Churchill accepted Eden's views. On 24 September he told Eden 'not to be so violent with him, for he was only trying to help me'.[18] Two days earlier he had received from Chamberlain another offer of resignation and the confession that 'I am a good deal more pessimistic about my own future than I was.'[19] This prompted Churchill to sound Eden out about the possibility of his taking the Foreign Office; but again, he was reluctant to do so. However, the idea of his joining the War Cabinet in another post was not rejected.

What scuppered Eden's chances was what ensured that the reshuffle remained limited – the influence of Chamberlain. Although fatally ill, the 'King over the water' was still a power in Tory politics. His remark to Sir Kingsley Wood that Churchill would be 'wise to keep me as long as possible, because if I did get well enough, I could give him more support politically than anyone else' may have sounded odd in view of his extra-Parliamentary reputation; but both Wood and Churchill knew that he was referring to 'support' from the Tory Party. Chamberlain regarded replacing Halifax by

Eden as 'a change of policy & a condemnation of my policy'. He did not think that Eden 'had been a good Foreign Secretary before or would be a good one now', and he predicted that Churchill would 'have to face a good deal of criticism from Conservatives' if Halifax was 'dropped'. So no change was made. Wood, however, did not think that 'the present administration would be long-lived'.[20] The scarcity of 'Churchillian' Conservatives who were *papabile* obscured the question of what it was a 'Churchillian' Conservative Party would represent – apart from its leader and a commitment to 'victory at all costs'.

Chamberlain was a broken man, and Eden prone to idealism, but they were, perhaps for these reasons, at one in deploring the idea that Cabinet changes be made at such a time for 'political reasons'.[21] Churchill could not afford to assume that the war had banished politics, but he tended to act as though that was the case. It was left to men like Margesson and Wood to try to insist that the interests for which the Conservative Party stood were safeguarded.[22] Not everybody shared Churchill's assumption that everyone would imitate him by subordinating everything to the aim of winning the war, without asking what would happen next. Beaverbrook, whose dalliance with Labour pacifists in 1939 had not prevented him from performing wonders as Minister of Aircraft Production, did not let his sponsorship of the Socialists who had written *Guilty Men* keep him from being wary of the Labour Party. It was one thing to use Michael Foot to undermine Chamberlain, but Beaverbrook was too attached to his own wealth and the existing social order to welcome its subversion by the Labour Party. He told Churchill on 6 September that Labour was 'preparing to unhorse the Government as soon as it appeared to be tired'. Eden, who was inclined to concur, thought that it lacked the 'personalities' necessary to do so, but Churchill thought that Bevin and Herbert Morrison had been 'written up to fill the bill'.[23] But what Churchill missed was that it was not left-wing propaganda which was 'building up' Bevin and Morrison, but his own actions. His lack of interest in the home front is amply attested to by its almost complete absence from his six volumes on the war. Churchill was content to let Labour Ministers take on the major tasks on the home front, which, inevitably, gave them a high profile in the press and the public mind.

If the Labour Party did not occupy quite such a warm place in his regard as America, Churchill tended to look at both in the same light: what could they contribute towards his 'one aim', which was 'to destroy Hitler'?[24] The simple grandeur of that 'aim' was appropriate to the summer of 1940, but it hardly promised the long-suffering people much for the future. But Churchill was not much interested in a future in which he thought he would play little part. He was, he told Eden at the end of September, 'now an old man' and 'would not make Lloyd George's mistake of carrying on after the war'; the 'succession', and by implication the future, was Eden's.[25] However, whenever any Conservative tried to interest him in 'war aims' which said something more positive about the future, Churchill was sternly discouraging. His response to Eden's 'Four Power Plan' in October 1942 is indicative of his attitude on such matters. Eden was trying to interest him in a post-war international order, which would be dominated by a quadripartite Anglo– Soviet–American–Chinese alliance, but Churchill told him that such 'speculative studies should be entrusted mainly to those on whose hands time hangs heavy'. He commended to him the first line of Mrs Glasse's recipe for Jugged Hare: 'First catch your hare.'[26] But whilst he was catching his hare, the Labour Party was catching the imagination of the public.

The attacks on the 'Guilty Men' in June were one sign that Party politics had not been abolished by the war. The attacks made then on the 'old gang' were to form a staple part of Labour's attack on the whole of the old ruling elite; it was 'the beginning of the erosion' of the 'credibility' of the Conserva- tive Party.[27] But Labour was not content simply to smear Conservative leaders; its leaders had their own objectives. Chamberlain was concerned to hear that they wanted to abolish the Means Test and repeal the 1927 Trades Union Act,[28] but that was only the tip of the iceberg. The egalitarian spirit produced by rationing, government control of food and labour supply, and restrictions on all aspects of 'normal' life, provided an ideal spawning ground for the Labour Party's policies to breed in. By the end of 1942 the old Chamberlainite Conservatism had lost its hold as well as its leaders, and Churchill gave no countenance to those, like Butler, who wished to refurbish it.[29]

Chamberlain's influence helped ensure that the reshuffle which followed his resignation was of a limited character. Eden had to be content with vague promises that the 'future was mine anyway'.[30] That model of the modern civil servant, Sir John Anderson, took Chamberlain's place as Lord President of the Council, and that epitome of the arts of tadpole and taper, Sir Kingsley Wood, now entered the War Cabinet. This last balanced the promotion there of the new strong man of the home front, Ernie Bevin.[31] Chamberlain was not quite forgotten. Churchill offered to put his name forward for the Garter, but he preferred to 'die plain "Mr Chamberlain", like my father before me'; something he did a few weeks later on 9 November.[32] The press on 4 October provided the dying man with a comfortless foretaste of what the obituarists would soon be writing: 'Not one', he noted, 'shows the slightest sign of sympathy for the man, or even any comprehension that there may be a human tragedy in the background.'[33] His friends were inclined to say that he had died 'of a broken heart', by which they meant that he had 'felt so acutely all the attacks that he had no heart to try to overcome the physical trouble'; whatever the truth of that, Chamberlain died 'resigned and brave'.[34] He had hoped that 'the verdict of history' would justify him and show that 'I realised from the beginning our military weakness & did my best to postpone if I could not avert the war', whilst his Labour critics had been content to mouth the clichés of their Party; but he feared that they might 'succeed in covering up their tracks'.[35] His fears proved more prophetic than his hopes. Churchill delivered a noble funeral oration on 12 November, but the apocryphal remark, 'I could have done it the other way', was more indicative of the attitude he was to take in the future.[36]

If Churchill succeeded to Chamberlain's legacy and wrote its history from his own point of view, it was not the only part of Chamberlain's legacy he took over. The former Prime Minister's retirement had left the leadership of the Conservative Party open. Mrs Churchill may not have wanted her husband to have it, but he had waited too long for it to let it pass him by; he may have told Eden that he would not make Lloyd George's mistake of 'carrying on after the war', but he did not intend to make his 'mistake' of failing to provide himself with a firm political base, either. It was inconceivable, in the circumstances, that anyone else would put themselves forward. There had never been an obvious successor to Chamberlain. Hoare, who might, in other circumstances, have been considered, was now *degommé* as Ambassador in Madrid, and no one else of his seniority existed – save for Churchill. He told the Party meeting on 9 October that he had always 'faithfully served two supreme causes – the maintenance of the enduring greatness of Britain and her Empire and the historic certainty of our Island life'.[37] That 'star', which he had so long followed, had finally brought him imperishable glory, but at the cost of those two 'supreme causes' to which his career had been dedicated. There was a tragic irony at the heart of Churchill's career – and this was it.

Churchill, of course, did not think that it was going to take another five years to finish off the war. The defeat of the German attempt to gain air superiority over southern Britain and the abandonment of 'Operation Sealion' – the projected German invasion – in the autumn, both brought cheer. Churchill looked forward to 1941, when the British would, he thought, have 'ten divisions' which could undertake 'formidable raids on the Continent'. But Churchill did not see such 'butcher and bolt' raids as an end in themselves. They would give the British Army valuable experience, which would help equip it for larger-scale operations, including, perhaps, an invasion of Italy.[38] The extent to which such optimistic fantasies could take control of Churchill's mind was shown by his strong support for de Gaulle's 'Operation Menace'. The plan looked marvellous in conception: the appearance of a British fleet and French forces off French West Africa would suffice to rally Dakar, and perhaps other French colonies, to the Allied cause. The reality was a botched operation, French hostility and a dramatic loss of prestige for de Gaulle.[39] If the Government was forced back towards a covertly more friendly policy towards Vichy, de Gaulle would not be dropped, if only because he was one of the few allies Churchill had. The attempt to persuade the Soviets to adopt an attitude of benevolent neutrality by sending Cripps on a special mission to Moscow proved of no avail. Not even a British offer to extend *de facto* recognition to the Soviet conquests of the Baltic republics could wean Stalin from his alliance with Hitler.[40]

By the end of October Churchill knew, thanks to the fact that the German 'Ultra' code had been broken, that there would be no German invasion that year,[41] and in his 'autumn balance sheet' to the House on 5 November, he struck a note of cautious optimism. Britain had survived, she had reinforced Egypt and was sending aid to the Greeks, who had just been attacked by the Italians.[42] Churchill's 'pluck', 'courageous energy and magnificent English' impressed even Channon,[43] and for those who, like Nicolson, had come to admire him just this side of idolatry, it made them feel: 'Thank God we have a man like that!'[44] But what both of them, and Churchill, were thinking of on that 5 November was the polling which was taking place in America. Churchill had restrained himself from saying too much about his hopes for a Roosevelt victory, in case he lost, but privately he looked forward to it bringing an end to American hesitations and her swift entry into the war.[45] The hopes kindled by Roosevelt's victory were high, and it is a sign of the power of wishful-thinking that it was only Lothian, who as Ambassador in Washington had a better insight into the realities of the American position, who was sceptical of them.[46]

Lothian advised Churchill to place Britain's 'cards on the table', by putting before Roosevelt a complete exposé of Britain's financial straits and her military needs. Churchill was doubtful about such an approach, instinctively preferring to wait for the 'march of events' to take its course; but Lothian and then Halifax both worked hard to convince him that the 'march of events' needed a nudge in the right direction.[47] But Churchill was reluctant to appear in the guise of a mendicant. He wanted to concentrate upon Britain's need for more shipping rather than upon the fact that Britain's war chest was nearly bare.[48] He was, therefore, less than pleased to hear that Lothian, upon his arrival back in America on 23 November, had declared to the American press: 'Well, boys, Britain is broke; it's your money we want.'[49] The phrase, as thus recorded, may have been 'seriously misleading'[50] in the eyes of historians who have examined the files of the Lothian mission, but it represented a deeper truth. Lothian may not have used those precise words, but few Americans had any doubt that the British were, indeed, after their money.

Roosevelt had already been thinking about methods of keeping the British in the war against the day when they ran out of dollars. Congress would not let him give armaments to the British, even had he been inclined to do so, but there was nothing to prevent him 'leasing' equipment, and even before he received Churchill's long and frank letter of 8 December, he was pondering ways of doing this.[51] The American Treasury Secretary, Henry Morgenthau, told the Treasury representative in Washington, Sir Frederick Phillips, that he needed a complete list of British holdings in the western hemisphere, differentiated according to their liquidity: 'It is a matter of convincing the general public of the determination of just how far the English businessman is ready to go.'[52] That was as it might be, but to Englishmen who had been used to thinking of themselves as members of a proud and independent imperial race, it sounded awfully reminiscent of the tone of voice of a family solicitor just before the family silver was sold off. Roosevelt, when shown a list of British assets, reacted with the coolness of the WASP patrician: 'Well, they aren't bust – there's lots of money there.'[53]

Churchill's letter of 8 December reached Roosevelt whilst he was on a cruise on the USS *Tuscaloosa*.[54] It was in part an emotional appeal, laying emphasis upon the common British and American interest in securing the defeat of Hitler, but it was also an impressive balance-sheet of the deficits which stood in the way of Britain being able to carry on without American aid. In his negotiations with Phillips, Morgenthau, exasperated by the obstacles which, it seemed to him, were being put in the way of a complete disclosure of British assets, had told him that: 'It gets down to a question of Mr Churchill putting himself in Mr Roosevelt's hands with complete confidence. Then it is up to Mr Roosevelt to say what he will do.'[55] That, in effect, was what Churchill had now done.

There was no formal reply to Churchill's plea, but Roosevelt's press conference on 17 December was taken as such. Using the homely analogy of helping a neighbour whose house had caught fire, Roosevelt announced what was to become known as 'lend-lease'. It was, he stressed, in America's own 'selfish' interests that the British should be able to continue their policy of pouring capital into the building up of the American defence industry.[56] In the absence of an ambassador, Lothian having died suddenly on 11 December, there was no fulsome response to this; but it was not simply his absence which prevented the British from emitting more than a half-hearted cheer. Roosevelt had spoken about Britain having 'plenty of assets', and the way in which he intended those assets should be used was made patently clear when he told Phillips on 23 December that an American warship was going to be despatched to Cape Town to pick up £50 million worth of gold which formed part of Britain's final reserves.[57]

Beaverbrook's Canadian blood revolted as much as did his imperial instincts from what Churchill, in an early draft response, called 'the sheriff collecting the last assets of a helpless debtor'.[58] 'They have', Beaverbrook wrote indignantly on Boxing Day, 'conceded nothing. They have exacted payment to the uttermost for all they have done for us. They have taken our bases without valuable consideration. They have taken our gold', and in return the British had received virtually nothing. He thought that the time for a 'complete understanding' with America had come.[59] This was a feeling which Churchill shared so strongly that it took several drafts and plenty of argument from the Foreign Office to calm him down.[60] Grateful as he was for Roosevelt's promise on 29 December that America would become the 'arsenal of democracy',

Churchill was beginning to realise the price which had to be paid for her patronage. He had drafted a message for Roosevelt on Christmas Day in which he complained about the defects in the destroyers which Britain had received in return for her bases.[61] This horrified the diplomats at the British Embassy, who feared that a message which stressed how seriously Britain was being affected by the bombing, and which opposed the transfer of gold as 'unnecessary', would badly affect the Americans, reviving fears about British morale and her willingness to pay the full price for her lone stand.[62] In his memoirs Churchill prints a version of his 'tough' message to Roosevelt,[63] but it was never, in fact, sent. He yielded to the arguments of the Foreign Office and sent, instead, an 'unclouded message of fulsome praise'.[64] The price of freedom was eternal vigilance – to make sure that the Americans were not upset in any way.

Among those who was most prominent in urging caution on Churchill was the Foreign Secretary, but this fact could no longer be accounted a sign of Halifax's incorrigible love of 'appeasement', for that office was now, at last, held by Eden. Lothian's death had provided Churchill with an opportunity, finally, to get rid of a Foreign Secretary whom he found personally unsympathetic. His first thought had been to replace Lothian with Lloyd George. The potential 'Pétain' would have been well out of harm's way in Washington; or, to put it another way, one of the few figures with any prestige and a different policy to his own would be out of the way. But Lloyd George's doctors told him that, at the age of seventy-five, his health was not up to it.[65] If he could not get rid of one figure who might pose a political threat to him, Churchill would get rid of another – so Halifax was tipped for the black spot. He did not want to go, and Lady Halifax even went as far as bearding Churchill at Downing Street in an effort to avert the appointment.[66] But it was to no avail. Eden, the only real alternative, did not want the job, and Churchill wanted him at the Foreign Office. Thus it was that Halifax's tall, languid, aristocratic form was despatched across the Atlantic to become 'a sort of high-class political dustbin'.[67] Churchill may have had to truckle to Roosevelt, but he was finally master in his own house. The Chamberlainite ascendancy was over. Hoare was in Madrid, and popularly supposed to be uncertain whether he was more unsafe there or in London; Simon was in dignified and gilded obscurity on the Woolsack; Chamberlain was dead, and now Halifax was going off to impress the Americans with his hamburger-eating skills. Cadogan, who regretted the appointment, had little doubt that it was a 'plot to get rid of him';[68] and, thanks to Halifax's sense of *noblesse oblige*, and the fact that, as in May, he did not have the stomach to stand up to Churchill, it succeeded. The 'abyss', which Halifax noted in a pained fashion, between the language of public service and Churchill's talk of 'personal advantage'[69] was symbolic of more than Halifax thought: it represented the difference between a man who was prepared to sacrifice everything to one end, and one who was not. It was that quality which had made Churchill the essential man in May and June 1940. But during the next year a growing number of people were to come to the conclusion that what had been fitting in that glorious summer was not the best way of Britain and her Empire emerging from the war with anything except nominal independence. It was certainly better to be an American rather than a German protectorate, but given that the war was being fought to preserve Britain's independence and a balance of power, that reflection was of little comfort to many Englishmen.

39

'Rogue Elephant'

The glorious summer of 1940 may have obscured Churchill's previous career and reputation, and, eventually, have come to dominate it, but the 'medals' of the Dardanelles, Russian intervention and Narvik were never quite forgotten at the time, and the events of early 1941 were to revive their memory. In retrospect Hankey was apt to see Halifax's departure as the moment at which Churchill surrounded himself with 'yes men' and lacked anyone to 'provide ballast'; the 'Rogue elephant' had broken loose from his keepers.[1] There were many who were disposed to agree.

Churchill's 'thirst for talking military strategy' may have been 'unquenchable',[2] but when that talk turned to action, and the action turned to ashes, then old memories were speedily revived. Churchill's propensity to tell generals how to run their campaigns had been apparent during the Narvik campaign, but once he was Prime Minister and Minister of Defence, it was restrained only by the fact that, at least until 1942, there were not many theatres of operations where British troops were able to take the offensive. The only one of these was in the Middle East, and the Commander-in-Chief there, Sir Archie Wavell, was, accordingly, favoured with even more of the Prime Minister's opinions than might otherwise have been the case. Churchill, like other politicians, was apt to complain about the performance, or rather the lack of it, by Wavell during the summer of 1940, and this reached such a stage that Eden and Dill had to warn Churchill that they would resign if he continued to pass derogatory comments.[3] Eden thought that it might be a good idea to introduce Wavell to Churchill, but it turned out not to be.[4] Wavell was a taciturn man, and his reaction to a Defence Committee meeting on 12 August, when Churchill criticised his disposition of his troops and his lack of offensive spirit, was to tell Eden that he thought he ought to resign.[5] Eden dissuaded him, pointing out that it was only Churchill's manner; but there were to be many times over the next year when Wavell wished he had followed his initial inclination.

At the root of the problems between Wavell and Churchill was the fact that Churchill took the view that 'wars are won by superior will-power' and thirsted to 'throw off the intolerable shackles of the defensive'.[6] Wavell took the view that wars were won by superior fire-power and armaments, and he lacked both, in a theatre of operations which stretched from Persia to the western desert. When, after much badgering by Churchill, Wavell told him in early November that he was going to mount an operation against the Italians soon, the Prime Minister 'purred like six cats'.[7] But that was only after he had been barking for two months like a particularly bad-tempered bulldog. He regarded Wavell as over-cautious, Wavell regarded him as impetuous; to Churchill Wavell was a 'good average Colonel', an opinion which Eden regarded as the product of prejudice.[8] He was, of course, the blue-eyed boy when his offensive, 'Operation Compass', proved a success; it was not simply the greatest success that the British Army had had, but it was the only one. By the end of January over ten Italian divisions had been destroyed, 130,000 prisoners taken and the port of Tobruk captured.[9] But that was, for Churchill's inflamed imagination, only the beginning.

Even before 'Compass' Churchill had warned Wavell that there was a 'possibility' of the 'centre of gravity in the Middle East shifting suddenly from Egypt to the Balkans'.[10] 'Safety first', Churchill had told Eden in November when discussing the possibility of sending aid to the Greeks, 'is the road to ruin in war';[11] but he was about to prove that it was not the only one. Deciding that the gallant Greeks had to be helped in their struggle, especially now that the Germans were taking an interest in the campaign, Churchill ordered Wavell to give priority to helping them, rather than advancing any further in North Africa. It is well known that defeat is an orphan, and after the event no one wanted to claim paternity for the ill-fated operation to help the Greeks. But the operation bore all the hallmarks of a Churchill special. There were good political reasons for not letting the Greeks down: 'It would be', as Colville recorded in early January, 'disastrous to let the Greek triumph end in defeat, as did the victories of the Finnish army last winter.'[12] But Churchill, contemptuous of Wavell's timidity and convinced of the virtues of the offensive spirit, overestimated what could be done. He told the Defence Committee on 10 February 1941 that it would be 'wrong' not to help the Greeks. When Dill remonstrated with him that Wavell had no spare capacity, Churchill lost his temper, telling him: 'What you need out there is a Court Martial and a firing squad.'[13] It may only have been 'Churchill's way', but it represented a dangerously simplistic view of what operations were feasible.

Churchill became rather less keen on the operation when his 'Ultra' decrypts revealed that the Germans were sending troops to Tripoli, and he telegraphed to Eden, who was in Athens, on 20 February telling him 'not to feel obligated to the Greek enterprise if in your hearts you feel it will only be another Norwegian fiasco'.[14] But neither Eden nor Dill felt it would, and Churchill, having covered himself by the warning about another Norway, pressed ahead. Margesson, who had replaced Eden at the War Office in December, felt that it was not only another 'Norway' but also that 'Dunkirk and Dakar rolled into one' was looming 'threateningly before us';[15] he was correct. The Greeks and the British had both performed brilliantly when matched with the Italians, but the Germans were a different matter, and the

Allies were soon forced on the defensive, at the same time as the German troops in the western desert were proving what a bad decision it had been to weaken Wavell's army there. By mid-April the British were falling back on Crete in some confusion. Margesson had been correct.

The military failures were bound to give rise to questions about the soundness of Churchill's judgment, but these were asked in an atmosphere where doubts were also being expressed about his whole strategy of dependence upon America and its effects upon the Empire.

Lend-lease was welcome, but Roosevelt's plans had had to be approved by the House and the Senate, which involved the British in a long and unpleasant wait. It was bad enough having to put the destiny of the Empire in the hands of America's legislators, but the Senate hearings involved the British having to declare all their assets in a manner reminiscent of nothing so much as a bankrupt being dunned by his creditors. As Roosevelt told one member of his Cabinet: 'We have been milking the British financial cow, which had plenty of milk at one time but which has now about become dry.'[16] The British jibbed at having to pledge all their remaining assets in America against military supplies, but Morgenthau told Congress that they would do so, all the same.[17] On 10 March Halifax was given what amounted to an ultimatum. The British must sell one of their important companies in the next week as a mark of good faith; a major subsidiary of Courtaulds was sold, at a knock-down price.[18] Sceptics could have been forgiven for asking whether American policy was to help their neighbour – or beggar him. In order to try to meet payment for their orders until the Lend-Lease Bill was approved by Congress, the British were forced to scrape the bottom of every available crock of gold. The Czechs lent the British £7.5 million in October 1940, and the Canadians sold off British investments in Canada to help out. The Dutch and Norwegians refused to hand over any money, and de Gaulle had none save for what the British gave him. A Belgian loan of £60 million in February helped stave off the embarrassment of defaulting on payment.[19] In March the British were informed that another American warship was on its way to Cape Town to collect more South African gold. The return for all this humiliation, at least during 1941, was plenty of food, but very little in the way of war-making machinery.[20]

For Churchill to declare, as he did to the War Cabinet on 20 February, that 'we should receive from America far more than we could possibly give',[21] was a statement of optimism rather than fact. For Britain to be not only 'skinned but flayed to the bone' seemed to Churchill a small price to pay for American involvement in the war;[22] but there was actually precious little sign that she was going to get involved, and voices were beginning to query the wisdom of the Churchillian approach. Fears that the Lend-Lease Bill might be jeopardised led Churchill to swallow what he felt to be exorbitant American demands about the conditions upon which they would hold the bases which they had received in exchange for the destroyers (thirty-nine of which were still unusable).[23] Lord Lloyd had protested, declaring that it was all part of an American plan to supplant the British Empire. Such comments were unwelcome inside the Foreign Office, which seemed much happier now it had found someone else to appease. Lloyd declared that the Americans were 'gangsters and there is only one way to deal with gangsters'.[24] But the Foreign Office, like Churchill, was firmly committed to winning American 'goodwill', which meant accepting whatever the Americans chose to offer and pretending to be grateful. It was an odd definition of independence. Lloyd's promotion to the leadership of the House of Lords in January 1941 put him in a position from which he might have carried on his campaign for common sense with greater effect, but he was struck down by a rare blood disease and died in early February; he would not have cared to see what prices the British were going to have to pay.[25]

Churchill was always apt to invest a great deal of importance in personal relationships, and he had put himself out in January to impress Roosevelt's special envoy, Harry Hopkins. From one point of view this paid off. Hopkins, a lean, angular figure with the healthy distrust of all things British, which was part of the mental luggage of any good 'New Dealer', was impressed with the Prime Minister and reported to Roosevelt that he 'was the gov[ernmen]t in every sense of the word – he controls grand strategy and often the details'.[26] He certainly dominated his Cabinet in a way which had not been possible before December, but not everyone regarded this as a good thing. The Australian Prime Minister, Robert Menzies, who was visiting London in early 1941, turned to Eden after a Cabinet meeting on 14 April and asked: 'Has no one in this Cabinet a mind of his own?' Eden replied 'with doubtful modesty that I hoped I had!'[27] It was not only Eden's modesty which was open to doubt. Hopkins had thought little of Eden,[28] and he was in no doubt about Churchill's dominance, but he had noted that 'the politicians and upper crust pretend to like him';[29] for some the 'pretence' was becoming too difficult to keep up. After all, what, by April/May 1941, had been achieved under his leadership? Britain had survived, but at a tremendous cost and with no sign of any meaningful victory, or any sort of victory for that matter, on the horizon.

Menzies's visit to Britain acted as a catalyst. The big Australian had been in full accord with Churchill's policy in 1940, but what he saw of Churchill's conduct of the war on his visit helped convince him that 'his wildly aggressive policies threatened to destroy not only the Empire, but Britain itself'.[30] His sense of discontent was inflamed by Churchill's insistence upon sending Australian troops to Greece against his advice.[31] Menzies's view that the Cabinet was a set of 'yes men' was shared by Hankey, who thought that they left the running of the war to Churchill; and he was worried by the Prime Minister's dictatorial habits and the ascendancy which he had over the Chiefs of Staff.[32] Such fears had been expressed quietly for some time. Channon had noted back in November that Churchill was 'humorous but dictatorial', and that MPs were 'complaining openly that Winston trades on his position, on his immense popularity in the country, though his popularity is on the decline; but it is still high. Yet the country does not want a dictator.'[33] Churchill's dominance was firmly established by April, but it did not seem to be justifying itself by producing results.

Churchill himself was evidently thriving upon the challenges which faced him; at last his enormous energy was fully harnessed. Nicolson noticed in early April that he was looking 'better than I have seen him look for years. All that puffy effect has gone and his face is almost lean.'[34] Hopkins, whose reports dissipated much of the effect of Kennedy's reports, described him thus: 'a rotund – smiling – red-faced gentleman ... black coat – striped trousers – a clear eye and a mushy voice'.[35] The 'black coat' and 'striped trousers' were a concession to the sartorial standards which his visitor expected of an Englishman. But Churchill was not always so solicitous. Menzies was shocked to find him wearing 'what is called a Siren Suit; a dull, blue woollen overall, with a zip fastener up the front'.[36] Churchill had an aristocratic disregard for other people's views combined with a love of uniforms and unconventional garb; as Prime Minister and Minister of Defence he could indulge these tastes to the full. His 'siren suit', or 'rompers', was a convenient, if unconventional, garment, but he would alternate it with his favourite air marshal's uniform, or the uniform of an Elder of Trinity House – or, indeed, very little at all. One of John Martin's earliest experiences of what a 'character' his new chief could be was having 'an interview with him in his bedroom walking about clad in only a vest'.[37]

At long last Churchill could please himself – and his already eccentric character blossomed. He liked to work in bed, read his newspapers and do some work before rising, so his secretaries had to get used to seeing their chief in various states of undress. He would rise late in the morning and after lunch would retire for an hour's sleep.[38] This regime enabled him to survive the punishing responsibilities which fell upon him. Always easily satisfied with the best of everything, he was now in a position to be pampered in a way which released his full energies for the job in hand. There were times when, as he told Colville in August 1940, he was 'ashamed of the easy life he led'; he had, he said, 'never before lived in such luxury'. His objective was to 'preserve "the maximum initiative energy"'. He 'tried' himself by 'court martial' every night to see if he had 'done anything effective during the day. I don't mean just pawing the ground; anyone can go through the motions; but something really effective.' So effectively did he 'preserve' his 'initiative energy' that his staff had very 'different views on this question of an easy life!'[39] His late hours exhausted the Chiefs of Staff and others, who did not have the advantage of having an afternoon nap and all their wants supplied. Churchill had always dominated those about him by sheer force of personality;

445

now that he was caparisoned with full powers and armed with a still-massive prestige, other people, who had never loomed large in his imagination, became simply adjuncts. As Hankey put it:

It is a complete dictatorship. The War Cabinet and the War Committee on military matters consist of a long monologue by one man. The others are just 'yes men'. The Chiefs of Staff, worn out by incessant late night meetings of the Defence Committee, are reduced almost to the position of 'Joint Planners'. . . .

Hankey had 'no objection in war to dictatorship, provided the dictator is sound and does not over-centralise. But he needs wise counsellors.'[40] Menzies, who had come to the same opinion since his arrival in England in February, was driven to wonder whether there was any real basis for Churchill's constant reiteration of the theme that the Americans would soon enter the war: 'If the PM were a better listener and less disposed to dispense with all expert or local opinion I might feel a little easier about it. But there's no doubt about it; he's a holy terror.'[41] But the problem, as he saw it, was that Churchill could not be 'overruled, and his colleagues fear him. The people have set him up as something little less than God, and his power is therefore terrific.'[42]

This was where the problem lay for those who questioned Churchill's leadership; indeed, that is still where it lies for any historian bold enough to put forward a query about it. Questioning the ancestral gods of any nation has never been an enterprise rewarded by anything save calumny; trying to question the living god was one fraught with peril. Ironically, at a time when Churchill's dissatisfaction with de Gaulle's dictatorial tendencies was leading him towards the thought that the General might be put into 'commission' by being surrounded by some sort of national committee, the Prime Minister's own critics were seeking a similar solution to the problem which they felt he posed. Lloyd George suggested to Menzies that the real problem was that 'Winston is acting as the master strategist, without qualification and without really forceful Chiefs of Staff to guide him.' He wanted to see the War Cabinet meet every day, not at Churchill's whim, and he wanted to see strong Ministers in it who were not bogged down in their departmental duties. There was, he said, 'no imagination, or sweep or fire' except for that which Churchill provided. His suggestion that one of the 'couple of good men' needed to 'prop up' a Churchill who was not 'interested in finance, economics and agriculture', should be a 'Dominions man'[43] held an obvious appeal to Menzies, who had been attending the War Cabinet and whom the Beaverbrook press had been building up as just such a man.[44] Hankey liked the idea of Menzies becoming the 'Smuts' of the current war; but the problem of how to put all, or any of this to Churchill, remained unsolved.[45]

That old Jesuit on the Woolsack, Lord Simon, favoured getting Menzies to 'bell the cat', or, failing that, Hankey himself; he had not survived for so long in politics as a Liberal by volunteering for forlorn hopes.[46] With Egypt apparently on the verge of being lost and the British forces in full retreat from Greece, the time was, in one sense, ripe for such a move; but in another sense it was not – for it would be easy to portray any criticisms as unpatriotic carping at a great man. Moreover, Churchill was no *ingénu* to be out-manoeuvred by a 'Colonial' and disgruntled Ministers. No one could accuse him of the 'château mentality' prevalent amongst the generals of the last war. With the censorship reports beginning to show a 'certain amount of discontent', and a growing feeling that 'the "ruling classes" are doing well out of the war', Churchill's 'honeymoon period', as Bracken put it, was 'over and the "grim realities" of marriage had to be faced'. The following day, 24 April, Churchill set off for a tour of the areas worst affected by the bombing: if the people were 'sick of hearty propaganda of the "Are we downhearted?" kind, sponsored by the Government',[47] it was time for them to see their emblematic Prime Minister.

Lloyd George may have taken the view that 'Winston should be at the helm, instead of touring the bombed areas',[48] but Churchill knew what he was doing. One of Lloyd George's greatest defects as a leader had been his tendency to become insulated from people and to lose contact with his power-base in the Commons and the country; it was not a mistake Churchill was going to repeat. He had always been, essentially, a Westminster politician, but the war turned him into a great popular hero – and he used his contacts with the people almost in the way de Gaulle was to use his *bains de foules* to renew a quasi-mystical contract. In the days before television diminished politicians to a size where they would fit into the corners of the nation's living-rooms, they were remote figures, glimpsed, as though at a distance darkly, through the medium of the press. He knew what his 'public' wanted and, 'showman' that he was, he gave it to them. Stalking through the bomb-sites with taurine glares of defiance, massive cigar stuck firmly in his mouth, he became the mythical 'Good ole Winnie', something at once human and yet super-human; a symbol to a people battered almost beyond endurance that all would come right.[49] As he told them upon his return, in a broadcast on 28 April: 'I have come back not only reassured but refreshed'; 'morale' was 'most high and splendid' where the damage had been heaviest: 'I felt encompassed by an exaltation of spirit in the people which seemed to lift mankind and its troubles above the level of material facts into that joyous serenity we think belongs to a better world than this.'[50] As a statement about the actual morale of the devastated cities, such a remark is deeply suspect,[51] but as a description of the effect which Churchill and 'the nation' had on each other, it could hardly be bettered. He promised that he 'and my colleagues, or comrades, rather – for that is what they are – will toil with every scrap of life and strength . . . not to fail these people or to be wholly unworthy of their faithful and generous regard'.

But Churchill's broadcasts would not have had the effect which they did if he had confined himself simply to exhortations and promises. From the start, when he had promised 'blood' and 'toil', he had made a point of emphasising that the task before the nation was not an easy one – which was why it was a glorious one. With the Battle of the Atlantic going badly, with the Greek campaign going disastrously, and with discontent beginning to rear its head, Churchill had to offer some hope – so he bade them, in Longfellow's words, 'westward, look, the land is bright'. That may have helped sustain popular morale, but it did not answer his critics at Westminster.

Beaverbrook, who was always prone to resignation, was dissatisfied with both Churchill's subservience to the Americans and discontented by his domination of the Cabinet, and by April he was ready to hand in his resignation. His official reason was poor health. But as he told Sir Charles Wilson (soon to be, as Lord Moran, Churchill's physician): 'The Prime Minister needs tough men around him.'[52] But Menzies's approach to Churchill on 1 May about 'the help he needs in Cabinet' came to nothing.[53] His response to the argument was: 'You see the people by whom I am surrounded. They have no ideas, so the only thing to be done is formulate my own ideas.'[54] This, of course, simply compounded the problem for those who felt that Churchill was surrounding himself with 'yes men'. Far from the cat being 'belled', Churchill made it plain that he would regard the debate in the House on Greece as a test of confidence in him and his Government. That debate took place on 7 May, a year since Chamberlain had faced the debate which had brought his Government down, and gave Churchill's critics a chance to say to his face what they had been saying in private.

Lloyd George had been 'glad' that he had not joined the War Cabinet: 'With a stubborn mind like Winston's blind to every essential fact which does not fit in with his ambitions', he had felt he could 'do no good'.[55] 'Winston now feels that he is God & the only God,' he had told his mistress in October, adding that 'we have scriptural authority for believing that the one & only God is a jealous God'.[56] To what extent Lloyd George's own attitude was prompted by such feelings is a matter for speculation, but he had long held that Churchill was 'entirely in the hands of sycophants who feed & fan his illusions'.[57] When he compared his own War Cabinet with Churchill's, it was always to the disadvantage of the latter: Eden was a man of straw and men like Sir John Anderson were little more than bureaucrats; as for Cadogan at the Foreign Office, he was a 'dull dog if not actually a dead dog'. Britain could not 'win' the war, and it was 'wishful thinking' to suppose otherwise'.[58] He had tried tackling Churchill on the question of a negotiated peace, but had received no reply save: 'Never, never, never!'[59] Some of these things he now proclaimed on the floor of the Commons in what was to be his last major speech in the House which he had infuriated and adorned for half a century. 'Our position', he stated bluntly, was that 'we have practically no Ally at all. . . . We have to hold out until America is ready with her equipment, but it is most important not to exaggerate what we are going to get, or rather, how quickly we are going to get it.' He dismissed the idea of a British invasion of the Continent as 'fatuous' and, whilst recognising Churchill's 'very brilliant mind', called for a 'real War Cabinet'.[60]

Churchill appeared 'shaken', and during the speech rose and contradicted Lloyd George several times.[61] His response was confident and even (to one admirer) perhaps a 'trifle too optimistic',[62] but his comments about Lloyd George showed how much he had been stung by his old chief. He called his speech the kind of thing with which 'the illustrious and venerable Marshal Pétain might well have enlivened the closing days of M. Reynaud's Cabinet'.[63] Lloyd George never forgave the insult.[64] The Government won the debate easily by 447 to 3 votes. It was perhaps fortunate for Churchill that his critics had chosen to make their move when they did. Speeches are not victories in battle, and whilst Churchill was adept at supplying the former, the latter proved desperately elusive. Greece was followed in May by the fall of Crete, which gave rise to further criticism. Eden's private secretary, Oliver Harvey, thought that it was 'dangerous because it is bad if the Government loses credit – for who is there to replace them? Only L.G. and the Beaver. The Prime Minister casts his mighty mantle over everything and so it is *he* (and perhaps A.E.) who will take the blame.'[65] With the British Expeditionary Force being rechristened 'Back Every Fortnight' in honour of its recent flights, there was a 'noticeable slump' in Churchill's popularity, 'and many of his enemies, long silenced by his personal popularity,' were 'once more vocal'.[66] Churchill described the 'Opposition' as 'being formed out of the left-outs of all parties'[67] and clearly regarded his critics as an unpatriotic nuisance. He once more triumphed over them in a debate on 10 June, but if, as Duff Cooper thought, and his letter of 8 June to Randolph indicated, Churchill believed that discontent was confined to the House of Commons, he was taking the cheers which had greeted him in the bombed cities and the majority which he secured in the division lobbies altogether too seriously.[68]

There was a great deal of what might be termed 'passive discontent'. His critics were not, as he imagined, simply sniping at him for old times' sake. The fears and worries of men like Menzies, Hankey, Hore-Belisha and Lloyd George were shared by those closer to him; the only difference was that Eden and Lord Cranborne told others what they thought, and not Churchill. Eden told Cazalet in September that the central problem was that there was 'no real War Cabinet' and that Churchill did not want one, as he preferred to manage the war himself. After yet another Parliamentary triumph by Churchill in July, Cranborne (who was now Dominions Secretary) sounded a warning note in a letter to Emrys-Evans:

Ministers always tend to overestimate the importance of such parliamentary triumphs. They look grand, but unless they convince the critics, they do not really strengthen the position of the Government, at any rate at home. It is like a tree which looks sound from outside, but gradually becomes rotten at the core. Then one day it becomes subjected to a tremendous strain, and it crumbles away.

'That', he warned, 'was what happened to Neville – Winston should be very careful it doesn't happen to him.'[69]

Because Churchill was the dominant personality of his administration, it was only natural that men should have sought to lay blame, as well as praise, at his feet. Indeed, had it not been for the esteem in which he was still held, his problems could have been much greater. Colville agreed with another of Churchill's private secretaries, John Peck, that Churchill 'does not help the Government machine to run smoothly and his inconsiderate treatment of the service departments would cause trouble were it not for the great personal loyalty of the service Ministers to himself'.[70] With the 'Ultra' decrypts in his hands giving him a detailed picture of the German line of battle in Greece and in North Africa, Churchill's natural tendency to behave as though he were the general in command was enhanced; after all, he did actually know more than the generals on the spot – or at least he thought he did.[71] It had been Churchill's decision that Crete could be held, and he had overruled his military advisers to enforce his will; so the blame laid at his door was in the right place.[72] With Wavell having to conduct campaigns in Abyssinia, Iraq and Syria, Churchill decided that he could transform a limited push into Libya into 'a large-scale operation', to the horror of the Chiefs of Staff Committee. General Sir Alan Brooke, soon to be promoted to Chief of the Imperial General Staff, wondered: 'How can we undertake offensive operations on two fronts ... when we have not got sufficient for one?'[73] Poor Wavell found himself the object of ceaseless prodding from the Prime Minister, and Dill, the CIGS, was 'temperamentally unfitted to work with anyone as overwhelming and impulsive as Churchill'.[74] Churchill's attitude towards his generals was not dissimilar from that expressed in Beatty's famous remark about Jutland: 'There seems to be something wrong with our bloody ships today!'

The confidence which Churchill had never felt in Wavell had turned into positive distrust, and Dill was 'just a pleasant old gentleman'.[75] The most recent studies of Dill have tried to restore his reputation from the imputations of the 'Churchillians', but the very fact that the accounts of how tired and ineffective he had become by May and June 1941 came from that source is indicative of how the Prime Minister regarded him.[76] The fact that Dill's wife had been seriously ill since the winter certainly did nothing to help him bear the punishing routine which Churchill kept. The two men even disagreed on fundamental strategic priorities. As the Afrika Korps advanced in late April, the Chiefs of Staff considered the question of evacuating Egypt. When Churchill discovered the existence of such contingency plans, he was so 'infuriated' that the Chiefs of Staff 'had trouble calming him down'. He accused General Kennedy, the Director of Military Operations, of being 'amongst those "many generals who are only too ready to surrender, and who should be made examples of like Admiral Byng!"'[77] In Churchill's eyes Egypt was of such vital interest that it was second only to the defence of the home islands; Dill, on the other hand, accorded equal priority to Singapore and the Far East.[78] He was unable to impose his priorities on the Prime Minister and equally unable to protect Wavell from Churchillian admonitions.

Fortified by knowledge from 'Ultra' that the Afrika Korps were going to mount a major offensive in May, Churchill harried Wavell unmercifully to get in first – his sense of urgency all the greater in view of the risk he had taken in rushing a consignment of new tanks out to the Middle East. He regarded Wavell's unwillingness to mount an offensive as another sign of defeatism, and after his operations failed in June, he determined to remove him. Wavell was replaced by General Sir Claude Auchinleck, upon whose spare frame now fell the tremendous burden of Churchill's expectations. He had already shown a ruthless determination to change his generals if they failed to bring satisfaction; but his critics thought that the changes might usefully be made higher up the chain of command.

Churchill had survived Parliamentary criticism, and changing generals might change his fortunes, but he had to face the fact that a year after her 'finest hour', Britain was still alone and a pensioner of the United States. If Churchill's colleagues had little say in the strategic direction of the war, they had their worries over other aspects of his policy. The American attitude towards the bases which they had received in exchange for the destroyers had caused a great deal of resentment among some of his colleagues, particularly Beaverbrook and Cranborne. Churchill's attitude remained 'that America in providing us with credits will enable us to win the war which we could not otherwise do';[79] but by the summer of 1941 there was still no sign of America entering the war herself. Moreover, there was some discontent amongst Conservative backbenchers that 'much Socialistic legislation would be passed under [the] guise of war needs'.[80] Such fears received little countenance from the new regime. Churchill was simply not interested in such petty matters, and Eden had 'little sympathy' with the Tory Party or the 'men who composed it'.[81] By default the Conservative Party found itself adopting an Atlanticist foreign policy and an eclectic programme of government intervention at home.

Criticism at home and lack of success abroad were forcing Churchill towards reshuffling his political and military packs, but it was from that source which his hopes began to revive in early June 1941. 'Ultra' decrypts revealed that the Germans were building up their forces in the east. Colville could 'not see the sense of it from Hitler's point of view';[82] however, those with more knowledge of the dynamics of Nazism could. Hitler's search for

'*Lebensraum*' and his ideological imperatives had always posited a war against the Jewish–Bolshevik state; from this the campaign in the west had always been something of a sideshow. Now the time was approaching when the crusade would be launched. Between 1941 and 1944, three out of the four million troops in the German Army would be employed on the eastern front, and out of the 13,600,000 men the Germans lost, ten million would be lost there.[83] With Germany about to attack Russia, it was clear that, at last, some of the pressure would be lifted from Britain. It was, perhaps, an opportunity to rethink priorities and foreign policy; if so, then it was an opportunity which Churchill let slip. His only thought was that, at last, Britain was going to get an ally.

40

In the House of Rimmon

Churchill's reaction to the German invasion of Russia is too well-known to be omitted from any account of his life. When taxed by Colville with the fact that his support for Russia was inconsistent with his reputation as an anti-Bolshevik, he replied: 'that he had only one single purpose – the destruction of Hitler – and his life was much simplified thereby. If Hitler invaded Hell he would at least have made a favourable reference to the Devil!'[1] Now that Russia was at war and 'innocent peasants were being slaughtered', Britain should 'forget about Soviet systems or the Comintern and extend our hand to fellow human beings in distress'.[2] The picture which this paints is supported by Churchill's broadcast on the evening of 22 June, in which he spoke of having warned Stalin of what was coming, and, whilst not repudiating his previous views on Communism, he announced that 'we shall give whatever help we can to Russia' because that would fulfil 'our one aim and one, single, irrevocable purpose . . . to destroy Hitler'.[3] The portrait painted by the citation of such remarks is not the whole of the picture. If Churchill responded with enthusiastic rhetoric, he did so because, after dismissing his initial thoughts that a landing might be attempted on the Continent, there was very little more he could do. Moreover, if he committed himself to the support of Russia without thinking out the long-term consequences, that was partly because of his total immersion in the short-term aim of defeating Hitler, and partly because he did not expect there to be any long-term consequences. Churchill shared the views of his military advisers that the Russian Army would be defeated, and his aim was to postpone the evil day for as long as possible. Moreover, Churchill needed the Russians almost as much as they needed him.

A year after adopting the policy of 'victory' Britain was no nearer achieving that aim. In May, with defeat in Greece having ruined the prospect of constructing any 'Balkan front', the future looked grim. In the Middle East, which Churchill regarded as so essential, the British were on the defensive, and German pressure on Vichy to provide them with bases in Syria, and a German-inspired revolt in Iraq at the beginning of May, all seemed to presage a German pincer movement on Egypt. It also looked as though pressure by the Nazis on Franco might put Gibraltar in peril, which would totally close the Mediterranean to the British. Churchill pleaded with Roosevelt on 29 April to put the 'most extreme pressure' on Vichy to 'break with the Germans' if they 'violated' the neutrality of any of its territories; after all, he reminded the President, if these 'important areas' were lost now 'and if at a later period the United States becomes a belligerent, we should all have a much longer journey to take'.[4] But Roosevelt's response hardly indicated that becoming a 'belligerent' was very near. He rejected the idea of making any diplomatic moves either to Vichy, over Syria and Morocco, or to the Portuguese over the Cape Verde Islands and the Azores. General Kennedy had been blasted as 'defeatist' for even contemplating evacuating Egypt, but Roosevelt, who could not be excoriated in the same way, blithely commented that if 'additional withdrawals become necessary, they will all be part of the plan which, at this stage of the war, shortens British lines' whilst greatly 'extending Axis lines'; in 'the last analysis the Naval control of the Indian Ocean and the Atlantic Ocean will in time win the war'.[5]

Churchill had, in his own view, gone very near to 'begging' Roosevelt to 'do his utmost to get the United States . . . into the war as soon as possible'. He was, therefore, less than pleased to learn that the head of the British naval mission in Washington had refused, with Foreign Office approval, a suggestion from the Americans to move a substantial part of their Pacific Fleet to the Atlantic.[6] His protests cut little ice with Menzies, or with the Foreign Office, for whom the defence of the Pacific against possible Japanese aggression was more important than it was for Churchill. As Cadogan put it, the Prime Minister 'suffers from the delusion that any cold water thrown on any hare-brained US suggestion will stop the US coming into the war!'[7] Churchill's reaction to Roosevelt's cold douche regarding Vichy and the Middle East revealed that this was not the only 'delusion' from which the Prime Minister was suffering. He told Eden gloomily on 2 May that there appeared to have been 'a considerable recession across the Atlantic' and that, albeit 'unconsciously', 'we are being left very much to our fate'.[8] What Roosevelt's reply actually indicated was what Churchill refused to recognise, which was that the Empire which meant so much to him meant nothing to the Americans – except as a symbol of something which they disliked. But Colville had never seen the Prime Minister in a 'worse gloom'. Part of it may, indeed, have been brought on by a visit to Plymouth the day before, where the results of German bombing brought home the price which ordinary people were having to pay for 'victory at all costs'; but the idea that there had been a 'recession' across the Atlantic contributed more. Churchill 'sketched out' to Ismay, Colville and Roosevelt's special envoy, Averell Harriman, 'a world in which Hitler dominated all Europe, Asia and Africa and left the US and ourselves with no option but an unwilling peace'.[9]

Churchill's initial response to Roosevelt's telegram was to express something of his 'depression', but the final version was toned down for fear of giving the wrong signals to the Americans; no one wanted them to think that their protégés were becoming weary. Churchill told him on 3 May that he could not take such a sanguine view of the loss of the Middle East, and he made an impassioned appeal for the Americans to declare themselves 'belligerents'.[10] Roosevelt ignored this, but promised to expedite supplies.[11]

The German invasion of Russia offered Churchill the only road out of the impasse he was in: with 'victory' nowhere in sight and the Americans seemingly oblivious to the future of the British Empire, Russia offered him an ally and the hope that German pressure on Egypt and the Suez canal would be lifted. This was why Churchill hastened unheeding to the support of Stalin. It was, of course, necessary to discount, immediately, Communism and the Nazi–Soviet pact and to concentrate on the fact that Britain needed an ally, which explains the character of Churchill's rhetoric; but underneath it all was one simple fact: the Prime Minister's policy of 1940 had, in effect, failed. Far from securing Britain's independence, it had mortgaged it to America. Of real 'victory' there was no prospect, and the national unity which Churchill had forged in adversity in 1940 was beginning to buckle under the strain of a never-ending series of defeats. Like most of his advisers, Churchill held out no great hopes that the Russians would keep the Germans occupied for very long, but every day counted.[12] In his haste to secure short-term advantages, Churchill neglected to ask himself what political implications his generous rhetorical offers of help to the Soviets might carry. As with the Americans, he too readily assumed that the Russians would put aside other considerations in the common struggle; but of all the Allied leaders, he was the only one who consistently allowed his horizons to be bound entirely by short- and medium-term considerations. The result in this instance was that he failed entirely 'to profit from a buyer's market'.[13]

That there was a 'buyer's market' and an opportunity, for the first time since 1941, for Britain to regain some sort of initiative is plain. Thanks partly to the indiscretions of the British Ambassador in Moscow, Cripps, the fear which the Russians had long had, that the British intended to pull out of the war and leave Hitler to deal with them, had been revived with the flight to England in May of Hitler's deputy, Rudolph Hess.[14] The Soviets saw in Hess's flight the long-awaited sign that the wicked imperialists were about to consummate their design.[15] Churchill would have been well-advised to have profited from the Russian uncertainty rather than seeking to reassure her that she would not be left alone in the cage with Hitler. Unlike the British and the French, Stalin had not entered the war of his own volition, and unlike the British, he was not the recipient of any tempting peace offers from Hitler. Just as the Soviets had only entered the war when they were kicked into it, so they would remain in it only as long as they could not get out of it. Churchill's reassurances were to throw away recklessly a card which could have had some value. Eden and Cranborne reminded him on 22 June that 'half the country' regarded the Soviet Union as being 'politically . . . as bad as Germany', and they took the 'Tory standpoint' that aid should be 'purely military'.[16] This was Stalin's immediate demand, but as the British were in no position to launch an invasion of Europe, they resorted to diplomatic sops, such as promising that they would make no separate peace and offering the Russians a share in their own lend-lease aid.[17]

Churchill was an enthusiastic proponent of this policy, wishing, indeed, to go further than Eden.[18] But as it became clear that Russia would not be making a quick exit from the war, the political implications of a Russian alliance had to be faced. Stalin showed none of Churchill's reluctance to contemplate the nature of the post-war world.

Despite Churchill's dislike of formulating 'war aims', he had given some thought to the future. Having been convinced that war would come because Hitler was upsetting the balance of power, Churchill wished to restore that balance when the conflict was over. He talked about a 'European federation',[19] but the matter did not really interest him: he did 'not understand such things and he would be out of it'. He would 'retire to Chartwell and write a book on the war'.[20] He was, of course, not always sure that he would really retire. He told Eden in September 1941 that he was in a 'post-war dilemma': 'if he retired [the] Tory Party would say he had left 'em when he could most help 'em electorally', but he felt 'no enthusiasm for post-war problems'. He did not 'feel at one with the Socialists', but disliked Chamberlain's Conservative Party almost as much as did Eden, who felt 'no desire' to work with it and who even contemplated going to India as Viceroy. For all his disclaimers of interest in the post-war world, Churchill exhibited more 'spunk' for politics than did his Foreign Secretary, as the latter noted with a sort of fastidious envy: 'I thought as I listened to Max and Winston revelling at every move in these old games, and even Winston, for all his greatness, so regarding it all, that I truly hate the "game" of politics.'[21]

Churchill's relish for politics would never dim, but much as he enjoyed the 'game', he had found that purpose for which he had always believed destiny had marked him out. But in his determination to see Germany defeated, Churchill neglected to ask himself, until too late, what the result of the total destruction of German power would be upon the balance of power for which he had wished to fight in the 1930s. As the Soviets pressed for more aid, a 'second front' and an alliance, Churchill was inclined to be 'impressed by the strength of our hand in dealing with Stalin': 'His need of us is greater than our need of him' was the view he was taking in November. He was aware that Eden's attitude was somewhat different, but told him: 'It will not be long before you are in control. Then you can do as you like about relations with the Soviets.'[22] This was among the first of what was to become a volume of hints that he would soon stand down in Eden's favour, hints usually made at times when he and the Foreign Secretary were in disagreement over some important issue of policy.

For all his fastidiousness about the 'game' of politics, and his doubts as to whether he had the 'spunk' for it, and despite his distaste for the Tory Party, Eden's political ambitions were far from dead; but he found himself in a very difficult situation. On the one hand, Churchill was inclined to confide in him and to flatter him with assurances of how much he depended upon his support,[23] but on the other, he was as aware as anyone of Churchill's shortcomings as war leader. He was critical of Churchill's refusal to have an effective War Cabinet,[24] and was encouraged in his own leadership aspirations by Beaverbrook and Oliver Harvey, both of whom pushed him towards a more pro-Soviet policy than that favoured by Churchill.

Beaverbrook's political tergiversations were about to take another turn. Churchill had rescued him in the summer when Labour MPs had revealed that his Lordship had backed the idea of supporting 'peace' candidates at by-elections in late 1939 and early 1940.[25] Beaverbrook had certainly deserved well of Churchill for his feats in 1940 as Minister of Aircraft Production, but the Prime Minister paid a price for what was becoming the luxury of having his old crony by his side. Beaverbrook's frequent threats of resignation, like his 'continually changing his mind as to what he is prepared to do', added to Churchill's 'problems' and he was never 'even a fairly good collaborator'.[26] Dissatisfied with his current political position, and pining for the drama of 1940, Beaverbrook saw in the Russian alliance a chance to recreate the great days of the recent past – he could 'now produce tanks and munitions for Russia as in the previous year he had produced aircraft for fighter command'.[27] There was, moreover, a political dimension in Beaverbrook's sudden enthusiasm for the Russian cause. Most Chamberlainite Conservatives were somewhat apprehensive of the Soviets, but amongst the ranks of Labour there was, naturally, great enthusiasm for a Russian alliance. His own advocacy of the Russian cause brought him into alliance with the Socialists, and, given the fact that neither Attlee nor Bevin was more than half-hearted about the Soviets, Beaverbrook's political prospects were much improved thereby. Moreover, like many of the British ruling elite, he was apprehensive of a post-war world dominated by America. A committed tariff reformer, America's obvious hostility to protective tariffs and Roosevelt's enthusiasm for world free trade filled him with foreboding.[28]

A not dissimilar set of assumptions influenced the thinking of Oliver Harvey. Harvey, who had been Eden's private secretary before the war, had accepted a nominal demotion to occupy that position again. Harvey saw Eden, and encouraged him to see himself, as a man of the left.[29] Harvey's enthusiasm for all things Soviet, which resembled that of George Bernard Shaw and the Webbs, led him to advocate a full alliance with the Soviets from the moment of the German invasion, and he encouraged Eden in the same direction.[30] Given Eden's own distaste for the Tory Party and his hankering after a centre Party, the Soviet alliance was an obvious bridge towards the fulfilment of such ambitions.[31] Nor was Harvey deflected from his views by a glimpse of the 'Gulag Archipelago' when he accompanied Eden to Russia in December; he concluded, with all the smugness of a left-wing Wykehamist, that it was the price which had to be paid for the modernisation of the Soviet Union.[32] Harvey's attitude, like Eden's own, was shaped in part by their reaction to the growing dependence upon America.

Churchill's enthusiasm for the Americans made him a rare bird among the British ruling elite. The feeling of being supplanted by the Americans as a world power stimulated anti-American feeling in many quarters in Britain. The effects of this anti-Americanism still await study, but it is plain that it was one of the motives which impelled Donald Maclean, 'Kim' Philby and Anthony Blunt to spy for the Soviets, whom they, like John le Carré's Bill Haydon, considered by far the lesser of two evils.[33] Most Britons did not go so far, but there can be no doubt that men like Eden and Harvey saw in a Soviet alliance a vital counter-weight to American domination. The bitter pill of dependence upon America was sweetened with a thick coating of condescension. Roosevelt's ways of doing business seemed chaotic to the British, and, as Eden commented during a visit to Washington in March 1943, it was 'all like a mad house' and he 'felt more at home in the Kremlin. There at least they meant business. Here all is confusion and woolliness.'[34]

Churchill's addiction to the American connection had to be tolerated as long as there seemed no alternative to it, but the Russians offered that alternative. The dangers to be apprehended from Roosevelt staying out of the war and dictating a 'Wilsonian' peace along the lines of 1919 seemed amply demonstrated by the results of Churchill's first wartime meeting with Roosevelt at Placentia Bay off Newfoundland in August. Harvey dismissed the Atlantic Charter as a 'terrible woolly document full of the old clichés of the League of Nations period'. It aroused fears that Roosevelt's intention was to 'put the USA on top'. The moral to be drawn from it was clear: 'We must begin building fast ourselves with our Allies here.'[35] Of these only the Russians offered a real counterpoise to American power. The spectacle of 'an American President talking at large on European frontiers chilled' Eden with 'Wilsonian memories'.[36] Yet, both the Charter itself, and American diplomacy preceding the meeting between Roosevelt and Churchill, indicated a determination to control the form of the final peace settlement.

The possibility of the British coming to some 'deal' with the Soviets was one which perturbed the Americans. Lord Halifax's cavalier dismissal of the people of the Baltic states as not demanding 'much respect or consideration', and his blithe acceptance of the possibility of Britain recognising the Soviet conquest of the three Baltic republics, alarmed Roosevelt.[37] In a telegram on 14 July Roosevelt referred to 'rumors' 'regarding trades or deals' with some of the occupied countries.[38] What he had in mind were the sort of arrangements which the British and their allies had made during the Great War, and he urged upon Churchill the importance of making 'no post-war peace commitments as to territories, populations, or economics'. The Atlantic Charter embodied just such a commitment.

For Churchill the prospect of meeting Roosevelt had overshadowed everything else: 'He is as excited as a schoolboy on the last day of the term,' Colville noted.[39] Churchill had taken a good deal of trouble to cultivate Roosevelt, and, to Eden's distress, he was trying to establish a similar relationship with Stalin; he put a great deal of faith, perhaps too much, in the power of personal relationships, and to him, the meeting with Roosevelt at Placentia Bay was crucial. Harry Hopkins, who accompanied him on board the *Prince of Wales*, described his attitude thus: 'You'd have thought Winston was being carried up into the heavens to meet God!'[40]

On one level the meeting was an enormous success. Having wooed the President by epistolary means heretofore, Churchill hoped that he would be able to establish a warm personal friendship, and he certainly came away from the conference feeling that he had achieved this.[41] There was an initial *faux pas* when the Prime Minister could not recall a previous meeting which Roosevelt told him they had had in 1919, but thereafter the President seemed to succumb to the charm which the Prime Minister was capable of laying out when the occasion demanded it. Churchill had asked Harriman anxiously: 'I wonder if he will like me?'; the latter told Churchill's daughter-in-law (and his own future wife) that 'the President is intrigued and likes him enormously'.[42] Churchill was careful to 'give due precedence' to the President, who was, after all, a head of state, and he referred to himself, several times, as 'the President's lieutenant'.[43] Much of this was the politics of courtship and should be taken with an appropriate pinch of salt, but in part it reflects the crude realities of the situation in which Churchill found himself. In all relationships there is the pursuer and the pursued, and there could be no doubt of the position Churchill occupied. Churchill valued his correspondence with Roosevelt so much because he was convinced that through that medium he could secure more from the President than could be obtained by more conventional means. But there is little sign of this. Indeed, for all the Sunday morning prayer meeting and hymn singing on board the *Prince of Wales*, and for all Roosevelt's fascination with Churchill, the British came away from the meeting with little more than a propaganda coup; this might be taken as a paradigm of the Churchill–Roosevelt relationship.

Churchill had gone to the meeting with high expectations. As he had told the Queen before his departure: 'I do not think our friend would have asked me to go so far ... unless he had in mind some further forward step';[44] in this he had misjudged Roosevelt. Lloyd George once wrote that he was unable to see an obstacle without thinking of a way around it, but in comparison to Roosevelt he was an example of the direct approach. If Machiavelli had never written, the President could have supplied the want – always supposing that anyone could have tied him down for long enough to write so much and that he would have been willing to commit himself to firm opinions. It was not so much that Roosevelt was devious, he simply had a congenital inability to let his right hand even know of the existence of his left hand. His direct contacts with Churchill had been through the medium of Hopkins and then of Harriman. From them he had obtained opinions which supported his policy of giving aid to the British. But he was mindful of the strong strain of isolationism which existed at home, and aware of the misgivings of his advisers over the British obsession with the Middle East and of their view that the supplies promised to Russia could only be delivered at the expense of the British war effort in that theatre.[45] He had told Hopkins to warn Churchill not to expect to talk about American entry into the war or the nature of any post-war settlement, but soon broke his own embargo.[46] But the Atlantic Charter was hardly even a poor substitute for an American declaration of war, whilst a stiff Anglo-American declaration aimed at Japan was quickly watered down by the American Secretary of State, Cordell Hull. Churchill may have thought that he had obtained from Roosevelt contingency plans for how the Americans were to escort British shipping, but all he had in fact obtained was a plan for how this should be done *if* Roosevelt decided it should be done; but once back in Washington the President's silence on the matter was complete. Roosevelt had executed upon Churchill a manoeuvre to which he was particularly prone: exercising his own considerable charm, he had allowed his interlocutor to go away with the impression that he had agreed with everything which had been said; members of his Cabinet did not keep diaries to record the change of the seasons.

What Roosevelt wanted from the conference Roosevelt got. He wanted to still anxieties that America, by supporting Britain, was also supporting her Empire. This the Atlantic Charter enabled him to do. If it was not, as Castlereagh called the Holy Alliance, 'a sublime piece of mysticism and nonsense', then it was the next best thing. Sumner Welles had prepared an American draft, but, as ever, Roosevelt preferred to make others do the running. Expressing his desire on 9 August for a joint declaration of principles, Churchill had Cadogan draw up a draft the following morning. Harvey, back in London, may have thought it nothing but a set of old Wilsonian clichés, but Cadogan and Churchill were aware of the fact that this in itself would appeal to a President whose thinking on foreign policy might be described in similar terms.[47]

Most of the eight clauses in the final form of the press release amounted to little more than a declaration from a conference of bishops that they were against sin. Britain and America eschewed any form of 'aggrandisement' for themselves and set their faces against any territorial changes imposed by undemocratic means. They also pledged themselves to 'respect the right of all peoples to choose the form of government under which they will live' and to restore self-government to those deprived of it. The question of whether this applied to the countries of the British Empire was, to Churchill, self-evidently not worth asking – of course, it did not; but Roosevelt's view was not necessarily the same.[48] If this third clause was to raise a few British eyebrows, the fourth clause, inserted by Welles, raised British hackles, as it promised access on equal terms, but with 'due respect for their existing obligations', to the trade and raw materials of the world for all people. Amery, who had been opposing the American desire to make free trade a condition of lend-lease, had feared that 'American ignorance and our weak-kneed desire not to say "boo" to them' would 'once again wreck the peace settlement', and could only hope that the reference to 'existing obligations' would safeguard imperial preference, but he had no great expectation that Churchill would help: 'He isn't even capable of understanding what is at issue.'[49] At the insistence of the War Cabinet a fifth clause was added about the need to secure 'improved labour standards, economic advancements and social security' for all men; the sixth clause, assuring safety to all nations and freedom from fear and want to all men, was the sort of Wilsonian nonsense to which both Roosevelt and liberals everywhere could give adherence, without stopping to think how little governments can do to achieve such things. A pledge to ensure freedom of the seas would keep American opinion happy, but it was the final clause in which Churchill invested most hopes in the absence of an American declaration of belligerency. This provided for the disarmament of 'aggressor nations' as a prelude to general disarmament and, at Churchill's insistence, the President agreed to insert a phrase about the need for a 'wider and permanent system of general security'.

Churchill chose to interpret the last clause as an implicit promise of American entry into the war, but the question of whether Roosevelt's implicit promises were worth the paper upon which they were not written raised itself. Quite what Roosevelt said to Churchill at the conference is a matter of some debate. Roosevelt certainly hoped that the Atlantic Charter and the news of his meeting with Churchill would spark 'an upsurge of public willingness to take up arms', and may have been correspondingly free with implications that America would soon be entering the war, implications which he was quick to disavow when it became plain from opinion polls that seventy-four per cent of Americans still favoured staying out of the war.[50] Churchill certainly derived the impression that even if she was not attacked, America would enter a war in the Far East in the event of Japanese aggression. Moreover, in his report to the War Cabinet on 19 August, Churchill asserted that Roosevelt 'had said that he would wage war, but not declare it, and that he would become more and more provocative', adding that he would order the United States Navy to attack U-boats on sight and thus force an 'incident'.[51]

That Churchill should have laid stress when talking to his colleagues upon Roosevelt's belligerent intentions was only natural, given the general British disappointment that America seemed no nearer to entering the war, but there is no reason to suppose that he did much more than convey the impression which Roosevelt had contrived to leave him with.[52] Churchill was correspondingly depressed by Roosevelt's remarks on returning home that America was no nearer to entering the war and that he had not entered into any secret agreements with the British. Kingsley Wood told Dalton on 25 August that 'not everyone accepts the PM's view that the President is a great man. There is another view that says he is a yes man to all who speak to him',[53] and at the Cabinet meeting that day, both Beaverbrook, who had attended the latter stage of the Placentia Bay meeting, and Halifax, back from Washington, gave it as their view that although Roosevelt wanted to enter the war, there was no likelihood of America doing so in the near future.[54] Churchill's response was to tell Hopkins on 28 August that Roosevelt's comments had created a 'wave of depression in the Cabinet', and he warned that this might spread to the Commons and to public opinion as the propaganda effect of his meeting with Roosevelt fizzled out. He warned that 'if 1942 opens with Russia knocked out and Britain left alone, all sorts of dangers may arise'. With the Germans carefully avoiding U-boat attacks in the western hemisphere, there seemed to Churchill little chance of an 'incident', and he asked Hopkins if he 'could give me any sort of hope'.[55]

The 'only thing' which Roosevelt and Hopkins could 'make out of' the telegram was that 'Churchill is pretty depressed and takes it out on us in this fashion'. Hopkins told Roosevelt that 'not only Churchill but all the members of the Cabinet and all the British people . . . believed that ultimately we will get into the war on some basis or other' and that if they 'ever reached the conclusion that this was not to be the case that would be a very critical moment in the war and the British appeasers might have some influence on Churchill'.[56] Churchill himself, confident that he and the President had made a 'deep and intimate contact of friendship', was less 'depressed' than perplexed as to 'how the deadlock is to be broken and the United States brought boldly and honourably into the war'. He worried that America might assume that with Russia in the war, there was no need for 'Uncle Sam' to join in, and the scepticism of Beaverbrook and Halifax had had its effect upon his opinion of Roosevelt. As he told his son Randolph, who, having become MP for Preston in October, was now serving in the Middle East: 'The President, for all his warm heart and good intentions, is thought by many of his admirers to move with public opinion rather than to lead and form it'; but he 'thanked God . . . that he is where he is'.[57]

In fact, an 'incident' did occur on 4 September when the USS Greer was attacked by a U-boat off Iceland, which gave Roosevelt the excuse he had needed to announce that, in future, American naval patrols would accompany British convoys in the western hemisphere.[58] But as so often, as Roosevelt gave with one hand, he took away with the other. One of Churchill's primary objectives before their meeting had been to obtain from the Americans a joint declaration warning the Japanese against any further aggression in the Far East. Roosevelt's lackadaisical way of running his administration led American policy towards Japan into a tougher line than he intended. Talks with the Japanese had opened in February, and despite the advocacy by the 'hawks' of full economic sanctions, Roosevelt preferred to proceed by his usual crab-like methods, agreeing only to freeze Japan's assets if she actually invaded French Indo-China. However, bureaucrats in the Office of Export Control chose to interpret restrictions on the sale of oil to the Japanese in a such a manner that from 26 July a total oil embargo was in effect. Roosevelt did not discover this until September, by which time he decided that to relax it would be to send the wrong signals to Tokyo – so the embargo remained in force.[59]

On 21 July the War Cabinet approved Eden's arguments that Britain should support whatever policy the Americans decided upon, despite the risk of war with Japan; the argument that America was bound to become involved in such a war was accepted as axiomatic.[60] At Placentia Bay Churchill had persuaded Roosevelt to agree to a declaration committing America to war in the case of any such Japanese action. This, Cadogan believed, would 'give the Japanese a jar'.[61] However, for all Churchill's faith that Roosevelt would abide by the declaration, once he was back in Washington the President accepted Hull's decision that it was too 'provocative', and it was toned down to a general statement about protection of American rights in the Far East.[62] With both Roosevelt and Stalin, Churchill was to find that bowing in the House of Rimmon was almost a full-time activity.

41

Between the Millstones

The voyage on the *Prince of Wales* had provided Churchill with the first opportunity since the war began of having something approaching a rest. The prospect of meeting Roosevelt had put him in high good humour. Unusually for him he had arrived at Wendover station early, and during the journey to Thurso, he passed the time by asking Lindemann, newly ennobled as Lord Cherwell, to calculate the volume of champagne he had consumed during his life. When Cherwell answered that it would take up only part of the coach in which they were sitting, Churchill responded: 'I am very disappointed, I had hoped it would have taken several coaches.'[1] At the start of the voyage he was 'as excited as a boy, planning all the details of the entertainment of the other fellow – ordering grouse, ordering turtle and ordering a band'.[2] During the voyage he passed part of his time listening to Hopkins's report upon his recent visit to Stalin, and part of it beating the American at backgammon; he declined the offer to teach him gin rummy,[3] preferring instead the delights of the film theatre set up in the ward-room. On the first evening of the voyage he turned up in the Mess Dress of the Royal Yacht Squadron for a showing of *Pimpernel Smith*, 'which he quite obviously enjoyed very much. He had not done a stroke of work during the day and was in a thoroughly good temper.'[4]

Churchill's 'good temper' even survived the heavy seas of the following day, when he turned nurse-maid and gave his private secretary, John Martin, doses of patent medicine to ward off sea-sickness. He was enjoying the 'strange sense of leisure',[5] and when his detective found him relaxing by reading *Captain Hornblower RN*, he commented on the unusual spectacle of the Prime Minister without his red boxes, to which Churchill responded: 'I am getting a lot of benefit from the rest and the fresh air. And I certainly needed it. My brain, too, is getting a rest in reading.'[6] He had been given the book by Oliver Lyttelton, who had just been appointed Minister Resident in the Middle East, and he telegraphed to him, after finishing the novel, 'I find Hornblower admirable', which caused 'perturbation at Middle East Headquarters', where it was supposed that 'Hornblower' was the code word for some special operation of which they had not been notified.[7]

Churchill had always been easily satisfied with the best of everything, and as Hopkins had just returned from Russia, there were ample supplies of caviare. It was, Churchill said, 'good to have such caviare even though it meant fighting with the Russians to get it'. When Hopkins refused a second glass of brandy after dinner on 6 August, Churchill twitted him: 'I hope that, as we approach the US, you are not going to become more temperate.' After which they all trooped off to the ward-room to watch *The Devil and Miss Jones*.[8] The Prime Minister's taste in films may not have won the approval of 'high-brows' like the Permanent Under-Secretary at the Foreign Office, Sir Alec Cadogan, but Churchill knew what he liked and stuck to it – plenty of action, a dramatic story-line, and preferably a costume drama. His particular favourite was *Lady Hamilton*, which, although he saw it for the fifth time on 8 August, still moved him to tears. At the end of the film he declared: 'Gentlemen, I thought this film would interest you, showing great events similar to those in which you have been taking part.'[9]

Consciousness of taking part in great historical events never left Churchill during these years; if de Gaulle was potentially *'l'homme du destin'*, Churchill was the very incarnation of that figure. Hence the careful planning of the first meeting with that other 'great man', Roosevelt; everything had to be at the level which the importance of the event demanded. Nor did Churchill neglect the importance of symbols, particularly at a meeting where the concrete results were likely to be few. The centre-piece was the Divine Service on the *Prince of Wales* on Sunday morning. The service was, in Churchill's words, to be 'fully choral and fully photographic'.[10] Churchill chose well-known hymns of proven emotional power: 'Onward Christian Soldiers' and 'Eternal Father Strong to Save' (which Churchill, in a revealing slip, called 'For Those in Peril on the Sea' in his memoirs – the spirit and not the title was what mattered). Of the service itself, Inspector Thompson recalled that it 'could not have failed to make an impact upon the least religious man', whilst Martin commented that 'you would have had to be pretty hard-boiled not to be moved by it all'.[11] Indeed, even the usually cynical Cadogan found it 'Very impressive'.[12] With 250 American servicemen mixed in with their British counterparts, 'it seemed a sort of marriage service between the two navies'.[13] As the 'leaders of two great peoples' stood there singing, 'surrounded by a representative body of citizens', it seemed to at least one observer an acknowledgment that 'the ultimate fate of mankind lay in a recognition of the eternal and unchanging values'.[14] The service ended with 'O God, Our Help in Ages Past', which Churchill had chosen because it was the anthem chanted by the Ironsides as they had borne the body of John Hampden to its final resting-place. 'Every word seemed to stir the heart. It was a great hour to live,' Churchill recorded in his memoirs.[15]

This was where Churchill was the essential war leader; he realised the importance of emotion and symbols, and it was through their utilisation, via the medium of his oratory and the projection of his personality, that he had galvanised the British people in 1940. But as Amery, who had known him perhaps longer than anyone else, commented, 'both his strength and his weakness lie in the fact that he reflects the great moments and emotions of our history, and is at one with the fight against the Armada, or Louis XIV, or Napoleon'. It is hard to think of any other British leader, save perhaps Macmillan (who rather caught the habit from Churchill), who would have recalled that the Ironsides had chanted 'O God, Our Help in Ages Past', let alone one who would, himself, have drawn sustenance from it as the giant Antaeus is said to have drawn strength from the land on which he stood. Churchill's patriotism was autochthonous, rooted in the very soil and history of England. But, along with this, as Amery noted, went a weakness: '[He] had never been in touch with any of the currents of thought of our own time.' This was a trifle unfair, considering Churchill's role with Lloyd George from 1909 to 1911, but there was much in what Amery wrote. He had, Amery said, 'always hated Dominion self-government, even in the Dominions, and hates it still more as applied to India', and, having 'accepted Free Trade in early youth', he had 'never been able to understand the concept of national protection or of Empire Preference any more than he has been able to understand what socialism is about'. Those views which he had forged for himself by his own study in the long afternoons of late-Victorian India had stayed with him on his long journey. They had made him a Liberal in Edwardian Britain and a Conservative in the post-war era, but, as Amery noted, 'he has never fitted into any political party and his judgement on the political issues of the day has almost always been wrong'. But 'for a great battle he does represent the heart of old England'.[16]

Despite the denials of some professional historians, the study of history is of great utility to the statesman. Not only does it teach a proper humility, but it also gives a sense of perspective, and this Churchill had. It was his sense of Britain's destiny which inspired him in 1940; for him Britain could not be true to herself unless she took the lead in repelling Hitler. He was conscious of donning the mantle of Elizabeth at Tilbury, and of his greatest ancestor, Marlborough; like the Younger Pitt, he would be 'the pilot who weathered the storm', although, in his behaviour and political isolation, he bore a far more marked resemblance to Pitt's father, Lord Chatham. It was also, in part, his sense of the tides of history which inclined him to look towards America for salvation. But history has its limitations, and for all that some of his admirers have sought to portray him as a man of vision, it was precisely in this department that Churchill's most serious blind spot lay.

In constructing the great six-volume work on the Second World War, Churchill was seeking to comment upon the history which he had made, to put it into order, and this involved, most of all, painting a picture of the developing Anglo-American alliance as inevitable, and the alliance as it emerged as a wholly beneficent creation. As he told President Eisenhower in April 1953, 'I am most anxious that nothing should be published which might seem to others to threaten our current relations in our public duties, or to impair the sympathy and understanding which exist between our two countries.' He went through volume six to make sure 'that it contains nothing which might imply that there was in those days any controversy or lack of confidence between us'.[17] But it was not only over volume six that he took 'great pains' to ensure such things. The whole work has been accurately described as 'a political speech – in a direct line from his 1943 address at Harvard and his more famous 1946 speech at Fulton, Missouri'. In it he rewrote 'world history to serve his country';[18] but the actuality was a good deal more painful than he chose to depict it in retrospect.

Talking with Macmillan in Cairo in late 1943, Churchill suddenly asked him an unexpected question: 'Cromwell was a great man wasn't he?' Macmillan replied, 'Yes, sir, a very great man.' 'Ah,' said Churchill, 'but he made one terrible mistake. Obsessed in his youth by fear of the power of Spain, he failed to observe the rise of France. Will that be said of me?' Churchill made the remark apropos of Germany and Russia,[19] but it is capable of a wider application. As early as 1945 it was apparent that so far as Russia was concerned, the answer to Churchill's question was 'yes'; he had been so fixed upon the German menace to the balance of power that he had signally failed to notice that by destroying German power, he had helped raise up a new and equally sinister threat; yet as early as 1941 it was plain that Stalin's eyes were fixed upon an horizon more distant than the one Churchill's eyes were disposed to scan. But there were two other areas in which Churchill's vision had failed him. The first has already been touched upon, and that is in relation to America. The Americans had already given ample evidence that their objectives were, the defeat of Hitler apart, very different than those for which Churchill fought. The disagreement over the Middle East in 1941 was to foreshadow a debate which was to carry on through 1942 and 1943 until Churchill found even the strategy of the war wrested from his grasp, just as he had come to a clearer realisation of the dangers to the balance of power which were to be apprehended from the defeat of Germany. But by that stage it was not only precedence, but power, which Churchill had to yield to Roosevelt. 'I get a large number of favourable and friendly decisions' from Roosevelt, Churchill minuted on one occasion in April 1944,[20] but the balance sheet suggests that he paid heavily in diplomatic terms for what concessions Roosevelt, Churchill minuted on one occasion in April 1944,[20] but the balancegrowth of Soviet power, he had also imperfectly understood the dynamics of American power and its hostility to the Empire to which he had devoted so much of his life. The third area in which his vision failed him was in relation to domestic politics, as he neglected the Conservative Party and allowed the Socialists to secure a hold on power which would do much to weaken the social and political system of which he had always been such a resolute defender. Even by 1941 it was apparent that a price would be paid for these things.

It might be argued that the price was worth paying, but in his memoirs Churchill cleverly avoids, at least until the very end, any suggestion that one had to be paid. The final volume is entitled 'Triumph and Tragedy'. The 'triumph' is readily apparent, but it is less clear to the reader what the 'tragedy' consists of. Clearly it cannot simply be Churchill's own fall from power, as that would hardly warrant the use of a word so pregnant with association; moreover, Churchill was too careful a writer to use such a powerful word loosely. The tragedy would appear to be the breakdown of the 'Grand Alliance' and the onset of what, by the time the book was published, was known as the Cold War. But the seeds of these things lay back in the war itself and in the nature of the alliance, and the time to try to avert them was not in 1944 or 1945, but earlier; and it was here where Churchill's single-minded concentration on the matter in hand, and his sense of history, let him down. Despite Roosevelt's often repeated dictum that political matters could wait until a peace settlement,[21] neither he nor his advisers behaved as though this were true; nor did Stalin. Only Churchill did so.

Whether in relation to France, where he allowed the Americans to take the lead, or in places like Yugoslavia, where he allowed himself to be misled by bamboozled British agents into backing the Communist resistance forces, Churchill underestimated the extent to which decisions taken during the war would influence the post-war settlement. When Attlee argued in June 1944 that 'We have a much stronger stake in France than the USA' and should not, therefore, allow Roosevelt's hatred of de Gaulle to cloud British relations with him,[22] he was doing no more than articulate a feeling which Eden and the Foreign Office had nurtured for some time: that Churchill was sacrificing real British interests for what they believed to be the somewhat nebulous benefits of American 'goodwill'.[22] Yet, when it came to the Soviet Union, the roles tended to be reversed, with Eden wishing to concede to win Russian goodwill, and Churchill arguing against conceding too much. In part this reflects different priorities. Eden was looking towards Russia as Britain's major partner on the European Continent, and as one of the foundations of British foreign policy;[23] Churchill, who saw the Americans occupying this role, was correspondingly eager to do nothing with the Soviets which would seriously alienate the Americans. But what Churchill failed to see was what Eden and Beaverbrook had spotted as early as 1941, which was the domestic political implications of the Russian alliance. Indeed, it might even be argued that excellent as he was as an emblematic Prime Minister when Britain was fighting alone, Churchill showed less prowess at dealing with the demands made by alliances.

Censorship reports revealed what a survey of the press could have told Churchill, namely that the entry of Russia into the war had had a tremendous impact on British public opinion. Before Russia Britain lacked an ally who could stand up to Hitler; the French, the Yugoslavs and the Greeks had all, rather like the British themselves, been brushed aside as tiresome irrelevances to German military power. Now, at last, there seemed to be an ally who, whilst retreating to be sure, was not being defeated in a matter of weeks. Russia's continued resistance caused a 'great upward surge in public morale', and there was 'little reservation in the enthusiasm shown for Russia and practically no defeatism'.[24] The British Minister to the Polish Government-in-Exile, Sir Charles Dormer, was right to doubt whether 'English people understand the Russian mentality and Soviet duplicity'.[25] Churchill quickly became alarmed at the naïve surge of enthusiasm for Russia, and asked the Ministry of Information what could be done to 'counter the present tendency of the British public to forget the dangers of Communism in their enthusiasm over the resistance of Russia'.[26] But the Ministry's take-over of many of the local committees set up to sponsor Anglo-Soviet friendship, rather like Mrs Churchill's leading role in Anglo-Soviet friendship groups, did nothing to counter the tendency which Churchill had noted with such alarm.

If the Ministry's intervention was designed to prevent home-grown Communists using such organisations as 'fronts', its own whitewashing of Russia did the job which it was trying to prevent British Communists from doing. The all-pervasive 'good old Uncle Joe' mood was capitalised on by Beaverbrook in late 1941 and 1942 to agitate for a 'second front now', much to Churchill's embarrassment,[27] and from being a bogey, Russia now became our gallant ally. This situation produced some pretty ironies, such as the staunchly right-wing T. S. Eliot rejecting the equally staunchly left-wing George Orwell's *Animal Farm* on the grounds that it was 'not the right point of view from which to criticise the political situation at the present time'.[28] Those who, like Bernard Shaw and H. G. Wells, had always praised the Soviet Union as a great example to everyone of what the 'progressive state' could do and could be, were now loud in their own praises as Communist Russia showed herself to have more stamina than her Tsarist predecessor; the fact that her Tsarist predecessor was not being heavily supplied by her allies was, in the prevailing atmosphere, conveniently ignored. The popularity of Russia certainly worked in favour of the Labour Party and against the Conservative Party, and many Conservatives lamented the total lack of interest in their Party by its leader.[29]

Given the hostility which both Churchill and Eden felt towards the still Chamberlainite-dominated Conservative Party, it was hardly surprising that some of its members should, even as early as 1941, have been expressing alarm at the way the world seemed to be going. On 6 August Eden received a deputation from the 1922 Committee led by that old stalwart of the India Defence League, Colonel Gretton. Its members complained that 'only left-wingers in the Foreign Office could now hope for promotion ... and that Maisky would soon make the country Bolshevik'. Eden shrugged off such complaints, regarding them as symptomatic of the large section of the Party which he detested;[30] but they were expressive of more than that. J. F. Crowder, the MP for Finchley and Secretary of the 1922 Committee, put the matter plainly to Amery on 18 December when he told him that the 'feeling of restlessness about the Government in our party was getting acute', not only about the conduct of the war, 'but also because they did not feel that there was anyone inside the Cabinet who stood for the Conservative point of view at all'. Indeed, there was 'a considerable regret in many quarters that Winston had been made leader of the Party for it deprived the party of someone who could speak on its behalf to Winston'.[31]

This lack of confidence in Churchill's war leadership, and feeling that he was ignoring the interests of the Party, was to grow acute during 1942, but it persisted throughout 1941. Although the putative challenge from Menzies had come to naught, Churchill's attempt to defuse criticism by restructuring his Cabinet in July had had a marked lack of success. The removal of Duff Cooper from the Ministry of Information was welcomed, but his replacement by Bracken smacked of 'cronyism', as did the elevation of Lindemann to the peerage and the promotion of his son-in-law, Duncan Sandys; John Peck, one of Churchill's secretaries, offered Colville £5 to suggest to Churchill that his other son-in-law, Vic Oliver, should be Cooper's replacement.[32] The old criticism that he surrounded himself with 'yes men' was not stilled; indeed, his brother Jack and Desmond Morton both discerned a 'rising annoyance in the House' in August, with Churchill's 'personal resentment at criticism – which is meant to be helpful – and the offence which he has given to many people, including Ministers, by his treatment of them'.[33] Of course Ministers who are replaced resent the fact, which accounts for much of the criticism levelled at Churchill by Lords Hankey and Reith, who both lost their jobs in the reshuffle, but Churchill's treatment of his old friend, Bob Boothby, over his involvement in convoluted dealings over Czech gold seemed to many to go beyond what was required.[34] Hankey, who had been demoted in the reshuffle to Paymaster-General, noticed the atmosphere in Cabinet when he made one of his increasingly rare appearances there on 8 October: 'No feeling of a happy team of comrades, such as I have been accustomed to. A crowd of silent men and the usual monologue by Churchill.'[35] Even allowing for the asperity of a Minister on the way down, there can be little doubt that Hankey was not far wrong in his feeling that Churchill was surrounded by men whom he had made and who feared to say 'boo' to him; even Eden, who would have resisted the suggestion that he was a 'yes man', could not deny that Churchill neither had, nor wanted to have, an effective War Cabinet.[36]

Eden had been less than pleased to see Churchill trying to start up a correspondence with Stalin similar to the one which he had with Roosevelt; this, he felt, was the Prime Minister engrossing too much of the Foreign Secretary's province to his own domain.[37] He acted at the beginning of July to nip any such attempt in the bud, and Churchill apologised to him for cutting him out.[38] Eden, henceforth, tried to make Russia as much his province as Churchill had succeeded in making America his. But from the start Russian demands, and Britain's lack of ability to meet the one for a 'second front now', created difficulties. The question of supplies for Russia had been broached at Placentia Bay, and in joint negotiations in Moscow in October, in which Beaverbrook and Harriman represented their respective Governments, it was agreed that the British would, in effect, forego some of their supplies under lend-lease in order to accommodate the Russians.[39] But whilst the Russians were perfectly happy when concessions were being made to them, they proved demanding allies.

The question of political and diplomatic collaboration was much thornier than the question of supplies, and Stalin soon showed himself adept at exploiting British guilt about being unable to provide a second front in order to extract from them diplomatic concessions. The British were anxious for an agreement between the Polish Government-in-Exile and their new allies, but from the start the Soviets made it plain that they would only accept an agreement upon their own terms, and in early July raised for the first, but not the last, time the threat of sponsoring their own Polish Government, if an agreement was not reached. Thus it was that Eden found himself putting immense pressure on the Government of the country for which Britain had declared war to make concessions to a country which had, in alliance with Hitler, raped it.[40] Eden and Harvey both regarded the Poles in Britain as tiresomely stubborn over questions which, to them, were of far less moment than the Russian alliance. The Russian offer to recognise Poland's 'ethnographic frontiers' raised in Polish minds all sorts of suspicions about Stalin's intentions, but when the British seemed to hesitate, Stalin pushed in a preposterous request for the establishment of second fronts in France and the Arctic.[41] The British were, of course, unable to oblige, but they were all the more eager to offer up diplomatic concessions instead. An agreement was reached at the end of July between the Soviets and the Poles which left open the question of the frontiers, but in which the former promised to release Polish prisoners held on Soviet soil. The number of Poles which the Russians claimed to have in captivity did not match the number which the Polish Prime Minister, General Sikorski, alleged had been taken in 1939, but for the moment that was a matter of small moment; Eden had secured an agreement between Britain's two allies.[42]

If reports of Maisky's conversations with British Communists on 22 July were to be believed, the agreement marked no change in Soviet policy, merely a pragmatic recognition that this was as much as could be obtained in the circumstances on that subject.[43] But this did not stop the Soviets pushing elsewhere, or prevent Churchill and Eden from giving in to demands which they felt were unjust. One area where Anglo-Soviet military co-operation could become a reality with some speed was Iran, where, after the British suppression of the pro-German revolt in Iraq in June, there was the suspicion that a similar event might occur. By the end of July Churchill had decided that Britain and Russia could co-operate in securing Iran and her oil supplies for the Allied cause, but his plans for diplomatic pressure to be followed by creeping control were frustrated when the Russians simply delivered an ultimatum to the Iranians in the middle of August. Thus it was that whilst the British and the Americans were spouting off about the Atlantic Charter the British were getting ready for what Harvey called 'our first act of "naked aggression"', something of which both Churchill and Eden were 'rather ashamed'.[44]

Despite the fact that they were only in the war because they had been forced into it, the Russians were to prove very adept at raising the spectre of a separate peace in order to exact concessions from the British – a tactic which proved more effective on Eden than it did on Churchill, but which had its effect even on him. On 4 September, with half of the Ukraine in German hands and Leningrad under siege, Maisky once more repeated Russian demands for an immediate second front, pointing out that if Russia were defeated, the British chance of winning the war might well be gone for ever. He also pressed for the forthcoming conference in Moscow about supplies to be extended to cover joint strategy, and for Britain to declare war on Finland. All in all it was a pretty bare-faced bit of cheek. The Russians were at war with the Finns because on 18 June they had renewed the assault which they had first made in 1939, and they were at war with Germany because the thieves had fallen out over their booty. Churchill thought that he discerned behind Maisky's remarks the threat of 'a separate peace'.[45] Churchill told him bluntly on the morning of 5 September that it was hardly for the Soviets, who only a few months earlier had been in alliance with the Germans, to criticise the British for not being able to do more to help Russia. But the Russians did extract from the British large concessions on the question of supplies, and, much against his own judgment, Churchill let Eden persuade him that the British would have to declare war on the Finns. He wrote to him on 4 December: 'An historic mistake is going to be committed all right. I take full responsibility for it.'[46] On 6 December Britain declared war on Finland, Hungary and Romania at Russia's behest.

In both Iran and Finland Churchill had taken decisions which made a mockery of the cause for which he had raised his standard in 1940. No doubt 'military necessity' at times demanded such sacrifices, and in the case of Iran such a defence may be entered, but with regard to Finland there was no such excuse. Churchill had conceded something which he knew was wrong simply in order to allow Eden to conciliate Stalin. The question of calling Stalin's bluff had not been raised, and perhaps, given the naïve excesses of public enthusiasm for the Soviets, this had been as well, but the fact remained that, with the Soviets on the ropes, Churchill had proved incapable of resisting Eden's pro-Soviet excesses. But there were limits to everything, and when

Eden went to Moscow in December to discuss the terms of Anglo-Russian co-operation and recommended accepting Stalin's demands that Russia's frontiers of June 1941 should be recognised, Churchill found that that limit had been reached. Churchill was more impressed with the strength of Britain's position vis-à-vis the Soviets than was Eden,[47] and by the time Eden was reporting back, Churchill had more reason than ever to be solicitous of American opinion.

The later half of 1941 had seen no great improvement from the British point of view in the progress of the war. Churchill replaced Dill with Alan Brooke in October in the hope of injecting more life into the British war effort, but whether in the Middle East or the Atlantic, the British showed as little sign of being able to win the war by themselves as ever. Macmillan, who had received a junior post at the Ministry of Supply as his great reward for his opposition to Chamberlain, wrote to Beaverbrook in October telling him that 'all the symptoms are developing which marked the end of the *Asquith* coalition (a coalition of parties) and the formation of the *Lloyd George* coalition (a coalition of personalities)'. The Commons was restive and the press critical; this was, he thought, partly because of 'our impotence to help Russia by direct military effort', but also due to a sense of dissatisfaction with the Government. The 'old gang', Simon, Kingsley Wood and company, were 'unpopular', whilst the 'new gang', especially Cooper, Greenwood and Attlee, were 'largely regarded as failures'. He did not want to get rid of Churchill, but he thought it essential that he should delegate power to a second-in-command who could look after the home front: 'If the Prime Minister does nothing, he will ride the immediate storm, but the Government will not last beyond the end of this year or the early part of next.'[48] This was not a bad prophecy, but one thing which it did not predict prevented, if only just, its fulfilment, and that was America's entry into the war.

Roosevelt had followed up his declaration of early September about convoys with amendments to the Neutrality Act in October, which allowed the arming of merchant ships and the carrying of war material directly to belligerents. The blockade on Japan had also remained strictly in force, but whilst this seemed to bring nearer the possibility of conflict between the two powers on the rim of the Pacific, it did nothing to hasten America's entry into Churchill's war. All Churchill's immediate hopes were vested in Auchinleck's offensive, 'Crusader', in November in Cyrenaica. If it went well, he foresaw the possible entry into the war of French North Africa under General Weygand, with consequences for Pétain and Vichy, as well as for Franco.[49] But the operation failed to live up to such expectations, and once again the British were reduced to hoping that somehow America would contrive to enter the war. Churchill combated the pessimism of some of his colleagues by reminding them of the 'difficulties which faced President Roosevelt as a result of the slow development of American opinion and the peculiarities of the American

Constitution', which provided that only Congress could declare war. The development of American opinion over the last year had been, he said, far greater than could have been anticipated. No one reminded the Prime Minister that it had been far less than his own anticipations of the previous year. It would, he told his colleagues, 'be a great error on his part to press President Roosevelt to act in advance of American opinion'.[50]

Churchill's spirits rose when Roosevelt warned him on 24 November that negotiations with the Japanese were going badly and that 'we must be prepared for real trouble, possibly soon'.[51] The possibility that the Japanese might attack only British possessions in the Far East, and that the Americans would not consider that a *casus belli*, was one which had haunted Churchill for some time; it was finally removed on 7 December when Churchill learnt that Roosevelt was prepared to consider a Japanese attack on any colonial possessions as constituting a reason for declaring war.[52] That evening Churchill had Harriman and the American Ambassador, Gil Winant, to dinner at Chequers. Harriman found the Prime Minister unusually silent and preoccupied.[53] Just before nine o'clock the butler, Sawyers, 'came in and said there was something in the news about a Japanese attack on the American fleet'.[54] Churchill told him to bring the wireless into the dining room. Once Churchill had digested the fact that the Japanese had attacked the American Fleet at Pearl Harbor, he ordered a call to be put through to Roosevelt. After a few minutes Roosevelt came through and Churchill asked him: 'Mr President, what's all this about Japan?' 'It's quite true,' he replied. 'They have attacked us at Pearl Harbor. We are all in the same boat now.' Roosevelt said that he was going to ask Congress to declare war on the morrow, and Churchill pledged himself to do the same in the Commons. Roosevelt then spoke to Winant before Churchill got the telephone back and declared: 'This certainly simplifies things. God be with you.'[55]

In his memoirs Churchill wrote: 'We had won the war. England would live.' Thus it was that after putting matters in train at the Foreign Office and the Service Ministries, and after telegraphing the Irish leader, De Valera, with a plea to join the war, 'Now or never! A nation once again!' (an appeal to which he remained deaf), Churchill retired to bed and, 'being saturated and satiated with emotion and sensation', he 'slept the sleep of the saved and thankful'.[56]

42

The Grand Alliance

Strictly speaking Churchill went to sleep under a false sense of security. It was all very well, quixotically, to declare war on Japan, but neither that nor the Japanese attack on Pearl Harbor actually brought America into the war against Germany. Indeed, it instead opened up a rather unpleasant scenario. If the Americans now began to mobilise fully for a war in the Pacific, not only would all the 1941 Staff talks about a 'Europe first' strategy and the plans based on them become so much waste paper, but the supply of lend-lease aid, already slowing down due to problems in American production and the demands of the Soviet Union, could be expected to dry up. That would have left Churchill high and dry. Unable to prosecute a war successfully against the Germans, Britain would have found herself committed to another one against Japan: strategic, diplomatic and military bankruptcy would have stared Churchill in the face, and, allied to financial bankruptcy, Macmillan's prophecy about the fate of the Government would have come true a good deal sooner than predicted.

The Prime Minister was rescued from this fate, far worse than death for Churchill, by one of Hitler's more inexplicable actions: on 11 December he obligingly declared war on America. This also rescued Roosevelt from a situation which, if prolonged, could have become acutely embarrassing. In his 'fireside chat' to the nation on 9 December, he had tried to persuade the American people that, despite the dastardly deed perpetrated by the Japanese (soon ubiquitously referred to as the 'Japs'), it was necessary to pursue a 'Germany first' strategy, since the attack on Pearl Harbor was part of a global plot by the Axis. Hitler's declaration of war saved him the difficult task of trying to peddle this line for very long in the absence of any German aggression on the United States. The exact reasons for Hitler's decision remain unclear, but he appears to have imagined that the Americans would concentrate on the Pacific war.[1] This was a reasonable assumption, given American anger at what the 'Japs' had done, but it was one Churchill was determined to prove false. On 9 December he proposed a meeting with Roosevelt to co-ordinate and discuss strategy.[2] The American leader was less keen on such a meeting, fearing that his opponents might portray it as a sign that he, and America, were in thrall to British imperial war aims, rather than the loftier objectives beloved of the fuzzy Wilsonianism which permeated what passed for American thinking on that topic.[3] But Churchill came all the same. He was as aware as anyone of the dangers of America adopting a 'Pacific first' strategy, and he was determined to capitalise on his relationship with Roosevelt to ensure that the Anglo-American talks of early 1941, which had foreshadowed a common 'Europe first' strategy, came to pass.[4]

With the American entry into the war a new phase had begun. From being the emblematic leader of an embattled island empire under siege, Churchill became, at least in his own eyes, the lynch-pin of the 'Grand Alliance', even as Marlborough had been two and a half centuries earlier. In going to meet the American President, Churchill had a number of advantages which he successfully pushed home as far as he could during the 'Arcadia' conference. Roosevelt's critics were to accuse him of having been bamboozled by Churchill into pursuing what became known as the 'Mediterranean strategy', one which, the same critics added, was dictated not by a concern for the defeat of Germany, but rather one to preserve the British Empire. There was something in this, but not very much. In the first place, whilst Roosevelt agreed to consider an invasion of North Africa ('Operation Gymnast'), he had by no means given up the idea, favoured by his own Chief of Staff, General Marshall, of launching an attack on Germany in 1942. But in dealing with the British he had to face up to a reality which dictated Churchill's priorities quite as much as any concern for the Empire did; this was the fact that any fighting in Europe in 1942 would be done mainly by the British, and the only place the British had any troops was in the western desert, which, perforce, became for the Allies what it had been for the British since the Italians had entered the war – the main theatre of land operations.

The fact that it would be British forces upon whom the burden of battle in 1942 would fall, placed Churchill in a strong position to press for an Allied invasion of French North Africa to coincide, it was hoped, with a successful British offensive in the western desert. As he sailed to America on the *Duke of York*, Churchill used the time which, on his previous Atlantic voyage, had been devoted to backgammon, to drawing up a comprehensive strategy for the future.[5] This was the second advantage which Churchill enjoyed in talking to the Americans. He knew what he wanted to do, whilst they were still immersed in debates over whether to go for a 'Pacific strategy'. American military thinking did not partake of the British love of peripheral operations. Where Churchill's thinking derived from the tradition of using sea-power to stretch a continental enemy's lines of communication by attacking it at any number of points along an exposed coastline, the strategy favoured by Marshall and those Americans who did not share Admiral Ernie King's desire to get at the 'Japs' first was one based on classic Clausewitzian principles of going straight for the heart of your main enemy. This difference, despite Roosevelt's agreement to adopt 'Gymnast', was papered over, rather than resolved, at 'Arcadia', and it was to rumble on through 1942 and 1943. Entangled with it was another difference of attitude based upon differing experiences. The British were well used to a 'make do and mend' attitude when it came to planning operations, and had become used to having to survey, often in a gloomy way which infuriated Churchill, the obstacles to any particular course of action. The Americans were apt to write this off as the British being obstructive. Their 'can do' attitude was based upon unlimited confidence in their own continental economy to produce whatever material the military needed in whatever quantities were required. This too was to complicate the course of Anglo-American relations.

Despite the dislike of his military advisers for Churchill's strategic preference for a descent on North Africa, Roosevelt had little alternative but to accept the Prime Minister's strategic priorities. When one of the Chiefs of Staff had queried the wisdom of taking the initiative in so forthright a fashion, and wondered whether a continuation of the previous 'kid-gloves' policy towards America might not be more in order, Churchill answered 'with a wicked leer in his eye, "Oh! that is the way we talked to her while we were wooing her; now that she is in the harem, we talk to her quite differently!"'[6] In fact, in his dealing with the President, he continued to show the same deference and delicacy of feeling as he had done on their previous meeting.

American susceptibilities were one of the considerations which led Churchill to resist the demands which were coming out of Moscow via Eden. At their meeting on 17 December, whilst Churchill was on his way to America, Stalin had put to Eden the Soviet conditions for an Anglo-Soviet agreement, which included recognition of Russia's frontiers as they had stood before the German invasion. This would involve the British recognising all the gains which the Soviets had made from their pact with Hitler, including the incorporation of Latvia, Lithuania and Estonia, the seizure of Bessarabia from Romania, and the territory seized from Finland; it also involved recognising the Soviet seizure of the eastern half of Poland.[7] Eden and Harvey were not averse to the sort of mass movements of population which Stalin's brutal redrawing of the map of eastern Europe would involve,[8] and in January Eden was to advocate accepting Stalin's terms on the grounds of *realpolitik*: if the Russians lost to the Germans, it would not matter; and if the Soviets won, they would be in a position to seize what they wanted anyway.[9] But for Churchill not only were Stalin's demands unacceptable in themselves, they were also contrary to the terms of the Atlantic Charter and, as such, likely to alienate the Americans. It would hardly help cement a 'Grand Alliance' for Britain to agree to such terms, and Churchill told Eden, and his colleagues, in no uncertain terms, that it would be better for the Foreign Secretary to leave Moscow without an agreement rather than agree to such proposals.[10] Thus it was that Eden did, indeed, return with no agreement.

Churchill could feel much happier about the results of his American sojourn. It might almost be said that he had established intimate relations with Roosevelt. Supreme power and responsibility allowed the more eccentric parts of Churchill's personality to flourish unchecked. His love of uniforms and unconventional garb became institutionalised in his 'siren suits', or 'rompers' as he (and others) were wont to call them, but it also blazed forth in a variety of military and quasi-military garb, complete with peaked cap, usually askew. His working habits took a similar path. Roused from sleep at about eight o'clock, Churchill would have his breakfast brought to him in bed, during which time the marmalade and the newspapers would compete for his attention. It was not just the 'threepenny edition of the *Daily Worker*', as he called *The Times*, which attracted his attention, but every newspaper, including the real *Daily Worker*. Having finished, and with newspapers scattered around the bedroom, he would light his first cigar of the day and sit back, attired in his favourite dressing-gown, which was green and gold with red dragons on it, looking for all the world like a mandarin. He would then get down to work on his red boxes.[11] Being a creature of habit, he liked to carry on this routine when abroad. Because it was thought too dangerous to take female secretaries on the hazardous voyage across the Atlantic, Churchill would be accompanied on these occasions by a male secretary, Peter Kinna. This gave him an even greater freedom to dictate his letters whenever he wished, even from the bathroom. One morning during the 'Arcadia' conference, Churchill, having bathed, was wrapped in an enormous towel and striding round the bedroom dictating letters. Eventually the inevitable happened and the towel fell to the ground, but Churchill, 'quite unconcerned', continued on his way, at which point Roosevelt entered the room. Churchill, who was seldom lost for words said: 'You see, Mr President, I have nothing to conceal from you.'[12]

If he had cemented his relationship with Roosevelt and secured from the Americans a commitment to the strategy he favoured, Churchill had also done his part in establishing the alliance on a wider basis. If the 'isolationists' distrusted him, to many other Americans Churchill had become a symbol of Britain's resistance, and he was determined to capitalise on this position; an alliance founded merely upon inter-governmental co-operation was not the force that one with its roots in a common purpose could be. In a speech to a joint session of Congress on Boxing Day 1941, Churchill adverted to his own ancestry by reminding his audience that: 'I cannot help reflecting that if my father had been American and my mother British, instead of the other way round, I might have got here on my own.' He went on to amplify the theme of his work on the *History of the English-Speaking Peoples*, which, nearly finished by 1939, had lain at Chartwell since then as its author went on to add another chapter to the story he had written. Aware of Britain's reputation in America for being a class-ridden society, Churchill declared himself in 'full harmony' with 'the tides which have flowed on both sides of the Atlantic against privilege and monopoly'. He stood by the ideal of the Gettysburg Address: 'government of the people by the people for the people'. It was a masterly performance, and the sort of thing which only Churchill could have done.[13]

But if the conference had gone well and the distant horizon seemed streaked with light, around Churchill's feet lay strewn the wreck of Britain's Empire in the Far East. All the plans made at the conference for the establishment of an American–British–Dutch–Australian ('ABDA') force, under the command of General Wavell, soon turned to dust. Even before Churchill had left for America there had been a portent of what was to come when the Japanese sank the ship on which he had previously crossed the Atlantic, the *Prince of Wales*, along with the *Repulse*. On Christmas Day they took Hong Kong, and the following day broke through British lines in Malaya. Whilst Churchill and Roosevelt were declaring the establishment of the 'United Nations' alliance (with twenty-six members, including Brazil and Ecuador) on New Year's Day 1942, the Japanese were engaged in hustling the Americans out of their last strongholds in the Philippines and in forcing the British to abandon Sarawak. A week later the central Malayan line of defence yielded to Japanese assaults, and on 21 January British forces there retreated to Singapore. On 23 January the thoroughly alarmed Australians appealed for assistance.

The impact of this *dégringolade* on Churchill's own position was considerable. No sooner had the British people become convinced that salvation was on its way than their armies suffered a series of defeats unprecedented in their history. When Churchill discussed matters with Eden and Beaverbrook after a meeting of the Defence Committee on 21 January, he seemed to the Foreign Secretary 'tired and depressed'.[14] It was no wonder. The Commons, according to Macmillan, was getting itself into a mood not dissimilar to that which had preceded the debate over Norway in 1940,[15] whilst the London newspapers were repeating, without comment, the statement from Sydney that 'if Singapore falls, Churchill will fall with it'.[16] Churchill, who was suffering from a heavy cold, was in a fatalistic mood, telling Eden that 'the bulk of the Tories hated him, that he had done all he could and would only be too happy to yield to another'. He seemed disinclined to take any action to ensure that in the forthcoming Commons debate on the war, pro-Government speakers were selected. He was not, he said, much interested in the future.[17]

But Churchill's mood was not solely due to the situation in the Far East and 'nagging' by the House of Commons. He had generally enjoyed robust health, and the strains which his working habits and his over-indulgence in food, drink and his work all induced, he seemed to take in a manner which was remarkable for any man, let alone an overweight workaholic of sixty-seven. However tough his constitution, it could not indefinitely carry uncomplainingly the burdens which he placed upon it. On the night of 26 December, whilst still in the White House, Churchill went to open his bedroom window, which required some force, and suddenly found himself short of breath and felt a dull pain over his heart. He asked his doctor, Sir Charles Wilson, the following morning whether he had had a heart attack. Wilson was in a dilemma. It was clear to him that the Prime Minister had had an attack of angina pectoris, and current medical wisdom prescribed a six-week rest in bed as part of the treatment. He knew his patient well enough to know that he would not accept such a remedy, and was well aware of the political ramifications which would follow the announcement that the Prime Minister had to rest for six weeks. So he fudged the issue, telling him that he had been 'overdoing it'. Churchill's response was what he had expected: 'Now, Charles, you're not going to tell me to rest. I can't. I won't. Nobody else can do this job.'[18] It is a measure of Churchill's toughness that he pursued a punishing schedule throughout the rest of the conference with no more ill-effects than a cold and some fatigue.

Churchill's heart attack remained a secret until Moran's diary was published, but his health had given his colleagues concern for a while – and, it must be said, that mingled with that concern was a hope that ill-health, albeit only of a temporary character, might relieve them of the problem of what to do about the Prime Minister. Back in August Harvey had noted, after listening to Eden castigating Churchill's conduct of the Defence Committee as 'a monologue – any opposition treated as fractious – policy and operations decided by impulse – no proper planning', that it seemed 'problematical whether the PM will survive the course. His health may fail – his headstrong qualities may outweigh his great abilities and he may have to go if we are to win the war.'[19] Cranborne's warning about Churchill taking Parliamentary sanction for approval, and thus treading the path of Chamberlain, seemed to be coming true. Amery, who was finding Churchill's 'die-hard' stance on making any concessions to Indian nationalist feeling 'intolerable',[20] and who shared the widespread doubts about his wisdom in combining the role of Prime Minister with that of Minister of Defence, told the Chief Whip, James Stuart, that it was his 'duty to be really frank with Winston' about the 'discontent in the Party'.[21]

Stuart, 'an intelligent reactionary' who had been 'very pro-Munich',[22] was, understandably, less than keen to tackle the Prime Minister. He faced the same dilemma as Amery and other 'friendly' critics. As Alan Brooke put it: 'God knows where we should be without him, but God knows where we shall go with him.'[23] Despite his 'deficiencies on the side of organisation and understanding of the way in which social and economic problems are developing', and despite mistakes and miscalculations in the conduct of the war, Amery did not see 'how we can do without him as a leader'; indeed, he took the view that Churchill had 'made such a name for himself that however many mistakes he made it would be impossible to displace him'.[24] The next few months were to prove that Amery's assessment was accurate, but as the criticism grew in proportion to the disasters which befell British arms, it seemed a damn close-run thing at times.

Churchill's critics were to seize upon his dual role as Minister of Defence and Prime Minister, and to argue that he should give up one of them. However, one reason for their ineffectiveness was that they were not unanimous as to which of these he should surrender; the other reason for their failure was that Churchill refused to give up either. Prior to the debate in the House on 27 January 1942, the small National Labour group, of which Nicolson was a member, was generally agreed that in order to win the war Churchill would have to go. But they could suggest no alternative save Cripps, who would soon be back from Moscow, and they were only too well aware of the damage which Churchill's fall would have on public morale. Nicolson, who, despite being sacked in the July reshuffle, still hero-worshipped Churchill, was 'disgusted' by their 'thinking in political and departmental terms' and ignoring the fact that 'Winston is the embodiment of the nation's will'.[25] But they were not unconscious of this fact, and nor were the others who were inclined to be critical of him as war leader. It was for this reason that Eden tended to confine his complaints to Harvey and his own diary, that Stuart feared to tackle Churchill, and, ultimately, why Churchill survived the disastrous first half of 1942. He had built up an enormous credit balance in the bank of public esteem and prestige; he was to draw lavishly upon it throughout 1942.

The reception which Churchill received upon his first appearance in the House after the 'Arcadia' trip on 20 January was, his son noted, 'Nothing like the reception Chamberlain got when he returned from Munich.'[26] Channon described his reception as hardly 'enthusiastic – civil, perhaps'.[27] Churchill was infuriated by the attitude of the Conservative Party, most of whom were, he told his PPS, Sir George Harvie-Watt, 'guilty' over Munich. He alone, he declared (not without reason), stood between the Party and its political extinction, and yet they had the nerve to complain.[28] He decided to call for an immediate vote of confidence, confronting his critics head on. Churchill opened the debate himself on 27 January and, as he spoke, 'the wind of opposition' could be felt 'dropping sentence by sentence'; by the time he finished it was 'clear that there is really no opposition at all'.[29] The initial lack of enthusiasm among MPs was dispelled by Churchill's own pugnacious performance and his detailed account of what had occurred at 'Arcadia'; even Channon was won over, describing the debate as 'one of the great days in parliamentary history'.[30]

Churchill's message to those who had been muttering against him was clear. If the Commons disapproved of his conduct of the war, MPs had a simple remedy to hand which they should use. Faced with the stark prospect of destroying the emblem of British defiance and the man of 1940, there were not many MPs who cared to do more than mutter into their gins in the smoking room. To get rid of Churchill, which was the only choice he was giving them if they were dissatisfied with his performance, would, of course, as his speech reminded MPs, have a world-wide impact just at the moment when, with the creation of the United Nations, Britain was 'no longer alone'. He did not seek to minimise the dangers of the situation in the Far East, or the probability that 'we shall have a great deal more' bad news from that region, but he concentrated on Russian successes and the immense potential which America's entry into the war brought to the Allied cause. It was a masterful performance, and if ninety minutes seemed a trifle long to some, Churchill had at once paid the Commons his usual compliment of taking it seriously, whilst at the same time emphasising to it the seriousness of the decision it was being asked to take.

Most of the speeches made against the Government were in minor key by minor MPs, but there were some exceptions. Sir John Wardlaw-Milne, the Chairman of the Conservative Foreign Affairs Committee, made two effective criticisms in an impressive speech on 28 January. It was, he said, wrong to table a motion of confidence, as that would give most MPs no choice other than to vote with the Government, which would give an entirely false impression of the state of feeling in the Commons. He also criticised the Government's lack of preparation for defending the Far East and made a swipe at the Government front bench, remarking that even after two years of lack of success, most of its inhabitants remained undisturbed in undistinguished tenure of their offices. Emmanuel Shinwell, who had been left out of the Government in May 1940, spoke for many when he said that he wished there could be two votes of confidence: one in the Prime Minister and the other in the Government.[31] The line of criticism was clear, and it resembled nothing so much as that advanced by the barons of medieval England against kings like Edward II, Richard II and Henry VI; the King was a great and good man, but he was surrounded by evil counsellors who should be removed.

The critics were met with a fighting speech from Randolph Churchill, who seized the chance offered by his election to defend his father on the floor of the Commons as fiercely as he would later defend him in print. The stormy relationship which Randolph had created, but failed to enjoy, with his father before the war detracted not one jot from his filial loyalty. The bright promise of the early 1930s was fast fading in a haze of drink and bellicosity. Clementine Churchill, who disapproved of his behaviour and lack of manners, hoped that 'he would lie down and be quiet. He makes his father and me anxious sometimes.'[32] The fierceness of his attack on his father's critics, and the personal nature of those attacks, illustrated one of the reasons for Clementine's anxieties. Even Nicolson, who considered Randolph 'amusing and brave', thought the speech 'rather unfortunate',[33] whilst Channon felt it 'added fuel to the fires of bitterness'.[34] Sir Archibald Southby, the MP for Epsom, and one of Churchill's sternest critics in the debate, made a comment about Randolph's being in uniform and in the Hose, which his father took to be an aspersion on his son's honour, and he confronted Southby in the corridor afterwards and, shaking his fist in his face, responded to his attempts to explain his words by shouting: 'Do not speak to me. You called my son a coward. You are my enemy. Do not speak to me.'[35] It was one of the great pities of Churchill's life that, despite the great love he bore for Randolph, they were never to have the sort of warm relationship that he wanted.

On the final day of the debate, 29 January, Churchill showed his son the best way to deal with criticism. He made no attacks on his opponents; indeed, he congratulated them on the excellence of their speeches. He defended his decision to concentrate on North Africa and aid to Russia at the expense of the Far East, and dwelt upon the advantages to be apprehended from the American alliance; he then placed his fate in the hands of the Commons.[36] 'Conciliatory' and 'tactful', Churchill was also successful,[37] winning by 464 votes to 1, with the Independent Labour MP, James Maxton, being the sole dissentient. It was a triumph in part because there was no alternative leader in sight, but Churchill's manner, and rumours that he was going to do something about reorganising his Government, had also played their part.[38] He was also fortunate in the timing of the debate. His decision to go for an immediate vote of confidence was not unconnected with the progress, or rather lack of it, of the war. On the very day that he secured the 'best repartee' to his critics, it was announced that the Germans had entered Benghazi and that the Japanese were only eighteen miles from Singapore.

The rumours about an impending reshuffle were evidence that Churchill did not take the result of the debate either for granted or complacently. In the edition of *Tribune* that Friday, the Socialist MP Aneurin Bevan declared that 'This is no National Government, and Churchill is no National leader!'[39] The reaction of a left-wing newspaper with a small circulation might be thought to have occasioned few worries in a Prime Minister who had just won a resounding victory in the Commons, but since the paper was backed by Beaverbrook and was pushing the twin causes of Sir Stafford Cripps and more aid to Russia, such an opinion would have stood in need of revision.

There was an irony in the fact that some of Churchill's critics during the debate had singled out his sponsorship of Beaverbrook for particular criticism since his Lordship had been giving the Prime Minister cause for concern for some time. At the root of the problem was Churchill's suspicions of the motives which had prompted Beaverbrook's fanatical display of loyalty to the Soviet Union. Russia was, of course, a great popular cause, and the newspaperman might be expected to follow as well as form opinion, but there had to be more to it than that. Given his constant threats to resign from the Government, and his obvious dissatisfaction with Churchill's methods, it was not fanciful to imagine that 'the Beaver' was manoeuvring himself into a situation where he could not only take advantage of the undertow of discontent with Churchill, but also encourage it for his own ends.[40] His sudden alliance with Cripps at the beginning of 1942, just as the war was going badly and criticism of Churchill becoming vocal, was hardly accidental.

Tall and austere in appearance, Sir Stafford Cripps looked like the teetotal vegetarian that he was. A wealthy barrister, he was Beatrice Webb's nephew by marriage and shared her taste for high thinking and plain living. During the 1930s he had gravitated, in a manner reminiscent of the performance of a later Labour MP with similar proclivities, if less intellect, Anthony Wedg-wood Benn, towards the extreme left of the Labour Party, actually being expelled from it in the late 1930s. His performance as Ambassador had been such that it was difficult to know who he had annoyed most, the Russians, the Foreign Office or Churchill.[41] 'Very brilliant and well-meaning, very unstable' and lacking in judgment, Cripps was, because of his associations with Russia, a man who could become a political danger if brought home; which was one reason why, in late 1941, Churchill showed no particular anxiety to bring him home.[42] Eden was surprised, when talking to Churchill on 14 November, to hear that the Prime Minister wanted Cripps home 'at once' – at least he was until he heard the reason: 'To put my fist in his face.'[43]

Unfortunately Churchill had to deprive himself of this pleasure, in favour of attempting to get Cripps inside the Government. This was not easily done. With his sudden popularity and the Beaverbrook press giving him elevated ideas of his own importance, Cripps wanted to make his adherence to the Government part of a deal whereby some of the 'old gang', such as Kingsley Wood and Margesson, would leave office. Churchill was not disposed to be dictated to and Cripps was not impressed by being offered a post in the Ministry of Supply.[44] With the vote of confidence in the bag, Churchill felt able to reject Cripps's demands to be made Minister of Supply with a seat in the Cabinet. To Beaverbrook's surprise, and consternation, his new ally was demanding his job and that he should be shunted off to Washington to co-ordinate supplies.[45] His response was to try to define his powers as Minister of Production in a way which would make him virtual dictator over the home front. But this brought him into direct conflict with the formidable Bevin, who complained to Eden on 4 February that Beaverbrook was 'impossible to work with. He was loyal to no-one, not even the Prime Minister.'[46]

Churchill could have done without all this intrigue, but it was inevitable given the fact that the Government was far less popular than the Prime Minister. The shifting political allegiances also created difficulty for Churchill in relation to defining the terms upon which the 'Grand Alliance' would be constructed. One set of colleagues wished to concede more to Russia than he thought was either desirable or acceptable to the Americans, whilst another set accused him of similar behaviour in respect to Roosevelt.

The division of opinion over Russia centred upon Eden's proposal of 5 January to accept Stalin's terms for an alliance. Churchill had not moved from his original reaction that the idea was unacceptable. On 28 January

Eden put up a paper to his colleagues arguing his case.[47] He was, naturally enough, supported by Beaverbrook, but also by Bevin and Herbert Morrison. Churchill, however, remained obdurate. When it came to America, the political divisions were elsewhere. The dislike of many Conservatives for the terms upon which the British had had to woo the Americans had not abated. At 'Arcadia' Churchill had thought it desirable to try to extract from Roosevelt a declaration that the 'bases for destroyers' deal had involved no transfer of sovereignty.[48] But Conservatives such as Amery felt that the terms upon which the Americans wished to conclude a 'master lend-lease' agreement, which included, as article VII, pledges to abolish Imperial Preference, were too severe. This, Amery and others argued, was a matter 'not of economics, but of political right of the British Commonwealth to be regarded as an entity and to make its own internal arrangements for economic co-operation as it pleases'. Amery felt that the American obsession with universal free trade would, even if it failed as 'a world policy', succeed 'as a policy for breaking up the British Empire and reducing it to an American *Lebensraum*'.[49]

Despite Amery's conviction that Churchill did not understand the importance of Imperial Preference, the Prime Minister was not much more enamoured of the American proposals than his Secretary of State for India; it was Eden who was the leading advocate of acceptance, but then he regarded Amery and the Protectionist wing of the Party as outdated and irrelevant to the new 'liberal' world order, and rather shared his American opposite number's preference for economic measures which would discourage autarchic regimes.[50] Churchill was inclined to dismiss article VII as one of Cordell Hull's fads, but he was disabused of this notion when Roosevelt telegraphed him on 4 February to urge him that 'further delay in concluding this agreement will be harmful to your interests and ours'.[51] In its most recent discussion of the matter the Cabinet had been against yielding to what was felt to be 'American blackmail',[52] and Churchill's response to Roosevelt's message reflected this feeling. It was not, he told Roosevelt, a question of free trade versus protection, for on the economic issue some compromise could be reached. What the British objected to was 'the inappropriateness in time and circumstances of our being forced to part with our freedom of honourable discussion with you on an issue, which in certain aspects, touches our sovereignty and independence'. This, he warned, might easily be represented as 'the acceptance by the British Government and by the British Empire as a condition of tutelage'.[53]

Stalin's demands, like those made by Roosevelt, brought out a number of points which Churchill preferred to avoid. The most important of these was the question of 'war aims'. On the immediate aim of defeating the Axis powers, all were agreed, but beyond that there was little agreement between Churchill and his allies, although the same was not true of Eden. Churchill's war aims were essentially conservative; he wished to preserve the world into which he had been born and with which he was happy. There might need to be social and economic reforms, but these were unglamorous topics which quite failed to distract his attention from the business of fighting the war. His views have been characterised as those of a 'paternalistic Whig aristocrat', and by 1941 he was seriously out of touch with opinion at home.[54] The advent into the war of Russia and America had given a great boost to those 'progressive' forces which, from the fall of the Chamberlain Government, had been drawing up schemes for a 'New Jerusalem'. The writer J. B. Priestley found that his broadcasts in 1940 were almost as popular as those of Churchill, and the reason for this was that, unlike the Prime Minister, he adverted to the sort of 'better world' which the British people deserved for their sacrifices in the war.[55]

Priestley was far from being the only figure who thought that popular opinion would be better mobilised by something more than calls to defiance and reminders of Britain's historic destiny. The demands made by Stalin and Roosevelt raised the whole question of the post-war order upon which peace and prosperity were to be founded. Eden, whose lack of sympathy with the Chamberlainite nature of his own Party was matched by a sympathy for those sections of the Labour Party which wanted to create a better world,[56] saw in both proposals foundation-stones upon which a 'centre party' could help to construct a new and better Britain. Given the 'amoral' nature of Soviet foreign policy, and the 'exaggeratedly moral' nature of that of America, 'at least where non-American interests are concerned', it was essential, Eden thought, for Britain to take the lead in co-ordinating a combined Allied policy; and this Churchill's obstinacy was preventing.[57] The American proposals would help to prevent any repetition of the events of post-1919, and Eden's own liberal views chimed nicely with the neo-Wilsonianism of Roosevelt and Hull. Churchill, who, as Halifax put it, was 'pretty bored with anything except the actual war',[58] preferred to postpone the discussion of such matters; in the natural course of events he did not imagine that he was going to play much part in the post-war world. However, he possessed enough power to frustrate Eden. The Foreign Secretary, who had been faced down time and again by Chamberlain, was soon to find himself in a similar situation with regard to Churchill and post-war planning.

In the international arena Churchill's preoccupation with the war and the short-term gave him a certain influence over the direction of Allied strategy in 1942 and 1943. But such was the nature of the balance of available military force that that influence would have been there for the taking without any need to concede to America and the Soviets the lead in planning for a post-war order. On the domestic front Churchill's lack of vision was first to lead to his having to try to conciliate Cripps, and, once his bubble had burst, it was to land him, in early 1943, with the problem of what to do about the Beveridge report and the brave new world which it promised. Because he reacted to it in much the same way he reacted to most manifestations of thought about the post-war era, the initiative passed, as it had done in international affairs, elsewhere, in this case to the Labour Party. With popular opinion galvanised by the example of the Soviets, and by the 'New Deal' rhetoric of the Americans, Conservatism of the old kind soon came to be at a discount, and it was Churchill's lack of interest in such matters which consolidated Labour's position and, ironically, helped render his own defeat in 1945 inevitable. There were Conservatives, most notably Eden and R. A. Butler, who would have liked, at least metaphorically, to have stolen Beveridge's clothes, a manoeuvre for which there were good precedents in the history of their Party, but Churchill's massive figure blocked the way. Too powerful a figure to remove, the essential war leader, Churchill was to become at once the necessity and the curse of the Conservative Party.

The inclusion of Cripps into the Government took place in a manner which marked a shift by the Government itself to the left,[59] even if the Prime Minister stayed firmly where he was. Cripps's refusal to take the Ministry of Supply resulted in Churchill 'ramping round' denouncing him with 'every kind of imprecation'.[60] Much as he might have liked to have punched Cripps on the nose, it was clear from public opinion surveys that he enjoyed a great deal of popularity and that his continued cries for more aid to Russia would prove a potent weapon against a Government which was already weak.[61] A limited reshuffle on 4 February, which brought Beaverbrook to the Ministry of Production, created more problems than it solved. 'The Beaver's' unpopularity with Labour, and particularly with Bevin, simply increased Churchill's problems. Then, on 15 February, in what Churchill was to call the greatest disaster in British military history, Singapore, with its garrison of 64,000 men, surrendered to a Japanese force inferior in numbers. The picture of General Percival and his fellow Britons surrendering to an Asiatic race was one which did more to undermine the British Empire than anything except the Americans. It also prompted Churchill to make a major effort to save his own bacon by offering Cripps a large enough enticement to enter the Cabinet.

In this he was helped by Beaverbrook finally acting on his repeated threats to resign. With his Lordship out of the way, Churchill could offer Cripps the post of Lord Privy Seal and Leader of the House, a measure clearly designed to placate those critics who alleged that the Cabinet was full of 'yes men' with no one to oversee the domestic front. But Churchill also took the opportunity to revenge himself on the Chamberlainite wing of the Party. He had told Eden back in October that 'in time all the Munich men would be driven out'.[62] The hostility of the 1922 Committee and of old Chamberlain loyalists like Southby made Churchill inclined to take the view that that time had now come. Margesson, Chamberlain's Chief Whip, was unceremoniously dismissed from the War Office, to be replaced by his own (and Churchill's former) Permanent Under-Secretary, James Grigg. He had not been considered effective at the War Office and was obviously a convenient scape-goat for Singapore, but Margesson had been damaged politically by attacks on the 'Baldwin–Chamberlain Old School Tie Clique',[63] and Churchill was not sorry to see him go. Sir Kingsley Wood, who had played such a notable part in Churchill's elevation in 1940, and upon whose advice he leant heavily when it came to economics, was demoted from the War Cabinet, to be replaced by Churchill's old friend, Oliver Lyttelton.

The reshuffle left the Cabinet, in Rab Butler's opinion, remarkably short of proper Conservatives: 'Churchill was not orthodox; Eden was not liked; Anderson had never called himself a Tory; Lyttelton nobody knew & he was regarded as a city shark!'[64] Nor was the situation to improve. After Wood's death in September 1943, Amery was able to lament, in terms so remarkably similar as to suggest that they were common currency among those Conservatives who distrusted Churchill and his works, that there was 'no real constructive Conservative in the Cabinet': 'Winston is a die-hard, mid-Victorian Whig. Anthony is a sentimental internationalist with no ideas on empire or economic questions. Cranborne is also rather of the same outlook, while Oliver [Lyttelton] is merely a merchant, thinking in terms of international consortia.'[65] The eclipse of the Conservative Party, about which Amery and others were to fret in 1943 and 1944, began with Chamberlain's death, but it received its greatest boost in Churchill's Cabinet reshuffle of February 1943.

The failure of any of the *soi-disant* anti-appeasers to establish themselves as either successful Ministers or as powers in the Party, left Churchill more reliant than ever on his own cronies such as Bracken, and upon Labour. The dissatisfaction which Labour Ministers expressed to Attlee over their failure to gain more from the reshuffle reflects their feeling that more was to be had. The 'staggering fact was', as Butler put it, that the 'revolt from the Right', represented by the Chamberlainite criticisms of Churchill, 'had brought about a War Cabinet more to the Left'.[66] But the questions were, had it all been enough to save Churchill, and how would he deal with the threat posed by Cripps?

43

Never Despair?

The changes in the Government had been forced upon Churchill, and the fact that the Chamberlainite Ministers had, as Cripps had wanted, been either removed or replaced, is a significant index of his influence, as well as of Churchill's dislike of the Conservative Party; but Churchill had had little choice in the matter. Cranborne had written to Eden on 16 February asking him whether he thought 'Winston has any idea how unpopular it [the Government] is.' He thought that the crux of the matter was one that Churchill was determined to ignore, namely the 'question of defence'. The best arrangement would be for Churchill to give the Defence post to Eden,[1] a view which the latter was inclined to share.[2] Cranborne wondered whether it was not time for the Ministers to do something drastic, like all handing in their resignations: 'I do feel most strongly that it is idle for him any longer to hide his head in the sand & say that everything politically is all right. It isn't. There is, as you know, grave disquiet even among the most docile of the Government's followers.' It was, of course, 'possible' for Churchill to 'make a magnificent speech & get an overwhelming vote of confidence with the Whips on', but that did not 'allay the discontent, it only increases it'.[3] Cazalet was inclined to agree: 'Winston thinks his majority being greater than after Crete denotes greater confidence in him personally. Of course it is not true, and he knows it – or perhaps he doesn't.'[4]

Churchill had asserted his mastery over the House at the end of January, but its resentment at his tendency to treat any criticism as 'fractious' had not vanished, and it spilled over in the aftermath of the fall of Singapore. His announcement of the disaster, although 'grim and not gay', somehow failed to strike the right note: 'Although he is not rhetorical,' Nicolson noted, 'he cannot speak in perfectly simple terms and cannot avoid the cadences of a phrase.'[5] By the time he came to speak to the House on the disaster, he also had to face the embarrassment of the fact that two German warships had escaped from Brest through the Channel, despite the efforts of the Navy. Churchill was beginning to wonder whether British soldiers were of the same calibre as their fathers were; with Cripps and Beaverbrook playing political games, a captious House and a string of military disasters to his credit, it was no wonder that Lady Violet Bonham-Carter found him, for the first time in their long acquaintanceship, 'depressed'.[6] This perhaps explains why he so badly misjudged his speech to the House on 17 February.

Churchill came into the House with his most taurine expression firmly fixed; he received no cheer. From the very start he seemed 'to have lost the House'.[7] A barrage of hostile questions rattled him, and he 'became irritable and rather reckless'. He accused his critics of 'anger and panic', which went down badly.[8] Amery thought that had he stuck to his original resolution to deny the House a debate, he might have found himself in serious trouble,[9] but as it was he got away with his worst performance in the House since becoming Prime Minister with only his prestige dented and his temper shaken. It was that performance which made coming to terms with Cripps inevitable, even at the price of putting Eden's nose out of joint by making him Leader of the House, a position from which, the Foreign Secretary feared, he might be able to launch a bid on the Premiership.[10] Harvey was not the only one who felt that 'it cannot go on like this or we shall lose the war', nor was he alone in thinking that 'either the PM must consent to reform his Cabinet including a separate Minister of Defence, or he must be got to go';[11] Hankey,[12] Lord Salisbury[13] and Eden himself held similar views. In the reshuffle Churchill gave ground politically, but on the issue of the Ministry of Defence he gave no ground at all. When Eden suggested appointing an assistant Minister of Defence, Churchill refused,[14] telling him a few days later that 'no one else could be Minister of Defence . . . as he was "soaked" in it'.[15]

The question of how the new Government would work, and whether Churchill would be able to hold on to his monopoly on defence matters, was one which dominated British politics for the rest of the year.

The Cabinet changes may have helped raise the popularity of the Government, especially with the hopes being placed in Cripps, but they did little to raise Churchill's morale. When his daughter Mary saw him on 27 February, she found him at 'a very low ebb'.[16] Others close to him, like Bracken and Eden, feared that his refusal to give up any of his workload might bring on a stroke. Bracken described him as 'most depressed now', sitting 'with his head in his hands' and talking of 'lasting only a few weeks'.[17] The 'wiseacres in the lobbies' were beginning to prophesy that it would not be long before 'the younger men, Cripps, A. E[den] and Lyttelton' would 'take over'; and with Churchill seeming to be 'losing both grip and ground', this appeared not unlikely.[18] Eden, who was aware of Wilson's warning to Churchill about his heart, wondered if it was wise of the Prime Minister to carry on consuming beer, three ports and three brandies over lunch, but he was impressed by Churchill's determination to go on 'till he dropped'.[19] The 'wiseacres' would have done well to ponder that determination, which had been in evidence throughout Churchill's long political career.

For a brief moment after the reshuffle it seemed, as Bevin put it to Eden on 25 February, that there was 'a much better balanced Cabinet'. When the issue of the Russian alliance came up that day, Eden found himself able to push the Prime Minister towards making the sort of concessions which he believed were necessary if, as he put it, Britain was to avoid 'just hand[ing] over to the Americans the conduct of Anglo-Soviet relations'.[20] But it was not long before the old complaints resurfaced. Any 'wiseacre' who had put money on the 'younger men' coming through to displace an ailing Churchill soon lost it. The hopes which Cripps had raised had always been extravagant ones – as Churchill put it when trying to keep him out of the Cabinet: 'What has he ever done?'[21] Far from reorganising the home front or pressing for aid to Russia, Cripps volunteered himself for the task of going out to India to try to sort out the constitutional and political deadlock which had arisen there in the face of the threatened Japanese invasion.[22] This, not unnaturally, quite convinced Churchill of his 'loyalty and integrity',[23] and he was happy to see the potential saviour take himself off into a political dead-end. If Cripps failed his backers, then, for quite different reasons, neither Lyttelton nor Eden 'came through' to replace Churchill.

Lyttelton failed to make the impact which would have allowed him to live down the rumours that he was a 'city shark', and his arrival in the House of Commons late in life meant that he lacked the experience and the debating skill necessary to dominate that assembly. This frustrated Eden's expectations that the three of them, in combination, could wield enough power to bring some order into the central direction of the war. Despite the initial hopes raised by the reshuffle, Eden was, by April, once more plunged into gloom at 'the direction and conduct of the war'. Churchill simply would not 'work with a War Cabinet'; he liked 'to move all the pieces himself'. There was, Eden lamented, 'no day to day direction of the war except by the Chiefs of Staff and Winston', with the Defence Committee rarely getting a look-in: 'I wouldn't object to this, if it gave results, but it doesn't.' But, as Eden recognised only too well, 'Winston is probably constitutionally incapable of working any other way', which presented him with a problem.[24]

Cranborne and his few other intimates urged Eden to use his position to try to secure the necessary reforms. Writing to him on 5 April, Cranborne argued that Churchill had only brought Cripps and Lyttelton in 'because of strong public pressure' and the move had been 'a sop', with 'the idea of making any fundamental change in the conduct of the war' not having occurred to Churchill. It was, he said, up to Eden to bring Lyttelton and Cripps together and put 'irresistible pressure on Winston'.[25] This was what Eden also heard from Harvey and Dick Law,[26] but matters were not that simple. One reason why changes had failed to be made was that Churchill did not want them, and Cranborne was right to suspect that he would fight 'tooth and nail' any proposals which would lessen his powers. Eden was not the man for such a fight. This was, as he himself recognised, partly because he lacked the 'spunk' of 'die-hard' politicos like Churchill and Beaverbrook,[27] but there was more to it than that. He admired Churchill's 'guts' and was flattered to be told by him: 'I regard you as my son.'[28] Nor was that all

Churchill seemed to regard him as, for on numerous occasions he had dropped more than hints that he thought of Eden as his designated successor.[29] For all his declared lack of political ambition, Eden was intensely conscious of his position as heir to Churchill, and he had not liked Cripps becoming Leader of the House, nor Attlee becoming Deputy Prime Minister, because he feared the effect of such moves on his own position.[30] But that position depended, as Churchill was not slow to remind him, on their relationship, and the Prime Minister was adept at dropping the odd hint that the succession was not cut and dried, arguing on occasion that the choice might be between Eden and Sir John Anderson.[31] Doubts about his own capacity, loyalty to Churchill, and self-interest all combined to make Eden a loyal (if complaining) lieutenant. He did not want to hazard the influence he believed he had with Churchill, or his future, in an effort to get rid of a leader who was bound to go at the end of the war.[32]

It was not Churchill's engrossment of power as such to which Eden and many others objected; it was the fact that it failed to deliver success in the war, and it was this same fact which continued to make Churchill vulnerable. That the Prime Minister should have been in a deep depression at the end of February was hardly surprising. On 23 February Stalin felt able to declare that Germany no longer possessed the military advantages which had been conferred upon her by 'Operation Barbarossa', and the achievements of the Soviet Army backed him up, yet everywhere British arms seemed to be failing. Was there, he began to wonder, something fundamentally wrong with the British armed forces?[33] Perhaps, as Nicolson feared, two post-war decades in which 'intellectuals' and liberals of all sorts had 'derided the principles of force upon which our Empire is built'[34] had taken their toll and undermined the old British fighting spirit. Moreover, where the Americans redeemed the loss of the Philippines by bombing Japan for the first time on 18 April, and then by halting the Japanese advance at the Battle of the Coral Sea in May, the British seemed incapable of such feats. On top of that Churchill was also faced with the price which alliances seemed to exact, in this instance the continuing Russian demand for a 'second front' and a treaty, and American demands for an invasion of Europe.

Churchill's doctor wondered whether it was a loss of the 'old crusading fire' which made Churchill more willing to contemplate making concessions to the Russians than he had been in December and January;[35] perhaps it was so, but it was more likely political necessity which pushed Churchill in a direction in which he was loath to go. After his resignation, Beaverbrook had dropped a 'broad hint that he now considered himself free to advocate his Russian views in his paper',[36] and this was what he proceeded to do. He told Churchill on 17 March that he wanted the Government to do three things: to recognise Russia's 1941 frontiers (with the exception of the one with Poland) 'irrespective of the decision of the United States'; to increase supplies of tanks and aircraft to Russia; and to mount an assault on the Continent.[37] That these were remarkably similar to the demands which the Soviets were making on the Government was not, perhaps, all that surprising given the close contacts between Beaverbrook and Maisky. Beaverbrook was emboldened in his advocacy of a 'second front' by the discovery, during a visit to Washington in March, that despite the decision made at 'Arcadia' for 'Operation Gymnast', the Americans were now taking the view that the British lack of success in the western desert had put that operation on the back-burner; in default of it Marshall had seized the opportunity to press for his preferred strategy of a direct assault on Europe.[38]

Churchill had glumly acknowledged that the shipping situation alone made 'Gymnast' impossible for 'several months'.[39] When he reflected on 'how I have longed and prayed for the entry of the United States into the war', he found it 'difficult to realize how gravely our Government affairs have deteriorated since December'.[40] In the circumstances he no longer, as he told Roosevelt on 7 March, felt that the principles of the Atlantic Charter should be construed so as to deny Russia her 1941 frontiers.[41] This did not mean that he agreed with Eden; merely that in the face of events, and the impossibility of acceding to demands for a 'second front now', diplomatic appeasement of the Russians was the only thing which he had left to offer.

But if Churchill was prepared to make concessions to Stalin, and to look to Roosevelt for approval for them, and if he was prepared to take advice from Eden on the subject, that did not mean that he was settling down under the new regime to a style of government more akin to collective Cabinet responsibility, or that there were not limits to his willingness to appease Roosevelt. He had given in, in late February, to American demands over the 'master lend-lease' agreement.[42] He was possibly genuinely under the impression that the Americans would be willing to allow the British Empire to keep its 'internal tariff', but even if he realised that this was not the case, he would have had little alternative but to sign.[43] But when it came to Roosevelt offering him half-baked advice on India, or when it came to accepting a more liberal policy on that subject, Churchill swiftly reverted to the rhetoric and attitudes of the India Defence League; indeed, he became a sort of one-man India Defence League in his own Cabinet.

Amery had found Churchill's views on India quite unchanged. Despite American disapproval, Churchill had made it plain that the terms of the Atlantic Charter did not apply to India; the most he was prepared to offer was a promise that the object of British policy was to confer Dominion Status on India at an unspecified date.[44] The Labour members of the Government were as unhappy with such a policy as were Amery and Eden, but until the threat of a Japanese invasion made the future of India a 'hot' political issue, they all preferred to steer clear of a topic on which the Prime Minister was known to have extreme views.[45] It was Roosevelt who, without perhaps realising what a nettle he had chosen to grasp, first raised with Churchill the possibility of giving independence. According to Churchill's memoirs, he reacted 'so strongly and at such length that he never raised it verbally again';[46] but if Roosevelt did not do so verbally, he certainly did bring up the topic again. The future status of India was also questioned by his own colleagues, many of whom favoured taking up a suggestion made in early January by the moderate Indian leader, Tej Baradhur Sapru, that India should be raised to Dominion Status at once and should be conceded much of the apparatus of self-government. Churchill's reaction to them was similar to his response to Roosevelt. As with so many other matters, Churchill simply did not want to consider something which he regarded as belonging to the province of questions to be dealt with after the war.[47]

Pressure from Amery and from his Labour colleagues, as well as the onward march of the Japanese, made it impossible for Churchill to maintain his attitude. In early February he decided that he would be prepared to concede some expansion in self-government, and declared his willingness to fly to India to put his proposals before the Indian politicians; he could, he told Eden, stop off in Cairo on his way home and try to sort out Auchinleck and the British command structure in the Middle East. For a sixty-seven-year-old man in uncertain health and under the pressures Churchill was under to propose such a thing struck Eden and Harvey as a 'gallant' act,[48] but the imminence of the downfall of Singapore put an end to the project. Amery's doubts as to whether Churchill had 'thought out the detailed implications' of the policy being proposed turned out to be correct.[49] Cripps's entry into the Government brought renewed pressure for the concession of Dominion Status, and Churchill was hardly in a position to oppose such a line of policy, especially when Roosevelt seemed to be expecting some movement on the part of the British.[50] When the newly created India Committee met to consider the question on 26 February, Amery felt, 'for the first time', not merely that Churchill was 'unbusinesslike' but that he was 'overtired and really losing his grip altogether'. He thought that a 'complete outsider' who knew nothing of Churchill's reputation 'would have thought him a rather amusing but quite gaga old gentleman who could not understand what was being talked about'.[51]

Churchill reassured Roosevelt on 4 March that the question of Dominion Status, which carried with it the right to secede from the Empire, was being actively considered.[52] But when Churchill put the India Committee's proposals before the Cabinet on 5 March, he did so 'with such an ill-grace' that it produced a revolt from Kingsley Wood and the Chamberlainite Conservatives which precipitated a political crisis.[53] Amery, who had thought that the only 'storm' was the one 'internal to Winston, who hated the idea of giving up all his most deeply ingrained prejudices merely to secure more American, Chinese and Left Wing support', found that others shared the same view. There was, of course, everything to be said for Amery's view of Churchill's reaction, and his description of it to the King was as amusing as it was accurate: 'He was undergoing all the conflicting emotions of a virtuous maiden selling herself for really handy ready money.'[54] It was an analogy which could have been applied across a whole range of topics.

Churchill did not much care if Cripps carried out his threats to resign, but the possibility that he would be accompanied by Attlee and company threatened the fate of the whole coalition. In 'his cups' on the evening of 5 March, Churchill told Eden that he was quite prepared to go himself and to advise the King that he should succeed him.[55] He repeated his threats of resignation in Cabinet on 7 March, and spoke of the 'strength of the Tory Party', a clear warning to any potential successors of the difficulty they would face pushing through a more liberal policy on India. But Cripps, for once, proved to be helpful. He was, he said, prepared to compromise on 'any basis except a statement that we have decided to do nothing', and he offered to go out to India himself. Churchill was impressed by this offer, but 'kept harking back to his position in the country, to our being jostled by Socialists', and to a theme which he seemed to have 'a strange hankering after' – the possibility of a return to Party Government.[56] Wisely Churchill accepted Cripps's offer.

Churchill was still under pressure from Roosevelt to concede independence to India. It is, perhaps, symbolic of the whole American approach to India that where, in the first draft of a message to Churchill on the subject, Roosevelt had candidly admitted that what followed was 'a purely personal thought based on very little first-hand knowledge on my part', the final version should have begun: 'I have given much thought to the problem of India';[57] it is not difficult to divine which version told the truth. Churchill made no direct reply to what was, even for Roosevelt, a half-baked idea. Basing himself on the analogy of the United States between 1783 and 1789, he came up with the idea that representatives from various parts of India could form a temporary 'Dominion Government' with a view to establishing something more permanent after the war. It was a measure of his respect for Roosevelt, as well as of his contempt for the silliness of the ideas he propounded, which prompted him to write in his memoirs that the document was of 'high interest' because it illustrated the 'difficulties of comparing situations in various centuries and scenes';[58] it also illustrated the price which had to be paid for 'ready money'.

The Americans were in a position to dictate both strategy and the delimitation of spheres of influence when it came to operational matters, and they were not slow to make this plain in the face of British failures. On 7 March Roosevelt made it clear to Churchill that unless the British agreed to mount an operation in Europe in 1942, America would have to shift her attention to the Pacific,[59] which, as he told the Prime Minister two days later, was to be regarded as an American responsibility. Britain, he was kind enough to say, had control of the area between Singapore and North Africa: 'But it is assumed that Operation "Gymnast", the landings in Northwest Africa, has been temporarily shelved.'[60] Marshall had now prevailed upon the President to adopt a 'Germany first' strategy, and plans were drawn up for an invasion of Europe in 1942, which would have, among its advantages, that of helping to relieve pressure from the Russians – without having conceded their demands about their 1941 frontiers.[61] Roosevelt sent Hopkins and Marshall to London at the beginning of April to explain his ideas to Churchill.[62] Marshall was slightly suspicious of the ease with which Churchill, after repeating the objections of his own advisers, gave in to the idea, but as the Americans had got what they came for, no one, it seemed, except the British military, had anything to complain about.

Marshall was right to be suspicious. Churchill had, in principle, no objection to the idea of an invasion of Europe in 1942, but he was convinced that it was quite impracticable; however, if it stopped the Americans turning towards the Pacific, it was worth saying 'yes' to Roosevelt's ideas – particularly if, as Churchill was convinced was the case, study of the operation and the 'march of events' would show it to be impossible.[63] In the meantime, the build-up of American troops in Britain could begin, ready for 1943, and if, as Stalin was demanding and Roosevelt expecting, an operation was needed for 1942, Churchill could always blow the dust off 'Gymnast'; he may have been old, tired and under strain, but he was never anybody's fool.[64]

The Hopkins visit saw the three main problems confronting Churchill all come to a head. On the question of strategy, Churchill made the required concessions, with his own unspoken caveats. On the question of the Soviet frontiers, Hopkins confirmed what telegrams from Washington had already made clear, that the Americans would not sign a treaty of the sort Stalin wanted, and that they regarded the promise of a cross-Channel operation in 1942 as taking 'the heat off Russia's diplomatic demands upon England'.[65] The American position was one which threatened acute embarrassment on two counts: in the first place, Churchill had indicated to Stalin at the same time as he had put the idea to Roosevelt in early March that Britain might be prepared to sign a treaty on his terms; and in the second place, it cut straight across the decision which the Cabinet had taken on 26 March, at Eden's bidding, to go ahead with the policy he favoured. Indeed, Roosevelt's attitude, in Eden's mind, raised the whole question of whether Britain was to have her own foreign policy or not: 'Whilst F.D.R. can legitimately claim that we should decide nothing without consultation with him,' Harvey wrote, echoing his master, 'he cannot properly claim that he can overrule our foreign policy or deny us a foreign policy at all.'[66] Churchill felt much the same way over the third bone of contention, India, when Roosevelt once more offered his 'advice' on what the British should do. On the Russian issue Eden got his way. It was, he told the Cabinet on 8 April, essential for Britain to be on good terms with a power whose post-war co-operation was essential, and so, with the exception of the Polish frontiers, the decision was reached to go ahead with, or without, Roosevelt.[67] On India, the President's intervention once more served to define the limits of Churchill's deference.

Cripps had arrived in India on 23 March with the Cabinet's offer. This amounted to a promise of Dominion Status after the war, but only after a request had been received from an elected constituent assembly. The Congress leaders refused to accept anything less than full independence immediately, whilst the Moslems would accept nothing which would leave them under Hindu rule.[68] Cripps, with the encouragement of Roosevelt's special representative, Colonel Johnson, proved willing to concede more than either the Viceroy, Linlithgow, or Churchill wanted, including an Executive Council, which, except for the Commander-in-Chief of the Army, would be entirely Indian and which would function, in effect, as a Cabinet. He was also prepared to transfer a large number of functions to an Indian-controlled defence department.[69] Hopkins denied, diplomatically rather than truthfully, that Johnson was acting with the President's approval, and Churchill angrily rebuked Cripps for exceeding his powers,[70] but the breakdown of negotiations on 11 April seemed to have saved the day for the Prime Minister.

Hopkins tried to play down Johnson's role because of the danger that, if and when the Cabinet turned down what had become known as the 'Cripps–Johnson proposals', Roosevelt would lose face because of the use Johnson had made of the President's name during the negotiations with the Indians.[71] Roosevelt's response to the breakdown of negotiations, and to Churchill's statement that public opinion in America would understand that the British had done their best, was 'unusually blunt and critical',[72] which lends credence to the suspicion (raised by the fact that Johnson received no rebuke) that the President's special representative had been his master's voice. He told Churchill that American opinion blamed the British for the deadlock and failed to understand their policy at all; he warned him that if India was lost to the Japanese and military setbacks for the Allied cause followed, 'the prejudicial reaction on American opinion can hardly be overestimated'. He urged Churchill to postpone his departure and put to the Americans the scheme which he, Roosevelt, had earlier suggested.[73]

The telegram, which was addressed to Hopkins, reached Chequers at three o'clock on Sunday morning, and it found Hopkins and Churchill still talking. The Prime Minister's reaction was explosive, and 'the string of cuss words lasted for two hours'.[74] He refused, point-blank, to follow a policy which, he was convinced, would lead to a Nationalist Government withdrawing India from the war. He was, he told Hopkins, 'quite ready to retire into private life if that would do any good in assuaging American public opinion', but British policy, he emphasised, would remain the same.[75] An edited and sanitised version of all of this was sent to Roosevelt later that day.[76]

Thus it was that Hopkins returned with agreement only on one topic, but as that was the major one, of Britain agreeing to a second front in Europe in

1942, he went home a happy man; he would have been less happy had he known of the mental reservation which the British had put on their acceptance of the American scheme at their joint meeting on 14 April. This, however, was something which Roosevelt was only to discover in June when Churchill came to Washington.

The Prime Minister was in a cheerier mood after his talks with Hopkins and Marshall, and when Eden lunched with him on 27 April, he found him 'in better form than I have known him for ages'.[77] He was under few illusions about his level of popularity: 'I am like a bomber pilot,' he told Malcolm MacDonald on 22 April. 'I go out night after night, and I know that one night I shall not return.'[78] But he still possessed the charisma, even when recounting a catalogue of disasters to the House, as he did on 23 April in a secret session, to inspire 'confidence' and a 'feeling of shame', at least in some, at having 'doubted him'.[79] But throughout April critical comments about the Prime Minister's running of the war were almost *de rigueur* in the press and the clubs of London. Most of the criticism centred around whether or not the Prime Minister should remain Minister of Defence. Hankey, who had been forced to retire from the Cabinet in March, had no doubt, drawing on his long administrative experience, that things needed shaking up. Speaking in the Lords on 25 March, he had urged the abolition of the Ministry of Defence and the placing of supreme control in the hands of the War Cabinet, assisted by the Chiefs of Staff; he had also called for an end to 'late night meetings'.[80] Another casualty of the reshuffle, Margesson's Under-Secretary, wrote an article in *The Times* in mid-April urging the creation of a 'Great General Staff', in which Churchill's role as Minister of Defence would be under the control of a collective body.[81] This 'Palace revolt', as Bevan called it hopefully, made little impact on Churchill, who, as Eden had feared and recognised,[82] would suffer no diminution of his responsibilities in defence matters; his sole recognition of the 'revolt' was a cavalier remark one evening that they had better finish the meeting of the Defence Committee before midnight or they would all incur Hankey's wrath.

But there were signs which indicated that Churchill might need to take some note of his critics, however loath he was to do so. On 25 March the Conservatives lost a by-election at Grantham on a swing of eight per cent to a candidate whose motto was 'total efficiency'; this was followed by the loss of Wallasey (with a swing of nearly thirty-six per cent against the Conservatives) and Rugby (with a swing of thirteen per cent) on 29 April.[83] Undoubtedly much of the voting reflected a reaction to the Chamberlain years, but a conjunction of discontent in the country and in Parliament unquestionably existed, and as Lord Salisbury (whose 'Watching Committee', set up in 1939, had started out as a rump of the 'Eden group') told the Foreign Secretary on 1 May, 'no *speech* by Winston, however brilliant, especially in Secret Session, will restore faith'. He thought that public and Parliamentary opinion was still 'attracted by Winston's leadership, his courage, and the broad lines of his strategic policy', but that it considered that 'he is taking on more than his strength or his *qualifications* can accomplish', and he warned that in 'the face of another disaster the position of the Government will rapidly deteriorate'.[84]

With Beaverbrook beginning to agitate for a 'second front now' and for more aid to Russia, and with his newspapers and others criticising not simply the Government, but even the Prime Minister himself, Churchill could ill afford another 'disaster'. He could also have lived happily without Roosevelt giving the Russians promises in May that a 'second front' would be opened in 1942.[85] That the Russians dropped their demands over recognition of their 1941 frontiers and accepted, instead, a simple twenty-year treaty of alliance, may have proved that Roosevelt was correct in thinking that this was really what Stalin had wanted all along, but it put Churchill, who was convinced that such an operation was impossible, in a difficult position.[86] He went to Washington in June to try to hammer out matters with Roosevelt, but whilst he was there news came through, on 21 June, of the fall of Tobruk. With this fresh disaster, Churchill's opponents decided that it was time to strike. With Roosevelt's sympathy ringing in his ears, Churchill returned to London to face what was bound to be a discordant symphony.

44

The End of the Beginning

The fact that the Germans had, once more, beaten the British to the offensive in the western desert was the latest in a long line of military failures, and the fact that it came on top of postponements in the British programme of convoys to the Soviets, who did, at least, seem to be able to defeat German armies, gave Churchill's critics ample room for complaint which they were not slow to make use of. Beaverbrook's campaign for a 'second front now' to help the Russians had just had its first great public meeting in Birmingham, and the press Lord, confident that he was riding a tide which had popular support, tried to engage Bevin in talks about the type of government which would succeed Churchill's. But, as on a later occasion when Labour colleagues tried to get him to intrigue against Attlee, Bevin would have none of it; he had not forgotten Beaverbrook's attempts to take over the home front earlier in the year.[1] But intrigue and speculation were rife as Churchill crossed the Atlantic once more. Five days after the fall of Tobruk a Beaverbrook journalist, Tom Driberg, standing on a platform of more aid for Russia and more efficient prosecution of the war, won the seat of Maldon in Essex with a swing of twenty-two per cent away from the Conservative Party.[2] A motion of no confidence was laid down in the order paper of the House in the name of Sir John Wardlaw-Milne, Sir Roger Keyes and Leslie Hore-Belisha.

They were hardly a formidable trio. Wardlaw-Milne, as Chairman of the Conservative Foreign Affairs Committee, was one of the leading back-benchers, a position which, Nicolson thought, had 'caused his head to swell badly'.[3] Keyes was an old friend of Churchill's, and the latter had helped him into Parliament and had given him the post, in 1940, of first director of Combined Operations. Keyes's appearance in the full-dress uniform of an Admiral of the Fleet during the Norway debate, when he had made a blistering attack on Chamberlain's running of the war, had played a notable part in sapping confidence in the Government, and, with a VC from the Great War, he was the sort of 'offensive-minded' figure whom Churchill admired; but his criticisms of the Chiefs of Staff had led to disputes with them, and in the autumn of 1941 Churchill had, albeit reluctantly, removed him from office.[4] Hore-Belisha, who, despite promises from Chamberlain after sacking him in January 1940, had never regained a place on the Government front benches, had, as revenge, constituted himself into one of that body's main critics.[5] The fate of their motion depended upon two things: whether the Government suffered any further military disasters before the House debated it on 1 July; and the presentation of their case.[6] In both areas Churchill's luck held.

Even before the debate opened the feeling was that the 'movement against Winston is subsiding'.[7] The insurmountable problem which the unlikely trio faced was one which had defeated all the Prime Minister's critics: 'there is no alternative to Winston'.[8] Wardlaw-Milne opened with reasoned criticisms of why Churchill should be relieved of the pressure of being Minister of Defence, but then totally lost the House when he suggested that what was needed was the appointment of a new Commander-in-Chief of the Army, the Duke of Gloucester. Neither the King nor his brothers was over-endowed with intellect, but the idea of the dimmest of them all taking over as commander of the armies brought a roar of 'disrespectful laughter',[9] and the 'buzz' went round the House, 'But the man must be an ass.'[10] Channon noticed Churchill's 'face light up, as if a lamp had been lit within him and he smiled genially. He knew now that he was saved.'[11] Wardlaw-Milne never recovered the ear of the House. Then came Keyes, whose criticisms were diametrically opposite to those made by Wardlaw-Milne. Churchill, he declared, did not interfere enough in the making of strategy and, with his adventurous disposition and inventive mind, he should do more. After this there was little the Government needed to do, but Lyttelton, who was put up to reply, managed to do even that badly. His inexperience in debate showed as, reading his speech (an unusual habit in those more enlightened days when MPs were expected to be able to speak without the aid of anything save their minds), he ploughed on, refuting all criticism and refusing to give way to other members. As he sat down Lyttelton turned to Eden and, 'visibly perspiring', said: 'I don't know if this is your idea of fun but it's not mine.'[12] He had done almost as much harm to his reputation as Wardlaw-Milne had to his cause.

It was some measure of Churchill's concern about the motion of censure that in the dining-room beforehand he had asked Boothby, whom he had sacked in disgrace eighteen months before, if he would speak for the Government. He did so, making a much better job of it than Lyttelton: 'When all is said and done,' he declared in a style which always held the House, 'this is the Government, and this is the Prime Minister, who "stood when earth's foundations fell"';[13] it was a line of argument which had already convinced most doubters where they must cast their vote.[14] Churchill applauded Boothby's effort, but, after that day, did not speak to him again for over a year. He walked out before the next contribution from Lord Winterton, who was 'old lace' to Shinwell's 'arsenic'. He made a direct attack on Churchill himself, whom he accused of being Britain's 'Führer'. Some of Churchill's critics may have thought, when the day ended at 2.40 a.m., that 'We've got the old bugger now!',[15] but they were wrong.

The following day Bevan and Hore-Belisha made up for the appalling performance of Wardlaw-Milne and company with devastating speeches. Bevan, whom Churchill was to describe as a 'squalid nuisance', was a variation on what was becoming a familiar pattern. A miner's son from South Wales, he had taken the trades union route out of the mines and into the Commons. A 'fire-brand' with a high-pitched voice, which an attractive Welsh lilt transformed into an effective vehicle for powerful oratory, Bevan was at his best when on the attack. His exalted principles were combined with a taste for high-living, which Beaverbrook, who enjoyed cultivating such things, encouraged to such an extent that Bevan became known as the 'Bollinger Bolshevik'. With the exceptions of Lloyd George and Mosley, British politics in the twentieth century has produced few more natural orators than Bevan, and on the afternoon of 2 July he turned the full contents of his armoury on Churchill. He criticised the Prime Minister for his decision to close rather than open the debate, which, he said, would deprive MPs of the chance to quiz him. How long, he asked, would the Prime Minister keep winning every debate and losing every battle? Churchill's ideas on strategy were out of date and he was, Bevan declared, surrounded by 'yes men'; it was up to the House to put Churchill 'under the clamp of strong men with no departmental interests'.[16] Hore-Belisha made an equally 'brilliant, eloquent and damning attack on the Government',[17] but in leaving his contribution until last Churchill showed that he had lost none of his Parliamentary cunning.

That morning Churchill had had what, with some irony, he called the 'advantage of considering a report from Sir Stafford Cripps'.[18] Cripps thought that the result at Maldon was 'undoubtedly largely due to results in Libya' and he came up with six points which needed dealing with, including the question of the supreme command of the war. Churchill was inclined to dismiss his strictures as 'all theory', growling that 'You can't run a war as if you were in a laboratory.' He did not, he thought, need the advice of Cripps on how to handle the Commons; nor did he.[19] As some of his critics noted, he did not actually deal with any of the substantive points made by his critics about the central direction of the war. He 'skated around dangerous corners', but, with his 'usual Churchillian gusto', ended by 'intoxicating his listeners'.[20] Having been accused by Hore-Belisha of glossing over British defeats, Churchill carefully outlined the gravity of the situation in the Middle East, where Rommel, the German commander, was only sixty miles from Alexandria and already beginning a major offensive. He offered no explanation for British failures in the region, but reminded the House that neither generals nor governments would take risks unless assured of backing at home: 'In wartime if you desire service you must give loyalty.' This was the centrepiece of his defence. What he was, in effect, saying to the House was 'trust me', drawing heavily upon the political and emotional capital which he had built up in 1940. He would not, he made plain, consent to any reduction in his powers or see them delegated to men who, unlike himself, were not responsible to the House of Commons, thus neatly turning aside Winterton's thrusts.[21] The Government won the division by 475 votes to 25, with about 20 abstentions.

At one level it was a great triumph and the Government had certainly been saved. Churchill had made a 'masterly debating speech',[22] but he had not really answered his critics, and even the devoted Nicolson noted that 'the impression left' by the debate was 'one of dissatisfaction and anxiety'.[23] Channon was not the only one who decided that he did not have the 'guts' to vote against the Government, and so trooped through the 'aye' lobby; one MP commented that never before had 'so many Members entered a division lobby with so many reservations in their minds'.[24] The situation remained, in effect, unchanged, as did the question of how much longer Churchill could go on 'losing every battle' and winning the debates.

Much, if not all, depended upon the subject Churchill had been torn away from discussing with the President – the launch of the 'second front'. Upon this subject enough has been written, as one commentator has it, to 'fill libraries'.[25] Because no second front in France was opened until 1944, and because Churchill was the foremost advocate of the 'Mediterranean strategy', volumes have been devoted to proving or disproving that he never really wanted an assault on mainland Europe. The reasons for such a case have been variously canvassed. American critics have focused upon his desire to maintain the British Empire as explaining his strategic preferences, whilst others have referred to his fear of another Dardanelles followed by another Somme offensive.[26] But viewed in the long perspective of Churchill's whole career, such speculations seem rather 'theoretical'. As the Dardanelles and the Russian intervention have shown, Churchill was readily able to convince himself that any military operation he favoured would be attended with speedy success and momentous consequences; so it was with the 'Mediterranean strategy'. There is no need to posit a concern with the Empire to explain his strategic preferences, for they were based upon the existence of that Empire. The only place in which the British had a large land force was the western desert – that is why he wanted to fight there, because it was the one place where the British could dominate proceedings and it was, as he tried to convince Roosevelt throughout the summer of 1942, the only theatre in which the promises to Stalin about a 'second front' in 1942 were capable of being fulfilled. Churchill did not think that an invasion of North-West Africa, to link up with a British offensive in the western desert, would rule out an invasion of Europe in 1943, but then he had thought that the appearance of a British fleet in the Sea of Marmora would lead to the collapse of Turkey, which, in turn, would knock out one of the 'props' upon which imperial Germany was resting. Of course, as so often, Churchill's prognosis was too optimistic by half, but that did not mean that he did not want a second front in Europe in 1943, merely that the 'march of events' ruled it out. If Churchill was a combination of 'Machiavelli' and Waugh's 'Brigadier Richie-Hook' (who liked to 'biff' the enemy), it was the latter who was the dominant force in his strategic thinking.[27]

Churchill had always 'accepted' Roosevelt's plan for an invasion of Europe in 1942 with caveats, and the more the British military tried to make such plans, the clearer it became, as he told Roosevelt at the end of May, that there were considerable obstacles in the way of such a scheme. But even whilst he was advising the President not to forget 'Gymnast', Churchill was pushing his staff to draw up plans for an invasion of Norway, 'Operation Jupiter', and he had not ruled out the possibility of a sudden attack on France, 'Operation Sledgehammer', if the situation on the Russian front made some such action necessary.[28] In short, in typically Churchillian fashion, he wanted to be able to leave his options open, believing that he would be able to combine a number of them in a way which would do 'such things' as he knew not what, but which would make the earth 'shake'. Having, as they thought, secured agreement to an invasion of Europe in 1942 back in April, and having promised Stalin as much, the Americans were naturally suspicious of this sudden change of mind, and out of those suspicions arose a host of possible explanations, each one more elaborate than the last; but viewed in the long perspective of Churchill's whole career, the Prime Minister's strategic thinking was entirely in character.

Churchill was well aware of the possibility of the Americans plumping for a 'Pacific first' strategy if they became convinced that the British were prevaricating over a cross-Channel operation in 1942, and during the summer of 1942 he used all the influence which his personal relationship with Roosevelt gave him to convince them that 'Gymnast' was the obvious operation to go for in 1942, and that it could be followed by the launch of a cross-Channel operation the following year. Marshall favoured such a tactic, but Roosevelt rejected it,[29] and after tough talks in London in late July, Churchill succeeded in convincing the Americans that Britain, which would have to bear the brunt of a cross-Channel operation, possessed neither the landing-craft nor the air superiority necessary for success.[30] Having convinced the Americans that a landing in North-West Africa was the only feasible major operation for 1942, Churchill now had to convince Stalin, who had been given the impression that a second front would be opened in Europe. It was not a prospect which Churchill relished, but he decided to go and do the job himself; an itinerary which included Cairo would give him the chance to sort out what he considered to be the mess there. Auchinleck may have succeeded in repelling Rommel's attack on Egypt, but he could give the Prime Minister no promises about when an offensive of his own would take place.[31] Churchill and his party set off from London on 3 August.

In his diary Oliver Harvey commented on the 'energy and gallantry of the old gentleman, setting off at 65 across Africa in the heat of mid-summer!'[32] Apart from the fact that Churchill was in his sixty-eighth year, there was much to be said for this point of view. Today Prime Ministers set off in jumbo jets provided with all the comforts of home. Churchill, however, had to make do with a couple of mattresses in the after-cabin of an unheated bomber, which, as his doctor remarked, was a rather 'feckless way of sending him'.[33] But, regardless of the cramped conditions, an ebullient Prime Minister 'lay on his bed in his underwear and held forth' to his advisers.[34] At least at the British Embassy in Cairo he was able to have an air-conditioned room. Before he had left Eden had asked him to see Canellopolous, the head of the Greek Government-in-Exile. Churchill, who had weightier matters on his mind, was not at all keen on the idea. Seeing Cadogan advancing up the stairs with a 'serious look' on his face, Churchill retreated, saying 'Can't-ellopolous', and when the Permanent Under-Secretary was summoned to the Prime Minister's bathroom a little later, he found him 'wallowing about like a porpoise, and throwing his sponge up and down to the chant of "Canellopolous! Can't-ellopolous! Canellopolous!"'[35] Although no doubt this would have been unamusing to the Greeks, and in these days of po-faced 'anti-racism' might even be considered reprehensible by the new puritans, it helps to explain the hold which Churchill was able to establish over his intimates. Who could be cross for long with a Prime Minister who sat in his bath throwing his sponge up and down looking, for all the world, like an overweight, bright-pink cherub?

The answer, of course, was those who fell foul of him when he was in one of his 'shoot Admiral Byng' moods, who could find him cruel. It was, after all, the same endearing figure who had come to Cairo in part to sack Auchinleck. 'The Auk' has found many defenders,[36] but at the time the Prime Minister wanted results and not alibis and he had had enough of 'the Auk'.[37] His first instinct was to offer the job to Brooke, but the latter, believing that he could be more use to the war effort by remaining with the Prime Minister and trying to restrain flights of fancy like 'Operation Jupiter', declined the honour. Instead, he pressed on Churchill the name of General Montgomery for command of the Eighth Army, but Churchill wanted General 'Strafer' Gott, who was already in the area and of whom he had heard good things.[38]

On the morning of 6 August Brooke was getting dressed when Churchill dashed into his room and, with the General 'practically naked', proceeded to unfold a plan for the reorganisation of the entire region; it was a good example of the strengths and weaknesses of Churchill as a warlord. The ideas showed the fertility of Churchill's mind, but the manner in which they were put forward, without any consultation with anyone, and with an immediate decision demanded, illustrated one of the reasons why the dour Ulsterman felt that he had better not take up the tempting offer of command in the Middle East. He was capable of standing up to Churchill, and he had had six months' experience in the job; would any successor be able to do the same, he wondered.[39]

What Churchill wanted was to divide up the old Middle East command.

There would be a 'Near East' command up to the Suez canal, which should, Churchill thought, come under Brooke himself, with Montgomery as his Eighth Army commander, whilst a 'Middle East' command, covering Syria, Palestine, Iraq and Persia, should come under Auchinleck, with General Alexander as his army commander.[40] What Churchill's plan ignored was the fact that Iraq and Palestine were both based, administratively, in Cairo, and that splitting the command in the way he proposed might well relieve Auchinleck's successor of the task of having to look over his shoulder, but at the cost of chaos. Brooke and the War Cabinet between them were able to talk him out of the scheme, but he would not be baulked of his plan of removing 'the Auk', and, with Brooke wishing to remain where he was, Churchill chose Gott as Eighth Army commander to serve under Alexander. But the following day Gott was shot down by enemy fire and killed whilst flying to Cairo, so, against his own first judgment, Churchill went for Montgomery.[41] Churchill took no pleasure in the replacement of Auchinleck; indeed, according to his doctor, he 'hated the thought',[42] but the fact was that the war was not being won, there was a widespread feeling that 'something was wrong', and replacing 'the Auk' was the quickest and easiest way to relieve some of the pressure on himself. But if the team of Alexander and Montgomery failed to deliver the goods, there might come a limit to the number of generals which one Prime Minister was allowed to run through.

Having sorted out the Middle East, at least to his own satisfaction, Churchill set off to see 'the Bear'. Unlike his first encounter with Roosevelt, this first meeting with Stalin was not one to which Churchill looked forward. He had to tell him that there would be no cross-Channel attack in 1942 and that, at least for the moment, British convoys to Russia would have to be suspended since the level of losses was unacceptably high. 'It was', he reflected in his memoirs, like 'carrying a large lump of ice to the North Pole'.[43] After being received by Molotov, Churchill retired to 'State villa no. 7', where, if the topic of ice had not already been on his mind, the plumbing would have put it there. In his memoirs he recalled the 'totalitarian lavishness' of the villa and of Soviet hospitality, but he had to suffer some discomfort before he could have the hot bath he longed for. Sybarite that he was, Churchill loved his hot baths, but having been looked after by batmen or valets for most of his life, he was curiously incapable of performing simple tasks like running a bath or boiling a kettle. The Russian 'mixer' tap was something which he had never come across, and the Cyrillic lettering on the tap-head was no help. His doctor heard loud curses coming from the bathroom, and when he went in he found the Prime Minister sitting in a large, lukewarm bath 'shivering and damning'. Making a guess as to how the tap worked, Wilson turned it, only to be 'damned for my incompetence' as a 'big gush of icy water' hit Churchill 'amidships'.[44] It was not a bad omen for what was to come over the next few days.

After a banquet of unsurpassed lavishness, Churchill went to see the Russian dictator at seven o'clock. Churchill plunged straight into the heart of the matter: there would be no assault on Europe in 1942 because there could not be. Stalin, who was understandably glum at the news, may well have wondered whether the wicked imperialists were about to do what he had done to them in 1939 and leave him to Hitler's mercy. He burst out indignantly through the interpreter asking why the British were afraid of the Germans and why they would not take risks? Churchill explained 'Torch' (as 'Gymnast' had been renamed) to him with the aid of a drawing of a crocodile and an analogy which became as famous as it was misleading; the western allies would, Churchill said, attack the 'soft underbelly' rather than the 'hard snout' of the beast. The meeting went on for four hours, and by the end of it Churchill felt that Stalin had grasped the strategic advantages of 'Torch'.[45]

Churchill thought that the rest of the meeting should be 'plain sailing'.[46] But, like Eden back in December, he was to find that one of the favourite gambits of the Soviet dictator was to blow alternately hot and cold. At their second meeting, on the night of 13 August, Stalin was in a boorish and downright insulting mood. Stalin handed Churchill a document setting out the Soviet point of view and then 'lay back puffing at his pipe, with his eyes half shut, emitting a stream of insults',[47] which included implying that the British Army was full of cowards. He complained that the British and the Americans were treating the Russian front as though it was unimportant and, after saying that he had received little in the way of help, had the nerve to accuse the British Navy of having 'turned tail' when the last convoy, PQ 17, had been decimated by U-boats. If the British would only try fighting, like the Russians, they might, he remarked, even find that they enjoyed it.[48] Perhaps fortunately, the interpreters were unable to keep up with the stream of insults, but Churchill gathered enough to anger him. The British, after all, had fought on against Hitler for a whole year – alone. He wisely forbore to mention, in an impassioned outburst, what the Soviets had been doing during that time. Instead, he talked of the need to establish true friendship and of the willingness of the western powers to sacrifice as many lives as necessary in the common cause – but not, he stressed, in futile operations which could not succeed. The interpreter, enthralled at the Prime Minister's words and quite unable to keep up with this flood of eloquence, put down his pencil at one point and, in response to Churchill's repeated cries of 'Did you tell him this?', stumbled along in the wake of his oratory. Stalin began to laugh and said: 'Your words are not important, what is vital is the spirit.'

Churchill went back to his room after the meeting 'downhearted and dispirited'.[49] Unable to believe that Stalin might have meant the insulting remarks (which Churchill could not bring himself to repeat in full in his memoirs), the Prime Minister and his entourage came up with an explanation for his behaviour, which says much for their ingenuity and ignorance of the

Soviet system and little for their common sense. Knowing from Harriman and Cadogan that such a 'hot and cold' technique had been used by Stalin on previous occasions, they produced the diverting theory that Stalin's 'Council of Commissars', which might have 'more power than we suppose', had taken the news less well than had Stalin the previous evening.[50] Thus fortified, Churchill decided that, despite the insults, he would stay for the banquet and meeting which were to be held on the morrow.

Whether the Soviet dictator knew that he had pushed Churchill a little too far, or whether he realised, as a pragmatist, that he was going to have to be satisfied with 'Torch', Stalin was in a mellower mood on the evening of 15 August when he fêted Churchill in Catherine the Great's state rooms in the Kremlin. If Churchill's normal diet was in some contrast to that endured by most of his fellow-countrymen, there was not the gulf between the two which existed inside the Kremlin. The 'vanguard of the people' did itself exceptionally well, but then it had no press to report upon what it was doing, or public opinion which could afford to become disaffected by reports of nineteen-course feasts. Stalin, in fine fettle from the innumerable toasts which were pledged, told Churchill: 'I am a rough man, not an experienced one like you,' which was as close as he came to either an explanation or an apology for the events of the previous day.[51] Such was the cordial atmosphere that Stalin even touched on the topic of Churchill's part in the Allied intervention in Russia after the Great War. He recounted the story of how, whilst on a visit to Moscow, Lady Astor and George Bernard Shaw had suggested that he should invite Lloyd George. When he had demurred because of Lloyd George's role in 1919–20, Nancy Astor had said that that had been all Churchill's fault, but that he was now 'finished'. Churchill acknowledged that there were some grounds for the last remark, but, Stalin claimed, he had said that if 'a great crisis comes, the English people might turn to the old war horse'. Churchill, who was easily moved, asked whether Stalin had forgiven him, to which the ex-seminarian responded: 'All that is in the past. It is not for me to forgive. It is for God to forgive.'[52] For the leader of an atheist state, Stalin was remarkably lavish in references to God at this time; but considering the position into which his own complacency had brought his country, perhaps that was not as surprising as Churchill found it.

Stalin was the life and soul of the party, but Churchill was clearly not enjoying himself, for reasons which were only later to become apparent to his doctor. Seeing this, Cadogan attempted to save the day by bringing the jollifications to a close, so he proposed a toast which had everyone on their feet: 'Gentlemen! I give you death and damnation to the Germans!' Afterwards Churchill and Stalin were photographed together, but the Prime Minister, who seemed still to be wrapped in his own thoughts, sat down and read a document whilst Harriman, Molotov and Stalin chatted. For once the Prime Minister was not in the mood for a late-night film show or chat, and he left at half-past one, telling Stalin that any differences which existed between them were ones of method only, and that he hoped to eliminate those. He set off for his car, his face 'set and resolute'. To Churchill's surprise, Stalin hurried after him, perhaps, as Wilson surmised, anxious lest he had 'gone too far'; when they parted Churchill said, 'Good-bye.'[53]

By the time Churchill came to give the Cabinet and Roosevelt a description of that evening he was in an altogether better frame of mind and more disposed to take a kindlier view of it, but that morning, driving back in the car, Churchill was 'like a bull in the ring, maddened by the pricks of the picadors'. Cadogan was astonished at the 'violence and depth of his resent-ment'. He did not, he stated angrily, know what he was supposed to be doing in Moscow and he would, he declared, go home on the morrow without seeing Stalin again. Back at the villa, Churchill speedily got into an argument with Cadogan over the communiqué which should be issued. To allow the Russian text, which referred in slighting terms to the failure of the western powers to keep their promises of a second front in 1942, would, the Prime Minister said, be 'calamitous'. Cadogan disagreed, at which Churchill repeated his claims, only to find the Permanent Under-Secretary repeating his. Sir Charles Wilson, who had stayed at Churchill's bidding, was astonished: 'I had never seen anyone talk to the PM like this.' Churchill told him grumpily that he could do as he liked, and at 3 a.m. the two men parted, on Churchill's side with an ill-grace. Wilson, who accompanied Churchill back to his room, then found out what had plunged the Prime Minister into such a black mood: 'Stalin didn't want to talk to me. I closed the proceedings down. I had had enough. The food was filthy. I ought not to have come.' The fact was that Churchill was suffering from frustration at not having been able to have the sort of intimate talk with Stalin that he could with Roosevelt. Pacing the room, clad by this point only in his silk underwear, Churchill told Wilson: 'I still feel I could work with that man if I could break down the language barrier. That is a terrible difficulty.' Stalin, he declared crossly, was a 'brigand', and he, Churchill, was not going to risk another snub from him, which was why he had deliberately said 'good-bye' and not 'good-night'. Any fresh moves could come from the Soviet leader. With that he got into bed, pulled his black eye-shade down, and went to sleep; it was a quarter to four.[54]

The Prime Ministerial slumbers did not last very long. He sent for his military assistant, Colonel Jacob, at nine o'clock to tell him that he had had second thoughts about leaving and that 'perhaps he had been unduly depressed and that Stalin had perhaps not meant to be as insulting as he had at first thought'; perhaps, he wondered, there had been some problems in translation?[55] At any rate, after talking with the British Ambassador, Sir Archie Clark-Kerr, Churchill decided that he would see Stalin again. This, however, proved more difficult to arrange than the diplomats had imagined, as the only response they received to their telephone calls to the Kremlin was

'Mr Stalin is out walking.'[56] It must have been an exceedingly long walk, for it was not until six o'clock that the news came through that the Soviet dictator would see Churchill in an hour. Having waited thus long, Churchill thought he might as well see him, but told Cadogan before leaving that he expected the meeting to be over in time for them to dine at half-past eight.

Churchill went in with a new, and better, interpreter, but at first it seemed that this was hardly needed. Stalin greeted Churchill's efforts at cordiality with no response, repeating his complaints about supplies and the lack of a second front. Churchill explained that the British intended to make a cross-Channel attack on a small scale in the near future just to make the Germans anxious that a full-scale invasion was imminent, but that failed to impress Stalin. At eight o'clock Churchill got up to leave, but Stalin, upon hearing that he was departing the next morning, then thawed and invited him back to his house for 'some drinks'. Churchill recorded that he 'said that I was in principle always in favour of such a policy'.[57] Whether by design or accident, Stalin had hit on the best way to touch Churchill's emotional nature. Back at Stalin's dacha Churchill met his daughter, Svetlana, and, with only the interpreters for company, they dined on until the small hours of the following morning. Realising that the Embassy would be wondering where on earth he had got to, he had his interpreter, Major Birse, telephone to give his apologies. Then the two men picked at the immense number of dishes which Stalin's housekeeper had brought to the table, and, in a relaxed mood with a good interpreter, Churchill felt that 'for the first time we got on easy and friendly terms'.[58]

Churchill's frustrations of the previous evening and of earlier that morning were assuaged as, at last, he felt that he was establishing a 'personal relationship'. He was a believer in what has been called the 'Great Men theory' of history. Such men could be recognised by the mark they made on their own and subsequent ages, and knowing himself to be one, Churchill enjoyed making contact with others of the same species. They talked about a possible meeting with Roosevelt and upon Churchill's pre-war advocacy of a 'Grand Alliance'. Stalin revealed that he had thought the Anglo-Soviet talks in 1939 had been designed only to 'intimidate Hitler, with whom the Western Powers would later come to terms'. With his love of historical analogy, Churchill referred back to the parallels between the current 'Grand Alliance' and that which his ancestor, Marlborough, had helped to organise during the War of the Spanish Succession. He must have felt that he was making 'real' contact when Stalin, continuing the historical analogies, said that it reminded him of the Napoleonic Wars. The conversation ranged over a host of issues, even to Stalin's policy of forced collectivisation. It had been, said Stalin with chilling brutality, necessary to have four years of terrible famine to avoid it ever happening in future; like his mentor Lenin, he did not think omelettes could be made without the sacrifice of a few eggs; and like many 'Great Men', he was not averse to equating human lives with eggs, even if fragility is the only thing which they have in common. But from the rarefied heights upon which the great ones of the ages dwell, such things are of small moment. After all, even Churchill, often the most kind-hearted of men, had expressed, at his first meeting with Stalin, a willingness to sacrifice 100–150,000 men on an assault on Europe if it would take the pressure off Russia. It might be added in mitigation that, unlike the Russian dictator, Churchill would have willingly made one of those lives his own had it been necessary. He had, as Boothby had said, stood firm when the earth was collapsing; Stalin, in similar circumstances, had simply gone to pieces.

At about 1 a.m. on Sunday, 16 August, Cadogan turned up with the text of a final communiqué, which expressed a common resolve to fight on in firm alliance until the final defeat of 'Hitlerism'. By the time the two leaders had agreed to it, it was half-past one and a 'considerable sucking pig' was brought in which Stalin 'fell upon' with relish.[59] When the talking finished, there was time only for a quick drink of coffee back at Churchill's villa before dashing off to the airport for half-past five. But, in sharp contradistinction to his mood at the same time the previous day, Churchill was elated, and it was after this that he sent his more optimisic message saying that he had, perhaps, been too pessimistic earlier.

Churchill's feelings of triumph as he returned to London via Tehran and Cairo were understandable. He had broken the news that there would be no second front without breaking the alliance, and he had, he felt, established a real personal relationship with Stalin; in the circumstances which he faced at home, these were real achievements, but it was possible to overrate them, and the signs are that Churchill did so. After all, Stalin had no alternative to carrying on the war; unlike the British, he had not been the recipient of any peace offers, and the scale of the conflict on the eastern front, so much greater than anything which would occur in the west, was a burden which had been thrust upon him by the dynamics of Nazism. In these circumstances there was no particular need for Churchill to be either as worried or as eager to conciliate Stalin as he was. He thought, he told Roosevelt and his colleagues back in London, that they would have to press ahead with 'Operation Jupiter'. Churchill had also shown little comprehension of the nature of Stalin's personal rule or of the Soviet system. Instead, he relied, as he did with Roosevelt, upon his personal relationship to make sure that everything came out right; the effects of this were not to be apparent for some time.

With Stalin pacified, Churchill now turned to getting a full commitment from Roosevelt to a 'Mediterranean strategy', although flattery led him to call it 'your great strategic conception', and he was not above encouraging Roosevelt's belief that the contacts which the Americans had cultivated in North Africa might ensure that the Allied landings there were unopposed.[60] This entailed conceding the command of the operation to an American,

General Eisenhower, and keeping de Gaulle and his Free French out of it; but they were both prices which Churchill was willing to pay for the firm American commitment which he secured in September. The Foreign Office was less happy on the last point. Churchill's attitude towards de Gaulle had cooled since the heady days of June 1940. In part this was due to de Gaulle's failure to rally much of the French Empire, and in part to the need, thereafter, to cultivate clandestine contacts with Vichy; but there was more to the estrangement than that. Unlike Churchill, who was willing to pay, in deference and flattery, the price which needed to be paid for American and Russian support, de Gaulle, who was far more dependent on the British than they were on their allies, steadfastly refused to show any gratitude; indeed, he turned the hand which fed him into his staple diet.[61]

After a particularly virulent display of Anglophobia from de Gaulle following the British invasion of Syria in mid-1941, relations between him and Churchill plummeted and, in a move strikingly similar to the one which some of Churchill's critics would have liked to have executed on the Prime Minister, the Foreign Office sought to restrain de Gaulle through the creation of a French National Committee.[62] But de Gaulle was as impatient of restraint as Churchill would have been, and the General dominated that, and any other body the British cared to create. By mid-1942 Churchill had become convinced that de Gaulle was a dangerous Anglophobe, whose accession to power in France would do Britain a great deal of harm.[63] Roosevelt, who listened to the voices of French exiles in America who had little time for the General whom they regarded as a Fascist, soon came to hold a similar view of the Frenchman, whose obsession with playing politics and representing himself as the personification of the French state the President came to regard as both tiresome and dangerous.[64] The Foreign Office and Eden, who were impressed with the 'symbolic role' which de Gaulle had taken on inside occupied France, were less keen on his being excluded from Allied counsels.[65] France, along with Russia, would, Eden thought, be one of the pillars of Britain's European policy after the war, and at a time when his mind was much on such matters, Eden wished to do nothing which might jeopardise Anglo-French relations.[66] Churchill's attitude on France, as on Russia and on Eden's ideas for the post-war era, was the same: it could all be left until the post-war era arrived.[67]

This did not imply that Churchill had no views on the post-war era, but those he had were rooted very firmly in the wartime alliance. He wanted the partners in the 'Grand Alliance' to stay out of Europe and for it to be 'run' by a Great Council of Great Powers, including Spain, Italy, Prussia and a Scandinavian federation.[68] With Churchill seeming to 'want to put the clock back to the Congress of Vienna', and Roosevelt wanting to put it back to 1919, there seemed to Eden a danger of Britain 'losing both the Old and the New World',[69] and in frustration at Churchill's attitude he even spoke, in early November, about the Prime Minister 'finding himself another Foreign Secretary'.[70] Nor was he the only member of the Cabinet who had become so discontented with the way policy was being run that thoughts of resignation had occurred to him; indeed, in the case of Cripps, he had already decided to act upon such thoughts.

Cripps's position may not have been helped by his involvement in Indian affairs, but in a series of dinners which he held over the summer, he did his best to get on better terms with Conservative MPs, to whom he had always been an object of mistrust; he made it clear that he saw Churchill being pushed aside, because of his lack of interest in the home front or post-war planning.[71] To Labour MPs he was even less discreet, and Dalton recorded him ruminating in late August over whether to resign and try to capitalise upon his popularity in order to promote the cause he supported, or whether to remain in order to take advantage of what he took to be the Prime Minister's inevitable 'fall'.[72] Dalton did not think that there was 'any point of contact ... between Cripps's reflections and reality', but there was one, and it lay in Cripps's decision in September to present Churchill with an ultimatum: either the Prime Minister agreed to his suggestions or he, Cripps, would resign.[73]

Cripps agreed to wait until the results of the campaigns in North-West Africa and the western desert were known before implementing his threat, but its existence meant that if either of those operations went wrong, Churchill's position might well be in jeopardy. Eden's friends and Beaverbrook all urged him to be 'more positive' about his 'position' as Churchill's heir-apparent, with Harvey, in particular, being anxious lest he was outflanked by Cripps or blocked by James Stuart, Kingsley Wood and the Chamberlainite caucus.[74] Eden felt he could 'do' the Premiership 'now', but he would take it only if Churchill fell.[75] Churchill was convinced that Cripps's resignation was part of some deep-laid plot to unseat him, and in early October he consulted Eden about the future.[76]

Eden was 'uneasy' because he 'agrees with much of Cripps's criticism', and he tried to convince Churchill at a meeting on 1 October that he had 'a case'. In an effort to avert a crisis, Eden brokered a deal between Cripps and Churchill whereby the former would take another post in the Government if necessary. But Churchill was under no illusions: 'If *Torch* fails, then I'm done for and must hand over to one of you.'[77] It was not so much that there would have been a great popular outcry for his removal; Churchill probably still had sufficient credit in that direction to have survived, but on what terms? As Bracken told Sir Charles Wilson, if the Allies suffered another defeat, 'important changes in the direction of the war would then be inevitable, and Winston will never submit to any curtailment of his powers. If we are beaten in this battle it's the end of Winston.'[78]

It was little wonder that Churchill described September and October 1942 as the 'most anxious months of the war'.[79] 'Torch' was his brain-child, and he had to work hard to ensure that the American planners did not cripple it by restricting it to landings inside the Mediterranean, which, in the event of a German move through Spain, would mean the Allied forces being cut off. But Montgomery's offensive at El Alamein in late October did not fail, and the Allied landings at Casablanca, Oran and Algiers on 8 November were an operational success. Two days later, at the Lord Mayor's banquet, a greatly relieved Churchill could rejoice in a 'definite victory', at last. In defiant mood he declared that: 'We mean to hold our own. I have not become the King's First Minister in order to preside over the liquidation of the British Empire.' It was not 'the end', or even 'the beginning of the end', but it was certainly the 'end of the beginning'.[80] He was right in the sense that it marked the end of an unrelieved succession of defeats, and thus the end of the threats to his Premiership. But there was another sense in which it was the 'beginning of the end'. The days of heroic defiance were ending and the new age which was dawning would demand more than the old virtues of courage and faith; the portents did not suggest that it would suit Churchill as well as the era that was passing.

45

The Road to Victory?

It may have been the 'end of the beginning' in Churchill's mind, but the next few months illustrated the dangers inherent in the Prime Minister's concentration on the short-term. In North Africa the arrangements which Eisenhower entered into with the Vichy chieftain, Admiral Darlan, raised a storm of protest in Britain and America and aroused fears there, and in Russia, that similar deals would be struck with other 'Quislings' once the invasion of Europe had taken place.[1] A similar determination to stand on old ways seemed to be evinced by Churchill's reaction to the publication on 19 December of the Beveridge report, which contained the germ of what became known as the Welfare State.[2] Churchill's handling of both topics showed his limitations in the new era which the 'turn of the tide' had opened.

General Dill, who had become the head of the British Joint Staff Mission in Washington in 1942, summed up both the problem caused by Darlan and the reasons why Eisenhower dealt with him thus:

The political trouble is that it is quite impossible to fit de Gaulle into the Darlan picture and whatever we may think of de Gaulle, he did stand firm when everything else in France crumbled and broke. However one can only live from day to day in this matter and Darlan is at the moment indispensable.[3]

Without his co-operation Eisenhower would not have been able to have ended the fighting in French North Africa by 13 November, as the Vichy troops, contrary to Roosevelt's expectations, remained loyal to Pétain and to Darlan as his representative. This, as Eisenhower stressed in his initial telegrams, was why he agreed to deal with the Admiral.[4] Roosevelt, advised by his special representative in Algiers, Robert Murphy,[5] was quite content to follow the advice of Eisenhower and of his own Chief of Staff, Admiral Leahy, that 'Eisenhower and his advisers . . . should be given a free hand in the matter'.[6] The reaction inside Britain was quite different. Eden, who had originally gone along with Churchill's line of supporting the President and Eisenhower, quickly changed his mind as Parliamentary, diplomatic and public opinion took the view which Harvey expressed to him on 14 November: 'It smells so much like Appeasement again. Compromise with Darlans and Pétains never pays. I want to keep our war clean!'[7] It was not simply public opinion which revolted at the idea of pushing aside de Gaulle in order to deal with a man who was closely associated with collaboration with the Germans. From his own staff Eden received warnings of the possible effect on the Russians of such deals; they, Gladwyn Jebb (one of the rising stars of the Foreign Office) warned Eden on 16 November, might conclude that the Allies had decided to base their 'future policy on an Anglo–American–Quisling combination directed against the Soviet Union'; warnings which were backed up by Clark-Kerr from Moscow.[8] From Attlee came warnings of the moral effect on the war effort and on Labour opinion of coming to any arrangement which left Darlan in charge in North Africa.[9] Even Bracken, who could usually be relied upon to support his boss, took the view, as Minister of Information, that if the Allies dealt with Darlan, 'a great storm will blow up in Parliament and the press' and that 'decent people everywhere will say that we have abandoned the brave men who tried to keep the spirit of France alive'.[10]

Bruised by a storm of protest which threatened to overshadow the victorious feats of arms, Churchill was persuaded by Eden to telegraph to Roosevelt to warn him of the 'very deep currents of feeling' which the 'arrangement with Darlan' had stirred up. His own feelings he expressed in the final paragraph: 'we should get on with the fighting and let that overtake the parleys',[11] which showed how little Churchill, engrossed in the question of the future direction of Allied strategy, understood those 'deep currents of feeling'. These were briefly calmed by Roosevelt's statement on 17 November that Darlan was a 'temporary expedient',[12] but it quickly became clear that by 'temporary', Roosevelt meant 'the duration of the war'.[13]

Churchill proved immune to further attempts by Eden to get him to remonstrate with the President. He had not exactly shown much enthusiasm for sending the telegram on 16 November, ending up at that morning's Cabinet with a 'tirade against de G[aulle]', whom he accused of 'battening on us' and of being 'capable of turning round and fighting with the Axis against us'.[14] This, as Cadogan, who was no uncritical admirer of the General, put it, was 'just untrue. Tiresome he may be, but sound on essentials.'[15] Eden argued against accepting the protocol which Eisenhower negotiated with Darlan on 20 November, but Churchill simply would 'not see the damage Darlan may do to the allied cause', and, when pressed, shouted at the Foreign Secretary: 'Well D[arlan] is not as bad as de Gaulle anyway.'[16] His anger against the General had, Eden suspected, been fuelled by words which the Frenchman and Clementine had had at lunch, when, in response to her asking whether the French Fleet would respond to Darlan's plea to rally to him, de Gaulle had said: 'Never, the Fleet's one ambition is to sink yours.' Clementine had replied with that prickliness which alienated some people: 'You have no right to speak like that in my house.' She had subsequently told Winston that de Gaulle hated the British and might fight with the Germans 'against us'.[17] Thus it was that Darlan consolidated his position, proclaiming himself, with Eisenhower's approval, *Chef d'Etat* of a North Africa which owed allegiance to Pétain;[18] it was an act which symbolised his determination to dig himself in and co-operate with the Allies as a power which could represent France.[19]

Churchill decided, for military reasons, to follow Roosevelt's line in a matter of policy which was crucial to the future direction of British foreign policy and to the cause for which many believed the war was being fought. Roosevelt thought that the French were a 'very silly people' and that de Gaulle did not 'really know what the opinion of France is or who represents France'. He thought that Darlan could be 'handled',[20] but shocked opinion in London and Washington by commenting to the Free French representatives in Washington on 20 November that he was quite prepared to use even someone like Pierre Laval, the very symbol of collaborationism, if it meant that the war would be won sooner.[21] What was even more worrying for Eden was to hear Churchill taking a similar view. At Cabinet on 3 December he took a 'disquieting line about Italy' and talked 'about making peace with a Government headed by [Count Dino] Grandi if such were set up'. The 'prospect', Eden lamented, 'of Darlan and Grandi Governments does not make an attractive Mediterranean'.[22] He was not alone in fearing the implications of dealing with European Vicars of Bray.

Eden and the Foreign Office were deluged with letters from Labour MPs and from trades unions protesting against the policy of dealing with Fascism.[23] With the Russians and the Allied Governments-in-Exile all expressing fears about the implications of the Darlan deal for the future,[24] Churchill's policy of backing Roosevelt at all costs threatened not the stability of his Government, but rather the nature of the cause for which he was fighting the war. As Cranborne put it to Eden on 11 December, the Allies had, ever since the Atlantic Charter, portrayed the war as a 'peoples' war' and a 'war for democracy'; if it was now to be turned (under the unlikely aegis of the neo-Wilsonian Roosevelt) into an old-fashioned 'balance of power' war, to be won by any means, the Government had better switch its propaganda line speedily.[25] Churchill did agree to press Roosevelt to let the British send Macmillan to Algiers to give Eisenhower advice on political matters,[26] but the Prime Minister steadfastly refused to put pressure on him to disown Darlan. Indeed, to meet the rising tide of discontent, Churchill had agreed to hold a secret session of the House on 10 December.

Churchill defended the deal as a 'temporary' expedient, putting the blame for it on Eisenhower, but claimed that it was necessary for the moment.[27] As far as it went it was a convincing argument, but it failed in its task because it ignored the fundamental questions about the future of British foreign policy which were raised by other MPs; moreover, his tactic of defending Darlan by attacking de Gaulle 'left an unpleasant taste in the mouth'.[28] He reminded the House that de Gaulle was 'no friend' to Britain and labelled him (in another passage omitted from the published version of the speech) 'one of those Frenchmen who have a traditional antagonism ... against the English';[29] if he had not been before all this, he certainly would have been afterwards. Churchill even looked, as he told the Cabinet on 21 December, to the possibility of Darlan's administration developing in a way which 'would overshadow the Fighting French Movement'.[30] He was only saved from the potentially damaging consequences of such a policy by the assassination of Darlan on Christmas Eve, which went to prove that Father Christmas had not missed Churchill out that year. The Prime Minister had, during the whole furore, been more concerned to decide the future of Allied strategy than he had been to attend to its consequences.

One reason why Eisenhower, Churchill and Roosevelt had been so ready to co-operate with Darlan was that despite what looked like an initial operational success, 'Torch' turned out to be a seriously flawed operation. This might have been expected from its genesis: foisted by Churchill, by a process of 'strategic natural selection',[31] upon the Americans in default of a cross-Channel operation which was pronounced unfeasible for 1942, in its final form it was a compromise. Sanguine as the Americans were about the French flinging up their arms and shouting 'Ah, bienvenus les Americains', they were paranoid about the possibility of getting cut off inside the Mediterranean and, at one stage, wanted to concentrate the operation at Casablanca and no further east than Oran. On small-scale maps this must have looked relatively simple, but it was a long way from Oran to Tunis on a single-track road that was unusable in bad weather, and Churchill had protested at the end of August that the 'whole pith' of the operation would be lost.[32] He had stressed then the need to get to Tunis before the Germans did, and whilst his advocacy had some effect, the most that the Americans would concede was that there should be a landing at Algiers. This had enabled Eisenhower to take advantage, as he saw it, of the fact that Darlan was there visiting his sick son in hospital, but the Admiral's writ had not run in Tunis and the French commander there, Admiral Esteva, had allowed the Germans to enter in force. This meant that by the time the Allied forces had managed to advance along the poor road to Tunisia, the Germans were well-ensconced, and, as Eisenhower was forced to conclude just before Christmas, the campaign in North Africa was going to last for some time.

It was the failure of 'Torch' to bring the hoped-for speedy result which did more than anything else to make a continuation of the 'Mediterranean strategy' possible. Churchill, with his usual optimism, had never thought that 'Torch' ruled out 'Operation Roundup' (the invasion of Europe) for 1943: 'I still hoped that French North-West Africa, including the Tunisian tip, might fall into our hands after a few months' fighting.'[33] Always able to convince himself that his favoured strategy would bring immense results and thus to underrate the difficulties in its way, Churchill was scornful of the advice of Brooke and the Chiefs of Staff, who predicted that 'Torch' would have precisely this effect.[34] The day after the Allied landings he told his planners that the operation was 'no excuse for lying down during 1943, content with descents on Sicily and Sardinia'.[35] Much of the debate over the 'second front' could be stilled if, instead of looking for Machiavellian stratagems on Churchill's part, historians would accept what a study of his career suggests to be the case, that this was, like the Dardanelles and Norway, another example of Churchillian optimism. 'Torch', he told his advisers on 18 November, was a 'springboard and not a sofa', and he saw no reason why they should not have 'closed down' the Mediterranean 'by the end of June with a view to "Roundup" in August'.[36]

That Churchill was in one of his moods of exaltation when everything appeared to be possible is confirmed by the telegram which he sent to Roosevelt that same day. He foresaw the 'swift success' in North Africa as being followed, once Tunis was secure, by an attack on Tripoli (perhaps made by Alexander's army), followed by the seizure of either Sardinia or Sicily, which would give the Allies a platform from which to bomb Rome or Naples and to secure air mastery of the Mediterranean. With a French army to be created in North Africa by the Allies, forces from Britain and their convoying escorts might be kept there instead of joining Eisenhower's army; an invasion of either Sardinia or Sicily could, after all, be mounted from Britain itself. The Prime Minister also looked forward to a 'supreme and prolonged effort' to bring Turkey into the war by the spring, which would, he thought, bring a great accession of strength to the Allies. Moreover, combined with the destruction of Rommel's forces and a Russian offensive in the Caucasus, this might well happen in a way which would open enormous possibilities for the Allied forces.[37] But even as he pressed for a meeting to discuss the matter, the failure of the Darlan strategy to deliver the goods and the German reinforcement of Tunis were blowing a blast of freezing air upon the Prime Minister's castles in the air. Churchill did not intend 'Torch' to rule out 'Roundup' for 1943, but that was what it did.

The possibility of 'Roundup' occurring in 1943 had, in any event, been endangered by the American decision to slow down the rate at which men and equipment were shipped to Britain. Marshall, who had a greater grasp of the logistics of the operation than did the British Prime Minister, continued to suspect, as he had since 1941, that Churchill's hankering after a 'Mediterranean strategy' had more to do with the British Empire than it had with winning the war, a misjudgment which has communicated itself to later historians.[38] Yet, as Churchill's protest to Roosevelt on 24 November against the slowing down of supplies shows, the Prime Minister was still prepared to argue that 'Roundup' could and should take place in 1943.[39] Churchill was certainly anxious lest the American decision portended a change towards a 'Pacific first' strategy,[40] but his arguments were those which he had used with his own planners earlier, and unless we posit the existence of some Machiavellian Churchill who has, hitherto, not revealed his cloven hoof, it seems more sensible to take the view which common sense dictates: the Prime

Minister believed what he said; he may have been wrong, but he was sincerely wrong. The fact that Marshall's fear that 'Torch' in 1942 would make 'Roundup' in 1943 impossible turned out to be correct, does not mean that this was the result desired by Churchill.[41]

Given Churchill's anxieties to ensure that the Americans were committed to 'Roundup', and given the pressure which Roosevelt was under to send more forces to the Pacific, it was little wonder that Churchill did not want to press him on the Darlan issue. But the fact remained that in return for hoped-for concessions on strategy, Churchill risked letting the Americans land the Allies with a very dubious ally running an even more dubious regime. Darlan's death saved him from this, and the Admiral's American-sponsored replacement, General Henri Giraud, was the very Hollywood image of what a French general should be; a man whose charm exceeded his intellect by a very long way, Giraud was an old-fashioned apolitical general, the very anti-thesis of de Gaulle and, as such, correspondingly welcome to Roosevelt.[42] Eden was anxious to see whether de Gaulle and Giraud could not be brought to co-operate, and the conference which Churchill was going to with Roosevelt at Casablanca early in the new year seemed to him the ideal opportunity to erase some of the damage done to the idea of a 'clean war' by the deal with Darlan.[43] Churchill pressed the idea of a Giraud–de Gaulle meeting on an unwilling President, but he, like Roosevelt, was more concerned with the determination of strategic priorities.

Churchill left London on 13 January 1943 and, as ever when travelling by air, the journey was both uncomfortable and dangerous. A mattress in the back of a bomber, improvised heating arrangements upon which he burnt his toes, and a blanket with which to keep out draughts, were hardly arrangements which commended themselves to Churchill's doctor, who travelled with him. Churchill was, Sir Charles Wilson noted, 'at a disadvantage in this type of travel, since he never wears anything at night but a silk vest. On his hands and knees, he cut a quaint figure with his big, bare white bottom.'[44] But the journey was always worth it. Away from the drabness of wartime London and the English winter, into the sunshine and brilliant blue skies of Morocco, Churchill could get away from the 'unending grind' and the 'feeling that there are more things to do in the twenty-four hours than can possibly be squeezed in'.[45]

But however precious the chance to do a little painting and some sightseeing, Churchill was at Anfa camp for business. It had been hoped that Stalin might be able to attend. The aftermath of 'Torch' had led to a worrying silence from 'Uncle Joe', which had been followed up by requests for greater aid, and it was, in part, the prospect of having to disappoint the Soviet leader, which led Churchill to press for 'Roundup' in 1943. He had told Stalin at the end of November not to worry 'about that rogue Darlan' and emphasised the operations which the western allies proposed to take in 1943.[46] But Stalin, whose armies were engaged in a crucial struggle around Stalingrad, could not come. So it was that the 'Emperor of the West' (Roosevelt) met with the 'Emperor of the East' without the 'Red Emperor'.[47] At the top of the agenda was what the western powers should do whilst the armies of 'Uncle Joe' took the brunt of the Nazi war-effort. From his villa Churchill telegraphed home: 'Conditions most agreeable. I wish I could say the same of the problems.'[48]

The decision reached at the conference to pursue the 'Mediterranean strategy' 'crucially affected the extent, justification, and character of the Soviet liberation/subjugation of Eastern and Central Europe'. Had the Allies mounted a successful invasion of France in 1943, then the armies of the western and eastern 'Emperors' might have met those of their 'Red' counterpart deep in eastern Europe, and 'the balance of power in central Europe would have been very different'; and countries which, only half a century later in the collapse of Soviet imperialism, grope unsteadily for 'freedom' might have been spared decades of tyranny.[49] Had Roosevelt not opted to declare that the Allies insisted upon 'unconditional surrender' from Germany, perhaps, then, some of the consequences which flowed from the strategic decisions taken might have been averted. The historian has to deal, of course, with events as they transpired, and to pose too many 'ifs' is to enter a looking-glass world, for one might equally ask what would have happened had the Allies tried 'Roundup' only to see it fail? Nevertheless, to ask 'what if?' at a few crucial points is to gain some sort of purchase on historical problems and helps to avoid the ever-present temptation to assume that what actually happened was inevitable and, therefore, automatically for the best.

Both Churchill and Roosevelt were at odds with their military advisers, but it was the latter and not the often impetuous Churchill who overruled his own experts. Churchill's writings on the subject of future strategy worried Brooke, as they seemed to him inconsistent.[50] This inconsistency has allowed historians to construct their own Churchill with regard to the course of operations in 1943. Brooke was convinced, as were the rest of the British Chiefs of Staff, that a Mediterranean offensive in 1943 would mean postponing 'Roundup' until the following year, but they considered that the 'Mediterranean gives us far better facilities for wearing down German forces both land and air, and of withdrawing [German] strength from Russia'.[51] Churchill, of course, found the first part of this formulation too pessimistic, but with Brooke telling him that there would not be enough troops or landing-craft for 'Roundup' in 1943, and with the Soviets to bear in mind, Churchill allowed himself to be persuaded.[52] But Brooke's conclusion that 'we had avoided the great danger of Winston siding with the Americans'[53] was wide of the mark, for Churchill had not given up believing that he could have his cake and eat it.

With Roosevelt rejecting the 'Pacific first' option, partly because of the inability of the American forces there to use the equipment already allocated to them, Marshall and his colleagues were firmly in favour of getting from the British a commitment to 'Roundup' in 1943.[54] On this too Roosevelt proved to have his own ideas. 'Roundup' could not have taken place until late in the year, Stalin had been encouraged to expect a 'second front in Europe' in 1943, and there were substantial numbers of troops and masses of equipment already in North Africa; in these circumstances it made more sense to exploit 'Torch' by an assault on Italian territory. After all, if Tunisia was cleared in the near future, the Allies could have 'Husky' (as the assault on Sicily was called) and possibly 'Roundup' too.[55] Churchill's investment in winning American 'goodwill' had paid a dividend, even if it was to Brooke and company. Not that Churchill believed this at the time, for, as his report on the conference to the War Cabinet on 20 January showed, he still believed that some sort of cross-Channel operation in 1943 would be possible.[56]

The initial reports to Stalin, combined with Roosevelt's declaration that the Allies intended to exact 'unconditional surrender' from their foes, led Stalin to believe that he was going to get his long-awaited second front, and he asked when it would come.[57] Churchill, who in a telegram to the Cabinet on 26 January had expressed the opinion that nothing less than a major invasion of Europe would satisfy the Soviet dictator,[58] was to prove correct.

At the final press conference on 24 January, a genial Churchill was photographed with an equally cheery Roosevelt, and both men were then photographed with Giraud and de Gaulle, which, along with the final communiqué which included the bombastic phrase that 'nothing like this' conference 'has ever occurred before', and Roosevelt's declaration about 'unconditional surrender', all served to give the impression that everything had gone well. But photographs can be misleading. Roosevelt and Churchill may have decided upon Allied strategy, but Giraud and de Gaulle were barely on speaking terms. Indeed, it had proved more difficult to persuade de Gaulle to attend the conference than it had to agree on strategy.

De Gaulle was invited to the conference on 15 January, with Roosevelt expressing the view that 'the banns must be read and the marriage concluded even if it proved to be a shotgun wedding', since 'failure to conclude the ceremony would be attributed to a difference of policy between the sponsors rather than between the parties'.[59] Despite Eden's best efforts to emphasise the embarrassment which his non-appearance would cause Churchill, it took nearly a week to persuade de Gaulle to go to the conference.[60] The General was reluctant to go because he did not want the British and Americans trying to interfere in French affairs, but the 'shotgun' which had persuaded him to go to Casablanca could not persuade him to accept Churchill's plan for a merger between his organisation and Giraud's.[61] In his fury at de Gaulle's behaviour, Churchill considered breaking with him and either dealing with one of his more amenable colleagues, or else following the American line of trying to build up Giraud. Macmillan persuaded against being so hasty,[62] but was horrified to discover, after the conference was over, that Roosevelt had signed agreements with Giraud, which, in effect, committed the Allies to such a policy.[63]

Churchill had been embarrassed by de Gaulle's initial refusal to come to the conference: 'The man must be mad to jeopardise the future of his movement with the United States', and he told Eden that if de Gaulle, in 'his fantasy of egotism', spurned this 'last chance', the whole basis of relations with him would be re-examined.[64] He had been equally cross with the General's behaviour once at Anfa, but it is doubtful whether he had known of the agreements which Roosevelt had signed with Giraud on the final morning of the conference – which is some sort of commentary on the President's way of doing business. For the British, France was a vital interest, and events inside occupied France and the part played by the Communist resistance suggested that the Allies should co-operate with a 'left-wing' rather than 'right-wing' Frenchman. With Roosevelt seeming determined to support a regime of the most reactionary character, this co-operation would be placed in danger. There were strong suspicions that Roosevelt's policy was to dismantle the French Empire; it looked as though 'what the Americans wanted to see after the war is an anti-communist, pro-American French Government under strong American influence'.[65] It proved possible to, in effect, nullify the accords, but the episode was a reminder to Eden and the Foreign Office that decisions taken now would have a profound influence upon the shape of the post-war era.

Churchill had managed to postpone discussion of another document which would indeed have a profound effect on the future, when, before going to Casablanca, he had cautioned his colleagues against too enthusiastic a reception of Beveridge's report on the future of the health and social services in Britain. Churchill's acquaintanceship with the author of the report went back to his days at the Board of Trade, when he had brought in Beveridge to help him in his own crusade for social reform, but, as his attitude to the report showed, those days were long behind him. At the heart of Beveridge's report was the proposal for a comprehensive system of social security, based upon subsistence-level benefits from 'the cradle to the grave'. Beveridge's flair for publicity and the press reaction to his report turned it into a sort of 'blueprint' for the 'brave new world' which Britain could become after the war.[66]

Coinciding as it did with the 'end of the beginning', Beveridge's proposals were seized upon by 'progressive' opinion in the country, but there was no good reason why the Conservatives should not have been able to jump on the bandwagon. Younger Conservatives like Butler and Eden welcomed them, and even older Conservatives like Amery could hope that 'our party will not be foolish enough to reject' it.[67] The Conservatives did not, but then nor did they show much enthusiasm for it, and the fault here was mainly Churchill's lack of interest. In his memoirs he devoted more space to the

British invasion of Madagascar than he did to Beveridge and social policy.

For Chamberlainites like Sir Kingsley Wood, the Beveridge scheme involved 'an impractical financial commitment' and an enormous increase in taxation; he was firmly against encouraging the notion that there might be a 'golden age' ahead. Cherwell was equally chilling, warning Churchill of the danger that the Americans might see such a generous scheme as a reason for withholding aid after the war.[68] It was by such advice that Churchill let himself be guided, despite arguments from Amery and others that the Conservatives needed to be able to match Labour when it came to showing a commitment to the creation of a better post-war world. Churchill, who thought Beveridge 'an awful windbag and a dreamer', did agree, on his return in January, to a compromise, forced on him largely by Labour, which committed the coalition to acceptance of the report in 'principle', but which promised nothing in the way of detailed legislation.[69] This line won the approval of the Chamberlainites, who felt that the Government had, if anything, gone too far. But when the matter was debated in February, forty-five Conservatives, including a group known as the Tory Reform Group, led by Quintin Hogg, the victor of the 1938 Oxford by-election, put down a motion calling for the creation of a Ministry of Social Security.[70]

Such calls left Churchill deaf, for on this issue, if on few others, he was at one with the bulk of his largely Chamberlainite Party. Butler urged Eden during the debate on 18 February to 'give a lead to our members & also show the country that our *intention* is to carry out a great & unprecedented policy of social reform'.[71] If, as one Conservative MP wrote in late 1942, the Party had become a 'cheap joke', and if it had 'ceased to exist' as 'an effective body of opinion either in the House or the Country',[72] the opportunity to begin to reverse that process had been lost by Churchill's failure to adopt even the right sort of rhetoric. Once again he preferred to leave post-war problems until after the war. This was all very well, but his refusal to let Eden or any other Conservative tackle them left Labour in possession of the field. If the road to victory was set, so too was the road to a 1945 in which Britain would be unable to harvest any reward abroad, and Labour would reap any available harvest at home. In September 1942 Beaverbrook had told Roosevelt that where the Great War had seen the end of the Liberal Party, this time it seemed that the Conservatives would be the main political casualty;[73] Churchill's unwillingness to let anyone else supply his defects helped to ensure a substantial degree of accuracy for his Lordship's prophecy.

46

Stresses and Strains

The Casablanca conference marked the high point reached by the tide of British influence, and from such a mark there can only be an ebb. It was not until late 1943 that it was apparent that the ebb-tide was moving, but after that the pace was swift: *facilis descensus averni*. Neither of Britain's great allies was satisfied with the results of the conference, and with the passage of time the balance of power shifted decisively in a direction which gave them the opportunity to alter the decisions reached there in a way which served their own interests. Stalin's discovery that the western powers did not intend to mount a major cross-Channel attack in 1943 exacerbated his suspicions that Russia was being left to do most of the fighting.[1] The decision reached at Casablanca did indeed leave the Russians, to all intents and purposes, fighting a separate war to the one in which her western partners were engaged. Where the Americans and the British were hoping to use the Mediterranean to hold down about twenty-five divisions, the Soviets were holding down some 214 divisions. At the end of the Tunisian campaign in May, the Allies rejoiced at the capture of 250,000 Axis troops; the Soviets, at the same time, were tackling over three million Axis troops.[2] But precisely because the Soviets were fighting a different war, there was little they could do to influence the war in the west except to exhort their allies to greater efforts. What Stalin could and did do was to use the embarrassment felt by his allies to press forward with his own political and diplomatic objectives. Churchill was soon to find that he could do as little to influence Soviet policy towards eastern Europe as Stalin could to bring forward the date of the second front in the west. By the time that event occurred, the Soviets were in a position to impose their wishes.

The Americans had only agreed to a continuation of the 'Mediterranean strategy' because they lacked any consensus amongst themselves on what to do next. Inaction in 1943 was clearly not an option, so, divided amongst themselves, they had followed the logic of having so many troops already in the Mediterranean theatre and had gone along with the British. However, that did not mean that they were happy with the decision or that they had rid themselves of suspicions that the British had, in effect, conned them.[3] Hitler's hopes that the unnatural alliance between British imperialism, American capitalism and Soviet Communism would break down under its inherent contradictions were wide of the mark, but only because they ignored the fact that he and his regime acted as the cement to keep it together; once he had vanished, his hopes would soon be fulfilled.[4] That they were not realised sooner owed much to Churchill's own efforts in his self-created role of facilitator.

At the conference Churchill had readily concurred in Roosevelt's declaration that the aim of the Allies was to secure the 'unconditional surrender' of their enemies. Churchill was later to claim that the President's statement had taken him by surprise,[5] but the phrase had been used in a telegram which Churchill had communicated to the Cabinet on 20 January, and it had certainly been aired beforehand. The phrase served two purposes; firstly, as a 'political and psychological substitute for a second front';[6] and secondly, as an assurance to those who feared that the Darlan deal would set a precedent for deals with Grandi or Field Marshal Hermann Goering.[7] In agreeing with Roosevelt, Churchill was making no great concession; he had never envisaged any other outcome to the war. Neither man stopped to enquire whether 'total victory is necessarily the surest foundation for a lasting peace'.[8]

Since the 'turn of the tide' Churchill's mood had become a good deal more optimistic, and in the Mediterranean sunshine it flourished like the green bay tree. He badgered an unwilling Cabinet into letting him go to Turkey, a visit which, he was convinced, would result in the Turks entering the war, which might even allow operations to be mounted in the eastern Mediterranean.[9] He suggested to Roosevelt that they might send a message to Stalin on Casablanca which included a pledge to mount a major operation across the Channel in August 1943.[10] His thoughts on the post-war era were also touched by the post-conference euphoria. Partly in order to encourage the Turks to enter the war, Churchill set down what he called his 'Morning Thoughts' on post-war security.[11] These 'Thoughts' derived in part from his earlier thoughts on the subject, and its ideas (if not its sonorous prose-style) owed something to Eden's recent writings on post-war security. It was hardly surprising that both men should have been in agreement on the broad outline of the post-war era, for the scenario which they envisaged was the only one which would enable Britain to come out of the war with any discernible gains to show for all her exertions.[12] Eden's idea of continuing the 'United Nations' into the post-war period and making it a 'world organisation for the preservation of peace' bulked large in Churchill's thoughts. The Great Powers who had won the victory would, he hoped, co-operate to win the peace, spurred on by the 'certainty' that, after all their current sufferings, 'a third struggle will destroy all that is left of culture, wealth and civilisation of mankind and reduce us almost to the level of wild beasts'. Alas that the thoughts generated by the morning should have evaporated as swiftly as the mist which often accompanies it after an over-heated day. The Turks, whilst being very polite, declined to enter the war; Stalin, after being very impolite, began the process of getting on with his own war; and the hopes of post-war co-operation began to founder as that process got under way.

One American verdict on Casablanca was 'we came, we listened and we were conquered';[13] it was an experience which they determined not to repeat. Macmillan summed up a common British attitude towards the Americans when he told one of his subordinates: 'We are the Greeks in the New Roman Empire.'[14] To a classically educated Englishman this reference spoke volumes. The Romans, of course, had the military prowess and the treasure with which to rule, but they were, so the stereotype had it, rather brainless and therefore in need of guidance from the subtle and better-educated Greeks. Of course the process had to be managed carefully, and it would never do for the 'Greeks' to reveal the power which they really possessed. During a visit to Washington in March, in which he discussed the shape of the post-war world with Roosevelt, Eden gained a good deal of amusement from the chaotic way in which the administration was run; he was less amused, but equally condescending, about the President's ideas on the future of Europe.[15] Such an attitude, understandable given the much greater experience and expertise which the British possessed in international diplomacy, was not altogether wise; it is usually a mistake to underestimate an opponent.

If Eden, and to an extent Churchill, underestimated the Americans, they, in turn, greatly overestimated the British. The American Chiefs of Staff and military planners were apt to credit the British with the co-ordinated strategic and diplomatic policy which they would have liked the President to pursue. The British, it was thought, wanted to pursue the 'Mediterranean strategy' not only because it would help them shore up their Empire, but because a long war, by leaving both Germany and Russia exhausted, might enable Britain to maintain a balance of power on the Continent.[16] Such a policy would certainly have been sensible, but it was far beyond anything which Churchill envisaged. It would have been a return to the 'limited liability' strategy pursued by Chamberlain and a repudiation of his own more heroic policy. But such fears on the part of the American planners made them determined never again to yield to Britain's strategic preferences. Like their British counterparts,[17] the American military nursed suspicions of the Soviets which were at variance with the rosy picture being painted by politicians and diplomats; but where the Foreign Office was dismissive of such views, the State Department was more receptive. One American official had concluded as early as December 1942 that 'the European civil war between the adherents or clients of the Anglo-Saxon powers on the one hand, and Russia on the other, has already begun'.[18] Such consideration made the Americans even more determined that their more direct approach to strategy in Europe should prevail, if only so that the German collapse did not find the Soviet armies 'alone on the continent'.[19] As early as March the Americans were pressing for clarification of the decisions reached at Casablanca, and by May they were ready to contest any continuation of the 'Mediterranean strategy'.

If the American pressure to shape the future of Allied strategy in their own image was one sign of the pressures which were beginning to impinge upon Britain, Stalin's demands in March for renewed discussion of the question of Soviet frontiers was another portent of what was to come. Eden, who still saw Russia as Britain's major partner in the post-war era, was well aware of the difficulties such questions posed, but believed that by discussing them on a tripartite basis, it might be possible to reach agreement on at least the broad outlines of a peace settlement. During Eden's absence in Washington, correspondence on the subject was shown to Churchill, who, upon seeing its subject, 'emitted a series of most vicious screams from his sickbed and ordained that the whole subject of post-war matters should be dropped at once like the hottest of hot bricks'.[20]

Churchill's outburst reflected not just the state of his health, but also that of his relationship with the Foreign Office. The Foreign Office was the one major department of state of which Churchill had not been the head, and his opinion of it, based partly upon its propagation of 'appeasement', was not high. The *bon mot* that 'the Home Office looks after things at home and the Foreign Office looks after the interests of foreigners' might be apocryphal, but it expresses an attitude which was often made explicit by Churchill. As he told Eden in May: 'it is said that if you read the odd paragraph numbers and the equal paragraph numbers in series, you get both sides of the case fully stated';[21] it was not meant as a compliment. Churchill had been angered at the attempt to stop him going to Turkey and told Eden that he must be allowed to go wherever he wanted to go: 'the Foreign Office were always on about small points like chrome and ships in Sweden'. Whatever truth there was in that comment ignored the fact that it was the Prime Minister's own edicts on things like post-war planning which confined the Foreign Office to such matters. With a flash of a line of argument he was to employ with Eden for the next decade and more, Churchill told the Foreign Secretary that he could not understand why he had tried to oppose his visit to the Turks: 'if he had been killed ... it would have been a good way to die and I should only have come into my inheritance sooner'.[22] Such a comment did not necessarily carry the flattering implication which its hearer might have assumed. As he had embarked for England, Churchill had told Colonel Jacob that whilst it would be a pity if an accident made him miss the end of 'such an interesting drama, it wouldn't be such a bad moment to leave. It is a straight run in now, and even the Cabinet could manage it!'[23]

The prospect of Eden entering into his inheritance and the Cabinet having to manage the 'straight run in' was raised by Churchill's falling ill soon after his return to England. On 11 February, when Churchill reported to the House on his journeyings, he had not looked well; the following day he was confined to bed with pneumonia, or, as Wilson called it (to Churchill's evident lack of amusement), 'the old man's friend'.[24] After Birkenhead's death in 1930, Churchill had sought to comfort his son with the reflection that he had gone both quickly and without much pain: 'Think of the great Duke of Marlborough – how he lingered on into surly decrepitude. How much better it would have been', he said, as he paced back and forth, 'had he been cut off in his brilliant prime ... a cannon ball at Malplaquet. ...'[25] Had the 'old man's friend' taken Churchill then, or later in the year when he was at Carthage, or had he failed to return from one of his heroic journeys by bomber, then he too would have been spared a descent into 'surly decrepitude'; but he would have missed an apotheosis enjoyed by few men in their lifetime. Eden and the Foreign Office would have enjoyed a greater freedom to get on with plans for the post-war era, but that, like the course of the war itself, had already been set by the decisions taken over the previous few months. Perhaps the course of domestic politics would have been different; certainly Eden and Butler would not have ignored the opportunity provided by Beveridge to escape from the shadows of 'appeasement'. But even on the international front Churchill was probably correct in assuming that one of his colleagues could have filled his position for the future, which is an index of how that position had changed since 1940.

From 1940 to 1941 Churchill, with all his faults, had been the essential man; without him those things which ought to have been done would not have been done, and perhaps could not have been done. Morale, as the battle for France had shown, was a vital component in military success: Churchill had been able to provide the former, even if he could not deliver much of the latter. During 1942 he had been able to exercise a decisive role in the determination of Allied strategy, and he had endeavoured to cultivate a relationship with Stalin which would do what the 'special relationship' with Roosevelt would do – namely to provide Britain with an influence upon the 'Grand Alliance' which her contribution to the war effort scarcely warranted. The next eighteen months revealed this line of policy to be based, in large measure, on an overestimation of what could be achieved by personal relationships.

One sign of the way that the future would develop came during Churchill's illness with Stalin's reply to the telegrams which he had been sent after Casablanca. The Soviet leader expressed his disappointment with the contribution being made to the war effort by the western powers, pointing out that since December the Germans had been able to transfer twenty-seven divisions to the eastern front. It was, he said, essential that a real second front in the west should be opened in the spring or early summer; to rub in his message he informed Churchill that his troops had just taken Kharkov.[26] Since all the western powers had to point to in riposte was the Germans breaking through Eisenhower's lines on 14 February, Churchill and Roosevelt were placed in a difficult situation by the Soviet démarche, especially since Maisky made it plain to Eden that the prospects of post-war collaboration depended upon all parts of the 'Grand Alliance' pulling their weight. Any hopes which Churchill was nurturing of playing the part of 'honest broker' between the Soviets and the Americans were shown up in the clear light thrown on Roosevelt's attitude to such matters by the fact that he did not wait to concert his reply to Stalin with Churchill. The President was conscious of the dangers of being seen to be 'ganging up' with the British against the Soviets, and on 22 February he sent his own reply to Stalin's message, emphasising American determination to invade Europe at the earliest possible moment.[27] On 4 March Churchill sent the President the text of a joint reply to Stalin, only to receive in response the text of Roosevelt's own earlier reply.[28] The Americans did not need 'Greeks' for their new 'Roman Empire'.

With no second front to deliver and with the convoys to Russia suffering from delays caused by U-boats and labour unrest at home, the British were not well-placed to withstand a fresh diplomatic offensive mounted by the Soviets in the aftermath of their victory at Stalingrad. When, at the end of March, Cadogan urged Churchill to warn the Russians that the poor state of Soviet-Polish relations was largely their fault, the Prime Minister responded that his 'influence was not supported by sufficient military contribution to the common cause to make any representations effective'.[29] To exercise any real influence upon the Soviets the British needed either a military lodgement on the mainland of Europe or American diplomatic support; in the absence of both Churchill could do nothing – except comment that 'the overwhelming preponderance of Russia remains the dominant fact of the future'.[30]

In view of this, and of the probability that neither Britain nor America would maintain large armies on the Continent after the war, Churchill looked towards the restoration of French power as a possible counterweight to any dangers which Russian 'preponderance' might cause;[31] but here he was faced with the problem of de Gaulle. As far as Eden and the Foreign Office were concerned, British policy was to bring about a union between Giraud and the temperamental de Gaulle, and this they pursued in North Africa through the agency of Macmillan.[32] To the Americans this was simply another case of the British pursuing political objectives under cover of the war, and Roosevelt did his utmost to break both de Gaulle and his connection with the British.[33] The differences between Churchill and Eden on the subject of the priority to be given to long-term objectives was nowhere more apparent than over de Gaulle. To Eden he was the price which had to be paid for the recreation of France as a Great Power;[34] but Churchill begged him not to 'allow our relations with the United States to be spoiled through our supposed patronage of this man ... whose accession to power in France would be a British disaster of the first magnitude'.[35]

Churchill was unable to force his American-led policy on the Foreign Office and the Cabinet, although he made a serious attempt to do so when he travelled to Washington in May for further discussions over the future direction of Allied strategy. Perhaps because of the difficulties he was having with the Americans on that front, he showed himself quite willing to sacrifice what Eden thought of as a major plank in Britain's post-war foreign policy. Roosevelt had prepared a long document outlining his own objections to de Gaulle and suggesting his replacement by Giraud;[36] Churchill simply concurred in his recommendations and told Eden that the time had come to break with the Frenchman.[37] The documents which Roosevelt had provided in support of his policy were, for the most part, tittle-tattle from anti-de Gaulle exiles in America and were rightly described by Harvey as 'a set of the most shaming *ex parte* arguments I have ever seen, from anyone else it would have been the telegram of a cad'.[38] Eden was able to use the argument that a de Gaulle–Giraud union was now so close that to break off relations with the former would be to inflict a major blow on French morale; moreover, it was, Eden argued, clear that de Gaulle now enjoyed so much support inside France that breaking off relations would '"make" him' in some circles, and that it would certainly 'make an enemy of him'.[39] Thus it was that the General, and with him an important part of Eden's policy for the future, survived. But it had been a close-run thing. Churchill's telegrams were not so much those of a 'cad' as those of a man watching power begin to slip away from his grasp.

Eden's visit to Washington had revealed something of American thinking about the post-war international order, and given Roosevelt's hostility to 'imperialism' and militarism, as well as his desire to leave the situation in Europe as fluid as possible for as long as possible, it was not difficult to divine what underlay his attitude towards de Gaulle. Eden and his advisers suspected that Roosevelt wanted a pro-American Government in post-war France, which would be willing to see the dismantling of the old French Empire. This would not only pose a threat to the British Empire, especially in the Far East, but it would also frustrate British attempts to play a leading role in Europe.[40] Eden had chided the Prime Minister for his indifference to post-war planning with the complaint that it meant 'America makes a policy and we follow', which was not, he wrote, 'a satisfactory role for the British Empire'.[41] What Eden had described as a possible danger in October, had become, by the middle of 1943, a real obstacle to an independent British foreign policy. Nor, so Churchill's Washington trip had revealed, was such a sacrifice to be rewarded by concessions on strategy. There would be no more Casablancas.

If the American connection created problems for Eden's policy towards post-war France, the Russian connection created even greater difficulties when it came to Britain's Polish allies. Unwilling as Churchill had been to raise their cause with the Soviets in March, the whole issue of Soviet-Polish relations was brought to the fore in late April with the revelation, by the Germans, that they had discovered the graves of 10,000 Polish officers at Katyn in eastern Poland. For nearly half a century British officialdom committed itself to the view, as morally obtuse as it was stupid, that there could be no certainty that these Poles had been killed by the Soviets. The Marxist intellectuals who staffed the Russian section of the Foreign Office Research Department certainly played their ignoble part in concocting and propagating a story which says as much about their politics as it does their intelligence, but the 'official' line on Katyn also reflected the stresses of the wartime alliance.[42]

The results of the Casablanca conference had placed a strain on the 'Grand Alliance' which the prolongation of the Tunisian campaign into May did nothing to relieve. With shortages of shipping and landing-craft making any cross-Channel operation in the summer doubtful,[43] Eisenhower then raised doubts, in April, whether even 'Husky' would be possible, as it seemed as though there were two German divisions on Sicily. Such 'pusillanimous and defeatist doctrines' brought forth a Churchillian outburst in which he declared that he did not 'see how the war can be carried on'.[44] Having just told the Russians that they would be getting no more convoys for a while because the shipping was needed for 'Husky', Churchill could 'not imagine' what Stalin would think of their abandoning that operation because of two German divisions – especially when his forces were dealing with 185 German divisions.[45] With the Americans making difficulties over Sicily, and with his own Chiefs of Staff coming to the gloomy conclusion that there could be no invasion of France until mid-1944,[46] there were enough problems besetting the 'Grand Alliance' without the Poles adding to the list.

The news of the grisly discovery at Katyn put Churchill in a dilemma – the first of many similar ones. He thought that the 'German revelations' were 'probably true', taking the view that the 'Bolsheviks can be very cruel',[47] but that was no foundation upon which to build a policy. It was clear that the Germans intended to use the discovery to drive a wedge between the British and their Soviet allies, using the Poles for that purpose. The Germans offered the Poles an independent enquiry by the Red Cross, a suggestion which, despite warnings from Churchill, their leader, General Sikorski, took up.[48] 'The attitude of the British Government was that the Katyn massacre was acutely embarrassing and should be ignored as much as possible.'[49] During his visit to Washington Eden had discovered that Roosevelt was in favour of trying to settle the question of the Polish frontier by Anglo-American intervention, and since he was no longer averse to recognising the 1941 frontiers (with suitable plebiscites in areas such as the Baltic states),[50] it seemed to Eden that the time was ripe for an attempt to solve the problem of the Polish frontier. Quite apart from the fact that Eden was over-optimistic in assuming that Roosevelt was ready to recognise the 1941 frontiers, the whole Katyn business aborted any such policy.[51] Stalin seized the opportunity of Sikorski's acceptance of the German proposal for an enquiry as an excuse to break off diplomatic relations with the London Poles.[52] Churchill pleaded with him not to carry out his decision and asked Roosevelt to intervene,[53] but the Prime Minister's own telegrams had no effect, and Roosevelt proved reluctant to get himself involved in an Anglo-Soviet quarrel.[54] Thus it was that the British now had a bitter foretaste of how their major allies would, in the future, decide policy by reference to their own priorities.

Stalin's attitude dealt a blow to Eden's hopes of building up a closer relationship with the Soviets, and, if necessary, consulting them before even the Americans on matters such as the future of eastern Europe.[55] It also raised the spectre of 'Soviet imperialism'. The question of whether the brave hopes of a new world in which the 'Grand Alliance' would 'win the peace', as it would the war, was one which exercised both partners in the western alliance. As Eden's visit to Washington had revealed, the Americans were less optimistic on this subject than were the British, perhaps because, unlike their allies, they could dare to glimpse a future without such co-operation. When Roosevelt had asked Eden whether he thought the Soviets intended to Communise the Continent, the Foreign Secretary had replied that he did not think so; and even if that were the case, 'we should make the position no worse by trying to work with Russia'.[56]

Without a degree of optimism about the possibility of Anglo-Soviet co-operation, it was difficult to see what, the defeat of Germany apart, the British could hope to gain from the war. The replacement of German by Soviet dominance of the Continent would hardly be the sort of result which would justify the sacrifices made to achieve it. Fears on the part of the Americans that the split between pro- and anti-Communist guerrillas in places such as Yugoslavia portended the opening of a 'civil war' between protégés of the 'Anglo-Saxons' and the Soviets[57] were not shared in Whitehall. The Foreign Office was aware of the danger that Stalin might try to dominate the Balkans as well as eastern Europe, but diplomats were far from 'convinced' that he would necessarily try to do so.[58] Alongside such a policy went Churchill's determination to subordinate everything to the war effort. On his way to Turkey in January, he had stopped off in Cairo, where he consulted with his former research assistant, now Captain Deakin of Special Operations Executive (SOE), and his superior, Colonel Keble, about the situation inside Yugoslavia.[59] It was as a result of that meeting, and the reports which SOE submitted, that Churchill decided to open direct contacts, through Deakin, with the Communist resistance under Tito.[60] This proved the first step on a road which led the British to abandon General Mihailovic and his Chetniks in favour of Tito – with momentous consequences for the post-war period.[61]

The Foreign Office was conscious of the fact that only by direct military intervention in the region could the western powers hope to have a major voice in the future of the Balkans.[62] It was, in part, the same line of thinking which led the Americans to decide that a cross-Channel invasion should take place as soon as possible; as Marshall warned Roosevelt on 30 March, if the Russians got to Germany before the western allies, 'there would be a most unfortunate situation immediately involved with the possibility of a chaotic condition quickly following'.[63] At the end of March Churchill had made a speech in which he had spoken of his ideas for a United Nations Organisation based upon regional federations, but the Americans had no intention of allowing either the British or the Russians to keep them from having a say in the affairs of Europe.[64] This Churchill discovered during his third conference in Washington in May.

Considerations of health made it necessary for Churchill to travel to America by sea. He may have resisted the attempts of the illness to 'befriend' him, but he had been very ill – as the suspension for a while of his 'red boxes' symbolised. Nothing save serious illness would have separated Churchill from his 'papers'. On the rare occasions when a matter was so important that it demanded his attention, he would dictate in a voice that was 'so weak' and a 'manner so gentle' that his secretariat 'longed for the old stamp and bark, the quick word of scorn, the snort of impatience and the final twinkle of forgiveness'.[65] In the American press, where such matters were ventilated with a freedom which the British press envied, the Prime Minister was hailed as 'the world's worst patient', and Roosevelt, who had been ill himself, pleaded with him not to 'overdo these days'.[66] This was speaking into the wind, but for once even Churchill's tremendous willpower bent before the storm. For nearly a week he did almost no work, and for the first time since his motor accident in 1930, he allowed himself to be confined to bed. But he did not 'believe in leaving things to nature' and badgered Sir Charles Wilson incessantly with the question: 'Can't you do anything else?'[67] Churchill's robust constitution, allied with Wilson's drugs, carried him through the illness, and it spared him yet another trip in the belly of a bomber.

The fact that the conference was in Washington meant that the Prime Minister and his party had a hectic schedule of social events to attend, and gave Churchill the chance to make a major speech to Congress; but it also gave the American Chiefs of Staff a chance to prove that they could be as skilful as the British in mounting a united front.[68] Churchill was confident of being able to talk Roosevelt into an extension of the 'Mediterranean strategy', but he was shaken to find that, whilst there were still some differences between the President and his staff, they were ones of method rather than substance.[69] At the first plenary session on 12 May Churchill used all his oratorical skills to portray the collapse of Italy as the 'great prize' awaiting the Allies after the invasion of Sicily. Drawing a parallel with the collapse of Bulgaria in 1918, which had portended that of imperial Germany, Churchill described an Italian surrender as the 'beginning' of Hitler's 'doom'. There was, he emphasised, no other way in which the Russians could be given 'relief'. To do nothing between 'Husky' and the invasion of Europe in 1944 ('Roundup') would place the western powers in Russia's 'debt', a 'position from which he would like to emerge'. A continuation of the 'Mediterranean strategy' opened up the prospect of an invasion of the Balkans, with prospects which no man could guess at.[70] It was all very persuasive stuff, but it cut across Marshall's wishes to 'close down' the Mediterranean.

Roosevelt was attracted by Churchill's ideas, but any gap between him and Marshall was purely tactical. The American Chiefs of Staff admitted the validity of Churchill's arguments about helping Russia, and the President saw any extension of the 'Mediterranean strategy' as being on a scale which would still allow for 'Roundup' by May 1944.[71] Indeed, as a result of Roosevelt's attitude, Hopkins now felt, for the first time, that he could be 'safely left alone with the Prime Minister'.[72] When Brooke and the British military indicated that 'Roundup' might not be possible until 1946, the Americans riposted with the threat of transferring their major war effort to the Pacific, which induced 'deep depression' in Brooke.[73] By 19 May the two sides had reached 'deadlock'. A compromise was not as difficult to reach as the Americans had made it appear. At an informal meeting of the Combined Chiefs of Staff on 19 May, the Americans appeared to concede a little by agreeing that a full-scale 'Roundup' for 1944 was impossible (something which they had always recognised), whilst the British, in turn, conceded that a major, 'Roundup'-type operation called 'Roundhammer' would take place.[74]

Having, after considerable debate, secured an agreement on strategy with Marshall, Brooke was horrified to find, on 24 May, that Churchill 'entirely repudiated' it. He argued instead for a commitment to an invasion of Italy and perhaps even the Balkans. Brooke described this as 'tragic', correctly perceiving that it would once more arouse American suspicions of Britain's motives for pursuing the 'Mediterranean strategy'.[75] In his diary, Admiral Leahy recorded that Churchill's attitude fitted well with the 'permanent' British policy of 'controlling the Mediterranean Sea regardless of what may be the result of the war'.[76] There were times when Churchill's attitude drove Brooke to 'desperation', and this was one of them. He described the Prime Minister's views on strategy in terms which merit quotation since they could be applied to any year of the war:

Thinks one thing at one moment and another at the next moment. At times the war may be won by bombing, and all must be sacrificed to it. At others it becomes necessary for us to bleed ourselves dry on the Continent because Russia is doing the same. At others our main effort must be in the Mediterranean directed against Italy or the Balkans alternately, with sporadic desires to invade Norway and 'roll up the map in the opposite direction Hitler did'. But more often than all he wants to carry out all operations simultaneously, irrespective of shortage of shipping.[77]

By selective quotation from his papers Churchill can be made to seem to be supporting almost any operation, but to adopt a phrase used by his father's biographer, 'he makes – and unmakes – sense from day to day'.[78] This is one reason why both Churchills require their opinions to be recorded in context.

On this occasion Churchill's stubbornness not only aroused American suspicions, but it brought from Roosevelt a firmness which surprised the Prime Minister. Feeling that Churchill was behaving like a 'spoilt boy', Roosevelt told him to 'shut up' and, with the assistance of Hopkins, succeeded in getting him to accept the Combined Chiefs of Staff's compromise in return for an agreement that he and Marshall could go to Algiers to discuss the possible invasion of Italy with Eisenhower. Sir Charles Wilson was puzzled by Churchill's attitude to Roosevelt that evening: 'Have you noticed that the President is a very tired man? His mind seems closed; he seems to have lost his wonderful elasticity';[79] he would have been less so had he been aware of what had happened earlier that day. If the words 'reluctance to accept my views' are substituted for 'loss of elasticity', then Hopkins's feeling that the President was not 'safe' when left alone with Churchill is as understandable as the latter's 'subdued' mood.[80]

It was true that the Americans had agreed to accept an extension of 'Husky', but their new attitude should have been sufficient warning that there would be no repetition of what had occurred after the first Washington conference in 1942. The Americans had now set a term to the 'Mediterranean strategy' by giving priority to the build-up for 'Roundhammer' and by reducing the forces available in that theatre. Over lunch at the British Embassy on 22 May, Churchill had given expression to his views on the post-war order: 'it was a plan to restore the world the Prime Minister loved the most – the nineteenth-century world of unabashed great-power politics'.[81] The question was whether Britain would be capable of operating on that level in the post-war period – and events since Casablanca suggested that the answer to that question would not be to the Prime Minister's liking.

47

Brave New Worlds

'Often, although the immediate objective may be a victory in common, there are long-term considerations that cannot be hidden away';[1] from the middle of 1943 the truth of this dictum was to become increasingly (and painfully) apparent. On the home front and abroad, the cement laid down in the cold climate provided by the danger of defeat proved friable in the balmier climate created by the anticipation of victory. The great coalition of 1940 still dominated British politics, and with victory certain, there were no cries for Churchill's removal. But his failure to provide a lead on the Beveridge report was to prove costly. The Conservatives already laboured under the disadvantages of being the Party of the 1930s, of slump, hunger marches and of Munich. At the time there had appeared to be no alternative to these things, but the war seemed to show, in retrospect, that more could have been done: Britain had fought, her economy had been fully mobilised, and her great allies provided, in their different ways, examples to be imitated. The Americans, with their 'can do' attitude to problems, provided proof that economic depressions and unemployment were not scourges sent from God, but things which could, with energy and initiative, be tackled. The Soviet Union, glamorised and mythologised by the efforts of the Ministry of Information and gullible publicists into a sort of 'workers' paradise', showed what could be achieved by a planned economy and an egalitarian ideology.

Before Beveridge, the Government had signally failed to provide anything to satisfy the cravings created by the 'peoples' war'. A war in which all were participants, in which all adults below the age of retirement were subject to military or industrial conscription, and in which food and other daily necessities were rationed, created a climate ripe for radical thinking. Priestley's 1941 broadcasts had reflected and fed this desire for a 'better world' after the war. With Beveridge came a blueprint – or so it seemed. The assumptions which underlay his report – that there would be full employment, and that there would be a free health service and an elimination of poverty – provided, Sir William claimed, a scheme which would, in the long-term, be self-financing. There was nothing in it which made it inevitable that Labour rather than the Conservatives would benefit from its tremendous popularity. It was not just 'progressive' younger Conservatives like Butler and Eden who wanted to seize the opportunity it afforded; even Tories of Churchill's generation, like Amery, realised that it offered a new rallying-cry. Beveridge was the only hope which the Conservatives were likely to have to lift the mortgage on their electoral chances left by their stewardship in the 1930s. But Churchill listened to Cherwell and Sir Kingsley Wood, who dilated on the expense of Beveridge, and, like them, failed to see the price that would have to be paid for not welcoming it.[2] Although the Conservatives were to adopt Beveridge, the manner in which they did so left few electors in doubt as to which Party was more likely to deliver the 'New Jerusalem' which everyone was to offer in 1945.

The Beveridge report, followed by White Papers on education and full employment, fed and reflected the hopes of a war-scarred population for a better tomorrow. One of the most searing indictments of Churchill's short-comings as a war leader was his failure to do anything to meet these aspir-ations; indeed it is doubtful if he realised that they existed. For him, 'victory' was enough of a war aim. That might have done for everyone in the heroic days of 1940, but by 1942 it was not enough to galvanise a weary nation. Churchill might have taken up the banner which Butler wished the Conserva-tives to raise, that of 'social reform'. Even had he done so, it would have been difficult for the Conservatives to have matched the appeal of Labour; but without doing so, the Conservatives became a 'cheap joke'.[3] Some of his critics liked to allege that, as a tactician, Churchill was careless of human life, but he was not more so than most leaders, and less so than either Roosevelt or Stalin; what he was careless of was what Roosevelt was careful of – that is the human material which every politician works with: the aspirations and dreams of the common people.

Churchill's concentration on 'victory rather than ideology'[4] also exacted a price abroad. The Washington conference, like the Quebec, Cairo and Tehran conferences which were to follow it, was to reveal the vanity of Churchill's hopes that the friendship which he had forged with Roosevelt, and which he sought with Stalin, could supply the place of real power to influence events.

The strongest element in what little thinking Churchill did about the post-war world order was the idea of Britain and America co-operating together in a 'fraternal association'. He saw in his own relationship with Roosevelt a microcosm of the 'special friendship' which should subsist between their two countries; without that, as he told Roosevelt in May, 'he could see small hope for the world'.[5] He looked forward to a 'common citizenship'; that 'mixing together', which he had spoken about in 1940, which would proceed apace until citizens of the one country might stand for office in the other. This was where the logic of the argument of his book, *A History of the English-Speaking Peoples*, led. England had carried the torch of freedom and democracy throughout the nineteenth century, but for her to do so in the twentieth, she needed to ally her power with that of the great nation which sprang from the same stock: the united 'English-Speaking Peoples' would be what Britain had been, the greatest force for good in the world.[6]

Churchill's generous rhetoric ignored the question of where, in such an association, power would lie, perhaps because of his conviction that 'he could convince the President of the wisdom of any course he wanted to pursue by written memoranda and by conversation'.[7] But the American attitude at and after the Washington conference of May 1943 not only belied Churchill's fond hopes, but also provided a more realistic answer to the question of who would wield the power.

Essential to Churchill's vision was the idea of an exclusive Anglo-American relationship, which was why he cleared his own telegrams to Stalin with Roosevelt; the President dreamed other dreams and saw different visions. The enigma of Soviet intentions intrigued him. Perhaps, in an 'intimate meeting', he could 'talk Mr Stalin out of his shell so to speak, away from his aloofness, secretiveness and suspiciousness until he broadens his views' and expresses a willingness to co-operate in forging a new world order; thus went the President's thoughts.[8] There was no place for Churchill at such a meeting. The British Prime Minister was an old-fashioned imperialist and would arouse the suspicions of Stalin. For a tripartite meeting to be held on British soil would be to invite suspicions in America that the President was being manipulated by Churchill. Roosevelt had already tried, and was continuing to try, to destroy de Gaulle, which, combined with a determination to take control of political matters after any invasion of Italy, would successfully stymie any British ambitions to control affairs in either country.[9] Churchill was a man of the past; Roosevelt saw himself and Stalin as the men of the future. It was partly such considerations which had kept the President from responding to Churchill's pleas for him to intervene in Polish-Soviet relations,[10] and they certainly played the major part in Roosevelt's attempts in May to fix up a private meeting with Stalin.

The need for some contact with the Soviet leader was shown by his angry response on 11 June to the news that there would be no cross-Channel operation in 1943: he accused the Allies of not keeping their promises; of leaving all the fighting to the Russians; and of combining to deny the Russians any say in the affairs of Italy.[11] Churchill, who had expected this 'castigation' as much as he resented it, promised to send an 'entirely good-natured' reply, laying stress upon the effects of the invasion of Italy and upon Allied willingness to co-operate with the Soviets. Imagining that Roosevelt was keen on a tripartite summit conference, Churchill expressed a willingness to travel anywhere, and suggested Scapa Flow as a possible venue.[12] Perturbed by the absence of any reaction from the President, Churchill told him on 18 June that he would send a reply to Stalin under his own name alone unless he heard further.[13] There was no need for this. Roosevelt alleged that he had not responded because he had not received Stalin's angry telegram until two days after the British; this was untrue.[14] The President had not replied because he had been contemplating the establishment of a policy towards the Soviets which would be distinctive from that adopted by the British. If Churchill wanted an exclusive Anglo-American relationship, Roosevelt hankered after a special relationship with the Soviets. He had been considering sending a reply to Stalin which 'generally took a softer and more pleading tone',[15] and whilst he eventually agreed to concur in Churchill's reply, Roosevelt had not abandoned the hope of a private meeting with Stalin. On 24 June Harriman gave Churchill the news that what Roosevelt wanted was the opportunity for an 'intimate understanding' with the Soviet leader;[16] Churchill's reaction was that of a jealous suitor who had just learnt that the object of his affections had arranged a date with a richer, more handsome man.

The prospect of Roosevelt and Stalin staging a latter-day re-enactment of the momentous meeting between Tsar Alexander I and Napoleon on a raft on the River Tilsit in 1807, at which they had (as they thought) settled the fate of the world, was not one which held much appeal to Churchill. In 1807 the British had possessed the wealth and power to upset the settlement thus reached; in 1943 this was evidently not the case. With the 'whole world expecting', and 'on our side' desiring, a 'meeting of the three great powers' in order to 'plan the future war moves' and 'search for the foundations of post-war settlement', it would, Churchill told Roosevelt on 25 June, be a 'pity' to 'draw U[ncle] J[oe] 7000 miles from Moscow for anything less'. A tripartite meeting would be 'one of the milestones of history' and 'if this is lost, much is lost', Churchill went on, excusing his frankness by reference to the 'gravity' of the 'issue'. He warned Roosevelt of the danger of Axis propaganda representing a Soviet-American meeting as a rift in the 'Grand Alliance'. There was, he wrote, no comparison with his own meeting with Stalin the previous year, which was 'on an altogether lower level': 'Nevertheless, whatever you decide, I shall sustain to the best of my ability.'[17]

Roosevelt 'flatly lied'[18] in his reply, when he credited 'Uncle Joe' with the idea of a Soviet-American meeting. Such a meeting would, Roosevelt told Churchill, have the advantages of avoiding pressure from Stalin for a second front, as well as enabling a clearer view to be obtained of Russian intentions as regards the war with Japan and the future of eastern Europe and her other 'post-war hopes and ambitions'. He promised a meeting with Churchill afterwards, to be followed by a tripartite summit conference.[19]

Any prospect of such a meeting was placed in jeopardy by Stalin's long and bitter telegram to the Allied leaders on 19 June, in which, after recapitulating their numerous assurances about a second front, he warned of the danger of a loss of 'confidence'.[20] This 'ugly message'[21] gave rise to fears in Churchill's mind that Stalin was contemplating some sort of deal with Hitler, and in the face of this he withdrew any opposition to a meeting between Roosevelt and Stalin.[22] It had taken considerable patience on his part for Churchill to send such a 'reasonable' reply to Stalin's complaints. He had not forgotten the part played by the Soviets during 1940, and he was 'getting rather tired of these repeated scoldings, considering that they have never been actuated by any-thing but cold-blooded self-interest and total disdain of our lives and fortunes'; he had asked Clark-Kerr to drop 'a friendly hint of the dangers of offending the two Western Powers', adding that 'Even my own long-suffering patience is not inexhaustible.'[23] He regarded Stalin's response as 'probably the end of the Churchill–Stalin correspondence from which I fondly hoped some kind of personal contact might be created between our countries',[24] and dropped heavy hints to Maisky on 2 July that 'he was getting rather tired of being scolded'. But he had still, as he told the Russian Ambassador, not given up the hope of building up Anglo-Soviet friendship.[25] On 12 July Eden urged upon Churchill the need for the creation of some organisation which would 'facilitate Anglo-US-Soviet collaboration;[26] and it was out of these exchanges that the plans grew for a meeting of the Allied leaders later in 1943.

Eden's initiative was part of what amounted to a defensive campaign to maintain some control for Britain over an independent foreign policy. Although the Cabinet had been able to deflect Churchill's wrath against de Gaulle in May, continued American pressure on the Prime Minister threat-ened the hopes which Eden still nurtured that British support for de Gaulle would one day produce dividends. Thanks to heroic efforts from Macmillan, de Gaulle and Giraud had finally agreed to form a French Committee of National Liberation (CFLN) on 3 June. The Foreign Office saw this as an embryonic French Government and wished to extend to it diplomatic recog-nition as such.[27] Churchill's visit with Marshall to discuss strategy with Eisen-hower in Algiers had coincided with the formation of the CFLN, and he had made an emotional and moving speech at a luncheon given by Admiral Cunningham on 4 June to celebrate the auspicious event. He referred, as did Eden, to the need for Anglo-French co-operation, whilst de Gaulle, in unexpectedly generous vein, paid tribute to the courage shown by Churchill and the British people.[28] The atmosphere in which to effect a reconciliation of sorts had been created. That it was swiftly destroyed was in part due to a crisis in which the Americans seized the chance to try to rid themselves of de Gaulle. Given the importance which Eden, the Foreign Office and Chur-chill all attached to Anglo-French relations, it might have been thought that the latter would have backed his Foreign Secretary's policy, but when a crisis arose over the command of the French forces in North Africa, he chose instead to back Roosevelt. Since Roosevelt took the view that North Africa was Giraud's fief,[29] and that Eisenhower had the right to tell the French what they could and could not do,[30] Churchill's support served only to damage Anglo-French relations and to infuriate his already irritable deputy.

Eden had been considering whether or not to accept the post of Viceroy of India, and one of the few reasons which compelled him towards a post which all his friends warned him would be the end of his political career was the consideration that he would be able to run 'a show of his own at last'.[31]

One argument in favour of staying was that he might be able to prevent 'gaffes' by the Prime Minister,[32] but that was easier to say than to do. Churchill had taken the view that the formation of the CFLN 'brings to an end my official connection with de Gaulle', and he had promised Roosevelt that he would do something to correct the pro-de Gaulle bias shown by the British press.[33] On arrival back in London, Churchill had drawn up a memorandum for the press which was so vitriolic about de Gaulle that at least one of those charged with distributing it, Osbert Lancaster, refused to do so.[34] In it Churchill described de Gaulle as a man of 'fascist and dictatorial tendencies',[35] and it spawned a plethora of anti-de Gaulle articles.[36] Churchill also sent a copy to Macmillan, with instructions to show it to General Georges and 'my friends' on the CFLN;[37] and with complete disregard for any semblance of unity on the Committee, Churchill wrote to Georges, whom he had known since the 1930s, and encouraged him to write back.[38]

Allied intervention simply made the crisis worse, as Giraud and his supporters thought that they could simply rely upon Churchill and Roosevelt for support, whilst de Gaulle, offended at foreign intervention, gave a passable imitation of Achilles sulking in his tent. Churchill, who nursed suspicions that Macmillan was a good deal more pro-de Gaulle than he ought to be, could not resist the opportunity provided by the prolonged crisis to score off him. On 15 June he sent him a telegram drawing his attention to St Matthew's Gospel, Chapter VII, verse 6: 'By their fruits shall ye know them.'[39] Macmillan hit back in kind, asking Churchill to look up Revelations, Chapter II, verses 2–4, where, at the end of a long passage, he found the words: 'Nevertheless I have somewhat against thee, because thou hast left thy first love.'[40] Egged on by Robert Murphy, who remained as anti-de Gaulle as ever, Roosevelt wanted to 'break' with the troublesome Frenchman, and he sent Eisenhower a telegram on 17 June which would, if put into effect, have achieved this result and committed both Britain and America to back Giraud and Georges.[41] Eden and the War Cabinet were horrified at this attempt to dictate Allied policy, and persuaded Churchill to advocate a less drastic course of action.[42] Fortunately the close friendship which had grown up between Eisenhower and Macmillan had already saved the day. They had shown one another telegrams from their respective leaders and then 'decided to interpret these instructions in our own way'.[43]

As a result of Macmillan's actions there was time for Eden's pressure on Churchill to pay off, and the crisis was satisfactorily resolved – for the moment. But the implication of the affair was disturbing to some within the Foreign Office. The Allies were about to invade Italy, and it was known that opinion within occupied Europe had moved to the left, yet at such a moment the Americans were willing to risk reviving memories of the deal with Darlan by breaking with de Gaulle in favour of men who had collaborated with Vichy. It almost seemed as though they wanted a return to 'a "comfortable" pre-war Europe of Pétains'.[44] 'Fed up with the way French policy' was 'taken out of his hands',[45] Eden pressed Churchill for immediate diplomatic recognition to be extended to the CFLN, but Churchill, who seemed to be 'crazy on the subject', refused to part company with Roosevelt.[46] When Eden 'retaliated' at a meeting of the Defence Committee on 8 July by saying that the 'Americans had mishandled' the French 'from the start', and that 'their treatment of de Gaulle would make him a national hero',[47] Churchill simply stuck to his position.

It was little wonder that India seemed to beckon Eden as a sort of haven where he could escape from the sometimes crushing burden of dealing with Churchill. According to Colville, although Eden 'frequently arrived [at No. 10] to protest, eyes ablaze and "at the end of his tether", he could never resist Churchill's paternal charm and he would return to the Foreign Office soothed and relaxed';[48] but such a version of events, whilst it might reflect the perspective from Downing Street, did not correspond with the view from the Foreign Office. Far from being 'soothed and relaxed', Eden was growing increasingly weary. He was a more sensitive plant than his Prime Minister, and his highly strung nature was not well-suited to Churchill's robust style of argument. When the Cabinet discussed French matters on 28 June, Churchill stubbornly refused to 'break with Roosevelt',[49] but, as Cadogan commented, 'Nobody wants him to, but he might reason with the man, or at least not out-Roosevelt with him.'[50] What the issue pointed up were the very different versions of post-war British foreign policy nurtured by Eden and Churchill. The Prime Minister clung to his vision of Anglo-American unity and, whilst recognising the importance of France, was not prepared to sacrifice the future to the ties of the past.

Churchill and Eden had a fierce argument on the subject on the night of 12/13 July. Eden put the case for a strong France and for an independent British foreign policy to Churchill, who agreed with both. But when pressed on the subject of immediate recognition for the CFLN, Churchill was 'adamant and said menacingly, "I will fight you to the death. You may get some support, but it won't last long!"' Churchill was 'in a crazy state of exultation', perhaps because of the 'incredible' quantity 'of liquor he consumed'. Faced with the prospect of a showdown in Cabinet, Eden elected instead for a policy of 'sapping and mining'.[51] He sent Churchill a long paper on 13 July in which he set out his vision of the future; it was, as was much of British planning, based upon a desire to avoid the mistakes of 1919–39. Britain's main concern at the end of this war would be what it had been at the end of the last war – namely how 'to contain Germany'; the Soviet alliance would do that in the east, but only a strong France could do so in the west. Such arrangements would be 'indispensable for our security whether or not the United States collaborate in the maintenance of peace on this side of the Atlantic', and they meant doing 'everything to raise French morale and promote French self-confidence'. This, Eden thought, was the point at which 'we ought not to allow our policy' to be governed by Roosevelt: 'Europe expects us to have a European policy of our own, and to state it.'[52]

Churchill too had decided to write a paper on the future of British foreign policy, and he did not let Eden's arguments change it. He was not willing to 'mar those personal relations of partnership and friendship . . . between me and . . . Roosevelt . . . by which . . . the course of our affairs has been most notably assisted', especially for a man like de Gaulle, a 'budding Führer', who would bring 'civil war' to France. He was, however, willing to allow Britain to deal with the CFLN as the *de facto* Government of France, but would go no further for fear of offending Washington; it all came down to the fact that 'The whole course of the war depends upon our cordial relations with the Americans.'[53] That evening he warned Eden that 'we might be coming to a break'.[54] But on the subject of the future of France the Cabinet was more 'Edenite' than 'Churchillian',[55] and by 21 July Churchill was willing to bow to pressure and ask Roosevelt whether the time had not come to recognise the CFLN.[56] But Roosevelt would have none of it, and where the President led, the Prime Minister followed.[57] Churchill's tendency to regard Anglo-American relations 'too exclusively in terms of his personal relations with Roosevelt'[58] was, Eden thought, endangering the whole future of Anglo-French relations – and with it any hope of a British foreign policy independent of America.[59]

Churchill's 'Atlanticist' bias made him quite willing to incur the perils of seeming to be Roosevelt's lieutenant, but this did not represent a sudden self-effacement on Churchill's part, quite the opposite; he was convinced that his personal contacts had brought, and would continue to bring him, great influence. That he could continue to believe this in the aftermath of the Washington conference and the signs of Roosevelt's desire for a closer relationship with Stalin is, in part, a testimony to the fact that he was 'so taken up with his own ideas that he is not interested in what other people think'.[60] He had arrived back from Algiers convinced that Marshall had changed his mind about not exploiting the 'Mediterranean strategy' after 'Husky'.[61] When, in early July, he learnt that Eisenhower was thinking of attacking Sardinia next instead of the Italian mainland, he told his military secretary, General Ismay, and the Chiefs of Staff that they could not 'allow the Americans to prevent our powerful armies from having full employment'; 'above all we must preserve to ourselves the full power to judge and launch [future operations] once we know what Sicily tastes like'.[62] With the successful campaign waged against the U-boats now releasing more shipping, and with decrypts revealing partisan activity against the Germans in the Balkans, Churchill's mind turned towards exploiting this situation once Sicily had been invaded.[63] He was, as Ismay once put it in a tone of exasperation, 'the greatest military genius in history. He can use one division on three fronts at the same time.'[64] With the success of 'Husky' after 9 July, this strain in Churchill's character combined with his misjudgment of Marshall's attitude to create a crisis in Anglo-American relations.

Much of Churchill's power derived from his use of words, and his method of argument left him prone to the belief that others had agreed with him. Sir Ian Jacob, Churchill's assistant military secretary, described this 'devastating' method:

> He would start by stating his case strongly. Often what he said could only be described as a half-truth.The strong emphasis would be on one particular sore point, and many of the surrounding factors would be disregarded or distorted. The result of this method of attack was that the person addressed didn't quite know whether to defend the particular point seized upon by the Prime Minister, or to deal with the distortions in order to try and get the emphasis restored.

His pugnacity in argument, and ability to 'browbeat, badger and cajole those who were opposed to him',[65] could win him many debates, but when used on military men, it often left him with a false impression. Admiral Lord Fisher had found it impossible to controvert Churchill in debate, and the Americans in the Second World War had similar problems. Hopkins told Sir Charles Wilson that Marshall had gone to Algiers to 'avoid controversy with Winston; we find he is too much for us', whilst Marshall himself said that he was sure that Churchill had heard what he had had to say, 'but he kept telling me what was going to happen'.[66]

The success of 'Husky' required another conference, this time at Quebec in August, and the Americans approached it full of suspicion about the Prime Minister's enthusiasms for further operations in the Mediterranean. The Secretary for War, Henry Stimson, saw British backing for de Gaulle, alongside their desire to secure control over the Allied Military Government in Occupied Territories (AMGOT), as further evidence that they were 'straining every nerve to lay a foundation throughout the Mediterranean area for their own Empire after the war is over'.[67] This was a view shared by Marshall, who told Roosevelt on 25 July that Churchill's strategy was based on a gamble which the Americans should not underwrite; it was, he said, 'Based on the speculation that a political and economic collapse could be brought about in the occupied countries especially in the Balkans. If that speculation proved to be faulty the Allies would be committed to a long-drawn-out struggle of blockade and attrition in Europe.'[68] With more experience of Churchill, Marshall would have realised that the place to seek explanations was in his impulsive character and not in Machiavellian theories. Stimson also had to resort to elaborate explanations for Churchill's attitude. He thought that the 'shadows of Passchendaele and Dunkerque' hung 'too heavily' over British heads for Churchill and Brooke to do more than 'render lip-service' to the idea of a cross-Channel operation: 'their heart is not in it'.[69]

Churchill, who was aware of the possibility that the Americans thought that 'we have led them up the garden path in the Mediterranean', took the view that as it had proved to be a 'beautiful path' with 'peaches here, nectarines there', they should be 'grateful'.[70] He had quite convinced himself that both Roosevelt and Eisenhower agreed with his strategy, and, as he told the South African leader, Jan Smuts, in a telegram on 16 July, 'I will in no circumstances allow the powerful British and British-controlled armies in the Mediterranean to stand idle'; if the Americans did not agree to 'march as far north as possible in Italy' whilst giving 'succour to the Balkan patriots' with 'our right hand', he would go it alone.[71] He misunderstood Marshall's agreement to follow up 'Husky' by invading Italy; in Churchill's mind it was the beginning of a strategy which would exploit the whole Mediterranean.[72] He was quite willing to envisage contemplating abandoning the cross-Channel attack ('Overlord') if success in Italy demanded the retention of all the divisions already in that theatre, and, with fine disregard for both logistics and the Americans, he thought that the dust might be blown off his favourite operation – 'Jupiter' – the invasion of Norway.[73] Churchill's willingness to abandon preconceived operations to exploit the march of events may have been 'opportunistic, in true Napoleonic style',[74] but it irritated his advisers and aroused deep suspicions amongst the Americans.

Crossing the Atlantic on the *Queen Mary*, Churchill was in high good humour, if a little apprehensive; the reasons were not far to seek.[75] On 25 July the news had come through that Mussolini had been dismissed, and whilst Italy remained in the war, the new leader, Marshal Badoglio, had begun clandestine talks with the Allies about a possible armistice. The prospects which this opened up – of Italy leaving the war, and of operations in the Dodecanese and the Balkans – all fired the Prime Minister's imagination. As Brooke put it, 'We had now arrived in the orchard and our next step should be to shake the fruit trees and gather the apples. Southern Europe was now threatened on all sides.'[76] But the memory of Roosevelt's firmness in May, and the argument which he had had with Stimson in mid-July, all cast a shadow over the 'garden path' down which Churchill wished to tread.[77] Churchill's apprehensions were more correct than his optimism, for the lessons of Washington were now to be driven home: 'the time had come to discipline the British and their formidable, unaccountable leader by the growing numerical power and superior wealth of the United States and the immense prestige of the President'.[78]

Churchill used the time afforded by the Atlantic crossing to prepare thoroughly for the conference. His fertile imagination had seized upon the notion that artificial harbours would need to be created if 'Overlord' was to be successful,[79] but the question of how these creations would work given the tidal flow in the Channel was one which he was able to think out with the aid of his advisers and a bath full of water. Ismay recalled the scene in

Churchill's cabin, as the Prime Minister sat there in 'a dressing-gown of many colours' surrounded by his advisers, with an admiral moving his hand in the bath to simulate the effect of waves and a brigadier stretching a lilo across the bath to show how it broke up the waves; it was, he reflected, 'hard to believe that this was the British High Command studying the most stupendous and spectacular amphibious operation of the war'.[80] It was entirely characteristic of Churchill to work on such a scheme even at a time when he was contemplating abandoning 'Overlord'; because his imagination played over so many options, it is always possible to adduce evidence to show that he was in favour of two or even three different operations at once. Had the Norwegian operation, 'Jupiter', been put into effect, then the biographer could, had it succeeded, have produced minutes to show that Churchill was its 'onlie begetter'; had it failed, evidence could be provided to demonstrate that it was only one of a number of Churchillian ideas, and that the reason it was put into effect was because others did not point out the defects in its planning. Heads Churchill wins, tails he does not lose. If the story of the 'Mulberry' harbours, as they came to be known, shows a resourceful Churchill backing a 'winner', then another scheme he fostered during the voyage, 'Habbakuk', illustrates his penchant for supporting eccentric ideas. The scheme to create aircraft carriers out of icebergs, and then to make artificial icebergs for this purpose, would sound incredible were it not for the facts that it existed and cost a lot of money before being proven a failure.[81] Convinced that all his geese were swans, the problem facing Churchill's advisers was to discern which of the many geese was a swan and then to convince the Prime Minister of this; it was a task which was beyond many. The Americans, however, were well-placed to perform such a service – the problem was that they seemed convinced that there were no swans at all in the Churchillian nest.

48

Between the Buffalo and the Bear

After the Tehran conference in November Churchill was to say to Lady Violet Bonham-Carter that it was there that he had realised 'for the first time what a small nation we are. There I sat with the great Russian bear on one side of me, with paws outstretched, and on the other side the great American buffalo, and between the two sat the poor little English donkey who was the only one . . . who knew the right way home';[1] that may have been so, but the preceding conferences at Quebec, Moscow and Cairo had all provided plenty of evidence of the limits of British power.

At Quebec the British had suffered setbacks on the two major issues of future strategy and relations with France. The Americans proved obdurate on 'Overlord' and its overriding priority, and if further operations in Italy were sanctioned, it was to be understood that they were subordinate to that priority; whilst there was life in his 'Mediterranean strategy' Churchill could hope, but after Quebec, even more than after Washington, he could do so only by closing his ears to what the Americans said and relying upon his personal influence with Roosevelt.[2] Eden had agreed to leave the question of the recognition of the CFLN until Quebec in the hope that face-to-face discussions would produce some movement on the part of the Americans, but despite a plea to Roosevelt from Churchill to 'go as far as you can',[3] the President turned his face against recognising the Committee as being equivalent to a French Government. Indeed, Roosevelt rather regretted Eden's presence at the conference; without him he thought he could have 'made much further headway with the Prime Minister'.[4] But under Eden's guidance, Churchill pressed Roosevelt hard, telling him on 22 August that 'all the liberal elements in the world' were in favour of recognition.[5] But it was to no avail. Roosevelt regarded de Gaulle as a menace to the principles for which the war was being fought, and the most he would agree to was the anodyne formula of recognising the CFLN as administering those territories which it actually held; and with that, and differing allied formulae, Eden had to rest discontented.[6]

Churchill did not share Eden's disappointment because he was, as he made clear to the Roosevelts at dinner at their country home, Hyde Park, on 14 August, still fixed on the hope that the 'fraternal relationship' between Britain and America would be 'perpetuated in peacetime'. Mrs Roosevelt's 'idealism' led her to express the fear that such an association might be 'misunderstood' by other nations,[7] and Russian reaction to the Quebec conference showed not only that there were grounds for her fear, but also the need for the Americans to convince the Soviets that they were not being threatened by an exclusive Anglo-American combination. Churchill and Roosevelt had agreed on 15 August to make a renewed bid to secure Stalin's presence at a tripartite meeting.[8] The Soviet leader had been even more than usually taciturn during the early summer, and a message of congratulation from him in July was followed up by a message of bitter complaint at the end of August. Referring to the lack of information about Anglo-American negotiations with Badoglio, Stalin declared on 24 August that he could no longer 'tolerate' being relegated to the position of 'passive observer', and he demanded the creation of a tripartite commission which would consider the whole question of how to deal with occupied territory. Both Churchill and Roosevelt were irritated by the tone of Stalin's message. Eden and Cadogan tried to convince them that they could not condemn Stalin for remaining aloof and then 'be dismayed with him because he rudely joins the party'. But Churchill 'would have none of it'. He foresaw, he said, 'bloody consequences in the future', using the word 'bloody' in a 'literal' sense. 'Stalin is an unnatural man. There will be grave troubles.' When Eden tried to suggest that it was 'not so bad', Churchill turned on him and snapped: 'There is no need for you to attempt to smooth it over in the Foreign Office manner.'[9] It was agreed that there would have to be a tripartite summit in the near future.

Churchill's exasperation reflected, at least in part, a general tiredness. By the end of August he was, in his doctor's eyes, 'unduly depressed by troubles that are not immediate and ... unable to shake them off'. Eden thought that he 'did not look at all well' when he saw him on 26 August.[10] But Churchill was, for once, able to enjoy something of a holiday, and he set off for the Lake of the Snows, some seventy-five miles from Quebec, where he devoted himself to fishing and relaxation. Given Churchill's routine the wonder was not that he looked out of sorts, but that he was able to keep going at such a pace at all; as one observer put it: 'No one who had a close acquaintanceship with the Prime Minister could fail to wonder how he maintained his remarkable energy and activity while leading the kind of life he did.'[11] His appetite for food was enormous, and whilst he seldom drank in the morning, he 'drank a good deal at lunch, often champagne followed by brandy'. After his regular afternoon nap he would have two or three glasses of 'iced whisky and soda' before dinner, at which he 'always had champagne, followed by several doses of brandy'; this would be followed by several whisky and sodas as the night wore on. Yet, to the astonishment of many, he would be none the worse for wear the next day and ready to indulge his great appetite for breakfast. Nor were the results of this over-indulgence burnt off by exercise. Churchill's 'relaxations were largely mental – conversation, reading and so on'.[12]

At the Lake of the Snows Churchill was content to do a little gentle fishing and left the exercise to others. He amused himself by singing the music-hall songs popular in his youth, alternating them with more recent ones by Noël Coward; he was 'in terrific form'.[13] His good humour was increased by the sight of his bodyguard, Inspector Thompson, falling out of his canoe; Churchill called across the lake to him: 'What are you trying to do, Thompson, commit suicide?'[14] Some, observing his life-style, might have asked the same of the Prime Minister, but when Eden came up to the lake on 26 August, he found Churchill happily splashing about in his bath by the light of one candle (the fuses having blown), eager to talk politics.[15] This was the sort of thing which endeared him to those colleagues who got close to him. And if he could be infuriating and inconsiderate to colleagues and those who worked for him, he could also show a solicitude which was all the more touching for being so rarely exercised. Hearing that his over-worked secretary, who was a Canadian, had received a visit from her mother who had travelled from Vancouver, Churchill made her a present of half the fare; such actions inspired 'feelings of real devotion in his staff'.[16]

Churchill's prolonged absence from London caused some anxiety back home, especially since his variations on the agreed programme made it difficult to keep him supplied with the secret decrypts through which he followed the inner movement of the war. After Canada he took himself back down to see the President at Hyde Park, where the two men agreed upon an invitation to Stalin, and Churchill's 'sleeping arrangements' became 'quite promiscuous', as he spent until 2 a.m. talking to Roosevelt and 'consequently spends a large part of the day hurling himself violently in and out of bed, bathing at unsuitable moments and rushing up and down corridors in his dressing gown'.[17] Clementine and their daughter Mary had accompanied him to Quebec, but the health of the former was by no means as robust as that of her husband; nor did she warm to Roosevelt, whose habit of calling people by their Christian names grated on her sense of what was proper. Her presence meant that Churchill was able to celebrate their thirty-fifth wedding anniversary at Hyde Park, with the President and Mrs Roosevelt joining in the junketing. Clementine confided to Mary that Winston had told her 'he loved her more and more each year';[18] something which it is to be hoped brought a little cheer to Clementine, who, having cracked her elbow, returned to London with her health no better than when she had left.

The aftermath of the Quebec conference had given Churchill an opportunity to escape from the harsh realities of his position; but the conferences which followed gave him no such relief: Cairo and Tehran drove home the message that not only was Britain the smallest of the 'Big Three', but also that the bonds of personal friendship could avail little against this fact, especially when Roosevelt seemed determined to use the opportunity of a meeting with Stalin to forge a new 'special relationship' at Churchill's expense.

Churchill had made plain his hopes for Anglo-American unity when he had received an honorary degree at Harvard on 6 September. Telling the American people that they could not 'escape world responsibility', Churchill stressed the 'ties of blood and history' which bound the British and American people together. He made a plea for the continuation of organisations such as the Joint Chiefs of Staff into the post-war era, and spoke with emotion of 'our common tongue' being the 'foundation of a common citizenship'; in Roosevelt's presence he called for them all to 'rise to the full level of our duty and of our opportunity'.[19] It was a public and frank declaration of his hopes for the future.

But Churchill's somewhat naïve hopes were not shared by Roosevelt. The Prime Minister might overlook Anglo-American differences for the sake of a wider vision, but the President's vision was of something wider still and did not involve turning a blind eye to British shortcomings. In one sense Churchill was the worst possible leader for the Americans to deal with since he confirmed so many of their prejudices about the British: old-fashioned, aristocratic, class-ridden, imperialistic – Churchill was all of these things, which is perhaps why the Americans took to him so quickly; he fitted their stereotype of an Englishman in a way that Eden or Attlee did not, but he also gave them a false impression of the character of the British administration and its aims. His continuing obsession, even after the Quebec conference, with developing operations in the eastern Mediterranean[20] simply made the Americans even more suspicious of his motives.[21] When, on 20 October, Churchill pressed for an Anglo-American meeting to take place in advance of the Tehran conference, Roosevelt was far from anxious for one;[22] he did not wish to appear to be 'ganging up' on Stalin. It was towards Russia that Roosevelt's face was set. The British were antediluvian imperialists with outdated ideas on the international order, but there was no reason why, if he could make contact at a personal level with Stalin, a Soviet-American axis should not dominate the 'Big Four' organisation which the President saw as the main force in the post-war world. What Roosevelt wanted was to get Stalin to concur in this vision, not to ally himself exclusively with an imperialist power which was, rather like its leader, past its peak.[23]

The conference of Foreign Ministers which took place in Moscow in October seemed to confirm that the Soviets were sympathetic to Roosevelt's idea, and there had even been indicators that Stalin might be willing to join in the war against Japan; unlike the British, the Russians had appeared to accept the American desire to have China as one of the 'Big Four'.[24] This was one good reason not to get together with Churchill before the Tehran conference; the other was the desire to avoid the British leader trying, once more, to secure backing for his Mediterranean ambitions.[25]

The Americans never did understand the root of Churchill's preoccupation with the Mediterranean. They continued to treat it as either a manifestation of British political ambitions in the region, or as deriving from a fear that an invasion of France would be followed by a repeat of the slaughter of the last war. What it actually stemmed from was Churchill's habitual over-optimistic opportunism. General Brooke watched with some frustration as the Prime Minister, in characteristic fashion, surveyed the scene advocating operations in the Dodecanese, against Rhodes and perhaps in the Balkans and the Adriatic; as in the last war, Churchill hoped that there might be a sudden collapse in enemy morale, and he was determined to exploit it if it came.[26] Sceptical of some of his master's dreams, Brooke was not, however, unhappy to have him as an advocate against the American desire to close up the Mediterranean. It would, he agreed, be a shame simply to stay on the defensive after November, when, according to the decisions reached at Quebec, seven divisions and their landing-craft would be moved to Britain in preparation for 'Overlord' in May; to do nothing for six months was, both Brooke and Churchill felt, a dreadful mistake, and it was for this reason that Churchill urged on Roosevelt the need for a meeting before Tehran.[27] Roosevelt, in pursuit of his own objective, which was to get Churchill to accept Chiang Kai-shek as one of the 'Big Four', eventually agreed to a meeting at Cairo in November, but only on condition that the Chinese leader was invited.[28] He then turned up two days later than agreed, which left conveniently little time for the discussion of strategy before they had to go to Tehran on 27 November. Roosevelt had out-manoeuvred Churchill and left the way open for an American-Soviet combination against him.

The Americans had been unsure whether the Soviets would want to back further operations in the Mediterranean, and they were correspondingly delighted to discover that Stalin was as forcefully behind 'Overlord' as they could have wished. Although on 27 and 28 November Churchill struggled to persuade the other leaders of his vision and its compatibility with 'Overlord', he did so in vain. Roosevelt declined to meet Churchill privately before he had had a chance to talk to Stalin, and by that time the British Prime Minister found himself outnumbered.[29] On every front the British suffered setbacks. 'Overlord' was confirmed as the major operation for 1944, and the date was fixed for the end of May. Although the Italian campaign was to continue, it was only to do so in so far as it contributed to 'Overlord', and there was to be an invasion of southern France, 'Anvil', in the summer of 1944 in preference to any Churchillian projects in the Adriatic.[30] Only one day was devoted to the question of the future international order, and Churchill was able to obtain no help from Roosevelt for his plans to try to help the London Poles improve their relations with the Soviet Union.[31]

Unsurprisingly, neither Churchill nor Eden in their respective memoirs dwelt upon the negative results of the conference. But as far as Churchill's ambitions were concerned, Tehran had been little short of disastrous. On his way to Cairo, Churchill had met Macmillan on 16 November to talk, in part, about the continuing problem of de Gaulle, but he had also complained that 'the Mediterranean position has not been exploited with vigour and flexibility', something which he put down to the Americans.[32] But at Tehran he had found himself faced with a combined American-Soviet front, not only on the great strategic question, but on a political and even a personal level; this was the reality of power, as opposed to Churchill's red, white and blue-tinted vision of Anglo-American unity. On the question of the future post-war United Nations, on Germany and on the issue of the French and Italian colonial empires, Roosevelt found common ground with Stalin; whilst on the question of Poland's frontiers and eastern Europe, Roosevelt was (partly for electoral reasons) willing to postpone a final decision, something which Stalin had no difficulty accepting. This commonality of interests, established in their private conversations, found some expression at Churchill's expense.

Churchill had felt unwell when he had left London, and neither his health nor his mood improved as the days passed. Roosevelt was a clever and subtle politician in a way Churchill never was. He was adept at giving his hearers the impression that he agreed with them without really saying very much himself, and he was a past master at avoiding committing himself until the last moment. Churchill was 'not at all clever at that sort of thing'; he spoke because he had strong views which he liked to express, and he had little concern with what his auditor had to say back.[33] At dinner on the evening of 29 November, Churchill pressed both his fellow leaders on the subject upon which he had been defeated earlier in the day, the 'Mediterranean strategy', which left him open to 'teasing' from Stalin. According to Harriman, Stalin 'kept needling Churchill without mercy', both on the subject of whether the British were really committed to 'Overlord' and on his views on the future of Germany.[34] Both Stalin and Roosevelt were in agreement that Germany should suffer some form of dismemberment and that her power should be destroyed once and for all. Churchill, who was well aware of the danger of having no other Great Power between Britain and Russia, was not so keen on the idea. Stalin accused him of being 'soft' on the Germans, and proposed that the entire German General Staff of 50,000 men should be shot. Churchill, whose perusal of reports on the Katyn massacre predisposed him to take a less jocular view of the subject than the President seemed to be adopting, protested against such barbarism and said that the British public would never tolerate it. In a 'heavy-handed attempt to break the tension', Roosevelt suggested shooting only 49,000 Germans, and when his son, Elliot, endorsed the idea, Churchill, who had had enough, got up from the table and went into the next room, only to be brought back by Stalin who claimed to have been joking. In the 'chaff', Churchill also denounced the idea, approved by both the other leaders, that strategic points such as Dakar and Bizerta should be under international control; Britain, he made plain, was not going to relinquish Hong Kong or Singapore.

It was little wonder that when Sir Charles Wilson went to see him after dinner, he found the Prime Minister in the grip of a 'black depression'. Sipping whisky with Eden and Clark-Kerr, Churchill was 'talking in a tired, slow voice, with his eyes closed'. He thought, he said, that there 'might be a more bloody war', but 'I shall not be there. I want to sleep for billions of years.' As he pondered the 'vast issues' before him, he said that he realised 'how inadequate we are'. Despite making an effort to throw off the mood of depression, Churchill 'could not rid himself of that glimpse of impending catastrophe: 'I believe man might destroy man and wipe out civilization. Europe would be desolate, and I may be held responsible.' The darkness of the vision gripped him: 'stupendous issues are unfolding before our eyes, and we are only specks of dust, that have settled in the night on the map of the world'. It was his sixty-ninth birthday and there was to be a party for him later that day: 'Do you think', he demanded abruptly, 'my strength will last out the war? I fancy sometimes that I am nearly spent.'[35]

Although this darkness was shaken off later that day, and at his birthday party Churchill told Stalin to call him 'Winston', it was never to disperse. The Prime Minister's fears about his health, whilst melodramatic, were not unfounded. Travelling to see Eisenhower after the conference, Churchill went down once more with pneumonia. But once more the old man proved to have remarkable powers of recuperation, and by 20 December he was sitting up in bed barking orders. From Macmillan's point of view this was not an unreservedly good thing, for the following day the CFLN ordered the arrest of some of the former Vichy Ministers who were still in Algiers, including the former Premier, Pierre-Etienne Flandin, who had become friendly with Randolph Churchill. Stirred up by Randolph, Churchill telephoned Macmillan and declared in excited tones that he would 'denounce the Committee' publicly.[36] He told Eden that Flandin's record was no worse than that of the 'majority of the Conservative Party',[37] and incited Roosevelt to intervene.[38] Although Macmillan managed to smooth things out before the new British Ambassador, Duff Cooper, arrived to take charge of relations with the French, Churchill's hostility not only proved that he had recovered his health, but it also put an end to Eden's hopes of being able to discuss with de Gaulle's Committee the planning of civil affairs following 'Overlord'.[39] With 'Overlord' only six months away, Eden was anxious to open talks with the French about civil affairs. He had been vexed by the American insistence that all civil affairs planning should take place in Washington rather than in the European Advisory Commission, which had been set up in London after the Moscow conference,[40] and this fresh example of Roosevelt's interference in French affairs did nothing to soothe his mood.

Tehran had confirmed the tendency of events since the third Washington conference, which was that power was passing to the Americans, but from Churchill's point of view it had added the disturbing dimension of an American-Soviet axis to the picture. Roosevelt's vision of the future was not, it should have been clear, the same as Churchill's. Where the Prime Minister wanted to see a continuation of the 'Grand Alliance', with an Anglo-American special relationship at its core, Roosevelt wanted a 'Big Four', which would have at its centre an American-Soviet special relationship. This would enable the President to avoid being contaminated by British imperialism, for which neither Chiang Kai-shek nor Stalin had any time. When it came to Europe Roosevelt was, despite the worries of some of his advisers, quite willing to envisage leaving the Soviets as the dominant military power.[41] He had told Stalin that he was determined to remove all American troops from the Continent, a sentiment with which, unsurprisingly, the Soviet dictator found himself in agreement.[42] When it came to Germany, Roosevelt, like Stalin, looked forward to her dismemberment. He thought that America should have control of north-western rather than south-western Germany, which would mean not having to deal with France or Italy. He was suspicious of British plans to rebuild France as a great power, seeing in it an example of imperialists sticking together; London would, he had told his advisers on the way to Tehran, 'undercut us in every move we make' in south-west Europe, hence his desire to avoid occupying a part of Germany which would make America dependent on either the British or the French for lines of communication.[43]

Roosevelt's suspicions of British intentions and ambitions were only increased by Churchill's seemingly endless quest for military operations in the Mediterranean. His dislike of imperialism led him towards the concept of international 'trusteeship' for former colonial territories, but he had already had sufficient experience of Churchill's attitude on that subject to know that he would get nowhere with the Prime Minister; but it might be otherwise with the Chinese and the Russians.[44] Stalin had little time for Churchill's concept of a 'Danubian federation' in south-eastern Europe, and Roosevelt, with his typically American distrust of the idea of power-blocs, tended to agree.[45] That Churchill might want some military power between himself and Stalin was not an objective with which Roosevelt had much sympathy. Equally, when it came to the frontiers of Poland and the Baltic states, Roosevelt wished to keep clear of European entanglements. He told Stalin jocularly on the last day of the conference that he 'wouldn't declare war' when the Soviets occupied these territories.[46] He was interested in the Polish issue only in so far as there were many Polish-American voters in places such as Chicago.[47] It was because there would be a Presidential election in 1944 that he was quite willing to leave that issue to be sorted out later, and did nothing to help Churchill when he raised the subject. The question of the Polish frontiers was one which the British did not want to be delayed much longer. Soviet troops were approaching former Polish territory, and once they were there, there would be even less room for negotiation than before;[48] but it was to no avail. Stalin welcomed Roosevelt's attitude. The Soviet leader was equally cheered at the idea of 'Overlord' and 'Anvil' occupying the Anglo-

American forces in 1944, which would put an end to Churchill's hankerings after an operation in the Adriatic. Stalin was not particularly anxious to have armies other than his own in central Europe.

Despite his moods of gloom during the conference, Churchill was not temperamentally disposed to accept it as anything more than a setback – and he was far happier when dwelling on the pleasant personal contacts with which it had ended and evidence of Soviet goodwill. At the start of his illness he had said to his bodyguard, 'Thompson, I am tired out in body, soul and spirit,' and he had given vent to the opinion: 'In what better place could I die than here – in the ruins of Carthage?'[49] But by Christmas Day he was up and about, wandering around in his dressing-gown, dictating minutes, ticking Macmillan off for being too pro-French, and generally on top form again;[50] as it was with his health, so it was with his attitude towards Tehran.

If Roosevelt had been unhelpful on the Polish question, Stalin at least had been clear what he wanted. The Russian leader had talked about Poland's eastern frontier being on the old 'Curzon line' of 1919–20, which was a more tactful way of referring to what Eden had called the 'Molotov–Ribbentrop' frontier; but it was the same thing. In return Stalin seemed willing to give the Poles German territory up to the River Oder. From the Russian point of view this had much to commend it: it pushed their frontier hundreds of miles to the west and, by giving the Poles and the Germans a permanent cause of conflict, it would ensure that the former remained on good terms with the Soviets.[51] It was an index of the British anxiety for good relations with Stalin that Churchill and Eden were also disposed to accept such a solution to the Polish problem. Churchill told Eden on 20 December to commend the idea to the Poles. There was a good deal of realism in this attitude. As Churchill told his Foreign Secretary, 'The Russian armies may in a few months be crossing the frontiers of pre-war Poland.'[52] The refusal of the Polish Government-in-Exile irritated Churchill, and he told Eden in early January 1944 that he contemplated making a public declaration that, although Britain had declared war for Poland, 'we have never undertaken to defend existing Polish frontiers'; the Poles, he exclaimed, 'must be very silly if they imagine we are going to begin a new war with Russia for the sake of the Polish eastern border'.[53] He told Stalin that he would do his best to bring the Poles to see reason.[54]

Churchill's views on Soviet policy fluctuated as much as did his views on strategy, and in both areas he was capable of being simultaneously optimistic and pessimistic. The worries of the summer of 1943 had given way to a different attitude. As he told Eden on 16 January, the 'tremendous victories of the Russian armies, the deep-seated changes which have taken place in the character of the Russian State and Government' and the 'new confidence which has grown in our hearts towards Stalin' had all disposed him to take a kindlier view than heretofore on the subject of the Baltic states. He thought that that subject had 'largely settled' itself by the advance of the Russian armies. But then, as so often, just as Churchill seemed to be about to make a definite declaration of policy, he did precisely what he had accused the Foreign Office of doing, namely holding back with one paragraph what he had seemed about to concede with another. He feared, he told Eden, that any 'pronouncement on the topic' might have 'disastrous effects' in America in election year, as well as exposing 'ourselves to embarrassing attacks in the Commons'.[55] Those so minded can take Churchill's lucubrations about an Adriatic front as evidence that he wanted to get to Vienna before the Communists, but viewed in the context of his post-Tehran attitude, this would appear most improbable. Like his pressure on Roosevelt for an operation at Anzio, it was a sign of his determination to exploit opportunities in the Mediterranean; neither he nor Roosevelt for that matter was planning for the Cold War – as Churchill's optimism about the Soviet Union illustrates. Both he and Eden agreed that since the Russian claims fell short of the imperial frontiers of 1914, it should be possible to accommodate Stalin's desires when it came to his future frontiers.[56]

If Churchill was not inclined to view Tehran as a diplomatic defeat, nor was he willing simply to accept that there could be no exploitation of opportunities in the Mediterranean. One of his reasons for going to Carthage had been to see Eisenhower to press on him what became known as 'Operation Shingle'. Once his health was recovered, Churchill lost no time persuading Roosevelt that an amphibious operation further up the 'leg' of Italy would draw in German armies and help the Allies to capture Rome – and all this by keeping fifty-six landing-craft where they were – which would not, Churchill thought, delay 'Overlord'.[57] Marshall warned the President that Churchill's request was probably part of another of his familiar campaigns to postpone the date of 'Overlord', but agreed to go along with it on the assurance that the date of that operation and the status of the decisions reached at Tehran remained unchanged. Thus it was that Roosevelt sanctioned the Anzio landings.[58] Marshall's caveats were wise, for the operation turned out to be a typically Churchillian affair, where the promised easy gains failed to materialise and the Allies found themselves bogged down in a situation which used far more men and equipment than had originally been envisaged.[59]

Anzio, like his correspondence with Eden over Russia, demonstrated that illness had done nothing to impair Churchill's capacity for over-optimism, and as he convalesced in the African sunshine, there were other indications of this. Being situated in North Africa had the advantage of placing the Prime Minister at the hub of the British war effort, and it must have seemed sometimes that all roads led to his villa. Beneš, the President of the Czech Government-in-Exile, came to lunch with him on 4 January to report on his visit to Moscow. The Czechs had just signed an agreement with the Russians, which included settling a new Russo-Czech frontier. In his optimistic mood Churchill accepted Beneš's assurances about the arrangement, without quite realising that this frontier had its effect on any new Polish-Soviet border;[60] but, as his comments to Eden show, it is unlikely that this would have disturbed him had he realised its implications.

Nor was Churchill worried about the implications of the support which he had been giving towards the Yugoslav Communist leader, Tito. Whilst convalescing Churchill wrote him a letter, to be delivered by his own son, Randolph, assuring him of continued British support. Churchill would have liked to have told him that he was breaking off relations with Mihailovic, but the Foreign Office was reluctant to do so; but he did tell Tito that he was ceasing to send any military aid to the Chetniks.[61] The implication of this, that Yugoslavia would be under Communist rule in the post-war world, appeared not to worry Churchill at all; his optimism about the Soviets blinded him to anything save the hope that backing Tito would be the best way to tie down German divisions.[62]

Churchill's presence in North Africa allowed him to take a personal interest in the politics of the Mediterranean campaign, but they also exposed him to an attempt by his old friend, Duff Cooper, to improve Anglo-French relations by arranging a meeting between the Prime Minister and General de Gaulle. Churchill had warned Cooper at the time of his appointment that de Gaulle was 'a man fascist-minded, opportunist, unscrupulous, ambitious to the last degree', whose advent to power would 'lead to great schisms'.[63] Cooper, who was a great francophile, took all this with a large pinch of salt and managed to arrange a luncheon party for both men on 14 January. Churchill, who had been irritated by the Frenchman's haggling over the date, told Cooper that he would not talk politics with him, but in a mellow, post-prandial haze, he broke his own rule.[64] Showing, for once, some tact in his dealings with Churchill, de Gaulle invited him to review French troops on the morrow. Much to Cooper's pleasure, Churchill was writing to Roosevelt by the end of January that he felt 'sorry' for de Gaulle, who was 'a bigger man in his way than those around him'.[65]

Churchill took advantage of his meeting with de Gaulle to deliver a lecture on his attitude towards his allies: 'Look here! I am the leader of a strong, unbeaten nation. Yet every morning when I wake my first thought is how I can please President Roosevelt, and my second is how I can conciliate Marshal Stalin.' Why, he asked the Frenchman, was it that his 'first waking thought' seemed to be 'how you can snap your fingers at the British and Americans'?[66] Anyone less egocentric than Churchill might have stopped to ask himself whether his early-morning thoughts of appeasement were bringing his country any greater dividends than a more Gaullist attitude might have done; but Churchill was content to bask in his own illusions, even after the experience in Tehran. Medicine could cure his pneumonia, but only the march of events could tackle his chronic over-optimism.

49

Appeasement Mk II

When Neville Chamberlain returned from Munich, having negotiated away another country's frontiers, Churchill had denounced him and called it a national humiliation; it was, after all, immoral to advise Czechoslovakia to submit to having part of her territory annexed. The questions at issue were whether a nation's 'independence is to be respected or not', whether any changes were to be as a result of 'the free consent and goodwill of the parties concerned' and whether 'the basis of international law is to be law or whether an exhibition of power politics is to be covered with our approval'; however, these words were not used about Czechoslovakia in 1938, they were used by the British Ambassador to the Poles in 1944. But the point which Sir Owen O'Malley put to Eden in January 1944 was exactly the same point that Churchill had been making to the Commons in October 1938: 'The real choice before us seems to me, to put it brutally, to be between on the one hand selling the corpse of Poland to Russia and finding an alibi to be used in evidence when we are indicted for abetting a murder' or else 'putting the points of principle to Stalin in the clearest possible way'.[1] The only difference between 1938 and 1944 was that this time it was Churchill who was participating in a national humiliation. Of course, he had the excuse that the Soviet Union was Britain's great ally, and there was nothing that Britain could actually do to help the Poles. But Churchill had not allowed Chamberlain the latter argument; he had called in aid against it the theory of the 'Grand Alliance', but now he realised what Chamberlain had always realised – the price that would have to be paid for such an alliance.

Chamberlain had never supposed that the Soviets would give their assistance free of charge, and one of his reasons for hesitating over the Soviet alliance in 1939 had been the knowledge of how much the Poles distrusted them. His policy had been predicated on a knowledge of the reality of British power; but it had been thrown over, first by himself and then by Churchill's policy of 'no surrender'. It had been resolved that Britain would be true to her glorious history and that she would 'conquer or die'. The only problem was that real life was never quite as simple as Churchill liked to make it seem; conquering or dying were not the only alternatives. Chamberlain had wanted to stay out of a war for a number of reasons, none of which changed just because Churchill had become Prime Minister. Firstly, Chamberlain was aware that another war would weaken the foundations of British power still

559

further; she could not, he had been told, afford to fight a long war, and she could not, militarily, win a short one. Secondly, war would push Britain into reliance upon the Americans, whose ideas would play an even greater part in shaping the peace settlement than they had in 1919; anti-imperialist and imbued with Wilsonian internationalism, the American brave new world was unlikely to hold much appeal, or much of a place, for Britain. Thirdly, Germany's sphere of expansion appeared to be in the east of Europe, a region where frontiers were blurred by history and racial minorities scattered about in the process; until Prague, Hitler's demands were less objectionable than the way he enforced them. Fourthly, any intervention in that region would require Soviet assistance, and the negotiations of 1939 had revealed what the price for that was likely to be; in the end it had proved easier for Hitler to settle the bill than it would have been for Britain and France.

Hence 'appeasement', denounced by Churchill as being unworthy of Britain's great history. Yet in January and February 1944 that same Churchill put pressure on the Poles to accept border changes which made the Munich settlement look like a simple frontier adjustment, and when the Poles resisted these demands, it was the man who had denounced Munich who told his colleagues on 15 February that he 'proposed to press them very strongly indeed'; in the final resort he would inform the Russians that he would support their claim to the Curzon line.[2] On 18 February he was able to inform Stalin that the Poles were ready to discuss their frontiers.[3] As he told Roosevelt, the deal with the Poles had achieved 'in essentials without actually saying so the settlement outlined at Teheran'.[4] The arguments he had used with the Poles were forceful ones: only the Russians could liberate Poland; 'if the Poles accepted, they had a decent prospect before them. If they refused, the Russian steam-roller would go over them.'[5] Had Chamberlain addressed such language to Beneš, it is not hard to imagine what Churchill would have said; but he was now discovering that moral indignation is a luxury which can only be enjoyed in opposition. Power brings hard choices. As Churchill told the Poles in early February, he 'did not intend to allow Anglo-Russian relations to be wrecked by the Polish Government if they refused what he regarded as a reasonable offer'; if they refused, he would 'conclude a direct agreement with Stalin'.[6] With Stalin demanding changes in the Polish Government before he would talk with it, thousands of square miles of Poland and East Prussia, Churchill was asking them to leave their future in the hands of the butcher of Katyn – and then he had the nerve to be annoyed when they cavilled at the notion: what would the man of 1938 have said of the Prime Minister of 1944?

Churchill's policy of 'glory' had been tried. It is not enough to say, as he later implied in his memoirs, that if it had been tried earlier, everything would have come out right – Churchill was always apt to think that this would happen if his ideas were implemented. The price of a Soviet alliance was as plain then as it was in 1941, 1944 or 1945. What Churchill had been unwilling to concede to the threat of German force, he gave to the threat of Soviet might. Although he had waxed lyrical about the changes in the Soviet system in the aftermath of Tehran, doubts crept in. At Cabinet on 25 January he asked whether the Russians really 'wanted an independent Poland', or 'had they in view a puppet Government under Russian control and a Soviet Republic?' He acknowledged Eden's fears that there were signs which pointed towards such a conclusion and added that, 'if there was any risk of this', they would have to 'consider carefully how far they could now press the Poles to go to meet the Russian viewpoint'.[7] Having thus, as he had in his telegrams to Eden, covered himself on both sides of the question, by expressing views which showed confidence in and suspicion of the Soviets, Churchill went ahead and pressed the Poles very hard indeed. After all, as he had said in Cabinet on 25 January, quarrels between the Poles and the Russians carried the risk of 'some degree of estrangement between Russia and the Western Powers. This would be calamitous, and might carry with it the seeds of future wars.' As one historian has commented, 'Here was the language which Churchill had condemned so strongly when used by the defenders of Munich', but there was one important difference – and that was that 'no informed man doubted that the great majority of the Sudetendeutsch had desired to belong to Germany; but there was every reason for doubting whether the people of eastern Poland wished to belong to Russia'.[8]

But appeasement paid no more dividends for Churchill than it had for Chamberlain. Having conceded the 'essentials' of Stalin's Tehran demands, the London Poles found that it was not enough. 'Uncle Joe' responded that 'such people' were not 'capable of establishing normal relations with the USSR',[9] which left Churchill trying to appease him still further by pointing out that the London Poles had conceded *de facto* most of what he had demanded.[10] The 'old' Churchill of 1938 showed through for a moment when he told Colville that he had felt like 'telling the Russians, "Personally I fight tyranny whatever uniform it wears or slogans it utters"'; but that was just rhetoric.[11] His suspicions of Soviet intentions flared up again, but he could do as little about Soviet designs on Poland as Chamberlain had been able to do about the Sudetenland.[12]

Even before Churchill's early-morning thoughts had turned to how to 'conciliate' Stalin, they had traversed the ground of how he was going to please the President of the United States; it was a humiliating position for a British Prime Minister who had been bent on glory and national honour to occupy, but given his hopes of Anglo-American unity, it was a necessary one. America's desire to occupy the north-western zones of Germany in order to avoid being dependent on the British and French for lines of communication presented the 'Overlord' planners with a delicate problem. American forces were due to land on the right flank of the invasion, and to get them to their zones of occupation would involve a complicated cross-over after landing, whilst to shift them to the left flank would involve delaying the operation. Roosevelt thought that the problem could be solved, but, as he told Churchill on 7 February, 'I am absolutely unwilling to police France and possibly Italy and the Balkans as well. After all, France is your baby and will take a lot of nursing.'[13] But having told the British to look after the French, Roosevelt frustrated all their efforts to reach an agreement with de Gaulle over civil affairs inside liberated France. As he told Churchill on 29 February, he preferred to leave such matters until later. But he could not, he warned, leave any troops in France, and he once again told Churchill that 'I denounce and protest the paternity of Belgium, France and Italy', and told him to 'bring up and discipline your own children. In view of the fact that they may be your bulwark in future days, you should at least pay for their schooling now!'[14] But to the frustration of Eden, and his foreign policy, the President continued to act as though France were to be ruled by a 'thorough-going A[llied] M[ilitary] G[overnmen]T' and could be 'treated as if she were Nicaragua';[15] and Churchill continued to follow his lead.

If Soviet inflexibility brought forth a glimpse of the Churchill of yesteryear, so too did any threat to any part of the British Empire or its interests. Roosevelt had been careful to keep off this subject since their correspondence over India in 1942, but in March 1944 he returned to the theme of trusteeship by sending Churchill a document which opposed any plans for Anglo-Russian spheres of influence in Persia in favour of international trusteeship; he was not, of course, heaven forbid, implying any American designs on Persian oil, and there was no connection between this and his urgent insistence that a conference to consider the subject of oil should be convened in Washington.[16] Churchill was glad to hear that America was not casting 'sheeps' eyes at our oilfields in Iran and Iraq' and disclaimed, for his part, any 'advantage, territorial or otherwise, as a result of the war'.[17] It was just as well, for it would have been difficult to point to any such 'advantages'. With lend-lease about to be scrutinised by Congress in an election year, Britain's financial weakness would once more be probed. The fact that Britain had now built up a dollar reserve worried Churchill, who felt that senators might not realise that, given the immense claims on Britain's sterling balances from India and Egypt, these were the only currency reserves which Britain had.[18] The role of indigent suitor precluded much in the way of dignity. It was little wonder that Churchill had concluded that: 'We certainly do have plenty to worry us now that our respective democracies feel so sure the whole war is as good as won.'[19]

This 'cryptic . . . sentence' was more than a reference to the 'thorny postwar problems that had begun to crop up';[20] it was prompted by the thought of elections. Although only Roosevelt was standing for re-election in 1944, Churchill had begun to wonder whether he might not have to do so.[21] If the sky above 10 Downing Street was dark, it was with the wings of chickens coming home to roost. If America and the Soviet Union were bidding fair to shape the post-war international order, forces other than Churchill's Conservative Party were doing the same on the home front. The domination of that front by Labour Ministers, Attlee, Morrison, Cripps and above all Bevin, had allowed the Labour Party to escape from the charge levelled against it after 1931, namely that it was (as it had proven itself then to be) unfit to govern. The egalitarianism of the war certainly favoured Labour more than it did the Conservatives, but the latter had missed their chance to seize any sort of initiative by being so lukewarm about the Beveridge report. The radicalisation of the British political climate by the war had little opportunity to show itself thanks to the electoral truce, but the growth of the Commonwealth Party and its performance in by-elections were a sign that the people wanted more 'advantages' out of a 'peoples' war' than simply victory.[22] The Conservatives felt little confidence in their leader, who had certainly taken little interest in the Party, or allowed others to do so.[23] In January the Party had lost Skipton in Yorkshire to the Commonwealth Party, but in February came an even bigger shock when the representative of the Devonshire clan, the Marquess of Hartington, failed to hold the family seat of West Derby-shire: 'In what was virtually an open party contest, the electorate had demon-strated their preference for the commitment to social reform.'[24] Churchill was not only surprised by the result, but 'very depressed' by its implications. He told Eden that he would 'like to go to the country'.[25] His very public intervention on behalf of Hartington had produced even less effect than a letter of support to a candidate in the Brighton by-election a fortnight earlier; it did not say much for popular gratitude. Just when national unity was essential 'with great events pending', it 'began to look as if democracy had not the persistence to go through with it'.[26] He told Eden that 'in '40 one could put up with anything because one felt one had the country behind one. Now the people were not united.'[27]

Churchill knew that some sort of reconstruction of the Tory Party was necessary and he liked the idea of 'young warriors' as candidates,[28] but Hart-ington had fitted into that category and he had still lost. Lord Cranborne, who shared Eden's distaste for the Chamberlainite nature of the existing Parliamentary Party, took the view that 'bad as . . . [it] was there was no better 'ole';[29] the problem was that neither Churchill nor Eden had the confidence of the Party, and neither of them possessed the time or the energy to do anything about its electoral chances. Churchill could only turn and appeal to the tattered banner of national unity and hope that the coalition would hold; of positive ideas he was bereft. Nor was this surprising.

Eden thought that Churchill looked 'tired and "knocked about"',[30] and in the aftermath of his illness, the burden which Churchill had borne now began to tell. His concentration would wander at times, and his conduct of Cabinet meetings, which had never been a model of orderly chairmanship, got worse.[31] Nearing 'the point of breakdown' himself, Eden sought some relief from his labours by trying to divide them, but Churchill was not happy with the idea of having the pernickety and obstinate Cranborne as his Foreign Secretary, so Eden had to remain where he was.[32] But there were times, as he told Harvey at the beginning of March, when he found Churchill's interfering and meddling in foreign policy almost too much to bear.[33] Thus it was that the Government remained unchanged. Churchill could make extensive references to Beveridge and the Government's record on social policies, as he did in a broadcast on 26 March, but the public could have little doubt from whom they were more likely to receive a 'New Jerusalem' if it came to choosing between the two main Parties in the coalition.[34]

But it was not only at home that Churchill's capacity to build a brave new world was doubtful. Stalin's response to his efforts in early March to persuade him that the London Poles really had conceded all the essential points was to complain that there had been leakages to the press. Since Churchill believed that these had come from the Russian Embassy itself, Stalin's response was not thought to be helpful, and Churchill had to ponder whether he would have to make a statement to the House saying that there would be no Soviet-Polish agreement.[35] Stalin chose to interpret this as a 'threat' and blamed Churchill for not standing by what had been agreed at Tehran.[36] Churchill hoped, as he told Roosevelt on 1 April, that 'the bark may be worse than its bite'[37] – which was a suitable sentiment for All Fools' Day. By the time 'Overlord' was launched on 6 June, Britain's relations with the two powers whom Eden regarded as the pillars of his post-war foreign policy in Europe, Russia and France, were still in a state of uncertainty which threatened to rob the military operation of any possible political or diplomatic gains.

Stalin's minatory despatch of 23 March, which had characterised Churchill's remonstrances about Poland as 'full of threats concerning the Soviet Union',[38] had set alarm bells ringing in London. Churchill's memoirs, like Eden's, were written under the shadow of the Cold War; both men took the occasion offered by the task of composition to reveal that they had been just as prescient about that 'war' as they had been about 'appeasement'. Eden was able to quote a minute written just after Stalin's message to good effect in this way: 'I confess to growing apprehension that Russia has vast aims and that these may include the domination of Eastern Europe and even the Mediterranean and the "communizing" of much that remains.'[39] Churchill, too, was able to cite his preoccupation with operations in the Balkan region as evidence of his foresight. However, as was the case with 'appeasement', matters are not that simple. Both men wrote copiously, and, as Churchill's memoranda in January on the subject of Soviet-Polish relations show, contradictory opinions could be expressed in different paragraphs; by judicious selection, both Churchill and Eden can be made to appear far-sighted or short-sighted. No simple disconnected narrative account can put these discreet quotations in context. Whatever doubts Eden allowed himself to express in the privacy of his minutes and his diaries, British foreign policy remained firmly committed to the view that provided the Soviets did not 'suspect us of having designs hostile to her security', they would 'welcome a prolonged period of peaceful relations' and would 'constitute no menace to British strategic interests'.[40]

Not everyone agreed with this view. From Duff Cooper, in Algiers, came at the end of May a document which deserves, for its prescience, to be ranked with the great 'state papers' of British diplomacy. Cooper's 'finest hour' had been his resignation after the Munich settlement. Cooper, like Eden, had pursued a pragmatic line after his resignation, keeping himself well clear of Churchill; in both cases prudence became its own reward.[41] As Minister of Information, Cooper had been a round peg in a square hole, whilst his brief spell as Minister Resident in the Far East had associated him (unjustly) with British imperial failure. Appointing him as British Ambassador with the CFLN (the rank of 'ambassador' being one conferred upon Cooper personally – the Committee was not a government and, therefore, the British representative to it did not automatically carry that rank) had been an inspired idea on Churchill's part, even if he had almost immediately regretted it.[42] A man of immense erudition and civilisation, Duff Cooper was also a diplomat of unusual quality.

Cooper had begun his professional career in the atmosphere of the Edwardian Foreign Office, with its fears of Germany and of the destruction of the balance of power. It had been this early experience which had shaped his perceptions of Nazi Germany, and which had made him one of the first to warn Churchill of the dangers to be apprehended from Hitler. It was also this experience, and the expertise gained by long study of foreign policy, which prompted Cooper to warn Eden and Churchill of the dangers which the Soviet Union might come to pose to the concept of the balance of power.[43] As he had proved by resigning over Munich, Cooper was a man who was prepared to place honour before his career, and he had not hesitated to tell Eden back in 1942 that there had been 'no more brutal and indefensible act of aggression than Russia's occupation' of the Baltic states;[44] now he cast his gaze to the wider canvas of which that had been but a detail. If Eden had a failing as Foreign Secretary, it was that he was apt to become so engrossed in the diplomatic minutiae that he neglected the broader themes;[45] Cooper's failing was the opposite – combined they would have made the ideal Foreign Secretary.

Cooper deplored the hand-to-mouth nature of British diplomacy; disguising it under the euphemism 'pragmatism' would not, he thought, get Britain very far in the post-war era. Taking as his theme the idea which had dominated Churchill's thinking in the 1930s – the balance of power – Cooper thought that the 'ineluctable logic of events compels us to acknowledge that in the period which follows the war Great Britain must beware of Russia'. This, he stressed, had little to do with Communism (although that gave the Soviets potential fifth columns in the west); it had everything to do with the fact that Russia would have the largest army on the Continent. The biographer of Talleyrand could not forget the fears which the presence of Cossacks in

Paris had created in 1814. It might be that Russia would be too exhausted to use her forces, or it might be that her honeyed words were genuine manifestations of intention: 'But two world wars should have sufficed to convince us that the safety of the British Empire should be based on more solid foundations than kind words and scraps of paper can provide.' To guard the future, Britain should sponsor a 'union' of the 'nations situated on the western seaboard of Europe', starting with a Franco-British alliance. That Britain was well-placed to do this, no one could doubt. The Belgian Foreign Minister, Paul-Henri Spaak, had raised the subject of a British-led European Union with Eden in early 1944, and with so many émigré governments having spent the war in London, the time and the atmosphere for such a development was ripe.[46] But Cooper's vision was wrecked upon the rocks of the hopes nurtured by Eden and Churchill.

For all the fears he may sometimes have expressed at this time, Eden still based his hopes for the future on the Soviet alliance, and he felt that the sort of European Union proposed by Cooper would 'increase' any 'danger' from Russia '(if it exists)' rather than 'diminish it'.[47] He did agree with Cooper about the importance of Anglo-French relations; the idea of a Franco-British alliance fitted well into Eden's policy of, in effect, reconstructing the Triple Entente of yesteryear. In his eyes, as in those of so many others, the principal post-war problem would be what it had been after 1918 – how to contain Germany; for this a Franco-British-Soviet combination would be ideal. However, even this attenuated strand of Cooper's thinking was blocked by Churchill.

Churchill was able to avert the dangers of having Cranborne to deal with at the Foreign Office by persuading Eden that all would be well with him if he went on holiday for most of April. Thus it was that the sexagenarian Premier took on the Foreign Office himself. The alarm bells which had been rung by Stalin's attitude towards the London Poles were given another ring by the Soviet Government expressing support, in mid-April, for pro-Communist mutineers amongst Greek forces in Cairo. Churchill told the Soviet Foreign Minister, Vyacheslav Molotov, sharply on 16 April that, 'This is really no time for ideological warfare. I am determined to put down mutiny'; but he followed this up with an indication that this was more than his usual policy of 'everything for the war'. Churchill wished the Soviets 'all success' in their negotiations for a Soviet-Romanian treaty, in which, he said, 'we consider you are the predominant power'.[48] The Russians responded by accusing the British of using their SOE agents in Romania to work against Soviet interests. Churchill dismissed Molotov's complaints as a 'mare's nest', but did acknowledge that, as the British had not actually informed the Soviets of the presence of the SOE mission, it was probably that fact alone which prompted the allegation.[49]

On 4 May, following Eden's return, Churchill asked him for a short paper on 'the brute issues between us and the Soviet Government which are developing in Roumania, in Bulgaria, in Yugoslavia, and above all in Greece': 'Broadly speaking the issue is: are we going to acquiesce in the Communization of the Balkans and perhaps of Italy? I am of the opinion on the whole that we ought to come to a definite conclusion about it'; if 'our conclusion is that we resist the Communist infusion and invasion we should put it to them pretty plainly at the first moment that military events permit. We should of course have to consult the United States first.'[50] The 'Bolsheviks', he had reminded Eden two days earlier, 'are crocodiles'.[51] He now thought that 'we are approaching a show-down with the Russians about their Communist intrigues in Italy, Yugoslavia and Greece'.[52] Those looking for an anticipation of the 'Iron Curtain' speech and for the origins of the 'Cold War warrior' might reasonably be pardoned for thinking that in such comments they had found their Grail. But what Churchill was proposing was something which was more analogous to Munich than it was to Fulton, Missouri. During May Eden consulted the Russians about the possibility of extending current 'understandings' into something more specific: Britain had 'recognised' Soviet 'predominance' in Romania; now, in return, the Soviets might like to acknowledge that Greece was within the British sphere.[53] That the Soviets agreed with such a proposal occasions as little surprise as the fact that neither Eden nor Churchill mentioned it in their respective memoirs. The Russians, however, were well aware of where power now lay in the western alliance, and they asked Churchill whether the Americans had agreed to his ideas of respective spheres of influence.[54]

The very idea of 'spheres of influence' was anathema to American diplomacy, reeking as it did of imperialism and the 'old diplomacy' which carved up the map of the world without heed to the wishes of 'the people'; so when Churchill put the idea to Roosevelt, he explicitly denied any intention of carving 'up the Balkans into spheres of influence'. Churchill explained that the 'arrangement' would prejudice neither a future peace settlement nor current tripartite co-operation; it was merely a 'useful device for preventing any divergence of policy' between Russia and Britain 'in the Balkans'.[55] The Foreign Office had already raised the question with the State Department, but had neglected to mention what Churchill's telegram revealed – namely that the matter had already been discussed with the Soviets, something which rang American alarm bells.[56] American diplomatic naïveté covered only Soviet motives, not those of the British. Roosevelt told Churchill on 11 June that the 'natural tendency' for military decisions to have political implications would be 'strengthened' by any Anglo-Soviet pact; this would 'certainly result in the ... division of the Balkan region into spheres of influence despite the declared intention'.[57] Churchill was 'much concerned' by the President's attitude; but given his vision of Anglo-American union, he would have to find a way to circumvent it that did not alarm Roosevelt.

If Anglo-Soviet relations were little clearer just after D-day, nor were those between Britain and France – even if events on that momentous day made explicit some of the assumptions upon which Churchill's thinking was based.

In the months before the invasion Churchill had continued to be concerned at the American attitude towards continuing the Italian campaign, but with the invasion of 'Fortress Europe' at hand, his attention turned from old worries to new prospects. It was characteristic of Churchill that he should have assumed that he was going to be able to accompany the Allied forces on the landings in Normandy, but colleagues, and eventually the King, stepped in to put an end to his fun. George VI told Churchill that if he went, he must be accompanied by the King. Unwilling to endanger his monarch, Churchill elected to stay in England – but moved himself as close to the action as he could get.

He went down to the south coast in a special train and inspected part of the embarkation process, which lifted his spirits immensely.[58] He then settled down to work on the train. Eden described it as 'an imaginative but uncomfortable exercise' on Churchill's part: 'The accommodation was limited and there was only one bath, adjoining his [Churchill's] compartment, and one telephone. Mr Churchill seemed always to be in the bath and General Ismay always on the telephone.'[59] Eden's new private secretary, Pierson Dixon (whose son was to marry Churchill's grand-daughter), found dinner on the evening of 3 June a 'very pictorial scene'. Churchill changed from one picturesque costume – that of an elder of Trinity House – to another – 'the cooler drill of a Colonel of the Hussars' – and made part of a tableau alongside his old friend Field Marshal Smuts and the 'fat, gross, Ernie Bevin'; the elegantly slim form of Eden made a striking contrast to Churchill and Bevin. If the accommodation was uncomfortable, the food was good and the drink – 1926 champagne and then vintage brandy – was even better.[60] As was often the case on such occasions, the conversation was dominated by the Prime Minister and the recollection of great events from the past. Churchill was aware of the fact that parts of his audience might have heard his tales before, but he did not let this trouble him unduly; as he said to Commander Thompson on an earlier occasion: 'You will bear witness that I do not repeat my stories so often as my dear friend the President of the United States.'[61] But on this occasion, with Smuts present, the talk went back to a topic unfamiliar to most of those present – Anglo-Boer relations at the turn of the century. It was a convivial evening, with Churchill telling Bevin and Eden by the end of the evening that he was willing to hand over the leadership to either of them.

Eden might well have been forgiven if he had hoped that such an event would come to pass sooner rather than later. With Anglo-Russian relations seemingly at Roosevelt's whim, Anglo-French relations had not escaped that baleful influence. Eden had warned Churchill on 9 May that unless the British recognised the French Committee as the body with whom the Allies would deal once inside France, there would be a 'real estrangement' with de Gaulle.[62] Duff

Cooper, who was well aware that Churchill's policy derived from Roosevelt's, asked him whether he could 'be sure that having sacrificed [French] . . . friendship and the hegemony of Europe out of friendship to the United States, the latter will not return to a policy of isolation?'[63] It was a good question to which Churchill had no real answer. Cadogan's view that 'we are nearly 3000 miles closer' to Europe 'than is President Roosevelt' predominated in the Foreign Office.[64] But Churchill remained obstinate: 'We ought not to quarrel with the President for fear of offending de Gaulle [who] . . . for all his magnitude, is the sole obstacle to harmonious relations between Great Britain and America on the one hand, and the skeleton and ghost of France on the other.'[65] Under pressure from Eden, Churchill, as on previous occasions, did ask Roosevelt if he would modify his policy,[66] but when Roosevelt refused, Churchill remained in step with him.[67] In an effort to offset the damage to Anglo-French relations, Eden persuaded Churchill to invite de Gaulle to England for D-day, but the General, offended at not being invited for formal talks (and unaware that D-day was about to be launched), stood on his dignity and declined to visit England; it was only after prolonged pressure from Cooper and his own colleagues that de Gaulle changed his mind.[68]

This kind of behaviour by de Gaulle was just the sort of thing which added an edge of personal resentment to Churchill's hostility towards the unbending Frenchman. Harriman warned Roosevelt that Churchill 'promises he will faithfully follow your line about de Gaulle but warns that the Foreign Office and some members of his Cabinet are insistent on going further . . . he really needs your help';[69] this the President was more than willing to provide. D-day was due to take place on 4 June, but bad weather necessitated its postponement; nevertheless, de Gaulle arrived in the siding at Portsmouth on 4 June for what was to be a classic encounter between the two men.

In his account, de Gaulle has Churchill use words which the Prime Minister's admirers (who would rather not believe that he held such language) deny;[70] but since the offending words were an unambiguous statement of Churchill's preference for the American alliance over any other, the argument is a storm in a tea-cup. If de Gaulle came away thinking that Churchill had said 'Anytime I have to choose between you and Roosevelt, I will always choose Roosevelt,' he can hardly be said to have come away with a false idea of Churchill's priorities. Churchill was offended by de Gaulle's refusal to fall in with his plans for him to make a broadcast to the French people, as well as by his generally ungrateful demeanour. De Gaulle, in turn, was offended by almost everything about the meeting. The presence of Smuts was like a red rag to a bull. Back in November Smuts had made a well-publicised speech in which he had said that France was finished as a Great Power;[71] nothing could have been better calculated to offend de Gaulle.[72] Nor did de Gaulle care for suggestions that if he 'were to express the wish to visit the President, he would be made most welcome'. The General felt that such a procedure was 'humiliating' and complained that the Allies had not responded to French plans for an agreement on civil affairs. Nothing could have been better calculated to irritate Churchill than such a display of unbending national pride. He told de Gaulle 'bluntly' that 'if, after every effort had been exhausted the President was on one side and the French Committee of National Liberation on the other, he, Mr Churchill, would almost certainly side with the President'. According to Eden's account, Churchill declared that 'if it came to the point he would always side with the United States against France',[73] which was exactly what de Gaulle understood the Prime Minister to have said. The luncheon which followed took place in a 'deplorable' atmosphere, with Eden trying to smooth de Gaulle's ruffled feathers. He and Bevin both told the General that Churchill's views were not necessarily definitive.[74]

Whatever words Churchill used, neither Eden nor de Gaulle was in any doubt of his preferences when it came to foreign policy; the American alliance came before everything. De Gaulle did not help matters much by his behaviour over the next few days. Offended by the terms of Eisenhower's proclamation to occupied France, the General refused to give a broadcast and, at one point, refused to allow French liaison officers to go to Normandy. When de Gaulle relented on the last point, he complained that 'he was always making concessions but ... nobody ever made them to him' – which piece of effrontery prompted Churchill to minute: 'Good Lord!'[75] Furious with the General, Churchill declared that 'de Gaulle must go'. When Brendan Bracken tried to calm Churchill down, he was told brusquely that he 'knew nothing about diplomacy',[76] whilst Eden found himself accused of trying to 'break up the Government' when he told the Prime Minister that the Cabinet supported the idea of making a civil affairs agreement with the French. Churchill told Eden that the 'Commons would back me against de Gaulle' and 'any of the Cabinet' who sided with the Foreign Secretary: 'F.D.R. and he [Churchill] would fight the world.'[77]

Bracken had used the argument: 'Why should the future relationship of France and Britain be prejudiced by the President's pique?';[78] it was a good question, and one which was relevant to a wider sphere than Anglo-French relations. Under pressure from the Cabinet and public opinion, Churchill once more begrudgingly asked Roosevelt to modify American policy towards the intransigent Frenchman, and the crisis slowly receded – having left a permanent mark on Anglo-French relations. But the President's wishes were also stalling Anglo-Soviet relations, affecting British policy in Italy and preventing any further exploitation of the military campaign there. Even Churchill's stock of patience with Roosevelt began to run low under the great strains which the President insisted on placing on it; it was almost as though he were testing the limits of Churchill's subservience.

50

'Stand Up and Beg?'

In a letter to Eden in August 1943, his Minister of State, Dick Law, wrote:

So beset are we with difficulties, domestic and international alike, that it is possible that the part we have played in this war will appear to the historian as the last brilliant flare-up which illuminates the darkness of the decline of British power and influence.[1]

The last year of the war provided nothing to contradict this sombre vision. Churchill, who shared this feeling of the 'old order changing', put a different gloss on it: 'The pomp and vanity must go; the old world will have had the honour of leading the way into the new'; Colville took this to be a 'reference to himself'.[2] But whilst there had been 'honour' in 1940, there was not much of it in the 'new world'. This was something which was borne in increasingly on Churchill in the period after D-day.

It was not just on policy towards France and Russia that British foreign policy found itself subordinated to American interests. Allied forces entered Rome on 5 June, and Churchill was astonished when, a few days later, the Government of Marshal Badoglio was replaced by one headed by Signor Bonomi and other liberals. Churchill had been only too happy to deal with Badoglio and King Victor Emmanuel after Mussolini's downfall; this satisfied not only his natural conservatism, but also his more urgent wish to wage war and to forget about politics.[3] The Americans interpreted this as another sign that the British were trying to build up a sphere of influence in the Mediterranean, and Roosevelt and Hull favoured the claims of old liberals like Count Sforza and the philosopher-historian, Benedetto Croce.[4] Churchill regarded the former as a 'useless, gaga, conceited politician', whose political objectives were motivated by personal ambition,[5] and dismissed the latter as a 'dwarf professor'.[6] But American patronage of the liberals placed them in a position to destabilise the Badoglio Government and to urge for the abdication of the King. When Roosevelt pressed for their demands to be granted, in early March 1944, Churchill continued to defend Badoglio, commenting that everything could be sorted out when Rome was taken.[7] Then, in June, he found himself out-manoeuvred, as neither the British representative of the Allied Control Council, General Mason-Macfarlane, nor the British Ambassador in Rome, Sir Noel Charles, did anything to support Badoglio when the liberals refused to join any Government unless he resigned. All Churchill could do was to fulminate against Charles ('A hopeless kind of person') and

Macfarlane ('never to be employed again'),[8] and tell Roosevelt that it was a 'great disaster that Badoglio should be replaced by this group of aged and hungry politicians';[9] but the damage was done, and the road which would lead to the end of the Italian monarchy had begun.

Back in 1942 Churchill had at least been able to excuse any diplomatic price which had to be paid to Roosevelt by pointing to the strategic advantages which such concessions enabled him to win; but this situation no longer obtained. Despite the agreement which had been reached at Tehran to follow 'Overlord' by an attack on southern France, 'Anvil', Churchill had never regarded the latter as being inevitable, and he had not given up hope of exploiting the Italian campaign further. He soon discovered the limits of British power when he tried to challenge the American decision to implement 'Anvil'. On 13 June the British Chiefs of Staff settled with their American counterparts that the advance in Italy would go no further than the Apennines, after which either 'Anvil', or amphibious operations in the Bay of Biscay or the Adriatic, would be attempted.[10] Brooke was happy to have kept these options open, but any cheerfulness he felt was soon to be dissipated by a combination of Churchill, General Alexander and Roosevelt.

On 18 June Alexander told Churchill that provided his forces were not weakened, he could 'split the German army in half and eliminate the German forces in Italy', after which there would be 'nothing to prevent me marching on Vienna' unless the Germans sent reinforcements on a large scale – which, of course, would certainly help the progress of 'Overlord'.[11] He sent Macmillan to London to be his advocate with the Prime Minister and Chiefs of Staff. Churchill was in bed when Macmillan was ushered in to see him; unsurprisingly, the scheme which was unfolded before the Prime Minister attracted his support. In the eyes of two separate groups of commentators, Churchill's backing for the unappealingly named 'Operation Armpit' had taken on two different sorts of significance. In American eyes it raised the spectre of the 'Mediterranean strategy' and, alongside British policy towards Italy, France and the Balkans, it formed part of a coherent alternative strategy.[12] To Churchill's defenders, it was not only this, but, foreshadowing the 'Iron Curtain speech', it was evidence of Churchill's foresight: he saw the dangers of Communist expansion and wished to forestall them by mounting an advance into central Europe.[13] Neither theory stands up to examination.

The mere sight of Churchill once more advocating an extension of the Mediterranean campaign was, as the editor of Brooke's diaries put it, enough to arouse 'all Marshall's own suspicions of Britain's Balkan designs';[14] those suspicions filtered through to the American historians who wrote immediately after the war. Such allegations were always stoutly denied by Churchill, and, as this account has shown, there was justice in these denials: Churchill never thought that one operation should cancel out another. But for those faced with the task of salvaging something from the wreckage of British foreign policy, a variation of the old American legend became invaluable. Churchill certainly favoured Alexander's operation, so was this not then evidence of his vision? If only the Americans had listened, the western powers would not have conceded control of eastern Europe to the Soviets: during the Cold War era this was a powerful pit-prop for Churchill's reputation. Britain, it could be argued, had been far-sighted, but she was too weak to impose her will on the short-sighted Americans; Churchill may have had to acquiesce in Russian designs, but he had attempted to stop them.

But there is little evidence to show that Churchill's support for 'Armpit' was based upon political motives; indeed, given his hostility to mixing politics with military objectives, the odds would seem to be against such an argument. Macmillan's diary makes it plain that when Churchill took up the idea, he did so for the reason which any student of his career will be familiar with – it fired his imagination. After the meeting with Brooke and the Chiefs of Staff on 22 June, when the details of the plan were outlined, Churchill kept Macmillan up until 2 a.m. discussing it: 'He is clearly getting very worked up and interested in the immense strategic and political possibilities of "Armpit".'[15] The political interest followed the strategic concept rather than inspiring it.

Alexander's strategic plans did not, alas, fit into a coherent British grand strategy for the Mediterranean – for there was no such beast. In Yugoslavia British support for Tito had put him in a position where he had not only displaced Mihailovic, but from which he also threatened the position of King Alexander II, whom Churchill supported. Churchill was, by June 1944, trying to secure some political support for the King by employing the services of Ivan Subasić, the Ban of Croatia;[16] but far from British policy in Yugoslavia helping to establish a sphere of influence there, it was bidding fair to hand the place over to the Communists.[17] Churchill's proposal of 11 June, that the Americans should agree to a 'trial of three months' for his suggestion to Stalin about spheres of influence in Romania and Greece, had aroused all the State Department's fears about Britain wanting to make the Mediterranean a 'British sea', even at the cost of 'making deals with the Soviet Union'.[18] Given this suspicion it was hardly surprising that the Americans reacted unfavourably to Churchill's attempt to reopen the strategic debate. On 12 June Roosevelt had agreed to giving Churchill's ideas about 'spheres of influence' *during* the war a trial,[19] but Hull, who had not realised this, drafted a telegram which the President sent on 22 June; this poured cold water on the idea.[20] To Churchill, who had no knowledge of the confusion within the American Government, this looked like a shift in policy. Churchill protested on 23 June. He could not, he retorted, 'admit that I have done anything wrong in this matter'. The Russians were 'the only power that can do anything in Roumania', whilst the same applied to Britain in the case of Greece. It would, Churchill commented (with a barbed reference to events in Italy, and perhaps Yugoslavia), 'be quite easy for me, on the general slithering to the left, which is so popular in foreign policy, to let things rip when the King of Greece would probably be forced to abdicate'; only by getting the Soviets to restrain the 'National Liberation Front' (EAM), the Communist-led resistance movement, could the British avoid this state of affairs.[21]

Alexander's strategy did not arise out of this diplomatic hodge-podge, but it did offer Churchill a way of making some sense out of it. With troops on the ground in northern Yugoslavia, and possibly in Greece, the British would clearly be in a better position to make their voice prevail. On 25 June, at Chequers, Churchill worked on a long paper for the Chiefs of Staff outlining the advantages of the operation. After his labours, Churchill retired to the sitting-room, where Macmillan came across him: 'I am an old and weary man. I feel exhausted,' Churchill commented. Clementine tried to cheer her husband up by remarking, 'But think what Mussolini and Hitler feel like!', to which Churchill replied, 'Ah but at least Mussolini has had the satisfaction of murdering his son-in-law.' This reference to the recent shooting of Count Ciano on charges of treason, and the prospect of Vic Oliver or Duncan Sandys sharing the same fate, 'so pleased him' that Churchill 'went for a walk and appeared to revive'.[22]

But just as Churchill and the British Chiefs of Staff were coming round to the conclusion that 'Armpit' was viable (although Brooke had his doubts about some of Churchill's more optimistic forecasts of what the operation would produce in the way of results),[23] the American Joint Chiefs were coming down firmly against it. 'Overlord' had not gone as speedily as the Allies had hoped, and Eisenhower was worried about the prospect of getting bogged down in France. On 23 June he had telegraphed to the Combined Chiefs of Staff strongly urging that 'France is the decisive theater'; resources would not, he thought, allow for attacks in the Adriatic as well: 'Anvil' might draw off German troops from the north and it must go ahead.[24] The Chiefs of Staff agreed, and on 24 June telegraphed to London in this sense.[25] It was their arguments which Churchill now sought to controvert.[26]

Churchill's appeal was, he told Roosevelt, 'a purely personal communication between you and me in our capacity as heads of the two western democracies'.[27] Brooke's scepticism about the possibilities of mounting Alexander's offensive in the near future had sobered down the content of the long telegram which was sent to Roosevelt on the evening of 28 June.[28] There was no explicit request for 'Armpit', but rather a reasoned argument against the idea of not exploiting the Italian campaign further. 'Overlord' was 'naturally ... accorded ... supreme priority', but doubt was expressed as to whether a landing at either Bordeaux or near Marseilles would do very much to help Eisenhower in the near future. Churchill thought that the question of whether 'we should ruin all hopes of a major victory in Italy and all its fronts and condemn ourselves to a passive role in that theatre' for the 'sake of ANVIL with all its limitations' was 'indeed a grave' one: 'Let us', Churchill warned in his most portentous vein, 'resolve not to wreck one great campaign for the sake of winning the other. Both can be won.'

The conclusion was typically Churchillian, but the cautious tone of the argument reflected Brooke's worries about arousing American fears, as well as his doubts about 'Armpit'. Nor was there, for once in a piece of Churchillian advocacy, the grand hopes held out for what one of his favoured operations could achieve – that was left for the Cold War warriors. Even before Churchill's 'personal' plea had been received, Roosevelt had sent a telegram upholding the American point of view.[29] The fact that the Prime Minister had chosen to place an emphasis upon their personal relationship did nothing to change the President's mind – so much for Churchill's fantasies about what his influence with Roosevelt might achieve for Britain. Brooke characterised the American reply as 'a rude one at that!',[30] whilst Macmillan called it 'not only a brusque but even an offensive refusal'.[31]

The President called in aid Stalin's opposition to any extension of the Mediterranean campaign, as well as the agreements reached at Tehran. Five divisions, the Americans claimed, could be withdrawn at once without in any way prejudicing Alexander's offensive, whilst the argument that there was not enough air cover for both 'Anvil' and Alexander was controverted. An Adriatic assault, it was pointed out, would be quite as difficult as Churchill alleged an advance up the Rhone valley would be, and it would employ only six Allied divisions and provide no help for the thirty-six engaged in 'Overlord'. Roosevelt warned that unless the Allies could agree on a directive for 'Anvil' by 1 July, 'we must communicate with Stalin immediately'. The President himself added to the bald statements drafted by the Joint Chiefs of Staff: in the first place, he told Churchill, 'At Teheran we agreed upon a definite plan of attack. Nothing has occurred to require any change'; in the second place, he added, assuming in turn his most solemn tone: 'history will never forgive us if we lose precious time and lives in indecision and debate'; and finally, Roosevelt reminded Churchill that he was facing an election in 1944 – and 'would never survive even a slight setback in OVERLORD if it were known that fairly large forces had been diverted to the Balkans'.[32]

Churchill was 'so enraged' by this rejection of his pleas that 'he thought of replying to the President in very strong terms'. Macmillan's comment was, if anything, an understatement.[33] Churchill was furious. He told Roosevelt that Alexander's campaign was being 'ruined' for the dubious gains which might be anticipated five months hence from an advance up the Rhone valley. With the Americans simply changing the timings of operations and taking such a stance, Churchill did not, he told Roosevelt,

know where I am or what orders should be given to the troops. If my departure from the scene would ease matters by tendering my resignation to The King, I would gladly make this contribution, but I fear that the demand of the public to know the reasons would do great injury to the fighting troops.

Wisely, Churchill allowed himself to be persuaded against sending this threat to the President; it is hard to see that it would have achieved any result.[34] He did think of flying to Washington to try the effect of personal contact, but Brooke was correct in surmising that once he had thought about it, 'Winston will realise there is nothing more to be gained by argument.'[35] Nor was there. Macmillan found him that evening 'anxious and a little harassed'. The realities of power had sunk in. With the Americans having more than twice as many men under arms as the British, and with the latter dependent upon American supplies, Churchill realised that 'we should have to give in if Eisenhower and Marshall insisted upon *Anvil*'.[36] They did. On 1 July the British agreed that 'Anvil' would be put into operation in August.[37]

Macmillan recorded after the event that: 'We can fight up to a point, we can leave on record for history to judge the reasoned statement of our views';[38] but then, as Auden had it, 'history' could only say 'alas' to the defeated. Once politicians start appealing to 'history' to vindicate them, it is a clear sign that they are in a position of powerlessness. Yet Macmillan had a point, for when the historians writing in the shadow of the Cold War came to look at such debates, some of them would decide that the Americans had made a mistake and that Churchill had been far-sighted. The truth is more prosaic. Churchill had, as in the previous two years, made a bid to influence Allied strategy, this time putting his relationship with the President on the line to do so – and he had failed. It was in the mood engendered by such defeats that he was to ask Roosevelt at the second Quebec conference in September 1944, during a discussion of lend-lease: 'What do you want me to do – stand up and beg like Fala [the President's dog]?'[39]

The fears expressed by men like Duff Cooper and Eden were now to come to pass; what did it profit Britain to efface herself and her interests in the hope of American goodwill? Churchill had had to yield over 'Anvil', but he had conceded over a range of diplomatic issues because he thought the cause of Anglo-America co-operation warranted it. But what had the British gained by conceding the lead to America over policy towards France and Italy, and by allowing Roosevelt to pronounce upon policy towards the Soviets? The next few months were to provide answers to such questions. Duff Cooper minuted with irritation on Eden's cautious response to his pleas for the formation of a western European bloc that it amounted to saying that, whilst it was a 'good idea', there were 'two insuperable obstacles to it – (1) It is difficult; (2) It is dangerous. It might irritate Russia and not wholly please the USA, therefore we prefer to wait and see what policies those countries intend to favour – and meanwhile do nothing.'[40] It was a cruel, and not altogether inaccurate or unfair, comment upon where Churchill's policies had brought the British Empire. As Cooper told Eden in August, Britain would 'emerge from this war with greater honour than any other country', and the 'leadership of Europe' would await her: 'But we may miss the opportunity of acquiring it if we hesitate to adopt a positive foreign policy through fear of incurring the suspicion of Russia on the one hand, or the disappointment of America on the other.'[41] Cooper's line of policy had a good deal of support within the Cabinet, particularly from the man whom Churchill had not wanted as his Foreign Secretary, Lord Cranborne;[42] but it had no support from the two men who counted – Churchill and Eden.

Eden had listened with some impatience to Churchill's comments to de Gaulle on 4 June about his priorities in foreign policy. Now he had to sit by whilst Britain had to 'give way to the US' on strategy and foreign policy; Churchill's decision on 1 July to support the American demand that the British recall their Ambassador to Argentina to protest against the policies of the new Government under Juan Perón was yet another blow to the Foreign Secretary: 'I wish I could persuade Winston to be more vigorous in favour of my French thesis. We are', Eden recorded in his diary, 'in the right there and have a right to have our say.'[43] But it was little use asking the Prime Minister to put himself out of step with the President, even when indications were that Roosevelt might well be moving towards unilateral recognition of de Gaulle's Committee now that it was clear that the General had support inside France.[44]

Both Foreign Secretary and Prime Minister were, as Eden himself later acknowledged, tired men, 'marked by the iron of five years of war'.[45] Eden had been able to take a holiday in April, but Churchill, instead of resting, had taken on the Foreign Office; Eden did not find that the Prime Minister's 'busman's holiday' had done him much good. The first Cabinet after the Foreign Secretary's return found Churchill at his most 'discursive', with most of the agenda not being reached, and Cranborne and Oliver Lyttelton both told Eden that they were 'worried by Winston's health and increased discursiveness'. Lyttelton told Eden that 'the Cabinet was on the verge of mutiny about late hours and length of sittings'.[46] But Eden's attempts to persuade Churchill to mend his ways had no effect. Smuts had warned Eden, in Churchill's hearing, that the Prime Minister 'may be mentally the man he was ... but he certainly is not physically. I fear that he overestimates his strength ... and he will wear himself out if he isn't careful.'[47] Eden allowed himself to quote this passage from his diary in his memoirs, but some examples of Churchill's behaviour at this time were too revealing to quote in full. Eden records one 'deplorable evening' at the Defence Committee on 6 July, but the account he gives in his memoirs is much edited.

In the published version Eden describes how Brooke 'reproached' Churchill for 'lack of confidence in his generals', but the diary account is more revealing and has Brooke saying: 'If you would keep your confidence in your generals for even a few days, I think we should do better.' In his memoirs Eden described Churchill as 'hurt and indignant', but omits Brooke's angry diatribe at the Prime Minister:

'I have listened to you for 2 days on end undermining the Cabinet's confidence in Alex[ander] until I felt I could stand no more. You asked me questions, I gave you answers. You didn't accept them and telegraphed to Alex who gave the same answers' – and more in the same vein.

Such a 'deplorable evening could not', Eden recorded, 'have happened a year ago'.[48] Brooke thought that Churchill now looked 'very old and tired', and that the Prime Minister was 'failing fast'.[49] Habits that had seemed endearing back in the heroic days of 1940, now struck tired men as irritating. Churchill's love of late-night meetings was not shared by diplomats like Cadogan, who had not had the advantage enjoyed by the Prime Minister of a sleep during the afternoon. When Churchill was in charge at the Foreign Office, his unbusiness-like methods annoyed Cadogan, who recorded one occasion when the Prime Minister's verbosity kept him away from his own work for three hours: 'How does he get through his work?' Cadogan wondered. 'Between 11 p.m. and 3 a.m.' was, he supposed, the answer.[50] But increasingly the real answer was that Churchill was not getting through all his work.[51]

Such accounts must, of course, be taken in context, and if the 'Moran thesis' is taken to mean that Churchill agreed to things such as the Yalta agreement because he was a tired man, then there is nothing in it. That Churchill was a man who was, at times, exhausted, is undeniable, but this was not why the final phase of the war was a diminuendo after the crescendo of 1940. The Prime Minister's aim had been 'victory', and on that objective he had kept a steady eye; but now subjects which he had put off until the end of the war were crowding in on his canvas. It was as difficult as ever to get the Prime Minister to contemplate long documents on the post-war era,[52] but his old ally, 'the march of events', was now against him. American help was conspicuous by its absence.

Any hopes which Churchill had nurtured that the visit of the Polish Premier, Stanislaw Mikolajcik, to Washington in June would help resolve the impasse in Soviet-Polish relations were disappointed. Roosevelt was lavish in promises of moral support – it was, after all, election year and there were all those Polish voters in Chicago to consider – but was barren in practical aid or suggestions.[53] As Eden put it, 'The poor Poles are sadly deluding themselves if they place any faith in these vague and generous promises'[54] – and so it proved. Churchill asked Stalin about the possibility of Mikolajcik visiting Moscow, and by the end of July Churchill was inclined to take a more cheerful view of the prospects for Soviet-Polish relations than was Eden.[55] Churchill told the Cabinet on 25 July that the Poles on the newly established 'Lublin Committee', who were co-operating with the Russians, were, 'neither Quislings nor Communists',[56] which said more for his optimism than his judgment. Under considerable pressure from Churchill, Mikolajcik agreed to go to Moscow for talks with Stalin. Churchill saw real hopes of a union of the London Poles with those backed by Stalin, and when the Soviet leader told him that the Russians were not recognising the Lublin Poles as a Government, and that he was willing to work for an agreement, Churchill described the message as 'the best ever received from U[ncle] J[oe]'.[57] Eden hoped that Churchill was right, but thought that 'like many communist messages, it is capable of several interpretations'.[58]

At first it seemed as though Eden's gloomy prognostications were unjustified. Stalin's talks with Mikolajcik went better than Churchill had expected, and Churchill described the Soviet leader's mood as 'more agreeable than we have sometimes met'.[59] Stalin's words certainly seemed to point in the right direction. He had told Mikolajcik that he wished for an independent Poland and that he had no intention of Communising the country, all of which was what the British wanted to hear.[60] On 1 August the Polish underground army in Warsaw began an uprising against the Germans; with the Red Army advancing on Warsaw the Poles wanted to ensure that the Soviets did not claim all the credit for the liberation of the Polish capital. Moscow radio had encouraged the uprising, and the Poles naturally expected help from the Soviets.[61]

The Polish underground army had unrealistic expectations of the help which the western allies could provide,[62] and any hopes that the Soviets, who were much nearer, would help, were soon falsified. Stalin claimed that his lines of communication were over-stretched and that German reinforcements made it impossible for the Red Army to advance further. In response to appeals from Churchill for help, Stalin stigmatised the underground army as 'adventurers'.[63] Whatever the truth of Stalin's military situation, his refusal to do anything to help the Poles, or to allow the western allies to do so, naturally led to suspicions that the Soviet leader was not averse to seeing the Nazis destroy the flower of the Polish resistance. With Warsaw levelled to the ground and more than 150,000 Poles killed, the 'best, the most dedicated of the young Polish generation' was decimated and the spirit of the Home Army crushed; Soviet promises, it seemed, were worth nothing.[64]

For Churchill the Soviet inaction was 'an episode of profound and far-reaching gravity', and he wanted to send a joint message with Roosevelt to put pressure on Stalin to help the Poles. Churchill hoped that Allied victories in Normandy might at last make it possible for Britain and America to take a tougher line with the Soviets.[65] But Roosevelt was interested only in 'preserving the image of Allied and Soviet support',[66] and when Churchill suggested on 25 August that they should send a joint message to Stalin telling him that British and American planes trying to supply Warsaw would, if necessary, land on Soviet territory,[67] the President took fright. Such action might seriously damage his hopes of long-term co-operation with the Soviets, and he told Churchill on 26 August that he did not 'consider it advantageous to the long-range general war prospect' to join in Churchill's message.[68]

Given the problems facing the alliance, and the growing divergence of policy, Churchill felt that it was time for another face-to-face meeting with Roosevelt, and from early August pressed him to fix a date and a place for another conference.[69] Roosevelt, who was anxious not to create the impression that the Russians were being left 'out in the cold', was less than keen on the idea of a meeting with Churchill so near the election, but he eventually gave in to the idea of another conference at Quebec – the eighth such, and so code-named 'Octagon'.[70]

Before attending 'Octagon', Churchill took himself off on another of his tours of the front line; but this one had a wider purpose than simply allowing him to get close to the troops and observe the launch of 'Operation Dragoon' (as 'Anvil' had been renamed). The 'short-termism' which had marked British foreign policy during the war was now having to be paid for. In both Yugoslavia and Greece the British had committed themselves to supporting autochthonous resistance movements which had strong Communist elements, but in both areas Britain was also committed to the support of monarchist Governments-in-Exile. The Foreign Office had, in Eden's words, often warned Churchill of 'the clash between our short- and long-term interests';[71] now, as the 'long term' arrived, the conflict in interests had to be faced. Eden told the Cabinet in June that indications were that the Soviets were 'generally speaking, out for a predominant position in S. E. Europe and are using Communist-led movements in Yugoslavia, Albania and Greece as a means to an end. . . . If anyone is to blame for the present situation in which Communist-led movements are the most powerful elements in Yugoslavia and Greece, it is we ourselves.' British agents had, Eden commented, done the work of the Russians 'for them'.[72] With British agents in Yugoslavia, including Churchill's son Randolph, all praising Tito, the Prime Minister had, as recently as April, been talking about recognising his movement as the Government of Yugoslavia unless King Peter came to terms with him.[73] Churchill used his tour of the Mediterranean to try to cobble together some form of agreement between the monarchists and the Communists – an enterprise which was fatally flawed from the start. Tito did not think that he had to make any compromises, whilst the monarchists, behind whom Churchill now flung his support, were hardly the most popular part of the Yugoslav resistance.

Churchill met Tito and the head of the Yugoslav Government, Subasić, on 12 and 13 August. His aims were what they had always been, and he exhorted both Croats to 'combine their resources so as to weld the Yugoslav People into one instrument in the struggle against the Germans'.[74] If Churchill really expected Tito or the monarchists to take such a naïve view, he was totally out of touch with the situation in the Balkans; with the Germans about to retreat, the struggle for power would begin, and no paper agreements would count for anything. Tito made all the proper noises: he did not want to introduce a Communist system into Yugoslavia, nor did he have anything against King Peter; he just wanted to let 'the people' decide on their future form of government. Under considerable pressure he even agreed to make public declarations to this effect.[75] Churchill may have gone away satisfied, but as Eden reminded him on 15 September, the extent to which Tito would keep his promises depended upon the Russians – and it was time to discover what Soviet objectives were in the Balkans.[76]

It was already clear from the American attitude in Italy and Greece that the British could expect no help from the Americans in establishing their influence in the Balkans. If Yugoslavia seemed in danger of falling into civil war through the divergent aims of the various resistance groups, then Greece, whose future was of even more concern to the British because of her strategic importance and because of the events of 1941, seemed even more likely to fall victim to a Communist-inspired coup. The 'National Peoples' Liberation Army' (ELAS) was the military arm of EAM, a 'front' organisation for the Greek Communist Party.[77] The Government of King George II, which the British backed, was detested by the Communists, who used the King's support for the pre-war dictatorship to discredit him. The British, who had tried to promote unity amongst the Greeks, were fearful that when the Germans withdrew, ELAS–EAM would use the opportunity to seize power; ELAS had certainly proved itself capable of waging war against the non-Communist resistance. It had been hoped that a British invasion of the Balkans would give the Allies the military force to combat any Communist rising, but now that (courtesy of the Americans) no such action would take place, the British, as Churchill told Roosevelt on 17 August, thought that it was essential that a British force should get into Athens as soon as possible after the German withdrawal.[78]

The State Department saw Churchill's telegram as yet another part of a malevolent British attempt to establish a sphere of influence in the Balkans, and Cordell Hull was less than keen to sanction it.[79] The American representative on the Allied Control Commission in Italy, Robert Murphy (of Darlan fame), opposed any attempt to reach an agreement between the Allies and the Greek Government prior to the return to Greece.[80] It was a week before Roosevelt responded to Churchill's telegram – and then, unexpectedly, he agreed to Britain sending a force to Greece.[81] Finally it looked as though the Americans might endorse British policy in part of the Mediterranean; but like the agreement which was reached between the resistance movements in September, this was short-lived.

It was not, however, only on the international front that Churchill's 'short-termism' was exacting a price. Although the war in the Far East was expected to carry on into 1947 or even 1948, for most Britons it was the war in Europe which counted, and as it was patently obviously coming to an end in the near future, speculation grew about when an election would take place. The great question was whether the coalition would continue after the war. As in most other areas, anticipations of the future were governed by what were to be perceived to be the lessons of the past. If British foreign policy was trying to guard against the dangers of another German revival, and if economists were planning to avoid another post-war 'boom and slump', then the politicians were thinking about whether there would be a 'coupon election' on the 1918 model. There were many politicians who shared Eden's view that 'those who had been working together' should not 'set about attacking each other'.[82] Labour, which feared Churchill doing a 'Lloyd George' – that is, going to the country as 'the man who won the war' – had good reason to want the coalition to continue; few shared Macmillan's prescience in September 1944 in prophesying that the Conservatives would be 'lucky to retain a hundred seats at the election'.[83]

Churchill's own mood about the political prospects fluctuated. When lunching with Eden on 17 July, he teased him that when the 'coalition broke up we should have two or three years of opposition and then come back together to clear up the mess!';[84] there was not much sign here of his wanting to retire. In more serious vein, before leaving for Quebec in early September, Churchill made it plain that he did not think that the life of the current House of Commons could be prolonged much further; he thought that there ought to be an election soon, perhaps in February before 'the glamour wears off'.[85] Eden did not share Churchill's evident relish for an election. But if Churchill imagined that he could fight on a 'Lloyd George platform', then, as in other areas, his vision was defective. The desire for a 'better world', nurtured by the hopes derived from the Beveridge report and by the sufferings of the war, would not be appeased by the 'glamour' of a successful war leader, and Churchill had nothing more to offer. Churchill 'no longer felt he had a "message" to deliver'; all he felt that he could do was to 'finish the war' and get the troops home 'and to see that they had houses to which to return'. But 'materially and financially the prospects were black'. Churchill had little faith in Beveridge and company, taking the view that 'the idea that you can vote yourself into prosperity is one of the most ludicrous that was ever entertained'.[86] He would not make an inspiring leader in an election which would be about the 'new world'.

Churchill was, himself, so obviously a part of the old world, and whatever affection he might be held in by the population and however well-equipped he might be to garner the votes of those who had traditionally voted Conservative, there was not very much in him to attract that substantial section of the electorate which would be voting for the first time at the next election. It was a decade since the last general election, and those who had come on to the electoral rolls since then would expect something more from a leader in peacetime than exhortations to blood, toil, tears and sweat. It was true that the Conservatives were as much committed, at least rhetorically, to the creation of a 'New Jerusalem' as Labour, but it took little more than common sense to see which Party was more likely to deliver the goods. Churchill's Conservatism was hostile to planning and government intervention, and yet, as the example of Russia showed, these things could win the peace as well as the war. Churchill himself had shown little interest in the Conservative Party or its organisation. As in the international field, he was apt to rely upon the impact of his personality to deal with any problems: in both cases he was to find that he had overestimated the impact of his own personality.

51

Victory at all Costs?

Churchill called the final volume of his war memoirs 'Triumph and Tragedy'; it is obvious what the 'triumph' is, but the 'tragedy' requires a little explication. 'I have a very strong feeling that my work is done. I have no message. I had a message';[1] Churchill's comments to his doctor after the Quebec conference encapsulate the 'tragedy' which followed his 'triumph'. In 1940 his message had been 'victory at all costs'; now the time had come to begin paying the costs. Anxious about Churchill's health, Colville hoped that he would live to see 'victory, complete and absolute', but he thought that it might be 'as well that he should escape the aftermath'.[2] It is not for nothing that in the most powerful legends the hero dies at the moment of triumph. What would Moses have done in the Promised Land? Would Alexander's myth have endured so long had he not died exhausted at thirty after having tried to hold together the Empire which he had conquered? Churchill, like his great ancestor, Marlborough, was to be granted no such boon. With 'no message' for the 'brave new world' in which he did not believe, it was Churchill's fate to have to usher it in. During the 1930s men like Churchill and Lord Lloyd had claimed that the Empire could be saved by an assertion of imperial willpower. In 1940 Churchill had a chance to show what could be achieved by an act of will; by 1944 it was clear enough that the grey men who had peddled the Baldwin/Chamberlain line on imperial and foreign policy had had a point. Britain, they had claimed, could not afford to fight another war; even if she came out on the winning side, it would, they had thought, be difficult to talk of 'victory'. It was hard to gainsay them.

Churchill could bring only one asset to bear on the situation facing him with regard to his great allies – his personal influence. If British power was in precipitate decline, its extent was not yet obvious, and whilst Churchill remained at the head of affairs, some façade could still be maintained. It remained to be tried what could be achieved by his influence.

At Quebec Churchill was able once more to renew his personal contact with that other heroic figure, 'F.D.R.'. The President looked thinner, and his concentration seemed even worse than Churchill's, but simply to be in his company again was to lift the Prime Minister up once more to that Olympian plane upon which the great ones of the ages dwell. Certainly the matters facing Churchill and Roosevelt required a view from Olympus. What should be the fate of defeated Germany? Should France once more become a Great

Power, even at the cost of admitting de Gaulle to the foothills of the sacred mountain? What organisation should there be to guarantee the future peace of the world? Olympian power as well as an Olympian vantage-point would be needed to sort out the future of a world in chaos.

The 'Olympus' metaphor might be in danger of being overworked, but before it is discarded it may be as well to recall that the gods of the ancient Greeks were themselves richly endowed with the frailties of the humans in whose lives they interfered; which makes it all the more applicable to Churchill and Roosevelt at Quebec. Neither the President nor the Prime Minister had read their carefully prepared briefing documents on the future of Germany, which provided for the economic and political rehabilitation of the country. The American Treasury Secretary, Henry Morgenthau, had little time for such 'soft' treatment, and as the President's remarks at Tehran had shown, he was little inclined towards undue leniency. When Morgenthau presented him with a plan which would dismember Germany and reduce her economy to an agrarian base, the President expressed his agreement with it, and he showed it to Churchill on 13 September.[3]

Churchill's initial response to what became known as the 'Morgenthau Plan' was similar to the way he had responded to Stalin's teasing at Tehran. Where Roosevelt was prepared to talk crudely about having either to 'castrate the German people or . . . treat them in such a manner so they can't just go on reproducing people who want to continue the way they have in the past', Churchill 'agree[d] with Burke. You cannot indict a whole nation.'[4] The evening finished with Churchill and Roosevelt taking opposite views, and yet, on the morrow, Churchill initialled the Morgenthau Plan. In his memoirs he implies that he agreed to the plan only with reluctance because he needed Morgenthau's support when it came to Britain getting further lend-lease.[5] It might indeed be that this was another example of Churchill having to yield to the President's ideas through mendicancy, but the enthusiasm with which he strengthened the language of the joint memorandum suggests that Moran was correct when he described how the Prime Minister was 'converted' by Cherwell's argument that the plan would benefit the British economy.[6] Churchill's understanding of modern economics was limited, and if 'the Prof.' told him that the impoverishment of the 'Hun' would mean a better future for the British people, then Churchill was quite willing to believe it. He was not particularly pleased when Eden remonstrated with him in front of the President on 15 September, but the Foreign Secretary and the Cabinet had their way in the end.[7]

Eden was less fortunate when it came to the eternal problem of persuading Churchill to part company with the President over France. The fact that back in July Roosevelt had stolen a march on the British by announcing that he recognised the French Committee as the *de facto* ruling body in France had annoyed Eden, who had seen it coming.[8] When he came to write his memoirs,

Eden was asked by one of his research assistants how he could 'explain' the fact that all the American leaders and Churchill had so disliked de Gaulle; his reply was short: 'I can't.'[9] In the American case it was partly the result of de Gaulle occupying the islands of St Pierre and Miquelon off Newfoundland in December 1941 in defiance of Hull's wishes, and partly a fear that de Gaulle was some sort of Fascist; but there was also a strong element of not wanting a British puppet to be installed in Paris. Anyone less likely to fill such a role than de Gaulle is difficult to imagine, and it was the General's ingratitude which stung Churchill perhaps more than anything else. As he told Sir Charles Wilson on the way home from Quebec: 'I must not let de Gaulle come between me and the French nation. He is an enemy of the English people. I must not let him have the revenge of putting me wrong with France.'[10] The British naval attack on French ships at Mers-el-Kebir in July 1940 had already done that job with part of the French nation; what Churchill's continued adherence to the President's line had done was to prevent the British taking the lead in securing French support for some sort of western European bloc. As Eden had fulminated back in July, 'Can't we really have a foreign policy of our own?'[11] Having received what by now must have been the expected response to this question from the Americans, it remained to be seen whether the Soviets would return a better answer.

The need for another conference with 'Uncle Joe' was even more urgent than that for one with Roosevelt; after all, most of the problems which beset the British in the Balkans would be more amenable to Soviet than to American aid. It was in this situation that the origin of what Churchill called his 'naughty document' lay. At Quebec Churchill had once more raised the question of a 'right-handed movement, with the purpose of giving the Germans a stab in the Adriatic armpit'; this, he told Marshall, would not only allow the Allies to get to Vienna more quickly, but it would also help to deal with the 'dangerous spread of Russian influence' in the Balkans.[12] The need for some immediate action in the region was emphasised by the news on 12 September that the Russians had entered Bulgaria: 'Even if they do not penetrate into Greek territory,' Eden telegraphed, 'their presence in the Balkans is bound to produce strong political reactions.' Eden warned that unless British troops made an early appearance in the region, 'the influence of Great Britain will suffer seriously'.[13] Churchill agreed with him and thought that there was 'a general feeling among the Staffs that we ought to have a showdown with the bear pretty soon'.[14] The Chiefs of Staff endorsed the earlier British desire to land troops in Greece as soon as possible. However, such action by itself could hardly ensure that British interests in the region were adequately protected; only an agreement with Stalin could do that.

It was not far to seek for the lines which such an agreement might take. It had already been agreed that the Russians should exercise a predominant role in Romania and Bulgaria; indeed, there was not very much anyone could do to stop them. In return, Stalin had seemed agreeable to the idea of Britain doing something similar in Greece and Yugoslavia. If this could be formalised, and if, at the same time, some arrangement could be reached over Poland, then not only would the threat of a Soviet 'tide' be stemmed, but the future of Anglo-Soviet relations would look brighter. It was with such hopes that Churchill went to Moscow in early October for the 'Tolstoy' conference.[15]

The conference has been described as the 'only time undisguised power politics predominated at a major wartime conference';[16] and so it was. Roosevelt's attitude at Tehran had shown Stalin that he was little interested in the fate of the Balkans and eastern Europe, an impression no doubt strengthened by the commitment to 'Anvil'.[17] A past master at allowing his interlocutor to believe that he agreed with him, Roosevelt had left Churchill with the impression after 'Octagon' that he accepted the need to stem the 'dangerous spread of Russian influence'.[18] In fact, as his response to the proposed Churchill–Stalin meeting showed, the President was 'essentially indifferent to the details of any settlement in eastern Europe, so long as they did not become issues in the presidential election'.[19] Before his advisers intervened, Roosevelt was tempted simply to wish Churchill 'every success'.[20] It was pointed out to Roosevelt that 'the Soviet Government would regard the absence of an American representative as a clear indication that the US Government has authorised the British Prime Minister to speak for both Governments'. The prospect of finding himself committed to 'a division of Europe into spheres of influence on a power political basis' in election year was enough to worry Roosevelt into sending Harriman as an observer – and making it clear to Stalin that any discussions should be 'preliminary to a meeting of the three of us'.[21]

What Stalin made of Roosevelt's windy Wilsonian rhetoric and documents such as the Atlantic Charter is a matter for amused speculation, but the language which Churchill held at their first meeting on 9 October was the sort that the old Georgian bandit understood; it was doubtless so much easier when 'imperialists' behaved like imperialists. In relaxed vein the two men talked about their mutual concerns in the Balkans. Churchill 'hoped Marshal Stalin would let him have the first say about Greece in the same way as Marshal Stalin about Roumania'. Stalin was quite willing to agree to this. Churchill told him that it was 'better to express these things in diplomatic terms and not to use the phrase "dividing into spheres", because the Americans might be shocked'; but 'as long as he and the Marshal understood each other he could explain matters to the President'.[22] There could be no better example of Churchill's faith in 'personal' diplomacy, or of his diplomatic methods.

Stalin showed some puzzlement about Roosevelt's message, which he 'did not like'. The President's statement that the current talks should be 'of a preliminary nature' seemed 'to demand too many rights for the United States leaving too little for the Soviet Union and Great Britain, who, after all, had a treaty of common assistance'. But if the Soviet leader was trying to drive a wedge between the two western allies, he was wasting his time. Still, given the original British version of what happened next, Stalin could be forgiven for thinking that there was a chance of dividing and ruling. The official version referred to the 'need to work in harmony' in the various Balkan countries and spoke about respective British and Soviet 'interests' there; but the British Ambassador's original draft gave an altogether more atmospheric version of the tone of the conversation:

PRIME MINISTER then produced what he called a 'Naughty document' showing a list of Balkan countries and the proportion of interest in them of the Great Powers. He said the Americans would be shocked if they saw how crudely he had put it. Marshal Stalin was a realist. He himself was not sentimental while Mr Eden was a bad man.[23]

Just how 'realistic' the 'naughty document' was is a moot point. What, for example, was '10%' of 'influence' in Romania worth when the Soviets had '90%'? How would the British exercise their share of a '25%' interest in Bulgaria? It was easier to see how Stalin might be able to use his '10%' interest in Greece, given the influence of ELAS and the Greek Communists, than it was to imagine what the '50–50%' split in Hungary and Yugoslavia was going to mean.[24] What was wrong with the 'percentages agreement' was not that it was 'rather cynical', but that it was as naïve a document as ever sought to pass muster as *realpolitik*; still, at least it was in a language that Stalin could understand, which was more than could be said for the modes of discourse preferred by Roosevelt, which might mean anything.

But perhaps it was not Stalin who was seeking to divide and rule. Was Churchill trying to 'use the Soviet Union against the United States and vice-versa in order to maintain the form if not the substance of the British Empire'?[25] The notion is intriguing, but does not quite chime either with the 'air of desperation' of the meetings, or with their substance. Churchill was not trying to 'use' the Soviets, except in the sense that he was trying to come to an arrangement which would allow the British to rescue some chestnuts from the fire. British troops had landed in Greece on 4 October and were due in Athens on the 14th; if Stalin had any influence over ELAS–EAM, it was essential that he did not use it against the British-sponsored Greek Government. Bulgaria and Romania were already lost causes and, thanks to Churchill's insistence on backing Tito, Yugoslavia bade fair to go the same way. Lord Randolph had, in his day, queried the wisdom of the Palmerstonian policy of keeping the Straits at Constantinople closed to the Russians, but it fell to his son to be the British Prime Minister who conceded the age-old Russian demand. The pre-war Treaty of Montreux, which governed the closure of the Straits, was, Churchill agreed with Stalin, an 'anachronism'.

According to the editor of the Churchill–Roosevelt correspondence, the perennial question of Poland 'took a back seat to the more pressing issue of maintaining British dominance in the Mediterranean';[26] this is so if 'back seat' is a euphemism for 'the Poles were considered expendable'. Before Stalin and Churchill got on to the subject of spheres of influence, it had been necessary to touch on the Polish problem; 'the impression left by Churchill's comments was that of a statesman willing to give the Soviets their way in Poland in return for their collaboration elsewhere'.[27] When the Soviets had agreed to allow some relief flights for Warsaw in early September, Churchill had considered it a 'great triumph', and he had told Eden that the time was ripe to 'push ahead with this Russo-Polish business'; he would get Mikolajcik to dismiss the Polish Commander in Chief, General Soznkowski, whom the Soviets blamed for the Warsaw uprising, and then persuade him to visit Stalin.[28] It had taken until the end of September to get rid of Soznkowski. Still, as Churchill reminded Stalin at their first meeting on 9 October, that deed had been done, and if Stalin wanted it, Mikolajcik could be brought to Moscow for discussions. When Stalin queried whether he would have authority to deal with the Lublin Committee, Churchill said that he was not sure. If, however, they were all in Moscow at the same time, 'they could, with British and Russian agreement, be forced to settle' – each side 'would bring pressure to bear on their Poles'. The 'difficulty about the Poles', Churchill concluded, 'was that they had unwise political leaders. Where there were two Poles there was one quarrel.' Stalin went even further, remarking that 'where there was one Pole he would begin to quarrel with himself through sheer boredom'.[29] Mikolajcik was put under pressure to go to Moscow, where he found himself in a most unenviable situation.

When Stalin and Churchill came to discuss Germany, the Prime Minister showed himself in favour of a harsh, Morgenthau-type policy. Although Churchill remained against mass executions, he was all in favour of putting the Germans to work to repair the damage they had done. Stalin thought that they would need to have a long occupation of Germany, but Churchill did not think that the Americans would 'stay very long'; a 'United Poland' might, however, be so employed. Churchill was quite happy to talk in terms of moving the populations of East Prussia and Silesia westwards in order to allow Poland's frontiers to encompass these parts of Germany. If the word 'appeasement' is to be used to describe Neville Chamberlain's attitude at Munich, a new coinage is needed to describe Churchill's at Moscow.

Churchill's defenders have been swift to use the argument that he 'had no choice', but it is an argument which their hero denied Chamberlain. Churchill had been swift to point out in 1938 that the very nature of Hitler's regime showed that he could not be trusted; a regime which imprisoned its opponents without trial and murdered them, and which broke its pledged word as easily as it gave it, could not be trusted to abide by international agreements, however freely entered into. Germany, Churchill had said, was a menace to the balance of power and it was obvious that her ambitions were greater than Hitler admitted; she must be stopped. Now she had been. But in order to do so Churchill had been forced to bankrupt Britain and to mortgage her future to the United States – and, in the process, he had helped raise the spectre of a menace which was even greater than the one he had destroyed, if only because there was now no balance of terror on the Continent. Hitler had had to keep an eye on the Soviet Union; who did Stalin have to keep an eye upon? This, then, was where the road to victory led.

Of course, if Stalin's words could be trusted despite the nature of the regime which he led, the British had at least salvaged something from the wreckage. Churchill told Roosevelt that 'we have found an extraordinary atmosphere of goodwill here'.[30] Churchill's 'naughty document' and some of the language which he had used with Stalin were omitted from the official record on the grounds that they might 'give the impression to historians that these very important discussions were conducted in a most unfitting manner'.[31] Apart from the prissiness of the English bureaucrat, the thing which is most likely to strike the historian about the whole business is a certain air of surrealism. On the morrow Eden and Molotov haggled about 'percentages', with the Foreign Secretary trying to increase Britain's 'share' in Bulgaria to '20%'. Churchill was cross with Eden for spoiling the 'good atmosphere' created by the previous day's discussions, but the Foreign Secretary explained that 'this was a real battle and I could not and would not give way'.[32] In fact, it was a profoundly unreal battle. Churchill saw in the 'percentages' a method of trying to co-operate with the Soviets in a manner which would also allow the Balkan (and other) states to choose their own Government. He tended to underrate the significance of Communist ideology, believing, naïvely, that 'the differences between our systems will tend to get smaller'.[33]

But even if Churchill's optimism about such matters had been realised, the fate of the Poles at Moscow showed how the new European order would have had to be created. Mikolajcik's position was little better than that occupied by President Hacha of Czechoslovakia in 1939; if no one used overt threats of force to him, the air of menace was undeniable. As so often, the British records provide an alibi for the Government. In discussions on 11 October, Churchill emphasised Britain's commitment to the country for whose sake she had entered the war,[34] but when it came to discussions with Mikolajcik and his Foreign Minister, Tadeusz Romer, on 13 October, it became clear what this meant in practice. Stalin wanted Mikolajcik to agree to a coalition which would be dominated by the Lublin Poles and he wanted him to agree to the Curzon line as a frontier; Churchill told Mikolajcik that he agreed with Stalin. Churchill tried to persuade Mikolajcik by pointing out the advantages which Poland would receive in the form of German territory in the west, and he warned the Pole not to 'estrange' the British Government. Mikolajcik, who was well aware of how his colleagues in London would regard the sacrifice of large slices of Polish territory, remained obdurate. Churchill then showed how little he understood Stalin's position by proposing that the Poles should accept the Curzon line as a compromise frontier until the peace conference. Stalin stated 'categorically' that he could never accept such a formula.

Churchill told Mikolajcik later that he was arguing for acceptance of the Russian proposals 'not because Soviet Russia is strong but because she is right'. This tends to detract from the excuse that Churchill had 'no choice'. Over the next three days Churchill and Eden put a great deal of pressure on Mikolajcik and his colleagues to give in to Stalin's demands, arguing that if they did, they would 'enjoy our full support';[35] they evidently did not see the irony in their own remarks. Churchill and Eden were wise not to specify what their 'support' would be worth in such circumstances; whatever 'percentage' of influence they may have thought they had in Poland, it was not proving to be worth even the proverbial bucket of warm spit which the American Vice-Presidency is said to be worth. Eventually Mikolajcik agreed to accept the Curzon line, provided that it was publicly stated that he did so under British duress, and the road seemed to be open for a Polish coalition.[36] Whatever it was, 'Tolstoy' was not Churchill's finest hour; had some other Premier negotiated such an agreement, his language can be guessed at.

At a private meeting with Mikolajcik on 14 October, Churchill had berated him with caring only about 'your own miserable interests', and of trying to wreck the Anglo-Soviet alliance: 'It is cowardice on your part.' He accused the Pole of refusing to face facts; 'never in my life have I seen such people'. Churchill accused Mikolajcik of being motivated by nothing more than 'hatred' of the Soviets, and quoted at him the words of General Anders to the effect that 'after having beaten the Germans we shall beat the Muscovites'. It was no doubt inconvenient to the Prime Minister that the 'unrealistic' Poles did not wish to surrender, but then it had been equally inconvenient for Hitler that an 'unrealistic' British Prime Minister had refused to do so in 1940. The Poles were certainly stubborn, but Mikolajcik was right to fear that his colleagues in London would never accept the terms – they did not, and he had to resign in November. It was odd that Churchill of all people was unable to understand an attitude of unreason based on national pride.[37] But Mikolajcik was not as unreasonable as the Prime Minister's reaction to the Polish Government's rejection of the Moscow plan made it appear. It was all very well offering Poland large slices of Germany, but that would mean permanent Polish–German enmity and force any government in Warsaw into dependence upon the Soviets in the future. In terms of *realpolitik* there was, perhaps, nothing else Churchill could have done, but he could have avoided making himself an accomplice to Stalin's ambitions; but then as he left Moscow in buoyant mood, he can hardly be said to have pressured the Poles because he 'had no choice'.

Upon his departure from Russia, Churchill sent a message telling Stalin that he was 'refreshed and fortified by the discussions', which had proved that 'there are no matters which cannot be adjusted between us when we meet together in frank and intimate discussion'.[38] Churchill left Russia still making 'his plans in the faith that Stalin's word is his bond'.[39] It made Chamberlain at Heston airport sound positively pessimistic. There was, of course, the question of how the Americans would react when they learnt of the agreements. But since Harriman had been present at few meetings and he was never officially informed of the 'percentages', Roosevelt could pursue his favourite line of appearing to agree with whatever his allies had decided. It was only in December, when the Greek Communists attempted a coup, that the American attitude became clear.

One diplomatic problem had been settled whilst Churchill was in Moscow. Eden had always feared that, at the end of the day, the Americans would steal a march on the British when it came to finally recognising the French Committee as the Government of France, and so it proved. Churchill, at Eden's behest, had put the arguments for such a course of action to Roosevelt on 14 October.[40] The President was being advised by Hull that the British would use America as a scapegoat for not recognising the Committee at an earlier date, and the Secretary of State was now advocating recognition. It is symptomatic of Roosevelt's casual approach, as well as of the sloppiness of American diplomacy, that whilst the President was telling Churchill on 19 October that recognition should not be granted yet,[41] Hull was telling the American Ambassador in Paris that such action was imminent.[42] The confusion arose from the fact that Roosevelt's condition for recognition was the declaration by de Gaulle of a 'zone of the interior', that is of a return to civilian rule; Roosevelt thought that this was going to happen some time in the future, whilst Hull was aware that it was imminent – and assumed that Duff Cooper would be receiving similar instructions. But Cooper, of course, was bound by Churchill's adherence to Roosevelt's line, and he was suitably shocked to discover on 20 October that the Americans would be extending recognition to de Gaulle almost immediately.[43] By a series of undignified scrambles, the British eventually caught up with the Americans. There was a moment of high farce at the last minute when an out-of-touch Roosevelt sent Churchill a telegram on 22 October which implied that recognition was still some days away, and the Prime Minister, with Cooper primed for the morrow, tried to withdraw to the President's now untenable position.[44] But the episode simply went to show how far Churchill would go to stay in step with Roosevelt, even when he was confused and out of date. On 23 October the Committee was recognised as the Provisional Government.

This action cleared the way for Churchill to make a formal visit to Paris in an attempt to rescue something from the quagmire of his relations with de Gaulle; for a man who put such store on personal relationships as being the stuff which oiled the wheels of diplomacy, Churchill had let his with de Gaulle reach a point of no return – and for nothing. De Gaulle hoped that the visit to Paris would mark the start of France's rehabilitation as a Great Power, but Churchill was determined that it should be nothing more than a ceremonial occasion – and he banned, in advance, any discussion of the idea of a 'western bloc'.[45] De Gaulle was, in consequence, 'much offended at what he regards as the neglect of France and at the extent of co-operation between the PM & Stalin & the President'.[46] The march down the Champs Elysées was an emotional moment for Churchill, but as a sign of anything for the future it was barren of significance. When it came to a choice between Europe and the Atlantic, Churchill had already cast his lot in with the Americans.

Churchill's American policy had two objectives, and the rhetoric which he habitually employed skilfully disguised the fact that only one of them was ever achieved. He wanted American support to defeat Germany, but he also wanted it to maintain British power; the Americans were only willing to give it for the first objective. Churchill's assumption that at bottom Anglo-American interests were the same in war and peace, was simply that – an assumption. The extent to which this was based upon Churchill's own relationship with Roosevelt was shown by his 'indescribable relief' when the President was victorious on 7 November. This meant that 'our comradeship will continue and will help to bring the world out of misery'.[47] But 'comradeship' did not mean to Roosevelt what it meant for Churchill, as events towards the end of the year showed.

The most famous example of Anglo-American disagreement, and the most public, came in December over British armed intervention in Greece to crush a Communist-inspired attempt at a coup, but this was only one of a number of issues which caused Anglo-American acrimony. At the international civil aviation conference at Chicago in November, British delegates refused to concede American demands for complete freedom of competition between airlines on all routes. When an impasse was reached, Roosevelt reminded Churchill of the effect which British obstinacy might have upon the progress of future lend-lease legislation through Congress;[48] in the face of such a threat, the British gave way. A similar fate awaited Churchill over the long-running American demand that the British should help them to put pressure on the Perónist regime in Argentina by cutting their supplies of beef from that source. That the Americans should have been willing, for political reasons, to reduce the already exiguous food supplies of their major ally, was as clear a sign as anyone could have wanted of the reality of the Anglo-American relationship. At American insistence the British had agreed not to negotiate any long-term food contract with the Argentines, but when the State Department seemed to be threatening the British with trade sanctions for not fully complying with American wishes, even Churchill was moved to protest.[49]

By themselves such matters would have amounted to no more than a few straws in the wind, but the signs were that there were whole haystacks beginning to be thrown about by the turbulence. Churchill's response to Roosevelt's warning over the civil aviation agreement showed the extent to which the Prime Minister was hoping that the Americans would behave as honorary Englishmen. He told Roosevelt on 28 November that he could not agree to American demands in full, and pleaded for American generosity: 'You will have the greatest navy in the world,' he told Roosevelt, and along with it the 'greatest air force', the 'greatest trade' and 'all the gold'; but these things did not 'oppress my mind with fear because I am sure the American people under your re-acclaimed leadership will not give themselves over to vainglorious ambitions, and that justice and fair-play will be the light that guides them'.[50] In other words Churchill was hoping that the Americans would behave in a way different to any other Great Power in history. It was a sorry ending for the man who had preached the virtues of the balance of power, but he had not then understood Chamberlain's reluctance to call in America to rectify that balance; Churchill was now in a better position to appreciate his predecessor's dilemma.

As Churchill surveyed the range of issues upon which American co-operation was vital, he became increasingly concerned that the co-operation seemed to be on their terms; it was not, as he told Smuts on 3 December, 'so easy as it used to be for me to get things done'.[51] Whether it was in the Far East, a sphere which the Americans had always dominated and where they showed little liking for the British-led campaign in Burma, or whether it was in Europe, where the Allied advances in Italy and north-west France were slowing down, the 'war-situation' was 'serious and disappointing'. His hopes for another meeting with Roosevelt having been dashed by the latter's insistence on a tripartite meeting, Churchill was reduced to sending him long telegrams on the various points at issue. Churchill had not liked the American tactic of advancing on a broad front in north-west Europe, but he had gone along with it, nor had he liked the American insistence on 'Anvil/Dragoon', but that too had gone through; now the Allied armies were stuck. Great plans for assaults in the Bay of Bengal on the Japanese, or across the Adriatic, had 'equally been set back'. When 'these realities' were contrasted with 'the rosy expectations of our peoples in spite of our joint efforts to dampen them down', the question arose: '"What are we going to do about it?"'[52] Hamstrung in so many areas by dependence upon America, Churchill was about to discover that even in those areas where he still felt able to exercise the right to unilateral action, the disapproval of his allies could be a hindrance.

Since 'Tolstoy' Churchill had happily proceeded on the basis that 'having paid the price we have to Russia for freedom of action in Greece, we should not hesitate to use British troops to support the Royal Hellenic Government'.[53] Thus it was that when, on the evening of 4 December, news came through from Athens of what looked like an attempted Communist coup, Churchill did not hesitate. His mood towards the Communists in Greece and Italy had hardened as a result of his 'deal' with Stalin; indeed, so 'vehement' were his 'denunciations of Communism, and in particular of ELAS and EAM in Greece' that Mrs Churchill sent him a note before lunch on 4 December 'begging him to restrain his comments'.[54] But there was no restraining him later that day when the news from Athens reached him. Pierson Dixon showed him a Foreign Office draft to the British commander, General Scobie, but the Prime Minister dismissed it as 'not nearly strong enough'. The time had come, he declared, for Scobie 'to take over law and order and to disarm the ELAS by force'. He cleared this with Eden and then 'settled down to draft his instructions, sitting gyrating in his armchair and dictating on the machine to Miss Layton, who did not bat an eyelid at the many blasphemies with which the old man interspersed his official phrases'. Churchill was in 'a bloodthirsty mood, and did not take kindly to suggestions that we should avoid bloodshed if possible'.[55] He did not finish dictating until 4 a.m., and Colville did not think that 'these late hours' improved 'the quality of his work'.[56] He told Scobie to treat Athens 'as if you were in a conquered city where a local rebellion is in progress', and that whilst it 'would be a great thing for you to succeed in this without bloodshed if possible', he should not hesitate to shed blood if it were necessary.[57] In a phrase which typified his attitude towards such matters, Churchill told the British Ambassador, Rex Leeper, that 'This is no time to dabble in Greek politics or to imagine that Greek politicians of varying shades can affect the situation.'[58]

Whatever Greek 'politicians' could or could not do, such an attitude, and the subsequent use of force by Scobie, outraged American politicians. Cordell Hull's long sojourn at the State Department had ended on 27 November, and he had been replaced by a protégé of Hopkins, Edward Stettinius. The choice of Stettinius in place of the politically more independent James Byrne was taken as an indication of Roosevelt's 'intention to conduct his own foreign policy'. Young, 'jovial' and 'energetic', Stettinius was the 'exemplar of glad-handing, back-slapping, vigorous American executive', a welcome contrast to the 'tired old men' and the 'Europeanised diplomats so abhorrent to American people'.[59] A man of 'vast affability' and a 'sincere desire to be a friend of all the world',[60] Stettinius reacted to the British intervention in Greece with an indignation which accurately reflected the feelings of his fellow Americans; high morality and ignorance make a powerful cocktail. American public opinion was not only critical of such a display of power-politics, but it also suspected that the British wished to 'impose a specific – more or less reactionary – pattern upon Europe'.[61] On 5 December the State Department issued a communiqué which criticised the British for interfering in the internal politics of Italy, by trying to prevent Count Sforza being made Italian Foreign Minister, and for intervening in Greece. To judge from Churchill's reaction, thoughts of straws and camels' backs cannot have been far from his mind.

On the same day (6 December) as Churchill sent Roosevelt his jeremiad about the state of the Allied war effort, he found himself sending a protest about the 'strictures' of the State Department. Churchill told Roosevelt that as a result he would have to answer questions in Parliament, 'and I hope you will realise that I must have all liberty in this matter'. It proved impossible to resist the temptation of contrasting his own behaviour with that of the State Department: 'I feel . . . entitled to remind you that on every single occasion in the course of this war I have loyally tried to support any statements to which you were personally committed.' Churchill had indeed supported the President over Darlan, over Russian demands for a share of the Italian Fleet and on other occasions; now he could see what reward he would receive. He was, he told Roosevelt, 'much astonished at the ascerbity [*sic*] of the State Department's communiqué'. For the Americans to issue such a 'public rebuke' to the British, when they had never said anything so harsh about the Soviets, was hardly fair.[62]

Churchill's attitude towards the Soviet Union at this time is a subject of some interest in view of his later role as the fugleman of the Cold War. Moran records him as 'havering', but has his attitude hardening by the end of the year;[63] the truth would seem to be more complex. Churchill placed a good deal of reliance upon the engagements into which he and Stalin had entered at Moscow. He was not, of course, certain that the Soviet leader would stand by them, but he was well aware of how much depended upon whether or not Stalin could be trusted. The resignation of Mikolajcik, and the failure of his own attempts to broker a Soviet-Polish settlement, had not shaken Churchill's faith in the Soviet alliance. In the light of events in Athens Eden wanted Churchill to open talks with the Soviets, but Churchill preferred to rely upon the 'Tolstoy' settlement. There was, Churchill told the Cabinet on 7 December, 'little question' that 'under present circumstances, Communist influence, under Russian patronage, was in due course, even without specific action by Russia, likely to establish itself throughout the Balkan peninsula, save possibly in Greece'.[64] Back in October 1942, when he had been resisting Eden's efforts to get him to think about the post-war world, Churchill had written: 'of course we shall have to work with the Americans in many ways, and in the greatest ways'; it would, he had added, 'be a measureless disaster if Russian barbarism overlaid the culture and independence of the ancient states of Europe'.[65] Now Britain was in sight of such a 'disaster', and events in Greece and their aftermath hardly suggested that 'working with the Americans' was going to provide a way out. Churchill had wanted 'victory at all costs'; now he seemed about to get what he had wanted, at the cost of everything he had stood for.

52

Anglo-America?

'Suspicion of British despotism in Europe is now thoroughly awakened,' the British Embassy in Washington reported on 10 December;[1] it was not only in America that such suspicions were aroused. American identification of British policy with Churchill was, in many ways, unfortunate – if only because it was likely to give rise to such suspicions. Churchill's partiality for monarchy as a form of government was not shared by Eden and many of his colleagues. Churchill was inclined to blame 'American and modernising pressure' in 1919 for making the Allies drive out the Hapsburgs and Hohenzollerns and thus creating a vacuum which 'gave the opening for the Hitlerite monster to crawl out of the sewer on to the vacant thrones'; he was aware that his views were probably 'very unfashionable', but he held on strongly to them.[2] Eden and the Foreign Office worried that Churchill's attitude would land them in trouble in a Europe radicalised by the experience of German occupation and total war. The Foreign Secretary had argued that King George II should agree to a Regency long before British troops entered Greece,[3] but he was thwarted by Churchill, who described himself as the King's 'friend'.[4] With the British backing the King, ELAS–EAM could (and did) claim that an attempt was being made to force a 'reactionary regime' on Greece; this was a view easily shared by liberal public opinion on both sides of the Atlantic.

The cruel realities of the situation in the Balkans, where the Communists used their position to fight other resistance groups, had never been brought before an Allied public opinion nurtured on tales of derring-do by heroic resistance fighters – which made the spectacle of British troops firing at such people all the more disturbing.[5] Attlee wrote to Eden on 7 December questioning Leeper's reports from Athens,[6] and the liberal press in both Britain and America attacked British policy, especially after the contents of Churchill's message to Scobie on 5 December were 'leaked'. But 'British policy' was not quite what Churchill's attitude made it seem. Churchill's view, which was that the King should be restored and that Scobie should put down any 'rebellion', was not actually shared by many of his own colleagues. The Prime Minister was able to suppress any rebels in the Commons, but he could not do so in a manner which satisfied many of his supporters; and, as Dalton noted, many Labour MPs were 'unduly sensitive to manner, as against substance'.[7]

Sir Richard Acland, the leader of the Commonwealth Party which had won by-elections at the Government's expense, put down an amendment to the King's speech which regretted that it contained no assurances that British forces would not be used to 'disarm the friends of democracy in Greece'. When the debate was held on 8 December, Churchill had a good answer to this, but it was one which on his lips failed to disarm all criticism. He was on ground common to all in declaring, picturesquely, that 'Democracy is no harlot to be picked up in the street by a man with a tommy gun', but his own obvious support for George II failed to erase Labour suspicions that Britain was supporting monarchists against Republicans.[8] Churchill seemed 'in rather higher spirits than the occasion warranted', and Harold Nicolson did not think that 'he quite caught the mood of the House, which at its best was one of distressed perplexity, and at its worst one of sheer red fury'.[9] Macmillan described Churchill's speech as a 'superb Parliamentary performance', but as not very 'profound'.[10] The Prime Minister was fortunate that his opponents had framed their censure motion to include the whole of British policy in Europe rather than simply in Greece, which might have created more trouble; the Government won with only thirty MPs voting for the motion of censure.

However, that solved none of Churchill's real problems. Despite the advice of Macmillan, Eden and General Alexander that negotiations for a Regency should be opened, Churchill persisted in maintaining that the crisis could be solved by military means.[11] But this laid him open to continuing criticism – and made him vulnerable to an order from the American, Admiral King, that none of his vessels should be used in ferrying British troops and their supplies to Greece.[12] Worried by the Anglo-American schism which was beginning to open, Churchill had sought once more to use Harry Hopkins as an intermediary. He told him not to be 'misled' by the fact that fewer than 300 MPs had voted for the Government: 'I could have had another 80 by sending out a three-line whip.' The British had been 'set upon, and we intend to defend ourselves'. Churchill felt that he had 'a right to the President's support in the policy we are following. . . . It grieves me very much to see signs of our drifting apart at the time when unity becomes even more important.'[13] His fury at the news of Admiral King's actions knew no bounds. Churchill drafted a message to Roosevelt which was tougher than anything he had written since the American decision to go ahead with 'Operation Dragoon'. King's decision might, he warned, 'produce a disaster of the first magnitude, which might endanger all the relations between Great Britain and the United States'; he went on to say that he was sure 'you have never seen these orders'.[14] But he was persuaded to tone down the terms of the telegram and, before sending it, decided to telephone Hopkins directly; he thought that there was less risk in doing this than 'in leaving matters in their present condition'. Churchill thought that it was unlikely that they would be listened in to by the Germans, 'but even if we are what can they do that would be worse than the American ships being cut out of the traffic and an open breach between Britain and the United States becoming known?'[15]

The telephone line was so bad that Hopkins could not make out 'what the Prime Minister was talking about', but he 'sounded as though he was very angry and stirred up about something'.[16] What Churchill was trying to tell Hopkins was that he wanted some 'word of approval spoken by the United States in favour of the Allied intervention in Athens';[17] but that was just what he was not going to get. Hopkins enquired into the business of Admiral King's order and told Halifax that he was sure that Roosevelt had never seen it. Hearing that Churchill was likely to be making a 'very strong protest' to the President, Hopkins asked Halifax to make sure that it was not sent. It would, Hopkins said 'serve no useful purpose but merely complicate the Greek situation further'; he added, for good measure, that 'public opinion about the whole Greek business in this country was very bad and that we felt that the British Government had messed the whole thing up pretty thoroughly'.[18] Roosevelt telegraphed on 13 December that his 'role in this matter' was 'that of a loyal friend and ally', but that 'limitations' were imposed upon the 'help' he could give by 'the traditional policies of the United States' and by 'the mounting adverse reaction of public opinion'. With an 'ally' like that, Churchill scarcely needed opponents. The best Roosevelt could do was to suggest that the King should approve the establishment of a Regency.[19]

It was just this solution which Eden was trying to foist upon the Prime Minister, and he received help from Macmillan, who persuaded Alexander to telegraph that a military solution was out of the question; the only solution, he telegraphed on 11 December, was to get the Archbishop of Athens, Damaskinos, appointed as Regent.[20] But Churchill would not buy this solution from Eden, Alexander or even Roosevelt, and it was largely due to his own pig-headedness that the crisis went on as long as it did. Churchill still wanted to solve the crisis by using the military, and he feared that the Archbishop would simply be used as a tool of the left – although whence he derived this idea is unclear.[21] Macmillan was soundly rebuked for recommending a Regency,[22] whilst Roosevelt was told that George II would not be deserted by the British.[23] To the growing frustration of the Foreign Office, Churchill continued to state with 'vehemence opinions based on no ascertained facts' such as, ' "I won't instal a Dictator – a Dictator of the Left". '[24] As Churchill 'rambled on' in this way at Cabinet on 21 December Eden, who was becoming infuriated at his attitude, told him that if the Cabinet had no confidence in Leeper, 'they had better say so and say the same of [the] Foreign Secretary at the same time'. Churchill replied, 'rather mournfully for him, that there was no doubt of Cabinet's support of Foreign Secretary. What was in doubt was Cabinet's confidence in him.'[25]

That this should have been so was hardly surprising. Leeper, Macmillan, Alexander and the Foreign Office were all advising in favour of a Regency and Churchill, with the sole support of Field Marshal Smuts, was holding out against it. Indeed, as Cadogan told Colville on 21 December, the 'PM was creating a deplorable impression in Cabinet now because he would not read his papers and would talk on and on'; Churchill was 'hopelessly overtired', and Colville feared that 'at seventy his powers of recuperation may not be very good'.[26] In fact, as Churchill had already proved, his powers of recuperation were remarkable, but there can be no doubt that as the realities of the 'brave new world' were borne in upon him, he fought them with a growing sense of weariness. Churchill believed in monarchy, the new age did not. In pursuit of his romantic dreams the Prime Minister was provoking a crisis with his Foreign Secretary and with the Americans.

Churchill's tiredness contributed to further complications in Anglo-American relations when he made a statement in the House about the state of Polish affairs on 15 December. Preoccupied by Greece, Churchill 'couldn't think of anything new to say' on Poland 'and so inserted long quotations from his own earlier speeches and a certain amount of padding about the Sybilline books'; he then decided not to give a speech at all, changing his mind yet again the following morning.[27] The 'Sybilline books' remained, but so did a passage which gave offence to the Americans. Churchill's efforts to persuade Stalin to exercise a moderating effect on the Lublin Poles, following Mikolajcik's resignation, had fallen upon the usual stony ground. Stalin had replied on 9 December accusing Mikolajcik of being a front-man for 'émigré' terrorists. He had dismissed the 'émigré Government' as unworthy of 'serious attention' and advocated building up 'the national Committee in Lublin'.[28] Churchill made plain to the House his support for the Soviet proposals about future frontiers, and he regretted that the 'attitude of the United States has not been defined with the same precision which His Majesty's Government have thought it wise to use'.[29]

It was clear from the British Embassy reports that what prevented even those American newspapers which were worried about the 'Red Menace' from supporting British policy in Greece were suspicions that Churchill himself wanted to restore George II to his throne.[30] Now his remarks on Poland produced a similarly 'mixed reaction', with the 'Russophobes' who supported Britain on Greece recoiling from the 'betrayal' of Poland.[31] Roosevelt was not best pleased to find himself at the centre of a political storm which he had steered hard to avoid. Hopkins told Churchill that 'public opinion here has rapidly deteriorated' as a result of the Greek situation and his own statement on Poland. Hopkins said that he did not know what Roosevelt and Stettinius 'may be compelled to say publicly', but warned that 'it is quite possible that one or both of them will have to proclaim their determination in unequivocal terms to do everything we can to seek a free world and a secure one'.[32] Hopkins was a useful channel for both Churchill and Roosevelt to express feelings which would have been out of place in a more formal telegraphic exchange. Roosevelt warned Churchill that he might come under 'strong pressure' to make the American position clear, and asked whether there would be any point in his trying to persuade Stalin not to recognise the Lublin Government.[33] Roosevelt released to the press the text of a letter which he had sent to Mikolajcik on 17 November, which gave a 'broad outline' of the 'general position of the United States'.[34] This was accompanied by an official statement which tried to square all possible circles. For the 'Russophobes' and the Polish vote, there was a ringing declaration that America 'stands unequivocally for a strong, free, and independent Polish state with the untrammeled right of the Polish people to order their internal existence as they see fit'; but for the British and the Russians there were paragraphs about America recognising frontier agreements entered into by 'the United Nations directly concerned'. The vagueness about whether America agreed to the principle of compensating Poland at Germany's expense distressed the British, but it was all they were going to get out of Roosevelt before another summit meeting.[35]

The need for such a summit meeting was obvious, but Stalin had steadfastly refused to be drawn from Russia; so, just before Christmas, Churchill and Roosevelt agreed to meet him at Yalta in the Crimea.[36] If the 'Big Three' were (somewhat blasphemously) to be compared with the Trinity, then Churchill was 'the Holy Ghost' – 'because he flies around so much,' as one wag put it. No sooner had he covenanted to go to Yalta than the septuagenarian Prime Minister decided that he was going to go to Greece. Alexander had reinforced his own earlier advice that a purely military solution was impossible, and with Churchill still unwilling to accept Damaskinos as sole regent, the only way out of an impasse was to go to Athens himself. Eden made it clear that King George II was concealing evidence about the state of opinion inside Athens, which shook the Prime Minister's confidence in his 'friend'.[37] Thus it was that Churchill and Eden found themselves in Athens on Christmas Day.

Churchill's own concentration on the position of the King and his unjustifiable suspicions of the Archbishop were the chief obstacles in the way of Britain acting as power-broker in Greek politics. Churchill's main concern was that 'if the powers of evil prevail in Greece . . . we must be prepared for a quasi-Bolshevised Russian-led Balkan peninsula', which might spread to Italy and Hungary.[38] But he had already conceded, in effect, Bulgaria and Romania to Russia, and there seemed little likelihood of Tito not coming out on top in Yugoslavia, so, despite his anti-Bolshevik rhetoric, what the Prime Minister was engaged upon was an exercise in damage limitation. Thus far Stalin had, so it appeared, kept to his word on Greece, as ELAS–EAM seemed to be getting no help from that source. Once in Athens, Churchill's penchant for conducting diplomacy in terms of personalities proved a welcome salvation for Eden's policies. The Prime Minister immediately took to the tall, heavily built Damaskinos, and by Christmas night Macmillan was recording in his diary that 'Winston seemed to like the Archbishop and to have got over his distrust of my recommendations'.[39] The forthright denunciation by Damaskinos of the atrocities committed by ELAS converted Churchill to his cause, and he asked him to preside over a conference the following day at the British Embassy.[40]

There was some doubt as to whether ELAS would agree to take part in any conference, but soon after Churchill began speaking at its opening session, 'three shabby desperadoes' arrived. It was a dramatic scene, illuminated by the chiaroscuro glow of the hurricane lamps, which provided the only source of light. Churchill in air commodore's uniform, with his cigar firmly in place, sat there, overshadowed by the massive figure of the Archbishop, who was made all the more imposing by his tall head-dress and his great flowing beard. Facing them in the crowded and ill-lit room were the shabby but grim figures representing the other protagonists in a civil war which was bitter, even by Greek standards. The background 'music' was provided by the noise of 'bursting mortar shells without'. Churchill left the ELAS representatives in no doubt as to his determination to pursue a military solution to the problem if necessary, but, as was so often the case with him once he actually met his opponents, his belligerent attitude softened somewhat. Churchill 'made it clear to the politicians that he did not mean us to be used for a reactionary policy'. He told his audience that Stalin had agreed with the British intervention (so much for the main hope of the Communists) and 'went a long way to suggest that Roosevelt also agreed' (so much for their other hope). Churchill left the Greeks to talk, telling them to come to an agreement – and to the surprise of Moran, who had heard the Prime Minister say that he would not shake hands with anyone from ELAS, Churchill proceeded to do just that before departing.[41]

Although Churchill had come to Athens in order to try to sort out a political dispute, the fact that the city was the scene of military action had its attractions for the Prime Minister. The night before the conference he had slept on HMS *Ajax* from which it was possible to see 'the smoke of battle in the street fighting west of the Piraeus', as well as to watch British aircraft 'strafe' ELAS strongholds on the hills outside Athens.[42] Churchill was dictating to one of his secretaries after lunch when shells landed near the ship: '"There – you bloody well missed us!" he cried. "Come on – try again!"'[43] There was further shelling when he got back to the *Ajax* after the conference, and Churchill could not resist ordering the captain to return fire: 'I bear the olive branch between my teeth. But far be it from me to interfere with military necessity.'[44]

Having been able to exercise his belligerent instincts in an entirely legitimate matter, Churchill was in fine fettle at a hastily convened press conference on 27 December. With thirty correspondents crowded into a small room at the Embassy, Churchill's secretary, Elizabeth Layton, had to sit behind him 'with my ear almost on his shoulder'; but even from that position she found it difficult to take down his words, such was the din of battle outside and the speed at which the Prime Minister spoke.[45] But his message was clear enough: Britain sought no selfish advantage from Greece, simply an end to anarchy. If the Greeks did not provide that before the 'Big Three' met early in the New Year, they were likely to find a temporary solution imposed upon them. Miss Layton was working on transforming her notes of all this into a communiqué when Colville told her that the Prime Minister wanted her at once. She found him sitting in an armchair 'wearing his coat and with a rug over his knees', whilst the 'mighty figure of the Archbishop' sat nearby. Damaskinos told Churchill that although he had done his best with their delegates, ELAS would only enter a coalition on terms which would allow them to dominate; it was a situation familiar from Poland, and one which was to become increasingly so in the years to come. Thus it was that Churchill did what the Foreign Office had been pleading with him to do for some time, which was to tell George II that the British would back Damaskinos as Regent – a solution which could have been adopted long before, had it not been for Churchill himself.[46]

If Greece provided an example of 'better late than never', the next meeting of the 'Big Three' was to provide an illustration that 'late' could mean 'never'. Churchill disliked the use of the term, the 'Big Three', and 'ticked off' Eden for using it; nor was the reason far to seek: 'It suggests [a] reminder of the Roman triumvirate, and Winston does not like to be regarded as Lepidus.'[47] Yet Lepidus he was, with Roosevelt cast as Mark Antony and Stalin as Augustus. With the onset of the Cold War, Yalta came to be condemned as a 'betrayal' by the western powers of Poland and eastern Europe. For this some explanations were proffered: Roosevelt was a tired, sick, old man, near unto death; whilst Churchill, who was also a tired man, was, according to taste, either too exhausted or too powerless to influence events.[48] But the pattern for Yalta had been set at Tehran, and the roots of Churchill's powerlessness lay in his own earlier decision to concentrate exclusively upon fighting the war; he had chosen to put all his eggs in the American basket, so it hardly behoved him to complain when the Americans ignored him. 'Surely the United States has never had a more persistent courtier than Churchill,' is how one commentator has put it;[49] but if Churchill had studied women the way he had studied warfare, he might have understood that ardent wooing is not always accompanied by a reciprocity of ardour. Just as he had before Tehran, Roosevelt rebuffed Churchill's desire for an Anglo-American meeting prior to Yalta; once more, under pressure, he yielded, but again, only to the extent of allowing a brief encounter.[50] If there was little place for Lepidus, that was partly his own fault.

Roosevelt's sight was fixed upon his vision of a United Nations Organisation, which, through the participation of the Great Powers on what would become the Security Council, would be an effective instrument for world peace. After all, with the destruction of the power of Europe, where the last two world wars had begun, the concentration of military power mainly in American and Russian hands was a welcome development. If America and Russia could stand together as friends, that would be enough to prevent another world war. Churchill's selfish imperial interests counted for nothing next to this vision, and Roosevelt certainly did not want to endanger it by seeming to be colluding with the old imperialist. The President's State of the Union address gave some indication of these things. American public opinion, to which Roosevelt was even more sensitive than most Presidents, had not liked the way in which their allies had behaved in Warsaw and Athens respectively; by late October only forty-seven per cent of Americans believed that it would be possible to trust Russia after the war – compared with fifty-six per cent in June.[51] The fears expressed by Hopkins to Churchill about American public opinion reacting adversely to British intervention in Greece were not imaginary. Roosevelt feared that his fellow Americans might react as they had at the end of the last world war and withdraw into isolation. He warned them of the dangers of such a course of action in his State of the Union address – that way lay 'the road to a third world war'. He dwelt upon the danger of 'power-politics' and cautioned the public against exaggerating the differences which existed between the Allies, and against simplifying the solutions to the complicated problems of Greece and Poland. In true Rooseveltian fashion, he spoke in terms of high-sounding generalities; despite pleas from Stettinius, there was no unequivocal statement that America would remain involved in world affairs. *Festine lente* remained the President's motto. Yalta would be an opportunity to establish a mood, to set the tone for post-war co-operation; there was no need for a complicated agenda or detailed advance discussions of the sort which the British wanted.[52] Roosevelt never lacked self-confidence; as he said to a friend apropos of Stalin and Yalta, 'I think if I give him everything I possibly can and ask for nothing from him in return, noblesse oblige, he won't try to annex anything and will work with me for a world of democracy and peace.' This is easily represented as simple-minded naïveté, but it reflected the 'style rather than the substance of Roosevelt's diplomacy';[53] Yalta would establish the 'mood music' for future Soviet-American relations.

Churchill had mortgaged Britain's future to his vision of Anglo-American co-operation. His whole policy, from 1929 onwards, had been predicated on the assumption that Britain was a Great Power and possessed the prestige first to hold on to her Empire, and then to organise a coalition against Hitler. The events of 1940 had delivered a shattering blow to these hopes, but Churchill had continued to insist that Britain behaved like the Great Power he was convinced she was. Like Canning, he would 'call in the new world to redress the balance of the old', but unlike Canning, Churchill really needed to do that. All the careful cultivation of Hopkins and Roosevelt, all the deference shown, even under severe strain, to the President, had been constituent parts of that policy. At Tehran, to Churchill's evident shock, Roosevelt had preferred to isolate him and to deal with Stalin directly. Lack of American support had pushed Churchill towards the 'percentages' deal with Stalin. The tone of the State of the Union address was a further cause of anger. '"What is all this about power-politics?"' Churchill asked irritably, opining that only the Americans actually practised that art. He was equally irritated to find that British behaviour in Greece had been bracketed with Soviet actions in Poland.[54] There was no sign either here, or in leakages in the American press which described Roosevelt as rebuking the British for their 'imperialism', of any 'special relationship'. And if there was no such thing, then Churchill had mortgaged the future for a chimera. During his so-called 'wilderness years' Churchill had accused first Baldwin and then Chamberlain of lacking the will to assert British power; 1940 had provided, in special circumstances, a demonstration of what willpower could achieve. But it could no more hold back the tide than could the commands of King Canute. Sceptical of 'these ideas of what is called a "Western bloc"',[55] Churchill had cultivated America and, with no support forthcoming from that source, he had been forced to appease Stalin over eastern Europe. Unless he could change this situation, he would have to continue in like vein. Those who talked about being 'Greeks in the new Roman Empire' would have done well to remember that the Greeks were, after all, slaves in that imperium.

The failure of the Americans to respond to his ideas of a 'special relationship' had left Churchill with no choice but to appease Stalin. The 'percentages' deal seemed to provide a *modus vivendi*, as Churchill told Eden in December: 'Considering the way the Russians have so far backed us up over what is happening in Greece, which must throw great strain on their sentiments and organisation, we really must not press our hand too far in Roumania.'[56] Churchill acknowledged that 'Communist influence' would dominate the Balkans, except in Greece;[57] Yalta would be just one more step towards the inevitable.

In May 1944, referring to the prospect of the 'communization of the Balkans', which Churchill feared, Eden pointed out that British policy in Greece and Yugoslavia had rather contributed to this end. 'We must', he had argued then, 'think of the after-war effect of these developments, instead of confining ourselves as hitherto to the short-term view of what will give the best dividends during the war and for the war.'[58] Implicit in this was a fundamental critique of British foreign policy during the war, and what frustrated Eden was the fact that that policy was far more a reflection of Churchill's views than his own. Churchill's interventions in foreign affairs were 'a series of romantic improvisations', and much though he might 'adore' Churchill, Eden was 'harassed by his interference'.[59] Churchill's waning powers matched those of the nation which he led – force of will was not, after all, a sufficient condition of success.[60] Much of his alarm at Roosevelt's State of the Union address stemmed from the fact that he had not read it properly,[61] and Churchill's combination of willpower and ignorance galled his highly strung Foreign Secretary. Eden himself was under immense pressure, and Sir Alexander Cadogan's criticisms of him were remarkably like his own observations about Churchill: 'He strides about the room, gabbling, and I, at least, can't hear what he says.'[62] A minute from Churchill which appeared to support Lord Cherwell against himself threw Eden into a paroxysm of rage. He threatened to resign if 'inexpert, academic opinions were sought on subjects to which he had given so much thought', and he 'ranted in a way' which Churchill had never 'heard him before'.[63] The Prime Minister managed to calm him down, but it was a sign of the strain which Eden was under.

The Foreign Secretary was particularly worried by what might happen at Yalta. With 'Stalin being the only one of the three who has a clear view of what he wants' and a 'tough negotiator' to boot, whilst Churchill was 'all emotion' and Roosevelt 'vague and jealous of others', a conference which took place without agendas or preliminary meetings would probably be 'chaotic'.[64] He pressed Churchill to get Roosevelt to agree to a meeting of Foreign Secretaries beforehand, on the model of the Moscow meeting before Tehran, and sent him a long list of topics which needed to be discussed. Eden foresaw 'dangers' in Roosevelt's habitual procrastination: 'Europe will take shape or break up while he stands by and it will be too late afterwards to complain. . . .'[65] But Roosevelt would go no further than to agree that there might be a meeting of Foreign Secretaries at Malta a few days before the conference; and with that the British had to be satisfied.[66]

The problem for Eden was that 'Europe' was already taking 'shape' – a shape determined in part by military actions, but also in part by Churchill's decisions. In late December, despite appeals from both Roosevelt and Churchill, Stalin decided to recognise the Lublin Poles as the Government of Poland; with the Red Army dominant in eastern Europe there was not much that the western powers could have done about this – even had they shared the same views.[67] In Yugoslavia, where Churchill's protégé, Tito, was now in a splendid political position, with the support of the Red Army adding steel to his demands, King Peter was forced, despite his own strong objections, to endorse an agreement between Tito and the Ban of Croatia, which lent a 'cloak of respectability' to what was likely to be a 'Communist dictatorship'.[68] With most of eastern Europe likely to come within Stalin's orbit, the only question was about the method by which this should happen. Nearly a decade before, Sir Nevile Henderson, the British Ambassador in Berlin, had argued that Germany's objectives in seeking to dominate central and eastern Europe were 'not in conflict with any direct British interest';[69] for this he had been condemned as 'naif'.[70] Now Churchill was assenting to the same proposition, substituting the name 'Stalin' for that of 'Hitler'. As in Henderson's case a caveat was entered: such ambitions must be secured 'peacefully'.[71] Yalta would help to determine whether what had not been possible with Hitler would be possible with Stalin.

The road had been a long one from Churchill's grandiose ideas of 1938 to the Chamberlain-like compromises of 1945, but after hard lessons, Churchill had learnt what Chamberlain had known then – which was that Britain unaided no longer possessed the power to determine the course of history. Chamberlain had tried to avoid becoming dependent upon America because he did not trust Roosevelt, nor did he think American aims were congruent with the interests of the British Empire. With his habitual impetuosity Churchill had sought to deny these things; he had discovered that he had been wrong. It remained only to be seen what could be saved from the wreckage. Henderson had observed in 1938 that, 'Right for right's sake doesn't count for anything any more, everything depends on the -ism or the -ology'; a 'conflict of philosophies' would be, he had told Halifax, 'almost as big a menace to world peace as the ambitions of dictators'.[72] At Moscow Churchill had gambled that the '-ology' and the '-ism' could be laid aside in a common pursuit of *realpolitik*. Eastern Europe was lost, but the west could still be saved. There were those in his Cabinet who would still fight the ideological battle of the 1930s and, having uprooted Fascism in Italy and Germany, wanted to go on to deal with its Iberian manifestations; Churchill gave them short shrift. The war had been fought to prevent the spread of German power, and there were already enough signs to suggest that too great a price might have been paid for that, but Churchill had no intention of pursuing Franco in Spain or Salazar in Portugal. Churchill feared that destabilising Franco would mean a Communist triumph in Spain, which would lead to the 'infection' spreading. But this was another powerful reason for keeping in well with Stalin:

At this time, every country that is liberated or converted by our victories is seething with communism. All are linked together and only our influence with Russia prevents their actively stimulating this movement, deadly as I conceive it to peace and also to the freedom of mankind.[73]

It was, perhaps, wise not to ask where the victory was in substituting for the undoubted menace of Fascism the equally deadly 'infection' of Communism.

That Churchill should have been 'rather depressed' in early January 1945 was, therefore, hardly surprising; the 'end of the war and the problems it will bring with it' were 'depressing'.[74] Attempts to persuade the Americans to launch some sort of offensive in the Balkans came to nothing,[75] whilst an offensive by the Germans in the Ardennes (the 'Battle of the Bulge') raised the prospect of the war in Europe dragging on into the summer. Roosevelt's evasiveness about a meeting between the two of them before Yalta hardly served to lift Churchill's gloom. When Hopkins came to London in early

January, it was almost possible to measure the difference in the temperature of Anglo-American relations from what it had been in the heady days of 1942. Then Hopkins had come as Roosevelt's right-hand man, and Churchill had used that relationship to try to establish his own close contacts with the President, but now Hopkins was a sick man whose influence with the President had waned. There was a symbolism in sending him to London to reassure Churchill in the aftermath of the differences between the two countries over Greece; it hardly suggested that the British occupied a very large place in the American view of the post-war world – nor did they.[76]

That the British had swapped 'appeasement' of Germany for 'appeasement' of America and Russia was not a perception confined to later historians. In a leading article on 30 December, the *Economist* had demanded that 'an end be put to the policy of appeasement'; if 'British policies and precautions' were to be 'traded against American promises, the only safe terms are cash and delivery'. The article described the Americans as thinking that the British spent 'half their time imitating Lord North [the Prime Minister who had lost the American colonies] and the other half of their time imitating Dr Schacht [Hitler's Minister of Economics who believed in a policy of national self-sufficiency]'.[77] American press opinion accused the British of being 'much too touchy', expressing the view that it all showed that the British felt 'for the first time politically and economically weak and inferior to the United States' – a 'bitter pill which the British still cannot bring themselves to swallow'.[78] Stettinius made the same point when he told Roosevelt that the article represented 'what is in the minds of millions of Englishmen ... the underlying cause is the emotional difficulty which anyone, and especially an Englishman, has in adjusting himself to a secondary role after having always accepted a leading role as his national right'.[79] These were the realities behind Churchill's diplomacy. The war which he had wanted to wage in order to assert Britain's role as a Great Power in stopping Fascism had served to expose the slenderness of the foundations upon which that power was based. For realising this and going to Munich, where he thought he could trust Hitler, Neville Chamberlain's reputation was blasted; for not realising it, and travelling the long road to Yalta, where this fundamental truth was once more revealed, even Churchill's immense prestige was to take a knock; but Stettinius was right in implying that what the British people were really protesting against was the realisation of their own powerlessness. Churchill had looked to 'Anglo-America' to redress the balance; what he got was Yalta.

53

Winston and the Argonauts

Yalta, or the Crimean conference as it was called officially, received the code-name 'Argonaut' – a classical reference to the tale of Jason and the Argonauts, who sailed beyond the Straits to Colchis where Medea and the Golden Fleece were to be found. Jason returned with the Golden Fleece; the latter-day Argonauts were to return with golden illusions. For Roosevelt, who had wanted Soviet participation in the United Nations and in the Far Eastern war against Japan, the conference seemed to have delivered the goods; if it was less successful for Churchill, who was unable to prevent his allies deciding on a large reparations bill to be paid by Germany, it still seemed to have produced agreements on Poland and on how to restore democracy to Europe.

Two images lodged immediately in the minds of the British delegation upon arrival at Yalta: the devastation of the Crimea by the war; and the frail, haggard appearance of the President. Roosevelt looked 'old and thin and drawn ... Everyone was shocked by his appearance and gabbled about it afterwards.'[1] At Vienna in 1815 Tsar Alexander I, Metternich of Austria and Castlereagh from England were the presiding deities as the survivors of the *ancien régime* redrew the map of Europe according to dynastic convenience. Their successors in 1919 at Versailles were President Wilson, Clemenceau and Lloyd George, when an attempt had been made to crown the triumph of a century of nationalism by creating a new Europe in its image. The double-edged nature of that weapon had been demonstrated by the rise of Hitler. Now three old men met by the sea-side to recreate a world out of the ruins of European civilisation. All Churchill's efforts to secure Anglo-American solidarity had come to naught and, on the eve of victory, it seemed doubtful what Britain was to gain from the 'Grand Alliance'. At the dinner on the first evening of the conference, 4 February, Churchill 'remarked that he was constantly being "beaten up" as a reactionary but that he was the only one of the three representatives present who could be thrown out of office at any time by the votes of his own people'. Stalin, to whom the idea of losing a general election must have come as something of a novelty, remarked that Churchill evidently feared the election results. Churchill 'replied that not only did he not fear them but he was proud of the right of the British people to change their government whenever they wished to do so'.[2] This was one of a number of shadows under whose pall Churchill worked at Yalta.

The war with Germany was expected to end by the summer, but the conflict with the Japanese would, it was thought, last another eighteen months – hence Roosevelt's eagerness to get the Soviets to enter that war. The Labour Party conference in December had approved a continuation of the coalition until the 'end of the war';[3] but did that mean the Japanese war? In September Churchill had been thinking in terms of an 'immediate election to follow Germany's surrender, his one remaining ambition being to run an election as a Conservative leader'.[4] With the analogy of Lloyd George's victory in 1918 very much in everyone's mind, the general expectation was that Churchill would win such an election; few Conservatives shared Macmillan's view that not only would the Conservatives lose,[5] but that it would do them good to do so, as defeat would allow them to 'come back reinvigorated'.[6] Churchill had no doubts about his fitness to fight an election, but others were not so certain. Amery, who had a longer experience of sitting in Cabinets than any Minister other than Churchill himself, did not find the Prime Minister an efficient chairman. Lloyd George, who shared Churchill's predilection for not reading his Cabinet papers in advance, had had 'an uncanny faculty for divining what it was about' after listening to one or two Ministers, but Churchill's self-absorption did not allow him to follow suit: 'Winston neither reads the papers or tries to collect opinions systematically and is a good deal slower on the uptake than L[loyd] G[eorge].' The consequence was that when Churchill was not talking himself, 'the thing is rather a bear garden' – with no one having any clear idea about what had been decided.[7] Amery was not alone in holding such views.

Churchill's habit of becoming obsessed with one issue became even worse in December when he was preoccupied with Greece, and it was partly this which drove the tidy-minded Attlee to protest to Churchill in January about the conduct of Cabinets. Quiet and unobtrusive, Attlee was the British equivalent of those grey men like Bormann and Molotov who also served more charismatic figures; but the comparison, by its absurdity, is more instructive for the differences which it reveals between the British political system and the others. Attlee was an easy man to underestimate, as Churchill's apocryphal comment that 'an empty taxi drew up and Attlee got out' reveals. Even within his own Party Attlee was overshadowed by his colleagues: the loud and extrovert Dalton, the ascetic-looking Sir Stafford Cripps, the ebullient cockney, Herbert Morrison, who would have been his own worst enemy had it not been for the heavyweight figure of the burly union leader, Ernie Bevin – these were all men who caught the public eye. In comparison, Attlee seemed a dull little man. But even dull little men have their uses; indeed, bureaucracies were invented by such people to give them a *raison d'être*. It was Attlee's unobtrusive efficiency as chairman of the various Cabinet committees on domestic policy that had allowed the coalition to articulate proposals on national health, unemployment and education which were to become the basis of a new consensus to which both Parties were to adhere in the future.

His civil servant's mind recoiled at the 'bear garden' which Cabinet meetings had become, and so, on 19 January, he sent Churchill a letter describing the 'present position' as 'inimical to the successful performance of the tasks imposed on us as a Government and injurious to the war effort'.[8]

It was characteristic of the man that Attlee should have typed the letter himself; his desire was to improve efficiency, not to create a political row. By typing the letter himself he ensured maximum secrecy for it – as well as minimum typing standards. Attlee accused Churchill of showing scant respect for his colleagues' views on domestic political matters. He complained of the long delays before the reports of Cabinet committees were discussed, and of the fact that, when they were, the Prime Minister had frequently not taken the trouble to read them. Time was then wasted in having to explain to Churchill what should already have been apparent to him, and 'not infrequently a phrase catches your eye which gives rise to a disquisition on an interesting point only slightly connected with the subject matter'; nor did Churchill's propensity to listen to advice from Bracken and Beaverbrook find favour in Attlee's eyes. These were comments with which Eden, Amery and Cadogan would have agreed; indeed, as Colville put it: 'Greatly as I love and admire the PM I am afraid there is much in what Attlee says, and I rather admire his courage in saying it.'[9] If the letter was typical of Attlee, the response to it said much about Churchill.

Churchill 'exploded'. He denounced Attlee's letter as a 'Socialist conspiracy' and drafted a 'sarcastic reply' in which he referred to the over-representation of the Socialists in the Government. Having discussed the letter with Clementine, Churchill then read it over the telephone to Beaverbrook. As 'John Martin said, "that is the part of the PM which I do not like"'. The fact that Clementine agreed with Attlee's comments merely made Churchill more morose. But after a good dinner his mood lightened, and with a film show in prospect he bade his staff to 'cast care aside' and 'not bother about Atler or Hitlee'.[10] 'And for the rest of the weekend the sun shone.'[11] Sarcastically, Churchill replied to Attlee's long letter by saying that he would always 'endeavour to profit by your counsels';[12] but as this would have meant a personality transplant, there was little chance of Churchill doing so. The bumptious schoolboy had grown into the insubordinate subaltern and then into the brash, self-confident politician, who believed that whatever he set his hand to he could achieve. Churchill remained the same 'Rogue elephant' who had been the despair of his friends and of two generations of civil servants; a man whose genius was, in Asquith's words, a 'zig-zag streak of lightning in the brain'. When set beside Balfour, Campbell-Bannerman and Asquith, let alone Baldwin and Attlee, Churchill was an 'exotic' on the British political scene, to be compared only with Lloyd George.

Lloyd George had beeen 'glad' that he was not in the War Cabinet; its members were 'yes men' compared to those with whom he had worked in the last war. Churchill was, he thought, 'blind to every essential fact which does not fit in with his ambitions'.[13] But this was a partial judgment. Lloyd George had always been prone to jealousy of Churchill's talents – and with both of them believing that they were 'watched over' and preserved for some 'great work', there was between them at once a bond and a sense of rivalry.[14] The 'Welsh Wizard' had stood aside in 1940, awaiting a recall to power, but on this occasion it was the turn of Churchill's 'guardian angel' to work overtime. Lloyd George's task in 1919 had been to try to create some sort of order out of chaos, and he had not found President Wilson much of a help; Churchill was now facing a not dissimilar situation. In 1939 the British had gone to war, more out of a sense of moral outrage than as the product of rational thought. Churchill had long been urging Britain's rulers to live up to their responsibilities and he had been dismissive of the constraints which Chamberlain had claimed restricted his power to act. Yet it had transpired that Chamberlain had been correct in supposing that Britain and France would find it difficult to win a war, and Tehran had showed what Yalta now confirmed, that the old Prime Minister had been right in thinking that the war would hand over power to the barbarian Soviets and the naïve Americans. Churchill may have had no choices available to him at Yalta, but since it was the outcome of a set of events which he had initiated, and since he had preached reliance on the Americans and alliance with the Soviets, it is difficult to have much sympathy for the predicament in which he found himself.

In the long, post-war triumph of the Churchillian version of the 1930s no episode came in for greater moral condemnation than Chamberlain's actions at Munich. How naïve of the Prime Minister to think that he could trust Hitler, and how weak and foolish of him to connive at handing over Czech territory to the evil regime of the Nazi dictator – thus went the line laid down in *The Gathering Storm* and a dozen or so imitators. Yet, on his return from Yalta, Churchill declared that Stalin was a 'person of great power, in whom he had every confidence'; Stalin, he declared, was not the man to embark on 'any adventures'.[15] The man of Yalta was ill-situated to comment on the man of Munich – the decline in British power was not something which a mere act of will could reverse.

Churchill had written to Eden on 25 January that the 'only hope for the world is the agreement of the Great Powers. If they quarrel, our children are undone.'[16] The chance of any combined Anglo-American agreement on the political matters to be discussed at Yalta went once it became clear, after Roosevelt's arrival in Malta on 2 February, that the President intended to maintain his pose as the 'honest broker'. Eden found that although he and Stettinius were 'in complete agreement on all major points', there was a crucial caveat to be added. The Americans were obsessed with the future 'World Council' and regarded the British preoccupation with Poland with suspicion; but as Eden saw clearly, 'unless the Russians can be persuaded or compelled to treat Poland with some decency there will not be a world council that is worth much'.[17] Churchill was able to get the military conversations to take on a political tone when he argued against the Combined Chiefs of Staff recommendation that the Allies should not advance beyond the frontiers of Italy. 'We should', he argued, 'occupy as much of Austria as possible as it was undesirable that more of Western Europe than necessary should be occupied by the Russians.'[18] The President showed little interest in the matter and, like his colleagues, doubted whether British fears that Poland's independence was at stake were justified.[19]

The flight to Russia was followed by a six-and-a-half-hour car journey to Yalta, by the end of which the western contingents were thoroughly tired. However, at the Vorontsov villa, where the British delegation was housed, there was a welcome in true comradely style – 'the table groaned with caviare and the pop of champagne bottles went on all the time like machine-gun fire'.[20] The magnificence of the architecture and the munificence of the rations were not matched by the domestic offices. Bedrooms were in short supply and there was only one bath and three wash-basins for the whole party, which meant that Churchill's secretaries found themselves queueing with 'impatient Generals and embarrassed Admirals, all carrying their shaving kit and wishing that their dressing-gowns had been long enough to cover their bare ankles'.[21] The Prime Minister's quarters were naturally more commodious, but it was not long before he was wishing that the dressing-gown with which he had clothed Anglo-American relations was a little less scanty.

The first plenary meeting took place on the afternoon of 5 February and, as it was mainly concerned with the military situation, it passed off well.[22] The most satisfying news to Stalin's ears was also the one which worried Churchill most – Roosevelt announced that he was going to withdraw all American troops from Europe within two years of the end of the war. Since the Allies had already decided that Germany was to be partitioned (even if they had not agreed on how this was to be done) into zones of occupation, this raised for Churchill the alarming prospect of Britain having to occupy the whole of western Germany by herself. It was to this pass that four years' devoted wooing of the Americans had brought the most Americanophile British Prime Minister of the century.[23] Nor were matters to improve materially when the conference turned to more political matters on the morrow.

The conference dinner that evening was the usual sumptuous affair at which it rained champagne and caviare – no London wartime rationing in the workers' state – but the atmosphere was not as good as usual. Roosevelt, who was looking both tired and ill, made a diplomatic *faux pas* when he told Stalin jovially that they all referred to him as 'Uncle Joe'. The old mass-murderer clearly felt that his dignity was being encroached upon and took umbrage.[24] Churchill was a great deal more good-natured about the verbal 'beating up' to which Roosevelt and Stalin subjected him as a 'reactionary', and he made what was possibly the only humane and sensible remark which any of the 'Big Three' uttered at the whole conference. Eden noted that Stalin's 'attitude to small countries' was 'grim, not to say sinister';[25] Churchill's comment on the subject was to the point: 'The eagle should permit the small birds to sing and care not wherefor they sang.'[26]

Churchill never did cotton on to the fact that his imperialism was as foreign to the Americans as the Soviet attitude towards the 'small birds' was to himself. The President's main concern was the one which occupied much of the time at the second plenary meeting on 6 February – the composition of the United Nations Organisation. In this concept Wilsonian Utopianism had come again. The Dumbarton Oaks conference at the end of 1944 had put in a good deal of the spade-work, but the Soviets had not agreed upon the question of voting rights in the proposed Security Council. Because of the experience of the League of Nations, the architects of this new piece of Utopian idealism wished to ensure that the Great Powers would be able to take effective action to keep world peace – hence the idea of a Security Council upon which they would be represented. But who should 'they' be? To Roosevelt's evident pleasure, Stalin expressed himself in favour of the new organisation; his only doubts, he said, were about how to prevent any future conflict between the Great Powers. Agreement was thus reached about the operation of any veto and about membership of the United Nations, with the two Soviet republics of Byelorussia and the Ukraine being allowed to join in their own right.[27]

The meeting on 6 February also discussed the question of the future of Poland. To say that Churchill's position was not a strong one would be a gross understatement. It was not simply that the Red Army was already in Poland and that Roosevelt began the discussion by saying that he had a 'distant view' on the Polish question, because even before Yalta Churchill had in fact ceded the moral high ground.[28] The pressure which had been put on Mikolajcik following the Moscow conference had led to his resignation since many of his compatriots felt that they had already conceded quite enough under British 'persuasion'. The British were now asking the London Poles to agree to a coalition with the Lublin 'Government', having already stated that they recognised the Curzon line as the eastern frontier, with Lvov going to the Soviets. It was hard to see what gnats there were for the British to strain at since they had already masticated several tough 'camels'. There is a sense in which what the British wanted at Yalta was the Soviets to save what was left of their face by agreeing to some sort of 'democratic' government, but there was, behind that, the strong feeling that Soviet behaviour over Poland would act as a touchstone with regard to Soviet intentions in the future.[29]

Stalin had all the cards in his hand. Not only were his troops in Poland and his allies clearly not agreed upon their policy on the subject, but the Americans were talking about withdrawing their troops from Europe within two years of the end of the war. Churchill declared in his most ringing tones that he rated the 'frontier question as less important' than the establishment of a 'strong, free and independent Poland'. He 'trusted' Stalin's assurances that he wanted the same objectives and hoped that they could, together, work out a solution to the problem.[30] Roosevelt wrote to Stalin after the meeting telling him 'in all frankness what is on my mind'. As might have been expected, the President's thoughts were dominated by the fact that if agreement was not reached, 'it puts all of us in a bad light throughout the world', and it would lead 'our people to think there is a breach between us, which is not the case'.[31] To a master of *realpolitik* like Stalin there was nothing very much here to resist him. If, as was suggested by some historians during the Cold War era, that event was precipitated by the Americans and the British misunderstanding innocent Soviet desires for security as something more menacing, it can hardly be alleged that Yalta gave Stalin much food for thought. Despite the fact that they raised the issue at eight or nine of the plenary sessions, the most the western allies could extract from the master of the Kremlin was the vague promise that 'all democratic and anti-Nazi parties' would have the right to participate in 'free and unfettered elections' based on universal suffrage and the secret ballot.[32]

Churchill expressed anxiety about stuffing the 'Polish goose so full of German food that it died of indigestion'; but since Stalin saw an end of Polish Governments being able to balance between Russia and Germany, he was not disposed to take such fears very seriously. Nor was that seared conscience much touched by Churchill's reservations about having to move masses of Germans to the west; '[He] observed that there were no Germans in these areas, as they had all run away.'[33] That Churchill and Roosevelt could still convince themselves that Stalin would allow really 'free and unfettered elections' in Poland after such remarks is more a testimony to the power of self-delusion than to anything else. Eden was not impressed with either his chief or yet with Roosevelt. The latter had arrived at the conference in an aeroplane aptly named the 'Sacred Cow'. After the event there were plenty of voices raised to the effect that it was a shame that Roosevelt had been in declining health, but Eden observed nothing to make him think that Roosevelt's decisions or actions were distorted by the state of his health.[34]

The refusal to concert action in advance with Churchill was, along with his desire to act as 'honest broker', a typical Rooseveltian manoeuvre. On his pet subject, the United Nations, he proved capable of ensuring that he got his way. Moreover, without telling the British or the Chinese, he negotiated an agreement with the Soviets to cover their entry into the war in the Far East.[35] If the President seemed 'vague' and appeared not to have done his homework on the documents before him, there was nothing very new about either phenomenon – they were part and parcel of the way Roosevelt habitually worked. He had supreme confidence in his ability to conjure up a satisfactory post-war settlement. But Roosevelt's talents were not displayed to their best advantage in detailed negotiation with a man like Stalin, who knew what he wanted. Much the same could be said of Churchill. As Eden delicately put it, 'Winston Churchill's strengths lay in his vigorous sense of purpose and his courage. . . . He was also generous and impulsive, but this could be a handicap at the conference table.' Churchill was apt to behave as he did in Cabinet: he liked to do most of the talking without listening to the views of others, and he 'found it difficult to wait for, and seldom let pass, his turn to speak. The spoils in the diplomatic game do not necessarily go to the man most eager to debate.'[36] Stalin, 'hooded, calm, never raising his voice', was a match for either of the western leaders. His objectives needed to be fixed only by reference to himself – there was no public opinion and no free press to bother the leader of the 'workers' state'.

At the fourth plenary session on 8 February the western leaders put their view on Poland to the Soviets, with Roosevelt agreeing that the proposed frontier on the Western Neisse (rather than the Eastern Neisse) would, indeed, give the Poles too much German territory, but the Soviets chose to ignore this and plug away at the question of recognition of the Lublin Government. Churchill launched on a long and emotional appeal. Failure to agree upon recognition of a single Polish Government would 'stamp this conference with the seal of failure'. Information available to the British did not support the Soviet contention that the Lublin Government enjoyed popular support. There is no reason to doubt the sincerity of Churchill's comments, but it is difficult not to feel that the kernel of his concern was the fear that 'His Majesty's Government would be charged in Parliament with having forsaken altogether the cause of Poland' if he acceded to Soviet demands for the recognition of the Lublin Government.[37] Stalin's response was to reiterate Soviet opinion about the popularity of the Lublin Government and to compare it with de Gaulle's Government, which, although unelected, had been recognised by the Great Powers. Sweet reason incarnate, Stalin told Churchill that 'if they approached the matter without prejudice they would be able to find a common basis. The situation was not as tragic as the Prime Minister thought and the question could be settled if too much importance was not attached to secondary matters and if they concentrated on essentials.' With Stalin taking such a line, and with Roosevelt anxious to secure Soviet agreement to a 'Declaration on Liberated Europe', which would act as a sort of moral lever on their actions in the future,[38] it was unsurprising that Churchill had to settle for the terms of the final communiqué.

Roosevelt's attitude did not please Churchill, but there was nothing he could do about that. He was a good deal happier with Stalin's behaviour. Churchill was always apt to personalise his politics, and the fact that he and the Russian leader clearly admired each other was an encouraging omen for the future – as was Stalin's refusal to lend any aid to the Communists in Greece; perhaps the agreement reached at Moscow would work.[39] Everything depended on how 'Uncle Joe' behaved with regard to the promises he had made about Poland and liberated Europe. Both the American and the British delegations came away from Yalta with something approaching euphoria in their mental luggage.

The first reaction in America to the Yalta communiqué was 'extremely favourable', not least because of the skilful way in which Roosevelt ensured that his version of events was the first to reach the press.[40] The War Cabinet was equally jubilant, sending a telegram to Churchill and Eden congratulating them on the 'skill and success' with which they had conducted discussions.[41]

The end of the conference provided Churchill with the chance for a little relaxation. In contrast to Moran's gloomy accounts of his mood,[42] other observers found Churchill in good form despite 'drinking buckets of Caucasian champagne which would undermine the health of any ordinary man';[43] indeed, it might have been that the champagne conduced to Churchill's good spirits. Bracken told him that the reception accorded to Yalta in *The Times* was such that 'I might have written the article myself', whilst Beaverbrook, equally ebullient, told Churchill that 'you now appear to your countrymen to be the greatest statesman as well as the greatest warrior'.[44] Only the London Poles and a few dissident Conservatives were inclined to dissent as the Prime Minister took himself off to see the battlefield at Balaclava. Having looked forward to the journey home through the Dardanelles, which would at last give him a chance to see the Straits which would be forever linked with his name, Churchill decided instead that events in Greece demanded his presence in Athens. There he received the sort of hero's reception which matched anything which Beaverbrook thought his fellow countrymen should accord him. In one sense the process of secular canonisation was under way.

The 'emblematic Churchill' was already assured of historical immortality, and the enthusiasm which the crowds in Paris in November and now in Athens accorded to him was a foretaste of what was to come; but the real Winston Churchill was facing problems which threatened to tarnish the legend even before it became set. Yalta was not universally welcomed, and on 28 February the House voted by 396 votes to 25 against an amendment condemning the final agreement as a breach of the Atlantic Charter. At one level this was just another minor revolt to be shrugged off; indeed, since the rebels were old-time Chamberlainites like Sir Archibald Southby and Chamberlain's former PPS, Lord Dunglass, it might even be argued that its significance was minimal. Eden, contemplating the idea of an election with no enthusiasm, did not see how he could ask people to vote for 'the men of Munich'. But such an attitude, however much it may have foreshadowed the fate which the Chamberlainites were to suffer at the hands of the Churchillian memoir-writers, ignored brute political facts of which it would have been wiser to have taken cognisance.

Churchill was a good deal more robust than Eden about the prospect of fighting an election; descending from his pedestal and plunging into the maelstrom of politicking did not appear to worry him. Churchill had always 'seen things in blinkers', or, as Clementine Churchill put it, 'His eyes are focused on the point he is determined to attain. He sees nothing outside that beam.'[45] Without that habit Churchill could never have been the man of 1940, but the price to be paid for this was gradually becoming apparent. Events between Tehran and Yalta had revealed something of that price in international affairs, but there was equally one to be paid on the domestic front. The war had 'exaggerated the isolation in which [Churchill] had dwelt apart during his political life'.[46] He had never had any knowledge of the lives of ordinary people, and the amount of attention which he had paid to the domestic front was minimal. Where Roosevelt never took his eyes off the electorate, Churchill, whilst paying homage to the democratic system, had totally ignored it. The story of how Churchill, after hearing complaints about rationing, asked to see the rations and, upon being shown them, commented, 'That seems enough for a good meal,' received the reply, 'Yes, Prime Minister, but that is the ration for a week,' encapsulates this, as does his astonishment that Rab Butler could actually want to go off and be President of the Board of Education during a war.[47] The reckoning for these things was not far to seek.

Churchill had been content to leave the Socialists (and Butler) to look after the domestic front, where the former had been able to slough off their reputation of being unfit to govern. Even before the Beveridge report one Conservative MP, Lord William Scott, had told the Chief Whip that 'throughout the country the Conservative Party has become a cheap joke', adding that Conservative MPs were well aware of Churchill's unflattering views of the majority of the Party,[48] and this situation did not change. Churchill's only contribution to rethinking the future of the Party was to suggest that they should 'put up' plenty of 'VCs' at the next election – but since one of those was amongst the dissentients over Yalta,[49] this was was not quite the positive thought which the Prime Minister imagined. The fact of the matter was that the bulk of the Conservative Party, of which Churchill was the leader, was made up of unreconstructed Chamberlainites. Churchill had given no thought to how the election which he would welcome was to be won. Experience suggested that the man who 'won the war' would win the peace, but there were many reasons why such a sanguine view might not be enough when the hour came. Whatever tendency existed amongst younger voters to cast their franchise in an idealistic fashion could, in the circumstances of 1945, expect to be greatly intensified, and Churchill had nothing to offer such people. It was true that the Conservatives, as partners in the coalition, had signed up for Beveridge, full employment and the other paraphernalia of what was to become known as Keynesianism, but a contest between Churchill and Labour over who was more likely to offer 'the People' a 'New Jerusalem' could well end in tears for the Prime Minister.

The debate on the Yalta agreement was not without its piquant side, as Chips Channon pointed out when he commented on the 'inconsistency' of those MPs who had abused Chamberlain in 1938 and were now 'meekly' accepting 'this surrender to Soviet Russia'.[50] Churchill was not in the least inclined to add a white sheet to his collection of exotic outfits. He had told the War Cabinet on 19 February that he was 'sure' that Stalin 'meant well to the world and to Poland' and that he had been 'sincere'.[51] Churchill and Eden were both 'well satisfied – if not more' by Yalta.[52] Addressing Ministers outside the War Cabinet on 23 February, Churchill spoke 'very warmly of Stalin', saying that as long as he 'lasted, Anglo-Russian friendship could be maintained'. He said that 'Poor Neville Chamberlain believed he could trust Hitler. He was wrong, but I don't think I'm wrong about Stalin.'[53] Yet the analogy clearly played on Churchill's mind, for by that same evening he was 'rather depressed, thinking of the possibilities of Russia one day turning against us, saying that Chamberlain had trusted Hitler and he was now trusting Stalin'. The 'shadows of victory' were now upon Churchill. In 1940 the issue 'was clear and he could see distinctly what was to be done', but now things were more complex. With the end of the European war in sight it was becoming impossible for Churchill to maintain his tunnel-vision. Whilst Churchill had been at Yalta the destruction of Dresden had taken place, but what would be left when 'Bomber' Harris had completed the 'destruction of Germany, "What will lie between the white snows of Russia and the white cliffs of Dover?" '[54] Churchill was right to ask, but it would have been better had he done so sooner. However, in the debate on 28 February he was as reassuring as he had been to Ministers. He had brought back with him from the Crimea the impression that Stalin wished 'to live in honourable friendship and equality with the Western democracies'. Churchill told the House that he knew 'of no Government which stands to its obligations, even in its own despite, more solidly than the Russian Soviet Government'.[55] Colville thought that Churchill was 'trying to persuade himself that all is well', but if Chamberlain's words after Munich appeared naïve in retrospect, it is difficult to know quite what adjective to use to describe Churchill's remarks.

If Churchill was 'trying to convince himself', he was doing a bad job. On the second day of the Yalta debate he telegraphed to Roosevelt warning him that whilst the Government would win the vote, 'there is a good deal of uneasiness in both parties that we are letting the Poles down etc.'. It was of the 'utmost importance' that Mikolajcik and other 'representative Poles' should be invited 'as soon as possible to the consultations in Moscow'.[56] The Foreign Office telegrams that evening showed that in Romania the Russians were 'intimidating the King and Government and setting about the establishment of a Communist minority government with all the technique familiar to students of the Comintern'. Eden and Churchill reacted to such a development in very different ways. The Foreign Secretary, who was inclined to place his faith in Yalta and the 'Declaration on Liberated Peoples', was concerned at such breaches of the Yalta spirit. Churchill was less impressed by such considerations. He told Eden on 28 February that there was 'nothing' he could do: 'Russia had let us go our way in Greece; she would insist on imposing her will in Roumania and Bulgaria. But as regards Poland we would have our say.'[57] Eden took the view that the peace settlement was indivisible,[58] but Churchill still took his stand on the spirit of the 'percentages' deal. He rebuked Eden on 5 March for trying to interfere in Romania, arguing that it might lead to charges that 'we have broken our faith about Roumania after taking advantage of our position in Greece'.[59] The difference between the two men was noticed by Harold Nicolson after the Yalta vote on 28 February. Churchill was 'overjoyed' and 'behaved like a schoolboy'. Eden's reaction revealed a better sense of perspective. Far from being 'overjoyed', he told Nicolson, 'My God, what a mess Europe is in! What a mess!'[60]

Publicly committed to faith in Russia's goodwill, Churchill quickly found that commodity in short supply. At the War Cabinet on the evening of 6 March Eden reported that Molotov had refused to allow Mikolajcik to enter Russia and that the Soviets were insisting on a Polish Government formed entirely of their own nominees. This put Churchill in an embarrassing position and he was anxious lest he should be charged with deceiving the Commons. He had, he thought, been 'fully entitled' to take the line which he had in the debate, since 'we were bound to assume the good faith of an Ally in the execution of an agreement so recently signed', but if it became clear that the Soviets were 'not going to carry [it] out', 'it would be necessary to give the whole story to Parliament'. Churchill thought that 'we were ... entitled to expect the full support of the US' in telling the Russians that their Polish proposals were unacceptable.[61] The doubts which had festered whilst he spoke so confidently in public now came to the surface – all the more strongly for being half-suppressed. The news the following day that the Soviets might be about to remove the former Romanian Prime Minister, General Nicholae Radescu, from his British sanctuary by force, brought an abrupt about-turn by Churchill on non-interference in Romania. Having reprimanded Eden on 5 March for interfering in Romania, by 7 March Churchill was telling him that 'our honour is at stake'. Both men now feared that 'our willingness to trust our Russian ally may have been vain and they look with despondency to the future'.[62] It was time to turn once more to America for aid. Such was the result of the war which had been fought to maintain British independence and to prevent the balance of power in Europe from being overthrown. Only the 'New World' could redress the balance of the old – but would it be willing to do so?

54

A 'Sad Wreck'

In the ten days after 8 March Churchill sent Roosevelt ten telegrams urging him towards a firmer line on the Soviet Union. Some historians have seen in this evidence of a determination to embroil America in British quarrels – something which can be regarded as good or bad depending upon the point of view adopted. Those who think that Churchill had with some foresight spotted the onset of the Cold War might be inclined to praise him for trying to alert the Americans to what was afoot; those who think that such warnings were a contributory factor in the causes of the Cold War take a different view.[1] Others see Churchill as playing a 'tricky game', trying to get Roosevelt to be firm with the Soviets at least in part so that he could play the role of mediator.[2] Yet another version of events has Churchill, in effect, using the Soviet threat as an instrument for forging Anglo-American unity anew as the end of the war threatened to destroy what was left of that commodity.[3] What all these sophisticated accounts have in common is that they suggest a degree of calculation in Churchill's actions for which there is little evidence. What evidence there is suggests that Colville was speaking for Churchill as well as himself when he wrote: 'God knows we have tried to march in step with Russia towards the broad and sun-lit uplands. If a cloud obscures the sun when we reach them, the responsibility is with Moscow.' With the word 'appeasement' once more being whispered aloud, Churchill could not afford to sit silent.

Churchill's understanding of both the Soviet system and the dynamics of eastern European politics was limited. Beneš was 'Beans' and the Commander of the Polish Army, Soznkowski, was 'sozzle something';[4] Czechoslovakia and Poland were both (to adapt a phrase) far-away countries of which neither Churchill nor the British knew very much. But there was a resonance to the name of Poland, for it had been the proximate cause of Britain entering the war. Churchill had been willing to make concession after concession to Stalin; indeed, he had staked much of his prestige after Yalta on the fact that Stalin could be trusted. Now he reacted to evidence to the contrary in just the way that Neville Chamberlain had reacted to the invasion of Prague – he grew angry and disillusioned. There were certainly plenty of illusions to be lost. Churchill persisted with his belief that Roosevelt would allow himself to be used by the British to bring pressure on Stalin over Romania and Poland, and, for much of the time, he also persisted with the idea that Stalin was not to blame for the harder line which the Soviets were taking.

Churchill was not pursuing some deep, long-term policy; he was facing what Eden called the 'sad wreck' of British foreign policy[5] – and trying desperately to rescue something from the wreckage. He did not 'want to be left alone in the cage with the Bear'.[6] Churchill had thought that the Moscow meeting and Yalta had given him guarantees which he could trust; Soviet refusal to give him any evidence to show his critics that he had been right produced in the old man a change of mood. As the blinkers of war were removed, Churchill began to perceive the magnitude of the mistake which had been made. Britain had gone to war in 1939 in a spasm of self-righteous indignation, convinced that as a Great Power it was her duty to defeat Nazi Germany, even if no other power (except France) cared to take on the task. The battle of France had cruelly exposed Anglo-French pretensions. By a combination of stubbornness and good fortune Britain's bacon had been saved first by Soviet entry into the war and then by that of the United States. Churchill had imagined that the 'Grand Alliance' could pursue the war single-mindedly. He could not conceive that the Americans might have different war aims, still less that they might 'gang up' on British imperialism with the Soviets. Together the Anglo-American alliance could restore a balance of power to the world order, and, united, the two countries could lead a reformed Soviet Union towards those same 'sun-lit uplands' which Churchill had foreseen back in 1940. When the Americans proved less than willing to underwrite this vision, Churchill had turned towards a little *realpolitik* with Stalin; but with 'Uncle Joe' seeming to be playing false, Churchill had nowhere else to turn than back to the Americans. The prospect of winning the war but losing the peace was now a very real one.

But Churchill faced a problem in remonstrating with Stalin. He himself had told Eden on 5 March that they had no grounds for interfering with events inside Romania, yet the evidence which was available then was not vastly different from that which was available three days later when he sent his first telegram to Roosevelt. What had changed was the picture in Poland, but that was hardly a ground for protesting about events in Romania. Churchill was, as he told Roosevelt, anxious not to provoke Stalin into responding with a *tu quoque* about Greece. It was for this reason that Churchill wanted the Americans to take up the Romanian question with the Soviets – 'we', he assured the President, 'will, of course, give you every support'. He referred Roosevelt to the discontent being felt in all political circles in Britain at the application of the 'well-known Communist technique' in Poland, and asked 'how would the matter go in the United States?' With Molotov clearly basing himself on the view that the Lublin Poles were the legitimate Polish Government and refusing to let Mikolajcik into the country, 'If we do not get things right now, it will soon be seen by the world that you and I by putting our signatures to the Crimea settlement have under-written a fraudulent prospectus.' He sent Roosevelt the text of a telegram which he proposed to send to Stalin, which asked him to live up to the promises made at Yalta.[7]

The American Ambassador in Moscow, Harriman, was disposed to view the Soviet tactics as part of a strategy which would allow the Lublin regime to become 'more and more the Warsaw Government and the ruler of Poland', but neither he nor Roosevelt was inclined to overreact in the way Churchill was doing.[8] The Americans were quite willing to try to keep the Soviets to the spirit of the Yalta accords, but only to the extent of getting Harriman to ask them to request the rival political groups to 'adopt a political truce in Russia'. At Yalta a tripartite commission had been set up to oversee the formation of a new government of 'national unity', and Harriman now requested that the Soviets allow it to approve the names of those Poles who were to take part in the negotiations – including Mikolajcik.[9] But of interference in the affairs of Romania the Americans would have no part. Churchill himself had hithertofore been careful to keep the Balkan areas, covered by the 'percentages' deal, separate from eastern Europe, which was not; his attempts to persuade the Americans to make a linkage which he did not himself want to make was unsuccessful.

On 10 March Churchill urged Roosevelt to postpone sending the message from Harriman,[10] and in another telegram sent details of a long list of violations of the 'spirit of Yalta', emphasising the necessity of the Soviets allowing British and American observers into Poland.[11] Much of this information was not new and all of it was derived from the London Poles, so what had changed Churchill's mind? It is hard not to conclude that the answer to this was 'the Parliamentary climate'. Churchill warned Roosevelt in the first of the 10 March telegrams that 'the feeling here is very strong. Four ministers have abstained from the divisions and two have already resigned.' He may have been as 'amused' as Harold Nicolson that 'the warmongers of the Munich period have now become the appeasers, while the appeasers have become the warmongers' on 27 February,[12] but the first signs of evidence that he might have been as wrong about Stalin as Chamberlain had been about Hitler were enough to send him scurrying to the Americans. To find oneself being accused of appeasement by Chamberlain's former PPS was enough to make even Churchill think hard.

The tone of Roosevelt's replies to his telegrams did not please Churchill.[13] Although he had no alternative but to agree to the despatch of Harriman's note to Molotov, he doubted whether it would produce the desired effect. 'We can, of course, make no progress at Moscow without your aid,' he told Roosevelt, 'and if we get out of step the doom of Poland is sealed.' This was the basic fact which determined British policy. But, warned Churchill, a 'month has passed since Yalta and no progress of any kind has been made. Soon I will be questioned in Parliament on this point and I shall be forced to tell them the truth.' The fact was that 'Poland has lost her frontier'; the question which would be asked in the Commons was 'Is she now to lose her freedom?' Churchill said that he did not want to 'reveal a divergence between the British and United States Governments', but if questioned in the Commons 'it would certainly be necessary for me to make it clear that we are in the presence of a great failure and an utter breakdown of what was settled at Yalta, but that we British have not the necessary strength to carry the matter further';[14] it was to this position that the proud hopes of 1940 had dwindled. Even now Churchill would not acknowledge that powerlessness to intervene effectively dictated a policy of non-interference; the ghosts of Munich stalked his memory and Churchill of 1938 sought to dictate that Churchill of 1945 still acted as though British action could avail.

Roosevelt was unimpressed. The only difference which he could perceive between himself and the British was over tactics, where he was convinced that Churchill was wrong. He pointed out that Harriman had had instructions to act since 9 March and had been prevented from acting on them by Churchill's anxieties. He saw no 'breakdown' of Yalta.[15] Churchill expressed his relief at Roosevelt's response, agreed that the main difference was over tactics and then pressed for firmer action.[16] He was clearly aware of the danger of his importunities 'becoming a bore' to Roosevelt, for he followed up these telegrams with one in his best sentimental vein. 'Our friendship', he told Roosevelt on 17 March, 'is the rock on which I build for the future of the world.' He 'always' thought of 'those tremendous days when you devised Lend-Lease, when we met at Argentia' – and so on and so forth.[17] It is unlikely that these appeals to a glorious past had any effect on the ailing President, but they were a sign of how desperate Churchill was to hang on to the clouds of glory trailed from those days.

Another sign that the demands of the brave new world could be ignored for little longer was the persistence of talk of a general election. The Labour conference in October had pronounced that the Party would fight the next election on its own programme, but there had been no announcement of when that election would be. Now, with the British and American armies across the Rhine and with the Nazi Reich clearly doomed, the question of when the election would be held was one which exercised minds at Westminster.

For those watching the straws in the wind to see when there were enough of them to make a bale of hay, Churchill's address to the Conservative Party conference at the Central Hall, Westminster, was a significant moment. This was the first time since he had become leader of the Party that he had addressed a Party rally. He praised the Conservatives for their 'patriotic restraint' from 'Party activity' despite the 'provocations from that happily limited class of left-wing politicians to whom Party strife is the breath of their nostrils'. He warned his listeners that because of the attitude of the other Parties an election following victory in Europe was highly likely. The whole tenor of the speech gave warning of what was to come. Churchill would rest his case to the 'people' on his wartime achievements and seek a mandate for the future on that basis; in the process he would seek the aid of 'men of good will of any Party or no Party'. He would also, it was plain, attack what he called the 'stay-at-home left-wing intelligentsia', who were advocating a 'brave new world' to be ready for the returning soldiers when they 'disembark at Liverpool'. But Churchill's vision of the soldiers wanting, as their 'heart's desire', to see 'old England' playing its part in 'the forefront of all the nations in battle against tyranny', was a reflection of how out of touch the Prime Minister was with public opinion. He sincerely believed that the people would be willing to wait to see what form a new society would take, and he was as wrong in believing that as he was in supposing that they would entrust the job to the Conservatives on no better security than his promise.[18]

The Labour Cabinet Ministers were not very pleased with Churchill's slighting references to the main difference between the two Parties: nationalisation. At Cabinet on 22 March Bevin accused Churchill of implying that Labour was going back on its commitment. To Churchill's mind this showed the 'growing difficulties' in the way of continued co-operation – although to Eden it simply showed that Churchill was more in favour of breaking up the coalition than he was himself.[19] The reception given to Churchill's speech to the Conservative Party conference had been an enthusiastic one, and with the precedent of 1918 and Lloyd George in mind, most Conservatives felt confident about the outcome of such an election.

As minds turned towards the future, but looked to the past for guidance upon how to act, there came to Churchill a poignant reminder of that past: on 26 March 1945 David Lloyd George died. The 'tremendous days' of the partnership of the 'heavenly twins' were long in the past, and the final phase of the Lloyd George–Churchill relationship was clouded by their differences in 1940–41. However, the last stage had been marked by a generous act on Churchill's part. Since his wife's death in 1941 Lloyd George had aged rapidly. In 1943 he had finally married Frances Stevenson, thus regularising her position, but at the cost of perpetuating family feuds. To fight another election in his eighty-second year would have been a formidable enough undertaking for anyone, but given Lloyd George's state of health by late 1944, it was becoming an impossibility for the 'Welsh Wizard'. Plans that he should stand unopposed for the seat which he had held for fifty years came to nothing, and it looked as though the former Prime Minister would have no forum to give his views on the peace settlement. It was a predicament which touched Churchill's generous heart and, on 18 December 1944, he wrote to Lloyd George offering him an earldom. Thus it was that in the New Year's Honours List that scourge of the House of Lords joined it as The Earl Lloyd-George of Dwyfor and Viscount Gwynedd.[20]

Churchill paid a notable tribute to his old comrade in the Commons on 28 March, but Colville noted that it was not as well done, ironically, as the eulogy which Churchill had delivered on Chamberlain four years earlier.[21] Churchill was certainly scornful of Lloyd George's 'farm-cart' funeral, preferring to reserve for himself a great state occasion.[22] Certainly people could hardly help comparing the two war leaders. To Amery's mind the main difference between them was that Lloyd George was 'purely external and receptive', whilst Churchill was 'literary and expressive of himself with hardly any contact with other minds'. At bottom Churchill was a 'restrospective Whig of the period 1750–1850, with very little capacity for looking forward', whilst Lloyd George had been 'a constructive Radical'.[23] Churchill, as his speech to the Conservative conference revealed, could have badly done with something creative, whether radical or not.

Churchill's main concern as the prospect of victory over Germany grew nearer was not with the war or the election, but rather with Russia. Attempts to read the runes in late March 1945 were uncannily like the attempts which had been made to do so with regard to Hitler after Munich. The British Ambassador, Clark-Kerr, quite acknowledged that Russian behaviour since Yalta had given little ground for optimism, but there were what might be called contra-indications. To build up a 'black record' on the basis of the past few weeks and to conclude that the Kremlin had 'turned away from the policy of co-operation with the West' would be a 'mistake'. In a despatch on 27 March Clark-Kerr reminded Churchill and Eden that there had been 'similar setbacks and disappointments' after previous conferences with the Soviets. After all there was no reason why the Soviets should have supposed that they could not fulfil their objectives in the Balkans, provided that they paid due attention to British interests in Greece and Yugoslavia – which they seemed to be doing. When it came to Poland, the Russians lacked 'the niceness of feeling which we cherish about an ally for whom we went to war', and, 'incapable of measuring the weight which lies behind public opinion', the Soviets were probably baffled as to why the British were taking such a close interest in a question 'in which no direct British interest is involved'. Besides that, there was the fact that neither the British nor the Americans had given Stalin any reason to suppose that they would not rest content with the Soviet interpretation of 'democracy' and 'free elections'.[24]

Clark-Kerr's points were almost too pertinent for comfort. After all, if Churchill and Roosevelt had really believed that the Soviet interpretation of the words of the Yalta declaration would be the same as their own, they were guilty of, at best, naïveté, and at worst culpable negligence. Churchill had given Stalin every encouragement at the Moscow conference to think that the crudest sort of 'spheres of influence' deal was on offer, and for him now to take Russia's attitude towards Poland as a 'pointer to general Soviet policy' was a little perverse. As Clark-Kerr reminded his masters, the 'word "co-operation", like the word "democracy", has different meanings in the Soviet Union and in the West'. There was, none the less, a worrying build-up of bad omens. On 21 March the Soviets resiled from their previous decision to send Molotov to San Francisco for the conference which would inaugurate the United Nations. This followed the denunciation on 19 March of the Soviet-Turkish treaty of friendship – an ominous prelude to the renegotiation of the 1936 treaty governing control of the Straits. Moreover, the agreements reached at Yalta regarding the exchanges of prisoners of war did not seem to be being observed by the Soviets. The question arose whether it was not time to have some sort of 'showdown' with the Soviets.[25] As Eden commented in his diary on 23 March, 'I take the gloomiest view of Russian behaviour everywhere. . . . Altogether our foreign policy seems a sad wreck and we may have to cast about afresh.'[26]

It was difficult to see what 'casting about afresh' could mean; the only road open to the British was the one upon which they were already travelling – to obtain support from the Americans. On 23 March Molotov made it plain that in the Soviet view acceptance of Yalta implied dealing with the Lublin Poles, and that the presence of Mikolajcik was not wanted.[27] The task of persuading the Americans to take action after this was made easier by Soviet allegations that they were being left to shoulder the major burden of the war. This was prompted by Russian suspicions at talks which they were aware were going on with the German SS commander in Italy. The Germans had for some time been advocating an alliance with the western allies against the Soviet menace, and in February General Wolff approached American agents with the suggestion that German forces in Italy might surrender. The Americans refused to let the Russians participate in talks in Bern in Switzerland, which raised their suspicions.[28] Churchill was inclined to think that the Soviets might well have a 'legitimate', if misplaced, fear,[29] but Roosevelt was not prepared to let the Soviets into what he regarded as an American sphere of influence.

On 27 March Churchill put his fears before Roosevelt. The Russian attitude over Poland amounted to allowing them a veto over candidates proposed by London or Washington whilst permitting the Lublin regime to establish itself in power – either way the Soviets were, Churchill thought, breaking the spirit of the Yalta accords. He reminded Roosevelt that both he and Eden were 'pledged to report' to the Commons if they were 'defrauded by Russia'. Then there was the delicate question of the fact that he had himself advised critics of Yalta to 'trust Stalin', which meant that if he had to make a statement to the House 'of facts', the 'whole world will draw the deduction that such advice was wrong'. Warning that Britain and America must not 'become parties to imposing on Poland' and other parts of eastern Europe 'the Russian version of democracy', Churchill thought that the time had come for 'a message from us both on Poland to Stalin'. There was, after all, no use setting up a 'new world organisation' on 'foundations of sand'.[30]

Roosevelt was receiving equally firm advice from Harriman, who warned him on 25 March that the Soviets clearly had no intention of inviting London-based Poles to join the Lublin Government. His response to this was to bang his fist on his wheelchair and to exclaim, 'Averell is right; we can't do business with Stalin. He has broken every one of the promises he made at Yalta.'[31] In his reply to Churchill, Roosevelt reminded him that they had agreed to place 'somewhat more emphasis on the Lublin Poles' than on other groups, but he acknowledged that this did not mean that that group had a veto over who should and should not be allowed to join the negotiations to widen the basis of the Polish Government. He thought that the detailed negotiations could be left to Harriman and Clark-Kerr on the commission, but he agreed that the time had come to take up the 'broader aspects of the Soviet attitude' directly with Stalin.[32] In his message to Stalin Roosevelt referred to the need not to disappoint the great expectations and hopes raised by Yalta and expressed his lack of understanding of the Soviet attitude on Poland. Any solution which resulted in the present regime simply continuing in power would not, Roosevelt said, be acceptable to the western allies, and he suggested that they should allow the tripartite commission to determine who should take part in discussions, with no side having an absolute veto; he also thought that British and American representatives should be allowed to visit Poland. He reminded Stalin of the great role which public opinion played in America in determining governmental policy.[33]

Churchill's message was even stronger. He thought Roosevelt's telegram a 'grave and weighty document', but he did not consider that it went far enough.[34] In his own message to Stalin he made it clear that he considered that Stalin had broken both the 'spirit' of Yalta and, at some 'points, the letter'. He blamed Soviet intransigence for holding up even the preliminary negotiations concerning the shape of the final government and for going back on an earlier promise to allow observers to go to Warsaw. Referring to his own advocacy of the Soviet cause before the Commons, and the possible electoral consequences if it transpired that he had been wrong, Churchill concluded his message by saying that he made his appeal as a 'sincere friend of Russia' not to 'smite down the hands of comradeship in the future guidance of the world which we now extend'.[35] Roosevelt made amendments in his message to Stalin to bring it more into line with Churchill's, and on 1 April both leaders sent their telegrams to the Soviet dictator.

But if there was now a greater measure of agreement on the diplomatic front, it transpired that this did not extend to the military one. Churchill had enjoyed himself with a visit to the front in the third week of March – an experience which he always found exhilarating – but he was less than happy when he discovered on 30 March that, contrary to his expectations, Eisenhower was not intending to advance directly to Berlin, but planned to move southwards towards Dresden. Churchill disliked the idea of leaving Berlin to the Soviets. The fall of Berlin would have a 'profound psychological effect' on German resistance, and on political grounds it was desirable not to have the German capital 'liberated' by the Soviets alone.[36] Churchill warned Roosevelt that it might increase the Soviet feeling that they had been the 'overwhelming contributor to our common victory' to such an extent as to lead them into 'a mood which will raise grave and formidable difficulties in the future'.[37] But Roosevelt would have none of this. Eisenhower's battle-plan, like the Allied discussion of the division of Germany into zones, did not provide for the western powers to be in Berlin, and Roosevelt was not willing to strain relations with Stalin further.[38]

Churchill was now facing the prospect that Russia could not be counted upon to exercise a 'beneficent influence in Europe', or to be a 'willing partner in maintaining the peace of the world'. Yet the result of the war was bound to leave the Soviets in a 'position of preponderant power and influence'. America had also built up an enormous power base; indeed, she was suggesting that an American economic mission to Greece might be part of a major role which she would play in European reconstruction. How was Britain to maintain her own in such company? Churchill put his answer to a meeting of the War Cabinet on 3 April at which representatives of the Dominion and Indian Governments were present: 'by our superior statecraft and experience'.[39] It was polite of those present not to ask how it was that 'superior statecraft' had managed to produce such a situation.

Still, the Anglo-American unity which Churchill's pleas to Roosevelt had failed to produce was being stimulated by Stalin's actions. The President had already moved towards a firmer line in his telegram of 1 April and the message which he received from Stalin pushed him further in that direction. The Soviet leader accused the Americans of entering into an agreement with General Wolff, which would not only deliver Italy into western hands but allow the Allied armies to advance further east – all in return for a promise to ease the peace terms which Germany would suffer. He accused the British of being behind the scheme and asked why it had been kept secret from Russia.[40] Stalin's motives for sending such a maladroit telegram are open to speculation. Perhaps he feared that he would be served by the British as he had served them in 1939 – those who cannot be trusted are always inclined to distrust others, just as those who habitually engage in duplicity are apt to attribute their own sin to others. If the Allies took the advice which Goebbels was offering them to ally with Germany, the rosy future which the Tehran, Moscow and Yalta conferences had opened up for the Soviet Union would have to be revised. Roosevelt expressed his 'astonishment' at Stalin's allegation, which he firmly denied before going on to express his 'bitter resentment' at the 'vile misrepresentations of my actions'.[41] To have driven Roosevelt closer to Churchill could hardly have been accounted a triumph for Stalin.

Churchill himself was so infuriated by Stalin's accusations that he refused to leave his bed until he had drafted a 'counterblast', even though this made him late for his meeting with the King of Norway.[42] There was, of course, the possibility that these suspicions explained why the Russians had been behaving so unco-operatively, but Churchill was 'anxious lest the brutality of the Russian messages' foreshadowed 'some deep change of policy for which they are preparing'. He was inclined, as he told Roosevelt on 5 April, to 'think it is no more than their natural expression when vexed or jealous'. It was therefore of the 'highest importance that a firm and blunt stand' should be made at this juncture in order that 'the air may be cleared' and the Soviets 'realize there is a point beyond which we will not tolerate insult'. Churchill thought that 'this is the best chance of saving the future'.[43] But none of this amounted to a settled determination to regard the Soviets as irredeemably hostile. Churchill wanted American help in case 'the Bear' turned out to have malevolent intentions, but he was prepared to be mollified by soft answers.

Because Churchill telegraphed so copiously, selective quotation can be used to prove almost anything. Those historians who seek to locate a change of policy by Roosevelt as part of the origins of the Cold War are apt to attribute this to Churchill's pressure. Certainly Roosevelt's reply to Churchill's comments on Stalin's message not only approved of the Prime Minister's tone but also added that 'our Armies will in a very few days be in a position that will permit us to become "tougher" than has heretofore appeared advantageous to the war effort',[44] but this was not necessarily a sign that Roosevelt had 'reconsidered his conciliatory and independent approach towards Russia'.[45] The telegram was despatched within two hours of the receipt of Churchill's message and was written by the President's Chief of Staff, Admiral Leahy, who, like Harriman, was in favour of taking a 'tougher' line. By this stage Roosevelt was paying even less attention to the detail of business than was his wont.[46] Stalin's replies were unconciliatory and made it plain that only Poles who wanted 'friendly relations between Poland and the Soviet Union' would be acceptable as members of a government in Warsaw.[47] However, by 7 April Stalin was denying that he had meant to cast aspersions upon Anglo-American integrity,[48] and Roosevelt was able to tell Churchill on 11 April that he would 'minimize the general Soviet problem as much as possible because these problems, in one form or another, seem to arise every day and most of them straighten out';[49] that was the authentic Rooseveltian touch – things would always 'straighten out'.

Churchill was concerned about reports of the President's ill-health, and he had warned the Foreign Office in mid-March not to 'overwhelm him with telegrams about business which I fear may bore him'.[50] But it still came as a profound shock when, at midnight on 12 April, Churchill was informed that President Roosevelt had died earlier that day. On a purely personal level Churchill was naturally 'very distressed', but on a political level the implications of such an untoward event were incalculable.[51] Churchill liked to conduct diplomacy as an extension of a personal relationship and, for all its ups and downs, he had succeeded in establishing one with Roosevelt which he believed would serve his own country well. Roosevelt had, after all, unrivalled experience as President and his prestige was immense. The British may not have been as well aware as they might have been of the fierce partisan emotions which Roosevelt aroused, but to lose, at the climax of the war in Europe, a man of such weight was, as Churchill told the House on 17 April, a 'melancholy event'.[52] In place of the self-assured and immensely skilful Roosevelt there now came to power a Missouri haberdasher called Harry Truman. In the usual tradition of American politics the Vice-President was a man who had brought strength to the Presidential 'ticket' in the elections, but he had been kept entirely uninformed by Roosevelt of his policies and plans and so came to power as a novice. Churchill's 'first impulse' was to fly over to America for the funeral, something of which Halifax approved, adding that he did not 'overlook the value ... of your seeing Truman'; nor did Churchill.[53] But with Attlee, Lyttelton and Cranborne already in America for the San Francisco conference, and with Eden preparing to go there, Churchill decided that he could not be spared. He received a 'very nice telegram' from Truman hoping that they would meet soon, but it was a decision which Churchill was always to regret.[54] The rock upon which he had sought to build his hopes was gone – but then Churchill's hopes of Roosevelt had always been over-sanguine. It remained to be seen what, if anything, could be saved from the 'sad wreck' of British foreign policy.

55

Failure and Apotheosis: II

Roosevelt was fortunate in the timing of his death. Such was his charisma that he was able to leave the legend that somehow he would have been able to 'straighten things out', which resulted in his successor being landed with the blame (or praise, according to taste) for starting the Cold War (or, if one prefers, 'standing up to' the Russians). He was also relieved of the task of trying to bring the unravelling strands of Allied diplomacy together. Churchill was not so fortunate. The Prime Minister felt 'much pain' when he saw how unequal Britain and America were in power,[1] and the Americans were well aware that the first and last maxim of Churchill's diplomacy was 'co-operation with the United States'.[2] But with Soviet armies in eastern Europe and Austria, with Tito's Yugoslavia looking towards Moscow, with Romania and Bulgaria firmly in the Soviet sphere, and with Stalin seeming increasingly incalculable, it was difficult to see quite what 'victory' would mean for the British outside the narrow definition of avoidance of defeat.

Churchill was conscious of Britain's impoverished state. Simply in order to make up for the overseas investments which had been sold Britain would need to export seventy-five per cent more than she had in 1938–9, and no one could say where the resources for that were going to come from. Britain's overseas liabilities amounted to more than £300 million and were increasing at the rate of £600 million every year.[3] Back in 1944 Churchill had been inclined to think that these sums could be written off against the moral debt which he conceived that the rest of the world owed to Britain,[4] but by 1945 he was not so sure.[5] Nor was it likely that the coalition Government would be the body which would deal with the parlous situation which would face a victorious Britain. The war with Japan might go on for another two years, but no one was thinking in terms of waiting that long before facing the electorate. As Churchill wrote to his wife on 6 April, everyone was resigning themselves to the 'unpleasant fact' that the election might come 'at the end of June or July'.[6]

The Prime Minister's tremendous energy was now flagging, and his inattention to his 'red box' and the papers therein made him an 'administrative bottleneck'.[7] Churchill's attention to matters which did not interest him had always been slight and, as fatigue and anxiety took their toll, it became even slighter.

One source of anxiety was, however, soon removed. Truman seemed more willing than Roosevelt to take a firm line with the Soviets. On 18 April Churchill concurred in sending a joint telegram to Stalin setting out their position on Poland. It was firmly stated that whilst conceding a predominant role to the Lublin Poles, Britain and America did not and could not accept that the Yalta accords had given them a veto over who should or should not take part in discussions. Truman and Churchill set out a list of the various Poles who should be invited to take part in discussions in Moscow, expressing their willingness that the Government headed by the Communist, Boleslaw Bierut, should be the first to arrive.[8] Truman himself made plain his dissatisfaction with the Soviet position over Poland when he talked to Molotov at the San Francisco conference on 23 April.[9] Stalin's reply to this barrage was unconciliatory. He asked Churchill and Truman to bear in mind that 'Poland borders on the Soviet Union, which cannot be said about Great Britain or the USA. Poland is to the security of the Soviet Union what Belgium and Greece are to the security of Great Britain.' He did not, he went on, know if the Greek and Belgian Governments were 'genuinely democratic' since no one had consulted him on the matter, but he could not 'understand why in discussing Poland no attempt is made to consider the interests of the Soviet Union in terms of security as well'. He did not see why they could not take Yugoslavia as a precedent: there Tito's men formed the core of the Government, so why not in Poland?[10]

Although Churchill was disappointed by this reply, he was still capable of being influenced by kind words from 'Uncle Joe'. With the Germans in disarray and rumours of surrender imminent, Churchill took good care to keep Stalin informed of the attempts by the German commander in Italy to surrender to the Allies, telling him that only unconditional surrender would be acceptable. Stalin replied on 25 April approving Churchill's language and expressing his determination to continue to put pressure on Berlin 'in the interests of our common cause'. This 'fascinated Churchill',[11] who, 'not altogether sober to begin with',[12] held forth for an hour and a half on the subject. Colville, who was present, commented that his 'vanity was astonishing' and that it was a good thing that Stalin did not know 'what effect a few kind words, after so many harsh ones, might well have on our policy towards Russia'. Colville need not have worried. However susceptible Churchill might be to flattery, he was not disposed to back down on the issue of Poland.

That Churchill's attitude was largely shaped by what might be called the 'shadow of Munich' was clear from the long telegram which he sent to Stalin on the night of 28–29 April.[13] He blamed the Soviets for the lack of progress which had been made since Yalta, pointing out that the names which the British had put forward were not even meant for inclusion in the final Government, but were simply meant to be representatives of the London groups which could enter into negotiations. Churchill also rejected the Yugoslav 'precedent', not least because he did not feel that the Tito regime gave Britain 'the feeling of a fifty–fifty interest and influence as between our two countries'. Churchill had accepted the fact that Yugoslavia was becoming a 'one-party regime', but Poland was a different matter. He was 'shocked' that Stalin could imagine that he wanted an anti-Soviet regime in Poland, but he pleaded with him to understand the place which Poland held in British hearts. The British, he said, had not gone to war out of 'calculation' but for 'sentiment'. After Hitler had broken the promises he had given at Munich and then attacked Poland 'there was a flame in the hearts of men like that which swept your people in their noble defence of their country'. He asked Stalin to understand that 'this British flame burns still among all classes and parties in this Island . . . and they can never fear this war will have ended rightly unless Poland has a fair deal', which meant 'sovereignty, independence and freedom on the basis of friendship with Russia'. Britain wanted to be 'friends on equal and honourable terms with the mighty Russian Soviet Republic', but there had to be a satisfactory settlement on Poland. Churchill rejected analogies with Greece or Belgium and sought to make it plain that Anglo-American agreement on Poland was not the result of concerted action but rather of an identity of view. He also referred to the difficulties created by rumours coming out of Poland, such as the one concerning a Polish delegation of sixteen which had gone to Russia the previous month and which had now vanished. It was ironic that six years after Neville Chamberlain had determined that Poland should be the acid test of Hitler's intentions, Churchill should have been doing the same thing with regard to Stalin. He found 'little comfort' in the prospect of a confrontation between a Soviet-dominated bloc and 'the English-speaking nations and their associates'. Churchill told Stalin that a 'quarrel' between the two groups 'would tear the world to pieces and that all of us leading men on either side who had anything to do with that would be shamed before history'. Even a long period of distrust and 'abuse and counter-abuse' would 'be a disaster' because it would hamper the 'recovery of the world economy'. Churchill concluded by hoping that there was 'no word or phrase in this out-pouring of my heart to you which unwittingly gives offence', and he begged his 'friend Stalin' not to 'underrate the divergencies which are opening up about matters which you may think are small to us but which are symbolic of the way the English-speaking democracies look at life'.

It was indeed a 'masterly' telegram,[14] and Churchill hoped that a 'complete understanding between the English-speaking world and Russia will be achieved and maintained'.[15] But the Churchill of 1938 had limited the room for manoeuvre of the Churchill of 1945, especially one facing an imminent election. For much of the war Churchill had given Stalin the impression that he was prepared to recognise Russia's special interests in Poland, but now that it was plain that Stalin intended to dominate the Warsaw Government without giving even a fig-leaf to cover the nakedness of that control, Churchill was faced with an insoluble dilemma. In practice, as he recognised, there was nothing which the British could do about the situation in Poland – just as little, in fact, as Chamberlain had been able to do in 1939. But, partly under his own advocacy, Poland had become a symbol, and Churchill was stuck with that fact in 1945. There was, in all truth, little that was surprising about Stalin's demands in Poland. With the Red Army the most powerful military force on the Continent, it would have been surprising if the Soviets had not seized a unique opportunity to mould the 'social structure' and the Governments of eastern Europe to eliminate 'all potential hostile influences' – particularly in Poland.[16]

What Churchill was asking for may have looked reasonable to him, but to Stalin it was unwonted and unwanted interference in his own sphere of influence. 'Sentiment' had led Churchill to advocate that Britain should interfere in the affairs of eastern Europe in 1938–9, and even though that policy had brought near disaster, he was at it again in 1945. Intellectually he may have realised that Britain was now the smallest of the 'Big Three', but he could not bring himself to follow the logic of that position. He sought to bring Stalin to heel over Poland, but, as Stalin had asked of the Pope at Yalta, 'How many divisions has he?' What, after all, was the implication of Stalin insisting upon a Polish regime which was subservient to him? If the British chose to interpret it as a sign that Stalin had hostile intentions, they would be moving towards just that sort of 'quarrel' which Churchill claimed would be a 'disaster' for the world. There was an incongruity between the cause and the effect which Churchill either did not appreciate or which the forthcoming election meant that he was unable to appreciate. At the end of a war in Europe which had been fought to stop one power dominating the Continent, a situation existed in which just that had come to pass. It did not say much for the 'superior statesmanship' upon which Churchill had said the British must depend to supply the place of actual power.

Stalin's response showed that the dictator still looked towards the 'percentages' deal as a model for the future and expressed his puzzlement at what he saw as a change of attitude by Churchill. In the aftermath of Churchill's message the Soviets accepted Mikolajcik as a candidate for consultation, but Molotov implied to Eden that future co-operation should be on the basis of Britain allowing Russia a 'free hand in Poland in return for the continuance of Russian non-interference in our own spheres of interest'.[17] Stalin's response to Churchill on 7 May contained the same implication. He made it plain that only a pro-Soviet Government would be tolerated in Warsaw and admitted that fifteen of the Poles had been arrested for anti-Soviet activity. If the British and Americans refused to accept the Warsaw Government as the basis for a future Polish regime, then that would preclude the possibility of an agreement over Poland.[18] Stalin could hardly have made his position plainer than that. Churchill told Truman that it was now essential for the 'Big Three' to meet as soon as possible. In the meantime it was necessary to 'hold firmly to the existing positions obtained or being obtained by our armies'. Although he was anxious to avoid 'giving the impression of "ganging up" against Stalin', that was precisely what Churchill wanted to do.[19]

On 7 May Churchill received the news of the German surrender. The fate of Hitler was still uncertain. Rumour and report had it that he had perished 'fighting with his last breath against Bolshevism'[20] – something which had an ironic ring about it considering Churchill's correspondence with Truman. He had, in fact, shot himself on the afternoon of 30 April, and even as Stalin was digesting Churchill's warnings, the corpse of the man whose vainglory had plunged Europe into chaos was burning in the wasteland of Berlin. But what did 'Victory in Europe' mean for the British?

With his 'blinkers' now firmly removed, Churchill did not like what he saw. He told Eden on 4 May that he feared that 'terrible things have happened during the Russian advance through Germany to the Elbe', and he now believed that if the Allies stuck to the agreed zonal division of Germany, it would mean 'the tide of Russian domination sweeping forward 120 miles on a front of 300 or 400 miles. This would be an event which, if it occurred, would be one of the most melancholy in history.' It was rather late in the day to have come to that conclusion. He now saw the prospect of Russia's frontier running from the Baltic to the Adriatic, including 'all the great capitals of middle Europe'. This, he thought, 'constitutes an event in the history of Europe to which there has been no parallel'. Churchill felt that the Great Powers needed to discuss the matter. His own proposals for dealing with the situation were unlikely to make it any better. He thought that the Anglo-American armies should remain where they were until 'we are satisfied about Poland and also about the temporary character of the Russian occupation of Germany, and the conditions to be established in the Russianized or Russian-controlled countries'. But the question of whether Britain could afford to do this was a vexed one. Time was not on her side. 'All these matters can only be settled before ... the United States Armies withdraw from Europe'. An 'early and speedy showdown' was essential.[21]

Another 'early and speedy showdown' was now likely on the electoral front. Stalin and Truman wanted to postpone the announcement of 'Victory in Europe' until 9 May, but on the evening of 7 May crowds in the London streets were 'beyond control' and victory was proclaimed on the following day.[22] 'Victory in Europe day' was a time for unconfined rejoicing and witnesses the apotheosis of Churchill as war hero. At 3 p.m. he broadcast the news of the German surrender to the nation from 10 Downing Street, and as he came out to go to the House the staff lined the path to the garden door to applaud him. His eyes brimming with tears, Churchill left for the Commons.[23] Horse Guards Parade, Birdcage Walk and Great George Street were, like Parliament Square itself, packed with crowds, and all along the way the Prime Minister was greeted with cries of 'good old Winnie'. It took half an hour to travel a quarter of a mile, and every minute of every yard was filled with the outpouring of the emotions of relief, pride and thankfulness – Churchill had won the war – and historical immortality.

Just before half-past three Churchill entered the Chamber; MPs 'yelled and yelled and waved their Order Papers'.[24] He read out the statement which he had just delivered over the radio and then, setting aside his spectacles, he did something which he rarely essayed – he spoke impromptu, thanking the House for its 'noble support', adding that 'the strength of the Parliamentary institution has been shown to enable it at the same moment to preserve all the title-deeds of democracy while waging war in the most stern and protracted form'. He concluded by doing what Lloyd George had done a quarter of a century before, proposing that the House adjourn to St Margaret's Church to 'give humble and reverent thanks to Almighty God for our deliverance from the threat of German domination'.[25] After the ceremony Churchill went back through Central Hall, once more the target of the plaudits of the crowd. From the balcony of the Ministry of Health overlooking Whitehall he saluted the people, telling them, 'This is your victory!' This brought the only note of disagreement of the day as the crowd roared back, 'No – it is yours.' It was, Churchill declared, 'the victory of the cause of freedom in every land'. And that was the note which the British people took to heart – even if, to the peoples of Poland and of eastern Europe, such words would have a hollow ring. This was not what the British people in their hour of triumph wished to hear. That evening Churchill once more saluted and was saluted by the crowds outside Downing Street. His words enshrined the apotheosis of the national achievement. It was, Churchill proclaimed, the 'victory of the great British nation as a whole'. Britain, 'this ancient island', had been the first to 'draw the sword against tyranny' and, never 'downhearted', even at the blackest times, the nation had come through the fires of war to victory. There was, he reminded his listeners, still the war against Japan to win, but they were more interested in singing 'Land of Hope and Glory'.[26]

At the end of his speech on the radio Churchill had said, 'we must now devote all our strength and resources to the completion of our task, both at home and abroad'; but to do this required political stability. At Cabinet on 4 May Bevin had taken exception to remarks by Churchill which implied that an election was imminent, pointing out that Labour had not definitely decided that the coalition should be broken up. But Churchill, pointing out the 'obvious drawbacks of a Government under sentence of execution', made it 'quite clear that he means to put an end to the Coalition, one way or another, before the end of the month'.[27] He sought Eden's opinion as to whether the election should come in June or October, and the Foreign Secretary, whilst he would have preferred to see the Government continue until the defeat of Japan, gave it as his opinion that it was better not to perpetuate the present uncertainty.[28] But as relations with the Soviets deteriorated, Churchill began to wonder whether an early election was really the best option.[29]

The prospect of American forces beginning to withdraw from Europe worried Churchill profoundly, as he told Truman on 11 May. An 'iron curtain' had been 'drawn down' upon the Russian front. It was, he thought, 'vital now to come to an understanding with Russia, or see where we are with her', and he renewed his call for a conference with Stalin.[30] The most obvious area where tension was building up was in the Venezia Giulia, where Tito's regime had designs on Trieste. Churchill had urged on Truman the importance of seizing the city, but when General Alexander began to occupy it on 1 May he found that Tito's forces were already in parts of the suburbs.[31] Truman agreed with Churchill in wanting to prevent a 'land grab' in advance of the peace conference. 'If we stand firm on this issue, as we are doing on Poland,' Truman told Churchill on 12 May, 'we can hope to avoid a host of similar encroachments.'[32] Churchill saw this as a triumph for his policy of enlisting American aid against the Soviets, but once again he was too sanguine.[33]

Truman and his advisers were aware of the advantages to Britain of a Soviet 'bogey', which could be used to induce them to keep American forces in Europe, and they were by no means convinced of Churchill's case; there was also some anxiety that a conflict over Trieste might drag America into 'war against Belgrade and Moscow'.[34] Churchill, Truman feared, was 'trying to make me the paw for the cat that pulled the chestnuts out of the fire'.[35] He had little intention of letting such a state of affairs come to pass. But nor, as he made clear to Churchill, did he intend to let Tito get away with anything in Trieste.

The prospect of conflict over Trieste made Churchill reconsider the prospects for an election. As he told Eden on 12 May, they could hardly ask for Labour's support in 'so serious a venture' and then 'immediately break up the Government'.[36] On 18 May Churchill wrote formally to the Labour and Liberal leaders presenting them with the alternatives of an immediate election or continuing the coalition until Japan was defeated. As a sop to Attlee and Labour Churchill promised that the Government would try to implement the Beveridge report and policies to ensure full employment.[37]

The Labour leaders knew that Churchill was under 'very heavy pressure from the Tory Party' to 'take' the election 'quickly'; indeed, he had told Bevin on 11 May that the Tories knew 'they can't win without me'.[38] Bevin and Attlee would have preferred to postpone an election, but the Labour Party conference at Blackpool on 19 May settled the matter the other way. On 21 May Attlee surprised Churchill by rejecting his proposal. The Prime Minister was 'hurt at the unnecessarily waspish and even offensive tone of Attlee's reply'.[39] Harold Macmillan and Randolph Churchill, who were both at dinner with Churchill at Chequers when Attlee's reply arrived, were not displeased to have placed on Labour the onus of breaking up the great coalition, but

Colville did not think that Churchill was happy.[40] He did not look forward to coming down from the pantheon of heroes into the arena of electoral strife, particularly at such a juncture.[41] But just as Labour had made the Churchill coalition, now it broke it. Churchill wrote to the King on 22 May requesting a dissolution of Parliament and after going to the Palace the following day, it was announced that a general election would be held.

Churchill was not only not desirous of descending into becoming a mere politician again, he had little love for the prospect of forming a purely Conservative Government to preside over the country until the election. The task of forming the 'Caretaker Government' gave him the opportunity to reward old friends and to try to solicit Liberal support. At dinner with Eden and Bracken on 24 May the latter criticised Churchill's choice of Ministers, which brought 'an explosion' from Churchill and provoked a shouting match between the two men. Bracken 'flounced out', refusing to take the Board of Trade until he knew whether Churchill was going to accept the agreements reached at Bretton Woods about the convertibility of sterling. Beaverbrook was then sent for, and he also refused to serve. Poor Eden, who was suffering from an ulcer, was not edified: 'I loathe these scenes, they are a hideous waste of time.'[42] But by 26 May the lineaments of the Government were plain. Bracken agreed to take the Admiralty and Macmillan received his first Ministerial office at the Air Ministry. Lord Dunglass, despite having been Chamberlain's PPS and having spoken against Yalta, was sent to the Foreign Office as Eden's Under-Secretary. The coalition nature of the Government was maintained by the presence in it of Liberals such as Lloyd George's son Gwilym and of Leslie Hore-Belisha, finally rescued from the wilderness to which Chamberlain had condemned him in 1940. Sir John Anderson at the Exchequer and Lord Woolton as Lord President of the Council maintained a 'non-Party' element. Beaverbrook, who had been active in promoting an election, now turned to Woolton and asked if he had 'any views yet on what election issues should be put forward? Outside of Churchill?'[43] There were other 'issues', but anyone could have been forgiven for believing that the only real Conservative policy was 'let Churchill finish the job'.

Woolton, who had made a great name for himself as Minister of Food, was alive to the danger that people would 'wonder whether the great war leader will be a good peace leader'. As he told Beaverbrook on 31 May, he found the most common question on everyone's lips was '"Is he really interested in reconstruction and social reform?"', which made it essential for the Conservatives to 'come out with a statement of what we intend to do about these things'. What the Government wanted, Woolton thought, was a mixture of 'Churchill the war-winner, Churchill the bull-dog breed in international conferences, and Churchill the leader of a Government with a programme of social reform'.[44] Woolton was right, but it is doubtful whether even that would have produced a markedly different election result. As it was, the

Conservatives chose to emphasise the first two of Woolton's points rather than the last – and that ensured defeat.

Labour entered the election with much trepidation. Few of its MPs expected to win, and there were some who thought that they would be fortunate to be able to make a dent in the 1935 election result.[45] Herbert Morrison, who was the shrewdest of the Labour tacticians, was one of the few who thought that Labour could win. If the Conservatives were blinded by Churchill's prestige and relied upon it to win, Labour were equally affected by it. A cartoon in the *Daily Express* summed up the mood of the Conservative campaign. It depicted Bracken in an admiral's uniform and Beaverbrook in a dockyard looking at a gigantic figurehead carved in the form of Churchill, with one saying to the other: 'We have a captain and we have a figure-head. If we shout loudly enough perhaps no one will notice that we don't have a ship.' This was cruel and unkind, but it contained a kernel of truth.

The Conservatives did have a manifesto and in its contents it was not that different from Labour's – which is not surprising considering that both Parties were campaigning on the promises made during the coalition, but the title and the layouts of the manifestoes gave the game away. The Conservative one was entitled, with splendid eighteenth-century style, 'Mr Churchill's Address to the Electors', and it opened with passages about foreign policy and the importance of maintaining Britain's prestige abroad. Only later did it get on to the domestic issues such as housing and employment, which, as Woolton had correctly spotted, were what the electorate was really interested in. Labour did not make the same mistake. Their manifesto was entitled 'Let us Face the Future', and it went on to do just that, putting housing, health and employment at the forefront of its concerns. However Churchill and the Conservatives had conducted their campaign, they were unlikely to have succeeded, having started out pointing it in the wrong direction.

It was with some sadness that Churchill witnessed the break-up of what he liked to call 'the Grand Coalition'. He gave a party for its members at Downing Street on the afternoon of 28 May and, 'with tears running down his cheeks', saluted his former colleagues, saying that 'the light of history will shine on all your helmets'. Then, with an oblique reference to the Russian troubles which were on his mind, he added that he was sure that 'if ever such another mortal danger threatened, we would all do the same again'. He would, he said, take 'my good friend Clem Attlee' with him to the conference with Truman and Stalin which was to take place in Potsdam. They all dispersed into the gardens for photographs and Churchill, in high good humour as the rain began to fall, called proceedings to a close with the remark, 'We'd better finish this or my political opponents will say this is a conspiracy on my part to give them all rheumatism.'[46] Churchill's precipitous descent into the worst sort of electioneering came as a great shock after all this friendliness.

Churchill's first election broadcast on 4 June was listened to with great anticipation, but by the end most listeners shared Amery's sense of depression. Churchill 'jumped straight off his pedestal as world statesman to deliver a fantastical exaggerated onslaught on Socialism', and Amery feared that Bracken and Beaverbrook 'have completely collared' Churchill.[47] Moran was told bluntly that Churchill's speech was 'cheap' – it had certainly missed the mark.[48] Churchill chose to concentrate on the issue of 'Socialism versus Individualism', and he declared that 'no Socialist Government conducting the entire life and industry of the country' could afford to dispense with 'some form of Gestapo'. Given the revelations from Buchenwald and Dachau this was, to put it mildly, an insensitive and foolish comment. If Churchill expected people not to wonder how it was that men with whom he had been happy to co-operate the week before had suddenly been so transformed, he was wrong. He launched into a blistering attack on Socialism as 'abhorrent to the British ideas of freedom'. It was, he warned, 'inseparably interwoven with Totalitarianism and the abject worship of the State'. There was, as many staunch Conservatives agreed, much to be said for this point of view, but however much former Chief Whips like Margesson and right-wingers like Channon were cheered by Churchill's attacks, Amery was right to think that it would put off a lot of uncommitted voters.[49]

Churchill's preoccupation with the threat of totalitarianism and with external threats was understandable given the situation in which Britain found herself, but after the euphoria of V-E Day the British people did not want to hear about problems with Russia over Poland. For four years the British propaganda machine had worked overtime to create the image of 'Uncle Joe' and 'our Russian allies', so few perceived Russia as any threat. Moreover, to have confessed that at the end of a long and ruinous war Britain was still facing a threat to the balance of power in Europe would, indeed, have been to have confessed failure. The result was a contest fought on two levels. Labour campaigned on the promise of building the 'New Jerusalem' whilst Churchill, banking on the hope that the 'desire for a new world' was nothing like as universal as the 'gratitude' to himself,[50] hammered away at 'Socialism' and got on with trying to ensure the support of the Americans against any Russian threat.

Truman's response to Churchill's telegrams about the 'iron curtain' was not everything which Churchill could have wished. Robust as the President was about Trieste, he told Churchill that it was impossible to forecast the future in Europe.[51] Then in late May came something like a revival of Roosevelt's approach as Truman attempted to mediate between his two allies. Hopkins, although sick and ailing, was sent to Moscow to talk to Stalin and the former American Ambassador to Moscow, Joseph Davies, was sent to see Churchill. Hopkins assured Stalin that America wished to 'work together' with Russia in peace as well as war, but public opinion, which had been almost universally sympathetic to the Soviets, was now disturbed by events since Yalta; indeed, the 'deterioration ... had been so serious as to affect adversely the relations between our two countries'. If things continued along their current path, the hopes which Roosevelt had always nurtured would be 'destroyed'.[52] Six conversations with Stalin between 26 May and 6 June seemed to produce what months of telegraphing and co-operation with the British had failed to – some movement on Stalin's part. He agreed to invite non-Lublin Poles for consultation in Moscow and even to contemplate their inclusion in a Polish government. Stalin also advocated the convening of a peace conference to settle outstanding questions.[53] Perhaps he was reassured by Hopkins's willingness to promise that America wanted a 'Poland friendly to the Soviet Union'; he was certainly encouraged by the fact that he was not facing an Anglo-American front. Stalin told Hopkins at dinner on 31 May that 'he believed that Churchill had misled the Americans' as regards events inside Poland and that the British wished to 'manage the affairs of Poland'.[54]

Although Churchill did not know what was going on in Moscow, he had become aware of a declension in American resolve even before Hopkins had left America. Truman's telegram on 14 May advocating a 'wait and see' attitude to the future was the forerunner of a series of cautious telegrams, which culminated in one warning that America could not get involved in fighting over Trieste unless the British were actually attacked.[55] Since Churchill was having troubled with Field Marshal Alexander, who was doubtful whether British troops would be willing to fight the Soviets and the Yugoslavs over an Italian city, this was the last thing which the Prime Minister wished to hear.[56] He was even less impressed by the arrival of Joseph Davies on 26 May.

Churchill had not been consulted about the Hopkins mission, but it and the arrival of Davies, a well-known sympathiser with the Soviet system, could hardly portend any good for the prospect of a firm Anglo-American stand over Poland. At his first meeting with the Prime Minister on 26 May, Davies told him that Hopkins was going to propose a tripartite meeting to Stalin; Truman wondered whether Churchill would have any objection to his having a meeting with Stalin first? Nothing could have been further from Churchill's desire. His conversations with Davies were the most unsettling Churchill ever had with an American. He told Davies that he was not willing to be excluded from a Truman/Stalin meeting and that he objected to the implication that 'the new disputes now opening up with the Soviets lay between Britain and Russia'.[57] He then, according to Davies's account, launched into a bitter attack on the Soviets which astonished the American.[58] Churchill attacked de Gaulle and Tito for their ingratitude towards him and then criticised the whole idea of unconditional surrender, saying, according to Davies, that had it not been for that he could have made peace with Hitler. Whilst much of this sounds like Churchill, particularly after 11 p.m., the last remark sounds more like a corruption of something which Davies himself said. Listening to Churchill's comments about the dire state of Europe and the Soviet threat, Davies said that he wondered whether Churchill was now 'willing to declare to the world that he and Britain had made a mistake in not supporting Hitler, for, as I understood him, he was now expressing the doctrine which Hitler and Goebbels had been proclaiming and reiterating for the past four years in an effort to break up Allied unity'.[59] It was little wonder that Churchill disliked Davies.

Churchill's evident desire to keep American troops in Europe to serve what Davies saw as purely British interests shocked the American and certainly contributed to Truman's neo-Rooseveltian policy of mediating between his two allies.[60] At his second meeting with Davies on 27 May, Churchill endeavoured to get him to see that Britain and the United States were 'united . . . upon the same ideologies, namely, freedom, and the principles set out in the American Constitution'.[61] Churchill's problem was one which he set out in a note of his conversation for Eden's benefit. He could not 'readily bring himself to accept the idea that the position of the United States is that Britain and Soviet Russia are just two Foreign Powers, six of one and half a dozen of the other, with whom the troubles of the late war have to be adjusted'. It was a most revealing statement and summed up the fundamental flaw in Churchill's diplomacy. He had always acted as though British and American interests were identical and latterly as though the Americans needed to be reminded of this; the revelation that this was not the case naturally disturbed him a great deal. There was, he thought, 'no equality between right and wrong'.

Churchill had, in fact, worked himself up into an ideological rage, and this was vented against Davies, the Soviets and the Labour Party; the bitterness of his 'Gestapo speech' cannot be understood purely in its domestic context. Churchill's note to Eden on 28 May reveals how little he had learnt from the war. Although he expressed his desire for a 'real friendship between the peoples of Russia and those of Great Britain', he showed less than no comprehension of what Stalin saw as his legitimate demands. As Stalin saw things, a friendly Poland was a *sine qua non* and he simply did not understand what the British interest in that country consisted of. For Churchill it was a 'matter of honour'. Britain had gone to war over Poland even though she had been 'ill-prepared'; she was now 'better armed'. If this rambling meant anything, it signified a willingness to take up arms once more for Poland's 'independence and sovereignty'; it was little wonder that Davies was worried about Churchill's state of mind. But the British were not, according to Churchill, just concerned with Poland. The 'rights of Czechoslovakia are very dear to the hearts of the British people' (who, presumably, had changed their views since 1938), as was the 'position of the Magyars' and of Austria. The Balkan countries too 'had the right to live'. Churchill did not want Truman to 'dismiss all these topics in the desire to placate the imperialistic demands of Soviet Communist Russia'. This was Churchill at his most unrealistic, and he was wise not to send these sentiments to Truman as they stood. Whatever he said about wanting Soviet friendship, Churchill was clearly not willing to pay any price for it and equally clearly wanted American troops to remain in Europe to avoid a price being extracted. Those who feared that Churchill was going to 'embroil us in a stew with Russia' were not far from the truth.[62] On 27 May he warned the Chiefs of Staff not to be too hasty in their demobilisation.[63]

Churchill, mindful of what he considered to be Chamberlain's weakness before the war, now wished to be 'firm' with Stalin. The Americans were not so convinced that Stalin's aims were either illegitimate or incompatible with world peace. In his memoirs Churchill reproduces the draft note which he had prepared after talking to Davies and says that he sent it to Truman, but he did not do so.[64] Viewed against the backdrop of the Cold War, which was in full force by the time Churchill's memoirs were written, his comments seem prescient, but viewed against the circumstances of May 1945, they seem more designed as a self-fulfilling prophecy. In his telegram to Truman on 29 May Churchill expressed his disappointment that the proposed conference would not take place in London, and he set his face against a preliminary Truman/Stalin meeting, but he expressed a willingness to meet at Potsdam.[65] In a further message on 31 May Churchill said that he had had 'agreeable talks with Mr Davies' – this might have been described by the young Churchill as a 'terminological inexactitude', for he confessed to others that 'after his talk with Davies he needed a bath to get rid of the ooze and the slime'.[66] What the Davies talks had revealed was the distance between Churchill and the Americans.

Churchill's bitterness against the totalitarian threat spilled out into his election campaign. For the Conservatives Churchill was the election issue. With Eden incapacitated by his ulcer, the main burden of the campaign fell on Churchill's shoulders, and this was not necessarily an advantage. Eden might have been able to make a more effective appeal to the centre ground; Churchill's appeal was firmly to Conservative supporters and those who shared his view of the international situation. The opinion polls demonstrated a swing towards the Government during the election campaign, which throws some doubt on the idea that Churchill's campaign style alienated voters. It certainly alienated many intellectuals, and even Harold Nicolson, who worshipped Churchill, thought his first broadcast 'disastrous'.[67] Churchill's face glowered down defiantly from every Conservative husting in the land, and the casual observer could have been forgiven for wondering how many seats the Prime Minister was standing for. Given their pre-war record and the fact that Churchill had made no efforts during the war to revitalise the Party, the Conservatives were perhaps wise to concentrate on the Prime Minister as their main card. It was true that their manifesto committed them to the establishment of a national health service and full employment just as Labour's did, but when it came to the question of which Party could be trusted to deliver the 'New Jerusalem', few would put their money on the Tories; and here Churchill simply confirmed existing opinions – no one could argue that he was vastly interested in post-war reconstruction.

The difference in style between the two leaders could hardly have been more marked. Churchill, the great war leader, accompanied by his entourage, would address one or two main meetings, whilst Attlee, driven in the family car by his wife, would stop off at the road-side, where he was photographed eating a packed lunch. In 1945 the 'image-makers' of modern politics were not yet thought of, but as an image of who was more 'down to earth' and concerned with the 'common people', Saatchi and Saatchi would have been hard-pressed to have come up with anything better. Churchill was more concerned with what he saw to be the most worrying European situation which he had ever seen,[68] but the electorate, screened from these concerns, was preoccupied with building a better Britain and a brighter future. When the election came on 5 July, older voters still cast their vote for the Conservatives and for the national saviour, but more middle-class voters than ever before voted Labour, as did the first-timers. Churchill was usually an enthusiastic campaigner, but this time his heart did not seem to be in things.[69] Certainly contemplation of Potsdam and the Russian problem distracted his attention from domestic political disputes, but there was more to it than that. During the election campaign Churchill was rather like a deep-sea diver entering a decompression chamber. During the war Churchill had been treated as a privileged being, admired and cosseted in his great struggle, but now, as Moran put it, 'he will be treated like other men. It is going to be a big drop to earth. It will hurt him. He will hate it'; it did and Churchill did.[70]

By polling day Churchill was exhausted, yet he still had Potsdam to come.[71] Because the election result was not expected for a fortnight, Churchill took Attlee to Potsdam with him – a circumstance which amused Stalin, who could not imagine losing an election. On 15 July Churchill finally met Truman and, of course, set about trying to charm him in order to build up the same relationship that he had enjoyed with Roosevelt.[72] He asked Truman bluntly at their first meeting whether those states which had passed into Russian control were 'free and independent or not'. But Truman was not going to be manoeuvred into an anti-Soviet front by Churchill, and whilst he said that he was not willing to see the eastern European states become mere satellites of the Soviet Union, he wanted to grant Stalin's legitimate demands.[73] During the conference Truman strove to mediate between his two allies; however little Churchill felt that he ought to be equating Britain and Russia, that was just what he did. Eden found Churchill's performance at the first plenary session on 17 July 'very bad'. Not only had the Prime Minister obviously not read his briefs, but this fact was clear to others. And, meeting Stalin once more, Churchill seemed captivated by him: 'I like that man.'[74] Tough negotiations over Poland and the future of Germany served to disenchant Churchill a little.

On the evening of 23 July Churchill telephoned Beaverbrook in London to check on his estimate of the election result – 'the PM would have a comfortable majority' was the press baron's opinion.[75] The following day was spent in hard bargaining with the Soviets over the future of Poland, but Churchill was now preoccupied with the election result. He did not have long to wait. On 26 July the first results came through. Bracken was 'out', Macmillan was 'out', then so were Randolph and Leo Amery. Churchill offered one of his staff a brandy for every Conservative gain – the man received three glasses during the course of the day.[76] It was a landslide exceeded only by that which had buried the Conservatives in 1905–6. Labour had 393 seats compared to the Conservatives 213. Labour had a clear majority for the first time in British history. In his memoirs Eden wrote that whilst there had been 'much gratitude to W[inston] as war leader, there is not the same enthusiasm for him as PM of the peace', and, in the privacy of the diary, he went on to add, 'and who shall say that the British people were wrong in this?'[77] He had a point.

The Aftermath

It was a shattering blow. Even in his own constituency where an 'independent' had stood against him, 10,488 votes had been cast against Churchill. A premonition had come to him in the night, but nothing could have prepared him for the scale of the defeat. When Clementine tried to comfort him by saying that it was probably a blessing in disguise, Churchill could only grunt that it was very well disguised.[1] The King offered him the Order of the Garter, but just having received the 'order of the boot' from the electorate Churchill did not feel much inclined to accept it. He resigned on 26 July. On the afternoon of 27 July he held a final Cabinet meeting. As they left he commented to Eden: 'Thirty years of my life have been passed in this room. I shall never sit in it again.'[2] Eden comforted Churchill by reminding him that his place in history was secure. Eden, who had heard during the campaign that his eldest son had been killed in action and whose marriage was breaking up, was not sad to be out of office – though he sympathised with Churchill. At the end of August, looking at photographs of Potsdam, Eden could only feel 'thankful that I was out of it'. He felt no desire to 'go back', and, 'fond as I am of W[inston], I do not feel I have the strength to undertake life or work with him again, it is too much of a strain and struggle'.[3] Both men would have been surprised, and Eden horrified, if they had been told that they would be back in harness again in 1951 and that Churchill would not retire until April 1955.

But Churchill's ejection from office marked a watershed. As Moran put it, 'the ten years that followed added little to his stature', and he would have done better to have followed Clementine's advice to stand down.[4] But if Churchill's political actions in the next decade added little to his stature, his other activities lent lustre to his fame. The 'iron curtain' speech at Fulton, Missouri, in 1946 confirmed his reputation as a 'visionary', whilst the six volumes of his history of the Second World War set an imprint on the historical record from which historians, even today, cannot quite escape.[5] Churchill expunged the defeat of 1945 with a narrow victory in 1951, but he long outstayed his welcome by not retiring until April 1955, by which time it was rumoured that he was 'gaga'. In retirement the legend grew as the man faded. Indeed, as Britain's decline as a Great Power proceeded apace, so did the need for Churchill grow. Whilst he lived, trailing clouds of glory, the fame of the Empire for which he had stood was not quite dimmed. There were books, such as Brooke's diaries and those of Moran, which seemed to the worshippers to tarnish the legend, but nothing could dim Churchill's glory. He died on 24 January 1965, seventy years to the day since the death of Lord Randolph Churchill, and when he was buried they buried the Empire with him. *The Times*'s headline read simply: 'The Greatest Englishman of His Time' – and there were those who thought that the personal pronoun should have been replaced by the word 'all'.

For a scapegrace schoolboy and a lieutenant of hussars to become a world-renowned statesman, and the winner of the Nobel Prize for Literature, was by any standards a remarkable feat, yet his admirers could not be content with this. As the layers of varnish settled on the portrait, something was lost. Churchill's admirers were jealous of his fame, disliking books which cast any unfavourable light upon the great man – Inspector Thompson's memoir and that of Eisenhower's aide, Captain Butcher, were early victims of this process. Starting after his father's death Randolph Churchill began a multi-volumed entombment of the mythological figure, and after 1968 Martin Gilbert applied the steadier hand of the historian to the task, completing what must be seen as the last of the great Victorian biographies some twenty years later. Gladstone rated three volumes written over five years, Disraeli got six, spread out over twenty, whilst Joseph Chamberlain also got six, but spread out over thirty years; it seemed entirely appropriate that Churchill should get eight volumes spread out over twenty years.

Yet the theme of the official biography, 'he shall be his own biographer', militates against analysis of the final achievement. Churchill, after all, had already very successfully been his own biographer in some dozen or so tomes, and whilst it is handy to have an accumulation of even more material from every available source, that is not quite the same as a portrait of Churchill or an analysis of his work. That he was a great man cannot be doubted, but his flaws too were on the same heroic scale as the rest of the man. By the end of the war even Churchill was beginning to wonder what he had achieved and he was resting all his eggs in the basket of American help. His attitude was already making Stalin suspicious of British intentions, and the change in his willingness to contemplate satisfaction of Soviet desires said little for his sense of reality. In 1938–9 he had advocated Britain forming a 'Grand Alliance' to prevent Hitler dominating Europe, and he had grossly overestimated Britain's capacity to fight that war – a mistake not made by his predecessor. At the end of that war he was, once again, faced with what looked like an attempt by one power to dominate the Continent, an odd result for so much expenditure of treasure and manpower, and yet again he sought an alliance to prevent it. Life had become a perpetual struggle, one long round of war. Churchill had nothing to offer the British people in 1945, and no one has been prepared seriously to argue that he did. His thinking on foreign and domestic policy was stuck firmly in the past. Even when he grasped new ideas like 'Europe', it was to do little more than deliver impressive speeches.

Surveying the situation in July 1945 it was hard to argue that Britain had won in any sense save that of avoiding defeat; indeed, Churchill's remarks to Joseph Davies seem to reflect some inkling of this. He had destroyed the awful tyranny of Hitler, but what had risen in its place? Perhaps his own comments to Macmillan in Cairo in 1943 about Cromwell indicate a degree of self-knowledge: 'he made one terrible mistake. Obsessed in his youth by fear of the power of Spain, he failed to observe the rise of France. Will that be said of me?'[6] If 'Germany' is substituted for 'Spain' and 'Russia' for 'France', then the answer to Churchill's rhetorical question might well be 'yes'. In the final volume of his memoirs he strove to avert any such charge, showing how early he had feared the 'iron curtain', but it could be said that he was both too slow and too quick to act: too slow in the sense that the time not to make concessions was 1941–3; too fast in the sense that having made concessions it was foolish to take umbrage so quickly in February/ March 1945; but by that stage Churchill was desperate to maintain the American alliance, and this was the only means of doing so.

Churchill stood for the British Empire, for British independence and for an 'anti-Socialist' vision of Britain. By July 1945 the first of these was on the skids, the second was dependent solely upon America and the third had just vanished in a Labour election victory. An appropriate moment to stop, for it was indeed the end of glory.

Notes

1: The Subaltern's Star

1 Austen Chamberlain Mss., letters to his sisters, AC 8, Austen to Ida Chamberlain, 2 November 1930
2 M. Gilbert (ed.), *Winston S. Churchill, vol. V, companion vol. 2: The Wilderness Years, 1929–35* (1981) (hereinafter *Churchill V, companion vol. 2*), Barnes to Churchill, 26 October 1930, pp. 210–11
3 *Ibid.*, Churchill to Maurice Ashley, 13 July 1931, p. 18
4 Randolph S. Churchill, *Winston S. Churchill, vol. I: companion vol. 2* (1967) (hereinafter *Churchill I, companion vol. 2*), p. 924
5 J. Ramsden, *The Age of Balfour and Baldwin* (1979), p. 98
6 R. R. James, *Churchill: A Study in Failure* (1970), pp. 14–15
7 W. S. Churchill, *The River War* (1899), p. 37
8 James, p. 5. This also seemed to be the message of the film *Young Winston*. See also, M. Gilbert, *Winston S. Churchill, vol. VIII* (1988) (hereinafter *Churchill VIII*), pp. 365–72
9 A. J. P. Taylor (ed.), *Churchill: Four Faces and the Man* (1969), p. 207 ff.
10 Lord Moran, *Winston Churchill: The Struggle for Survival 1940–65* (1966), p. 400
11 *Ibid.*, p. 123
12 Randolph S. Churchill, *Winston S. Churchill, vol. I* (1968) (hereinafter *Churchill I*), p. 352
13 Moran, p. 778
14 *Churchill V, companion vol. 2*, Lady Leslie to Churchill, 22 October 1930, p. 206
15 R. F. Forster, *Lord Randolph Churchill* (1981 edn), pp. 30–2, for this
16 Churchill, *The River War*, p. 33
17 Moran, p. 621
18 *Ibid.*, p. 123
19 Randolph S. Churchill, *Winston S. Churchill, vol. I: companion vol. 1* (1967) (hereinafter *Churchill I, companion vol. 1*), p. 154
20 *Ibid.*, pp. 154, 168–9
21 *Ibid.*, pp. 168–9.
22 E. D. W. Chaplin (ed.), *Winston Churchill and Harrow* (1941), p. 2
23 Moran, p. 123
24 Chaplin (ed.), pp. 11–16
25 *Churchill I*, p. 202
26 *Churchill I, companion vol. 1*, p. 328
27 *Ibid.*, p. 338
28 *Ibid.*, p. 353

29 W. S. Churchill, *My Early Life* (1974 edn), pp. 43–4; *Churchill I*, p. 189
30 *Churchill I, companion vol. 1*, pp. 385–7
31 *Ibid.*, pp. 390–1
32 *Ibid.*, p. 457
33 *Churchill I*, pp. 248–50
34 *Ibid.*, p. 371
35 Churchill, *My Early Life*, p. 76; *Churchill I*, p. 211
36 Churchill, *ibid.*
37 *Churchill I, companion vol. 1*, p. 583
38 *Ibid.*, p. 585
39 Chaplin (ed.), p. 16
40 *Churchill I, companion vol. 1*, p. 585
41 *Churchill I*, p. 349
42 *Churchill I, companion vol. 1*, p. 600
43 *Ibid.*, p. 666
44 M. & E. Brock (eds), *H. H. Asquith, Letters to Venetia Stanley* (1982) (hereinafter *Asquith Letters*), p. 415
45 *Churchill I*, pp. 297–8
46 *Ibid.*, p. 293
47 *Churchill I, companion vol. 1*, pp. 816–17
48 Moran, p. 405

2: A Victorian Frame of Mind

1 R. R. James, *Victor Cazalet: A Portrait* (1976), diary, 28 March 1922, pp. 76–7
2 J. Barnes & D. Nicholson (eds), *The Empire at Bay: Leo Amery Diaries 1929–55* (1988) (hereinafter *Amery Diary II*), 5 August 1929, p. 49
3 *Churchill I, companion vol. 2*, p. 799
4 W. S. Churchill, *Savrola* (1974 edn), p. 34
5 *Ibid.*, p. 115
6 M. Cowling, *Religion and Public Doctrine in Modern England* (1980), p. 289
7 *Churchill I, companion vol. 2*, p. 815
8 Churchill, *Savrola*, p. 165
9 Cowling, pp. 30–1
10 Churchill, *Savrola*, p. 118
11 *Ibid.*, p. 79
12 *Ibid.*, pp. 78–9
13 *Churchill I, companion vol. 1*, p. 760
14 *Ibid.*, p. 767
15 Churchill, *Savrola*, p. 115
16 *Churchill I, companion vol. 2*, p. 751
17 *Ibid.*, p. 734
18 *Ibid.*, p. 751
19 *Ibid.*, p. 828
20 *Ibid.*, p. 811
21 *Ibid.*, p. 784

22 *Churchill I*, pp. 364–5
23 *Ibid.*, p. 381
24 *Ibid.*, pp. 380–2
25 *Churchill I, companion vol. 2*, p. 946
26 *Ibid.*, p. 863
27 *Ibid.*, p. 864
28 Moran, p. 773
29 *Churchill I, companion vol. 2*, p. 750
30 *Ibid.*, p. 938
31 *Ibid.*, p. 903
32 *Ibid.*, p. 807
33 *Ibid.*, p. 823
34 *Ibid.*, p. 938
35 *Ibid.*, p. 828
36 Lord Birkenhead, *Churchill 1874–1922* (1989), pp. 83–4
37 *Churchill I, companion vol. 2*, p. 950
38 *Ibid.*, Churchill to his mother, 22 December 1897, p. 839
39 *Ibid.*, p. 933
40 *Ibid.*, pp. 999–1001
41 *Churchill I*, pp. 420–1
42 *Churchill I, companion vol. 2*, pp. 813, 858
43 *Ibid.*, p. 862
44 *Ibid.*, pp. 954–5
45 *Ibid.*, p. 996
46 *Ibid.*, p. 1003
47 *Ibid.*, p. 812
48 A. Storr, 'The Man', in Taylor (ed.), *Churchill: Four Faces and the Man*, p. 225
49 Churchill, *My Early Life*, pp. 311–15
50 *Churchill I*, pp. 443–8
51 *Ibid.*, pp. 462–505
52 *Churchill I, companion vol. 2*, memo. by Churchill, c. 1912, pp. 1094–9
53 *Ibid.*, Churchill to Aylmer Haldane, 5 October 1990, pp. 1106–8
54 M. Gilbert (ed.), *Winston S. Churchill, vol. V, companion vol. 1* (1979) (hereinafter *Churchill V, companion vol. 1*), Churchill to the Prince of Wales, 27 October 1900, p. 1067
55 James, *Churchill*, p. 304
56 *Churchill V, companion vol. 2*, Churchill to Lord Knutsford, 28 October 1930, p. 213
57 *Churchill I*, p. 545
58 *Ibid.*, pp. 536–9

3: A Dissident Unionist

1 Randolph S. Churchill, *Winston S. Churchill, vol. II, companion vol. 1* (1969) (hereinafter *Churchill II, companion vol. 1*), p. 48
2 *Churchill I, companion vol. 2*, Chamberlain to Lady Randolph, 12 October 1900, p. 1208
3 *Ibid.*, St John Broderick to Churchill, 2 October 1900, p. 1204
4 James, *Victor Cazalet*, diary, 7 December 1924, p. 101
5 *Ibid.*; see also Balfour Papers, Add. Mss. 49694, Churchill to Balfour, 2 December 1911, fos 62–3
6 Forster, pp. 383–6, for a brilliant account; James,

Churchill, p. 16; M. Ashley, *Churchill as Historian* (1968), Chap. 5
7 *Churchill II, companion vol. 1*, pp. 1–21
8 Churchill, *The River War, passim*
9 W. S. Churchill, *The Malakand Field Force* (1898), *passim*
10 *Churchill I, companion vol. 1*, p. 1162
11 W. S. Churchill, *Mr Brodrick's Army* (1974 edn), pp. 1–11
12 *Ibid.*, p. 12
13 *Ibid.*, p. XIII
14 *Ibid.*, p. 40
15 *Churchill II, companion vol. 1*, Chamberlain to Churchill, 15 August 1903, p. 219
16 *Ibid.*, Morley to Churchill, 30 June 1902, p. 149
17 P. Gordon (ed.), *The Red Earl: The Papers of the Fifth Earl Spencer, vol. II: 1885–1906* (Northampton, 1986), p. 300
18 *Churchill II, companion vol. 1*, Churchill to Rosebery, 10 October 1902, p. 168
19 W. S. Churchill, *Great Contemporaries* (1937), pp. 3–4
20 Gordon (ed.), pp. 44–6
21 *Churchill II, companion vol. 1*, Cecil to Churchill, 28 December 1901, p. 112
22 *Ibid.*, Churchill to Rosebery, 20 October 1902, p. 168
23 Northcliffe Papers, Add. Mss. 62156, Churchill to Harmsworth, 26 August 1903, fo. 5
24 R. F. Mackay, *Balfour* (1985), p. 146
25 Northcliffe Papers, Add. Mss. 62156, Churchill to Harmsworth, 1 September 1903, fos 7–8
26 *Churchill II, companion vol. 1*, Churchill to Cecil, 5 June 1903, p. 197; Churchill to Devonshire, 13 July 1903, p. 211
27 *Ibid.*, Cecil to Churchill, 31 August 1903, p. 222
28 Churchill, *Great Contemporaries*, pp. 154–8. The whole story is in R. S. Churchill, *Lord Derby* (1959), pp. 79–81
29 *Churchill II, companion vol. 1*, Churchill to Cecil, 24 October 1903, pp. 242–4 This is the first of what would make up a fine library of revealing letters Churchill never sent.
30 *Ibid.*, Travis-Clegg to Churchill, 11, 14, 17 October 1903, pp. 232, 237–8, 239–40
31 *Ibid.*, Cecil to Churchill, 27 October 1903, pp. 244–5
32 *Ibid.*, Finnemore to McKenna, 2 December 1903, p. 257; Moore-Bayley to Churchill, 7 December 1903, pp. 259–61
33 Gordon (ed.), p. 317
34 *Churchill II, companion vol. 1*, Travis-Clegg to Churchill, 29 December 1903, pp. 275–6
35 *Ibid.*, Cecil to Churchill, December 1903, pp. 267–8
36 *Ibid.*, p. 267
37 Gordon (ed.), pp. 318–21
38 *Ibid.*, Spencer to Campbell-Bannerman, 12 January 1904, p. 323
39 R. R. James, *Churchill Speaks* (1981), p. 60
40 *Churchill II, companion vol. 1*, pp. 264–5, 269–71, 285–94, 303–5

41 Balfour Mss. 49694, Churchill to Balfour, 22 January 1904, fos 43–6
42 *Ibid.*, Balfour to Churchill, 1 February 1904, fo. 47
43 *Ibid.*, Churchill to Balfour, 2 February 1904, fo. 49
44 *Ibid.*, Churchill to Sandars, 5 February 1904, fo. 52
45 *Churchill II, companion vol. 1*, pp. 326–31
46 *Ibid.*, Churchill to Cecil, 1 January 1904, p. 283
47 *Ibid.*, pp. 342–7
48 *Ibid.*, Hicks-Beach to Churchill, 12 April 1904, p. 333
49 *Ibid.*, Churchill's correspondence with Laski, May 1904, pp. 354–9
50 *Ibid.*, Churchill letter, March 1904, p. 319
51 *Ibid.*, Churchill to Cecil, 2 June 1904, p. 346
52 *Ibid.*, Churchill to Moore-Bayley, 17 October 1904, p. 366
53 J. Vincent (ed.), *The Crawford Papers* (Manchester, 1984) (hereinafter *Crawford Papers*), entry for 2 August 1904, p. 76
54 *Churchill II, companion vol. 1*, p. 389
55 *Ibid.*, pp. 394–6
56 R. S. Churchill, *Winston S. Churchill, vol. II* (1967) (hereinafter *Churchill II*), p. 87
57 *Crawford Papers*, entry for 26 July 1905, p. 83
58 *Churchill II, companion vol. 1*, Morley to Churchill, 29 November 1905, p. 406
59 R. Hyam, *Elgin and Churchill at the Colonial Office* (1968), pp. 41–3
60 J. Wilson, *Sir Henry Campbell-Bannerman* (1973), p. 459

4: Son of his Father?

1 Forster, epilogue
2 W. S. Blunt, *My Diaries 1884–1914* (1932 edn), p. 489
3 *Ibid.*, p. 518
4 *Crawford Papers*, diary, 26 July 1905, p. 83
5 Moran, p. 745
6 D. Jablonsky, *Churchill: The Great Game and Total War* (1991), p. 24
7 Churchill, *Savrola*, p. 35
8 Jablonsky, p. 18
9 *Churchill II*, p. 329
10 Storr, 'The Man', in Taylor (ed.), *Churchill: Four Faces and the Man*, for this and much else
11 Hyam, p. 490
12 *Churchill II, companion vol. 1*, pp. 496–500, 504–9, 518–22
13 *Churchill II*, p. 147
14 A. L. Friedberg, *The Weary Titan: Britain and the Experience of Relative Decline 1895–1905* (Princeton, 1988), for a recent study
15 Chamberlain at the 1902 Colonial conference
16 D. G. Boyce, *The Crisis of British Power: The Imperial and Naval Papers of the Second Earl of Selborne 1895–1910* (1990) (hereinafter *Selborne Papers II*), Selborne to Midleton, 20 July 1905, p. 206
17 Ged Martin, *The Durham Report* (Cambridge, 1975)

18 *Churchill II, companion vol. 1*, p. 498
19 *Churchill II*, pp. 165–70
20 *Churchill II*, p. 167
21 Lord Birkenhead, *The Speeches of Lord Birkenhead* (1929), p. 5
22 *Churchill II, companion vol. 1*, pp. 532–3
23 *Churchill II*, pp. 182–3
24 *Ibid.*, p. 185
25 *Ibid.*, p. 187
26 *Churchill II*, p. 155
27 *Ibid.*, p. 185
28 Moran, p. 185
29 Lord Birkenhead, *F.E.* (1959), pp. 21–58; J. Campbell, *F. E. Smith* (1984), Chaps 1–4
30 *Churchill II*, pp. 222–3
31 *Churchill II, companion vol. 1*, p. 563
32 *Churchill II*, pp. 192–3
33 *Churchill II, companion vol. 1*, p. 571
34 Hyam, pp. 501–2
35 *Churchill II, companion vol. 2*, p. 730
36 *Ibid.*, p. 689
37 Birkenhead, *Churchill*, p. 171
38 *Churchill II, companion vol. 2*, p. 689
39 J. Wilson, pp. 589–91
40 Blunt, pp. 140, 639
41 Blunt, p. 140
42 S. Koss, *Haldane* (1969), p. 54
43 V. Bonham-Carter, *Winston Churchill as I Knew Him* (1966 edn), p. 142
44 H. V. Emy, *Liberals, Radicals and Social Politics 1892–1914* (Cambridge, 1973), pp. 173–9
45 Bonham-Carter, p. 153
46 Birkenhead, *Churchill*, p. 150
47 *Ibid.*, pp. 150–1
48 *Churchill II*, p. 243

5: The 'New' Liberal

1 G. R. Searle, *The Quest for National Efficiency* (1972), is still the outstanding book on these topics. G. L. Bernstein, *Liberalism and Liberal Politics in Edwardian England* (Mass., 1986), Emy, *op. cit*, and M. Bentley, *The Climax of Liberal Politics* (1987), cover these divisions within the Party.
2 Emy, pp. 167–73
3 *Churchill II, companion vol. 1*, p. 104
4 Emy, p. 11
5 N. & J. Mackenzie (eds), *The Diaries of Beatrice Webb, vol. III* (1984) (hereinafter *Webb Diary*), 9 February 1906, p. 25
6 *Ibid.*, 30 October 1907, p. 75
7 *Ibid.*, 10 June 1904, pp. 326–7
8 Bentley, p. 112
9 W. S. Churchill, 'The Untrodden Field in Politics', *The Nation*, 7 March 1907
10 *Webb Diary*, 8 July 1903, p. 287
11 N. Mackenzie (ed.), *The Letters of Sidney and Beatrice Webb. vol. II* (1978) (hereinafter *Webb Letters II*), Beatrice to Mary Playne, 2 February 1908, p. 281
12 *Ibid.*, Beatrice to Sidney Webb, 21 February 1908, p. 285

Notes

13 *Ibid.*, pp. 219–20, 281
14 *Churchill II, companion vol. 1*, p. 755
15 Emy, pp. 154–6, 166–7
16 *Ibid.*, pp. 167–73
17 *Churchill II*, pp. 254–7
18 W. S. Churchill, *Liberalism and the Social Problem* (1974 edn), pp. 193–202
19 The most recent study is B. B. Gilbert, *Lloyd George, vol. 1* (1989). See also the first two volumes of John Grigg's biography of Lloyd George and P. Rowland, *Lloyd George* (1975)
20 Churchill, *Liberalism and the Social Problem*, pp. 152–4; *Webb Letters II*, pp. 217–20
21 Emy, pp. 162–5, 167, 173, 184; Bentley, pp. 110–16
22 Bentley, pp. 74–88
23 Emy, p. 157
24 *Ibid.*, p. 158
25 *Webb Diary*, 10 February 1908, p. 88
26 Birkenhead, *Churchill*, p. 182
27 *Webb Diary*, 16 October 1908, p. 100
28 *Churchill II, companion vol. 2*, pp. 862–4
29 Churchill, *Liberalism and the Social Problem*, pp. 220–1
30 *Churchill II, companion vol. 2*, pp. 863–4
31 *Webb Diary*, 11 March 1908, p. 90
32 Bonham-Carter, p. 163
33 J. M. McEwan (ed.), *The Riddell Diaries 1908–23* (1986) (hereinafter *Riddell Diary*), 17 October 1908, p. 20
34 Churchill College, Cambridge, Blanche Lloyd diary, April 1908
35 Mary Soames, *Clementine Churchill* (1979), pp. 41–3
36 *Ibid.*, p. 44
37 Churchill, *My Early Life*, p. 385
38 Soames, pp. 50–3; *Churchill II*, pp. 352, 357 for examples
39 *Riddell Diary*, June 1911, p. 24
40 *Churchill II, companion vol. 2*, Churchill to Asquith, 26 December 1908, p. 861
41 *Webb Letters II*, Beatrice to Mary Playne, 27 February 1908, p. 287
42 *Churchill II, companion vol. 2*, Churchill to Asquith, 26 December 1908, p. 861
43 E. David (ed.), *Inside Asquith's Cabinet* (1977), 27 July 1908, p. 73
44 A. J. A. Morris, *The Scaremongers: The Advocacy of War and Rearmament 1896–1914* (1984), pp. 168–83
45 *Webb Diary*, July 1903, p. 288
46 A. J. Marder, *From Dreadnought to Scapa Flow, vol. 1* (1961) (hereinafter Marder I), pp. 137–8; Koss, pp. 56–7; M. V. Brett (ed.), *Journals and Letters of Reginald, Viscount Esher, vol. II* (1934) (hereinafter *Esher II*), pp. 324–5
47 Koss, p. 57
48 *Churchill II*, pp. 511–14
49 Marder I, p. 140
50 *Ibid.*, pp. 145–7
51 *Ibid.*, pp. 147–56; Morris, pp. 175–7
52 Asquith Mss. 21, Lloyd George to Asquith, 2 February 1909, fo. 61 ff.

53 Marder I, Knollys to Esher, 10 February 1909, p. 160
54 *Ibid.*, Esher to Knollys, 12 February 1909
55 *Esher II*, 12 February 1909, p. 370
56 Marder I, Asquith to Mrs Asquith, 20 February 1909, p. 161
57 Asquith Mss. 21, undated note by Asquith, fo. 167
58 Emy, pp. 212–13

6: The Limits of Radicalism

1 P. de Mendelssohn, *The Age of Churchill: Heritage and Adventure 1874–1911* (1961), pp. 423–4
2 *Ibid.*, p. 420
3 *Ibid.*, p. 490
4 Bonham-Carter, p. 186
5 *Churchill II, companion vol. 2*, pp. 1132–3
6 *Ibid.*, p. 1136
7 *Ibid.*, p. 967
8 *Churchill II*, pp. 240–5
9 *Ibid.*, pp. 262–3
10 Emy, p. 216
11 *Ibid.*, p. 213
12 *Webb Diary*, 20 December 1909, p. 132
13 *Churchill II, companion vol. 2*, Cabinet memo., 14 February 1910, pp. 968–71
14 Asquith Mss. 23, Grey to Asquith, 25 March 1910, fo. 82
15 S. Koss, *Asquith* (1976), pp. 120–2
16 *Ibid.*, p. 121–2
17 *Churchill II*, pp. 367–72
18 *Churchill II, companion vol. 2*, Lloyd George to Churchill, 25 September 1910, pp. 1023–4
19 *Riddell Diary*, 2 July 1912, pp. 46–7
20 W. S. Churchill, *Thoughts and Adventures* (first pub. 1932, 1974 edn), pp. 39–40
21 Lord Beaverbrook, *Men and Power 1917–18* (1956), p. XVII
22 *Churchill II, companion vol. 2*, Churchill to Lloyd George, 6 October 1910, pp. 1024–5
23 Sandars Mss. 760, Sandars to Esher, 10 August 1910
24 *Crawford Papers*, 9 May 1910, p. 153
25 *Riddell Diary*, 2 March 1912, p. 34
26 Churchill, *Thoughts and Adventures*, p. 44
27 Mendelssohn, p. 503
28 *Riddell Diary*, 8 February 1913, p. 55
29 *Ibid.*, November 1911, p. 25
30 *Churchill II*, p. 379
31 Sir Edward Grey, *Twenty-Five Years, vol. 1* (1925), pp. 72–6
32 H. Nicolson, *Portrait of a Diplomatist Being the Life of Sir Arthur Nicolson First Lord Carnock, and a Study of the Origins of the Great War* (1930) (hereinafter *Carnock*), pp. 177–8
33 Wilson, pp. 541–4
34 K. Wilson, *The Policy of the Ententes* (1989), pp. 116–18
35 Sandars Mss. 764, Balfour to Sandars, 21 September 1911, fos 97–8
36 W. S. Churchill, *The World Crisis, vol. 1, 1911–14* (1974 edn), (hereinafter *World Crisis I*), pp. 51–3

37 *Ibid.*, pp. 60–6
38 Marder I, pp. 244–5; S. R. Williamson, *The Politics of Grand Strategy* (Harvard, 1968), pp. 188–93
39 Marder I, p. 250; Williamson, p. 194
40 Marder I, pp. 248–9; Koss, *Asquith*, pp. 58–9
41 Williamson, p. 195
42 David (ed.), *Inside Asquith's Cabinet* (1977), Charles Hobhouse diary (hereinafter Hobhouse diary), 13 August 1912, p. 120
43 Marder I, p. 252

7: Young Man in a Hurry

1 *Churchill II, companion vol. 2*, Sandars to Balfour, 14 December 1911, pp. 1357–8
2 *Riddell Diary*, November 1911, p. 27
3 Marder I, p. 250
4 Koss, *Asquith*, p. 148
5 M. V. Brett (ed.), *Journals and Letters of Reginald, Viscount Esher, vol. III* (1938) (hereinafter *Esher III*), 4 October 1912, p. 61
6 Unpublished Esher papers, Churchill College, 4 October 1912
7 Marder I, p. 250
8 Sir Austen Chamberlain, *Politics from the Inside* (1937), p. 485
9 Hobhouse diary, 16 November 1912, p. 108; Williamson, pp. 198–200
10 Hobhouse diary, *ibid.*
11 Williamson, Chap. 7
12 Sandars Mss. 764, memo., 24 November 1911, fos 206–7
13 Williamson, pp. 203–4; Morris, pp. 302–3
14 *Esher III*, 24 November 1911, p. 74
15 Marder I, pp. 246–51; *World Crisis I*, pp. 83–8; *Churchill II, companion vol. 2*, p. 1303 ff.
16 Marder I, p. 252
17 *Esher III*, 24 November 1911, p. 74
18 Morris, p. 315
19 *Ibid.*, p. 295
20 Blunt, 30 January 1912, p. 792
21 Williamson, pp. 250–2; *Churchill II, companion vol. 3*, Churchill to Cassel, 7 January 1912, p. 1492
22 Grey, p. 252
23 *World Crisis I*, pp. 95–6
24 *Ibid.*, pp. 100–1
25 Morris, pp. 313–15
26 Koss, *Asquith*, p. 147
27 Marder I, p. 25
28 E. T. S. Dugdale (ed.), *German Diplomatic Documents, vol. IV: The Descent to the Abyss, 1911–14* (NY, 1931) (hereinafter GD IV), Widenmann to Tirpitz, 28 October 1911, p. 43
29 *Esher II*, 12 February 1909, p. 370
30 Hobhouse diary. Chap. 3 is entitled 'Lloyd George the Irresponsible'.
31 *Esher II*, 12 February 1909, p. 370
32 Sandars Mss. 760, Spender to Esher, 10 August 1910, fo. 267; J. Barnes & D. Nicholson (eds), *The Leo Amery Diaries 1896–1929* (1980) (hereinafter *Amery Diary I*), F. S. Oliver to Amery, 8 November 1910, pp. 71, 343
33 *Riddell Diary*, 15 June 1912, p. 44
34 *Ibid.*, 2 July 1912, p. 46
35 *Ibid.*, 27 July 1912, p. 48
36 Bonham-Carter, p. 239
37 *Riddell Diary*, 31 March 1912, p. 40
38 Bonham-Carter, p. 239
39 Marder I, p. 163
40 *Ibid.*, pp. 216–18
41 *World Crisis I*, p. 38
42 Marder I, p. 169
43 Morris, p. 319
44 *Ibid.*, pp. 319–20, 369–71
45 Williamson, p. 266
46 R. S. Churchill, *Winston S. Churchill, vol. II, companion vol. 3* (1969) (hereinafter *Churchill II, companion vol. 3*), Churchill to Haldane, 6 May 1912, pp. 1548–9
47 Hobhouse diary, 10 May 1912, p. 114
48 Williamson, pp. 268–70; Nicolson, *Carnock*, pp. 270–2
49 Hobhouse diary, 21 June 1912, pp. 115–16; Williamson, p. 276
50 *Esher III*, Esher to M. V. Brett, 2 July 1912, p. 99
51 Morris, p. 317
52 *Churchill II, companion vol. 3*, Churchill memo., 22 June 1912, pp. 1570–2
53 Williamson, pp. 276–7
54 *Churchill II, companion vol. 3*, Churchill memo., 25 June 1912, p. 1573–8
55 Williamson, p. 278
56 *Ibid.*, p. 279
57 *Ibid.*
58 Morris, p. 168
59 Marder I, p. 294
60 *Churchill II, companion vol. 3*, Churchill to Lord Roberts, 12 July 1912, pp. 1594–5
61 Hobhouse diary, 6 July, pp. 116–17
62 Williamson, p. 279
63 Hobhouse diary, 6 July (recording the events of 4 and 5 July), p. 117
64 *Ibid.*; Williamson, p. 280
65 Marder I, Esher to Knollys, 5 July 1912, p. 294
66 Hobhouse diary, 10 July 1912, p. 117
67 *Ibid.*, 17 July 1912, p. 118
68 *Ibid.*; Williamson, pp. 280–1; Marder I, pp. 295–6
69 Balfour Mss. 49694, Churchill to Balfour, 16 July 1912, fo. 84
70 Williamson, p. 282; Hobhouse diary, 17 July 1912, p. 118
71 K. Hamilton, *Bertie of Thame: Edwardian Ambassador* (Suffolk, 1990), pp. 283–4; Nicolson, *Carnock*, pp. 267–9; Williamson, pp. 261–3
72 Nicolson, *ibid.*, p. 269
73 Hamilton, pp. 283–4
74 *Ibid.*, pp. 290–1; Williamson, p. 287; Marder I, p. 304
75 *Churchill II, companion vol. 3*, Churchill to Grey and Asquith, 23 August 1912, pp. 1638–9
76 Hamilton, p. 291
77 *Ibid.*, p. 293; Marder I, p. 307
78 Hamilton, pp. 293–4
79 *Churchill II, companion vol. 3*, Churchill to Grey and Asquith, 23 August 1912, p. 1639

80 Hamilton, p. 293; Williamson, pp. 291–2
81 Hamilton, pp. 295–6; Williamson, p. 297
82 Williamson, p. 297
83 *Ibid.*, pp. 297–8
84 Hamilton, p. 296
85 Nicolson, *Carnock*, p. 420
86 *Ibid.*, p. 272
87 Morris, Chap. 13
88 Soames, p. 75
89 *Ibid.*
90 *Ibid.*, p. 81
91 *Ibid.*, p. 92

8: An Isolated Liberal

1 *World Crisis I*, p. 183
2 Marder I, pp. 253–5
3 Hobhouse diary, 13 August 1912, p. 121
4 *Ibid.*, 17 July 1912, p. 118
5 Moran, *passim*, and also E. Nel, *Mr Churchill's
   Secretary* (1958)
6 James, *Churchill*, p. 14
7 Bonham-Carter, p. 16
8 Soames, *passim*
9 Marder I, pp. 263–4
10 *Ibid.*, p. 253
11 *Crawford Papers*, 5 December 1912, p. 291; Marder
   I, pp. 258–9; Morris, p. 336
12 Hobhouse diary, 6 July 1912, p. 117; Marder I,
   pp. 254–5
13 Marder I, pp. 264–5
14 *Ibid.*, p. 82
15 *Ibid.*, pp. 163–5; Morris, pp. 166–84
16 Marder I, pp. 266–70
17 *Ibid.*, pp. 263–4
18 *Crawford Papers*, 27 November 1912, p. 319
19 Blunt, 21 October 1912, p. 815
20 Bonham-Carter, pp. 17–18
21 Hobhouse diary, 24 June 1913, p. 140
22 *Churchill II*, p. 344
23 *Asquith Letters*, p. 7
24 Chamberlain, p. 414
25 *Asquith Letters*, pp. 7–8
26 *Churchill II*, pp. 469–70
27 *Ibid.*, p. 473
28 R. Blake, *The Unknown Prime Minister* (1955),
   pp. 156, 160–5
29 *Ibid.*, pp. 171–2
30 *Asquith Letters*, pp. 36–7; Koss, *Asquith*, pp. 151–2
31 *Churchill II, companion vol. 3*, Churchill to Asquith,
   5 December 1913, pp. 1818–24
32 *Ibid.*, Churchill to Asquith, 18 December 1913,
   p. 1834
33 *Asquith Letters*, 17 December 1913, p. 38
34 Hobhouse diary, 20 December 1913, p. 153
35 *Churchill II, companion vol. 3*, pp. 1818–24, 1825–
   32
36 Hobhouse diary, 20 December 1913, p. 154
37 Hobhouse diary, ed. comment, p. 153
38 *Churchill II*, p. 659
39 Hobhouse diary, 20 December 1913, p. 154
40 Marder I, p. 318
41 *Ibid.*, p. 319

42 *Churchill II, companion vol. 3*, p. 1842
43 *Ibid.*, Churchill to Asquith, 19 January 1914,
   p. 1850
44 Hobhouse diary, 23 January 1914, p. 155
45 *Ibid.*, p. 156
46 *Ibid.*, 26 January 1914, pp. 157–8
47 *Churchill II, companion vol. 3*, Churchill to Lloyd
   George, 26 January 1914, pp. 1854–5
48 *Ibid.*, Lloyd George to Churchill, 27 January 1914,
   p. 1856. The whole correspondence is at Asquith
   Mss. vol. 25.
49 Hobhouse diary, 27 January 1914, p. 158
50 Asquith Mss. 25, Beauchamp to Asquith, 29 January 1914, fos 170–7
51 *Ibid.*, Simon to Asquith, undated, fos 148–9
52 *Churchill II, companion vol. 3*, Asquith to Churchill,
   1 February 1914, pp. 1859–60
53 Hobhouse diary, p. 160
54 Blake, p. 185
55 *Churchill II*, p. 488
56 *Ibid.*, pp. 488–90; Blake, p. 185
57 *Asquith Letters*, 17 March 1914, p. 55
58 Blake, p. 188
59 *Churchill II*, pp. 497–9
60 Blake, p. 189
61 Chamberlain, letter of 23 March 1914, p. 631;
   Blake, pp. 198–9, for debates
62 *Churchill II*, p. 501

9: War Lord at Sea

1 *Riddell Diary*, 16 January 1914, p. 77
2 *Ibid.*, 25 January 1914, p. 79
3 *Ibid.*
4 *World Crisis I*, pp. 185–6
5 Hobhouse diary, 18 July 1914, p. 174
6 *Asquith Letters*, 26 July 1914, p. 126
7 *Ibid.*, 28 July 1914, p. 129
8 *World Crisis I*, p. 193
9 *Asquith Letters*, 24 July 1914, p. 123
10 The best recent examination is offered by M.
   Brock, 'Britain Enters the War', in R. J. W. Evans
   & H. Pogge von Strandmann, *The Coming of the
   First World War* (Oxford, 1988), pp. 145–78; other
   accounts consulted are: Wilson, *The Policy of the
   Ententes*; C. Hazlehurst, *Politicians at War* (1971);
   Williamson, *The Politics of Grand Strategy*; J. Joll, *The
   Origins of the First World War* (1985); Z. A. Steiner,
   Britain and the Origins of the First World War (1977).
11 *World Crisis I*, p. 200
12 *Churchill II, companion vol. 3*, p. 1989
13 *Riddell Diary*, November 1911, p. 27
14 M. Gilbert, *Winston S. Churchill, vol. III* (1971)
   (hereinafter *Churchill III*), pp. 11–12; Hazlehurst,
   p. 41
15 *Asquith Letters*, 31 July 1914, p. 138; Nicolson,
   Carnock, p. 303
16 *Asquith Letters*, 1 August 1914, p. 140
17 *Ibid.*; J. Grigg, *Lloyd George: From Peace to War
   1912–16* (1985), pp. 144–8
18 *Asquith Letters*, 2 August 1914, p. 146
19 Hazlehurst, pp. 56–60
20 *Asquith Letters*, 1, 2 August 1914, pp. 140, 146

21 Hobhouse diary, August 1914, p. 179
22 *Churchill II, companion vol. 3*, pp. 1196–7
23 Nicolson, *Carnock*, pp. 303–5
24 J. Charmley, *Lord Lloyd and the Decline of the British Empire* (1987), pp. 233–5, for an account of Cambon's actions
25 Hazlehurst, p. 88
26 *Asquith Letters*, 3, 4 August 1914, pp. 148, 150; Brock, pp. 159–60
27 Viscount Grey, *Twenty-Five Years, vol. II* (1925) (hereinafter Grey II), pp. 14–16
28 Hazlehurst, pp. 44–8, 52–3
29 Williamson, pp. 351–2, 361–6; *Churchill III*, pp. 7–9
30 *Riddell Diary*, 10 October 1914, p. 91
31 *Ibid.*, November 1911, p. 27
32 *Ibid.*, 10 October 1914, pp. 91–2
33 *World Crisis I*, pp. 221–7, 247–56
34 R. Prior, *Churchill's 'World Crisis' as History* (Kent, 1983), pp. 1–8; A. J. Marder, *From Dreadnought to Scapa Flow, vol. II* (1965) (hereinafter Marder II), pp. 20–41; R. Hough, *Former Naval Person* (1985), pp. 59–60
35 *Churchill III*, p. 14
36 Soames, p. 107
37 *Ibid.*, pp. 107–8
38 *Churchill III*, p. 84; Marder II, p. 48
39 *Asquith Letters*, 19 August 1914, p. 179
40 Hobhouse diary, 21 August 1914, p. 183
41 *Churchill III, companion vol. I*, p. 47
42 *Asquith Letters*, 26 August 1914, p. 197; S. Roskill, *Hankey: Man of Secrets, vol. I* (1970) (hereinafter Roskill I), pp. 143–4
43 Bonham-Carter, p. 329; *Churchill III*, pp. 67–8
44 Prior, pp. 16–18; Marder II, pp. 50–5
45 *Asquith Letters*, 22 September 1914, p. 253
46 Marder II, p. 83
47 *World Crisis I*, p. 322
48 The account which follows is based upon: *World Crisis I*, Chap. 15; *Churchill III*, Chap. 4; *Churchill III, companion vol. I*, pp. 158–86; Prior, Chap. 4; Marder II, pp. 83–4; Hobhouse diary, pp. 193–7; *Asquith Letters*, pp. 260–8.
49 Grey II, p. 79
50 *Asquith Letters*, 3 October 1914, p. 260
51 *Churchill III, companion vol. I*, pp. 160–1; *World Crisis I*, pp. 344–5
52 *Churchill III, companion vol. I*, p. 163
53 *Asquith Letters*, 10 October 1914, p. 277
54 Marder II, p. 85
55 *Asquith Letters*, p. 277
56 *Riddell Diary*, 10 October 1914, p. 92
57 Prior, p. 30
58 *Ibid.*, pp. 34–6
59 *Asquith Letters*, 7 October 1914, pp. 266–7
60 *Ibid.*, 13 October 1914, pp. 275–6

10: 'Ninepins'

1 Sandars Mss. 766, Balfour to Sandars, 22 September 1914, fo. 145
2 M. Hankey, *The Supreme Command, vol. I* (1961), p. 186

3 *Asquith Letters*, 14 September 1914, p. 238
4 *Ibid.*, 16 September 1914, p. 243
5 A. J. P. Taylor (ed.), *Lloyd George: A Diary by Frances Stevenson* (1971) (hereinafter *Stevenson Diary*), 23 October, 5 November 1914, pp. 6, 10
6 Hobhouse diary, 15 October 1914, p. 198
7 Byron Farwell, *The Great War in Africa 1914–18* (NY, 1987), Chap. 11, for a full account of the East African imbroglio
8 *Riddell Diary*, 22 October 1914, p. 92
9 *Churchill III*, pp. 132–3
10 *Asquith Letters*, 27 October 1914, p. 287
11 *Ibid.*, 28–29 October 1914, pp. 290–7; *Churchill III, companion vol. I*, pp. 220–33; *World Crisis I*, pp. 401–2; Marder II, pp. 87–91
12 *World Crisis I*, p. 403
13 *Ibid.*, p. 402
14 *Ibid.*, p. 403
15 *Asquith Letters*, p. 294
16 Prior, pp. 11–15; Marder II, pp. 101–28; Bonham-Carter, pp. 345–6
17 Marder II, p. 184
18 *Churchill III*, pp. 20–1
19 *Ibid.*, pp. 52–3
20 *Ibid.*, p. 58
21 *Ibid.*, p. 140
22 Prior, p. 46
23 Marder II, p. 187
24 *Churchill III, companion volume I*, pp. 343–5
25 Prior, p. 46; Marder II, pp. 189–98
26 Marder II, pp. 183–4
27 W. S. Churchill, *The World Crisis, vol. II* (1923) (hereinafter *World Crisis II*), p. 42
28 Balfour Mss. 49703, Hankey to Balfour, 21 January 1915, fo. 152
29 Marder II, p. 181
30 *World Crisis II*, pp. 46–8
31 Balfour Mss. 49703, fos 127–30, for Hankey's memo., which is also reproduced in *Churchill III, companion vol. I*, pp. 335–43
32 *Churchill III, companion vol. I*, pp. 350–6
33 *Ibid.*, p. 346
34 *Ibid.*, p. 242
35 James, *Churchill*, p. 64, for example
36 *Churchill II, companion vol. I*, p. 278
37 Blanche Dugdale, *Arthur James Balfour, vol. II* (1936) (hereinafter Dugdale II), p. 130, Balfour to Hankey, 2 January 1915
38 Balfour Mss. 49703, Hankey to Balfour, 2 January 1915, fo. 142
39 Dugdale II, Fisher to Balfour, 4 January 1915, pp. 128–9
40 *Ibid.*, p. 184
41 *Asquith Letters*, pp. 325–9; *Churchill III, companion vol. I*, pp. 296–312
42 *Asquith Letters*, 4 December 1914, p. 325
43 *Ibid.*, 20 December 1914, p. 331
44 Balfour Mss. 49703, Hankey to Balfour, 21 January 1915, fo. 152
45 *Ibid.*, Hankey to Balfour, 29 December 1914, fo. 126; Marder II, pp. 191–3
46 *Churchill III, companion vol. I*, p. 299
47 Dugdale II, p. 129

48 *Asquith Letters*, 7 January 1915, p. 396
49 *Churchill III, companion vol. 1*, p. 297
50 Marder II, p. 189
51 *Churchill III, companion vol. 1*, pp. 360–1
52 *Ibid.*, p. 367
53 Marder II, p. 204; James, *Churchill*, p. 65
54 *Churchill III, companion vol. 1*, pp. 371–2
55 *Ibid.*, p. 380
56 *Ibid.*, p. 381
57 Prior, pp. 54–6; *World Crisis II*, pp. 97–9; James, *Churchill*, pp. 65–6
58 *World Crisis II*, pp. 101–2
59 *Ibid.*, p. 102
60 Marder II, p. 206
61 Prior, pp. 56–7; Marder II, p. 206
62 Marder II, pp. 184, 189
63 *Churchill III, companion vol. 1*, Fisher to Jellicoe, 19 January 1915, p. 430
64 *Ibid.*, p. 395
65 *Ibid.*, Churchill to Kitchener, 20 January 1915, p. 433
66 *Asquith Letters*, 20 January 1915, p. 387
67 *Churchill III, companion vol. 1*, pp. 429–30; Balfour Mss. 47903, Hankey to Balfour, 21 January 1915, fo. 152
68 *Churchill III, companion vol. 1*, p. 430
69 *Ibid.*, p. 428
70 *Ibid.*, pp. 451–4
71 *World Crisis II*, pp. 159–62, where the date is incorrectly given as 27 January
72 *Churchill III, companion vol. 1*, Fisher to Asquith, 28 January 1915, pp. 461–2
73 *World Crisis II*, p. 162; *Churchill III, companion vol. 1*, p. 462; *Asquith Letters*, 28 January 1915, p. 405; Marder II, p. 210; Prior, pp. 61–2; Mackay, *Balfour* (1985), pp. 258–9
74 *Churchill III, companion vol. 1*, pp. 463–5
75 Balfour Mss. 49712, Balfour's memo., 1 February 1915, fos 144–7
76 Balfour Mss. 49703, Hankey to Balfour, c. 4 February 1915, fo. 160

11: Dire Straits

1 *Churchill III, companion vol. 1*, pp. 468–70
2 Marder II, p. 227
3 *Ibid.*, pp. 223–8
4 *Churchill III, companion vol. 1*, Fisher to Jellicoe, 21 January 1915, p. 436
5 Balfour Mss. 49703, Hankey to Balfour, 10 February 1915, fo. 165
6 *Churchill III, companion vol. 1*, pp. 506–12
7 *World Crisis II*, pp. 177–8
8 *Churchill III, companion vol. 1*, pp. 527–34
9 *Ibid.*, pp. 518–19
10 Hobhouse diary, 16 February 1915, p. 222
11 *Stevenson Diary*, 15 May 1915, p. 50
12 *Churchill III, companion vol. 1*, pp. 535–44
13 *Asquith Letters*, 23 February 1915, p. 445, wrongly dated as 24 February in *Churchill III, companion vol. 1*, p. 554
14 *World Crisis II*, p. 184
15 *Ibid.*, pp. 183–9
16 *Ibid.*, pp. 175–6, 188
17 *Churchill III, companion vol. 1*, p. 558
18 *Ibid.*, pp. 559–60
19 *Ibid.*, pp. 567–77
20 *Asquith Letters*, 26 February 1915, p. 445
21 Hobhouse diary, 23 March 1915, p. 231
22 *Stevenson Diary*, 21 January 1915, p. 23
23 *Churchill III, companion vol. 1*, pp. 517–22
24 *Ibid.*, Margot Asquith diary, 25 January 1915, p. 454
25 Peter Clarke, 'Asquith and Lloyd George Revisited', in J. M. W. Bean (ed.), *The Political Culture of Modern Britain* (1987), pp. 154–5
26 *Churchill III, companion vol. 1*, p. 584
27 *Ibid.*, p. 586
28 *Ibid.*, pp. 591–2
29 *Ibid.*, pp. 610–18
30 *Ibid.*, pp. 628–9
31 *Ibid.*, p. 634
32 *Asquith Letters*, 1 March 1915, p. 456
33 *Churchill III, companion vol. 1*, Birdwood to Kitchener, 5 March 1915, pp. 637–8
34 *Ibid.*, pp. 646, 652, 653, 656, 661–2; Prior, pp. 90–1; Marder II, pp. 240–3
35 *Churchill III, companion vol. 1*, p. 643
36 *Ibid.*, pp. 665–73
37 *World Crisis II*, p. 216
38 Marder II, pp. 263–5
39 *Churchill III, companion vol. 1*, pp. 677–8
40 *World Crisis II*, pp. 196–7
41 *Churchill III, companion vol. 1*, p. 681
42 *Ibid.*, p. 694
43 Roskill I, p. 163
44 I have based my account on *World Crisis II*, Chap. 11, and Marder II, pp. 246–7
45 *World Crisis II*, pp. 234–7
46 Balfour Mss. 49702, Balfour to Lord Sydenham, 23 March 1915, fo. 301
47 *Churchill III, companion vol. 1*, p. 710
48 *Ibid.*, pp. 710–13
49 Prior, p. 95
50 *World Crisis II*, pp. 233–4
51 Prior, p. 91
52 *World Crisis II*, p. 234
53 *Churchill III*, pp. 365–6
54 *Churchill III, companion vol. 1*, pp. 728–30
55 *World Crisis II*, p. 244
56 *Ibid.* pp. 244–7
57 Roskill I, pp. 164–5
58 *Churchill III, companion vol. 1*, p. 774
59 *Ibid.*, pp. 747, 751–3
60 *Ibid.*, Esher diary, 20 March 1915, p. 719
61 *Ibid.*, pp. 720–2
62 *Stevenson Diary*, 8 April 1915, p. 41
63 *Churchill III, companion vol. 1*, Churchill to Balfour, 8 April 1915, p. 780
64 *Ibid.*, pp. 781–5
65 *Ibid.*, p. 792
66 *Ibid.*, p. 794
67 *Ibid.*, p. 807
68 *Asquith Letters*, 25 March 1915, p. 508

12: Dropping the Albatross

1 *Asquith Letters*, 25 March 1915, p. 508
2 *Ibid.*, 29 March 1915, p. 517
3 *Ibid.*, 30 March 1915, p. 523
4 Hazlehurst, p. 252
5 Hazlehurst, pp. 227–39, 251–2, argues that Churchill was not involved in any conspiracy; Koss, in *Haldane*, Chap. 7, and *Asquith*, argues the contrary; I am not convinced by him.
6 *Churchill III, companion vol. 1*, pp. 732–8, 741, 753, 755–6
7 *Ibid.*, pp. 759–60
8 *Ibid.*, pp. 760, 764–5, 769, 770; Roskill I, pp. 170–2
9 *Churchill III, companion vol. 1*, p. 817
10 *Asquith Letters*, 25 March 1915, p. 508
11 *Ibid.*, 30 March 1915, pp. 521, 523–4; *Stevenson Diary*, 26 March 1915, p. 56
12 Hazlehurst, pp. 265–70; Koss, *Haldane*, pp. 184–95; Blake, pp. 241–3
13 *Churchill III, companion vol. 2*, pp. 855–6
14 *Ibid.*, pp. 859–61
15 *Ibid.*, p. 862
16 *Ibid.*, p. 864; Roskill I, pp. 173–4
17 *Ibid.*, Fisher to Jellicoe, 13 May 1915, p. 869
18 *Ibid.*, pp. 872–87
19 *Ibid.*, pp. 888–9
20 *Esher III*, diary, 15 May 1915, p. 235
21 *Ibid.*, 17 May 1915, pp. 236–7; Blake, pp. 243–4; *Churchill III, companion vol. 2*, pp. 897–8
22 *Churchill III, companion vol. 2*, pp. 896–7; Marder II, pp. 270–2
23 Birkenhead, *Churchill*, p. 383
24 Koss, *Asquith*, pp. 181–2
25 A. Gollin, 'Asquith: A New View', in M. Gilbert (ed.), *A Century of Conflict 1850–1950* (1966), pp. 112–13; Koss, *Asquith*, pp. 186–90
26 A. J. P. Taylor, 'Politics in the First World War', in his *Essays in English History* (1976), pp. 218–54; A. Gollin, *Proconsul in Politics: A Study of Lord Milner in Opposition and in Power, 1854–1905* (1964), pp. 260–2
27 *Stevenson Diary*, 15 May 1915, p. 50
28 *Churchill III, companion vol. 2*, Churchill to Asquith, 17 May 1915, p. 898
29 *Ibid.*, Churchill to Asquith, 18 May 1915, pp. 902–3
30 *Stevenson Diary*, 19 May 1915, p. 52
31 Roskill I, p. 175
32 Marder II, p. 241
33 *Churchill III, companion vol. 2*, Churchill to Law, 19 May 1915, p. 908
34 Blake, p. 245
35 *Churchill III, companion vol. 2*, p. 910
36 Asquith Mss. vol. 27, Emmot to Asquith, 20 May 1915, fo. 176
37 *Ibid.*, Pringle to Asquith, 20 May 1915, fo. 178. This volume also contains all the correspondence on Churchill's replacement.
38 *Churchill III, companion vol. 2*, pp. 914–15
39 *Stevenson Diary*, 19 May 1915, p. 52
40 *Riddell Diary*, 19 May 1915, p. 114

41 *Stevenson Diary*, 19 May 1915, p. 114
42 *Churchill III, companion vol. 2*, Clementine Churchill to Asquith, 20 May 1915, p. 921
43 *Ibid.*, Churchill to Law, 21 May 1915, pp. 922–4
44 *Ibid.*, Law to Churchill, 21 May 1915, p. 924
45 *Ibid.*, Churchill to Asquith, 21 May 1915, pp. 925–6
46 *Ibid.*, Asquith to Churchill, 21 May 1915, pp. 926–7
47 *Ibid.*, Churchill to Asquith, 21 May 1915, p. 926
48 *Ibid.*, Churchill to Asquith, 21 May 1915, p. 927
49 Churchill, *Great Contemporaries*, p. 92
50 Birkenhead, *Churchill*, p. 393
51 *Riddell Diary*, 20 May 1915, p. 115
52 *Ibid.*, p. 116
53 *Ibid.*, 23 May 1915, p. 118
54 Dugdale II, p. 184
55 W. S. Churchill, *The Second World War, vol. 1: The Gathering Storm* (1974 edn) (hereinafter *Gathering Storm*), pp. 411–16
56 *Churchill III, companion vol. 2*, pp. 956–7
57 *Riddell Diary*, 26 May 1915, p. 119
58 Soames, p. 122
59 Balfour Mss. 49694, Churchill to Balfour, 2 December 1911, fo. 62
60 *Churchill III, companion vol. 2*, p. 964
61 *Ibid.*, pp. 1003–4
62 *Churchill III*, p. 495
63 *World Crisis II*, pp. 433–4; Prior, pp. 160–1
64 *Churchill III, companion vol. 2*, pp. 1041–2
65 Blake, p. 265
66 D. G. Boyce (ed.), *The Crisis of British Unionism: The Domestic Political Papers of the Second Earl of Selborne, 1885–1922* (1987) (hereinafter *Selborne Papers I*), Selborne to Bonar Law, 7 July 1915, pp. 130–2
67 *Churchill III, companion vol. 2*, p. 1140
68 *Ibid.*, pp. 1151–5
69 *Churchill III, companion vol. 2*, p. 1042
70 *Stevenson Diary*, 15 September 1915, pp. 59–60
71 *Ibid.*, p. 57
72 *Churchill III, companion vol. 2*, p. 1184, gives a misleading impression of Churchill's views. These can be studied at the Public Record Office (hereinafter PRO), Cab. 42/3/28.
73 Prior, pp. 173–4
74 *Churchill III, companion vol. 2*, pp. 1193–9
75 Blake, pp. 268–9
76 *Churchill III*, pp. 559–60
77 *Ibid.*, p. 562
78 *Churchill III, companion vol. 2*, p. 1183
79 *Churchill III*, p. 563
80 *Churchill III, companion vol. 2*, pp. 1249–50
81 *Stevenson Diary*, 24 May 1915, p. 53
82 *Asquith Letters*, 25 March 1915, p. 508
83 *Churchill III*, p. 569
84 Blake, p. 234
85 Hobhouse diary, 13 August 1912, p. 121
86 Blunt, 21 October 1912, p. 815
87 *Churchill III, companion vol. 1*, Violet Asquith to Churchill, 13 November 1915, pp. 1254–5

Notes

13: Wilderness Politics

1 *Churchill III*, Chaps 18–21, for Churchill at the front

2 *Churchill III, companion vol. 2*, Churchill to Curzon, 8 December 1915, p. 1320

3 D. Fraser (ed.), *In Good Company: The First World War Letters and Diaries of the Hon. William Fraser* (1990), 8 January 1916, p. 79. I am grateful to Piers Mackesy for drawing my attention to this source.

4 *Ibid.*, 23 January 1916, p. 80

5 *Churchill III*, pp. 605–11

6 *Churchill III, companion vol. 2*, pp. 1290–1, 1384

7 *Ibid.*, pp. 1333, 1366 for example

8 *Ibid.*, Churchill to Mrs Churchill, 28 January 1916, p. 1402

9 *Churchill III*, pp. 707–10

10 *Ibid.*, pp. 716–23; Bonham-Carter, pp. 450–3

11 *Churchill III, companion vol. 2*, Churchill to Balfour, 8 March 1916, p. 1444; Bonham-Carter, pp. 452–4

12 *Selborne Papers I*, p. 187

13 *Churchill III*, letter to Churchill, 30 December 1915, p. 623

14 *Churchill III, companion vol. 2*, Churchill to Mrs Churchill, 30 December 1915, p. 623

15 *Ibid.*, pp. 1352, 1363, 1365–6, 1383

16 *Ibid.*, pp. 1365, 1369

17 *Ibid.*, letter to Mrs Churchill, 6 January 1916, p. 1359

18 *Ibid.*, letter to Mrs Churchill, 4 January 1916, p. 1357

19 *Ibid.*, letter to Mrs Churchill, 2 January 1916, p. 1352

20 *Ibid.*, letter to Mrs Churchill, 1 February 1916, p. 1409

21 *Amery Diary I*, F. S. Oliver to Amery, 23 July 1915, p. 123

22 *Ibid.*, July 1915, pp. 126–7; Taylor, *Politics in Wartime*, pp. 25–31; Gollin, pp. 320–5

23 *Riddell Diary*, 26 February, 19 March 1916, pp. 147–8, 149

24 Blake, pp. 280–2

25 Campbell, pp. 430–2

26 *Churchill III, companion vol. 2*, letter from Mrs Churchill, 13 March 1916, p. 1453, fn. 1; letter from Carson, 23 March 1916, p. 1462

27 *Churchill III*, pp. 753–4; Campbell, p. 430

28 *Churchill III, companion vol. 2*, letter to Mrs Churchill, 28 March 1916, p. 1467

29 *Stevenson Diary*, 15 September 1915, p. 60

30 *Churchill III, companion vol. 2*, letter to Mrs Churchill, 8 April 1916, p. 1482

31 *Ibid.*, Churchill to Lloyd George, 10 April 1916, p. 1485

32 *Stevenson Diary*, 19 April 1916, p. 72

33 *Churchill III*, pp. 778–85

34 *Ibid.*, pp. 778–83

35 *Churchill III, companion vol. 2*, p. 1530

36 Lord Beaverbrook, *Politicians and the War 1914–16, vol. II* (1932), p. 290

37 *Churchill III, companion vol. 2*, p. 1545

38 *Riddell Diary*, 10 December 1916, p. 179

39 *Ibid.*, 11 December 1916, p. 179

40 Beaverbrook, *Politicians and the War* p. 324

41 *Churchill III, companion vol. 2*, p. 1357

42 Taylor (ed.), *Politics in Wartime*, p. 37

43 M. Gilbert, *Winston S. Churchill, vol. IV: 1917–22* (1975) (hereinafter *Churchill IV*), pp. 11–13; M. Gilbert, *Winston S. Churchill, vol. IV, companion vol. I* (1977) (hereinafter *Churchill IV, companion vol. I*), pp. 42–5

44 *Riddell Diary*, 18 February 1917, p. 186

45 *Churchill IV*, p. 16

46 *Churchill IV, companion vol. I*, p. 60

47 *Stevenson Diary*, 19 May 1917, p. 158

48 *Churchill IV*, p. 17

49 *Ibid.*, p. 11

50 *Churchill IV, companion vol. I*, pp. 48–9, 76

51 *Ibid.*, p. 68

52 *Ibid.*, p. 70

53 *Ibid.*, pp. 71–2

54 *Ibid.*, pp. 73–5

55 Blake, p. 360

56 *Churchill IV*, pp. 28–30

57 Blake, p. 361; Lord Beaverbrook, *Men and Power 1917–18* (1956), pp. 125–36

58 *Amery Diary I*, 18 July 1917, p. 164

59 L. P. Arnn, *Winston S. Churchill as Minister of Munitions* (unpublished Oxford D. Phil. thesis, 1977), p. 35

14: Master and Servant

1 R. Boothby, *Recollections of a Rebel* (1978), p. 52

2 Roskill I, diary, 22 July 1917, p. 415

3 Beaverbrook, *Men and Power*, p. 140

4 Blake, p. 361

5 Roskill I, diary, 17 August 1917, p. 425

6 Arnn, pp. 85–99, for his relations with organised labour

7 *Churchill IV*, p. 47; R. Blake (ed.), *The Private Papers of Douglas Haig, 1914–19* (1952), 12 September 1917, p. 254

8 Beaverbrook, *Men and Power*, p. 126

9 *Churchill IV, companion vol. I*, Churchill to Lloyd George, 4 May 1918, pp. 309–10

10 *Ibid.*, Churchill to Lloyd George, 15 May 1918, pp. 311–16

11 For the Maurice affair see Koss, *Asquith*, pp. 233–4; Roskill I, pp. 539–45; Beaverbrook, *Men and Power*, pp. 250–60; E. David, 'The Liberal Party Divided, 1916–18', *Historical Journal* (1970)

12 A. J. P. Taylor, 'Lloyd George', in *Essays in English History* (1976), p. 129

13 Beaverbrook, *Men and Power*, p. 260

14 John Ramsden, *The Age of Balfour and Baldwin* (1979), p. 122

15 *Ibid.*, pp. 132, 136

16 *Riddell Diary*, 17 November 1918, p. 249

17 Ramsden, p. 142

18 Beaverbrook, *Men and Power*, p. 325

19 *Selborne Papers I*, Selborne to Austen Chamberlain, 18 March 1918, p. 213

20 Ramsden, p. 136

21 P. Williamson (ed.), *The Modernisation of Conservative Politics: The Diaries and Letters of William Bridgeman, 1904-35* (1988) (hereinafter *Bridgeman Diary*), February 1918, pp. 127–8

22 Blake, *The Unknown Prime Minister*, pp. 387–8

23 Churchill, *Thoughts and Adventures*, p. 38

24 *Churchill IV*, pp. 159–60

25 *Ibid.*, pp. 161–2

26 *Ibid.*, pp. 163–5

27 *Riddell Diary*, 17 November 1918, p. 249

28 *Churchill IV, companion vol. 1*, Beaverbrook to Churchill, 26 November 1918, pp. 426–7

29 Ramsden, p. 133

30 Moran, 7 December 1947, p. 327

31 *Churchill IV, companion vol. 1*, Churchill to Lloyd George, 26 December 1918, pp. 443–7

32 *Riddell Diary*, 26 January 1919, p. 255

33 *Amery Diary I*, letter to Lloyd George, 27 December 1918, p. 248

34 *Riddell Diary*, 25 December 1918, p. 252

35 *Churchill IV*, p. 175

36 Beaverbrook, *Men and Power*, p. 127

37 K. Middlemas (ed.), *Whitehall Diary, vol. I: 1916-25* (1969) (hereinafter Jones diary I), Jones/Hankey corr., 17, 18 January 1919, p. 72

38 *Churchill IV, companion vol. 1*, Henry Wilson diary, 10 January 1919, p. 451; Churchill to Midleton, 14 January 1919, p. 453

39 K. Jeffrey, *The British Army and the Crisis of Empire, 1918-22* (Manchester, 1984), pp. 12–13

40 *Amery Diary I*, 29 December 1918, p. 248

41 K. O. Morgan, *Consensus and Disunity: The Lloyd George Coalition Government 1918-22* (1979), pp. 29–30, 34–40

42 *Churchill IV, companion vol. 1*, Churchill to Curzon, 16 January 1919, p. 458; *Stevenson Diary*, 9 March 1919, pp. 170–1

43 *Ibid.*, Lloyd George to Churchill, 18 January 1919, p. 461

44 *Ibid.*, Churchill to Lloyd George, 20 January 1919, p. 470

45 Jeffrey, p. 14

46 *Churchill IV, companion vol. 1*, pp. 481–2

47 Jeffrey, pp. 15–16; *Churchill IV, companion vol. 1*, Churchill to Lloyd George, 27 January 1919, pp. 483–4

48 W. S. Churchill, *The World Crisis, vol. IV: The Aftermath* (1st pub. 1929, 1974 edn) (hereinafter *World Crisis IV*), p. 73

49 *Ibid.*, pp. 53–6; *Churchill IV*, pp. 181–90

50 Morgan, pp. 49–51, 108–12, 134–5; James, *Churchill*, pp. 105–7

51 K. Jeffrey (ed.), *The Military Correspondence of Field Marshal Sir Henry Wilson 1918-22* (1985) (hereinafter *Wilson Corr.*), p. 83

52 *Churchill IV, companion vol. 1*, Churchill to Lloyd George, 27 January 1919, p. 487

53 James, *Churchill*, pp. 107–9, and the War Cabinet minutes at PRO Cab. 23/11/15 give the full picture, unlike Gilbert at *Churchill IV, companion vol. 1*, pp. 525–7, who prints only extracts which support his contention.

54 James, *Churchill*, pp. 107–9

55 *Riddell Diary*, 11 April 1919, p. 267

56 D. Lloyd George, *The Truth about the Peace Treaties, vol. I* (1937), p. 368

57 *Ibid.*, Kerr to Lloyd George, 15 February 1919, p. 531

58 *World Crisis IV*, pp. 171–2

59 *Churchill IV*, pp. 245–6; *Churchill IV, companion vol. 1*, Kerr to Lloyd George, 15 February 1919, p. 530

60 *Churchill IV*, pp. 248–51

61 *Riddell Diary*, 16 February 1919, p. 257

62 *Churchill IV, companion vol. 1*, Lloyd George to Churchill, 16 February 1919, pp. 538–9

63 Jeffrey, *The British Army and the Crisis of Empire*, p. 18

64 *Churchill IV, companion vol. 1*, Chamberlain to Churchill, 5 February 1919, pp. 512–14

65 Jones diary I, pp. 71–2; Jones to Lloyd George, 8 February 1919, on 'industrial unrest', pp. 73–4; Morgan, pp. 50–2, 134–6

66 *Churchill IV, companion vol. 1*, pp. 540–1

67 *Wilson Corr.*, pp. 83–6

68 *Churchill IV*, p. 259

69 *Riddell Diary*, 11 April 1919, p. 267

70 R. R. James (ed.), *Memoirs of a Conservative: J. C. C. Davidson's Memoirs and Papers, 1910-37* (1969) (hereinafter *Davidson Memoirs*), p. 53

71 PRO Cab. 23/15, minutes of 4 March 1919

72 *Churchill IV, companion vol. 1*, Churchill to Lloyd George, 8 March 1919, pp. 581–2

73 *Ibid.*, Churchill to Lloyd George, 26 April 1919, pp. 624–6

74 PRO Cab. 23/15, minutes of 14 May 1919; James, *Churchill*, p. 112

75 James, *ibid.*, p. 111

76 *Churchill IV, companion vol. 1*, Churchill to Wilson, 8 June 1919, p. 678

77 *Ibid.*, pp. 685–8

78 *Ibid.*, pp. 699–701

79 M. Gilbert, *Winston S. Churchill, vol. IV, companion vol. 2* (1977) (hereinafter *Churchill IV, companion vol. 2*), p. 728

80 *Ibid.*, Wilson diary, 10, 11 July 1919, pp. 739–40

81 *Churchill IV, companion vol. 1*, unsent letter to Lloyd George, 17 February 1919, pp. 544–6

82 *Churchill IV*, p. 305

83 *Churchill IV, companion vol. 2.*, p. 759

84 *Ibid.*, p. 771

85 *Ibid.*, Churchill to Lloyd George, 24 August 1919, pp. 816–17

86 *Ibid.*, Lloyd George to Churchill, 30 August 1919, pp. 826–7

87 *Ibid.*, Lloyd George memo., 30 August 1919, pp. 827–8

88 *Ibid.*, Churchill to Lloyd George, 6 September 1919, pp. 843–4

89 *Ibid.*, Churchill to Lloyd George, 20 September 1919, p. 865

90 *Ibid.*, Lloyd George to Churchill, 22 September 1919, pp. 867–9

91 *Ibid.*, Churchill to Lloyd George, 22 September 1919, pp. 869–72

92 James, *Churchill*, pp. 120–2

93 *Riddell Diary*, 11 April 1919, p. 267

15: Fusion and Fissures

1 *Churchill IV, companion vol. 2*, p. 594
2 *Ibid.*, Wilson diary, 8 July 1919, p. 734
3 James, *Churchill*, pp. 124–5
4 S. Roskill, *Hankey: Man of Secrets, vol. II: 1919–31* (1972) (hereinafter Roskill II), p. 110
5 *Churchill IV, companion vol. 2*, Wilson diary, 11, 12 July 1919, pp. 739, 741
6 *Ibid.*, Churchill to Lloyd George, 8 July 1919, p. 735
7 Koss, *Asquith*, p. 247
8 Lord Beaverbrook, *The Decline and Fall of Lloyd George* (1963), p. 9
9 Beaverbrook, *Men and Power*, pp. 230–8
10 *Ibid.*, p. 238
11 *Bridgeman Papers*, 4 July 1919, p. 141
12 Blake, pp. 413–15
13 *Churchill IV*, pp. 365–6
14 *Selborne Papers I*, Selborne to Younger, 27 February 1920, pp. 224–5
15 Morgan, pp. 177–85
16 *Riddell Diary*, 10 January 1920, p. 301
17 *Ibid.*, 1 February 1920, p. 304
18 Campbell, pp. 530–5
19 *Riddell Diary*, 22 January 1920, p. 303
20 Ramsden, p. 143; Blake, pp. 416–17; Morgan, pp. 183–4
21 Morgan, p. 185
22 *Ibid.*, pp. 185–7
23 Blake, pp. 416–17; Ramsden, p. 145
24 *Stevenson Diary*, 17 January 1920, p. 197
25 Beaverbrook, *Men and Power*, pp. 10–11
26 *Riddell Diary*, 24 January 1920, p. 303
27 *Stevenson Diary*, 20 January 1920, p. 198
28 Blake, p. 235
29 *Wilson Corr.*, Wilson to Milne, 2 December 1919, pp. 134–5
30 *Ibid.*
31 *Churchill IV, companion vol. 2*, Churchill memo., 1 August 1919, pp. 780–4; Churchill to Lloyd George, 4 August 1919, p. 791
32 James, *Victor Cazalet*, p. 77
33 Roskill II, 25 August 1919, p. 107
34 PRO Cab. 24/78, 3 May 1919
35 Jeffrey, *The British Army and the Crisis of Empire*, p. 19
36 PRO Cab. 23/15, 606A, meeting 5 August 1919
37 *Churchill IV, companion vol. 2*, Churchill memo., 1 August 1919, pp. 780–6
38 Jeffrey, *The British Army and the Crisis of Empire*, p. 20
39 *Ibid.*, pp. 20–6
40 W. S. Churchill, *India* (1974 edn), Introduction, p. VI
41 Lord Birkenhead, *Frederick Edwin Earl of Birkenhead, vol II: The Last Phase* (1935), p. 245
42 Churchill, *India*, pp. VI–VII
43 *Ibid.*, p. 437, speech on Amritsar
44 *Churchill IV, companion vol. 2*, Wilson diary, 23 January 1920, p. 1017
45 Jeffrey, *The British Army and the Crisis of Empire*,

Churchill to Lloyd George, 11 October 1919, p. 80
46 *Churchill IV, companion vol. 2*, Wilson diary, 11, 12 May 1920, pp. 1090, 1091–2
47 *Wilson Corr.*, Wilson to Milne, 14 May 1920, p. 170
48 *Churchill IV, companion vol. 2*, Churchill to Lloyd George, 13 June 1920, pp. 1119–20; to Cabinet, 15 June, pp. 1121–2
49 Jeffrey, *The British Army and the Crisis of Empire*, pp. 27–8
50 *Riddell Diary*, 6, 11 June 1920, p. 314
51 The correspondence is in *Wilson Corr.*, nos 125–9, 132, 134, 136–8; the quotation is from no. 137, Churchill to Wilson, 14 July 1920, pp. 188–9.
52 *Ibid.*, Churchill to Wilson, 25 June 1920, pp. 181–2
53 *Churchill IV, companion vol. 2*, Wilson diary, 12 July 1920, p. 1142
54 Jones diary I, p. 118; *Churchill IV*, p. 457
55 *Churchill IV, companion vol. 2*, Wilson diary, 30 August 1920, pp. 1194–5
56 *Ibid.*, Churchill to Wilson, 18 September 1920, pp. 1209–11
57 *Ibid.*, Churchill to Lloyd George, 8 July, 13 August 1919, pp. 735–6, 805; Wilson diary, 15 August 1919, p. 808
58 *Churchill IV, companion vol. 2*, Churchill to Lloyd George, 24 August 1919, pp. 1184–7
59 *Ibid.*, Churchill memo., 3 November 1919, pp. 1229–30
60 *Ibid.*, Churchill memo., 16 November 1919, pp. 1237–41
61 *Ibid.*, Birkenhead to Churchill, pp. 1241–2
62 *Ibid.*, Churchill to Lloyd George, 24 March 1920, pp. 1253–5
63 *Ibid.*, Churchill to Lloyd George, 4 December 1920, pp. 1260–2
64 *Ibid.*, Wilson diary, 23 January 1921, p. 1319
65 *Ibid.*, Montagu to Lloyd George, 26 October 1920, p. 1222
66 R. S. Churchill, *Lord Derby*, pp. 383–4
67 *Churchill IV, companion vol. 2*, Churchill to Lloyd George, 4 January 1921, pp. 1289–91
68 *Ibid.*, Churchill to Lloyd George, 31 August 1920, p. 1199
69 *Ibid.*, Churchill to Lloyd George, 9 January 1921, pp. 1295–6
70 *Amery Diary I*, Amery to Sir Henry Wilson, 1 August 1918, pp. 330–2; Amery to Smuts, 16 August 1918, pp. 233–4; M. L. Dockrill and J. D. Goold, *Peace without Promise: Britain and the Peace Conferences 1919–23* (1981), pp. 133–5
71 The literature on this is voluminous; this account is based on E. Monroe, *Britain's Moment in the Middle East* (1963), and on E. Kedourie, *In the Anglo-Arab Labyrinth* (Cambridge, 1976).
72 Dockrill, p. 141
73 *Churchill IV, companion vol. 2*, Churchill to Sir Percy Cox, 16 January 1921, p. 1311
74 M. Brown (ed.), *The Letters of T. E. Lawrence* (1988), Lawrence to his mother, 20 March 1921, p. 185

16: Decline

1 *Churchill IV, companion vol. 2*, Churchill to Lloyd George, 25 January 1921, p. 1324
2 Morgan, pp. 241–4
3 M. Cowling, *The Impact of Labour* (Cambridge, 1971), p. 57
4 Morgan, Chap. 10
5 *Riddell Diary*, 23 May 1920, p. 312
6 R. S. Churchill, *Lord Derby*, p. 388
7 *Crawford Papers*, 30 January 1921, p. 409; *Churchill IV, companion vol. 2*, Wilson diary, 20 January 1921, p. 1317
8 *Churchill IV, companion vol. 2*, Derby to Churchill, 17 December, 23 December 1921, pp. 1270–1, 1273
9 R. S. Churchill, *Lord Derby*, Derby to Sassoon, 23 December 1921, p. 388
10 *Crawford Papers*, 17 March 1921, p. 410
11 Halifax Papers, Halifax to Baldwin, August 1937
12 C. Wrigley (ed.), *Warfare, Diplomacy and Politics* (1986), p. 2
13 Beaverbrook, *Men and Power*, p. XIII
14 Ramsden, pp. 149–51
15 *Stevenson Diary*, 26 April 1921, p. 210
16 Beaverbrook, *The Decline and Fall of Lloyd George*, p. 33
17 *Churchill IV*, p. 581
18 *Stevenson Diary*, 26 April 1921, p. 210
19 Beaverbrook, *The Decline and Fall of Lloyd George*, p. 34
20 *Ibid.*, pp. 35–7; Campbell, p. 539; *Riddell Diary*, 21 December 1920, p. 330
21 Beaverbrook, *The Decline and Fall of Lloyd George*, pp. 38–9; India Office Record Library (hereinafter IORL), Montagu Papers, Mss. EUR, 523/23, correspondence with Sir George Lloyd, 1921, for Montagu's criticisms
22 Beaverbrook, *The Decline and Fall of Lloyd George*, p. 251
23 Earl of Ronaldshay, *The Life of Lord Curzon, vol. III* (n.d. but 1928), p. 254
24 A. J. P. Taylor, *Beaverbrook* (1972), p. 184
25 *Riddell Diary*, 24 April 1921, p. 342; 14 May 1921, p. 343; Cowling, *The Impact of Labour*, pp. 120–1
26 *Stevenson Diary*, 25 May 1921, p. 219
27 *Ibid.*, 31 May 1921, p. 219
28 *Ibid.*, 1 June 1921, p. 219
29 Beaverbrook, *The Decline and Fall of Lloyd George*, Chap. 4
30 *Ibid.*, p. 61
31 Cowling, *The Impact of Labour*, pp. 115–21
32 Beaverbrook, *The Decline and Fall of Lloyd George*, Churchill to Lloyd George, 9 June 1921, pp. 272–3
33 *Ibid.*, Churchill to Lloyd George, 15 June 1921, pp. 277–8
34 *Ibid.*, p. 68
35 *Crawford Papers*, diary, 21 May 1921, p. 411
36 Cowling, *The Impact of Labour*, pp. 72, 120–3
37 *Crawford Papers*, diary, 14 August 1919, p. 402
38 *Stevenson Diary*, 20 June 1921, p. 223

39 *Ibid.*, 22 June 1921, p. 223
40 Campbell, p. 544
41 Beaverbrook, *The Decline and Fall of Lloyd George*, pp. 73–4
42 Campbell, p. 545
43 *Stevenson Diary*, 24 June 1921, pp. 223–4
44 *Selborne Papers I*, Selborne to Salisbury, 13 June 1921, pp. 228–9
45 Beaverbrook, *The Decline and Fall of Lloyd George*, pp. 76–7
46 *Selborne Papers I*, Salisbury to Selborne, 6 July 1921, pp. 229–30
47 Campbell, pp. 556–7
48 *Ibid.*, p. 557
49 *Churchill IV*, pp. 667–8
50 *Churchill IV, companion vol. 2*, Curzon to Lloyd George, Curzon to Churchill, 13 June 1921, pp. 1502–4; Cabinet notes, 4 July 1921, pp. 1542–3
51 *Ibid.*, Churchill to Lloyd George and Curzon, 25 June 1921, pp. 1521–2
52 *Ibid.*, Churchill to Montagu, 8 October 1921, pp. 1644–5
53 *Ibid.*, Churchill/Lloyd George corr., 1, 8 October 1921, pp. 1637–8, 1642–3
54 *Churchill IV*, pp. 670–2
55 *Ibid.*, p. 673
56 *Ibid.*, pp. 674–5
57 *Selborne Papers I*, Selborne to Salisbury, 29 July 1921, pp. 231–2
58 *Stevenson Diary*, 8 November 1921, pp. 226–7
59 *Ibid.*, 9 November 1921 p. 236
60 *Churchill IV, companion vol. 2*, Churchill to Lloyd George, 9 November 1921, pp. 1666–7
61 *Churchill IV*, p. 670
62 Birkenhead, *Birkenhead II*, p. 163
63 Campbell, p. 567
64 *Churchill IV, companion vol. 2*, Churchill to Curzon, 29 September 1921, p. 1635
65 *Churchill IV*, pp. 678–81
66 *Bridgeman Papers*, Bridgeman to his wife, 16 December 1921, pp. 153–4; Blake, *The Unknown Prime Minister*, pp. 434–5
67 *Selborne Papers I*, Salisbury to Selborne, 15 November 1921, p. 233
68 Beaverbrook, *The Decline and Fall of Lloyd George*, pp. 124–5; Blake, *The Unknown Prime Minister*, pp. 436–7
69 Ramsden, pp. 157–8; Campbell, pp. 586–7
70 Campbell, p. 587
71 Ramsden, pp. 159–60
72 Beaverbrook, *The Decline and Fall of Lloyd George*, Lloyd George to Chamberlain, 10 January 1922, pp. 290–1
73 Morgan, p. 275
74 *Ibid.*, pp. 272–4; Beaverbrook, *The Decline and Fall of Lloyd George*, pp. 290–1; Ramsden, p. 160; Campbell, pp. 588–9; Blake, *The Unknown Prime Minister*, p. 439; Cowling, *The Impact of Labour*, pp. 133–4
75 *Churchill IV, companion vol. 2*, Churchill to Mrs Churchill, 4 January 1922, p. 1712
76 Morgan, pp. 268–70

77 *Churchill IV*, pp. 765–6
78 *Ibid.*, p. 769
79 *Churchill IV, companion vol. 2*, Wilson diary, 25 January 1922, pp. 1734–5
80 *Wilson Corr.*, Wilson to Allenby, 4 January 1922, p. 332
81 *Ibid.*, Wilson to Rawlinson, 15 February 1922, p. 339
82 James, *Victor Cazalet*, 11 April 1922, p. 77
83 *Churchill IV, companion vol. 2*, Churchill to Curzon, 24 December 1921, p. 1699
84 Beaverbrook, *The Decline and Fall of Lloyd George*, p. 292; Morgan, pp. 309–10
85 *Stevenson Diary*, 3 February 1922, p. 241
86 *Churchill IV*, p. 770
87 *Riddell Diary*, 3 February 1922, p. 362
88 Campbell, pp. 581–6; *Selborne Papers I*, pp. 233–5
89 *Churchill IV, companion vol. 2*, Lloyd George to Churchill, 15 June 1921, p. 1511
90 *Churchill IV*, pp. 691–3
91 *Bridgeman Papers*, memo., 1922, p. 156
92 *Churchill IV, companion vol. 2*, Churchill to Mrs Churchill, 7 February 1922, p. 1757
93 Cowling, *The Impact of Labour*, p. 151
94 Morgan, pp. 271–2
95 *Churchill IV, companion vol. 2*, Churchill to Lloyd George, 27 February 1922, pp. 1786–7
96 *Ibid.*, Churchill/Montagu corr., 31 January–2 February 1922, pp. 1743–9
97 *Ibid.*, H. A. L. Fisher diary, 28 February 1922, p. 1791
98 *Ibid.*, Churchill to Lloyd George, 27 February 1922, pp. 1786–7
99 *Ibid.*, Lloyd George to Chamberlain, 27 February 1922, pp. 1788–90; Cowling, *The Impact of Labour*, pp. 154–5
100 *Churchill IV, companion vol. 2*, Churchill to J. Philip, 7 March 1922, p. 1795; Cowling, *ibid.*, pp. 156–7

17: The Fall and After

1 Beaverbrook, *The Decline and Fall of Lloyd George*, p. 140
2 *Churchill IV, companion vol. 2*, Sassoon to Esher, 6 March 1922, p. 1794
3 *Churchill IV*, p. 772; R. R. James, *Churchill Speaks* (1981), pp. 411–12, speech on 'the Socialist peril' at Loughborough; pp. 414–16, 'Plea for National Unity', Northampton, 25 March 1922; pp. 417–19 on 'Socialism' at Dundee, 8 April 1922
4 Morgan, pp. 332–5; Cowling, *The Impact of Labour*, pp. 158–60
5 A. J. P. Taylor (ed.), *My Darling Pussy: The Letters of Lloyd George and Frances Stevenson 1913–41* (1975), Lloyd George to Frances Stevenson, 21 March 1922, p. 39
6 *Churchill IV, companion vol. 2*, Beaverbrook to Lloyd George, 15 March 1922, pp. 1807–8
7 Taylor (ed.), *My Darling Pussy*, Lloyd George to Frances Stevenson, 22 March 1922, p. 40
8 *Churchill IV*, pp. 773–4

9 *Churchill IV, companion vol. 2*, Churchill to Lloyd George, 18 March 1922, pp. 1810–12
10 *Ibid.*, Chamberlain to Lloyd George, 21 March 1922, pp. 1814–15
11 Beaverbrook, *The Decline and Fall of Lloyd George*, p. 139
12 *Ibid.*, Lloyd George to Horne, 22 March 1922, p. 293
13 *Churchill IV, companion vol. 2*, Lloyd George to Chamberlain, 22 March 1922, p. 1818
14 *Ibid.*, Chamberlain to Lloyd George, 23, 25 March 1922, pp. 1820, 1827–8; Chamberlain to Curzon, 24 March 1922, pp. 1820–1
15 Morgan, p. 310; *Churchill IV*, p. 778
16 Cowling, *The Impact of Labour*, p. 166
17 James, *Churchill Speaks*, speech at Northampton, 25 March 1922, pp. 415–16
18 R. Blake, *The Conservative Party from Peel to Churchill* (1970), pp. 205–9; Ramsden, pp. 160–1
19 *Selborne Papers I*, pp. 234–5; *Davidson Memoirs*, pp. 111–12
20 Blake, *The Unknown Prime Minister*, pp. 440–1
21 *Churchill IV*, pp. 735–7
22 Morgan, pp. 311–12, 337–8; Beaverbrook, *The Decline and Fall of Lloyd George*, pp. 142–5
23 The brilliant account by G. R. Searle in his *Corruption in British Politics* (1987) will remain the definitive work on this subject
24 *Amery Diary I*, 2 August 1922, p. 290; *Crawford Papers*, diary, 3 August 1922, pp. 428–9
25 *Amery Diary I*, 3 August 1922, p. 290
26 *Crawford Papers*, diary, 3 August 1922, p. 429
27 Campbell, pp. 602–3; *Bridgeman Papers*, diary, 1922, pp. 158–9
28 *Amery Diary I*, 2 August 1922, p. 290
29 *Churchill IV, companion vol. 1*, Churchill memo., 16 December 1920, pp 1267–9; *Churchill IV, companion vol. 2*, Churchill to Lloyd George, 9 August 1921, p. 1584; Churchill memo., 26 September 1921, pp. 1628–9
30 Beaverbrook, *The Decline and Fall of Lloyd George*, pp. 151–2
31 Morgan, pp. 321–2
32 *Churchill IV, companion vol. 2*, Churchill to Balfour, 12 September, pp. 1984–5; Campbell, p. 605; Cowling, *The Impact of Labour*, p. 191
33 Beaverbrook, *The Decline and Fall of Lloyd George*, Lloyd George to Curzon, 15 September, p. 296; *Crawford Papers*, diary, 15 September, pp. 435–6; *Churchill IV, companion vol. 2*, Cabinet minutes, 15 September, pp. 1988–92
34 This, of course, was the motto of *The Second World War*, but Churchill originally meant it as an inscription for a war memorial.
35 *Churchill IV*, pp. 801–7
36 *Churchill IV, companion vol. 2*, p. 1989
37 Jones diary I, 26 October 1922, pp. 218–19
38 Beaverbrook, *The Decline and Fall of Lloyd George*, p. 160
39 *Churchill IV, companion vol. 2*, p. 1989
40 M. Kinnear, *The Fall of Lloyd George: The Political Crisis of 1922* (1973), Chap. 5; Morgan, pp. 322–4; James, *Churchill*, pp. 141–4; Beaverbrook, *The*

Decline and Fall of Lloyd George, pp. 160–3; Campbell, pp. 606–7

41 *Churchill IV*, p. 829

42 *Amery Diary I*, 18 September 1922, p. 291

43 *Ibid.*, 27 September 1922, p. 291

44 A. Clark (ed.), *'A Good Innings': The Private Papers of Viscount Lee of Fareham* (1974) (hereinafter *Lee Papers*), 23 September 1922, p. 229

45 *Churchill IV, companion vol. 2*, Churchill to Archie Sinclair, 25 September 1922, pp. 2029–30

46 *Ibid.*, Churchill to Dominion Prime Ministers, 24, 25 September 1922, pp. 2025–6, 2030–1

47 Roskill II, Hankey diary for 23–27 September 1922 (written 4 October), pp. 289–90

48 *Churchill IV, companion vol. 2*, Churchill to Harington, 27 September 1922, pp. 2043–4

49 Roskill II, p. 289

50 *Churchill IV, companion vol. 2*, Cabinet minutes, 29 September 1922, meeting at 10 p.m., p. 2053

51 *Ibid.*, Curzon to Chamberlain, 29 September 1922, p. 2054

52 Roskill II, pp. 291–2

53 *Crawford Papers*, diary, 30 September 1922, p. 438

54 *Ibid.*, p. 439

55 *Ibid.*

56 *Lee Papers*, 1 October 1922, p. 229

57 *Ibid.*, *Crawford Papers*, diary, 30 September 1922, pp. 439–40

58 *Crawford, ibid.*, p. 440

59 Campbell, p. 607

60 *Crawford Papers*, diary, 1 October 1922, pp. 440–1

61 *Churchill IV, companion vol. 2*, Churchill to Dominion Prime Ministers, 7 p.m. 1 October 1922, pp. 2062–6

62 *Crawford Papers*, diary, 6 October 1922, p. 445

63 *Ibid.*, p. 446

64 Blake, *The Unknown Prime Minister*, pp. 447–8

65 *Selborne Papers I*, Salisbury to Selborne, 26 September 1922, pp. 235–6

66 Blake, *The Unknown Prime Minister*, pp. 448–9; *Davidson Memoirs*, pp. 114–15

67 *Selborne Papers I*, Salisbury to Selborne, 12 October 1922, pp. 236–7; *Bridgeman Papers*, Bridgeman to his wife, 17 October 1922, p. 160; *Amery Diary I*, 10 October 1922, p. 293; Kinnear, pp. 87–8; Cowling, *The Impact of Labour*, p. 194

68 Austen Chamberlain Mss., AC 33/2/52, Chamberlain to Birkenhead, 12 October 1922; also quoted in Campbell, p. 608

69 Cowling, *The Impact of Labour*, pp. 196–212, gives the most detailed and involved account of these events; see also Blake, *The Unknown Prime Minister*, pp. 450–4, and Kinnear, pp. 117–30.

70 *Crawford Papers*, diary, 20 October 1922, p. 455

71 Campbell, pp. 612–13; Kinnear, Chap. 10

72 *Churchill IV, companion vol. 2*, Churchill to J. C. Robertson, 27 October 1922, pp. 2092–4

73 Kinnear, pp. 130–2

74 *Ibid.*, pp. 136–8

75 F. W. S. Craig (ed.), *British Parliamentary Election Results 1918–49* (1977 edn), p. 715, for an analysis of the results

76 *Churchill IV*, pp. 876–7

77 *Ibid.*, p. 880

78 *Ibid.*, pp. 882–3

79 *Churchill IV, companion vol. 2*, Churchill to Lloyd George, 2 November 1922, pp. 2114–16

80 Kinnear, pp. 151–4

81 *Churchill V, companion vol. 1*, Churchill to Spears, 18 November 1922, pp. 3–4

82 *Crawford Papers*, diary, 17 November 1922, p. 467; Campbell, pp. 613–18

83 Cowling, *The Impact of Labour*, pp. 262–4

84 *Ibid.*, pp. 224–34

85 *Riddell Diary*, 30 May 1923, p. 388

86 M. Gilbert, *Winston S. Churchill, vol. V: 1922–39* (1976) (hereinafter *Churchill V*), pp. 7–8; *The Times*, 5 May 1923, reporting Churchill at the Aldwych Club, 4 May; Cowling, *The Impact of Labour*, pp. 221–2; James, *Victor Cazalet*, 5 January 1923, pp. 87–8

87 Blake, *The Unknown Prime Minister*, pp. 507–12; *Davidson Memoirs*, pp. 147–8

88 Blake, *Conservative Party*, p. 214; Ramsden, pp. 175–6

89 *Churchill V, companion vol. 1*, Chamberlain to Churchill, 31 October 1923, p. 92

90 James, *Churchill Speaks*, p. 425

91 *Churchill V*, pp. 17–21

92 *Churchill V, companion vol. 1*, Churchill letter to *The Times*, 17 January 1924, pp. 94–7

93 *Churchill V*, pp. 24–7

18: Reforging a Reputation

1 *Churchill IV, companion vol. 1*, Churchill to Mrs Churchill, 27 March 1920, p. 1059

2 Soames, Chap. 15

3 *Ibid.*, pp. 123–5

4 *Churchill III*, pp. 622–3, 626–7

5 *Churchill V, companion vol. 1*, Mrs Churchill to Churchill, 24 February 1924, pp. 110–12

6 *Churchill III, companion vol. 3*, Churchill to Mrs Churchill, 10, 13, 19, 24 January 1916, pp. 1365–6, 1368–70, 1383–4, 1394–5; *Stevenson Diary*, 15 September 1915, pp. 59–60

7 *Churchill IV, companion vol. 2*, Churchill to Mrs Churchill, 16 February 1921, p. 1354

8 M. Gilbert (ed.), *Winston S. Churchill, vol. V, companion vol. 3: The Coming of War 1936–9* (1982) (hereinafter *Churchill V, companion vol. 3*), Neville Chamberlain to Churchill, 6 October 1938, pp. 1204–5

9 *Churchill IV*, p. 914

10 D. Jablonsky, *Churchill, the Great Game and Total War* (1991), pp. 33–9, 66–9

11 *Churchill IV*, pp. 914–15

12 Lord Cecil of Chelwood Papers, Add. Mss. 51073, Churchill to Cecil, 23 March 1924, fo. 108

13 Ramsden, pp. 190–2

14 Austen Chamberlain Mss., AC 35/9, Chamberlain to Birkenhead, 26 February 1924

15 *Bridgeman Papers*, Bridgeman to his wife, 9 March 1924, p. 176

16 *Churchill V, companion vol. 1*, Churchill to Baldwin, 7 March 1924, p. 119

17 Chaplin (ed.), pp. 21–2
18 *Amery Diary I*, 24 February 1924, p. 372
19 *Churchill V, companion vol. I*, Chamberlain to Churchill, 3 March 1924, pp. 115–16
20 *Amery Diary I*, 4 March 1924, p. 372
21 *Ibid.*, 5 March 1924, p. 372
22 *Ibid.*, 7 March 1924, p. 373
23 *Ibid.*, 8 March 1924, p. 373
24 Campbell, pp. 658–61; Ramsden, pp. 179–80
25 Cowling, *The Impact of Labour*, pp. 338–9
26 *Ibid.*, Amery to Geoffrey Dawson, 9 January 1924, p. 341
27 *Ibid.*, p. 389
28 *Amery Diary I*, 8 March 1924, p. 373
29 Cowling, *The Impact of Labour*, p. 398; *Amery Diary I*, 14 March 1924, p. 373
30 *Ibid.*, pp. 395–6
31 *Ibid.*, pp. 390–1, 395, 399
32 *Churchill V*, p. 35
33 *Ibid.*, p. 34
34 *Bridgeman Papers*, Bridgeman to his wife, 9, 15 March 1924, p. 176
35 *Churchill V, companion vol. I*, Derby to Rawlinson, 19 March 1924, p. 125
36 17th Earl of Derby Papers, 920.Der/17/33, Churchill to Derby, 13 April 1924
37 *Churchill V, companion vol. I*, Churchill to Balfour, 3 April 1924, pp. 138–40
38 Lord Birkenhead, *Contemporary Personalities* (1924), pp. 116–18
39 *Churchill V, companion vol. I*, Birkenhead to Derby, 28 March 1924, p. 135
40 James, *Churchill Speaks*, pp. 431–4
41 C. Cook, *The Age of Alignment: Electoral Politics in Britain 1922–9* (1975), p. 224
42 Cowling, *The Impact of Labour*, p. 401
43 *Churchill V*, pp. 43–4
44 *Churchill V, companion vol. I*, Goschen to Churchill, 5 August 1924, pp. 172–3
45 *Ibid.*, Churchill to Goschen, 11 August 1924, pp. 174–5
46 *Churchill V*, p. 48
47 *Churchill V, companion vol. I*, Churchill to Goschen, 11 September 1924, pp. 197–8
48 Cook, pp. 293–309
49 Neville Chamberlain Mss. (hereinafter NC), NC 2/21, diary, 28 March 1924
50 D. Dilks, *Neville Chamberlain, vol. I* (1984), p. 398
51 Jones diary I, 4 November 1924, p. 302
52 NC 2/21, diary, 5 November 1924
53 Dilks, p. 398
54 NC 2/1, diary, 5 November 1924
55 *Churchill V*, p. 57
56 *Ibid.*, p. 59
57 NC 2/21, diary, 6 November 1924
58 *Churchill V, companion vol. I*, Austen Chamberlain to Baldwin, 6 November 1924, p. 237
59 *Amery Diary I*, 7 November 1924, p. 390
60 NC 2/21, diary, 20 November 1924
61 Cowling, *The Impact of Labour*, pp. 406–8
62 Jones diary I, 8 November 1924, p. 303
63 For Baldwin's Conservatism see Ramsden, pp. 203–4, 207–15; Cowling, *The Impact of Labour*,
pp. 407–9, 414–15; S. Baldwin, *An Interpreter of England* (1935)
64 Cowling, *ibid*, p. 407
65 Ramsden, p. 208
66 'A Gentleman with a Duster', *The Conservative Mind* (1924), pp. 46–7
67 Charmley, *Lord Lloyd*, pp. 72–4, for this
68 *Crawford Papers*, diary, 25 August 1935, p. 564
69 *Bridgeman Papers*, introduction, pp. 1–10
70 J. Parry, 'High and Low Politics in Modern Britain', *Historical Journal* (1986), pp. 768–9
71 Cowling, *The Impact of Labour*, p. 415
72 Jones diary I, 8 November 1924, p. 303

19: 'A Cabinet of Faithful Husbands'

1 *Davidson Memoirs*, Davidson to F. S. Jackson, 18 November 1923, p. 188
2 Campbell, Salisbury to Baldwin, 26 January 1924, pp. 658–9
3 Dilks, pp. 406–9
4 NC 2/21, diary, 18 November 1923
5 *Ibid.*, 26 November 1924
6 Lord Birkenhead, *The Speeches of Lord Birkenhead* (1929), p. 217
7 Campbell, p. 641
8 Dilks, p. 405
9 Parry, p. 769
10 See Dilks I, *passim*, for much of this estimate, which is also based on Neville's letters to his family; see especially NC 18/1/1006, Neville to Hilda Chamberlain, 30 May 1937.
11 Dilks, p. 407
12 Campbell, p. 717
13 *Ibid.*, p. 641. I hope this will not be taken as a criticism of Dr Campbell's superb biography; it is simply that he and the present author approach the problem from different perspectives.
14 F. Woods, *A Bibliography of the Works of Sir Winston Churchill, KG. OM. CH.* (1979 edn), pp. 216, 241
15 Churchill, *Great Contemporaries*, p. 109
16 IORL, Reading papers, Mss. EUR F118/100, Birkenhead to Reading, 21 January 1925
17 Austen Chamberlain Mss., AC 53/553, Sir William Tyrrell to Chamberlain, 11 March 1926; Lord Lloyd Papers, GLLD 13/3, Chamberlain to Lloyd, 1, 21 April 1925, Chamberlain to Lloyd, 11 May 1925
18 *Churchill V, companion vol. I*, Churchill to Rosebery, 8 November 1924, pp. 239–40
19 Jones diary I, 28 November 1924, p. 307
20 *Churchill V, companion vol. I*, Churchill to Baldwin, 28 November 1924, pp. 271–2
21 Ramsden. pp. 268–9; *Bridgeman Papers*, diary, 1925, pp. 179–80; *Davidson Memoirs*, pp. 211–13
22 P. J. Grigg, *Prejudice and Judgement* (1948), p. 195
23 Boothby, p. 46
24 Jones diary I, 17 May 1925, p. 315
25 Grigg, p. 174
26 *Churchill V, companion vol. I*, Churchill to Baldwin, 15 December 1924, pp. 303–7
27 *Davidson Memoirs*, pp. 211–12

28 *Bridgeman Papers*, diary, 1925, pp. 179–80
29 *Ibid.*, Bridgeman to Geoffrey Dawson, 13 February 1925, p. 181; *Amery Diary I*, 27 February 1925, p. 397; *Davidson Memoirs*, p. 212
30 *Bridgeman Papers*, Bridgeman to Baldwin, 11 February 1925, p. 180; *Davidson Memoirs*, p. 212
31 *Churchill V, companion vol. 1*, Churchill to Viscount Cecil, 20 January 1925, p. 350
32 *Ibid.*, Churchill to Baldwin, 15 December 1924, pp. 303–7; to Bridgeman, 15 December 1924, pp. 307–9; Churchill Cabinet memo., 29 January 1925, pp. 395–8
33 *Ibid.*, Churchill to Baldwin, 15 December 1924, pp. 306, 307
34 Roskill II, p. 404
35 *Gathering Storm*, p. 55
36 *Ibid.*, p. 32
37 *Davidson Memoirs*, p. 219
38 *Ibid.*, p. 213
39 *Amery Diary I*, 15 July 1925, p. 416; *Bridgeman Papers*, Bridgeman to his wife, 15 July 1925, p. 187
40 *Bridgeman Papers*, diary, 22 July 1925, p. 183
41 *Ibid.*, Bridgeman to his wife, 22 July 1925, p. 188; *Davidson Memoirs*, pp. 216–17
42 Ramsden, p. 271
43 James, *Victor Cazalet*, diary, 7 December 1924, pp. 100–1
44 NC 2/21, diary, 1 May 1925
45 James, *Victor Cazalet*, diary, 7 December 1924, pp. 100–1
46 *Churchill V, companion vol. 1*, Baldwin to King George V, 18 December 1924, pp. 310–11
47 *Ibid.*, Baldwin to King George V, 28 April 1925, pp. 472–3
48 Jones diary I, 17 May 1925, pp. 315–16
49 James, *Churchill*, pp. 161–3
50 *Churchill V, companion vol. 1*, Churchill to Sir Otto Niemeyer, 2 January 1925, pp. 329–30, and also 22 February, pp. 411–12
51 Boothby, p. 46; James, *Churchill*, pp. 158–63
52 Grigg, pp. 180–6
53 Dilks, pp. 430–1
54 Grigg, p. 182
55 *Churchill V*, pp. 80–2

20: Staking Out a Claim

1 *Churchill V*, p. 116
2 Ramsden, pp. 272–4
3 *Churchill V, companion vol. 1*, Churchill to Baldwin, 22 February 1925, pp. 409–10
4 Ramsden, pp. 276–7
5 *Churchill V, companion vol. 1*, Churchill to Mrs Churchill, 8 March 1925, pp. 423–5
6 Birkenhead, *Contemporary Personalities*, p. 114
7 *Churchill V, companion vol. 1*, Baldwin to King George V, 1 May 1925, pp. 476–8
8 Jones diary I, July 1925, pp. 321–5; Ramsden, pp. 281–3; Dilks, pp. 437–9
9 *Churchill V*, pp. 130–3
10 K. Middlemas (ed.), *Whitehall Diary, vol. II: 1926–30* (Oxford, 1969) (hereinafter Jones diary II),

p. IX; Ramsden, pp. 281–4; *Churchill V*, pp. 149–51; Campbell, pp. 771–3; *Davidson Memoirs*, pp. 226–330
11 *Davidson Memoirs*, p. 227
12 NC 1/26/361, Chamberlain to his wife, 1/2 May 1926
13 NC 2/22, diary, May 1926; Jones diary II, 3 May 1926, p. 33, records a more moderate version of this.
14 *Bridgeman Papers*, diary, May 1926, pp. 194–5
15 NC 1/26/361, Churchill to Mrs Churchill, 1/2 May 1926
16 NC 2/22, diary, May 1926
17 *Ibid.*; *Davidson Memoirs*, p. 231; Jones diary II, pp. 32–6
18 *Churchill V*, p. 151
19 *Davidson Memoirs*, Davidson to Lord Irwin, 14 June 1926, pp. 242–3
20 *Ibid.*, pp. 236–7; *Churchill V*, pp. 152–3
21 *Davidson Memoirs*, pp. 238–9
22 Jones diary II, 4 May 1926, p. 36
23 Taylor, *Beaverbrook*, p. 232
24 *Davidson Memoirs*, p. 242
25 Jones diary II, 7 May 1926, p. 41
26 *Ibid.*, 9 May 1926, p. 44
27 *Ibid.*, for Grigg's comment, and 10 May 1926, p. 46, for the suggestion about union funds
28 Dilks, p. 473
29 NC 1/26/365, Churchill to his wife, 9 May 1926
30 *Davidson Memoirs*, p. 244
31 *Ibid.*, p. 246
32 *Ibid.*, pp. 254–5; *Bridgeman Papers*, Bridgeman to Baldwin, 7 September 1926, pp. 200–1
33 *Amery Diary I*, 11 May 1926, p. 454
34 *Churchill V, companion vol. 1*, Baldwin to King George V, August 1926, pp. 739–40
35 NC 2/22, diary, 10 August 1926
36 *Churchill V, companion vol. 1*, George Lane-Fox to Lord Irwin, 18 August 1926, p. 742
37 *Davidson Memoirs*, p. 231
38 James, *Victor Cazalet*, pp. 93–4
39 Churchill, *Great Contemporaries*, p. 112
40 R. S. Churchill, *Twenty-One Years* (Cambridge, 1965), pp. 66–7
41 *Ibid.*, p. 94
42 Campbell, pp. 712–13
43 Churchill, *Great Contemporaries*, p. 115
44 James, *Victor Cazalet*, 17 October 1916, pp. 15–16
45 *Ibid.*, 5 January 1923, p. 86
46 *Ibid.*, pp. 94–5
47 J. Charmley, *Duff Cooper: The Authorised Biography* (1986), p. 47
48 Boothby, pp. 41–4
49 C. E. Lysaght, *Brendan Bracken* (1979), p. 58
50 *Ibid.*, pp. 67–70
51 Charmley, *Lord Lloyd*, for Lloyd's history
52 *Ibid.*, pp. 120–1
53 *Churchill V, companion vol. 1*, Churchill/Chamberlain corr., 21 May 1926, pp. 724–5
54 *Ibid.*, Hoare to Irwin, 18 June 1926, p. 732
55 *Bridgeman Papers*, November 1929, pp. 233–4
56 Churchill, *Thoughts and Adventures*, p. 23
57 *Davidson Memoirs*, p. 202

58 Baldwin Papers, vol. 43, Chamberlain to Baldwin, 30 August 1925
59 Dilks, p. 440
60 *Ibid.*, p. 499, quoting Chamberlain to Irwin, 15 August 1926
61 *Bridgeman Papers*, diary, 1929, p. 232
62 Dilks, pp. 447–9
63 *Ibid.*, p. 448
64 *Ibid.*
65 *Ibid.*, p. 500; *Bridgeman Papers*, diary, November 1929, pp. 230–1
66 Dilks, p. 499
67 *Churchill V, companion vol. 1*, Churchill to Mrs Churchill, 4 February 1926, 20 March 1926, pp. 641, 677
68 *Bridgeman Papers*, diary, November 1929, p. 233
69 *Churchill V*, p. 91

21: Bidding for the Leadership

1 *Churchill V, companion vol. 1*, Hoare to Irwin, 29 April 1926, p. 689
2 Grigg, pp. 196–9; *Churchill V, companion vol. 1*, Churchill to King George V, 8 April 1927, pp. 979–83
3 *Ibid.*, Amery to Baldwin, 9 April 1927, pp. 983–4
4 *Ibid.*, Baldwin to King George V, 12 April 1927, pp. 984–6
5 Jones diary II, 12 April 1926, p. 98
6 James, *Victor Cazalet*, diary, 2 January 1927, p. 115
7 *Churchill V, companion vol. 1*, Winterton to Irwin, 6 June 1927, pp. 1005–6
8 *Ibid.*, Sir Arthur Steel-Maitland to J. C. C. Davidson, 8 September 1926, pp. 819–20
9 *Davidson Memoirs*, Patrick Gower to Davidson, 2, 4 September 1926, p. 256
10 NC 2/22, diary, 1 July 1927
11 *Ibid.*, 7 October 1927
12 *Ibid.*, 28 March 1928
13 *Churchill V, companion vol. 1*, Baldwin to Irwin, 15 September 1927, p. 1050
14 Dilks, pp. 425–6
15 *Churchill V, companion vol. 1*, Churchill to Baldwin, 6 June 1927, pp. 1006–10
16 Dilks, pp. 426–7, 491–3, 511–14
17 *Churchill V, companion vol. 1*, Churchill to Chamberlain, 7 June 1927, pp. 1010–11
18 *Ibid.*, Chamberlain to Churchill, 10 June 1927, p. 1015
19 NC 2/22, diary, 16 June 1927
20 Dilks, pp. 534–5
21 *Churchill V, companion vol. 1*, Chamberlain to Churchill, 14 October 1927, p. 1061
22 *Ibid.*, Churchill to Chamberlain, 18 October 1927, p. 1063
23 *Bridgeman Papers*, Bridgeman to Baldwin, 21 October 1927, p. 211
24 *Churchill V, companion vol. 1*, Churchill to Chamberlain, 2 November 1927, p. 1086
25 *Ibid.*, Churchill memo., 12 December 1927, pp. 1128–37; 20 January 1928, pp. 1187–94

26 Dilks, p. 539, Chamberlain to Hilda Chamberlain, 11 December 1927
27 *Churchill V, companion vol. 1*, Chamberlain to Irwin, 25 December 1927, p. 1155
28 *Ibid.*, Chamberlain to Churchill, 24 December 1927, pp. 1153–4
29 *Ibid.*, Chamberlain to Irwin, 25 December 1927, pp. 1154–5
30 *Ibid.*, Churchill to Chamberlain, 29 December 1927, p. 1157
31 Dilks, pp. 541–5; *Churchill V*, pp. 259–75
32 R. R. James (ed.), *Chips: The Diaries of Sir Henry Channon* (1967) (hereinafter *Channon Diary*), 8 July 1936, p. 69
33 *Churchill V, companion vol. 1*, Macmillan to Churchill, 1 January 1928, pp. 1158–61
34 H. Macmillan, *The Middle Way* (1936), is the classic statement of his beliefs; for their genesis see A. Horne, *Macmillan, vol. I: 1894–1957* (1988), Chaps 4–5; and H. Macmillan, *Memoirs, vol. I: Winds of Change* (1966), Chaps 15–16.
35 *Churchill V, companion vol. 1*, Churchill to Baldwin, Churchill to Macmillan, 5 January 1928, pp. 1172–3
36 *Ibid.*, Churchill memo., 20 January 1928, pp. 1194–7
37 *Ibid.*, Churchill to Irwin, 25 December 1927, p. 1155
38 *Ibid.*, Grigg to Churchill, 6 March 1928, p. 1220
39 *Ibid.*, Macmillan to Churchill, 1 January 1928, p. 1160
40 *Ibid.*, Chamberlain to Churchill, 24 December 1927, pp. 1153–5; Dilks, pp. 543–4
41 NC 1/26/384, Chamberlain to Mrs Chamberlain, 25 January 1928
42 *Churchill V, companion vol. 1*, Churchill memo., 9 March 1928, pp. 1221–5
43 Dilks, p. 547
44 *Churchill V, companion vol. 1*, Churchill to Chamberlain, 13 March 1928, pp. 1227–8
45 NC 7/9/23, Chamberlain/Churchill corr., Chamberlain to Churchill, 14 March 1928
46 NC 2/22, diary, 21 March 1928
47 Dilks, p. 549
48 Those with a taste strange enough to encompass the details of this arid and arcane subject can indulge it by following the papers and proceedings of the Policy Committee in PRO Cab. 27/364. Dilks summarises them, pp. 548–50.
49 NC 2/22, diary, 28 March 1928
50 Dilks, pp. 549–50; *Churchill V*, pp. 275–7
51 *Churchill V, companion vol. 1*, Hoare to Irwin, 30 March 1928, p. 1242
52 NC 2/22, diary, 4 April 1928
53 Campbell, p. 804
54 NC 2/22, diary, 28 March 1928
55 *Ibid.*, 30 March 1928
56 *Churchill V, companion vol. 1*, Churchill to Mrs Churchill, 5 April 1928, p. 1247
57 *Ibid.*, Churchill to Baldwin, 7 April 1928, pp. 1251–2
58 Baldwin Mss., vol. 5, Chamberlain to Baldwin, 12 April 1928; Dilks, pp. 552–3

59 *Churchill V, companion vol. 1*, Baldwin to Churchill, 14 April 1928, p. 1260
60 *Ibid.*, Churchill to Mrs Churchill, 15 April 1928, pp. 1260–1
61 NC 2/22, diary, 19 April 1928
62 *Ibid.*, PRO Cab. 23/57, meeting of Cabinet, 20 April 1928
63 NC 2/22, diary, 19 April 1928
64 Ramsden, pp. 290–1
65 Charmley, *Duff Cooper*, pp. 48–51
66 *Churchill V, companion vol. 1*, Sir Austen Chamberlain to Lady Ivy Chamberlain, 11 February 1929, p. 1423
67 *Ibid.*, Churchill to Baldwin, 2 September 1928, pp. 1332–3
68 *Ibid.*, Chamberlain to Irwin, 12 August 1928, p. 1327
69 *Amery Diary I*, 12 December 1928, p. 574
70 *Ibid.*, 21 July 1928, p. 557
71 *Ibid.*, 27 February 1929, p. 590
72 *Churchill V, companion vol. 1*, Churchill to Mrs Churchill, 10 August 1928, p. 1326
73 *Amery Diary I*, 19, 20 February 1929, pp. 587–8
74 NC 2/21, diary, 5 December 1924
75 *Amery Diary I*, 12 December 1928, p. 574
76 Charmley, *Lord Lloyd*, pp. 142–6
77 PRO, Nevile Henderson Mss., FO 800/261, Sir Walford Selby to Sir William Tyrrell, 1 September 1927, fos 225–8
78 Lord Cecil of Chelwood Papers, Add. Mss. 51079, Cecil to Sir Austen Chamberlain, 18 August 1927
79 *Ibid.*, Add. Mss. 51082, Cecil to Irwin, 7 June 1927
80 *Churchill V, companion vol. 1*, CID minutes, 4 December 1924, pp. 286–7, for an example
81 *Ibid.*, Churchill memo., 20 July 1927, p. 1033
82 Jones diary II, 25 February 1929, p. 172; NC 2/22, diary, 11 March 1929
83 *Churchill V, companion vol. 1*, Irwin to Baldwin, 28 March 1929, p. 1452
84 NC 2/22, diary, 11 March 1929
85 *Churchill V, companion vol. 1*, Churchill to Rothermere, 14 November 1928, pp. 1376–7
86 Jones diary II, 6 March 1929, p. 175

22: *Shooting at Santa Claus*

1 Beaverbrook, *Men and Power*, p. XXIII
2 Charmley, *Lord Lloyd*, Chap. 22, for detailed references to support the contention that there was a conspiracy against Lloyd
3 Austen Chamberlain Mss., AC 55/315, Lindsay to Chamberlain, 17 June 1929
4 PRO FO 794/14, minute by Lindsay, June 1929; Henderson to MacDonald, 29 June 1929, fos 25–8
5 *Ibid.*, minute by Lindsay, 2 July 1929, fo. 32 – the underlining is on the original
6 Lloyd Mss., Lloyd to Lady Lloyd, 7 July 1929
7 *Churchill V*, p. 337
8 *Ibid.*; *Hansard Parliamentary Debates* (hereinafter *Hansard*), 5th series, vol. 230, cols 1301–2
9 British Library of Political and Economic Science,

Dalton Mss., diary, vol. 10, 24 July 1929, fo. 163; this extract is not in the published version: B. Pimlott (ed.), *The Political Diary of Hugh Dalton, 1918–40* (1986) (hereinafter *Dalton Diary*)
10 NC 18/1/663, Neville to Ida Chamberlain, 28 July 1929
11 Lloyd Mss., Churchill to Lloyd, 28 July 1929
12 Dalton Mss., diary, vol. 10, 26 July 1929, fo. 165
13 NC 18/1/663, Neville to Ida Chamberlain, 28 July 1929
14 Lloyd Mss., Lady Lloyd's diary, 26 July 1929, p. 198
15 NC 1/27/98, Austen to Neville Chamberlain, 9 August 1929
16 Lloyd Mss., Churchill to Lloyd, 28 July 1929
17 *Churchill V, companion vol. 2*, Churchill notes, c. July 1929, p. 26
18 S. Ball, *Baldwin and the Conservative Party: the Crisis of 1929–31* (Yale, 1988), pp. 11–16, for Baldwin's failings
19 *Churchill V, companion vol. 2*, Churchill notes, p. 26
20 See Ball, *passim*, for the crisis; also Charmley, *Duff Cooper*, pp. 62–5, and *Lord Lloyd*, pp. 171–9
21 Ball, p. 17
22 Lloyd of Dolobran Papers, GLLD 13/19, Croft to Lloyd, 1 August 1929
23 Ramsden, p. 298
24 *Amery Diary II*, pp. 1–14
25 *Churchill V, companion vol. 2*, Churchill to Baldwin, 29 June 1929, p. 11.
26 *Amery Diary II*, 3 August 1929, p. 49
27 *Ibid.*, 23–25 October 1929, p. 52; Taylor, *Beaverbrook*, pp. 275–7; *Bridgeman Papers*, diary, July 1930, pp. 236–7; Ball, pp. 48–9
28 *Davidson Memoirs*, Davidson to Irwin, 9 November 1929, pp. 308–10
29 *Bridgeman Papers*, Bridgeman to his wife, 23 November 1929, p. 235
30 *Amery Diary II*, introduction, p. 6; Ball, p. 111, appears to support this view, but hedges his bets in places. C. Bridge, *Holding on to the Empire* (1986), pp. 33–6, also appears to accept it.
31 IORL, Irwin Papers, Mss. EUR C 152/18/1/298, Hoare to Irwin, 13 November 1929
32 *Amery Diary II*, introduction p. 6; James, *Churchill*, p. 187
33 Taylor, *Beaverbrook*, p. 267
34 Ball, p. 49
35 *Ibid.*, p. 114
36 *Ibid.*, p. 116
37 *Ibid.*
38 *Churchill V, companion vol. 2*, Churchill to Irwin, 1 January 1930, p. 112
39 James, *Churchill*, p. 196, quoting Churchill in the Commons, 23 December 1929
40 *Churchill V, companion vol. 2*, p. 114
41 Lord Birkenhead, *Last Essays* (1930), p. 33
42 *Ibid.*, p. 49; Campbell, pp. 822–5, for more
43 GLLD 17/26 for these
44 *Churchill V, companion vol. 2*, Lord Lytton to Irwin, 20 November 1929, pp. 114–15
45 Bridge, p. 31

46 *Davidson Memoirs*, Irwin to Davidson, 15 December 1929, pp. 310–11
47 Bridge, pp. 21–30, for example
48 James, *Churchill*, p. 195, for a classic statement of the correct liberal thinking
49 N. Nicolson (ed.), *Harold Nicolson: Diaries and Letters, vol. I: 1930–9* (1966) (hereinafter *Nicolson Diary I*), 23 January 1930, p. 41
50 K. Young (ed.), *The Diaries of Sir Robert Bruce Lockhart, vol. I: 1915–38* (1973) (hereinafter *Lockhart Diary*), 21 January 1930, p. 113
51 *Amery Diary II*, 7 November 1929, p. 64
52 *Nicolson Diary I*, 23 January 1930, pp. 41–2
53 *Amery Diary II*, 15, 27 February 1930, pp. 64–5
54 *Ibid.*, introduction, pp. 11–17; 3 March 1930, p. 65; Ball, pp. 59–63
55 Ball, pp. 69–77; *Davidson Memoirs*, pp. 334–41
56 *Davidson Memoirs*, Ball to Davidson, 14 August 1930, p. 341
57 Ball, pp. 79–81
58 NC 8/10/6, Bridgeman to Chamberlain, 3 October 1930
59 *Amery Diary II*, 26 May 1930, p. 72

23: Birkenhead's Legatee

1 *Churchill V, companion vol. I*, Churchill to H. C. Osborne, 22 December 1924, pp. 312–13
2 *Ibid.*, Irwin to Cosmo Gordon Lang, 15 April 1929, p. 1462
3 *Ibid.*, Irwin to Chamberlain, 15 April 1929, pp. 1462–3
4 *Ibid.*, John Buchan to Churchill, 19 March 1929, pp. 1448–9
5 James, *Victor Cazalet*, 7 December 1924, pp. 100–1
6 *Churchill V, companion vol. I*, Churchill to Balfour, 26 July 1926, p. 742
7 *Ibid.*, Balfour to Churchill, 6 March 1929, pp. 1438–9
8 *Ibid.*, Churchill to Mrs Churchill, 19 August 1924, p. 178; Churchill to Rosebery, 4 December 1924, p. 290
9 *Churchill V, companion vol. 2*, Churchill to W. Lints Smith, 5 July 1929, pp. 12–13, puts the figure at £5,000, but a letter from Churchill to his wife on 19 September puts it at £6,000, p. 86
10 *Ibid.*, Churchill to Thornton Butterworth, 30 August 1929, p. 64
11 *Ibid.*, Baldwin to Churchill, 4 September 1930, p. 181
12 *Ibid.*, Churchill to Baldwin, 24 September, p. 186
13 Woods, pp. 60–1
14 *Churchill V, companion vol. 2*, Churchill to Mrs Churchill, 19 September 1930, pp. 85–6
15 *Churchill V, companion vol. I*, T. E. Shaw (Lawrence) to Churchill, 18 March 1929, p. 1446
16 *Churchill V, companion vol. 2*, T. E. Shaw to Churchill, 7 September 1930, p. 183
17 Churchill, *My Early Life*, pp. 238–9. Joining in the campaign for Churchill in 1899 by waving red ribbons was one of my grandmother's earliest memories; red was the (patriotic) Unionist colour, she would explain; no doubt she was right, but I have always wondered if the ribbons were orange – perhaps someone can enlighten me?
18 *Ibid.*, pp. 370–1
19 *Ibid.*, p. 372
20 James, *Churchill*, p. 390
21 Churchill, *Great Contemporaries*, 'Morley', p. 61, first published in 1929
22 *Ibid.*, 'Rosebery', p. 10, first published in 1929
23 *Ibid.*, 'Balfour', p. 150, first published in April 1931
24 *Ibid.*, 'Joseph Chamberlain', p. 35, first published in February 1930
25 Birkenhead, *Frederick Edwin Earl of Birkenhead, vol. I*, foreword by Churchill, p. 16
26 Lord Birkenhead, *F.E.* (1959), p. 551
27 Campbell; Chap. 26 is entitled 'Burned Out'
28 *Ibid.*, p. 836
29 *Churchill V, companion vol. 2*, Churchill to Beaverbrook, 23 September 1930, pp. 185–6
30 NC 8/10/16 (c), Chamberlain to Bridgeman, 1 November 1930
31 NC 8/10/16b (1), Chamberlain to Bridgeman, 18 November 1930
32 *Amery Diary II*, intro., pp. 32–3; 7–8 August 1930, pp. 78–9; 30 September 1930, pp. 80–1; Ball, pp. 98–100
33 *Bridgeman Papers*, Chamberlain to Bridgeman, 8 October 1930, p. 241
34 NC 8/16(a), Churchill to Bridgeman, 18 October 1930
35 *Churchill V, companion vol. 2*, Churchill to Baldwin, 14 October 1930, pp. 191–3
36 *Ibid.*, Baldwin to Churchill, 14 October 1930, pp. 193–4
37 *Ibid.*, Churchill to Baldwin, 16 October 1930, p. 194
38 *Ibid.*, Baldwin to Irwin, 16 October 1930, p. 195
39 NC 8/10/16(c), Chamberlain to Bridgeman, 1 November 1930
40 *Churchill V, companion vol. 2*, Austen Chamberlain to Churchill, 20 October 1930, p. 200
41 *Ibid.*, Churchill to Baldwin, 24 September 1930, p. 186
42 *Ibid.*, memo. by Prince Bismarck, 20 October 1930, p. 199
43 Bridge, pp. 51–3
44 *Ibid.*, pp. 55–6
45 Sir John Simon Papers, vol. 67, Simon to Lord Inchcape, 21 November 1930; to Lord Peel, 20 November 1930; to Neville Chamberlain, 27 November 1930; NC 2/22, diary, 21, 23 November, 5 December 1930
46 *Davidson Memoirs*, Baldwin to Davidson, 23 October 1930, p. 354
47 *Ibid.*, Baldwin to Davidson, 13 November 1930, p. 255
48 Bridge, pp. 40–2; Ball, pp. 119–21
49 James (ed.), *Churchill Speaks*, pp. 514–15
50 *Davidson Memoirs*, Baldwin to Davidson, 15 December 1930, p. 356
51 *The Times*, leading article, 13 December 1930

52 *Churchill V, companion vol. 2*, Sir Malcolm Hailey to Irwin, 13 December 1930, pp. 232–3
53 Ball, pp. 120–3
54 *Hansard*, 5th series, Commons debates, 26 January 1931
55 *Churchill V, companion vol. 2*, Churchill to Randolph Churchill, 8 January 1931, p. 243
56 AC 6/1/785, Austen to Ivy Chamberlain, 2 February 1931; also compare the similar account in NC 18/1/724, Neville to Hilda Chamberlain, 31 January 1931
57 *Churchill V, companion vol. 2*, Churchill to Baldwin, 27 January 1931, pp. 250–1; Baldwin to Churchill, 28 January 1931, p. 251
58 *Amery Diary II*, 30 January 1931, p. 146
59 See n. 56 above for the Chamberlains; Lane-Fox is at *Churchill V, companion vol. 2*, letter to Irwin, 28 January 1931, pp. 252–3
60 *Churchill V*, pp. 385–7
61 Ball, p. 118; Ramsden, p. 304, puts the figure at fifty-two
62 James (ed.), *Churchill Speaks*, 30 January 1931, p. 525
63 Ball, p. 119
64 *Amery Diary II*, 9 February 1931, p. 147
65 *Churchill V, companion vol. 2*, Churchill to Rothermere, 10 February 1931, p. 265
66 *Ibid.*, Churchill to Randolph Churchill, 7 February 1931, p. 264
67 Lysaght, Bracken to Randolph Churchill, 13 February 1931, p. 113
68 NC 2/22, diary, 23 February 1931
69 Baldwin Mss. vol. 166, Topping to Chamberlain, 25 February 1931, fos 50–3
70 AC 5/1/532, Austen to Ida Chamberlain, 28 February 1931
71 *Amery Diary II*, editor's introduction, p. 114
72 James (ed.), *Churchill Speaks*, 23 February 1931, pp. 528–33
73 *Churchill V, companion vol. 2*, Churchill to Mrs Churchill, 26 February 1931, pp. 280–1; *The Times*, 25 February 1931
74 *Davidson Memoirs*, pp. 357–8; *Bridgeman Papers*, notes, c. 10 March 1931, pp. 243–4; Ramsden, pp. 311–12
75 *Bridgeman Papers*, notes, March 1931, p. 244

24: Scalped by Baldwin

1 *Bridgeman Papers*, notes, March 1931, p. 244
2 Ball, p. 139
3 Charmley, *Duff Cooper*, pp. 63–5
4 GLLD 19/5, Lloyd to Baldwin, 2 March 1931
5 *Ibid.*, Lloyd memo., 4 March 1931
6 *Churchill V, companion vol. 2*, Spender-Clay to Irwin, 5 March 1931, p. 292; Davidson to Irwin, 5 March 1931, p. 292, fn. 1
7 *Amery Diary II*, 9 March 1931, p. 154
8 *Ibid.*, 5 March 1931, p. 151; cf. NC 2/22, diary, 8 March 1931
9 *Ibid.*, 6 March 1931, p. 152
10 NC 2/22, diary, 8 March 1931
11 *Churchill V, companion vol. 2*, Jones diary, 11 March 1931, p. 295
12 *Bridgeman Papers*, diary, 28 March 1931, p. 245
13 *Amery Diary II*, 12 March 1931, p. 155; Ball, p. 143
14 Charmley, *Duff Cooper*, p. 66
15 *Ibid.*, p. 65
16 *Ibid.*, Churchill to Lady Diana Cooper, 20 March 1931, p. 67
17 *Churchill V, companion vol. 2*, Davidson to Irwin, 6 March 1931, p. 293
18 *Lockhart Diary*, 10 March 1931, pp. 156–7
19 Charmley, *Lord Lloyd*, p. 176
20 *Ibid.*, Chaps 24–8
21 *Amery Diary II*, 26 March 1931, p. 158
22 NC 8/10/34, Churchill to Chamberlain, 9 April 1931
23 *Churchill V, companion vol. 2*, Churchill to Oliver Locker-Lampson, 22 March 1931, p. 308
24 Churchill, *India*, passim
25 *Churchill V, companion vol. 2*, Churchill to Thornton Butterworth, 17 July 1931, p. 346
26 *Nicolson Diary I*, 21 July 1931, p. 81
27 *Ibid.*, 31 August 1931, p. 89
28 N. Mosley, *Rules of the Game* (1982), p. 152
29 *Churchill V, companion vol. 2*, Hoare to Chamberlain, 31 August 1931, p. 354
30 IORL Mss. EUR E240/1, Hoare to Willingdon, 2 September 1931
31 Churchill Papers, CHAR 2/197, telephone message from Lloyd to Churchill, 20 April 1933, fo. 28
32 IORL Mss. EUR E240/1, Hoare to Willingdon, 3 December 1931
33 *Ibid.*, Hoare to Willingdon, 10 December 1931
34 *Churchill V, companion vol. 2*, Churchill to Reeves Shaw, 29 November 1931, p. 380. It was not published in England until 1933.
35 *Ibid.*, Churchill to Esmond Harmsworth, 28 December 1931, p. 385
36 *Ibid.*, Churchill to Randolph Churchill, 5 January 1932, pp. 390–2
37 *Ibid.*, Churchill to Sir James Hawkey, 1 February 1932, pp. 397–8
38 *Ibid.*, Churchill to Boothby, 6 February 1932, pp. 399–400
39 *Churchill V*, pp. 429–30
40 *Ibid.*, p. 433
41 *Ibid.*, pp. 433–4, attributes the letter to Hoare, whilst *Churchill V, companion vol. 2*, pp. 448–9, has it from Baldwin to MacDonald
42 *Morning Post*, 7 October 1932
43 IORL Mss. EUR E240/3, Hoare to Willingdon, 10 February 1933
44 *Morning Post*, 7 October 1932
45 *Churchill V, companion vol. 2*, Churchill to Lord Sydenham, 7 January 1933, p. 513
46 Bridge, p. 94
47 IORL Mss. EUR E240/3, Hoare to Willingdon, 1 March 1933
48 *Ibid.*, Hoare to Willingdon, 10 February 1933
49 *Ibid.*, Hoare to Willingdon, 17 February 1933
50 Baldwin Mss. vol. 106, Hoare to Baldwin, 9 January 1933

51 Bridge, p. 95
52 IORL Mss. EUR E240/3, Hoare to Willingdon, 10 March 1933
53 *Ibid.*, Hoare to Willingdon, 31 March 1933
54 *Amery Diary II*, 27 March 1933, p. 291
55 IORL Mss. EUR E240/3, Hoare to Willingdon, 31 March 1933
56 NC 18/1/822, Neville to Hilda Chamberlain, 1 April 1933
57 IORL Mss. EUR E240/3, Hoare to Willingdon, 31 March 1933
58 *Ibid.*, Hoare to Willingdon, 17 March 1933
59 Charmley, *Lord Lloyd*, pp. 175–6
60 Bridge, p. 99
61 *Churchill V, companion vol. 2*, H. A. Gwynne to Churchill, 4 April 1933, p. 563
62 IORL Mss. EUR E240/3, Hoare to Willingdon, 16 April 1933
63 *Hansard*, House of Commons, 13 April 1933; also in James (ed.), *Churchill Speaks*, pp. 562–5
64 Churchill, *Great Contemporaries*, p. 165
65 Ramsden, pp. 303–5; Ball, pp. 22–5

25: Colonel Blimp's Last Stand

1 *Davidson Memoirs*, p. 384
2 GLLD 19/5, Derby to Lloyd, 18 June 1934
3 GLLD 11/1, press statement by Lloyd, 2 May 1933
4 *Churchill V, companion vol. 2*, Burnham to Churchill, 7 April 1933, p. 580; *Churchill V*, p. 478
5 4th Marquess of Salisbury Papers, Mss. S (4) 205/141, E. Cadogan to Salisbury, 12 March 1934
6 *Bridgeman Papers*, diary, October 1933, p. 256
7 *Churchill V, companion vol. 2*, Churchill to Ormsby-Gore, 10 April 1933, p. 584
8 *Churchill V*, pp. 478–9
9 Bridge, p. 103
10 *Davidson Memoirs*, pp. 383–4
11 James, *Victor Cazalet*, 19 April 1933, p. 154
12 *Churchill V, companion vol. 2*, Linlithgow to Churchill, 1 May 1933, pp. 589–90
13 *Ibid.*, Churchill to Linlithgow, 2 May 1933, p. 591
14 *Ibid.*, Churchill to Linlithgow, 7 May 1933, p. 595
15 Bridge, p. 103
16 IORL Mss. EUR E240/3, Hoare to Willingdon, 19 May 1933
17 *Amery Diary II*, 28 June 1933, p. 297
18 *Ibid.*, p. 298
19 *Churchill V*, p. 483; IORL Mss. EUR E240/3, Hoare to Willingdon, 30 June 1933
20 Bridge, p. 109
21 *Ibid.*
22 IORL Mss. EUR E240/3, Hoare to Willingdon, 19 May 1933
23 *Amery Diary II*, 6 October 1933, p. 304
24 NC 18/1/845, Neville to Hilda Chamberlain, 7 October 1933
25 Charmley, *Lord Lloyd*, p. 192
26 Charmley, *Duff Cooper*, p. 75
27 e.g. *Churchill V, companion vol. 2*, Churchill's draft press statement, 7 September 1933, pp. 650–2
28 *Ibid.*, Churchill to Sir M. O'Dwyer, 31 October 1933, p. 677
29 Charmley, *Lord Lloyd*, p. 192
30 Bridge, pp. 113–18
31 *Churchill V*, pp. 512–13
32 *Amery Diary II*, 16 April 1934, p. 379
33 *Churchill V, companion vol. 2*, Churchill to T. O'Connor, 11 April 1934, pp. 749–52, for the text
34 *Stevenson Diary*, 14, 20 April 1934, pp. 268–9
35 Derby Papers, 920. Der/17/33, contains much of the material quoted in the account given here
36 C. Bridge, 'Churchill, Hoare, Derby and the Committee of Privileges, April to June 1934', *Historical Journal* (1979), pp. 215–27; Bridge, pp. 112–31
37 *Churchill V, companion vol. 2*, Churchill to Mr Speaker, 15 April 1934, pp. 755–8
38 *Stevenson Diary*, 7 May 1934, p. 270
39 IORL Mss. EUR E240/7, Hoare to Willingdon, 20 April 1934
40 IORL Mss. EUR E240/73, evidence of the Secretary of State for the Select Committee; Parliamentary Papers (PP) 1933–4, Committee of Privileges Reports (hereinafter CPR), pp. 20–3, for summary of evidence
41 The full report is in the Derby Papers, vol. 33, and is summarised in Bridge, p. 127
42 Derby Papers, vol. 33, notes of a meeting at the India Office, 26 April 1934; also reproduced in *Churchill V, companion vol. 2*, p. 776
43 IORL Mss. EUR E240/3, Hoare to Willingdon, 20 October 1933
44 *Ibid.*, Hoare to Willingdon, 3 November 1933
45 Derby Papers, vol. 33, paper by Barlow, 11 October; Barlow to Derby, 21, 27 October; Hoare to Derby, 3 November; Bridge, pp. 128–9, gives additional evidence
46 *Churchill V*, pp. 531–2
47 *Stevenson Diary*, 11 May 1934, p. 271
48 *Churchill V, companion vol. 2*, Hoare to Sir George Stanley (Derby's brother), 17 May 1934, p. 793
49 *Ibid.*, p. 789
50 *Ibid.*, O'Connor to Churchill, 5 June 1934, pp. 799–801
51 *Amery Diary II*, 12 June 1934, p. 381
52 *Churchill V*, pp. 539–42
53 *Amery Diary II*, 13 June 1933, pp. 382–3
54 James, *Churchill*, pp. 214, 289–91
55 I. Berlin, *Mr Churchill in 1940* (n.d.), p. 8
56 *Ibid.*, p. 9
57 Charmley, *Duff Cooper*, p. 78
58 Bridge, p. 131
59 M. Cowling, *The Impact of Hitler* (Cambridge, 1975), p. 59
60 *Churchill V, companion vol. 2*, Churchill in *The Times*, 1 July 1934
61 *Evening Standard*, 24 January 1934
62 *Churchill V, companion vol. 2*, Churchill to Linlithgow, 7 May 1933, p. 595
63 *Churchill V*, p. 486
64 James, *Churchill*, p. 214
65 *Churchill V*, pp. 502–3
66 *Ibid.*, p. 507
67 PRO Cab. 23/79 29 (34)3, 18 July 1934

68 *Churchill V*, pp. 554–6
69 Bridge, p. 133
70 IORL, Brabourne Papers, Mss. EUR F97/2, Hoare to Lord Brabourne, 28 November 1934; Bridge, pp. 134–5
71 IORL Mss. EUR E240/4, Hoare to Willingdon, 9 November 1934
72 *Ibid.*, Hoare to Willingdon, 29 November 1934; *Churchill V*, pp. 573–6
73 *Amery Diary II*, 4 December 1934, p. 389
74 Charmley, *Lord Lloyd*, p. 192
75 *Churchill V*, pp. 594–5
76 GLLD 11/1, Lloyd to Wolmer, 19 February 1935
77 Salisbury Papers, Mss. S(4) 208/30–2, Salisbury to Lord Wolmer, 28 February 1935

26: The Prophet Jeremiah?

1 *Amery Diary II*, 5 June 1935, p. 395
2 A. Duff Cooper, *Old Men Forget* (1953), p. 171
3 *Gathering Storm*, Chap. 5
4 *Churchill V*, p. 616
5 *Churchill V, companion vol. 2*, Churchill/Baldwin corr., 6, 7 October 1935, pp. 1288–9
6 *Ibid.*, Churchill to Lord Stonehaven, 12 October 1935, p. 1291
7 *Churchill V*, pp. 685–7
8 The literature on this is voluminous. The most important works are: N. H. Gibbs, *Grand Strategy vol. I* (1976) (hereinafter *Grand Strategy I*); G. Peden, *British Rearmament and the Treasury 1932–9* (Edinburgh, 1979); R. A. C. Parker, 'British Rearmament 1936–9', *English Historical Review* (1981); G. Peden, 'A Matter of Timing: The Economic Background to British Foreign Policy, 1937–9', *History* (1984)
9 Ashley, p. 213
10 *Gathering Storm*, p. 505
11 Woods, pp. 119–20
12 See n. 8 above for the most important works. P. M. H. Bell, *The Origins of the Second World War in Europe* (1986) provides a useful summary of the new orthodoxy.
13 *Churchill V, companion vol. 2*, Irwin to Davidson, 31 March 1931, p. 312
14 Bridge, p. 157
15 *Ibid.*, pp. 159–62
16 *Churchill V, companion vol. 2*, Linlithgow to Churchill, 19 May 1933, p. 603
17 PRO, Halifax Mss., FO 800/328, Hal/38/38, Halifax to Sir Roger Lumley, 21 March 1938
18 *Ibid.*, Hal/38/101, Hoare to Mrs Lindsay, November 1938
19 R. A. Butler Papers, Mss. RAB G9/13, Butler to Ian Black, 21 April 1938
20 Bridge, pp. 157–61, for India. W. N. Medlicott et al. (eds), *Documents on British Foreign Policy, 1919–39, Second series, vol. XIX* (1984–5) (hereinafter DBFP), no. 336, for Halifax using the same approach to Hitler at their meeting in 1937. This theme is explored further in my *Chamberlain and the Lost Peace* (1989)

21 IORL Mss. EUR C152/28, Lloyd to Irwin, 31 July 1929
22 *Churchill V, companion vol. 2*, Churchill to Linlithgow, 7 May 1933, p. 595
23 *Ibid.*, Churchill to Rothermere, 12 May 1935, pp. 1169–70
24 *Ibid.*, Churchill to G. M. Trevelyan, 3 January 1935, p. 985
25 *Davidson Memoirs*, Davidson to Baldwin, 29 February 1932, p. 390
26 *Churchill V, companion vol. 2*, Birla to Gandhi, 25 August 1935, pp. 1243–5, is very revealing on Churchill's limitations
27 *Ibid.*, Hoare to Brabourne, 4 March 1935, p. 1101
28 Bridge, pp. 159–61
29 *Churchill V, companion vol. 2*, Churchill's notes for a broadcast, 16 January 1934, pp. 702–13
30 Bridge, pp. 161–2
31 James (ed.), *Churchill Speaks*, p. 579 ff.; *Churchill V*, pp. 505–10, 549–80
32 *Churchill V*, pp. 623–53
33 *Hansard*, House of Commons, 22 May 1935
34 M. Ceadel, 'The First British Referendum: The Peace Ballot 1934–5', *English Historical Review* (1980)
35 This is the theme of my *Chamberlain and the Lost Peace*, although it was obviously too obscure for any of the reviewers to pick it up.
36 NC 2/23A, diary, 2 August 1935
37 *Grand Strategy I* gives a full account
38 *Ibid.*, pp. 440–50; Charmley, *Duff Cooper*, pp. 86–7, for the arguments with the War Office
39 PRO Cab. 23/79, Cabinets 29, 31 (34) of 18 and 31 July 1934; Chamberlain's proposed cuts are given in detail in the Defence Requirements Committee minutes, Cab. 16/111, DC (M) (32), 20 June 1934
40 *Churchill V*, pp. 554–5
41 *Davidson Memoirs*, pp. 403–4, for this interpretation
42 Parliamentary Papers, Cmd 4827, Statement Relating to Defence, published 4 March 1935
43 J. Terraine, *The Right of the Line: The Royal Air Force in the European War 1939–45* (1985), pp. 27–8
44 *Ibid.*, p. 30
45 *Churchill V, companion vol. 2*, memo. by Lord Weir, August 1935, pp. 1241–2
46 Terraine, pp. 17–19
47 *Churchill V*, pp. 625–36
48 James, *Churchill*, pp. 234–5
49 *Churchill V, companion vol 2*, Hoare to Willingdon, 1 March 1935, pp. 1091–2; Hoare to Brabourne, 4 March 1935, pp. 1099–101
50 Cowling, *The Impact of Hitler*, pp. 43–5
51 *Stevenson Diary*, 30 November 1934, pp. 293–4; *Churchill V, companion vol. 2*, Churchill to Mrs Churchill, 2, 10 March 1935, pp. 1097, 1115
52 *Stevenson Diary*, 10 January 1935, p. 298
53 *Hansard*, House of Commons, 11 March 1935
54 *Churchill V, companion vol. 2*, Churchill to Mrs Churchill, 2 March 1935, p. 1097
55 Cowling, *The Impact of Hitler*, pp. 59–60; *Davidson Memoirs*, p. 408; S. Roskill, *Hankey: Man of Secrets*,

vol. III: 1931–63 (1974) (hereinafter Roskill III), pp. 162–3, for the tart

56 *Channon Diary*, 12 September 1937, pp. 137–8

57 *Ibid.*; Ramsden, pp. 328–9; Cowling, *The Impact of Hitler*, pp. 41–62

58 *Churchill V, companion vol. 2*, Londonderry to Churchill, 30 December 1934, p. 974

59 *Ibid.*, MacDonald to Sir Austen Chamberlain, 10 January 1935, p. 987

60 Roskill III, pp. 144–6

61 *Churchill V*, pp. 649–53

62 *Ibid.*, pp. 616–17

63 *Churchill V, companion vol. 2*, Churchill to Mrs Churchill, 2, 10 March 1935, pp. 1097, 1115

64 *Stevenson Diary*, 10 January 1935, p. 298

65 NC 18/1/1133A, Neville to Ida Chamberlain, 3 December 1939, for a considered and long-held opinion

66 *Churchill V, companion vol. 2*, Thomas Jones to a friend, 2 June 1935, p. 1187

67 *Ibid.*, Churchill to Cyril Asquith, 8 August 1934, p. 843

68 T. Stannage, 'The East Fulham By-election of 25 October 1933', *Historical Journal* (1971)

69 R. A. C. Parker, 'British Rearmament 1936–9', *English Historical Review* (1981)

70 NC 2/23A, diary, 2 August 1935

71 Ceadel, 'The First British Referendum', for the details; *Davidson Memoirs*, p. 408

72 *Churchill V, companion vol. 2*, recollections, 27 June 1935 (but surely much later in composition?), pp. 1202–3

73 Cowling, *The Impact of Hitler*, Neville to Hilda Chamberlain, 9 November 1935, p. 63

74 *Nicolson Diary I*, 21 August 1935, p. 211

75 Lord Templewood, *Nine Troubled Years* (1954), for Hoare's view of his speech

76 *Churchill V, companion vol. 2*, Churchill to Sir Abe Bailey, 31 October 1935, p. 1308

77 *Ibid.*, Churchill/Baldwin corr., 6, 8 July 1935, pp. 1207–8

78 *Ibid.*, Simon to Churchill, 11 July 1935, p. 1210

79 Derby Papers, Mss. 920. Der/17/33, Churchill to Derby, 27 September 1935

80 *Churchill V, companion vol. 2*, Baldwin to Churchill, 6 October 1935, p. 1288 and fn. 1

81 *Ibid.*, Churchill to Stonehaven, 12 October 1935, p. 1291 and fn. 1

82 *Ibid.*, Law to Churchill, 16 October 1935, pp. 1294–5

83 *Ibid.*, Churchill recollections, 14 November 1935, p. 1324

84 *Churchill V*, p. 687

85 *Churchill V, companion vol. 2*, Churchill, unsent letter to *The Times*, 28 November 1935, p. 1335

27: Fortune's Vicissitudes

1 *Churchill V, companion vol. 2*, Morton to Churchill, 26 October (November ?) 1935, pp. 1301–2

2 Soames, pp. 218–20

3 *Churchill V, companion vol. 2*, Churchill to Mrs Churchill, 25 August 1934, p. 856

4 *Ibid.*; but Riddell to Churchill, 20 August 1934, mentions £2,500, pp. 251–2

5 *Ibid.*, Churchill to Riddell, 18 October 1932, p. 484

6 *Ibid.*, Riddell to Churchill, 30 July 1932, pp. 459–60

7 *Ibid.*, Churchill to Marsh, 5 August 1932, p. 463

8 *Ibid.*, William Blackwood to Churchill, 1 August 1934, p. 834

9 *Colliers*, 17 December 1932, 25 February 1933; the latter was republished in Riddell's *Sunday Chronicle* as three articles, whilst it also appeared in *Pictorial Magazine*, 17 February 1934, see Woods, p. 230

10 *Churchill V, companion vol. 2*, Bracken to Churchill, 22 August 1931, p. 350

11 *Ibid.*, p. 468, fn. 4

12 *Ibid.*, p. 874, fn. 3

13 *Ibid.*, Churchill to Mrs Churchill, 25 August 1934, p. 856

14 *Ibid.*, Churchill to Korda, 24 September 1934, pp. 876–7

15 *Ibid.*, Churchill to Mrs Churchill, 1 January 1935, p. 982

16 *Ibid.*, Churchill to Feiling, 22 September, pp. 874–5

17 *Ibid.*, Churchill to Harrap, 25 September 1932, p. 425

18 *Ibid.*, Scribner to Churchill, 8 August 1935, p. 1229

19 *Ibid.*, Churchill to Harrap, 2 October 1935, p. 1287

20 Woods, pp. 68–9

21 *Churchill V, companion vol. 2*, Churchill to Scribner, 17 August 1935, p. 1238

22 *Ibid.*, Churchill to Mrs Churchill, 26 December 1935, pp. 1363–4

23 R. S. Churchill, *Twenty-One Years*, pp. 114–15

24 *Ibid.*, pp. 129–31

25 *Ibid.*, p. 94

26 *Ibid.*, p. 120

27 *Churchill V, companion vol. 2*, Londonderry to Churchill, 30 December 1934, p. 974

28 *Ibid.*, Churchill to Mrs Churchill, 13 April 1935, p. 1139

29 *Ibid.*, Churchill to Randolph Churchill, 3 November 1931, p. 369

30 Soames, pp. 242–3

31 *Ibid.*, p. 245

32 *Ibid.*

33 *Churchill V, companion vol. 2*, Birla to Gandhi, 25 August 1935, p. 1243

34 *Ibid.*, Churchill to Mrs Churchill, 31 December 1934, p. 978

35 Soames, p. 261; the full texts as in *Churchill V, companion vol. 2*, p. 979 ff.

36 *Ibid.*, pp. 266–7

37 Charmley, *Duff Cooper*, p. 88

38 *Nicolson Diary I*, 10, 11, 13 December 1935, pp. 230–2; *Channon Diary*, 17 December 1935, pp. 47–8; *Amery Diary II*, 10 December 1935, p. 404

39 *Churchill V, companion vol. 2*, Bracken to Churchill, 11 December 1935, p. 1348
40 Cowling, *The Impact of Hitler*, pp. 99–102
41 *Churchill V, companion vol. 2*, Randolph Churchill to Churchill, 17 December 1935, p. 1353
42 Cowling, *The Impact of Hitler*, pp. 101–2
43 *Stevenson Diary*, 22 November 1934, p. 292
44 *Davidson Memoirs*, p. 405
45 J. A. Cross, *Lord Swinton* (1982), is the most recent study
46 Baldwin Mss. vol. 47, Cunliffe-Lister to Baldwin, 8 June 1935
47 *Churchill V*, pp. 660–2
48 Roskill III, pp. 234–6 and Appendix 2, for some sense on all this
49 *Churchill V, companion vol. 2*, Churchill memo., 23 July 1935, ADR21, pp. 1215–24
50 Lysaght, p. 68
51 R. Harrod, *The Prof* (1959), p. 87
52 James, *Churchill*, pp. 241–4, is excellent here
53 *Churchill V, companion vol. 2*, Churchill to Swinton, 8 August 1935, pp. 1229–30
54 Peden, *British Rearmament*, Appendix III, for the figures in detail
55 *Churchill V, companion vol. 2*, Swinton to Churchill, 12 August 1935, pp. 1231–2
56 Peden, *British Rearmament*, p. 83
57 Roskill III, pp. 196–7; *Churchill V, companion vol. 2*, Weir to Swinton, 22 August 1935, pp. 1241–2
58 Peden, *British Rearmament*, pp. 82–3
59 *Ibid.*, pp. 80–1
60 PRO Cab. 16/112, DRC 37, 21 November 1935, vol. I
61 Peden, *British Rearmament*, Appendix III; Roskill III, Appendix A, gives the figures for what was actually spent, which creates a misleading impression; Peden, pp. 120–1, for the increased emphasis on bombers
62 *Churchill V*, p. 651
63 *Churchill V, companion vol. 3*, Churchill to Mrs Churchill, 8 January 1936, p. 5
64 GLLD 5/5, Lord Lloyd to David Lloyd, 25 March 1935
65 Roskill III, pp. 202–7
66 Charmley, *Duff Cooper*, Chaps 12–13
67 Liddell Hart Mss., section 11, notes of conversation with Duff Cooper, 18 January 1936
68 *Hansard*, House of Commons, 26 March 1936
69 *Churchill V, companion vol. 2*, Hoare's record of conversation with Eden and Churchill, 21 August 1935, pp. 1239–40
70 *Churchill V, companion vol. 3*, Churchill to Cecil, 9 April 1936, pp. 93–4

28: Searching for Allies

1 *Hansard*, House of Commons, 10 March 1936
2 Peden, *British Rearmament*, p. 83
3 *Hansard*, House of Commons, 23 April 1936
4 *Churchill V, companion vol. 3*, Weir to Churchill, 28 April 1936, p. 121

5 PRO Cab. 21/435, Hankey to Inskip, 19 April 1936
6 Earl of Avon, *The Eden Memoirs, vol. I: Facing the Dictators* (1962) (hereinafter *Eden I*), p. 346
7 *Nicolson Diary I*, 10 March 1936, pp. 248–9, supports the view in Eden's memoirs, as does 'Baffy' Dugdale's diary, 12 March 1936, see N. Rose (ed.), *Baffy: The Diaries of Blanche Dugdale* (1973) (hereinafter *Dugdale Diary*), p. 8
8 *Churchill V, companion vol. 3*, 29 July 1936, pp. 290–1
9 *Ibid.*, Londonderry to Churchill, 4 May 1936, pp. 129–31
10 *Ibid.*, Churchill to Londonderry, 6 May 1936, pp. 142–3
11 *Ibid.*, Cecil to Churchill, 22 April 1936, p. 112
12 *Dugdale Diary*, *passim*, for this connection
13 *Churchill V*, p. 739
14 *Dugdale Diary*, 12 March 1936, p. 8
15 *Nicolson Diary I*, 23 March 1936, p. 254
16 R. Griffiths, *Fellow-Travellers of the Right* (1975), for this
17 *Nicolson Diary I*, 16 July 1936, p. 269
18 *Churchill V, companion vol. 3*, Spier recollections, pp. 160–2
19 *Ibid.*, Lady Violet Bonham-Carter to Churchill, 19 May 1936, pp. 162–3
20 *Nicolson Diary I*, 20 September 1936, p. 273
21 *Ibid.*, 28 April 1936, p. 259
22 *Churchill V*, p. 738
23 *Churchill V, companion vol. 3*, Thomas Jones diary, 22 May 1936, p. 166
24 *Channon Diary*, 26 May 1936, p. 61
25 *Dugdale Diary*, 30 September 1936, p. 29
26 *Channon Diary*, 28 May 1936, p. 62
27 *Davidson Memoirs*, p. 410
28 *Ibid.*, pp. 410–11
29 *Churchill V, companion vol. 3*, meeting of 29 July 1936, pp. 291–2; see also Cowling, *The Impact of Hitler*, pp. 147–8
30 James, *Churchill*, p. 268, for a discussion
31 Charmley, *Duff Cooper*, pp. 87, 98
32 *Churchill V*, Neville to Hilda Chamberlain, 15 February 1936, p. 706
33 *Churchill V, companion vol. 3*, Hankey to Churchill, 29 January 1936, pp. 26–7
34 *Ibid.*, Churchill to Hankey, 31 January 1936, p. 29
35 *Ibid.*, Warburton to Churchill, 27 March 1936, pp. 80–2
36 *Ibid.*, Churchill to Morton, 31 March 1936, p. 85; Morton to Churchill, 3 April 1936, pp. 87–8
37 *Ibid.*, Swinton to Hankey, 9 June 1936, pp. 188–9
38 *Ibid.*, Churchill to Hankey, 26 February 1936, pp. 58–9
39 *Churchill V*, p. 745
40 Roskill III, p. 231
41 *Churchill V, companion vol. 3*, Swinton to Hankey, 26 June 1936, pp. 216–17
42 PRO Cab. 21/426, Hankey to Inskip, 29 June 1936; also at Roskill III, p. 232
43 *Churchill V*, pp. 733–8, 742

44 *Churchill V, companion vol. 3*, Hankey to Baldwin, 29 June 1936, p. 223, for an example
45 *Amery Diary II*, 3 April 1936, pp. 412–13 and following entries
46 Cowling, *The Impact of Hitler*, pp. 140–1
47 PRO Cab. 23/85, 6 July 1936; extracts printed in *Churchill V, companion vol. 3*, pp. 233–6
48 PRO Prem. 1/193 for the full texts, extracts of which are given in *Churchill V, companion vol. 3*, pp. 265–77, 277–94
49 *Churchill V, companion vol. 3*, p. 283
50 PRO Prem. 1/193, Swinton memo., August 1936
51 D. Irving, *Churchill's War, vol. I* (Australia, 1987), pp. 59–61. It is perhaps necessary to say that Mr Irving is cited only when his sources have been checked and seem reliable. It should not be necessary to say such things, as Mr Irving's sources, unlike the conclusions which he draws from them, are usually sound, but such is the hatred (and that is not too strong a word) which Mr Irving arouses, that it is necessary for a biographer taking a non-hagiographical view of Churchill to do so. The current author admires Mr Irving's assiduity, energy and courage, even if he differs from him in his conclusions.
52 *Churchill V, companion vol. 3*, A. H. Richards memo., 29 July 1936, pp. 295–6
53 *Churchill V*, pp. 747–8
54 D. Dutton, *Austen Chamberlain* (1985), p. 307
55 James, *Victor Cazalet*, p. 186
56 *Dugdale Diary*, 19 March 1936, p. 10
57 *Churchill V, companion vol. 3*, Churchill to N. B. Foot, 7 August 1936, p. 308
58 *Ibid.*, 15 October 1936, pp. 362–4
59 *Ibid.*, Churchill to Randolph Churchill, 13 November 1936, p. 401
60 N. Thompson, *The Anti-Appeasers: Conservative Opposition to Appeasement in the 1930s* (1971), p. 130
61 Charmley, *Lord Lloyd*, pp. 188–92
62 *Churchill V, companion vol. 3*, Lady Houston to Churchill, 6 November 1936, p. 388
63 *Hansard*, House of Commons, 5 November 1936
64 *The Times*, 25 October 1936
65 *Churchill V, companion vol. 3*, Churchill to Lady Violet Bonham-Carter, 25 May 1936, p. 172
66 *Ibid.*, 3 December 1936, pp. 449–50
67 Duff Cooper diary, 16 November 1936. My copy of this was taken whilst the Cooper papers were in my custody, so I have not cited the reference number to it in the Cooper Papers, which are now in Churchill College, Cambridge.
68 James, *Churchill*, p. 270
69 *Churchill V*, p. 816
70 *Churchill V, companion vol. 3*, Churchill notes, December 1936, pp. 450–4.
71 Cooper diary, December 1936
72 *Lockhart Diary*, 4 December 1936, p. 359
73 *Churchill V, companion vol. 3*, Churchill statement, 5 December 1936, pp. 457–9
74 *Nicolson Diary I*, letter, 7 December 1936, p. 282
75 *Amery Diary II*, 4 December 1936, p. 431
76 *Ibid.*, 7 December 1936, p. 432
77 Boothby, p. 125
78 *The Times*, 8 December 1936
79 *Nicolson Diary I*, 9 December 1936, p. 284
80 *Dugdale Diary*, 8 December 1936, p. 34

29: Churchill and Chamberlain: I

1 *Churchill V, companion vol. 3*, Churchill to Bernard Baruch, 1 January 1937, p. 521
2 *Churchill V*, p. 832
3 *Amery Diary II*, 10 December 1937, p. 433
4 *Nicolson Diary I*, 10 December 1937, p. 286
5 NC 7/7/5, Chamberlain to Lothian, 10 June 1936
6 PRO Cab. 24/266 CP326(36), 3 December 1936; 334(36), 11 December; 337(36), 14 December 1936, for the arguments
7 Peden, *British Rearmament*, p. 128, whose figures differ slightly from those in Roskill III, p. 259
8 *Churchill V, companion vol. 3*, notes of Churchill's speech, 8 December 1936, pp. 468–70
9 *Ibid.*, Churchill memo., 20 December 1936, pp. 500–2
10 *Ibid.*, memo., 7 January 1937, pp. 531–4
11 Peden, *British Rearmament*, pp. 128–9
12 *Churchill V, companion vol. 3*, Hankey to Inskip and Baldwin, 1 March 1937, pp. 585–6
13 Peden, *British Rearmament*, p. 129
14 *Ibid.*, pp. 129–30
15 PRO Cab. 16/136, DPRC meeting, 11 June 1936
16 Peden, *British Rearmament*, pp. 153–5
17 *Churchill V, companion vol. 3*, Scribner to Churchill, 4 June 1936, p. 168, fn. 2
18 *Churchill V*, p. 835, fn. 1
19 *Churchill V, companion vol. 3*, Churchill to Stanley Williams, 28 December 1936, p. 456
20 *Churchill V*, p. 835, fn. 1
21 *Churchill V, companion vol. 3*, Churchill to Mrs Churchill, 2 February 1937, p. 575
22 *Churchill V*, p. 844
23 *Hansard*, House of Commons, 4 March 1937
24 NC 8/24/1, Margesson to Chamberlain, March 1937
25 NC 8/24/14, Hoare to Chamberlain, 6 May 1937
26 *Churchill V, companion vol. 3*, Churchill to Sir Abe Bailey, 17 May 1937, p. 673
27 Derby Papers, Mss. 920. Der/17/33, Derby to Churchill, 28 May 1937
28 *Channon Diary*, 31 May 1937, pp. 129–30
29 *Churchill V, companion vol. 3*, p. 685, fn. 1
30 IORL Mss. EUR F97/22B, Butler to Lord Brabourne, 14 December 1938
31 *Ibid.*, Butler to Brabourne, 9 March 1938
32 Peden, *British Rearmament*, p. 87 ff.; *Grand Strategy I*, Chap. 8
33 NC 18/1/1003, Neville to Hilda Chamberlain, 25 April 1937
34 NC 18/1/1010, Neville to Ida Chamberlain, 4 July 1937; DBFP XIX, no. 15, minutes of CID meeting, 5 July, p. 22 ff.
35 NC 2/23A, diary, 27 April 1937
36 NC 18/1/1001, 1014, Neville to Hilda Chamberlain, 10 April, 1 August 1937
37 *Churchill V, companion vol. 3*, Angell to Churchill, 15 March 1937, pp. 620–2

38 NC 18/1/1043, Neville to Hilda Chamberlain, 27
March 1938, and the letters at n. 36 above for
this; see also my *Chamberlain*, pp. 4–5, 8–10, 23–
5, 74
39 W. S. Churchill, *Marlborough, vol. II* (1974 edn,
vol. III of the 1936 edn), preface, p. 22
40 *Churchill V*, pp. 859–64
41 *Ibid.*, Thomas Jones diary, 14 June 1937, p. 860
42 R. J. Minney (ed.), *The Private Papers of Hore-
Belisha* (1960) (hereinafter *Hore-Belisha Papers*),
p. 130
43 Peden, *British Rearmament*, p. 66, quoting Chamberlain to his sister, 14 November 1936
44 *Ibid.*, p. 87
45 PRO Cab. 23/93, minutes, 6 April 1938
46 Peden, *British Rearmament*, pp. 90–4, for a full
coverage of the economic issues
47 *Hore-Belisha Papers*, pp. 87–91
48 PRO Cab. 64/9, Air Ministry note, 22 October
1937
49 PRO Cab. 64/3, Hankey to Inskip, 27 September
1937
50 Peden, *British Rearmament*, pp. 131–2
51 DBFP XIX, no. 401, Cabinet meeting, 22
December 1937
52 Charmley, *Chamberlain*, pp. 17–21, 24–8, for
these
53 *Churchill V, companion vol. 3*, Wilson to Grigg, 31
January 1938, which does not include the figure
'8', which is in *Churchill V*, p. 896
54 J. Harvey (ed.), *The Diplomatic Diaries of Oliver
Harvey 1937–40* (1970) (hereinafter *Harvey Diary*),
19–23 December 1937, 1–13 January 1938,
pp. 65, 67; DBFP XIX, no. 410, Eden to Chamberlain, 1 January 1938; no. 418, Eden to Chamberlain, 9 January 1938
55 DBFP XIX, Appendix I, Chamberlain diary, 19
February 1938; no. 415, Chamberlain to Eden, 7
January 1938
56 PRO FO 800/328, Hal/38/38, Hoare to Sir Roger
Lumley, 21 March 1938
57 NC 18/1/1040, Neville to Hilda Chamberlain, 27
February 1938; also NC 1/17/9, Neville to Ivy
Chamberlain, 3 March 1938
58 *Gathering Storm*, p. 162
59 Ramsden, p. 366
60 *Churchill V, companion vol. 3*, Churchill to Eden, 21
February 1938, p. 914
61 Charmley, *Chamberlain*, pp. 52–4, 57; D. Carlton,
Anthony Eden (1981), pp. 141–3
62 *Nicolson Diary I*, Nicolson to his wife, 2 March
1938, p. 328
63 *Ibid.*, Nicolson to his wife, 25 February 1938,
p. 326
64 *Amery Diary II*, 22 February 1938, p. 457; *Channon
Diary*, 21 February 1938, p. 145
65 R. S. Churchill (ed.), *Step by Step* (1974 edn),
p. 219
66 *Amery Diary II*, 20 February 1938, p. 456
67 *Eden I*, pp. 585–6; *Harvey Diary*, 18, 20 February
1938, pp. 93, 97; Cooper diary, 19, 20 February
1938; James, *Victor Cazalet*, Cazalet to Baldwin, 24
February 1938, pp. 198–9

68 Carlton, pp. 132–4; Charmley, *Chamberlain*,
pp. 52–9
69 *Amery Diary II*, 22 February 1938, pp. 457–8;
Channon Diary, 21, 22 February 1938, pp. 145–6;
Charmley, *Chamberlain*, pp. 59–61
70 *Amery Diary II*, 22 February 1938, p. 458
71 *Ibid.*, 22 February 1938, p. 458; *Channon Diary*, 22
February 1938, p. 146
72 James, *Victor Cazalet*, Cazalet to Baldwin, 24 February 1938, p. 200

30: 'Cads Like the Apostles' or 'Cavemen'?

1 Thompson, p. 228
2 Paul Emrys-Evans Papers, Add. Mss. 56247,
Emrys-Evans to Amery, 1 July 1954, fos 22–3
3 *Dalton Diary*, 8 April 1938, p. 227
4 *Hansard*, House of Commons, 14 March 1938
5 W. Murray, *The Change in the European Balance of
Power, 1938–9* (Princeton, 1984), p. 159. A similar
line is taken in C. Barnett, *The Collapse of British
Power* (1972), pp. 474, 505, 509–12
6 NC 18/1/1041, Neville to Hilda Chamberlain, 13
March 1938
7 NC 18/1/1043, Neville to Hilda Chamberlain, 27
March 1938
8 DBFP I (1949), no. 86, Newton to Foreign Office,
15 March 1938
9 T. Taylor, *Munich: The Price of Peace* (1979),
pp. 662–6
10 DBFP II, nos 708, 761, Viscount Chilston to
Foreign Office, 29 August, 4 September 1939
11 Charmley, *Chamberlain*, pp. 63–4, 96–7
12 *Gathering Storm*, p. 160
13 C. A. MacDonald, *The United States, Britain and
Appeasement 1936–9* (1980), Chap. 5; D. Reynolds,
The Creation of the Anglo-American Alliance 1937–41
(1981), pp. 16–18 and ff.
14 NC 18/1/1032, Neville to Hilda Chamberlain, 17
December 1937
15 Charmley, *Chamberlain*, pp. 40–5, and the authorities cited there
16 PRO FO 800/328, Hal/38/38, Halifax to Sir Roger
Lumley, 21 March 1938
17 *Harvey Diary*, 16, 19 March 1938, pp. 125–9
18 PRO Cab. 27/623, FP(36)27, 18 March 1938
19 *Ibid.*, FP(36)27, 21 March 1938
20 *Ibid.*, FP(36)26, 27, 18, 21 March 1938; Cab. 23/
93, 15(38), 28 March 1938
21 *Churchill V, companion vol. 3*, Irene Noel-Baker to
Churchill, 16 March 1938, p. 939
22 Emrys-Evans Papers, Add. Mss. 58247, Emrys-
Evans to Amery, 1 July 1954
23 *Nicolson Diary I*, 16 March 1938, p. 332
24 *Ibid.*, 17 February 1938, p. 323
25 DBFP I, pp. 95–7
26 NC 18/1/1043, Neville to Hilda Chamberlain, 27
March 1938
27 *Hansard*, House of Commons, 24 March 1938
28 NC 18/1/1043, Neville to Hilda Chamberlain, 27
March 1938
29 *Amery Diary II*, editorial notes, pp. 466–7
30 *Ibid.*, p. 471

31 *The Times*, 1 June 1938, for a report of a speech by Churchill in Sheffield. His meeting with Henlein on 13 May is at *Churchill V, companion vol. 3*, pp. 1021–4

32 PRO Cab. 27/623, FP(36)27, 21 March 1938

33 *Churchill V, companion vol. 3*, Violet Pearman to N. B. Foot, 10 February 1938, p. 907

34 *Churchill V*, p. 919; *Churchill V, companion vol. 3*, Churchill notes, 19 March 1938, p. 950

35 *Churchill V, companion vol. 3*, pp. 972–6

36 *Ibid.*, R. J. Thompson to Churchill, 24 March 1938, pp. 957–8

37 *Churchill V*, pp. 919–20

38 *Nicolson Diary I*, 7 April 1938, p. 333

39 *Dalton Diary*, 7 April 1938, p. 226

40 Irving, p. 104

41 *Ibid.*, Chap 6

42 Taylor, *Beaverbrook*, Beaverbrook to Frank Gannett, 9 December 1938, p. 387

43 The *samizdat Comrade* published by the 'Friends of O. M.' continues this line even now

44 *Churchill V, companion vol. 3*, Violet Pearman to Cazalet, 16 February 1938, p. 907, fn. 2

45 *Churchill V*, p. 683

46 PRO Prem. 1/252, Fisher to Chamberlain, 2 April 1938

47 *Churchill V*, p. 920

48 Roskill II, p. 320, muddles the figures up as usual, and I have preferred to use those given by R. Overy, 'German Pre-War Aircraft Production Plans', *English Historical Review* (1975), and in Peden, *British Rearmament*, p. 156

49 Peden, *ibid.*

50 *Ibid*, p. 155

51 *Churchill V, companion vol. 3*, Chamberlain/Churchill corr., 18, 26 April 1938, pp. 996, 1007

52 R. S. Churchill (ed.), *Step by Step*, pp. 253–9

53 *News of the World*, 1 May 1938

54 Charmley, *Duff Cooper*, p. 115

55 *Hansard*, House of Commons, 12 May 1938

56 NC 18/1/1051, Neville to Ida Chamberlain, 13 May 1938; Cross, pp. 212–15

57 NC 18/1/1051, Neville to Ida Chamberlain, 13 May 1938

58 *Churchill V*, p. 941; *Churchill V, companion vol. 3*, Colonel Ismay to Inskip, 23 May 1938, pp. 1040–2

59 *Ibid.*, Page-Croft to Churchill, 28 April 1938, pp. 1009–10

60 *Hansard*, House of Commons, 5 May 1938

61 *Channon Diary*, 3 May 1938, p. 155

62 *Hansard*, House of Commons, 24 March 1939

63 James, *Churchill*, p. 322

64 *Churchill V, companion vol. 3*, Churchill to Hore-Belisha, 4 June 1938, pp. 1052–4

65 Not 28 June, as Mr Gilbert asserts, *Churchill V*, p. 952

66 *Hore-Belisha Papers*, pp. 125–7

67 *Harvey Diary*, 2 July 1938, p. 157

68 *Dugdale Diary*, 22 May 1938, pp. 90–1

69 *Nicolson Diary I*, 17 May 1938, p. 341

70 *Harvey Diary*, 19 May 1938, p. 140

71 IORL, Mss. EUR F97/22B, Butler to Lord Brabourne, 24 April 1938

72 *Harvey Diary*, 22 April 1938, p. 128

73 NC 18/1/1053–4, Neville to Hilda and Ida Chamberlain, 22, 28 May 1938, for Chamberlain's reaction; Charmley, *Chamberlain*, pp. 79–81

74 *Hore-Belisha Papers*, p. 125

75 PRO Prem. 1/283, Simon to Chamberlain, 14 July 1938

76 *Hore-Belisha Papers*, p. 128

77 NC 18/1/1058, Neville to Ida Chamberlain, 4 July 1938

78 *Churchill V, companion vol. 3*, Eden to Churchill, 28 April 1938, pp. 1010–11

79 *Channon Diary*, 22 March 1938, p. 153

80 *Amery Diary II*, 24 March 1938, pp. 499–500

81 *Hansard*, House of Commons, 22 February 1938

82 Earl of Avon, *The Eden Memoirs, vol. 2: The Reckoning* (1965) (hereinafter *Eden II*), pp. 31–2

83 *Nicolson Diary I*, 9 November 1938, p. 377

84 *Churchill V, companion vol. 3*, Acland to Churchill, 23 May 1938, pp. 1038–9

85 *Ibid.*, Churchill to Acland, 26 May 1938, p. 1043

31: The Myths of Munich

1 *Daily Telegraph*, 26 July 1938; also in R. S. Churchill (ed.), *Step by Step*, p. 226

2 *Churchill V, companion vol. 3*, notes of interview with Foerster, 14 July 1938, p. 1101

3 *Daily Telegraph*, 'Thoughts on Germany's big-scale manoeuvres', 18 August 1938

4 *Daily Telegraph*, 'Can Europe stave off war?' 15 September 1938; also in R. S. Churchill (ed.), *Step by Step*, p. 284

5 *Churchill V, companion vol. 3*, p. 1155.

6 DBFP II, nos, 822, 834, 855, 857–8, 907, Phipps to Halifax, 10, 13, 14, 17 September 1938; also PRO FO 800/311, Phipps to Halifax, 14 September 1938, for the French

7 Charmley, *Chamberlain*, pp. 96–9, for more detail

8 See n. 1, above

9 *Churchill V, companion vol. 3*, Randolph Churchill to Churchill, 15 September 1938, p. 1159

10 *Harvey Diary*, 15 September 1938, p. 180

11 *Nicolson Diary I*, 14 September 1938, p. 360

12 *Amery Diary II*, 16 September 1938, pp. 509–10

13 *Harvey Diary*, 17 September 1938, p. 185

14 *Nicolson Diary I*, 19 September 1938, pp. 369–70

15 Cooper diary, 11 September 1938

16 PRO Cab. 23/95, 39(38), 17 September 1938; Cooper diary, 17 September 1938

17 *Amery Diary II*, 19 September 1938, p. 510

18 *Dugdale Diary*, 18, 20 September 1938, pp. 98–110

19 D. Dilks (ed.), *The Diaries of Sir Alexander Cadogan 1938–45* (1971) (hereinafter *Cadogan Diary*), 19 September 1938, p. 101

20 DBFP II, no. 928, for the British record; G. Weinberg, *The Foreign Policy of Hitler's Germany, vol. II* (1980), pp. 439–42, for Daladier

21 *Churchill V, companion vol. 3*, Crossley diary, 20 September 1938, p. 1170

22 PRO FO 800/314, Churchill to Halifax, 31 August 1938

23 *Nicolson Diary I*, 15 September 1938, p. 360

24 *Churchill V, companion vol. 3*, Boothby to Churchill, 31 August 1938, p. 1130

25 *Amery Diary II*, 19 September 1938, p. 510

26 *Ibid.*, 20 September 1938, p. 511

27 *Nicolson Diary I*, 22 September 1938, pp. 363–4

28 R. S. Churchill (ed.), *Step by Step*, p. 284

29 *Churchill V, companion vol. 3*, Page-Croft to Churchill, 31 October 1938, pp. 1251–2

30 *Nicolson Diary I*, 22 September 1938, p. 365

31 R. A. Butler, *The Art of the Possible* (1971), Chap. 4 summarises the argument which is also used by Hoare in his memoirs

32 DBFP II, no. 1033; PRO Cab. 23/95, 42(38), 24 September 1938

33 *Churchill V, companion vol. 3*, press statement, 26 September 1938, p. 1177; *Nicolson Diary I*, 26 September 1938, p. 367

34 *Cadogan Diary*, 24 September 1938, p. 103

35 Cooper diary, 24 September 1938

36 *Ibid.*, 25 September 1938; PRO Cab. 23/95, 43(38), 25 September 1938; Lord Birkenhead, *Halifax: The Life of Lord Halifax* (1965), pp. 400–1

37 DBFP II, nos 1043, 1044, 1058, Halifax to Butler, Halifax to Chamberlain, 23 September 1938; Butler Mss. RAB G10/26, character sketch of Halifax

38 PRO FO 800/309, H/VI/81, Amery to Halifax, 24 September 1938

39 *Ibid.*, H/VI/82, Spears *et al.* to Halifax, 24 September 1938

40 *Eden II*, pp. 25–7; *Harvey Diary*, 17 September 1938, p. 184

41 *Amery Diary II*, 26 September 1938, p. 517

42 *Nicolson Diary I*, 26 September 1938, p. 367

43 *Amery Diary II*, 26 September 1938, p. 517

44 *Ibid.*, 26, 27 September 1938, pp. 517–18; *Nicolson Diary I*, 26, 27 September 1938, pp. 367–8; *Dugdale Diary*, 26, 27 September 1938, pp. 104–5; *Harvey Diary*, 26, 27 September 1938, pp. 198–200; *Channon Diary*, 25–27 September 1938, pp. 164–5; *Crawford Papers*, diary, 25–27 September 1938, p. 589

45 A. Bryant (ed.), *In Search of Peace* (1938), pp. 274–6, for the text

46 *Amery Diary II*, 28 September 1938, p. 520

47 Charmley, *Chamberlain*, pp. 134–5

48 *Channon Diary*, 28 September 1938, p. 171

49 *Amery Diary II*, 28 September 1938, p. 521

50 *Nicolson Diary I*, 28 September 1938, pp. 369–70

51 *Churchill V*, pp. 986–7; *Eden II*, p. 28

52 *Eden II*, p. 28

53 L. S. Amery, *My Political Life, vol. III: The Unforgiving Years 1929–40* (1955), p. 280; Macmillan, p. 506

54 *Amery Diary II*, 28 September 1938, pp. 520–1; the manuscript version is the same

55 *Channon Diary*, 28 September 1938, p. 171

56 *Nicolson Diary I*, 29 September 1938, p. 372

57 *Ibid.*, 28 September 1938, p. 371

58 *The Times*, 29 September 1938

59 *Churchill V*, p. 987

60 *Amery Diary II*, 28 September 1938, p. 521

61 *Nicolson Diary I*, 28 September 1938, p. 371

62 *Gathering Storm*, p. 200

63 *Churchill V, companion vol. 3*, Crossley to Churchill, 28 September 1938, p. 1185. The reference given in *Churchill V, companion vol. 3*, p. 1184, to supporting evidence on p. 1188, is to the published Nicolson diaries, which support only the contention that Nicolson remained seated.

64 *Ibid.*, press statement, 28 September 1938, pp. 1184–5

65 Charmley, *Duff Cooper*, pp. 121–2; *Cadogan Diary*, 27 September 1938, p. 107, is equally clear that it was Chamberlain who gave the order that afternoon.

66 Cooper diary, 29 September 1938. It is an odd example of scholarly editing that Mr Gilbert should cite his source for this at *Churchill V, companion vol. 3*, p. 1189, as 'Norwich papers' when he has never seen them. What Mr Gilbert saw was the extract from his diary which Duff sent to Churchill in 1953 for his approval. Churchill replied that he preferred it not to be published. A 'great scholarly editor', as one reviewer called Mr Gilbert, would, it might be thought, have given his actual source, rather than creating a misleading impression.

67 *Nicolson Diary I*, 29 September 1938, p. 372

68 *Amery Diary II*, 30 September 1938, p. 523

69 *Dugdale Diary*, 29 September 1938, p. 108

70 *Amery Diary II*, 30 September 1938, p. 523

71 *Churchill V, companion vol. 3*, p. 1189

72 Charmley, *Duff Cooper*, pp. 88–9

73 Cooper diary, 29 September 1938

74 Charmley, *Chamberlain*, pp. 144–8

75 *Dugdale Diary*, 30 September 1938, p. 109

76 *Amery Diary II*, 3 October 1938, pp. 524–5

77 *Churchill V, companion vol. 3*, Nicolson diary, 3 October 1938, pp. 1196–7

78 Charmley, *Duff Cooper*, pp. 127–30

79 *Churchill V, companion vol. 3*, Churchill to Cooper, p. 1189, but surely not dated '30 Sept.' as the 'great scholarly editor' has it. Homer is nodding rather vigorously at this point. The meeting at Bracken's house on 5 October, which Gilbert places after Churchill's speech in *Churchill V*, p. 1002, was, as Nicolson implies and both Amery and Dugdale make plain, *before* that speech.

80 *Amery Diary II*, 3 October 1938, p. 525

81 *Dugdale Diary*, 4 October 1938, pp. 110–11

82 *Amery Diary II*, 5 October 1938, p. 526; cf. *Dugdale Diary*, 5 October 1938, p. 111

83 *Nicolson Diary I*, 5 October 1938, p. 375

84 *Hansard*, House of Commons, 5 October 1938

85 *Nicolson Diary I*, 6 October 1938, p. 375

86 *Amery Diary II*, 6 October 1938, pp. 527–8

87 *Nicolson Diary I*, 6 October 1938, pp. 375–6

88 *Churchill V, companion vol. 3*, Hoare to Chamberlain, 5 October 1938, p. 1202; PRO FO 800/328, Halifax to Chamberlain, 11 October 1938

89 NC 18/1/1174, 1175, Neville to Hilda Chamberlain, 28 October, 6 November 1938

90 NC 18/1/1071, Neville to Ida Chamberlain, 9 October 1938

32: *The Winter of Discontent*

1 Charmley, *Duff Cooper*, p. 132
2 *Amery Diary II*, 11 October 1939, p. 530
3 Cecil Papers, Add. Mss. 51081, Cranborne to Cecil, 16 October 1938
4 NC 18/1/1071, Neville to Ida Chamberlain, 9 October 1938
5 NC 18/1/1075, Neville to Hilda Chamberlain, 6 November 1938
6 *Churchill V, companion vol. 3*, Boothby to Churchill, 10 October 1938, pp. 1209–10
7 *Ibid.*, Churchill to Boothby, 11 October 1938, p. 1210
8 NC 18/1/1071, Neville to Ida Chamberlain, 9 October 1938
9 *Churchill V, companion vol. 3*, Chamberlain to Churchill, 6 October 1938, pp. 1204–5
10 *Churchill V*, p. 1012
11 Macmillan, p. 569; *Dalton Diary*, editor's notes, p. 247
12 *Nicolson Diary I*, 9 November 1938, p. 378
13 *Gathering Storm*, Cooper to Churchill, 19 November 1938, p. 208
14 *Ibid.*, Churchill to Cooper, 22 November 1938, p. 209
15 Nicolson diary, Mss., Balliol College, Oxford, 27 October 1938; *Amery Diary II*, 29 November 1938, p. 537
16 *Hansard*, House of Commons, 17 November 1938
17 *Daily Telegraph*, 17 November 1938
18 Weinberg, pp. 514–17
19 Butler Mss. RAB G11/130, Makins to Butler, 11 October 1938 (not, as in the catalogue, Haking to Butler, 1940!)
20 DBFP III, no. 179, Henderson to Halifax, 11 October 1938
21 NC 1/20/1/186, Cadogan to Mary Endicott Chamberlain, 5 November 1938
22 NC 18/1/1074, Neville to Ida Chamberlain, 22 October 1938
23 Weinberg, pp. 515–16; W. K. Wark, *The Ultimate Enemy* (1985 edn), p. 113
24 NC 18/1/1076, Neville to Ida Chamberlain, 13 November 1938
25 PRO Cab. 27/627, FP(36), 32nd meeting, 14 November 1938
26 PRO Prem. 1/327, Cadogan to Perth, 12 December 1938, fo. 70
27 Charmley, *Chamberlain*, p. 151, for details
28 IORL Mss. EUR F97/22B, Butler to Brabourne, 14 December 1938
29 *Harvey Diary*, 10–13 October 1938, pp. 211–13
30 Nicolson diary, Mss., 30 November 1938
31 *Nicolson Diary I*, 18 July 1938, p. 406
32 NC 18/1/1081, Neville to Ida Chamberlain, 8 January 1939
33 Charmley, *Chamberlain*, pp. 155–7, for details
34 NC 18/1/1085, Neville to Ida Chamberlain, 12 February 1939

35 NC 18/1/1084, Neville to Hilda Chamberlain, 5 February 1939
36 IORL, Marquess of Zetland Mss., Mss. EUR D609/11, Zetland to Linlithgow, 29 January 1939; NC 18/1/1085, Neville to Ida Chamberlain, 12 February 1939
37 Templewood, p. 328
38 NC 18/1/1089, Neville to Ida Chamberlain, 12 March 1939
39 Charmley, *Chamberlain*, Chap. 16; C. Hill, *Cabinet Decisions on Foreign Policy October 1938–June 1941* (Cambridge, 1991), Chap. 2, surveys the various views; A Prażmowska, *Britain, Poland and the Eastern Front, 1939* (Cambridge, 1987), takes a somewhat different view.
40 *Nicolson Diary I*, 5 December 1938, p. 382
41 *Churchill V, companion vol. 3*, letter published in *The Times*, 13 December 1938, p. 1308
42 *Ibid.*, Churchill to Mrs Churchill, 29 December 1938, p. 1329
43 *Ibid.*, Churchill to Mrs Churchill, 19 December 1938, pp. 1316–17
44 *Ibid.*, Churchill to Mrs Churchill, 22 December 1938, p. 1323
45 *Churchill V*, pp. 1043–4
46 *Churchill V, companion vol. 3*, pp. 1389–91
47 *Ibid.*, Churchill to Sir Douglas Hacking, 18 March 1939, pp. 1394–6, not sent
48 Cmd 6106, Blue Book on the outbreak of war, doc. 9.
49 Charmley, *Chamberlain*, pp. 166–75
50 Macmillan, p. 593
51 *Nicolson Diary I*, 11 April 1939, p. 397
52 *Amery Diary II*, 21 March 1939, p. 549
53 *Churchill V*, p. 1052
54 *Ibid.*, pp. 1052–3
55 *Churchill V, companion vol. 3*, pp. 1436–9, for details
56 NC 18/1/1094, Neville to Hilda Chamberlain, 15 April 1939
57 NC 18/1/1093, Neville to Ida Chamberlain, 9 April 1939
58 NC 18/1/1095, Neville to Ida Chamberlain, 23 April 1939
59 NC 18/1/1094, Neville to Hilda Chamberlain, 15 April 1939
60 *Ibid.*
61 DBFP V, nos 1 & 2, conversations with Beck
62 *Ibid.*, nos 278, 279, 285
63 Weinberg, p. 550
64 Charmley, *Chamberlain*, pp. 180–91; Prażmowska, pp. 72–4, 137–47; Hill, pp. 57–70
65 Charmley, *ibid.*, p. 171; Prażmowska, pp. 72–7; Hill, pp. 42–3
66 Charmley, *ibid.*, pp. 172–4
67 *Churchill V, companion vol. 3*, broadcast, 28 April 1939, p. 1478
68 R. S. Churchill (ed.), *Step by Step*, p. 9 of the preface
69 PRO Prem. 1/304, Chamberlain to Lord Francis Scott, 12 June 1939
70 *Churchill V, companion vol. 3*, Churchill to Halifax, 11 June 1939
71 Irving, pp. 164–72, seems to come close to this
72 *Nicolson Diary I*, 14 June 1939, p. 403

73 *Churchill V*, p. 1075
74 See Chap. 34 below
75 *Churchill V*, Chap. 52
76 NC 18/1/1107, Neville to Hilda Chamberlain, 15 July 1939
77 *Churchill V, companion vol. 3*, Churchill/Halifax corr., 3, 6 February 1939, pp. 1363, 1366
78 *Ibid.*, speech, 21 June 1939, p. 1529
79 Charmley, *Chamberlain*, p. 189
80 *Churchill V, companion vol. 3*, Stafford Cripps diary, 22 June 1939
81 NC 18/1/1102, Neville to Ida Chamberlain, 10 June 1939
82 *Churchill V, companion vol. 3*, Camrose notes, 3 July 1939, pp. 1544–6
83 Channon Diary, 4 July 1939, p. 204
84 *Churchill V, companion vol. 3*, Hoare to William Astor, 11 July 1939, p. 1562
85 *Ibid.*, Churchill to Rothermere, 19 July 1939, pp. 1569–70
86 *Ibid.*, Wolmer to Churchill, 31 July 1939, p. 1580
87 NC 18/1/1111, Neville to Ida Chamberlain, 5 August 1939
88 *Eden II*, pp. 57–8
89 Cooper diary, 29 August 1939
90 *Churchill V*, pp. 1106–7
91 *Amery Diary II*, 2 September 1939, p. 570
92 Charmley, *Chamberlain*, pp. 207–8, for details
93 *Churchill V, companion vol. 3*, Churchill to Chamberlain, 2 September 1939, pp. 1605–6
94 Cooper diary, 2 September 1939
95 *Churchill V*, p. 1111
96 *Hansard*, House of Commons, 3 September 1939
97 *Churchill V*, p. 1112
98 *Amery Diary II*, 3 September 1939, p. 571
99 *Churchill V*, p. 1113

33: Churchill and Chamberlain: II

1 *Churchill V, companion vol. 3*, Churchill to Thornton-Kemsley, 13 September 1939, p. 1622
2 *Nicolson Diary I*, 8 December 1937, p. 314
3 Roskill III, Hankey to Lady Hankey, 3 September 1939, p. 419
4 NC 18/1/1116, Neville to Ida Chamberlain, 10 September 1939
5 NC 18/1/1125, Neville to Hilda Chamberlain, 15 October 1939
6 A. Marder, 'Winston is back', in *From the Dardanelles to Oran* (1974); R. Lamb, *Churchill as War Leader* (1991), pp. 24–9
7 NC 18/1/1121, Neville to Hilda Chamberlain, 17 September 1939
8 NC 18/1/1124, Neville to Ida Chamberlain, 8 October 1939
9 NC 18/1/1126, Neville to Ida Chamberlain, 22 October 1939
10 NC 18/1/1094, Neville to Hilda Chamberlain, 15 April 1939
11 *Churchill V, companion vol. 3*, Camrose notes of conversation with Chamberlain, 3 July 1939, pp. 1544–6

12 Carlton, p. 151; not, as Mr Lamb imagines (p. 16), Secretary of State for War
13 *Churchill V, companion vol. 3*, Amery to Churchill, 4 September 1939, pp. 1618–19; *Amery Diary II*, 4 September 1939, p. 571
14 *Amery Diary II*, 5 September 1939, p. 572
15 Lord Macaulay, *History of England, vol. II* (1967 edn), p. 25
16 Naval historians are a fierce sub-species of the genus historian, which is, goodness knows, ferocious enough. Arthur Marder in the essay cited in n. 6 above, took the view that Churchill did not 'run roughshod' over Pound (p. 169). Captain Roskill, *au contraire*, thought that this was just what Churchill did: *Journal of the Royal United Services Institute* (1982), no. 4, vol. 117. R. Hough, in *Former Naval Person*, takes a more balanced view. Lamb, who ignores other writers on the subject, is a Roskillite.
17 Hough, p. 136
18 PRO, Admiralty Papers, ADM 205/2, notes on conference, 4 September 1939. The words quoted were underlined by Churchill. See also M. Gilbert, *Winston S. Churchill, vol. VI: Their Finest Hour* (1983) (hereinafter *Churchill VI*), p. 7
19 J. R. M. Butler, *Grand Strategy, vol. II* (1957), pp. 249–50; A. F. Wilt, *War from the Top* (1990), pp. 10–11
20 Hough, p. 136
21 Sir E. L. Spears, *Assignment to Catastrophe, vol. I: July 1939–May 1940* (1954)(hereinafter Spears I), p. 216
22 *Amery Diary II*, 5 September 1939, p. 572; see also editorial notes, pp. 559–60
23 PRO ADM 199/1928, Churchill memo., 12 September 1939
24 PRO ADM 205/4, Pound note, 20 September 1939
25 *Ibid.*, Churchill note, 20 September 1939
26 Marder, *From the Dardanelles to Oran*, p. 142
27 PRO ADM 199/1929, Pound to Churchill, 3 December 1939
28 *Ibid.*, Churchill to Pound, 5 December 1939
29 PRO Cab. 65/2, WM(39)111, 11 December 1939
30 Marder, *From the Dardanelles to Oran*, p. 145
31 *Ibid.*, p. 147
32 *Churchill VI*, Hoare to Beaverbrook, 1 October 1039, p. 47
33 N. Nicolson (ed.), *Harold Nicolson: Diaries and Letters, vol. II: 1939–45* (1967) (hereinafter *Nicolson Diary II*), 26 September 1939, p. 37
34 Sir John Colville, *The Fringes of Power: The Downing Street Diaries 1939–55* (1985) (hereinafter *Colville Diary*), 28 September 1939, p. 27
35 *Ibid.*, 9 November 1939, p. 50
36 C. Eade (ed.), *The War Speeches, vol. I: 1938–41* (1975 edn) (hereinafter *War Speeches I*), pp. 119–23
37 *Colville Diary*, 13 November 1939, p. 51
38 Charmley, *Chamberlain*, p. 211; see also D. Dilks, 'The Twilight War and the Fall of France: Chamberlain and Churchill in 1940', in D. Dilks (ed.), *Retreat from Power, vol. II: After 1939* (1981), p. 49
39 Sir L. Woodward, *British Foreign Policy in the Second World War, vol. I* (1970) (hereinafter Wood-

ward I), pp. 13, 20–2; *Churchill VI*, pp. 55–6

40 *Gathering Storm*, p. 316

41 PRO FO 800/310, Churchill to Halifax, 20 October 1939

42 PRO Cab. 65/1, WM(39)58, 24 October 1939; see also Carlton, pp. 158–9, and *Churchill VI*, pp. 67–8

43 *Harvey Diary*, 30 October 1939, p. 326

44 *Churchill VI*, Churchill to Halifax, 10 September 1939, p. 23

45 *Ibid.*, Hoare diary, 7 September 1939

46 NC 18/1/1121, Neville to Hilda Chamberlain, 17 September 1939

47 *Gathering Storm*, pp. 311–12

48 NC 18/1/1124, Neville to Ida Chamberlain, 8 October 1939; see also NC 7/9/63, memo by Sir Horace Wilson, 3 October 1939

49 PRO Cab. 65/2, WM(39) 116, 117, 15, 16 December 1939; *Gathering Storm*, note on the Norway iron-ore traffic by Churchill, 16 December 1939, pp. 351–2; Marder, *From the Dardanelles to Oran*, pp. 148–50; Dilks (ed.), *Retreat from Power, vol. II*, pp. 45–7

50 *Gathering Storm*, p. 352

51 PRO Cab. 83/1, MC(39) 10[th meeting], 20 December 1939

52 *Ibid.*

53 PRO Cab. 65/4, WM(39)122, 22 December 1939

54 *Ibid.*; *Gathering Storm*, p. 352

55 PRO Cab. 65/11, Confidential Annexe, WM(40) 1, 2, 10, of 2, 3, 10 January 1940; Woodward I, pp. 53–69

56 PRO FO 800/328, Churchill to Halifax, 13 January 1940

57 Dilks (ed.), *Retreat from Power, vol. II*, p. 52

58 NC 1/18/1149, Neville to Hilda Chamberlain, 6 April 1940

59 Dilks (ed.), *Retreat from Power, vol. II*, pp. 50–1

60 *War Speeches I*, pp. 146–7

61 *Churchill VI*, pp. 136–8

62 PRO FO 800/328, Halifax to Churchill, 20 January 1940

63 *Ibid.*, Churchill to Halifax, 20 January 1940

64 PRO Cab. 65/12, WM(40)68, 14 March 1940

65 PRO FO 800/328, Churchill to Halifax, 14 March 1940

66 Butler Mss. RAB G11/1, 'Narvik', 11 January 1940

67 PRO FO 800/316, Butler to Halifax, 17 July 1940

68 *Churchill VI*, p. 190

69 PRO Cab. 65/6, WM(40)67, 13 March 1940; Woodward I, pp. 169–70

70 Lamb, p. 19, whose addiction to the old myths detracts from the value of this section of his book

71 *Churchill VI*, pp. 203–4

72 NC 18/1/1150, Neville to Ida Chamberlain, 13 April 1940

34: Failure and Apotheosis: I

1 PRO Cab. 99/3, 28 March 1940

2 *Gathering Storm*, pp. 371–2

3 Woodward I, pp. 114–15

4 *Gathering Storm*, p. 375

5 J. L. Moulton, *The Norwegian Campaign of 1940* (1966), pp. 56–7; Woodward I, p. 114, fn. 1

6 PRO Cab. 65/6, WM(40)84, 8 April 1940

7 *Colville Diary*, 9 April (not 8 April as in *Churchill VI*, p. 172), p. 99

8 PRO Cab. 65/6, WM(40)85, 9 April 1940

9 Moulton, p. 71

10 PRO Cab. 99/3, S[upreme] W[ar] C[ouncil] 7(40), 9 April 1940; Cab. 83/3, MCC(40)17, 9 April 1940

11 Piers Mackesy, 'Churchill on Narvik', *Journal of the Royal United Services Institute* (1970), p. 28. I should like to thank Piers Mackesy for his help in commenting on an earlier draft of this chapter.

12 NC 18/1/1150, Neville to Ida Chamberlain, 13 April 1940

13 *Gathering Storm*, pp. 376–7

14 NC 18/1/1150, Neville to Ida Chamberlain, 13 April 1940

15 Moulton, pp. 148–9

16 *Ibid.*, p. 149

17 R. Macleod and D. Kelly (eds), *The Ironside Diaries 1937–40* (1962) (hereinafter *Ironside Diary*), pp. 257–8

18 *Nicolson Diary II*, 11 April 1940, p. 70

19 *Colville Diary*, 11 April 1940, p. 101

20 *Churchill VI*, p. 230

21 *Ibid.*, pp. 230–1

22 C. Stuart (ed.), *The Reith Diaries* (1975) (hereinafter *Reith Diary*), p. 245

23 PRO Prem. 1/404, memo. by Sir Edward Bridges, 25 April 1940

24 NC 18/1/1151, Neville to Hilda Chamberlain, 20 April 1940

25 PRO Prem. 1/404, memo. by Sir Horace Wilson, 25 April 1940; *Churchill VI*, pp. 246–7

26 Lamb, pp. 39–40

27 Moulton, pp. 155–6

28 PRO Prem. 1/404, minute by Hankey, 17 April 1940

29 *Gathering Storm*, pp. 394–5

30 *Ibid.*, p. 395

31 *Ibid.*, Piers Mackesy, 'Churchill on Narvik', pp. 29–33, for the counter-arguments; also Piers Mackesy to the author, 17 January 1992

32 *Churchill VI*, p. 251

33 PRO ADM 199/1029, Cork to Churchill, 18 April 1940

34 *Ibid.*, Mackesy to London, 19 April 1940

35 PRO Cab. 65/12, WM(40), 19 April 1940

36 *Churchill VI*, Churchill to Chamberlain, 24 April 1940, 'not sent', pp. 264, 267

37 *Colville Diary*, 25 April 1940, p. 108

38 NC 18/1/1152, Neville to Ida Chamberlain, 27 April 1940; also *Churchill VI*, Chamberlain to Churchill, 24 April 1940, p. 267

39 NC 18/1/1152, Neville to Ida Chamberlain, 27 April 1940

40 *Colville Diary*, 25 April 1940, p. 108

41 NC 18/1/1152, Neville to Ida Chamberlain, 27 April 1940

42 *Churchill VI*, p. 277
43 *Channon Diary*, 30 April 1940, p. 243
44 *Colville Diary*, 1 May 1940, p. 115
45 *Ironside Diary*, 3 May 1940, p. 293
46 *Ibid.*, 4, 5 May 1940, pp. 294, 295
47 *Channon Diary*, 1 May 1940, p. 244
48 *Colville Diary*, 3 May 1940, p. 116
49 Spears I, p. 112
50 *Ibid.*, p. 115
51 *Nicolson Diary II*, 1 May 1940, pp. 74–5
52 *Ibid.*, 3, 4 May 1940, p. 75
53 *Nicolson Diary I*, 8 December 1937, p. 314
54 *Channon Diary*, 7 May 1940, p. 244
55 *Dugdale Diary*, 7 May 1940, p. 168
56 *Nicolson Diary II*, 7 May 1940, pp. 76–7
57 *Dugdale Diary*, 7 May 1940, p. 168
58 *Hansard*, House of Commons, 7 May 1940; *Amery Diary II*, 7 May 1940, p. 592
59 *Channon Diary*, 7 May 1940, p. 245
60 Spears I, p. 122
61 *Hansard*, House of Commons, 8 May 1940
62 *Dalton Diary*, 8 May 1940, p. 341
63 *Hansard*, House of Commons, 8 May 1940
64 *Channon Diary*, 8 May 1940, p. 246
65 *Amery Diary II*, 8 May 1940, pp. 610–11
66 Dilks, (ed.), *Retreat from Power, vol. II*, pp. 55–6, puts forward an argument which possesses more ingenuity than power of persuasion. Spears, p. 124; *Amery Diary II*, 8 May 1940, p. 610; *Nicolson Diary II*, 8 May 1940, p. 78, all have no doubt what the Prime Minister meant, nor did *Channon Diary*, 8 May 1940, p. 245.
67 *Nicolson Diary II*, 8 May 1940, p. 79
68 *Amery Diary II*, 8 May 1940, p. 611
69 *Channon Diary*, 8 May 1940, p. 246
70 *Dalton Diary*, 9 May 1940, pp. 343–4; *Colville Diary*, 9 May 1940, p. 120
71 *Dalton Diary*, 8, 9 May 1940, pp. 342–4; *Channon Diary*, 9 May 1940, pp. 247–8; James, *Victor Cazalet*, diary, 9 May 1940, p. 227; *Nicolson Diary II*, 9 May 1940, pp. 80–1
72 *Dalton Diary*, 9 May 1940, p. 343
73 *Eden II*, diary, 9 May 1940, pp. 96–7
74 Moran, diary, 7 December 1947, p. 323
75 Spears I, p. 131
76 Taylor, *Beaverbrook*, p. 409, who does not believe it any more than I do.
77 NC 18/1/1155, Neville to Ida Chamberlain, 11 May 1940; see also Halifax's account as given to Cadogan, in *Cadogan Diary*, 9 May 1940, p. 280, which bears out the account in Chamberlain's letter.
78 *Gathering Storm*, p. 426
79 Halifax diary, 9 May 1940, in Birkenhead, *Halifax* (hereinafter Halifax diary), p. 454
80 *Ibid.*, pp. 454–5
81 NC 18/1/1155, Neville to Ida Chamberlain, 11 May 1940
82 *Churchill VI*, pp. 310–11; *Nicolson Diary II*, 19 May 1940, p. 82
83 PRO Cab. 65/7, WM(40)119, 10 May 1940
84 *Churchill VI*, p. 313
85 *Gathering Storm*, p. 427
86 *Churchill VI*, pp. 314–15
87 *Gathering Storm*, p. 428

35: Walking with Destiny

1 *Channon Diary*, 13 May 1940, p. 252; *Nicolson Diary II*, 13 May 1940, p. 85
2 NC 13/17/68, Patrick Donner to Chamberlain, 13 May 1940
3 NC 13/17/57, E. C. Cobb to Chamberlain, 10 May 1940
4 NC 18/1/1155, Neville to Ida Chamberlain, 11 May 1940
5 *Amery Diary II*, 11 May 1940, p. 615
6 *Dalton Diary*, 11 May 1940, p. 346
7 W. S. Churchill, *The Second World War, vol. II: Their Finest Hour* (1975 edn) (hereinafter *Finest Hour*), p. 11, for a complete list
8 James (ed.), *Churchill Speaks*, speech on his eightieth birthday, 30 November 1954, p. 965
9 PRO FO 800/328, for reams of stuff from these; also *Crawford Papers*, diary, 15 November 1939, pp. 607–8
10 Hill, pp. 136–41
11 PRO Prem. 4/25/2, fos 106–7
12 *Crawford Papers*, diary, 15 December 1939, p. 610
13 Taylor, *Beaverbrook*, p. 405
14 NC 18/1/1155, Neville to Ida Chamberlain, 11 May 1940
15 B. Pimlott (ed.), *The Second World War Diary of Hugh Dalton, 1940–45* (1986) (hereinafter *Dalton Diary II*), 28 May 1940, p. 26
16 W. F. Kimball (ed.), *Churchill & Roosevelt: The Complete Correspondence, vol. I: The Alliance Emerging, October 1933–November 1942* (Princeton, 1984) (hereinafter *Churchill & Roosevelt I*), Churchill to Roosevelt, 15 May 1940, p. 37
17 *Ibid.*, Churchill to Roosevelt, 18 May 1940, p. 39; Churchill to Roosevelt, 20 May 1940, p. 40
18 Hill, p. 149, who is very good on all of this
19 *War Speeches I*, p. 181
20 Berlin, p. 16
21 PRO Cab. 65/7, WM(40)132, 21 May 1940
22 PRO, C[hiefs] O[f] S[taff] Memoranda, Cab. 80/11, COS 394; Cab. 65/13, WM(40)140, 26 May 1940. See also the excellent discussion of this in Hill, pp. 156–8, and D. Reynolds, 'Churchill and the British "Decision" To Fight on in 1940: Right Policy, Wrong Reasons', in R. Langhorne (ed.), *Diplomacy and Intelligence during the Second World War*, pp. 147–67.
23 *Cadogan diary*, 27 May 1940, p. 291
24 PRO Cab. 65/13, WM(40)141, 11.30 a.m., 27 May 1940
25 Halifax diary, 27 May 1940, p. 458
26 PRO Cab. 65/13, WM(40)142, 4.30 a.m., 27 May 1940
27 NC 2/24A, diary, 26 May 1940
28 PRO Cab. 65/13, WM(40)142, 27 May 1940
29 Halifax diary, 27 May 1940, p. 548
30 *Cadogan Diary*, 27 May 1940, p. 291
31 Halifax diary, 27 May 1940, p. 548

32 *Churchill VI*, pp. 414–16; PRO Cab. 65/7, WM(40)144, 28 May 1940
33 Cab. 65/13, WM(40)145, 28 May 1940 (not 29 May as Mr Gilbert has it at *Churchill VI*, p. 419)
34 Reynolds, pp. 152–4, puts, I think, too much store by Churchill's hesitations
35 *Reith Diary*, 28 May 1940, p. 254
36 *Dalton Diary II*, 28 May 1940, p. 27
37 H. Dalton, *The Fateful Years* (1957), p. 336. This is slightly different to the one given in the diary, p. 28, but I have preferred it because it is more dramatic!
38 *Dalton Diary II*, 28 May 1940, pp. 336–7
39 Hill, pp. 175–7
40 *Amery Diary II*, 28 May 1940, p. 619
41 PRO Cab. 65/13, WM(40)145, 7 p.m., 28 May 1940
42 *Gathering Storm*, p. 69
43 *Ibid.*, Churchill to Reynaud, 28 May 1940, pp. 84–5
44 J. Martin, *Downing Street: The War Years* (1991), 30 May 1940, p. 11
45 *Cadogan Diary*, 24 May 1940, p. 292
46 *Reith Diary*, 1 June 1940, p. 256
47 *Ibid.*, 28 May 1940, p. 255
48 Borthwich Institute, Hickleton Mss., Halifax diary, 30 May 1940
49 *Colville Diary*, 10 May 1940, p. 122
50 *Channon Diary*, 29 May 1940, p. 255
51 Roskill III, Hankey to Hoare, 12 May 1940, p. 468

36: Giving Destiny a Helping Hand

1 *Churchill VI*, p. 428
2 Spears I, p. 295
3 Lord Ismay, *The Memoirs of General The Lord Ismay* (1960), p. 133
4 PRO Cab. 99/3, SWC(40) 13th meeting, 31 May 1940; Spears I, pp. 295–316, for the full account
5 Spears I, p. 314
6 *Ibid.*, pp. 316–17
7 *Finest Hour*, p. 107
8 *Hansard*, House of Commons, 4 June 1940
9 *Amery Diary II*, 4 June 1940, p. 620
10 *Nicolson Diary II*, 4 June 1940, p. 93
11 *Dalton Diary*, 4 June 1940, p. 35
12 *Reith Diary*, 5 June 1940, p. 256
13 *Colville Diary*, 4 June 1940, p. 97
14 Reynolds, *The Creation of the Anglo-American Alliance*, pp. 106–13
15 Sir E. L. Spears, *Assignment to Catastrophe, vol. II* (1954) (hereinafter Spears II), p. 48
16 *Nicolson Diary II*, Vita Sackville-West to Harold Nicolson, 5 June 1940, p. 93
17 *Churchill & Roosevelt I*, p. 42
18 *Ibid.*, Churchill to Roosevelt, 10 June 1940, p. 43
19 *Ibid.*, Churchill to Roosevelt, 12 June 1940, pp. 44–5
20 *Ibid.*, Roosevelt to Churchill, 13 June 1940, pp. 45–6
21 PRO Prem. 4/43B/1, Churchill to Mackenzie King, 5 June 1940

22 Reynolds, *The Creation of the Anglo-American Alliance*, pp. 108–13, for the American reaction
23 Spears II, pp. 131–2
24 *Churchill VI*, p. 500
25 Spears II, p. 140. My account is based on Spears II, pp. 139–58, and PRO Cab. 99/3, SWC(40)14, 11 June 1940
26 Spears II, p. 161
27 PRO Cab. 99/3, SWC(40)15, 12 June 1940; Spears II, pp. 167–71
28 PRO Cab. 65/7, WM(40)163, 12 June 1940; *Colville Diary*, 12 June 1940, p. 153
29 PRO Cab. 99/3, SWC(40)16, 13 June 1940; Spears II, pp. 199–218; *Finest Hour*, pp. 119–21; *Churchill VI*, pp. 528–35
30 PRO Cab. 65/7, WM(40)165, 13 June 1940; *Colville Diary*, 13 June 1940, p. 155
31 *Churchill & Roosevelt I*, Churchill to Roosevelt, 14 June 1940, pp. 46–7
32 *Ibid.*, Roosevelt to Churchill, 14 June 1940, pp. 47–8
33 PRO Cab. 65/7, WM(40)166, 14 June 1940
34 Spears II, pp. 257–8
35 *Ibid.*, pp. 266–7; *Harvey Diary*, 15 June 1940, pp. 390–1
36 *Harvey Diary*, 16 June 1940, p. 391
37 Spears II, pp. 291–7; D. Thompson, *The Anglo-French Union* (1966)
38 Spears II, p. 323
39 *Churchill & Roosevelt I*, Churchill to Roosevelt, 15 June 1940, pp. 49–51
40 Reynolds, 'Churchill and the British "Decision" . . .', pp. 160–2
41 P. Addison, *The Road to 1945* (1975), pp. 111–12
42 NC 2/24A, 5, 10 June 1940
43 *Ibid.*, 9 September 1940
44 NC 18/1/1155, Neville to Ida Chamberlain, 11 May 1940
45 NC 2/24A, 28 May 1938; House of Lords Record Office, Lloyd George Mss. G/4/5/48, Churchill to Lloyd George, 29 May 1940
46 NC 2/24A, 5 June 1940
47 *Amery Diary II*, 18 June 1940, p. 626
48 NC 2/24A, diary, 18 June 1940
49 *Hansard*, House of Commons, 18 June 1940
50 *Colville Diary*, 18 June 1940, p. 164
51 *Channon Diary*, 20 June 1940, p. 259
52 *Ibid.*, 18 June 1940, p. 258
53 Martin, 21 June 1940, p. 12
54 *Nicolson Diary II*, 19 June 1940, p. 97
55 *Dalton Diary II*, 18 June 1940, p. 42

37: The Struggle for Survival

1 Woodward I, p. 301; F. Kersaudy, *Churchill and de Gaulle* (1981), Chap. 1
2 Woodward I, pp. 321–30; R. T. Thomas, *Britain and Vichy* (1978), Chaps 1–3
3 Woodward I, p. 321, draft declaration by de Gaulle, 19 June 1940
4 J. Charmley, *British Policy towards General de Gaulle, 1942–4* (unpublished Oxford D. Phil. thesis, 1982), Chap. 1, for all this

5 *War Speeches I*, pp. 209–17

6 Reynolds, *The Creation of the Anglo-American Alliance*, pp. 103–18

7 Reynolds, 'Churchill and the British "Decision"...', pp. 156–61; R. A. C. Parker, *Struggle for Survival: The History of the Second World War* (Oxford, 1989), pp. 151–2

8 Reynolds, *ibid.*, p. 167

9 Irving, pp. 299, 305, 344–5 and *passim*

10 Terry Coleman's article, 'Was This our Finest Hour?' in *The Independent*, 1 September 1990, was greeted with outrage by some of that newspaper's readers: my quotations are from letters published in *The Independent*, 5 September 1990. The reaction in the East Anglian press to an article of mine in similar vein, as well as the attitude of the national press to Clive Ponting's *1940: Myth and Reality* (1990), illustrates the enduring hold which the myth has.

11 Parker, p. 45. It is with some reluctance that I disagree with my friend and former supervisor, Alastair Parker, on this point.

12 Ponting, p. 112

13 A. Howard, *Rab: The Life of R. A. Butler* (1987), p. 97

14 Ponting, p. 113; PRO Cab. 65/7, WM(40)171, 18 June 1940, item 5, is 'closed'

15 *Cadogan Diary*, 18 June 1940, p. 304

16 PRO FO 800/323, Halifax to Hoare, 19 June 1940

17 NC 18/1/1163, Neville to Hilda Chamberlain, 29 June 1940

18 NC 18/1/1162, Neville to Ida Chamberlain, 21 June 1940

19 PRO FO 800/322, Churchill to Halifax, 25 June 1940

20 *Ibid.*, Butler to Halifax, 26 June 1940

21 Butler Mss. RAB G11/80, Halifax to Churchill, 27 June 1940

22 *Cadogan Diary*, 2 July 1940, p. 309

23 Hill, p. 185

24 K. Jefferys, *The Churchill Coalition and Wartime Politics, 1940–45* (Manchester, 1991), pp. 47–8

25 Macaulay, pp. 548–9

26 NC 18/1/1162, Neville to Ida Chamberlain, 21 June 1940

27 NC 18/1/1163, Neville to Hilda Chamberlain, 29 June 1940

28 Roskill III, Hankey to Hoare, 19 July 1940

29 *Dalton Diary II*, 25 June 1940, p. 48

30 Jefferys, p. 47

31 NC 18/1/1162, Neville to Ida Chamberlain, 21 June 1940

32 Butler Mss. RAB G11/108, Butler to Cripps, 12 August 1940

33 J. W. Wheeler-Bennett, *Action This Day: Working with Churchill* (1968), Chap. 1, for this view, which is also reflected in Colville's diary for May and June

34 *Colville Diary*, 10 May 1940, p. 122

35 Roskill III, Hankey to Hoare, 12 May 1940

36 NC 1/23/80, Chamberlain to Dorothy Lloyd, 18 May 1940

37 NC 18/1/1158, Neville to Ida Chamberlain, 25 May 1940

38 NC 2/24A, 10 June 1940

39 NC 18/1/1161, Neville to Hilda Chamberlain, 15 June 1940

40 PRO FO 800/323, Halifax to Hoare, 19 June 1940

41 *Cadogan Diary*, 11 May 1940, p. 281, also editorial notes on p. 301

42 Alex Danchev, 'Dill', in J. Keegan (ed.), *Churchill's Generals* (1991), pp. 55–7. Danchev says that Dill did 'stand up' to Churchill, but not in the 'right fashion' – the result was the same as the more widely accepted version that Dill could not stand up to Churchill.

43 See above, Chap. 34, for the discussion on this point between Marder and Roskill – it is noticeable that Marder strictly applies his caveats about Pound not being a 'door-mat' only to the period before Churchill became Prime Minister, Marder, *From the Dardanelles to Oran*, pp. 171–8.

44 C. Barnett, *Engage the Enemy More Closely* (1991), takes this view.

45 Butler Mss. RAB G11/108, Butler to Cripps, 12 August 1940

46 Birmingham University Library, Avon Mss., AP 20/1/20A, Eden diary, 18 May 1940

47 *Ibid.*, 20 August 1940

48 *Ibid.*, 21 August 1940

49 Soames, pp. 291–2

50 *Churchill VI*, pp. 568–9, 574

51 J. Gooch, 'An Emblematic Prime Minister', *The Times Higher Education Supplement*, 1 July 1983, p. 13

52 NC 18/1/1161, Neville to Hilda Chamberlain, 15 June 1940

53 NC 2/24A, diary, 19 May 1940

54 PRO FO 371/24240, A3858/131/45, Churchill to Lothian, 17 June 1940

55 PRO Prem. 3/476/10, Lothian to Foreign Office, 27 June 1940; see also Reynolds, *The Creation of the Anglo-American Alliance*, pp. 112–13

56 T. Garton Ash, 'In the Churchill Museum', *The New York Review of Books*, 7 May 1987, p. 22

57 Reynolds, *The Creation of the Anglo-American Alliance*, p. 86. It will be obvious how indebted I am to Dr Reynolds's brilliant account, even if I take a more pessimistic view of the Americans than he does.

58 *Ibid.*, p. 114

59 *Ibid.*, pp. 115–20; also David G. Haguland, 'George C. Marshall and the Question of Military Aid to England, May–June 1940', in W. Laqueur (ed.), *The Second World War: Essays in Military and Political History* (1982), pp. 142–57

60 *Colville Diary*, 28 June 1940, p. 175

61 *Churchill VI*, Churchill to Lothian, 28 June 1940, p. 607

62 PRO FO 371/24240, A3852/3853/131/45, Lothian's telegram of 17 June, Foreign Office comments, and Churchill's correspondence with Halifax, 24, 28 June 1940; Foreign Office to Lothian, 30 June 1940

63 Reynolds, *The Creation of the Anglo-American Alliance*, pp. 116–18
64 *Churchill & Roosevelt I*, draft telegram, 5 July 1940, pp. 53–4
65 Reynolds, *The Creation of the Anglo-American Alliance*, pp. 23–5, 124–6
66 *Ibid.*, pp. 126–7
67 *Churchill & Roosevelt I*, Churchill to Roosevelt, 31 July 1940, pp. 56–7
68 PRO Cab. 66/10, WP(40)276, 18 July 1940
69 Reynolds, *The Creation of the Anglo-American Alliance*, pp. 122–3
70 *Hansard*, House of Commons, 20 August 1940
71 Reynolds, *The Creation of the Anglo-American Alliance*, pp. 127–31

38: The Liquidation of the British Empire

1 W. S. Churchill, *War Speeches, vol. II* (1975 edn) (hereinafter *War Speeches II*), p. 344
2 PRO Cab. 66/11, WP(40)324, memo. by Sir Kingsley Wood, 21 August 1940
3 Reynolds, *The Creation of the Anglo-American Alliance*, pp. 147–50
4 P. Rowland, *Lloyd George* (1975), p. 777
5 *Ibid.*, Lloyd George to the Duke of Bedford, 14 September 1940, p. 779
6 Lloyd George Mss. G81, memo., 12 September 1940; NC 2/24A, diary, 24 September 1940, for the Government intercepting his letters
7 NC 2/24A, diary, 26 July 1940
8 AP 20/1/20A, Eden diary, 25 August 1940, recording a conversation with Churchill on 22 August, part of which is in *Eden II*, p. 134
9 *Ibid.*, 21 August 1940
10 *Ibid.*, 22 August 1940, also in *Eden II*, p. 134
11 *Ibid.*, 2 September 1940
12 Boothby, pp. 166–7
13 *Amery Diary II*, editorial notes, pp. 603–8; *Colville Diary*, 26, 28, 29 July 1940, pp. 201, 203–4
14 Templewood Papers, XIII/7, Beaverbrook to Hoare, 14 July 1940. Butler Mss. RAB G11/108, Butler to Cripps, 12 August 1940
15 Templewood Papers, XIII/7, Butler to Hoare, 20 July 1940
16 AP 20/1/20A, Eden diary, 7 August 1940
17 *Ibid.*, 19 September 1940
18 *Ibid.*, 24 September 1940; also *Eden II*, p. 138 in part
19 NC 7/9/97, Chamberlain to Churchill, 22 September 1940
20 NC 2/24A, diary, 24 September 1940
21 *Ibid.*; Eden diary, 2 September 1940
22 Eden diary, 2 September 1940
23 Eden diary, 6 September 1940
24 *Colville Diary*, 10 August 1940, p. 215
25 Eden diary, 30 September 1940
26 PRO, Avon Mss., FO 954/7, M461/2, Churchill to Eden, 18 October 1942
27 Addison, p. 112
28 NC 2/24A, diary, 24 September 1940
29 Addison, Chap. 5, 'New Deal at Dunkirk', for this; see also Jefferys, pp. 54–6
30 Eden diary, 20 September 1940
31 Jefferys, p. 51
32 NC 7/9/101, 102, Churchill/Chamberlain corr., 30 September, 1 October 1940
33 NC 2/24A, diary, 4 October 1940
34 PRO FO 800/323, Halifax to Hoare, 29 November 1940
35 NC 18/1/1158, Neville to Ida Chamberlain, 25 May 1940
36 *War Speeches I*, pp. 299–301
37 *Colville Diary*, 9 October 1940, p. 259
38 *Ibid.*, 9 August 1940, p. 214
39 A. J. Marder, *Operation Menace* (Oxford, 1976), for this
40 G. Gorodetsky, *Stafford Cripps' Mission to Moscow 1940-42* (Cambridge, 1984), pp. 52–8
41 *Churchill VI*, pp. 889–90
42 *Hansard*, House of Commons, 5 November 1940
43 *Channon Diary*, 5 November 1940, p. 272
44 *Nicolson Diary II*, 5 November 1940, p. 125
45 *Colville Diary*, 1 November 1940, p. 283
46 Reynolds, *The Creation of the Anglo-American Alliance*, p. 150
47 PRO Prem. 3/486/1, fos 299–35, for the various drafts; *Cadogan Diary*, 11 November 1940, p. 335; Reynolds, *ibid.*, pp. 150–1
48 *Ibid.*; also *Churchill & Roosevelt I*, pp. 87–101
49 *Cadogan Diary*, p. 335
50 Reynolds, *The Creation of the Anglo-American Alliance*, p. 336, referring to p. 152, J. Lash, *Roosevelt and Churchill 1939-41: The Partnership that Saved the West* (NY, 1976), pp. 260–1, takes a different view, and his argument is, to my mind, more compelling than that of Dr Reynolds.
51 Lash, pp. 259–61; Reynolds, *ibid.*, pp. 153–4
52 Lash, p. 263
53 Reynolds, *The Creation of the Anglo-American Alliance*, p. 154
54 *Churchill & Roosevelt I*, Churchill to Roosevelt, 7 December 1940, pp. 102–9
55 Reynolds, *The Creation of the Anglo-American Alliance*, p. 156
56 Lash, pp. 263–4
57 PRO Prem. 4/17/1, Wood to Churchill, 23 December 1940; also Reynolds, p. 159
58 *Ibid.*; also in *Churchill & Roosevelt I*, p. 120
59 Taylor, *Beaverbrook*, Beaverbrook to Churchill, 26 December 1940, p. 439
60 *Churchill & Roosevelt I*, draft messages, Churchill to Roosevelt, 28, 31 December 1940, pp. 121–3
61 *Ibid.*, draft from Churchill to Roosevelt, 25 December 1940, p. 119
62 Reynolds, *The Creation of the Anglo-American Alliance*, pp. 159–60
63 *Finest Hour*, p. 366; Mr Gilbert, pp. 975–7, makes the same error
64 Reynolds, *The Creation of the Anglo-American Alliance*, p. 159
65 *Ibid.*, pp. 175–6; Rowland, p. 781; *Churchill & Roosevelt I*, pp. 114–16
66 Reynolds, *The Creation of the Anglo-American Alliance*, pp. 176–7; Birkenhead, *Halifax*, pp. 467–70; *Cadogan Diary*, 18–20 December 1940,

pp. 341–2; Halifax Mss. A7.8.3. Halifax diary, 17, 19, 20, 23 December 1940
67 Reynolds, *ibid.*, p. 176
68 *Cadogan Diary*, 20 December 1940, p. 342
69 Halifax Mss. A7.8.3. diary, 20 December 1940

39: 'Rogue Elephant'

1 Halifax Mss. A 4.410.5, Hankey to Halifax, 1 May 1941
2 *Colville Diary*, 20 September 1940, p. 245
3 *Eden II*, p. 129
4 *Ibid.*, pp. 129–30
5 AP 20/1/20A, Eden diary, 13 August 1940
6 Ismay, p. 195
7 *Finest Hour*, p. 344
8 *Eden II*, p. 132
9 Lamb, *Churchill as War Leader*, pp. 84–6, for a short and incisive account
10 *Finest Hour*, p. 347
11 *Ibid.*, Churchill to Eden, 3 November 1940, p. 345
12 *Colville Diary*, 6 January 1941, p. 330
13 Lamb, p. 88
14 W. S. Churchill, *The Second World War, vol. III: The Grand Alliance* (1975 edn) (hereinafter *The Grand Alliance*), Churchill to Eden, 20 February 1941, p. 47
15 *Colville Diary*, 5 March 1941, p. 361
16 Ponting, p. 212
17 Reynolds, *The Creation of the Anglo-American Alliance*, p. 162
18 *Ibid.*, pp. 164–5; A. P. Dobson, *US Wartime Aid to Britain 1940–46* (1986), p. 29
19 Ponting, pp. 213–14
20 Reynolds, *The Creation of the Anglo-American Alliance*, p. 167
21 PRO Cab. 65/17, WM(41)6, 20 February 1941
22 PRO Prem. 4/17/2, Churchill to Sir Kingsley Wood, 20 March 1941
23 *Churchill & Roosevelt I*, pp. 139–41; Reynolds, *The Creation of the Anglo-American Alliance*, pp. 169–73
24 Charmley, *Lord Lloyd*, p. 253
25 *Ibid.*, pp. 256–7; Reynolds, *The Creation of the Anglo-American Alliance*, pp. 169–70
26 R. Sherwood, *Roosevelt and Hopkins: An Intimate History* (NY, 1948), p. 243
27 AP 20/1/21, Eden diary, 14 April 1941
28 Sherwood, p. 237
29 *Ibid.*, p. 243
30 D. Day, *Menzies and Churchill at War: A Controversial New Account of the 1941 Struggle for Power* (Australia, 1986), p. 23
31 Lord Hankey Papers, diary, 22 April 1941
32 *Ibid.*, 28 April 1941
33 *Channon Diary*, 6 November 1940, p. 273
34 *Nicolson Diary II*, 1 April 1941, p. 155
35 Sherwood, p. 238
36 Day, p. 61
37 Martin diary, 2 June 1940, p. 11
38 *Ibid.*; E. Nel, *Mr Churchill's Secretary* (1961 edn), pp. 27–8
39 *Colville Diary*, 27 August 1940, p. 231

40 Halifax Mss. A4.410.5, Hankey to Halifax, 1 May 1941
41 Day, Menzies diary, 22 February 1941, p. 612
42 *Ibid.*, 14 April 1941, p. 127
43 *Ibid.*, 26 April 1941, pp. 152–3
44 *Ibid.*, pp. 154–5
45 Hankey Papers, diary, 1 May 1941
46 *Ibid.*
47 *Colville Diary*, 23 April 1941, p. 377
48 Day, Menzies diary, 26 April 1941, p. 152
49 W. H. Thompson, *I Was Churchill's Shadow* (1952), pp. 43, 61–5, for descriptions of some of these visits
50 *War Speeches II*, p. 389
51 Ponting, pp. 164–72, paints a more accurate portrait. See also P. Fussell, *Wartime* (Oxford, 1989), Chaps 2 and 11
52 Moran, Beaverbrook to Wilson, 19 April 1941, pp. 795–6
53 Day, Menzies diary, 1, 2 May 1941, pp. 166–7; Hankey Papers, diary, 1 May 1941
54 Hankey Papers, diary, 2 May 1941
55 Taylor (ed.), *My Darling Pussy*, Lloyd George to Frances Stevenson, 4 October 1940, p. 239
56 *Ibid.*, Lloyd George to Frances Stevenson, 22 October 1940, p. 245
57 *Ibid.*, p. 242
58 Day, Menzies diary, 26 April 1941, pp. 152–3
59 Rowland, p. 785
60 *Hansard*, House of Commons, 7 May 1941
61 *Channon Diary*, 7 May 1941, p. 303
62 *Nicolson Diary II*, 8 May 1941, p. 165
63 *Hansard*, House of Commons, 7 May 1941
64 Rowland, p. 786
65 Emrys-Evans Mss. 58235, Harvey to Evans, 3 June 1941, fo. 76
66 *Channon Diary*, 6 June 1941, p. 307
67 *Churchill VI*, Winston to Randolph Churchill, 8 June 1941, pp. 1104–6
68 *Nicolson Diary II*, 10 June 1941, p. 171; coming from so devoted an admirer of Churchill's this confirms the testimony in every other diary and set of correspondence
69 Emrys-Evans Mss. 58240, Cranborne to Emrys-Evans, 31 July 1941, fo. 36
70 *Colville Diary*, 19 June 1941, p. 402
71 Lamb, p. 126
72 *Ibid.*, pp. 93–7
73 A. Bryant, *The Turn of the Tide 1939–43* (1957) (hereinafter Alanbrooke diary I), 17 June 1941, p. 255
74 *Ibid.*
75 Eden diary, 24 September 1940
76 Danchev, 'Dill', in Keegan (ed.), *Churchill's Generals*, esp. p. 56
77 Alanbrooke diary I, 27 April 1941, p. 254
78 Danchev, p. 57
79 *Colville Diary*, 5 March 1941, p. 360
80 AP 20/1/21, Eden diary, 5 September 1941
81 *Ibid.*, 2 January 1941
82 *Colville Diary*, 12 June 1940, p. 399
83 Wilt, p. 154

40: In the House of Rimmon

1 *Colville Diary*, 21 June 1941, p. 404
2 *Ibid.*, 22 June 1940, p. 406
3 *War Speeches I*, pp. 452–3
4 *Churchill & Roosevelt I*, Churchill to Roosevelt, 29 April 1941, p. 176
5 *Ibid.*, Roosevelt to Churchill, 1 May 1941, pp. 178–80
6 *Churchill VI*, p. 1075
7 *Cadogan Diary*, 1 May 1941, p. 375
8 PRO Prem. 3/469, Churchill to Eden, 2 May 1941, fo. 350
9 *Colville Diary*, 2 May 1941, p. 382
10 PRO Prem. 3/469, draft fos 351–4, text printed in *Churchill & Roosevelt I*, pp. 181–2; it was sent to Roosevelt on 3 May
11 *Churchill & Roosevelt I*, Roosevelt to Churchill, 10 May 1941
12 S. Lawlor, 'Britain and the Russian Entry into the War', in Langhorne (ed.), *Diplomacy and Intelligence*, pp. 171–3
13 Gooch, p. 13
14 Gorodetsky, pp. 115–16
15 *Ibid.*, pp. 132–5
16 *Colville Diary*, 22 June 1941, p. 405
17 J. Beaumont, *Comrades in Arms* (1986), pp. 28–31
18 *Harvey Diary*, 9 July 1941, p. 17; *Cadogan Diary*, 9 July 1941, p. 392
19 *Colville Diary*, 12 December 1940, p. 310
20 *Ibid.*, 13 December 1940, p. 312
21 AP 20/1/21, Eden diary, 5 September 1941
22 *Ibid.*, 14 November 1941
23 For example *ibid.*, 8, 10 October 1941
24 James, *Victor Cazalet*, diary, 20 September 1941, p. 264
25 *Colville Diary*, 4 July 1941, p. 410
26 AP 20/1/21, Eden diary, 14 July 1941
27 Taylor, *Beaverbrook*, p. 475
28 *Ibid.*, pp. 476, 480–2
29 Carlton, pp. 184–5
30 *Ibid.*, J. Harvey (ed.), *The War Diaries of Oliver Harvey 1941–5* (1978) (hereinafter *Harvey Diary II*), 11 August 1941, p. 30, for one of many examples
31 *Harvey Diary II*, 8, 9 July 1941, pp. 16–17
32 British Library, Harvey Mss. diaries, 56398 (provisional number), 24 December 1941, for a passage which, unsurprisingly, is not in the published version
33 J. Costello, *Mask of Treachery* (1988), pp. 243–4
34 *Harvey Diary II*, 13 March 1943, p. 229
35 *Ibid.*, 12 August 1941, p. 31
36 *Eden II*, quoting his diary, 21 July 1941, p. 273
37 Lash, pp. 366–8
38 *Ibid.*, p. 336
39 *Colville Diary*, 1 August 1941, p. 423
40 Sherwood, p. 351
41 PRO Cab. 65/19, WM(41)84, 19 August 1941
42 W. Averell Harriman & E. Abel, *Special Envoy to Churchill and Stalin 1941–6* (NY, 1975), p. 75
43 Lash, p. 394
44 *Churchill VI*, p. 1148
45 Reynolds, *The Creation of the Anglo-American Alliance*, pp. 210–11; R. Dallek, *Franklin D. Roosevelt*

and American Foreign Policy 1932–45 (NY, 1979), pp. 277–80; Lash, pp. 391–2
46 *Churchill & Roosevelt I*, p. 227
47 *Cadogan Diary*, 10 August 1941, pp. 398–9; PRO Prem. 3/485/1, Churchill to Foreign Office, 11 August 1941
48 The text is at PRO Prem. 3/485/7, fo. 73
49 *Amery Diary II*, 10 August 1941, for the quotation, and 11 and 14 August 1941, p. 710
50 Dallek, pp. 284–5
51 *Churchill & Roosevelt I*, p. 229
52 *Ibid.*, pp. 229–30; Dallek, pp. 285–7; Lash, pp. 401–4
53 Dalton Diary, Mss., vol. 25, 25 August 1941
54 PRO Cab. 65/19, WM(41)84, 25 August 1941
55 PRO Prem. 3/224/2, Churchill to Hopkins, 28 August 1941, fo. 37; Sherwood, p. 373; Lash, p. 403; Reynolds, *The Creation of the Anglo-American Alliance*. p. 215
56 Sherwood, pp. 373–4
57 *Churchill VI*, Winston to Randolph Churchill, 29 August 1941
58 Dallek, pp. 287–8
59 Reynolds, *The Creation of the Anglo-American Alliance*, pp. 234–6; Dallek, pp. 300–3
60 Reynolds, *ibid.*, p. 237
61 *Cadogan Diary*, 11 August 1941, p. 399
62 Reynolds, *The Creation of the Anglo-American Alliance*, pp. 238–9

41: Between the Millstones

1 Thompson, *Churchill's Shadow*, p. 68; Martin, 3 August 1941, p. 56
2 Martin, 4 August 1941, p. 57
3 Sherwood, p. 350
4 *Churchill VI*, p. 1155
5 Martin, 5 August 1941, p. 57
6 Thompson, p. 69
7 *The Grand Alliance*, p. 282
8 *Cadogan Diary*, 6 August 1941, p. 396
9 *Ibid.*, 8 August 1941, pp. 396–7
10 Martin, 10 August 1941, p. 58
11 *Ibid.*
12 *Cadogan Diary*, 10 August 1941, p. 398
13 Martin, 10 August 1941, p. 58
14 Thompson, p. 73
15 *The Grand Alliance*, p. 284
16 *Amery Diary II*, 25 November 1941, p. 750
17 P. G. Boyle (ed.), *The Churchill–Eisenhower Correspondence 1953–5* (N. Carolina, 1990), Churchill to Eisenhower, 9 April 1953, p. 40
18 Garton Ash, 'In the Churchill Museum', p. 22
19 *Churchill II*, p. 283
20 PRO Prem. 3/177/1, M447/4, Churchill to Lord Cranborne, 20 April 1944
21 Franklin D. Roosevelt Library (hereinafter FDRL), Roosevelt Mss., Leahy to Roosevelt, 15 November 1944; Berle Mss., Box 58, Berle to Hull, September–December 1942, for expressions of this view
22 PRO, Avon Mss, FO 954/9, Fr/44/105, Attlee to Eden, 31 May 1944

23 PRO Prem. 3/182/4, Eden to Duff Cooper, 25 July 1944, for a full statement of Eden's policy
24 *Colville Diary*, 13 August 1941, p. 425
25 R. Douglas, *New Alliances 1940–41*, p. 79
26 Addison, p. 135
27 Taylor, *Beaverbrook*, p. 495 ff.
28 Addison, p. 137
29 *Ibid.*, pp. 138–41
30 AP 20/1/21, Eden diary, 6 August 1941
31 *Amery Diary II*, 18 December 1941, p. 754
32 *Colville Diary*, 16 July 1941, p. 415
33 *Ibid.*, 18 August 1941, p. 428
34 R. R. James, *Bob Boothby: A Portrait* (1991), Chap. 11, for a full account
35 Roskill II, diary, 15 October 1941, p. 529
36 James, *Victor Cazalet*, diary, 20 September 1941, p. 264
37 *Harvey Diary II*, 9 July 1941, p. 17
38 *Ibid.*, 12 July 1941, p. 19
39 Beaumont, pp. 53–7
40 *Eden II*, pp. 270–2; *Harvey Diary II*, July 1941, pp. 16–24; Douglas, pp. 76–7
41 *Harvey Diary II*, 20 July 1941, p. 22
42 Douglas, pp. 80–1
43 *Ibid.*, p. 79
44 *Harvey Diary II*, 25 August 1941, p. 36
45 PRO Cab. 65/23, WM(41)90, 5 September 1941
46 PRO Prem 3/170/1, Churchill to Eden, 4 December 1941, fo. 38
47 *Eden II*, diary, 14 November 1941, p. 282
48 Taylor, *Beaverbrook*, Macmillan to Beaverbrook, 13 October 1941, pp. 494–5
49 *Churchill & Roosevelt I*, Churchill to Roosevelt, 20 October 1941, pp. 252–7
50 PRO Cab. 65/24, WM(41)112, 12 November 1941
51 *Churchill & Roosevelt I*, Roosevelt to Churchill, 24 November 1941, pp. 275–6
52 *Churchill VI*, p. 1266
53 Harriman, p. 111
54 Accounts of that evening vary. Churchill's, in *The Grand Alliance*, p. 397, and Harriman, pp. 111–12, have a nice dramatic piece about Churchill mishearing the news, to which they had all been listening. I have preferred to follow the account at Martin, 7 December 1941, pp. 66–7, which, unlike the others, was written at the time.
55 *Churchill & Roosevelt I*, p. 281
56 *The Grand Alliance*, pp. 398–9

42: The Grand Alliance

1 *Churchill & Roosevelt I*, p. 283 and evidence cited there
2 *Ibid.*, Churchill to Roosevelt, 9 December 1941, pp. 283–4
3 *Ibid.*, pp. 284–6
4 *The Grand Alliance*, pp. 423–31, for Churchill's objectives
5 M. Howard, *Grand Strategy, vol. IV* (1972), introduction, for a brilliant survey of this topic
6 Alanbrooke diary I, p. 282
7 *The Grand Alliance*, p. 412; *Eden II*, pp. 295–7
8 *Harvey Diary II*, 22 September, 25 October 1941, pp. 45, 55
9 *Eden II*, pp. 318–19
10 *The Grand Alliance*, Churchill to Attlee, Churchill to Eden, 20 December 1941, p. 413
11 Nel, p. 27, for this
12 M. Gilbert, *Winston S. Churchill, vol. VII: The Road to Victory, 1941–5* (1986) (hereinafter *Churchill VII*), p. 28
13 *War Speeches II*, p. 145
14 *Eden II*, diary, 21 January 1942, p. 318
15 *Amery Diary II*, 16 January 1942, p. 763
16 G. M. Thompson, *Vote of Censure* (1968), p. 88
17 *Eden II*, p. 318
18 Moran, diary, 27 December 1941, pp. 17–18
19 *Harvey Diary II*, 3 August 1941, p. 26
20 *Amery Diary II*, 24 November 1941, p. 749
21 *Ibid.*, 23 December 1941, p. 755
22 *Harvey Diary II*, 10 October 1941, p. 51
23 Thompson, *Vote of Censure*, p. 92
24 *Amery Diary II*, 31 December 1941, pp. 758–9
25 *Nicolson Diary II*, 14 January 1942, p. 205
26 *Ibid.*, 20 January 1942, p. 206
27 *Channon Diary*, 20 January 1942, p. 317
28 Jefferys, pp. 89–90
29 *Nicolson Diary II*, 27 January 1942, p. 207; the speech itself is at *Hansard*, House of Commons, 27 January 1942
30 *Channon Diary*, 27 January 1942, p. 318
31 *Hansard*, House of Commons, 28 January 1942
32 Derby Mss., 920. Der/17/33, Clementine Churchill to Derby, 12 October 1942
33 *Nicolson Diary II*, 28, 29 January 1942, pp. 208–9
34 *Channon Diary*, 28 January 1942, p. 319
35 *Nicolson Diary II*, 29 January 1942, p. 209
36 *Hansard*, House of Commons, 29 January 1942
37 *Channon Diary*, 29 January 1942, p. 319
38 *Amery Diary II*, 29 January 1942, p. 767
39 Thompson, *Vote of Censure*, p. 99
40 *Harvey Diary II*, 21 October 1941, p. 54
41 Addison, pp. 195–220
42 *Harvey Diary II*, 17 September 1941, p. 43
43 AP 20/1/21, Eden diary, 14 November 1941
44 *Harvey Diary II*, 20 January 1942, p. 87
45 Taylor, *Beaverbrook*, p. 508
46 AP 20/1/22, Eden diary, 4 February 1942; *Harvey Diary II*, 4 February 1942, p. 91
47 *The Grand Alliance*, pp. 412–13; *Eden II*, pp. 318–20
48 *Churchill & Roosevelt I*, Churchill memo., 14 January 1942, p. 323
49 *Amery Diary II*, 31 December 1941, p. 757
50 *Harvey Diary II*, 2–6 February 1942, pp. 90–1
51 *Churchill & Roosevelt I*, Roosevelt to Churchill, 4 February 1942, pp. 344–5
52 *Amery Diary II*, 2 February 1942, p. 767
53 *Churchill & Roosevelt I*, Churchill to Roosevelt (not sent), 5 February 1942, pp. 345–6
54 Reynolds, *The Creation of the Anglo-American Alliance*, p. 255, for an excellent discussion
55 Addison, Chap. 4
56 *Harvey Diary II*, 3 August, 11 August, 10 October

1941, 20 January, 2–7 February 1942, pp. 26, 30, 51, 87, 90–2; AP 20/1/21, Eden diary, 5 September, 10 October 1941

57 *Eden II*, pp. 318–19

58 PRO FO 954/29A, Halifax to Eden, 5 January 1942

59 Jefferys, pp. 92–3

60 *Dalton Diary II*, 5 February 1942, p. 362

61 Jefferys, pp. 92–3

62 AP 20/1/21, Eden diary, 8 October 1941

63 Butler Mss, RAB G14, Butler to Hoare, 23 February 1942

64 K. Jefferys (ed.), *Labour and the Wartime Coalition: From the Diary of James Chuter Ede, 1941–5* (1987) (hereinafter *Chuter Ede Diary*), 23 February 1942, p. 54

65 *Amery Diary II*, 27 February 1944, p. 969

66 *Chuter Ede Diary*, 27 February 1942, p. 60

43: *Never Despair?*

1 Avon Mss. AP 20/39/151, Cranborne to Eden, 16 February 1942

2 *Harvey Diary II*, 12–16 February 1942, pp. 94–6

3 AP 20/39/151, Cranborne to Eden, 16 February 1942

4 James, *Victor Cazalet*, mid-February 1942, p. 273

5 *Nicolson Diary II*, 15 February 1942, p. 211

6 *Ibid.*, 12 February 1942, p. 211

7 *Channon Diary*, 17 February 1942, p. 322

8 *Nicolson Diary II*, 17 February 1942, p. 212

9 *Amery Diary II*, 17 February 1942, p. 775

10 *Harvey Diary II*, 17, 18 February 1942, pp. 97–8

11 AP 20/39/150, Harvey to Eden, 13 February 1942

12 Hankey Papers, Mss., HNKY 4/34, Hankey to Hoare, 12 March 1942; Roskill III, pp. 549–53

13 Thompson, *Vote of Censure*, p. 146

14 AP 20/1/22, Eden diary, 9 February 1942

15 *Harvey Diary II*, 16 February 1942, p. 97

16 Soames, p. 314

17 Eden diary, 27 February 1942

18 *Harvey Diary II*, 27 Feburary 1942, p. 102

19 Eden diary, 9 February 1942; *Harvey Diary II*, 9 February 1942, p. 93

20 Eden diary, 25 February 1942

21 *Ibid.*, 18 February 1942

22 Addison, pp. 202–6; Jefferys, p. 95; R. I. Moore, *Churchill, Cripps and India 1939–45* (Oxford, 1979), Chaps 3 and 4, for the details

23 Eden diary, 9 March 1942

24 Eden diary, 7 April 1942

25 AP 20/39/153, Cranborne to Eden, 5 April 1942

26 *Harvey Diary II*, 19 February 1942, p. 99

27 AP 20/1/21, Eden diary, 5 September 1941

28 *Harvey Diary II*, 9 October 1941, p. 50

29 AP 20/1/21, Eden diary, 5 September, 14 November 1941; AP 20/1/22, Eden diary, 18 February 1942

30 Eden diary, 16, 18 February 1942

31 *Harvey Diary II*, 18 February 1942, p. 98

32 *Ibid.*, 17 February 1942, p. 95

33 *Nicolson Diary II*, 12 February 1942, p. 211

34 *Ibid.*, 27 February 1942, p. 214

35 Moran, p. 32

36 AP 20/1/22, Eden diary, 28 February 1942

37 Taylor, *Beaverbrook*, p. 523

38 *Ibid.*, p. 525; Howard, *Grand Strategy IV*, for details of the American change of heart

39 *Churchill & Roosevelt I*, Churchill to Roosevelt, 4 March 1942, p. 380

40 *Ibid.*, Churchill to Roosevelt, 5 March 1942, p. 381

41 *Ibid.*, Churchill to Roosevelt, 7 March 1942, pp. 394–5

42 *Churchill & Roosevelt II*, p. 359

43 *Churchill & Roosevelt I*, Churchill/Roosevelt corr., 10, 11, 12 February 1942, pp. 356–60; see also Reynolds, *The Creation of the Anglo-American Alliance*, Chap. 10

44 Moore, pp. 36–42

45 *Ibid.*, pp. 43–6; *Amery Diary II*, pp. 606–10, 728–30

46 W. S. Churchill, *The Second World War, vol. IV: The Hinge of Fate* (1975 edn) (hereinafter *The Hinge of Fate*), p. 137

47 *Amery Diary II*, p. 729

48 *Harvey Diary II*, 9 February 1942, p. 93

49 *Amery Diary II*, 6 February 1942, p. 769

50 Harriman, p. 129; Moore, p. 63

51 *Amery Diary II*, 26 February 1942, p. 779

52 *Churchill & Roosevelt I*, Churchill to Roosevelt, 4 March 1942, pp. 374–5

53 *Harvey Diary II*, 5 March 1942, p. 105; *Cadogan Diary*, 5 March 1942, p. 440

54 *Amery Diary II*, 4 March 1942, p. 783

55 *Harvey Diary II*, 6 March 1942, p. 106

56 AP 20/1/22, Eden diary, 7 March 1942

57 *Churchill & Roosevelt I*, pp. 400–4

58 *The Hinge of Fate*, p. 140

59 *Churchill & Roosevelt I*, Roosevelt to Churchill, 7 March 1942, pp. 390–3

60 *Ibid.*, Roosevelt to Churchill, 9 March 1942, pp. 398–9

61 Howard, p. XVI; K. Sainsbury, *The North African Landings 1942* (1977), p. 87; Sherwood, pp. 518–60

62 *Churchill & Roosevelt I*, Roosevelt to Churchill, 1 April 1942, p. 437

63 Sherwood, pp. 523–4

64 Sainsbury, pp. 94–6; Howard, pp. XVI–XVIII

65 Sherwood, p. 526; *Harvey Diary II*, 9, 15, 26 March, 1, 8, April 1942, pp. 107–9, 113–15

66 *Harvey Diary II*, 15 March 1942, p. 109

67 *Cadogan Diary*, p. 443

68 Moore, pp. 83–116

69 *Ibid.*, pp. 110–16; *Amery Diary II*, pp. 734–6

70 Moore, p. 118

71 Sherwood, p. 524

72 *Churchill & Roosevelt I*, p. 445

73 *Ibid.*, Roosevelt to Churchill, 11 April 1942, pp. 446–7

74 *Ibid.*, p. 447

75 *Ibid.*, pp. 447–8; Sherwood, pp. 530–1

76 *Churchill & Roosevelt I*, p. 447

77 *Eden II*, diary, 27 April 1942, p. 326

78 *Nicolson Diary II*, 22 April 1942, p. 223

79 *Ibid.*, 23 April 1942, pp. 223–4
80 Roskill II, pp. 549–52
81 Thompson, *Vote of Censure*, pp. 144–5
82 *Ibid.*, p. 144
83 Jefferys, p. 224, for the figures; Thompson, *ibid.*, pp. 147–9
84 AP 20/39/118, Salisbury to Eden, 1 May 1942
85 *Eden II*, pp. 327–30; Sherwood, pp. 556–60, 563–9, 577–9; *Cadogan Diary*, pp. 449–56, entries for May and early June 1942
86 *The Hinge of Fate*, Chap. 20

44: The End of the Beginning

1 Thompson, *Vote of Censure*, pp. 174–5; Taylor, *Beaverbrook*, p. 530, doubts whether such a meeting took place.
2 Addison, pp. 206–7
3 *Nicolson Diary II*, 1 July 1942, p. 231
4 P. Halpern (ed.), *The Keyes Papers, vol. III: 1939–45* (1981), pp. 83–5
5 *Hore-Belisha Papers*, pp. 289–91
6 *Harvey Diary II*, 25 June 1942, p. 135
7 *Channon Diary*, 25 June 1942, p. 333; *Nicolson Diary II*, 24 June 1942, p. 230
8 *Channon Diary*, 24 June 1942, p. 333
9 *Ibid.*, 1 July 1942, p. 334
10 *Nicolson Diary II*, 1 July 1942, p. 231
11 *Channon Diary*, 1 July 1942, p. 231
12 Thompson, *Vote of Censure*, pp. 198–9
13 James, *Boothby*, p. 310
14 *Channon Diary*, 30 June, 2 July 1942, pp. 333–4; Jefferys, pp. 99–100
15 Thompson, *Vote of Censure*, p. 203
16 *Ibid.*, pp. 205–7
17 *Channon Diary*, 2 July 1942, p. 334
18 *The Hinge of Fate*, pp. 256–7
19 Moran, pp. 42–3
20 *Channon Diary*, 2 July 1942, p. 334
21 *The Hinge of Fate*, pp. 259–64
22 Moran, p. 43
23 *Nicolson Diary II*, 2 July 1942, p. 232
24 Jefferys, p. 100, quoting Cuthbert Headlam
25 Garton Ash, 'In the Churchill Museum', p. 23
26 The most recent works on this are: Mark A. Stoler, *The Politics of the Second Front* (NY, 1977); W. S. Dunn, *Second Front Now – 1943* (Alabama, 1980); and J. Grigg, *1943: The Victory That Never Was* (1980)
27 Garton Ash, 'In the Churchill Museum', p. 25
28 *The Hinge of Fate*, pp. 210–11, 220–23; *Churchill & Roosevelt I*, Churchill to Roosevelt, 28 May 1942, pp. 494–500
29 Sherwood, pp. 603–5; *Churchill & Roosevelt I*, p. 533; Howard, pp. 398–400; Sainsbury, pp. 108–14
30 *The Hinge of Fate*, pp. 289–92; Sherwood, pp. 607–12; Sainsbury, pp. 115–18; Howard, pp. 401–3; *Churchill & Roosevelt I*, Churchill to Roosevelt, 27 July 1942, pp. 541–3
31 P. Warner, 'Auchinleck', in Keegan (ed.), *Churchill's Generals*, pp. 138–40
32 *Harvey Diary II*, 30 July 1942, p. 145

33 Moran, diary, 3 August 1942, p. 49
34 *Cadogan Diary*, Cadogan to his wife, 3 August 1942, p. 466
35 L. Rowan, in Wheeler-Bennett (ed.), *Action This Day*, p. 265; *Eden II*, p. 339
36 For Auchinleck's defence see J. Connell, *Auchinleck* (1959), pp. 674–85; also Warner, 'Auchinleck', pp. 138–41
37 Alanbrooke diary I, p. 479; D. Fraser, *Alanbrooke* (1982), pp. 281–2; *The Hinge of Fate*, p. 297
38 Alanbrooke diary I, pp. 439–41; Fraser, pp. 283–4
39 Alanbrooke diary I, 6 August 1942, pp. 444–5
40 *Ibid.*; *The Hinge of Fate*, Churchill to Attlee, 6 August 1942, pp. 299–300
41 *Ibid.*, *The Hinge of Fate*, pp. 300–1; Fraser, pp. 285–6
42 Moran, diary, 4 August 1942, p. 50; see also *The Hinge of Fate*, p. 303
43 *The Hinge of Fate*, p. 308
44 Moran, diary, 12 August 1942, p. 54; cf. *The Hinge of Fate*, pp. 308–9
45 *The Hinge of Fate*, pp. 309–13
46 Moran, diary, 13 August 1942, p. 56
47 *Ibid.*, p. 57
48 Harriman, pp. 156–7. The official British version is at PRO Prem. 3/76A/12, fos 81–90. Churchill gives a sanitised version in *The Hinge of Fate*, pp. 315–16; Harriman gives a fuller one in *Special Envoy*, which is elaborated upon in *Churchill VII*, p. 185.
49 Moran, diary, 13 August 1942, p. 57
50 *The Hinge of Fate*, pp. 316–17
51 Moran, diary, 14 August 1942, pp. 58–9; other accounts upon which the following paragraphs are based are: Harriman, pp. 161–4; *The Hinge of Fate*, pp. 318–19; *Cadogan Diary*, p. 473
52 Harriman, p. 161
53 *The Hinge of Fate*, Churchill to Attlee and Roosevelt, 17 August 1942, p. 319; Moran, diary, 14 August 1942, p. 59
54 Moran, *ibid.*, pp. 60–1
55 *Churchill VII*, p. 193
56 Moran, diary, 15 August 1942, p. 63
57 *The Hinge of Fate*, p. 320. The official account and the interpreter's account of the formal and the informal meeting are in PRO Prem. 3/76A/12, fos 11–15, 35–7; I have also drawn on Moran's account of what Churchill told him, p. 63.
58 *Churchill & Roosevelt I*, Churchill to Roosevelt, 18 August 1942, p. 571
59 *The Hinge of Fate*, p. 322
60 *Churchill & Roosevelt I*, Churchill to Roosevelt, 26 August 1942, pp. 575–7
61 Charmley, *British Policy Towards General de Gaulle 1942–4*, pp. 2–6; Kersaudy, Chaps 6–8
62 Kersaudy, pp. 154–67
63 PRO Prem. 3/120/7, Churchill memos, 11 April, 30 May 1942, fos 285, 283
64 A. L. Funk, *Charles de Gaulle: The Crucial Years* (Oklahoma, 1959), Chap. 1
65 *Harvey Diary II*, 18 September, 2 October 1942, pp. 158, 166
66 PRO Prem. 4/100/7 ff., FM/42/229, Eden to

Churchill, 19 October 1942; Sir L. Woodward, *British Foreign Policy in the Second World War, vol. V* (1976) (hereinafter Woodward V), pp. 2–18

67 *Harvey Diary II*, 15, 19 October 1942, pp. 168, 170; PRO Prem. 4/100/7, M461/2, Churchill to Eden, 18 October 1942

68 Woodward V, pp. 18–19; *Harvey Diary II*, 3 November 1942, p. 175

69 *Harvey Diary II*, 23 October 1942, p. 171

70 *Ibid.*, 3 November 1942, p. 176

71 Butler Mss. RAB G14, fos 58–60, Butler notes, July 1942

72 *Dalton Diary II*, 24 August 1942, pp. 479–80

73 *The Hinge of Fate*, pp. 356–8

74 *Harvey Diary II*, 13 August 1942, pp. 149–50

75 *Ibid.*, 24 August 1942, p. 152

76 *Eden II*, pp. 342–3

77 *Harvey Diary II*, 2 October 1942, p. 165

78 Moran, diary, 30 September 1942, p. 76

79 *Ibid.*, p. 71

80 *War Speeches II*, pp. 342–4

45: The Road to Victory?

1 Charmley, *British Policy towards General de Gaulle 1942–4*, pp. 7–12; *The Hinge of Fate*, Chap 35; *Eden II*, pp. 353–9

2 Addison, pp. 215–23; Jefferys, pp. 117–21; K. Jefferys, 'British Politics and Social Policy during the Second World War', *Historical Journal* (1987); and the controversial discussion in C. Barnett, *The Audit of War* (1986).

3 Admiral Cunningham Papers, Add. Mss. 52570, Dill to Cunningham, 1 December 1942, fo. 137

4 D. Chandler *et al.* (eds), *The Eisenhower Papers, vol. II* (Baltimore, 1970), doc, 622–5, 689, FDRL, Roosevelt Mss., Map Room Papers, Box 105, TORCH (1) sec. 2, folder 4, tel. 518, Eisenhower to Marshall, 14 November 1942; *Churchill & Roosevelt II*, pp. 3–4

5 FDRL, Henry Wallace diary, microfilm, vol. 16, 12 November 1942

6 *Ibid.*, Map Room Papers, Box 167, folder 6, Warfare, NW Africa, 'TORCH', Leahy to Roosevelt, 15 November 1942

7 *Harvey Diary II*, Harvey to Eden, 14 November 1942, pp. 184–5

8 PRO FO 371/32139, Z9013/8325/17, Jebb minute, 16 November 1942 and accompanying correspondence

9 PRO FO 954/8, Attlee to Eden, 12 November 1942

10 *Ibid.*, Bracken to Eden, 14 November 1942

11 *Churchill & Roosevelt II*, Churchill to Roosevelt, 16 November 1942, p. 7

12 Sherwood, p. 653

13 FDRL, Map Room Papers, Casablanca conference, folder 6, Office of War Information, memo., Percy Winner to R. E. Sherwood, 1 January 1943

14 PRO Cab. 65/32, WM(42)156, 16 November 1942

15 *Cadogan Diary*, 14 November 1942, p. 469

16 *Eden II*, diary, 20 November 1942, pp. 350–1

17 AP 20/1/22, Eden diary, 20 November 1942, omitted from the version published in Eden's memoirs

18 *The Times*, 2 December 1942

19 PRO, War Office Papers, WO 204/303, Darlan to Leahy, 19 November 1942

20 PRO FO 954/29, pt II, Lyttelton's record of a meeting with Roosevelt, November 1942, fo. 673

21 Quai d'Orsay, Archives of the Free French Movement, CNF, vol. 130, fos 147–59

22 AP 20/1/22, Eden diary, 3 December 1942; needless to say this is not in the memoirs

23 PRO FO 371/32144, Z9714/8325/17 is full of such protests; see also *Hansard*, House of Commons, 26 November 1942; *The Times*, 2 and 3 December 1942; and *Daily Mirror*, 2 and 3 December 1942

24 PRO Cab. 66/32, WP(42)576, Eden to the Cabinet, 11 December 1942; FO 371/32146, Z10138, 10180, 10083/8325/17

25 PRO FO 954/16, pt I, Cranborne to Eden, 11 December 1942, fo. 213 ff.

26 *Churchill & Roosevelt II*, Churchill to Roosevelt, 11 December 1942, p. 71; for the circumstances surrounding the appointment of Macmillan see J. Charmley, 'Macmillan and the Making of the French Committee of Liberation', *International History Review* (1982)

27 *Nicolson Diary II*, 10 December 1942, pp. 266–7

28 *Harvey Diary II*, 11 December 1942, p. 198

29 PRO Prem. 3/422/12, fos 531–67. The published version is in C. Ede (ed.), *Secret Session Speeches* (1946), pp. 76–96. Because there is no *Hansard*, it is impossible to be sure which parts of the speech were delivered, but it is clear from the Harvey and Nicolson diaries that the passages about de Gaulle, omitted from Ede, were. *Churchill VII*, pp. 277–8, confirms this.

30 PRO Cab. 65/32, WM(42)171, 8 December 1942

31 *The Hinge of Fate*, p. 224

32 *Ibid.*, Churchill to Roosevelt, 27 August 1942, p. 341

33 *Ibid.*, p. 419

34 Howard, pp. 207–16

35 *The Hinge of Fate*, Churchill memo., 9 November 1942, p. 420

36 *Ibid.*, p. 421

37 *Churchill & Roosevelt II*, Churchill to Roosevelt, 18 November 1942, pp. 10–15

38 *Ibid.*, p. 20

39 *Ibid.*, Churchill to Roosevelt, 24 November 1942, pp. 38–9

40 *Ibid.*, p. 38

41 Garton Ash, pp. 24–5, comes to a similar conclusion after making very heavy weather of it all

42 H. Macmillan, *War Diaries* (1984), Macmillan to Churchill, 12 February 1943, p. 23

43 PRO FO 371/36199, Z117, Z474/117/69, Eden to Halifax, 2, 14 January 1943; *Harvey Diary II*, 25 December 1942, 5 January 1943, pp. 203–4, 209

44 Moran, diary, 13 January 1943, p. 79

45 *Ibid.*, 19 January 1943, pp. 79–80

46 *Churchill & Roosevelt II*, Churchill to Roosevelt, 2 December 1942, pp. 49–52
47 Macmillan, letter to Lady Dorothy Macmillan, 26 January 1943, p. 8
48 Howard, p. 241
49 T. Garton Ash, 'From World War to Cold War', *The New York Review of Books*, 11 June 1987, p. 45
50 Alanbrooke diary I, 3 December 1943, p. 529; cf. *The Hinge of Fate*, pp. 423–5
51 Alanbrooke diary I, 11 December 1942, pp. 534–5
52 *Ibid.*, 15, 16 December 1942, p. 535; *The Hinge of Fate*, p. 434
53 Alanbrooke diary I, p. 535
54 *Churchill & Roosevelt II*, pp. 117–18
55 *Ibid.*; Alanbrooke diary I, pp. 534–51
56 *The Hinge of Fate*, pp. 441–2
57 *Churchill & Roosevelt II*, p. 132
58 *Churchill VII*, p. 313
59 PRO Prem. 3/442/6, Macmillan to Eden, 17 January 1943
60 *Cadogan Diary*, 17–19 January 1943, pp. 504–5; *Harvey Diary II*, 18–20 January 1943, pp. 209–11
61 PRO Prem. 3/442/3, Churchill memo., 16 January 1943
62 PRO, Papers of the British Minister Resident at Allied Forces headquarters in Algiers, FO 660/86, Macmillan diary, 17–18 January 1943
63 *Ibid.*, memo., probably by Macmillan, on the 'Giraud–Roosevelt Arrangements', not dated but probably 28 January 1943. For the texts see A. L. Funk, 'The "Anfa Memorandum"', *Journal of Modern History* (1954)
64 PRO FO 371/36247, Z1269/1266/69, Churchill to Eden, 18 January 1943 from which the quotations are taken; they are omitted from the version in *The Hinge of Fate*, p. 440
65 PRO FO 371/36118, Z1648/5/69, minute by William Strang, February 1943
66 Addison, pp. 215–20; Jefferys, *Wartime Politics*, pp. 113–19
67 *Amery Diary II*, 30 November 1942, p. 848
68 Addison, p. 221
69 Jefferys, p. 119
70 Addison, p. 224
71 AP 20/10/679, Butler to Eden, 18 February 1943
72 Addison, pp. 230–1
73 FDRL, Private Secretary's Files, Box 49, Gt Britain, 1942, Beaverbrook to Roosevelt, 15 September 1942

46. Stresses and Strains

1 M. Kitchen, *British Policy towards the Soviet Union during the Second World War* (1986), pp. 145–8; Wilt, p. 94
2 Wilt, pp. 167–8
3 *Churchill & Roosevelt II*, p. 121; Howard, pp. 271–5; Wilt, pp. 197–200; Stoler, pp. 77–8
4 Wilt, p. 96
5 *The Hinge of Fate*, pp. 442–3
6 Stoler, p. 77
7 Howard, pp. 282–3
8 *Ibid.*, p. 285
9 *Churchill VII*, pp. 314–15
10 *Churchill & Roosevelt II*, Churchill to Roosevelt, 3 February 1943; Howard, p. 328
11 *Churchill & Roosevelt II*, Churchill to Roosevelt, 2 February 1943, pp. 129–32
12 *Eden II*, pp. 365–6
13 Stoler, p. 77
14 *Dalton Diary II*, 1–2 January 1944, p. 693
15 *Harvey Diary II*, 13–19 March 1943, pp. 228–34
16 Stoler, pp. 79–83
17 Kitchen, pp. 171–2
18 Stoler, p. 86
19 *Ibid.*, p. 88
20 Kitchen, p. 150
21 Sir L. Woodward, *British Foreign Policy in the Second World War, vol. II* (1971) (hereinafter Woodward II), M602/4, Churchill to Eden, 22 May 1944, p. 540
22 Eden, p. 364
23 *Churchill VII*, Jacob diary, 6 February 1943, p. 335
24 *Nicolson Diary II*, 11 February 1943, p. 279; Moran, p. 88
25 Birkenhead, *F.E.*, p. 551
26 Howard, pp. 328–9
27 *Churchill & Roosevelt II*, Roosevelt to Churchill, 5 March 1943, pp. 153–4
28 *Ibid.*, Churchill to Roosevelt, 4 March 1943, pp. 151–3
29 Kitchen, quoting Churchill to Cadogan, 2 April 1943, p. 153
30 *Ibid.*, p. 150
31 *Ibid.*, p. 151
32 J. Charmley, 'Harold Macmillan and the Making of the French Committee of Liberation', *International History Review* (1982), for the details
33 FDRL, Hopkins Mss., Sherwood Coll., Box 330, book 7, Murphy to Hopkins, 20 February 1943; Roosevelt to Eisenhower, 22 February 1943; Memorandum on Eden's visit to Washington, March 1943
34 PRO FO 371/36013, Z2933/51/17, PM/43/41, Eden to Churchill, 2 March 1943
35 *Ibid.*, M81/3, Churchill to Eden, 28 February 1943
36 FDRL, Map Room, Box 166, folder 3, pt II, tel. 805, 8 May 1943; *Churchill & Roosevelt II*, pp. 209–11
37 *Harvey Diary II*, 21 May 1943, p. 259; PRO FO 371/36047, Z6026/148/17, Churchill to Eden, 23 May 1943
38 *Harvey Diary II*, 24 May 1943, p. 260
39 *Ibid.*, pp. 259–60; PRO Cab. 65/38, WM(43)75, Eden to Churchill, 23 May 1943
40 PRO FO 371/36036, Z4105/77/17, minutes by various Foreign Office officials, early April 1943, outline British views of America's policy towards France
41 PRO Prem. 4/100/7, PM/42/229, Eden to Churchill, 19 October 1942
42 Kitchen, pp. 159–60
43 Howard, pp. 358–60
44 *Ibid.*, pp. 368–9
45 *Ibid.*, D72/3, Churchill to Chiefs of Staff, 8 April 1943, p. 369

46 *Churchill VII*, pp. 382–3
47 *Cadogan Diary*, p. 521
48 Kitchen, p. 153
49 *Ibid.*, pp. 154
50 *Harvey Diary II*, 16 March 1943, pp. 231–2; Sherwood, pp. 709–10
51 Woodward II, p. 625
52 *Ibid.*, pp. 626–7
53 *Ibid.*, p. 628; *Churchill & Roosevelt II*, Churchill to Roosevelt, 25 April 1943, pp. 193–5
54 *Churchill & Roosevelt II*, Churchill to Roosevelt, 28 April 1943, pp. 199–202
55 G. Ross, *The Foreign Office and the Kremlin* (Cambridge, 1984), Eden to Clark-Kerr, 4 February 1944, pp. 121–3
56 *Eden II*, p. 373
57 Stoler, p. 86
58 Ross, pp. 117–20
59 *Churchill VII*, pp. 317–18
60 Lamb, pp. 251–5
61 *Ibid.*, pp. 256–65; P. Auty & R. Clogg (eds), *British Policy towards Wartime Resistance in Yugoslavia and Greece* (1975), Chaps 3 & 4
62 Ross, pp. 119–20
63 Stoler, p. 90
64 Sherwood, pp. 717–18
65 Nel, p. 95
66 *Churchill & Roosevelt II*, Roosevelt to Churchill, 17 March 1943, pp. 156–7
67 Moran, p. 88
68 Stoler, p. 92
69 Moran, p. 96
70 *The Hinge of Fate*, pp. 512–15; Stoler, pp. 92–3; Alanbrooke diary I, 12 May 1943, pp. 613–14
71 Stoler, p. 93
72 Moran, p. 96
73 Alanbrooke diary I, p. 619; Stoler, pp. 93–4; Howard, pp. 423–34
74 Alanbrooke diary I, pp. 620–1; Stoler, pp. 93–4
75 Alanbrooke diary I, 24, 25 May 1943, pp. 626–7
76 Stoler, p. 95
77 Alanbrooke diary I, 24 May 1943, p. 626
78 Forster, p. 4
79 Moran, 25 May 1943, p. 97
80 *Ibid.*, p. 96
81 *Churchill & Roosevelt II*, p. 222

47: Brave New Worlds

1 Sir Ian Jacob, in Wheeler-Bennett (ed.), *Action This Day*, p. 206
2 Addison, pp. 220–5; Barnett, *Audit of War*, pp. 46–9
3 Addison, p. 230
4 Sir John Colville, in Wheeler-Bennett (ed.), *Action This Day*, p. 90
5 *Churchill & Roosevelt II*, memo. of meeting, 22 May 1943, pp. 225–6
6 *Ibid.*; Colville, in Wheeler-Bennett (ed.), *Action This Day*, pp. 95–7
7 Jacob, in *ibid.*, p. 207
8 Harriman, pp. 216–17; Dallek, pp. 403–4; K. Sainsbury, *The Turning Point* (1985), pp. 9–10

9 *Churchill & Roosevelt II*, Roosevelt to Churchill, 14, 17 June 1943, pp. 251, 255–7
10 *Ibid.*, unsent draft letter, Roosevelt to Churchill, 30 April 1943, pp. 203–5 and editorial notes
11 *Ibid.*, pp. 244–5
12 *Ibid.*, Churchill to Roosevelt, 12, 13 June 1943, pp. 245–7
13 *Ibid.*, Churchill to Roosevelt, 18 June 1943, p. 259
14 *Ibid.*, Roosevelt to Churchill, 18 June 1943, p. 261
15 *Ibid.*, p. 259
16 Harriman, pp. 216–17; Dallek, p. 403
17 *Churchill & Roosevelt II*, Churchill to Roosevelt, 25 June 1943, pp. 278–9
18 *Ibid.*, 28 June 1943, p. 283
19 *Ibid.*, Roosevelt to Churchill, 28 June 1943, pp. 283–4
20 *Ibid.*, Roosevelt to Churchill, 29 June 1943, pp. 285–8
21 *Harvey Diary II*, 26 June 1943, p. 269
22 *Churchill & Roosevelt II*, Churchill to Roosevelt, 28 June 1943, p. 285
23 Woodward II, Churchill to Clark-Kerr, 16 June 1943, p. 556
24 *Ibid.*, Churchill to Clark-Kerr, 29 June 1943, p. 561
25 *Ibid.*, p. 562
26 Ross, Eden to Churchill, 12 July 1943, pp. 133–4
27 PRO FO 371/36177, Z6247/30/69, Eden to Halifax, 29 May 1943
28 Macmillan, *War Diaries*, 4 June 1943, pp. 109–10
29 *Churchill & Roosevelt II*, Roosevelt to Churchill, 4 June 1943, pp. 229–30
30 *Ibid.*, Roosevelt to Churchill, 10 June 1943, pp. 235–7
31 *Harvey Diary II*, 12 May 1943, p. 256
32 *Ibid.*, 7 June 1943, p. 265
33 *Churchill & Roosevelt II*, Churchill to Roosevelt, 6 June 1943, pp. 231–2
34 Nicolson Mss., Balliol College, diary, 30 June 1943 and inset letter, Sir Osbert Lancaster to Nigel Nicolson, 19 April 1960
35 PRO FO 371/36178, Z7066/30/69, Churchill memo., June 1943
36 PRO Prem. 3/121/1, note, June 1943, fo. 15
37 PRO Prem. 3/181/7, T791/3, Churchill to Macmillan, 11 June 1943
38 PRO FO 954/8, T745/3, Churchill to Macmillan, 6 June 1943
39 PRO Prem. 3/181/7, tel. 926, Churchill to Macmillan, 15 June 1943
40 *Ibid.*, tel. 957, Macmillan to Churchill, 18 June 1943
41 *Churchill & Roosevelt II*, Roosevelt to Churchill, 17 June 1943, pp. 255–7
42 *Ibid.*, Churchill to Roosevelt, 18 June 1943, pp. 257–8; *Cadogan Diary*, 18 June 1943, p. 537
43 Macmillan, *War Diaries*, 18 June 1943, p. 125
44 *Harvey Diary II*, 14 June 1943, pp. 266–7
45 *Ibid.*, 6 July 1943, p. 271
46 *Ibid.*, Eden II, p. 396
47 *Eden II*, diary, 8 July 1943, p. 397

48 Colville, in Wheeler-Bennett (ed.), *Action This Day*, p. 108

49 PRO Cab. 65/35, WM(43)89, 28 June 1943

50 *Cadogan Diary*, 28 June 1943, p. 539

51 *Harvey Diary II*, 13 July 1943, p. 274

52 PRO FO 954/8, Fr/43/128A, Eden to Churchill, 13 July 1943; *Eden II*, pp. 397–8

53 PRO Prem. 3/181/8, Churchill draft Cabinet paper, 13 July 1943. There is an edited version at W. S. Churchill, *The Second World War, vol. V: Closing the Ring* (1975 edn) (hereinafter *Closing the Ring*), pp. 114–15

54 *Eden II*, p. 398

55 King's College, London, Alanbrooke Mss. 5/7, 28 June 1943, fo. 51 ff.

56 *Churchill & Roosevelt II*, Churchill to Roosevelt, 21 July 1943, pp. 354–6

57 *Ibid.*, Roosevelt to Churchill, 22 July 1943, pp. 339–40

58 PRO FO 371/36301, Z8226/6504/69, minute by William Strang, 15 July 1943

59 *Ibid.*, Z8250/6504/69, Eden minute, 25 July 1943

60 Moran, pp. 103–6

61 *Ibid.*, pp. 101–3; *Closing the Ring*, pp. 28–9

62 *Closing the Ring*, p. 415, Churchill to the COS, 2 July 1943

63 *Churchill VII*, pp. 439–41

64 Harriman, p. 216

65 Jacob, in Wheeler-Bennett (ed.), *Action This Day*, p. 185

66 Moran, p. 103

67 Stoler, quoting Stimson to Roosevelt, 1 July 1943, p. 99

68 Howard, p. 561

69 *Ibid.*, pp. 561–2

70 Stoler, p. 100

71 *Churchill VII*, pp. 442–3

72 *Ibid.*, p. 443

73 *Ibid.*, Churchill to COS, 19 July 1943, pp. 444–5; Howard, pp. 564–5

74 Howard, p. 564

75 Moran, p. 109

76 Alanbrooke diary I, p. 683

77 Moran, p. 109

78 Alanbrooke diary I, p. 687

79 *Closing the Ring*, pp. 49–51

80 Ismay, p. 308

81 Alanbrooke diary I, pp. 695–6

48: Between the Buffalo and the Bear

1 Jacob, in Wheeler-Bennett (ed.), *Action This Day*, p. 96

2 Howard, pp. 569–72; Alanbrooke diary I, pp. 698–718; J. Ehrman, *Grand Strategy, vol. V* (1956), pp. 53–63; Stoler, pp. 112–23; *Closing the Ring*, pp. 56–7

3 PRO Prem. 3/181/9, Churchill to Roosevelt, 15 August 1943 (this is not in the Kimball edition, the only case I can find of Homer nodding)

4 Foreign Relations of the United States (FRUS), *Conferences at Washington and Quebec* (Washington, 1970), p. 953, fn. 1

5 PRO FO 371/36303, Z9219/6504/69, Churchill to Attlee, 22 August 1943

6 PRO FO 371/36304, Z9382/6504/69, for the final texts, 26 August 1943

7 Harriman, p. 222

8 *Churchill VII*, p. 471

9 Harriman, pp. 225–6

10 *Eden II*, p. 404; see also *Cadogan Diary*, 27 August 1943, p. 556

11 Jacob, in Wheeler-Bennett (ed.), *Action This Day*, p. 182

12 *Ibid.*, pp. 183–4

13 *Cadogan Diary*, 29 August 1943, p. 556

14 Thompson, *I was Churchill's Shadow*, p. 119

15 *Eden II*, diary, 26 August 1943, p. 404

16 Nel, p. 114

17 *Cadogan Diary*, Cadogan to Lady Cadogan, 4 September 1943, p. 559

18 Soames, p. 340

19 *War Speeches II*, pp. 510–15

20 *Churchill & Roosevelt II*, Churchill memo., 9 September 1943, pp. 443–5

21 Sherwood, pp. 765–7; Sainsbury, *Turning Point*, pp. 128–30

22 *Churchill & Roosevelt II*, Churchill to Roosevelt, 20 October 1943, pp. 543–4

23 Sainsbury, *Turning Point*, pp. 126–7, 135–6, 138–41; Dallek, pp. 418–20, 423–6

24 Sainsbury, *ibid.*, pp. 91–3, 110, 115–19

25 *Ibid.*, pp. 124–6

26 A. Bryant, *Victory in the West* (1959), pp. 48–53; Ehrman, pp. 89–93; *Churchill VII*, Chap. 31

27 *Churchill & Roosevelt II*, Churchill to Roosevelt, 20, 23 October 1942, pp. 543–4, 555–8

28 Sainsbury, *Turning Point*, pp. 124–6, 130–4

29 *Ibid.*, pp. 222–4; *Churchill & Roosevelt II*, pp. 610–11

30 Ehrman, pp. 173–83; Sainsbury, *ibid.*, pp. 228–30, 242–6

31 Dallek, pp. 437–9; Sainsbury, *ibid.*, pp. 273–7

32 Macmillan, *War Diaries*, 16 November 1943, p. 294

33 Moran, p. 126

34 Harriman, p. 273; other accounts are at *Closing the Ring*, pp. 238–9; Sherwood, p. 790; and Moran, p. 141

35 Moran, diary, 29 November 1943, pp. 139–40

36 PRO FO 954/8, Fr/43/187, Macmillan to Eden, 21 December 1943

37 PRO FO 371/36136, Z12598/5/69, Churchill to Eden, 21 December 1943

38 *Churchill & Roosevelt II*, Churchill to Roosevelt, 21 December 1943, pp. 625–6

39 PRO Prem. 3/182/3, Churchill to Eden, 23, 24 December 1943

40 PRO FO 371/40390/U/93, 97/93/74; PRO, Committee on Armistice and Civil Affairs, Cab. 87/83, ACA(43)23, 20 December 1943, for the details

41 Harriman, pp. 227, 272–5; Stoler, pp. 153–4

42 Sainsbury, *Turning Point*, pp. 163–4, 225–7

43 Foreign Relations of the United States, *Conferences at Cairo and Tehran, 1943* (Washington, 1961), pp. 253–6; Stoler, p. 138

44 Dallek, pp. 434–5
45 Sainsbury, *Turning Point*, pp. 277–8
46 Dallek, p. 436; Sainsbury, *ibid.*, pp. 273–4
47 Sherwood, p. 796; Sainsbury, *ibid.*
48 Kitchen, pp. 176–7; Woodward II, pp. 649–52
49 Thompson, *I Was Churchill's Shadow*, pp. 129–31
50 *Ibid.*, pp. 131–2; Martin, pp. 131–2; *Colville Diary*, 25, 26 December 1943, p. 457; Macmillan, *War Diaries*, 25 December 1943, p. 338
51 Woodward II, pp. 650–1
52 *Ibid.*, p. 655; *Churchill VII*, pp. 614–15
53 Kitchen, p. 177
54 *Ibid.*, pp. 177–8
55 PRO Prem. 3/399/6, Churchill to Eden, 16 January 1944; Sir L. Woodward, *British Foreign Policy in the Second World War, vol. III* (1971) (hereinafter Woodward III), pp. 112–13
56 PRO Prem. 3/339/6, PM/44/21, Eden to Churchill, 25 January 1944
57 *Churchill & Roosevelt II*, Churchill to Roosevelt, 26 December 1943, pp. 632–3; Ehrman, pp. 215–19
58 *Ibid.*, Roosevelt to Churchill, 27 December 1943, p. 636
59 Ehrman, pp. 226–9
60 *Colville Diary*, 4 January 1944, p. 462; Woodward III, pp. 156–7; *Churchill & Roosevelt II*, Churchill to Roosevelt, 6 January 1944, pp. 650–1
61 *Churchill & Roosevelt II*, Churchill to Roosevelt, 10 January 1944, pp. 660–1
62 Lamb, pp. 261–3; Woodward III, pp. 308–11
63 PRO Prem. 3/273/1, Churchill to Cooper, 14 October 1943
64 PRO FO 954/9, Cooper to Eden, 16, 17 January 1944
65 *Churchill & Roosevelt II*, Churchill to Roosevelt, 30 January 1944, pp. 691–3
66 *Churchill VII*, p. 646

49: Appeasement Mk II

1 PRO FO 954/20A, O'Malley to Eden, 22 January 1944
2 PRO Cab. 65/45, WM(44)21, 15 February 1944
3 *Churchill & Roosevelt II*, Churchill to Roosevelt, 20 February 1944, pp. 735–9
4 *Ibid.*, Churchill to Roosevelt, 20 February 1944, p. 735
5 *Harvey Diary II*, 8 February 1944, p. 330
6 *Ibid.*
7 PRO Cab. 65/45, WM(44)11, 25 January 1944
8 R. Douglas, *From War to Cold War 1942–8* (1981), p. 28
9 W. Kimball (ed.), *Churchill & Roosevelt. The Complete Correspondence, vol. III: The Alliance Declining, February 1944–April 1945* (Princeton, 1984) (hereinafter *Churchill & Roosevelt III*), Churchill to Roosevelt, 4 March 1944, p. 21
10 *Ibid.*, Churchill to Roosevelt, 7 March 1944, pp. 29–30
11 *Colville Diary*, 4 March 1944, p. 476
12 *Harvey Diary II*, 29 February, 2, 10 March 1944, pp. 334–5
13 *Churchill & Roosevelt II*, Roosevelt to Churchill, 7 February 1944, p. 709
14 *Ibid.*, Roosevelt to Churchill, 29 February 1944, pp. 766–7
15 PRO FO 371/40363, U2718/14/74, minute by J. G. Ward, 5 April 1944
16 *Churchill & Roosevelt III*, Roosevelt to Churchill, 29 February, 3 March 1944, pp. 3–10, 14
17 *Ibid.*, Churchill to Roosevelt, 4 March 1944, pp. 17–18
18 *Ibid.*, Churchill to Roosevelt, 9 March 1944, pp. 35–7
19 *Ibid.*, Churchill to Roosevelt, 4 March 1944, p. 18
20 *Ibid.*, p. 17
21 *Colville Diary*, 18 February 1944, p. 474
22 Jefferys, *Wartime Politics*, pp. 150–6; Addison, pp. 248–50
23 AP 20/1/24, Eden diary, 16, 24 March 1944
24 Jefferys, p. 157
25 AP 20/1/24, Eden diary, 18 February 1944
26 *Colville Diary*, 18 February 1944, p. 474
27 AP 20/1/24, Eden diary, 18 February 1944
28 *Ibid.*, 18 January 1944
29 *Ibid.*, 24 January 1944
30 *Ibid.*, 18 February 1944
31 *Cadogan Diary*, editor's note, p. 612
32 *Ibid.*
33 *Eden II*, p. 449; *Harvey Diary II*, 10, 28 March, 7 April 1944, pp. 335, 337; *Colville Diary*, 22 March 1944, p. 479
34 *War Speeches III*, pp. 104–15
35 Woodward III, p. 181
36 *Ibid.*, p. 182
37 *Churchill & Roosevelt III*, Churchill to Roosevelt, 1 April 1944, pp. 68–9
38 *Ibid.*, pp. 69–70
39 *Eden II*, p. 439
40 Ross, 'Foreign Office Paper on Post-War Soviet Policy', 29 April 1944, pp. 147–55
41 Charmley, *Duff Cooper*, Chap. 16
42 *Ibid.*, pp. 165–9
43 *Ibid.*, pp. 184–6, for a summary of WP(44)409
44 PRO FO 954/25A, Cooper to Eden, 22 April 1942, fo. 112
45 J. Charmley (ed.), *Descent to Suez: The Diaries of Sir Evelyn Shuckburgh 1951–6* (1987), pp. 12–15
46 *Ibid.*, p. 184; also J. Charmley, 'Duff Cooper and Western European Union', *Review of International Studies* (1985)
47 PRO Cab. 66, WP(44)409, Eden to Cooper, 31 July 1944
48 Carlton, pp. 236–7
49 *Churchill VII*, pp. 753–4
50 Woodward III, M497/4, Churchill to Eden, 4 May 1944, pp. 115–16
51 *Churchill VII*, M483/4, Churchill to Eden, 2 May 1944, p. 754
52 Woodward III, M498/4, Churchill to Eden, 4 May 1944, p. 116
53 *Ibid.*
54 *Ibid.*
55 *Churchill & Roosevelt III*, Churchill to Roosevelt, 31 May 1944, pp. 153–4

56 Woodward III, p. 117
57 *Churchill & Roosevelt III*, Roosevelt to Churchill, 10 June 1944, p. 177
58 *Churchill VII*, p. 787
59 *Eden II*, p. 452
60 P. Dixon (ed.), *Double Diploma: The Life of Sir Pierson Dixon* (1968), diary, 3 June 1944, pp. 89–90
61 *Colville Diary*, 1 January 1944, p. 461
62 PRO Prem. 3/177/3, PM/44/327, Eden to Churchill, 9 May 1944
63 PRO FO 371/42134, Z3307/1/69, Cooper to Churchill, 25 April 1944
64 PRO FO 371/41879, Z3306/12/17, Cadogan to Eden, 9 May 1944
65 PRO Prem. 3/177/3, M541/4, Churchill to Eden, 10 May 1944
66 *Churchill & Roosevelt III*, Churchill to Roosevelt, 26 May 1944, p. 145
67 *Ibid.*, Roosevelt to Churchill, 27 May 1944, p. 146
68 Duff Cooper, pp. 327–9
69 FDRL, Map Room, Box 31, 011, French Civil Affairs, tel. M18783, Harriman to Roosevelt, 29 May 1944
70 *Closing the Ring*, p. 404, gives Churchill's account; de Gaulle's is at C. de Gaulle, *Mémoires de Guerre, tome II, l'unité* (Paris, 1956), pp. 223–4. The official British account is at PRO FO 371/42000, Z4379/3636/17.
71 J. van der Poel (ed.), *Selections from the Smuts Papers, vol. VI* (Cambridge, 1973), pp. 456–60
72 *Eden II*, p. 453
73 *Ibid.*
74 *Ibid.*; also Pierson Dixon Papers, Dixon Mss., diary, 4 June 1944 (courtesy of Mr Pierson Dixon)
75 PRO Prem. 3/177/4, Churchill minute, 7 June 1944, fo. 488
76 Dixon diary, 6 June 1944
77 PRO FO 954/9, Fr/44/175, Dixon to Eden, 6 June 1944; see also AP 20/1/24, Eden diary, 6, 7 June 1944
78 PRO FO 954/9, Fr/44/125, Bracken to Eden, 6 June 1944

50: 'Stand Up and Beg?'

1 AP 20/10/680A, Dick Law to Eden, 8 August 1943
2 *Colville Diary*, 2 April 1944, p. 482
3 *Churchill & Roosevelt II*, Roosevelt to Churchill, 20 September 1977 [*sic* for 1943], 21 September, 6 November 1943, pp. 456, 458–9, 587
4 *Ibid.*, editorial notes, p. 697
5 Woodward II, Churchill minute, 12 October 1943, p. 512
6 *Churchill & Roosevelt III*, Churchill to Roosevelt, 8 March 1944, pp. 31–3
7 *Ibid.*, Roosevelt to Churchill, 7 March 1944, pp. 28–9; Churchill to Roosevelt, 8 March 1944, pp. 31–3
8 PRO Prem. 3/243/12, M.705/4, Churchill to Eden, 10 June 1944; Churchill to Charles, 10 June 1944; Churchill to Macfarlane, 11 June 1944

9 *Churchill & Roosevelt III*, Churchill to Roosevelt, 10 June 1944, pp. 176–7
10 A. Bryant (ed.), *Triumph in the West 1943–6* (1959) (hereafter Alanbrooke diary II), 13 June 1944, pp. 215–17; Ehrman, pp. 268–9
11 Macmillan, *War Diaries*, p. 470, for text; Ehrman, pp. 266–7, for context
12 *Churchill & Roosevelt III*, editorial notes, pp. 197–8; C. Wilmot, *The Struggle for Europe* (1952), is the *locus classicus* for this view
13 F. W. D. Deakin, 'The Myth of an Allied Landing in the Balkans during the Second World War . . .', in Auty and Clogg (eds), *British Policy towards Wartime Resistance in Yugoslavia and Greece*, pp. 93–4; this was also the theme of the third programme of Martin Gilbert's 'Television biography' of Churchill, shown on the BBC on 29 January 1992
14 Alanbrooke diary II, p. 222
15 Macmillan, *War Diaries*, notes, 22 June 1944, p. 473
16 Woodward III, pp. 324–32; E. Barker, 'British Decision-making over Yugoslavia', in Auty & Clogg (eds), *British Policy towards Wartime Resistance in Yugoslavia and Greece*, pp. 46–8; *Churchill & Roosevelt III*, Churchill to Roosevelt, 18 May 1944, pp. 131–2
17 Lamb, pp. 264–75
18 *Churchill & Roosevelt III*, editorial notes, p. 178
19 *Ibid.*, Roosevelt to Churchill, 12 June 1944, p. 182
20 *Ibid.*, Roosevelt to Churchill, 22 June 1944, p. 201
21 *Ibid.*, Churchill to Roosevelt, 23 June 1944, pp. 202–3
22 Macmillan, *War Diaries*, note, 25 June 1944, p. 474
23 Alanbrooke diary II, p. 222–3
24 Ehrman, pp. 349–50
25 *Ibid.*, p. 350
26 *Churchill & Roosevelt III*, Churchill to Roosevelt, 25 June 1944, p. 207
27 *Ibid.*, Churchill to Roosevelt, 28 June 1944, pp. 212–13
28 *Ibid.*, Churchill to Roosevelt, 28 June 1944, pp. 214–20
29 *Ibid.*, Roosevelt to Churchill, 28 June 1944, p. 213
30 Alanbrooke diary II, 28 June 1944, p. 224
31 Macmillan, *War Diaries*, note, 28 June 1944, p. 476
32 *Churchill & Roosevelt III*, Roosevelt to Churchill, 29 June 1944, pp. 221–3
33 Macmillan, *War Diaries*, p. 476
34 *Churchill & Roosevelt III*, draft letter from Churchill to Roosevelt, 30 June 1944, pp. 225–6
35 Alanbrooke diary II, 30 June 1944, p. 226
36 Macmillan, *War Diaries*, p. 476
37 *Churchill & Roosevelt III*, Churchill to Roosevelt, 1 July 1944, pp. 227–9; Ehrman, pp. 355–8
38 Macmillan, *War Diaries*, p. 476
39 J. M. Blum, *From the Morgenthau Diaries, vol. III: Years of War 1941–5* (NY, 1967), p. 373, cited by Garton Ash in 'In the Churchill Museum', p. 25
40 PRO, Papers of the British Minister Resident in North Africa and the British Ambassador in Algiers 1944, FO 660/199, Cooper's marginalia
41 Charmley, *Duff Cooper*, pp. 186–7

42 *Ibid.*, pp. 187–8

43 AP 20/1/24, Eden diary, 1 July 1944

44 Charmley, *British Policy towards General de Gaulle 1942–4*, Chap. 16

45 *Eden II*, p. 462

46 AP 20/1/24, Eden diary, 24 April 1944

47 *Ibid.*, 1 May 1944; also at *Eden II*, p. 442

48 *Ibid.*, 6 July 1944, for the full account, which is bowdlerised at *Eden II*, pp. 461–2

49 Alanbrooke diary II, 1 May 1944, p. 185

50 *Cadogan Diary*, 12 April 1944, p. 618

51 *Ibid.*, 19 April 1944, p. 621

52 *Ibid.*, 7 July 1944, pp. 645–6; AP 20/1/24, Eden diary, 6–7 July 1944

53 Woodward III, pp. 191–2; *Churchill & Roosevelt III*, editorial notes, p. 234

54 *Eden II*, p. 464

55 AP 20/1/24, Eden diary, 1 July 1944

56 PRO Cab. 65/47, WM(44)95, 24 July 1944

57 *Churchill & Roosevelt III*, Churchill to Roosevelt, 29 July 1944, pp. 261–2

58 AP 20/1/24, Eden diary, 30 July 1944

59 *Churchill & Roosevelt III*, Churchill to Roosevelt, 10 August 1944, pp. 269–70

60 Woodward III, pp. 201–2

61 *Ibid.*, pp. 203–4, footnote; Ehrman, pp. 369–70; J. Garliński, *Poland in the Second World War* (1985), pp. 280–3

62 *Churchill & Roosevelt III*, pp. 259–60

63 *Ibid.*, Churchill to Roosevelt, 18 August 1944, pp. 281–2

64 Garliński, pp. 293–4

65 *Churchill & Roosevelt III*, Churchill to Roosevelt, 18 August 1944, p. 282

66 *Ibid.*, editorial notes, p. 283

67 *Ibid.*, Churchill to Roosevelt, 25 August 1944, p. 295

68 *Ibid.*, Roosevelt to Churchill, 26 August 1944, p. 296

69 *Ibid.*, Churchill to Roosevelt, 5 August 1944, p. 265

70 *Ibid.*, editorial notes, p. 266

71 *Eden II*, p. 459

72 Barker, 'British Decision-making over Yugoslavia', in Auty & Clogg (eds), *British Policy towards Wartime Resistance in Yugoslavia and Greece*, citing WP (44)304, 7 June 1944, p. 48

73 Woodward III, pp. 324–5

74 *Churchill & Roosevelt III*, Churchill to Roosevelt, 14 August 1944, p. 275

75 Woodward III, pp. 339–42; Macmillan, *War Diaries*, 12, 13 August 1944, pp. 501–2

76 Woodward III, Eden to Churchill, 15 September 1944, p. 344

77 *Ibid.*, pp. 386–7

78 *Churchill & Roosevelt III*, Churchill to Roosevelt, 17 August 1944, pp. 278–9

79 *Ibid.*, editorial notes, p. 278

80 Macmillan, *War Diaries*, 25 July 1944, p. 491

81 *Churchill & Roosevelt III*, Roosevelt to Churchill, 26 August 1944, p. 297

82 *Eden II*, diary, 30 June 1944, p. 465

83 *Channon Diary*, 6 September 1944, p. 393

84 *Eden II*, diary, 17 July 1944, p. 463

85 *Ibid.*, diary, 4 September 1944, p. 473

86 *Colville Diary*, 7 September 1944, p. 510

51: Victory at all Costs?

1 Moran, diary, 20 September 1944, p. 183

2 *Colville Diary*, 9 September 1944, p. 511

3 *Churchill & Roosevelt III*, editorial notes, p. 317; Moran, diary, 13 September 1944, pp. 177–9; W. S. Churchill, *The Second World War, vol. VI: Triumph and Tragedy* (1975 edn) (hereinafter *Triumph and Tragedy*), p. 101

4 Moran, diary, 13 September 1944, p. 177

5 *Triumph and Tragedy*, p. 101; *Churchill & Roosevelt III*, p. 317

6 Moran, pp. 177–9

7 *Eden II*, p. 476

8 AP 20/1/24, Eden diary, 11 July 1944

9 *Ibid.*, loose page, undated, inserted in the diary, but obviously dating from the time when Eden was composing his memoirs

10 Moran, diary, 22 September 1944, p. 185

11 *Harvey Diary II*, 15 July 1944, p. 348

12 *Churchill VII*, p. 959

13 *Ibid.*, Eden to Churchill, 12 September 1944, p. 963

14 *Ibid.*, Churchill to Eden, 13 September 1944, p. 963

15 D. Dilks, 'British Political Aims in Central, Eastern and Southern Europe, 1944', in F. W. Deakin *et al.* (eds), *British Political and Military Strategy in Central, Eastern and Southern Europe in 1944* (1988), pp. 33–7

16 *Churchill & Roosevelt III*, editorial notes, pp. 348–9

17 K. Sainsbury, 'Central and Eastern Europe at the Quebec Conference', in Deakin *et al.* (eds), *British Political and Military Strategy...*, pp. 55–8

18 PRO Prem. 3/329/7, Churchill to the War Cabinet, 12 September 1944

19 *Churchill & Roosevelt III*, editorial notes, p. 343; Sainsbury, pp. 60–2; Douglas, pp. 43–4

20 *Churchill & Roosevelt III*, unsent draft, Roosevelt to Churchill, 4 October 1944, p. 343

21 *Ibid.*, Roosevelt to Churchill, 4 October 1943, p. 344; Douglas, p. 44

22 Ross, *The Foreign Office and the Kremlin*, p. 176, for the official text; the full record is at PRO Prem. 3/434/7 and at FO 800/302. Churchill gives an anodyne version at *Triumph and Tragedy*, pp. 149–50; see also G. Ross, 'The Moscow Conference of October 1944', in Deakin *et al.* (eds), *British Political and Military Strategy...*, pp. 72–3.

23 Ross, p. 177

24 *Triumph and Tragedy*, p. 150, for the percentages

25 *Churchill & Roosevelt III*, editorial notes, p. 351

26 *Ibid.*, p. 350

27 *Ibid.*

28 A. Polonsky (ed.), *The Great Powers and the Polish Question 1941–5* (1976), p. 220

29 PRO, Inverchapel Papers, FO 800/302, 9 October 1944

30 *Churchill & Roosevelt III*, Churchill to Roosevelt, 11 October 1944, p. 353
31 *Churchill VII*, p. 992, fn. 1
32 *Eden II*, diary, 10 October 1944, p. 483
33 *Triumph and Tragedy*, pp. 152–3
34 Polonsky, Eden to Foreign Office, 12 October 1944, pp. 220–1
35 *Ibid.*, pp. 221–4
36 *Churchill & Roosevelt III*, Churchill to Roosevelt, 18 October 1944, pp. 358–61
37 *Documents on Polish-Soviet Relations, 1941–5, vol. II* (1967), pp. 423–4
38 *Triumph and Tragedy*, p. 159
39 Moran, diary, 16 October 1944, pp. 202–3
40 *Churchill & Roosevelt III*, Churchill to Roosevelt, 14 October 1944, pp. 355–6
41 *Ibid.*, Roosevelt to Churchill, 19 October 1944, p. 362
42 *F[oreign] R[elations] [of the] U[nited] S[tates] 1944: vol. III* (1968), pp. 741–2
43 PRO FO 660/281/403/20–22/44, minutes by Peake and Cooper, 20, 21 October 1944; FO 660/221, 83/20/44, Cooper to Foreign Office, 21 October 1944.
44 *Churchill & Roosevelt III*, Roosevelt to Churchill, 22 October 1944, p. 366; FDRL Map Room Papers, Box 011, France (1) sec. 2, civil affairs, memo. by Hopkins, 23 October 1944
45 *Harvey Diary II*, 11 November 1944, pp. 365–6
46 British Library, Harvey Mss., Harvey to Pierson Dixon, 4 November 1944
47 *Churchill & Roosevelt III*, Churchill to Roosevelt, 8 November 1944, p. 385
48 *Ibid.*, Roosevelt to Churchill, 24 November 1944, pp. 407–8
49 *Ibid.*, Churchill to Roosevelt, 26 November 1944, pp. 413–16
50 *Ibid.*, Churchill to Roosevelt, 30 November 1944, pp. 424–5
51 *Churchill VII*, p. 1081
52 *Churchill & Roosevelt III*, Churchill to Roosevelt, 6 December 1944, pp. 434–6
53 *Churchill VII*, M1070/4, Churchill to Eden, 4 November 1944, p. 1055
54 *Colville diary*, 4 December 1944, p. 532; the text of the letter is at *Churchill VII*, p. 1085
55 Dixon diary, 4 December 1944
56 *Colville Diary*, 4 December 1944, p. 533
57 *Triumph and Tragedy*, pp. 188–9
58 *Ibid.*, p. 189
59 H. G. Nicholas (ed.), *Washington Despatches 1941–5* (1981), 27 November 1944, pp. 464–5
60 *Ibid.*, 2 December 1944, p. 468
61 *Ibid.*, 10 December 1944, p. 472
62 *Churchill & Roosevelt III*, Churchill to Roosevelt, 6 December 1944, pp. 437–9
63 Moran, pp. 206–7
64 PRO Cab. 65/48, WM (44) 162, 7 December 1944
65 *The Hinge of Fate*, Churchill to Eden, 21 October 1942, pp. 360–1

52: Anglo-America?

1 Nicholas, p. 474
2 PRO Prem. 4/33/5, M311/5, Churchill to Eden, 8 April 1945
3 Woodward III, pp. 409–11
4 PRO Prem. 3/212/9, Churchill to Eden, 6 October 1944
5 *Colville Diary*, 7 December 1944, p. 533
6 PRO FO 954/11, Attlee to Eden, 7 December 1944
7 *Dalton Diary II*, 8 December 1944, p. 814
8 *Hansard*, House of Commons, 8 December 1944
9 *Nicolson Diary II*, Nicolson to his sons, 8 December 1944, p. 416
10 Macmillan, *War Diaries*, 8 December 1944, p. 599
11 *Ibid.*, 8–10 December 1944, pp. 599–601; Woodward III, pp. 414–18
12 *Churchill & Roosevelt III*, Churchill to Roosevelt, 10 December 1944, pp. 453–4
13 *Ibid.*, Churchill to Hopkins, 10 December 1944, p. 451
14 PRO Prem. 3/212/5, draft message, Churchill to Roosevelt, 10 December 1944. This is not in the Kimball edition, which makes it only the second case of Homer nodding that I have found.
15 *Ibid.*, note 'dictated by PM', 10 December 1944
16 Sherwood, p. 840
17 *Churchill & Roosevelt III*, Churchill to Hopkins, 11 December 1944, p. 452
18 Sherwood, p. 841
19 *Churchill & Roosevelt III*, Roosevelt to Churchill, 13 December 1944, pp. 455–6
20 PRO FO 954/11, Macmillan to Eden, 11 December 1944; Macmillan, *War Diaries*, 11 December 1944, p. 602
21 PRO Cab. 65/48, WM(44)169, 16 December 1944; Woodward III, pp. 415–17
22 Woodward III, p. 417
23 *Churchill & Roosevelt III*, Churchill to Roosevelt, 15 December 1944, pp. 457–8
24 *Cadogan Diary*, 21 December 1944, p. 689
25 *Eden II*, diary, 21 December 1944, pp. 499–500
26 *Colville Diary*, 21 December 1944, p. 537
27 *Ibid.*, 14 December 1944, pp. 535–6
28 Polonsky, Churchill/Stalin corr., pp. 230–2
29 *Hansard*, House of Commons, 15 December 1944, not 14 December as in *Churchill VII*, p. 1104
30 Nicholas, 17 December 1944, pp. 476–7
31 *Ibid.*, 24 December 1944, p. 483
32 Sherwood, p. 842
33 *Churchill & Roosevelt III*, Roosevelt to Churchill, 15 December 1944, pp. 462–3
34 Polonsky, Roosevelt to Mikolajcik, 17 November 1944, pp. 227–8
35 *Ibid.*, US press release, 18 December 1944, and fn. 1; Woodward III, pp. 241–2
36 *Churchill & Roosevelt III*, Roosevelt to Churchill, 23 December 1944, p. 469
37 Woodward III, pp. 422–4; *Eden II*, pp. 500–2; *Triumph and Tragedy*, pp. 203–4
38 *Triumph and Tragedy*, Churchill to Smuts, 22 December 1944, p. 203

39 Macmillan, *War Diaries*, 25 December 1944, pp. 616–17
40 *Eden II*, p. 501; *Colville Diary*, Colville to John Martin, 26 December 1944, p. 540
41 Macmillan, *War Diaries*, 26 December 1944, pp. 617–18; *Colville Diary*, letter to Martin, p. 541; Moran, diary, 26 December 1944, pp. 212–13; Dixon diary, 26 December 1944. The official British record is at PRO FO 954/11.
42 *Colville Diary*, letter to Martin, 26 December 1944, p. 540
43 *Churchill VII*, p. 1121
44 *Ibid.*, p. 1126
45 Nel, p. 162
46 Woodward III, pp. 428–33
47 K. Young (ed.), *The Diaries of Sir Robert Bruce Lockhart, vol. II: 1939–65* (1980) (hereinafter *Lockhart Diary II*), 13 January 1945, p. 390
48 H. Feis, *Churchill, Roosevelt and Stalin* (New Jersey, 1957), for a classic account. Moran, Chap. 24, 'Yalta diary', for the *locus classicus* of the 'sick Roosevelt' argument; Dallek, pp. 503–20, has a very different version of Roosevelt's behaviour. Douglas, pp. 62–72, compares Yalta to Munich. Two more recent accounts are R. Edmonds, *Setting the Mould: The United States and Great Britain 1945–50* (Oxford, 1986), pp. 33–43; and F. J. Harbutt, *The Iron Curtain: Churchill, America, and the Origins of the Cold War* (1986), pp. 81–99, takes a line similar to the one presented here.
49 Harbutt, p. *XI*
50 *Churchill & Roosevelt III*, pp. 493–6
51 Dallek, p. 503
52 *Ibid.*, pp. 505–7; Sherwood, pp. 844–5; Harbutt, pp. 41–3
53 Harbutt, p. 42
54 *Lockhart Diary II*, 7 January 1945, p. 387
55 Charmley, *Duff Cooper*, p. 190
56 PRO Prem. 3/374A, M1207/4, Churchill to Eden, 11 December 1944
57 PRO Cab. 65/64, WM(44)164, 11 December 1944
58 Kitchen, p. 206
59 *Lockhart Diary II*, 6 January 1945, p. 386
60 *Colville Diary*, 21 December 1944, p. 537
61 *Lockhart Diary II*, 7 January 1945, p. 387
62 *Cadogan Diary*, 8 January 1945, p. 693
63 *Colville Diary*, 9 January 1945, p. 550
64 AP 20/1/25, Eden diary, 4 January 1945
65 *Eden II*, p. 505
66 *Churchill & Roosevelt III*, Churchill to Roosevelt, 6 January 1945; Roosevelt to Churchill, 6 January 1945; Churchill to Roosevelt, 8, 9 January 1945; Roosevelt to Churchill, 9 January 1945, pp. 495–6, 501–3
67 *Ibid.*, Roosevelt to Churchill, 30 December 1944, pp. 482–4
68 *Eden II*, p. 506; Woodward III, pp. 358–62
69 W. Medlicott (ed.), *Documents on British Foreign Policy, vol. XIX* (1985), no. 16, Henderson to Eden, 5 July 1937, p. 32
70 *Ibid.*, Vansittart minute, 22 July 1937, p. 37
71 *Ibid.*, no. 53, Henderson to Sargent, 20 July 1937

72 PRO FO 800/313, Henderson to Halifax, 5 April 1938
73 Harbutt, p. 78
74 *Colville Diary*, 8 January 1945, p. 550
75 *Churchill & Roosevelt III*, Roosevelt to Churchill, 2 January 1945, p. 490
76 *Ibid.*, p. 517; Sherwood, pp. 846–9
77 *Economist*, 'Noble Negatives', 30 December 1944
78 Nicholas, 7 January 1945, p. 494
79 Edmonds, p. 36

53: Winston and the Argonauts

1 Moran, diary, 3 February 1945, p. 218
2 Sherwood, p. 852
3 *Dalton Diary II*, 11 December 1944, p. 815
4 *Amery Diary II*, 4 September 1944, p. 998
5 *Channon Diary*, 6 September 1944, p. 393
6 *Amery Diary II*, 6 September 1944, p. 998
7 *Ibid.*, 23 November 1944, p. 1012
8 Attlee Mss., Churchill College, Cambridge, ATLE 2/2, Attlee to Churchill, 19 January 1945
9 *Colville Diary*, 20 January 1945, p. 554
10 *Ibid.*
11 Jacob, in Wheeler-Bennett (ed.), *Action This Day*, p. 117
12 Attlee Mss., Churchill to Attlee, 22 January 1945
13 Taylor (ed.), *My Darling Pussy*, Lloyd George to Frances Stevenson, 4 October 1940, p. 239
14 *Riddell Diary*, 21 May 1913, 18 January 1914, pp. 65, 78
15 PRO Cab. 65/51, WM(45)22, 19 February 1945
16 *Churchill VII*, p. 1170
17 *Eden II*, diary, 1 February 1945, p. 510
18 *Triumph and Tragedy*, p. 224
19 Moran, diary, 3 February 1945, p. 219
20 Martin, 5 February 1945, p. 179
21 Nel, pp. 167–8
22 *Triumph and Tragedy*, pp. 228–31; Sherwood, pp. 852–3; *Eden II*, p. 513
23 *Triumph and Tragedy*, p. 230
24 Moran, diary, 4 February 1945, p. 223
25 *Eden II*, diary, 4 February 1945, p. 512
26 Sherwood, p. 852
27 *Triumph and Tragedy*, pp. 232–3
28 *Ibid.*, p. 239
29 *Churchill & Roosevelt III*, pp. 521–30
30 Polonsky, Eden to Churchill, 1 February 1945, pp. 240–2; *Eden II*, pp. 515–17; Moran, diary, 3 February 1945, p. 219
31 Polonsky, Roosevelt to Stalin, 6 February 1945, pp. 242–3
32 *Ibid.*, Yalta final communiqué, 11 February 1945, pp. 249–50
33 *Ibid.*, Churchill memo., 8 February 1945, pp. 246–7; *Triumph and Tragedy*, p. 243
34 *Eden II*, p. 513
35 *Churchill & Roosevelt III*, p. 527
36 *Eden II*, p. 514
37 PRO Cab. 66/63, WP(45)57, record of 4th Plenary Meeting
38 Harbutt, pp. 86–9, is, it seems to me, convincing on this point

39 Moran, diary, 11 February 1945, pp. 230–3
40 Nicholas, report dated 17 February 1945, p. 515; Harbutt, pp. 91–2
41 PRO Cab. 65/51, WM(45)18, tel. to Churchill and Eden, 12 February 1945
42 Moran, pp. 226–33
43 *Cadogan Diary*, letter, 9 February 1945, p. 707
44 *Eden II*, p. 522
45 Moran, p. 247
46 *Ibid*.
47 Butler, p. 90
48 Addison, pp. 230–1
49 *Colville Diary*, 19 February 1945, p. 561
50 *Channon Diary*, 28 February 1945, pp. 398–9
51 PRO Cab. 65/51, WM(45)22, 19 February 1945
52 *Cadogan Diary*, letter to Halifax, 20 February 1945, p. 717
53 *Dalton Diary II*, 23 February 1945, p. 836
54 *Colville Diary*, 23 February 1945, pp. 562–3
55 *Hansard*, House of Commons, 27 February 1945
56 *Colville Diary*, 27 February 1945, p. 565
57 *Ibid*., 28 February, p. 565
58 PRO FO 945/23, Eden to Churchill, 5 March 1945
59 *Ibid*., Churchill to Eden, 5 March 1945
60 *Nicolson Diary II*, Nicolson to Vita Sackville-West, 1 March 1945, p. 439
61 PRO Cab. 65/51, WM(45)26, 6 March 1945
62 *Colville Diary*, 7 March 1945, p. 570

54: A 'Sad Wreck'

1 T. H. Anderson, *The United States, Great Britain and the Cold War 1944–7* (Columbia, 1981), takes, on the whole, a favourable view of Churchill's motives
2 *Churchill & Roosevelt III*, p. 545
3 Harbutt, Chaps 1 & 2 *passim*, takes this line.
4 Garton Ash, 'From World War to Cold War', p. 47
5 *Eden II*, p. 525
6 Garton Ash, 'From World War to Cold War', p. 48
7 *Churchill & Roosevelt III*, Churchill to Roosevelt, 8 March 1945, pp. 547–51
8 Harriman, pp. 427–8
9 Polonsky, Harriman to Molotov, 19 March 1945, pp. 255–8
10 *Churchill & Roosevelt III*, Churchill to Roosevelt, 10 March 1945, pp. 551–2
11 *Ibid*., Churchill to Roosevelt, 10 March 1945, pp. 553–9
12 *Nicolson Diary II*, 27 February 1945, p. 437
13 *Churchill & Roosevelt III*, Roosevelt to Churchill, 11 March 1945, pp. 560–3
14 *Ibid*., Churchill to Roosevelt, 13 March 1945, pp. 564–6
15 *Ibid*., Roosevelt to Churchill, 15 March 1945, pp. 568–9
16 *Ibid*., Churchill to Roosevelt, 16 March 1945, pp. 571–2
17 *Ibid*., Churchill to Roosevelt, 17 March 1945, p. 574
18 *The Times*, 16 March 1945
19 *Eden II*, diary, 23 March 1945, pp. 524–5

20 Rowland, pp. 795–6
21 *Colville Diary*, 28 March 1945, p. 580
22 Moran, diary, 7 December 1947, p. 326
23 *Amery Diary II*, 26 March 1945, p. 1034
24 Ross, Clark-Kerr to the Foreign Office, 27 March 1945, pp. 193–9
25 *Ibid*., Orme Sargent minute, 2 April 1945, pp. 199–203; Woodward III, pp. 511–19; *Cadogan Diary*, pp. 724–5
26 *Eden II*, p. 525
27 *Churchill & Roosevelt III*, p. 585
28 *Ibid*., pp. 585–6
29 *Churchill VII*, p. 1261
30 *Churchill & Roosevelt III*, Churchill to Roosevelt, 27 March 1945, pp. 587–9
31 Anderson, p. 47
32 *Churchill & Roosevelt III*, Roosevelt to Churchill, 29 March 1945, pp. 593–4
33 *Ibid*., Roosevelt to Churchill, 29 March 1945, pp. 595–7
34 *Ibid*., Churchill to Roosevelt, 30 March 1945, p. 598
35 *Ibid*., Churchill to Roosevelt, 31 March 1945, pp. 599–600
36 *Churchill VII*, pp. 1274–6
37 *Churchill & Roosevelt III*, Churchill to Roosevelt, 1 April 1945, pp. 603–5
38 *Ibid*., Roosevelt to Churchill, 4 April 1945, pp. 607–9
39 PRO Cab. 65/52, WM(45)39, 3 April 1945
40 *Churchill & Roosevelt III*, Roosevelt to Churchill, 4 April 1945, pp. 609–10
41 *Ibid*., Roosevelt to Churchill, 4 April 1945, pp. 611–12
42 *Colville Diary*, 5 April 1945, p. 582
43 *Churchill & Roosevelt III*, Churchill to Roosevelt, 5 April 1945, p. 613
44 *Ibid*., Roosevelt to Churchill, 6 April 1945, p. 617
45 Anderson, p. 49
46 *Churchill & Roosevelt III*, editorial note, p. 617
47 *Ibid*., p. 622
48 *Ibid*., p. 624
49 *Ibid*., Roosevelt to Churchill, 11 April 1945, p. 630
50 *Ibid*., p. 619
51 *Colville Diary*, 12 April 1945, p. 587
52 *Triumph and Tragedy*, p. 305
53 *Churchill VII*, p. 1291
54 *Ibid*., pp. 1293–5; *Triumph and Tragedy*, p. 308

55: Failure and Apotheosis: II

1 *Churchill VII*, p. 1283
2 *Churchill & Roosevelt III*, p. 633
3 PRO Cab. 66/53, WP(44)360, paper by Keynes, circulated 1 July 1944
4 PRO Cab. 65/43, WM(44)93, 14 July 1944
5 *Churchill VII*, p. 1282
6 *Ibid*., p. 1284
7 *Colville Diary*, 24 April 1945, p. 592
8 Polonsky, Truman and Churchill to Stalin, 18 April 1945, pp. 265–7
9 *Ibid*., Truman to Stalin, 23 April 1945, pp. 267–8

Notes

10 *Ibid.*, Stalin to Churchill, 24 April 1945, pp. 268–9
11 *Colville Diary*, 26 April 1945, p. 593
12 *Churchill VII*, p. 1315, quoting the Colville diaries. The published text cited at fn. 11 has neither this passage nor an ellipsis to illustrate its removal – an interesting comment on Colville's editing.
13 Woodward III, pp. 532–6, for the full text, part of which is given by Churchill in *Triumph and Tragedy*, pp. 317–19
14 *Colville Diary*, 26 April 1945, p. 592
15 *Churchill VII*, p. 1320
16 Ross, Clark-Kerr to Foreign Office, 27 March 1945, p. 196
17 Woodward III, p. 539
18 *Ibid.*, pp. 543–4
19 PRO FO 954/20, Churchill to Truman, 6 May 1945
20 *Colville Diary*, 5 May 1945, p. 596
21 PRO FO 945/20, Churchill to Eden, 4 May 1945
22 *Churchill VII*, p. 1338
23 Nel, pp. 176–7
24 *Nicolson Diary II*, letter, 8 May 1945, pp. 486–7
25 *Hansard*, House of Commons, 8 May 1945
26 *The Times*, 9 May 1945
27 *Amery Diary II*, 4 May 1945, p. 1040
28 *Eden II*, p. 535
29 M. Gilbert, *Winston S. Churchill, vol. VIII: Never Despair 1945–65* (1988) (hereinafter *Churchill VIII*), pp. 5–6
30 PRO Cab. 120/186, Churchill to Truman, 12 May 1945
31 *Triumph and Tragedy*, pp. 354–5
32 *Churchill VIII*, p. 8
33 *Ibid.*, Gilbert is equally over-sanguine
34 Anderson, pp. 62–4
35 *Ibid.*, p. 65
36 PRO Prem. 4/65/4, Churchill to Eden, 12 May 1945
37 *Ibid.*, drafts to James Stuart, 18 May 1945
38 *Dalton Diary II*, 11 May 1945, pp. 858–9
39 Macmillan, *War Diaries*, 21 May 1945, p. 762
40 *Colville Diary*, 26 May 1945, p. 601
41 *Dalton Diary II*, 11 May 1945, p. 859
42 AP 20/1/25, Eden diary, 24 May 1945
43 Bodleian Library, Woolton Mss., vol. 20, fo. 19, undated note to Woolton
44 *Ibid.*, Woolton to Beaverbrook, 31 May 1945, fos 17–18
45 *Dalton Diary II*, 26 May 1945, p. 864
46 *Ibid.*, 28 May 1945, p. 865
47 *Amery Diary II*, 4 June 1945, p. 1046
48 Moran, diary, 4 June 1945, p. 453

49 *Churchill VIII*, p. 34; *Channon Diary*, 5 June 1945, p. 408; *Nicolson Diary II*, Vita Sackville-West to Nicolson, 22 June 1945, p. 472; Addison, pp. 265–6
50 Moran, diary, 20 May 1945, p. 251
51 Anderson, pp. 66–7
52 Sherwood, p. 889
53 *Ibid.*, pp. 890–903
54 *Ibid.*, p. 909
55 *Triumph and Tragedy*, pp. 357–8
56 *Churchill VIII*, pp. 15–17
57 PRO Prem. 3/430/1, for Churchill's account. Davies's official account is at *Foreign Relations of the United States: Potsdam I*, pp. 64–81
58 Anderson, pp. 69–70, quotes extensively from the account in the Davies papers
59 Woodward III, p. 580, fn. 2; see also Anderson, p. 70
60 Anderson, pp. 70–1; Harbutt, pp. 106–7
61 PRO Prem. 3/430/1, M529/5, Churchill to Eden, 28 May 1945, also partly quoted at Woodward III, p. 583
62 *Lockhart Diary II*, 26 May 1945, p. 440
63 *Churchill VIII*, p. 26
64 *Triumph and Tragedy*, pp. 370–1; but see PRO Prem. 3/430/1 and Woodward III, p. 583
65 PRO Prem. 3/430/1, Churchill to Truman, 29, 31 May 1945
66 *Lockhart Diary II*, 3 June 1945, p. 443
67 *Ibid.*, 7 June 1945, p. 446
68 Alanbrooke diary II, 11 June 1945, pp. 470–1
69 Moran, diary, 14 June 1945, pp. 253–4
70 *Ibid.*, 20 May 1945, p. 252
71 Alanbrooke diary II, 4 July 1945, p. 465
72 PRO Prem. 3/430/8, record of Churchill/Truman conversation, 18 July 1945
73 PRO Prem. 3/430/8, Churchill's record of meeting with Truman, 17 July 1945
74 AP 20/1/25, Eden diary, 17 July 1945
75 Moran, diary, 23 July 1945, p. 283
76 *Churchill VIII*, p. 106
77 *Eden II*, p. 551; the full text is at AP 20/1/25, Eden diary, 26 July 1945

The Aftermath

1 *Triumph and Tragedy*, p. 432
2 *Eden II*, diary, 27 July 1945, p. 551
3 AP 20/1/25, Eden diary, 31 August 1945
4 Moran, p. 786
5 Ashley, pp. 159–60
6 *Churchill II*, p. 283

Bibliography

(Place of publication for all books is London unless otherwise stated.)

1. MANUSCRIPT SOURCES

Public Record Office Kew (PRO):

a) *Admiralty Papers*

b) *Foreign Office*

FO 371	Foreign Office, General Correspondence
FO 800	Private Papers Series:
	Sir Alexander Cadogan
	Lord Cranborne
	Lord Halifax
	Sir Nevile Henderson
	Lord Inverchaple (Clark-Kerr)
	Sir Orme Sargent
FO 954	Avon Papers
FO 434	Confidential Print, S.E. Europe
FO 1011	Papers of Sir Percy Loraine

c) *Prime Minister's Papers*

Prem. 1	Neville Chamberlain
Prem. 3	Winston Churchill
Prem. 4	Winston Churchill

d) *Cabinet Office Papers*

Cab. 2	Committee of Imperial Defence
Cab. 21	Registered Files
Cab. 23	Cabinet Meetings, Minutes
Cab. 24	Cabinet Meetings, Memoranda
Cab. 27	Cabinet Committee on Foreign Policy
Cab. 42	Dardanelles Committee
Cab. 53	Chiefs of Staff Committee
Cab. 55	Joint Planning, Sub-Committee
Cab. 63	Hankey Papers

Cab. 64	Ministry for the Co-ordination of Defence Papers
Cab. 65	War Cabinet Minutes
Cab. 66	War Cabinet Memoranda
Cab. 83	Military Co-ordination Committee Files
Cab. 99	Supreme War Council

e) *Treasury*

T 160	Finance Files
T 161	Supply Files
T 188	Leith-Ross Papers

2. PRIVATE PAPERS

Leo Amery Diaries	Courtesy of the Rt Hon. Julian Amery MP
Asquith Papers	Bodleian Library, Oxford
Baldwin Papers	Cambridge University Library
Lord Balfour Papers	British Library
Beaverbrook Papers	House of Lords Record Office
A. A. Berle Papers	F. D. Roosevelt Library, Hyde Park
Lord Brabourne Papers	India Office Record Library
R. A. Butler Papers	Trinity College, Cambridge
Cadogan Papers	Churchill College, Cambridge
Lord Cave Papers	British Library
Lord Cecil of Chelwood	British Library
Austen Chamberlain	Birmingham University Library
Neville Chamberlain	Birmingham University Library (Courtesy of Dr B. Z. Benedikz)
Lord Cherwell	Nuffield College, Oxford
Churchill Papers	Churchill College, Cambridge
Duff Cooper Papers	Churchill College, Cambridge
Viscount Crookshank	Bodleian Library, Oxford
Admiral Lord Cunningham	British Library
17th Earl of Derby	Liverpool City Library
Anthony Eden	Birmingham University Library
Paul Emrys-Evans	British Library
Halifax Papers	Churchill College, Cambridge
Lord Hankey	Churchill College, Cambridge
Harry Hopkins Papers	F. D. Roosevelt Library, Hyde Park
Lord Ismay Papers	King's College, London
Sir H. Knatchbull-Hughessen	Churchill College, Cambridge
Liddell Hart Papers	King's College, London
Linlithgow Papers	India Office Records Library

Lloyd George Papers	House of Lords Record Office
Lloyd of Dolobran	Churchill College, Cambridge
Lord Margesson Papers	Churchill College, Cambridge
Henry Morgenthau Papers	F. D. Roosevelt Library, Hyde Park
Viscount Northcliffe	British Library
Sir H. Page-Croft	Churchill College, Cambridge
Sir E. Phipps	Churchill College, Cambridge
Franklin D. Roosevelt	F. D. Roosevelt Library, Hyde Park
4th Marquess of Salisbury	Hatfield House
Sir Robert Sandars	Bodleian Library, Oxford
Sir John Simon	Bodleian Library, Oxford
Sir L. Spears	Churchill College, Cambridge
Sir R. Storrs	Pembroke College, Cambridge
Sir W. Strang	Churchill College, Cambridge
Templewood Papers	Cambridge University Library
Sir R. Vansittart	Churchill College, Cambridge
Lord Woolton	Bodleian Library, Oxford
Sir L. Worthington-Evans	Bodleian Library, Oxford
Zetland Papers	India Office Record Library

3. BOOKS BY CHURCHILL

a) *Autobiographica/biographica*
(NB All my quotations are taken from the *Centenary Collected Edition* published 1974–5 in thirty-four volumes, the pagination of which generally follows that of the American edition.)

The Malakand Field Force (1898)
The River War (1899)
Lord Randolph Churchill (2 vols) (1906)
The World Crisis (5 vols) (1923–31)
My Early Life (1930)
India (1931)
Thoughts and Adventures (1932)
Marlborough (4 vols) (1933–8)
Great Contemporaries (1937)
Savrola (1974 edn)

b) *Collections of Speeches*

Arms and the Covenant (1938)
Step by Step (1939)
Into Battle (1941)
The Unrelenting Struggle (1942)

The End of the Beginning (1943)
Onwards to Victory (1944)
The Dawn of Liberation (1945)
Victory (1946)
Secret Session Speeches (1946)
The Sinews of Peace (1948)
Europe Unite (1950)
In the Balance (1951)
The Unwritten Alliance (1961)
Mr Brodrick's Army (1974 edn)
The War Speeches (2 vols) (1975 edn)

c) *The Second World War*, 6 vols (1948–54)

The Gathering Storm (1948)
Their Finest Hour (1949)
The Grand Alliance (1950)
The Hinge of Fate (1951)
Closing the Ring (1952)
Triumph and Tragedy (1954)

d) *A History of the English-Speaking Peoples*, 4 vols (1956–8)

4. THE OFFICIAL BIOGRAPHY

Winston S. Churchill, 8 vols (1966–88)
(Vols 1 & 2 by R. S. Churchill, the remainder by M. Gilbert)
Each of the first five volumes is accompanied by companion volumes, for which see section 6 (a).

Vol. I: Youth. 1874–1900 (1966)
Vol. II: Young Statesman. 1900–14 (1967)
Vol. III: 1914–16 (1971)
Vol. IV: 1917–22 (1975)
Vol. V: 1922–39 (1976)
Vol. VI: Their Finest Hour 1939–41 (1983)
Vol. VII: The Road to Victory 1941–5 (1986)
Vol. VIII: Never Despair 1945–65 (1988)

5. BIOGRAPHIES/STUDIES OF CHURCHILL

(NB There are so many of these that I have included only the most useful.)

M. Ashley, *Churchill as Historian* (1968)
I. Berlin, *Mr Churchill in 1940* (n.d.)
Lord Birkenhead, *Churchill 1874–1922* (1989)

V. Bonham-Carter, *Winston Churchill as I Knew Him* (1966 edn)

P. Brendon, *Churchill: An Authentic Hero* (1984)

L. Broad, *Winston Churchill* (1941)

R. Callahan, *Churchill: Retreat from Empire* (Delaware, 1984)

E. D. W. Chaplin (ed.), *Winston Churchill and Harrow: Memoirs of the Prime Minister's Schooldays 1888–92* (1941)

J. Colville, *The Churchillians* (1981)

M. Gilbert, *Churchill's Political Philosophy* (Oxford, 1981)

P. Guedalla, *Mr Churchill: A Portrait* (1941)

R. Hough, *Former Naval Person: Churchill and the Wars at Sea* (1985)

R. Hough, *Winston and Clementine: The Triumph of the Churchills* (1990)

R. Hyam, *Elgin and Churchill at the Colonial Office* (1968)

D. Irving, *Churchill's War: The Struggle for Power* (1987)

D. Jablonsky, *Churchill, The Great Game and Total War* (1991)

R. R. James, *Churchill: A Study in Failure* (1970)

R. R. James (ed.), *Churchill Speaks* (1981)

D. Kavanagh, *Crisis, Charisma and British Political Leadership: Winston Churchill as the Outsider* (1974)

F. Kersaudy, *Churchill and De Gaulle* (1981)

R. Lamb, *Churchill as War Leader* (1991)

J. P. Lash, *Roosevelt and Churchill 1939–41: The Partnership that Saved the West* (NY, 1976)

W. Manchester, *The Caged Lion: Winston Spencer Churchill 1932–40* (1988)

W. Manchester, *The Last Lion: Winston Spencer Churchill: Visions of Glory 1874–1932* (1983)

Sir J. Marchant (ed.), *Winston Spencer Churchill: Servant of Crown and Commonwealth* (1954)

P. de Mendelssohn, *The Age of Churchill: Heritage and Adventure 1874–1911* (1961)

S. M. Miner, *Between Churchill and Stalin* (N. Carolina, 1988)

R. I. Moore, *Churchill, Cripps and India* (1979)

Lord Moran, *Winston Churchill: The Struggle for Survival 1940–65* (1966)

E. Murray, *Churchill's Bodyguard* (1988)

E. Nel, *Mr Churchill's Secretary* (1958)

H. Pelling, *Winston Churchill* (1974)

R. Prior, *Churchill's 'World Crisis' as History* (Kent, 1983)

M. P. Schoenfeld, *The War Ministry of Winston Churchill* (Iowa, 1972)

A. Seldon, *Churchill's Indian Summer: The Conservative Government, 1951–5* (1981)

A. J. P. Taylor (ed.), *Churchill: Four Faces and the Man* (1969)

R. W. Thompson, *The Yankee Marlborough* (1963)

W. H. Thompson, *I Was Churchill's Shadow* (1952)

M. Weidhorn, *Sir Winston Churchill* (Boston, Mass., 1979)

J. Wheeler-Bennett, *Action This Day: Working with Churchill* (1968)

F. Woods, *A Bibliography of the Works of Sir Winston Churchill KG. OM. CH* (1979 edn)

K. Young, *Churchill and Beaverbrook* (1966)

6. PUBLISHED PRIMARY SOURCES

a) *Churchill Papers*

Companions to the official biography

Edited by Randolph S. Churchill:
Winston S. Churchill, vol. I, companion vol. 1: 1874–96 (1967)
Winston S. Churchill, vol. I, companion vol. 2: 1896–1900 (1967)
Winston S. Churchill, vol. II, companion vol. 1: 1901–7 (1969)
Winston S. Churchill, vol. II, companion vol. 2: 1907–11 (1969)
Winston S. Churchill, vol. II, companion vol. 3: 1911–14 (1969)

Edited by Martin Gilbert:
Winston S. Churchill, vol. III, companion vol. 1: August 1914–April 1915 (1972)
Winston S. Churchill, vol. III, companion vol. 2: May 1915–December 1916 (1972)
Winston S. Churchill, vol. IV, companion vol. 1: January 1917–June 1919 (1977)
Winston S. Churchill, vol. IV, companion vol. 2: July 1919–March 1921 (1977)
Winston S. Churchill, vol. IV, companion vol. 3: April 1921–November 1922 (1977)
Winston S. Churchill, vol. V, companion vol. 1: The Exchequer Years (1979)
Winston S. Churchill, vol. V, companion vol. 2: The Wilderness Years, 1929–35 (1981)
Winston S. Churchill, vol. V, companion vol. 3: The Coming of War, 1936–9 (1982)

R. R. James (ed.), *Churchill Speaks: Collected Speeches, 1897–1963* (1981)

b) *Other Sources*
i) *Documents on British Foreign Policy*
C. P. Gooch & H. Temperley, *Documents of the Origins of the War*, 13 vols (1924–38)
W. N. Medlicott *et al.* (eds), *Documents on British Foreign Policy, 1919–39, Second series, vols, XVIII, XIX* (1984–5)
E. L. Woodward *et al.* (eds.) *Documents on British Foreign Policy, 1919–39, Third series, vols I–VII* (1946–54)

ii) *Documents on German Foreign Policy*
E. T. S. Dugdale (ed.), *German Diplomatic Documents, vol. IV: The Descent to the Abyss, 1911–14* (NY, 1931)
D. C. Watt *et al.* (eds), *Documents on German Foreign Policy 1933–45. Series D., vols V–VIII* (1953–5)

iii) *Miscellaneous*
F. W. S. Craig (ed.), *British Parliamentary Election Results 1918–49* (1977 rev. edn)

Documents on Polish-Soviet Relations 1941–5, 2 vols (1961, 1967)
Hansard's Parliamentary Debates, House of Commons, 5th series
A. Polonsky (ed.), *The Great Powers and the Polish Question 1941–5* (1976)
G. Ross (ed.), *The Foreign Office and the Kremlin: British Documents on Anglo-Soviet Relations 1941–5* (Cambridge, 1984)

c) *Letters and Private Papers*
Lord Birkenhead, *The Speeches of Lord Birkenhead* (1929)
R. Blake (ed.), *The Private Papers of Douglas Haig, 1914–19* (1952)
D. G. Boyce (ed.), *The Crisis of British Unionism: The Domestic Political Papers of the Second Earl of Selborne, 1885–1922* (1987)
D. G. Boyce (ed.), *The Crisis of British Power: The Imperial and Naval Papers of the Second Earl of Selborne 1895–1910* (1990)
P. G. Boyle (ed.), *The Churchill–Eisenhower Correspondence 1953–5* (N. Carolina, 1990)
M. V. Brett (ed.), *Journals and Letters of Reginald, Viscount Esher, vol. II: 1903–10* (1934)
M. V. Brett (ed.), *Journals and Letters of Reginald, Viscount Esher, vol. III: 1910–15* (1938)
M. & E. Brock (eds), *H. H. Asquith, Letters to Venetia Stanley* (1982)
M. Brown (ed.), *The Letters of T. E. Lawrence* (1988)
A. Bryant (ed.), *In Search of Peace* (1938)
D. Chandler *et al.* (eds), *The Eisenhower Papers, vol. II* (Baltimore, 1970)
A. Clark (ed.), *'A Good Innings': The Private Papers of Viscount Lee of Fareham* (1974)
R. Cockett (ed.), *My Dear Max: The Letters of Brendan Bracken to Lord Beaverbrook, 1925–58* (1990)
H. E. Craster (ed.), *Speeches on Foreign Policy by Viscount Halifax* (1940)
D. Fraser (ed.), *In Good Company: The First World War Letters and Diaries of the Hon. William Fraser* (1990)
D. Garnett (ed.), *The Letters of T. E. Lawrence* (1938)
P. Gordon (ed.), *The Red Earl: The Papers of the Fifth Earl Spencer, vol. II: 1885–1906* (Northampton, 1986)
D. Haig, *The Private Papers of Douglas Haig, 1914–19* (1952)
P. G. Halpern (ed.), *The Keyes Papers: Selections from the Private and Official Correspondence of Admiral of the Fleet Baron Keyes of Zeebrugge, vol. II: 1919–38* (1980)
P. G. Halpern (ed.), *The Keyes Papers: Selections from the Private and Official Correspondence of Admiral of the Fleet Baron Keyes of Zeebrugge, vol. III: 1939–45* (1981)
R. R. James (ed.), *Memoirs of a Conservative: J. C. C. Davidson's Memoirs and Papers, 1910–37* (1969)
K. Jeffrey (ed.), *The Military Correspondence of Field Marshal Sir Henry Wilson 1918–22* (1985)

W. F. Kimball (ed.), *Churchill & Roosevelt: The Complete Correspondence, vol. I: The Alliance Emerging, October 1933–November 1942* (Princeton, 1984)

W. F. Kimball (ed.), *Churchill & Roosevelt: The Complete Correspondence, vol. II: Alliance Forged. November 1942–February 1944* (Princeton, 1984)

W. F. Kimball (ed.), *Churchill & Roosevelt: The Complete Correspondence, vol. III: Alliance Declining. February 1944–April 1945* (Princeton, 1984)

N. Mackenzie (ed.), *The Letters of Sidney and Beatrice Webb, vol. II: Partnership 1892–1912* (1978)

R. J. Minney (ed.), *The Private Papers of Hore-Belisha* (1960)

H. G. Nicholas (ed.), *Washington Despatches 1941–5* (1981)

J. van der Poel (ed.), *Selections from the Smuts Papers, vol. VI* (Cambridge, 1973)

B. McL. Ranft (ed.), *The Beatty Papers: Selections from the Private and Official Papers of Admiral of the Fleet Earl Beatty, vol. I: 1902–18* (1989)

A. J. P. Taylor (ed.), *My Darling Pussy: The Letters of Lloyd George and Frances Stevenson 1913–41* (1975)

A. Temple-Patterson (ed.), *The Jellicoe Papers: Selections from the Private and Official Correspondence of Admiral of the Fleet Jellicoe, vol. II: 1913–35* (1968)

P. Williamson (ed.), *The Modernisation of Conservative Politics: The Diaries and Letters of William Bridgeman, 1904–35* (1988)

7. PUBLISHED DIARIES

J. Barnes & D. Nicholson (eds), *The Leo Amery Diaries 1896–1929* (1980)

J. Barnes & D. Nicholson (eds), *The Empire at Bay: The Leo Amery Diaries 1929–55* (1988)

W. S. Blunt, *My Diaries 1884–1914* (1932 edn)

A. Bryant (ed.), *The Turn of the Tide 1939–43* (1957)

A. Bryant (ed.), *The Triumph in the West 1943–6* (1959)

J. Charmley (ed.), *Descent to Suez: The Diaries of Sir Evelyn Shuckburgh 1951–6* (1987)

Sir John Colville, *The Fringes of Power: The Downing Street Diaries, 1939–55* (1985)

E. David (ed.), *Inside Asquith's Cabinet* (1977)

D. Dilks (ed.), *The Diaries of Sir Alexander Cadogan 1938–45* (1971)

P. Dixon (ed.), *Double Diploma: The Life of Sir Pierson Dixon* (1968)

T. Evans (ed.), *The Killearn Diaries* (1972)

J. Harvey (ed.), *The Diplomatic Diaries of Oliver Harvey 1937–40* (1970)

J. Harvey (ed.), *The War Diaries of Oliver Harvey 1941–5* (1978)

R. R. James (ed.), *Chips: The Diaries of Sir Henry Channon* (1967)

K. Jefferys (ed.), *Labour and the Wartime Coalition: From the Diary of James Chuter Ede 1941–5* (1987)

N. & J. Mackenzie (eds), *The Diaries of Beatrice Webb, vol. III* (1984)

R. Macleod & D. Kelly (eds), *The Ironside Diaries 1937–40* (1962)

H. Macmillan, *War Diaries* (1984)

J. Martin, *Downing Street: The War Years* (1991)

J. M. McEwan (ed.), *The Riddell Diaries 1908–23* (1986)

P. Moon (ed.), *Wavell, The Viceroy's Journal* (1973)

K. Middlemass (ed.), *Whitehall Diary, vol. I: 1916–25* (Oxford, 1969)

K. Middlemass (ed.), *Whitehall Diary, vol. II: 1926–30* (Oxford, 1969)

N. Nicolson (ed.), *Harold Nicolson: Diaries and Letters, vol. I: 1930–39* (1966)

N. Nicolson (ed.), *Harold Nicolson: Diaries and Letters, vol. II: 1939–45* (1967)

N. Nicolson (ed.), *Harold Nicolson: Diaries and Letters, vol. III: 1945–62* (1968)

B. Pimlott (ed.), *The Political Diary of Hugh Dalton, 1918–40* (1986)

B. Pimlott (ed.), *The Second World War Diary of Hugh Dalton, 1940–45* (1986)

N. Rose (ed.), *Baffy: The Diaries of Blanche Dugdale* (1973)

C. Stuart (ed.), *The Reith Diaries* (1975)

A. J. P. Taylor (ed.), *Lloyd George: A Diary by Frances Stevenson* (1971)

J. Vincent (ed.), *The Crawford Papers* (Manchester, 1984)

K. Young (ed.), *The Diaries of Sir Robert Bruce Lockhart, vol. I: 1915–38* (1973)

K. Young (ed.), *The Diaries of Sir Robert Bruce Lockhart, vol. II: 1939–65* (1980)

P. Ziegler (ed.), *Personal Diary of Admiral The Lord Louis Mountbatten, Supreme Allied Commander South-East Asia 1943–7* (1988)

8. MEMOIRS

L. S. Amery, *My Political Life, vol. I: England Before the Storm 1896–1914* (1953)

L. S. Amery, *My Political Life, vol. II: War and Peace 1914–29* (1953)

L. S. Amery, *My Political Life, vol. III: The Unforgiving Years 1929–40* (1955)

Duchess of Atholl, *Working Partnership* (1958)

Earl of Avon, *The Eden Memoirs, vol. I: Facing the Dictators* (1962)

Earl of Avon, *The Eden Memoirs, vol. II: The Reckoning* (1965)

Lord Birkenhead, *Law, Life and Letters, vol. I* (1927)

Lord Birkenhead, *Law, Life and Letters, vol. II* (1927)

R. Boothby, *I Fight to Live* (1947)

R. Boothby, *Recollections of a Rebel* (1978)

R. A. Butler, *The Art of the Possible* (1971)

R. A. Butler, *The Art of Memory* (1982)

Sir Austen Chamberlain, *Politics from the Inside* (1937)

Lord Chandos, *The Memoirs of Lord Chandos* (1962)

R. S. Churchill, *Twenty-One Years* (Cambridge, 1965)

A. Duff Cooper, *Old Men Forget* (1953)

Sir H. Page-Croft, *My Life of Strife* (1948)

H. Dalton, *The Fateful Years* (1957)

Lord Eccles, *By Safe Hand: Letters of Sybil & David Eccles 1939–42* (1983)

Charles de Gaulle, *Mémoires de Guerre: tome II, l'unité* (Paris, 1956)

Sir Edward Grey, *Twenty-Five Years, 2 vols* (1925)

P. J. Grigg, *Prejudice and Judgement* (1948)

Earl of Halifax, *Fulness of Days* (1957)

W. Averell Harriman & E. Abel, *Special Envoy to Churchill and Stalin 1941–6* (NY, 1975)

Sir Nevile Henderson, *Failure of a Mission* (1940)

Lord Home, *The Way the Wind Blows* (1976)

Lord Ismay, *The Memoirs of General The Lord Ismay* (1960)

V. Lawford, *Bound for Diplomacy* (1963)

Harold Macmillan, *Memoirs, vol. I: Winds of Change* (1966)

M. Muggeridge (ed.), *Ciano's Diplomatic Papers* (1948)

Sir W. Selby, *Diplomatic Twilight* (1953)

Lord Simon, *Retrospect* (1953)

Sir W. Strang, *Home and Abroad* (1956)

Lord Templewood, *Nine Troubled Years* (1954)

Sir R. Vansittart, *The Mist Procession* (1958)

Earl of Woolton, *The Memoirs of The Rt Hon. The Earl of Woolton* (1959)

Lord Zetland, *'Essayez': The Memoirs of Lawrence, Second Marquess of Zetland* (1956)

9. SECONDARY SOURCES

a) *Biographies*

C. F. Adam, *Life of Lord Lloyd* (1948)

Lord Birkenhead, *Frederick Edwin Earl of Birkenhead, vol. I: The First Phase* (1933)

Lord Birkenhead, *Frederick Edwin Earl of Birkenhead, vol. II: The Last Phase* (1935)

Lord Birkenhead, *Lady Eleanor Smith: A Memoir* (1953)

Lord Birkenhead, *F.E.* (1959)

Lord Birkenhead, *Halifax: The Life of Lord Halifax* (1965)

R. Blake, *The Unknown Prime Minister* (1955)

J. Campbell, *F. E. Smith* (1984)

D. Carlton, *Anthony Eden* (1981)

J. Charmley, *Duff Cooper: The Authorised Biography* (1986)

J. Charmley, *Lord Lloyd & the Decline of the British Empire* (1987)

R. S. Churchill, *The Rise & Fall of Sir Anthony Eden* (1959)

R. S. Churchill, *Lord Derby* (1959)

I. G. Colvin, *Vansittart in Office* (1965)

J. Connell, *Auchinleck* (1959)

C. Coote, *A Companion of Honour* (1963)

P. Cosgrave, *An English Life: R. A. Butler* (1981)

J. A. Cross, *Sir Samuel Hoare* (1977)

J. A. Cross, *Lord Swinton* (1982)

R. Dallek, *Franklin D. Roosevelt and American Foreign Policy 1932–45* (NY, 1979)

D. Dilks, *Neville Chamberlain, vol. I* (1984)

B. E. C. Dugdale, *Arthur James Balfour, First Earl of Balfour 1906–30*, 2 vols (1936)

D. Dutton, *Austen Chamberlain* (1985)

K. Feiling, *Neville Chamberlain* (1946)

R. F. Forster, *Lord Randolph Churchill* (1981 edn)

D. Fraser, *Alanbrooke* (1982)

A. L. Funk, *Charles de Gaulle: The Crucial Years* (Oklahoma, 1959)

B. B. Gilbert, *Lloyd George, vol. I* (1989)

A. M. Gollin, *Proconsul in Politics: A Study of Lord Milner in Opposition and in Power, 1854–1905* (1964)

J. Grigg, *Lloyd George: From Peace to War 1912–16* (1985)

K. Hamilton, *Bertie of Thame: Edwardian Ambassador* (Suffolk, 1990)

M. Hankey, *The Supreme Command, vol. I* (1961)

R. Harrod, *The Prof* (1959)

R. V. F. Heuston, *Lives of the Lord Chancellors* (1964)

A. Horne, *Harold Macmillan, vol. I: 1894–1957* (1988)

A. Howard, *Rab: The Life of R. A. Butler* (1987)

R. R. James, *Anthony Eden* (1987)

R. R. James, *Victor Cazalet: A Portrait* (1976)

R. R. James, *Bob Boothby: A Portrait* (1991)

S. Koss, *Haldane* (1969)

S. Koss, *Asquith* (1976)

C. E. Lysaght, *Brendan Bracken* (1979)

R. F. Mackay, *Balfour* (1985)

J. Lees-Milne, *Harold Nicolson: A Biography, 1930–68* (1981)

J. Lees-Milne, *The Enigmatic Edwardian: The Life of Reginald, 2nd Viscount Esher* (1986)

N. Mosley, *Rules of the Game* (1982)

N. Mosley, *Beyond the Pale: Sir Oswald Mosley 1933–80* (1983)

Lord Newton, *Lord Lansdowne: A Biography* (1929)

H. Nicolson, *Portrait of a Diplomatist Being the Life of Sir Arthur Nicolson First Lord Carnock, and a Study of the Origins of the Great War* (1930)

H. Nicolson, *Curzon: The Last Phase 1919–25. A Study in Post-War Diplomacy* (1937)

A. R. Peters, *Anthony Eden at the Foreign Office 1931–8* (Aldershot, 1986)

Sir Charles Petrie, *The Life and Letters of The Rt Hon. Sir Austen Chamberlain, vol. I* (1939)

B. Pimlott, *Hugh Dalton* (1985)

Earl of Ronaldshay, *The Life of Lord Curzon*, 3 vols (1928)

N. Rose, *Vansittart: Portrait of a Diplomat* (1978)

S. Roskill, *Hankey: Man of Secrets, vol. I: 1877–1918* (1970)

S. Roskill, *Hankey: Man of Secrets, vol. II: 1919–31* (1972)

S. Roskill, *Hankey: Man of Secrets, vol. III: 1931–63* (1974)

S. Roskill, *Admiral of the Fleet, Earl Beatty* (1980)

P. Rowland, *Lloyd George* (1975)

R. Sherwood, *Roosevelt and Hopkins: An Intimate History* (NY, 1948)

R. Skidelsky, *Oswald Mosley* (1975)

M. Soames, *Clementine Churchill* (1979)

A. J. P. Taylor, *Beaverbrook* (1972)

H. A. Taylor, *Smith of Birkenhead, Being the Career of the First Earl of Birkenhead* (1931)

G. Waterfield, *Professional Diplomat: Sir Percy Loraine* (1980)

J. Wilson, *Sir Henry Campbell-Bannerman* (1973)

P. Ziegler, *Mountbatten: The Official Biography* (1985)

b) *General Works*

A. Adamthwaite, *France and the Coming of the Second World War* (1977)

P. Addison, *The Road to 1945* (1975)

T. H. Anderson, *The United States, Great Britain and the Cold War, 1944–7* (Columbia, 1981)

S. R. Ashton, *British Policy towards the Indian States, 1905–39* (1982)

S. Aster, *1939: The Making of the Second World War* (1973)

P. Auty & R. Clogg (eds), *British Policy towards Wartime Resistance in Yugoslavia and Greece* (1975)

S. Ball, *Baldwin and the Conservative Party: The Crisis of 1929–31* (Yale, 1988)

E. Barker, *Churchill and Eden at War* (1978)

C. Barnett, *The Audit of War* (1986)

C. Barnett, *The Collapse of British Power* (1972)

C. Barnett, *Engage the Enemy More Closely* (1991)

M. Baumont, *The Origins of the Second World War* (1978)

J. M. W. Bean (ed.), *The Political Culture of Modern Britain* (1987)

J. Beaumont, *Comrades in Arms* (1986)

Lord Beaverbrook, *Politicians and the War 1914–16, vol. I* (1928)

Lord Beaverbrook, *Politicians and the War 1914–16, vol. II* (1932)

Lord Beaverbrook, *Men and Power 1917–18* (1956)

Lord Beaverbrook, *The Decline and Fall of Lloyd George* (1963)

P. M. H. Bell, *The Origins of the Second World War in Europe* (1986)

M. Bentley, *The Climax of Liberal Politics* (1987)

G. L. Bernstein, *Liberalism and Liberal Politics in Edwardian England* (Mass., 1986)

Lord Birkenhead, *America Revisited* (1924)

Lord Birkenhead, *Contemporary Personalities* (1924)

R. Blake, *The Conservative Party from Peel to Churchill* (1970)

C. Bridge, *Holding on to the Empire* (1986)

B. Bond, *British Military Policy between the Two World Wars* (1980)

D. Butler & D. Stokes, *Political Change in Britain* (1st edn. 1969, 2nd edn. 1974)

J. R. M. Butler, *Grand Strategy, vol. II* (1957)

A. Cairncross, *The Price of War: British Policy on German Reparations 1941–9* (Oxford, 1986)

J. Charmley, *Chamberlain and the Lost Peace* (1989)

R. S. Churchill (ed.), *Step by Step* (1974 edn)

C. Cook, *The Age of Alignment: Electoral Politics in Britain 1922–9* (1975)

J. Costello, *Mask of Treachery* (1988)

M. Cowling, *The Impact of Labour* (Cambridge, 1971)

M. Cowling, *The Impact of Hitler* (Cambridge, 1975)

M. Cowling, *Religion and Public Doctrine in Modern England* (1980)

R. Dallek, *Franklin D. Roosevelt and American Foreign Policy 1932–45* (NY, 1979)

D. Day, *Menzies and Churchill at War: A Controversial New Account of the 1941 Struggle for Power* (Australia, 1986)

D. Dilks (ed.), *Retreat from Power, vol. I: 1906–39* (1981)

D. Dilks (ed.), *Retreat from Power, vol. II: After 1939* (1981)

D. Dilks & C. Andrew (eds), *The Missing Dimension: Governments and Intelligence Communities in the Twentieth Century* (1984)

A. P. Dobson, *US Wartime Aid to Britain 1940–46* (1986)

M. L. Dockrill & J. D. Goold, *Peace without Promise: Britain and the Peace Conferences, 1919–23* (1981)

R. Douglas, *1938: In the Year of Munich* (1977)

R. Douglas, *The Advent of War* (1978)

R. Douglas, *From War to Cold War 1942–8* (1981)

R. Douglas, *New Alliances, 1940–41* (1982)

W. S. Dunn, *Second Front Now – 1943* (Alabama, 1980)

R. Edmonds, *Setting the Mould: The United States and Great Britain 1945–50* (Oxford, 1986)

J. Ehrman, *Grand Strategy, vol. V* (1956)

J. T. Emmerson, *The Rhineland Crisis* (1977)

H. V. Emy, *Liberals, Radicals and Social Politics 1892–1914* (Cambridge, 1973)

B. Farwell, *The Great War in Africa 1914–18* (NY, 1987)

H. Feiss, *Churchill, Roosevelt and Stalin* (New Jersey, 1957)

D. French, *British Economic and Strategic Planning 1905–15* (1982)

A. L. Friedberg, *The Weary Titan: Britain and the Experience of Relative Decline 1895–1905* (Princeton, 1988)

L. W. Fuchser, *Neville Chamberlain and Appeasement* (1982)

F. R. Gannon, *The British Press & Germany 1936–9* (1971)

J. Garliński, *Poland in the Second World War* (1985)

N. H. Gibbs, *Grand Strategy, vol. I* (1976)

M. Gilbert, *The Roots of Appeasement* (1966)

M. Gilbert, *First World War Atlas* (1970)

G. Gorodetsky, *Stafford Cripps' Mission to Moscow 1940–42* (Cambridge, 1984)

R. Griffiths, *Fellow-Travellers of the Right* (1975)

J. Grigg, *1943: The Victory That Never Was* (1980)

P. Haggie, *Britannia at Bay: The Defence of the British Empire against Japan 1931–41* (1981)

F. J. Harbutt, *The Iron Curtain: Churchill, America and the Origins of the Cold War* (1986)

J. Haslam, *The Soviet Union and the Struggle for Collective Security* (1984)

C. Hazlehurst, *Politicians at War* (1971)

C. Hill, *Cabinet Decisions on Foreign Policy October 1938–June 1941* (Cambridge, 1991)

M. G. Hitchens, *Germany, Russia and the Balkans: Prelude to the Nazi–Soviet Non-Aggression Pact* (1983)

J. D. Hoffman, *The Conservative Party in Opposition 1945–51* (1964)

R. F. Holland, *Britain and the Commonwealth Alliance 1918–39* (1981)

M. Howard, *The Continental Commitment* (1972)

M. Howard, *Grand Strategy, vol. IV* (1972)

M. Howard, *War and the Liberal Conscience* (Oxford, 1981)

D. Irving (ed.), *Breach of Security* (1968)

W. Jackson, *Britain's Defence Dilemma* (1990)

R. R. James, *Gallipoli* (1965)

K. Jefferys, *The Churchill Coalition and Wartime Politics, 1940–45* (Manchester, 1991)

K. Jeffrey, *The British Army and the Crisis of Empire 1918–22* (Manchester, 1984)

J. Joll, *The Origins of the First World War* (1985)

D. E. Kaiser, *Economic Diplomacy and the Origins of the Second World War* (Princeton, 1977)

P. M. Kennedy, *The Realities behind Diplomacy* (1980)

P. M. Kennedy, *The Rise of the Anglo-German Antagonism 1860–1914* (1980)

P. M. Kennedy, *The Rise and Fall of the Great Powers* (1988)

M. Kinnear, *The Fall of Lloyd George: The Political Crisis of 1922* (1973)

M. Kitchen, *British Policy towards the Soviet Union during the Second World War* (1986)

G. Kolko, *The Politics of War: Allied Diplomacy and the World Crisis of 1943–5* (1969)

S. Koss, *The Rise and Fall of the Political Press in Britain, vol. II* (1984)

P. Kyba, *Covenants without Swords: Public Opinion and British Defence Policy* (Ontario, 1983)

R. Langhorne (ed.), *Diplomacy and Intelligence* (1983)

W. Scott Lucas, *Divided We Stand: Britain, the US and the Suez Crisis* (1991)

C. A. MacDonald, *The United States, Britain and Appeasement 1936–9* (1980)

A. J. Marder, *From Dreadnought to Scapa Flow, vol. I: The Road to War, 1904–14* (1961)

A. J. Marder, *From Dreadnought to Scapa Flow, vol. II: The War Years to the Eve of Jutland, 1914–16* (1965)

A. J. Marder, *Operation Menace* (Oxford, 1976)

G. Martel (ed.), *The Origins of the Second World War Reconsidered* (1986)

E. May (ed.), *Knowing One's Enemies* (Princeton, 1984)

B. J. C. McKercher, *The Second Baldwin Government and the United States 1924–9* (Cambridge, 1984)

W. N. Medlicott, *Britain and Germany* (1969)

R. K. Middlemas, *The Diplomacy of Illusion: The British Government and Germany 1937–9* (1972)

W. J. Mommsen & L. Kettenaker (eds), *The Fascist Challenge and the Policy of Appeasement* (1984)

G. Monger, *The End of Isolation: British Foreign Policy 1900–7* (Edinburgh, 1963)

R. J. Moore, *Churchill, Cripps and India 1939–45* (Oxford, 1979)

K. O. Morgan, *Consensus and Disunity: The Lloyd George Coalition Government 1918–22* (1979)

A. J. A. Morris, *The Scaremongers: The Advocacy of War and Rearmament 1896–1914* (1984)

J. L. Moulton, *The Norwegian Campaign of 1940* (1966)

W. Murray, *The Change in the European Balance of Power, 1938–9* (Princeton, 1984)

L. B. Namier, *Diplomatic Prelude* (1948)

L. B. Namier, *In the Nazi Era* (1952)

S. Newman, *March 1939: The British Guarantee to Poland* (Oxford, 1976)

R. Ovendale, *Appeasement and the English-Speaking World* (Cardiff, 1975)

R. Ovendale, *The English-Speaking Alliance 1945–51* (1985)

R. A. C. Parker, *Struggle for Survival: The History of the Second World War* (Oxford, 1989)

G. Peden, *British Rearmament and the Treasury 1932–9* (Edinburgh, 1979)

C. Ponting, *1940: Myth and Reality* (1990)

L. R. Pratt, *East of Malta, West of Suez: Britain's Mediterranean Crisis 1936–9* (Cambridge, 1975)

A. Prażmowska, *Britain, Poland and the Eastern Front, 1939* (Cambridge, 1987)

J. Ramsden, *The Age of Balfour and Baldwin* (1979)

D. Reynolds, *The Creation of the Anglo-American Alliance 1937–41* (1981)

K. Robbins, *Munich 1938* (1968)

E. M. Robertson (ed.), *The Origins of the Second World War* (1971)

W. R. Rock, *British Appeasement in the 1930s* (NY, 1977)

S. Roskill, *British Naval Policy between the Wars*, 2 vols (1968, 1976)

A. L. Rowse, *All Souls and Appeasement* (1961)

H. Butterfield Ryan, *The Vision of Anglo-America* (Cambridge, 1987)

K. Sainsbury, *The North African Landings 1942* (1977)

K. Sainsbury, *The Turning Point* (Oxford, 1985)

G. Schmidt, *The Politics and Economics of Appeasement* (1986 edn)

G. R. Searle, *The Quest for National Efficiency* (1972)

G. R. Searle, *Corruption in British Politics* (1987)

B. Semmel, *Liberalism and Naval Strategy* (Boston, 1986)

R. Shay, *British Rearmament in the Thirties* (Princeton, 1977)

Sir E. L. Spears, *Assignment to Catastrophe, vol. I: July 1939–May 1940 & vol. II: June 1940* (1954)

Z. A. Steiner, *Britain and the Origins of the First World War* (1977)

M. A. Stoler, *The Politics of the Second Front* (NY, 1977)

A. J. P. Taylor, *The Origins of the Second World War* (1961)

T. Taylor, *Munich: The Price of Peace* (1979)

J. Terraine, *The Right of the Line: The Royal Air Force in the European War 1939–45* (1985)

R. T. Thomas, *Britain and Vichy* (1978)

G. M. Thompson, *Vote of Censure* (1968)

N. Thompson, *The Anti-Appeasers: Conservative Opposition to Appeasement in the 1930s* (1971)

C. Thorne, *The Approach of War* (1967)

C. Thorne, *Allies of a Kind* (1978)

N. Waites (ed.), *Troubled Neighbours: Franco-British Relations in the Twentieth Century* (1971)

J. D. Wallin, *By Ships Alone: Churchill and the Dardanelles* (Carolina, 1981)

W. K. Wark, *The Ultimate Enemy* (1985)

D. C. Watt, *Personalities and Policies* (1965)

D. C. Watt, *Too Serious a Business* (1975)

D. C. Watt, *Succeeding John Bull* (Cambridge, 1984)

G. Weinberg, *The Foreign Policy of Hitler's Germany*, 2 vols (Carolina, 1970, 1980)

J. W. Wheeler-Bennett, *Munich: Prologue to Tragedy* (1948)

J. W. Wheeler-Bennett (ed.), *Action This Day: Working with Churchill* (1968)

S. R. Williamson, *The Politics of Grand Strategy* (Harvard, 1968)

C. Wilmot, *The Struggle for Europe* (1952)

K. Wilson, *Empire and Continent* (1987)

K. Wilson, *The Policy of the Ententes* (1989)

A. F. Wilt, *War from the Top* (1990)

Sir L. Woodward, *British Foreign Policy in the Second World War, vol. I* (1970)

Sir L. Woodward, *British Foreign Policy in the Second World War, vol. II* (1971)

Sir L. Woodward, *British Foreign Policy in the Second World War, vol. III* (1971)

Sir L. Woodward, *British Foreign Policy in the Second World War, vol. IV* (1976)

10. COLLECTIONS, ESSAYS, ARTICLES AND THESES

L. P. Arnn, *Winston S. Churchill as Minister of Munitions* (unpublished Oxford D. Phil. thesis, 1977)

T. Garton Ash, 'From World War to Cold War', *The New York Review of Books* (1987)

T. Garton Ash, 'In the Churchill Museum', *The New York Review of Books* (1987)

S. Ball, 'Failure of an Opposition? The Conservative Party in Parliament 1929–31', *Parliamentary History* (1985)

E. Barker, 'Problems of the Alliance: Misconceptions and Misunderstandings', in F. W. Deakin *et al.* (eds), *British Political and Military Strategy in Central, Eastern and Southern Europe in 1944* (1988)

Lord Birkenhead, *Last Essays* (1930)

C. Bridge, 'Churchill, Hoare, Derby and the Committee of Privileges, April to June 1934', *Historical Journal* (1979)

C. Bridge, 'Conservatism and Indian Reform 1929–39', *Journal of Imperial and Commonwealth History* (1974–5)

M. Brock, 'Britain Enters the War', in R. J. W. Evans & H. Pogge von Strandmann, *The Coming of the First World War* (Oxford, 1988)

K. D. Brown, *Essays in Anti-Labour History* (1974)

A. Bryant (ed.), *In Search of Peace* (1938)

M. Ceadel, 'The First British Referendum: The Peace Ballot 1934–5', *English Historical Review* (1980)

J. Charmley, *British Policy towards General de Gaulle 1942–4* (unpublished Oxford D. Phil. thesis, 1982)

J. Charmley, 'Harold Macmillan and the Making of the French Committee of Liberation', *International History Review* (1982)

J. Charmley, 'Duff Cooper and Western European Union', *Review of International Studies* (1985)

E. David, 'The Liberal Party Divided, 1916–18', *Historical Journal* (1970)

D. Dilks, 'British Political Aims in Central, Eastern and Southern Europe, 1944', in F. W. Deakin *et al.* (eds), *British Political and Military Strategy in Central, Eastern and Southern Europe in 1944* (1988)

A. L. Funk, 'The "Anfa Memorandum"', *Journal of Modern History* (1954)

S. Ghosh, 'Decision-making and Power in the British Conservative Party: A Case Study of the Indian Problem 1929–34', *Political Studies* (1965)

M. Gilbert (ed.), *A Century of Conflict 1850–1950: Essays for A. J. P. Taylor* (1966)

J. Gooch, 'An Emblematic Prime Minister', *The Times Higher Education Supplement*, 1 July 1983

G. Gorodetsky, 'Churchill's Warning to Stalin: A Reappraisal', *Historical Journal* (1986)

G. Gorodetsky, 'The Hess Affair and Anglo-Soviet Relations on the Eve of "Barbarossa"', *English Historical Review* (1986)

J. P. Harris, 'The British General Staff and the Coming of War, 1933–9', *Bulletin of the Institute of Historical Research* (1986)

P. Hennessy & A. Seldon (eds), *Ruling Performance* (Oxford, 1987)

D. Hunt, 'British Military Planning and Aims in 1944', in F. W. Deakin *et al.* (eds), *British Political and Military Strategy in Central, Eastern and Southern Europe in 1944* (1988)

K. Jefferys, 'British Politics and Social Policy during the Second World War', *Historical Journal* (1987)

J. Keegan (ed.), *Churchill's Generals* (1991)

P. M. Kennedy, 'Appeasement and British Defence Policy in the Inter-War Years', *British Journal of International Studies* (1978)

L. Kettenacker, 'The Anglo-Soviet Alliance and the Problem of Germany', *Journal of Contemporary History* (1982)

M. Kitchen, 'Winston Churchill and the Soviet Union during the Second World War', *Historical Journal* (1987)

W. Laqueur (ed.), *The Second World War: Essays in Military and Political History* (1982)

S. Lawlor, 'Britain and the Russian Entry into the War', in R. Langhorne (ed.), *Diplomacy and Intelligence* (1983)

W. R. Louis (ed.), *The Origins of the Second World War: A. J. P. Taylor and his Critics* (1971)

W. R. Louis & H. Bull (eds), *The 'Special Relationship'* (Oxford, 1986)

Piers Mackesy, 'Churchill on Narvik', *Journal of the Royal United Services Institute* (1970)

A. J. Marder, *From the Dardanelles to Oran* (1974)

R. Overy, 'German Pre-War Aircraft Production Plans', *English Historical Review* (1975)

R. A. C. Parker, 'British Rearmament 1936–9', *English Historical Review* (1981)

R. A. C. Parker, 'Economics, Rearmament and Foreign Policy', *Journal of Contemporary History* (1975)

R. A. C. Parker, 'The Pound Sterling, the American Treasury and British Preparations for War 1938–9', *English Historical Review* (1983)

J. Parry, 'High and Low Politics in Modern Britain', *Historical Journal* (1986)

G. Peden, 'The Burden of Imperial Defence and the Continental Commitment Reconsidered', *Historical Journal* (1984)

G. Peden, 'A Matter of Timing: The Economic Background to British Foreign Policy, 1937–9', *History* (1984)

G. Peele & C. Cook (eds), *The Politics of Reappraisal 1918–39* (1975)

G. Peele, 'St George's and the Empire Crusade', in C. Cook, *By-elections in British Politics* (1969)

G. Peele, 'Revolt over India', in G. Peele & C. Cook (eds), *The Politics of Reappraisal* (1975)

A. J. Prażmowska, 'War over Danzig?' in *Historical Journal* (1983)

D. Reynolds, 'Churchill and the British "Decision" To Fight on in 1940: Right Policy, Wrong Reasons', in R. Langhorne (ed.), *Diplomacy and Intelligence during the Second World War* (Cambridge, 1985)

K. Robbins, 'Britain, 1940 and "Christian Civilisation"', in D. Beales & G. Best (eds), *History, Society and the Churches* (Cambridge, 1985)

K. G. M. Ross, 'Foreign Office Attitudes to the Soviet Union 1941–5', *Journal of Contemporary History* (1981)

K. G. M. Ross, 'The Moscow Conference of October 1944', in F. W. Deakin *et al.* (eds), *British Political and Military Strategy in Central, Eastern and Southern Europe in 1944* (1988)

K. Sainsbury, 'Central and Eastern Europe at the Quebec Conference', in F. W. Deakin *et al.* (eds), *British Political and Military Strategy in Central, Eastern and Southern Europe in 1944* (1988)

T. Stannage, 'The East Fulham By-election of 25 October 1933', *Historical Journal* (1971)

A. J. P. Taylor, *Politics in Wartime* (1964)

A. J. P. Taylor, *Essays in English History* (1976)

P. Tsakaloyannis, 'Moscow Puzzle', *Journal of Contemporary History* (1986)

J. Turner (ed.), *The Larger Idea* (1988)

P. Warner, 'Auchinleck', in J. Keegan (ed.), *Churchill's Generals* (1991)

P. Williamson, 'Safety First: Baldwin, the Conservative Party and the 1929 General Election', *Historical Journal* (1982)

P. Williamson, 'A Banker's Ramp? Financiers and the British Political Crisis of 1931', *English Historical Review* (1984)

K. M. Wilson, *Imperialism and Nationalism in the Middle East* (1983)

C. Wrigley (ed.), *Warfare, Diplomacy and Politics* (1986)

J. W. Young (ed.), *The Foreign Policy of Churchill's Peacetime Administration 1951–5* (Leicester, 1988)

Index

I should like to thank the staff of the Churchill Memorial in Fulton, Missouri, for their help and their assistance in preparing this index; I owe a particular debt to Judith Pugh, Judith Bell, Warren Hollrah and Kevin Mathis.